W9-APL-030
THE
American
Century
Thesaurus

THE American Century Thesaurus

Laurence Urdang

A Time Warner Company

The American Century Thesaurus. Warner Books Paperback Edition

Previously published by Oxford University Press, Inc. with example sentences as *The Oxford Desk Thesaurus: American Edition* and with the addition of an index as *The Oxford Thesaurus: American Edtion.*

Reprinted by permission of Oxford University Press, Inc.

Cover design by Jerry Pfeiffer

Warner Books, Inc.
1271 Avenue of the Americas
New York, NY 10020

Visit our Web site at
www.warnerbooks.com

A Time Warner Company

Printed in the United States of America

First Warner Books Printing: August, 1996
Reissued: August, 1997

15 14 13 12

INTRODUCTION

In its narrowest sense, a synonym is a word or phrase that is perfectly substitutable in a context for another word or phrase. People who study language professionally agree that there is no such thing as an ideal synonym, for it is virtually impossible to find two words or phrases that are identical in denotation (meaning), connotation, frequency, familiarity, and appropriateness. Indeed, linguists have long noted the ***economy of language,*** which suggests that no language permits a perfect fit, in all respects, between any two words or phrases. Many examples of overlapping can be cited; the more obvious ones in English are those that reflect a duplication arising from Germanic and Romance sources, like ***motherly*** and ***maternal, farming*** and ***agriculture, teach*** and ***instruct.*** In such pairs the native English form is often the one with an earthier, warmer connotation. In some instances, where a new coinage or a loanword has been adopted inadvertently duplicating an existing term, creating "true" synonyms, the two will quickly diverge, not necessarily in meaning but in usage, application, connotation, level, or all of these. For example, scientists some years ago expressed dissatisfaction with the term ***tidal wave,*** for the phenomenon was not caused by tides but, usually, by submarine seismic activity. The word ***tsunami*** was borrowed from Japanese in an attempt to describe the phenomenon more accurately, but it was later pointed out that ***tsunami*** means 'tidal wave' in Japanese. Today, the terms exist side by side in English, the older expression still in common use, the newer more frequent in the scientific and technical literature.

Any synonym book must be seen as a compromise that relies on the sensitivity of its users to the idiomatic nuances of the language. In its best applications, it serves to remind users of words, similar in meaning, that might not spring readily to mind and to offer lists of words and phrases that are alternatives to and compromises for those that might otherwise be overused and therefore redundant, repetitious, and boring.

1. Selection of Headwords

Two criteria have been employed: first, headwords have been selected because of their frequency in the language, on the assumption that synonyms are more likely to be sought for the words that are most used; second, some headwords of lower frequency have been included because it would be otherwise impossible to find a suitable place to group together what are perceived as useful sets of synonyms. Obvious listings have been omitted on the grounds that users of ***The American Century Thesaurus*** can easily find synonyms for, say, ***abdication*** by making nouns out of the verbs listed under ***abdicate.*** This deliberate attempt to avoid duplication is mitigated in the case of very common words. For the convenience of the user, both ***shy*** and ***bashful*** are main entries, as are ***method, manner,*** and ***mode,*** which, though much the same in some respects, differ in detail and application. In contrast to other books, however, ***mitigate*** is a main entry but not ***mitigation, mistake*** and ***mistaken*** are main entries but not ***mistakenly,*** etc. Where it is determined that such derivations are neither automatic nor semantically obvious, separate listings have been provided.

2. Synonym Lists

Each main entry is followed by one or more sense groupings. An effort has been made to group the synonyms semantically as well as syntactically and idiomatically: that is, each synonym listed within a given set should prove to be more or less substitutable for the main entry.

In some instances, idiomatic congruity may, unavoidably, become strained; where it is felt to be stretched too far—though still properly listed among its accompanying synonyms—a semicolon has been inserted to separate subgroups of synonyms. Such subgroupings have been confined largely to distinctions between literal and figurative uses, between transitive and intransitive verbs, and between synonyms that differ in more subtle aspectual characteristics of meaning or syntax.

Not all senses of all words are covered for either or both of the following reasons: the sense, though it exists, is relatively rare in ordinary discourse and writing or there are no reasonable synonyms for it. Thus, this sense of ***mercy,***

> an affecting or moving of the mind in any way; a mental state brought about by any influence; an emotion or feeling

is not covered for the first reason, as it is a literary and somewhat archaic usage. The same can be said for the sense,

> a bodily state due to any influence

and for other senses listed in the largest dictionaries but rarely encountered except in literary contexts. Even in such contexts it would be unusual to need a synonym for this word and others like it.

3. Cross References

There are very few cross references between main listings in the *Thesaurus,* for it seemed desirable to avoid unnecessary duplications of listings. Where such cross references do occur, they are simple and straightforward:

> **superior** *adj.* . . . 3 See **supercilious,** above. —*n.* 4 See **supervisor,** below.

A number of cross references occur within entries, between variant forms of an expression. At the entry for *take,* for example, as one can say either *take* or *take it* in the sense of 'understand,' etc., the option is shown in the following way:

take *v.* . . . **19** °understand, °gather, °interpret, °perceive, apprehend, °deduce, conclude, °infer, °judge, deem, °assume, °suppose, °imagine, °see

33 ***take it.*** **(a)** withstand *or* tolerate *or* survive punishment *or* abuse, °survive **(b)** See **19,** above.

In a few entries, the form "See also" is used.

A unique feature of the *Thesaurus* is the cross reference system between synonyms and main entries: every word listed as a synonym that also appears as a main entry is preceded by a degree mark (°). Users seeking additional synonyms or a different aspect or nuance of meaning of a synonym so marked are at once alerted to the fact that it has its own main entry and can look it up directly.

locale *n.* °site, °location, °spot, °place, °setting, venue, °neighborhood, °situation, locality

When a degree mark precedes a term beginning with a word or words in parentheses, the cross reference is to the word following the parentheses. Thus, in the following example, the degree marks refer the reader to the entries for ***play, show, piece, production,*** and ***scenario.***

drama *n.* **1** °play, stage play, photoplay, screenplay, °(stage) show, °(theatrical) piece, °(stage) production; °scenario

Some words that are main entries are not marked when they appear in a phrase, for reference to them would not yield useful synonyms. In the following entry, for example, marking the words ***take, pleasure, put, edge,*** and ***enjoyment*** would be misleading, hence they are unmarked:

overshadow *v.* . . . **2** °spoil, °blight, °ruin, °mar, take (all) the pleasure from, put a damper on, take the edge off, °impair, take the enjoyment out of

4. Labels

A. All words and phrases that are recognized as belonging to a particular variety of English, whether geographical or stylistic, are labeled. The labels used are those commonly encountered in ordinary dictionaries:

Colloq Colloquial; informal; used in everyday conversation and writing, especially in the popular press and in dramatic dialogue; sometimes avoided where more formal language is felt to be appropriate, as in business correspondence, scholarly works, technical reports, documents, etc.

Slang Belonging to the most informal register and characteristic chiefly of spoken English; often originating in the cult language of a particular sociocultural group. Not sufficiently elevated to be used in most writing (aside from dialogue), but often found in the popular press and frequently heard on popular radio and television programs.

Taboo Not used in polite society, usually because of the risk of offending religious, sexual, or cultural sensibilities; occasionally encountered on latenight television and radio (chiefly in dialogue from a script but not usually tolerated on call-in shows where it is edited out by time-delay devices); often occurring in graffiti and in dialogue in novels, plays, and films.

Archaic Describing an obsolete word or phrase (like *coxcomb, lounge lizard*) that is used deliberately to invoke the feeling of a bygone time.

Old-fashioned Used of a synonym (like *comfit*) that is no longer current but might occasionally be encountered among older speakers and in older writing.

Technical Used of a somewhat specialized word that is not commonly encountered in ordinary, everyday English, like *defalcator,* which appears as a synonym under *swindler.*

Literary Describes a word, like *euchre* 'cheat,' that is not usually met with in everyday language, even of the formal genre, but may be found in poetry and other literary works.

Brit, US, Australian, Canadian, New Zealand Marks a word or phrase that occurs typically in the designated variety.

The meanings of other labels are self-evident.

B. All labels can occur in combination. Usage labels always take precedence over dialect labels. For example,

> **pushover** *n.* **1** °sure thing, *Colloq* °piece of cake, child's play, °snap, °picnic, walkover, *US* °breeze, *Slang* cinch, *Brit* doddle, *US* lead-pipe cinch

Here, "sure thing" is standard universal English. All words and phrases following *Colloq* up to the *Slang* label are colloquial: "piece of cake, . . . walkover" are universal colloquial English, "breeze" is US colloquial. All synonyms following the *Slang* label are slang: "cinch" is universal English slang, "doddle" is confined to British slang, and "lead-pipe cinch" is confined to American slang.

> **talented** *adj.* . . . *Colloq* ace, °crack, top-notch, *Brit* wizard, whizzo, *US* crackerjack

In this entry, all synonyms shown are colloquial, "ace, crack, topnotch" being universal English, "wizard, whizzo" British, and "crackerjack" US.

It must be emphasized that such labels are to some extent impressionistic and are based in the *Thesaurus* on a consensus of several sources: that is, there is no implication that "breeze" is never used in the sense of "pushover" except in the US, nor should such an inference be made.

C. Comments regarding what might be viewed as "correct" in contrast to "incorrect" usage are generally avoided. For example, the nonstandard use of ***between*** in contexts referring to more than two of anything or of ***among*** in contexts involving fewer than three goes unmarked. However, if the usage question is confined to what can easily be represented in a "lexical" environment, then suitable treatment is accorded it; thus "infer" is labeled *Nonstandard* under ***imply*** but, because the substitution of ***imply*** for ***infer*** is not attested, there is no reciprocal listing under ***infer***. To take another example, "different to," in the typically British usage ***His house is different to mine,*** is rarely encountered in American English; in American English, purists condemn "different than," as in ***His house is different than mine,*** which is increasingly heard in British English; purists on both sides of the Atlantic prefer "different from." Such matters are best left to usage books and to usage notes in dictionaries and are not treated in the *Thesaurus*.

D. Main entry words and subentries are not labeled, only the synonyms. Thus, under ***push*** appears the idiomatic expression, ***push (up) daisies,*** which is not labeled:

> **push** *v.* . . . **12** ***push (up) daisies.*** be dead (and buried), be six feet under

The idiom is not labeled because it is assumed that the user has looked it up to find a substitute for it, hence needs no information about it other than a listing of its alternatives (which are labeled, when appropriate). Should users need more detailed information about a given word or phrase, they should resort to a dictionary, the proper repository for such information. A rare exception to the foregoing occurs where a headword has one meaning in American English and quite a different meaning in another regional variety. Thus, in the following entry, the labels apply to the different senses of the main entry word, not to the synonyms following (since "tunnel," for example, has the same meaning in British and American English):

> **subway** *n.* **1** *Brit* °underground (railway), tube **2** *US* °tunnel, underpass

E. Synonyms bearing any kind of label appear at the end of the set in which they are listed, except in the case described immediately above.

5. Spelling and Other Variants

The spellings shown throughout are those preferred by most modern American writers. American variant spellings are shown; if they are variants of the main entry word, they appear as the first word in the set(s) of synonyms following:

mousy *adj.* 1 mousey, . . .
movable *adj.* moveable, . . .

Such variants are also shown when they appear within an entry:

investigate *v.* enquire or inquire into, . . .

Common British spelling variants (*humour, traveller, unravelled*) are not shown, but less common ones are listed for convenience. Where both forms are variants in American spelling, they are described by "*or US also*":

. . . accouterments *or US also* accoutrements, . . .
. . . phony *or US also* phoney, . . .

This should be understood to mean "the normal American spelling is *accouterments* (or *phony*)" but that alternative spellings occur occasionally.

6. Substitutability

A. The purpose of a synonym book is to provide the user with a collection of words that are as close as possible in meaning to a designated word. For example:

porous *adj.* spongy, spongelike, permeable, pervious, penetrable

It is possible to substitute for *porous* any of the words given as synonyms without any adjustment of grammar or phrasing. That is not to suggest that the synonyms are identical: "permeable" and "pervious" are far less frequent in English than "spongy, spongelike." Some might argue that "penetrable" is not synonymous with the other listed words; but it is the function of this book to provide synonyms for the main entries, not for the other synonyms listed. No claim is made—nor could it be made—that synonyms are identical, either to one another or to another word, merely that they fall well within the criteria of what, for practical purposes, is viewed as synonymy in the language.

It is certainly true that substituting for *porous* any of the five listed synonyms will yield five standard English sentences.

B. Some judgment is required of the user in determining the syntax and idiomaticity with which a given word or expression can be substituted: words are rarely as readily interchangeable in a context as might be components in a chemical or mathematical formula. Moreover, while such formulae are reflective of science, language offers its users the virtually infinite variety available only in art, with each individual speaker of any language being presented with the opportunity to become an artist.

In the following example, all terms can be substituted for *adjoining* when it precedes the noun that it modifies; to create idiomatic parallels in constructions where *adjoining* follows the noun it modifies, the parenthetical prepositions must be used:

adjoining *adj.* °neighboring, contiguous (to), adjacent (to), abutting, bordering; next (to)

Interpreting this, the following are all idiomatic: ***adjoining land, neighboring land, contiguous land, adjacent land, abutting land,*** and ***bordering land.*** But if the context requires the adjective to come after ***land,*** then the parenthetical words must be added to yield constructions that are idiomatic, like ***land adjoining the supermarket, land neighboring the supermarket, land contiguous to the supermarket, land adjacent to the supermarket, land abutting the supermarket, land bordering the supermarket,*** and ***land next to the supermarket.***

As this is intended as a synonym book and not a work on English collocations, the matter of idiomaticity cannot be taken much further.

C. Often, the semicolon may be used to separate transitive uses of a verb from intransitive:

preach *v.* . . . **2** moralize, sermonize, °advise, °counsel, admonish, °reprimand, °lecture, °harangue, pontificate; °urge, inculcate, °advocate

Because of the behavior of verbs in English, different synonyms may be required depending on what the object of the verb is and, often, whether the object is a word or phrase or a clause:

predict *v.* foretell, °prophesy, °forecast, °foresee, augur, °prognosticate, forewarn, presage, vaticinate; portend, °foreshadow, foretoken, forebode; °intimate, °hint, °suggest

D. Wherever possible, the proper prepositional or adverbial particle normally accompanying a verb in a certain sense has been supplied, though it must be emphasized that the one offered is the most frequently used and not, necessarily, the only one acceptable in standard usage. Particles used with some words may vary considerably, owing not only to dialect variation but also to whether the verb is used actively or passively as well as to which nuance of meaning, sometimes far too subtle to be dealt with adequately in a book of this kind, is to be expressed. The following entry illustrates the full treatment that can be accorded to words that occur in a wide variety of grammatical environments:

persevere *v.* Often, ***persevere in*** *or* ***with*** *or* ***at.*** °persist, °resolve, °decide, °endure, °continue, carry on *or* through, keep at *or* on *or* up, be steadfast *or* staunch *or* constant, keep going, stand fast *or* firm, °see through, be *or* remain determined *or* resolved *or* resolute *or* stalwart *or* purposeful *or* uncompromising, be tenacious *or* persistent *or* constant *or* pertinacious *or* assiduous *or* sedulous, be tireless *or* untiring *or* indefatigable, show determination *or* pluck or grit, be plucky, be patient *or* diligent *or* stubborn *or* inflexible *or* adamant *or* obstinate *or* obdurate, show *or* exhibit *or* demonstrate patience *or* diligence *or* stubbornness *or* inflexibility *or* obstinacy *or* obduracy, remain dogged, pursue doggedly, be intransigent *or* intractable, cling to, stick to, °support, stop at nothing, sustain, *Colloq* °stick with, stick (it) out

E. In some adjective senses, a split might occur between attributive and predicative uses, though in most such cases, where the syntax is open, only one, usually common illustration is given. For example, *alone* is used only predicatively or postpositively, not attributively; that is, one cannot say *An alone woman. . . .* In this particular case, the normal attributive form would be *lone,* but *lone* is not listed as a synonym for *alone* because they are not mutually substitutable. It is acknowledged that the detailed description of the special syntactic ways in which certain words (like *alone, agog, galore*) behave lies outside the province of this book.

A

abandon *v.* **1** give up *or* over, °yield, °surrender, °leave, °cede, let go, °deliver (up), °turn over, °relinquish **2** °depart from, °leave, °desert, °quit, go away from **3** °desert, °forsake, °jilt, walk out on **4** °give up, °renounce; °discontinue, °forgo, °drop, desist, abstain from —*n.* **5** recklessness, intemperance, wantonness, lack of restraint, unrestraint

abandoned *adj.* **1** left alone, °forlorn, forsaken, °deserted, neglected; rejected, shunned, cast off *or* aside, jilted, dropped, °outcast **2** °bad, °immoral, amoral, °wicked, °sinful, °evil, °corrupt, unprincipled, unrestrained, °uninhibited, °reprobate; °loose, °wanton, debauched, °wild, °dissolute, dissipated, °profligate; depraved, °lewd, °lascivious, flagitious

abbreviate *v.* **1** °shorten, compress, °contract, truncate, °trim, °reduce, °curtail **2** °shorten, °cut, condense, °abridge, °abstract, °digest, epitomize, summarize, *US* synopsize

abbreviated *adj.* skimpy, °brief, revealing

abbreviation *n.* initialism; acronym; shortening, contraction

abdicate *v.* °give up, °renounce, disclaim, °waive, disown, °surrender, °yield, °relinquish, °abandon, °resign, °quit

abduct *v.* °kidnap, °carry off, make away *or* off with, °seize, *Slang US* °snatch, °grab

abet *v.* **1** °encourage, °urge, instigate, °incite, °provoke, egg on, °prod, goad; °aid, °help, °assist **2** countenance, °approve (of), °support, °endorse, °second, °sanction, condone; °further, °advance, °promote, °uphold

abeyance *n.* ***in abeyance.*** °pending, abeyant, °reserved, °in reserve, shelved, pushed *or* shoved *or* shunted aside, postponed, °put off, suspended, *US* tabled; temporarily inactive, °dormant; latent; *Colloq* in a holding pattern, on the back burner; *Slang* on hold, in the deep freeze, on the shelf, on ice, hanging fire

abhor *v.* °hate, °loathe, °detest, abominate, execrate; regard *or* view with horror *or* dread *or* fright *or* repugnance *or* loathing *or* disgust, shudder at, recoil *or* shrink from; be *or* stand aghast at

abhorrent *adj.* °hateful, detestable, abhorred, °abominable, °contemptible, odious, °loathsome, horrid, heinous, execrable, °repugnant; °repulsive, °repellent, °revolting, °offensive, °disgusting, horrifying, °obnoxious

abide *v.* **1** °stand, °endure, °suffer, °submit to, °bear, °put up with, °accept, °tolerate, °brook **2** °live, °stay, reside, °dwell, °sojourn **3** °remain, °stay, °continue, °tarry; °linger, °rest **4** ***abide by.*** °consent to, °agree to, comply with, °observe, °acknowledge, °obey, °follow, °submit to, conform to, keep to, remain true to, stand firm by, adhere to, hold to

abiding *adj.* °lasting, °permanent, °constant, °steadfast, °everlasting, unending, °eternal, °enduring, °indestructible; unchanging, °fast, hard and fast, °fixed, °firm, immutable, °changeless

ability *n.* **1** adeptness, °aptitude, °facility, °faculty, °capacity, °power, °knack, °proficiency, *Colloq* know-how **2** °talent, °skill, cleverness, °capacity, °wit, °gift, °genius, °capability **3** ***abilities.*** °faculty, faculties, talent(s), gift(s), skill(s)

ablaze *adj.* **1** aflame, afire, °burning, °on fire, alight, blazing **2** lit up, alight, brilliantly *or* brightly lit, sparkling, gleaming, aglow, °bright, °brilliant, °luminous, illuminated, °radiant

able *adj.* **1** °capable, °qualified, °competent, °proficient **2** °talented, °clever, skilled, °masterful, masterly; °adept, °skillful, °gifted, °superior, °expert, °accomplished

abnormal *adj.* **1** °deviant, deviating, °irregular, °unusual, unconventional, aberrant, *Psych jargon* °exceptional **2** °peculiar, °unusual, °odd, °strange, °queer, freakish, °unnatural, °extraordinary, °weird, °eccentric, °bizarre, anomalous, aberrant, °perverse, °deviant, °irregular, *Colloq* off-beat, *Slang* oddball, °kinky, °weirdo

abnormality *n.* **1** irregularity, unconformity, unusualness, °singularity, °eccentricity, unconventionality, uncommonness, deviation, aberration, idiosyncrasy **2** distortion, anomaly, malformation, deformity

abode *n.* °residence, °dwelling, dwelling place, °house, °home, °domicile, habitation, °quarters, °lodging, °accommodations, *Military* billet; *Colloq Brit* digs, diggings

abolish *v.* °eliminate, °end, put an end to, °terminate, °destroy, annihilate, annul, °void, make void, °demolish, do away with, nullify, °repeal, °cancel, °obliterate, liquidate, °destroy, °stamp out, °quash, °extinguish, °erase, °delete, expunge; eradicate, extirpate, deracinate, °uproot

abolition *n.* elimination, °end, °termination, annulment, nullification, repudiation, °cancellation; °destruction, annihilation

abominable *adj.* **1** °offensive, °repugnant, °repulsive, °vile, °monstrous, °loathsome, odious, execrable, detestable, °despicable, °base, °disgusting, °nauseous, nauseating, °foul, °abhorrent, horrid, °deplorable **2** °terrible, unpleasant, °disagreeable; °awful, °distasteful, in bad taste, °horrible, °frightful, *Colloq Brit* °beastly

aboriginal *n.* °native, indigene, autochthon; *Colloq Australian* Abo, *Offensive Australian* aborigine, *Slang Australian contemptuous* boong

abound *v.* **1** °prevail, °thrive, °flourish **2** ***abound in.*** be crowded *or* packed *or* jammed with, be abundant *or* rich in, proliferate (in *or* with) **3** ***abound with.*** teem *or* swarm *or* throng with, be filled *or* infested with, overflow with

about *adv.* **1** °round, °around, close *or* near by, on every side **2** °approximately, °around, °nearly, °roughly, more or less, °almost, close to *or* upon; give or take **3** to and fro, up and down, back and forth, here and there, hither and yon, °far and wide, hither and thither **4** here and there, °far and wide, hither and yon, hither and thither, °helter-skelter **5** °around, °prevalent, in the air **6** °approximately, °nearly, °close to, not far from, °almost, just about, °around —*prep.* **7** °around, °surrounding, encircling **8** °round, °around, all round, °everywhere, in all directions, all over **9** °near, °nearby, adjacent to, °beside, alongside, °close by, nigh **10** with, °at hand, *Colloq* on **11** °touching, °concerning, connected with, involving, in *or* with reference to, in *or* with regard to, °regarding, in the matter of, with respect to, respecting, °relative to, relating to, apropos, *Formal* anent

about-face *n.* °reversal, °reverse, °turnabout, turnaround, U-turn, volte-face, *Brit* about-turn

above *adv.* **1** °overhead, on high, °aloft, in the sky *or* heavens **2** upstairs —*prep.* **3** on, on (the) top of, upon, °over, atop **4** °over, more than, °exceeding, in excess of, beyond, greater than, °surpassing **5** insusceptible to, unaffected by, out of reach of, not susceptible *or* vulnerable *or* exposed to, superior to **6** ***above all.*** before *or* beyond everything, first of all, °chiefly, °primarily, in the first place, °mainly, essentially, °at bottom

aboveboard *adv.* **1** °openly, candidly, °freely, publicly, frankly, straightforwardly, plainly, for all to see, out in the open, in the open —*adj.* **2** °open, °candid, °frank, °straight, °direct, °honorable, straightforward, °forthright, guileless, undeceiving, °artless, °ingenuous, undeceptive, undeceitful, °straight from the shoulder; °honest, °genuine

abridge *v.* °shorten, °reduce, condense, °cut, °abbreviate, °cut back, °trim, °curtail, °pare down, °contract, compress, °digest, summarize, epitomize, °abstract, *US* synopsize

abridgment *n.* **1** shortening, reduction, °abbreviation, condensation, contraction, truncation, trimming **2** curtailment **3** °digest, condensation, °epitome, compendium, concise edition *or* version, cut edition *or* version; °synopsis, °abstract, °summary, °précis, °outline, °résumé

abroad *adv.* **1** °overseas, in foreign lands *or* parts **2** broadly, °widely, °at large, near and far, °far and wide, °everywhere, extensively, publicly **3** °outside, out-of-doors, away, out and about

abrupt *adj.* **1** °sudden, °hasty, °quick, °precipitate, °snappy; unexpected, unannounced, unplanned, °unforeseen, unanticipated **2** °precipitous, °steep, °sheer, °sudden **3** °curt, °short, °brusque, °blunt, °bluff, °gruff, uncivil, °rude, °discourteous, °impolite, unceremonious, °snappish

absence *n.* **1** nonattendance, nonpresence, nonappearance, truancy **2** °lack, °want, deficiency, nonexistence; insufficiency, scantiness, paucity, °scarcity, °dearth

absent *adj.* **1** away, °out, °off, °elsewhere, not present, missing, gone **2** missing, lacking, °wanting, °deficient —*v.* **3** ***absent (oneself) from.*** keep *or* stay away from; withdraw *or* retire from

absent-minded *adj.* °preoccupied, °inattentive, unattentive, °absorbed, unmindful, °absent, °off, °withdrawn, unheeding, °heedless, unheedful, °inadvertent; distracted, abstracted, daydreaming, in a brown study, in the clouds, °unaware, °oblivious, in a trance, distrait(e), mooning, (far) away (somewhere), stargazing, woolgathering

absolute *adj.* **1** °perfect, °complete, °total, finished, °thorough, through and through, consummate, °flawless, °faultless, unadulterated, °pure, unmixed, unalloyed, °undiluted; °rank **2** °complete, °outright, °downright, °genuine, °real, °pure, °out-and-out, °transparent, °unmitigated, °categorical, °unqualified, unconditional, utter, °veritable, unconditioned **3** unrestricted, unrestrained, unconstrained, °unlimited, °unmitigated, °arbitrary, °despotic, °dictatorial, °totalitarian, °supreme, almighty, °arbitrary, autocratic, °tyrannical **4** °positive, °certain, °sure, unambiguous, °unquestionable, °authoritative, verifiable, uncompromised

absolutely *adv.* **1** unqualifiedly, unconditionally, unreservedly, unexceptionally, unequivocally, unquestionably, °positively, °definitely, °really, genuinely, decidedly, °surely, °truly, certainly, categorically **2** °totally, °utterly, °completely, °entirely, fully, °quite, °altogether, °wholly —*interj.* **3** certainly, assuredly, °positively, °definitely, °of course, °naturally, indubitably, yes, to be sure

absorbed *adj.* engrossed, °lost, wrapped up, occupied, °engaged, immersed, buried, °preoccupied, concentrating, °rapt

absorbing *adj.* engrossing, °engaging, °riveting, captivating, fascinating, °spellbinding, gripping

abstract *adj.* **1** °theoretical, unapplied, notional, ideational, conceptual, metaphysical, unpractical, °intellectual **2** nonrepresentational, °symbolic, nonrealistic —*n.* **3** °summary, °epitome, °synopsis, °essence, °digest, condensation, °survey, conspectus, °extract; °outline, °précis, °résumé —*v.* **4** epitomize, °abbreviate, °digest, summarize, condense, °shorten, °abridge, °cut, °cut down, *US* synopsize

absurd *adj.* **1** °ridiculous, °silly, °nonsensical, °senseless, °outlandish, °preposterous, °farcical, °mad, °stupid, °foolish, idiotic, imbecilic *or* imbecile, moronic, °childish;

laughable, °ludicrous, risible, °inane, *Colloq* °crazy, nutty, nuts, *Chiefly Brit* °daft **2** asinine, °senseless, illogical, irrational, unreasoned, °unreasonable, °incongruous, °paradoxical, °unsound, °meaningless

absurdity *n.* **1** °folly, silliness, ridiculousness, foolishness, ludicrousness, °nonsense, senselessness, meaninglessness, illogicality, irrationality, unreasonableness, incongruity, °stupidity, *Colloq* craziness, nuttiness, *Chiefly Brit* daftness **2** °paradox, self-contradiction, °error, °fallacy

abundance *n.* overflow, °superfluity, overabundance, superabundance, °excess, °surplus, oversupply, °glut, °satiety, oversufficiency; °plenty, plenteousness, plentifulness, plenitude, copiousness, °profusion, *Formal* nimiety

abundant *adj.* **1** °plentiful, overflowing, °ample, copious, oversufficient, superabundant, plenteous, °profuse, °inexhaustible, °replete, °bountiful, bounteous **2** abounding (in), °full (of), °rich (in), °luxuriant, °lavish

abuse *v.* **1** °misuse, misemploy, °pervert, misapply, °exploit **2** maltreat, ill-use, °injure, °wrong, °hurt, °mistreat, °manhandle, °ill-treat; °damage **3** malign, revile, censure, °upbraid, assail, objurgate, °lambaste, °berate, °rebuke, °scold, reproach, °disparage, traduce, defame, °insult, swear at, °curse (at), calumniate, °slander, °libel, decry, deprecate, °vilify, rail against —*n.* **4** °misuse, misusage, misemployment, °perversion, misapplication, misappropriation, *Rhetoric* catachresis **5** addiction, dependence **6** maltreatment, ill-treatment, ill-use, °fault **7** °self-abuse, self-pollution, masturbation, °violation, defilement; corruption **8** revilement, reviling, execration, vituperation, malediction, imprecation, °tongue-lashing, calumny, calumniation, vilification, obloquy, scurrility, invective, maligning, upbraiding, berating, objurgation, scolding; billingsgate

abused *adj.* **1** misused **2** maltreated, ill-treated, mistreated, °hurt

abusive *adj.* **1** insulting, °scurrilous, °vituperative, calumnious, °offensive, °slanderous, libelous, defamatory, censorious, opprobrious, disparaging, deprecatory, depreciatory, °derogatory, °derisory, derisive, reviling, vilifying, °vituperative, °reproachful; °profane; °rude, °filthy, °dirty, °foul, °vulgar, °obscene, smutty, °vile, thersitical **2** °perverted, misapplied, °improper, °wrong, °incorrect; exploitive, exploitative, exploitatory; °brutal, °cruel, °injurious, °hurtful, °harmful, °destructive **3** °corrupt, °venal, °dishonest, °crooked

abysmal *adj.* **1** °awful, appalling, °dreadful, °terrible, °profound **2** abyssal, °bottomless, °profound, unfathomable, unfathomed

abyss *n.* °deep, abysm, bottomless gulf, yawning chasm, gaping void, unfathomable cavity, impenetrable depth(s)

academic *adj.* **1** scholastic, collegiate; °scholarly, °learned, °lettered, erudite **2** °theoretical, °hypothetical, conjectural, °speculative, °abstract; ivory-tower, °visionary, °idealistic; °impractical, °unrealistic, unpractical

accent *n.* **1** °emphasis, °stress, °force, °prominence, accentuation; °intensity, inflection; °cadence, °beat **2** diacritic, diacritical mark, °mark, accent mark **3** °pronunciation, articulation, °intonation, speech pattern, inflection —*v.* **4** accentuate, °emphasize, °stress, give prominence to, °mark, underline, underscore, °distinguish, highlight, set off *or* apart

accept *v.* **1** °receive, °take, °allow, °permit **2** accede (to), °agree (to), assent (to), °consent (to), °acknowledge, °admit, °allow, °recognize **3** °assume, °undertake, take on *or* up, agree to bear **4** reconcile oneself to, °suffer, °undergo, °experience, °stand, °withstand, °stomach, °endure, °bear, °resign oneself to, °brook, °allow, °tolerate, °take

acceptable *adj.* **1** °satisfactory, °adequate, °tolerable, all right, °sufficient, admissible, °passable, *Colloq* O.K. *or* okay **2** °agreeable, °pleasing, °welcome, °satisfying, °delightful, °pleasant

accessible *adj.* approachable, °open, °available, attainable, obtainable, reachable, °ready, °at hand, *Colloq* get-at-able

accessory *n.* **1** °extra, °addition, adjunct, °attachment, component, °frill, *Slang* bells and whistles, doodah, *US and Canadian* doodad **2** accessary, °accomplice, helper, °assistant, confederate, °colleague, abettor, °aide, collaborator, conspirator, coconspirator, fellow criminal, associate *or* partner in crime —*adj.* **3** °extra, °subordinate, °auxiliary, additional, ancillary, supplemental, °supplementary, °secondary, adventitious, *Formal* adscititious

accident *n.* **1** °mishap, °misfortune, mischance, misadventure, °blunder, °mistake; °casualty, °disaster, °catastrophe, °calamity **2** °chance, °fortune, °luck, fortuity, °fluke; serendipity **3** °nonessential, accessory *or* accessary, °extra, °addition

accidental *adj.* °chance, fortuitous, °lucky, unlucky, serendipitous; undesigned, °unpremeditated, uncalculated, unintended, unintentional, unwitting, °inadvertent; unexpected, unplanned, °unforeseen, unanticipated, adventitious; °casual, °random

accommodate *v.* **1** °fit, °suit, °adapt, °adjust, °modify; customize **2** harmonize, make consistent, °reconcile, °adapt **3** °equip, °supply, °provide, °furnish **4** °put up, °house, °lodge, °shelter, °quarter, *Military* billet **5** °suit, °oblige, convenience, °serve

accommodating *adj.* **1** °obliging, cooperative, °helpful, °hospitable; °considerate, conciliatory, easy to deal with, pliant, °yielding, compliant, °polite, °friendly, complaisant, °kind, °kindly **2** °pliable, °accessible, corruptible, subornable, get-at-able; bribable

accommodation *n.* **1** °adaptation, °adjustment, modification, °change, °alteration, conformation, conformity **2** °settlement, °treaty, compromise **3** convenience, °favor

4 Usually, ***accommodations.*** lodging(s), room(s), °quarters, °shelter, °housing; °facility, premises, *Brit* digs **5** °loan, (financial) assistance *or* aid; °grant, grant-in-aid

accompany *v.* **1** convoy, °escort, chaperon *or* chaperone, °go along with; °attend; usher, °squire **2** go (along) with, come with, be associated with, belong with, go together with, be linked with

accomplice *n.* accessory *or* accessary, partner in crime, confederate, °ally, °associate, °colleague, °fellow, °henchman, collaborator, conspirator, coconspirator, abettor, °assistant, fellow criminal, *Colloq US* °cohort

accomplish *v.* °fulfill, °perform, °achieve, °carry out, °execute, °carry off, do, °complete, °carry through, °finish, °effect, bring to an end, conclude, °wind up, °end; attain, °reach, °gain; *Colloq* °bring off, °knock off, °polish off, *Slang* °pull off, *US* °swing, °hack, °cut

accomplished *adj.* consummate, °perfect, °expert, °adept, °skillful, °proficient, °practiced, °gifted, °talented, skilled, °professional

accomplishment *n.* **1** °fulfillment, °consummation, °completion, °realization, attainment, °achievement, conclusion, culmination, °realization **2** coup, °feat, °exploit, °triumph, tour de force **3** °skill, skillfulness, °talent, °gift, °ability

accord *v.* **1** °agree, harmonize, concur, be at one, °correspond, °agree, be in harmony, be consistent, °go (together), °coincide, °conform —*n.* **2** °agreement, unanimity, concord, °reconciliation, °harmony, mutual understanding, conformity, accordance, °rapport, concert **3** °agreement, °treaty, °pact, °contract **4** °agreement, °harmony, congruence; correspondence

accordingly *adv.* **1** °hence, °therefore, °consequently, °thus, in consequence (where)of, (and) so **2** suitably, in conformity, in compliance; conformably, °appropriately, compliantly

according to *adv. phr.* **1** on the authority of, consistent with, in conformity *or* agreement with, as said *or* believed *or* maintained, etc. by **2** conformable to, consistent with, in conformity with, commensurate with

account *v.* **1** ***account for.*** °explain, give a reason for, give *or* render a reckoning for, °answer for, °justify, reckon for —*n.* **2** °calculation, accounting, °reckoning, computation, °(financial) statement; enumeration **3** °interest, °profit, °advantage, °benefit, °favor; °sake **4** °explanation, °statement, °description, °report, °recital, °narrative, °history, °chronicle **5** °consideration, °use, °worth, °importance, consequence, °note, value, °merit; °standing, °significance, °estimation, °esteem **6** °story, °narration, °narrative, °report, °tale, °relation, °description **7** ***take into account*** *or* ***take account of.*** °notice, take note of, °consider, take into consideration, allow for

accountability *n.* answerability, °responsibility, °liability, culpability, accountableness

accountable *adj.* answerable, °responsible, °liable, °obliged, obligated

accumulate *v.* °collect, °gather, °amass, °mass, pile *or* heap up, aggregate, cumulate; °assemble, °store, °stock, °hoard, stockpile, put *or* lay away

accumulation *n.* **1** collecting, amassing, °gathering, aggregation, heaping *or* piling up **2** °growth, °increase, buildup **3** °heap, °pile, °mass, °collection, °hoard, °store, stockpile, °stock, aggregation; assemblage

accuracy *n.* exactness, correctness, *Loosely* °precision, preciseness

accurate *adj.* **1** °exact, °correct, error-free, °precise **2** °careful, °meticulous, °nice, with an eye to *or* for detail, °scrupulous, °conscientious **3** unerring, on target, *Colloq* on the mark, *Brit* spot on (target)

accusation *n.* °charge, °allegation, indictment, citation, arraignment, °complaint; °imputation, incrimination, denunciation, impeachment

accuse *v.* **1** ***accuse*** **(*of or with*).** °blame, censure, hold responsible (for), °charge (with), °denounce (for), point the finger (at), cite, call to account **2** ***accuse*** **(*of or with*).** °charge, °indict, °impeach, arraign, °incriminate; °attribute, °impute

accustom *v.* °familiarize, °acquaint, habituate, °train, °season; acclimatize *or* acclimate

accustomed *adj.* **1** °customary, °habitual, °usual, °traditional, °normal, °regular, °set, °routine, °ordinary, °familiar, wonted, °common, habituated **2** °used

ache *v.* **1** °pain, °hurt, °smart, throb, °pound; °sting **2** °yearn, °long, °hunger, °hanker, pine; crave —*n.* **3** °pain, °pang, throbbing, pounding, smarting, soreness **4** °pang, °pain; °distress; °longing

achieve *v.* **1** °accomplish, °carry out, °execute, °succeed in, °complete, °fulfill, bring off *or* about; °realize, °effect **2** °accomplish, attain, °reach, °gain, °get, °acquire, °win, °obtain

achievement *n.* **1** attainment, °accomplishment, °acquisition, acquirement **2** °accomplishment, attainment, °feat, °deed, °exploit, °victory **3** °fulfillment, °realization, °accomplishment, attainment, °completion

acknowledge *v.* **1** °admit, °confess, °allow, °concede, own, °recognize, °accept, accede, acquiesce; own up to **2** °answer, reply to, °respond to, react to

acknowledgment *n.* **1** acknowledging, confessing, admitting, owning, °admission, confession, avowal, affirmation **2** °approval, acceptance, °recognition, °allowance **3** °reply, °response, °answer, °recognition

acme *n.* °peak, apex, °top, °summit, °pinnacle, °zenith; °climax, culmination

acquaint *n.* ***acquaint with.*** familiarize with, inform of *or* about, make aware of, apprise of, advise of

acquaintance *n.* **1** °familiarity, °knowledge, acquaintanceship, °understanding, awareness; °experience **2** °associate, °fellow, °colleague

acquainted *adj.* **1** known to each other *or* one another, familiar with each other *or* one another, on speaking terms **2** ***acquainted with.*** °familiar with, known to, aware of, informed of, knowledgeable of, conversant with

acquire *v.* °get, °obtain, °gain, °win, °earn, °procure, °secure, come by *or* into; °receive, come into possession of; °buy, °purchase

acquisition *n.* **1** obtaining, getting, acquiring, acquirement, °gain, procurement **2** possession(s), °property, °purchase; °object

act *n.* **1** °deed, °action, °undertaking, °operation, °step, °move; °feat, °exploit; °accomplishment, °achievement **2** °performance, °show, °bit, skit, °stand, °routine, °turn, sketch, *Colloq* °thing, *Slang US* shtick **3** °performance, °pretense, °posture, °stance, feigning, °front, °fake, °dissimulation, °show, °deception, °hoax, °affectation **4** °bill, °law, °decree, edict, statute, °order, ordinance, °command, mandate, °resolution, °measure, enactment —*v.* **5** °behave (oneself), °carry on, deport oneself, comport oneself, °conduct oneself **6** °perform, °play, do **7** °portray, °represent, impersonate, act out, °personify, take *or* play the part *or* role of, personate **8** feign, °pretend, °counterfeit, °fake, dissemble, °make believe, °sham, simulate, °dissimulate, °posture **9** °take effect, °work, °operate, °function, °perform

action *n.* **1** °activity, °performance, °movement, °motion, °energy, liveliness, vim, °vigor, °spirit, °vitality; °enterprise, °initiative **2** °influence, °effect, °power, °force, °strength **3** °deed, °act, °undertaking, °exertion, °exercise **4** °remedy, °proceeding, °process **5** fighting, °combat **6** °fight, °battle, °engagement, °encounter, °clash, °fray, sortie, °skirmish, affray **7** °effect, effectiveness, °activity, °function, °performance, functioning, °reaction **8** ***actions.*** °behavior, °conduct, deportment, demeanor, ways, °manner, °manners

activate *v.* °move, actuate, set in motion, get started, °energize, get *or* set going, °start, °initiate, switch *or* turn on, trigger; °motivate, °rouse, °arouse, °prompt, °stimulate, °stir, °mobilize, °animate, impel, galvanize, *Colloq US* light a fire under

active *adj.* **1** °strenuous, °vigorous, °full, °dynamic, °physical; °energetic, °lively, °busy, °brisk, bustling, occupied, °on the move, *Colloq* on the go, °running **2** acting, °effective, °efficacious, °effectual, working, functioning, °operative, °potent, °influential; °powerful **3** °energetic, °lively, hyperactive, °animated, spry, °nimble, °quick, °agile, °sprightly

activity *n.* **1** °action, °movement, °motion, °vigor, vim, °energy, liveliness, bustle **2** °pursuit, °occupation, °vocation, °work, °function, °operation, °job, °labor, °endeavor, °enterprise, °project, °undertaking, °venture, °interest

actual *adj.* **1** existing, existent, °real, °genuine, °factual, °true, °authentic, verified, verifiable, true-to-life, °manifest, realized, °realistic, *Colloq* °solid **2** °present, °current, existent, °real, °genuine, °physical, °tangible

actually *adv.* °really, °in reality, °in fact, in actuality, in point of fact, °in truth, °absolutely, as a matter of fact, °indeed, °truly, °literally

acute *adj.* **1** °sharp, °pointed, °narrow **2** °severe, °intense, °critical, °crucial, °dangerous, °grave, °serious, °severe **3** °sharp, °cutting, °intense, °severe, °violent, °penetrating, °exquisite, °excruciating, °fierce, shooting, stabbing, °piercing, °sudden **4** °keen, °sharp, °sensitive **5** °keen, sharp-witted, °shrewd, °clever, °ingenious, °astute, °sharp, canny, °incisive, discerning, °perceptive, perspicacious, °intelligent, °penetrating, insightful, percipient, °wise, °sensitive, °discriminating; °alert, °aware, on the qui vive

adapt *v.* **1** °suit, °fit, make suitable, °qualify **2** °alter, °modify, °change, remodel, °tailor, reshape, °shape, °fashion; °adjust, °accommodate, °accustom, acclimatize *or* acclimate, habituate

adaptable *adj.* °flexible, °pliable, pliant, compliant, accommodative, °tractable, malleable, ductile, °versatile; alterable, °changeable

adaptation *n.* **1** °fitting, suiting, modifying, adjusting, conversion **2** modification, °change, °adjustment, °accommodation, reworking, customization, °alteration

add *v.* **1** °join, °unite, °combine, annex **2** °total, °sum, °sum up, °combine, count up, °reckon, *US* tote (up), *Brit* °tot (up) **3** °continue, °go on **4** ***add to.*** °increase, °enlarge, °amplify, augment, °supplement

addict *n.* **1** °(habitual) user, *Slang* junkie, dopefiend, doper, °head, pothead, acid-head, pill popper, tripper, *Chiefly US* hophead **2** °devotee, aficionado, °fan, °admirer, °follower, adherent, °supporter, °enthusiast, *Colloq* buff, °hound, °fiend, groupie, *Slang* °freak, °bug, nut, teeny-bopper

addition *n.* **1** adding, joining, putting together, uniting, combining **2** totaling, adding up, summing up, summation, counting up, °reckoning, *US* toting up, *Brit* totting up **3** addendum, appendix, appendage, °supplement, °increment, augmentation, °extension **4** °extension, ell, *US* annex, wing, *Brit* annexe —*prep.* **5** ***in addition to.*** as well as, °besides, beyond, over and above —*adv. phr.* **6** ***in addition.*** °moreover, furthermore, additionally, °besides, withal, °to boot, in *or* into the bargain, too, also, as well

address *n.* **1** °speech, °talk, discourse, °oration, °lecture; °sermon **2** °location, °whereabouts —*v.* **3** speak *or* talk to; deliver *or* give a speech to; °lecture **4** °greet, °hail, accost, °approach **5** ***address oneself to.*** devote *or* direct *or* apply oneself to

adept *adj.* **1** °versed, °proficient, skilled, well-skilled, °expert, °accomplished, °skillful, adroit, dexterous *or* dextrous, °able,

°masterful, masterly, °polished —*n.* 2 °expert, °master, °specialist, °authority, *Colloq* °dab hand, old hand

adequate *adj.* 1 °sufficient, °enough, °ample; °satisfactory, °fitting, °equal, °suitable 2 °passable, °fair, fair to middling, middling, °average, °tolerable, °(barely) acceptable, °(barely) satisfactory, all right, °competent, not (at all) bad, °so-so, *Colloq* OK *or* okay, up to snuff, not that *or* too bad, no great shakes 3 °equal, °suitable, suited, °fitted, up, °proper, °qualified, °competent, good enough

adjoining *adj.* °neighboring, contiguous (to), adjacent (to), abutting, bordering; next (to)

adjust *v.* 1 set right, °arrange, °settle, harmonize, °reconcile, °resolve, set *or* put to rights; arbitrate, mediate; redress, °rectify, °correct, °patch up 2 °change, °alter, °modify, °regulate, °set 3 °adapt (to), accommodate (oneself) (to), accustom (oneself) (to); get used (to), acclimatize *or* acclimate (to), reconcile (oneself) (to) 4 put in order, °arrange, rearrange, close *or* fasten *or* zip *or* button (up)

adjustment *n.* 1 adjusting, altering, °alteration, °setting, regulating, °regulation, setting *or* putting right *or* aright *or* to rights, correcting, °correction, calibrating, calibration; tuning 2 °arrangement, °balance, coordination, °order, alignment, °harmony, harmonization

administer *v.* 1 administrate, °manage, °control, °run, °direct, °conduct, superintend, °supervise, °oversee 2 °execute, °carry on, °carry out; °apply, °implement, °prosecute 3 °dispense, °supply, °furnish, °give (out), °provide (with), mete out, °distribute, °deliver, °deal, °hand out

administration *n.* 1 °management, °direction, °conduct, supervision, °oversight, superintendence, °regulation, °charge 2 °authority, °management, *US* °government 3 dispensation, administering, supplying, furnishing, °provision, °delivery, °distribution, °application

admirable *adj.* wonderful, awe-inspiring, °excellent, °estimable, °splendid, °marvelous, °superior, °first-rate, first-class, °of the first water, °great, °fine, *Colloq* top-drawer, rip-snorting, A-1 *or* A-one, *Brit* smashing, °magic

admiration *n.* °wonder, awe; °delight, °pleasure; °esteem, °regard, °appreciation, °respect

admire *v.* 1 wonder *or* marvel (at), °delight in 2 °esteem, regard *or* respect highly, °look up to, °revere, °idolize, °venerate, °worship

admirer *n.* 1 °devotee, aficionado, °fan, °supporter, °enthusiast, adherent, °follower, *Slang* groupie 2 beau, °suitor; °lover, °sweetheart, °darling

admission *n.* 1 access, °admittance, entrée, °entry 2 °reception, acceptance, °appointment, °institution, induction, °installation, investiture 3 acknowledging, °acknowledgment, allowing, °allowance, admitting, °admittance, conceding, concession 4 °acknowledgment, confession, concession, °profession, °declaration, disclosure, affirmation, concession, divulgence *or* divulgement, °revelation 5 ticket, (entry *or* entrance) fee, °tariff

admit *v.* 1 °let in, allow to enter, take *or* allow in; °accept, °receive 2 °allow, °permit, °grant, °brook, °tolerate 3 °accept, °concede, acquiesce, °allow, °grant, °accept, °recognize, take cognizance of 4 °confess, own, °concede, divulge, °reveal, °acknowledge, °declare

admittance *n.* leave *or* permission to enter, °entry, entering, °entrance, access, entrée

adolescent *n.* 1 °teenager, °youth, °juvenile, °minor, °stripling, youngster, *US* teen, *Colloq* kid; *Slang* teeny-bopper —*adj.* 2 teenaged, °young, youthful, maturing, pubescent; °immature, °puerile, °juvenile

adopt *v.* 1 °take (in), °accept, take *or* accept as one's own 2 °take, take up *or* on *or* over, °embrace, espouse; arrogate, °appropriate

adorable *adj.* °lovable, °beloved, loved, °darling, °sweet, °dear; °delightful, appealing, °attractive, charming, captivating, °fetching

adore *v.* 1 °esteem, °honor, °respect, °admire; °idolize, dote on 2 °worship, °venerate, °reverence, °revere, °exalt; °hallow 3 °love, be in love with, °cherish, °fancy, °revere, adulate, *Colloq* have a crush on, carry the *or* a torch for

adult *adj.* 1 °mature, grown up, full-grown, matured, of age —*n.* 2 grown-up

adulterate *v.* °falsify, °corrupt, °alloy, °debase, °water (down), °weaken, °dilute, bastardize, °contaminate, °pollute, °taint, *Colloq* °doctor; *Slang US* °cut

advance *v.* 1 move *or* put *or* push *or* go forward; °approach 2 °further, °promote, °forward, °help, °aid, °abet, °assist, °benefit, °improve; °contribute to 3 go *or* move forward, °move (onward), °go on, °proceed, °get ahead 4 °hasten, accelerate, °speed 5 move up, °promote 6 prepay, °lend —*n.* 7 °progress, °development, forward movement; °improvement, betterment; °headway 8 °rise, °increase, °appreciation 9 prepayment, °deposit; °loan 10 ***in advance.*** (a) beforehand, °ahead (of time), °before (b) °before, °in front (of), °ahead (of), beyond

advantage *n.* 1 °superiority, °upper hand, dominance, °edge, head start; °sway; *Colloq US and New Zealand* °drop 2 °gain, °profit, °benefit, °interest; °asset, betterment, °improvement, advancement; °use, °usefulness, utility, °help, °service 3 ***to advantage.*** °better, °(more) favorably, advantageously

advantageous *adj.* °profitable, °worthwhile, °gainful, °opportune, °beneficial, °favorable, °useful, valuable

adventure *n.* 1 °exploit, escapade, °danger, °peril; °affair, °undertaking, °feat, °deed; °experience, °incident, °event, °occurrence,

°happening, °episode 2 °speculation, °hazard, °chance, °risk, °venture, °enterprise —*v.* 3 °venture, °hazard, °risk, imperil, °endanger, °jeopardize, °threaten 4 °dare, wager, °bet, °gamble, °stake, try one's luck, *Brit* punt

adventurer *n.* 1 adventuress, soldier of fortune, swashbuckler, °hero, °heroine, °daredevil; °mercenary 2 adventuress, °cheat, °swindler, charlatan, trickster, °rogue, °scoundrel, knave; cad, bounder, °philanderer, fortune hunter, opportunist

adventurous *adj.* °daring, °rash, °brash, °reckless, devil-may-care, °bold, °foolhardy, °hazardous, °risky, °daredevil, °venturesome, adventuresome, temerarious, °audacious, °bold, °intrepid, °brave, °courageous

adversary *n.* 1 foe, °enemy, °opponent, °antagonist, °competitor, °rival —*adj.* 2 °opposed, °hostile, antagonistic, competitive

advertisement *n.* 1 °notice, handbill, blurb, broadside, °bill, °circular, °brochure, °poster, placard, *affiche,* classified, commercial, °spot (announcement), *US* car card, billboard, *Colloq* ad, °plug, *Brit* advert 2 advertising, °promotion; publicity; °propaganda, ballyhoo, hoopla, *Colloq* hype, beating the drum, *US* puffery

advice *n.* 1 °counsel, °guidance, °recommendation, °suggestion, °opinion, °view; °warning, admonition, *Technical* paraenesis 2 °information, °news, °intelligence, °notice, notification; communication

advisable *adj.* recommendable, °expedient, °prudent, °practical, °sensible, °sound, °seemly, °judicious, °wise, °intelligent, °smart, °proper, °politic

advise *v.* 1 °counsel, °guide, °recommend, °suggest, commend; °caution, admonish, °warn; °urge, °encourage 2 °tell, °announce (to), °inform, apprise, °register, °make known (to), °intimate (to), °notify

adviser *n.* °counselor, mentor, °guide, cicerone, °counsel, °consultant, confidant(e)

advisory *adj.* 1 consultive, consultative, counseling, hortatory, monitory, admonitory, *Technical* paraenetic(al) —*n.* 2 °bulletin, °notice, °warning, admonition, °prediction

advocate *v.* 1 °support, °champion, °back, °endorse, °uphold, °recommend, stand behind, °second, °favor, speak *or* plead *or* argue for *or* in favor of —*n.* 2 °supporter, °champion, °backer, upholder, °second, exponent, °proponent, °patron, defender, apologist 3 °lawyer, °counsel; intercessor; *US* attorney, counselor-at-law, *Brit* barrister, solicitor

aesthete *n.* connoisseur, art lover, lover of beauty, aesthetician *or* esthetician, *US* tastemaker

aesthetic *adj.* 1 artistic, °tasteful, °beautiful; in good *or* °excellent, etc. taste 2 °sensitive, artistic, °refined, °discriminating, °cultivated

affair *n.* 1 °matter, °topic, °issue; °business, °concern, °interest, °undertaking, °activity 2 °concern, °business, *US slang* beeswax 3 °event, °business, °occurrence, °happening, °proceeding, °incident, °operation 4 Also, *affaire.* °love affair, amour, °romance, °intrigue, °fling, °liaison, °relationship, *affaire d'amour, affaire de coeur*

affect[1] *v.* 1 °attack, act upon, °lay hold of, °strike 2 °move, °stir, °impress, °touch, °strike; °perturb, °upset, °trouble, °agitate 3 °influence, °sway, °change, °transform, °modify, °alter

affect[2] *v.* 1 °assume, °adopt, °put on, °pretend (to), feign, °sham, °fake, °counterfeit 2 °choose, °select; °use, °wear, °adopt

affectation *n.* 1 affectedness, pretentiousness, artificiality, insincerity, posturing 2 °pretense, simulation, false display, °show, °front, °pose, °pretension, façade; °act, °airs

affected *adj.* 1 °unnatural, °artificial, °specious, °stilted, °stiff, °studied, °awkward, nonnatural, contrived, °mannered 2 °pretended, simulated, °hollow, °assumed, feigned, °fake, faked, °false, °counterfeit, °insincere, °spurious, °sham, °bogus, *Colloq* phoney *or US also* phony 3 °pretentious, °pompous, high-sounding, °mincing, niminy-piminy, *Colloq* la-di-da 4 attacked, seized, afflicted, °stricken, gripped, touched; °diseased, laid hold of 5 afflicted, moved, touched, stirred, distressed, troubled, °upset, °hurt; influenced, swayed, impressed, struck, played *or* worked *or* acted upon

affection *n.* goodwill, °(high) regard, °liking, fondness, °attachment, loving attachment, tenderness, °warmth, °love

affectionate *adj.* °fond, loving, °tender, caring, °devoted, doting, °warm

affiliated *adj.* associated; °attached, connected, combined, °united, joined

affinity *n.* 1 °relationship, °kinship, closeness, °alliance, connection *or Brit* connexion; °sympathy, °rapport 2 friendliness, fondness, °liking, °leaning, °bent, °inclination, °taste, °partiality, attractiveness, °attraction

afflict *v.* °affect, °bother, °distress, °oppress, °trouble, °torment

affliction *n.* 1 °hardship, °misery, °misfortune, °distress, °ordeal, °trial, tribulation, adversity, °suffering, °woe, °pain, °grief, °torment, wretchedness 2 °curse, °disease, °calamity, °catastrophe, °disaster, °plague, °scourge, tribulation, °trouble

afford *v.* 1 have the means, be able *or* rich enough, °manage, bear the expense, °pay, °provide 2 °give, °spare, °give up, °contribute, °donate; °sacrifice 3 °yield, °give, °supply, °produce, °provide, °furnish, °grant, °offer; give forth

afoul *adv.* ***afoul of.*** entangled with, in trouble with, in conflict with, at odds with

afraid *adj.* 1 °fearful, frightened, °scared, intimidated, apprehensive, lily-livered, white-livered, terrified, °panic-stricken, °faint-hearted, weak-kneed, °timid, timorous, °nervous, °anxious, jittery, °on edge, edgy, °jumpy; °cowardly, pusillanimous, craven,

Colloq yellow **2** °sorry, °unhappy, °regretful, °apologetic, rueful

age *n.* **1** lifetime, duration, length of existence; lifespan **2** °maturity, °discretion; °majority, adulthood, seniority **3** °period, °stage, °time **4** long time, aeon *or, esp. US,* eon; years **5** °era, epoch, °period, °time *—v.* **6** grow old(er), °mature, °ripen

aged *adj.* °old, °elderly, superannuated, °ancient, age-old, °gray, °venerable

agency *n.* °means, °medium, instrumentality; intervention, intercession, °action, intermediation; °operation, °mechanism, °force, °power, °activity, working(s), °energy

agent *n.* **1** °representative, °intermediary, °go-between, °proxy, emissary, °delegate, spokesman, spokeswoman, spokesperson, °deputy, °substitute, surrogate, °advocate, emissary, legate, °envoy, °factor **2** °factor, °agency, °cause, °means, °force, °instrument, °power, °vehicle, °ingredient, catalyst

aggravate *v.* **1** °worsen, °intensify, exacerbate, °heighten, °magnify, °increase; °inflame **2** °exasperate, °frustrate; °anger, incense, °infuriate; °provoke, °irritate, nettle, rile, vex, °annoy, °harass, hector, °bother; embitter, °rankle, *Colloq* peeve, needle, get on one's nerves; *Slang Brit* give (someone) aggro

aggression *n.* **1** aggressiveness, °hostility, belligerence, combativeness, *Slang Brit* aggro **2** °attack, °assault, onslaught, °invasion, encroachment

aggressive *adj.* **1** combative, °warlike, °martial, °belligerent, bellicose, °pugnacious, °quarrelsome, disputatious, litigious; °hostile, unfriendly **2** °forward, °assertive, °forceful, °bold, *Colloq* °pushy

aggressor *n.* °assailant, attacker, instigator, initiator, provoker; °belligerent

agile *adj.* **1** °nimble, °quick, °brisk, °swift, °active, °lively, lithe, limber, spry, °sprightly **2** °keen, °sharp, °alert, dexterous *or* dextrous, °resourceful, °acute

agitate *v.* **1** °excite, °arouse, °rouse, °move, °perturb, °stir up, disquiet, °fluster, °ruffle, °rattle, disconcert, °discomfit, unsettle, °upset, °rock, °unnerve, °shake (up), *Colloq* discombobulate **2** °push, °press, °campaign; °promote **3** °stir (up), churn, °disturb, °shake, roil

agitated *adj.* moved, stirred (up), shaken (up), rattled, °disturbed, °upset, °nervous, perturbed, jittery, °jumpy, uneasy, °ill at ease, fidgety, disquieted, discomfited, ruffled, flustered, °unsettled, unnerved, wrought-up, discomposed, °disconcerted, aroused, roused, °excited, *Colloq* discombobulated

agitation *n.* **1** shaking, °disturbance, churning, °stirring, turbulence **2** °excitement, arousal, rabble-rousing, °provocation, stirring-up, °incitement, °ferment, stimulation, overstimulation, commotion

agitator *n.* activist, °rabble-rouser, incendiary, *agent provocateur,* insurrectionist, °troublemaker, demagogue, firebrand

agog *adj.* °eager, avid, °keen, °enthusiastic, °expectant, °impatient, °breathless

agonizing *adj.* °painful, distressful, distressing, °harrowing, torturous, racking, °excruciating, tortured, tormented

agony *n.* °anguish, °trouble, °distress, °suffering, °misery, wretchedness, °pain, pangs, °woe, °torment, throes, torture, °affliction

agree *v.* **1** concur, °conform, come *or* go together, °coincide, °correspond, harmonize, °reconcile; °accord, °tally, *Colloq* jibe **2** Often, ***agree on or upon or to.*** °consent to, °favor, acquiesce in *or* to, °approve of, accede to, settle (on *or* upon), assent to **3** °concede, °grant, °consent, °admit, °approve, °allow, °accept, concur; accede (to), acquiesce (in *or* to), assent (to), see eye to eye **4** ***agree with.*** °suit

agreeable *adj.* **1** °pleasing, °pleasant, enjoyable, °pleasurable, °favorable, °delightful, °satisfying, °satisfactory, °good, °nice, °acceptable; to one's liking *or* taste **2** in favor, approving, °willing, consenting, acquiescent, complying, compliant, in agreement *or* accord, concurring, amenable, °sympathetic, well-disposed; °accommodating, accommodative

agreement *n.* **1** °understanding, covenant, °treaty, °pact, °accord, °compact, °settlement, concordat; °contract, °bargain, *Colloq* °deal **2** concord, °harmony, compatibility, °unity, concurrence, unanimity

ahead *adv.* **1** at the *or* in front, °in advance, in the lead *or* vanguard, up ahead, °before, to the fore **2** °winning **3** °onward, °forward, on

aid *v.* **1** °help, °support, °assist, °facilitate, °back, °abet, °uphold, °promote; succor, °relieve, °subsidize *—n.* **2** °help, °support, °assistance, °backing, °relief, °benefit, °service, succor, °comfort **3** funding, °subsidy, subvention; grant money, °grant, grant-in-aid, °scholarship

aide *n.* aide-de-camp, °assistant, helper, coadjutor; good *or* strong right arm, right hand, right-hand man; °colleague, °partner, °ally, °comrade, comrade-in-arms, *US* °cohort, *Colloq* man Friday, girl Friday, *US* gal *or* guy Friday

ail *v.* **1** °trouble, °afflict, °affect, °bother, °distress, °upset, °worry, make ill *or* sick, °pain, °hurt **2** °suffer, be *or* feel ill *or* sick *or* poorly *or* unwell *or* indisposed, *US* be sick

ailment *n.* °illness, sickness, °affliction, °disease, °disorder, indisposition, malady; °disability, °infirmity; malaise, queasiness

aim *v.* **1** °direct, °point, °focus, °train, °level **2** ***aim at.*** focus on, have designs on, °aspire to, plan for *or* on, set one's sights on, °seek, strive for, try for, °wish, °want **3** °seek, °intend, °plan *—n.* **4** °direction, pointing, °focus, focusing *or* focussing, sighting **5** °purpose, °goal, °ambition, °desire, °aspiration, °object, °end, °objective, °target, °intent, °intention, °plan

aimless *adj.* **1** °purposeless, °pointless, °frivolous 2 undirected, °erratic, °chance, °haphazard, °random, vagrant, wayward; °wanton

air *n.* 1 °atmosphere, ambiance *or* ambience, aura, °climate, °feeling, °sense, °mood, °quality 2 °breeze, zephyr, °current, °draft; °breath, °puff, °wind 3 °manner, °style, °appearance, °aura, °feeling, °bearing, °quality, flavor 4 °melody, °tune, °song, music 5 ***airs.*** °pretension, °pretense, °show, affectedness; haughtiness, hauteur, °arrogance, °superiority, superciliousness —*v.* 6 ventilate, °freshen, °refresh, aerate 7 °show off, °parade, °display, °exhibit; °publish, °broadcast, °circulate, °publicize, make public *or* known, °reveal, °expose, °disclose, divulge, °tell, °express, °declare

akin *adj.* ***akin (to).*** °related (to), allied *or* connected *or* affiliated (to *or* with), associated (with), germane (to), °like, °alike, °similar (to)

alarm *n.* 1 °warning, °alert, danger *or* distress signal; tocsin, bell, gong, °siren, whistle, horn 2 °fear, °fright, apprehension, °dismay, trepidation, °terror, °dread, °anxiety, °excitement, °panic, consternation, °distress, nervousness, uneasiness, °discomfort —*v.* 3 °frighten, °scare, °daunt, °startle, °terrify, °panic; °unnerve, °dismay, °disturb, °upset

alcohol *n.* °spirits, °liquor, °the bottle, the cup that cheers, demon rum, John Barleycorn, *Colloq* °booze, hard stuff, °juice, °moonshine, firewater, *Slang* rotgut, *US and Canadian* hooch

alcoholic *adj.* 1 °intoxicating, inebriating —*n.* 2 drunkard, °drunk, dipsomaniac, sot, toper, drinker, winebibber, serious *or* problem drinker, tippler, *Colloq* barfly, °soak, *Slang* boozer, alchy *or* alkie *or* alky, dipso, °stew, rummy, *US and Canadian* °lush, boozehound, wino

alert *adj.* 1 °awake, wide-awake, watchful, °vigilant, °attentive, heedful, °wary, °cautious, on the qui vive, °aware, on guard, on the lookout, °observant, *Colloq* on the ball, on one's toes 2 °active, °nimble, °lively, °agile, °quick, spry, °sprightly, °vivacious —*n.* 3 °lookout 4 °alarm, °warning, °signal, °siren —*v.* 5 °warn, °caution, °advise, °alarm, forewarn, °signal, °notify

alibi *n.* 1 °excuse, °explanation —*v.* 2 °excuse, °explain

alien *adj.* 1 °foreign, °strange, °exotic, °outlandish, °unfamiliar —*n.* 2 °foreigner, °stranger, outlander, °outsider, nonnative, °immigrant, °newcomer

alienate *v.* 1 Usually, ***alienate from.*** disabuse (of *or* from), wean away (from), °detach (from), °distance (from) 2 °distance, estrange

alike *adj.* 1 °similar, °akin, resembling *or* like one another, akin to *or* similar to one another, showing *or* exhibiting a resemblance —***adv.*** 2 in like manner, in the same manner *or* way, similarly, equally, uniformly, identically

alive *adj.* 1 living, °live, breathing, among the living, in the land of the living 2 ***alive to.*** sensitive *or* alert to, aware *or* conscious of, cognizant of 3 °alert, °active, °lively, °vivacious, °quick, °spirited, °animated, °brisk, spry, °sprightly, °vigorous, °energetic 4 astir, teeming, swarming, thronging, crowded, °packed, buzzing, crawling, jumping, bustling, humming, *Colloq* °lousy

allegation *n.* °charge, °accusation, °complaint; °assertion, avowal, asseveration, °claim, °declaration, °statement, deposition

allege *v.* °declare, aver, °state, assert, °charge, affirm, avow, asseverate, depose, °say

alleged *adj.* described, designated; claimed, avowed, stated; purported, °so-called, suspected, °supposed, °assumed, presumed; °hypothetical, conjectural

alliance *n.* 1 °union, confederation, °combination, °federation, °pact, °league, °association, coalition, affiliation, °connection, °bond; °unity, °affinity 2 °marriage, °affinity

allot *v.* °distribute, apportion, allocate, earmark, °assign, parcel *or* dole out, °deal (out), °divide, °share (out), °dispense

allotment *n.* °share, apportionment, °ration, °portion, °quota, °allowance, °measure

allow *v.* 1 °acknowledge, °admit, °grant, °concede, own 2 °agree to, °concede, cede to, °admit, °permit, °authorize, °entertain, °consent to 3 °permit, °let, °suffer 4 °tolerate, °stand (for), °brook, °sanction, countenance, °permit, °consider, °put up with 5 °give, let (someone) have, °appropriate, °grant, budget, earmark, °assign, allocate, °approve 6 make allowance *or* concession for, set apart *or* aside, °put aside, take into account *or* consideration; °add; °deduct

allowance *n.* 1 °permission, toleration, °tolerance, sufferance, °admission, concession, °sanction; allowing, permitting, tolerating, °suffering, sanctioning, brooking, countenancing 2 °payment, recompense, °remuneration, reimbursement, °remittance 3 °stipend, °dole, pin *or* pocket money, °quota, °ration; °pension, annuity, allocation 4 °deduction, °discount, reduction, °rebate; °credit; tret; tare 5 excuse(s), concession, °consideration

alloy *n.* 1 °mixture, °mix, °combination, °compound, composite, °blend, °amalgam, admixture; aggregate —*v.* 2 °contaminate, °pollute, °adulterate, °debase, °diminish, °impair, °vitiate 3 °change, °modify, °temper, °alter, °moderate, allay

ally *n.* 1 °comrade, confederate, collaborator, coadjutor; accessory *or* accessary, °accomplice; °associate, °partner, °friend —*v.* 2 °league, °combine, °unite, °join (up), °team (up), °side, °band together, °associate, affiliate, °collaborate, confederate

almost *adv.* °nearly, °about, °approximately, °practically, °virtually, well-nigh, bordering on, on the brink of, verging on, °on the verge of, little short of; not quite, all but; °barely, °scarcely, °hardly; *Colloq* damn near

aloft *adv.* °above, °overhead, (up) in the air, in flight, up (above); on high; heavenward, skyward
alone *adj.* **1** °unaccompanied, unescorted, °solitary, by oneself, *tout(e) seule,* °solo, unattended, unassisted; °abandoned, °desolate, °deserted **2** unequaled, °unparalleled, °unique, °singular, unexcelled, unsurpassed, without equal, °peerless, °matchless —*adv.* **3** solitarily, by oneself, °solo **4** °only, solely, exclusively, °simply, °just, °merely
aloof *adv.* **1** °apart, away, at a distance, °separate; at arm's length —*adj.* **2** °private, °reticent, °reserved, °withdrawn, °haughty, °supercilious, °standoffish, °formal, unsociable, °unsocial; °distant, °remote **3** °standoffish, °distant, °remote, °cool, °chilly, unresponsive, unfriendly, antisocial, °unapproachable; °unsympathetic, apathetic, °indifferent, undemonstrative
alter *v.* °change, °revise, °modify, °vary, °transform; °adjust, °adapt, °convert, remodel
alteration *n.* °change, modification, °revision, °transformation; °adjustment, °adaptation, conversion, remodeling
alternate *v.* **1** °rotate, °exchange, °change, interchange, °take turns, go *or* take, etc. in turn, *US* change off, interexchange **2** °succeed, be in succession *or* rotation —*adj.* **3** in rotation, °successive; every other, every second **4** °alternative, °second, other —*n.* **5** °variant, °alternative, °(second) choice, *US and Canadian* °substitute, °deputy, °stand-in, backup, °understudy; pinch hitter, *Baseball* designated hitter
alternation *n.* rotation, °succession; °exchange, interchange
alternative *adj.* **1** °alternate, °variant, (an)other, °different, additional; °substitute, surrogate —*n.* **2** °alternate, °variant, °choice, °option, °selection; °possibility; °substitute, surrogate
altogether *adv.* °entirely, °utterly, °completely, °wholly, °totally, fully, in all respects, °absolutely, °perfectly, °quite; all in all, in all
altruism *n.* selflessness, self-sacrifice, unselfishness, °philanthropy, generosity, °charity, charitableness, humanitarianism, humaneness, °benevolence, °humanity, public-spiritedness
always *adv.* **1** at all times, again and again, on all occasions, every *or* each time, each and every time, without exception, unexceptionally; °often, many times, °usually **2** °forever, continually, °ever, perpetually; unceasingly, unendingly, eternally, evermore, ever after, everlastingly, till the end of time, in perpetuity **3** °in any case, as a last resort
amalgam *n.* °mixture, °blend, °combination, °alloy, °mix, composite, admixture, °amalgamation; °compound
amalgamate *v.* °blend, °combine, °unite, °mix, °join, consolidate, °compound, °integrate, °merge
amalgamation *n.* °blend, fusion, °combination, °mixture, mingling, admixture, composite, °compound, blending, joining, consolidating, consolidation, compounding, commingling, fusing, coalescing, coalescence, °union, uniting, unification, integration, °merger, °association, °composition
amass *v.* °accumulate, °mass, pile *or* heap *or* rack up, °collect, °gather (together), °assemble, aggregate, cumulate, stock *or* store up, °hoard, °set aside
amateur *n.* **1** layman, nonprofessional, lay person, tyro; dabbler, °dilettante, bungler; *Colloq US* bush leaguer —*adj.* **2** °lay, nonprofessional, untrained; °unpaid; °dilettante, amateurish, °unprofessional, unskilled, inexpert, unskillful, °clumsy, °mediocre, °inferior, °crude, bungling, second-rate; *Colloq US* bush league
amaze *v.* °astound, °astonish, °surprise, awe, °stun, °stagger, °take aback, °floor, dumfound *or* dumbfound, confound, °nonplus, stupefy, *Colloq* flabbergast, °dazzle
amazement *n.* °astonishment, °surprise, awe, °wonder, stupefaction
amazing *adj.* astonishing, astounding, surprising, wonderful, °remarkable, °extraordinary, °marvelous, °fabulous, °stunning, °dazzling, staggering, °awesome
ambassador *n.* °envoy, °delegate, legate, emissary, °minister, plenipotentiary, diplomat; °agent, °deputy, °representative, (papal) nuncio, °messenger
ambiguity *n.* **1** equivocalness, equivocacy, amphibology *or* amphiboly; vagueness, indistinctness, uncertainty, indefiniteness, imprecision, inconclusiveness **2** equivocation, double-talk, doublespeak, equivoque; °pun, double entendre, amphibologism
ambiguous *adj.* **1** °equivocal, amphibological, amphibolic *or* amphibolous; misleading **2** °doubtful, dubious, °questionable, °obscure, °indistinct, unclear, °indefinite, indeterminate, °uncertain, undefined, °inconclusive, °uncertain, °vague, °misty, foggy, unclear; °cryptic, delphic, enigmatic(al), oracular, °mysterious, °puzzling; confusable *or* confusible **3** °unreliable, undependable
ambition *n.* **1** °hunger, °thirst, craving, °appetite, arrivisme **2** °drive, °enterprise, °energy, °initiative, °vigor, °enthusiasm, zeal, avidity, *Colloq* get-up-and-go **3** °goal, °object, °aim, °aspiration, °hope, °desire, °dream, °objective, °wish, °purpose
ambitious *adj.* **1** aspiring, °hopeful; °enthusiastic **2** °energetic, °enterprising, °vigorous, zealous, °enthusiastic, °eager **3** °greedy, °avaricious, overzealous, overambitious, *Colloq* °pushy, yuppie
ambush *n.* **1** °trap, ambuscade *or Archaic* ambuscado —*v.* **2** lie in wait, °trap, °waylay, ensnare, entrap, °lurk, ambuscade, °intercept, *Colloq* lay in wait, *US* bushwhack
amend *v.* **1** °reform, change for the better, °improve, °better, ameliorate **2** °correct, emend, emendate, °rectify, set to rights, °repair, °fix, °revise
amendment *n.* **1** °correction, emendation, reformation, °change, °alteration, rectifica-

tion, °repair, °reform, °improvement, amelioration, betterment, enhancement **2** °attachment, °addition, addendum; clause, paragraph; °alteration

amends *n.* ***make amends.*** °compensate, °pay, °repay, make reparation *or* restitution, recompense, redress, °remedy, °requite

amiable *adj.* °friendly, well-disposed, °kindly, °kind, °amicable, °agreeable, congenial, °genial, °warm, winsome, °winning, affable, °agreeable, °pleasant, °obliging, °tractable, approachable, °benign, °good-natured, good-hearted, kindhearted; °affectionate

amicable *adj.* °friendly, °amiable, congenial, °harmonious, °brotherly, kindhearted; °warm, °courteous, °cordial, °polite, °civil, °pleasant; °peaceful, °peaceable

amid *prep.* mid, in *or* into the middle *or* midst *or* center of, amongst, °among, surrounded by, in the thick of, *Literary* amidst

amiss *adj.* **1** °wrong, °at fault, awry, °out of order, °faulty, °defective, °improper, °untoward; astray, °erroneous, fallacious, °confused, °incorrect, °off *—adv.* **2** °wrong, awry, °badly, °poorly, imperfectly; inopportunely, unfavorably, unpropitiously **3** wrongly, improperly, °badly; incorrectly, inappropriately **4** ***take or think (it) amiss.*** °mistake, °misinterpret, °misunderstand, °take offense (at)

among *prep.* **1** amongst, °amid, amidst, mid, in the midst *or* middle *or* center of, surrounded by **2** amongst, to each *or* all (of)

amount *v.* **1** ***amount to.*** **(a)** add up to, °total, aggregate, come (up) to **(b)** °become, develop into *—n.* **2** °quantity, °volume, °mass, °expanse, °bulk, °supply, °lot; °number; °magnitude **3** °(sum) total, aggregate, °extent, °entirety

ample *adj.* **1** °broad, °wide, °spacious, °extensive, °expansive, °great **2** wide-ranging, °extensive, °broad **3** °abundant, °extensive, °fruitful **4** °abundant, °full, °complete, °plentiful, copious, °generous, °substantial; °sufficient, °adequate, °enough **5** °liberal, unsparing, unstinted, unstinting, °generous, °substantial, °large, °lavish **6** copious, °full, °broad, °detailed, °extensive, extended, °thorough

amplify *v.* **1** broaden, °widen, °extend, °increase, °expand (on), °enlarge (on), expatiate on, °detail; °add to, augment, °supplement **2** °exaggerate, °overstate, °magnify, °stretch **3** °enlarge (on), °elaborate (on), °stretch, °lengthen, °detail, °embellish, embroider

amply *adv.* **1** °widely, broadly, extensively, greatly, expansively **2** to a great extent, °largely, fully, abundantly **3** abundantly, fully, copiously **4** fully, °well, liberally, unstintingly, generously, °richly, °substantially, lavishly; sufficiently

amulet *n.* °charm, °talisman, good-luck piece; °fetish

amuse *v.* **1** °divert, °entertain, please, °beguile, °interest, °occupy **2** make laugh, °delight, °cheer, *Colloq* °tickle

amusement *n.* **1** °entertainment, °diversion, °recreation, °pleasure, °relaxation, °distraction, °enjoyment, °fun, °sport, °joke, °lark, beguilement **2** °entertainment, °diversion, divertissement, °recreation, °distraction, °pastime; °game, °sport

anachronism *n.* misdate, misdating, misapplication; antedate, antedating, prochronism; postdate, postdating, parachronism

analysis *n.* **1** °examination, °investigation, °study, °scrutiny, enquiry *or* inquiry, dissection, assay, °breakdown, °division **2** °interpretation, °opinion, °judgment, °criticism, critique; °review

analyze *v.* **1** take apart *or* to pieces, °separate, dissect, °break down, anatomize **2** °examine, °investigate, °study, °scrutinize, °interpret; assess, °evaluate, critique, °criticize, °review; °estimate, assay, °test

ancestor *n.* forebear, forefather; °forerunner, °precursor, antecedent, *Formal* °progenitor, primogenitor

anchor *n.* **1** mooring **2** °stability, °security, °mainstay, °support, stabilizer, holdfast, sheet anchor *—v.* **3** °attach, affix, °secure, °moor, °fix, °fasten; °pin, rivet, °glue

ancient *adj.* **1** °old, °bygone, °past, °former, earlier, *Literary* olden **2** °old, °antique, antediluvian, °primitive, °prehistoric, primeval, primordial, Noachian, *Literary* Ogygian **3** °old, °old-fashioned, archaic, °timeworn, °aged, aging, °obsolescent, °antiquated, °elderly, °venerable, °gray, hoary, superannuated, °obsolete, fossil, fossilized

anger *n.* **1** °rage, wrath, ire, °fury, pique, spleen, choler; °antagonism, irritation, vexation, °indignation, °displeasure, °annoyance, irritability, °resentment, °outrage *—v.* **2** °enrage, °infuriate, °madden, pique, incense, raise one's hackles, make one's blood boil, rile, °gall; °annoy, °irritate, vex, nettle, °displease, °exasperate, °provoke

angle[1] *n.* **1** °slant, °oblique, corner, °edge, intersection; °bend, cusp, °point, apex, °projection **2** °slant, °point of view, °aspect, °viewpoint, °standpoint, °approach, °position, °side, °perspective

angle[2] *v.* ***angle for.*** fish for; °look for, °seek, be after, try for, °hunt for

angry *adj.* **1** enraged, °furious, irate, °resentful, ireful, wrathful, piqued, incensed, infuriated, fuming; irritated, °irritable, annoyed, vexed, irascible, provoked, °indignant, exasperated, splenetic, *Literary* wroth, *Colloq* livid, hot under the collar, on the warpath, (all) steamed up, up in arms, °mad **2** °inflamed, irritated, °sore, smarting

anguish *n.* **1** °suffering, °pain, °agony, °torment, torture, °misery **2** °suffering, °grief, °distress, °woe, °anxiety *—v.* **3** °disturb, °upset, °distress, °afflict, °trouble; °torment, torture

animal *n.* **1** °creature, being, mammal, °organism **2** °beast, °brute, °savage, °monster *—adj.* **3** zoological, zooid, animalistic **4** °physical, fleshly, °sensual, °gross, °coarse,

°unrefined, uncultured, uncultivated, °rude, °carnal, °crude, bestial, beastlike, subhuman

animate *v.* **1** °activate, °enliven, invigorate, °stimulate, inspirit, °excite, °stir, °vitalize, °spark, vivify, revitalize, breathe life into, innervate **2** °inspire, inspirit, °stimulate, actuate, °move, °motivate, °incite, °rouse, °arouse, °excite, °fire (up), °encourage, °energize, °vitalize, spur (on *or* onward(s)) —*adj.* **3** °lively, °spirited, °vivacious, °animated, °quick **4** °alive, °moving, breathing, *Archaic* °quick

animated *adj.* **1** °lively, °quick, °spirited, °active, °vivacious, °energetic, °vigorous, °excited, °ebullient, °enthusiastic, °dynamic, vibrant, °ardent, enlivened, °passionate, °impassioned, °fervent **2** °mechanical, automated, °lifelike, °moving

animation *n.* **1** °spirit, spiritedness, °vitality, °dash, élan, °zest, °fervor, °verve, liveliness, °fire, °ardor, ardency, exhilaration, °intensity, °energy, °pep, °dynamism, °enthusiasm, °excitement, °vigor, vivacity **2** enlivenment, liveliness, energizing, invigoration, enlivening, innervation

animosity *n.* °hostility, °antagonism, antipathy, °ill will, malevolence, enmity, hatred, animus, °loathing, detestation, °contempt; bad blood, malice, °bitterness, acrimony, °resentment, °rancor

announce *v.* **1** °proclaim, °make public, °make known, set *or* put forth, °put out, °publish, advertise, °publicize, promulgate, °broadcast, herald; °circulate; °tell, °reveal, °disclose, divulge, °declare, °propound **2** °intimate, °suggest, hint at, °signal **3** °declare, °tell, °state, aver, assert, asseverate; °notify; °confirm **4** foretell, betoken, augur, portend, presage, °harbinger, herald, °signal; °precede

announcement *n.* **1** °declaration, °pronouncement, °proclamation, °statement **2** notification, °notice, °word **3** commercial, °advertisement, advert, ad, °spot **4** °report, °bulletin, communiqué, disclosure

announcer *n.* presenter, master of ceremonies, MC, emcee, *Literary or Brit hist* Master of the Revels; °reporter, anchorman, anchorwoman, anchorperson, °anchor; newsreader, newscaster, sportscaster, weatherman, weatherperson

annoy *v.* **1** °irritate, °bother, °irk, vex, nettle, get on (someone's) nerves, °exasperate, °provoke, incense, rile, °madden, *Colloq* °get at **2** °pester, °harass, harry, badger, °nag, °plague, °molest, bedevil, *Colloq* °bug, needle, hassle, *Slang* get up someone's nose

annoyance *n.* **1** irritation, °bother, vexation, exasperation, pique, aggravation, *Colloq* botheration **2** °nuisance, °pest, irritant, °bore, *Colloq* °pain, pain in the neck *or US* ass *or Brit* arse

answer *n.* **1** °reply, °response; rejoinder, °retort, riposte, *Colloq* comeback **2** *Law* °defense, counter-statement, °plea, °explanation; *Technical* °declaration, replication, rejoinder, surrejoinder, rebutter *or* rebuttal, surrebutter *or* surrebuttal **3** °solution, °explanation —*v.* **4** °reply, °respond; °retort, rejoin, riposte **5** °satisfy, °fulfill, suffice for, °meet, °suit, °serve, °fit, °fill, conform to, correlate with **6** ***answer back.*** talk back (to) **7** ***answer for.*** **(a)** be accountable *or* responsible *or* answerable for, be to blame for; take *or* undertake responsibility for; °sponsor, °support, °guarantee **(b)** make amends for, atone for, suffer the consequences of **(c)** take *or* accept the blame for

antagonism *n.* **1** °opposition, °animosity, enmity, °rancor, °hostility, antipathy **2** °conflict, °rivalry, °discord, °dissension, °friction, °strife; contention

antagonist *n.* °adversary, °opponent, °enemy, foe; contender, °competitor, °competition, °opposition

anticipate *v.* **1** °forestall, °intercept, °preclude, obviate, °prevent; nullify **2** foretell, °forecast, °predict, °prophesy, foretaste, °foresee **3** °expect, °look forward to, prepare for; count *or* reckon on

anticipation *n.* **1** °expectation, expectancy; °hope **2** foreknowledge, precognition; °intuition, presentiment, °feeling; °foreboding, apprehension

antidote *n.* antitoxin, antiserum, antivenin; counteractant, counterirritant; °cure, °remedy, °specific; medication, °medicine, °drug, medicament, *Technical* alexipharmic

antiquated *adj.* °old, °old-fashioned, outmoded, °passé, out-of-date, dated, archaic, °obsolescent, °antique, °obsolete, °quaint, °ancient, antediluvian, mediaeval *or* medieval, °primitive; °extinct; *Colloq* old hat

antique *adj.* **1** °old, °old-fashioned; °antiquated, outmoded, °passé, out-of-date, °obsolete —*n.* **2** collectable *or* collectible, collector's item, bibelot, objet d'art, objet de vertu, object *or* article of vertu, heirloom, curio, °rarity

anxiety *n.* **1** °solicitude, °concern, uneasiness, disquiet, nervousness, °worry, °dread, angst, apprehension, °foreboding **2** °appetite, °hunger, °thirst, °desire, °eagerness, °longing, °ache, °concern

anxious *adj.* **1** troubled, uneasy, disquieted, °uncertain, apprehensive; °solicitous, °concerned, °worried, distressed, °disturbed, °nervous, °tense, °fretful, °on edge, °restless, edgy, perturbed, °upset; °wary, °cautious, °careful, watchful **2** °desirous, °eager, °keen, °enthusiastic, °ardent, °agog, avid, yearning, °longing, aching, °impatient

apart *adv.* **1** aside, to one side, by oneself, at a distance, °separate, °separately **2** °separately, distinctly, °individually, °singly, °alone, independently **3** to *or* into pieces, asunder **4** ***apart from.*** °except for, excepting, separately from, aside from, °besides, but for, not including, excluding, not counting

aperture *n.* °opening, °space, °gap, cleft, °chink, °crevice, °crack, fissure, °hole, chasm

apologetic *adj.* °regretful, °sorry, contrite,

°remorseful, °penitent, rueful, °repentant, conscience-stricken

apologize *v.* **1** beg *or* ask pardon, express regret(s), feel sorry *or* regretful *or* remorse(ful) **2** make *or* give excuses *or* explanation(s), °defend, °justify, °vindicate, espouse

appall *v.* °dismay, °shock, °discomfit, °unnerve, °intimidate, °terrify, °frighten, °scare, °horrify, °alarm, °startle, °daunt

apparatus *n.* °equipment, requisites, °tool, °instrument, utensil, °device, °implement, °machine, machinery, °gear, °paraphernalia, °tackle, °outfit; appliance, *Colloq* °contraption, gadgetry, °gadget

apparel *n.* clothing, attire, °clothes, °dress, raiment, °garments, *Colloq* °gear, °rags, glad rags, duds, *Slang US* threads

apparent *adj.* **1** °evident, °plain, °clear, °obvious, °patent, unmistakable; °conspicuous, °marked, °manifest, °visible, °discernible **2** appearing, °seeming, °illusory, ostensible, °superficial, °outward

apparently *adv.* **1** °evidently, plainly, °clearly, °obviously, patently, °manifestly **2** °seemingly, °ostensibly, superficially, °outwardly

appeal *v.* **1** entreat, supplicate, °solicit, °plead, °petition, °apply, °sue; °beseech, °beg, implore, °pray **2** °attract, be attractive to, allure, please; invite, °tempt, °beguile, °fascinate, °interest —*n.* **3** °application, °suit; entreaty, °call, °request, °supplication, solicitation, °petition, °plea; °prayer **4** °attraction, °lure, allurement, °charm, °fascination

appear *v.* **1** come forth, become visible *or* manifest, put in an appearance, °materialize, °surface, °emerge, °rise, °arise, °come up, enter (into) the picture, show oneself, °turn up, °arrive, °come, *Colloq* crop *or* show up; *Slang* °show **2** °perform, °act, °play, take the role *or* part of **3** °occur, °happen, °come up, be included, °figure, °arrive **4** °seem, be clear *or* evident *or* plain *or* manifest; °look **5** be published, °come out, become available

appearance *n.* **1** °arrival, advent; °presence; °publication **2** °aspect, look(s), °form; mien, °air, demeanor; °bearing, °manner **3** °display, °show **4** °semblance, °show, °hint, °suggestion; °illusion

appetite *n.* **1** °desire, °inclination, proclivity, °tendency, °disposition, °bent, °preference, °liking, predilection, °zest, fondness, °love, zeal; °enthusiasm; °taste, °relish; *Formal* appetency, appetence **2** craving, °hunger, °thirst, °desire, keenness, hankering, yearning, °longing, °passion, °demand, *Formal* edacity

applaud *v.* **1** °approve, express approval, °clap, °cheer, give (someone) a hand, *Colloq* °root (for) **2** express approval of, °praise, °laud, °hail, commend

applause *n.* clapping, acclamation, acclaim, éclat; cheering, cheers; °approval, commendation, approbation, °praise, °kudos, plaudit(s)

applicable *adj.* °fit, °suitable, suited, °appropriate, °proper, apropos, °fitting, °befitting, °pertinent, apt, germane, °right, °seemly, °relevant, apposite

application *n.* **1** °use, °employment, utilization, °practice, °operation **2** relevancy, °relevance, °reference, pertinence, germaneness, appositeness; °bearing **3** °attention; diligence, industriousness, °effort, °perseverance, °persistence, assiduity, °devotion, °dedication, commitment, attentiveness, *Colloq* stick-to-itiveness; °industry **4** °request, solicitation; °appeal, °petition, °claim

apply *v.* **1** °fasten, °fix, affix, °stick, °cement, °glue **2** °administer, rub in *or* on, embrocate **3** °appropriate, °assign, °allot, °credit; °use, utilize, °employ, put to use **4** °bear, have bearing; be relevant, °refer, °pertain, appertain, °relate, °suit **5** °devote, °dedicate, °commit, °focus, °concentrate, pay attention, °address; do, °attend, °tend, *Colloq* buckle down (to) **6** °seek, go after; °register, °bid, try out, °put in; audition, °interview, make application **7** °petition, °solicit; °appeal, °request

appoint *v.* **1** °fix, °set, °settle, °determine, ordain, °authorize, °establish, °destine, °arrange, °assign, °allot, °prescribe, °decree **2** °name, °designate, °nominate, °elect; °assign, °delegate, commission, deputize; °select, °choose **3** °equip, fit out, °furnish, °decorate

appointment *n.* **1** °meeting, °date, rendezvous, °engagement; assignation, tryst **2** nomination, °election; °assignment, designation; °selection, °choice **3** °job, °position, °post, °situation, °office, °place, °assignment, *Colloq* berth, °slot

appreciate *v.* **1** value, find worthwhile *or* valuable; °esteem, °cherish, °enjoy, °admire, rate *or* regard highly, °prize, °treasure, °respect **2** increase *or* rise *or* gain in value *or* worth **3** °understand, °comprehend, °recognize, °perceive, °know, be aware *or* cognizant *or* conscious of

appreciation *n.* **1** °gratitude, thankfulness, gratefulness, °thanks; °acknowledgment; °obligation **2** °increase, °rise, °advance, °growth, enhancement, °gain; aggrandizement **3** °understanding, comprehension, °perception, °recognition, °knowledge, awareness; °realization, °enjoyment; °admiration

apprentice *n.* **1** °novice, tyro, °learner, starter, beginner, °greenhorn, *Colloq US* rookie —*v.* **2** indenture, °contract, °bind

approach *v.* **1** °near, °advance, draw *or* come near *or* nearer *or* close *or* closer, *Formal* come nigh **2** °approximate, nearly equal, come close to, °compare with **3** make advances *or* overtures to, °proposition, propose to, °sound out, make (a) proposal to, °solicit, *Colloq* °chat up —*n.* **4** *approaches.* advances, overtures, proposals, propositions **5** access, °passage, °way, °path, °course; °entry **6** °advance, °movement **7** °method, °procedure, modus operandi, °way, °technique, °style, °manner, °attitude, *Slang US* MO (= 'modus operandi')

appropriate *adj.* **1** °suitable, apt, °fitting, °fit, °proper, °right, °meet, °becoming, °befitting, °seemly, suited, apropos, °correct, germane, °pertinent, °happy, felicitous *—v.* **2** °take, °take over, °seize, expropriate, arrogate, annex, impound; commandeer; °steal, °pilfer, filch, usurp, make away *or* off with, *Colloq* °pinch, °lift, *Brit* °nick, *US* °boost **3** set aside *or* apart, °devote, °assign, earmark, °allot, apportion

appropriately *adv.* fittingly, suitably, °properly, correctly, aptly, rightly, becomingly, meetly

approval *n.* °sanction, approbation, °blessing, °consent, °agreement, concurrence; °endorsement, acceptance, imprimatur, affirmation, éclat, confirmation, mandate, authorization; °license, °leave, °permission, rubber stamp, *Colloq* OK *or* okay, °go-ahead, green light

approve *v.* **1** Often, ***approve of.*** °allow, countenance, condone, °permit, °sanction, °authorize, °endorse, put one's imprimatur on, °agree (to), °accept, assent (to), °go along with, *Colloq* OK *or* O.K. *or* okay, give the green light *or* go-ahead *or* one's blessing (to), rubber-stamp **2** °confirm, affirm, °support, °ratify, °uphold, °subscribe to, °second, give the stamp of approval to; °favor, commend, °recommend **3** ***approve of.*** °sanction, consider fair *or* good *or* right, °accept, °favor, °respect, be partial to, °like, have regard for, have a preference for, °tolerate, reconcile oneself to

approximate *adj.* **1** °rough, °inexact, °loose, °imprecise, estimated, *Colloq* guesstimated, ballpark *—v.* **2** °near, °approach, come close to, °verge on **3** °resemble, °approach, look *or* seem like; simulate

approximately *adv.* **1** approaching; °nearly, °almost, °close to, °about, °around, give or take, °roughly, °generally

aptitude *n.* **1** °fitness, suitability, appropriateness, °relevance, applicability, suitableness, aptness **2** °tendency, propensity, °disposition, predilection, °bent, proclivity; °talent, °gift, °ability, °capability, °facility, °faculty, °flair **3** °intelligence, quick-wittedness, °intellect; °capacity, aptness

arbitrary *adj.* **1** °capricious, varying, °erratic, °uncertain, °inconsistent, °doubtful, unpredictable, °whimsical, irrational, °chance, °random, °inconsistent, °subjective, unreasoned, *Colloq* chancy, iffy **2** °absolute, °tyrannical, °despotic, °authoritarian, magisterial, °summary, °peremptory, autocratic, °dogmatic, imperious, uncompromising, °inconsiderate, highhanded, °dictatorial, *Rare* thetic(al)

arch *adj.* **1** °chief, °principal, °prime, °primary, °preeminent, °foremost, °first, greatest, consummate, °major **2** °clever, cunning, °crafty, roguish, °tricky, °shrewd, °artful, °sly, °designing **3** waggish, saucy, °mischievous, prankish

ardent *adj.* °eager, °intense, zealous, °keen, °fervent, fervid, °passionate, avid, °fierce, °impassioned, °hot, °warm; °enthusiastic

ardor *n.* °eagerness, °desire, zeal, fervency, burning desire, keenness, °fervor, °passion, °heat, °warmth; °enthusiasm

arduous *adj.* **1** °laborious, °difficult, °hard, °tough, °strenuous, onerous, °burdensome, backbreaking, °painful, *Formal* operose; tiring, °exhausting, wearisome, fatiguing, taxing, grueling, °trying, °formidable **2** °energetic, °strenuous, °vigorous

area *n.* **1** °space, °room **2** °extent, °limit, compass, °size, square-footage, acreage **3** °space, °field, °region, °tract, °territory, °district, °zone, °stretch; °section, °quarter, °precinct, arrondissement, °neighborhood, locality, bailiwick, *US* °block **4** °scope, °range, °extent, °breadth, compass, °section **5** court, courtyard, °enclosure, °close, yard; °square, °ground, arena, °field, parade ground, °parade

argue *v.* **1** °dispute, °debate, °disagree, °bicker, wrangle, °quarrel, squabble, °spar, °fight, remonstrate, altercate, *Colloq chiefly Brit* °row, °scrap **2** °discuss, °reason, °debate, wrangle **3** make a case, °talk, °plead, °debate, contend **4** °prove, evince, °indicate, °denote, °demonstrate, °show, °establish, °suggest, °signify, betoken **5** °say, assert, °hold, °maintain, °reason, °claim, contend **6** ***argue into or out of.*** persuade *or* dissuade, talk out of *or* into, °prevail upon; °convince

argument *n.* **1** °debate, °dispute, °disagreement, °quarrel, °controversy, polemic, wrangle, squabble, °tiff, spat, altercation; °conflict, °fight, °fracas, affray, °fray, donnybrook, °feud, *Colloq* °row, falling-out, °scrap, barney **2** °point, °position, °(line of) reasoning, °logic, °plea, °claim, pleading, °assertion, contention, °case; °defense

argumentative *adj.* °quarrelsome, disputatious, °belligerent, combative, contentious, litigious, disagreeable, °testy

arise *v.* **1** °rise, °get up, °stand up, get to one's feet; °wake up, get out of bed, °awake **2** °rise, °go up, °come up, ascend, °climb; °mount **3** °come up, be brought up, be mentioned, *Colloq* crop up **4** °spring up, °begin, °start (up), °originate, °come up, *Colloq* crop up

aroma *n.* **1** °smell, °odor, °fragrance, °scent, °perfume, °savor, °bouquet; redolence **2** °smell, °odor, °character, °aura, °atmosphere, °flavor, °hint, °suggestion

aromatic *adj.* °fragrant, °spicy, perfumed, °savory, °pungent

around *adv.* **1** °about, °approximately, °nearly, °almost, °roughly; circa **2** °about, °everywhere, in every direction, on all sides, all over, °throughout **3** 'round, °round, °about, in a circle *or* ring, on all sides **4** 'round, °round, °about, for everyone *or* all **5** 'round, °round, °about, all about, °everywhere, here and there, hither and thither, hither and yon, °far and wide **6** in perimeter *or* periphery *or* circumference **7** 'round, °round, from beginning to end, from start to finish, °through **8** 'round, °round, °about, in the neighborhood *or* vicinity *or* (general) area **9** 'round, in a circle *or* circuit, in *or* by a circular *or* circuitous route *or* path, circuitously, in a roundabout way *—prep.* **10** 'round, °round, °about, °surrounding, encompassing, enveloping, encircling, on all sides of, in all directions from, enclosing; orbiting **11** °about, 'round, °approximately, °roughly; circa **12** 'round, °round, here and there in, °about, °throughout, all over, everywhere in **13** 'round, °about, °nearby, in the neighborhood *or* vicinity *or* (general) area of

arouse *v.* **1** °awaken, °raise (up), °wake up, waken, °rouse, °revive, °stir (up) **2** °excite, °stir up, °stimulate, °awaken, °summon up, °spark, *Colloq* °turn on **3** °provoke, °encourage, °quicken, °foster, °call forth, °stir up, °kindle, °foment

arrange *v.* **1** °order, °dispose, array, °organize, °sort (out), systematize, °group, °set up, °rank, °line up, align, °form, °position **2** °settle, °plan, °set (up), °organize, orchestrate, °manipulate, choreograph; predetermine, °decide, °prepare, °determine, prearrange, °devise, °bring about, contrive; fix it **3** orchestrate, °score, °adapt

arrangement *n.* **1** °order, °disposition, grouping, °organization, array, °display, °structure, structuring, ordering, alignment, line-up, *Colloq* °setup **2** °structure, °combination, construction, contrivance, °affair, °setup **3** °settlement, °agreement, °terms, °plan, °contract, covenant, °compact **4** orchestration, °score, instrumentation, °adaptation, °interpretation, °version **5** ***arrangements.*** °preparations, plans; °groundwork, planning

arrest *v.* **1** °stop, °halt, °check, °stall, °forestall, detain, °delay, °hinder, °restrain, °obstruct, °prevent, °block, °interrupt **2** °catch, °capture, °seize, apprehend, °take, °take in, take into custody, detain, *Colloq* °nab, °pinch, collar, bust, °run in, *Brit* °nick **3** °slow, °retard, °stop *—n.* **4** °seizure, °capture, apprehension, °detention; °restraint, *Colloq* bust, *US* collar **5** °stop, stoppage, °check, cessation **6** ***under arrest.*** in custody, under legal restraint, in the hands of the law, imprisoned, arrested

arresting *adj.* °striking, °shocking, °remarkable, °impressive, electrifying, °stunning, °extraordinary, surprising, °dazzling

arrival *n.* **1** coming, advent, °appearance **2** °newcomer; °immigrant; °traveler, °passenger; °tourist; *Australian* °migrant, new chum

arrive *v.* **1** °come, make one's appearance, °appear, °turn up, *Colloq* °show up; *Slang* °hit (town), blow in **2** °succeed, °prosper, °get ahead (in the world), reach the top, *Colloq* °make it, °make the grade, get somewhere, get there **3** ***arrive at.*** come *or* get to, °reach; attain

arrogance *n.* self-assertion, °impertinence, insolence, °presumption, °nerve, °effrontery, °gall, presumptuousness, self-importance, °conceit, egotism, hauteur, haughtiness, loftiness, °pride, hubris, pompousness, pomposity, °pretension, pretentiousness, °bluster, °snobbery, snobbishness, *Colloq* snottiness, *Slang Brit* °side

arrogant *adj.* **1** °presumptuous, assuming, self-assertive, °conceited, °egotistical, °pompous, °superior, °brazen, bumptious, cavalier **2** °haughty, °overbearing, imperious, highhanded, overweening, °disdainful, °contemptuous, °scornful, °snobbish, °supercilious, °lofty, swaggering, *Brit* toffee-nosed; *Colloq* uppity, on one's high horse, high and mighty, snotty

art *n.* **1** °skill, skillfulness, °ingenuity, °aptitude, °talent, artistry, craftsmanship; °knowledge, °expertise; °craft, °technique, adroitness, °dexterity, *Colloq* know-how **2** artistry; °taste, tastefulness **3** °craft, °technique, °business, °profession, °skill **4** °knack, °aptitude, °faculty, °technique, mastery; °dexterity, adroitness **5** °trickery, craftiness, cunning, wiliness, slyness, guile, °deceit, duplicity, artfulness, cleverness, astuteness **6** ***arts.*** wiles, schemes, stratagems, artifices, subterfuges, tricks; maneuvers

artful *adj.* **1** °scheming, °wily, °sly, cunning, °foxy, °tricky, °crafty, °deceitful, underhand *or* underhanded, double-dealing, guileful, °disingenuous **2** °ingenious, °clever, °astute, °shrewd, °dexterous

artifice *n.* **1** °skill, cunning, °trickery, °craft, craftiness, artfulness, guile, duplicity, °deception, °chicanery, underhandedness, shrewdness, slyness, wiliness, trickiness **2** °stratagem, °device, °maneuver, °trick, contrivance, °wile, °ruse, °subterfuge, °expedient, contrivance, *Colloq* °dodge

artificial *adj.* **1** °unnatural, °synthetic, man-made, manufactured, simulated, °imitation, °plastic **2** made-up, concocted, °bogus, °fake, °sham, °false, °counterfeit, *Colloq* phoney *or US also* phony **3** °affected, °unnatural, °forced, °pretended, high-sounding, feigned, °assumed, contrived, °factitious; meretricious, °insincere, °sham, faked, *Colloq* phoney *or US also* phony

artless *adj.* **1** °innocent, °sincere, guileless, °ingenuous, °true, °natural, °open, unartificial, °genuine, °simple, °direct, °candid, °frank, °honest, straightforward, °aboveboard, uncomplicated, undevious, undeceptive, *Colloq* °up front, °on the level, on the up and up **2** unpretentious, unassuming, °unaffected, °natural, °simple, naive *or* naïve, °unsophisticated, °plain, °ordinary, °humble **3** unskilled, untalented, unskillful, unpracticed, °inexperienced, inexpert, °primitive, unproficient, °incompetent, °inept, °clumsy, °crude, °awkward, bungling

ashamed *adj.* °embarrassed, abashed, humiliated, chagrined, mortified, blushing, °shamefaced, °sheepish, red-faced

ask *v.* **1** °question, interrogate, °query, °quiz; inquire *or* enquire (of) **2** °demand, °require, °expect, °request **3** °beg, °apply (to), °appeal (to), °seek (from), °solicit (from), °petition, °plead (to), °beg, °beseech, °pray, entreat, implore **4** invite, °bid, °summon **5** ***ask after*** *or* ***about.*** inquire *or* enquire after *or* about **6** ***ask for.*** **(a)** invite, °attract, °encourage, °provoke **(b)** °request, °seek

aspect *n.* **1** °viewpoint, °point of view, °position, °standpoint, °side **2** complexion, °light, °angle, °interpretation, mien, °face **3** °exposure, °prospect, °outlook, °orientation **4** °side, °feature, °attribute, °characteristic, °quality, °detail, °angle, facet, °manifestation, °element, °circumstance

aspersion *n.* °slander, °libel, false insinuation, calumny, °imputation, °allegation, detraction, °slur, obloquy, defamation, disparagement

aspiration *n.* °desire, °longing, yearning, craving, hankering, °wish, °dream, °hope; °ambition, °aim, °goal, °objective, °purpose, °intention, °plan, °scheme, °plot

aspire *v.* ***aspire to.*** °desire, °hope, °long, °wish, °aim, °yearn; dream of

assailant *n.* attacker, assaulter, mugger

assault *n.* **1** °attack, onslaught, °onset, °charge, °offensive, blitzkrieg, blitz, °strike, °raid, incursion, sortie; °aggression, °invasion **2** beating, battering, °holdup, mugging; °rape, °violation, molestation; *Law* battery —*v.* **3** °attack, assail, set *or* fall upon, °pounce upon, °storm, °beset, °charge, °rush, °lay into **4** °rape, °violate, °molest **5** °beat (up), °batter, °bruise, °harm, °hit, °strike, °punch, smite

assemble *v.* **1** convene, °gather, call *or* bring *or* get together, convoke, °summon, °muster, marshal, °rally, levy, °round up, °collect, congregate, forgather *or* foregather; °meet **2** °accumulate, °gather, °amass, °collect, bring *or* group *or* lump together, °compile, °unite, join *or* draw together **3** °construct, put together, °erect, °set up, fit *or* join *or* piece together, °connect, °fabricate, °manufacture, °make

assembly *n.* **1** °gathering, °group, °meeting, assemblage, °body, °circle, °company, congregation, °flock, °crowd, °throng, multitude, °host; horde **2** convocation, °council, °convention, congress, °association, conclave; °diet, synod **3** construction, putting together, erection, °connection, setting up, °setup, fitting *or* joining *or* piecing together, °fabrication; °manufacture, making

assertion *n.* **1** °statement, °declaration, affirmation, contention, asseveration, averment, avowal, °pronouncement; *Law* affidavit, deposition **2** insistence, °proclamation, °representation, affirmation, confirmation

assertive *adj.* declaratory, affirmative, asseverative; °definite, °certain, °sure, °positive, °firm, °emphatic, °bold, °aggressive, °confident, °insistent; °dogmatic, doctrinaire, °domineering, °opinionated, °peremptory, *Colloq* °bossy, °pushy

asset *n.* **1** Also, ***assets.*** °property, °resources, °possessions, holdings, °effects, °capital, °means, valuables, °money, °wealth **2** °talent, °strength, °advantage, °resource, °benefit

assign *v.* **1** °allot, allocate, apportion, consign, °appropriate, °distribute, °give (out), °grant **2** °fix, set (apart *or* aside), °settle (on), °determine, °appoint, °authorize, °designate, ordain, °prescribe, °specify **3** °appoint, °designate, °order; °name, °delegate, °nominate, °attach; °choose, °select; *Brit* °second **4** °attribute, ascribe, accredit, °put down; °refer

assignment *n.* **1** °allotment, allocation, apportionment, giving (out), °distribution **2** °task, °obligation, °responsibility, chore, °duty, °position, °post, °charge, °job, °mission, commission; °lesson, homework **3** °appointment, designation, naming, nomination **4** designation, °specification, ascription

assist *v.* **1** °aid, °help, °second, °support **2** °further, °promote, °abet, °support, °benefit, °facilitate **3** °help, succor, °serve, work for *or* with; °relieve

assistance *n.* °help, °aid, °support, succor, °backing, °reinforcement, °relief, °benefit

assistant *n.* **1** helper, helpmate *or* helpmeet, °aid, °aide; aide-de-camp, °second **2** °deputy, °subordinate, °subsidiary, °auxiliary; underling

associate *v.* **1** ***associate (with).*** **(a)** ally with, °link, join *or* unite (with), combine *or* confederate (with), °connect (with), conjoin (with) **(b)** °see, be seen with, socialize *or* fraternize (with), mix *or* mingle (with), go (out) with, consort with, have to do with, *Colloq* hang out with, *Brit* pal with *or* about, pal up (with), *US* pal around (with) —*n.* **2** °colleague, °partner; °fellow, fellow worker **3** confederate, °ally, collaborator; °accomplice, accessory *or* accessary **4** °comrade, °companion, °friend, °mate, buddy; confidant(e) —*adj.* **5** °subsidiary, °secondary **6** allied, affiliate, °affiliated, associated; accessory *or* accessary

association *n.* **1** °society, °organization, confederation, confederacy, °federation, °league, °union, °alliance, guild, coalition, °group; °syndicate, °combine, consortium, cooperative **2** °connection, °link, affiliation, °relationship, °bond, °tie, linkage, linking, pairing, joining, conjunction, bonding **3** °fellowship, intimacy, °friendship, camaraderie, comradeship, °relationship

assortment *n.* **1** °group, °class, °category, °batch, °set, °lot, classification, grouping **2** °collection, °potpourri, °mixture, mélange, array, agglomeration, conglomeration, °medley, farrago, °variety, °miscellany, °jumble, salmagundi, gallimaufry, °mishmash, *Colloq* mixed bag

assume *v.* **1** °accept, °adopt, °take, °use, °employ; arrogate, °appropriate, take over *or* up, °undertake **2** °take on (oneself), take upon (oneself), put *or* try on, don, °adopt;

°acquire **3** °presume, °suppose, °believe, °fancy, °expect, °think, °presuppose, °take, take for granted, °surmise, *Chiefly US* °guess **4** pretend to, feign, °sham, °counterfeit, simulate, °sham, °affect, °fake

assumed *adj.* **1** appropriated, °taken, usurped, expropriated, preempted, seized **2** °pretended, °put on, °sham, °false, feigned, °affected, °counterfeit, simulated, °spurious, °bogus, °fake; pseudonymous, made-up, *Colloq* phoney *or US also* phony **3** °taken, taken for granted, presumed, °supposed, accepted, expected, presupposed; °hypothetical, °theoretical, suppositional

assurance *n.* **1** °promise, °pledge, guarantee *or* guaranty, °warranty, commitment, °bond, surety; °word, word of honor, °oath, °vow **2** °certainty, °confidence, °trust, °faith, reassurance, surety, assuredness, certitude; °security **3** audacity, °impudence, °presumption, boldness, brazenness, °nerve, °effrontery, insolence, *Colloq* °brass, °gall, cheek, chutzpah **4** °self-confidence, self-reliance, °confidence, steadiness, intrepidity, self-possession, °poise, aplomb, coolness, °control, °self-control, °resolve, *Colloq* °gumption, °guts, gutsiness

assure *v.* **1** °secure, stabilize, °settle, °establish, °confirm, °certify, °warrant, °guarantee, °ensure, be confident of, make *or* be sure *or* certain **2** °encourage, inspirit, °reassure, hearten **3** °convince, °persuade, °reassure, make (someone) certain; °ensure **4** assert, °state, asseverate, °promise

astonish *v.* °amaze, °surprise, °shock, °astound, °stun, °stagger, dumbfound *or* dumfound, bowl over, °floor, stupefy, °daze, *Colloq* flabbergast

astonishment *n.* °amazement, °surprise, °shock, stupefaction, °wonder, wonderment

astound *v.* °surprise, °shock, °astonish, °stun, °stagger, dumbfound *or* dumfound, bowl over, °floor, stupefy, °bewilder, °overwhelm, *Colloq* flabbergast

astute *adj.* **1** °shrewd, °subtle, °clever, °ingenious, adroit, °wily, cunning, °calculating, canny, °crafty, °artful, °arch, °sly, °foxy, guileful, underhand, underhanded; *Rare* astucious **2** °sharp, °keen, °perceptive, °observant, °alert, °quick, °quick-witted, °sage, sagacious, °wise, °intelligent, insightful, perspicacious, discerning, °knowledgeable

atmosphere *n.* **1** °air, heaven(s), °sky, aerosphere **2** °air, ambiance *or* ambience, °environment, °climate, °mood, °feeling, °feel, °spirit, °tone

atone *v.* expiate, °make amends, °pay, °repay, °answer, °compensate; redress, °remedy, propitiate, °redeem

atonement *n.* °amends, propitiation, reparation, repayment, compensation, °payment, °restitution, recompense, expiation, °penance, °satisfaction

atrocious *adj.* **1** °cruel, °wicked, iniquitous, °villainous, °fiendish, execrable, appalling, °abominable, °monstrous, °inhuman, °savage, barbaric, °brutal, barbarous, heinous, °dreadful, °flagrant, flagitious, °gruesome, °grisly, °ruthless, °ghastly, unspeakable, horrifying, °horrible, °awful, °infamous, °infernal, °satanic, hellish **2** °awful, °terrible, °bad, °rotten, horrid, appalling, °frightful, horrendous, *Colloq* °lousy

atrocity *n.* **1** °enormity, wickedness, flagitiousness, iniquity, °infamy, cruelty, heinousness, °horror, °evil, inhumanity, °barbarity, savagery **2** °evil, °outrage, °crime, villainy, °offense

attach *v.* **1** °fasten, °join, °connect, °secure, °fix, affix; tack *or* hook *or* tie *or* stick on, °pin, rivet, °cement, °glue, °bond, solder, °weld, braze; °unite; *Nautical* °bend **2** °connect, °associate, °assign, affiliate, °enlist, °join, °add, subjoin, *Brit* °second **3** endear, °attract **4** °fix, affix, °pin, °apply, ascribe, °assign, °attribute, °put, °place **5** adhere, °cleave, °stick **6** °seize, °lay hold of, °confiscate, °appropriate

attached *adj.* **1** connected, joined, *Brit* seconded **2** °united, fastened, °fixed **3** Often, ***attached to.*** °devoted (to), °partial (to), °fond (of) **4** °spoken for, married, unavailable, °engaged, betrothed

attachment *n.* **1** °fastening; °connection, °tie, °link, °bond **2** attaching, °fastening, linking, joining, affixing, fixing, °connection **3** °affection, °regard, fidelity, faithfulness, °devotion, °liking, fondness, °affinity, friendliness, °loyalty, °admiration, tenderness, °partiality, °friendship, °love **4** adjunct, °addition, accessory *or* accessary, °device, appliance, °extra, accoutrement *or US also* accouterment, appendage, °part; °ornament, °decoration; *Colloq* °gadget

attack *v.* **1** assail, °assault, fall *or* set *or* pounce upon; °charge, °rush, °raid, °strike (at), °storm; °engage (in battle), °fight; *Colloq* °mug, °jump **2** °criticize, censure, °berate; °abuse, revile, inveigh against, °denounce, °condemn, malign, denigrate, decry, °disparage, deprecate, °vilify **3** °begin, °start; °approach, °undertake **4** °affect, °seize; infect **5** °waste, °devour, °destroy, °eat; °erode, corrode, °decompose, °dissolve —*n.* **6** °assault, °onset, °offensive, onslaught, incursion, °raid, °strike, °inroad, °invasion **7** °criticism, censure; °abuse, denunciation, revilement, denigration, decrial, disparagement, deprecation, vilification **8** °seizure, °spell, °spasm, °paroxysm; °fit, °bout **9** °destruction, wasting; °erosion, corrosion

attempt *v.* **1** °try, °essay, °undertake, °take on, °venture; °endeavor, °strive, *Colloq* have *or* take a crack at, try on, have a go *or* shot at —*n.* **2** °endeavor, °try, °essay; °effort, °undertaking, °bid, *Colloq* °crack, °go, °shot **3** °attack, °assault

attend *v.* **1** be present (at), go to, be at, °appear (at), put in an appearance (at), °turn up (at), °haunt, °frequent; °sit in (on), *US and Canadian* audit **2** °turn to, pay attention to, °serve, tend to, °take care of, °deal with, °handle, °heed, °fulfill **3** Also, ***attend to.*** watch over, wait on *or* upon, °care for, °take care of, °minister to, occupy oneself with, °look after, look out for, devote oneself to **4** °escort, °accompany, °conduct, convoy, °squire, usher, °wait upon, °follow; chaperon *or* chaperone **5** be associated with, °accompany, result in *or* from, °give rise to

attendance *n.* **1** °presence, °appearance, being **2** audience, °crowd, °assembly, assemblage, °gathering, °turnout, °gate, °house **3** ***in attendance.*** waiting upon, attending, serving

attendant *adj.* **1** waiting upon, accompanying, following; resultant, resulting, °related, consequent, concomitant, depending, accessory *or* accessary —*n.* **2** °escort, °servant, °menial, helper, usher *or* usherette, chaperon *or* chaperone; °aide, °subordinate, underling, °assistant; °follower, *Denigrating* lackey, °flunky, °slave; *Colloq US* °cohort

attention *n.* **1** °heed, °regard, °notice; concentration **2** publicity, °notice, °distinction, acclaim, °prominence, ***réclame,*** °notoriety; limelight

attentive *adj.* **1** heedful, °observant, °awake, °alert, °intent, watchful, concentrating, assiduous; °mindful, °considerate **2** °polite, °courteous, courtly, °gallant, °gracious, °accommodating, °considerate, °thoughtful, °solicitous, °civil, °respectful, deferential

attest *v.* °bear witness (to), °bear out, °swear (to), °vow, °testify, °certify, °vouchsafe, °declare, assert, asseverate, aver, affirm, °confirm, °verify, °substantiate, vouch for, *Law* depose, depose and say, depone

attitude *n.* **1** °posture, °position, °disposition, °stance, °bearing, °carriage, °aspect, demeanor **2** °posture, °position, °disposition, °opinion, °feeling, °view, °point of view, °viewpoint, °approach, °leaning, °thought, °inclination, °bent, °tendency, °orientation

attract *v.* °draw, invite; °entice, °lure, allure, appeal to, °charm, °captivate, °fascinate, *Colloq* °pull

attraction *n.* **1** °draw, °appeal; °magnetism; gravitation, *Colloq* °pull **2** °draw, °lure, °enticement, attractant, °inducement; °show, °entertainment, °presentation, °performance, *Colloq* °come-on, crowd-puller, crowd-pleaser

attractive *adj.* attracting, °drawing, pulling, captivating, °taking, °fetching, appealing, luring, °inviting, enticing, °seductive, °engaging, charming, °interesting, °pleasing, °winning, alluring, good-looking, °pretty, °handsome

attribute *n.* **1** °quality, °character, °characteristic, °property, °feature, °trait, °virtue —*v.* **2** ascribe, °impute, °assign, put down to, trace to, °charge, °credit

attribution *n.* °assignment, ascription, °credit

audacious *adj.* **1** °daring, °bold, °confident, °intrepid, °brave, °courageous, °adventurous, °venturesome, °reckless, °rash, °foolhardy, °daredevil, devil-may-care, °fearless, doughty, mettlesome **2** °presumptuous, °shameless, °bold, °impudent, °pert, saucy, °defiant, °impertinent, °insolent, °brazen, °unabashed, °rude, °disrespectful, °cheeky, °forward

aura *n.* °air, °atmosphere, °feeling, ambiance *or* ambience, °spirit, °character, °quality, °odor, °aroma, emanation

auspices *n.* aegis, sponsorship, °authority, °protection, °support, °backing, supervision, °guidance, °patronage, °sanction, °approval, °control, °influence

authentic *adj.* °genuine, °real, °actual, °bona fide, °factual, °accurate, °true, °legitimate, °authoritative, °reliable, °veritable, °trustworthy, °faithful, °undisputed

authenticate *v.* °verify, validate, °certify, °substantiate, °endorse, vouch for, °confirm, corroborate

author *n.* °creator, originator, inventor, °father, °founder, framer, initiator, maker, prime mover, architect, °designer; °writer, novelist, littérateur

authoritarian *adj.* °dictatorial, imperious, °totalitarian, autocratic, °arbitrary, °absolute, °dogmatic, °domineering, °strict, °severe, unyielding, °tyrannical, °despotic, *Colloq* °bossy

authoritative *adj.* **1** °official, valid, °authentic, documented, certified, validated, °legitimate, sanctioned; conclusive **2** °scholarly, °learned, °authentic, valid, °sound, °veritable, verifiable, °accurate, °factual, °faithful, dependable, °reliable, °trustworthy, °true, °truthful

authority *n.* **1** °power, °jurisdiction, °dominion, °right, °control, °prerogative, authorization; hegemony **2** °word, °testimony, °evidence, *Colloq* °say-so **3** °expert, °specialist, °scholar, °sage, °judge, arbiter **4** ***authorities.*** °government, °establishment, officials, officialdom, °powers that be, °police

authorize *v.* empower, commission; °sanction, °approve, countenance, °permit, give leave, °allow, °license, °entitle, consent *or* subscribe to, °endorse, *Colloq* OK *or* okay, give the green light *or* go-ahead to

automatic *adj.* **1** self-acting, self-governing, self-regulating, °mechanical, °robot, automated **2** °mechanical, °involuntary, °unconscious, instinctive *or* instinctual, °natural, °spontaneous, °impulsive, conditioned, reflex, robotlike, *Slang* knee-jerk **3** °unavoidable, °inevitable, inescapable, ineluctable

auxiliary *adj.* **1** °helping, assisting, °supportive, aiding, abetting; °helpful, accessory *or* accessary, °supplementary **2** °subordinate, additional, °subsidiary, °secondary, ancillary, °extra, °reserve; °accessory —*n.* **3** °help, °assistance, °aid, °support, °accessory **4** helper, °assistant, °aide, alter ego, °supporter, *Colloq* man Friday, girl Friday

available *adj.* at *or* to hand, at one's disposal, °accessible, °handy, °present, °ready, (readily) obtainable, °convenient, °nearby,

°close by, within reach, °on tap, at one's fingertips *or* elbow

avant-garde *adj.* innovative, advanced, °progressive, °experimental, °original, °new, ground-breaking, pioneering, precedent-setting; °revolutionary, °extreme, extremist, *Colloq* far-out, °way-out

avarice *n.* °greed, acquisitiveness, cupidity, craving, covetousness, °desire, greediness, °rapacity, selfishness; stinginess, meanness, miserliness, parsimony, tightfistedness, closefistedness, niggardliness, penuriousness

avaricious *adj.* °greedy, acquisitive, °grasping, covetous, °mercenary, °selfish; penny-pinching, stingy, °miserly, °mean, parsimonious, tightfisted, closefisted, niggardly, °penurious, °tight

average *n.* **1** °mean, °norm, °usual, °standard **2** ***on average.*** °in the main, °generally, normally, °usually, °ordinarily, typically, customarily, °as a rule, °for the most part —*adj.* **3** °normal, °common, °usual, °customary, °general, °typical, °ordinary, °regular **4** °mediocre, middling, °run-of-the-mill, commonplace, °common, °ordinary, °undistinguished, unexceptional, *Colloq* °so-so

averse *adj.* °disinclined, unwilling, °reluctant, °resistant, °loath, °opposed, anti, antipathetic, ill-disposed, °indisposed

aversion *n.* **1** °dislike, abhorrence, repugnance, antipathy, °antagonism, °animosity, °hostility, °loathing, hatred, odium, °horror; disinclination, unwillingness, °reluctance, °dislike, °distaste **2** °dislike, hatred, °hate, °loathing

avoid *v.* °shun, keep (away) from, keep off, leave alone, keep *or* steer clear of, °refrain from, °dodge, circumvent, °sidestep, °elude, °escape, °evade

awake *v.* **1** °wake (up), °awaken, °get up, rouse *or* bestir oneself **2** °awaken, °animate, °arouse, °rouse, °stimulate, °revive, °incite, °excite, °activate, °alert, °stir up, °fan, °kindle, ignite, °fire **3** ***awake to.*** awaken to, wake up to, °realize, °understand, become aware *or* conscious of —*adj.* **4** up, aroused, roused, wide-awake, up and about, °alert, on the alert, on the qui vive, watchful, on guard, °attentive, °conscious; heedful, °alive

awaken *v.* See **awake, 1, 2,** above.

award *v.* **1** °grant, °give, °confer, °bestow, present, °accord, °furnish, endow with; °assign, apportion —*n.* **2** °prize, °trophy, °reward **3** °grant, bestowal, °presentation, °endowment, awarding

aware *adj.* **1** °informed, apprised, °knowledgeable, °knowing, posted, in the know, °enlightened, *au fait, au courant,* cognizant, *Slang* °hip, hep, °wise **2** °sensitive, °sensible, °conscious

awesome *adj.* awe-inspiring, °awful, °imposing, °amazing, wonderful, breathtaking, °marvelous, wondrous, °moving, °stirring, affecting, °overwhelming, °formidable, daunting, °dreadful, °fearsome, °fearful, °frightening, horrifying, °terrifying, °terrible; °unbelievable, °incredible; alarming, °shocking, °stunning, stupefying, astounding, astonishing

awful *adj.* **1** °bad, °terrible, °inferior, °base, °abominable, °rotten, °horrible, horrid; °tasteless, °unsightly, °ugly, °hideous, °grotesque, *Slang* °lousy, *Brit* naff **2** °frightful, °shocking, execrable, unpleasant, °grotesque, °nasty, °ghastly, °gruesome, horrendous, horrifying, horrific, °horrible, unspeakable

awfully *adv.* °very (much), °badly, °terribly, °extremely, greatly, remarkably, in the worst way, dreadfully, extraordinarily, °exceedingly, excessively, °really, °fearfully, inordinately; incomparably

awkward *adj.* **1** °clumsy, ungainly, °left-handed, ham-handed, ham-fisted, blundering, bungling, maladroit, uncoordinated, undexterous, inexpert, gauche, unhandy, °inept, oafish, unskilled, unskillful, *Colloq* °all thumbs, butterfingered, *Brit* cack-handed **2** °ungraceful, ungainly, inelegant, °wooden, gawky **3** °embarrassed, °shamefaced, uncomfortable, °ill at ease, uneasy, °out of place, discomfited, °confused **4** °dangerous, °hazardous, °risky, °precarious, °perilous **5** °difficult, °touchy, °sensitive, °embarrassing, °delicate, unpleasant, uncomfortable, °ticklish, °tricky, °trying, °troublesome, *Colloq* °sticky

B

babble *v.* **1** °prattle, twaddle, °jabber, gibber, °chatter, °gurgle, burble, gabble, *Colloq* °blab, blabber, °gab, yak, natter, witter, *Brit* rabbit **2** divulge, °tell, °disclose, °repeat, °reveal, °tattle, °gossip, °blurt (out), *Colloq* °blab —*n.* **3** °gibberish, °nonsense, twaddle, °prattle, chatter(ing), gibber, °jabber, gibber-jabber, °drivel, °rubbish, *bavardage*; °murmur, hubbub

baby *n.* **1** infant, neonate, newborn, babe, babe in arms, °child, toddler, °tot —*v.* **2** cosset, °coddle, °pamper, mollycoddle, °indulge, °spoil, °pet

back *v.* **1** invest in, wager *or* bet on **2** Also, ***back up.*** **(a)** °support, °uphold, stand behind, °promote, °encourage, °help, °uphold, °second, °side with, °endorse, °aid, °abet, °assist; °sponsor, °subsidize, °underwrite, subvene, °finance, *Slang US and Canadian* bankroll **(b)** °reverse, go *or* move in reverse, go *or* move backward(s) **3** ***back down (from) or off (from) or away (from)***

or out (*of*) *or* **up.** °withdraw (from), °retreat (from), °abandon, °retire (from), backtrack (from), shy away (from), °recoil (from), °turn tail (from) *—n.* **4** backside, °rear, *Technical* dorsum **5** ***at the back of*** *or* ***at someone's back.*** behind, following, pursuing, chasing, *US* in back of **6** ***behind the back of*** *or* ***behind someone's back.*** surreptitiously, °secretly, clandestinely, privately, furtively, sneakily, slyly; treacherously, traitorously, perfidiously, deceitfully, insidiously **7** ***break the back of.*** **(a)** °overcome, °master **(b)** *US* °crush, °ruin, bankrupt, °destroy, °defeat, vanquish, *Colloq* °break **8** ***on (someone's) back.*** *US* weighing (down) on *or* upon (someone), burdening (someone), lodged with (someone), resting with (someone) **9** ***turn one's back on*** *or* ***upon.*** °abandon, °forsake, °ignore, °disregard, °repudiate, °reject, °cast off, disown, °deny **10** ***with one's back to*** *or* ***against the wall.*** hard pressed, struggling (against odds), without hope, with little *or* no hope, °helpless, in dire straits, in (serious) trouble *—adj.* **11** °rear; °service, servants' **12** *US and Australian and New Zealand* °outlying, °remote, °isolated, °distant; °undeveloped, °primitive, °raw, °rough, °uncivilized **13** in arrears, °overdue, past due, °late; behindhand *—adv.* **14** to *or* toward(s) the rear, rearward(s), backward(s); away **15** in return *or* repayment *or* requital *or* retaliation; again **16** ago, in time(s) past **17** behind, behindhand, in arrears, °overdue **18** ***go back on.*** °renege, °fail; °deny, disavow, °break, °repudiate

backbone *n.* **1** °spine, spinal column **2** °mainstay, chief *or* main support, °buttress, °pillar **3** resoluteness, sturdiness, firmness, °determination, °strength (of character), mettle, purposefulness, °resolution, °courage, °fortitude, °resolve, °will, willpower, °strength, °stability, °stamina, staying power, °grit

backer *n.* **1** °supporter, °advocate, promoter, °sponsor, °patron **2** investor, benefactor *or* benefactress, °supporter, underwriter, *Colloq* angel **3** °bettor, *Brit* punter

background *n.* **1** °history, °experience, °qualifications, credentials, grounding, training; °breeding, °upbringing, °family; curriculum vitae, *Colloq* CV **2** °distance, offing, °horizon, °obscurity **3** ***in the background.*** °inconspicuous, °unnoticed, °unobtrusive, °behind the scenes, out of the limelight *or* spotlight, unseen, out of the public eye, backstage

backing *n.* **1** °support, °help, °aid, °assistance, succor; °approval, °endorsement, °patronage, sponsorship **2** investment, °money, °funds, funding, °subsidy, °grant; sponsorship

backlash *n.* °reaction, °repercussion, °recoil, counteraction, °rebound, °kickback, backfire; °boomerang

backward *adj.* **1** °bashful, °shy, °reticent, diffident, °retiring, °coy, °timid, unwilling, °loath, chary, °reluctant, °averse **2** °slow, dimwitted, °dull, °stupid, slow-witted, °dumb, °feebleminded, *Colloq Brit* gormless, °dim **3** °slow, °late, behindhand, retarded **4** rearward; to the rear, behind; to the past **5** retrograde, retrogressive, °reverse, regressive *—adv.* **6** backwards, rearward(s), in reverse, regressively, retrogressively; withershins *or* widdershins, *Brit* anticlockwise, *US* counterclockwise **7** backwards, in reverse; back to front

bad *adj.* **1** °poor, °wretched, °inferior, °defective, °awful, °worthless, °miserable, egregious, execrable, substandard, °unsatisfactory, °disappointing, °inadequate, nonstandard, *Colloq* °lousy, °rotten, crummy, *Slang Brit* grotty, naff **2** °corrupt, polluted, vitiated, debased, °base, °vile, °foul, °rotten, miasmic, noxious, mephitic, °unhealthy, °poisonous, °injurious, °dangerous, °harmful, °hurtful, pernicious, deleterious, °ruinous **3** °evil, °ill, °immoral, °wicked, °vicious, °vile, °sinful, depraved, °awful, °villainous, °corrupt, amoral, °criminal, °wrong, unspeakable **4** unpleasant, °offensive, °disagreeable, °inclement, °severe, °awful, unfavorable, adverse, °inclement, *Colloq* °lousy, °rotten **5** unfavorable, unlucky, unpropitious, °unfortunate, °inauspicious, troubled, °grim, distressing, discouraging, unpleasant **6** °off, tainted, spoilt *or* spoiled, °moldy, °stale, °rotten, decayed, putrefied, °putrid, contaminated **7** irascible, ill-tempered, grouchy, °irritable, °nasty, °peevish, °cross, crotchety, crabby, °cranky, curmudgeonly **8** °sorry, °regretful, °apologetic, contrite, rueful, °sad, conscience-stricken, °remorseful, °upset **9** °sad, depressed, °unhappy, °dejected, °downhearted, disconsolate, °melancholy; °inconsolable **10** °naughty, ill-behaved, misbehaving, °disobedient, °unruly, °wild; °mischievous **11** distressing, °severe, °grave, °serious, °terrible, °awful, °painful

badly *adv.* **1** °poorly, defectively, insufficiently, inadequately, unsatisfactorily, carelessly, ineptly, shoddily, deficiently **2** unfortunately, unluckily, unsuccessfully, unfavorably, °poorly **3** incorrectly, faultily, defectively, °poorly, improperly, inaccurately, erroneously, unacceptably; ineptly, inartistically, amateurishly, °awfully **4** immorally, wickedly, viciously, mischievously, naughtily, shamefully, improperly, villainously **5** °dangerously, °severely, gravely, critically, grievously, °seriously **6** unkindly, cruelly, harshly, °severely, wretchedly, dreadfully, improperly, atrociously, horribly, unspeakably **7** unfavorably, damagingly, critically **8** very much, greatly, °seriously **9** distressfully, emotionally, °hard

bag *n.* **1** °sack, shopping bag, reticule, string bag, *Chiefly Brit* carrier bag, *Scots and dialectal* °poke, °pocket **2** baggage, °luggage, valise, satchel, °grip, °suitcase, overnight bag, carry-on luggage *or* bag, Gladstone bag, carpetbag, portmanteau, toilet kit *or* case, sponge bag; brief case, attaché case, dispatch *or* despatch case **3** °purse, handbag, evening bag, °wallet, *Scots Highland dress* sporran **4** crone, °hag, °beast, ogress, gorgon, nightmare, °witch, harridan, *Archaic* beldam, *Slang* old bat, dog, °monster, *US* two-bagger **5** °occupation, °hobby, avocation, °business, °vocation, °department, °concern, °affair, *Colloq* °lookout, °worry, *Slang* °thing *—v.* **6** °catch, °trap, ensnare, °snare, entrap, °capture, °land; °kill, °shoot

balance *v.* **1** °weigh, °estimate, °ponder, °consider, °deliberate, assess, °compare, °evaluate **2** °steady, °poise; °equalize, stabilize, °level, °match, even out *or* up **3** °compensate (for), °make up for, counterbalance, °offset, °match, °equal; counterpoise *—n.* **4** scale(s), steelyard **5** °control, °command, °authority, °weight, °preponderance **6** equilibrium, °stability, steadiness, °footing; equiponderance; °equality, °harmony **7** °remainder, °residue, °rest; °excess, °surplus, °difference

ban *v.* **1** °prohibit, °forbid, °outlaw, proscribe, interdict, °bar, disallow, debar *—n.* **2** °prohibition, °taboo, proscription, interdiction, interdict; °embargo, °boycott

banal *adj.* trite, hackneyed, stereotyped, clichéd, stereotypical, commonplace, old hat, °stock, °common, °everyday, °ordinary, °pedestrian, °humdrum, °tired, unoriginal, unimaginative, platitudinous; trivial, °petty, jejune, *Slang* corny

band[1] *n.* **1** °strip, ribbon, °belt, bandeau, fillet, °tie; °stripe, °line, °border *—v.* **2** °line, °stripe, °border **3** °tie, °keep, °bind

band[2] *n.* **1** °company, troop, °platoon, °corps, °group, °body, °gang, horde, °party, °pack, °bunch **2** °group, °ensemble, °combination, orchestra, *Colloq* combo *—v.* **3** ***band together.*** °unite, confederate, gather *or* join *or* league together, °team up, affiliate, °merge, federate

banish *v.* **1** °exile, expatriate, deport, extradite, °transport, °eject, oust, °expel, rusticate, send to Siberia, drive out *or* away, °dismiss, excommunicate, °outlaw, °ostracize **2** °drive, drive out *or* away, °expel, °cast out, °dismiss, °reject

banner *n.* **1** °standard, °flag, °pennant, ensign, burgee, gonfalon, pennon, °streamer, banderole; °symbol *—adj.* **2** °leading, °foremost, °momentous, °memorable, °notable, °important, °noteworthy

banquet *n.* **1** °feast, sumptuous repast *or* meal, ceremonial dinner, lavish dinner *—v.* **2** °feast, °indulge, wine and dine, °regale, °carouse

banter *n.* °raillery, badinage, persiflage, pleasantry, jesting, joking, °repartee; chaffing, teasing, °chaff; *Colloq* kidding, ribbing

bar *n.* **1** °rod, °shaft, °pole, °stick, °stake **2** °strip, °stripe, °band, °belt; °streak, °line **3** °barrier, °obstacle, °obstruction, barricade, °hindrance, °block, °deterrent, °impediment; °ban, °embargo **4** sandbar, °shallow, shoal, bank, sandbank **5** °tribunal, court, courtroom, law court, bench **6** barroom, saloon, public house, °café, °lounge, cocktail lounge, tavern, taproom, canteen, *Brit* °local, wine bar; *Colloq* °pub; *Slang* boozer, gin mill **7** °counter *—v.* **8** °fasten, °close up, °secure, °shut up; °lock, °lock up, padlock **9** °block, °obstruct, °stop, °stay, °hinder, °keep (out), °shut out, °exclude, °prevent, °forbid, °prohibit, °set aside; °forestall, °impede, °hamper, °retard, balk, barricade; °ban, °embargo *—prep.* **10** °except (for), excepting, excluding, °barring, °outside (of), save for, aside from, but

barbarian *n.* **1** °savage, °brute **2** °boor, lowbrow, lout, oaf, °clod, churl, °philistine, ignoramus, °yahoo; hooligan, vandal, ruffian, °tough, *Brit slang* yob, yobbo, skinhead *—adj.* **3** °uncivilized, uncultivated, uncultured, °philistine, °savage; barbarous, barbaric, °coarse, °vulgar, uncouth, °rude; °boorish, loutish, oafish, °crude, °rough, insensitive, churlish, uncivil

barbarity *n.* cruelty, inhumanity, ruthlessness, savagery, brutishness, barbarousness, heartlessness, viciousness, coldbloodedness, bloodthirstiness

bare *adj.* **1** unclothed, °naked, °nude, stark-naked, unclad, exposed, uncovered, undressed, hatless, unshod, discalced, *Brit* starkers; *Colloq* in the altogether, in one's birthday suit, in the buff; *Slang US* bareass **2** unconcealed, °undisguised, °open, revealed, °literal, bald, °manifest, °out-and-out, °overt, uncovered, straightforward, °direct, °unvarnished, unembellished, °cold, °hard, °plain, °unadorned, °basic, °simple **3** unfurnished, undecorated, °vacant, stripped, °empty **4** denuded, stripped, leafless, defoliated, shorn, °barren; bared **5** °plain, °mere, °simple, °minimal, °essential, °absolute, °basic; °meager, scant, °scanty *—v.* **6** °expose, °lay bare, uncover, °reveal, °open; undress, °unveil **7** °disclose, °reveal, °lay bare, uncover, divulge, °unfold, °tell, °expose, unmask, °bring to light **8** °strip, °divest, denude; defoliate

barefaced *adj.* **1** unconcealed, °open, °undisguised, °blatant, °manifest, °unmitigated, °outright, °downright, °out-and-out, °sheer, unalloyed, °undiluted **2** °audacious, °impudent, °shameless, °insolent, °impertinent, °immodest, °bold, arrant, °unabashed, °forward, °brazen, °brassy, saucy, °pert, unblushing, *Colloq* °cheeky

barely *adv.* °scarcely, °only, °just, not quite, °hardly, only just, no more than

bargain *n.* **1** °agreement, °contract, °understanding, °arrangement, covenant, °pact, °compact, °settlement, °transaction, °deal **2** good deal, *Colloq* giveaway, *US* °steal *—v.* **3** °negotiate, °trade, °haggle, barter, °dicker, chaffer **4** ***bargain for.*** °expect, °count on, °anticipate, °foresee, °take into account, allow for, be prepared for

barren *adj.* **1** °sterile, childless, °infertile **2** unproductive, °sterile, °bare, °infertile;

°fruitless, °dry, unfruitful, °unprofitable, °poor

barrier *n.* **1** °bar, °fence, railing, °wall; ditch, ha-ha **2** °obstacle, °bar, °obstruction, °block, °impediment, °hindrance **3** °boundary, boundary line, °limit, °frontier

barring *prep.* excluding, °exclusive of, °bar, omitting, leaving out, excepting, °except (for), save for, aside from, °besides, but

base[1] *n.* **1** °bottom, foot, °support, °stand, °pedestal **2** °groundwork, °background, fundamental principle, °principle, °foundation, underpinning; infrastructure, °basis **3** °root, °theme, °radical, °stem, °core **4** °home, °station, °camp, starting point, point of departure, °post, °center —*v.* **5** °establish, °found, °secure, °build, °ground, °anchor, °fix, hinge, °form; °derive, °draw **6** °establish, headquarter, °post, °station, °position, °place

base[2] *adj.* **1** °low, undignified, °cowardly, °selfish, °mean, °despicable, °contemptible, °filthy, °evil **2** degraded, °degrading, °menial, °inferior, °mean, °unworthy, °lowly, °low, °groveling, °servile, slavish, subservient, °downtrodden, abject, °miserable, °wretched, °sordid, undignified, ignoble, °dishonorable, °disreputable, °vile, °scurrilous, °wicked, *Colloq* infra dig **3** °mean, °cheap, °sorry, °common, °poor, °shabby, °shoddy **4** °sordid, °offensive, °lewd, °lascivious, °obscene, °profane, °rude, °raw, ribald, °unseemly, °vulgar, °coarse, °dirty, °indecent, °evil-minded, °filthy, °pornographic **5** °poor, °shoddy, °cheap, °fake, pinchbeck, °inferior, °counterfeit, °fraudulent, debased, forged, °spurious, °worthless, °bad **6** °wicked, °evil, °wretched, °corrupt, °shameful, currish, °loathsome, °scurvy, °insufferable, °villainous

bashful *adj.* **1** °shy, °retiring, °embarrassed, °meek, abashed, °shamefaced, °sheepish, °timid, diffident, self-effacing, unconfident; °ill at ease, uneasy, uncomfortable, °nervous, °self-conscious, °awkward, °confused, *Colloq* in a tizzy, *US and Canadian* discombobulated **2** °modest, °coy, unassuming, unostentatious, demure, °reserved, restrained, *Rare* verecund

basic *adj.* °fundamental, °essential, °key, °elementary, underlying, °prime, °primary, °root; °principal, °central, °focal, °vital

basis *n.* **1** °foundation, °base, °bottom, °heart, °footing, °principle, underpinning; infrastructure **2** °essence, main ingredient *or* constituent, point of departure

batch *n.* **1** °quantity, °lot; °amount, °volume **2** °set, °group, °number, °quantity, °assortment, °bunch, °pack, °collection

batter *v.* **1** °beat, °hit, °strike, clout, °belabor, °pound, pummel *or* pommel, °pelt, bash, smite, thrash, *Colloq* wallop, clobber **2** °bombard, °attack, °assault **3** maltreat, °mistreat, °ill-treat, °abuse; maul, °bruise, °harm, °mangle, disfigure

battle *n.* **1** °fight, °conflict, °combat, °action, °encounter, °clash, °engagement, °struggle, donnybrook, °fray, *Law* affray; °brawl, °fracas, melee *or* mêlée; °contest; duel, hand-to-hand encounter **2** °argument, °dispute, altercation, °quarrel, °war; °contest, °competition; °struggle, °fight, °crusade, °campaign —*v.* **3** Usually, ***battle against.*** °fight, contend *or* struggle *or* fight with *or* strive against, °combat

bauble *n.* °gewgaw, trinket, °ornament, °trifle, °toy, bagatelle, knickknack, °plaything, kickshaw

bawdy *adj.* °lewd, °obscene, °taboo, °vulgar, °dirty, smutty, °filthy, °coarse, °earthy, °gross, °raw, scatological, °rude, °lascivious, salacious, indelicate, °indecent, indecorous, °broad, °crude, ribald, °risqué, °suggestive, Rabelaisian, °uninhibited, unrestrained, °lusty, *Literary* lubricious *or* lubricous

bawl *v.* **1** °shout, °bellow, vociferate, °roar, °yell, trumpet, °thunder, *Colloq* holler **2** °cry, wail, °weep, °keen, squall, blubber, whimper; yelp, *Colloq* yammer **3** ***bawl out.*** °scold, °reprimand, °upbraid

beach *n.* **1** shore, lakeshore, bank, seashore, seaside, strand, °coast, °margin, *Formal* littoral —*v.* **2** °ground, run aground, strand; °careen

beacon *n.* °signal, °sign, °fire, °light, bonfire, °flare, signal fire, Very light, °rocket; lighthouse, pharos

beam *n.* **1** °timber, scantling, girder, rafter; °bar, °brace, °plank, °board, stud, trestle **2** °ray, °gleam; °shaft; pencil —*v.* **3** °radiate, °shine; smile radiantly

beamy *adj.* °broad, °wide, broad in the beam; °big, °heavy, °chubby, chunky, °fat, °obese

bear *v.* **1** °carry, °transport, convey, °move, °take, *Colloq* tote **2** °carry, °support, °sustain, °shoulder, °hold up, °uphold; °suffer, °undergo, °experience, °endure **3** °merit, be worthy of, °warrant; °provoke, invite **4** °stand, °abide, °tolerate, °brook, °survive, °endure, °stand up to; reconcile oneself to, admit of, *Colloq* °put up with **5** °have, °carry, °show, °exhibit, °display, °sustain **6** °produce, °yield, °develop, °breed, °generate, engender; give birth to, °spawn, °bring forth **7** °entertain, °harbor, °wish **8** ***bear on or upon.*** relate *or* have relevance *or* be relevant to *or* pertain to, touch on *or* upon, °affect, °concern, have a bearing on *or* upon, °influence **9** ***bear out.*** °confirm, °support, corroborate, °substantiate, °uphold, °back up **10** ***bear up.*** **(a)** °survive, °hold out, °stand up, °hold up, °withstand **(b)** °support, °cheer, °encourage **11** ***bear with.*** °put up with, be patient with, make allowance(s) for

bearable *adj.* °tolerable, °supportable, endurable, °acceptable, °manageable

bearing *n.* **1** °carriage, deportment, °manner, °behavior, °conduct, °aspect, demeanor, °posture, °stance, °air, °attitude, mien, °presence **2** sustaining, supporting, °endurance, °enduring **3** °aspect; °relation, °reference, °relationship, correlation, pertinence, °relevance, °connection, relevancy, applicability, °application, germaneness, °significance **4** Often, ***bearings.*** °direction, °orientation, °(relative) position

beast *n.* **1** °animal, °creature, being **2** °brute, °savage, °animal, °monster

beastly *adj.* **1** °uncivilized, uncultivated, uncivil, °rude, °crude, °boorish, °unrefined, °coarse; °cruel, °inhuman, °savage, barbaric, barbarous, bestial, °brutal **2** °abominable, intolerable, °offensive, unpleasant, °awful, °terrible, °ghastly, horrid, °disagreeable, °horrible, °hateful, execrable; °foul, °vile, °nasty, °rotten, °dirty, °filthy

beat *v.* **1** °strike, °pound, bash, smite, °batter, pummel *or* pommel, °belabor, °pelt, clout, thrash, give (someone) a thrashing *or* beating, drub, °manhandle, thump, whack, cane, °scourge, °whip, bludgeon, °club, cudgel, fustigate; °whip, °flog, °lash, *Colloq* clobber, wallop, give (someone) a once-over **2** °defeat, °best, worst, win (out) over, vanquish, trounce, °rout, °outdo, °subdue, °overcome, °overwhelm, °preempt; °surpass, °conquer, °crush, °master, *US* beat out **3** throb, °pulsate, palpitate, °pound, thump **4** *Nautical* °tack **5** hammer, °forge, °shape, °form, °fashion, °make, °mold **6** °mix, °whip, °stir, °blend **7** tread, °wear, °trample **8** ***beat it.*** °depart, °leave, abscond, run off *or* away, *Slang US* take it on the lam, lam out of here, *US* hit the road **9** ***beat off.*** drive off *or* away, °rout —*n.* **10** °stroke, °blow **11** °rhythm, °tempo, °measure; °pulse, throb, °stress, pulsation **12** °course, °round, °tour, °route, °circuit, °run, °path; °area, bailiwick —*adj.* **13** dead beat, °exhausted, °spent, drained, worn-out, °weary, bone-tired, °fatigued, fagged

beautiful *adj.* **1** °attractive, charming, °comely, °lovely, good-looking, °fair, °pretty, alluring, appealing, °handsome, °radiant, °gorgeous, *Formal* pulchritudinous, *Scots* °bonny; *Colloq* smashing **2** °excellent, °first-rate, unequaled, °skillful, °admirable, °magnificent, well done; °superb, spectacular, °splendid, °marvelous, wonderful, °incomparable, °superior, °elegant, °exquisite, °pleasant, °pleasing, °delightful, *Colloq* smashing

beautifully *adv.* **1** attractively, chicly, fashionably, delightfully, charmingly, splendidly, magnificently, *Colloq* smashingly **2** admirably, superbly, excellently, wonderfully, marvelously, splendidly, spectacularly, magnificently, *Colloq* smashingly

beautify *v.* adorn, °embellish, °decorate, °ornament, titivate, °elaborate, garnish, deck (out), bedeck

beauty *n.* **1** loveliness, attractiveness, handsomeness, pulchritude **2** belle, *Colloq* looker, °knockout, °dream, dreamboat, stunner **3** °attraction, °strength, °advantage, °asset

beckon *v.* °signal, °gesture, °motion; °summon, °bid, °call

become *v.* **1** turn *or* change *or* transform into **2** grow *or* develop *or* evolve into; mature *or* ripen into **3** °enhance, °suit, °fit,

befit, be proper *or* appropriate for, °behoove **4** °grace, adorn **5** ***become of.*** come of, happen to

becoming *adj.* enhancing, beautifying, °seemly; °attractive, °comely, °fetching, °chic, °stylish, °fashionable, °tasteful; °appropriate, °fitting, °fit, °meet, °befitting, °proper, °suitable

bedlam *n.* °pandemonium, °uproar, hubbub, commotion, °confusion, °tumult, turmoil, °furor, °chaos; madhouse

bedraggled *adj.* soiled, °dirty, °muddy, muddied, °untidy, stained, disheveled, scruffy, messy; °wet, °sloppy, soaking *or* sopping *or* wringing wet, soaked, drenched, *Colloq Brit* gungy, *US* grungy

befitting *adj.* °fitting, °becoming, °due, suitable *or* suited (to), °appropriate (to), apropos, °proper (to), °seemly (for)

before *adv.* **1** °previously, earlier, already, beforehand; °formerly, in the past; °once **2** °ahead, °in advance, °in front, in the forefront, °first, in the vanguard, *Colloq* °up front **3** °ahead, in the future, to come —*prep.* **4** ahead of, in advance of, in front of, forward of **5** in front of; in the presence of **6** °preceding, previous *or* anterior to, °prior to; on the eve of **7** in preference to, rather than, sooner than, more willingly than —*conj.* **8** previous to *or* preceding the time when

beg *v.* **1** entreat, °beseech, °plead (with), crave, implore, importune, °wheedle, °cajole, supplicate (with), °pray; °ask for, °request **2** °solicit, sponge, *Colloq* cadge, °scrounge, *US* panhandle

beggar *n.* **1** mendicant, °supplicant, suppliant, almsman, sponger, °tramp, vagrant, °pauper, *Colloq* cadger, scrounger, *US* panhandler —*v.* **2** impoverish; °want, °challenge, °defy, baffle

begin *v.* **1** start (out *or* off *or* in *or* on), °initiate, enter on *or* upon, set out *or* about, set out on *or* upon, *Somewhat formal* °commence **2** °start (off), °inaugurate, °originate, °open, °launch, °create, °establish, °found, °set up; °go into **3** °arise, °start, °originate, *Somewhat formal* °commence

beginning *n.* **1** °start, commencement, °outset, °onset, inception, °dawn, dawning, °birth, genesis, °origin, °creation, day one; origination, °source, wellspring **2** °opening, °start, inception, commencement

begrudge *v.* **1** °resent, °envy, °grudge **2** give (be)grudgingly *or* unwillingly *or* reluctantly, °deny, °refuse

beguile *v.* **1** delude, °deceive, °cheat, °swindle, °dupe, °fool, °mislead, °hoodwink, bamboozle, °take in **2** °defraud (of), °deprive (of), cheat (out of *or* into), °swindle (out of) **3** °charm, °divert, °amuse, °distract, °fascinate, engross, °engage, allure

behalf *n.* ***on*** *or* ***US in behalf of, or on*** *or* ***US in one's behalf.*** °for, as a representative of, in place of, °instead of, in the name of, on the part of; in the interest of, for the benefit *or* advantage of

behave *v.* °act, °react, °function, °operate, °perform, °work, conduct *or* deport *or* comport *or* bear (oneself); act obediently, act properly, be good

behavior *n.* °conduct, demeanor, deportment, °bearing, °manners, comportment; action(s)

behead *v.* decapitate, guillotine, *Archaic* decollate

behold *v.* °see, °look at, °regard, set *or* lay eyes on, descry, °notice, °note, espy, °perceive, discern, °remark, °view

beholden *adj.* °obliged, obligated, °indebted, °grateful, °in debt, under (an) obligation

behoove *v.* be required of, be incumbent on, be proper of, be fitting of *or* for, befit; be advisable for, be worthwhile for, be expeditious for *or* of, be advantageous to *or* for, be useful to *or* for, be beneficial to *or* for

belabor *v.* thrash, °beat, pummel *or* pommel, buffet, °pelt, °lambaste

belated *adj.* °late; behind time, behindhand, °out of date; delayed, detained

belief *n.* **1** °trust, dependence, °reliance, °confidence, °faith, °security, °assurance **2** acceptance, credence; assent **3** °tenet, °view, °idea, °sentiment, °conviction, °doctrine, dogma, principle(s), axiom, °maxim, °creed, °opinion, °persuasion **4** °intuition, °judgment

believe *v.* **1** °accept, put faith *or* credence in *or* into, find credible, find creditable; °allow, °think, °hold, °maintain, °feel; °take it, °suppose, °assume **2** ***believe in.*** trust to *or* in, rely upon *or* on, have faith *or* confidence in, put one's trust in, be convinced of, °swear by, °credit **3** ***make believe.*** °pretend, °suppose, °imagine, °fancy, conjecture, °assume

belittle *v.* °diminish, °minimize, °disparage, °slight, decry, °detract from, °depreciate, °trivialize, deprecate, °degrade, denigrate, °downgrade, deemphasize, °discredit, °criticize, derogate; °reduce, °mitigate, lessen, undervalue, °underestimate, underrate, °minimize, *Colloq* °play down, pooh-pooh

belligerent *adj.* **1** warring; °warlike, °militant, warmongering, hawkish, jingoistic, bellicose, °martial **2** °quarrelsome, °pugnacious, contentious, disputatious, °truculent, °aggressive, °hostile, combative, antagonistic, bellicose —*n.* **3** warring party, °antagonist, °contestant; warmonger, hawk, jingoist, °militant

bellow *v.* **1** °roar; °yell, °shout, °blare, trumpet, °howl, *Colloq* holler —*n.* **2** °roar; °yell, °shout, *Colloq* holler

belong *v.* **1** be a member (of), be affiliated *or* associated *or* connected (with), be attached *or* bound (to), be a part (of) **2** have a (proper) place (in), be proper (to) **3** ***belong to.*** be owned by, be the property *or* possession of

belonging *n.* °association, °connection, °alliance, °relationship, °affinity, °relation

belongings *n.* °(personal) property, °effects, °possessions, °goods, °things, chattels

beloved *adj.* **1** loved, cherished, adored, °dear, dearest, °darling, °precious, treasured; admired, worshiped, revered, esteemed, idolized, respected; valued, prized —*n.* **2** °sweetheart, °darling, dearest, °love; °lover, °paramour, inamorata *or* inamorato, *Colloq* °flame

below *adv.* **1** lower down, farther down, further down **2** °beneath, underneath, °under; downstairs, *Nautical* below-decks, *Brit* below-stairs **3** on earth, here, in this world, under the sun —*prep.* **4** °under, underneath, °beneath **5** less *or* lower *or* cheaper than **6** deeper *or* farther down than **7** °under, °beneath, underneath **8** lower *or* less than, °under **9** inferior *or* subordinate to, lower than **10** inferior *or* secondary to, °under, °beneath, lower than **11** °beneath, °unworthy of, unbefitting, not worth

belt *n.* **1** sash; *Literary* girdle, cestus, cincture, °zone **2** °zone, °band, °strip, °circuit, °perimeter; °area, °swath, °tract, °region, °district —*v.* **3** °strike, °hit, °punch; °beat, thrash **4** ***belt out.*** sing *or* perform stridently *or* loudly; put over *or* across

bemoan *v.* °lament, mourn *or* grieve *or* weep *or* moan for

bemuse *v.* **1** °confuse, °muddle, °mix up, addle, befuddle, °perplex, °bewilder, °puzzle, *Colloq US and Canadian* discombobulate **2** stupefy, benumb, °numb, °paralyze

bend *n.* **1** curve, °turn, turning, corner; °bow, °angle, crook, °hook, curvature, flexure —*v.* **2** °arch, °bow, curve, crook **3** °bow; curtsy *or* curtsey; °kowtow, salaam; kneel, genuflect **4** °incline, °channel, °focus, °direct, °steer, °set; °fix **5** °submit, °bow, °yield, °give way, be pliant *or* subservient *or* tractable **6** °incline, °turn, °deflect

bender *n.* *Colloq* °drunk, °spree, °bout, °revel, carousal, °carouse, bacchanal; *Slang* binge, °jag, *US* toot

beneath *adv.* **1** low *or* lower down, °below, °under, underneath **2** °below, underneath, °under; °underground —*prep.* **3** °under, underneath, °below **4** °below, °unworthy of, unbefitting, undeserving of, not (even) meriting, lower than

benefactor *n.* °patron, °supporter, °sponsor, °donor, °philanthropist; °backer, investor, °supporter, *Colloq* angel

beneficial *adj.* **1** °advantageous, °serviceable, °useful, °profitable, °helpful, °supportive, °favorable, °constructive, °good **2** healthful, °healthy, salutary, salubrious; °efficacious, °effective

benefit *n.* **1** °advantage, °profit, °good, °sake, °gain, °aid, °help, °service **2** Often, ***benefits.*** perquisite(s), emolument(s), allowance(s), extra(s), fringe benefit(s), *Colloq* perk(s) —*v.* **3** °improve, °aid, °help, °better, °promote, °further, °advance, °forward **4** °profit, °gain

benevolence *n.* **1** °charity, °kindness, kindliness, °humanity, humanitarianism, beneficence, charitableness, goodness, °altruism, goodwill, unselfishness, °philanthropy, generosity, magnanimity **2** °gift, °grant, contribution, °donation, beneficence

benevolent *adj.* °charitable, well-disposed, °gracious, °good, °kind, °kindly, humane, °humanitarian, well-wishing, °thoughtful, °considerate, °sympathetic, caring, kindhearted, warmhearted, compassionate, °benign, benignant; °liberal, °generous, magnanimous, openhanded; °beneficial, °helpful, salutary

benighted *adj.* unenlightened, naive *or* naïve, °uninformed, °ignorant

benign *adj.* **1** °kindly, °gracious, °good, °kind, kindhearted, °benevolent, benignant, °warm, warmhearted, °cordial, °genial, congenial, °tender, tenderhearted, compassionate, °sympathetic, °softhearted **2** °bland, °gentle, °mild, °warm **3** °kind, °favorable, °fortunate; salutary, salubrious, °mild, congenial, °propitious **4** nonfatal, nonmalignant, nonvirulent, curable, °harmless

bent *adj.* **1** curved, deflected, bowed, °crooked, distorted, twisted, warped **2** °strange, °weird, °peculiar, twisted, °deviant, warped, °wry, awry, °corrupt, corrupted; °perverted, °perverse, °abnormal **3** °dishonest, °crooked, °illegal **4** °determined, °intent, °set, resolved, °resolute, °decided, °set —*n.* **5** °turn, °inclination, °direction, °disposition, predisposition, °tendency, °bias, °leaning, proclivity, propensity, °partiality, °prejudice; °ability, °aptitude, °talent, °gift

bequeath *v.* °leave, °make over, °will, °pass on, hand down *or* on, °transmit, *Law* °devise

bequest *n.* legacy, °inheritance

berate *v.* °scold, chide, °rate, °upbraid, revile, °abuse, rail at, excoriate, °castigate, objurgate; °harangue

bereave *v.* °deprive; °strip, °rob, °dispossess

berserk *adj.* amok, °mad, °violent, °wild, crazed, frenzied, °maniacal

beseech *v.* supplicate, entreat, implore, °plead (with), °beg, importune, obsecrate

beset *v.* encompass, °surround, °besiege; assail, °attack, °harass, harry, hector, °bother, °afflict, °trouble

beside *prep.* **1** alongside, °near, next to, with, °close to, hard by, °nearby, °by **2** away from, wide of, °apart from, unconnected with, °off **3** ***beside oneself.*** out of one's mind *or* wits, at the end of one's tether, °overwrought, °agitated, °upset, °crazy, °mad

besides *adv.* **1** °in addition, additionally, also; °further, furthermore, °moreover, as well, too; °to boot, on top of everything else, into the bargain —*prep.* **2** over and above, above and beyond, °in addition to, additionally to, as well as; aside from, °barring, excepting, °except for, excluding, °exclusive of, not counting *or* including, beyond, °apart from, other than

besiege *v.* **1** lay siege to, beleaguer **2** blockade, °block, block off *or* up, hem in, °cut off; °surround, crowd round **3** importune, °sue, °petition, assail, *Brit* pressurize *or US* pressure, °press, °overwhelm, inundate

best *adj.* **1** °superlative, unexcelled, finest, °preeminent, °first, °superb, unsurpassed, °superior, °excellent, °paramount, °first-rate, *Colloq* A-1 *or* A-one **2** kindest, most beneficent, nicest **3** °foremost, choicest, °preeminent, most suitable, most appropriate, most qualified, most talented, most desirable, most outstanding **4** largest, most, greatest **5** richest, wealthiest; first-class, upper-crust, °upper-class —*n.* **6** finest; °first **7** °finery, best clothes, *Colloq* best bib and tucker **8** greatest *or* maximum effort —*adv.* **9** most excellently, to the fullest extent, in the most suitable way, most adroitly, most skillfully, most superbly, most artistically **10** with greatest satisfaction, most successfully —*v.* **11** win (out) over, °conquer, °beat, °surpass, °overpower, get the better of, °subdue, °defeat, worst, vanquish, trounce, °rout, °crush, °master, °outdo, °overwhelm, °overcome, °outwit

bestow *v.* °confer; °give, °award, °present, °donate, °grant

bet *n.* **1** wager, °stake, °gamble, °risk, °venture, °speculation, *Brit* punt, *Colloq Brit* °flutter —*v.* **2** wager, °stake, °gamble, °risk, °hazard, °play, lay (a bet *or* stake *or* wager), °put, °chance, °speculate, °venture, *Brit* punt

betray *v.* **1** be *or* prove false *or* disloyal to, °sell out, break faith with, °let down, °fail, °inform on, *Colloq* sell down the river, *Slang Brit* °shop **2** °reveal, °disclose, divulge, °impart, °tell; °expose, °lay bare **3** °lead astray, °mislead, misguide, °deceive, °dupe, °fool, °hoodwink

betrayal *n.* **1** treachery, treason, disloyalty, °perfidy, traitorousness, faithlessness, bad faith, breach of faith, *Slang* °sell out **2** °revelation, divulging, disclosure, divulgence

better *adj.* **1** °superior **2** more; greater, larger, bigger **3** wiser, safer, °well-advised, more intelligent **4** healthier, haler, heartier, less ill *or US* sick, improved; cured, recovered —*adv.* **5** preferably, °best; more wisely, more advisedly, more safely **6** ***better off.*** **(a)** improved, happier, °well-advised **(b)** wealthier, richer **7** ***think better of.*** reconsider, think twice, change one's mind —*n.* **8** °advantage, mastery, °superiority, °control **9** ***betters.*** superiors —*v.* **10** °improve, ameliorate, °advance, °raise, elevate **11** °surpass, °excel, °outdo, °outstrip, °beat, °improve

bettor *n.* gambler, speculator, wagerer, gamester, °player, *Brit* °better, punter, *Colloq* crapshooter, °sport

bewail *v.* °lament, °mourn, °bemoan, moan *or* mourn over, shed tears *or* whimper over, weep *or* cry *or* keen over, beat one's breast over

beware *v.* take heed, be careful, be wary, be cautious, be on one's guard, exercise caution, °mind, watch out, °look out, take care

bewilder *v.* °confuse, confound, °perplex, °puzzle, °mystify, befuddle, baffle, °bemuse

bewitch *v.* °enchant, °entrance, spellbind, °charm, °fascinate, °beguile, cast a spell over, °captivate, °enrapture

bias *n.* **1** °prejudice, °partiality; °inclination, °leaning, °bent, °disposition, propensity, °tendency, predilection, predisposition, proclivity **2** °angle, °slant, diagonal **3** °influence, impulse, °weight —*v.* **4** °influence, affect unduly *or* unfairly, °sway, °incline, °prejudice, °color, °taint, predispose

biased *adj.* biassed, °prejudiced, °partial; warped, distorted, °jaundiced

bicker *v.* °dispute, °quarrel, wrangle, °argue, squabble, °tiff, *Colloq* spat

bid *v.* **1** °offer, make an offer (for), °tender, proffer **2** *Archaic or literary* °ask, °pray, °press, entreat, °beg, °request, °suggest, invite **3** *Formal* °command, °demand, °order, °tell, enjoin, °dictate

bidding *n.* **1** °invitation, summons **2** °command, °order, °dictate, °direction, °instruction, °demand

big *adj.* **1** °large, °great, °grand; °huge, °enormous, °immense, °gigantic, °giant, tremendous, °colossal, Brobdingnagian, °jumbo, *Colloq Brit* socking *or* whacking big *or* great, *US* humongous **2** °ample, °hefty, °huge, °bulky, °fat, °obese; °large, °hulking, beefy, °burly, °brawny, strapping, gargantuan, elephantine, °enormous, °gigantic, °immense, °monstrous **3** °tall, grown, °mature, grown up, °large **4** °important, °significant, °outstanding, °weighty, consequential, °major, °grave, °momentous, °notable, °noteworthy, °telling **5** °important, °prominent, °illustrious, °noteworthy, °notable, °renowned, °eminent, °distinguished, esteemed **6** °generous, magnanimous, °charitable, °unselfish, giving **7** *Colloq* °popular, °famous, °well-known, °successful **8** °large, °capital, upper-case, majuscule —*adv.* **9** *Colloq* pompously, boastfully, conceitedly, arrogantly, pretentiously **10** successfully, °well, outstandingly, effectively

bigoted *adj.* °prejudiced, °intolerant, °biased, °jaundiced, °one-sided, °partial

bigotry *n.* °prejudice, °intolerance, °bias, °partiality

bigwig *n.* **1** °boss, kingpin, °king, °queen, nabob, VIP (= 'very important person'), *Colloq* big shot, big gun, big cheese, big wheel, hotshot, °chief, brass hat, *US* (chief) honcho, Mr. Big **2** ***bigwigs.*** °brass, brass hats

bilious *adj.* ill-tempered, bad-tempered, ill-natured, °peevish, °testy, °cross, °petulant, tetchy, choleric, dyspeptic, °angry, wrathful

bill¹ *n.* **1** invoice, °account; °tally, °reckoning, tabulation, *US* °(restaurant) check, *Colloq US* °tab **2** *US and Canadian* °note, banknote, paper money, *Colloq* folding money —*v.* **3** invoice, °charge

bill² *n.* beak, neb, nib, pecker; jaws

bind *v.* **1** °tie, °fasten, °secure, make fast, °tie up **2** constrain; °hold, °oblige, °obligate **3** gird, °encircle, wreathe, °wrap, °cover, °swathe, bandage **4** °cement, °stick, cause to adhere; °attach, °connect —*n.* **5** *Colloq US* °dilemma, °predicament, tight spot, °(difficult) situation, *Colloq* pickle, °fix, °jam **6** *Brit* °annoyance, irritant, °bother, °bore, °trial, °ordeal, irritation, vexation, *Colloq* pain (in the neck *or* arse)

birth *n.* **1** childbirth, °delivery, *Technical* parturition, *Old-fashioned* confinement **2** °origin, °creation, °emergence, °beginning, °start, origination **3** nativity, °origin, °extraction; °parentage, °line, °lineage, ancestry, descent, °family, blood

bisexual *adj.* **1** hermaphrodite *or* hermaphroditic(al), androgynous **2** *Colloq* AC/DC, swinging both ways, *Facetious* ambisextrous —*n.* **3** androgyne, hermaphrodite

bit *n.* **1** °morsel, °piece, °scrap, °fragment, °shred, °particle, °grain, °crumb **2** °jot, tittle, whit, scintilla, °trace, °touch, °hint, °suggestion, °suspicion, °particle, iota, °speck, atom **3** °moment, °minute, °second, °flash, *Colloq* two shakes (of a lamb's tail) **4** °piece, °share, °equity, °segment, °portion, °part, fraction

bitch *n.* **1** °shrew, °nag, termagant, virago, harpy, °fury, spitfire, °scold **2** whore, °prostitute, bawd, harlot, call girl, trollop, strumpet, trull, °drab, °tart, floozy, streetwalker, *Colloq* bimbo, pro, *US* hooker, °tramp, hustler —*v.* **3** °complain, °object, °protest, grumble, *Colloq* °gripe **4** °bungle, °botch, °ruin, °spoil

bite *v.* **1** °nip; °chew, °gnaw **2** °sting —*n.* **3** °mouthful, °morsel, °scrap, °bit, °piece, °taste; °snack, *Slang* nosh **4** °sting

biting *adj.* °severe, °harsh, °cutting, °piercing, °penetrating, °keen, °sharp, °bitter; °cold, °wintry, °freezing

bitter *adj.* **1** °harsh, acerbic, acrid, °sharp, °caustic, mordant **2** unappetizing, °distasteful, °unsavory, unpleasant, hard (to swallow *or* take), irritating, °obnoxious, °disagreeable, °nasty, °painful, °unwelcome, °unpalatable **3** °miserable, °grievous, dispiriting, distressing, °cruel, distressful **4** °resentful, °embittered, °rancorous; °hateful **5** stinging, °cutting, °biting, °harsh, °reproachful, °vicious, acrimonious, °virulent; °cruel, °unkind, unpleasant, °nasty **6** °sharp, °keen, °cutting, °severe, °biting, °cold, °wintry, °freezing

bitterness *n.* **1** harshness, acerbity, acrimony, acrimoniousness, spleen, *Literary* gall and wormwood **2** °animosity, hatred, °resentment; °hostility, °antagonism

bizarre *adj.* **1** °eccentric, °unusual, unconventional, °extravagant, °whimsical, °strange, °odd, °curious, °peculiar, °queer, °offbeat, °fantastic, °weird, °incongruous, °deviant, °erratic, *Slang* °kinky **2** °grotesque, °irregular, °nonconformist, nonconforming, °outlandish, °outré, °quaint, °fantastic, unconventional

blab *v.* °broadcast, °tattle, °babble, °betray, °reveal, °disclose, divulge, °expose

blabbermouth *n.* telltale, babbler, chatterer, °gossip, *Colloq* °blab, tattletale, bigmouth

black *adj.* **1** jet, jet-black, coal-black, inky, sooty, swart, °swarthy, raven, ebony, °dusky, *Literary* ebon **2** Negro, negroid, colored, dark-skinned **3** °dark, °pitch-black, jet-black, coal-black, Stygian; starless, moonless **4** °dark, °somber, °dusky, °gloomy, °menacing, glowering, louring *or* lowering, °threatening, °funereal **5** °malignant, baleful, baneful, °deadly, deathly, °sinister, °dismal, °hateful, °disastrous **6** °bad, °foul, iniquitous, °wicked, °evil, diabolical, °infernal, hellish, °atrocious, °awful, malicious, °abominable, °outrageous, °vicious, °villainous, flagitious, °vile, °disgraceful, °unscrupulous, °unconscionable, unprincipled, blackguardly, knavish, °perfidious, insidious, nefarious, dastardly, treacherous, unspeakable, °shameful, °scurvy, °criminal, felonious **7** °angry, wrathful, °furious, frowning, bad-tempered, sulky, °resentful, clouded, °threatening, glowering

blacken *v.* **1** darken, smudge, begrime **2** °slander, °libel, asperse, cast aspersions on, traduce, °smear, °sully, °soil, besmirch, °taint, °tarnish, defame, revile, malign, °vilify, °discredit, denigrate

blackleg *n.* scab, strikebreaker

blackmail *n.* **1** extortion, °ransom, °tribute, *US* °graft —*v.* **2** extort money from; °force, coerce, compel, °make

blade *n.* **1** °knife, cutting edge **2** *Literary* sword, rapier, sabre, °dagger, poniard, stiletto, cutlass, bayonet, °knife, penknife, jackknife **3** leaf, °leaflet, frond, °shoot **4** *Somewhat old-fashioned* °playboy, ladies' man, man about town, fop, °dandy

blame *v.* **1** find fault with, censure, °criticize, °fault; °accuse, °charge, °indict, °condemn, °point to, point (the finger) at, °rebuke, °reprimand, recriminate, reproach, °scold, reprehend, °reprove **2** hold responsible, fix (the) responsibility upon *or* on, put *or* place *or* lay (the) blame on, lay at someone's door, °denounce, °incriminate —*n.* **3** censure, °criticism, °reproof, °rebuke, °recrimination, °disapproval, disapprobation, reproach, objurgation, condemnation, reprehension **4** culpability, °responsibility; °guilt, *Slang* °rap

blameless *adj.* °faultless, guiltless, °innocent, °irreproachable, unimpeachable

bland *adj.* **1** °gentle, °soothing, °smooth, °mild, °suave, urbane, °cool, unruffled, °calm, composed, unemotional, °nonchalant, insouciant **2** insipid, °boring, °dull, uninteresting, ennuyant, °tasteless, *Colloq US* plain vanilla; *Slang US* blah

blank *adj.* **1** °empty, °plain, °bare **2** unornamented, °unadorned, undecorated, °void **3** °vacant, °empty **4** °passive, °impassive, expressionless, emotionless, vacuous, °mindless, unexpressive **5** °disconcerted, discomfited, nonplussed, °confused, °helpless, resourceless, perplexed, dazed, bewildered **6** unrelieved, °stark, °sheer, utter, °pure, unmixed, °absolute, °unqualified —*n.* **7** °space; °line, °box **8** °nothing, °zero, °nil; °void, °emptiness

blare *v.* **1** °blast, °bellow, trumpet, °ring, °boom, °thunder, °roar, bray; °resound, °echo, reverberate, resonate —*n.* **2** °blast, °bellow, °ring, °roar, °boom, °noise, °sound, clamor

blasé *adj.* **1** bored, °jaded, °weary, unimpressed, ennuyé **2** °indifferent, °cool, °superior, °supercilious, °sophisticated, °unmoved, °nonchalant, emotionless, °phlegmatic, apathetic, pococurante, °carefree, lighthearted, insouciant, devil-may-care

blaspheme *v.* **1** °curse, °swear, imprecate, execrate, °profane, °damn **2** °abuse, malign, calumniate, defame, °disparage, revile, °put down, decry, deprecate, °depreciate, °belittle

blasphemous *adj.* °profane, °impious, °irreverent, °disrespectful, °sacrilegious, irreligious, °sinful, °wicked, °evil, iniquitous

blast *n.* **1** °blow, °gust, °wind, °gale **2** °blare, °sound, °noise, °racket, °din, °bellow, °roar; °boom **3** °explosion, °burst, °eruption, °discharge; detonation **4** (*at or in*) ***full blast.*** fully, at full tilt, at the maximum, °completely, °thoroughly, °entirely, maximally, *Slang* with no holds barred, *US* to the max —*v.* **5** °blow up, °explode, dynamite, °demolish, °destroy, °ruin, °waste, °lay waste, °shatter, °devastate **6** defame, °discredit, °denounce, °criticize, °attack; °ruin, °destroy **7** °curse, °damn

blatant *adj.* **1** °obvious, °flagrant, palpable, °obtrusive, arrant, °shameless, unashamed, °brazen, °overt, °glaring **2** °noisy, clamorous, °loud, bellowing, °strident, vociferous, °rowdy, °boisterous, °obstreperous, °uproarious

blaze *n.* **1** °flame, °fire, °holocaust, inferno, conflagration **2** °outburst, °eruption, flare-up **3** °light, brightness, °brilliance, brilliancy, °glow —*v.* **4** °burn, °flare up, °flame **5** ***blaze away*** (*at*). °fire, °shoot, open fire, °blast; °bombard, °shell

bleach *v.* **1** whiten, °lighten, °fade, blanch, blench, *Technical* etiolate —*n.* **2** whitener, chlorine

bleak *adj.* **1** cheerless, °dreary, depressing, °dismal, °gloomy, °somber, °melancholy, °sad, °unhappy, °mournful **2** °cold, °chilly, °raw, °bitter **3** °barren, °bare, exposed, windswept, °desolate

blemish *v.* **1** °deface, °mar, °scar, °impair, disfigure **2** °tarnish, °stain, °sully, °spoil, °mar, °flaw, °harm, °damage, °scar, °injure, °bruise, besmirch —*n.* **3** disfigurement, °scar, °mark, °impairment, °stain, °smear, °blot; °defect, °flaw, °error, °fault, °imperfection, °error, erratum

blend *v.* **1** °mix, °mingle, °combine, meld, commingle, intermingle **2** °shade, °grade, gradate, °graduate, °merge, coalesce, °fuse,

°unite —*n.* 3 °mixture, °mix, °combination, mingling, meld, commingling, intermingling

bless *v.* 1 consecrate, °hallow, °sanctify; °extol, °glorify, °praise, °revere, °adore 2 °give, make happy or fortunate, endow, °favor, °furnish, °provide, °supply, °grace

blessing *n.* 1 benediction, °prayer, consecration 2 °boon, °favor, °advantage, good fortune, °godsend, °luck, °profit, °gain, °help, °asset, °gift, °bounty

blight *n.* 1 °affliction, °disease, °plague, infestation, °pestilence, °scourge 2 °misfortune, °curse, °trouble, °woe, °calamity —*v.* 3 °afflict, °infest, °plague, °scourge; wither, °mar, °taint, °blast

blind *adj.* 1 sightless, eyeless, unsighted, purblind, stone-blind 2 imperceptive, °slow, insensitive, °thick, °dense, °obtuse, °stupid, weak-minded, dull-witted, slow-witted, dimwitted, *Colloq Brit* gormless 3 °indiscriminate, undiscriminating, °heedless, °reckless, °rash, °impetuous, °inconsiderate, unreasoning, °mindless, °senseless, °thoughtless, °unthinking, irrational, delusional 4 ***blind to.*** unaware *or* unconscious of, impervious *or* insensible to, unaffected *or* untouched *or* unmoved by —*v.* 5 °deceive, blindfold, blinker; bamboozle, °hoodwink, °fool 6 °conceal, °hide, °eclipse, °overshadow; °dazzle, blindfold —*n.* 7 °shade, curtain, °screen, °cover, shutter(s), awning 8 °pretense, °pretext, °front, °cover, smoke screen, °stratagem, °subterfuge, °ruse, °trick, °deception, *Colloq* °dodge; *Slang* scam

blindly *adv.* recklessly, heedlessly, deludedly, indiscriminately, rashly, impetuously, irrationally, thoughtlessly, mindlessly, senselessly, unthinkingly

blink *v.* 1 wink, °flicker, *Technical* nictitate 2 °twinkle, °flicker, °gleam, glimmer, °shimmer, °flash, °sparkle, scintillate, coruscate 3 °flinch, wince, °shrink, quail, blench, °recoil, °start, °move 4 ***blink at.*** wink at, °ignore, °overlook, °disregard —*n.* 5 wink, °flicker 6 ***on the blink.*** *Colloq* °out of order, °broken, in disrepair, not working *or* operating, not operational, *Slang US* out of whack, on the fritz

bliss *n.* °happiness, blitheness, gladness, °joy, blessedness, °delight, felicity, °glee, °enjoyment, °pleasure, joyousness, °cheer, exhilaration, °gaiety, blissfulness, °rapture, °ecstasy

blithe *adj.* 1 blissful, °happy, °cheerful, joyous, °merry, lighthearted, well-pleased, °delighted, °gay, °joyful, °elated, jubilant 2 happy-go-lucky, insouciant, °heedless, °carefree, unconcerned, °blasé, °casual, °detached, °indifferent, uncaring, °careless

bloated *adj.* °swollen, distended, full, puffy; puffed-up, °overgrown, °inflated, °pompous

blob *n.* °gob, gobbet, globule, °drop, droplet, °bit, gout, °lump, °dab, *Colloq* glob, *Chiefly US and Canadian* smidgen *or* smidgin

block *n.* 1 °piece, chunk, hunk, °lump, °slab; °stump; °brick, cube 2 °bar, °obstacle, °obstruction, °hindrance, °stumbling block, °deterrent, °impediment, °barrier —*v.* 3 °obstruct, °close off, barricade; °bar, °shut off; °hinder, °hamper, balk, °impede, °prevent 4 ***block out.*** (a) °rough out, °design, °outline, sketch, °lay out, °plan (b) °mask, °screen, °blank (out), °erase, °eliminate, °exclude, °blot out, °deny 5 ***block (up).*** °stuff (up), congest, °clog, *Colloq Brit* bung up

bloodshed *n.* °slaughter, °carnage, butchery, °killing, °murder, bloodletting; °violence; genocide

bloodsucker *n.* leech, extortionist, extortioner, blackmailer; °parasite, barnacle, *Colloq* sponge, freeloader, °scrounge, scrounger; *Slang US* moocher

bloodthirsty *adj.* °murderous, °homicidal, °savage, feral, °cruel, °ruthless, pitiless, °vicious, °brutal, °sadistic, °ferocious, °fierce, *Formal* °sanguinary, *Literary* °fell

blot *n.* 1 °stain, °spot, °mark, smudge, blotch, °blemish, disfigurement, °smear, smirch, °scar, *Colloq* splodge *or US also* splotch —*v.* 2 °stain, °spot, °spatter, smudge, °mark, °blur 3 ***blot one's copybook.*** °err, destroy *or* ruin *or* mar *or* spoil one's reputation, commit an indiscretion, °transgress, °sin 4 ***blot out.*** (a) °obscure, °conceal, °cover (up), °hide, °eclipse, °dim (b) °obliterate, °destroy, °erase, °demolish, efface, annihilate, °delete, rub *or* wipe out

blow[1] *v.* 1 °breathe, °puff, °exhale; °expel 2 °waft, °puff, whistle, whine, °blast 3 °bungle, °botch, make a mess of, muff, mismanage, *Colloq* °screw up, °mess up, °fluff, °bugger up, *Taboo* fuck up 4 *Colloq* °spend, °lavish, squander, °waste, throw out or away 5 short-circuit, burn out 6 ***blow hot and cold.*** vacillate, °hesitate, dither, *Colloq* °shilly-shally 7 ***blow out.*** (a) °extinguish (b) °explode, °burst (c) short-circuit, burn out 8 ***blow up.*** (a) become furious *or* angry *or* enraged, °flare up, lose one's temper, *Slang* blow one's top *or US also* stack, flip one's lid *or Brit* top (b) °explode, °burst, °shatter, *Colloq* bust; detonate, dynamite, °destroy, °blast (c) °enlarge, °inflate, embroider, °magnify, °expand, °exaggerate, °overstate (d) °enlarge, °magnify, °amplify, °expand, °increase (e) °inflate; distend, °swell —*n.* 9 °gale, °storm, °tempest, °whirlwind, tornado, cyclone, °hurricane, typhoon, northeaster, nor'easter

blow[2] *n.* 1 °stroke, °punch, clout, whack, °hit, °knock, thump, thwack, *Colloq* wallop 2 °shock, °surprise, °bombshell, °jolt, bolt from the blue, °revelation

blue *adj.* 1 depressed, low-spirited, dispirited, °sad, °dismal, down, °down in the mouth, °gloomy, °unhappy, °glum, downcast, crestfallen, chapfallen, °dejected, °melancholy, °despondent, °downhearted, morose 2 °obscene, °vulgar, °indecent, titillating, °pornographic, °dirty, °filthy, °lewd, smutty, °risqué, °bawdy, °sexy, X, X-rated, 18, *US* XXX; indelicate, °suggestive, °off-color, °erotic, °coarse, °offensive, °improper

bluff[1] *v.* **1** °deceive, °hoodwink, °dupe, °mislead, delude, °trick, cozen, °fool, *Colloq* bamboozle **2** °pretend, feign, °bluster, °fool, *Colloq* kid; *Slang* bullshit —*n.* **3** °bombast, °bravado, boasting, bragging, °bluster, °show, puffery; °deception, °blind; *Literary* rodomontade, gasconade; *Colloq* °hot air

bluff[2] *adj.* **1** blustering, °gruff, °rough, °abrupt, °blunt, °curt, °short, °crude **2** °frank, °open, °hearty, straightforward, °plain, plain-spoken, °outspoken, affable, approachable, °good-natured, °friendly —*n.* **3** °cliff, escarpment, °precipice, scarp, headland, promontory, palisades

blunder *v.* **1** °stumble, °flounder —*n.* **2** °mistake, °error, gaffe, faux pas, °slip, slip-up, °howler, *Colloq* boo-boo, screw-up, °fluff, boner, *US* goof, goof-up

blunt *adj.* **1** °dull, °worn **2** °abrupt, °curt, rough-spoken, plain-spoken, °short, °direct, °candid, °frank, unceremonious, undiplomatic, °inconsiderate, °thoughtless, °brusque, °outspoken, °bluff, °brash, indelicate, °rude, uncivil, °ungracious, °discourteous, °impolite; straightforward, °straight, uncomplicated, uncompromising —*v.* **3** °dull, take the edge off **4** °soften, °mitigate, mollify, soothe; efface, °dim, °obscure, °blur, °weaken

blur *n.* **1** indistinctness, dimness, haziness, cloudiness, fogginess **2** °fog, haze, *Brit* fuzz —*v.* **3** °dim, °befog, °obscure, bedim; efface **4** °obscure, °hide, °conceal, °veil, °mask; °weaken

blurt *v.* Usually, ***blurt out.*** burst out with, utter; °reveal, °disclose, °give away, divulge, *Colloq* °blab

blush *v.* be *or* act ashamed, redden, °flush, °color

bluster *v.* **1** °storm, °rage, °harangue **2** °swagger, °strut, °talk big, °boast, °brag, blow one's own horn *or* trumpet, °show off, crow —*n.* **3** swaggering, storming, raging, °raving, haranguing, °tumult; °hot air, puffery, °bravado, grandiloquence, *Literary* rodomontade

board *n.* **1** °plank, scantling, °timber **2** °table, gaming *or* game table *or* surface **3** °food, meals, °provisions **4** °council, °committee, directors, directorship, °management, °cabinet, panel, trustees, advisers *or* advisors **5** ***on board.*** aboard, on —*v.* **6** go aboard, ship aboard; °enter, °embark on **7** °feed; °eat, take meals; °accommodate, °lodge, °house, billet, °quarter; °lodge, °stay, °live, °room; *Colloq* °put up

boast *n.* **1** °brag, bragging —*v.* **2** °brag, vaunt, crow, °showoff, *Colloq US* blow *or* toot one's (own) horn *or* trumpet; *Slang* lay it on thick, °talk big

boastful *adj.* °ostentatious, showoffish, bragging, vainglorious, °egotistical, °vain, °conceited

boat *n.* [See also **ship, 1.**] °vessel, °craft, skiff, small craft, motorboat, speedboat, knockabout, runabout, yacht, motor yacht, sailing yacht, *Brit* rowing boat, sailing boat, *US* rowboat, sailboat, *Colloq* °ship

bode *v.* portend, °promise, augur, betoken, forebode, presage; °foreshadow

body *n.* **1** °corpse, °cadaver, °remains, carcass, *Slang* °stiff **2** °trunk, torso **3** main part *or* portion, °hull, fuselage **4** °substance, essentials, main part, °essence, °heart, °center, °core **5** °majority, °bulk, main part *or* portion, mass(es) **6** °association, °league, °band, °corps, confederation, °fraternity, °society; °committee, °council; °group, assemblage, °assembly, congress, °company **7** richness, °substance, firmness, consistency, solidity, thickness, density, fullness, viscosity

bog *n.* **1** °swamp, fen, °marsh, quagmire **2** ***bog down.*** °impede, °slow, °hamper, °encumber, °stymie, °stick, °handicap, °clog, °check, °set back, °hold back

bogus *adj.* °counterfeit, °spurious, °fake, °false, °fraudulent, °sham, °imitation, °fictitious, *Colloq* phoney *or US also* phony

Bohemian *adj.* °nonconformist, unconforming, unconventional, °unorthodox, °casual, free-and-easy

boil[1] *v.* **1** °bubble, °seethe; °simmer, °stew, steam **2** °seethe, °fume, sizzle, °smolder, °chafe, fulminate, °ferment, sputter, splutter, °bluster

boil[2] *n.* abscess, carbuncle, pustule, *Technical* furuncle

boisterous *adj.* °rowdy, clamorous, °rough, °noisy, °lively, °exuberant, °unruly, °wild, °undisciplined, °tempestuous, °stormy, turbulent, *Colloq* rambunctious

bold *adj.* **1** °courageous, °brave, plucky, °confident, stouthearted, lionhearted, °daring, °enterprising, °audacious, °fearless, unafraid, °intrepid, °resolute, °dauntless, undaunted, valiant, °stout, valorous, °stalwart, °adventurous, °venturesome; °reckless, °foolhardy, incautious, °daredevil, °rash **2** °audacious, °presumptuous, °forward, °immodest, °brazen, °impudent, temerarious, °impertinent, °shameless **3** °pronounced, °outstanding, °striking, °vigorous, °clear, °strong, °vivid, °distinct, °conspicuous

bolster *v.* °support, °prop (up), °brace, shore up, °buttress, °uphold, °back (up), °reinforce, °aid, °help, °assist, °further, °advance

bolt *n.* **1** arrow, dart, °projectile, °missile, *Historical* °quarrel **2** °pin, °bar, °rod, °catch; latch **3** machine screw **4** °roll, °length **5** lightning flash, thunderbolt, *Formal* fulguration **6** ***bolt from or out of the blue.*** °surprise, °shock, °bombshell, °bomb, °blow, °revelation, eye-opener, *Colloq* shocker **7** ***shoot one's bolt.*** exhaust *or* use up one's resources, *Slang* burn out, *US* poop out —*v.* **8** °spring, dart, shoot off, °take flight, °run (away *or* off), °rush (off *or* away), °break away, °flee, decamp, abscond, °escape, °fly, °dash (off *or* away), *Colloq* skedaddle, scram, *Brit* scarper, do a bunk, do a moonlight flit, *US* take a (runout) powder **9** °gulp (down), swallow whole **10** °fasten,

°lock, latch, °secure **11** °fix, °attach, °fasten, °connect, make fast to —*adv.* **12** ***bolt upright.*** °erect, °straight, rigidly, stiffly

bomb *n.* **1** °bombshell, °shell, °explosive —*v.* **2** °bombard, °shell, °batter, °blow up

bombard *v.* **1** °batter, °bomb, °shell **2** assail, °attack, °assault, °set upon; °besiege

bombast *n.* pretentious language, flatulence, °bluster, °show, grandiloquence, magniloquence, °hot air, °bravado, °boast, boasting, *Literary* gasconade, rodomontade; *Colloq* puffery

bombastic *adj.* high-flown, °extravagant, °pompous, °grandiose, grandiloquent, magniloquent, °inflated, fustian, flatulent, turgid, *Literary* euphuistic

bombshell *n.* °surprise, °shock, eye-opener, °bomb, °blow, °revelation, bolt from *or* out of the blue, *Colloq* shocker

bona fide *adj.* °genuine, °authentic, attested, °real, °veritable, °legitimate, °true, valid; in good faith, °sincere, °honest

bond *n.* **1** tie(s), °shackles, chains, fetters, °manacles, °handcuffs, °trammels, thongs, cord(s), rope(s); restraint(s), constraint(s), check(s), control(s), rein(s) **2** covenant, °pact, °contract, °agreement, °engagement, °compact, °treaty **3** °connection, °link, linkage, °union, °tie, °relationship —*v.* **4** °cement, °bind, hold together, °stick, cohere

bondage *n.* °slavery, °servitude, °subjection, subjugation, enslavement, serfdom, thralldom; vassalage, villeinage

bonny *adj.* °beautiful, °comely, °attractive, °pretty, °lovely

bonus *n.* °reward, °largess, handout, °perquisite, °extra, °honorarium, °tip, gratuity, °remuneration, compensation, *Colloq* °perk

book *n.* **1** °volume, tome, °work, °publication; hardcover, softcover, paperback **2** libretto, °words, °lyrics **3** rules, laws, regulations —*v.* **4** °engage, °reserve; earmark, ticket; °order, °register, °enroll, °list, °enlist, log, °record, °post

bookkeeper *n.* clerk; accountant, *Brit* chartered accountant, CA, cashier; *US* CPA, certified public accountant

bookworm *n.* bibliophile, booklover, inveterate *or* ardent reader, *Formal* bibliophage

boom *v.* **1** °sound, °resound, resonate, °blast, rumble, °thunder, °roar, bang, °explode **2** °prosper, °thrive, °flourish, °progress, °grow, °increase, burgeon *or* bourgeon —*n.* **3** °blast, rumble, °explosion **4** °prosperity, profitability; °growth, °increase, burgeoning *or* bourgeoning

boomerang *v.* °rebound, °recoil, backfire, °miscarry, redound

boon *n.* °gift, °favor, °award, °reward, gratuity, °present; °blessing, °benefit, °advantage

boor *n.* **1** °rustic, °peasant, yokel, (country) bumpkin, °provincial, backwoodsman, *US* hayseed, hillbilly, Juke, Kallikak, *Slang* hick **2** °barbarian, °yahoo, oaf, °clod, clodhopper, °philistine, °clown, grobian; hoyden, *Colloq* lummox, *Slang* galoot, °slob, *US* goop, slobbovian

boorish *adj.* °rustic, °barbarian, °rude, °crude, °ill-mannered, uncultured, °coarse, clownish, uncouth, loutish, oafish, gawky, °vulgar, ill-bred

boost *n.* **1** °lift, shove *or* push up *or* upward(s), *Colloq* leg up; °rise, °raise **2** °encouragement, °help, °aid, °assistance, °support **3** °increase, °rise, *US* °raise, hike —*v.* **4** °lift, shove *or* push up *or* upward(s), °raise **5** °encourage, °promote, °help, °aid, °support, °assist, °improve **6** °increase, °raise

boot *n.* **1** ***to boot.*** °in addition, into the bargain, °besides, °moreover, as well, also, too, additionally **2** shoe, riding boot, bootee —*v.* **3** °eject, °expel, shove, °propel, °push, *Colloq* °kick **4** *Literary* °profit, avail, °help, be in aid of

booth *n.* **1** °stall, °stand **2** °compartment, cubicle, °box, *Brit* kiosk

bootless *adj.* °pointless, unavailing, °vain, °purposeless, °useless, °futile, °worthless, unproductive, °ineffective, °inefficacious, °fruitless, °unprofitable, profitless, unremunerative, unrewarding, °wasteful, time-wasting, Sisyphean

booty *n.* °plunder, °gain, spoil(s), contraband, takings, °loot, *Slang* swag, boodle, °(hot) goods, °take

booze *n.* **1** °drink, °(hard) liquor, spirit(s), whisk(e)y, °alcohol, *US* demon rum, John Barleycorn, mountain dew, white lightning, white mule; *Slang* rotgut, °poison, firewater, mother's ruin, *US and Canadian* °sauce, °juice, hooch, red-eye —*v.* **2** °drink, tipple; *Humorous* bibulate; *Slang* hit the bottle, *US* hit the sauce

border *n.* **1** °edge, °margin, hem, binding, trimming, °trim, edging, °periphery, purfle, purfling **2** Usually, ***borders.*** limit(s), bound(s), confines **3** °boundary, °frontier **4** °frame, frieze, molding; dado, wainscot *or* wainscoting *or* wainscotting **5** borderline, °edge, °verge, °brink **6** bed, flowerbed, herbaceous border —*v.* **7** °edge, °trim, °bind, °fringe, purfle **8** °resemble (closely), °approach (closely), verge upon *or* on **9** lie alongside, adjoin, abut (on *or* upon), verge upon *or* on, °touch, be adjacent to

bore[1] *n.* **1** °hole, drill-hole, bore-hole —*v.* **2** °pierce, °perforate, °drill, °penetrate, °puncture, °tap, °punch, °stab, °prick; °sink, °tunnel, °dig (out), °gouge (out); hollow out

bore[2] *n.* **1** °annoyance, °nuisance —*v.* **2** °weary, °wear out, °tire, °exhaust, °jade

boredom *n.* dullness, dreariness, ennui, °tedium, monotony

boring *adj.* °dull, °monotonous, °tedious, °humdrum, °tiresome, °dreary, °flat, °dead, uninteresting, unexciting, ennuyant, °stale, °tired, °dry, dry as dust, arid; tiring, wearying, wearisome, °exhausting, soporific; °repetitious, °wordy, prolix, unending, long-drawn-out

borrow *v.* °take, °appropriate, °draw, °adopt, °refer to, °obtain, *Colloq* sponge, cadge, touch (someone) for, *US* °bum; *Slang* mooch

bosom *n.* **1** °breast, °chest, bust; *Slang* boobs, knockers, tits, titties, °pair, jugs, bazoom(s), *Brit* Bristols **2** °midst, °interior, °heart, °core, °center **3** °soul, °heart, heart of hearts, °bowels, blood, *Colloq* °gut *—adj.* **4** °close, °intimate, °dear, °beloved, cherished, °boon, °special, °confidential

bosomy *adj.* big-busted, busty, well-endowed

boss *n.* **1** °chief, °supervisor, °head, administrator, °manager, °foreman, °superintendent, °overseer; °employer, °director, °proprietor, °owner, *Brit* managing director, *US* president, *Dialect* himself, *Colloq* supremo, *Brit* governor, gov, gaffer, *US* °super, °leader, kingpin, big cheese, the man, *Slang* honcho, head *or* chief honcho, Mr. Big, prexy *or* prex *—v.* **2** °supervise, °head, °manage, °run, °oversee, °overlook, °direct, °control, superintend, °command, take charge, be in charge **3** domineer, push *or* shove around *or* about, °dominate, order about, °lord it over

bossy *adj.* °overbearing, °domineering, °dictatorial, °tyrannical, °despotic, imperious, lordly

botch *v.* °bungle, mismanage, °spoil, *Colloq* screw *or* louse up, °blow, °mess up, °muck up, make a mess *or* hash *or* muddle of; *Slang Brit* bollocks *or* ballocks *or US* bollix up

bother *v.* **1** °annoy, °pester, °worry, °irritate, °trouble, hector, °harass, °hound, dog, °nag, °plague, needle, *Colloq* hassle; *Slang US* °nudge **2** °trouble (about), °fuss (at), make a fuss (about), concern oneself (with), °burden **3** °confuse, °bewilder, °perplex, °perturb, °upset, disconcert, °discomfit *—n.* **4** °trouble, °inconvenience **5** °worry, °annoyance, vexation, °nuisance, irritation, °trouble, °effort, °disturbance, °upset, *Slang* hassle **6** dither, °flutter, *Colloq* tizzy, °pet, °stew, °lather, °sweat **7** °pest, irritant, °nag, °nuisance, *Colloq* °pain, pain in the neck *or Brit taboo* arse *or US taboo* ass; *Slang US* °nudge **8** °disturbance, to-do, ado, commotion, °fuss, °trouble, °disorder, °stir, hubbub

bottle *n.* **1** flask, container; decanter **2** °courage, °nerve, manliness, manfulness, °grit, °backbone, °gumption, mettle, °pluck, Dutch courage, *Slang* °guts; *Colloq* °spunk, starch, *US* moxie **3** ***the bottle.*** °alcohol, alcoholic drink, spirit(s), °liquor, °booze, °sauce *—v.* **4** ***bottle up.*** **(a)** °contain, °restrain, °hold back, °control, °suppress, °repress, hold *or* keep in check, °stifle **(b)** °trap, °cut off, hem in, °box in

bottom *n.* **1** °seat, °buttocks, °rear, behind, rear end, derrière, rump, °posterior, hindquarters, breech, fundament, gluteus maximus, *Colloq* backside, °butt, buns, prat, *Brit* °bum, *US* can, °duff, keister *or* keester, hinie; *Taboo Brit* arse, *US* ass; *Slang US* tokus *or* tochis *or* tuchis, tushie *or* tushy *or* tush **2** °base, foot, °foundation, °groundwork, substructure, °footing, underpinning, fundament **3** °basis, °foundation, °source, °origin, °cause, °heart, °nub **4** °depths, Davy Jones's locker; bed **5** ***at bottom.*** basically, fundamentally, in the final *or* last analysis, °really, °in reality, °truly, °in truth, essentially **6** ***Bottoms up!*** Prosit!, To your (very good) health!, Cheers!, Here's to—!, Skoal!

bottomless *adj.* unfathomed, unfathomable, abyssal, °abysmal, °inexhaustible, °unlimited, °immeasurable, unplumbable

bounce *n.* **1** °bound, °leap, °hop, °recoil, ricochet, °rebound **2** °vitality, °energy, °verve, °zest, vivacity, liveliness, °animation, °dynamism, °life, *Colloq* °pep, zip, °go, get-up-and-go *—v.* **3** °bound, °rebound, °hop; °recoil, ricochet

bound[1] *n.* **1** Usually, ***bounds.*** °boundary, boundary line, limit(s), °extent, border(s), confines *—v.* **2** °limit, °restrict, confine, delimit, °define, circumscribe

bound[2] *n.* **1** °leap, °jump, vault, °spring; °bounce, °hop **2** ***by leaps and bounds.*** See **leap, 7,** below. *—v.* **3** °leap, °jump, °hop, °spring, vault, gambol, °caper, romp, °frolic, °bounce, *Colloq* galumph

bound[3] *adj.* **1** tied, °fast, °fixed, fastened, confined, secured **2** °obliged, obligated, required, constrained, °forced, compelled **3** °determined, resolved **4** °likely, °certain, °sure, °destined, predestined, °fated, °doomed **5** °destined, scheduled, booked; headed, directed

boundary *n.* border(s), limit(s), frontier(s); bound(s), confines, °perimeter

boundless *adj.* °limitless, unbounded, °unlimited; illimitable, °vast, °endless, unending, °infinite, °immense, °enormous, °immeasurable, incalculable, measureless, unrestricted, unchecked, °inexhaustible, unstoppable, unbridled, °uncontrolled, *Literary* vasty

bountiful *adj.* **1** °generous, beneficent, munificent, °liberal, unsparing, unstinting, °charitable, eleemosynary, magnanimous, *Literary* bounteous **2** °ample, °abundant, plenteous, °plentiful, copious, °rich, *Literary* bounteous

bounty *n.* **1** generosity, liberality, munificence, charitableness, °philanthropy, °charity, unselfishness, beneficence, goodness **2** °gift, °present, °largess, °grant, °subsidy, °endowment, subvention **3** °reward, °award, °premium, °bonus, gratuity

bouquet *n.* **1** nosegay, posy, °bunch, °arrangement, °spray **2** °aroma, °scent, °odor, °fragrance, °perfume **3** compliment(s), °praise, commendation

bourgeois *adj.* **1** middle-class, °conventional, °philistine, capitalistic, propertied; °materialistic, °greedy, money-grubbing, money-hungry **2** working-class, proletarian, °plebeian

bout *n.* **1** °turn, °round, °time, °occasion, °spell, °period, °session **2** °chance, °spree, °stint, °opportunity, innings **3** °contest,

°match, boxing match, prizefight, °meet, set-to, °struggle, °encounter, °engagement; duel

bow *n.* **1** °nod; curtsy *or* curtsey, salaam, °kowtow, genuflection, °prostration, °obeisance —*v.* **2** °defer, °yield, °submit, °give in, °bend, bow down, °capitulate **3** °bend, °incline, °lower **4** °weigh down, °crush, °overload, bend down, °burden **5** °nod, curtsy *or* curtsey, salaam, °kowtow, genuflect, °prostrate oneself, make obeisance

bowels *n.* °interior, °insides, °depths; °heart, °center, °core, intestines, viscera, vitals, belly, °gut, *Colloq* innards, °guts

bowl[1] *v.* °move, trundle, °wheel, °roll, °spin

bowl[2] *n.* dish; basin, °pan

box[1] *n.* **1** °case, °receptacle, crate, carton, container, °casket, coffer, caddy, °chest —*v.* **2** crate, encase, °package **3** ***box in or up.*** °trap, confine, °bottle up, hem in, °enclose, °surround; °pin down

box[2] *v.* **1** °fight, engage in fisticuffs, °spar, °battle **2** °strike, buffet, °punch, °hit, *Colloq* slug, sock, whack, thwack, clout, °belt, thump, °lambaste, whomp —*n.* **3** °blow, buffet, °punch, °hit, °strike, *Colloq* slug, sock, whack, thwack, clout, °belt, thump, whomp

boy *n.* **1** °lad, °youth, young man, °stripling, youngster, schoolboy, °fellow, urchin, brat, *Colloq* kid, °guy, small fry, little shaver **2** °servant, houseboy, °attendant; lackey, °slave, *Archaic* knave, varlet, °rogue, °wretch, caitiff **3** ***old boy.*** (in Britain) (public) schoolmate; °friend, °chum, °pal, *Archaic* old bean, old egg, old crumpet, dear boy; crony

boycott *v.* **1** blacklist, °embargo; °avoid, °refuse, °shun, °reject, eschew, pass over *or* by —*n.* **2** °embargo, blacklist, blacklisting, °ban

boyish *adj.* **1** °young, youthful, °juvenile, °adolescent **2** °childish, °puerile, °juvenile, °immature

brace *n.* **1** °bracket, stiffener, °reinforcement, reinforcer, °support, °buttress, °prop, °stay, °strut, truss **2** °drill **3** °clasp, °clamp, °buckle, fastener, °clip, holdfast, °catch, coupler, coupling **4** °pair; °couple, °span, °team (of two) —*v.* **5** °steady, °reinforce, °support, °strengthen, prop *or* shore up **6** ***brace oneself.*** steady *or* gird *or* prepare oneself; hold *or* hang on

bracing *adj.* °invigorating, °tonic, °stimulating, °refreshing, °exhilarating, fortifying, restorative

bracket *n.* **1** °support, corbel, °console **2** shelf **3** °category, °class, °set, °group, grouping, classification, °division, °level; °order, °grade, °rank —*v.* **4** classify, °rank, °group; °unite, °combine, °join, °link

brag *v.* °boast, crow, trumpet, vaunt, °strut, °swagger, °show off, *Colloq* °talk big, blow *or* toot one's own horn *or* trumpet, go on about

braggart *n.* boaster, bragger, braggadocio, windbag, peacock, °showoff, Scaramouch *or* Scaramouche, *Slang* bigmouth, loudmouth, gasbag

braid *n.* **1** plait **2** trimming, embroidery, soutache, °lace, fillet, °band, ribbon —*v.* **3** plait, intertwine, interlace, °weave, °twist

brain *n.* **1** brains, °intelligence, °intellect, °understanding, °sense, °thought, °imagination, °capacity, perspicacity, perceptiveness, °perception, percipience; °wisdom, sagacity, °wit, discernment, acumen; °knowledge, cognition **2** °genius, °mastermind, °intellectual; °leader, planner

brake *n.* **1** °curb, °check, °restraint, °restriction, constraint, °control, °rein —*v.* **2** °slow, slow up *or* down, put on *or* apply the brakes, reduce speed, decelerate, slacken, °hold up

branch *n.* **1** °offshoot, arm; limb, bough, °stem, °shoot, °twig, sprig **2** °department, °section, subsection, °division, subdivision, °office, °part, °ramification; affiliate, °subsidiary; spinoff —*v.* **3** ramify, °divide, subdivide, °diverge; °diversify

brand *n.* **1** °kind, °make, °type, °sort, °variety; brand name, °manufacturer, maker, trade name, trademark, °label, °mark, marque, *Chiefly US and Canadian* name brand —*v.* **2** °mark, °stamp, °identify, °tag, °label, trademark **3** °label, °characterize; °stigmatize, °discredit, °disgrace

brand-new *adj.* °new, °unused, °fresh, firsthand, °mint, virgin

brash *adj.* **1** °hasty, °rash, °impetuous, °precipitate, °impulsive, headlong, °reckless **2** °impudent, °rude, °impertinent, °disrespectful, °insolent, °forward, °audacious, °brassy, °brazen, °bold, °tactless, undiplomatic, °presumptuous, *Colloq* °cheeky, °fresh

brass *n.* °effrontery, °gall, °nerve, temerity, °impudence, insolence, rudeness, *Colloq* cheek, °nerve

brassy *adj.* **1** °impudent, °forward, °insolent, saucy, °brash, °rude, °brazen, °shameless; °coarse, °flashy, florid, °flamboyant; *Colloq* °cheeky, °fresh **2** °harsh, °strident, °tinny, °grating, dissonant, °shrill, °loud

bravado *n.* boldness, °bluster, boasting, braggadocio, °swagger, °front, self-assurance, *Literary* rodomontade, gasconade; °arrogance, pretentiousness, *Colloq* °machismo, *Slang Brit* °side

brave *adj.* **1** °fearless, °intrepid, °bold, °courageous, °daring, °gallant, °stout, stouthearted, valiant, valorous, °stalwart, plucky, °staunch, undaunted, °dauntless, unafraid, unfearing, °indomitable, °heroic, *Colloq* °macho; *Slang* gutsy **2** °fine, °handsome, °grand, °splendid, °showy, colorful, spectacular, °smart —*v.* **3** °challenge, °defy, °dare; °brazen (out), °face, confront, °encounter, °meet

bravery *n.* °daring, °courage, valor, heroism, °fortitude, fearlessness, intrepidity, intrepidness, °pluck, °determination, staunchness, firmness, resoluteness, °resolution, indomitability, stalwartness, *Colloq* °machismo

brawl *n.* **1** °fight, melee *or* mêlée, °battle, battle royal, donnybrook, °fray, wrangle,

°dispute, °disorder, brannigan, °fracas, °row, °quarrel, squabble, *Colloq* punch-up, free-for-all, °scrap, ruckus —*v.* **2** °fight, wrangle; °row, °quarrel, squabble, *Colloq* °scrap

brawn *n.* muscle(s), °strength, robustness, brawniness, °might, °power, *Colloq* huskiness

brawny *adj.* °muscular, °strong, °tough, °robust, °mighty, °powerful, °burly, strapping, beefy, °hefty, °bulky, *Colloq* °husky

brazen *adj.* °brassy, °shameless, °barefaced, °brash, °outspoken, °forward, °immodest, unashamed, °audacious, °candid, °open, °unabashed, brazenfaced; °rude, °impudent, °impertinent, °insolent, saucy, *Colloq* °cheeky, °fresh, *US* sassy

breach *n.* **1** °break, °violation, infraction, disobedience, nonobservance, °infringement, contravention **2** °break, °rift, °gulf, °split, breakup, °separation, °rupture, severance, °schism, °split, alienation, estrangement **3** °gap, fissure, °crack, °split, °hole, °opening; chasm —*v.* **4** °rupture; °break through, invade

breadth *n.* **1** °width, wideness, broadness, °beam, °span, °spread, thickness **2** °extent, °magnitude, °degree, °amount, °scope, °expanse, °range, °area, °depth, °detail **3** liberality, largeness, catholicity, latitude

break *v.* **1** break apart *or* up *or* asunder, °fracture, °rupture, break into bits, °come apart, °shatter, °shiver, °crack, °crash, °splinter, °fragment, °split, °burst, °explode, *Colloq* bust **2** °reveal, °announce, °disclose, divulge, °tell, °make public **3** °relax, ease up, °improve, ameliorate, change for the better **4** °demolish, smash, °destroy, °crush, °ruin, °defeat, °foil, °frustrate **5** °ruin, bankrupt **6** °weary, °exhaust, °wear out, °weaken, debilitate **7** °crush, °overcome; cow, °cripple, °demoralize, °weaken, °undermine, °discourage **8** °break in, °tame, °discipline, °train, °condition **9** °violate, °transgress, °disobey, contravene, °defy, °infringe, fail to observe, °ignore, °disregard, °flout **10** °break off, °discontinue, °interrupt, °sever, °cut off; °give up, °suspend, °disrupt **11** °break up, °divide, °disperse, °scatter **12** break loose *or* away *or* forth, separate from, °break out (of), °escape (from), °depart (from) **13** break forth, burst forth; emerge *or* come out suddenly **14** demote, *Colloq* bust **15** ***break away.*** °leave, °depart, °separate (oneself) **16** ***break down.*** **(a)** °demolish, °destroy **(b)** °decompose, °break up; °analyze **(c)** °collapse, °give way, °disintegrate, be crushed, be prostrated **17** ***break ground.*** °initiate, °begin, °commence, °found, °set up, °establish, °inaugurate, be innovative, innovate, *Colloq* °break the ice, take the plunge, start the ball rolling **18** ***break in.*** **(a)** °interrupt, interpose, interject, burst in, °intrude, °intervene, °interfere, °disturb **(b)** °train, °educate, °prepare; °accustom, °condition, habituate, °wear. See also **8,** above. **(c)** °rob, burgle, burglarize, break and enter **19** ***break off.*** **(a)** °discontinue, °stop, °cease, °end **(b)** °disengage; °sever, °detach. See also **10,** above. **20** ***break out.*** **(a)** °escape; °emerge, °appear **(b)** °erupt, come out in, break out in *or* into **21** ***break the ice.*** See **17,** above. **22** ***break through.*** °penetrate, force *or* get through **23** ***break up.*** See also **11, 16(b),** above. **(a)** °disband, °disperse; °disintegrate **(b)** °fracture, °fragment, comminute **(c)** See **24(a),** below. **24** ***break with.*** **(a)** °break up (with), separate from, °leave, °depart from **(b)** °renounce, °repudiate, disavow —*n.* **25** °fracture, °split, °separation, °rupture, °breach, °rift, °schism **26** °gap, °opening, °hole; °crack, °slit **27** °interruption, discontinuity, discontinuation, hesitation, °suspension, hiatus, °gap, lacuna, unevenness, irregularity **28** °rest, °respite, rest period, coffee break, tea break, °intermission, °interlude, °lull, °pause, playtime, *US* °recess, *Colloq* breather **29** °chance, stroke of luck, °opportunity, °opening

breakdown *n.* **1** °collapse, °downfall, °failure, foundering; °destruction, °ruin **2** °(mental) collapse, nervous breakdown, *Colloq* crackup **3** °analysis, °rundown, detailing, °review; decomposition, itemization, classification, dissection, distillation, fractionation

breakneck *adj.* °reckless, °dangerous, °daredevil; °excessive, °careless, headlong, °rash, *Colloq* hell-for-leather

breast *n.* **1** °chest, °bosom, bust; teat, *Technical* mamma, *Slang* boob, knocker, tit, titty **2** °soul, °core, °heart, heart of hearts

breath *n.* **1** °gust, zephyr, °breeze, °puff, whiff, °stirring, °stir **2** °hint, °suggestion, °indication, °touch, °murmur, °whisper, soupçon **3** ***take one's breath away.*** °astound, °astonish, °surprise, °amaze, °dazzle, °startle, °shock, °stagger

breathe *v.* **1** °live, °exist **2** inhale and exhale, respire, suspire **3** °exhale, °expel, °puff, °blow **4** °whisper, °murmur, °hint (at), °suggest, °tell, °speak, °say

breathless *adj.* **1** panting, out of breath, winded, gasping, °exhausted, °spent, worn-out, tired out, *Colloq Brit* puffed **2** surprised, amazed, astonished, astounded, awestruck, staggered **3** °eager, °agog, °feverish, in suspense

breed *n.* **1** °kind, °sort, °type, °variety, species; °race, °lineage, °stock, °family, °strain —*v.* **2** °produce, °generate, °bring forth, °create, engender, °hatch, beget, °give rise to, °develop, °cause **3** °raise, °rear, °cultivate, °propagate **4** °arise, °originate, °appear; °develop, °grow, °increase, multiply

breeding *n.* **1** rearing, bringing-up, raising, cultivation, °development, propagation **2** °(good) upbringing, °(good) manners, °civility, politeness, politesse, gentility, °(good) behavior

breeze *n.* **1** °breath, °puff, zephyr, °wind, °draft, °gust, *Nautical* cat's-paw **2** easy *or* simple job *or* task, °nothing, *Colloq* °snap, *Slang* cinch, *US* lead-pipe cinch

breezy *adj.* 1 airy, °fresh, °windy, drafty, °brisk, gusty 2 °casual, °carefree, light-hearted, °cheerful, cheery, airy, °lively, °spirited, blithesome, °buoyant

brevity *n.* shortness, briefness, conciseness, concision, terseness, succinctness, pithiness, compactness, laconicism *or* laconism, °economy

brew *v.* 1 °ferment, cook, °boil; infuse 2 concoct, °devise, °plan, *Colloq* cook up; contrive, °prepare, °bring about, °cause, °produce, °hatch 3 °start, °go on, °hatch, °begin, °form; °stew, °simmer, *Colloq* cook —*n.* 4 beer, ale, °stout; tea; beverage, °drink; concoction, °mixture

bribe *n.* 1 °graft, °inducement, *Colloq* °kickback, *Chiefly US* payola, *US* plugola —*v.* 2 pay *or* buy off, °buy; °corrupt, suborn, *Colloq* °fix; *Slang* °oil, grease (someone's) palm, *Brit* nobble

bric-a-brac *n.* bric-à-brac, curiosities, knick knacks, collectables *or* collectibles, trinkets, gewgaws, gimcracks; bibelots, curios, objets d'art, objets de vertu

brick *n.* 1 °block, cube, chunk, hunk, °slab; stone 2 °pal, °comrade, °friend, *Colloq* °chum, *US and Canadian* buddy

bridal *adj.* °nuptial, °wedding; conjugal, connubial, °marriage

bridge *n.* 1 °span 2 °link, °connection, °tie, °bond —*v.* 3 °span, °cross (over), go *or* pass over, °traverse 4 °connect, °link, °unite, °join, °tie

bridle *n.* 1 °restraint, °curb, °check, °control —*v.* 2 °curb, °check, °restrain, °hold in, °control 3 °bristle, draw oneself up, be *or* become indignant, take offense *or* umbrage *or* affront (at), be affronted *or* offended (by)

brief *adj.* 1 °short, °momentary, °little, °fleeting; °short-lived, transitory, °transient, evanescent, °passing, °temporary, ephemeral, °fugitive 2 °short, °concise, °succinct, °to the point; condensed, shortened, °cut, curtailed, °abbreviated, compressed, abridged, °thumbnail, compendious 3 °curt, °abrupt, °terse, °short, °blunt, °brusque —*n.* 4 °summary, °outline, °digest, °précis, °résumé, compendium, °abstract, condensation, °abridgment, °synopsis, °extract 5 *in brief.* °briefly, concisely, in sum, in summary, to sum up, succinctly, °in a word —*v.* 6 °advise, °inform, °fill in, °coach, °instruct, °enlighten; °explain, run through *or* down

briefly *adv.* 1 concisely, tersely, succinctly, °in a word, °in short; bluntly, curtly, in a nutshell, in a few words, to sum up 2 momentarily, for a few moments *or* seconds *or* minutes, fleetingly, hurriedly, °hastily, °quickly

bright *adj.* 1 °light, shining, gleaming, °radiant, °brilliant, resplendent, glittering, flashing, *Formal* refulgent, effulgent, fulgent, fulgid, fulgorous; alight, aglow, beaming, °dazzling, °glowing, °luminous, lambent, °incandescent, ablaze with 2 °clear, cloudless, °fair, unclouded 3 °shiny, °polished, °lustrous, °glossy, sparkling 4 °hopeful, °optimistic, °favorable, °propitious, auspicious, °promising, °rosy 5 °brilliant, °vivid, °intense, fluorescent, *US trademark* Day-Glo 6 °intelligent, °clever, °quick-witted, °witty, °brilliant, keen-minded, sharp-witted, °gifted, °astute, °ingenious, °alert, °smart; °precocious; *Colloq* brainy, on the ball 7 °illustrious, °glorious, °splendid, °magnificent, °distinguished, °outstanding 8 °cheerful, °gay, °happy, °exuberant, °lively, °animated, °vivacious, °spirited

brighten *v.* 1 °illuminate, °enliven, °lighten, cheer up, liven up, *Colloq* °perk up 2 °shine, °polish, burnish

brilliance *n.* 1 brightness, °radiance, °luster, °splendor, magnificence, °sparkle, °dazzle, °glitter, effulgence, °light 2 °intelligence, °wit, °intellect, keenness, sharpness, acuteness, °genius, °talent, sagacity; precocity

brilliant *adj.* 1 °bright, shining, °lustrous, °radiant, resplendent, °dazzling, °luminous; °incandescent, glittering, sparkling, °scintillating, coruscating, °twinkling, *Formal* effulgent 2 °splendid, °magnificent, °superb, °beautiful, °distinguished, °striking, °glorious, °remarkable, °exceptional, °outstanding 3 °illustrious, °famous, °noted, °celebrated, °eminent, °prominent, °renowned, °accomplished 4 °intelligent, °clever, °gifted, °bright, °talented, °smart, °expert, °masterful, °accomplished, °ingenious, °imaginative, °creative; °quick-witted, sharp-witted, keen-witted, °enlightened; °resourceful, discerning, °able, °competent

brim *n.* 1 °edge, °margin, lip, °rim; °brink —*v.* 2 be full *or* filled, overflow

bring *v.* 1 °carry, °bear, °fetch, °get, °take; °deliver 2 °lead, °conduct, convey; °escort, invite, °accompany 3 °draw, °attract, °lure, allure 4 °carry, °bear, convey; °report 5 °bring on, °bring about, °occasion, °give rise to, be the source *or* cause of, °create, °cause, engender, °produce; °contribute to 6 °institute, °advance; invoke 7 *bring about.* °occasion, °cause, °bring on, °accomplish, °effect, °achieve, °produce 8 *bring around.* (a) °revive, resuscitate, bring to; °restore (b) °persuade, °win over, °convince, °influence 9 *bring down.* (a) °overthrow, depose, oust, unseat, dethrone, °overturn, °topple (b) °reduce, lessen, °diminish, cut (back *or* down) 10 *bring forth.* (a) °bear, give birth to, °produce; °yield (b) °set forth, bring out *or* in *or* up, °introduce, present, °produce, °put out, °submit, °offer, °advance 11 *bring in.* (a) °earn, °yield, °produce, °realize, °fetch, °return, sell for (b) See 15, below. 12 *bring off.* °succeed (in), °carry out, °achieve, °accomplish, do, carry out *or* off, °perform, °succeed, °pull off; *Colloq* °put over 13 *bring on.* (a) °produce, °put on, °introduce, °bring in (b) °induce, °produce, °occasion, °bring about 14 *bring out.* (a) °display, °feature, focus on, °illuminate, °set off, make noticeable *or* conspicuous, °emphasize, °develop (b) °publish, °issue, °release, make known *or* public, °produce; °put on, °stage **15** ***bring up.*** **(a)** °rear, °raise, °care for, °look after, nurture, °breed; °educate, °teach, °train, °tutor **(b)** °introduce, °broach, °bring in, °raise, °pen (up), °set forth, °mention, °touch on, °talk about, °discuss; reintroduce, °recall **(c)** °raise, elevate **(d)** °vomit, °throw up, °regurgitate, disgorge

brink *n.* **1** °edge, °brim, °rim, °margin, lip, °border **2** °verge, °point

brisk *adj.* **1** °active, °lively, °busy, °vigorous **2** °quick, °animated, °sprightly, spry, °energetic, °spirited **3** °strong, °steady, °fresh, °refreshing, °bracing, °invigorating, °stimulating, °crisp, °biting, °bracing, °keen, nippy, °chill, °chilly, °cool, °cold **4** °energetic, vibrant, °invigorating, °stimulating

bristle *n.* **1** °hair, whisker, barb, °prickle, °thorn, quill, *Technical* seta *—v.* **2** °prickle, °rise, °stand up, *Formal* horripilate **3** °seethe, become angry *or* infuriated *or* furious *or* maddened, °boil, °flare up, see red, °bridle **4** °teem, °crawl, be thick, °swarm, be alive

brittle *adj.* **1** °fragile, frangible, breakable; friable **2** °frail, °weak, °delicate, °sensitive, °fragile, °insecure

broach *v.* °introduce, °raise, °open (up), °suggest, °mention, hint at, touch on *or* upon, bring up *or* in, °talk about, °advance

broad *adj.* **1** °wide, °expansive, °large, °extensive; °spread out, °ample, °spacious **2** °bright, °plain, °open, °full; unshaded **3** °plain, °clear, °obvious, °emphatic, °explicit, °pronounced, °direct, unconcealed, °undisguised, unsubtle, °evident **4** °main, °general, generalized, °rough, unspecific, nonspecific, °approximate, °sweeping **5** plainspoken, °outspoken, °forthright, °direct, unreserved, °frank, °candid, unrestrained **6** °inclusive, °general, widely applicable, °extensive, wide-ranging, °comprehensive, wholesale; °vague, °imprecise, °indefinite, unfocused, nonspecific, unspecified **7** °liberal, °tolerant, °catholic, ecumenical, latitudinarian **8** °dirty, °blue, °coarse, °rude, °indecent, °vulgar, °improper, indelicate, °off-color, °loose, °gross, °obscene, °lewd, °lascivious, °filthy, °pornographic; inelegant, °unrefined, unladylike, ungentlemanly, titillating *—n.* **9** °woman, °girl, *Slang* dame, cookie *or* cooky, skirt, bimbo, bird, chick, °number, doll, °piece (of baggage)

broadcast *v.* **1** °air, °transmit, relay; °radio; televise, telecast **2** °announce, advertise, °publish, °proclaim; disseminate **3** °sow, °scatter, °seed *—n.* **4** °program, °show; °transmission, telecast

brochure *n.* °pamphlet, booklet; catalog; folder, °leaflet; °tract

broil *v.* grill, barbecue

broke *adj.* penniless, °indigent, °down-and-out, poverty-stricken, °penurious, °impoverished, °insolvent, °destitute, °poor, °needy, bankrupt, ruined, *Colloq* on one's beam ends, °on one's uppers, strapped, flat *or* dead *or* stony broke, °hard up, °short, up against it, *US* °flat, on the skids; *Slang Brit* skint

broken *adj.* **1** fragmented, shattered, shivered, splintered, ruptured, cracked, °split, smashed, pulverized, disintegrated, destroyed, demolished **2** fractured **3** enfeebled, weakened, crushed, defeated, beaten, ruined; dispirited, °dejected, discouraged, demoralized, °subdued, debilitated, *Colloq* licked **4** tamed, trained, disciplined, °obedient, docile, domesticated, °subdued; conditioned **5** violated, transgressed, disobeyed, contravened, defied, flouted, disregarded, ignored, infringed **6** interrupted, °disturbed, discontinuous, °disjointed, °disconnected, fragmented, °fragmentary, °intermittent, °erratic, °sporadic **7** Also, ***broken down.*** out of order *or* commission, not working *or* functioning, in disrepair, *Slang* °on the blink, out of kilter, kaput, *US* on the fritz, out of whack

brokenhearted *adj.* °heartbroken, depressed, °downhearted, °dejected, devastated, crushed, overwhelmed, heartsick, downcast, °upset; °forlorn, °sorrowful, disconsolate, °inconsolable, grief-stricken, °miserable, °wretched, °melancholy, heavy-hearted, °sad, °doleful, dolorous, woeful, °woebegone, °gloomy, morose, °glum, cheerless, *Colloq* down

broker *n.* stockbroker; °agent, °dealer, middleman, °intermediary, °go-between, *Brit* stockjobber

brooch *n.* °clasp, °pin; °fastening

brood *n.* **1** °young, °offspring, °progeny; children, °family *—v.* **2** °incubate, °hatch, °set, °sit, °cover **3** Also, ***brood on or over.*** ponder (on *or* over), meditate (on *or* over), °contemplate, ruminate (on *or* over), muse (on *or* over) **4** mope, °sulk, °pout, pine, eat one's heart out, °fret, °worry, agonize, °despair

brook[1] *n.* °stream, rivulet, °run, runnel, rill, *US, Canadian, Australian, and New Zealand* creek; *No. England dialectal* beck, gill *or* ghyll, *Northern, Midwestern, and Western US* crick; *Scots* °burn

brook[2] *v.* °endure, °tolerate, °stand, °abide, °put up with, °suffer, °allow

broth *n.* °stock, bouillon, consommé; soup; decoction

brothel *n.* bordello, whorehouse, house of ill fame *or* ill repute, bawdyhouse, bagnio; seraglio, harem, *Obsolete* °stew, *Colloq US* sporting house, *Slang Brit* knocking-shop, *US* cathouse

brother *n.* sibling; °relation, °relative, °kin, kinsman; °fellow, fellow man, fellow clansman, fellow citizen, fellow countryman, fellow creature; °associate, °colleague, confrère, °companion, *Colloq* °pal, °chum, *Brit and Australian* °mate, *US* buddy

brotherhood *n.* **1** brotherliness, °fellowship, °companionship, °alliance, °friendship, comradeship, camaraderie, °kinship **2** °fraternity, guild, °society, °association, °order, °league, °union, °organization, °club, community, °circle, °set, °clique

brotherly *adj.* °fraternal, °kind, °affectionate, °cordial, °friendly, °amicable, °amiable, °neighborly, °loyal, °devoted

browbeat *v.* °bully, °intimidate, °threaten, badger, °dominate, cow, °frighten, °discourage, °tyrannize, hector, °harass, keep after, °nag, *Colloq* hassle

browse *v.* look over *or* through, °skim (through), °scan, thumb *or* flip *or* flick through

bruise *n.* **1** °injury, °hurt, contusion, °bump, °welt, °scrape, abrasion, °scratch, °wound, black-and-blue mark, blotch, °blemish, °mark, °spot, discoloration, °damage, *Technical* ecchymosis —*v.* **2** °injure, contuse, °hurt, °scrape, °harm; °wound, °damage

bruiser *n.* prizefighter, boxer, fighter; °tough, ruffian, bodyguard, °thug, °hoodlum, bouncer, *Colloq* hooligan, tough guy, toughie, *Brit* °minder, *US* roughneck, hood, gorilla, plug-ugly, torpedo, enforcer

brunt *n.* °(full) force, °burden, onus, °weight, °impact; °shock, °stress, °violence, onslaught

brush[1] *n.* **1** brushwood, shrubs, undergrowth, branches, °scrub, °brush, bracken, brambles, underbrush, underwood **2** °thicket, °brake, copse, grove, boscage

brush[2] *n.* **1** hairbrush, toothbrush, clothesbrush, shoebrush, nailbrush, paintbrush; broom, dustbroom, besom, *US* whiskbroom **2** See **brush-off. 3** °encounter, °engagement, °skirmish, *Colloq Brit* spot of bother —*v.* **4** °scrub, °clean; °groom, curry; °sweep, °whisk, °gather **5** graze, °touch **6** ***brush aside or away.*** °disregard, °dismiss, °put aside, shrug off **7** ***brush off.*** °dismiss, °ignore, °rebuff, send off *or* away *or* packing **8** ***brush up (on).*** °review, restudy, °go over, °refresh, °study, *Archaic* con

brushoff *n.* °dismissal, °rebuff, °rejection, snub, *Colloq* cold shoulder, putdown, °slap in the face, the (old) heave-ho; *Slang US and Canadian* walking papers

brusque *adj.* °blunt, °rude, °overbearing, °impolite, uncivil, °discourteous, °ungracious, °ill-mannered, unmannerly; churlish, °gruff, °abrupt, °short, °curt, °sharp, °terse, °brash, °bluff

brutal *adj.* **1** °inhuman, °savage, °cruel, pitiless, °harsh, °severe, barbaric, barbarous, °beastly, bestial, °sadistic, °murderous; inhumane, °heartless, hard-hearted, °unkind, °fierce, stonyhearted, insensitive, unfeeling, °coldblooded, °unsympathetic, °remorseless, °ruthless, °ferocious, °atrocious, Draconian *or* Draconic, *Literary* °fell **2** °rude, °ill-mannered, °coarse, °unrefined, °boorish, ill-bred, °rustic, crass, uncouth, uncultured, uncultivated, °rough, °crude

brute *adj.* **1** brutish, °dull, unfeeling, °senseless, °blind, unintelligent, °unthinking, °thoughtless, °mindless, unreasoning, irrational, °instinctive, °physical, °material; insensate, °unconscious —*n.* **2** °animal, °beast, °savage

bubble *n.* **1** blister, air pocket, globule, droplet **2** ***bubbles.*** °froth, °foam, suds, °lather, spume; effervescence, carbonation, °fizz —*v.* **3** °foam, °froth, °boil, °seethe, °fizz

bubbly *adj.* **1** °effervescent, foamy, frothy, fizzy, sparkling **2** °effervescent, °merry, °ebullient, bouncy, °animated, °vivacious, °cheerful, cheery, °lively, °excited —*n.* **3** champagne, sparkling wine, sparkling burgundy, asti spumante, *Colloq Brit* champers

bucket *n.* pail, scuttle

buckle *n.* **1** °clasp, fastener, °clip, °fastening, °hook, °catch —*v.* **2** °collapse, °cave in, °crumple, °bend, °warp, °distort, °twist, °bulge

bug *n.* **1** insect, beetle, larva, grub, caterpillar, butterfly, mosquito, °fly, spider, *Colloq Brit* creepy-crawly, *US* no-see-um **2** °microbe, °germ, virus; °disease, °affliction, °illness, sickness, °ailment, °disorder, malady, infection; °condition, °complaint, °infirmity, indisposition **3** °obsession, °craze, °fad, °mania, °rage **4** °enthusiast, faddist, °fan, °fanatic; hobbyist **5** listening device; microphone, transmitter, electronic eavesdropper, °tap **6** °fault, °error, °mistake, °failing, °shortcoming, *Colloq* hang-up, glitch —*v.* **7** °annoy, °irritate, °pester, °irk, °harass, °bother **8** °tap, °spy on

bugger *n.* **1** buggerer, sodomite. **2** °chap, °fellow, °man; °boy, °lad, °child, °tot; *Slang chiefly Brit* geezer, *US* °jerk; *Colloq* °guy, *Brit* bloke, °fool, idiot —*v.* **3** Also, ***bugger up.*** °ruin, °destroy, °botch, °bungle, °wreck; make a mess of, *Colloq* mess *or* screw up, *Brit* bollocks *or* ballocks up, balls up, make a balls-up of, cock up, *US* ball up, bollix up; *Taboo* fuck up **4** ***bugger about or around.*** **(a)** °fool about, waste time, °dawdle, *Colloq US* lallygag *or* lollygag; *Taboo* fuck about *or* around **(b)** cause complications for, create difficulties for **5** ***bugger off.*** °go away, °depart, °leave, clear off *or* out, *Colloq* make tracks, skedaddle, °beat it, *Slang* piss off; *Taboo* fuck off

build *v.* **1** °construct, °erect, °raise, °set up, °assemble **2** °found, °establish, °base **3** °develop **4** Also, ***build up.*** °intensify; °increase, °develop, °enlarge, °strengthen —*n.* **5** °physique, °figure, °body, °shape, *Slang* bod

building *n.* edifice, °structure, construction, erection

bulge *n.* **1** °lump, °hump, protuberance, °bump, °swelling, °projection —*v.* **2** °protrude, °stick out, °swell (out)

bulk *n.* **1** °volume, °magnitude, °mass, enlargement, largeness, °size **2** °majority

bulky *adj.* °large, °voluminous, °unwieldy, °awkward, ungainly, cumbersome, *Brit* chunky

bulletin *n.* °message, °notice, communication, °announcement, communiqué, dispatch *or* despatch, °report, °account, °flash, news item *or* flash

bully *n.* **1** persecutor, intimidator, °tyrant —*v.* **2** °persecute, °intimidate, °tyrannize, °torment, °browbeat, °daunt, awe, cow, terrorize; hector, °harass, °push around —*adj.* 3 *Old-fashioned* °jolly, °worthy, °admirable —*interj.* 4 Usually, ***Bully for (someone)!*** Bravo!, Great!, Fantastic!, Fabulous!, Marvelous!, Spectacular!; So what?, What of it?; *US* Peachy!, Dandy!, Neat-oh!; *Old-fashioned* Fantabulous!

bulwark *n.* 1 °defense, °safeguard, redoubt, bastion, buffer, °barrier, °rampart, fortification —*v.* 2 °defend, °protect, °shelter

bum *n.* 1 °buttocks, °posterior, hindquarters, fundament, behind, rump, °bottom, behind, derrière, rear end, backside, °seat, °rear, *Colloq Brit* arse, *US* fanny, can, hinie, tush, tushy *or* tushie, tokus *or* tochis *or* tuchis, keister *or* keester, ass 2 °tramp, panhandler, °beggar, vagrant, °loafer, °drifter, °vagabond, hobo, °derelict, gypsy; *Brit* caird, °tinker, °traveler; *US* (shopping) bag lady —*adj.* 3 °improper, unjustified, °false, °fraudulent, trumped-up, °untrue, fabricated, made-up, °bogus 4 °bad, °awful, unfair, °dishonest, °poor, °rotten, *Slang* °lousy, crummy —*v.* 5 °borrow, °beg, sponge, *Colloq* °scrounge, cadge, °touch, put the touch on, *US* mooch, °hit, °hit up

bump *n.* 1 °blow, °collision, °thud, °hit, °knock, buffet, clunk, whack 2 °lump, protuberance, °welt, °swelling, tumescence, °knob, °bulge —*v.* 3 °knock (against), °strike, °hit, °collide (with), °run into, °ram; smash, °crash, *Colloq* wallop 4 ***bump into.*** °meet, °encounter, run into *or* across, °come across, stumble over 5 ***bump off.*** °murder, °kill, °put away, assassinate, do away with, °execute, liquidate, dispatch *or* despatch, *Slang* °take for a ride, °destroy, °eliminate, °rub out, °wipe out, do in, *US* °waste, ice

bumpy *adj.* °lumpy, °rough, uneven, °irregular, knobby, knobbly, °pitted; potholed, bouncy, jarring, jerky, rutted

bunch *n.* 1 °bundle, °cluster, °batch, °clump; °bouquet, nosegay, posy, °spray 2 °crowd, °knot, °collection, °group, °lot, °gathering, °cluster, °clutch, °batch, °assortment, °mass —*v.* 3 °sort, °class, classify, °categorize, assort, group together, °bracket 4 ***bunch up.*** °gather; smock; °collect, °crowd, °group, °cluster

bundle *n.* 1 °bunch, °collection, °package, °parcel, °packet, °pack; bale, sheaf; *Archaic* fardel —*v.* 2 °gather (together), °tie up (together), °collect, °pack, °package 3 ***bundle off*** *or* ***out.*** dispatch *or* despatch, °pack off, hustle *or* hurry off *or* away, send away *or* off; decamp, scurry off *or* away, *Colloq Brit* do a moonlight flit

bungle *v.* °spoil, °botch, mismanage, °stumble, bumble, *Golf* foozle, *Colloq* foul *or* screw *or* louse up, °blow, mess *or* muck up, make a mess *or* hash *or* muddle of, muff, *Slang Brit* °bugger, *US* snafu, *Taboo* fuck up

buoy *n.* 1 (navigational *or* channel) mark *or* marker, °float; nun (buoy), can (buoy), bell (buoy), gong (buoy), °siren, °signal, mooring buoy, spar buoy, lollipop —*v.* 2 Often, ***buoy up.*** °lift, °raise, elevate, °support, hearten, °sustain, keep up

buoyant *adj.* 1 afloat, floating, floatable 2 °light, resilient, °lively, °vivacious, °bright, °cheerful, °carefree, °blithe, °animated, °jaunty, bouncy, °ebullient, lighthearted, *Colloq* peppy

burden *n.* 1 °load, °weight, gravamen; °strain, °pressure, °trouble, onus, millstone, °cross, albatross —*v.* 2 °load, °weigh down, saddle with, °encumber; °tax, °oppress

burdensome *adj.* onerous, cumbersome, °oppressive, °weighty, °troublesome, wearisome, bothersome, distressing, worrying, worrisome, vexatious, °irksome

bureau *n.* 1 *Brit* (writing) desk, *US* chest of drawers, °chest, dresser, chifferobe, chiffonier 2 °office, °agency, °department, °division, °section, subdivision, subsection, desk

bureaucracy *n.* officialdom, officialism, °government, red tape, °administration, °authorities

burglar *n.* housebreaker, °thief, °robber; sneak thief, cat burglar, *US* second-story man

burial *n.* interment, °funeral, entombment, obsequies, sepulture

burlesque *n.* 1 °caricature, °lampoon, spoof, °parody, °satire, °mockery, travesty, *Colloq* °takeoff; °(grotesque) imitation, vulgarization, °exaggeration 2 *US* striptease, strip show, nudie *or* girlie show —*v.* 3 °satirize, °take off, °lampoon, spoof, °parody, °caricature, travesty —*adj.* 4 °satirical, derisive, mock-heroic, mock-pathetic

burly *adj.* °stout, °sturdy, corpulent, °large, °big, °hefty, °stocky, thickset, °brawny, chunky, °heavy, beefy, °muscular, °strong, strapping, °rugged, °tough, *Colloq* °husky

burn *v.* 1 °blaze, °flame, °flare, °smolder 2 ignite, set on fire, °fire, °light, °kindle, incinerate, *Slang* torch 3 °desire, °yearn, °wish, °long, °itch 4 °waste, throw *or* fritter away, squander 5 overcook, °blacken, char, °singe

burning *adj.* 1 °flaming, blazing, °fiery; °ablaze, aflame, afire, °on fire 2 vehement, °ardent, °excited, °passionate, °fervent, fervid, °intense, °fiery, °enthusiastic 3 raging, °violent, parching 4 °hot, blazing, °scorching, seething, °withering

burrow *n.* 1 °excavation, °hole, warren, °tunnel —*v.* 2 °dig, delve, °tunnel, °bore; °excavate

burst *v.* °break (asunder), °rupture, °shatter, °explode, °blow up; °puncture; *Slang* bust

bury *n.* 1 inter, inhume, lay to rest 2 °abandon, °forget, consign to oblivion, eradicate, extirpate 3 °submerge (oneself), °exile (oneself), °plunge, become engrossed *or* absorbed 4 °conceal, °obscure, °hide, °cover up 5 °overwhelm, °overcome, inundate

business *n.* 1 °duty, °function, °occupation, °calling, °vocation, °trade, °profession, °work, °province, °area, °subject, °topic, °concern, °affair, °responsibility, °role, °charge, °obligation 2 °matter, °job, °task,

°subject, °question, °problem, °issue, °point, °affair 3 dealing, °transaction; °trade, °commerce, °traffic 4 °concern, °establishment °organization, °company, °firm, °house, °enterprise; corporation, partnership, proprietorship

busy *adj.* 1 occupied, °engaged, employed, °involved 2 working, °industrious, °active, °diligent; bustling, °hectic, °lively, hustling, °energetic 3 °ornate, °elaborate, °detailed, °complicated, complex, (over)decorated, °intricate, Baroque, Rococo —*v.* 4 °occupy, °involve, °employ, °divert, absorb, engross

busybody *n.* °pry, snoop(er), peep(er), °gossip, meddler, Paul Pry, *Colloq* Nosy Parker, *Slang US* buttinsky

butcher *n.* 1 °murderer, slaughterer, °killer, ripper, °cutthroat, executioner, annihilator 2 destroyer, bungler, muddler —*v.* 3 °slaughter, °massacre, °murder, cut *or* hack *or* hew to pieces, dismember, disembowel, °exterminate, annihilate, °kill, liquidate 4 °botch, °bungle, °foul up, *Colloq* °mess up, make a mess *or* hash of; *Slang* louse up, °screw up, *Brit* bollocks *or* ballocks up, *US* bollix up; *Taboo* fuck up

butt[1] *n.* °target, °end, °object, °prey, °victim, °dupe; gull, *Colloq* pigeon, °sucker; *Brit* Aunt Sally, *Slang US and Canadian* patsy

butt[2] *v.* 1 abut, °join, °meet 2 ***butt in or into.*** °interfere, °intrude, °interrupt, *Colloq US* kibitz; °meddle

buttocks *n.* °bottom, behind, derrière, °seat, °rear, rear end, backside, °posterior, hindquarters, fundament, *Colloq Brit* °bum, arse, *US* hinie, can, tush *or* tushy *or* tushie, tokus *or* tochis *or* tuchis, keister *or* keester, °butt, °tail, prat, ass; *Slang* cheeks, °duff

buttonhole *v.* 1 corner, detain, accost, importune, °waylay —*n.* 2 corsage, *US* boutonniere *or* boutonnière

buttress *v.* °sustain, °support, °strengthen, °prop (up), °brace, °reinforce, shore up

buxom *adj.* 1 °hearty, °healthy, °vigorous, °lusty, °attractive, °comely, °plump, *Colloq* °hefty 2 busty, °bosomy, chesty, well-endowed, big-busted

buy *v.* 1 °purchase; °acquire, °obtain, °get, °procure, °gain, °come by, °secure 2 °accept, °allow, °take, °believe, °swallow, °go for 3 °bribe, suborn, °pay off, buy off, °corrupt —*n.* 4 °purchase, °acquisition 5 Also, ***good buy.*** °bargain, *Colloq US and Canadian* °steal

buyer *n.* °customer, consumer, °client, purchaser

buzz *n.* 1 °hum, °murmur, drone, buzzing 2 °stir, °ferment, °talk, °undercurrent 3 phone call, °ring 4 °thrill, feeling of excitement, °sensation, stimulation, °kick, *Colloq* °high —*v.* 5 °hum, °murmur, drone 6 fly down on, zoom onto 7 °telephone, °ring (up), °call (up), phone; °summon, °signal, buzz *or* ring for

by *prep.* 1 °near, °beside, next to, °close to, alongside 2 via, °by way of, °through; °past 3 °by means of, on 4 °before, not later than, sooner than 5 during, at —*adv.* 6 Often, ***close by.*** °near, °nearby, °at hand, °close, °about, °around, *Literary* nigh 7 °past, °nearby 8 away, aside

bygone *adj.* °past, °former, olden; of old, of yore

bypass *v.* 1 °avoid, °evade, circumvent, °sidestep, skirt, go *or* get round, °detour; °ignore, *Slang* give the go-by —*n.* 2 °detour, alternative (way *or* route)

bystander *n.* °spectator, °onlooker, °observer, °witness, nonparticipant, passerby, °eyewitness

byword *n.* °proverb, proverbial saying, °parable, °maxim, adage, °motto, °slogan, apophthegm *or* apothegm, aphorism, catchword, catch phrase

C

cab *n.* °taxi, taxicab, *Obsolete* (horse-drawn) hackney, hansom (cab); *Old-fashioned US* °hack

cabal *n.* 1 °intrigue, °plot, °conspiracy, °scheme 2 junta *or* junto, °clique, °set, coterie, °faction, °band, °league; °unit, °party, caucus, °club; °ring, °gang —*v.* 3 °intrigue, °plot, conspire, connive, machinate

cabaret *n.* 1 nightclub, nightspot 2 floor show, °show, °entertainment, °amusement

cabin *n.* 1 °hut, °shack, °cottage, °cot, shanty; bungalow, °lodge, chalet; *Scots* bothy 2 stateroom, °compartment, berth

cabinet *n.* 1 cupboard, °bureau, chifferobe, commode, chiffonier, °chest (of drawers), chest-on-chest, tallboy, *US* highboy, lowboy 2 °council, °ministry, °committee, advisers *or* advisors, senate

cable *n.* 1 wire, °line, °rope, hawser, °chain, mooring, strand, °guy 2 °telegram, wire, cablegram, radiogram, *US* Mailgram —*v.* 3 telegraph, wire; °radio

cache *n.* 1 hiding place, °hole, vault, repository 2 °store, °hoard, °supply, °reserve, nest egg, stockpile, *Colloq US and Canadian* stash —*v.* 3 °hide, °store, °conceal, squirrel away, °secrete, °bury, *Colloq* stash (away)

cachet *n.* 1 °stamp, °feature, distinguishing mark, °identification 2 °distinction, °prominence, °importance, °prestige, °dignity

cadaver *n.* °corpse, °(dead) body, °remains, *Slang* °stiff

cadence *n.* °measure, °beat, °rhythm, °tempo, °accent, °pulse, meter, lilt, °swing

café *n.* coffee house, coffee bar, coffee shop, bistro, snack bar, brasserie; tearoom, lunchroom, restaurant, eating house, canteen; cafeteria, *US* diner, *Colloq* eatery; *Slang Brit* caff, *US* greasy spoon

cage *n.* **1** crate, °enclosure, °pen, °pound, coop, hutch —*v.* **2** Also, ***cage up or in.*** confine, °enclose, °pen, impound, °shut up, *or* in, coop (up), °imprison; °restrict, °restrain, hem in

cajole *v.* °wheedle, °coax, °beguile, °jolly (along), cozy along, °seduce, inveigle, °persuade, *Colloq* soft-soap, butter (up), °stroke, sweet-talk

cajolery *n.* wheedling, coaxing, blandishment, beguilement, jollying, °persuasion, seduction, inveigling, inveiglement, *Colloq* soft soap, buttering-up, sweet talk

cake *n.* **1** pastry, bun, *Brit* gateau **2** °piece, chunk, °bar, °block, cube, °lump, °loaf, °slab —*v.* **3** °harden, °solidify, °thicken, congeal, °dry, °coagulate, encrust, consolidate

calamitous *adj.* distressful, dire, °tragic, °disastrous, °destructive, °awful, °devastating, °fatal, °deadly, pernicious, cataclysmic, catastrophic, °ruinous, °dreadful, °terrible

calamity *n.* **1** °disaster, °destruction, °ruin, °catastrophe, cataclysm, devastation, °tragedy, misadventure, mischance, °mishap **2** °distress, °affliction, °trouble, °hardship, °misery, °tragedy, °misfortune, adversity, °reverse, °ruin, ruination, °desolation, wretchedness

calculate *v.* °compute, °reckon, add up, assess, °evaluate, °count, °figure (out), °estimate, °gauge, °determine, ascertain, °work out

calculated *adj.* **1** arranged, designed, planned, °prepared, adjusted, adapted, °fit, °fitted, intended, suited **2** °deliberate, °purposeful, °intentional, °premeditated, planned

calculating *adj.* °shrewd, conniving, °crafty, °sly, °scheming, °designing, Machiavellian, manipulative, canny, contriving

calculation *n.* **1** computation, °reckoning, counting, °estimation, figuring, determining **2** °answer, °product, °result, °figure, °count, °estimate, °amount **3** °estimate, °forecast, °expectation, °prediction, deliberation; circumspection, cautiousness, wariness, °caution, °prudence, °forethought, °discretion

calculator *n.* computer, adding machine; abacus

calendar *n.* **1** appointment book, °schedule, slate, *Brit* °diary, *US* datebook, *US law* docket **2** almanac, °chronology, °chronicle, annal(s)

caliber *n.* **1** diameter, °size, °bore, °gauge **2** °merit, °ability, °talent, °capability, competence, °capacity, °quality, °strength, stature **3** °degree, °measure, °stamp, °quality

calibrate *v.* °adjust, °graduate; °standardize

call *v.* **1** °shout, °cry (out), °hail, °yell, °roar, °bellow, call out, *Colloq* holler **2** °name, °designate, °denote, denominate, °term, °style, °nickname, °label, °title, °entitle, °tag, °identify, dub, °christen, baptize **3** °call up, °telephone, phone, °ring (up), dial, *Colloq* °buzz **4** °summon, invite, °assemble, convoke, convene, °bid, °gather, °collect, °muster, °rally **5** °visit, °attend; call in; °call on **6** °awake, °awaken, °wake up, °rouse, *Colloq Brit* °knock up **7** ***call down.*** **(a)** appeal to, invoke, °petition, °request, entreat, supplicate **(b)** °reprimand, °chastise, °castigate, °upbraid, °scold, °reprove, °rebuke **8** ***call for.*** **(a)** °demand, °request, °ask for, °order, °require, °claim **(b)** °pick up, °fetch, come for, °get, °accompany, *Colloq* °collect **9** ***call forth.*** °summon, invoke, draw on *or* upon, °evoke; °elicit, °inspire **10** ***call off.*** °cancel; °discontinue; °postpone **11** ***call on or upon.*** **(a)** request of, entreat, °ask, °address; apostrophize **(b)** supplicate, apostrophize, appeal to **(c)** °visit **12** ***call up.*** **(a)** °summon, °enlist, °recruit, conscript, *US* °draft **(b)** °call, °telephone, phone, °ring (up) —*n.* **13** °shout, °cry, °yell, °whoop, *Colloq* holler **14** summons, °invitation, °bidding, °notice, notification, °order, °request, °demand, °command; telephone call, phone call, *Brit* °ring; *Colloq* tinkle **15** °reason, justification, °cause, °need, °occasion, °right, °excuse; °requirement **16** ***on call.*** °ready, on duty, standing by, on standby, awaiting orders **17** ***within call.*** within earshot *or* hearing *or* (easy) reach

calling *n.* °vocation, °occupation, °profession, °business, °trade, °employment, °work, °line, °job, métier, °pursuit, °career, °area, °province, °(area of) expertise, °specialty, *Colloq* °racket

callous *adj.* hardened, °thick-skinned, unfeeling, uncaring, °insensible, insensitive, °hard, hardhearted, °tough, hard-bitten, °cold, °coldhearted, °heartless, °indifferent, °unsympathetic, apathetic, *Colloq* hard-boiled, hard-nosed

callow *adj.* °inexperienced, °immature, °juvenile, naive *or* naïve *or* naïf, °green, guileless, °unsophisticated, °innocent, °raw, °unfledged, °untried, *Colloq* (still) wet behind the ears

calm *n.* **1** °quiet, stillness, tranquillity, °serenity, °hush, °peace, peacefulness **2** calmness, composure, placidity, placidness, °peace, °repose, °sang-froid, coolness, °self-control, equanimity, self-possession —*adj.* **3** °quiet, °still, °tranquil, °serene, °peaceful, balmy, halcyon, °mild, undisturbed, unagitated, placid, pacific; motionless, °smooth, °even; windless **4** composed, °cool, coolheaded, self-controlled, °impassive, °dispassionate, °unmoved, unruffled, °serene, °tranquil, °sedate, °staid, °stoical, *Colloq* together —*v.* **5** Also, ***calm down.*** °quiet, quieten, °still, soothe, °hush, °lull, pacify; mollify, appease, placate, become *or* make quiet *or* pacified *or* less agitated, *Colloq* cool off *or* down

camouflage *n.* **1** °disguise, concealment, coverup, °cover, °guise, °cloak, °mask, °screen, °blind, °(false) front, °show, façade, °pretense, °trickery, °deception; protective coloring *or* coloration, *Technical* apatetic *or* aposematic *or* cryptic coloring *or* coloration

—*v.* 2 °disguise, °cloak, °mask, °cover (up), °hide, °conceal, °screen, °veil; °misrepresent, °falsify

camp[1] *n.* 1 camping ground, campground, bivouac, encampment, campsite; °settlement; camping site, *Brit* caravan site 2 °faction, °set, coterie, °clique, °group, °party, °body —*v.* 3 encamp, pitch camp, tent 4 °lodge, bivouac, °settle 5 ***camp out.*** *Slang* °crash

camp[2] *adj.* 1 °outré, °outrageous, exaggerated, °artless, °affected, inartistic, °extravagant, °artificial, dadaistic, °theatrical, °mannered, °flamboyant, °showy, °ostentatious, °effeminate, *Colloq* campy —*v.* 2 °exaggerate, °show off, °strut, °flaunt, °flounce, °prance, °posture, *Colloq* ham

campaign *n.* 1 operation(s), maneuver(s), °crusade, °action; °drive, °offensive, °push, °effort; °struggle 2 °competition, °contest, °rivalry, °race —*v.* 3 °run, °electioneer, °compete, *Brit* °stand; *US and Canadian* °stump; *Colloq* throw *or* toss one's hat in the ring

cancel *v.* 1 °void, annul, invalidate, nullify, °quash; °revoke, rescind, °redeem, °repeal, °abolish, °retract, °withdraw, °recall, °repudiate, abrogate, countermand, °deny 2 °delete, °obliterate, cross *or* strike *or* blot out, dele, °rub out, °erase, expunge, efface, eradicate, °quash, deracinate; °eliminate, do away with 3 Sometimes, ***cancel out.*** °neutralize, nullify, counterbalance, countervail, °compensate (for), °make up for, °offset, °counteract

cancellation *n.* 1 cancelation, canceling, annulment, nullification, rescinding, voiding, rescission, revocation, °abolition, abandonment, withdrawal, abrogation; °repeal 2 cancelation, invalidation, revocation, °abolition, discontinuance, °termination, °suppression 3 cancelation, elimination, °abolition; stoppage, cessation

candid *adj.* 1 °frank, °open, °plain, °sincere, °ingenuous, °straight, straightforward, °truthful, °forthright, °direct, unequivocal, plain-spoken, plain-speaking, °outspoken, °honest, °artless, °blunt, guileless, openhearted, °aboveboard, undeceitful, undeceiving, undeliberative, uncalculating, uncalculated, °unpremeditated, uncontrived, *Colloq* upfront 2 °just, °impartial, °objective, °fair, °equitable, unbiased, °unprejudiced, evenhanded; unbigoted 3 unposed, °informal, impromptu

candidate *n.* aspirant, seeker, officeseeker, °runner, °nominee; applicant, entrant; °prospect, °possibility

candor *n.* 1 openness, frankness, ingenuousness, °simplicity, naiveté *or* naïveté *or* naivety, outspokenness, unreservedness, forthrightness, °honesty, °sincerity, directness, straightforwardness, unequivocalness 2 impartiality, fairness, °justice, °objectivity, open-mindedness

candy *n.* sweet(s), bonbon(s), sweetmeat(s), confectionery

cannibal *n.* anthropophagite, man-eater

cant *n.* 1 °hypocrisy, insincerity, °sham, °pretense, humbug, sanctimony, sanctimoniousness, lip service, affectedness, °pretension 2 °jargon, °shop, shoptalk, argot, °vernacular, slang, °dialect, patois, creole, pidgin, gobbledegook *or* gobbledygook, *Colloq* °lingo

cantankerous *adj.* ill-natured, °quarrelsome, °perverse, °cross, choleric, cross-grained, crabby, curmudgeonly, crusty, grumpy, °surly, irascible, °snappish, bad-tempered, ill-tempered, bearish, °bilious, °peevish, °testy, °irritable, °touchy, °disagreeable, tetchy, °contrary, *Colloq* crotchety, grouchy, *US* °cranky

canvass *v.* 1 °solicit, °electioneer, °campaign, °poll, *US and Canadian* °stump 2 °survey, °poll, °study, °analyze, °examine, °investigate, °interview, °question —*n.* 3 solicitation, °campaign 4 °survey, °study, °investigation, °poll, °examination, °tally

canyon *n.* °gorge, °ravine, gully *or* gulley, °pass, defile, *Brit dialectal* gill *or* ghyll, *US and Canadian* coulee, gulch; *US* °gap, arroyo

cap *n.* 1 hat, head covering 2 lid, °top, °cover 3 ***cap in hand.*** humbly, meekly, servilely, submissively, subserviently, docilely, respectfully —*v.* 4 °surpass, °outdo, °outstrip, °better, °beat, °exceed, °top, °excel 5 °cover, °protect

capability *n.* °ability, °power, °potential, °capacity, °means, °faculty, wherewithal; °talent, °proficiency, °aptitude, adeptness, °skill, competence

capable *adj.* 1 °able, °competent, °efficient, °proficient, °qualified, °talented, °gifted, skilled, °skillful, °accomplished, apt, °adept, °clever, °effective, °effectual; °expert, masterly, °masterful 2 ***capable of.*** disposed to, inclined to, predisposed to

capacity *n.* 1 °volume, °content, °size, dimensions; °room, °space 2 °potential, °ability, °capability, competence, °intelligence, °wit, brain(s), °talent, °aptitude, acumen, °understanding, °sense, °judgment, perspicacity, perceptiveness, °perception, mother wit, °intellect, °genius, °skill, °gift, °faculty, °power, °potential, *Colloq chiefly US* right stuff, the goods 3 °position, °condition, °character, °place, °post, °role, °job, °office, °duty, °responsibility, °province, °sphere, °function; *Law* competency, °qualification

cape[1] *n.* headland, promontory, peninsula, neck, °point, *Archaic* ness

cape[2] *n.* °mantle, shawl, °stole, °cloak

caper *n.* 1 °skip, °leap, °spring, °frolic, °hop, gambol, °frisk, curvet, gambado 2 escapade, °stunt, °mischief, °prank, high jinks, *US* °crime, burglary, °robbery, *Colloq* shenanigan, dido, °lark, *Slang US and Canadian* °job —*v.* 3 °skip, °hop, °frolic, °leap, °jump, °frisk, romp, gambol, °prance, °cavort, curvet

capital *n.* 1 °head, °top, °crown, °cap 2

°seat (of government) **3** °money, °assets, °funds, finance(s), °cash, wherewithal; °wealth, °means, °property, °resources, °savings, °principal **4** majuscule, °upper case, large letter, °initial, *Colloq* °cap —*adj.* **5** °chief, °main, °major, °important, °cardinal, °central, °principal, °prime, °primary, °paramount, °preeminent, °foremost, °leading **6** first-class, °first-rate, °excellent, °superior, °matchless, °peerless, °choice, °select, °outstanding, °fine, °superb, °splendid, °marvelous, °extraordinary, *Colloq* smashing, °great, °super, *Brit* brill, *Old-fashioned* topping, top-hole, °ripping, ripsnorting

capitulate *v.* **1** °surrender, °yield, °give up, °submit, °succumb **2** acquiesce, °concede, °relent, °give in, °yield

capricious *adj.* °whimsical, °erratic, °flighty, °fickle, mercurial, unsteady, °variable, °unstable, wayward, unpredictable, undependable, °changeable, °impulsive, crotchety, quirky, °unreliable, °inconstant, °fanciful, °wanton

capsize *v.* °upset, °overturn, turn turtle *or* upside down, °tip (over), keel over, invert

captivate *v.* enthral *or US* enthrall, °enslave, °fascinate, °hypnotize, °entrance, °beguile, °charm, enamor, °enchant, °bewitch, °enrapture, °dazzle, infatuate, °attract, allure, °seduce, °win

captive *n.* **1** °prisoner, °convict, °hostage, detainee, internee; °slave, bondman *or* bondsman, bondservant —*adj.* **2** imprisoned, incarcerated, confined, caged, locked up, under lock and key

captivity *n.* confinement, °imprisonment, internment, °detention, °custody, incarceration, °restraint; °bondage, °slavery, thralldom, enslavement, °servitude; *Archaic* durance

capture *n.* **1** °seizure, °taking, °catching, °arrest, apprehension, *Slang* °pinch, collar —*v.* **2** °seize, °take, °catch, lay *or* take hold of, °grab, apprehend, °arrest, *Slang* °pinch, collar, °nab, *Brit* °nick

car *n.* **1** °(motor) vehicle, motorcar, automobile, passenger car, *Old-fashioned or slang* motor; *Chiefly US* auto; *Colloq* jalopy, °heap, °pile, crate, °machine, buggy, °transport; *Slang* wheels **2** °(railway) carriage

card *n.* **1** playing card, *Slang* pasteboard **2** calling card, visiting card, *carte de visite,* business card **3** greeting card, Christmas card, birthday card, anniversary card, condolence card, Easter card, New Year card **4** postcard, *US* postal card **5** index card, file card **6** membership card; press card; union card **7** dance card **8** credit card; bank card **9** identity *or* identification card, ID (card) **10** °joker, prankster, practical joker, °wag, humorist, °comedian, funnyman **11** ***in or, esp Brit on the cards.*** °destined, °fated, slated, in the offing; °likely, °probable, °possible, °liable **12** ***play one's cards right, well, badly, etc.*** °act, °behave, take action; °plan, use strategy **13** ***put or lay one's cards on the table or show one's cards.*** act openly, reveal all, be forthright, be direct, be open, be honest, be unsecretive, *Colloq* °come clean

cardinal *adj.* °important, °chief, °key, °special, °main, °central, °principal, °prime, °primary, °essential, °necessary, °fundamental; °supreme, °paramount, highest, °first, °foremost, °leading, °preeminent

care *n.* **1** °anxiety, °worry, °trouble, °anguish, disquiet, °distress, °grief, °sorrow, dolor, °sadness, °suffering, °misery, °woe, tribulation **2** °concern, °regard, °vigilance, mindfulness, °heed, °solicitude; heedfulness, °attention, °pains, carefulness, meticulousness, punctiliousness; °caution, circumspection **3** °responsibility, °charge, °protection, guardianship, °custody, keeping, °safekeeping; °control, °direction, supervision **4** ***take care of.*** °look after, °attend to, be responsible for, take charge of, take responsibility for; °tend, °nurse —*v.* **5** be concerned, trouble oneself, feel interest, °worry, °fret, °trouble, *Brit* °mind **6** ***care for.*** **(a)** °look after, °tend, °attend (to), watch over, °protect, °take care of, °provide for; °nurse **(b)** °like, °fancy, be attracted to, be fond of, °love, be keen on, be enamored of

careen *v.* heel over, keel over; *US loosely* °career, °sway, °tip, °pitch, veer, °swerve, °lurch

career *n.* **1** °employment, °occupation, °calling, °vocation, °pursuit, °(life's) work, °job, °business, livelihood; °profession, °trade, °craft, métier —*v.* **2** °speed, °race, °rush, °dash, °fly, °tear, °hurtle, °bolt, °shoot, *Colloq* zoom

carefree *adj.* °nonchalant, °easy, easygoing, insouciant, lighthearted, °blithe, happy-go-lucky, °breezy, airy; °blasé, °indifferent, unconcerned, unworried, trouble-free, worry-free, contented, °happy

careful *adj.* **1** °cautious, °wary, circumspect, chary, °prudent, watchful, °aware, °alert, °vigilant **2** °meticulous, °painstaking, °attentive, punctilious, (well-)organized, °systematic, °precise, °fastidious, °thorough, °scrupulous, °conscientious, °particular, °finicky, finical, °fussy

careless *adj.* **1** unconcerned, untroubled, unworried, °casual, °indifferent, °heedless, °thoughtless, °inconsiderate, uncaring, devil-may-care, °irresponsible, °cursory, °lackadaisical, °perfunctory **2** °inattentive, negligent, °thoughtless, °absent-minded, neglectful, °remiss; unobservant, °unthinking, °imprudent, unmindful, incautious, °unwary, °reckless, slapdash, °rash **3** °inaccurate, °imprecise, °inexact, °incorrect, °wrong, error-ridden, °erroneous, *Colloq* °sloppy **4** unstudied, °ingenuous, °artless, °casual, °nonchalant

caress *n.* **1** °pat, °stroke, fondling, blandishment; °cuddle, °embrace, °hug; nuzzle, °kiss —*v.* **2** °touch, °pat, °pet, °fondle, °stroke; °cuddle, °embrace, °hug; nuzzle, °kiss

cargo *n.* shipment, consignment, shipload,

truckload, wagonload, °load, trainload, *US* carload; °freight, °goods, °merchandise

caricature *n.* **1** cartoon, °parody, °burlesque, °lampoon, °satire, pasquinade, *Colloq* °takeoff, spoof, *Brit* sendup —*v.* **2** °parody, °satirize, °lampoon, °burlesque, °ridicule, °mock, °distort, *Colloq* °take off, *Brit* °send up

carnage *n.* °slaughter, butchery, °massacre, blood bath, °holocaust, °killing, *Shoah, Churban* or *Hurban*

carnal *adj.* fleshly, °sensual, °animal, bodily, °lustful, °voluptuous, libidinous, °lecherous, concupiscent, °sexual, °erotic, °lascivious, licentious, °lewd, °prurient

carouse *v.* **1** °make merry, °revel, *Colloq* °party, pub-crawl, make whoopee, go on a bender *or* tear *or* binge *or* toot, °paint the town red, binge, °booze —*n.* **2** °revel, °spree, °fling, wassail, carousal, °drunk, bacchanal, *Colloq* binge, °bender, °booze, boozer, *Brit* knees-up, *US* °tear, toot

carp *v.* °find fault, °criticize, °cavil, °complain, °nag, °pick at, °pick on, °bully, bullyrag *or* ballyrag, *Colloq* °knock, pick holes (in), °gripe, *Brit* whinge

carriage *n.* **1** °(railway) coach, *US* °car **2** °bearing, mien, °air, °manner, deportment, °conduct, demeanor, °attitude, °posture, °stance, °presence, °behavior, comportment **3** °freight, freightage, transportation, cartage, shipping; postage

carrier *n.* **1** bearer, °porter; transporter, drayman, shipper, hauler *or Brit* haulier; carter **2** transmitter, *Immunology* vector, *US* typhoid Mary

carry *v.* **1** °transport, convey, °bear, °lug, °drag, °cart, °move, *Colloq* tote, *Slang US* schlep **2** °conduct, convey, °lead, °take, °transport, °transfer, °transmit **3** °drive, impel, °conduct, convey, °take, °move **4** °support, °maintain, °finance **5** °bear, °hold up, °uphold, °maintain **6** °win, °take, °sweep, °capture, °gain, °secure **7** °stock, °sell, °offer; °display **8** °broadcast, disseminate, °offer, °release; °communicate, °present, °read, °report, °announce; °give **9** ***carry away.*** °transport, °excite, °enrapture, °delight **10** ***carry off.*** **(a)** °win, °gain, °capture, °secure **(b)** abscond with, °kidnap, °take, purloin, *Colloq Brit* °pinch, °nick **(c)** °accomplish, °perform, °effect, do, °succeed, handle *or* manage successfully, °bring off, °carry out **(d)** °kill, be *or* cause the death of, cause to die **11** ***carry on.*** **(a)** °continue, °proceed, °go on, °persist, keep on *or* at, °persevere **(b)** °manage, °conduct, °operate **(c)** °misbehave, *Colloq* act up, °fool around, *Brit* °play up **12** ***carry out or through.*** °perform, °effect, °implement, °complete, °execute, °accomplish, °continue, conclude

cart *n.* **1** handcart, pushcart, trolley, barrow, wagon *or Brit also* waggon —*v.* **2** °carry, convey, °move, °lug, °drag, tote, °transport, °bring, °haul, *Colloq US* schlep

carte blanche *n.* °license, °permission, °sanction, free rein, °authority, °discretion

carve *v.* **1** hew, °cut, sculpt, °sculpture, °shape, °chisel, °model, °fashion, °engrave, incise, °grave, °whittle, °chip **2** Often, ***carve up or out.*** °divide (up), °cut (up), subdivide, apportion, °parcel out, °allot, °partition

case[1] *n.* **1** °instance, °example, °event, °occurrence; °happening, °occasion, °circumstance, °state, °situation **2** °action, °suit, lawsuit, °dispute; °cause **3** °patient, °invalid, °victim **4** °specimen, °instance, °example **5** ***in any case.*** °in any event, come what may, °at all events, anyhow, anyway **6** ***in case.*** **(a)** lest, for fear that **(b)** if, in the event that, if it happens *or* proves *or* turns out that, if it should happen *or* prove *or* turn out that **7** ***in case of.*** in the event of; for fear of **8** ***the case.*** the fact, the actuality, the truth, the reality, what really happened *or* took place

case[2] *n.* **1** °box, container, carton, crate; °chest, holder, °receptacle; °trunk, °suitcase, °casket **2** covering, °cover, °protection, casing, envelope, °wrapper —*v.* **3** encase, °box, crate, °pack, °package, containerize

cash *n.* **1** °money, currency, bills, °notes, banknotes, °change, hard cash *or* money, specie, coin of the realm, legal tender, *Slang* moolah, dough, bread, °loot, spondulix *or* spondulicks, *Brit* lolly, °ready, °readies, *US* °scratch, gelt, mazuma —*v.* **2** Also, ***cash in.*** °change, °sell, liquidate, °exchange; °realize

casket *n.* **1** °chest, °box, container, °case, coffer, °receptacle **2** °coffin; sarcophagus

cast *n.* **1** °throw, °toss, °pitch, °shy, °lob, °thrust, chuck **2** dramatis personae, actors and actresses, players, performers, troupe, °company **3** °form, °shape, °mold; °formation, formulation, °arrangement **4** °model, casting, °mold; °stamp, °type **5** °twist, °turn, irregularity, °warp; squint **6** °turn, °inclination, °bent, °hint, °touch; tinge, °tint, coloring —*v.* **7** °throw, °toss, °pitch, °fling, °sling, °hurl, °dash, °send, *Colloq* chuck, °shy **8** °assign, °delegate, °appoint, °designate, °name, °nominate, °choose, °pick, °select **9** °form, °mold, °found **10** ***cast about for.*** °search for, °look for, °seek **11** ***cast aside.*** °reject, °discard, cast *or* throw away *or* out, °get rid of. See also **14,** below. **12** ***cast away.*** °maroon, shipwreck. See also **11,** above. **13** ***cast off.*** °throw off, °shed, doff **14** ***cast out.*** °expel, drive out, °throw out, °evict, °eject, oust, °exile, °remove. See also **11,** above.

castaway *n.* °reject, castoff, °outcast, pariah, °exile

caste *n.* °(social) class, °rank, °order, °level, °stratum, °standing, °position, °station, °status, °estate

castigate *v.* °chastise, °punish, °correct, °penalize, °discipline, °rebuke, °reprimand, read the riot act (to), keelhaul, °chasten, °criticize, *Colloq* °tell off, °dress down, *Chiefly Brit* tick off, *Brit* carpet, haul over the coals,

US and Canadian °chew out, rake over the coals, put *or* call on *or* on to the carpet

castle *n.* **1** fortress, °stronghold, citadel **2** mansion, °palace, manor house, °hall, chateau

casual *adj.* **1** °accidental, °chance, °random, fortuitous, unexpected, °unforeseen, °unpremeditated, unplanned, unforeseeable, unpredictable, serendipitous **2** °uncertain, unsure, °haphazard, °occasional, °random, °irregular, unsystematic, °sporadic, °erratic **3** °indifferent, °nonchalant, °offhand, insouciant, apathetic, °cool, unconcerned, uninterested, pococurante, °dispassionate, °blasé, °relaxed, °lackadaisical **4** °informal; °lounge **5** °offhand, happy-go-lucky, °natural, °easy, easygoing, devil-may-care, unconcerned, °relaxed, dégagé, unconstrained

casualty *n.* **1** °disaster, °catastrophe, °calamity, °accident, mischance, misadventure, °mishap **2** **(a)** °victim, °fatality, *Colloq* statistic **(b)** Usually, ***casualties.*** *Chiefly military* wounded, injured, missing, missing in action, °dead, fatalities, *US* MIA(s), body count

catastrophe *n.* **1** °disaster, °calamity, cataclysm **2** °misfortune, bad luck, °shock, °blow, °tragedy, °disaster; °mishap, mischance, misadventure, °accident, °fiasco, °failure

catch *v.* **1** °capture, °seize, apprehend, take *or* get (hold of), °grab, °grip, °grasp, take captive, °hold, °arrest, take prisoner, *Colloq* °nab, °pinch, collar, *Brit* °nick **2** °trap, ensnare, entrap, °snare, °net, °bag, °hook, °round up, corral **3** °take, get on *or* on to, °board **4** °surprise, °discover, °find **5** be seized *or* taken hold of by *or* with, °come down with, be afflicted by *or* with, °contract, °get, °suffer from **6** °strike, °hit, °deliver, °fetch, °box **7** °tangle, become entangled *or* stuck *or* trapped *or* hooked **8** °restrain, °stop, °check, °curb **9** °intercept, °grab, °seize, °snatch **10** °understand, °see, °comprehend, °grasp, apprehend, °fathom, °perceive, discern, °follow, °take in, °gather, *Colloq* °figure out, °get, °catch on (to), get the drift (of), *Brit* °twig **11** °captivate, °charm, °bewitch, °enchant, °fascinate, °seduce, °attract, °entice, allure **12** °attract, °draw **13** ***catch on.*** **(a)** °understand, °grasp, °see (through), °comprehend, °get (it), *Brit* °twig **(b)** take hold, °succeed, become popular *or* fashionable **14** ***catch up.*** **(a)** absorb, °involve, enthrall, °immerse **(b)** °reach, °overtake, °overhaul —*n.* **15** °capture, °take, °bag, °prize, °trophy **16** °acquisition; °conquest **17** °clasp, °hook, °pin, °clip, °fastening, fastener **18** °trick, °disadvantage, °hitch, °snag, °fly in the ointment, catch-22, °trap, °problem, °drawback, *Colloq US* hooker

catching *adj.* **1** contagious, °infectious, transmissible, transmittable, communicable **2** °attractive, captivating, fascinating, °enchanting, bewitching, entrancing, °winning, enticing, alluring, °fetching

categorical *adj.* °direct, °explicit, °express, unconditional, °firm, °positive, unreserved, unrestricted, °absolute, °outright, °downright, unequivocal, unambiguous, °specific; °emphatic, °unqualified, °authoritative, °dogmatic, *Technical* apodeictic *or* apodictic

categorize *v.* classify, °class, °sort, °organize, assort, °rank, °order, °section, departmentalize, °group, °arrange

category *n.* °class, classification, °type, °sort, °kind, °variety, °group, grouping, listing, °rank, ranking, °list, °grade, °department, °division, °section, sector, °area, °sphere; °head, heading

cater *v.* **1** °provision, victual; purvey, °provide **2** ***cater for or to.*** °indulge, °humor, °serve, dance attendance on, °pamper, °baby, °coddle, °minister to, °spoil, mollycoddle, cosset, °pander to

catholic *adj.* °universal, °general, (all-)inclusive, °broad, °wide, °comprehensive, widespread, all-embracing, eclectic, °liberal

cattle *n.* livestock, °stock, beef; cows, bulls, bullocks, steers, bovines, oxen

cause *n.* **1** °origin, °occasion, °source, °root, genesis, °agent, prime mover, wellspring **2** originator, °creator, °producer, °agent, °agency **3** ground *or* grounds, justification, °reason, °basis, °call, °motive **4** °case, °matter, °issue, °concern; °movement, °undertaking; °ideal, °belief —*v.* **5** °make, °induce **6** °effect, bring on *or* about, °give rise to, °result in, °produce, °create, °precipitate, °occasion, lead to, °induce, °generate, °provoke, °promote; engender; °motivate, compel

caustic *adj.* **1** °burning, corrosive, °destructive, mordant, astringent **2** °sarcastic, °biting, acrimonious, °sharp, °bitter, °sardonic, °cutting, °trenchant, °critical, °scathing, acid, °harsh, °pungent, °virulent

caution *n.* **1** °warning, admonition, admonishment, caveat, monition, °advice, °counsel, °injunction **2** wariness, °prudence, °care, °vigilance, °forethought, °heed, watchfulness, alertness, circumspection, °discretion —*v.* **3** °warn, admonish, forewarn, °tip (off); °advise, °counsel

cautious *adj.* °wary, heedful, °careful, °prudent, circumspect, watchful, °vigilant, °alert, °discreet, °guarded

cave *n.* **1** cavern, grotto, °hollow, °hole, °cavity, den —*v.* **2** ***cave in.*** **(a)** °collapse, °break down, °give way, °subside, fall in *or* inwards **(b)** °yield, °submit, °give way; °surrender; *Colloq* °buckle, knuckle under

cavil *n.* **1** °quibble, °complaint —*v.* **2** °carp, °quibble, split hairs, °complain, °find fault, censure, °criticize, °dispute, °object, demur, *Colloq* nitpick

cavity *n.* °pit, °hole, °hollow, °opening, crater, °gap; °space

cavort *v.* curvet, °prance, °caper, °frisk, °bound, gambol, romp, °skip, °leap, °jump, °dance

cease *v.* **1** °stop, °end, °finish, °leave off, °terminate, °halt, °discontinue, desist (from), °break off (from), °refrain (from)

—*n.* 2 ***without cease.*** ceaselessly, endlessly, unendingly, incessantly, interminably, continuously, continually, constantly, ad infinitum, infinitely, perpetually, °forever, eternally, everlastingly, °nonstop, unremittingly
cede *v.* °yield, °give way, °give up, °grant, °give, °surrender, deliver up, turn *or* make *or* hand over, convey, °transfer, °relinquish, °abandon, °renounce, °abdicate
celebrant *n.* officiant, °official; °priest
celebrate *v.* 1 °hold, °perform, solemnize, ritualize, °observe, °keep, °honor, officiate at; °sanctify, °hallow, consecrate, °dedicate 2 rejoice (in *or* at), °memorialize; have a party, °revel, °make merry, wassail, *Colloq* °party, °paint the town red, whoop it up 3 °extol, °praise, °exalt, °glorify, °laud, °eulogize, °honor; lionize 4 °publicize, advertise, °broadcast
celebrated *adj.* °famous, °renowned, °well-known, famed, °prominent, °noted, °eminent, °noteworthy, °distinguished, °illustrious, acclaimed
celebration *n.* 1 °observance, °observation, °performance, solemnization, hallowing, sanctification, memorialization, commemoration 2 praising, extolling, honoring 3 °party, °fête, °gala, °festivities, °frolic, °revelry, merrymaking
celebrity *n.* 1 °renown, °fame, repute, °reputation, °prominence, eminence, °distinction, °prestige, famousness, °popularity, notability, stardom; °notoriety 2 °notable, °dignitary, °star, luminary, toast of the town, °personage, °name, °personality, superstar
celestial *adj.* 1 °heavenly, °divine, °spiritual, °godly, paradisiac(al) *or* paradisaic(al), °sublime, empyrean, elysian, ethereal, °immortal, °supernatural 2 astronomical, astral
celibacy *n.* 1 bachelorhood, spinsterhood, singleness 2 °chastity, virginity, continence, (self-)restraint, abstinence, °purity
celibate *adj.* 1 °unmarried, °single, unwed 2 abstinent, abstemious, continent, ascetic; virgin(al), °pure, °chaste, unsullied, undefiled, °virtuous, °immaculate —*n.* 3 bachelor, spinster
cell *n.* °chamber, °room, apartment, cubicle; °stall
cellar *n.* basement, vault
cement *n.* 1 mortar, °bond, °glue, gum, paste, solder; adhesive —*v.* 2 °stick, °glue, paste, solder, °weld, braze, °bond; °join, °bind, °combine, °unite; cohere, °hold, °cling, adhere
center *n.* 1 °middle, °core, °heart; °nucleus, focal point, °hub, °pivot, nave; midpoint —*v.* 2 °focus, °converge, °meet, °concentrate, °cluster
central *adj.* 1 °middle, medial, median; inner, °inside 2 °main, °principal, °important, °chief, °key, °leading, °dominant, °prime, °primary, °preeminent, °cardinal, °significant, °essential
ceremonial *adj.* 1 °ritual, celebratory, commemorative 2 °formal, °solemn, °stately, °dignified; °ceremonious, august —*n.* 3 °rite, °ritual, °formality, °ceremony, °service, °observance
ceremonious *adj.* 1 °ceremonial, °formal, °dignified, °solemn, *Colloq* °stuffy, °stiff, starchy 2 courtly, °courteous, °polite, °civil, °correct, °proper, °conventional, punctilious, °careful
ceremony *n.* 1 °rite, °observance, °solemnity, °service, °ceremonial, °ritual, °formality, °function; obsequies 2 motions, formalities *or* formality, conventions *or* convention, niceties, proprieties, °form, °protocol; lip service, appearances, proformas, °etiquette, °decorum
certain *adj.* 1 °determined, °set, °fixed, °predetermined, °decided, settled, °firm, °stable, °invariable, established, °standard, °constant, unchanging, °steady, unfluctuating, nonfluctuating, °traditional 2 °sure, unerring, °definite, dependable, °trustworthy, unfailing, °infallible, °reliable, assured, guaranteed 3 °sure, °inevitable, inescapable, °destined, predestined, ineluctable, inexorable, °unavoidable, °definite, °firm; unchanging, °changeless, °infallible, °permanent, *Colloq* on the cards, a sure thing, *US* °in the cards 4 indubitable, °indisputable, °undisputed, undoubted, °sure, °doubtless, unequivocal, incontestable, undeniable, °incontrovertible, °absolute, irrefutable, °unquestionable, unquestioned, unarguable, valid 5 °confident; assured, °sure, °positive, °definite 6 °specific, °particular, °definite; unnamed, unspecified, nonspecified, nonspecific
certainty *n.* 1 °fact, actuality, °reality, °truth, *Colloq* sure thing 2 °assurance, self-assurance, definiteness, °confidence, °conviction, °faith, authoritativeness, positiveness, certitude 3 ***for a certainty.*** assuredly, °definitely, certainly, °surely, °positively; °undoubtedly, indubitably, without (a) doubt, undeniably, unquestionably, °absolutely, *Colloq* for sure
certify *v.* 1 °confirm, °attest (to), °verify, °testify (to), affirm, aver, asseverate, corroborate, °substantiate, °endorse, °guarantee, °warrant; °swear (to), °bear witness (to), °vouchsafe, °vouch (for) 2 °declare, classify, °establish, °confirm
chafe *v.* 1 °rub, °warm (up), °heat (up) 2 °rub, abrade, °fret, °gall, °irritate, make sore 3 °fume, °rage, °seethe; °ruffle, vex, °fret, °irritate —*n.* 4 °sore, abrasion, °bruise, soreness, irritation
chaff *n.* 1 °banter, °raillery, °ridicule, badinage, joking, teasing, twitting, *Colloq* kidding, ragging, *Chiefly US and Canadian* joshing —*v.* 2 °banter, °tease, °twit, rail at, *Colloq* kid, °rag, *Chiefly US and Canadian* josh
chain *n.* 1 °string, series, °combination; °sequence, °succession, °train, °course, °set, concatenation 2 °restraint, °check, °trammel, °control, confinement, fetter, °bond, °manacle, °shackle, gyve —*v.* 3 °shackle,

°secure, °fasten, °bind, gyve; confine, fetter, °restrain, °restrict, °tie, °limit

chair *n.* **1** °seat, armchair, stool, bench, easy chair, rocking chair **2** throne, bench, °position, cathedra, °authority; professorship, directorship **3** chairperson, chairman, chairwoman, presiding officer, °leader, °moderator —*v.* **4** °preside, °lead, °govern, °moderate, °run, °direct, °manage, °oversee

challenge *v.* **1** °question, °dispute, °defy, object to, °take exception to, °contest, °doubt, call into doubt, call into *or* to question, impugn **2** invite, °dare, °summon, call out, °provoke **3** °brave, °dare, confront, °defy, °contest —*n.* **4** °question, °dispute, °doubt **5** °invitation, °dare, summons, °provocation, confrontation, defiance; °ultimatum **6** °problem, °demand, stimulation, °trial, °test

chamber *n.* **1** °assembly, °body, legislature, judicature, °house, congress, judiciary, senate, °diet; consortium **2** meeting hall, reception room, assembly room **3** °compartment, °niche, °nook, °cavity **4** °room, apartment; bedroom, bedchamber

champion *n.* **1** °victor, °winner, conqueror, titleholder, prizewinner, titleist **2** defender, °guardian, °protector, °hero, °supporter, °backer, °protagonist, °advocate **3** fighter, combatant, °hero, warrior, campaigner, °veteran —*v.* **4** °defend, °protect, °guard; °support, °back, °stand up for, fight for, °maintain, °sustain, °uphold; espouse, °forward, °promote, °advocate

chance *n.* **1** °fortune, °luck, °fate **2** °opportunity, °time, °turn; °occasion **3** Also, ***chances.*** °likelihood, °probability, °prospect, °odds, °certainty, predictability; conceivability, °possibility **4** Also, ***chances.*** °risk, °speculation, °gamble **5** ***by chance.*** **(a)** accidentally, unintentionally, inadvertently **(b)** °perhaps, °maybe, °possibly, conceivably —*adj.* **6** °casual, °incidental, °accidental, unintentional, °inadvertent; unplanned, °unpremeditated, unexpected, °unforeseen; unlooked-for —*v.* **7** °happen; °occur, °come to pass, °take place, °come about; befall, betide **8** °risk, °hazard; imperil, °endanger, °jeopardize, °stake, °bet, wager

change *n.* **1** °substitution, replacement, °exchange, interchange, °switch **2** °variation, °difference, °switch, °variety, °novelty **3** °variation, °alteration, changeover, °mutation, °shift, modulation, modification, °transformation, metamorphosis, °revolution **4** coin(s), coppers, °silver; °(hard) cash —*v.* **5** °exchange, interchange, °switch, °trade; °replace (with), °substitute, *Colloq* swap *or* swop **6** °modify, °alter, °modulate; mutate, °transform, metamorphose **7** °fluctuate, °shift, °vary; vacillate **8** ***change to or into.*** °turn into, °become, °transform, mutate, transmute, °convert, metamorphose

changeable *adj.* **1** °variable, mutable, °protean, °inconstant, °unstable, °unsettled, shifting, °uncertain, °irregular, uneven, unpredictable, labile, °capricious, °erratic, °fickle, °unreliable, undependable, mercurial, °volatile **2** alterable, modifiable, transformable, convertible

changeless *adj.* **1** unchanging, unvaried, °eternal, °permanent, °fixed, °stable; unchangeable, immutable, unalterable, °inevitable, °uniform **2** °abiding, °permanent, °constant, °perpetual, °everlasting, °steadfast, unvarying, unchanging

channel *n.* **1** watercourse, canal, waterway, ditch, aqueduct, sluice, trench, trough, gutter, moat; riverbed, streambed **2** °strait, °narrows, neck **3** °furrow, °groove, flute **4** °course, °means, °way, °approach, avenue, °medium, °path, artery, conduit —*v.* **5** °direct, convey, °pass, °guide, °lead, °conduct

chant *n.* **1** °song, psalm, hymn, canticle, plainsong, plainchant, mantra, paean, dirge, monody, descant, carol; singsong —*v.* **2** °sing, intone, descant, carol

chaos *n.* formlessness, °disorder, °confusion; °pandemonium, °bedlam, turmoil, °tumult; entropy

chaotic *adj.* **1** formless, °shapeless, °incoherent, disordered, °disorderly, disorganized, unorganized, unsystematic, unsystematized, unmethodical, °haphazard, °irregular, °helter-skelter, °confused, °topsy-turvy, jumbled, higgledy-piggledy, *Brit* shambolic **2** °tumultuous, °noisy, clamorous, °uproarious, °wild, °riotous, frenzied, °hectic, turbulent, unstuck

chap *n.* °fellow, °lad, °man, °boy, *Colloq* °guy, geezer, °customer, gink, *US* buddy, *Brit* bloke, *Australian* cove, *Old-fashioned US* gazabo *or* gazebo; *Old-fashioned Brit* (old) egg, (old) bean, (old) crumpet, °(old) boy; *Slang US* bozo

character *n.* **1** °brand, °stamp, °mark, °symbol, monogram, insigne, badge, °emblem, °sign, °seal, °label; °letter, °number, °figure, °type, °sort, °arbitrary, °peculiar, rune, hieroglyphic *or* hieroglyph **2** °characteristic, °quality, °distinction, °trait, °feature, °mark; °sort, °kind, °type, °nature, °description, °attribute; idiosyncrasy, °peculiarity **3** °morality, °honesty, °integrity, respectability, °rectitude, °honor, °courage, goodness **4** °person, °personage, °personality, °individual **5** °role, °part, °personality, characterization, dramatis persona **6** °eccentric, °card, *Colloq* oddball, nut, nutter, loony, bat, °weirdo, nutcase, screwball, crackpot, fruitcake, *Australian or old-fashioned Brit* cove **7** °role, °position, °status, °capacity **8** ***in character.*** °fitting, °proper, °suitable, in keeping, °typical, °normal, expected, °characteristic **9** ***out of character.*** untypical, atypical, uncharacteristic, °abnormal, unexpected, unfitting

characteristic *adj.* **1** °typical, °representative; °emblematic, °symbolic, °distinctive, idiosyncratic, °symptomatic —*n.* **2** °mark, °trait, °attribute, °feature, °quality, °property, °peculiarity, idiosyncrasy, °character, earmark

characterize *v.* delineate, °describe, °portray, depict, °represent, °define, °brand, °label, °mark, °note, °identify

charade *n.* travesty, °absurdity, °mockery, farce, °parody

charge *n.* **1** °load, °burden, °weight, onus, °impediment; °care, °concern, °obligation **2** °price, °fee, °cost **3** °debt, debit, °expense, assessment, °liability **4** °care, °custody, °protection, guardianship, wardship, supervision, °jurisdiction, °control, °responsibility, °safekeeping **5** °order, mandate, °injunction, °precept, °command, °dictate, °direction, °instruction, °demand, exhortation **6** °accusation, °imputation, indictment, °allegation **7** °attack, °onset, °action, °assault, sally, °raid, foray, sortie —*v.* **8** °fill, imbue, °load, °instill, pervade, °permeate, °saturate, °suffuse **9** °burden, °entrust, commission, °assign; °afflict, °tax **10** °command, °order, °bid, enjoin, exhort, °urge, °require, °instruct, °direct **11** °blame, censure, °accuse; °indict, cite, °name; °allege, assert **12** °bill, invoice, assess, debit **13** °ask, °demand, °claim, °require, °expect **14** °attack, °assault, °storm, assail, do battle (with)

charitable *adj.* **1** °generous, °liberal, °bountiful, munificent, °unselfish, openhanded, bighearted, magnanimous, °philanthropic, public-spirited, unsparing, eleemosynary **2** well-disposed, °kindly, °kind, beneficent, °benevolent, well-wishing, °lenient, °tolerant, °forgiving, °indulgent, °understanding, compassionate, humane, °sympathetic, °considerate, well-meaning, °good

charity *n.* **1** generosity, almsgiving, munificence, liberality, openhandedness, magnanimity, beneficence, °philanthropy, unselfishness, °humanity, humanitarianism, goodwill **2** leniency, bigheartedness, largeheartedness, °benevolence, magnanimity, °indulgence, considerateness, °consideration, compassion, °understanding, °sympathy, kindheartedness **3** alms, °donation, contribution, largess *or* largesse, *Colloq Brit* °dole, *US* °welfare, °relief

charm *n.* **1** °amulet, °talisman, °fetish, rabbit's foot, good-luck piece **2** attractiveness, °appeal, °fascination, allure, °magnetism, desirability, °elegance, urbanity, °sophistication, sophisticatedness, suavity, °grace, °refinement, cultivatedness, cultivation, °culture, °polish; °magic, °enchantment, °spell, °sorcery **3** ***charms.*** °beauty, attractiveness, pulchritude, prettiness, handsomeness, °appeal, allure, °magnetism, °pull, °draw **4** ***like a charm.*** successfully, °perfectly, miraculously, marvelously, extraordinarily, especially well —*v.* **5** °influence, °control, °subdue, °bind, put a spell on, °bewitch, °enchant, °seduce, °hypnotize, mesmerize, enthral *or US* enthrall, °captivate, °delight, °fascinate, *Literary* °enrapture **6** °overcome, °subdue, °calm, soothe, allay, assuage, °hypnotize, mesmerize

charmed *adj.* **1** bewitched, spellbound, °enchanted, magical **2** fortified, protected **3** pleased, °delighted, °enchanted, °happy

charmer *n.* enchanter, enchantress, °sorcerer, sorceress, °magician; vamp, °siren, Circe, Cleopatra, Lorelei, °temptress, °seductress; °seducer, Romeo, Valentino, Don Juan, Lothario, Casanova, lady-killer, ladies' man; °flatterer; smooth talker, *Colloq* °(big-time) operator, con artist *or* man, *Old-fashioned* smoothie, wolf

chart *n.* **1** sea-chart, map **2** map, °table, tabulation, graph, diagram; blueprint —*v.* **3** °plot, °plan, map (out), °design

charter *n.* **1** °document, °contract, °compact, °agreement, covenant **2** °permit, °permission, °license, °authority, franchise, °right, °privilege, concession **3** °lease, °contract —*v.* **4** °license, °authorize, °document, commission, °approve, °certify, franchise, °qualify; °recognize **5** °let, °lease, °rent, °hire, °engage, °contract

chase *n.* **1** hunting, °hunt, °pursuit **2** °run after, °follow, °pursue, °track, go (out) after; court, woo **3** ***chase away, off, out, etc.*** °rout, °put to flight, °hound; drive away, °off, °out, etc.

chaste *adj.* **1** °pure, virginal, virgin, °celibate, abstinent, continent, °virtuous, undefiled, stainless, unstained, unsullied, unblemished, °decent, °clean, °good, °wholesome, °moral **2** °subdued, °severe, restrained, °unadorned, austere, unembellished, °simple, °pure, undecorated, °clean

chasten *v.* **1** °discipline, °correct, °chastise, °punish, °castigate **2** °moderate, °temper, °subdue, °curb, °restrain, °repress, °tame, °suppress

chastise *v.* °punish, °beat, thrash, °belabor, °spank, °whip, °flog, °scourge, birch, cane; °discipline, °chasten, °correct, censure, °berate, °scold

chastity *n.* °purity, continence, virginity, maidenhood, maidenhead, °virtue, °celibacy, abstinence, abstention, abstemiousness, °restraint, self-restraint, forbearance

chat *n.* **1** °conversation, colloquy, °talk, small talk, °gossip, °palaver, chitchat, °tête-à-tête, heart-to-heart, *Colloq* °gab, *Chiefly Brit* chinwag, confab, *Brit* witter, natter, *US and Canadian* °rap, gabfest, bull session —*v.* **2** °converse, °gossip, °talk, chitchat, *Colloq* °gab, chew the fat *or* the rag, jaw, *Brit* witter, natter; *Slang US and Canadian* °rap, bullshit **3** ***chat up.*** flirt *or* dally with, °persuade, °induce, °prevail upon, °tempt, °lure, °entice, inveigle, °seduce, °proposition

chatter *v.* **1** °prattle, gabble, °jabber, prate, °patter, gibber, cackle, gibber-jabber, *Brit* chaffer, *Colloq* °gab, jaw, *Brit* natter, witter, rabbit on *or* away, °waffle **2** clatter, °rattle —*n.* **3** °prattle, prate, °patter, °gossip, cackle, jabbering, chattering

cheap *adj.* **1** °inexpensive, low-priced, bargain-priced, low-cost, sale-priced, cut-price, °reasonable; °economy, budget (-priced) **2** °economical; reduced **3** °shoddy, °base, °shabby, °tawdry, °sleazy, tatty, °seedy; °inferior, low-grade, °poor, second-rate, trashy, °worthless, *Brit* twopenny *or* tuppenny; *Colloq* °tacky, *Brit* tinpot, *Slang US* two-bit, °lousy, chintzy **4** stingy, °miserly, °penurious, niggardly, penny-pinching, cheeseparing, °frugal, °tight, tight-fisted, Scroogelike, skinflinty *—adv.* **5** inexpensively, cheaply, °for a song, *Brit* for twopence *or* tuppence **6** cheaply, °easily, reasonably, °for a song, *Brit* for twopence *or* tuppence *—n.* **7** ***on the cheap.*** inexpensively, reasonably, cheaply, at *or* below cost, °for a song, *Brit* for twopence *or* tuppence; *Slang* for peanuts

cheat *n.* **1** °swindler, deceiver, °impostor, °fraud, faker, °fake, °swindler, trickster, confidence man, con man, °operator, charlatan, mountebank, °rogue, shark, *Colloq* phoney *or US* phony, snake-oil artist *—v.* **2** °swindle, °deceive, bilk, °trick, °take, °fleece, °defraud, euchre, °hoax, °hoodwink, *Colloq* con, °take in, rook, flimflam, finagle, diddle, °fiddle, move the goal posts, bamboozle, °take for a ride; *Slang* °rip off

check *v.* **1** °stop, °arrest, °stay, °halt, °obstruct, °block, °limit; °retard, °slow, °brake, °curb, °hinder, °hamper, °impede, °thwart **2** °restrain, °control, °repress, °stay, °inhibit, °contain, °curb, °restrict **3** °authenticate, °verify, °confirm, °substantiate, validate, corroborate, °check into, °check out, °check up on **4** enquire about *or* after *or* into, °check into, check (up) on, °examine, °investigate, °inspect, make sure of, °verify, °monitor, °test, °study, °scrutinize **5** °correspond, °coincide, °agree, jibe, °tally, °conform, °check out, °fit, °mesh; °compare **6** ***check in.*** °arrive, °report **7** ***check in or into.*** °register, sign in *or* on, °enroll, log in **8** ***check into.*** °investigate, °check out, °check up on, °verify, °check **9** ***check off.*** tick (off), °mark, °check **10** ***check out.*** **(a)** °depart, °leave; °go **(b)** °investigate, °research, °explore, enquire into, look into *or* at *or* over, °scrutinize, °examine, °inspect, °probe, °survey, °check up on, °check, °check into, check over **(c)** °pass, pass muster *or* scrutiny, meet approval, be verified, °check **(d)** *Slang* cash in one's checks *or* chips, kick the bucket, croak **11** ***check over or out.*** °review, °verify, °authenticate, °check **12** ***check up (on).*** **(a)** °investigate, do research, °probe, °explore, °check **(b)** °determine, °discover, °find out, °look into, °check *—n.* **13** °stop, stopping, °cease, surcease, hesitation, cessation, stoppage, °interruption, °break, °pause, balk *or* baulk, discontinuity, discontinuation, discontinuance, °suspension **14** °restraint, °repression, °inhibition, limitation, °curb, °restriction, °control, constraint, °hindrance, °obstruction, °impediment, damper **15** °control, °test, inspection, °examination, °scrutiny, verification, substantiation, authentication, confirmation, validation, corroboration **16** tick, °mark, °dash, X **17** °token, °receipt, counterfoil, °stub; voucher, chit, certificate **18** °chip, °counter **19** °tab, charge(s), *Chiefly Brit* °bill

checkered *adj.* **1** checkerboard, checked; °patchwork; plaid, tartan **2** °variegated, diversified, alternating, °variable, good and bad, varying, fluctuating, up and down; °uncertain

cheeky *adj.* °impudent, °impertinent, °insolent, °audacious, °disrespectful, °rude, uncivil, °forward, °brazen, °pert, saucy

cheer *n.* **1** °disposition, °frame of mind, °spirit **2** cheerfulness, gladness, °mirth, °joy, °gaiety, blitheness, °happiness, buoyancy, lightheartedness, merrymaking **3** °comfort, °solace, °encouragement, consolation **4** °shout, °cry, hurrah, rah, huzzah, hurray *or* hooray *—v.* **5** °comfort, °console, °solace, °encourage, inspirit, °warm, *Colloq* buck up **6** °gladden, °enliven, cheer up, hearten, °buoy up, °brighten, elate, uplift, °lift up **7** °applaud, °shout, hurrah, °clap, °yell; *Colloq Brit, Australian, New Zealand* barrack for

cheerful *adj.* **1** joyous, °glad, gladsome, blithesome, °blithe, °happy, cheery, of good cheer, °joyful, °jolly, °exuberant, jubilant, °gleeful, °gay, lighthearted, °merry **2** cheering, gladdening, animating, °bright, enlivening, cheery, °gay, °buoyant, °invigorating

cherish *v.* **1** °treasure, hold *or* keep dear, °prize **2** °foster, °tend, °cultivate, °preserve, °sustain, nurture, °nourish, °nurse, cosset

chest *n.* **1** °box, coffer, °trunk, strongbox, caddy, °casket, °case **2** °breast; thorax

chew *v.* **1** masticate, °grind, °munch; °bite, °gnaw **2** ***chew the fat or rag.*** °gossip, °palaver, °chat, °converse, °talk, *Slang US and Canadian* bullshit **3** ***chew out.*** °scold, °rebuke, °reprimand **4** ***chew over.*** think about *or* on *or* over, °consider, °review, °ponder, ruminate on, meditate on *or* over

chic *adj.* **1** °stylish, °fashionable, à la mode, modish, °smart, °tasteful, °elegant; °sophisticated; *Colloq* °trendy *—n.* **2** °style, °fashion, good taste, tastefulness, °elegance, stylishness, modishness

chicanery *n.* °trickery, sophistry, °deception, quibbling, sharp practice, cheating, deviousness, duplicity, pettifoggery, double-dealing, °artifice, skulduggery

chief *n.* **1** °head, °leader, °principal, °superior, °supervisor, °superintendent, °manager, °overseer, captain, °master, ringleader, chieftain, *Dialect* himself, *Colloq* °boss, bossman, *Brit* governor, gov, supremo, *US* °man, kingpin, (head *or* chief) honcho, number one, numero uno, head man, big White Chief, big Chief, Great White Father, big Daddy, °super; *Slang* big cheese, *Brit* gaffer, *Chiefly US* Mr. Big *—adj.* **2** °head; °leading, ranking, °superior, °supreme, °foremost, °premier, °first, greatest, °outstanding **3** °principal, most important, °essential, °key, °paramount, °(first and) foremost, °primary, °prime, °main

chiefly *adv.* °mainly, °in particular, °especially, °particularly, °above all, most of all, °preeminently, °principally, °primarily, mostly, predominantly, °largely, by and large, °on the whole, °in the main, °generally, in general, °usually, °as a rule

child *n.* **1** °offspring, °descendant, son *or* daughter, little one, youngster, *Formal* °progeny, °issue, *Colloq* kid, nipper, *Slang Brit* sprog **2** fetus, newborn, neonate, infant, °baby, babe, toddler, boy *or* girl, lad *or* lass, °stripling, youngster, °youth, °juvenile, °adolescent, °teenager, young man *or* woman, young gentleman *or* lady, *Chiefly Scots* laddie *or* lassie

childhood *n.* °infancy, babyhood, boyhood *or* girlhood, °youth, °puberty, minority, adolescence, teens

childish *adj.* °childlike, °juvenile, °puerile, °infantile, babyish; °immature, °inexperienced, naive *or* naïve *or* naïf, °undeveloped, underdeveloped, retarded; °silly, *US* sophomoric

childlike *adj.* youthful, °young, °innocent, trustful, °ingenuous, °unsophisticated, naive *or* naïve, °trusting, credulous, °open, undissembling, unassuming, guileless, °artless

chill *n.* **1** coldness, °cold, coolness, sharpness, °nip **2** °cold, flu, influenza, (la *or* the) grippe, ague, *Technical* coryza, *Colloq* (the) sniffles, sneezles and wheezles **3** coolness, iciness, frigidity, aloofness; unfriendliness, °hostility —*adj.* **4** °cold, °cool, numbing, chilling, °chilly, °raw, °penetrating, °icy, °frigid, °wintry, frosty, arctic, °polar, glacial **5** shivering, chilled (through), °numb, numbed, numbing, benumbed **6** °cold, °coldblooded, °aloof, °indifferent, insensitive, unemotional, °unsympathetic; °chilly —*v.* **7** °cool, °freeze, °refrigerate, ice **8** °dampen, dispirit, °depress, deject, dishearten, °distress

chilly *adj.* **1** °cool, coldish, °cold, °frigid, nippy, frosty, °icy, °crisp, °chill **2** °chill, °unenthusiastic, unresponsive, unreceptive, frosty, unwelcoming, °crisp, °cool, °cold, unfriendly, °hostile; °distant, °aloof

chime *n.* **1** bell, set of bells, carillon, °ring, °peal **2** ringing, °peal, chiming, tolling, tintinnabulation, clanging, ding-dong, °striking; tinkle, °jingle, °jangle —*v.* **3** °ring, °peal, °toll, °sound, tintinnabulate, clang, °strike **4** °mark, °denote, °indicate, °announce **5** ***chime in.*** **(a)** join in, °blend, harmonize **(b)** °interrupt, intercede, °intrude, °interfere, °break in, *Colloq* °chip in; *Slang* °butt in

chink *n.* fissure, °rift, °crack, °crevice, °gap, °opening, cleft, °slit, °aperture, °cranny

chip *n.* **1** °fragment, °piece, shard *or* sherd, °splinter, °flake, °sliver, °scrap, °morsel, °bit **2** °counter, marker, °token; °plaque, *US* °check —*v.* **3** °chisel, °whittle, hew **4** ***chip in.*** **(a)** °contribute; °participate **(b)** °interrupt, °break in, °intrude, °interfere, intercede, interpose, *Colloq* °chime in

chirp *v.* **1** tweet, °peep, °twitter, chirrup, warble, trill, cheep, chitter, chirr, °pipe —*n.* **2** tweet, °peep, °twitter, chirrup, warble, trill, cheep, chitter, chirr

chisel *v.* **1** °carve, °cut, °pare, °groove, °shape, °engrave, °grave **2** °cheat, °defraud, °swindle, bilk, °trick, °fool, °dupe, gull, *Colloq* bamboozle

chivalrous *adj.* courtly, °gracious, °courteous, °polite, °gallant, °noble, knightly, gentlemanly, °considerate, °kind, °charitable, magnanimous

chivalry *n.* knight-errantry; °honor, °bravery, °courage, °courtesy, politeness, courtliness, gallantry, °nobility, virtuousness, righteousness, justness, fairness, impartiality, equitableness

choice *n.* **1** °selection, °election, °preference, choosing, °pick, acceptance **2** °option, realm of possibilities; °alternative, °voice, °determination **3** °pick, elite *or* élite, °flower, °best, °select, cream, *crème de la crème* —*adj.* **4** °select, °exquisite, °special, °superior, °prime, high-quality, °excellent, °preeminent, °best, °prize, °first-rate, °exceptional, preferred, °desirable, °ideal, °rare, *Colloq Brit* plummy **5** selected, °select, handpicked, well-chosen, °fit, °appropriate, °fitting

choke *v.* **1** suffocate, asphyxiate, °smother, °stifle, strangle, throttle, garrotte *or* garrote *or* garotte, burke **2** °stop, °fill (up), °block (up), °obstruct, congest, °clog, dam (up), constrict **3** Also, ***choke off.*** °smother, °suppress, °stifle, °prohibit, °frustrate, °deny, obviate, °cut off, °stop, put a stop to; dissuade, °discourage **4** ***choke back or down.*** °suppress, °repress, °stifle, °restrain

choose *v.* °select, °elect, °pick (out), °determine, °judge; °decide, °prefer, opt, settle upon *or* on

choosy *adj.* °selective, °discriminating, discerning, °fastidious, finicky *or* finical, °particular, °fussy, °demanding, °exacting, °difficult, hard to please, *Colloq* picky

chop *v.* **1** Also, ***chop away or down or off.*** °cut, °hack, hew, °lop, crop, °cleave, °sever **2** Also, ***chop up.*** mince; dice, cube; °hash —*n.* **3** °cut, °blow, °stroke

christen *v.* **1** baptize, anoint **2** °name, °call, dub

chronic *adj.* **1** longlasting, longstanding, °lingering, inveterate, °persistent, continuing, °lasting, long-lived **2** inveterate, °persistent, dyed-in-the-wool, confirmed, °habitual, hardened

chronicle *n.* **1** °record, °history, °diary, °chronology, °account, °narrative, °description, °report, °register, annal(s), archive —*v.* **2** °record, °register, °list, °enter, archive, °document, °describe; °tell, °recount, °narrate, °report, °relate, retail

chronology *n.* °account, °record, °calendar, almanac, °journal, log; °sequence

chubby *adj.* podgy *or US* pudgy; stumpy, stubby, chunky, tubby, °plump, °dumpy, thickset, heavyset, °heavy, °ample, overweight

chuckle *v.* **1** °laugh, chortle, crow, snigger, °giggle, °titter —*n.* **2** chuckling, °laugh, chortle, crowing, °giggle; °laughter, snigger, sniggering

chum *n.* 1 °friend, °comrade, °companion; confidant(e), °familiar; °fellow, °colleague, *Colloq* °pal, sidekick, *Chiefly Brit, Australian, New Zealand* mate, *Chiefly US and Canadian* buddy —*v.* 2 Often, *chum around.* °associate, *Colloq* °pal (around) 3 *chum up with.* ally (oneself) with, be friendly with, °go with, °associate with, *Colloq* pal (up *or* about *or* around) with, *US* team up with

chummy *adj.* °friendly, °sociable, °intimate, °close, °thick, *Colloq* pally, *US* palsy-walsy, buddy-buddy

chute *n.* 1 °waterfall, °rapid 2 °slide, °shaft, °channel, °ramp, runway, trough, °incline

circle *n.* 1 disc *or chiefly US* disk, °ring, hoop, °loop, °band, °wheel, annulus, ringlet; cordon 2 °set, coterie, °clique, °class, °division, °group, °crowd; °society, °fellowship, °fraternity, °company —*v.* 3 °encircle, circumambulate, go round *or* around, °tour; circumnavigate 4 °encircle, °surround, gird, °enclose, circumscribe

circuit *n.* 1 compass, circumference, °perimeter, °periphery, °girth, °border, °boundary, °edge, °limit, ambit, °margin, °outline, confine(s), °bound, °pale 2 °round, °tour, ambit, °circle, °orbit, °course, °lap

circular *adj.* 1 °round, disc-shaped *or chiefly US* disk-shaped, disklike *or* disclike, discoid; ring-shaped, ringlike, hooplike, hoop-shaped, annular 2 °roundabout, °indirect, circuitous, °tortuous, twisting, twisted, anfractuous; periphrastic, circumlocutory; °devious 3 illogical, °inconsistent, °redundant, fallacious, irrational, *Formal* sophistic *or* sophistical

circulate *v.* 1 move *or* go about *or* round *or* around, °orbit, °flow, °course, °run, °circle 2 °spread, °distribute, disseminate, °issue, °publish, °air, °announce, °proclaim, °make known, noise abroad, bruit about, °report, °broadcast, °reveal, divulge, advertise, °publicize, promulgate, °put about, bring *or* put out, pass out *or* round *or* around 3 °spread, go around *or* round, be bruited about, °come out

circulation *n.* 1 °circuit, °course, °orbit, °flow, flowing, °motion 2 °spread, spreading, dissemination, °transmission, °passage, °distribution, diffusion, °publication, °advertisement, °announcement, issuance, issuing, °pronouncement, °proclamation, promulgation, °broadcast, broadcasting

circumstance *n.* 1 Often, *circumstances.* °situation, condition(s), °state (of affairs); °status, °station, °resources, °income, °finances 2 °event, °incident, °episode, °occurrence, °affair, °happening, °occasion

circumstantial *adj.* 1 °indirect, °presumptive, evidential *or* evidentiary, interpretive, deduced, presumed, °presumptive, presumable, implicative, implied, inferred, inferential 2 °accidental, °incidental, hearsay, °indirect, unimportant, adventitious, °provisional, °secondary, unessential, °nonessential, fortuitous, °chance, °extraneous 3 °detailed, °particular, °precise, °explicit, °specific

citizen *n.* 1 voter; °native; householder, °resident, °inhabitant, °denizen, dweller, freeman; *Brit* patrial, ratepayer; *US* taxpayer 2 city dweller, town dweller, townsman, townswoman, villager, burgess, oppidan

city *n.* °metropolis, °municipality, borough, burgh; conurbation, megalopolis; *Brit* urban district; °see, diocese, bishopric; *New Zealand* urban area; *Colloq* °town, *US* burg

civil *adj.* 1 civilian, nonmilitary, °lay, laic, laical, °secular 2 °domestic, °internal; °public 3 °polite, °courteous, °respectful, well-mannered, °proper, civilized, °cordial, °formal, courtly, urbane, °polished, °refined

civility *n.* °courtesy, politeness, °respect, comity, urbanity, amiability, °consideration, courteousness, cordiality, °propriety, °tact, °diplomacy, politesse, °protocol

civilization *n.* 1 °culture, °refinement, cultivation, enlightenment, °edification, °sophistication, °polish 2 °culture, mores, custom(s)

civilize *v.* 1 °enlighten, °refine, °polish, edify, °educate, acculturate 2 °tame, domesticate; broaden, elevate, acculturate

claim *n.* 1 °demand, °assertion, °request, °requisition, °petition, °application; °requirement 2 right(s), °call, °title —*v.* 3 °demand, °seek, ask *or* call (for), °exact, insist (on *or* upon), °require, °command, be entitled to 4 °declare, assert, °allege, °state, put *or* set forth, affirm, contend, °maintain

clammy *adj.* 1 °moist, °sticky, gummy, °pasty, viscous, °slimy 2 °moist, °damp, °humid, °close, °muggy, °wet, °misty, foggy

clamp *n.* 1 °clasp, °vice, °brace, °clip, fastener —*v.* 2 °fasten (together), °clip (together), °bracket, make fast, °clasp

clan *n.* 1 °tribe, °family, °dynasty, °line, °house 2 °fraternity, °brotherhood, °party, °set, °clique, coterie, °circle, °crowd, °group, °fellowship, °society, °faction, °family, °tribe; °band, °ring, °gang

clap *v.* 1 °applaud; °cheer, acclaim 2 °slap, °strike, °pat 3 °put, °place, °slap, °fling, °toss, °cast, *Colloq* °stick 4 °impose, °lay, °apply —*n.* 5 °crack, °slap, °report, °crash, bang, °snap

clapper *n.* °tongue

clarify *v.* 1 elucidate, make clear, °simplify, make plain, °clear up, °explain, shed *or* throw light on *or* upon, °illuminate, explicate 2 °clear, °purify, °clean

clarity *n.* 1 clearness, transparency, limpidity, pellucidity 2 lucidity, °definition, definiteness, distinctness; comprehensibility, understandability, intelligibility, unambiguousness

clash *n.* 1 °crash, clang, clank, clangor 2 °collision, smash, °(hostile) encounter, °conflict, °engagement, °fight, °battle, °disagreement, °difference, °argument, °dispute, altercation, °quarrel, squabble —*v.* 3 °conflict, °fight, °battle, °disagree, °differ, °argue, °dispute, °quarrel, squabble, °feud, wrangle, cross swords **4** °conflict, disharmonize, °jar, be at odds *or* out of keeping

clasp *n.* **1** fastener, °fastening, °hook, °catch, °clip, °pin, °brooch **2** °embrace, °hug, °hold, °grasp, °grip —*v.* **3** °fasten, °secure, °close, °hold, °hook, °clip, °pin, °clamp **4** °hold, °embrace, take hold of, °hug, °enclose, °envelop **5** °grab, °grasp, °seize, °clutch, °grip

class *n.* **1** °rank, °grade, °level, °order, °stratum; °caste, °lineage, °birth, °pedigree, °stock, °extraction, descent **2** °category, °division, classification, °group, °genre, °league, °realm, °domain; °kind, °sort, °type **3** °excellence, °merit, °refinement, °elegance, °prestige, °importance, °taste, discernment, °distinction, °bearing, °presence, °savoir-faire, °savoir-vivre, °breeding **4** year, °form, *US* °grade —*v.* **5** classify, °group, °arrange, assort, °type, °categorize, °rank, °grade, °rate, °order

classic *adj.* **1** °standard, °leading, °outstanding, prototypical, °definitive, °model, °ideal, archetypal, paradigmatic **2** °legendary, °immortal, °enduring, °deathless, ageless, °timeless, undying, °venerable, °time-honored; °outstanding, °first-rate, °superior, °excellent, °noteworthy, °notable, °exemplary —*n.* **3** °paragon, °epitome, outstanding example, exemplar, °model, paradigm, °prototype **4** °masterpiece, masterwork

classical *adj.* **1** °standard, °model, °exemplary, °traditional, established, °influential, °authoritative, °serious, °weighty **2** Greek, Latin, Roman

claw *n.* **1** talon, °nail —*v.* **2** °scratch, °tear, °scrape, °rake, °slash **3** °grapple, °grab, °catch, °scrape, scrabble

clean *adj.* **1** °pure, undefiled, unsullied, unmixed, unadulterated, uncontaminated, unpolluted, uninfected, °unspoiled, °sanitary, disinfected; antiseptic, decontaminated, purified, °sterile **2** unsoiled, untainted, unstained; unsullied; cleansed, cleanly, (freshly) laundered *or* washed, scrubbed; °spotless, °immaculate **3** clean-cut, °neat, °simple, °definite, uncomplicated, °smooth, °even, °straight, °trim, °tidy **4** °innocent, °blameless, °inoffensive, °respectable; °decent, °chaste, °pure, °honorable, °good, undefiled, °virtuous, °moral **5** nonradioactive **6** °unarmed, weaponless —*adv.* **7** °completely, °entirely, °thoroughly, fully, °totally, °wholly, °altogether, °quite, °utterly, °absolutely **8** ***come clean.*** °confess, °acknowledge, make a clean breast, °admit, make a revelation, °reveal, *Colloq* own up, °spill the beans; *US dialect* fess up; *Slang* °sing —*v.* **9** °cleanse, °wash, lave, °(take a) shower, sponge, mop, °scrub, °scour, °sweep, dust, vacuum, °polish, °launder, dry-clean, *Brit* hoover; °tidy, °neaten, do up, straighten up *or* out, unclutter; *Brit* bath; *US and Canadian* bathe **10** ***clean out.*** **(a)** °exhaust, deplete **(b)** °empty, leave bare, °clear out, °evacuate **11** ***clean up.*** **(a)** °clean, °cleanse, °wash, °(take a) shower, *Brit* bath; *US* take a bath, bathe, wash up **(b)** °purge, °purify, °disinfect, depollute, decontaminate, °clear, sanitize

cleanse *v.* **1** °clean, absterge, deterge, °wash, °scour, °scrub **2** °purify, depurate: °purge, °wash away, expiate

clear *adj.* **1** unclouded, cloudless, °sunny, °fair, sunlit, °fine **2** °transparent, limpid, crystalline; translucent, uncloudy, unclouded, pellucid **3** °bright, °lustrous, shining, °shiny, sparkling, *Formal* nitid **4** °bright, °fresh, unblemished, unscarred **5** °distinct, °sharp, well-defined, °definite; °legible, °readable; °acute, °vivid **6** understandable, °intelligible, perspicuous, lucid, comprehensible, apprehensible, °discernible, °plain, °obvious, unambiguous, unequivocal, °explicit, °definite, unmistakable, °indisputable, °undisputed, °unquestionable, °incontrovertible **7** °distinct, unclouded, unconfused, °explicit, °plain, °definite, clear-cut, palpable **8** °evident, °plain, °obvious, °patent, °manifest, °apparent **9** °perceptive, °acute, °sensitive, perspicacious, discerning, °keen **10** °certain, °sure, convinced, °confident, °positive, °determined, °definite, assured **11** °pure, unwavering, well-defined, °distinct, clarion, bell-like **12** °pure, guileless, °unsophisticated, °innocent, °blameless, °faultless; not guilty **13** unencumbered, °free, °net **14** °unlimited, °unqualified, unquestioned, °unquestionable, °absolute, °complete, °entire; °pure, °sheer, °perfect **15** disengaged, disentangled, unentangled, °free, freed, °rid, °quit, °loose, unencumbered, released **16** °open, unencumbered, °free, unblocked, unobstructed, °unimpeded, °direct —*adv.* **17** brightly, effulgently, radiantly, luminously, lambently **18** distinctly, °clearly, starkly, perceptibly, discernibly, understandably, prominently **19** °completely, °utterly, °entirely, cleanly, °clean, °wholly, °totally —*v.* **20** °clarify, °cleanse, °clean, °purify **21** exonerate, absolve, acquit; °excuse, °forgive **22** Also, ***clear up.*** become fair *or* cloudless *or* sunny **23** °open (up), °free; unblock, unclog, unstop; disencumber, dislodge **24** °empty **25** Also, ***clear away or out.*** °remove, °eliminate, °take; cut away *or* down **26** disburden, unburden, °purge, °free, °rid **27** leap *or* jump over, vault **28** Also, ***clear up.*** °settle, °discharge, °pay, °square, °defray, °satisfy **29** ***clear off or out.*** °leave, °depart, decamp, go *or* run off, get out, °withdraw, *Slang* °beat it, scram, *Taboo Brit* sod off, *Chiefly Australian* shoot through, *US and Canadian* take a (runout) powder **30** ***clear up.*** **(a)** °eliminate, °remove, °settle; °clarify **(b)** °tidy (up), °neaten (up), put *or* set in order **(c)** °explain, elucidate, explicate, °clarify, make plain *or* clear, disambiguate. See also **22, 28,** above. —*n.* **31** ***in the clear.*** °innocent, not guilty; exonerated, forgiven, absolved; unburdened, disburdened, unencumbered, °free

clearance *n.* **1** °space, °gap, °hole, °interval, °separation, °room, °margin, °leeway, °allowance **2** °approval, °endorsement, authorization, °consent; °license, °leave, °permission

clearly *adv.* **1** distinctly; starkly, plainly **2** °evidently, °apparently, °manifestly, °obviously, certainly, °definitely, °positively, unequivocally, unquestionably, incontestably, without doubt, °undoubtedly, indubitably, demonstrably, °absolutely, °utterly **3** audibly, distinctly, understandably

cleave *v.* °split, °divide, °cut, cut *or* chop *or* hew in two *or* asunder, bisect, halve, °separate, °slit, rive

clergyman *n.* **1** clergywoman, ecclesiastic, churchman, churchwoman, cleric, reverend, °divine, man of the cloth, holy man, °priest, °minister, chaplain, °father, rabbi, °pastor, parson, rector, vicar, dean, canon, presbyter, prebendary *or* prebend, deacon, sexton, sacristan, guru, ayatollah, imam **2** °monk, friar, °brother, monastic, °religious **3** °preacher, gospeler, evangelist, revivalist, °missionary, sermonizer

clerical *adj.* **1** ecclesiastical, churchly, °pastoral, sacerdotal, °priestly, hieratic, rabbinical, ministerial, monastic, apostolic, prelatic, papal, pontifical, episcopal, canonical **2** white-collar, °office, °professional, secretarial, stenographic, accounting, bookkeeping

clever *adj.* **1** skilled, °talented, °skillful, adroit, °dexterous, °gifted, °agile, °quick-witted, °intelligent, °perceptive, discerning, °sharp, sharp-witted, °adept, °able, *Colloq* brainy **2** °shrewd, cunning, guileful, canny, °artful, °crafty, °sly, °wily, °foxy **3** °intelligent, °wise, °sage, sagacious; °ingenious, °original, °resourceful, Daedalian, inventive, °creative, °smart, °imaginative **4** deft, adroit, nimble-fingered, °dexterous, °handy, °skillful

cliché *n.* stereotype, bromide, trite saying, old saw *or* maxim, °truism, platitude, commonplace, banality, *Colloq* chestnut

client *n.* °customer, °patron, shopper; °patient

clientele *n.* clients, patrons, customers; °custom, °business, °trade, °patronage, following

cliff *n.* °precipice, °bluff, escarpment, scarp, °crag, rock face, cuesta, scar *or Scots* scaur

climate *n.* **1** °weather, *Literary* clime **2** °atmosphere, ambiance *or* ambience, °air; °feeling, °mood, °aura, °milieu, °feel

climax *n.* **1** culmination, °height, °acme, apex, °summit, °zenith, apogee, °peak, high point, °maximum, supreme moment **2** turning point, °crisis, crossroads **3** orgasm —*v.* **4** culminate, °peak, °crest, come to a head

climb *v.* **1** Also, ***climb up.*** °mount, ascend, °go up, °scale, °shin (up), clamber up, *US* shinny (up) **2** °creep, °trail, °twine; °grow **3** °rise, °arise, ascend, °go up, °mount; °advance **4** ***climb along.*** °creep, °edge, clamber, °crawl, inch **5** ***climb down.*** **(a)** °descend, °go down **(b)** Usually, ***climb down from.*** °retreat (from), °withdraw (from), back away (from), °give up, °abandon, °renounce —*n.* **6** °grade, °incline, °route, °pitch; ascent; descent

clinch *v.* **1** °secure, °settle, °confirm, °determine, conclude, °dispose of, °complete, °wind up, °finalize, *Colloq* sew up —*n.* **2** close quarters, °hug, °clasp, °embrace; °cuddle

clincher *n.* finishing touch, °payoff, punch line, coup de grâce, final *or* crowning blow

cling *v.* **1** °stick, adhere, °attach, °fasten, °fix **2** °favor, be *or* remain devoted *or* attached to, °embrace, hang onto, °retain, °keep, °cherish **3** ***cling together or to one another.*** °embrace, °hug, cleave to one another, clasp one another, clutch one another, hold (fast) to one another, grasp one another

clip[1] *v.* **1** °clasp, °fasten, °fix, °attach, °hold, °clinch; °staple —*n.* **2** °clasp, fastener

clip[2] *v.* **1** °trim (off), °lop (off), °cut (off), crop, bob, °snip **2** °shorten, °reduce, °abbreviate, °diminish, °cut (short) **3** °strike, °hit, °punch, smack, °box, cuff, whack, *Colloq* wallop, clout; *Slang* sock **4** °cheat, °swindle, bilk, overcharge, *Slang* rook —*n.* **5** °segment, °interval, °section, °part, °portion, °extract, °cutting, °excerpt, °bit, snippet, °scrap, °fragment **6** °blow, cuff, °punch, °hit, °strike, smack, whack, °box, *Colloq* wallop, clout; *Slang* sock **7** °pace, °rate, °speed

clique *n.* °set, coterie, °crowd, °circle, °group

cloak *n.* **1** °mantle, °cape, °robe, °wrap, poncho; °coat, overcoat **2** °mantle, concealment, °cover, °screen, °shroud, °veil —*v.* **3** °conceal, °hide, °mask, °screen, °veil, °shroud, °cover up; °disguise

clod *n.* **1** °lump, °mass, °gob, °wad, hunk, chunk; piece of sod *or* turf; *Colloq* glob **2** idiot, °fool, °dolt, blockhead, simpleton, dunce, °dope, oaf, lout, ass, °boor, °clown, ninny, ninnyhammer, bumpkin, clodhopper, *Slang* vegetable, *US and Canadian* °jerk

clog *v.* °hamper, °encumber, °impede; °obstruct, °choke (up), °block, congest, °jam

close *v.* **1** °shut, °close up, °seal; °close off, °lock, padlock, °secure, °fasten **2** make inaccessible, °shut, *Chiefly US* place off limits **3** conclude, °end, °finish, °complete, bring to a close *or* end, °terminate, °climax, *Colloq* °wind up **4** conclude, °sign, °seal, °make, °settle, °clinch, °agree, °arrange, °work out, °establish **5** Also, ***close down.*** °discontinue, °terminate, °stop, °suspend, °shut down, go out of business, cease operation(s), °close (up), *Colloq* °wind up, shut up shop, put up the shutters **6** Also, ***close off.*** °seal, make inaccessible, °shut (off), °obstruct, obturate **7** ***close one's eyes to.*** °ignore, °overlook, °disregard **8** ***close up.*** **(a)** °close, °shut (up), °lock up, °close (down) **(b)** °close, come *or* draw *or* bring together, °unite, °join; °connect —*adj.* **9** °near; adjacent, proximate, proximal **10** closed, °shut (up), °fixed, °fast, °secure, °tight **11** °dense, °compact, °tight,

°cramped, compressed, °tiny, minuscule, °minute **12** °stuffy, °musty, °stale, fusty, confining, °oppressive, airless, unventilated, confined, stifling, suffocating **13** nearly equal *or* even, close-matched, neck and neck, °tight **14** °careful, assiduous, °precise, °detailed, concentrated, °strict, rigorous, °minute, searching, °attentive, °alert, °intent, °intense, °thorough, °painstaking **15** °attached, °intimate, °devoted, °familiar, inseparable, close-knit, °solid, °confidential; °fast; *Colloq* °thick, thick as thieves, pally, *US and Canadian* palsy-walsy, buddy-buddy **16** °private, °privy, °secret, °guarded, closely guarded, °confidential **17** °secretive, °reticent, °taciturn, °reserved, closemouthed, °tight-lipped, °silent **18** stingy, °mean, °miserly, niggardly, tightfisted, closefisted, parsimonious, °penurious, penny-pinching, cheeseparing, Scroogelike, skinflinty, *Colloq* °near, *Brit* mingy **19** °secluded, concealed, shut up *or* away, °hidden —*adv.* **20** °near, in the neighborhood (of), not far (from), adjacent (to); alongside; °at hand, °nearby, °close by **21** ***close to** or **on** or **onto.*** °nearly, °almost, °about, °practically, °approximately, nigh onto, approaching —*n.* **22** °end, °termination, conclusion, °finish, °completion, cessation; culmination

cloth *n.* **1** °fabric, °material, textile, *Chiefly Brit* °stuff **2** ***the cloth.*** the clergy, the (religious) ministry, the priesthood

clothe *v.* **1** °dress, attire, garb, °apparel, °outfit, fit out *or* up, accoutre *or US also* accouter, *Brit* kit out *or* up, *Colloq* tog up *or* out **2** endow, °invest, caparison, endue

clothes *n. pl.* clothing, °apparel, attire, °wear, °dress, °garments, raiment, °wardrobe, °outfit, °ensemble, vestment(s), *Old-fashioned* duds, *Colloq* togs, °gear, get-up, *Slang* glad rags, *Brit* clobber; *Slang US* (set of) threads

clown *n.* **1** jester, °fool, °zany, °comic, °comedian, funnyman **2** buffoon, °boor, °rustic, °yahoo, oaf, lout, °clod, °dolt, bumpkin, clodhopper, °provincial, °peasant, yokel, *Colloq* lummox; *Slang chiefly US* °jerk; *Old-fashioned* galoot *or* galloot; *Slang chiefly US and Canadian* hick —*v.* **3** Often, ***clown around** or **about.*** °fool (around), play the fool, horse around *or* about, °caper, cut a caper *or* capers, engage in high jinks *or* hijinks, *US* °cut up, cut didos

club *n.* **1** cudgel, bat, bludgeon, mace, billy, truncheon, baton, °staff, °stick; cosh, *Chiefly US and Canadian* blackjack **2** °association, °society, °organization, °fraternity, sorority, °fellowship, °brotherhood, sisterhood, °federation, °union, guild, °lodge, °alliance, °league, °order, consortium, °company **3** clubhouse **4** nightclub, °cabaret, *Colloq* nightspot —*v.* **5** °beat, cudgel, bludgeon, bat, °belabor; °lambaste, baste, thrash, trounce **6** Often, ***club together.*** band *or* join *or* league (together), °team (up), join forces, °combine, °ally, °associate, confederate, °cooperate

clue *n.* **1** °hint, °suspicion, °trace, intimation, °suggestion, °inkling, °indication, °pointer, °lead, °tip, tip-off, °evidence, °information, °advice; °key, °answer, °indicator —*v.* **2** ***clue someone in** or Brit also **up.*** °hint, °suggest, °imply, °intimate, °inform, °advise, °indicate

clump *n.* **1** °lump, °mass, °clod, chunk, hunk, °wad, °gob, *Colloq* glob **2** °bunch, °cluster; °thicket, copse; wood, *Chiefly Brit* spinney —*v.* **3** °lump, °mass, °heap, °collect, °gather, °bunch, °pile

clumsy *adj.* °awkward, ungainly, °unwieldy, °ungraceful, gawky, maladroit, unhandy, unskillful, °inept, bungling, bumbling, cloddish, oxlike, bovine, uncoordinated, lubberly, oafish; gauche, *Colloq* butterfingered ham-fisted, ham-handed, cack-handed

cluster *n.* **1** °collection, °bunch, °clutch, tuft, °bundle **2** °collection, °bunch, °group, °knot, °body, °band, °company, °gathering, °crowd, °assembly, congregation, °throng, °flock, assemblage, °swarm —*v.* **3** °collect, °bunch, °group, °band, °gather, °crowd, congregate, °throng, °assemble, °accumulate °mass, aggregate

clutch *v.* **1** °seize, °snatch, °grab, °grasp, take *or* lay hold of; °hold; *US* °snag —*n.* **2** ***clutches.*** **(a)** grasp, °hold; °embrace **(b)** °influence, °control, °power, °domination dominance, °possession

clutter *n.* **1** °mess, °litter, °jumble; °mishmash, olla podrida, °confusion, °hash, gallimaufry, hotchpotch *or US also* hodgepodge, °muddle, farrago, °medley **2** °confusion, °tangle, °chaos, disarray —*v.* **3** Often, ***clutter up.*** °mess up, °litter, °strew, make a shambles of

coach *n.* **1** °carriage, bus, omnibus, motorcoach **2** °tutor, trainer, °instructor, °teacher, mentor, *Brit* crammer —*v.* **3** °tutor, °train, °instruct, °guide, °direct, °drill, °prepare, °prompt, °school, °exercise, *Brit* °cram

coagulate *v.* congeal, gel, °jell, jellify, clot curdle, °set

coarse *adj.* **1** °rough, uneven, °scratchy, °prickly, bristly; °crude, rough-hewn, unfinished, °unrefined **2** °rude, °boorish, loutish, °crude, °ill-mannered, unpolished, °rough, uncouth, °impolite, uncivil, °unrefined **3** °rude, °indecent, °improper, indelicate, °obscene, °lewd, °vulgar, °gross, smutty, °dirty, °filthy, °foul, °offensive, °lascivious, ribald, °bawdy; foulmouthed **4** °inferior, low-quality, second-rate, °shoddy, °tawdry, trashy; kitschy

coast *n.* **1** seaside, seashore, shore, °seacoast, strand, °beach, littoral, coastline, seaboard —*v.* **2** °glide, °skim, °slide, °sail

coat *n.* **1** overcoat, greatcoat; jacket, anorak, parka, *Brit* cagoule *or* kagoul *or* kagoule, *Colloq Brit* cag **2** coating, layer, covering, overlay; °film —*v.* **3** °cover, °paint, °spread

coax *v.* °persuade, °urge, °wheedle, °cajole

°beguile, °charm, inveigle, °jolly, °manipulate

cocky *adj.* °overconfident, °arrogant, °haughty, °conceited, °self-important, °egotistical, °proud, °vain, prideful, cocksure, saucy, °cheeky, °brash

coddle *v.* °pamper, °baby, cosset, mollycoddle, °indulge, °humor, °spoil, *Brit* cocker

code *n.* **1** law(s), regulation(s), rule(s), jurisprudence, jus canonicum (= 'canon law'), jus civile (= 'civil law'), jus divinum (= 'divine law'), jus gentium (= 'universal law'), jus naturale (= 'natural law'), corpus juris (= 'body of law'), pandect, lex, non scripta (= 'common law, unwritten law'), lex scripta (= 'written law') **2** cipher *or* cypher, cryptogram **3** °system, practice(s), convention(s), standard(s), criterion (criteria), principle(s), rule(s), maxim(s), custom(s), pattern(s), °structure, tradition(s), °organization, °protocol, orthodoxy —*v.* **4** encode, encipher *or* encypher, encrypt

coffin *n.* °casket, °pall, °(pine) box; sarcophagus

cog *n.* **1** tooth, geartooth, sprocket, ratchet **2** underling, °pawn, °subordinate, nonentity, °zero, cipher *or* cypher, °nothing, °nobody, small fry

cognizance *n.* °knowledge, awareness, °perception, °notice, consciousness, mindfulness

coherent *adj.* **1** °consistent, °orderly, organized, well-organized, °logical, °rational, °reasonable, well-ordered **2** understandable, °sensible, comprehensible, °intelligible, articulate, lucid, °clear

cohort *n.* **1** troop, °squad, squadron, °platoon, brigade, °unit, cadre, wing, legion, °detachment, contingent **2** °company, °band, °group, °faction, °set, °body, °corps **3** °companion, confederate, °accomplice, °associate, °fellow, °comrade, °friend, confrère

coil *v.* **1** °wind, °twist, °snake, °wrap, enwrap, °spiral, *Nautical* fake *or* flake (down) —*n.* **2** winding(s), circle(s), °loop, whorl, °spiral, helix, °twist

coin *n.* **1** specie, °money, currency; °change, °cash, °silver —*v.* **2** °mint, °stamp **3** °invent, °create, °conceive, °originate, °start, °make up, °fabricate, °frame, concoct, think *or* dream up **4** ***coin money.*** earn *or* make money, become wealthy, enrich oneself, *Colloq* °rake it in

coincide *v.* fall *or* come *or* go together, °line up, co-occur, °correspond, synchronize, °match, °tally, °agree, °(be in) accord, °equal, jibe

coincidence *n.* **1** co-occurrence, simultaneity, correspondence, concurrence, consistency, contemporaneity, synchronism, synchrony, coextension, coevality, coinstantaneity **2** congruence, °matching, jibing, °agreement, concord, °accord, °harmony, accordance, conformity, congruity, consonance, concomitance **3** chance occurrence, °fluke, °chance, °accident, °luck, fortuity, fortuitousness, *US and Canadian* happenstance

coincidental *adj.* °chance, lucky *or* unlucky, fortuitous, °accidental, unexpected, unpredicted, unpredictable, °unforeseen

cold *adj.* **1** °chill, °chilly, frosty, °icy, °keen, nippy, °freezing, °frigid, ice-cold, stone-cold, °bitter (cold), °raw, °biting, biting-cold, numbing, gelid; °wintry, hibernal, brumal; arctic, glacial, °polar, hyperborean *or* hyperboreal, Siberian **2** °chilly, chilled; unheated, heatless **3** °indifferent, apathetic, °chilly, chilling, °cool, °icy, °dispassionate, °unsympathetic, °aloof, unresponsive, spiritless, unfriendly, uncordial, °lukewarm, °frigid; °cold-blooded, insensitive, uncaring, unemotional, undemonstrative, °reserved, °unmoved, spiritless, °callous, °remote, °distant, standoffish, °unapproachable, stonyhearted, emotionless, unfeeling, °coldhearted **4** depressing, cheerless, chilling, °gloomy, dispiriting, deadening, disheartening, °bleak, °dismal, discouraging **5** unmoving, °stale, trite, stereotyped; °dead **6** °weak, °faint, °stale, °old, °dead **7** °unprepared, unready **8** Often, ***getting cold.*** °far, °distant, °remote, off the track —*n.* **9** coldness, frigidity, iciness **10** head *or* chest *or* common cold, influenza, ague, (the *or* la) grippe, *Technical* coryza, gravedo, *Colloq* sniffles, the flu, °bug, sneezles and wheezles —*adv.* **11** °completely, °thoroughly, °entirely, °absolutely, unhesitatingly, °promptly, °immediately, unreservedly, abruptly

coldblooded *adj.* **1** *Technical* poikilothermic *or* poikilothermal **2** unexcited, unemotional, °cool, unimpassioned, unfeeling, °callous, °thick-skinned, insensitive, °heartless, uncaring, °stony, °steely, stonyhearted, °coldhearted, imperturbable, °unmoved, °indifferent, unresponsive, °unsympathetic, apathetic, °dispassionate **3** °cruel, °brutal, °savage, °inhuman, barbarous, °vicious, barbaric, °merciless, pitiless, °ruthless

coldhearted *adj.* insensitive, °unsympathetic, apathetic, °indifferent, unfeeling, uncaring, °callous, °thick-skinned, °cold, °cool, °frigid, hardhearted, °heartless, °unkind, °thoughtless, unthoughtful, uncharitable, °ruthless, pitiless, °unmerciful, °cruel, °merciless, °mean

collaborate *v.* °cooperate, °join (forces), work together, °team up

collapse *v.* **1** fall (down *or* in *or* apart), °crumple, °cave in, deflate, °crumble, tumble down, °break down, °go **2** °fail, °(come to an) end, °fall through, °peter out, °disintegrate, °dissolve, °fall flat, °founder, come to naught *or* nought, break up *or* down; °decline, °diminish; °disappear, °evaporate, go up in smoke, go bankrupt, °go under, *Brit* °go to the wall, *Colloq* °fizzle out **3** °pass out, °faint, °drop, *Colloq* keel over; *Old-fashioned or literary* swoon **4** °break down (mentally), have a (nervous) breakdown, °go to pieces, come *or* fall apart, *Colloq* crack up, *US also* °crack —*n.* **5** cave-in,

°breakdown **6** °failure, °downfall, °ruin; disappearance, disintegration, °dissolution, bankruptcy **7** °(mental) breakdown, °prostration, *Colloq* crackup

colleague *n.* teammate, fellow worker, coworker; °associate, °comrade, °ally, confrère, °mate, consociate, *Chiefly Brit and Australian* °mate, *US* buddy

collect *v.* **1** °gather (together), get *or* bring *or* come together, °amass, °accumulate, °assemble, °compile, °pile up, heap up, rack up; convene, congregate, °converge, °rally, °meet **2** °summon (up), °draw (up), °muster, °gather (up), °concentrate

collected *adj.* °calm, °serene, controlled, °cool, °sedate, composed, °nonchalant, °poised, unruffled, unperturbed, at ease, °comfortable, °tranquil, unexcited; imperturbable; °confident

collection *n.* **1** collecting, °gathering, solicitation, garnering, gleaning, °accumulation, amassment, aggregation, *Colloq Brit* whipround **2** °accumulation, °hoard, °store, assemblage, omnium-gatherum; anthology, chrestomathy

collector *n.* gatherer, accumulator; connoisseur, art lover

collide *v.* **1** °crash, strike *or* dash together **2** ***collide with.*** crash into, smash into, °run into, °bump into, smack into

collision *n.* smashup, smash, °crash, °wreck, °pileup, *Colloq Brit* prang; *US* crackup

color *n.* **1** °hue, °tint, tincture, °shade, °tone, °cast, tinge, pigmentation; pigment, dye **2** ***colors.*** **(a)** °flag, ensign, °standard, °pennant, °banner, burgee **(b)** °device, badge, °emblem, insigne *or pl.* insignia, symbol(s), °identification; °identity, °appearance, °face; loyalties —*v.* **3** °tint, dye, °stain, °paint, crayon, tincture, tinge; pigment **4** °influence, °affect, °distort, °falsify, °taint, °warp, °twist, °slant, °pervert, °bias **5** °blush, redden, °flush **6** °falsify, °distort, °misrepresent, °disguise, °mask, °conceal

colorless *adj.* **1** °pale, pallid, blanched, °white; °wan, ashen, sallow, waxen, °sickly, °washed-out **2** °dull, °drab, uninteresting, vacuous, °vapid, °lifeless, °boring, °tedious, spiritless, °dry, dry as dust, °dreary, characterless, insipid, °bland, namby-pamby, °lackluster, uninspiring, uninspired

colossal *adj.* **1** °huge, °vast, °enormous, °gigantic, °giant, mammoth, °massive, gargantuan, cyclopean, Brobdingnagian, °immense, °monumental, titanic, herculean, elephantine, °jumbo **2** spectacular, stupendous, wonderful, awe-inspiring, staggering, °extraordinary, °incredible, °overwhelming, °unbelievable

combat *n.* **1** °fight, °encounter, °engagement, duel, °battle, °conflict, °war, warfare; °skirmish **2** °struggle, °contest, °strife, °controversy, °dispute, °quarrel, °disagreement, altercation, °vendetta, °feud **3** °opposition, °difference, confrontation **4** °action, fighting, °battle, °war —*v.* **5** °fight, °(do) battle, °war, °clash, contend, duel, joust, °wrestle, come to blows, °spar, °grapple (with) **6** °fight, struggle *or* strive against, °contest, °oppose, °defy, enter the lists against, °withstand

combination *n.* **1** °union, conjunction, °mixture, °mix, grouping, °set, array **2** °association, °alliance, coalition, °union, °federation, confederation, °combine, syndication, °syndicate, consortium, °trust, bloc, cartel, °party, °society, °organization, °league, °cabal, °conspiracy, °clique; claque **3** °mixture, °amalgam, °compound, compounding, °mix, °alloy, conglomerate, conglomeration, aggregate, aggregation, °amalgamation, °blend, emulsion, °suspension, colloid, °solution, °composition, *Technical* parasynthesis, parathesis; mosaic, °patchwork

combine *v.* **1** °unite, °unify, °join, °connect, °relate, °link, conjoin, °band, °ally, °associate, °integrate, °merge, °pool **2** °blend, °mix, °amalgamate, °mingle, consolidate, °compound, °incorporate, put together **3** °blend, °fuse, synthesize, °bind, °bond, °compound, °unite, coalesce, come together, commingle, °mingle

come *v.* **1** °approach, °advance, °(draw) near, °move, *Archaic and literary* draw nigh **2** °arrive, °appear, make *or* put in an appearance, *Colloq* blow in, °report (in), turn *or* show up, °check in, sign in, clock on *or* in, °roll in **3** °enter **4** ***come about.*** **(a)** °occur, °happen, °take place, °come up; befall, *Loosely* °transpire **(b)** *Nautical* °tack, °go about **5** ***come across.*** **(a)** °find, °discover, °encounter, meet (up *or* up with), run across *or* into, happen *or* chance upon *or* on, hit *or* light on *or* upon, stumble upon *or* on, *Colloq* °bump into **(b)** °pay (up), °settle; °yield, °give up, °submit **(c)** be communicated *or* understandable, °penetrate, °sink in **6** ***come along.*** °fare, do, °progress, move along **7** ***come apart.*** °disintegrate, °crumble, fall *or* fly to pieces, °separate, break (apart *or* up *or* down) **8** ***come at.*** °attack, °assault, °charge, °rush (at), fly at, descend upon *or* on, *Colloq* go *or* make for **9** ***come by.*** **(a)** °acquire, °obtain, °get, °procure, °secure, °find, take *or* get possession of, get *or* lay hold of, get *or* lay *or* put (one's) hands *or US also* fingers on; be given **(b)** °win, °earn, attain; be awarded **10** ***come clean.*** See **clean, 8,** above. **11** ***come down on or upon.*** pounce on *or* upon, °rebuke, °criticize, revile, °reprimand, bear down on, °blame **12** ***come down with.*** succumb to, °contract, °catch, be stricken *or* afflicted with, °acquire **13** ***come in.*** **(a)** °win, °succeed; *Colloq* °finish (in the money) **(b)** be, °prove, turn out *or* prove to be **(c)** °finish, end up, °arrive **(d)** °enter **14** ***come off.*** **(a)** °occur, °happen, °come to pass, °take place, *Loosely* °transpire **(b)** °emerge, result as **15** ***come out.*** **(a)** be revealed, become public *or* common knowledge, become known, get about *or* around, get *or* leak out, °emerge **(b)** be published *or* issued *or* produced *or* distributed, be shown, be in print, °première (c) °end, conclude, °turn out, °terminate, °finish **16** *come over.* **(a)** °go over, °communicate, °come across, be communicated, °succeed, be received **(b)** °affect, °influence, °possess **(c)** °visit, drop *or* stop by *or* in **17** *come through.* **(a)** °recover (from), °recuperate (from), get well *or* better **(b)** conclude *or* end (up) *or* finish *or* wind up successfully *or* satisfactorily, °succeed, °arrive, not fail *or* disappoint **18** *come to.* **(a)** °amount to, add up to, °total, aggregate **(b)** regain *or* recover consciousness, awake(n), °revive, °wake up, come (a)round **(c)** °regard, °concern, °relate to, be a question of, °involve, be relevant to, be involved **19** *come up.* **(a)** °arise, °surface, present itself, be brought up, be broached, °come about, °turn up, °rise, *Colloq* crop up **(b)** °grow, °thrive, °appear **(c)** °rise, °arise

comedian *n.* comedienne, humorist, °comic, °wit, °wag, jokesmith; °clown, buffoon, funnyman, funster, jester, °fool, °zany, merry-andrew

comely *adj.* good-looking, °pretty, °bonny, °lovely, °fair, °beautiful, °handsome, °attractive, appealing, °wholesome, winsome, °buxom

come-on *n.* °lure, °attraction, °enticement, °inducement, °temptation, bait; loss leader

comfort *v.* **1** °console, °solace, soothe, assuage, °reassure, °relieve, hearten, °cheer, °gladden —*n.* **2** consolation, °solace, °relief, °cheer **3** °ease, °luxury, °security, °abundance, °plenty, opulence

comfortable *adj.* **1** at ease, °easy, °tranquil, °serene, °relaxed, contented, untroubled, undisturbed **2** °well-off, °carefree, insouciant, contented, satisfied; self-satisfied, complacent, °smug **3** °likable, °easy, congenial, °amiable, °cordial, °warm, °pleasant, °agreeable, enjoyable, relaxing **4** °suitable, °acceptable, °adequate, °satisfactory, °reasonable

comic *adj.* **1** °funny, droll, comical, °humorous, °hilarious, sidesplitting, mirthful, jocose, jocular, °witty, waggish, °clever, facetious, amusing —*n.* **2** See **comedian.**

command *v.* **1** °order, °direct, °bid, enjoin, °charge, °request, °require, °demand, °instruct; °say, °prescribe, °decree **2** °control, °dominate, have *or* maintain *or* wield authority *or* control *or* sway *or* influence over, hold sway over; °lead, °rule, °govern, have under one's thumb, call the tune; °head (up) **3** °master, draw upon *or* on, °control, °summon **4** °attract, °earn; °exact, compel, °demand **5** °dominate, °control, °overlook, °look down on; °have, °enjoy, °possess —*n.* **6** °order, °direction, behest, mandate, °charge, °bidding, °instruction **7** °control, °authority, °power, °sovereignty, °dominion, °regulation, °direction, °management, °government, °oversight, °leadership, °charge, °sway, stewardship, °jurisdiction **8** mastery, °control, (thorough) grasp *or* knowledge

commemorate *v.* °memorialize, °remember, °celebrate, °observe, °dedicate, consecrate, solemnize, °sanctify, °hallow, °reverence, °revere, °honor, °venerate, pay tribute *or* homage to, °salute; °immortalize

commence *v.* **1** °begin, enter upon, °start, °initiate, °launch, embark on *or* upon **2** °begin, °start, °open **3** °begin, °start, °initiate, °launch, °inaugurate, °establish

comment *n.* **1** °remark, °reference, animadversion, °note, annotation, °criticism, °exposition, °explanation, °expansion, elucidation, clarification, footnote **2** commentary, °opinion, °remark, °view, °observation, °reaction —*v.* **3** °remark, °observe, opine, °say **4** *comment on or about.* °discuss, °talk about, remark on; °reveal, °expose

commerce *n.* °trade, °business, mercantilism, marketing, merchandising, °traffic, trafficking

commit *v.* **1** °entrust, consign, °transfer, °assign, °delegate, °hand over, °deliver, °give; °allot, °pledge, allocate **2** °sentence, °send (away), confine, °shut up, intern, °put away, °imprison, incarcerate **3** °perpetrate, do, °perform, °carry out **4** *commit oneself.* °pledge, °promise, covenant, °agree, °assure, °swear, give one's word, °vow, °vouchsafe, °engage, °undertake, °guarantee, bind oneself

committee *n.* °council, °board, °cabinet, panel, °body, commission

common *adj.* **1** °ordinary, °everyday, commonplace, °prosaic, °usual, °familiar, °customary, °prevalent, °frequent, °run-of-the-mill, °general, °normal, °standard, °conventional, °regular, °routine, °stock, °average, °proverbial; °plain, °simple, garden-variety, common-or-garden, workaday, °undistinguished, unexceptional **2** °mutual, °reciprocal, °joint, shared **3** low-class, °ordinary, °plain, °simple, °plebeian, °bourgeois, proletarian, °run-of-the-mill, °vulgar, °unrefined **4** °inferior, low-grade, °mean, °cheap, °base **5** °public, °general, community, communal, collective, nonprivate, °universal; well-known **6** trite, °stale, hackneyed, worn-out, °banal, °tired, overused, stereotyped, clichéd, stereotypical

communicate *v.* **1** °make known, °impart, °confer, °transmit, °transfer, hand on *or* down, °share, pass on *or* along, send on, °spread; °tell, divulge, °disclose, °reveal, °announce, °transmit, promulgate, proffer, °tender, °offer, convey, °deliver, present, °give, °yield, °supply **2** Also, *communicate with.* be in communication (with), °converse (with), °talk (with), °chat (with); °correspond (with); °associate (with), be in contact *or* touch (with), °reach **3** get *or* put across, make understandable; get through to, °reach, be of one mind, be in tune, °relate, be in *or* en rapport, make oneself understood, *Slang* be *or* vibrate on the same frequency *or* wavelength

compact *adj.* **1** °packed, compacted, closely

knit, condensed, concentrated, consolidated, compressed; °dense, °solid, °firm, °thick **2** °tight, °small, °snug, °little **3** condensed, °terse, laconic, °close, pithy, °succinct, °concise, °brief, compendious, °epigrammatic, aphoristic

companion *n.* **1** °fellow, °associate, °comrade, °colleague, confrère, *Colloq chiefly Brit and Australian* °mate, *US and Canadian* buddy **2** °vade mecum, °manual, handbook, °guide, reference book, enchiridion **3** °escort, chaperon(e), °attendant, (in Spain, Portugal) duenna

companionship *n.* °fellowship, camaraderie, comradeship, °company, °society, amity, °friendship, °fraternity

company *n.* **1** °companionship, °society, °fellowship; °attendance, °presence; associates, friends, companions, comrades **2** assemblage, °party, °band, °group, °retinue, entourage, °suite, °train, coterie, °ensemble, troop, followers, following, °flock; °circle, °assembly, °gathering, °convention, °body, °crowd, °throng, *Theater* troupe, °cast, players, actors, performers **3** guest(s); visitor(s), caller(s) **4** °firm, °business, °house, °concern, °institution, °establishment, °enterprise; proprietorship, partnership, corporation, *Brit* public limited company, plc, *Australian and New Zealand and South African* private limited company, Pty

compare *v.* **1** °liken, °associate, make (an) analogy (with), °refer, analogize **2** ***compare with.*** °resemble, be *or* look like, be on a par with, be in a class *or* the same class with, °correspond, °match, °parallel, °approach, °approximate, bear *or* merit comparison (with); °rival, compete with *or* against, be a match for **3** °contrast, measure against, °weigh, juxtapose, set side by side, °relate, correlate

comparison *n.* **1** contrasting, °contrast, juxtaposing, juxtaposition, balancing, °balance, weighing **2** °match, similarity, °resemblance, °likeness, comparability, °relation, °relationship, commensurability, °kinship, point of agreement *or* correspondence

compartment *n.* °division, °section, °partition, °part, °space, °chamber, bay, alcove, °cell, pigeonhole, locker, cubbyhole, °niche, cubicle, °slot

compensate *v.* **1** recompense, °make up (for), make restitution *or* reparation, °offset, °make good, indemnify, °repay, °reimburse, redress, °requite; expiate, °atone, °make amends (for) **2** °balance, counterpoise, counterbalance, °equalize, °neutralize, °even (up), °square, °offset **3** °pay, remunerate, °reward, °repay, recompense

compensatory *adj.* compensative, remunerative, restitutive *or* restitutory, expiatory, reparative *or* reparatory, piacular

compete *v.* contend, °vie, °struggle, °strive, °conflict, joust, °fence; °fight, °battle, °clash, °collide

competent *adj.* **1** °adequate, °suitable, °sufficient, °satisfactory, °acceptable, all right, *Colloq* OK *or* okay **2** °qualified, °fit, °capable, °proficient, °able, °prepared

competition *n.* **1** °rivalry, contention, striving, °struggle **2** °contest, °match, °meet, °game, °tournament, °event; championship **3** See **competitor.**

competitor *n.* °rival, °opponent, °competition, °opposition, °adversary; °antagonist, °contestant, contender

compile *v.* °collect, put together, °gather, °accumulate, °assemble, °amass, collate, °organize, °order, systematize; anthologize, °compose

complain *v.* grumble, °moan, °groan, wail, grouse, °carp (at), whimper, °cry, °lament, °bemoan, *Colloq* °gripe, °squawk, grouch, *Brit* whinge, *Slang* °bitch, beef, *US* °kick

complaint *n.* grumble, °grievance, *Colloq* °gripe, °squawk, *Slang* beef, *US* °kick

complement *v.* **1** °completion, °perfection, confirmation, finishing touch, °consummation **2** °crew, °team, °company, °band, °outfit; °quota, °allowance, quorum —*v.* **3** °complete, °perfect, round out *or* off, °set off, top off; °flesh out **4** °supplement, °enhance, °add to

complete *adj.* **1** °entire, °whole, °intact, uncut, unbroken, °undivided, °unabridged, °full, undiminished, unabated, unreduced **2** finished, ended, concluded, °over, done, °accomplished, terminated; settled, executed, performed **3** °entire, °total, °thorough, °absolute, utter, °unqualified, unmixed, unalloyed, °pure, °unmitigated, °rank **4** °perfect, consummate, °exemplary, °ideal, °model, °superior, °superlative, °superb, °faultless, °flawless —*v.* **5** conclude, °finish, °end, bring to an end, °accomplish, °achieve, do, *Colloq* °wrap up; °finalize **6** °round out, °round off, °perfect; °crown, culminate

completely *adv.* **1** °entirely, fully, °quite, °wholly, °totally, °altogether, in toto, °thoroughly, °perfectly, °exactly, °precisely, down to the ground, from start to finish, from beginning to end, from A to Z, from the word "go," in full; °lock, °stock, and barrel; °hook, line and sinker; heart and soul; °root and branch; en masse **2** unqualifiedly, unconditionally, °thoroughly, °utterly, °totally, °absolutely, °quite, °altogether, unreservedly **3** °clearly, °expressly, explicitly, unambiguously, °entirely, fully, °totally, °wholly, °altogether, unequivocally, °truly, categorically, flatly

completion *n.* **1** conclusion, °end, °close, °termination, °fulfillment, °consummation, culmination, °realization, °accomplishment, °finish **2** finishing, finalization, windup, finishing-off, completing

complexity *n.* **1** °complication, convolution **2** intricacy, involvement, complicatedness; inscrutability

complicate *v.* **1** °mix up, °entangle, °snarl, °tangle, confound, °muddle, °confuse **2** make complicated *or* complex, make involved *or* intricate, make a shambles *or* mess *or* muddle of, °mess up, *Colloq* °screw up

complicated *adj.* °involved, °intricate, complex, °compound, °elaborate; °ornate, Byzantine, Daedalian, tangled, knotty, °confused, °labyrinthine

complication *n.* **1** °complexity, involvement, intricacy, convolution **2** °difficulty, °problem, °predicament, °dilemma, °obstacle, °obstruction, °snag, °drawback

compliment *n.* **1** °praise, °homage, commendation, °honor, °tribute, °flattery, °bouquet, °favor **2** Usually, ***compliments.*** °respects, °regards, good *or* best wishes, felicitations, salutations, °greetings *—v.* **3** °honor, °praise, pay homage *or* tribute to, commend, °laud, °congratulate, felicitate; °flatter

complimentary *adj.* **1** °laudatory, commendatory, encomiastic, panegyrical, eulogistic, congratulatory, °flattering **2** °free, gratis, °on the house

comply *v.* °agree, °obey, °conform, °consent, acquiesce, concur, °submit, °yield, accede; °accord

compose *v.* **1** constitute, °form, °make (up), be a constituent *or* ingredient *or* component *or* element of, be a part of **2** °write, °create, °imagine, °think up, °originate, °frame, °formulate, °make (up), °author, °devise; contrive; set to music, °arrange **3** ***be composed of.*** consist of *or* in, comprise, be formed *or* made (up) of, be constituted of **4** ***compose oneself.*** °calm (down), quiet *or* *Chiefly Brit* quieten (down), pacify, control oneself, get control of *or* over oneself

composition *n.* **1** °theme, °essay, article, °paper, °story **2** °combination, °makeup, °structure, °form, °assembly, °setup, °organization, layout, °arrangement, configuration, shaping; °balance, °harmony, °proportion, °placement, placing, construction **3** °combination, aggregate, °mixture, °compound, compounding, °mix, formulation, °formula, composite, °amalgam, °alloy, mélange, °medley **4** °creation, origination, formulation, fashioning **5** °makeup, constitution

compound *v.* **1** put together, °combine, °mix, concoct, °compose, °make (up), °formulate, °blend **2** °blend, °merge, coalesce, °combine, °unite, fuse *or US also* fuze, come *or* go together **3** °aggravate, °intensify, exacerbate, °heighten, augment, °add to, °worsen, °increase; °enhance, multiply *—adj.* **4** °intricate, complex, °involved, °complicated; composite, multiple, multiform, multifaceted, *Technical* parasynthetic, parathetic *—n.* **5** composite, °blend, °synthesis, °combination, consolidation, *Technical* parasynthesis, parathesis; °mixture, °amalgam, °alloy, merging, °merger, °mix

comprehend *v.* °understand, °see, °grasp, °conceive, °take in, apprehend, °realize, °fathom, °perceive, discern, absorb, assimilate, °appreciate

comprehensive *adj.* °inclusive, encompassing, °thorough, °extensive, °full, °exhaustive, °complete, °sweeping, °wide, °broad, encyclopedic *or* encyclopaedic

compulsive *adj.* compelling, °obsessive, coercive, °urgent, °forceful, °overwhelming, constrained

compunction *n.* **1** °remorse, contrition, °regret, uneasiness of mind, pang *or* pricking of conscience, self-reproach **2** hesitation, °reluctance, °reserve, disinclination, °qualm, °misgiving, unwillingness, °fear

compute *v.* °calculate, °reckon, °figure (out), °work out, °determine, ascertain, °estimate

comrade *n.* °colleague, °associate, °friend, °companion, crony, confrère, *Colloq* °pal, °chum, *Chiefly Brit and Australian* °mate, *Australian* cobber, *US* buddy

conceal *v.* **1** °hide, °secrete, °bury, °cover, °disguise, °camouflage **2** keep secret *or* hidden, keep quiet about, °disguise, not reveal; dissemble

concede *v.* **1** °admit, °allow, °grant, °acknowledge, °confess, own (up *or* to *or* up to), °accept **2** °grant, °yield, °surrender, °cede, °give up, °submit, °resign, °relinquish, °abandon, °waive

conceit *n.* **1** °vanity, °pride, egotism, °self-esteem, self-admiration, self-love, narcissism, vainglory, *amour-propre;* °arrogance **2** °fancy, whim, caprice **3** elaborate figure (of speech), °affectation, strained *or* far-fetched metaphor

conceited *adj.* °vain, °egotistical, self-centered, egocentric, self-admiring, narcissistic, prideful, °proud, °arrogant, self-involved, °self-important, self-satisfied, °smug, complacent, vainglorious, °snobbish, *Colloq* stuck-up; *Slang* snotty

conceive *v.* **1** °have, °bear, beget, sire, °father, give birth to; become pregnant (with) **2** °formulate, °devise, °plan, contrive, °create, °plot, °hatch, °develop, evolve, °fabricate, think *or* make up, °form, °frame, °design **3** °think (up), °imagine, °speculate (on), °perceive, °see, °understand, °realize, °comprehend, °envision, °envisage, conjure up, dream up, hypothesize, postulate, °posit, °suggest, °suppose

concentrate *v.* **1** °focus, °direct, °center, centralize, °converge, consolidate **2** condense, °reduce, distill, °intensify, °refine, °strengthen **3** °gather, °collect, congregate, draw *or* bring together, °crowd, °cluster, °group **4** °think, focus one's thoughts *or* attention, apply oneself

conception *n.* **1** °birth, °beginning, genesis, inception, commencement, °emergence, °start, inauguration, °initiation, °launch, launching, °origin, origination, °formation, formulation, introduction **2** °idea, °notion, °inkling, °clue, concept; *idée reçu;* °understanding, °knowledge, °appreciation, comprehension **3** °design, °plan, °scheme, °proposal, °outline

concern *v.* **1** refer *or* relate to, have relation

or reference to, be about, pertain *or* appertain to, be pertinent or relevant to, °regard, apply to, be connected *or* involved with, °bear on, be germane to, °involve, °touch (on) **2** °affect, have (a) bearing *or* (an) influence on, °involve, °touch; °interest, be of importance *or* interest to **3** °worry, °trouble, °disturb, °bother, °perturb, unsettle, °upset, °distress —*n.* **4** °business, °affair, °problem; °responsibility, °duty, °charge, °task, involvement, *Colloq* °thing; *Slang* °bag, shtick **5** °interest, °regard, °consideration, °care, °thought, awareness, °attention **6** °anxiety, °worry, °solicitude, apprehension, °distress, apprehensiveness, uneasiness, malaise, disquiet, disquietude **7** °business, °firm, °company, °house, °establishment, °enterprise, °organization **8** °matter, °affair, °issue

concerned *adj.* **1** °involved, °responsible, °interested, °active; caring, °solicitous **2** troubled, vexed, °anxious, °worried, distressed, uneasy, perturbed, bothered, °upset, °disturbed

concerning *prep.* °about, °regarding, relative *or* relating to, referring to, with *or* in reference to, as regards, in *or* with regard to, with an eye to, with respect to, respecting, apropos (of), as to *or* for, in the matter of, on the subject of, re, *Formal* anent

concise *adj.* °brief, °terse, laconic, °compact, °direct, °succinct, °epigrammatic, cogent, pithy, compendious, °summary, °trenchant, compressed, condensed, °short; shortened, abridged, curtailed, °abbreviated

concrete *adj.* °real, °actual, °literal, °realistic, °authentic, valid, °genuine, °bona fide, °reliable; °specific, °particular, °definite, °definitive, clear-cut, °material, °physical, °tangible, °substantial

condemn *v.* **1** censure, °blame, °criticize, remonstrate with *or* against, °denounce, °disparage, reproach, °rebuke, °reprove, °scold, °reprimand, °upbraid **2** °convict, find guilty; °sentence, °doom **3** Usually, ***condemned.*** °doomed, damned, °destined, °fated, ordained, foreordained; consigned

condescend *v.* °stoop, °deign, lower *or* humble *or* demean oneself, come down off one's high horse

condescending *adj.* patronizing, belittling, °disdainful, °contemptuous, °pompous, °overbearing, high-handed, imperious, °snobbish, °haughty, *Colloq* snooty, *Brit* toffee-nosed, *Slang* snotty

condition *n.* **1** °state; circumstance(s), °shape **2** °stipulation, °proviso, °demand, °requirement, °term, °qualification, contingency, requisite, °prerequisite **3** working order, °fitness, °shape, °form, fettle; °health **4** ***conditions.*** °circumstances; °quarters; °environment —*v.* **5** °ready, get *or* make ready, °prepare, °equip, °outfit, fit (out *or* up), °adapt, °modify **6** °train, °educate, °teach; brainwash; °influence, °mold, °persuade **7** °accustom, inure, °adapt, acclimate, acclimatize; mithridatize

conduct *n.* **1** °behavior, action(s), demeanor, °manners, deportment, comportment, °attitude **2** °guidance, °direction, °management, supervision, °leadership, °administration, °government, °running, handling, °control, °command, °regulation, °operation —*v.* **3** °guide, °direct, °supervise, °manage, °carry on, °run, °control, °administer, °regulate, °operate **4** °lead, °guide, °escort, show (in *or* out), usher **5** °channel, °carry, °transmit, convey; °direct **6** ***conduct oneself.*** °behave, °act, demean, deport, comport, acquit

confer *v.* **1** °converse, °consult, °deliberate, °talk (over), °discuss, take counsel **2** When transitive, ***confer on.*** °give, °grant, °present, °award; °bestow (on)

conference *n.* °meeting, °convention, symposium, congress, seminar, forum, colloquium; °discussion, °talk, colloquy, *US* bull session

confess *v.* °disclose, °acknowledge, °admit, own (up *or* to *or* up to), °declare, avow, make a clean breast (of); °reveal, divulge, °confirm, °concede, affirm, aver, °testify; disbosom oneself, *Colloq* °come clean

confidence *n.* **1** °trust, °reliance, °faith; °belief **2** °assurance, °self-confidence, self-assurance, self-reliance, °poise, aplomb, coolness; °conviction, certitude, boldness, °courage, °nerve **3** ***in confidence.*** °in secrecy, in privacy, privately, confidentially, intimately, *Colloq* on the Q.T.

confident *adj.* **1** °secure, °sure, °certain, assured, °positive, convinced **2** °self-confident, self-assured, °self-possessed, reliant, self-reliant, °dauntless, °bold, °cool, cocksure, °fearless, °courageous, *Colloq* °cocky

confidential *adj.* °private, °secret, °intimate; classified; *Colloq* hush-hush

confirm *v.* **1** °ratify, °sanction, °authorize, °endorse, °support, °sustain, °approve, °uphold, °back up, validate, °verify, °recognize; °authenticate, accredit **2** °establish, °settle, affirm, °ensure, °clinch, °substantiate, °guarantee, °bind, °seal **3** °strengthen, °encourage, °fortify, °reinforce, corroborate, °substantiate, °buttress, °prove

confiscate *v.* °appropriate, °seize, impound, sequester, sequestrate, expropriate, °take (away), commandeer

conflict *n.* **1** °fight, °battle, °combat, °engagement, °struggle, °war, °fray, °fracas, affray, °brawl, donnybrook **2** °dispute, °argument, °controversy, wrangle, contention, °disagreement, altercation, °feud, °quarrel, °row; squabble, °tiff, *Colloq* spat **3** °clash, °antagonism, °difference, °opposition, °disagreement, °variance, °discord —*v.* **4** °clash, °disagree, °differ, be incompatible *or* at odds *or* at variance, be in opposition (to)

conform *v.* **1** °comply (with), °follow, °observe, °obey, °respect, °abide by, adapt *or* adjust (to) **2** °accord (with), °agree (with), concur (with), °coincide (with), °correspond (with), harmonize (with), °square (with), °match, °tally (with), °fit (in with), be consistent (with), be in accord *or* in accordance (with), ring true

confuse *v.* **1** disconcert, °perplex, °puzzle, °bewilder, °mystify, baffle, °bemuse, befuddle, °discomfit, confound, °fluster, °flummox, °upset, disorient, °embarrass, abash, °shame, °dismay, *Colloq* °rattle, °throw, *Chiefly US* discombobulate, *US and Canadian* buffalo **2** °disorder, confound, disorganize, throw into disarray, °muddle, °mix up, °snarl (up), ensnarl, °tangle (up), °entangle, °botch, *Colloq* °mess up, make a mess of, °screw up, *Brit* make a balls-up of, *US* ball up **3** °mix up, confound, °muddle, °jumble, °snarl (up), ensnarl; °blur

confused *adj.* **1** mixed up, jumbled, disordered, disorganized, °disorderly, muddled, muddle-headed, snarled (up), messy, baffling, confusing, mystifying, °puzzling, °perplexing; °contradictory, °ambiguous, misleading, °inconsistent, mixed up, botched (up), *Colloq* higgledy-piggledy **2** bewildered, perplexed, puzzled, baffled, (be)fuddled, mystified, disoriented, discomposed, at sea, flummoxed, dazed, muddled, bemused, mixed up, nonplussed, °disconcerted, abashed, °put off, °put out, °disturbed, flustered, °ill at ease, °upset, at sixes and sevens, at a loss, *Rare* metagrobolized, *Colloq* screwed up, muzzy, out of it, not with it, *Chiefly US* discombobulated, fouled up; *Slang* (all) balled up, *Brit* (all) bollocksed *or* ballocksed (up), *US* (all) bollixed (up), *US and Canadian* snafu **3** jumbled, mixed up, muddled, °disorderly, confusing, messy, disorganized, °topsy-turvy; °miscellaneous, motley, *Brit* shambolic

confusion *n.* **1** °disorder, °mix-up, °mess, °jumble, °muddle, disarray, disarrangement, °chaos, °shambles **2** °tumult, commotion, °disorder, turmoil, °pandemonium, °bedlam, °chaos **3** °mix-up, confounding; °ambiguity, ambiguousness, °misunderstanding, contradiction, inconsistency **4** mixing, combining, mixing-up, intermingling **5** °assortment, °mixture, °potpourri, gallimaufry, hotchpotch *or US and Canadian also* hodgepodge **6** °embarrassment, discomfiture, mortification, abashment, shamefacedness, chagrin

congested *adj.* (over)crowded, blocked (up), jammed, crammed, plugged, stopped *or* stuffed (up), choked

congratulate *v.* felicitate, °compliment

congratulations *interj.* Felicitations!, Best wishes!, Well done!, Many happy returns!, *Colloq* Nice going!, Good show!

connect *v.* **1** join *or* link *or* tie (together), °unite **2** °associate, affiliate, °link, °relate, °league, °tie (in) **3** °fasten, °bind, °unite, °tie, °link, °join, °attach, °couple, put together, °secure, °fit, °fix, affix, °stick, °anchor, °lock; rivet, °weld, braze, solder, °screw, °nail, stitch, °sew, °pin, °hook, °staple, °tack, °glue, °cement, °fuse, °seal, °buckle, strap, °bolt, °lash, °chain, °moor

connection *n.* **1** uniting, joining, linking, connecting, coupling; °union, °bond, °joint, °link **2** °link, °tie, (inter)relation(ship), interplay, °bearing, °reference, °relevance, appropriateness, correlation, °tie-in; coherence, consistency, °association **3** Often, ***connections***. °contact, °ally, °acquaintance, °friend (at court); °influence, *Colloq* °pull; *US slang* °drag **4** ***connections***. relatives, °relations, °family, °kin, kith and kin

conquer *v.* **1** °overcome, vanquish, °beat, °defeat, °subdue, °crush, °subjugate **2** °capture, °seize, °win, °gain, °acquire, °obtain; °occupy, annex, °overrun **3** °overcome, triumph *or* prevail over, °beat, surmount, °master, win out (over)

conquest *n.* **1** vanquishment, subjugation, °defeat, °domination, °subjection **2** °victory, °triumph, mastery, °win

conscience *n.* °morality, °morals, °judgment, fairness, sense of right and wrong, ethics, °honor, standards, °principles, scruples

conscientious *adj.* **1** °scrupulous, °principled, °fair, °moral, °ethical, °strict, °righteous, right-minded, upstanding, °upright, °honorable, °just, °responsible, high-minded; incorruptible **2** °cautious, °careful, °scrupulous, °exacting, °meticulous, punctilious, °painstaking, °diligent, °particular, rigorous, °thorough **3** °prudent, °discreet, °politic, °careful, circumspect, heedful, °attentive, °serious

conscious *adj.* **1** °aware, °awake, °alert **2** °deliberate, °intentional, purposive, °purposeful, °willful, °studied

consent *v.* **1** °agree, °comply, concur, accede, acquiesce, °concede, °yield, °submit, °cede, °conform, °give in **2** ***consent to***. °permit, °allow, °agree to, give in to, °approve, °authorize —*n.* **3** °approval, assent, °permission, °sanction, authorization, imprimatur, seal of approval, *Colloq* °OK *or* okay, °go-ahead **4** °agreement, acceptance, acquiescence, compliance, °approval, concurrence

consequently *adv.* so, °therefore, as a result *or* consequence, °accordingly, ergo, °hence, °thus

conservation *n.* °preservation, °protection, °safekeeping, °maintenance, °upkeep, °management, safeguarding; husbandry, °economy

conservative *adj.* **1** °reactionary, °right, right-wing, rightist, Tory **2** °cautious, °careful, °prudent, °moderate, °temperate, middle-of-the-road, °sober, °stable; unprogressive, °orthodox, °traditional, conformist, °hidebound, °conventional, °standard, fundamentalist, trueblue, dyed-in-the-wool —*n.* **3** °reactionary, rightist, right-winger, Tory, fundamentalist; °moderate, middle-of-the-roader

conserve *v.* **1** °keep, °preserve, hold on to, °save, °spare, °reserve **2** °preserve, °maintain, keep up, °take care of

consider *v.* **1** think about *or* over, take into

or under consideration, deliberate (over *or* about), contemplate (on *or* over), °weigh, °ponder, mull over, cogitate on, meditate (on *or* upon *or* over), reflect (on *or* upon), ruminate (on *or* over), °chew over, °study, °examine **2** °heed, °mark, take into account *or* consideration, °reckon with, °bear in mind, °note, °observe, make allowance for; °esteem, °respect, have regard for **3** °regard, look upon; °judge, deem, take to be, °think, °believe, °gauge, °rate, °estimate, °reckon

considerable *adj.* **1** sizeable *or* sizable, °substantial, °large, °big, °great; appreciable, °respectable, °noticeable, largish, biggish, °goodly, °decent, °fair, *Colloq* °tidy **2** °important, °worthy, of consequence, of distinction, °distinguished, °illustrious, °noteworthy, °notable, °remarkable, °estimable, °influential, °respectable

considerate *adj.* °thoughtful, °kind, °kindly, kindhearted, goodhearted, °helpful, °friendly, °neighborly, °gracious, °obliging, °accommodating, °charitable, °generous, °unselfish; °sympathetic, compassionate, °sensitive; °attentive; °solicitous

consideration *n.* **1** °regard, °concern, attentiveness, °solicitude, thoughtfulness, compassion, °kindness, kindliness, kindheartedness, considerateness, °respect, caring, °care **2** °reward, compensation, °remuneration, °fee, °payment, recompense, emolument, °tip, gratuity, *pourboire*, baksheesh *or* backsheesh; °honorarium **3** °thought, deliberation, °reflection, contemplation, rumination, cogitation, °study, °examination

considering *prep.* °in view of, in (the) light of, bearing in mind, making allowance for, taking into consideration *or* account, looking at, all in all, all things *or* everything considered, inasmuch as, insomuch as

consistent *adj.* **1** agreeing, in agreement, in harmony, in keeping, °harmonious, in concordance, conforming, in conformance, accordant, compatible, in accord *or* accordance, consonant **2** dependable, °regular, °predictable, undeviating, °steady, °steadfast, unchanging, °uniform, unswerving, °constant

consistently *adv.* **1** steadily, constantly, regularly, uniformly, °daily, day by day **2** dependably, unswervingly, staunchly, devotedly, °firmly, resolutely, faithfully, uniformly, unfailingly

console *v.* °comfort, soothe, °calm, assuage, °solace, °cheer (up)

conspicuous *adj.* **1** °obvious, °clear, °evident, °plain, palpable, °perceptible, °patent, °prominent, °apparent, clear-cut, °unquestionable, incontestable, °incontrovertible **2** °obvious, unmistakable, °prominent, °outstanding, °noticeable, °impressive, °vivid, °obtrusive; °striking, °showy, °garish, °gaudy, °loud, °tawdry, °blatant, °lurid, °vulgar, °flashy, °ostentatious **3** °notable, °noteworthy, °exceptional, °outstanding, °eminent, °unusual, °marked, °extraordinary, °remarkable, °distinguished, °impressive, °awesome, awe-inspiring, °glorious

conspiracy *n.* °plot, °scheme, °stratagem, °intrigue, collusion, °cabal, connivance, °foul play, dirty work

constable *n.* policeman, policewoman, °(police) officer, *US* patrolman, *Colloq* cop, copper, *Brit* bobby; *Slang* flatfoot, fuzz

constant *adj.* **1** °resolute, °immovable, °steadfast, °firm, dependable, unshakeable *or* unshakable, °determined, unswerving, undeviating, persevering, unwearying, unwearied, °untiring, indefatigable, °tireless, unflagging, unwavering, unfailing, unfaltering, °persistent; °loyal, °true, tried and true, °devoted, °staunch, trusty, °faithful **2** incessant, unceasing, ceaseless, °perpetual, °persistent, uninterrupted, °steady, °regular, °invariable, unremitting, unvarying, °relentless, unrelenting, °continuous, °continual; unending, °endless, never-ending, °nonstop, °perennial, °eternal, °everlasting, *Literary* sempiternal **3** unchanging, unchanged, °invariable, unvarying, °fixed, °uniform, unalterable, immutable, °changeless, °persistent

construct *v.* **1** °build, °erect, °make, put together, °frame, °set up, °put up, °assemble **2** °fabricate, °devise, °create, °forge, °invent, °formulate, °compose, °shape, °set up, °fashion

constructive *adj.* **1** °helpful, °useful, °practicable, °advantageous, °practical, °productive, °beneficial, °positive **2** °virtual, inferential, °implicit, inferred, derived, deduced

consult *v.* **1** Often, ***consult with.*** °confer (with), °discuss (with), °deliberate (with), °talk over (with), inquire *or* enquire of, seek advice from, °ask (of), °question, interrogate, take counsel (with *or* of) **2** °refer to, °look up, seek information from

consultant *n.* **1** °physician, °doctor, °specialist, °expert **2** adviser *or* advisor, °expert, counsellor *or US* counselor

consume *v.* **1** °devour, °eat (up), °gulp (down), °swallow, °drink (up), °put away, gobble (up); °digest **2** °use up, °exhaust, deplete, °drain, °expend, °diminish, °reduce **3** °waste, °occupy, squander, °fritter away, °dissipate, absorb, °lose, °throw away, °lavish, *Slang* °blow **4** °destroy, °ruin, °(lay) waste, °demolish, °wreck, °gut, °raze, *Slang US and Canadian* °total **5** °overcome, °overwhelm, °devastate, °destroy, annihilate, °ravage, °(lay) waste, °wear out, °ruin, eat up, °devour, do in; preoccupy, °obsess

consummation *n.* **1** °completion, °accomplishment, °fulfillment, °finish, °end, °realization, attainment, °achievement, °success; completing, accomplishing, fulfilling, finishing, ending, realizing, attaining, achieving **2** °acme, °perfection, °peak, culmination, finishing touch, conclusion, grand finale, °climax

contact *n.* **1** °junction, conjunction, °connection **2** °acquaintance, °friend, °connection, *Colloq US* in **3** °touch, communication, °association —*v.* **4** get in touch with, °communicate with, °reach, get hold of; phone, °ring (up), °telephone, speak to *or* with, write to, correspond with

contain *v.* **1** °hold, have in it; °bear, °carry **2** °hold, have the capacity for, °accommodate, °admit, °carry; °seat **3** °restrain, °restrict, confine, °repress, °control, hold back *or* in, °curb, °bridle, keep under control, °suppress, °check, °stifle

contaminate *v.* defile, °sully, °pollute, °corrupt, °rot, °stain, °soil, °taint, infect, °poison, °foul, °spoil, befoul; °debase, °adulterate, °vitiate

contemplate *v.* **1** look *or* gaze at *or* on *or* upon, °behold, °view, °survey, °observe, °regard, °eye; °scan, °scrutinize, °inspect **2** ruminate (over), ponder (on *or* over), °deliberate (over), muse (on *or* over), meditate *or* reflect (on), think (about *or* over), mull over, cogitate (over), turn over in one's mind, brood on *or* over, chew on *or* over, °consider, °study, °examine **3** °plan, °intend, think of *or* about, °consider, entertain the idea *or* notion of

contemporary *adj.* **1** of the time, contemporaneous, coeval, coexistent, concurrent, concomitant, °parallel, synchronous, synchronic, °coincidental, coetaneous **2** °modern, °current, present-day, °new, up-to-date, °stylish, °fashionable, modish, à la mode, °latest, in; °novel, newfangled, *Colloq* °trendy

contempt *n.* °loathing, abhorrence, hatred, odium, °hate; °scorn, disdain, contumely, °disgust

contemptible *adj.* °despicable, °loathsome, detestable, °scurvy, °low, °mean, °base, °inferior, currish, °wretched, °vile, abject, ignominious, °unworthy, °shabby, °shameful

contemptuous *adj.* °scornful, °disdainful, sneering, derisive, insulting, contumelious, °insolent

content[1] *n.* **1** °capacity, °volume, °size, °measure **2** Usually, ***contents.*** ingredients, components, constituents; °load **3** °substance, subject matter; °significance, purport, °import, °essence, °text, °theme, °topic, °thesis

content[2] *n.* **1** °pleasure, °satisfaction, °gratification, °happiness, contentment, contentedness, felicity, °delight **2** °ease, °comfort, tranquillity, °serenity, °peace, peacefulness, contentedness —*adj.* **3** pleased, satisfied, °happy, °delighted, contented, gratified, °glad, °cheerful; °comfortable, fulfilled —*v.* **4** °satisfy, please, °gratify, soothe, °cheer, °gladden, °delight

contest *n.* **1** °competition, °match, °tournament, championship, tourney, °meet, °game, °rivalry, °trial **2** °strife, °controversy, °dispute, contention, °debate, altercation, °argument, velitation; °conflict, °struggle, °fight, °battle, °combat, °war —*v.* **3** contend, °argue, °dispute, °debate; °challenge, °(call into) question, °oppose, °counter, confute, object to, refute

contestant *n.* contender, °competitor, °opponent, °rival, °adversary, entrant, °player, °participant

context *n.* °structure, framework, °environment, °situation, circumstance(s); ambiance *or* ambience, °surround, surroundings, °frame (of reference), °setting, °background

continual *adj.* °constant, incessant, °perpetual, °nonstop, °persistent, uninterrupted, °regular, °steady, unbroken, unceasing, ceaseless, °constant, °eternal, unremitting, interminable, °endless, unending; *Loosely* °continuous

continue *v.* **1** °carry on, °proceed (with), keep up *or* on *or* at, °go on (with), °pursue, °persist (in), °persevere (in) **2** °endure, °last, °go on, °persist, be prolonged, °remain **3** °maintain, °keep (on), °prolong, °perpetuate, °carry on (with), persist in *or* with, °sustain, °extend **4** °resume, °pick up, °take up, °carry on (with) **5** °proceed, °go (on), °extend

continuous *adj.* **1** connected, unbroken, uninterrupted **2** incessant, °persistent, °perpetual, °nonstop, unceasing, ceaseless, °constant, unremitting, interminable, °endless, unending; *Loosely* °continual

contract *n.* **1** °agreement, °understanding, °deal, °bargain, °arrangement, °pact, commitment, °obligation, °compact —*v.* **2** °engage, °agree, °promise, covenant, °undertake **3** °catch, °acquire, °get, °come down with, °develop, become infected with, *Brit* go down with **4** °diminish, °shrink, draw together, °roll (oneself), °narrow, °squeeze, constrict, compress, condense, °decrease, °reduce **5** °wrinkle, °knit, crease, corrugate, °pucker

contradict *v.* **1** °deny, gainsay, °dispute, controvert, argue against; °oppose **2** contravene, belie, refute, disallow, °forbid, disaffirm, °counter, abrogate, nullify, annul, °reverse, °counteract

contradictory *adj.* °inconsistent, °paradoxical, °incongruous, conflicting, °incompatible, discrepant; °ambiguous, ambivalent

contraption *n.* contrivance, °device, °gadget, °mechanism, °apparatus, *Colloq* widget, thingumabob *or* thingamabob, thingumajig *or* thingamajig, thingummy, whatsit, doodah, thingy, *US* gizmo *or* gismo, Rube Goldberg (invention), whatchamacallit, *Colloq Brit* gubbins

contrary *adj.* **1** °opposite, °opposing, °opposed, °different, °contradictory, conflicting, antagonistic **2** antagonistic, °perverse, contrarious, °hostile, unfriendly, inimical, cross-grained, refractory, contumacious, °self-willed, °argumentative, unaccommodating, antipathetic, *Literary* froward **3** adverse, unfavorable, °inauspicious, unlucky, °unfortunate, unpropitious, °untoward, °inopportune, °bad, °foul —*n.* **4** °opposite, °reverse —*adv.* **5** perversely, oppositely, contrariwise, contrarily, in opposition to

contrast *v.* **1** juxtapose, °oppose, °compare, °distinguish, °differentiate, °discriminate, set *or* place against; °set off **2** °conflict, differ *or* diverge *or* deviate (from) —*n.* **3** °comparison; °difference, °distinction, °disparity, °dissimilarity

contribute *v.* **1** °give, °furnish, °donate, °bestow, °grant, °present, °provide, °supply **2** ***contribute to.*** °add to, °promote, °advance, °help, °aid, °support, °forward, have a hand in, play a part *or* role in

control *v.* **1** °command, °dominate, °direct, °steer, °pilot, hold sway over, °rule, exercise power *or* authority over, °govern, °manage, °lead, °conduct, be in control (of), call the tune, °guide, °oversee, °supervise **2** °check, hold back *or* in check, °curb, °repress, °contain **3** °suppress, °put down, °master, °subdue, °restrain, °curb, °manage —*n.* **4** °command, °direction, °power, °authority, °leadership, °management, °guidance, supervision, °oversight, °charge; °sway, °rule, °jurisdiction **5** °restraint, °check, °curb, mastery, °command, dominance, °domination **6** °knob, button, dial, °handle, lever, °switch; °device, °mechanism

controversial *adj.* **1** °debatable, °disputable, °questionable, °moot, °doubtful, °unsettled **2** polemical, dialectic, litigious, °factious **3** disputatious, °argumentative, contentious; °provocative

controversy *n.* **1** °dispute, °debate, contention, °argument, argumentation, disputation, wrangling, confrontation, questioning, °disagreement **2** °argument, °dispute, °disagreement, °quarrel; squabble, °tiff, *Colloq* spat

convalesce *v.* °recover, °improve, get better, °recuperate

convenient *n.* **1** °suitable, commodious, °useful, °helpful, °handy, °serviceable, °expedient, °opportune, °advantageous **2** °handy, °nearby, within (easy) reach, at one's fingertips, close at hand, °available, °accessible; °(at the) ready

convention *n.* **1** °assembly, °meeting, °gathering, congregation, congress, °conference, symposium, °council, conclave, °diet, synod, seminar **2** °rule, °practice, °custom, °tradition, °usage, °formality, conventionalism

conventional *adj.* °customary, °habitual, °usual, °normal, °regular, °standard, °orthodox, °traditional, established, °ordinary, °everyday, °common, commonplace, °accustomed, received, agreed; °reactionary, °old-fashioned, °stodgy, °stuffy, old hat

converge *v.* come *or* go together, °meet, °join, °unite, °merge, °coincide; °blend

conversation *n.* °discussion, °talk, °chat, °dialogue, colloquy, °parley; chitchat, °gossip, discourse, °palaver, *Colloq chiefly Brit* chinwag

conversationalist *n.* deipnosophist

converse *v.* °discuss, °talk, °speak, °chat, °parley, discourse, °gossip, °chatter

convert *v.* **1** °change, °modify, °alter, °transform, transmute, mutate, transfigure, transmogrify, remodel, remake, metamorphose **2** proselytize, °switch, °change (over) —*n.* **3** proselyte; neophyte, catechumen, °disciple

convict *v.* **1** find *or* prove guilty, *Slang* °nail —*n.* **2** °prisoner, °captive, *Slang* con, jailbird *or Brit also* gaolbird, °lag

conviction *n.* **1** proof of guilt **2** °belief, °opinion, °view, °persuasion, °position **3** °certainty, sureness, positiveness, °confidence, °assurance, certitude

convince *v.* °win over, °talk into, °persuade, bring (a)round, °sway

cool *adj.* **1** °chilly, °chill, chilling, cooling, unheated; chilled, °cold, °refreshing, °fresh **2** °calm, °serene, °collected, °levelheaded, °quiet, unexcited, unemotional, undisturbed, unexcitable, unruffled, unflappable, coolheaded, °relaxed, controlled, under control, °self-possessed, self-controlled, unperturbed, °phlegmatic, composed, imperturbable **3** °dispassionate, °cold, °coldblooded, emotionless, °deliberate, °coldhearted, °calculated, °willful, °premeditated, °purposeful, purposive **4** uninvolved, °distant, °remote, °aloof, °detached, removed, uninterested, unconcerned, °unsympathetic, apathetic, °cold, °coldhearted, °coldblooded **5** °lukewarm, °distant, uncordial, unfriendly, unsociable, °unapproachable, °standoffish, °forbidding, unwelcoming, °cold, °frigid **6** °bold, °audacious, °brazen, °overconfident, °presumptuous, °shameless, °unabashed, °impertinent, °impudent, °insolent —*n.* **7** coolness, °chill, chilliness, *Colloq* coolth **8** aplomb, °poise, sedateness, °control, °self-control, composure, °sang-froid —*v.* **9** °chill, °refrigerate, ice **10** °diminish, °reduce, lessen, abate, °moderate

cooperate *v.* **1** °collaborate, work together, °join, °unite, interact, °team up, join forces, act jointly *or* in concert **2** °participate, °contribute, lend a hand, °help, °assist

cooperation *n.* **1** collaboration, teamwork, interaction, synergism *or* synergy **2** °support, °help, °aid, °assistance, °patronage, °backing, advocacy, °favor, helping hand, °friendship, °blessing, sponsorship, °auspices, backup

coordinate *v.* **1** °organize, classify, °order, °arrange, systemize, systematize, codify, °categorize, °group, °match (up), °dispose, °rate, °rank, °grade **2** harmonize, correlate, °unify, °mesh, synchronize, °integrate, *Colloq* pull together —*adj.* **3** °equivalent, °parallel, °correspondent, complementary, correlative, °equal, °reciprocal, coordinating, coordinative, *Technical* paratactic

cope *v.* **1** °manage, get along *or* by, °make do, °survive, subsist, °come through **2** ***cope with.*** be a match for, °withstand, contend with *or* against, °handle, °deal with, °dispose of

copy *n.* **1** °reproduction, °replica, °facsimile, °likeness, °imitation, °double, °twin, duplication, °duplicate, °transcript, replication, carbon (copy), photocopy, °print **2** °example, °sample, °specimen **3** °text, °writing —*v.* **4** °reproduce, °duplicate, replicate, °transcribe, *Colloq* °knock off **5** °imitate, °mimic, impersonate, emulate, ape, °parrot, °echo

cord *n.* °string, °line, °twine; °rope

cordial *adj.* °friendly, °warm, affable, °amiable, °kindly, °genial, °gracious, welcoming, °pleasant, °good-natured, °nice; °courteous, °polite

core *n.* **1** °center, °heart, °middle, °nucleus, inside(s) **2** °essence, marrow, °heart, °pith, °gist, °quintessence, sum and substance —*v.* **3** °pit, °seed

corps *n.* body of men *or* women, troop, cadre, °unit, °detachment, °cohort, °division, battalion, brigade, °platoon, °squad, column, squadron

corpse *n.* °body, °remains, °cadaver, *Slang* °stiff; (of an animal) carcass

correct *v.* **1** °right, set *or* put right, °amend, redress, °rectify, °remedy, °repair, °fix, right wrongs; °cure **2** °scold, admonish, °rebuke, °reprimand, °berate, chide, °reprove; censure, °blame **3** °punish, °chastise, °chasten, °discipline, °castigate **4** °reverse, °offset, °counteract, counterbalance, °neutralize, nullify, °make up for, annul, °cancel; °adjust, °change, °modify **5** °mark, °grade —*adj.* **6** °proper, °decorous, °decent, °appropriate, °suitable, °fit, °right, °meet, °fitting, °befitting, apt, *de rigueur, comme il faut, Old-fashioned Brit* tickety-boo **7** °conventional, established, °set, °standard, °normal, °orthodox, approved, °in order, *de rigueur, comme il faut,* °usual, °natural, °customary, °traditional, done, °right, *Old-fashioned Brit* tickety-boo **8** °accurate, °right, °precise, °exact, °factual, valid, °true, °proper, °fitting, apt, °suitable, °appropriate; °faultless, °perfect, unimpeachable

correction *n.* **1** °improvement, emendation, rectification, redress, °remedy, reparation, °amendment; corrigendum **2** °punishment, castigation, chastisement

correspond *v.* **1** °agree, °conform, °tally, °comply, °accord, harmonize, be congruous, °match, °coincide **2** °write, °communicate, be in touch *or* contact

correspondent *n.* newspaperman, newspaperwoman, pressman, presswoman, °journalist, °reporter, stringer, newsman, newsperson

corridor *n.* °hall, hallway, °passage, passageway

corrupt *adj.* **1** °dishonest, untrustworthy, °dishonorable, underhand(ed), °venal, *Colloq* °crooked **2** debased, depraved, °perverted, subverted, °evil, °wicked, °degenerate, degraded —*v.* **3** °debase, °pervert, °subvert, °degrade, deprave, °warp **4** °adulterate, °contaminate, °pollute, °taint, defile, infect, °spoil, °poison **5** °bribe, suborn, °buy (off)

cost *n.* **1** °price, °outlay, °payment, °charge, °expense, °expenditure, °rate, °tariff —*v.* **2** sell for, °get, °fetch, °bring in, *Colloq* set (someone) back

costume *n.* °dress, clothing, attire, °clothes, garb, °apparel, raiment, °garments, °outfit, vestment, livery, °uniform, °kit, *Colloq* °gear, togs, get-up; *Slang* °rags, *US* threads

cot *n.* bed, crib; cradle, bunk

cottage *n.* °hut, °shack, °cabin, bungalow, shanty, *Literary* °cot; *US and Canadian* °lodge, chalet

couch *n.* **1** sofa, settee, °settle, divan, love seat, chaise (longue); daybed; °tête-à-tête, siamoise; *US* davenport —*v.* **2** embed, °frame, °style, °express, °phrase

council *n.* **1** °assembly, °meeting, conclave, °conference, synod, consistory, °convention, congress, congregation, °gathering, convocation, *US* caucus **2** °board, °ministry, directors, °cabinet, panel, °committee, °body, directorate, directory, caucus

counsel *n.* **1** °advice, °judgment, °direction, °opinion, °guidance, °instruction, °recommendation, exhortation, *Technical* paraenesis **2** consultation, °discussion, deliberation, °consideration **3** adviser *or* advisor, °guide, °counselor; °lawyer, *Brit* barrister; *US* attorney —*v.* **4** °advise, recommend to, suggest to, °instruct; °guide

counselor *n.* adviser *or* advisor, °counsel, °lawyer, *Brit* counsellor-at-law, barrister, *US* counselor-at-law, attorney

count *v.* **1** count up *or* off, °enumerate, °number, °calculate, add up, °total, °reckon, °compute, °tally, °figure up, quantify, *Colloq* °figure out **2** °include, °consider, °regard, deem, °judge, look on *or* upon **3** ***count on or upon.*** rely on *or* upon, depend on *or* upon, be sure of, °trust, bank on, be confident of, *Chiefly Brit (dialectal in US)* reckon on *or* upon, *Chiefly US* figure on *or* upon

counter *n.* **1** °token, disk *or* disc, °chip, °piece, marker **2** °table, °bar

counteract *v.* counterbalance, °neutralize, °correct, annul, nullify, °cancel, °oppose, °mitigate

counterfeit *adj.* **1** forged, °fake, °fraudulent, °imitation, °bogus, °spurious, *Colloq* phoney *or US also* phony **2** make-believe, °sham, °pretended, °pretend, feigned, °insincere, °fake, faked, °false, °artificial, meretricious, pseudo, °factitious, °synthetic, °unreal, simulated —*n.* **3** °fake, °imitation, °forgery, °reproduction, *Colloq* phoney *or US also* phony —*v.* **4** °forge, °copy, °reproduce, °falsify, °imitate; *Slang* hang paper **5** feign, °pretend, simulate, °put on, °fake

counterfeiter *n.* *Slang* paperhanger

country *n.* **1** °nation, °state, °power; °territory, °realm **2** °(native) land, homeland, °fatherland, motherland, mother country **3** countryside, rural area *or* surroundings, °provinces, hinterlands; mountains, woods, wilderness, outback, *Colloq* sticks, *US* boondocks, boonies

couple *n.* **1** °pair, duo, twosome; °brace, °span, yoke, °team **2** ***a couple of.*** a few, °several, a handful (of), one or two, three or four —*v.* **3** °join, °link, yoke, °combine, °unite, match up, °connect

courage *n.* °bravery, valor, boldness, intrepidity, gallantry, dauntlessness, °daring, fearlessness, heroism, °nerve, *Colloq* °grit, °guts, °pluck, °spunk, *US* moxie, sand, *Slang Brit* °bottle

courageous *adj.* °brave, valiant, valorous, °bold, °intrepid, °gallant, °dauntless, °daring, °fearless, °heroic, *Colloq* plucky

course *n.* **1** °path, °way, °orbit, °route, °run, °track, ambit, °line, °circuit, °passage **2** °movement, °progress, °headway, °advance, °progression; °speed **3** °procedure, °process, °performance, °routine, °conduct, °order, °practice, dispatch *or* despatch, °execution **4** °direction, °tack **5** °class, °lecture, seminar, °program **6** ***of course.*** °naturally, °surely, certainly, °positively, °obviously, °definitely, assuredly, °by all means; °undoubtedly, indubitably, without (a) doubt, no doubt, *Colloq US* °sure

courteous *adj.* °polite, well-mannered, well-behaved, gentlemanly, °ladylike, °well-bred, °polished, urbane, civilized, °respectful, °civil, courtly, °proper, °decorous, °tactful, °considerate, °diplomatic

courtesy *n.* politeness, °elegance, courtliness, politesse, courteousness, °respect, respectfulness, good manners, °formality, °civility, °ceremony; red-carpet treatment

cover *v.* **1** °protect, °shelter, °shield, °screen; °guard, °defend, °command **2** Also, ***cover up or over.*** °conceal, °hide, °bury, °mask, °shroud, °obscure; dissemble; °enclose, °envelop **3** overlie, spread over, overspread, lie on, layer, °coat, blanket **4** °wrap, swaddle **5** °dress, °clothe, garb, attire, °robe, sheathe **6** extend *or* stretch over, °occupy, engulf, inundate, °submerge **7** °include, °comprehend, °provide for, comprise, extend over, °contain, °embody, °incorporate, °account for, °take into account, °take in, °deal with **8** °act, take responsibility *or* charge, stand *or* sit in, °substitute, °take over, run things, °double **9** °traverse, °complete, pass *or* travel over, °travel, °cross **10** compensate for, °defray, be enough *or* sufficient for, °counter, °offset, counterbalance, °make up for, insure *or* protect against —*n.* **11** lid, °top, °cap, covering **12** binding, boards, °wrapper, dust jacket, jacket **13** Often, ***covers.*** blanket, quilt, eiderdown, duvet, bedclothes, bedding, °(bed) linen; coverlet, counterpane; *US* comforter **14** °shelter, °protection, concealment, hiding place, hideout, °retreat, °refuge; °hide, *US and Canadian* °blind; *Colloq Brit* hidey-hole **15** °cloak, °screen, °disguise, concealment, °pretense, °front, °camouflage, smoke screen, coverup, °mask, covering

coward *n.* poltroon, craven, dastard, sissy *or* cissy, °baby, mouse, °milksop; Scaramouch *or* Scaramouche; *Colloq* chicken, *Slang* yellow-belly; *US and Canadian* milquetoast

cowardice *n.* cowardliness, chicken-heartedness, faintheartedness, timidity, timorousness, pusillanimity

cowardly *adj.* °timid, °fearful, frightened, °afraid, °scared, °fainthearted, timorous, chicken-hearted, chicken-livered, lily-livered, white-livered, craven, namby-pamby, dastardly, pusillanimous, vitelline, *Slang* yellow, yellow-bellied

coy *adj.* °shy, °modest, diffident, demure, °timid, °bashful, °self-conscious, °sheepish, timorous, unassuming, unpretentious; °reserved, self-effacing, °retiring, °evasive, °reluctant, °recalcitrant

cozy *adj.* **1** °comfortable, °snug, °warm, °restful, °secure, relaxing, °easy, *Colloq* comfy **2** °convenient, °expedient, self-serving, underhand(ed)

crack *n.* **1** °break, °fracture, °chink, °crevice, °rift, °gap, °flaw, °split, fissure, °slit, cleft, °split, °check, °rupture, °breach **2** °snap, °report, bang, °clap, °shot **3** °moment, °instant, °time, °second —*v.* **4** °snap **5** °break, °fracture, °rupture; °shiver, °shatter, smash **6** fissure, °craze, crackle, *US* alligator

craft *n.* **1** °skill, °ability, artisanship, handiwork, °ingenuity, skillfulness, °art, °talent, °dexterity, cleverness, mastery, expertness, °expertise, °flair, °genius, *Colloq* know-how **2** °deceit, guile, cunning, °fraud, °trickery, wiliness, foxiness, artfulness, craftiness, duplicity **3** °trade, °occupation, °calling, °vocation, métier; °profession **4** °vessel, °ship, °boat; hovercraft; aircraft, airplane, °plane; spaceship, spacecraft, °rocket —*v.* **5** °make, °fashion, °fabricate

crafty *adj.* °artful, cunning, °clever, °shrewd, °foxy, canny, °wily, °sly, °scheming, °calculating, °designing, plotting, °tricky, °sneaky, °deceitful, °shifty, °dodgy, guileful, insidious, double-dealing, °two-faced, duplicitous, treacherous

crag *n.* °cliff, °bluff, tor, °peak, °rock, escarpment, scarp, °precipice, *US* palisade

cram *v.* **1** °pack, °stuff, overstuff, overcrowd, °jam, °fill **2** °study, burn the midnight oil, *Literary* lucubrate, *Colloq* °grind, *Brit* swot

cramped *adj.* °tight, crowded, incommodious, uncomfortable, °close

crank *n.* **1** °eccentric, °character, °oddity, *Colloq* nut; *Brit slang* nutter, nutcase **2** monomaniac, °zealot, °fanatic

cranky *adj.* **1** °eccentric, °odd, °weird, °strange, °queer, °peculiar, quirky, °capricious, °whimsical **2** °testy, grouchy, crabby, °short-tempered, °surly, irascible, °waspish, churlish, °gruff, curmudgeonly, °cantankerous, choleric, °snappish, °petulant, °peevish, contentious, °querulous, °irritable, splenetic, *Colloq* crotchety

cranny *n.* °chink, °crevice, °crack, fissure, °check, °fracture, °break, °furrow, °split, cleft

crash *v.* **1** °fall, °topple **2** °force, °drive, °run, smash **3** bang, °boom, °explode —*n.* **4** °boom, bang, smash, °explosion, °blast **5** °disaster, °collapse, °failure

crawl *v.* **1** °creep, worm, °wriggle, wiggle, °squirm; °edge **2** inch, °creep, °drag **3** cower, °cringe, grovel, toady, fawn **4** °teem, °abound, °swarm, be overrun *or* swamped

craze *n.* °fad, °fashion, °trend, °enthusiasm,

°rage, °mania, °thing, °obsession; last word, *dernier cri*

crazy *adj.* **1** °mad, °insane, demented, °deranged, °unbalanced, unhinged, lunatic, *non compos mentis,* °daft, certifiable, °mental, touched (in the head), out of one's mind *or* head, mad as a March hare *or* hatter, maddened, crazed, *Colloq* balmy, cuckoo, cracked, crackers, crackbrained, dotty, daffy, dippy, gaga, goofy, crackpot, loony, off one's rocker, have a screw loose, screwy, batty, bats, bats-in-the-belfry, *Brit* barmy (in the crumpet), potty, bonkers, round the bend *or* twist, off one's chump, doolally, *US* off one's trolley, out of one's gourd, screwball, nuts, nutty (as a fruitcake); *Slang* bananas, *US* out to lunch, meshuga, flaky, flaked-out, (plumb) loco **2** °silly, °absurd, °foolish, °nonsensical, °inane, °ridiculous, °preposterous, laughable, risible, °ludicrous, asinine, °stupid, moronic, imbecile *or* imbecilic, idiotic, °feebleminded, °harebrained, *Colloq* crackpot **3** °impractical, °impracticable, unworkable, °unsound, °pointless, °imprudent, °rash, °reckless, ill-considered **4** °enthusiastic, °eager, avid, zealous, °keen, °excited **5** °infatuated, keen on *or* about, °wild, °mad, *Colloq* dotty, *US* nuts, nutty; *US slang* ape

create *v.* **1** °make, °produce, °form, bring into being, °originate, °conceive; sire, °father **2** engender, beget, °spawn, °generate, °invent, °imagine, °think up, °frame, °forge, °fashion, °fabricate, °manufacture, °develop, °design, contrive, °devise, °produce, dream up, °initiate

creation *n.* **1** °beginning, °origin, °birth, °start, inception, genesis, making, °formation **2** the world, the universe, the cosmos

creative *adj.* °imaginative, inventive, originative, artistic, °original, °ingenious, °resourceful

creator *n.* **1** originator, °author, initiator, °founder, °father, inventor, architect, °designer, framer, maker, prime mover **2** God, Supreme Being, the Deity

creature *n.* **1** being, °organism, °entity, living thing **2** ***creature comforts.*** (physical *or* bodily *or* material *or* mundane *or* superficial *or* nonspiritual) luxuries

credit *n.* **1** °belief, °faith, °trust, credence **2** creditation, °acknowledgment, °attribution, ascription **3** °trust, °confidence, faithfulness, reliability, trustworthiness, °honesty, °probity, dependability; solvency **4** °honor, commendation, °praise, °tribute, acclaim, °esteem, °recognition, °merit —*v.* **5** °believe, °trust, hold accountable, put *or* place one's faith *or* confidence in, have faith *or* confidence in, °rely on, °accept, depend on *or* upon **6** ascribe, °acknowledge, °attribute, °assign; °impute

creed *n.* °tenet, dogma, °doctrine, credo, teaching, °principles, °belief, set of beliefs

creek *n.* **1** (*in Brit. usage*) inlet, bay, cove, °harbor **2** °(*in US and Canadian usage*) stream, streamlet, °brook, rivulet, rill, runnel, °run, °burn

creep *v.* **1** °crawl, °slither, inch, °squirm, °wriggle, wiggle **2** °crawl, °drag **3** °steal, °sneak; °slink, skulk, tiptoe, *Colloq* °pussyfoot

crescent *n.* **1** demi-lune, semi-lune, lune, lunette —*adj.* **2** crescent-shaped, demilune, semi-lune, biconcave, concavo-concave

crest *n.* **1** °top, °summit, °pinnacle, °peak, °head, °ridge **2** °seal, °device, °figure, badge, °emblem, insigne, °symbol, °design —*v.* **3** °top, °crown, surmount, °cap **4** culminate, °reach, °top, *US* top out

crevasse *n.* °gorge, chasm, °abyss, °ravine, fissure, °crack, °furrow

crevice *n.* °crack, fissure, °chink, cleft, °cranny, °groove, °furrow, °break, °split, °rift

crew *n.* °group, °company, °band, troupe, °party, °gang, °team, °corps, °body

crime *n.* °offense, °violation, °misdeed, °wrong; felony, misdemeanor; lawlessness

criminal *adj.* **1** °illegal, °unlawful, °illicit, °lawless, °dishonest, *Colloq* °crooked **2** °wicked, °evil, °bad, °wrong, °corrupt, °vile, °black, °immoral, amoral, °sinful, °villainous, iniquitous, flagitious, depraved; °disgraceful, reprehensible —*n.* **3** °felon, °convict, lawbreaker, °outlaw, °culprit, °offender, °miscreant, malefactor, wrongdoer, °villain, °scoundrel, knave, blackguard; °gangster, mafioso, desperado, °racketeer; °hoodlum, °thug, hooligan, °tough, ruffian, °terrorist, *Colloq* roughneck, bad guy, black hat, bad hat, baddie *or* baddy, crook; *Slang* hood, *US* mobster

cringe *v.* **1** cower, wince, °flinch, quail, °recoil, blench, °tremble, °quiver, quake *or* shake in one's boots *or* shoes, °shrink **2** °defer, °kowtow, grovel, °crawl, fawn, bootlick, *US* apple-polish; *Slang* kiss someone's *Brit* arse *or US and Canadian* ass, *Taboo slang* brown-nose

cripple *n.* **1** amputee, paralytic —*v.* **2** disable, °lame, °incapacitate, °handicap, °maim; °impair, °damage, °weaken, debilitate, emasculate, °enervate

crippled *adj.* **1** °disabled, °lame, handicapped, incapacitated; weakened, °weak, debilitated **2** damaged, immobilized, inoperative

crisis *n.* **1** turning point, critical time *or* moment **2** °disaster, °emergency, °calamity, °catastrophe, °danger

crisp *adj.* **1** °brittle, crunchy, friable, breakable, crumbly, frangible **2** curly, crispy, crinkly, frizzy, frizzled

critical *adj.* **1** carping, °faultfinding, censorious, disparaging, depreciatory *or* depreciative, depreciating, deprecatory *or* deprecative, deprecating, judgmental **2** °crucial, °important, °essential, °basic, °key, decisive, °pivotal, °vital, °momentous **3** °grave, °serious, °dangerous, °uncertain, °perilous, °severe, touch-and-go, °ticklish, °sensitive, °touchy, *Colloq* °parlous

criticism *n.* **1** °judgment, °evaluation, appraisal, °analysis, assessment, °estimation, valuation **2** censure, °disapproval, condemnation, disparagement **3** critique, °review, commentary

criticize *v.* **1** °judge, °evaluate, value, assess, appraise, °estimate; °discuss, °analyze **2** censure, °find fault (with), °carp (at), °cavil (at), °condemn, °attack, °denounce, °disapprove (of), animadvert on *or* upon, °put down, impugn, °blast, °lambaste, *Colloq* °pan, °knock, *Brit* slate

crooked *adj.* **1** °criminal, °dishonest, °illegal, °unlawful, °illicit, °wrong, °perverse, *Brit slang* °bent **2** °bent, bowed, askew, awry, °deformed, distorted, contorted, °lopsided, twisted, °misshapen, °disfigured, warped, °gnarled

cross *n.* **1** crucifix, rood **2** °hybrid, crossbreed, °mongrel; °blend, °combination —*v.* **3** *cross off or out.* °strike out, °erase, °cancel, °rub out, °delete, °wipe out **4** °meet, intersect, °join **5** cross over, go across, °pass over, °span, °traverse —*adj.* **6** °peevish, irritated, annoyed, piqued, °irritable, °testy, °snappish, irascible, °surly, choleric, splenetic, grouchy, huffish *or* huffy, pettish, °cranky, grumpy, °touchy, °moody, fractious, vexed, curmudgeonly, °petulant, °waspish, °querulous, °cantankerous, crusty, °short-tempered, on a short fuse, °hot-headed, *Colloq* crotchety, *Slang Brit* shirty **7** annoyed, irritated, °angry, irate, °furious

crouch *v.* °bend (down), squat (down), hunker down, °stoop (down)

crowd *n.* **1** °throng, multitude, horde, °swarm, °mass, °press, °flood, °mob, °flock, °pack **2** °company, °set, °circle, °lot, °bunch, °group, coterie, °clique, claque, °faction —*v.* **3** °throng, °swarm, °herd, °pour, °pile, °press, °cluster, °gather, °get together, °flood, °flock, °assemble, congregate **4** °push, °press, °drive, shove, °thrust, °force, °load, °pack, °cram, °jam, corral **5** compress, °squeeze, °pack, °jam, °cram, °collect; °stuff

crown *n.* **1** coronet, diadem, wreath, fillet, circlet, tiara **2** °sovereignty, °rule, °dominion, °authority, °government, °realm, rulership, °jurisdiction **3** °monarch, ruler, °sovereign, potentate; °king, °queen, emperor, empress, His *or* Her Majesty, His *or* Her Highness —*v.* **4** enthrone, *Colloq US* coronate **5** °cap, °top, surmount, culminate, °climax, consummate, °fulfill, °reward

crucial *adj.* °critical, decisive, °pivotal, °vital, °momentous, °major, °important, °essential

crude *adj.* **1** °unrefined, °raw, °natural, °original, unprocessed **2** °rough, unpolished, °rudimentary, °immature, °undeveloped, °primitive, °unrefined, unfinished **3** °rough, °coarse, °rude, °unrefined, uncouth, crass, °gross, °rustic, uncivil **4** °blunt, °brusque, °unsophisticated, °inconsiderate, °tasteless, indelicate, °offensive, °improper, °vulgar

cruel *adj.* **1** °merciless, pitiless, hard-hearted, °harsh, stonyhearted, °heartless, unsparing, °callous, °beastly, °coldblooded, °ruthless, °unkind, °hard **2** °ferocious, °inhuman, barbaric, barbarous, °brutal, °savage, °bloodthirsty, °vicious, °sadistic, °fiendish, diabolical, hellish, °atrocious, Neronian *or* Neronic *or* Neroic

cruise *v.* **1** °sail, °coast, °travel, °journey, voyage; yacht —*n.* **2** °sail, voyage, °journey, boat *or* yachting trip

crumb *n.* °fragment, °morsel, °bite, °scrap, °particle, °shred, snippet, °sliver, °bit, °speck, scintilla, mote, molecule, atom

crumble *v.* °disintegrate, °fragment, break apart, °break up, °shiver, come to pieces

crumple *v.* °wrinkle, °crush, crease, °rumple, °mangle, crinkle

crunch *v.* **1** °chew, °bite, °crush, °grind, °munch —*n.* **2** moment of truth, decision time, °crisis, critical moment, °showdown, crux, °juncture

crusade *n.* **1** °campaign, °expedition, holy war; jihad *or* jehad —*v.* **2** °campaign, °war, °battle; take up a cause, °lobby, °fight

crush *n.* **1** °break, smash, °crunch, °pulverize, °shiver, °splinter, °pound, °grind **2** °crumple, °wrinkle, crease, crinkle, °rumple, °mangle **3** squash, °pulp, mash, °squeeze, compress, °press **4** °overcome, °defeat, °conquer, vanquish, °beat, thrash; °subdue, °put down, °quash, °quell, °overwhelm, °squelch, °suppress, °repress **5** abash, °embarrass, °shame, °mortify, °depress, °devastate, °humiliate, °disgrace —*n.* **6** °press, °pressure, °crowd

cry *v.* **1** °weep, °sob, wail, °keen, °bawl, shed tears **2** whimper, °snivel, pule, mewl, whine, °moan, °groan, °fret, *Colloq* turn on the waterworks, *Brit* grizzle **3** *cry out for.* °demand, °need, °call for, beg for, °plead for —*n.* **4** °scream, °shriek, wail, °howl, yowl **5** °shout, °whoop, °yell, °howl **6** °call, °sound, °note **7** war cry, battle cry, °slogan, watchword **8** *a far cry.* a long way, quite a distance, °remote, °distant, very different; not, not quite

crypt *n.* °tomb, vault, mausoleum, °sepulcher, °grave, catacomb; °cellar, basement

cryptic *adj.* **1** °secret, °occult, °mystical, °hidden, esoteric, mystic, cabalistic **2** °obscure, °mysterious, unclear, °nebulous, °vague, inscrutable, °recondite, arcane, enigmatic, °puzzling

cuddle *v.* **1** snuggle up (to), nestle *or* huddle (against) **2** °caress, °embrace, °fondle, °hug, °pet, bill and coo, make love (to), *Colloq* neck, smooch, *Australian and New Zealand* smoodge *or* smooge, *Slang US* °make out (with), watch the submarine races —*n.* **3** °hug, °embrace, °snuggle

cue *n.* **1** °prompt, °hint, °reminder, °signal, °sign —*v.* **2** °signal, °prompt, °remind

culprit *n.* **1** accused, °prisoner **2** °offender, °criminal, malefactor, wrongdoer

cultivate *v.* **1** °till, °plow, °farm, °work **2** °grow, °raise, °tend, °produce **3** °develop, °promote, °further, °encourage, °foster, °advance **4** woo, make advances to, ingratiate oneself with, court, pay court to, curry favor with, *Colloq* °work on, *Slang* suck up to, butter up, *US* shine up to; *Taboo slang* brown-nose

cultivated *adj.* °sophisticated, cultured, °educated, °refined, °elegant, soigné(e), civilized, °polished, aristocratic, urbane, °suave, cosmopolitan

culture *n.* **1** cultivation, °refinement, °sophistication, urbanity, suavity, °elegance, °(good) breeding, °background, erudition, °education, enlightenment, °learning, °taste, °discrimination, °savoir-faire, °savoir-vivre, discernment **2** °civilization, mores, °customs, life-style, way of life, (sense of) values

curb *n.* **1** °check, °restraint, °control —*v.* **2** °check, °restrain, °bridle, °control, °contain, °repress, °subdue, °suppress

cure *n.* **1** course of treatment, °therapy, °remedy, medication, medicament, °medicine, °drug, °prescription; cure-all, nostrum, panacea —*v.* **2** °heal, °mend, restore to health *or* working order, °remedy, °rectify, °correct, °repair, °fix **3** smoke, pickle, °dry, °salt, °preserve, corn, marinate

curiosity *n.* **1** inquisitiveness, °interest **2** snooping, prying, peeping, intrusiveness, meddlesomeness, °interference, *Colloq* nosiness, Nosy Parkerism **3** curio, °oddity, °rarity, conversation piece, *objet de virtu* or *vertu*, *objet d'art*, found object; bric-a-brac *or* bric-à-brac, knickknack, °bauble, trinket, °gewgaw

curious *adj.* **1** °inquisitive, inquiring, °interested **2** snooping, prying, °intrusive, meddlesome, interfering, *Colloq* °nosy **3** °odd, °peculiar, °eccentric, °strange, °outré, °queer, °unusual, °outrageous, °offbeat, °weird, °bizarre, unconventional, freakish, °exotic, °singular, °out of the ordinary, °extraordinary, °erratic, pixilated, °quaint, °outlandish, °grotesque, aberrant, °abnormal, °singular, °irregular, °deviant, °deviate, *Colloq* °kinky, nuts, nutty; *Slang Brit* barmy

current *adj.* **1** °contemporary, °ongoing, °present, contemporaneous, °simultaneous, coeval **2** °prevalent, °prevailing, °common, °popular, accepted, known, widespread, reported, in circulation, going round *or* around, bruited about, widely known, in the air, present-day **3** °fashionable, °stylish, à la mode, modish, in vogue, °latest, up-to-date, *Colloq* °trendy **4** *US* °up to date, in the know, °informed, advised, in touch, °aware, posted, *au courant, au fait,* on the qui vive —*n.* **5** °stream, °flow, °undercurrent **6** °course, °progress, °tendency, °tenor, °drift, °trend, °inclination, mainstream

curse *n.* **1** malediction, imprecation, denunciation, damnation, execration, °oath **2** °evil, bane, °misfortune, °affliction, °torment, °harm, °scourge, cross to bear, hex, *Colloq* °jinx **3** °profanity, °oath, blasphemy, obscenity, bad language, dirty word, swearword, curse word —*v.* **4** °damn, execrate, °blast, °denounce, anathematize, excommunicate **5** swear at, blaspheme at **6** °burden, saddle, °weigh down, °handicap

cursory *adj.* °superficial, °hasty, °hurried, °passing, °quick, slapdash, °perfunctory, °rapid, °summary

curt *adj.* °abrupt, °short, °terse, °brief, laconic, °concise; °blunt, °gruff, °harsh, °brusque, unceremonious, °snappish, °rude, crusty

curtail *v.* °shorten, °abbreviate, °cut short, °abridge, °diminish, °reduce, °cut, °cut back, °cut down

cushion *n.* **1** pillow, °bolster, °pad —*v.* **2** °soften, absorb, °mitigate, °reduce, buffer, °insulate, mollify, lessen

custody *n.* **1** °care, custodianship, °safekeeping, °protection, °charge, guardianship, keeping **2** °imprisonment, °detention, incarceration, confinement

custom *n.* **1** °practice, °habit, °usage, °fashion, °way, wont, °tradition, °routine, °convention, °form **2** ***customs.*** °toll, °duty, impost, °tax, excise, levy, °dues, °tariff **3** °patronage, °support, °business, °trade —*adv.* **4** °specially, °especially, °expressly, exclusively, °particularly; to order

customary *adj.* **1** °usual, °normal, °conventional, °routine, °everyday, °common, commonplace, °ordinary **2** °accustomed, °habitual, °regular, °traditional, wonted

customer *n.* **1** °client, °patron, °buyer, purchaser; consumer **2** °chap, °fellow, °character, °person, °guy, *Colloq Brit* bloke

cut *v.* **1** °gash, °slash, °slit; °open **2** °slice, °cut off, °carve **3** Often, ***cut up.*** °hurt, °wound, °pain, °upset, °grieve, °distress, aggrieve, °slight, °insult, °offend, affront **4** °trim, °snip, °lop, °clip, crop, °shorten, shear, °chop off; °mow; °dock **5** °abbreviate, °shorten, crop, condense, °abridge, °edit, °cut back, °reduce, °cut down; epitomize, °abstract, °digest, summarize, °curtail **6** °dilute, °thin, °water (down), °weaken; °degrade, °adulterate **7** °avoid, fail to attend, eschew **8** °lower, °reduce, lessen, °cut back (on), °cut down (on), °slash, °diminish, °decrease, retrench (on), °curtail **9** conclude, °settle, °agree **10** °prepare, °draw, °write, °sign **11** ***cut back.*** **(a)** See **5,** above. **(b)** See **8,** above. **12** Often, ***cut dead.*** snub, °slight, °spurn, °shun, °ignore, give the cold shoulder (to) **13** ***cut down.*** **(a)** °fell, chop *or* hew down **(b)** °kill, °cut off, °murder, assassinate **14** ***cut in.*** °interrupt, °intrude, °interfere, *Colloq* °butt in **15** ***cut off.*** **(a)** °cleave, °sever, chop *or* lop *or* hack off **(b)** °intercept, °interrupt, °discontinue, °end, °stop, °terminate, °break off **(c)** °separate, °sever, °split, estrange **(d)** disinherit, disown, °reject **16** ***cut out.*** **(a)** °delete, °remove, excise, strike *or* cross out, °edit out, °omit, °cut, °kill, *Technical* dele **(b)** °extract, excise, °remove, resect **(c)** °stop, °cease, desist (from), °quit **(d)** °suit, °equip, °fit **(e)** °plan, °prepare, °ready, °organize, °destine **17** ***cut up.*** **(a)** °chop (up), dice, cube, mince, °cut, °divide (up), °carve (up)

(b) °misbehave **18** ***cut up rough.*** get angry, lose one's temper, show resentment —*n.* **19** °gash, °slash, °incision, °nick, °wound **20** °share, °portion, °percentage, °piece, dividend, commission **21** reduction, cutback, curtailment, °decrease **22** deletion, excision, °omission **23** affront, °insult, °offense, °slight, snub, °dig, jibe, °slap in the face, cold shoulder **24** °engraving, °plate **25** artwork, °picture, °illustration, °plate, °drawing, line cut, line engraving, halftone —*adj.* **26** separated, °detached, severed **27** abridged, °abbreviated, cut-down, shortened, edited, curtailed **28** reduced, diminished, lowered, discounted **29** ***cut and dried.*** **(a)** clearcut, settled, arranged, °decided, °predetermined, prearranged **(b)** °stale, unoriginal, trite, hackneyed, °old; °dull, °boring **(c)** manufactured, °automatic, unchanging, unchanged

cute *adj.* **1** °pretty, °attractive, °adorable, °dainty, °lovely, °beautiful, *Colloq US* cunning **2** °clever, °shrewd, °ingenious, adroit, °crafty, cunning

cutthroat *n.* **1** °murderer, °pirate, °killer, °thug, hatchet man, gunman, assassin, *Slang US* gunsel, torpedo, hit man —*adj.* **2** °merciless, °ruthless, °unmerciful, unprincipled, °relentless, pitiless, °brutal, °coldblooded, °coldhearted **3** °murderous, °homicidal, °lethal, °deadly, barbaric, °fierce, °cruel, barbarous, °savage, °inhuman, °brutal, brutish, °violent, °ferocious, °bloodthirsty, °sanguinary, bloody, feral, °vicious, °truculent

cutting *adj.* **1** °severe, °biting, °chill, °cold, °icy, °frigid, °freezing, °raw, °piercing, °penetrating **2** °sarcastic, °sardonic, °bitter, °scornful, sneering, acid, °scathing, acerb(ic), wounding, °stern, °harsh, °caustic, mordant, acrimonious, °contemptuous; malevolent, malicious, invidious, °vicious, °venomous —*n.* **3** scion, °slip, clipping

cycle *n.* **1** °round, rotation, °circle, °course; series, °sequence, °run, °succession, °pattern —*v.* **2** °recur, °return, °rotate, recycle, °circle

D

dab *v.* **1** daub, °pat, °tap, tamp, °touch —*n.* **2** °touch, °drop, °trace, °bit, mite, °hint, °suggestion, °pinch, °dash, °spot, tinge, *Colloq* dollop, smidgen **3** daub, °poke, °pat, °tap, °touch

dabble *v.* **1** °dip, °splash, °spatter, sprinkle, bespatter, besprinkle, bedabble **2** ***dabble in or with or at.*** °tinker, °trifle (with), putter *or Brit* potter, dally, *Colloq* fool (around *or* about *or* with *or* about with)

dab hand *n. phr.* past master, °expert, °master, °adept, °authority, wizard, *Colloq* ace

daft *adj.* **1** °foolish, °silly, °giddy, °senseless, °absurd, °ridiculous, °stupid, °nonsensical, fatuous, fatuitous, imbecile *or* imbecilic, idiotic, moronic, °obtuse, cretinous, boneheaded, fatheaded, dimwitted, witless, asinine, attocerebral, weak-minded, simpleminded, brainless, °feebleminded, featherbrained, rattlebrained, °harebrained, slow-witted, °half-witted, fatwitted, addlepated, addlebrained, *Brit* gormless, *Colloq* °dumb, dopey *or* dopy, daffy; *Slang* cockeyed, *US* cockamamie *or* cockamamy, running on empty **2** See **crazy, 1,** above. **3** ***daft about.*** °mad about, infatuated with, besotted by *or* with, °sweet on, *Colloq* nuts about, crazy about

dagger *n.* °knife, poniard, skean, short sword, stiletto, dirk, °blade, kris, bowie knife, bayonet

daily *adj.* **1** °diurnal, circadian, °everyday, quotidian **2** °ordinary, °common, commonplace, °everyday, °routine, °regular —*adv.* **3** constantly, °always, habitually, day after day, regularly, every day, continually, continuously

dainty *adj.* **1** °delicate, °graceful, °fine, °elegant, °exquisite, °neat **2** °fastidious, °sensitive, °squeamish, finicky *or* finical, overnice, overrefined, °genteel, °mincing **3** °choice, °delicious, delectable, °tasty, appetizing, palatable, toothsome —*n.* **4** °delicacy, sweetmeat, °treat, comfit, tidbit *or Brit* titbit, °morsel

damage *n.* **1** °harm, °injury, °hurt, °impairment, mutilation, °destruction, devastation **2** °expense, °price, °cost; °bill, invoice, *US* °check **3** ***damages.*** compensation, reparation, °indemnity —*v.* **4** °harm, °hurt, °injure; °wound; °mutilate, disfigure, °mar, °deface; °wreck, °ruin, °spoil, °impair

damn *v.* **1** °condemn, °criticize, find fault with, °berate, °castigate, °upbraid, °attack, °blast, °reprimand, °reprove, remonstrate, °denounce; °blame **2** °doom, °condemn, °sentence **3** °curse (at), °swear (at), execrate —*n.* **4** jot or tittle, brass farthing, *Slang* hoot, two hoots (in hell), tinker's damn *or* cuss **5** ***give a damn.*** °care, °mind, be concerned, °worry, *Slang* give a hoot

damnable *adj.* °awful, °terrible, °horrible, horrid, °atrocious, °abominable, °dreadful, °hideous, execrable, accursed, cursed, detestable, °hateful, °abhorrent, °despicable, °loathsome, °wicked, °sinful, °offensive, heinous, pernicious, °infernal, malicious, malevolent, °outrageous, °foul, °rotten, °base, °vile, odious

damp *adj.* **1** °clammy, °moist, wettish; °humid, dank, °misty, dewy, °steamy, °muggy —*n.* **2** moistness, moisture, dampness, clamminess, humidity

dampen *v.* **1** °damp, moisten, sprinkle, bedew **2** °stifle, °deaden, °damp, °check, °chill, °cool, °restrain, °retard, lessen, °diminish, °reduce, °suppress, abate, °moderate, allay, °subdue, °temper, °dull, °discourage

dance *v.* **1** °cavort, gambol, °caper, °skip, °leap, romp, trip the light fantastic (toe), *US* cut a rug, sashay, *Colloq* bop, hoof it —*n.* **2** ball, °social, dancing party, *thé dansant, US* tea dance, °promenade, *Colloq* shindig *or* shindy, °hop, bop, *US and Canadian* prom

dandy *n.* **1** fop, coxcomb, °(gay) blade, beau, °gallant, lady-killer, ladies' *or* lady's man, °rake, *Colloq* °swell, clotheshorse, *Brit* toff, blood, *US* °dude —*adj.* **2** °fine, °splendid, °first-rate, °great, °marvelous, °neat, spectacular

danger *n.* **1** °peril, °risk, °threat, °hazard, °jeopardy **2** ***in danger of.*** °likely (to be), °liable (to be)

dangerous *adj.* **1** °risky, °perilous, °hazardous, unsafe, °precarious, °rickety, *Colloq* chancy, iffy **2** °threatening, °menacing, °harmful, treacherous

dangerously *adv.* **1** perilously, hazardously, unsafely, precariously, recklessly **2** ominously, alarmingly

dangle *v.* **1** °hang (down), °droop, °depend, °swing, °sway **2** °flaunt, brandish, °wave, °flourish **3** °wait, *Slang* cool one's heels

dapper *adj.* °neat, °spruce, °smart, °trim, well-dressed, well-turned-out, °stylish, °fashionable, °elegant, °chic, °dressy; *Colloq* got up *or* dressed to the nines, dressed to kill, swanky *or* swank, ritzy; *Slang* snazzy, °nifty, °sharp, °swell, classy, *US and Canadian* spiffy

dapple *adj.* **1** spotted, dotted, °mottled, °speckled, °flecked, dappled; brindled; pied, piebald, skewbald, °paint, fleabitten, *US* pinto —*v.* **2** °spot, °dot, mottle, speckle, bespeckle, stipple

dare *v.* **1** °challenge, °defy, °provoke; throw down the gauntlet **2** °risk, °hazard, °gamble, °venture, °face, make bold, be so bold as —*n.* **3** °challenge, °provocation, °taunt; °ultimatum

daredevil *n.* **1** exhibitionist, °showman, stuntman, stuntwoman; °adventurer, soldier of fortune, *Colloq* °showoff —*adj.* **2** °reckless, °rash, death-defying, °impulsive, °daring, °dashing, °impetuous, incautious, °imprudent, °wild, °foolhardy, madcap, devil-may-care; °audacious, °bold, °brave, °fearless, °gallant, °courageous, °intrepid

daring *n.* **1** °courage, boldness, °bravery, valor, intrepidity, fearlessness, °grit, °pluck, °spirit, mettle, adventurousness, derring-do, *Colloq* °guts, °spunk, °nerve; *Slang Brit* °bottle —*adj.* **2** °bold, °audacious, °courageous, °brave, valorous, °intrepid, °fearless, unafraid, plucky, mettlesome, °adventurous, °venturesome, °hardy; °rash, °reckless, *Colloq* gutsy, *US* nervy

dark *adj.* **1** unlit, unlighted, unilluminated, ill-lighted, ill-lit, °sunless; °black, stygian, pitch-dark, inky, jet-black **2** °dim, °murky, tenebrous, °shady, °shadowy **3** °gloomy, °dismal, °dreary, °dull, °drab, subfuscous, subfusc, °bleak, cheerless, °mournful, °dour, °pessimistic, °somber, °doleful, °joyless, °grim, °sad, °melancholy, °sorrowful **4** °evil, °wicked, °vile, °base, °foul, iniquitous, nefarious, blackhearted, °villainous, °sinister, °satanic, °devilish, hellish **5** °murky, °overcast, cloudy, °threatening, °black, °dusky, lowering *or* louring; foggy, °misty; *US* glowering **6** °mysterious, °deep, °profound, °incomprehensible, enigmatic, °puzzling, impenetrable, unfathomable, abstruse, °recondite, arcane, °obscure **7** °hidden, concealed, °secret, °occult, mystic(al), °cryptic **8** brunette; °black, °swarthy, brown; (sun-) tanned, *Old-fashioned* swart **9** °ignorant, unenlightened, °benighted —*n.* **10** °night, nighttime, nightfall **11** darkness, blackness, °gloom, gloominess, murk, murkiness **12** °obscurity, °ignorance

darling *n.* **1** °sweetheart, °beloved, °love, °dear, dearest, truelove **2** °pet, °favorite, apple of (someone's) eye, *Brit* blue-eyed boy; *US* fair-haired boy —*adj.* **3** °beloved, loved, cherished, adored, °dear, °precious, treasured **4** °pleasing, °fetching, °attractive, °adorable, °enchanting, °lovely, alluring, °engaging, bewitching, charming

dash *v.* **1** °crash, smash, °shatter, °break °shiver, °fragment, °split; °destroy, °ruin, °spoil, °frustrate, °obliterate **2** °hurl, °toss, °throw, °fling, °cast, °pitch, *Colloq* chuck **3** °rush, °run, dart, °spring, °bolt, °bound, °race, sprint; °hasten, °fly, °hurry, °speed **4** ***dash off.*** scribble —*n.* **5** dart, °bolt, °rush, °run, °spurt, °spring, °bound, sprint **6** °flourish, élan, °flair, liveliness, °style, °panache, °spirit, brio, °verve, °zest, °spice; °ardor, °fervor, °vigor, °energy **7** °bit, °pinch, soupçon, °hint, °suggestion, °touch, °trace, tinge, °taste, °drop, °piece, *Colloq* smidgen, *US* tad

dashing *adj.* **1** °spirited, °lively, °impetuous, °energetic, °vigorous, °dynamic, °animated, *Colloq* peppy **2** °fashionable, °stylish, °chic, à la mode, modish, °smart, °elegant, °dapper, *Colloq Brit* °swish **3** °flamboyant, °showy, °ostentatious, °pretentious

data *n.* °facts, °information, statistics, figures, °details, °matter, observations, material(s); °text; °evidence

date *n.* **1** °time, year, °season, °period, °day; °age, °era, epoch, °stage, °phase **2** °appointment, °meeting, °engagement, rendezvous, assignation, tryst; °fixture **3** °escort, °companion, °friend, boyfriend, girlfriend, °girl, °woman, °boy, °man, swain, beau, °lover, *Colloq* °steady **4** ***out of date.*** °old-fashioned, °old, °ancient, archaic, °antiquated, dated, °passé, outmoded, °obsolete, °obsolescent, *Colloq* old hat **5** ***up to date.*** °modern, °latest, °current, °contemporary, à la mode, °fashionable, *Colloq* °trendy —*v.* **6** show one's age, make obsolete *or* obsolescent *or* old-fashioned **7** °entertain, °escort, °go out (with), °go steady (with)

daunt *v.* °intimidate, cow, °discourage, dishearten, dispirit, °unnerve, °shake, °upset, disconcert, °discomfit, °put off, awe, °overawe, °appall, °alarm, °threaten, °frighten, °terrify, °scare, terrorize

dauntless *adj.* °fearless, undaunted, unafraid, unflinching, °stalwart, °brave, °courageous, °bold, °audacious, °intrepid, valorous, °daring, °gallant, °heroic, °venturesome, plucky, stouthearted, valiant

dawdle *v.* °linger, loiter, °straggle, °delay, °procrastinate, dally, °lounge, laze, °idle, °lag, lie about, waste time, *Colloq* dillydally, °shilly-shally

dawn *n.* **1** daybreak, sunrise, break of day, crack of dawn, first light, dawning, cockcrow *or* cockcrowing, *Literary* aurora, dayspring, *US* sunup **2** dawning, °beginning, commencement, °start, °birth, awakening, inception, genesis, °outset, °onset, °origin, °appearance, °arrival, advent, °emergence, inauguration, °rise, first occurrence —*v.* **3** °gleam, °break, °brighten, °lighten **4** °begin, °originate, °commence, °arise, °appear, °emerge, °start, °arrive, °develop, °unfold **5** ***dawn on or upon.*** °occur to, come to mind, become apparent *or* evident to

day *n.* **1** daytime, °daylight, broad daylight, light of day **2** °time, hour, °age, °period, °era, epoch, °date, °prime, heyday; lifetime

daydream *n.* **1** °reverie, woolgathering, °fantasy, °fancy, °dream, musing, castle in the air *or* in Spain, pipe dream —*v.* **2** °fantasize, °imagine, °fancy, °envision, °dream

daylight *n.* **1** sunlight, °sun, sunshine, °light **2** °open, broad daylight, light of day, full view, full knowledge, °clarity

daze *v.* **1** °stun, stupefy, °blind, °dazzle, bedazzle, °shock, °stagger, °startle, °astonish, °astound, °amaze, °surprise, °overcome, °overpower, °dumbfound, benumb, °paralyze, *Colloq* bowl over, °floor, flabbergast; *Slang* blow one's mind **2** befuddle, °confuse, °bemuse, °bewilder, °puzzle, °mystify, baffle, °perplex, °nonplus, °blind —*n.* **3** °confusion, °flurry, °spin, whirl **4** ***in a daze.*** stupefied, in a trance, bewildered, °confused, perplexed, disoriented, °dizzy, dazzled, bedazzled, °overcome, overpowered, nonplussed, befuddled, flustered; startled, surprised, shocked, stunned, astonished, astounded, amazed, staggered; bemused, baffled, puzzled, mystified, *Colloq* flabbergasted, bowled over, floored

dazzle *v.* **1** °impress, °bewitch, °enchant, °charm, °beguile, °intrigue, °captivate, °fascinate, spellbind, °entrance, °hypnotize, mesmerize **2** See **daze, 1,** above. —*n.* **3** °brilliance, °splendor, magnificence, °sparkle, °glitter, *Slang* razzle-dazzle, razzmatazz

dazzling *adj.* °bright, °brilliant, resplendent, blinding, bedazzling, °radiant, °splendid, °magnificent, °glorious, sparkling, °scintillating; °stunning, °overwhelming, °overpowering, stupefying, dizzying; °gorgeous; *Colloq* splendiferous, mind-boggling

dead *adj.* **1** deceased, °defunct, °extinct, gone, departed, °late, °lifeless, no more, *Colloq* done for, *Slang* pushing up daisies, *Brit* gone for a burton **2** insensate, °insensible, °numb, paralyzed, benumbed, unfeeling **3** °insensible, °unconscious, °out, dead to the world, deathlike, deathly **4** insensitive, unemotional, unfeeling, emotionless, apathetic, °lukewarm, °cool, °cold, °frigid, unresponsive, °unsympathetic, °indifferent, unconcerned, uninterested; °numb, °wooden, °callous, hardened, impervious, inured, °inert **5** °out, smothered, extinguished **6** °inanimate, °lifeless, °inert, inorganic **7** °extinct, °obsolete, perished, °past, outmoded, °disused, expired, °passé **8** °barren, unfruitful, °infertile, unproductive **9** °tired (out), °exhausted, worn-out, °fatigued, °spent, collapsing, in a state of collapse, *Slang* bushed, °beat, *Brit* knackered, *US and Canadian* pooped **10** °dull, lusterless, °flat, °neutral, °vapid, °empty, °bland, °colorless, °gray, beige, °dun **11** °stagnant, motionless, °still, °standing, °static, °inert, unmoving, °inactive, °quiet, °calm **12** °boring, °dull, °tedious, °tiresome, °monotonous, °prosaic, uninteresting, °run-of-the-mill, °ordinary, commonplace, °dry, insipid, °bland, °flat, two-dimensional, °lifeless, °stiff, °rigid, °stony **13** °dull, muffled, deadened, anechoic, unresounding, nonresonant **14** °complete, °entire, °total, °absolute, °downright, °thorough, through and through, utter, all-out, °out-and-out, °unqualified, unrelieved, unbroken, °categorical, °outright **15** °profound, °deep **16** °sudden, °abrupt, °complete, °full **17** °certain, °sure, unerring, °exact, °precise, °accurate, °crack —*adv.* **18** °completely, °entirely, °absolutely, °totally, °utterly, categorically, °thoroughly, unconditionally, unqualifiedly **19** °completely, °entirely, °absolutely, °totally; abruptly, °suddenly **20** °directly, °exactly, °precisely —*n.* **21** depth(s), °extreme, °midst, °middle

deaden *v.* **1** °numb, benumb, °paralyze, anesthetize, desensitize, °dull; °damp **2** °weaken, °moderate, soothe, °mitigate, assuage, °reduce, lessen, °diminish, alleviate, °cushion, °soften, mollify, °blunt, °dull

deadlock *n.* **1** °standstill, °impasse, °stalemate, standoff, °draw, stoppage, *Colloq US* Mexican standoff —*v.* **2** bring *or* come to a standstill *or* impasse, °stall, °stop, °halt

deadly *adj.* **1** °lethal, °fatal; °dangerous, pernicious, °poisonous, noxious, toxic; baleful, °harmful, nocuous **2** °mortal, °implacable, °ruthless, °savage **3** °murderous, °homicidal, °bloodthirsty, °brutal, °vicious, °ferocious, barbarous, barbaric, °savage, °inhuman, °coldblooded, °heartless, °ruthless, pitiless, °merciless **4** deathly, deathlike, °pale, pallid, °ghostly, cadaverous, °ghastly, °wan, °white, livid, ashen **5** °boring, °excruciating, °dull, °tiresome, °tedious, °dreary, °humdrum, °lackluster, wearying, wearisome **6** °exact, °precise, °accurate, °true, unerring, unfailing

deaf *adj.* 1 hard of hearing, stone-deaf 2 unhearing, unheedful, °heedless, °insensible, insensitive, impervious, °indifferent, °oblivious, unresponsive, °unmoved, unconcerned, unyielding

deal *v.* 1 °distribute, dole out, °give out, °parcel out, mete out, °allot, apportion, °administer, °dispense 2 buy and sell, °handle, °stock, do business, °trade, °traffic 3 °behave, °act, °conduct oneself 4 ***deal with.*** °treat, °handle, °take care of, have to do with, °attend to, °see to, °reckon with, °grapple with, act on; °practice, °administer, °engage in —*n.* 5 °transaction, °arrangement, °negotiation, °agreement, °contract, °bargain, °understanding 6 Often, ***great deal.*** (large *or* great) amount, °lot, (large *or* huge) quantity; °extent

dealer *n.* °trader, businessman, businesswoman, °merchant, °tradesman, retailer, shopkeeper, vendor, merchandiser; wholesaler, jobber, distributor, stockist, supplier; °broker, °agent, salesman, *US* storekeeper

dealings *n. pl.* °business, °commerce, °exchange, °trade, °traffic, °transactions, negotiations; °relations, relationships, affairs

dear *adj.* 1 °beloved, loved, adored, °darling, °precious, cherished, prized, valued, treasured, °favored, °favorite, °pet, esteemed, admired, venerated, honored 2 °expensive, costly, high-priced, highly priced, *Colloq* °pricey —*n.* 3 °darling, °sweetheart, °beloved, °love, truelove, °sweet, honey, °precious, °pet, °favorite, °treasure, °precious, *Colloq* sweetie, sweetiepie, *Slang* °baby —*adv.* 4 °dearly; at great cost *or* expense, at a high *or* excessive price

dearly *adv.* 1 greatly, very much, °indeed, °sincerely 2 affectionately, °fondly, lovingly, tenderly 3 expensively, °dear, at great cost *or* expense, at a high *or* excessive price, punitively

dearth *n.* °scarcity, °want, °need, °lack, deficiency, sparseness *or* sparsity, scantiness, insufficiency, inadequacy, °shortage, paucity, exiguity, °poverty, exiguousness; °absence

death *n.* 1 demise, decease, °passing, °dying, °end 2 °end, °termination, cessation, °expiration, expiry 3 °end, °finish, °termination; extinction, °destruction, extermination, annihilation, eradication, obliteration, extirpation, liquidation, °ruin, °downfall, °undoing

deathless *adj.* °eternal, °everlasting, °immortal, undying, imperishable, °permanent, unending, °timeless, never-ending

debase *v.* 1 °lower, °degrade, devalue, °depreciate, °depress, demote, deprecate, °belittle, °diminish, °reduce, °disparage 2 °adulterate, °contaminate, °taint, °pollute, °corrupt, °mar, °spoil, °impair, °vitiate, abase, defile, bastardize; °poison

debatable *adj.* °controversial, arguable, °questionable, °doubtful, dubious, problematic *or* problematical, °disputable, open *or* subject to dispute *or* doubt *or* question, in dispute *or* doubt *or* question, °moot, polemic *or* polemical, unsure, °uncertain, °unsettled, undecided

debate *n.* 1 °discussion, °argument, °dispute, altercation, °controversy, wrangle, contention, polemic; argumentation 2 deliberation, °consideration, °(careful) thought, °reflection, cogitation, meditation, contemplation —*v.* 3 °argue, wrangle, °dispute, °contest, contend; °discuss, °moot, °question 4 °deliberate, °consider, °reflect (on), mull over, °ponder (over), °weigh, ruminate (over), meditate (on *or* over), think (over *or* on), think through

debonair *adj.* 1 °suave, soigné(e), °elegant, urbane, °refined, °dapper, °genteel, °well-bred, °courteous, °civil, mannerly, °gracious, °polite, affable, °obliging, °pleasant, *Colloq* °smooth 2 °carefree, insouciant, °gay, °nonchalant, lighthearted, °dashing, charming, °cheerful, °buoyant, °jaunty, °sprightly

debt *n.* 1 °obligation; °due, indebtedness, °liability, °responsibility, °accountability, °encumbrance 2 ***in debt.*** under obligation, owing, °accountable, °beholden, °indebted, °responsible, answerable for, °liable, encumbered, in arrears, °straitened, in dire straits, in (financial) difficulty *or* difficulties, in the red, *Colloq US and Canadian* in hock

debut *n.* 1 °première, introduction, °initiation, inauguration, launch *or* launching, coming out —*v.* 2 °launch, °come out, °enter, °appear

decadent *adj.* 1 declining, decaying, deteriorating, debased, degenerating, falling off, °on the wane, °withering, degenerative 2 °corrupt, °dissolute, °immoral, debauched, dissipated, °self-indulgent, °degenerate

decay *v.* 1 (a) decline, wane, ebb, dwindle, diminish, decrease (b) °decline, °waste away, atrophy, °weaken, wither, °degenerate, °deteriorate, °disintegrate; °crumble 2 °rot, °decompose, molder, °putrefy, °spoil; °turn, go bad, °go off —*n.* 3 °decline, weakening, °failing, fading, deterioration, decadence, degeneration, wasting, atrophy, dilapidation, disintegration, °collapse; °downfall 4 °rot, rotting, decomposition, °mold, putrefaction, mortification

deceit *n.* 1 °deception, deceitfulness, °fraud, fraudulence, cheating, °trickery, chicanery *or* chicane, °dissimulation, dishonesty, misrepresentation, double-dealing, duplicity, °hypocrisy, treachery, underhandedness, guile, °craft, slyness, craftiness, cunning, knavery, funny business, *Colloq* °hanky-panky, monkey business 2 °trick, °subterfuge, °stratagem, ploy, °ruse, maneuver, °artifice, °wile, °hoax, °swindle, °double-cross, misrepresentation, °pretense, °sham, contrivance, °shift, confidence trick, subreption, gloze, *Dialectal Brit and colloq US* flam; *Colloq* flimflam; *Slang* scam, con, con trick, con game

deceitful *adj.* °dishonest, underhand(ed), untrustworthy, misleading, °crooked, °insincere, °false, °fraudulent, °counterfeit, °disingenuous, °lying, mendacious, untruthful; °wily, °crafty, °sly, cunning, °scheming, guileful, °artful, °sneaky, double-dealing, °two-faced, °hypocritical, duplicitous, *Colloq* phoney *or US also* phony

deceive *v.* °mislead, delude, impose on *or* upon, °fool, °hoax, °trick, °cheat, °swindle, °betray, °double-cross, °lead on, lead up *or* down the garden path, °lead astray, pull the wool over (someone's) eyes, inveigle, °cajole, *Archaic* cozen; *Colloq* con, bamboozle, °take in, °take for a ride, two-time, move the goal posts; *Slang US* °take

decent *adj.* **1** °becoming, °suitable, °appropriate, °proper, °seemly, °fitting **2** °seemly, °decorous, °tasteful, °dignified, mannerly, °nice, °clean, °respectable, °polite, °modest, °presentable, °acceptable **3** °adequate, °acceptable, °passable, °fair, °competent, °mediocre, middling, fair to middling, °moderate, °respectable, not bad, °ordinary, °so-so, not outstanding, unimpressive, °average, neither here nor there, all right, °reasonable, °tolerable, °satisfactory, good enough, *Colloq* OK *or* okay **4** °courteous, °proper, °right, °fair, °honest, °honorable, °friendly, °considerate, °gracious, °nice, °thoughtful, °obliging, °kind, °generous, °accommodating **5** °chaste, °pure, °virtuous, °modest, °well-bred, °decorous, well-brought-up, °respectable, °nice

deception *n.* **1** duplicity, °deceit, °intrigue, °hypocrisy, °fraud, cheating, °trickery, chicanery *or* chicane, °dissimulation, double-dealing, °subterfuge, sophistry, treachery, knavery, tergiversation **2** °trick, °ruse, °artifice, °stratagem, °subterfuge, °maneuver, °wile, imposture, °hoax, °sham, °pretense

deceptive *adj.* **1** misleading, °false, °illusory, deceiving, °unreliable **2** °fraudulent, °deceitful, °dishonest, untruthful, °fake, °false, °shifty, fallacious, °specious, °spurious, °bogus, °counterfeit, pseudo, sophistical; °tricky, °dodgy, °evasive, °elusive, °slippery, *Colloq* phoney *or US also* phony

decide *v.* **1** °determine, °settle, °resolve, conclude, take *or* reach *or* come to a decision, reach *or* come to a conclusion, make up one's mind, arbitrate, °judge, adjudicate, referee, °umpire **2** ***decide on or upon.*** fix *or* fasten *or* settle on *or* upon, °choose, °select, °pick (out), °elect, opt (for), °commit oneself (to)

decided *adj.* **1** °definite, °pronounced, °marked, unmistakable, unambiguous, unequivocal, °certain, °sure, °absolute, °obvious, °clear, °evident, °unquestionable, unquestioned, °indisputable, °undisputed, undeniable, irrefutable, incontestable, °unqualified, unconditional, °incontrovertible, °solid **2** °fixed, °firm, °resolute, °determined, adamant(ine), °stony, °unhesitating, decisive, °definite, unfaltering, °assertive, asseverative, unswerving, unwavering

decipher *v.* **1** decode, decrypt; unravel, unscramble, disentangle, °translate, °work out, °explain, °solve, *Colloq* °figure out **2** °read, °interpret, °make out, *Colloq* °figure out

decision *n.* **1** °settlement, °determination, °resolution, settling, resolving, arbitration **2** °judgment, conclusion, °resolution, verdict, °sentence, ruling, °finding, °decree, °settlement, °outcome **3** °determination, firmness, decidedness, °resolve, decisiveness, conclusiveness, steadfastness, °purpose, purposefulness

declaration *n.* **1** °statement, °assertion, attestation, deposition, asseveration, affirmation, avowal, °announcement, °proclamation, °pronouncement, °profession **2** °proclamation, °announcement, °pronouncement, promulgation, pronunciamento, edict, ukase, manifesto, °notice

declare *v.* **1** assert, °say, °offer, °submit, affirm, °state, aver, asseverate, avow, avouch, °profess, °protest, °swear, °claim, °proclaim; °confirm, °certify, °ratify **2** °announce, °make known, °pronounce, °decree, °rule, °proclaim, herald, promulgate, °publish, °broadcast, trumpet (forth)

decline *v.* **1** °refuse, °turn down, °deny, °reject, demur, °forgo, °veto, °avoid, abstain from **2** °diminish, lessen, °decrease, °wane, °flag, °go down, fall *or* taper off, °subside, °ebb, abate, °dwindle, °shrink, °fade, *Colloq* °peter out, run out of steam, *US* run out of gas **3** slope *or* slant (downward(s)), °descend, drop *or* fall off, °dip, °sink **4** °deteriorate, °degenerate, °worsen, °fail **5** go *or* drop down, °settle, °dip, °sink, °set —*n.* **6** diminution, °decrease, lessening, °ebb, downturn, falloff, falling off, reduction, abatement, °slump, descent **7** degeneration, deterioration, °loss, diminution, weakening, debility, °weakness, worsening, °decay, °failing **8** declivity, (downward) slope *or* slant, descent, °downgrade, °incline

decompose *v.* **1** °disintegrate, °separate, fall *or* come apart, break up *or* down, take apart, dissect, anatomize, atomize, °resolve, decompound, °analyze **2** °rot, °disintegrate, °decay, molder, °putrefy; °spoil, go off *or* bad, turn sour

decorate *v.* **1** °embellish, adorn, °ornament, garnish, embroider, °elaborate, bedeck, deck (out), °trim, °dress (up), spruce *or* smarten up, °beautify, *Literary* caparison, *Colloq Brit* tart up **2** *Brit* °paint, wallpaper, redecorate, furbish, °refurbish, °renovate, °fix up, °restore

decoration *n.* **1** garnish, °trim, trimming, adornment, °embellishment, °ornament, ornamentation, garnishment **2** medal, laurel, °award, badge, °colors, °order, ribbon, °star, garter

decorous *adj.* °becoming, °dignified, °decent, °correct, mannerly, °seemly, °refined, °elegant, °polite, well-behaved, °genteel, demure, °polished, gentlemanly, °ladylike

decorum *n.* **1** °etiquette, proper behavior, °propriety, good form, mannerliness, politeness, °dignity, gentility, good manners, respectability, courtliness, deportment **2** correctness, °propriety, °protocol, punctilio, conformity

decoy *n.* 1 bait, °lure, °trap, °attraction, °enticement, °inducement, stool pigeon —*v.* 2 °lure, entrap, °entice, °attract, °induce, °seduce, bait, °trick, °tempt, ensnare, inveigle, allure

decrease *v.* 1 °diminish, °reduce, °decline, lessen, °lower, abate, °fall off, °shrink, °shrivel (up), °contract, °dwindle, °ebb, °subside, °wane, °taper off, de-escalate, slacken, °let up, ease (off *or* up), °curtail, cut (down *or* back), *Colloq* run out of steam, *US* run out of gas —*n.* 2 diminution, reduction, °decline, lessening, lowering, abatement, falling off, shrinking, shriveling, contraction, decrement, dwindling, °ebb, subsidence, tapering off, °wane, de-escalation, slackening, easing (off *or* up), curtailment, °cut, cutback

decree *n.* 1 °order, mandate, directive, ordinance, edict, °law, statute, °regulation, enactment, °act, ruling, dictum, °dictate, °injunction, °sanction, manifesto, °proclamation, promulgation, °determination, °decision, °judgment, rescript, °prescription, pronunciamento, firman, ukase, *Rom Cath Ch* decretal —*v.* 2 °order, °command, °direct, °rule, mandate, ordain, °dictate, °charge, enjoin, °proclaim, °pronounce, °prescribe, °decide, °determine, adjudge, *Scots law* decern

decrepit *adj.* 1 °feeble, enfeebled, °weak, weakened, °frail, °infirm, wasted, worn-out, unfit, debilitated, enervated, °disabled, incapacitated, °crippled, °doddering; out of shape, in bad shape; °aged, °old, °elderly, °ancient, superannuated, senescent, °senile, *Colloq* gaga 2 °dilapidated, deteriorated, crumbling, decayed, decaying, withered, wasted, °antiquated, tumbledown, broken-down, °rickety, °unstable, °shaky, °ramshackle, °derelict, creaking, creaky, °rundown

decrepitude *n.* 1 feebleness, °weakness, °infirmity, debilitation, enervation, incapacity, old age, superannuation, senescence, °senility, caducity, dotage 2 dilapidation, deterioration, °decay, °ruin

dedicate *v.* 1 °devote, consecrate, give (up *or* over), °yield, °offer, °surrender, °commit, °pledge, °assign 2 consecrate, °bless, °sanctify, °hallow 3 inscribe; °address, °assign

dedication *n.* 1 °devotion, °assignment, °pledge, commitment, allegiance, adherence, faithfulness, fidelity, °loyalty, devotedness, wholeheartedness, single-mindedness, fixedness, fealty 2 inscription, °address; °message 3 consecration, sanctification, hallowing

deduce *v.* conclude, °infer, °understand, °gather, °assume, °presume, °derive, °draw, °work out, °divine, glean, °take it, °suppose, °surmise, °suspect, *Brit slang* suss out

deduct *v.* °subtract, take away *or* out *or* off, take from, °remove, °withdraw, *Colloq* °knock off

deduction *n.* 1 subtraction, diminution, °decrease, reduction, withdrawal, °removal, abstraction 2 conclusion, °inference, °finding, °reasoning, °result

deed *n.* 1 °act, °action; °performance 2 °exploit, °feat, °achievement, °accomplishment 3 °title (deed), °document, °instrument, indenture, °contract, °agreement

deep *adj.* 1 °extensive, °bottomless, abyssal, unfathomable, °profound; °wide, °broad, yawning, chasmal *or* chasmic 2 °profound, arcane, °recondite, °difficult, abstruse, °obscure, esoteric, °incomprehensible, beyond *or* past comprehension, impenetrable, unfathomable, inscrutable, °mysterious, mystic(al), °occult, °weighty, °serious, *Colloq* °heavy 3 °wise, °learned, °sage, sagacious, °astute, perspicacious, °profound, discerning, °acute, °intense, °penetrating, °knowledgeable, °knowing 4 °rapt, °absorbed, engrossed, occupied, °preoccupied, °intent, °intense, °involved, °engaged, immersed, °lost, *Colloq* into 5 °devious, cunning, °shrewd, °crafty, canny, °clever, °knowing, °scheming, °artful, °designing 6 °profound, °intense, °sincere, °serious, °heartfelt, °earnest, °ardent, °fervent, °poignant, deep-rooted 7 °low, °resonant, booming, resounding, sonorous, rumbling 8 °rich, °dark, °intense, °strong —*n.* 9 ***the deep.*** the ocean, the main, the sea, the waters, the high seas, the briny (deep), the wave(s), Davy Jones's locker, Neptune's *or* Poseidon's kingdom *or* domain —*adv.* 10 °deeply, far down, °profoundly, intensely, earnestly, heavily

deepen *v.* 1 °dig out, °burrow, °sink, dredge, °excavate, °scoop (out) 2 °intensify, °increase, °concentrate, °strengthen, °expand, °magnify

deeply *adv.* 1 °deep, (far) downward(s) *or* inward(s), way down, deep down 2 °profoundly, intensely, strongly, powerfully, very much, acutely, keenly, gravely, greatly, to a great extent, °extremely, °thoroughly, °completely, °entirely, °seriously, °severely, irrevocably, unreservedly; passionately, heavily, emotionally

deface *v.* °mar, disfigure, °spoil, °ruin, deform, °blemish, °damage, °mutilate, °harm, °impair, °injure, °destroy

default *n.* 1 °failure, °fault, °defect, °neglect, °negligence, dereliction, °lapse, °oversight, nonperformance, nonfulfillment, inaction 2 nonpayment, delinquency —*v.* 3 °fail, °neglect, °dishonor, °lapse, °fall short, come (up) short

defeat *v.* 1 °overcome, °conquer, vanquish, be victorious over, get the better of, °beat, °subdue, °overwhelm, °overpower, prevail over, °triumph over, bring down, worst, thrash, °rout, °repulse, °overthrow, trounce, °whip, °crush, °destroy, do in, °best 2 °thwart, °frustrate, °disappoint, °check, balk, °stop, °terminate, °end, °finish, °foil —*n.* 3 °conquest, °overthrow, beating, °repulse, trouncing, °rout, vanquishment 4 frustration, °undoing, °failure, °miscarriage, °set back; Waterloo

defecate *v.* °void (excrement), move the bowels, excrete, °eliminate, °evacuate (the bowels), have a (bowel) movement *or* bm, open the bowels, relieve oneself, *Babytalk* do number two, *Euphemistic* go to the men's *or* ladies' (room), go to the toilet *or* bathroom *or* lavatory, °excuse (oneself), wash (one's) hands, go to the bathroom, go to the powder room; *Mincing* go to the little boys' *or* girls' room; *Colloq Brit* spend a penny, go to the loo, pass a motion, *Taboo slang* (take a) crap *or* shit

defect *n.* **1** °shortcoming, deficiency, °lack, °want, inadequacy, insufficiency, shortfall, °failure, °weakness, °frailty, °weak point, °imperfection, irregularity, °liability **2** °blemish, °imperfection, °failing, °weakness, °flaw, °fault, °mark, °stain, irregularity, °mistake, °error —*v.* **3** desert, change sides *or* loyalties, turn traitor, °go over; °escape

defective *adj.* **1** °imperfect, °faulty, °flawed, °deficient, °broken, °out of order, impaired, marred, *Colloq* °on the blink, *US* on the fritz **2** retarded, °simple, °feebleminded, (mentally) deficient *or* incompetent, °backward, subnormal, *Brit education* ESN (= 'educationally subnormal'), *US education* °exceptional

defector *n.* °deserter, apostate, °turncoat, °traitor, °renegade, *Colloq* rat

defend *v.* **1** °protect, watch over, °guard, °safeguard, °keep (safe), °shelter, °shield, °screen, °preserve; fight for **2** °fortify, arm, °secure; fend *or* ward off, parry **3** °plead for, speak *or* stand up for, °stick up for, go to bat for, °support, °uphold, °stand by, °champion, stand with *or* behind *or* beside, argue for *or* in behalf of, hold a brief for, espouse

defense *n.* **1** °shelter, °protection, °cover, °guard, °safeguard, °shield **2** fortification, armor, barricade, °screen, °bulwark, °rampart **3** °excuse, apology, °reason, apologia, °explanation; justification, vindication, °argument, °plea, advocacy, °support

defenseless *adj.* unprotected, exposed, °vulnerable, °unguarded; °helpless, °weak, °powerless, °impotent

defer[1] *v.* °put off, °postpone, °delay, °shelve, lay *or* put aside, adjourn, *US* °table; *Colloq Brit* kick into touch

defer[2] *v.* Often, ***defer to.*** give in (to), give ground *or* way (to), °yield (to), °submit (to), °bow (to), °capitulate (to), °cede (to), accede (to), acquiesce (to); °comply (with), °agree (to)

deference *n.* **1** °respect, °regard, politeness, °civility, °courtesy, °consideration, °esteem **2** °obeisance, °submission, acquiescence, °obedience, compliance

defiant *adj.* challenging, °bold, °brazen, °audacious, °daring; °rebellious, °disobedient, °stubborn, °recalcitrant, °obstinate, refractory, unyielding, °insubordinate, °mutinous, °unruly, °self-willed, °aggressive, headstrong, contumacious, °pugnacious, °hostile, °belligerent, antagonistic, *Slang* gutsy, spunky

deficient *adj.* **1** °wanting, lacking, °defective, °incomplete, unfinished, °short, °insufficient, °inadequate, °sketchy, skimpy, °scarce **2** °faulty, impaired, °flawed, °imperfect, °incomplete, °defective, °inferior, °unsatisfactory

deficit *n.* °loss, deficiency, shortfall, °shortage, °default

define *v.* **1** °determine, °establish, °fix, demarcate, mark off *or* out, delimit, °limit, lay *or* set down, circumscribe, °specify, °identify, delineate, °describe **2** °describe, °explain, °interpret, °spell out, °detail, °clarify, delineate, °expand on, expatiate on *or* upon; °characterize, °state, °name

definite *adj.* **1** °specific, °particular, °exact, °pronounced, °explicit, °express, °precise **2** °sure, °positive, °certain, assured, °fixed, settled, confirmed **3** °clear, °plain, well-defined, unambiguous, unequivocal, °distinct, clear-cut, °obvious

definitely *adv.* °positively, °absolutely, °surely, to be sure, assuredly, certainly, indubitably, °undoubtedly, categorically, unequivocally, unquestionably, decidedly, °finally, °once and for all; plainly, °clearly, °obviously, patently

definition *n.* **1** delineation, delimitation, demarcation, outlining; acutance, °resolution, distinctness, °clarity, sharpness, °focus, °precision **2** °description, °explanation, explication, clarification, °statement (of meaning), °sense, °meaning

definitive *adj.* **1** decisive, °final, conclusive, °ultimate **2** °thorough, through and through, °exhaustive, °ultimate, consummate, °complete, °authoritative, °reliable **3** clarifying, unambiguous, °categorical, °absolute, °unqualified, °accurate, °exact, °precise

deflect *v.* avert, turn away *or* aside, °deviate, °change, °swerve, °switch, °divert, °shy, veer, °sidetrack; °fend off

deformed *adj.* **1** °misshapen, malformed, distorted, twisted, °grotesque, °gnarled, °crooked, contorted, awry, warped, °bent **2** °disfigured, °crippled, °lame, °misshapen; °abnormal **3** distorted, warped, °bent, °perverted, twisted, °grotesque; °abnormal

defraud *v.* °cheat, °swindle, °trick, °beguile, cozen, °dupe, delude, °fool, bilk, °fleece, °victimize, °take in, °deceive, humbug, °hoodwink, flimflam, *Colloq* do, diddle, con, slip one over on, put (something) over on, pull a fast one on, fast-talk, °rope in, *US* °take; *Slang* °take for a ride, gyp, °rob, °rip off, rook; *Dialect* flam

defray *v.* °pay, °settle, °meet, °discharge, liquidate, °clear, °cover, °reimburse, *Colloq* pick up the bill *or* tab *or* *US* check (for), foot the bill (for)

defunct *adj.* **1** °dead, deceased, °extinct **2** inoperative, °inapplicable, °unused, unusable, °invalid, expired, °obsolete, °passé,

°dead, expired, °nonexistent, outmoded, °out

defy *v.* **1** °challenge, °dare, °face, confront, °brave, °stand up to, °flout, brazen out, °thumb one's nose at, *Colloq Brit* cock a snook at **2** °frustrate, °thwart, baffle, °resist, °withstand, °repel, °disobey, °repulse

degenerate *adj.* **1** debased, degraded, °corrupt, corrupted, vitiated, °decadent, depraved, °reprobate, °dissolute, ignoble, °base, °low, °inferior, °vile —*v.* **2** °decline, °deteriorate, °decay, °sink, °worsen; backslide, regress, retrogress, °weaken, go to the dogs, go to rack and ruin, *Colloq* go to pot —*n.* **3** °reprobate, debauchee, °wastrel, °profligate, °rake, rakehell, °roué; °pervert, °deviate

degradation *n.* **1** degeneracy, degeneration, deterioration, corruptness, corruption, vitiation, baseness, depravity, turpitude **2** disrepute, °discredit, °shame, °humiliation, ignominy, °dishonor, °disgrace, abasement, debasement

degrade *v.* **1** °downgrade, demote, °break, *Military* cashier, *Ecclesiastic* unfrock, *Law* disbar; depose, unseat; disfranchise *or* disenfranchise; *Military* drum out (of the corps), *esp naval* disrate; *US military* bust **2** °disgrace, °dishonor, °humble, °shame, °discredit, °debase, demean, abase; °humiliate, °mortify, °belittle, deprecate, °depreciate, cheapen, °reduce, °lower **3** °dilute, °adulterate, °weaken, °thin, °water (down), °alloy

degrading *adj.* demeaning, humiliating, °shameful, shaming, debasing, lowering, discreditable

degree *n.* **1** °grade, °level, °stage, °class, °caste, °rank, °order, °scale, °standing, °status, °station, °position, °situation, °estate, °condition **2** °measure, °magnitude, °extent, °limit, °point; lengths, °step **3** *by degrees.* little by little, bit by bit, °step by step, inch by inch, inchmeal, °gradually, slowly, (almost) imperceptibly **4** *to a degree.* **(a)** °rather, °somewhat, °quite **(b)** °substantially, considerably, °highly, decidedly, °exceedingly, to a considerable extent

deign *v.* °condescend, °stoop, °vouchsafe, °concede; °yield, °agree

deity *n.* °god, goddess, supreme being, °creator, demiurge

dejected *adj.* downcast, °downhearted, depressed, dispirited, discouraged, °despondent, down, °low, chapfallen, crestfallen, °melancholy, °sad, °unhappy, °gloomy, °glum, °miserable, °blue, low-spirited, in low spirits, °forlorn, °woebegone, disconsolate, °sorrowful, morose, °heartbroken, heavy-hearted, in the doldrums, *Colloq* down in the dumps, °down in the mouth

delay *v.* **1** °postpone, put off *or* aside, °defer, temporize, °suspend, °shelve, hold off *or* up (on), put on hold, hold in abeyance, put *or* keep in a holding pattern, pigeonhole, put on ice, put in *or* into the deepfreeze, *Colloq* put on the back burner, *Brit* kick into touch, *US* °table **2** hold up *or* back, detain, °impede, °hinder, °retard, °keep, °bog down, °set back, slow (up *or* down); °stop, °arrest, °halt, °check; °obstruct **3** loiter, °procrastinate, °hesitate, poke *or* drag (along), °tarry, °wait, °lag (behind), °dawdle, hang back, °stall, °linger, dally, mark time, putter *or* *Brit* potter; vacillate; *Colloq* dillydally, shilly-shally, °drag one's feet —*n.* **4** °postponement, deferral, deferment, °wait, °holdup; °setback **5** °lull, °interlude, hiatus, °interruption, °gap, °interval, lacuna, °stop, stoppage, °wait, waiting, °holdup, suspension **6** tarrying, loitering, dawdling, *Colloq* dillydallying, shilly-shallying

delectation *n.* °delight, °enjoyment, °amusement, °entertainment, °diversion, °pleasure, °satisfaction

delegate *n.* **1** °envoy, °agent, legate, °representative, °ambassador, plenipotentiary, °minister, emissary, commissioner, (papal) nuncio, (papal) internuncio, spokesperson, spokesman, spokeswoman, °go-between —*v.* **2** depute, commission, °appoint, °designate, °assign, °name, °nominate, accredit, °authorize, empower, mandate **3** °assign, °give, hand over *or* on, pass over *or* on, depute, °transfer, °entrust, °relegate, *Colloq* pass the buck for, *US* buck

delete *v.* °erase, °cancel, rub *or* cross out *or* off, °remove, °blot out, expunge, efface, °eliminate, °obliterate, °wipe out, eradicate, °strike out, cut *or* edit (out), *Publishing* blue-pencil; *Printing* dele

deliberate *adj.* **1** °intentional, planned, °studied, °willful, intended, °premeditated, °calculated, °conscious, prearranged, °purposeful, °preconceived, considered; °cold-blooded **2** °slow, °methodical, °careful, °unhurried, paced, °measured, °regular, °even, °steady, °sure, °unhesitating, unfaltering, °confident **3** °careful, °prudent, °cautious, °painstaking, °discreet, considered, °considerate, °thoughtful, well-thought-out, °thorough, °methodical, °systematic, °fastidious, °orderly, punctilious, °dispassionate, °cool, composed, °collected, °calm, °serene, unruffled —*v.* **4** °consider, °ponder, think (about *or* over), °weigh, °debate, meditate (on *or* over), reflect (on *or* over), cogitate (on *or* over), °study

deliberately *adv.* intentionally, °on purpose, purposely, willfully, consciously, wittingly, calculatedly, calculatingly, knowingly, pointedly, resolutely, of one's (own) free will, on one's own, with one's eyes (wide) open

delicacy *n.* **1** fineness, exquisiteness, gracefulness, °beauty, lightness, daintiness **2** fragility, fragileness, °frailty, frailness, °weakness, °infirmity, feebleness, tenderness; susceptibility **3** °sensitivity, °difficulty, ticklishness, °finesse, nicety, °sensibility **4** °luxury, sweetmeat, °dainty, tidbit *or* *Brit* titbit, °savory

delicate *adj.* **1** °fragile, breakable, °frail, °tender, frangible, °dainty; perishable, °flimsy **2** °fine, °exquisite, °dainty, °graceful,

°elegant, °subtle **3** °feeble, °weak, °sickly, °frail, debilitated, weakened, enfeebled, °unhealthy **4** °critical, °ticklish, °sensitive, °dangerous, °tricky, °precarious, °touchy, *Slang* °hairy; *Colloq* °sticky **5** °dainty, °squeamish, °queasy, °fastidious, °prudish, Victorian, °finicky, finical, °refined, °discriminating, discerning, °sensitive, puristic, °proper, °coy, °modest, demure **6** °gradual, °subtle, °nice, °precise, muted, °soft, °faint, °subdued

delicious *adj.* **1** delectable, °luscious, ambrosial, °savory, mouthwatering, toothsome; °choice, flavorful, °tasty, appetizing, palatable, *Colloq* scrumptious; *Slang* °yummy **2** enjoyable, °delightful, °pleasurable, °pleasing, °pleasant, °choice, °enchanting, fascinating; °agreeable, charming, °engaging; amusing, °entertaining

delight *v.* **1** please, °gratify, °satisfy, °gladden, °cheer, °tickle, °amuse, °entertain, °divert, °excite, °thrill, °captivate, °entrance, °fascinate **2** ***delight in.*** °enjoy, °appreciate, °like, °relish (in), °savor, °revel in, glory in; °love, °adore; *Colloq* get a kick from *or* out of; *Slang* °get off on —*n.* **3** °pleasure, °gratification, °joy, °satisfaction, °enjoyment, °delectation; °bliss, °ecstasy, °rapture

delighted *adj.* pleased, °happy, °charmed, thrilled, °enchanted, ***enchanté(e)***

delightful *adj.* **1** °pleasing, °agreeable, °pleasurable, enjoyable, °joyful, °pleasant, °lovely, amusing, °entertaining, diverting, °exciting, °thrilling **2** °attractive, congenial, °winning, winsome, charming, °engaging, °exciting; captivating, °ravishing, fascinating, °enchanting

delinquent *n.* **1** malefactor, (young *or* youthful) offender, wrongdoer, lawbreaker, °culprit, °criminal, °miscreant; hooligan, ruffian, roughneck —*adj.* **2** neglectful, negligent, °derelict, °remiss, °failing, defaulting **3** °overdue, past due, in arrears, °late, °unpaid

delirious *adj.* **1** °wild, °hysterical, distracted, °incoherent, °rambling, irrational, °raving, ranting, frenzied, °frantic, °disturbed, demented, °deranged, unhinged, °mad, °insane, °crazy, lunatic **2** °wild, °excited, crazed, thrilled, °ecstatic

deliver *v.* **1** °carry, °bring, convey, °distribute, give *or* hand out; purvey, take round; °cart, °transport **2** °hand over, °give, °surrender, °cede, °yield, °make over, °relinquish, give up *or* over, °commit, °transfer, °turn over, °resign **3** set free, °liberate, enfranchise, °extricate, °release, °save, °rescue; °emancipate, manumit, °redeem; disencumber, disburden, °ransom **4** °give, °present, utter, °read, °broadcast; °proclaim, °announce, °declare, °set forth, °communicate, °make known, °express, °publish, °hand over, °hand out, promulgate, °pronounce, °enunciate **5** °give, °administer, °inflict, °deal, °direct, °send, °launch, °impart, °throw; °cast, °hurl, °shoot, °discharge, °fire **6** °bring forth, °bear, give birth to, °bring into the world

delivery *n.* **1** °distribution, delivering, deliverance, conveyance, transportation, °transport **2** °liberation, °release, deliverance, emancipation **3** childbirth, parturition; confinement **4** °presentation, °performance; utterance, enunciation, articulation, °pronunciation, °expression, °execution

delusion *n.* **1** °deception, °trick, °stratagem, °artifice, °ruse, °pretense **2** false *or* mistaken impression, °fallacy, °illusion, °mistake, °error, °misconception, misbelief, °hallucination

demand *v.* **1** °require, °order, °bid, °call (for); °insist, °command **2** °claim, °ask (for), °require, insist on; °exact **3** °require, °call for, °need, °want, necessitate, °cry out for **4** °ask (for), inquire *or* enquire, °request; °requisition —*n.* **5** °request, °bid, behest, °requisition, °order, insistence; °outcry **6** °want, °need, °requirement, °desire; °market (demand), marketability; consumer *or* customer acceptance **7** ***in demand.*** wanted, needed, requested, coveted, °popular, sought after, desired, °desirable, *US* on request, *Brit* in request **8** ***on demand.*** °on call, on request, on presentation, when requested *or* required; °at once, °immediately, without delay

demanding *adj.* **1** °difficult, °hard, exigent, °tough, °exacting, °trying, taxing **2** °insistent, clamorous, °urgent, °nagging, °persistent

democratic *adj.* egalitarian, classless; republican, °representative, °popular, self-governing, autonomous

demolish *v.* **1** tear *or* pull down, dismantle, reduce to ruin(s), smash, pull to pieces, °knock down, °raze, °topple, °destroy, °level **2** °destroy, °end, bring to an end, make an end of, put an end to, °devastate, °terminate, annihilate, °overturn, °overthrow, °crush, °defeat, refute, °disprove, °dispose of, °suppress, °squelch, °quash

demon *n.* **1** °devil, evil spirit, °fiend, cacodemon *or* cacodaemon; °monster, ghoul, °ogre, harpy, vampire **2** °fanatic, °fiend, °enthusiast, °addict, *Colloq* °freak

demonstrable *adj.* provable, confirmable, attestable, verifiable; °evident, °self-evident, °obvious, undeniable, °apparent, °manifest, °indisputable, °unquestionable, °positive, °certain, conclusive

demonstrate *v.* **1** °show, °prove, make evident, °establish, evince, °evidence, °exhibit, °manifest **2** °display, °explain, °expose, °describe, °present; °illustrate **3** °picket, °march, °parade, °rally, °protest

demonstration *n.* **1** °proof, °evidence, °testimony, confirmation, verification, substantiation; °manifestation, °exhibition, °display, °illustration, °indication **2** °presentation, °display, °show, °explanation, °description, clarification, elucidation, °exposition, *Colloq* demo **3** picketing, °march, °parade, °protest, °rally, sit-in, *Colloq Brit* demo

demonstrative *adj.* **1** °open, unrestrained,

unconstrained, unreserved, °expansive, °effusive, °emotional, °warm, °tender, °affectionate, loving **2** illustrative, indicative, °representative, probative, evidential; provable, °evident

demoralize *v.* **1** dispirit, °daunt, dishearten, °discourage, °defeat; °weaken, °cripple, °enervate, devitalize, °depress, °subdue, °crush **2** °corrupt, °pervert, deprave, °vitiate, °debase, debauch **3** °bewilder, °discomfit, °unnerve, °shake (up), °confuse, °fluster, disconcert, °perturb, °disturb, °upset, *Colloq* °rattle

denial *n.* **1** contradiction, negation, repudiation, refutation, disavowal, disclaimer, disaffirmation **2** retraction, recantation, renunciation, withdrawal **3** °refusal, °rejection, negation; °veto

denizen *n.* °inhabitant, dweller, °occupant, frequenter, °resident; °citizen

denomination *n.* **1** °sect, °persuasion, °school, church, °order **2** °sort, °kind, °type, °nature, °variety, °unit, °size, value; °grade, °class, genus, species, °order, classification **3** designation, appellation, °name, °identification, °style, °title, °tag, °term; designating, naming, identifying, styling, classifying, titling, entitling, tagging, terming, denominating

denote *v.* **1** °indicate, °specify, °designate, °distinguish, °signify, °mark, °note **2** °mean, °name, °symbolize, °represent, betoken

denounce *v.* **1** °accuse, °brand, °stigmatize, °charge, °blame, °incriminate, °implicate, complain about **2** °betray, °inform against, °report, °reveal **3** °criticize, °condemn, decry, denunciate, °attack, assail, censure, impugn, declaim *or* rail (against), °vituperate, revile, °vilify, inveigh against; °ridicule, °(hold up to) shame, pillory, °(heap) scorn (upon), cast a slur on

dense *adj.* **1** °compact, °thick, compressed, condensed, °close, °solid, °heavy, impenetrable **2** crowded, °packed, °tight, impenetrable, impassable **3** °stupid, °slow, slow-witted, thickheaded, °dull, thick-witted, °obtuse, °stolid, cloddish, °dim, dimwitted, °foolish, *Colloq* °thick, °dumb

deny *v.* **1** °contradict, gainsay, refute, controvert, disaffirm, disclaim, confute, negate, °dispute **2** °reject, °refuse, °withhold, °forbid, °turn down, °decline, disallow; °recall, °revoke, °recant **3** disavow, °repudiate, °renounce, disown, forswear, disclaim

depart *v.* **1** °go, go away *or* out *or* from *or* off, °leave, °quit, °retire (from), °retreat (from), °withdraw (from), °exit (from), set out *or* forth *or* off, decamp, get out, abscond, °fly, cut and run, °skip (out), run off *or* away *or* out, take to the road, take one's leave, °check out, °disappear, vanish, °evaporate, *Jocular* toddle off, *Imperative* Begone!, *Colloq* °beat it, scram, shove off, make oneself scarce, *Brit* scarper, *US* hit the road, be out of (someplace), *Slang* °split, *Imperative* get lost, *US* cut (on) out, vamoose, take a (runout) powder, lam (on) out, take it on the lam, *Brit* do a moonlight flit, *Usually imperative* °bugger off, buzz off, *Taboo imperative* fuck off **2** Often, ***depart from.*** °deviate (from), °change, °diverge (from), turn (aside *or* away) (from), °differ (from), °vary (from), °break away (from), °leave, °abandon, °stray (from), veer (from)

department *n.* **1** °division, subdivision, °branch, °office, °bureau, °section, °segment, °unit, °part **2** °responsibility, °concern, °worry, °sphere, bailiwick, °jurisdiction, °domain, °control, area *or* sphere of influence *or* activity

depend *v.* **1** ***depend (on or upon).*** be contingent *or* dependent *or* conditional on, °turn on, hinge on, pivot on, °hang on, be subject to, rest on, be influenced *or* determined *or* conditioned by **2** ***depend on or upon.*** °trust (in), °rely on, °count on, °reckon on, bank on, be sure of, put one's faith *or* trust in

deplorable *adj.* **1** °lamentable, °regrettable, °sad, woeful, °grievous, °wretched, °miserable, °unfortunate, °awful, distressing, °disturbing, troubling, upsetting, °grave, °serious, °oppressive, °difficult, °desperate, °hopeless, °tragic, °disastrous **2** °shameful, °disgraceful, °scandalous, °disreputable, °awful, °bad, appalling, °dreadful, °abominable, execrable, °terrible, reprehensible

deposit *v.* **1** °place, °leave, set *or* put *or* lay (down), °drop, *Colloq US* plunk down **2** °entrust, °leave, °lodge, consign, °keep, °place, °put; °store, °save, °set aside, bank, lay *or* put away, *Brit* pay in, *Colloq* stash away —*n.* **3** down payment, part *or* partial payment, advance payment **4** °precipitate, °sediment, °silt, alluvium, °dregs, lees, °accumulation, deposition

depreciate *v.* **1** devalue, devaluate, °decrease, °diminish, lessen, °reduce, °lower, °depress, cheapen, °mark down **2** °disparage, °diminish, °deride, decry, underrate, undervalue, °underestimate, °minimize, °belittle, °slight, derogate, deprecate, °discredit, denigrate, °run down, vilipend, *Colloq* °play down, *US* °talk down

depredation *n.* °plunder, plundering, °pillage, pillaging, despoliation, despoiling, ravaging, sacking, laying waste, devastation, °destruction; ransacking, °robbery, looting; °ravages

depress *v.* **1** deject, dispirit, °oppress, °sadden, °grieve, cast down, dishearten, °discourage, °dampen, cast a gloom *or* pall over, °burden, °weigh down **2** °weaken, °dull, debilitate, °enervate, °sap; °depreciate, cheapen, devalue, devaluate; °diminish, °lower, bring down, °reduce **3** °press (down), push (down) (on), °lower

depression *n.* **1** °indentation, dent, dimple, °impression, °pit, °hollow, °recess, °cavity, concavity, °dip **2** dejection, °despair, °gloom, downheartedness, °sadness, °melancholy, discouragement, despondency, gloominess, glumness, the blues, unhappiness; *Colloq* the dumps **3** °recession,

°slump, °(economic) decline, downturn, *US, Canadian* bust

deprive *v.* °withhold, °deny, °refuse; °withdraw, °remove, °strip, °dispossess, take away, expropriate, °divest; mulct

deprived *adj.* °needy, in want, in need, °impoverished, badly off, °destitute, °poor, poverty-stricken, *Euphemistic* underprivileged, disadvantaged

depth *n.* **1** deepness, °extent, °measure, °profundity, profoundness **2** °profundity, profoundness, abstruseness, °obscurity, reconditeness, °complexity, intricacy **3** °profundity, °wisdom, sagacity, sageness, °understanding, °perception, astuteness, perspicacity, perspicaciousness, °insight, °intuition, acumen, °penetration **4** °intensity, °profundity, °strength; vividness, °brilliance, brilliancy, brightness, richness **5** ***depths.*** deep(s), °abyss, abysm, chasm, bowels of the earth, °(bottomless) pit, nethermost reaches *or* regions, nadir **6** ***in depth.*** °thoroughly, comprehensively, °in detail, °profoundly, °deeply, extensively, intensively, concentratedly, probingly

deputy *n.* °substitute, replacement, surrogate, °stand-in, °reserve, °proxy; °agent, °operative, °representative, °go-between, °intermediary, spokesperson, spokesman, spokeswoman, °delegate, °ambassador, °minister, emissary, °envoy, legate, (papal) nuncio; *Chiefly US* °alternate

deranged *adj.* °mad, °insane, demented, lunatic, unhinged, °unbalanced, °berserk, °crazy, crazed, °psychotic, irrational, ***non compos mentis***, out of one's mind *or* senses *or* head, not all there, of unsound mind, crackbrained, mad as a hatter *or* March hare, off the rails, *Colloq* touched, dotty, °daft, cracked, bats, cuckoo, balmy, *US* have nobody home (upstairs), out to lunch, off the wall, *Brit* barmy (in the crumpet), potty; *Slang* bonkers, dippy, barmy *or* balmy, batty, screwy, loony, nuts, nutty, wacky, bananas, off one's rocker, off one's trolley, °mental, missing a few marbles, not having all one's marbles, kooky, with a screw loose, *Chiefly US* (plumb) loco, meshuga, *Chiefly Brit* off one's chump

derelict *adj.* **1** °deserted, °abandoned, forsaken, neglected; ruined, °dilapidated, °rundown, tumbledown **2** negligent, °remiss, neglectful, °delinquent, dilatory, °careless, °heedless, °lax, °slack, °irresponsible, °slipshod, slovenly, *Colloq* °sloppy —*n.* **3** vagrant, °tramp, °outcast, pariah, °loafer, °wastrel, °good-for-nothing, ne'er-do-well, malingerer, °vagabond, °slacker, °down-and-out, *US and Canadian* hobo, *Colloq US* °bum

deride *v.* °mock, °ridicule, °scoff (at), °jeer (at), °laugh (at), make fun *or* sport (of), °tease, °taunt, °twit, poke fun (at), make a laughingstock (of), °sneer (at), °scorn, °flout, disdain, pooh-pooh, °belittle, °diminish, °disparage, laugh off, *Brit* °rally, *Colloq* °knock, *Brit* take the mickey *or* micky out of

derision *n.* °ridicule, °mockery, °raillery, °laughter, °sarcasm, scoffing, °contempt, °scorn, contumely, °disrespect; °satire, °lampoon, pasquinade, °burlesque, °caricature, travesty

derisory *adj.* mocking, ridiculing, °scornful, derisive, °disdainful, °contemptuous, taunting, insulting, contumelious, jeering; °sardonic, °sarcastic, ironic(al), °satirical

derivation *n.* °origin, descent, °extraction, °source, °beginning, °foundation, ancestry, genealogy, etymology, °root

derivative *adj.* **1** derived, borrowed, procured, obtained, acquired; unoriginal, °secondhand, copied, imitative, plagiarized, plagiaristic —*n.* **2** °derivation, °offshoot, °development, spinoff, by-product

derive *v.* **1** °draw, °extract, °get, °obtain, °acquire, °procure, °receive, °secure, °gain, °elicit, °deduce, educe, °infer, °gather, °collect, °harvest, glean, cull, winnow **2** ***derive from.*** arise from *or* out of, originate in *or* with *or* from, emerge from *or* out of, come (forth) from *or* out of, arrive from, issue from, proceed from, develop from, spring from, flow from, emanate from, stem from, be traceable *or* traced to

derogatory *adj.* depreciatory, depreciating, depreciative, disparaging, abasing, debasing, lowering, denigrating, belittling, diminishing, demeaning, detracting, deflating, minimizing, °mitigating; uncomplimentary, °offensive, insulting

descend *v.* **1** come *or* go down, move down, °climb down, °get down **2** °decline, incline (downward(s)), °slope, °slant, °dip, °drop, °fall, °plunge, °plummet **3** °stoop, °condescend, °sink, lower oneself **4** ***descend on.*** °attack, °assault, invade, pounce on *or* upon, swoop down on *or* upon

descendant *n.* °offspring, °progeny, °issue, °heir, °posterity, °family; °child, son, daughter, grandchild, scion; °offshoot

describe *v.* **1** °tell (of), °recount, °relate, give an account (of), °narrate, °recite, °report, °chronicle; retail **2** °detail, °define, °explain, °specify, delineate **3** °characterize, °portray, °paint, depict, °identify, °label, °style; °represent **4** °trace, mark out, °outline, °traverse, °draw

description *n.* **1** portrayal, characterization, depiction, (thumbnail) sketch, °portrait **2** °account, °narrative, °story, °report, °representation, °statement, °definition; °explanation, commentary; °chronicle, °history, °record, °narration; °memoir **3** °sort, °kind, °nature, °character, °type, °variety, °brand, °breed, species, °category, genus, ilk, °genre, °class; °stripe, kidney, feather

desecrate *v.* °profane, defile, °blaspheme (against), °dishonor, °degrade, °debase, befoul, °contaminate, °pollute, °corrupt, °violate, °pervert, °vitiate

desert[1] *n.* **1** °waste, wilderness, wasteland, dust bowl —*adj.* **2** °barren, °desolate, °uninhabited, unpeopled, °lonely, °deserted; arid,

°bare, °vacant, °empty, °wild, uncultivated —*v.* **3** °forsake, °leave, °abandon; °jilt, °throw over; °maroon, strand, leave to twist (slowly) in the wind; *Colloq* run *or* walk out on, leave flat *or* in the lurch, leave high and dry **4** abscond, °quit, °run away (from), °defect, °abandon; *Military slang* go over the hill

desert[2] *n.* Often, ***deserts.*** payment, recompense, °requital, compensation, °due, °right; °retribution, °justice, *Slang* comeuppance, what's coming to one

deserted *adj.* °abandoned, °desolate, forsaken, neglected, °uninhabited, unpeopled, °vacant, vacated, unfrequented, unvisited, unoccupied, °empty; stranded, rejected, godforsaken, °isolated, °solitary, °lonely, friendless

deserter *n.* °runaway, °fugitive, escapee, absconder, °defector, °renegade, °outlaw; °traitor, °turncoat, *Colloq* rat

deserve *v.* °merit, °earn, be entitled to, be worthy of, °rate, °warrant, °justify

deserved *adj.* merited, earned, °just, °rightful, °suitable, °fitting, °fit, °appropriate, °proper, °right, °fair, °equitable, °meet, warranted, condign

deserving *adj.* °meritorious, °worthy, merited, commendable, °laudable, °praiseworthy, creditable, °estimable

design *v.* **1** °plan, °draw up, °think of, conceive of, °contemplate, °devise, °lay out, visualize, °envisage, °envision, sketch (out), °pattern, °set up **2** °plan, sketch (out), delineate, °outline, °draft, work *or* map *or* block out, °lay out, °devise, °invent, contrive, °create, °conceive, °originate, °think up, °develop, °organize, °frame, °shape, °mold, °forge, °make, °construct, °form, °fashion **3** sketch, °draft, °lay out, °draw; °form, °devise **4** °intend, °mean, °plan; °purpose, °destine; °scheme, °plot —*n.* **5** °plan, °scheme, °conception, °study, °project, °proposal, °undertaking, °enterprise; blueprint, °pattern, °chart, diagram, layout, map, °drawing, °draft, sketch, °model, °prototype **6** °form, °shape, configuration, °pattern, °style, °motif, °format, layout, °makeup, delineation, °arrangement, °organization, °composition, °structure, construction **7** °aim, °purpose, °intention, °objective, °object, °goal, °point, °target, °intent **8** ***designs.*** °plot, °intrigue, °stratagem, °cabal, °conspiracy, conniving, manipulation, connivance, evil intent *or* intentions

designate *v.* **1** °indicate, °specify, pinpoint, particularize, delineate, °point out, °identify, °state, °set forth, write *or* put down, °name **2** °appoint, °nominate, °name, °identify, denominate, °select, °pick, °choose, °elect, °assign, °appropriate, °delegate, depute **3** °mean, °stand for, °symbolize, °denote, °represent **4** °call, °name, °style, °term, °label, °christen, dub, °nickname, °entitle

designer *n.* **1** °creator, originator, architect, artificer, °author, deviser, inventor; (interior) decorator, artist; draftsman **2** intriguer, schemer, conniver, plotter, conspirator

designing *adj.* °scheming, plotting, conniving, conspiring, intriguing, °calculating, °wily, °tricky, cunning, °sly, underhand(ed), °crafty, °artful, °shrewd, Machiavellian, guileful, °deceitful, double-dealing, °devious, treacherous, *Colloq* °crooked

desirable *adj.* **1** sought-after, wanted, coveted, longed-for, looked-for, desired **2** °attractive, °pleasant, °pleasing, °agreeable, °winning, winsome, captivating, °seductive, alluring, °fetching **3** °good, °goodly, °excellent, °choice, °fine, °superior, °superb, *Colloq Brit* plummy **4** °profitable, °worthwhile, °beneficial, °advantageous, valuable, °worthy, °estimable, commendable, °admirable

desire *v.* **1** crave, °want, °fancy, covet, wish for, hope for, long *or* yearn for, pine *or* sigh for, °hanker after, have an eye *or* taste for, hunger *or* thirst for *or* after, die for, have one's heart set on, give one's eyeteeth for, *Colloq* have a yen for, *US slang* have the hots for **2** °ask for, °request, °order, °demand, °solicit, importune, °summon, °require —*n.* **3** °longing, craving, yearning, hankering, °hunger, °thirst, °appetite; °passion, °lust, libido, lustfulness, concupiscence, lecherousness, lechery, lasciviousness, salaciousness, prurience, *Slang* hot pants, *US* the hots; *Colloq* yen **4** °wish, °request, °urge, °requirement, °order, °requisition, °demand, desideratum; °appeal, entreaty, °petition

desirous *adj.* wishful, desiring, °longing, yearning, °hopeful, hoping

desolate *adj.* **1** °solitary, °lonely, °isolated, °deserted, °forlorn, forsaken, friendless, °alone, °abandoned, neglected; °desert, °uninhabited, °empty, unfrequented, °bare, °barren, °bleak, °remote **2** laid waste, ruined, devastated, ravaged, destroyed **3** °dreary, °dismal, °wretched, °joyless, cheerless, comfortless, °miserable, °unhappy, down, disconsolate, °sad, °sorrowful, °forlorn, °mournful, °woebegone, °gloomy, °brokenhearted, heavy-hearted, °inconsolable, °dejected, downcast, °downhearted, dispirited, low-spirited, depressed, °melancholy, spiritless, °despondent, °dismal, distressed, discouraged, °hopeless —*v.* **4** depopulate **5** °destroy, °devastate, °ruin, °lay waste, despoil, °ravage, °demolish, °obliterate, annihilate, °raze, °gut **6** °dismay, dishearten, °depress, °daunt, dispirit, °sadden, deject, °discourage

desolation *n.* **1** °destruction, °ruin, devastation, °waste, spoliation, despoliation, °sack, °depredation, extirpation, obliteration, ravagement, barrenness, °havoc, °chaos **2** °grief, °sorrow, dreariness, °despair, °gloom, °distress, °melancholy, °sadness, °misery, °woe, °anguish, wretchedness, dolor, dolefulness, unhappiness

despair *n.* **1** hopelessness, °desperation, discouragement, disheartenment, despondency, dejection, °depression, °gloom, gloominess, °misery, °melancholy, wretchedness, °distress, miserableness, °anguish; °resignation —*v.* **2** give up *or* lose hope; °surrender, °quit

desperate *adj.* **1** °reckless, °foolhardy, °rash, °impetuous, °frantic, frenzied, °panic-stricken **2** °careless, °hasty, devil-may-care, °wild, °mad, frenetic, °furious **3** °anxious (for), craving, °hungry (for), °thirsty (for), needful (of), °desirous (of), covetous (of), °eager (for), longing *or* yearning (for), wishing (for), hoping (for), aching (for), pining (for) **4** °urgent, °pressing, compelling, °serious, °grave, °acute, °critical, °crucial, °great **5** °precarious, °perilous, life-threatening, °hazardous, °dangerous, °tenuous, °hopeless, beyond hope *or* help **6** at one's wit's end, °forlorn, despairing, °despondent, °wretched, at the end of one's tether *or* rope, °frantic

desperation *n.* **1** recklessness, impetuosity, rashness, foolhardiness, imprudence, heedlessness **2** °despair, °anxiety, °anguish, anxiousness, despondency, °depression, dejection, discouragement, defeatism, pessimism, hopelessness, °distress, °misery, °melancholy, wretchedness, °gloom, °sorrow

despicable *adj.* °contemptible, below *or* beneath *or* beyond contempt *or* scorn *or* disdain, °mean, detestable, °base, °low, °scurvy, °vile, °sordid, °wretched, °miserable, ignoble, ignominious, °shabby; °shameful, °shameless, reprehensible

despise *v.* disdain, °scorn, look down on *or* upon, be contemptuous of, sneer at, °spurn, contemn; °hate, °loathe, °detest, °abhor

despite *prep.* °in spite of, °notwithstanding, undeterred by, °regardless of, in the face *or* teeth of, in defiance of, without considering, without thought *or* consideration *or* regard for, ignoring

despondent *adj.* °dejected, °sad, °sorrowful, °unhappy, °melancholy, °blue, depressed, down, downcast, °downhearted, °low, morose, °miserable, disheartened, discouraged, dispirited, low-spirited, °down in the mouth, *Colloq* down in the dumps

despot *n.* absolute ruler *or* monarch, °dictator, °tyrant, °oppressor, autocrat

despotic *adj.* °dictatorial, °tyrannical, °oppressive, °authoritarian, imperious, °domineering, °totalitarian, °absolute, autocratic, °arbitrary

despotism *n.* autocracy, monocracy, autarchy, totalitarianism, absolutism, dictatorship, °tyranny, °oppression, °suppression, °repression

dessert *n.* °sweet, *Brit* pudding, *Colloq Brit* pud, afters

destination *n.* journey's end, terminus, °stop, stopping place; °goal, °end, °objective, °target

destine *v.* **1** °fate, predetermine, predestine, ordain, foreordain, preordain; °doom **2** °design, °intend, °mean, °devote, °assign, °appoint, °designate, °purpose, °mark, earmark, °set aside

destined *adj.* **1** meant, intended, designed, °predetermined, foreordained, predestined, °fated; °doomed, written; *US* °in the cards **2** °certain, °sure, °bound, ineluctable, °unavoidable, °inevitable, inescapable

destiny *n.* °fate, °doom, °fortune, °lot, kismet, karma

destitute *adj.* **1** in want, °impoverished, poverty-stricken, °poor, °indigent, °down-and-out, °needy, °on one's uppers, badly off, penniless, °penurious, impecunious, °insolvent, bankrupt, *Colloq* °hard up, °broke, *US* on skid row **2** Usually, ***destitute of.*** bereft of, deficient in, deprived of, devoid of, lacking (in), °wanting (in), in need, needful (of), without

destroy *v.* **1** °demolish, tear *or* pull down, °raze, °wipe out, °ravage, °wreck, smash, °ruin, break up *or* down, annihilate, °crush, eradicate, extirpate, °exterminate, °devastate, commit mayhem, °lay waste, vandalize, *Slang US* °trash **2** °ruin, do away with, °end, make an end of, bring to an end, bring *or* put an end to, °terminate, °finish, °kill **3** °counteract, °neutralize, nullify, annul, °cancel (out), °reverse; °stop, interfere with **4** °disprove, refute, confute, °deny, °contradict, negate, °overturn, °overthrow, °ruin, °spoil, °undermine, °weaken, enfeeble, devitalize, °exhaust, disable, °cripple

destruction *n.* **1** demolition, razing, wrecking, °ruin, ruining, ruination, breaking up *or* down, °mayhem, °havoc, annihilation, devastation, tearing *or* knocking down, laying waste, ravagement; rack and ruin, *Colloq* wiping out **2** °slaughter, annihilation, °killing, eradication, °murder, extermination, °holocaust, liquidation, °massacre, extinction, genocide, assassination, slaying, putting to death, putting an end to, making an end of, doing away with, putting away, *Colloq* doing in, wiping out; *Slang US* rubbing out, rubout **3** °undoing, °end, °ruin, ruination, °downfall, °termination, breakup, °breakdown, °collapse

destructive *adj.* **1** °harmful, °injurious, baneful, pernicious, °dangerous, °hurtful, toxic, °poisonous, °virulent, noxious, °bad, °malignant, baleful, °unwholesome, damaging, °detrimental, deleterious, °devastating; °deadly, °fatal, °lethal, °fell, °killing, internecine **2** °negative, adverse, °opposing, °opposed, °contrary, °contradictory, antithetical, conflicting, unfavorable, condemnatory, °derogatory, disparaging, disapproving, °critical

desultory *adj.* shifting, °devious, unsteady, °irregular, wavering, °inconstant, °fitful, °spasmodic, unmethodical, °disconnected, unsystematic, °disorderly, disordered, unorganized, disorganized, °inconsistent, °random, °haphazard, °chaotic, °erratic, °shifty

detach *v.* °separate, uncouple, °part, disjoin, °disengage, disunite, °disconnect, disentangle, °free, unfasten, °undo, °cut off, °remove

detached *adj.* 1 °disconnected, °unattached, separate(d), °free, °isolated, disentangled, unfastened, removed, °cut off, divided, disjoined 2 °disinterested, °aloof, uninvolved, unemotional, °dispassionate, *dégagé(e)*, °reserved, °impersonal, °impartial, °neutral, °objective, unbiased, °unprejudiced

detachment *n.* 1 separating, unfastening, disconnecting, detaching, disengaging; °separation, disconnection, disengagement 2 aloofness, unconcern, °indifference, coolness, inattention, insouciance 3 See **detail,** 3, below.

detail *n.* 1 °particular, °element, °factor, °point, °fact, °specific, technicality, component, °item, °feature; °aspect, °respect, °count 2 ***details.*** °particulars, minutiae, niceties, fine points, specifics, technicalities 3 °detachment, °squad, °party, cadre, °duty, °fatigue, °group 4 ***in detail.*** specifically, °particularly, °thoroughly, °in depth, item by item, point by point, exhaustively, comprehensively, °inside out, °perfectly —*v.* 5 °specify, °spell out, °itemize, delineate, catalogue, °list, °tabulate, °enumerate, particularize, °recount, cite (chapter and verse) 6 °assign, °appoint, °charge, °delegate, °name, °specify, °send

detailed *adj.* 1 itemized, °exhaustive, °comprehensive, °thorough, °full, °complete, °inclusive, particularized, °precise, °exact, °minute, blow-by-blow, °circumstantial 2 °intricate, complex, °complicated, °elaborate, °ornate

detect *v.* 1 uncover, °find (out), °discover, °locate, °learn of, ascertain, °determine, °dig up, °unearth 2 °perceive, °note, °notice, °identify, °spot, °observe, °sense, °read, °scent, °smell, discern, °feel, °catch, °find

detective *n.* investigator, private investigator, CID man, policeman, °constable, *Colloq* private eye, °sleuth, sherlock, °snoop, snooper, *US* P.I., dick, Hawkshaw, *Brit* tec; *Slang* cop, copper, *US and Canadian* gumshoe, peeper

detention *n.* °custody, confinement, °imprisonment, °captivity, internment, incarceration, °restraint, *Literary, archaic* durance

deter *v.* dissuade, °discourage, °inhibit, °intimidate, °daunt, frighten off *or* from *or* away, scare off *or* from; °prevent, °stop, °obstruct, °check, °hinder, °impede

detergent *n.* 1 cleaner, cleanser, soap (powder *or* flakes *or* liquid); surfactant, surface-active agent, detersive —*adj.* 2 cleaning, cleansing, washing, purifying, detersive

deteriorate *v.* 1 °worsen, °decline, °degenerate, °degrade, °spoil, get worse, °depreciate, °slip, °slide, *Colloq* go to pot, go to the dogs, go downhill 2 °decay, °decline, °disintegrate, °fall apart, °decompose, °crumble, °erode

determination *n.* 1 resoluteness, °resolution, firmness, °resolve, steadfastness, °tenacity, °perseverance, °fortitude, doggedness, °persistence, constancy, single-mindedness, °will (power), *Colloq* °grit, °guts 2 °settlement, °resolution, resolving, °decision, °solution, °judgment, verdict, °outcome, °result, °upshot, conclusion, °end, °termination 3 fixing, settling, ascertainment, ascertaining, delimitation, °definition

determine *v.* 1 °settle, °decide, °clinch, arbitrate, °judge, adjudge, conclude, °terminate, °end 2 ascertain, °find out, °discover, conclude, °infer, °draw, °learn, °detect; °verify 3 °decide, °choose, °select, °resolve, make up one's mind, settle on *or* upon, fix on *or* upon 4 °affect, °influence, act on, °shape, °condition, °govern, °regulate, °dictate

determined *adj.* 1 °decided, °resolute, resolved, °purposeful, dogged, strong-willed, °strong-minded, °single-minded, °tenacious, °intent, °firm, unflinching, unwavering, °fixed, °constant, °persistent, persevering, °steady, unfaltering, °unhesitating, unyielding, °stubborn, °obstinate, adamant 2 °fixed, determinate, °definite, °exact, °precise, °distinct, °predetermined, ascertained, identified

deterrent *n.* °hindrance, °impediment, discouragement, disincentive, dissuasion, °check, °hitch, °obstacle, °obstruction, °stumbling block; °catch, °snag, °rub, °fly in the ointment, °bar, °drawback

detest *v.* °despise, °loathe, °hate, °abhor, execrate, abominate

detour *n.* 1 °diversion, deviation, circuitous route *or* way, roundabout way, °bypass —*v.* 2 °deviate, turn (away) from, °divert, °bypass

detract *v.* ***detract from.*** °diminish, °reduce, take away from, °subtract from, lessen, °depreciate, °disparage

detriment *n.* °disadvantage, °drawback, °liability; °damage, °harm, °ill, °impairment, °injury, °hurt, °loss

detrimental *adj.* disadvantageous, °harmful, °injurious, °hurtful, damaging, deleterious, °destructive, °prejudicial, adverse, unfavorable, inimical, pernicious

devastate *v.* 1 °lay waste, °ravage, °destroy, °waste, °sack, °raze, °ruin, °desolate, °spoil, °wreck, °demolish, °level, °flatten, °gut, °obliterate 2 disconcert, confound, °discomfit, °take aback, °nonplus, °shatter, °overwhelm, abash, °shock; °humiliate, °mortify, °embarrass, chagrin, *Colloq* °floor, *US* discombobulate

devastating *adj.* 1 °keen, °incisive, mordant, °penetrating, °trenchant, °telling; °sardonic, °sarcastic, °bitter, acid, °caustic, °savage, °satirical, °virulent, vitriolic 2 °ravishing, captivating, °enthralling, °stunning, °overpowering, bewitching, °spellbinding; spectacular

develop *v.* 1 bring out *or* forth, °advance, expand (on *or* upon), broaden, enlarge (on *or* upon), °amplify, evolve, expatiate (on *or* upon), elaborate (on *or* upon), °reveal, lay open, °expose, °unfold, °disclose, °bare, °(cause to) grow, realize the potential (of); °cultivate, °improve, °promote, °exploit, °strengthen 2 °(make) grow, °mature, °ripen, °age, °expand; °flower, blossom, bloom, °increase **3** °exhibit, °display, °show, °demonstrate, °manifest **4** °emerge, °arise, °appear, °come out, °come to light, evolve, °originate, °begin, °commence, °happen, °occur, °come about; come forth, °result

development *n.* **1** °occurrence, °happening, °event, °incident, °circumstance, °situation, °condition, °phenomenon **2** °evolution, °growth, evolvement, maturation, unfolding, maturing, °maturity, °increase, °expansion, enlargement, °increment; °advance, advancement, °progress; °improvement

deviant *adj.* **1** deviating, °divergent, °different, °abnormal, °strange, uncommon, °unusual, °odd, °peculiar, °curious, aberrant, °eccentric, idiosyncratic, °deviate, °queer, quirky, °weird, °bizarre, °offbeat, °singular, *Slang* °kinky, freaky, *Chiefly Brit* °bent **2** °perverse, °perverted, twisted, °unnatural, depraved, °degenerate, licentious, °lascivious, °lewd; °homosexual, °gay, lesbian, tribadistic, *Offensive and disparaging* °queer, homo, butch *—n.* **3** °homosexual, °gay, lesbian, tribade, sapphist, homophile; *All the following are offensive and denigrating* °pervert, °degenerate, °deviate, *Slang* °queer, homo, °queen, fairy, pansy, nancy (boy), nance, butch, (bull) dyke, *US and Canadian* °fag, faggot, °fruit, aunt, auntie, *Brit* poof, poofter, ginger (beer), *Caribbean* auntie man

deviate *v.* **1** turn aside *or* away, °swerve, veer, °wander, °stray, °drift, digress, °diverge; °divert *—adj., n.* **2** See **deviant, 1, 3,** above.

device *n.* **1** contrivance, °mechanism, °machine, machinery, °implement, utensil, °apparatus, °instrument, appliance, °tool, °gadget, °gimmick, *Colloq* °contraption, widget, thingamajig, *Brit* gubbins **2** °stratagem, °scheme, °trick, °artifice, °ruse, °plot, ploy, gambit, °strategy, °maneuver, °machination; machinery, °apparatus, °mechanism, contrivance, °gimmick, °tool, weapon **3** °design, °emblem, °figure, °(heraldic) bearing, insigne, cadency mark, mark of cadency, °hallmark, trademark, °symbol, badge, coat of arms, °seal, °crest, colophon, logotype, logo, monogram, °charge, °cognizance, signet; °motto, °slogan, °legend **4** *devices.* °pleasure, °disposition, °will, °inclination, °fancy, °desire, whim

devil *n.* **1** Satan, Lucifer, Mephistopheles, Beelzebub, Asmodeus, Abaddon, Apollyon, Belial, Lord of the Flies, prince of darkness, spirit of evil, evil spirit, cacodemon *or* cacodaemon, evil one, wicked one, archfiend, Fiend, deuce, *Scots* Clootie; *Colloq* Old Harry, (Old) Nick, *US* (Old) Scratch **2** °brute, °fiend, °demon, °beast, °ogre, °monster, °rogue, °scoundrel, °rake, knave, rakehell, °villain, ghoul, hellhound, vampire, °barbarian; °witch, hellcat, °shrew, termagant, vixen, virago, ogress, harpy, °hag, Xanthippe *or* Xantippe, crone **3** °fellow, °person, °chap, °wretch, bloke, °guy, °beggar, °unfortunate, *Colloq* °bugger, *Brit* sod **4** °imp, scamp, °rascal, fox, slyboots, sly dog, rapscallion, confidence man, trickster, *Colloq* °operator, smoothie, smooth *or* slick operator, con man, con artist **5** ***like the devil.*** °exceedingly, °extremely, excessively, violently, speedily, confoundedly, deucedly **6** ***—the devil.*** in heaven's name, the dickens, in the world, on God's green earth, in hell

devilish *adj.* diabolic(al), °satanic, Mephistophelian, °fiendish, demonic, cacodemonic, demoniac(al), °infernal, hellish, °villainous, °sinister, °wicked, °evil, iniquitous, °sinful, flagitious, heinous, malign, malevolent, °malignant, °cruel, maleficent; impish, °mischievous, prankish, °naughty, °crazy, madcap

devilry *n.* **1** deviltry, °mischief, mischievousness, roguery, naughtiness, rascality, roguishness, diablerie, archness, knavery, knavishness **2** deviltry, devilishness, wickedness, °evil, fiendishness, diablerie, cruelty, malice, malevolence, viciousness, perversity, iniquity, hellishness, villainy

devious *adj.* **1** °deceitful, underhand(ed), °insincere, °deceptive, misleading, subreptitious, °sneaky, furtive, °surreptitious, °secretive, double-dealing, treacherous, °dishonest, °shifty, °smooth, °slick, °slippery, °scheming, plotting, °designing, °foxy, vulpine, °wily, °sly, °crafty, °tricky, *Colloq* °crooked **2** °indirect, °roundabout, zigzag, °evasive, circuitous, °crooked, °rambling, °serpentine, °tortuous, sinuous, anfractuous

devise *v.* **1** concoct, °make up, °conceive, °scheme, contrive, dream up, °design, °draft, °frame, °form, °formulate, °plan, °arrange, °work out, °think up, °originate, °invent, °create, *Colloq* cook up **2** °bequeath, °will, convey, °hand down, °give, °assign, °dispose of, °transfer, °bestow

devote *v.* **1** °apply, °appropriate, °assign, °allot, °commit, allocate, set aside *or* apart, put away *or* aside, °dedicate, consecrate **2** °apply, °pledge, °dedicate, °commit, °give up

devoted *adj.* °faithful, °true, dedicated, committed, °devout, °loyal, loving, doting, °staunch, °tender, °steadfast, °constant; °ardent, caring, °fond, °earnest, zealous, °enthusiastic

devotee *n.* °fan, aficionado, adherent, votary, °enthusiast, °addict, *Colloq* buff, °fiend, *US* °hound; *Slang* °bug, nut, °freak, *US* °head, junkie, groupie

devotion *n.* **1** devotedness, devoutness, °reverence; earnestness, religiousness, °piety, religiosity, pietism, godliness, holiness, spirituality, °sanctity; °worship, °prayer, °observance, °ritual **2** °dedication, consecration, °attachment, °loyalty, devotedness **3** zeal, °ardor, °fervor, ardency, °intensity, °fanaticism, °eagerness, °enthusiasm, earnestness, °readiness, willingness; °love, °passion, infatuation, fondness, °affection °attachment, adherence, °loyalty, allegiance

devour *v.* **1** wolf (down), °gulp (down), °bolt, °swallow (up), °gorge, gobble (up) gormandize, °cram, °stuff, eat (up) greedily

Archaic gluttonize; *Colloq Brit* pig, *US and Canadian* pig out (on) **2** °consume, °waste, °destroy, °wipe out, °ravage, annihilate, °demolish, °ruin, wreak havoc upon, °devastate, °obliterate, eradicate **3** °relish, °revel in, absorb, be absorbed by; engulf, °consume, drink in, eat up, °swallow up, °take in; °swamp, °overcome, °overwhelm

devout *adj.* **1** °devoted, °pious, °religious, reverent, worshipful, °faithful, dedicated, °staunch, churchgoing; °holy, °godly, °saintly, °pure **2** devotional, reverential, °religious, °solemn **3** °earnest, °sincere, °genuine, °hearty, °heartfelt, °devoted, °ardent, zealous

dexterity *n.* **1** °touch, nimbleness, adroitness, deftness, °facility, °knack, °skill, °proficiency; sleight of hand **2** cleverness, °ingenuity, ingeniousness, °tact, astuteness, keenness, sharpness, shrewdness, cunning, guile, canniness, artfulness

dexterous *adj.* **1** dextrous, deft, lithe, °nimble, °supple, °agile, °quick, °skillful **2** °clever, °ingenious, °astute, °keen, °sharp, °shrewd, cunning, guileful, canny, °artful, °crafty, °slick

diabolic *adj.* **1** diabolical, °devilish, °satanic, Mephistophelian, demonic, demoniac(al), °fiendish, hellish, °infernal **2** diabolical, °cruel, °wicked, iniquitous, °evil, °fiendish, appalling, °dreadful, °inhuman, °atrocious, execrable, °abominable, °awful, °terrible, °damnable, accursed, horrid, °horrible, °hideous, °monstrous, odious, °vile, °base, °corrupt, °foul, depraved, flagitious, heinous, malicious, malevolent, malign, maleficent, °sinister, °sinful, °impious, °bad

diagnose *v.* °identify, °name, °determine, °recognize, °distinguish, pinpoint, °interpret; °analyze

dialect *n.* °speech (pattern), phraseology, °idiom, °accent, °pronunciation, patois, °vernacular; °jargon, °cant, slang, argot, °language, °tongue, creole, pidgin; brogue, burr, *Colloq* °lingo

dialogue *n.* **1** duologue, °conversation, °discussion, °conference, °talk, °chat, colloquy, communication **2** °parley, °conference, °meeting, °huddle, °tête-à-tête, colloquy, *Colloq US and Canadian* rap session

diary *n.* appointment book, datebook, °calendar, engagement book; °journal, °chronicle, log, °record, annal(s)

dicey *n.* °risky, °tricky, °dangerous, °difficult, °ticklish, unpredictable, °uncertain, unsure, °doubtful, *Colloq* iffy, chancy, °hairy

dicker *v.* **1** °bargain, °trade, barter, °deal, °haggle, °negotiate —*n.* **2** °bargain, °deal, °haggle, °negotiation

dictate *v.* **1** °say, °prescribe, ordain, °decree, °demand, °command, °lay down (the law), °order, °direct, °pronounce, °impose —*n.* **2** °decree, °demand, °command, °order, °direction, °instruction, °charge, °pronouncement, edict, fiat, ukase, mandate, caveat, °injunction, °requirement, °bidding, behest

dictator *n.* autocrat, absolute ruler *or* monarch, °despot, overlord, °oppressor, tsar *or* czar, °tyrant, Fuehrer *or* Führer

dictatorial *adj.* **1** °absolute, °arbitrary, °totalitarian, °authoritarian, autocratic, all-powerful, omnipotent, °unlimited **2** °despotic, °tyrannical, °authoritarian, iron-handed, °domineering, imperious, °overbearing, *Colloq* °bossy

diction *n.* **1** °language, °wording, (verbal *or* writing) style, °expression, °usage, expressiveness, °terminology, word choice, vocabulary, phraseology, phrasing, °rhetoric **2** articulation, °pronunciation, enunciation, °delivery, elocution, °oratory, °presentation, °speech, °intonation, inflection

dictionary *n.* lexicon, °glossary, wordbook; °thesaurus

die *v.* **1** lose one's life, lay down one's life, °perish, °expire, decease, suffer death, *Euphemistic* °depart, give up the ghost, be no more, (go to) meet one's maker, breathe one's last, go to the happy hunting grounds, go to one's reward, go to one's final resting place, go west, pay the debt of nature, pay one's debt to nature, pass through the pearly gates, pass away *or* on, join the majority, go the way of all flesh; *Slang* pop off, bite the dust, kick the bucket, croak, *Brit* snuff it, go for a burton, pop one's clogs, *US* turn up one's toes, cash in one's chips *or* checks **2** Often, ***die down or out or away.*** °dwindle, lessen, °diminish, °decrease, °ebb, °decline, °wane, °subside, wither (away), °wilt, °melt (away), °dissolve, °peter out, °fail, °weaken, °deteriorate, °disintegrate, °degenerate, °fade (away), °droop, molder, °sink, vanish, °disappear **3** °expire, °end, °stop, °cease **4** Usually, ***die off or out.*** become extinct, °perish **5** °long, pine, °yearn, crave, °hanker, °want, °desire, °hunger, °ache

diet[1] *n.* **1** °fare, °food, °nourishment, nutriment, °sustenance, °subsistence, victuals, intake, aliment **2** regimen, °regime —*v.* **3** °fast, abstain; °slim; °reduce

diet[2] *n.* °council, congress, °parliament, senate, legislature, °house, °chamber, °assembly

differ *v.* **1** °diverge, °deviate, be separate *or* distinct, be dissimilar *or* different, °contrast; °depart **2** °disagree, °conflict, °contradict, be contradictory, °vary, be at variance, °take issue, part company, °fall out, °quarrel, °argue

difference *n.* **1** °distinction, °dissimilarity, °discrepancy, unlikeness, °disagreement, inconsistency, °diversity, °variation, imbalance; °inequality, dissimilitude, incongruity, °contrast, contradistinction, contrariety **2** Often, ***differences.*** °dispute, °quarrel, °argument, °disagreement, °dissension, °conflict **3** °change, °alteration, metamorphosis, reformation, °transformation, conversion, °adjustment, modification **4** idiosyncrasy, °peculiarity, °characteristic, °character, °nature **5** °rest, °remainder, °leftover, °balance

different *adj.* **1** °unlike, unalike, °dissimilar, conflicting; °contrary, °discrete, contrastive, contrasting, disparate, °divergent, °diverse, °distinct, °opposite, °separate, distinguishable; another *or* other **2** °unique, °unusual, °peculiar, °odd, °singular, °particular, °distinctive, °personal, °extraordinary, °special, °remarkable, °bizarre, °rare, °weird, °strange, unconventional, °original, °out of the ordinary; °new, °novel, °exceptional, °unheard-of **3** assorted, °manifold, multifarious, numerous, °abundant, °sundry, °various, °varied, °divers, °many, °several

differentiate *v.* **1** °distinguish, °discriminate, contradistinguish, °separate, °contrast, °oppose, set off *or* apart, tell apart **2** °modify, specialize, °change, °alter, °transform, transmute, °convert, °adapt, °adjust

difficult *adj.* **1** °hard, °arduous, °toilsome, °strenuous, °tough, °laborious, °burdensome, onerous, °demanding; *US* like pulling teeth, *Brit* like drawing teeth; *Colloq US* tough sledding, hard going, *Chiefly Brit* hard slogging **2** °puzzling, °perplexing, baffling, enigmatic(al), °profound, abstruse, °obscure, °recondite, complex; °thorny, °intricate, °sensitive, knotty, problematic(al), °ticklish, scabrous **3** intractable, °recalcitrant, obstructive, °stubborn, unmanageable, °obstinate, °contrary, unaccommodating, refractory, unyielding, uncompromising; °naughty, ill-behaved; *Colloq Brit* bloody-minded **4** troubled, troubling, °tough, °burdensome, onerous, °demanding, °trying, °hard, °grim, °dark, unfavorable, straitening **5** °fussy, °particular, °demanding, °finicky, finical, °fastidious, °critical, °troublesome, *difficile,* °awkward, *Colloq* nitpicking

difficulty *n.* **1** °strain, °hardship, arduousness, laboriousness, formidableness, tribulation, painfulness **2** °hardship, °obstacle, °problem, °distress, °pitfall, °dilemma, °predicament, °problem, °snag, °hindrance; Gordian knot **3** Often, ***difficulties.*** °embarrassment, °plight, °predicament, °mess, strait(s), °trouble, °scrape, *Colloq* hot water, °jam, pickle, °fix; hot potato

diffuse *adj.* **1** spread (out *or* about *or* around), scattered, dispersed, widespread; °sparse, °meager, °thin (on the ground) **2** °wordy, verbose, prolix, long-winded, loquacious, °discursive, digressive, °rambling, circumlocutory, °meandering, °roundabout, circuitous, periphrastic, ambagious, diffusive, pleonastic —*v.* **3** °spread, °circulate, °distribute, °dispense, °disperse; dispel, °scatter, °broadcast, °sow, disseminate; °dissipate

dig *v.* **1** °excavate, °burrow, °gouge, °scoop, hollow out; °tunnel **2** °nudge, °thrust, °stab, °jab, °plunge, °force, °prod, °poke **3** °appreciate, °enjoy, °like, °understand **4** °notice, °note, °look at, °regard **5** ***dig into.*** °probe (into), delve into, go deeply into, °explore, °look into, °research, °study **6** ***dig out or up.*** °unearth, disinter, exhume, °bring up, °find, °obtain, °extract, ferret out, winkle out, °discover, °bring to light, °expose, dredge up, °extricate, come up with, *Australian* fossick —*n.* **7** °thrust, °poke, °jab, °stab, °nudge **8** °insult, insinuation, °gibe, °slur; °taunt, °jeer; *Colloq* °slap (in the face), °wisecrack, °crack, *US* low blow

digest *v.* **1** assimilate **2** °bear, °stand, °endure, °survive, assimilate, °accept, °tolerate, °brook, °swallow, °stomach **3** °comprehend, assimilate, °understand, °take in, °consider, °grasp, °study, °ponder, meditate (on *or* over), °reflect on, think over, °weigh **4** °abbreviate, °cut, condense, °abridge, compress, epitomize, summarize, °reduce, °shorten —*n.* **5** condensation, °abridgment, °abstract, °précis, °résumé, °synopsis, °summary, conspectus, °abbreviation

dignified *adj.* °stately, °noble, °majestic, °formal, °solemn, °serious, °sober, °grave, °distinguished, °honorable, distingué, °elegant, august, °sedate, °reserved; °regal, courtly, lordly, °lofty, °exalted, °grand

dignify *v.* °distinguish, ennoble, elevate, °raise, °exalt, °glorify, upraise, °lift, uplift, °enhance, °improve, °better, upgrade

dignitary *n.* °personage, °official, °notable, °worthy, magnate, °power, higher-up; °celebrity, lion, luminary, °star, superstar, *Colloq* VIP, °bigwig, big shot, big wheel, big name, big gun, hotshot, hot stuff, big noise, big White Chief, big Chief, big Daddy, *Brit* Lord *or* Lady Muck, high-muck-a-muck, *Slang* big cheese, *Chiefly US* Mr. Big, biggie, fat cat

dignity *n.* **1** °nobility, majesty, °gravity, gravitas, °solemnity, courtliness, °distinction, stateliness, °formality, °grandeur, eminence; hauteur, loftiness **2** °worth, worthiness, °nobility, nobleness, °excellence, °honor, honorableness, respectability, respectableness, °standing, °importance, greatness, °glory, °station, °status, °rank, °level, °position **3** °self-respect, self-regard, *amour-propre,* °self-confidence, °self-esteem, °pride, self-importance

digression *n.* **1** aside, departure, deviation, °detour, obiter dictum, parenthesis, apostrophe, excursus **2** digressing, deviating, divergence, going off at a tangent, °rambling, °meandering, straying, wandering, deviation

dilapidated *adj.* ruined, broken-down, in ruins, gone to rack and ruin, wrecked, destroyed, falling apart, °decrepit, °derelict, battered, tumbledown, °run-down, °ramshackle, crumbling, decayed, decaying, °rickety, °shaky, °shabby, *Brit* raddled

dilemma *n.* °predicament, °quandary, double bind, catch-22, °impasse, °deadlock, °stalemate; °plight, °difficulty, °trouble; °stymie, snooker; *Colloq* °bind, °box, °fix, °jam, °spot, pickle, °squeeze

dilettante *n.* dabbler, trifler, °aesthete, °amateur

diligent *adj.* persevering, °persistent, °industrious, assiduous, sedulous, °intent, °steady, °steadfast, focused, concentrated, °earnest, °attentive, °conscientious, hard-working, indefatigable, °tireless, °constant, °painstaking, °careful, °thorough, °scrupulous, °meticulous, punctilious

dilute *v.* °water (down), thin (down *or* out), °cut, °weaken, °doctor, °adulterate; °mitigate, lessen, °diminish, °decrease

dim *adj.* **1** °obscure, obscured, °vague, °faint, °weak, weakened, °pale, °imperceptible, °fuzzy, °indistinct, ill-defined, indiscernible, undefined, °indistinguishable, foggy, clouded, cloudy, °nebulous, blurred, blurry, unclear, °dull, °hazy, °misty, °dark, °shadowy, °murky, tenebrous, °gloomy, °somber, °dusky, crepuscular **2** °stupid, °obtuse, doltish, °dull, dull-witted, °foolish, slow-witted, dimwitted, °dense, *Colloq* °thick, °dumb —*v.* **3** °obscure, °dull, becloud **4** darken, bedim, °shroud, °shade

diminish *v.* **1** °decrease, °decline, abate, lessen, °reduce, °lower, °shrink, °curtail, °contract, °lop, crop, °dock, °clip, °prune, °cut, truncate, °cut down, °abbreviate, °shorten, °abridge, compress, condense, °pare (down), °scale down, boil down **2** °belittle, °disparage, °degrade, °downgrade, °discredit, °detract (from), °vitiate, °debase, deprecate, demean, derogate, °depreciate, vilipend, devalue, cheapen, °put down, °dismiss, °humiliate, demean, °reject **3** °wane, °fade, °dwindle, °ebb, die out *or* away, °peter out, soap out, °recede, °subside; slacken, °let up, °wind down, °slow (down), °ease (off), *Colloq* run out of steam

diminutive *adj.* °small, °tiny, °little, °miniature, °petite, °minute, minuscule, mini, °compact, °undersized, °pocket, pocket-sized, pygmy, °elfin, Lilliputian, midget, °wee, microscopic; micro, infinitesimal; *US* vest-pocket, vest-pocket-sized, *Colloq* teeny, teeny-weeny *or* teensy-weensy, itty-bitty *or* itsy-bitsy

din *n.* **1** °noise, clamor, °uproar, shouting, screaming, yelling, babel, clangor, clatter, commotion, °racket, °row, hullabaloo, hubbub, hurly-burly, °rumpus, °blare, blaring, bray, braying, °bellow, bellowing, °roar, °blast, roaring, °pandemonium, °tumult, *Colloq* hollering —*v.* **2** °instill, drum, hammer

dine *v.* °eat, °banquet, °feast, sup, break bread, breakfast, lunch, have a bite *or* snack, nibble, *Colloq* °feed, *Slang* nosh

dingy *adj.* °dark, °dull, °gloomy, °dim, °lackluster, faded, discolored, °dusky, °drab, °dreary, °dismal, cheerless, depressing, °gloomy, °shadowy, tenebrous, smoky, sooty, gray-brown, smudgy, grimy, °dirty, soiled

dip *v.* **1** °immerse, °plunge, °duck, dunk, douse, bathe, °submerge **2** °decline, °go down, °fall, °descend, °sag, °sink, °subside, °slump **3** *dip in or into.* °dabble in, °play at; °skim, °scan —*n.* **4** swim, °plunge; immersion; *Brit* bathe **5** lowering, °sinking, °depression, °drop, °slump, °decline

diplomacy *n.* **1** °tact, tactfulness, adroitness, °discretion **2** statecraft, statesmanship, °negotiation; °intrigue, Machiavellianism, °machination, maneuvering

diplomatic *adj.* °tactful, °discreet, °prudent, °wise, °sensitive, °politic, °courteous, °polite, discerning, °perceptive, perspicacious, °thoughtful

direct *v.* **1** °manage, °handle, °run, °administer, °govern, °regulate, °control, °operate, superintend, °supervise, °command, head up, °rule; *Colloq* °call the shots **2** °guide, °lead, °conduct, °pilot, °steer, show *or* point (the way), be at the helm; °advise, °counsel, °instruct, °mastermind; usher, °escort **3** °rule, °command, °order, °require, °bid, °tell, °instruct, °charge, °dictate, enjoin; °appoint, ordain **4** °aim, °focus, °level, °point, °train; °turn **5** °send, °address, °post, °mail —*adj.* **6** °straight, unswerving, shortest, undeviating, °through **7** uninterrupted, unreflected, unrefracted, without interference, unobstructed **8** unbroken, lineal **9** straightforward, °unmitigated, °outright, °matter-of-fact, °categorical, °plain, °clear, unambiguous, unmistakable, °to the point, without *or* with no beating about the bush, °unqualified, unequivocal, °point-blank, °explicit, °express **10** straightforward, °frank, °candid, °outspoken, plain-spoken, °honest, °blunt, °open, °uninhibited, unreserved, °forthright, °honest, °sincere, unequivocal; undiplomatic, °tactless

direction *n.* **1** directing, aiming, pointing, guiding, °guidance, conducting, °conduct, instructing, °instruction, managing, °management, administering, °administration, governing, °government, supervising, supervision, operating, °operation, °running, °leadership, directorship, directorate, °control, captaincy, handling, manipulation, °regulation, °rule, °charge **2** Often, ***directions.*** instruction(s), °information; °bearing, °road, °way, °route, avenue, °course

directly *adv.* **1** °straight, in a beeline, unswervingly, undeviatingly, as the crow flies **2** °immediately, °at once, °straightaway, right away, °quickly, °promptly, without delay, speedily, instantly, *Colloq US and Canadian* momentarily **3** °soon, later (on), anon, °presently, in a (little) while, °shortly **4** °exactly, °precisely, °just; °completely, °entirely —*conj.* **5** as soon as, when

director *n.* **1** °executive, administrator, °official, °principal; chairman, president, vice president; governor; °head, °chief, °boss, °manager, °superintendent, °supervisor, °overseer, °foreman, headman, *Colloq* kingpin, number one, numero uno, Mr. Big, the man; *Slang* top dog, top banana, *Brit* gaffer, *US* big cheese, head *or* chief honcho **2** °guide, °leader; steersman, helmsman, °pilot, °skipper, commander, commandant, captain; cicerone; maestro, concertmaster, conductor; impresario

dirt *n.* **1** °soil, °mud, °muck, °mire, °grime, slime, °sludge, °ooze, slop; dust, soot; excrement, ordure; °filth, °waste, °refuse, °trash, °garbage, °rubbish, offal, °junk, dross, sweepings; leavings, °scrap, orts; *Slang Brit* gunge, *US* grunge **2** °soil, °earth, loam, °ground, clay **3** indecency, obscenity, smut, °pornography, foulness, corruption, °filth, vileness **4** °gossip, °scandal, °talk, °rumor, inside information, *Colloq* °lowdown, °(inside) dope, *Slang US* scuttlebutt

dirty *adj.* **1** °foul, unclean, befouled, soiled, begrimed, sooty, grimy, °filthy, mucky, besmeared, besmirched, polluted, squalid, sullied, stained, spotted, smudged, slovenly, °unwashed, °bedraggled, slatternly, °untidy, *Slang Brit* gungy, *US* grungy **2** smutty, °indecent, °obscene, ribald, °off-color, °prurient, °risqué, salacious, °lewd, °lascivious, salacious, °pornographic, °coarse, licentious, °rude, °blue, scabrous **3** unfair, °unscrupulous, unsporting, °dishonest, °mean, underhand(ed), unsportsmanlike, °dishonorable, °deceitful, °corrupt, treacherous, °perfidious, °villainous, °disloyal; malicious, malevolent, °rotten, °filthy **4** °bad, °foul, °nasty, °stormy, rainy, °windy, blowy, blowing, squally, °sloppy **5** °bitter, °resentful, °angry, °furious, wrathful, smoldering **6** °sordid, °base, °mean, °despicable, °contemptible, ignoble, °scurvy, °low, °lowdown, ignominious, °vile, °nasty, °infamous —*v.* **7** °stain, °sully, befoul, °soil, begrime, besmirch, °pollute, °muddy, °smear, defile; °blacken, °tarnish

disability *n.* **1** °handicap, °impairment, °defect, °infirmity, disablement **2** °inability, incapacity, unfitness, °impotence, powerlessness, helplessness

disabled *adj.* incapacitated, °crippled, °lame; damaged, ruined, impaired, harmed, nonfunctioning, inoperative, *Slang Brit* scuppered

disadvantage *n.* **1** deprivation, °setback, °drawback, °liability, °handicap, °defect, °flaw, °shortcoming, °weakness, weak spot, °fault **2** °detriment, °harm, °loss, °injury, °damage; °prejudice, °disservice

disagree *v.* **1** °differ, dissent, °diverge **2** °conflict, °dispute, °quarrel, °argue, contend, °contest, °bicker, °fight, °fall out, squabble, wrangle, °debate

disagreeable *adj.* **1** unpleasant, unpleasing, °offensive, °distasteful, °repugnant, °obnoxious, °repellent, °repulsive, objectionable, °revolting, odious **2** °offensive, noxious, °unsavory, °unpalatable, nauseating, °nauseous, °nasty, sickening, °disgusting, °revolting, °repellent, °abominable, objectionable **3** bad-tempered, ill-tempered, disobliging, uncooperative, unfriendly, uncivil, °abrupt, °blunt, °curt, °brusque, °short, uncourtly, °impolite, bad-mannered, °ill-mannered, °discourteous, °rude, °testy, grouchy, splenetic, °cross, ill-humored, °peevish, morose, sulky, °sullen

disagreement *n.* **1** °difference, °discrepancy, °discord, discordance, discordancy, °dissimilarity, disaccord, °diversity, incongruity, nonconformity, incompatibility **2** dissent, °opposition, °conflict, contradiction, °difference, °disparity **3** °quarrel, °strife, °argument, °dispute, velitation, altercation, °controversy, contention, °dissension, °debate, °clash, *Colloq US* rhubarb

disappear *v.* **1** vanish, °evaporate, vaporize, fade (away *or* out), evanesce, *Poetic* evanish **2** die (out *or* off), become extinct, °cease (to exist), °perish (without a trace)

disappoint *v.* **1** °let down, °fail, dissatisfy **2** °mislead, °deceive, disenchant, *Colloq* °stand up **3** °undo, °frustrate, °foil, °thwart, balk, °defeat

disappointed *adj.* **1** frustrated, unsatisfied, °dissatisfied, disillusioned, °disenchanted, discouraged, °downhearted, disheartened, downcast, saddened, °unhappy, °dejected, °discontented, °let down **2** foiled, thwarted, balked, defeated, °undone, failed, °let down

disappointing *adj.* discouraging, dissatisfying, °unsatisfactory, unsatisfying, °disconcerting; °poor, second-rate, °sorry, °inadequate, °insufficient, °inferior, °pathetic, °sad

disappointment *n.* **1** frustration, nonfulfillment, unfulfillment, unsatisfaction, °dissatisfaction, °setback, °failure, °letdown, °defeat, °blow, °fiasco, °calamity, °disaster, °fizzle, *Brit* damp squib, *Colloq* °washout **2** dejection, °depression, discouragement, disenchantment, °distress, °regret, mortification, chagrin

disapproval *n.* disapprobation, condemnation, censure, °criticism, °reproof, reproach, °objection, °exception, °disfavor, °displeasure, °dissatisfaction

disapprove *v.* °condemn, °criticize, censure, object to, decry, °denounce, animadvert on *or* upon, put *or* run down, deplore, deprecate, °belittle, °look down on, frown on *or* upon, *Colloq* °knock, look down one's nose at, tut-tut

disarm *v.* **1** unarm; demilitarize, demobilize, °disband, deactivate **2** °win over, put *or* set at ease, mollify, appease, placate, pacify, °reconcile, conciliate, propitiate, °charm

disaster *n.* °catastrophe, °calamity, cataclysm, °tragedy, °misfortune, debacle, °accident, °mishap, °blow, act of God, adversity, °trouble, °reverse

disastrous *adj.* **1** °calamitous, catastrophic, cataclysmic, °tragic, °destructive, °ruinous, °devastating, appalling, °harrowing, °awful, °terrible, dire, horrendous, °horrible, horrifying, °dreadful, °fatal **2** °awful, °terrible, unlucky, °unfortunate, °detrimental, °grievous, °harmful

disband *v.* °disperse, disorganize, °scatter, °break up, °dissolve, demobilize, deactivate, °retire

discard *v.* **1** °get rid of, °dispense with, °dispose of, throw away *or* out, toss out *or* away, °abandon, jettison, °scrap, *Colloq* °trash, °dump, *Slang* ditch —*n.* **2** °reject, castoff

discernible *adj.* **1** °perceptible, °visible, seeable, perceivable, °apparent, °clear, °observable, °plain, detectable; °conspicuous, °noticeable **2** distinguishable, recognizable, identifiable, °distinct

discharge *v.* 1 °release, °let out, °dismiss, let go, send away; °pardon, exonerate, °liberate, °(set) free, acquit, °let off, absolve 2 °expel, oust, °dismiss, cashier, °eject, °give notice, *Colloq* °sack, give (someone) the sack, °fire, kick out 3 °shoot, °fire (off); set *or* let off, detonate, °explode 4 °emit, send out *or* forth, pour out *or* forth, °gush; disembogue; °ooze, °leak, exude; excrete, °void 5 °carry out, °perform, °fulfill, °accomplish, do, °execute 6 °pay, °settle, liquidate, °clear, °honor, °meet, °square (up) 7 °unload, offload, disburden, °empty —*n.* 8 °release, °dismissal 9 °expulsion, ouster, °dismissal, °ejection, °notice, *Colloq* the ax, °the sack, the boot, *Slang US and Canadian* one's walking papers, the bounce, the gate 10 shooting, firing (off), °report, °shot; salvo, fusillade, °volley; detonation, °explosion, °burst 11 emission, °release, °void, voiding, excretion, excreting, emptying, °flow; °ooze, oozing, pus, suppuration, °secretion, seepage 12 °performance, °fulfillment, °accomplishment, °execution, °observance, °achievement 13 °payment, °settlement, liquidation, squaring (up), °clearance 14 unloading, disburdening, offloading, emptying

disciple *n.* 1 °apprentice, °pupil, °student, proselyte, °learner, °scholar 2 °follower, adherent, °devotee, °admirer, votary; °partisan, °fan, aficionado

disciplinarian *n.* taskmaster, martinet, drill sergeant; °tyrant, °despot, °dictator

discipline *n.* 1 training, drilling, regimen, °exercise, °practice, °drill, inculcation, indoctrination, °instruction, °schooling 2 °punishment, °penalty, chastisement, castigation, °correction 3 °order, °routine, °(proper) behavior, °decorum 4 °direction, °rule, °regulation, °government, °control, °subjection, °restriction, °check, °curb, °restraint 5 °subject, °course, branch of knowledge, °area, °field, °specialty —*v.* 6 °train, °break in, °condition, °drill, °exercise, °instruct, °coach, °teach, °school, °indoctrinate, inculcate; edify, °enlighten, °inform 7 °check, °curb, °restrain, °bridle, °control, °govern, °direct, °run, °supervise, °manage, °regulate, hold *or* keep in check, *US* ride herd on 8 °punish, °chastise, °castigate, °correct, °penalize, °reprove, °criticize, °reprimand, °rebuke

disclose *v.* 1 °reveal, °impart, divulge, °betray, °release, °tell, °blurt out, °blab, °leak, °let slip, °report, °inform, *Colloq* °spill the beans, blow the gaff, *Slang* squeal, snitch, squeak, rat, peach, *US* fink 2 °bare, °reveal, °expose, uncover, °show, °unveil

discomfit *v.* 1 °embarrass, abash, disconcert, °disturb, °confuse, make uneasy *or* uncomfortable, discompose, °fluster, °ruffle, confound, °perturb, °upset, °worry, unsettle, °unnerve, *Colloq* °rattle, *US* faze, discombobulate 2 °frustrate, °foil, °thwart, baffle, °check, °defeat, trump, °outdo, °outwit, °overcome

discomfort *n.* 1 uneasiness, °hardship, °difficulty, °trouble, °care, °worry, °distress, vexation 2 °ache, °pain, °twinge, soreness, irritation; °bother, °inconvenience, °nuisance

disconcerted *adj.* discomposed, discomfited, ruffled, uneasy, put out *or* off, uncomfortable, °queasy, flustered, °agitated, °upset, shaken, °unsettled, perturbed, °confused, bewildered, perplexed, baffled, puzzled, *US* thrown off, *Colloq* rattled, *US* fazed, discombobulated; *Slang* (all) shook (up)

disconcerting *adj.* °awkward, discomfiting, off-putting, upsetting, unnerving, °unsettling, °disturbing, confusing, confounding, bewildering, °perplexing, baffling, °puzzling

disconnect *v.* °separate, disjoin, disunite, uncouple, °detach, unhook, °undo, °disengage, unhitch; cut *or* break off; cut *or* pull apart, °part, °divide, °sever

disconnected *adj.* 1 unconnected, °separate, °apart, °unattached; °split, separated 2 °incoherent, irrational, °confused, illogical, garbled, °disjointed, °rambling, mixed-up, unintelligible, uncoordinated, °random

discontent *n.* °displeasure, unhappiness, °dissatisfaction, discontentment, °distaste, uneasiness; malaise

discontented *adj.* displeased, °dissatisfied, °discontent, annoyed, vexed, °fretful, irritated, °testy, piqued, °petulant, °disgruntled, exasperated, *Colloq* fed up, *Slang* browned off, pissed off, *Brit* cheesed *or* brassed off

discontinue *v.* °cease, °break off, °give up, °stop, °terminate, put an end to, °quit, °leave off, °drop; °interrupt, °suspend

discord *n.* °strife, °dissension, °disagreement, °conflict, disharmony, contention, disunity, discordance, °division, incompatibility

discordant *adj.* 1 °contrary, disagreeing, °divergent, °opposite, °opposed, adverse, °contradictory, °incompatible, differing, °different, conflicting, °at odds, °incongruous, in conflict, in disagreement, °at variance, °dissimilar 2 inharmonious, dissonant, jarring, cacophonous, unmelodious, unmusical, °harsh, °strident, jangling, °grating

discount *v.* 1 °reduce, °mark down, °deduct, °lower, take *or* knock off 2 °diminish, lessen, °minimize, °detract from 3 °disregard, °omit, °ignore, pass *or* gloss over, °overlook, °brush off, °dismiss —*n.* 4 reduction, markdown, °deduction, °rebate, °allowance

discourage *v.* 1 dispirit, dishearten, °daunt, unman, °dismay, cow, °intimidate, awe, °overawe, °unnerve 2 °deter, °put off, dissuade, advise *or* hint against, talk out of, divert from; °oppose, °disapprove (of), °dampen, *Colloq* throw cold water on 3 °prevent, °inhibit, °hinder, °stop, °slow, °suppress, obviate

discourteous *adj.* uncivil, °impolite, °rude, unmannerly, °ill-mannered, bad-mannered, °disrespectful, misbehaved, °boorish, °abrupt, °curt, °brusque, °short, ungentlemanly, unladylike, °insolent, °impertinent, °ungracious

discover *v.* **1** °find (out), °learn, °perceive, °unearth, uncover, °bring to light, turn *or* dig up, smoke *or* search out, root *or* ferret out; °determine, ascertain, °track down, °identify; °locate **2** °see, °spot, catch sight *or* a glimpse of, lay eyes on, °behold, °view, °encounter, °meet (with); °notice, espy, descry, °detect, discern **3** °originate, °conceive (of), °devise, contrive, °invent, °make up, °design, °pioneer; come *or* chance *or* stumble upon

discovery *n.* **1** °finding, °recognition, uncovering, determining, ascertaining, unearthing; origination, °invention, °conception, °idea; °development **2** °exploration, disclosure, detection, °revelation

discredit *v.* **1** °detract, °disparage, defame, °dishonor, °disgrace, °degrade, bring into disfavor *or* disrepute, deprecate, demean, °lower, devalue, °depreciate, devaluate, °belittle, °diminish, °reduce; °slur, °slander, °vilify, calumniate, °sully, °smear, °blacken, °taint, °tarnish, besmirch, smirch, °stigmatize, asperse, malign, °libel **2** disbelieve, °deny, °dispute, °doubt, °question, raise doubts about, °distrust, °mistrust, give no credit *or* credence to **3** °disprove, °reject, refute, invalidate; °mock, °ridicule —*n.* **4** °dishonor, °degradation, °disfavor, disrepute, ill repute, °disgrace, ignominy, °infamy, odium, °stigma, °shame, °smear, °slur, °scandal, obloquy, opprobrium, °humiliation **5** °damage, °harm, °reflection, °slur, °aspersion, °slander, defamation, °blot, °brand, °tarnish, °blemish, °taint **6** °doubt, °skepticism, dubiousness, doubtfulness, °qualm, °scruple, °question, incredulity, °suspicion, °distrust, °mistrust

discreet *adj.* °careful, °cautious, °prudent, °judicious, °considerate, °guarded, °tactful, °diplomatic, circumspect, °wary, chary, heedful, watchful, circumspect

discrepancy *n.* °gap, °disparity, lacuna, °difference, °dissimilarity, deviation, divergence, °disagreement, incongruity, incompatibility, inconsistency, °variance; °conflict, discordance, contrariety

discrete *adj.* °separate, °distinct, °individual, °disconnected, °unattached, discontinuous

discretion *n.* **1** °tact, °diplomacy, °prudence, °care, discernment, sound judgment, circumspection, sagacity, common sense, good sense, °wisdom, °discrimination **2** °choice, °option, °judgment, °preference, °pleasure, °disposition, °volition; °wish, °will, °liking, °inclination

discriminate *v.* **1** °distinguish, °separate, °differentiate, discern, draw a distinction, tell the difference **2** °favor, °disfavor, °segregate, show favor *or* prejudice *or* bias for *or* against, be intolerant

discriminating *adj.* discerning, °perceptive, °critical, °keen, °fastidious, °selective, °particular, °fussy, °refined, °cultivated

discrimination *n.* **1** °bigotry, °prejudice, °bias, °intolerance, °favoritism, one-sidedness, unfairness, inequity **2** °taste, °perception, perceptiveness, discernment, °refinement, acumen, °insight, °penetration, keenness, °judgment, °sensitivity; connoisseurship, aestheticism

discursive *adj.* wandering, °meandering, digressing, digressive, °rambling, circuitous, °roundabout, °diffuse, long-winded, verbose, °wordy, prolix, °windy

discuss *v.* converse about, talk over *or* about, chat about, °deliberate (over), °review, °examine, consult on; °debate, °argue, thrash out

discussion *n.* °conversation, °talk, °chat, °dialogue, colloquy, °exchange, deliberation, °examination, °scrutiny, °analysis, °review; confabulation, °conference, powwow; °debate, °argument; *Colloq chiefly Brit* chinwag, *US and Canadian* bull session

disdainful *adj.* °contemptuous, °scornful, contumelious, derisive, sneering, °superior, °supercilious, °pompous, °proud, prideful, °arrogant, °haughty, °snobbish, lordly, °regal; jeering, mocking, °insolent, insulting, *Colloq* °hoity-toity, high and mighty, stuck-up, highfalutin *or* hifalutin; *Slang* snotty

disease *n.* **1** sickness, °affliction, °ailment, malady, °illness, infection, °complaint, °disorder, °condition, °infirmity, °disability, *Archaic* murrain, *Colloq* °bug **2** °blight, cancer, virus, °plague; contagion

diseased *adj.* °unhealthy, unwell, °ill, °sick, ailing, °unsound, °infirm, °out of sorts, abed, infected, contaminated; afflicted, °abnormal

disembark *v.* °land, alight, go *or* put ashore, get *or* step off *or* out, °leave; debark, detrain, deplane

disembodied *adj.* incorporeal, bodiless; °intangible, °immaterial, insubstantial *or* unsubstantial, impalpable, °unreal; °spiritual, °ghostly, °spectral, °phantom, wraithlike

disenchanted *adj.* disillusioned, disabused, undeceived, °disappointed; °blasé, °indifferent, °jaundiced, sour(ed), cynical

disengage *v.* °loose, °loosen, unloose, °detach, unfasten, °release, °disconnect, disjoin, °undo, disunite, °divide, °cleave (from), °separate, uncouple, °part, disinvolve, °extricate, get out (of), °get away (from), cut loose, °throw off, °shake (off), °get rid of, break (with *or* from), break (up) (with); unbuckle, unhitch, unclasp, unlatch, unbolt, unlock, unleash, unfetter, unchain, unlace, unhook, unbind, untie; °(set) free, °liberate, disentangle

disfavor *n.* **1** °disapproval, °dislike, °displeasure, disapprobation, unhappiness **2** disesteem, °discredit, °dishonor, °disgrace, disrepute —*v.* **3** °disapprove (of), °dislike, discountenance, frown on *or* upon

disfigured *adj.* marred, damaged, scarred, defaced, mutilated, injured, impaired, blemished, disfeatured, °deformed, distorted, spoilt *or* spoiled, ruined

disgrace *n.* **1** ignominy, °shame, °humiliation, °embarrassment, °degradation, debasement, °dishonor, °discredit, °disfavor, disrepute, vitiation, °infamy; disesteem, °contempt, odium, obloquy, opprobrium **2** °blemish, °harm, °aspersion, °blot, °scandal, °slur, °stigma, vilification, smirch, °smear, °stain, °taint, black mark —*v.* **3** °shame, °humiliate, °embarrass, °mortify **4** °degrade, °debase, °dishonor, °discredit, °disfavor, °vitiate, defame, °disparage, °scandalize, °slur, °stain, °taint, °stigmatize, °sully, besmirch, smirch, °tarnish, °smear, asperse, °vilify, °blacken, drag through the mud, reflect (adversely) on

disgraceful *adj.* **1** °shameful, humiliating, °embarrassing, °dishonorable, °disreputable, °infamous, ignominious, °degrading, debasing, degraded, debased, °base, °low, °vile, °corrupt, °bad, °wrong, °sinful, °evil, °mean, °despicable, °contemptible, opprobrious **2** °shameless, °outrageous, °notorious, °shocking, °scandalous, °improper, °unseemly, °unworthy; °indecent, °rude, °flagrant, °lewd, °lascivious, °delinquent, objectionable

disgruntled *adj.* displeased, °dissatisfied, irritated, peeved, vexed, °cross, exasperated, annoyed, °unhappy, °disappointed, °discontented, °put out; malcontent, °discontent, °testy, °cranky, °peevish, grouchy, grumpy, °moody, °sullen, sulky, ill-humored, bad-tempered, ill-tempered, *Colloq* fed up, *Slang* browned off, *Brit* cheesed off

disguise *v.* **1** °camouflage, °cover up, °conceal, °hide, °mask **2** °misrepresent, °falsify, °counterfeit, °fake, °deceive —*n.* **3** °guise, °identity, coverup, °camouflage, °appearance, °semblance, °form, °outfit, °costume **4** °pretense, °deception, °dissimulation, façade, °semblance, *Colloq* °front

disgust *v.* **1** °sicken, °offend, °nauseate, °repel, °revolt, °put off, °outrage, °appall, *Slang* gross out —*n.* **2** °revulsion, nausea, sickness, repugnance, fulsomeness, °outrage, °distaste, °aversion **3** °loathing, °contempt, hatred, abhorrence, odium, animus, °animosity, enmity, °antagonism, antipathy, °dislike

disgusted *adj.* °nauseated, sickened, °nauseous, °queasy; offended, outraged, *Colloq* fed up (with), °sick (of), sick and tired (of); *Slang US* grossed out

disgusting *adj.* nauseating, sickening, °offensive, °outrageous, sick-making, fulsome, °repulsive, °revolting, °repugnant, off-putting, °repellent, °obnoxious, °loathsome, °gross, °vile, °foul, °nasty; unappetizing, °unsavory, objectionable, °distasteful

dishonest *adj.* untrustworthy, underhand(ed), °dishonorable, °fraudulent, °fake, °counterfeit, deceiving, °deceptive, unfair, double-dealing, thieving, thievish, knavish, cheating, °deceitful, °lying, untruthful, mendacious, treacherous, °perfidious, °corrupt, °unscrupulous, unprincipled; °two-faced, °hypocritical; *Colloq* °crooked, °shady; *Chiefly Brit slang* °bent

dishonor *v.* **1** °insult, °abuse, affront, °outrage, °slight, °offend, °injure **2** °disgrace, °degrade, °shame, °debase, °humiliate, °mortify, abase, °vitiate, °humble **3** defile, °violate, °ravish, °rape, °seduce, deflower, debauch —*n.* **4** disesteem, °disrespect, irreverence, °slight, °indignity, ignominy, °disgrace, °shame, disrepute, °discredit, °insult, °offense, affront, loss of face, depreciation, belittlement, disparagement, detraction, derogation, obloquy **5** °aspersion, defamation, °libel, °slander, °blot, °slur, °smear, smirch, black mark, °blemish, denigration

dishonorable *adj.* **1** °disgraceful, °degrading, inglorious, ignominious, °shameful, shaming, °base, debased **2** unprincipled, °shameless, °corrupt, °unscrupulous, untrustworthy, treacherous, °traitorous, °perfidious, °dishonest, °hypocritical, °two-faced, duplicitous, °disreputable, discreditable, °base, °despicable; °disloyal, unfaithful, °faithless **3** °improper, °unseemly, °unbecoming, °unworthy, °outrageous, objectionable, reprehensible, °flagrant, °bad, °evil, °vile, °low, °mean, °contemptible, below *or* beneath criticism, °foul, heinous, °dirty, °filthy

disillusion *v.* disabuse, °disappoint, disenchant, break the spell, °enlighten, set straight, disentrance, disenthrall, undeceive

disinclined *adj.* °averse, °indisposed, °reluctant, unwilling, °loath, °opposed, unwilling; °hesitant

disinfect *v.* °clean, °cleanse, °purify, °purge, sanitize, °fumigate, decontaminate, °sterilize

disinfectant *n.* germicide, antiseptic, sterilizer, bactericide, sanitizer, fumigant, decontaminant, decontaminator, purifier, cleaner, cleanser

disingenuous *adj.* °clever, °artful, °crafty, °sly, on the qui vive, cunning, insidious, °foxy, °wily, °slick, °smooth; °insincere, °false, °dishonest, °tricky, °devious, °deceitful, underhand(ed), guileful, °shifty; double-dealing, °two-faced, duplicitous, °hypocritical, °scheming, plotting, °calculating, °designing, contriving

disintegrate *v.* break up *or* apart, °shatter, come *or* fall apart, come *or* go *or* fall to pieces, °crumble; °decompose, °rot, °decay, molder

disinterested *n.* unbiased, °impartial, °unprejudiced, altruistic, °objective, °fair, °neutral, open-minded, °equitable, °just, °dispassionate, °detached, evenhanded, °impersonal, uninvolved

disjointed *adj.* **1** disjoined, separate(d), °disconnected, unconnected, dismembered, disunited, divided, °split (up) **2** ununified, °loose, °incoherent, °confused, °aimless, directionless, °rambling, muddled, jumbled, mixed up, °fitful, discontinuous, disorganized, unorganized, °disorderly

dislike *v.* **1** be averse to, °mind, turn from, °disfavor, disesteem, be put *or* turned off by; °hate, °loathe, °scorn, °despise, contemn, °detest, abominate, execrate, *Brit* take a scunner (to) —*n.* **2** °aversion, °displeasure, °distaste, °disfavor, disesteem, disrelish, disaffection, disinclination; °loathing, hatred, animus, °animosity, antipathy, detestation, °contempt, execration, °ill will; °disgust, repugnance; °hostility, °antagonism, *Brit* scunner

disloyal *adj.* unfaithful, °faithless, °untrue, °false, untrustworthy, recreant; treasonable *or* treasonous, treacherous, °traitorous, unpatriotic, °subversive, °perfidious, °deceitful; °renegade, apostate, °heretical

dismal *adj.* depressing, °gloomy, cheerless, °melancholy, °somber, °dreary, °sad, °bleak, °funereal, lugubrious, °forlorn, morose, °solemn, °dark, °grim, °wretched, °woebegone, woeful, °black, °blue, °joyless, °doleful, dolorous, °unhappy, °miserable, lowering; °pessimistic

dismay *v.* **1** °alarm, °frighten, °scare, °terrify, appall *or* appal, °panic, °horrify, °petrify, °intimidate, cow, disconcert, °unnerve **2** unsettle, discompose, °upset, °discourage, °take aback, °startle, °shock, °put off, dishearten —*n.* **3** consternation, °alarm, °anxiety, °agitation, °terror, °panic, °horror, °shock, °fright, °fear, trepidation, apprehension, °dread, awe

dismiss *v.* **1** °discharge, oust, °release, °give notice (to), let go, °lay off, °throw out, toss out, °remove, *Chiefly military* cashier, *Old-fashioned military* drum out, *Brit politics* deselect, *Colloq* °fire, send packing, kick out, send to the showers, *Brit* °sack, give (someone) the sack, °boot (out), °turn off, *US* give (someone) (his/her) walking papers, give (someone) a pink slip, can; *Slang* give (someone) the (old) heave-ho **2** °reject, °set aside, °repudiate, °spurn, °discount, °disregard, lay aside, put out of one's mind, think no more of, °write off, °banish, have *or* be done with, °scorn, °discard, °ignore, shrug off; °belittle, °diminish, pooh-pooh **3** °disperse, °release, °disband, send away

dismissal *n.* **1** °discharge, °expulsion, °notice, *Colloq* firing, °bounce, marching orders, walking papers, *Brit* °sack, sacking, one's cards, *US* pink slip; *Slang* the (old) heave-ho, *Brit* the boot **2** °cancellation, adjournment, °discharge, °end, °release; congé

disobedient *adj.* **1** °insubordinate, °unruly, °naughty, °mischievous, °bad, ill-behaved, badly behaved, °obstreperous, unmanageable, refractory, fractious, °ungovernable, uncomplying, unsubmissive, wayward, noncompliant, incompliant, intractable, °defiant; °delinquent, °derelict, disregardful, °remiss, undutiful **2** °contrary, °perverse, °willful, headstrong, °stubborn, °recalcitrant, obdurate, °obstinate, contumacious, wayward, cross-grained, °opposed, °mutinous, °rebellious, °revolting, anarchic, *Colloq* pigheaded

disobey *v.* °defy, °break, contravene, °flout, °disregard, °ignore, °resist, °oppose, °violate, °transgress, °overstep, go counter to, °fly in the face of, °infringe, °thumb one's nose at, °snap one's fingers at, *Brit* cock a snook at; °mutiny, °rebel, °revolt, °strike

disorder *n.* **1** disarray, °confusion, °chaos, disorderliness, disorganization, untidiness, °mess, °muddle, °jumble, °hash, °mishmash, °tangle, hotchpotch *or US and Canadian also* hodgepodge, derangement, °shambles, °clutter **2** °tumult, °riot, °disturbance, °pandemonium, °upheaval, °ferment, °fuss, °unrest, °uproar, hubbub, hullabaloo, commotion, clamor, turbulence, turmoil, turbulence, °violence, °bedlam, free-for-all, °rumpus, brouhaha, °fracas, affray, °fray, °brawl, donnybrook, scuffle, °fight, melee *or* mêlée, battle royal, °battle, civil disorder, breach of the peace, *Colloq Brit* kerfuffle *or* carfuffle *or* kurfuffle, *Slang Brit* bovver **3** °ailment, °illness, sickness, °affliction, malady, °affection, °complaint, °disease —*v.* **4** °upset, disarrange, °muddle, °confuse, confound, unsettle, disorganize, discompose, °shake up, °disturb, °mix (up), befuddle, °jumble, °scramble, °tangle, °snarl

disorderly *adj.* **1** °confused, °chaotic, scrambled, muddled, disordered, °irregular, °untidy, messy, messed up, disarranged, disorganized, unorganized, jumbled, cluttered, °haphazard, in disarray, °pell-mell, °helter-skelter, *Colloq* °topsy-turvy, higgledy-piggledy **2** °unruly, °uncontrolled, °undisciplined, ungoverned, °disobedient, °mutinous, °rebellious, °lawless, °obstreperous, refractory, turbulent, °violent, °tumultuous, unrestrained, °boisterous, °noisy, °rowdy, °wild; unmanageable, °ungovernable, uncontrollable, intractable

disorientated *n.* °confused, bewildered, °lost, adrift, (all) at sea, mixed up, °uncertain, unsure, °insecure, disoriented, *Colloq* out of it, in a fog, *Brit* off (the) beam, *US* off the beam

disparage *v.* **1** °belittle, °diminish, °depreciate, devalue *or* devaluate, cheapen, °talk down, °discredit, °dishonor, decry, demean, °criticize, denigrate, deprecate, derogate, underrate, undervalue, °downgrade, °reduce, °minimize **2** °run down, °slander, °libel, defame, traduce, malign, backbite, °vilify, °insult, °stab in the back, *US* backstab; *Colloq* poor-mouth; *Slang US and Canadian* bad-mouth

disparity *n.* °difference, °discrepancy, °gap, °inequality, unevenness, imbalance, °dissimilarity, °contrast, imparity, inconsistency, incongruity

dispassionate *adj.* **1** °cool, °calm, composed, °self-possessed, unemotional, unexcited, unexcitable, unflappable, °levelheaded, °sober, self-controlled, even-tempered, unruffled, °unmoved, °tranquil, °equable, placid, °peaceful, °serene **2** °fair, °impartial, °neutral, °disinterested, °detached, °equitable, evenhanded, unbiased, °just, °objective, °unprejudiced, open-minded, °candid, °frank, °open

dispatch *v.* **1** send off *or* away *or* out, send on one's way **2** °send, °mail, °post, °transmit, °forward, °ship, °express, °remit, convey, *Chiefly US and Canadian* °freight **3** °kill, °murder, slay, °dispose of, put to death, °execute, do away with, do in, assassinate, liquidate, °finish (off), put an end to, °put away (for good), *Slang* °polish off, °bump off, °eliminate, gun down, °silence, °get, °erase, °rub out, °knock off, °bury, *US* ice, °hit, °take for a ride, °waste, °zap **4** °hasten, °hurry, °speed up, accelerate, get done, °accomplish, °get through, conclude, °finish off, °complete, °execute, do —*n.* **5** °haste, °speed, promptness, quickness, °expedition, expeditiousness, celerity, alacrity, swiftness, °hurry, °rapidity **6** communiqué, °report, °bulletin, °story, °news (item), communication, °message, °piece, °document, °instruction, °missive **7** °execution, °killing, °murder, disposal, assassination, dispatching, slaying

dispensable *adj.* °disposable, °nonessential, unessential, inessential, °unnecessary, unneeded, °expendable, °superfluous, °needless, °useless

dispense *v.* **1** °distribute, °give out, hand *or* pass out, °furnish, °supply, °provide, °give away, °deal (out), dole out, °parcel out, disburse, mete out, °share (out), °issue, apportion, allocate, °allot, °assign, *Colloq* dish out **2** °administer, °conduct, °direct, °operate, superintend, °supervise, °carry out, °execute, °discharge, °apply, °implement, °enforce **3** ***dispense with.*** **(a)** do without, °forgo, °give up, eschew, °relinquish, °refuse, °waive, forswear, abstain (from), °renounce, °reject **(b)** do away with, °get rid of, °eliminate, °dispose of, °abolish, manage *or* do without, °remove, °cancel, °ignore, render unnecessary *or* superfluous

disperse *v.* **1** °spread (out), °scatter, °broadcast, °distribute, °circulate, °diffuse, disseminate **2** °disband, °spread out, °scatter, °dissipate, °break up; °disappear, vanish; dispel, °dismiss, °rout, send off *or* away

displace *v.* **1** °move, °transfer, °shift, relocate, dislocate, misplace, °disturb, disarrange, °disorder, unsettle **2** °expel, unseat, °eject, °evict, °exile, °banish, depose, °remove, oust, °dismiss, °discharge, cashier, *Colloq* °fire, kick *or* throw out, *Brit* °sack **3** take the place of, °supplant, °replace, °supersede, °succeed

display *v.* **1** °show, °exhibit, °air, put *or* set forth, make visible, °expose, evince, °manifest, °demonstrate, °betray, °reveal, °unveil, °disclose; advertise, °publicize **2** unfurl, °unfold, spread *or* stretch *or* open out, °present **3** °show off, °flaunt, °parade, °flourish, vaunt, *Colloq* °flash —*n.* **4** °show, °exhibition, °exhibit, °presentation, array; °demonstration; °exposition, °manifestation, °revelation **5** °ostentation, °spectacle, °flourish, °show, °parade, °ceremony, °pageantry, °pageant, °splendor, array, panoply, magnificence, °grandeur, °pomp, °splash, éclat, élan, °dash

displease *v.* °offend, °put out, dissatisfy, °upset, °provoke, °exasperate, °worry, °trouble, vex, °annoy, °irritate, pique, °irk, nettle, peeve, °chafe, rile, °ruffle, °anger, °infuriate, °frustrate, get (someone's) goat, *Colloq* miff; *Slang US* °bug

displeasure *n.* **1** °dissatisfaction, °disapproval, °disfavor, discontentment, °distaste, °dislike, discountenance **2** °annoyance, irritation, vexation, chagrin, °indignation, dudgeon, ire, °anger, exasperation

disposable *adj.* **1** discardable, throwaway, nonreturnable, °paper, °plastic, biodegradable **2** °available, °liquid, spendable, usable, °expendable, obtainable

dispose *v.* **1** °place, °arrange, °move, °adjust, °order, array, °organize, °set up, °situate, °group, °distribute, °put **2** °incline, °influence, °persuade, °induce, °bend, °tempt, °move, °motivate, °lead, °prompt, °urge **3** ***dispose of.*** **(a)** °deal with, °settle, °decide, °determine, conclude, °finish (with) **(b)** throw away *or* out, °discard, °get rid of, jettison, °scrap, *Colloq* °dump, °junk, *US* °trash **(c)** °distribute, °give out, deal out, °give (away), °dispense, apportion, °parcel out, °allot, °part with, °transfer, °make over, °bestow, °sell **(d)** do away with, °finish off, °put away, °demolish, °destroy, °consume, °devour, °eat, *Slang* °kill (off), °knock off, °polish off

disposed *adj.* °likely, °inclined, apt, °liable, °given, tending *or* leaning toward(s), °prone, °subject, of a mind to, minded, °willing, °ready, predisposed

disposition *n.* **1** °character, °temper, °attitude, temperament, °nature, °personality, °bent, °frame of mind, °humor, °makeup, °spirit **2** °arrangement, °organization, °placement, disposal, ordering, grouping, °set, placing **3** °transfer, transference, dispensation, disposal, °assignment, °settlement, °determination, bestowal, parceling out, °distribution **4** °determination, °choice, disposal, °power, °command, °control, °management, °discretion, °decision, °regulation

dispossess *v.* °evict, °expel, oust, °eject, turn *or* drive out, dislodge, *Colloq* kick *or* throw out, *Brit* boot out, *US* °bounce

disproportion *n.* °inequality, unevenness, °disparity, imbalance, asymmetry, irregularity, lopsidedness, °dissimilarity, inconsistency, incongruity

disproportionate *adj.* °unbalanced, out of proportion, asymmetrical, °irregular, °lopsided, °dissimilar, °inconsistent, incommensurate, °incongruous; unfair, unequal, uneven, disparate

disprove *v.* refute, confute, invalidate, °contradict, negate, °rebut, °discredit, controvert, °puncture, °demolish, °destroy, *Colloq* shoot *or* poke full of holes

disputable *n.* °debatable, °moot, °doubtful, °uncertain, dubious, °questionable, °uncertain, undecided, °unsettled, °controversial; arguable

dispute *v.* **1** argue with *or* against, °question, °debate, °challenge, impugn, gainsay, °deny, °oppose, °fight (against), object to, °take exception to, disagree with, °contest, confute, quarrel with, °doubt, raise doubts about, dissent (from) **2** °argue (about), °debate, °discuss, quarrel about, wrangle over, differ (on *or* about) —*n.* **3** °argument, °debate, °disagreement, °difference (of opinion), °controversy, polemic, °conflict, °quarrel, wrangle, velitation; °discussion; *Colloq Brit* argy-bargy *or* argie-bargie *or* argle-bargle **4** °conflict, °disturbance, °fight, altercation, °row, °disagreement, °brawl, donnybrook, °feud, °rumpus, °fracas; °strife, °discord; °tiff, velitation, *US* spat

disqualify *v.* declare ineligible *or* unqualified, turn down *or* away, °reject, °exclude, °bar, debar, °rule out

disregard *v.* **1** °ignore, °overlook, pay little *or* no heed *or* attention to, take little *or* no notice *or* account of, dismiss from one's mind *or* thoughts, turn a blind eye *or* deaf ear to, °brush aside, °pass up, wink *or* blink at, °make light of, let go by, °gloss over, *Rare* pretermit **2** snub, °slight, turn up one's nose at, °disparage, °despise, contemn, disdain, °scorn, give the cold shoulder to, cold-shoulder, °cut; underrate, °underestimate, take little *or* no account of, undervalue, °minimize, °dismiss, °sneeze at, *Slang* °brush off, give the go-by —*n.* **3** °disrespect, °contempt, °indifference, inattention, nonobservance, °neglect, heedlessness, *Rare* pretermission; disdain, low regard, disesteem

disrepair *n.* °decay, °ruin, °collapse, dilapidation, deterioration, ruination

disreputable *adj.* **1** °low, °base, abject, °contemptuous, unrespectable, disrespectable, untrustworthy, discreditable, °dishonorable, °disgraceful, reprehensible, °shameful, °despicable, ignominious, °bad, °wicked, heinous, °vicious, iniquitous, °vile, opprobrious, °scandalous, louche, °questionable, dubious, *Colloq* °shady **2** disheveled, °unkempt, slovenly, °untidy, °shabby, disordered, messy, °dirty, °bedraggled, scruffy, °seedy, °threadbare, °tattered, *Brit* down at heel, raddled, *US* down at the heel(s), *Colloq* °sloppy, *Slang Brit* grotty

disrespect *n.* rudeness, impoliteness, discourtesy, °incivility, unmannerliness, irreverence, °impudence, °impertinence, insolence, indecorum, *Colloq* cheek

disrespectful *adj.* °impolite, °rude, °discourteous, uncivil, unmannerly, °ill-mannered, bad-mannered, °irreverent, °impudent, °insolent, indecorous, °pert, saucy, °forward, *Colloq* °fresh, °cheeky

disrobe *v.* undress, °strip, bare oneself

disrupt *v.* **1** °disorder, °upset, disorganize, °disturb, unsettle, °shake up, disconcert, °agitate **2** °interrupt, break in *or* into, °interfere (with)

dissatisfaction *n.* **1** °discontent, discontentment, unhappiness, °displeasure, nonfulfillment, °disappointment, frustration, °discomfort, uneasiness, disquiet, malaise **2** °annoyance, irritation, °dismay, °displeasure

dissatisfied *adj.* °discontented, displeased, °disappointed, unsatisfied, °discontent, °disgruntled, °unhappy, unfulfilled, ungratified, frustrated

dissension *n.* °disagreement, dissent, °discord, contention, °strife, °conflict, discordance, °friction

disservice *n.* °harm, °damage, °injury, °wrong, unkindness, °bad turn, °disfavor, °injustice

dissident *n.* **1** dissenter, °nonconformist, protester *or* protestor, heretic, °rebel, apostate, recusant; °revolutionary —*adj.* **2** disagreeing, °nonconformist, nonconforming, dissenting, dissentient, apostate, noncompliant, heterodox, °discordant, conflicting, contentious

dissimilar *adj.* °different, °unlike, unalike, °distinct, °separate, contrasting, °diverse, °unrelated, heterogeneous

dissimilarity *n.* °difference, dissimilitude, unlikeness, °disparity; °discrepancy

dissimulate *v.* °pretend, dissemble, feign, °disguise, °camouflage, °cover up, °conceal, °deceive, °misrepresent, °fake, °counterfeit

dissimulation *n.* °deception, misrepresentation, dissembling, °deceit, °deception, °hypocrisy, °sham, °pretense, duplicity, double-dealing

dissipate *v.* **1** °scatter, °spread (out), °disperse, be dispelled, °diffuse; disseminate, °sow, °distribute; °break up **2** spread thin, °evaporate, vanish, °disappear, vaporize, °peter out, °diminish **3** squander, °waste, °fritter away, °throw away, burn up, °use up, °exhaust, °run through **4** °revel, °carouse, °party, sow one's wild oats, burn the candle at both ends, roister, °make merry, debauch, go on a spree

dissipation *n.* **1** squandering, °waste, wastefulness, °profligacy, °abandon, abandonment, self-indulgence, self-gratification, overindulgence, intemperance, hedonism, fast *or* high living, *la dolce vita*, voluptuousness, sensualism, sybaritism, dissoluteness, °dissolution, excess(es), wantonness, debauchery, carousing, °prodigality, recklessness, °extravagance, rakishness **2** disappearance, dispersion, dispersal, diffusion, °scattering, vanishing **3** °distraction, °amusement, °diversion, °entertainment

dissociate *v.* °separate, °cut off, °sever, disassociate, disjoin, °disconnect, °abstract, °disengage, °detach, °isolate, °distance, °break off (from), °break up (with), °divorce, °set apart, °segregate

dissolute *adj.* dissipated, debauched, °abandoned, °corrupt, °degenerate, °rakish, °profligate, °wanton, rakehell, intemperate, °incontinent, °loose, licentious, overindulgent, carousing, °self-indulgent, hedonistic, pleasure-bound, °immoral, amoral, libidinous, unrestrained, depraved

dissolution *n.* **1** disintegration, °separation, breakup, °breakdown, °separation, breaking up, breaking down, °collapse, °undoing **2** °destruction, decomposition, °decay, °ruin, °overthrow, dissolving, disbandment, °dismissal, dispersal, disorganization, discontinuation; adjournment, ending, °end, °termination, conclusion, °finish

dissolve *v.* **1** °melt (away), liquefy, °disperse, °disintegrate, °diffuse, °decompose, °thaw (out), °fuse, deliquesce; °sublime; vanish, °disappear, °fade (away), °diminish, °decline, °peter out **2** °collapse, break into, °melt into **3** °break up, °disperse, °dismiss, °terminate, °finish, conclude, adjourn, °recess, °disband, °wind up; liquidate

distance *n.* **1** remoteness, °space, °gap, °interval, mileage, footage, °stretch **2** aloofness, °detachment, °reserve, coolness, haughtiness, hauteur, stiffness, rigidity —*v.* **3** °separate, °detach, °dissociate, disassociate

distant *adj.* **1** °far, far-off, °remote, °faraway, long-way-off; removed **2** away, °off **3** °aloof, °detached, °reserved, °cool, °cold, °haughty, °standoffish, °unapproachable, °inaccessible, °withdrawn, °reticent, °ceremonious, °formal, °stiff, °rigid, °frigid, unfriendly

distaste *n.* **1** °dislike, °disfavor, antipathy, disrelish, disinclination; °dissatisfaction, °displeasure, discontentment **2** °aversion, °revulsion, °disgust, nausea, abhorrence, °loathing, repugnance, °horror

distasteful *adj.* °disgusting, °revolting, sickmaking, nauseating, °nauseous, °repugnant, °repulsive, °loathsome, fulsome, °nasty, °disagreeable, °foul, off-putting, °unpalatable, °obnoxious, objectionable, °offensive, unpleasing, unpleasant, displeasing

distinct *adj.* **1** °clear, °perceptible, °plain, understandable, °vivid, °definite, well-defined, °precise, °exact, unmistakable *or* unmistakeable, °noticeable, recognizable, °obvious, °patent, °marked, °manifest, °evident, °apparent, °explicit, unambiguous, clear-cut, palpable, unequivocal, lucid, °sharp, pellucid, limpid, °transparent **2** °separate, °detached, °discrete, °different, °dissimilar, distinguishable, °distinguished; °individual, sui generis, °unique, °special, °singular; °peculiar, °unusual, uncommon, contrasting

distinction *n.* **1** differentiation, °discrimination, °difference, °contrast, °separation, °division, dividing line; distinctiveness **2** °honor, °credit, °prominence, eminence, °preeminence, °superiority, uniqueness, greatness, °excellence, °quality, °merit, °worth, value, °prestige, °note, °importance, °significance, consequence, °renown, °fame, repute, °reputation, °celebrity, °glory, °account

distinctive *adj.* distinguishing, °characteristic, °unique, °singular, °distinct, °individual, °typical, idiosyncratic, °peculiar

distinguish *v.* **1** °differentiate, °discriminate, tell the difference, tell apart, °determine, °judge, °decide, tell who's who *or* what's what **2** classify, °categorize, °characterize, individualize, °mark, °identify, °define, °designate, °denote, °indicate, °separate, °single out, °set apart; °grade, °group **3** °sense, °make out, °perceive, discern, °pick out, °recognize, °identify, °detect, °notice; °see, espy, descry; °hear; °smell; °taste; °feel **4** call attention to, °identify, °mark, °set apart, °separate, °segregate, °indicate, particularize

distinguished *adj.* **1** °celebrated, °famous, °illustrious, °noted, °renowned, °notable, °noteworthy, °preeminent, °eminent, °prominent, honored, respected, °honorable **2** °dignified, °noble, °grand, °stately, *distingué*, °royal, °regal, aristocratic

distort *v.* **1** °twist, °warp, deform, misshape, contort, gnarl, °bend, disfigure, °wrench **2** °twist, °warp, °slant, tamper with, °color, varnish, torture, °pervert, °misrepresent, °fabricate, °falsify, misstate, °alter, °change, °bend, °garble, °violate

distract *v.* **1** °divert, °deflect, °sidetrack, °turn aside, draw away **2** °divert, °amuse, °entertain, °gratify, °delight, °occupy, °interest, absorb, engross **3** °bewilder, °confuse, confound, °perplex, °puzzle, discompose, befuddle, °mystify, disconcert, °fluster, °rattle, °bemuse, °daze, °disturb, °agitate, °trouble, °bother

distraction *n.* **1** bewilderment, befuddlement, °disorder, °disturbance, °upset, °confusion, °agitation **2** °diversion, °entertainment, °amusement

distraught *adj.* distracted, °agitated, troubled, °disturbed, °upset, perturbed, wrought *or* worked up, °excited, °frantic, at one's wit's end, °overwrought, frenetic, °nervous, frenzied, °feverish, °wild, °hysterical, °delirious, irrational, °crazy, °mad, °insane, °berserk, run(ning) amok *or* amuck

distress *n.* **1** °anguish, °anxiety, °affliction, angst, °grief, °misery, °torment, °ache, °pain, °suffering, °agony, torture, °woe, woefulness, wretchedness; unhappiness, °sorrow, °sadness, °depression, heartache, °desolation **2** °calamity, °trouble, adversity, °catastrophe, °tragedy, °misfortune, °difficulty, °hardship, °straits, °trial, °disaster —*v.* **3** °bother, °disturb, °perturb, °upset, °trouble, °worry, harrow, harry, vex, °harass, °plague, °oppress, °grieve, °torment, torture, °afflict

distribute *v.* **1** deal *or* dole out, °parcel out, °give (out), mete out, °dispense, apportion, °allot, °share (out), °partition, °divide up, °assign, °issue, °circulate, °pass out, pass round *or* around, °hand out, °deliver, convey, *Colloq* dish *or* spoon out **2** °disperse, °scatter, °strew, spread (round *or* around *or* about), °diffuse, disseminate **3** °sort, classify, °class, °categorize, assort, °arrange, °group, °file, °order

distribution *n.* **1** apportionment, °allotment, allocation, °assignment, parceling out, sharing; deployment **2** issuance, °circulation, dissemination, giving (out), dispersal, dispensation; deployment **3** °arrangement, °disposition, grouping, classification, °order, ordering, °division, cataloging, codification; deployment

district *n.* °territory, °region, °section, sector, °division, °partition, °part, °precinct, locality, °area, °locale, °department, °province, community, °quarter, °neighborhood, °ward

distrust *v.* **1** °mistrust, °doubt, °question, be skeptical of, be circumspect *or* cautious about, °suspect, be suspicious *or* wary of, °discredit, disbelieve, *Colloq* smell a rat; *Colloq* be leery of —*n.* **2** °mistrust, °doubt, doubtfulness, uncertainty, misgiving(s), °skepticism, °suspicion, disbelief, incredulity, incredulousness, hesitation, °caution, wariness, °qualm, hesitancy

distrustful *adj.* distrusting, untrusting, mistrustful, doubting, chary, °wary, °cautious, °suspicious, °skeptical, °doubtful, dubious, cynical, disbelieving, °unbelieving, uneasy, °nervous, °hesitant, hesitating, unsure, °uncertain, *Colloq* °leery

disturb *v.* **1** °interrupt, °disrupt, °intrude (on), °inconvenience, °put out, °interfere (with); °bother, °pester, °annoy, °irritate, °irk, °upset, °plague, hector, harry, °harass, °worry, vex, °provoke, pique, peeve, get on (someone's) nerves, *Colloq* °bug, miff, get under (someone's) skin, get in (someone's) hair, drive nuts *or* crazy *or* bats *or* batty *or* bananas *or* up the wall, hassle **2** °agitate, stir *or* churn (up), °shake (up), unsettle, roil, °disorder **3** unsettle, °affect, °upset, °damage, °harm, °destroy **4** °trouble, disconcert, °discomfit, °perturb, °ruffle, °fluster, °upset, °agitate, °put off, °bother, discommode, °put out, unsettle, °distress; °alarm, *Colloq* °shake (up) **5** °affect, °upset, confound, °confuse, °change, °put off, °ruin, °destroy, °cancel, make ineffectual *or* ineffective, negate

disturbance *n.* **1** disruption, °disorder, disorganization, disarrangement, disarray; °upheaval, °interruption, °upset, intrusion, °interference **2** commotion, °disorder, °upset, °outburst, °tumult, turmoil, turbulence, °violence, hubbub, hullabaloo, hurly-burly, °uproar, brouhaha, °rumpus, °brawl, melee *or* mêlée, breach of the peace, donnybrook, °fray, affray, °fracas, °trouble, *Colloq* ruckus, *Brit* spot of bother, *Slang Brit* spot of bovver

disturbed *adj.* **1** °upset, uneasy, uncomfortable, discomfited, troubled, °worried, bothered, °agitated, °anxious, °concerned, apprehensive, °nervous **2** psychoneurotic, °neurotic, °unbalanced, psychopathic, °psychotic, maladjusted, °mad, °insane, °out of one's mind, depressed, *Colloq* °crazy, unable to cope, *Brit* bonkers, *Slang* nuts, screwy, batty, off one's rocker, off the deep end, messed up, screwed-up

disturbing *adj.* upsetting, off-putting, perturbing, troubling, °unsettling, worrying, °disconcerting, disquieting, alarming, distressing

disused *adj.* °abandoned, neglected, °unused; discontinued, °obsolete, archaic

diurnal *adj.* °daily, circadian; day-to-day, °regular, °everyday, quotidian; daytime

dive *v.* **1** °plunge, nose dive, °sound, °descend, °dip, °submerge, °go under, °sink; °jump, °leap, °duck; °swoop, °plummet —*n.* **2** °plunge, nose dive **3** °bar, saloon, nightclub, bistro, °club, *Colloq* nightspot, *Slang* °joint, *US* °dump, honky-tonk, juke joint

diverge *v.* **1** °separate, °radiate, °spread (apart), °divide, subdivide, fork, branch (off *or* out), ramify, °split **2** °deviate, turn aside *or* away, °wander, digress, °stray, °depart, °drift, divagate

divergent *adj.* differing, °different, °dissimilar, disparate, °variant, °separate, diverging, disagreeing, conflicting, discrepant

divers *adj.* °various, °several, °sundry; °miscellaneous, multifarious, °manifold, °varied, assorted, °variegated, differing, °different; some, numerous, °many

diverse *adj.* °different, °varied, diversified, multiform, °various, assorted, °mixed, °miscellaneous; °distinctive, °distinct, °separate, varying, °discrete, °dissimilar, differing, °divergent, heterogeneous

diversify *v.* °vary, variegate, °change, °mix; °spread, °distribute, °divide, °break up, °separate; branch out

diversion *n.* **1** °digression, deviation, departure, °distraction **2** °detour, °sidetrack, deviation, °bypass **3** °amusement, °distraction, °entertainment, °pastime, °recreation, divertissement, °game, °play, °relaxation

diversity *n.* **1** °difference, °dissimilarity, dissimilitude, unlikeness, °disparity, deviation, divergence, departure, distinctiveness, diverseness, °variation, °variety, individuality, inconsistency, contrariety, °discrepancy, °contrast **2** °variety, °range, °extent, heterogeneity, multiplicity, multifariousness, variegation, multiformity

divert *v.* **1** °switch, rechannel, redirect; °change, °alter, °deflect **2** turn away, °turn aside, avert, reroute, °deflect; change course, swerve (off *or* away), °shift, °sidetrack, °depart, °deviate **3** °entertain, °amuse, °distract, °interest, °beguile, °engage, °occupy, absorb

divest *v.* **1** °strip, denude, °rid, get rid, °relieve, disencumber, °deprive, °dispossess; despoil, mulct **2** ***divest oneself of.*** take *or* put off, doff, °remove; °disrobe, unclothe, undress

divide *v.* **1** °separate, °split (up), °break up, °cleave, cut up *or* asunder, °partition, °segregate, subdivide; °disconnect, disjoin, °detach, °sever, sunder, °part **2** Sometimes, ***divide up.*** °distribute, °share (out), °measure out, °parcel out, °partition, °dole (out), °deal (out), mete out, allocate, °allot, apportion, °dispense, °give (out) **3** °separate, °split, cause to disagree, °alienate, disunite, set at odds, sow dissension (among), pit *or* set against one another, disaffect **4** °branch (out), ramify, °split, °separate **5** °categorize, classify, °sort, assort, °grade, °group, °(put in) order, °rank, °organize, °arrange

divine *adj.* **1** °godlike, °godly, °holy, deiform, deific, angelic, °seraphic, °saintly; °heavenly, °celestial; °sacred, sanctified, hallowed, consecrated, °religious, °spiritual **2** °superhuman, °supernatural, °gifted, °preeminent, °superior, °excellent, °supreme, °exalted, °transcendent, °extraordinary **3** °great, °marvelous, °splendid, °superlative, °glorious, °superb, °admirable, wonderful, °awesome, °perfect, °excellent, °beautiful, *Colloq* °super, °great, °terrific, smashing, °fantastic, splendiferous, *Colloq Brit* ace, °magic —*v.* **4** intuit, °imagine, conjecture, °guess, °assume, °presume, °infer, °suppose, hypothesize, °surmise, °suspect, °understand, °perceive, °speculate, °theorize, °predict, foretell, have foreknowledge of; °determine, °discover —*n.* **5** holy man, °priest, °clergyman, cleric, ecclesiastic, °minister, °pastor, reverend, churchman, prelate

division *n.* **1** dividing, °split, splitting (up), breaking up, °partition, partitioning, partitionment, °separation, separating, diremption, segmentation, segmenting, compartmentation, sectioning, apportioning, apportionment, °allotment **2** °section, °compartment, °segment; °partition, °separation **3** °branch, °department, sector, °section, °unit, °group, arm; °part, °set, °category, °class, classification **4** °boundary (line), °border, borderline, °frontier, °margin, °line, dividing line **5** °discord, °disagreement, °upset, °conflict, °strife, disunity, disunion

divorce *n.* **1** °separation, °split, split-up, °dissolution, severance, disunion, breakup —*v.* **2** °separate, °divide, °split (up), °part, °sever, °detach, °dissociate, disassociate; °dissolve

dizzy *adj.* **1** °giddy, vertiginous, lightheaded, °faint, dazed, tottering, unsteady, reeling, tipsy, *Colloq* woozy **2** °confused, °silly, °giddy, empty-headed, °scatterbrained, muddled, befuddled, °flighty, featherheaded, featherbrained, rattlebrained, °harebrained, °frivolous

dock *n.* **1** wharf, °pier, berth, jetty, quay —*v.* **2** °(drop) anchor, berth, °tie up, °moor, °land, °put in

doctor *n.* **1** °physician, medical practitioner, M.D., general practitioner, G.P., *Colloq* medic, medico, doc, sawbones, bones; shrink —*v.* **2** °treat, °attend, medicate; °cure, °heal; practice medicine **3** °mend, °repair, °patch (up), °fix **4** °falsify, tamper with, °adulterate, °disguise, °change, °modify, °alter; °cut, °dilute, °water (down); °spike; °drug, °poison

doctrine *n.* teaching, body of instruction, °precept; °principle, °tenet, dogma, article of faith, canon, °conviction, °creed, °belief, credo, °opinion, °idea, concept, theory, °proposition, °thesis, postulate

document *n.* **1** °paper, certificate, °instrument, °report, °chronicle, °record —*v.* **2** °record, °chronicle, particularize, °detail, °describe; °verify, validate, °certify, °authenticate, corroborate, °substantiate

doddering *adj.* shaking, quaking, palsied, trembling, trembly, quivering, quavering, reeling, unsteady, °shaky, staggering, °shambling, °decrepit, faltering; °feeble, °weak, °frail, °infirm; °aged, °old, superannuated, °senile, anile

dodge *v.* **1** dart, °shift, move aside, °sidestep, °duck, bob, °weave, °swerve, veer **2** °avoid, °elude, °evade, escape from **3** escape from answering, °sidestep, °duck, °evade, hedge; °quibble, tergiversate, double-talk, *Colloq* °waffle —*n.* **4** °trick, °subterfuge, ploy, °scheme, °ruse, °device, °stratagem, °plan, °plot, °machination, chicane, °deception, prevarication, contrivance, °evasion, *Slang* wheeze, °racket

dodgy *adj.* °tricky, °dangerous, °perilous, °risky, °difficult, °ticklish, °sensitive, °delicate, °touchy, °dicey; °uncertain, °unreliable; °rickety, *Colloq* chancy, °hairy, *Brit* dicky

dogmatic *adj.* °arbitrary, °categorical, °dictatorial, imperious, °peremptory, °overbearing, doctrinaire, °authoritarian, °emphatic, °insistent, °assertive, °arrogant, °domineering; obdurate, °stubborn; °opinionated, °positive, °certain, *Rare* thetic(al), *Colloq* °pushy

dole *n.* **1** °portion, °allotment, °share, °quota, °lot, °allowance, °parcel; compensation, °benefit, °grant, °award, °donation, °gift, largess *or* largesse, alms, gratuity; *Slang* handout **2** °distribution, apportionment, allocation, dispensation —*v.* **3** °give (out), °deal (out), °distribute, °hand out, mete out, °share (out), °dispense, °allot, allocate, apportion, *Colloq* dish out

doleful *adj.* °sad, °sorrowful, °melancholy, °gloomy, °mournful, cheerless, °joyless, °somber, depressed, disconsolate, °blue, down, distressed, °dejected, °downhearted, °forlorn, °unhappy, lugubrious, dolorous, °wretched, °miserable, °woebegone, woeful, °dreary, *Colloq* °down in the mouth, down in the dumps; distressing, °funereal, depressing, °grievous, °harrowing

dolt *n.* °fool, ass, blockhead, dunce, dullard, idiot, nitwit, ignoramus, numskull *or* numbskull, donkey, nincompoop, ninny, ninnyhammer, simpleton, dunderpate, dunderhead, bonehead, simpleton, °twit, fathead, goon, moron, imbecile, *Colloq* °dope, dumbbell, dimwit, chump, °dummy, °half-wit, birdbrain, pinhead, clot, °clod, chucklehead, *Brit* muggins, *US* thimble-wit, °jerk, knucklehead, lunkhead, meathead, lamebrain, dingbat, ding-a-ling, °flake

domain *n.* **1** °realm, °dominion, °territory, °property, land(s), °province, °kingdom, empire **2** °province, °realm, °territory, °field, bailiwick, °area, °department, °sphere, °discipline, °specialty, specialization, °concern

domestic *adj.* **1** °home, °private, °family, familial; residential, household **2** °tame, domesticated, house-trained, housebroken **3** °home, °native, °indigenous, °internal, autochthonous —*n.* **4** °servant, °(hired) help, housekeeper, major-domo, steward

domicile *n.* **1** °dwelling (place), °residence, °abode, °home, habitation, °(living) quarters, °housing, accommodation(s), lodging(s), *Colloq Brit* digs, diggings, *Slang* °pad —*v.* **2** °locate, °quarter, °lodge, °settle, °establish, °situate, domiciliate

dominant *adj.* **1** commanding, °authoritative, controlling, governing, ruling, °leading, reigning, °influential, °assertive, °supreme, °superior, ascendant **2** °predominant, °chief, °main, °principal, °primary, °prevailing, °outstanding, °preeminent, °paramount

dominate *v.* **1** °command, °control, °govern, °rule, °direct, °lead, °reign (over), exercise command *or* authority *or* control *or* rule over, have the whip *or* upper hand (over), °run (things), be in *or* have under control, rule the roost *or* roast, *Colloq* call the shots *or* the tune, wear the trousers *or US* the pants, be in the driver's seat, rule with an iron hand, have under one's thumb **2** °overlook, look (out) over, tower over *or* above, rise above, °overshadow; °predominate

domination *n.* **1** °authority, °control, °rule, °power, °command, °influence, °sway, °supremacy, ascendancy, hegemony, the whip *or* upper hand, °preeminence, mastery **2** °oppression, °subjection, °repression, °suppression, subordination, enslavement, enthrallment; dictatorship, °despotism, °tyranny

domineering *adj.* °overbearing, imperious, °officious, °arrogant, autocratic, °authoritarian, highhanded, high and mighty, °masterful, °arbitrary, °peremptory, °dictatorial, °despotic, °tyrannical, °oppressive, °strict, °hard, °harsh, °tough, *Colloq* °bossy, °pushy

dominion *n.* **1** °rule, °authority, °control, dominance, °domination, °grasp, mastery, °grip, °command, °jurisdiction, °power, °sovereignty, °sway, ascendancy, °preeminence, primacy, °supremacy, hegemony **2** °domain, °realm, °territory, °region, °area, °country, °kingdom

donate *v.* °give, °provide, °supply, °present, °contribute, subscribe (to *or* for), °pledge, °award, °bestow, °confer, °grant, °vouchsafe, °will, °bequeath

donation *n.* **1** °gift, contribution, largess *or* largesse, °present, °grant, °award, alms, °offering, °bequest **2** giving, contribution, bestowal, °allotment, °provision, °offer

donor *n.* giver, provider, supplier, benefactor *or* benefactress, contributor, °supporter, °backer

doom *n.* °fate, karma, °destiny, °fortune, °lot, kismet; °downfall, °destruction, °death, °ruin, extinction, annihilation, °death, °end, °termination, terminus

doomed *adj.* **1** °fated, cursed, °condemned, damned, °destined, ordained, foreordained, predestined **2** accursed, bedeviled, ill-fated, luckless, star-crossed, bewitched, °condemned

dope *n.* **1** See **dolt**. **2** °narcotic, °drug, opiate, hallucinogen, psychedelic, *Slang* °upper, downer **3** °information, °data, °facts, °news, °details, °story, °scoop, *Slang* info, °lowdown, °score, *Brit* gen, *US and Canadian* poop

dormant *adj.* **1** asleep, sleeping, slumbering, resting, at rest, °quiet, °inactive, °still, °inert, unmoving, motionless, stationary, immobile, quiescent, comatose, °torpid, hibernating, slumberous, somnolent, °sleepy, °lethargic, °dull, sluggish **2** latent, °potential, °hidden, concealed, undisclosed, unrevealed, unexpressed

dose *n.* **1** °portion, °quantity, °amount, °measure, dosage —*v.* **2** °dispense, °administer, °prescribe

dot *n.* **1** °spot, °speck, °point, °jot, °mark, iota, fleck, °dab; decimal point, *Brit* full stop, *US* °period **2** ***on the dot.*** °exactly, °precisely, punctually, to the minute *or* second, °on time, *Colloq* on the button —*v.* **3** °spot, fleck, speckle, stipple, bespeckle

dote *v.* Often, ***dote on or upon.*** be fond of, be infatuated with, °love, °idolize, hold dear, °adore, °make much of; °coddle, °pamper, °spoil, °indulge

double *adj.* **1** twofold, paired, coupled, duplicate(d), doubled **2** folded *or* doubled *or* bent over, overlapped, two-ply **3** dual, twofold, °ambiguous, double-barreled **4** twice **5** °deceitful, °dishonest, treacherous, °traitorous, °insincere, °hypocritical, double-dealing, °false —*v.* **6** °duplicate, replicate; °copy; °increase, °enlarge; °magnify —*n.* **7** °twin, °duplicate, °copy, °replica, °facsimile, clone, °copy, counterpart, doppelgänger, °lookalike, °stand-in, °understudy, *Slang* (dead) ringer, spitting image *or* spit and image **8** ***at or on the double.*** °quickly, °on the run, at full speed *or* tilt, briskly, °immediately, °at once, without delay, *Slang* PDQ

double-cross *v.* °cheat, °defraud, °swindle, °hoodwink, °trick, °betray, °deceive, °mislead, play false with, *Colloq* two-time

doubt *v.* **1** disbelieve, °discredit, °mistrust, °distrust, have misgivings (about), °question, °suspect **2** °hesitate, waver, vacillate, °fluctuate, °scruple, be uncertain, entertain doubts, have reservations —*n.* **3** uncertainty, hesitation, °misgiving, reservation(s), °qualm, °anxiety, °worry, apprehension, disquiet, °fear **4** °distrust, °mistrust, °suspicion, incredulity, °skepticism, dubiousness, dubiety *or* dubiosity, lack of faith *or* conviction, irresolution **5** ***in doubt.*** See **doubtful,** below.

doubtful *adj.* **1** °in doubt, dubious, °questionable, open to question, °problematic, °debatable, °disputable, °uncertain, unpredictable, indeterminate, °unsettled, °unresolved, conjectural, °indefinite, unclear, °obscure, °vague, anybody's guess, *Colloq* up in the air **2** °skeptical, unconvinced, °distrustful, mistrustful, °suspicious, °uncertain, unsure, °hesitant, hesitating, vacillating, °indecisive **3** dubious, °questionable, °shady, louche, °disreputable, °controversial

doubtless *adv.* **1** doubtlessly, °undoubtedly, no doubt, indubitably, indisputably, unquestionably, °surely, for sure, certainly, for certain, °naturally, without (a) doubt, beyond *or* without (a *or* the shadow of) (a) doubt, °truly, °positively, °absolutely, *Colloq* absotively, posolutely, *US* make no mistake **2** °probably, most *or* very likely, in all probability, °supposedly, °presumably

dour *adj.* **1** °sullen, °sour, unfriendly, °cold, °gloomy, morose, °dreary, °grim, cheerless, °dismal, °forbidding **2** °hard, °tough, austere, °severe, °hardy, °inflexible, °obstinate, °stubborn, unyielding, uncompromising, °strict, °rigid, obdurate, °stern, °harsh, adamant, *Colloq* hard-nosed

dowdy *adj.* frowzy, frumpy, °drab, °dull, °seedy, °shabby, °unseemly, °unbecoming; slovenly, °sloppy, messy, °unkempt; °old-fashioned, unfashionable, *Colloq US* °tacky

down-and-out *adj.* **1** °indigent, poverty-stricken, °poor, penniless, °destitute, °impoverished, *Colloq* °broke, *US* on the skids, on skid row, on the bum, *Slang Brit* skint —*n.* **2** °derelict, °beggar, °outcast, °tramp, vagrant, °vagabond, *US* °bum

downfall *n.* °ruin, °undoing, debacle, °collapse, °degradation, °defeat, °overthrow, °breakdown

downgrade *v.* **1** demote, dethrone, °humble, °lower, °reduce, °displace, depose, °dispossess, disfranchise *or* disenfranchise, *US military* bust; *Colloq* bring *or* take down a peg **2** °belittle, °minimize, °play down, °disparage, decry, denigrate, °run down, *US and Canadian* downplay —*n.* **3** descent, °decline, declension, °(downward) slope, gradient, °grade, °inclination **4** ***on the downgrade.*** °on the wane, waning, declining, falling, slipping, falling off, losing ground, going downhill, *US and Canadian* on the skids

downhearted *adj.* discouraged, depressed, low-spirited, °miserable, °blue, °sad, downcast, °dejected

downpour *n.* rainstorm, deluge, inundation, cloudburst, thundershower, thunderstorm, torrential rain, °torrent; monsoon

downright *adj.* **1** °direct, straightforward, °plain, °frank, °open, °candid, plain-spoken, °explicit, °blunt, °brash, °bluff, not roundabout *or* circuitous, unambiguous, °out-and-out, °outright, °categorical, °flat, unequivocal, °outspoken, unreserved, °unabashed, unrestrained, unconstrained, °bold —*adv.* **2** °completely, °entirely, °totally, °thoroughly, certainly, °surely, (most) assuredly, °definitely, °absolutely, unconditionally, unequivocally; °very, °extremely, unqualifiedly, °perfectly, uncompromisingly, unmitigatedly, °utterly, unquestionably, °profoundly, °undoubtedly, indubitably

downtrodden *adj.* subjugated, oppressed, burdened, plagued, afflicted, exploited, overwhelmed, cowed, °overcome, beaten, °abused, mistreated, maltreated, tyrannized, *Colloq* °beat

downward *adj.* **1** declining, sliding, slipping, spiraling, descending, going *or* heading *or* moving down —*adv.* **2** downwards, down, °below, °lower

doze *v.* **1** Often, ***doze off.*** (take *or* have a) nap, catnap, drowse, °sleep, slumber, *Colloq* snooze, have forty winks, drop *or* nod off, grab some shuteye, *Chiefly Brit* (have *or* take a) zizz, *Brit* kip, *US* catch a few Z's —*n.* **2** °nap, catnap, siesta, °sleep; °rest; *Colloq* snooze, forty winks, shuteye, *Brit* zizz, kip, lie-down

drab *adj.* °dull, °colorless, °dreary, °dingy, °lackluster, lusterless, °dismal, cheerless, °gray, °somber

draft *n.* **1** °plan, sketch, °drawing, °outline, °rough (sketch), blueprint, diagram, °prospectus **2** bill of exchange, °check, money order, postal order; letter of credit **3** °breeze, °breath (of air), °(light) wind, °current (of air), puff (of air *or* wind) **4** °dose, °portion, °measure, °quantity, °drink, °swallow, °sip, °nip, °tot, potation, dram, °gulp, *Colloq* swig, tipple —*v.* **5** sketch, delineate, °outline, °design, °plan, °frame, °block out, °compose, diagram, °draw (up)

drag *v.* **1** °pull, °draw, °haul, °tow, °tug, °trail, °lug **2** °pull, °distract, °draw; °induce, °persuade, °coax, °wheedle **3** trudge, slog, °crawl, °creep, inch, °shuffle, shamble **4** °trail (behind), °linger, °dawdle, °lag (behind), °straggle, draggle, °putter, loiter, °poke (along), dillydally, *US* lallygag **5** (be) prolong(ed), (be) extend(ed), °(be)draw(n) out, (be) protract(ed), (be) stretch(ed) out, spin out *or* be spun out **6** ***drag one's feet or heels.*** °delay, °procrastinate, hang back; °obstruct, °block, °stall —*n.* **7** °bore, °nuisance, °annoyance; °pest; *Colloq* °drip, °pain (in the neck), °headache

drain *n.* **1** ditch, °channel, trench, culvert, conduit, °pipe, gutter, °outlet, watercourse, sewer, cloaca **2** depletion, reduction, sapping, °sap, °exhaustion, °strain, °drag; outgo, outflow, withdrawal, disbursement, °expenditure **3** ***down the drain.*** wasted, gone, thrown away, °lost, *Slang* °up the spout —*v.* **4** °draw off, °tap, °extract, °remove, take away, °withdraw, pump off *or* out; °empty, °evacuate, drink up *or* down, quaff, °swallow, °finish **5** °consume, °use up, °exhaust, °sap, deplete, bleed, °strain, °tax, °spend; °weaken, debilitate, °impair, °cripple **6** seep, °trickle, °ooze, °drip, °leave, go *or* flow from *or* out of, °disappear (from), °ebb

drama *n.* **1** °play, stage play, photoplay, screenplay, °(stage) show, °(theatrical) piece, °(stage) production; °scenario **2** dramaturgy, stagecraft, theater art(s), thespian *or* histrionic art(s); acting, °theater, dramatic art **3** histrionics, dramatics, theatrics, theatricalism, play-acting

dramatic *adj.* **1** theatric(al), dramaturgic(al), °thespian, histrionic, °stage **2** °vivid, °sensational, °startling, breathtaking, °sudden, °striking, °noticeable, °extraordinary, °impressive, °marked, °shocking, °expressive, °graphic, °effective; °complete, °considerable, °radical, °major **3** °flamboyant, °melodramatic, colorful, °showy, °stirring, spectacular; °theatrical, histrionic, exaggerated, overdone

dramatist *n.* °playwright, dramaturge, screenwriter, scriptwriter, scenarist, tragedian, melodramatist

dramatize *v.* °exaggerate, overplay, °overstate, °overdo, make a production *or* show (out) of, *Colloq* °lay it on (thick), °pile it on, ham (something *or* it) up

drape *v.* **1** °hang, festoon, °swathe, deck, array, bedeck, adorn, °ornament, °decorate —*n.* **2** °drapery, curtain; hanging, tapestry

drapery *n.* °drape, curtain; hanging, valance, pelmet, tapestry, arras, portière, lambrequin, °drop

drastic *adj.* °violent, °severe, °extreme, °strong, °powerful, °potent, puissant, °fierce, °forceful, °vigorous, rigorous, °harsh, °radical, Draconian, °desperate, dire

draw *v.* **1** °pull, °tug, °tow, °drag, °haul, °lug **2** pull *or* take out, °extract; unsheathe, unholster **3** °draw off; °pour; drain off *or* out **4** °attract, °gather, allure, °lure, bring out *or* forth, °elicit, *Colloq* °pull **5** depict, sketch, °portray, °outline, delineate, °design, limn, °paint **6** °devise, °draw up, °draft, °create, contrive, °frame, °compose, °prepare **7** °inhale, °breathe (in), °inspire; suck in **8** °draw out, °withdraw, °take, °receive, °get, °acquire, °obtain, °secure, °procure, °extract, °remove **9** °choose, °pick, °select, °take **10** ***draw back.*** °retreat, °recoil, °shrink (from), °withdraw **11** ***draw in.*** °arrive, °pull in **12** ***draw off.*** **(a)** °tap, °pour **(b)** °withdraw, draw *or* go away, °depart, °leave **13** ***draw on.*** **(a)** °employ, °use, make use of, °exploit, have resort *or* recourse to, °resort to, °fall back on, rely *or* depend on **(b)** come close *or* near, °near, draw nigh, °approach, °advance **14** ***draw out.*** **(a)** °extend, drag out, °prolong, protract, °lengthen, °stretch, °spin out **(b)** °elicit, °evoke, induce to talk **(c)** See **8**, above. **15** ***draw up.*** **(a)** °halt, °stop, pull up *or* over **(b)** °draft, °compose, °prepare, °put down (in writing), °frame, °compile, put together, °formulate **(c)** °arrange, deploy, °position, °order, °rank, marshal —*n.* **16** °magnetism, °attraction, °lure, °enticement, *Colloq* °pull, drawing power **17** °tie, °stalemate, dead heat, °deadlock

drawback *n.* °disadvantage, °hindrance, °stumbling block, °obstacle, °impediment, °hurdle, °obstruction, °snag, °problem, °difficulty, °hitch, °catch, °handicap, °liability, °flaw, °defect, °detriment, *Colloq* °fly in the ointment; *Taboo* nigger in the woodpile

drawing *n.* °picture, depiction, °representation, sketch, °plan, °outline, °design, °composition, black-and-white, monochrome

drawn *adj.* °haggard, °worn out, °tired, °fatigued, °strained, pinched, °tense, °exhausted

dread *v.* **1** °fear, be afraid of, apprehend, °anticipate, °flinch, shrink *or* recoil from, cringe *or* quail *or* blench *or* wince at, view with horror *or* alarm —*n.* **2** °fear, °fright, fearfulness, trepidation, apprehension, apprehensiveness, uneasiness, °anticipation, °alarm, nervousness, °qualm, queasiness, °misgiving, °dismay, °worry, °anxiety, consternation, °concern, °distress, perturbation, disquiet, °aversion, °horror, °terror, °panic, *Colloq* cold feet, butterflies (in the stomach), the jitters; *Slang* the heebie-jeebies, the willies, the collywobbles —*adj.* **3** feared, dreaded, °dreadful, °terrifying, °terrible

dreadful *adj.* **1** °bad, °awful, °terrible, *Colloq* °rotten, *Slang* °lousy **2** °grievous, dire, °horrible, horrendous, horrifying, horrid, °monstrous, °fearful, feared, °frightful, °dread, °frightening, °shocking, alarming, appalling, °fearsome, °hideous, °ghastly, °atrocious, heinous, °wicked, °evil, iniquitous, °villainous, flagitious, °fiendish, diabolical, °devilish, demonic, malevolent, maleficent, malefic, *Colloq* °scary

dream *n.* **1** °reverie, °daydream, °delusion, °fantasy, °hallucination, °illusion, °vision, mirage, pipe dream, °(flight of) fancy, °speculation —*v.* **2** °imagine, °fancy, conjure up, hallucinate

dreamer *n.* fantasizer, °visionary, idealist, °romantic, romanticist, idealizer, utopian; daydreamer, escapist, stargazer

dreamlike *adj.* °unreal, °fantastic, °unbelievable, phantasmagoric(al), hallucinatory *or* hallucinative *or* hallucinational, surreal, delusionary *or* delusional, illusionary *or* illusional, delusive *or* delusory, illusory *or* illusive, insubstantial *or* unsubstantial, °imaginary, chimeric(al), °fanciful, °fancied, °visionary

dreamy *adj.* **1** °dreamlike, °vague, °indefinite, °indistinct, undefined, °intangible, °misty, °shadowy, °faint **2** °absent-minded, °absent, °faraway, abstracted, °pensive, °thoughtful; daydreaming, musing, occupied, in a reverie, in a brown study, in the clouds; *Colloq* off somewhere **3** relaxing, °soothing, calming, lulling, °gentle, °tranquil, °peaceful, °peaceable, °quiet; °lazy, °sleepy, °drowsy

dreary *adj.* **1** °dismal, °joyless, cheerless, °gloomy, °bleak, drear, °somber, °doleful, depressing, °wretched; °sad, °melancholy, downcast, depressed, °funereal, °glum, °unhappy, °forlorn, °mournful, morose, °blue, °miserable **2** °boring, °lifeless, °colorless, ennuyant, °drab, °dull, arid, °dry, uninteresting, °dead, °monotonous, °prosaic, °tedious, °tiresome, tiring, wearisome, wearying,

°humdrum, °ordinary, °vapid, °run-of-the-mill, unstimulating, unexciting

dregs *n. pl.* **1** °sediment, °grounds, lees, °deposit, °residue, solids, °remains; °precipitate **2** outcasts, pariahs, °rabble, °riffraff, scum, tramps, down-and-outs, losers

drench *v.* °soak, °saturate, °wet, °flood, inundate, °immerse, °drown

dress *v.* **1** °clothe, put on (clothing *or* clothes), attire, °apparel, °outfit, fit out, garb, accoutre *or US also* accouter; array, bedeck, deck out, °rig out, smarten up **2** array, °equip, adorn, °decorate, deck out, °arrange **3** bandage, °treat, medicate, °doctor **4** ***dress down.*** °reprimand, °scold, °berate, °castigate, °rebuke, °reprove, °upbraid, *Colloq* °tell off, haul (someone) over the coals, *US and Canadian* °chew out, *US* rake (someone) over the coals, tee off on (someone), *Brit* tear (someone) off a strip **5** ***dress up.*** **(a)** put on dinner *or* formal clothes, put on one's (Sunday) best (clothes), *Colloq* put on one's best bib and tucker *or* one's glad rags **(b)** °(put on a) costume, °disguise, °masquerade, °camouflage, put on fancy dress —*n.* **6** frock, gown, °outfit, °costume, *Colloq* get-up

dressmaker *n.* seamstress, °tailor, couturier *or* couturière, modiste

dressy *adj.* **1** °formal, dressed-up, °elegant, °fancy, °chic **2** °elegant, °smart, °stylish, *Colloq* classy, ritzy, *Brit* °swish

drift *v.* **1** °coast, °float, °waft **2** °wander, °roam, °meander, °stray, rove, °ramble, *Colloq* mosey —*n.* **3** °trend, °tendency, °direction, °course, °current, °bias, °inclination, °flow, °sweep, °bent **4** °intention, °meaning, purport, °purpose, °aim, °object, °tenor, °tone, °spirit, °color, °essence, °gist, °significance, °import **5** °accumulation, °pile, °heap, °mass, bank, °mound, dune

drifter *n.* vagrant, °tramp, °vagabond, beachcomber, rambler, wanderer, *Colloq* knight of the road, *US* °bum, hobo

drill *v.* **1** °bore, °penetrate, °pierce, cut a hole **2** °rehearse, °train, practice, °exercise, °teach, °instruct, °school, °tutor, °coach, °indoctrinate; °discipline —*n.* **3** auger, °(brace and) bit, gimlet **4** °practice, training, °repetition, °exercise, °rehearsal; °discipline

drink *v.* **1** quaff, imbibe, °sip, °gulp, °swallow, °swill, guzzle, toss off, °lap (up), *Colloq* wet one's whistle, swig, knock back, *US* °belt **2** tipple, °nip, °indulge, tope, chug-a-lug, °carouse, *Colloq* °booze, bend the elbow, hit the bottle, go on a binge *or* bender, drown one's sorrows, *US and Canadian* go on a toot, *Chiefly Brit* pub-crawl **3** ***drink to.*** °toast, °salute, °celebrate, °pledge —*n.* **4** beverage, potation, liquid refreshment, °liquid, potable, °draft **5** °alcohol, °spirits, °liquor, the cup that cheers; stirrup cup; *Colloq* °booze, °the bottle, hard stuff, mother's ruin, eye-opener, nightcap, *US* hooch; *Slang* rotgut, *US* the sauce, red-eye **6** °tot, °nip, draft *or chiefly Brit* draught, schooner, pint, bumper, jigger, snifter, °sip, °taste, °glass, °gulp, °swallow, *Scots* (wee) deoch-an-doruis *or* doch-an-doris, (wee) dram, *Brit* sundowner; cordial, highball, shot, after-dinner drink, liquor, brandy, cognac, beer, wine; *Colloq* snort, slug, swig **7** ***the drink.*** the sea, the ocean, the main, °the deep, *Nautical* Davy Jones's locker, *Colloq* the briny

drip *v.* **1** dribble, °trickle, °drop; drizzle, sprinkle —*n.* **2** dribble, °trickle, °drop, dripping **3** °milksop, °bore, wet blanket, °killjoy, damper, *Colloq Brit* °wet, weed, *Colloq* wimp, *Slang* °pill, °drag, *US and Canadian* milquetoast

drive *v.* **1** °push, °propel, impel, °urge, °press, °thrust, °move, °motivate, actuate, °prod, °spur, goad, °urge, °force, °make, compel, coerce, constrain, °oblige, pressure *or Brit* pressurize, high-pressure, °induce, °require; °demand **2** °operate, °conduct, °maneuver, °manipulate, °handle, °steer, °control; °pilot **3** °ride, °travel, motor, °go, °move, °proceed, °journey, °tour, *Colloq* tool along **4** °stab, °plunge, °thrust, °sink, °push, °send, °dig, °ram **5** °herd, drove, °shepherd, ride herd (on) **6** ***drive at.*** °hint (at), °suggest, °imply, °intimate, allude *or* refer to, °intend, °mean, have in mind, °indicate, *Colloq* °get at —*n.* **7** °ride, °trip, °outing, °journey, °run, °tour, °excursion, *Colloq* °spin, whirl **8** °energy, °effort, °impetus, °vigor, vim, °spunk, °enterprise, °industry, °initiative, °ambition, ambitiousness, °determination, °persistence, °urgency, zeal, °enthusiasm, keenness, aggressiveness, *Colloq* get-up-and-go, °pep, zip, °push, °hustle **9** driveway, °approach, (private) road *or* street, lane, byway, °(scenic) route **10** °campaign, °effort, °appeal, °crusade

drivel *v.* **1** dribble, drool, slobber, °slaver **2** °babble, prate, °prattle, gibber, °jabber, burble, gabble, °chatter, blether *or US* blather, *Colloq* gibber-jabber, °gab, *US* run off at the mouth, *Brit* rabbit *or* witter *or* natter on —*n.* **3** °gibberish, °rubbish, °(stuff and) nonsense, twaddle, balderdash, hogwash, *Colloq* eyewash, tripe, °garbage, malarkey, hooey, °hot air, bosh, baloney *or* boloney, *Slang* crap, bull, bilge (water), codswallop, *US* horsefeathers, *Taboo* bullshit, balls, *Brit* (load of old) cobblers

droop *v.* **1** °sag, °hang (down), °wilt, °dangle **2** languish, °weaken, °flag, °wilt, wither, be limp, °slump, °sag

drop *n.* **1** globule, bead, °drip, droplet, °tear **2** °bit, °spot, °particle, °taste, dram, °sip, °nip, °pinch, °dash, °dab, *Colloq* smidgen **3** descent, °fall **4** °decline, °slope, fall-off, drop-off, declivity, °incline —*v.* **5** °drip, °trickle, dribble **6** °fall, °descend, °sink, drop away *or* down *or* off, °dive, °plunge, °plummet, °decline, °collapse **7** °desert, °forsake, °give up, °abandon, °leave, °quit, °throw over, °jilt, °discard, °reject, °repudiate, °renounce, *Colloq* chuck, ditch, °dump;

°relinquish, let go, °discontinue, °stop, °cease, °end **8** °release, let go of, °shed, °cast off, °discard, doff **9** °omit, °leave out, °exclude, °eliminate **10** °dismiss, let go, °fire, °discharge, oust, *Colloq chiefly Brit* °sack, give (someone) the sack **11** °decline, °decrease, drop *or* fall off, °diminish, slacken, slack *or* taper off, °subside, lessen **12** ***drop in (on).*** °visit, °call (on), °pop in (on), °come by, stop in **13** ***drop out.*** °withdraw (from), °leave; rusticate, °depart, decamp, go away *or* off, °take off, °turn off

drown *v.* **1** °flood, inundate, °swamp, deluge, °drench, °immerse, °submerge, engulf **2** °overwhelm, °overcome, °overpower, engulf, °swamp, deluge, inundate

drowsy *adj.* °sleepy, heavy-lidded, °groggy, somnolent, dozy, oscitant; °nodding, yawning; °torpid, sluggish, °tired, °weary, °listless, °lethargic, °lazy

drudgery *n.* toil, °labor, moil, travail, °(hack) work, donkey-work, chore, slog, slogging, °slavery, *Colloq* °grind, °sweat, *Brit* skivvying, °fag

drug *n.* **1** medication, °medicine, medicament, pharmaceutical, °remedy, °cure, °treatment; cure-all, panacea **2** opiate, °narcotic, °stimulant, °tranquilizer, antidepressant, hallucinogen(ic), psychedelic, hypnotic, soporific, °sedative, analgesic, pain-killer, *Slang* °dope, downer, °upper —*v.* **3** °dose, medicate, °treat **4** anesthetize, °dope, °deaden, °knock out, °sedate, stupefy, °numb, benumb, °dull, narcotize; °poison, *Slang* slip (someone) a Mickey (Finn)

druggist *n.* °pharmacist, apothecary, *Brit* chemist

drunk *adj.* **1** drunken, intoxicated, inebriated, besotted, tipsy, °groggy, sotted, crapulent *or* crapulous, in one's cups, °under the weather, °under the influence, °maudlin, ebriate, ebriose, ebrious, *Colloq* soused, pickled, °high (as a kite), °tight, boozed, boozy, lit (up), half seas over, three *or* four sheets to the wind, °out (cold), under the table, *Brit* squiffy; *Slang* pie-eyed, °loaded, stoned, stewed (to the gills), (well-)oiled, bombed (out of one's mind), crocked, plastered, tanked, sloshed, polluted, stinko, smashed, blotto, pissed, *Taboo slang chiefly US* shit-faced **2** exhilarated, °excited, °exuberant, invigorated, inspirited, °animated, °ecstatic; flushed, °feverish, °inflamed, aflame, °fervent, fervid, °delirious —*n.* **3** drunkard, drinker, toper, tippler, sot, °soak, bibber, winebibber; dipsomaniac, °alcoholic, problem drinker; *Colloq* guzzler, swiller, sponge, *Slang* wino, boozer, dipso, °lush, souse, alky, *US* juicer, juicehead, rummy **4** °carouse, bacchanal, carousal, bacchanalia, °revel, *Slang* °bender, °tear, °jag, bat, *US and Canadian* toot, *Chiefly Brit* pub-crawl

drunkenness *n.* intoxication, insobriety, intemperance, sottishness, bibulousness, inebriety, crapulence, crapulousness, tipsiness, ebriety; dipsomania, alcoholism, ebriosity; *Colloq* boozing, *Slang* hitting the bottle *or US* the sauce

dry *adj.* **1** dehydrated, desiccated, arid, sear, parched, waterless, moistureless; °barren, °bare, °fruitless **2** °dreary, °boring, °tedious, °tiresome, wearisome, wearying, tiring, °dull, uninteresting, °monotonous, °prosaic, commonplace, °stale, uninspired; °plain, °unadorned, unembellished **3** °witty, droll, °wry, cynical, °biting, °sarcastic, °cutting, °keen, °sly, ironic —*v.* **4** dehydrate, desiccate, °parch **5** dry up *or* out, wither, °shrivel, °shrink, °wilt

duck *v.* **1** bob, °dodge, °dip, °dive, °stoop, °bow, °bend, °crouch **2** °plunge, °submerge, °immerse, dunk **3** °avoid, °sidestep, °evade, °dodge, °elude, °shun, °steer clear of, shy away from; °shirk

dud *n.* **1** °failure, *Colloq* °flop, lead balloon, lemon, °washout, *Colloq US and Canadian* dog, clinker —*adj.* **2** °worthless, valueless, °broken, unusable, °useless, inoperative, nonfunctioning, malfunctioning, *Colloq* kaput, bust(ed), *Brit* °duff

dude *n.* **1** °dandy, fop, fancy dresser, Beau Brummell, popinjay, boulevardier, man about town, *Archaic* coxcomb, macaroni; *Slang* °swell, *Brit* toff **2** °man, °fellow, °chap, *Colloq* °guy

due *adj.* **1** °payable, owed, owing, °unpaid, °outstanding, in arrears **2** °fitting, °right, °rightful, °correct, °proper, °appropriate, apropos, apposite, °suitable, apt, °meet; °deserved, (well-)earned, merited, °just, justified **3** °necessary, needed, °adequate, °sufficient, °enough, °satisfactory; °ample, plenty of **4** expected, scheduled, anticipated —*adv.* **5** °directly, °exactly, °precisely, °straight

dues *n. pl.* (membership) fee, charge(s)

duff *adj.* °bad, °useless, °worthless, unworkable, inoperable, inoperative, °broken; °fake, °false, °counterfeit, *Colloq* °dud, phony *or Brit also* phoney

duffer *n.* °incompetent, blunderer, bungler, oaf, *Colloq* ox, lummox

dull *adj.* **1** °stupid, slow-witted, °dense, °stolid, bovine, cloddish, clodlike, °backward, °obtuse, doltish, crass, °dumb, *Colloq* °thick, °dim, dimwitted, *Brit* dim as a Toc H lamp **2** insensitive, °numb, °insensible, imperceptive *or* impercipient, unresponsive, °indifferent, unfeeling, °unsympathetic, °callous, hardened, °hard, inured, obtundent **3** °lifeless, °indifferent, unresponsive, sluggish, °slow, °listless, °inactive, °torpid **4** °boring, °tiresome, °tedious, °monotonous, uninspired, uninspiring, unoriginal, uninteresting, °humdrum **5** °dismal, °dreary, depressing, °somber, °gray, °dark, °murky, °gloomy, cloudy, clouded, °overcast, °sunless **6** blunted, °blunt; °obtuse **7** °hazy, blurry, °opaque, °drab **8** muffled, numbing, deadened, muted, °indistinct —*v.* **9** allay, assuage, °relieve, °mitigate, lessen, °reduce **10** °dim, °tarnish, °obscure, bedim, °blur, cloud, becloud **11** stupefy, narcotize, °numb, benumb, desensitize, °deaden, °blunt, obtund

duly *adv.* **1** °properly, fittingly, deservedly, °appropriately, suitably, befittingly, rightly, correctly, °accordingly **2** punctually, °on time

dumb *adj.* **1** °mute, °speechless, voiceless; °silent, °quiet, °taciturn, °mum, wordless; °inarticulate **2** °dull, °stupid, *Colloq* °thick

dumbfound *v.* dumfound, °amaze, °shock, °surprise, °startle, °astonish, °astound, °bewilder, °stagger, °stun, °floor, °nonplus, °confuse, confound, *Colloq* flabbergast, bowl over

dumbfounded *adj.* dumfounded, amazed, shocked, surprised, startled, astonished, astounded, bewildered, staggered, floored, nonplussed, overwhelmed, °speechless, stunned, °thunderstruck, dazzled, dazed, dumbstruck, taken aback, °confused, confounded, bemused, perplexed, baffled, °disconcerted, *Colloq* bowled over, flabbergasted, knocked out, thrown (off), *US* thrown for a loss, *Brit* knocked for six, knocked sideways

dummy *n.* **1** mannequin, manikin *or* mannikin, °model, °figure **2** °sample, °copy, reprint, °reproduction, °likeness, °substitution, °imitation, °sham, mock-up, simulation, *Colloq* phoney *or US also* phony **3** °fool, idiot, dunce, blockhead, ninny, ass, °dolt, numskull *or* numbskull, simpleton, *Colloq* dimwit, *US* thimble-wit **4** *US* pacifier

dump *v.* **1** °unload, offload, °empty, °drop, °deposit, throw *or* fling down, °tip **2** °get rid of, °throw away, °scrap, °discard, ditch, jettison, °dispose of, °reject, °tip, toss out *or* away, *Colloq* °junk, chuck out *or* away —*n.* **3** junkyard, rubbish heap, *US* garbage dump, *Brit* °tip

dumpy *adj.* °stocky, pudgy, squat, chunky, °chubby, tubby, °stout, °plump, portly, °fat

dun *v.* °press, importune, °solicit, °plague, °nag, °pester, *Slang US* °bug

dung *n.* manure, °muck, droppings, cowpats, fertilizer, guano, excrement, faeces *or US chiefly* feces, *US* cow *or* buffalo chips, horse apples, *Slang* cowflop, *Taboo* shit, horseshit, cowshit

dungeon *n.* donjon, °keep, °cell, °prison, lockup, oubliette, black hole, °stronghold

dupe *n.* **1** °fool, gull, °victim, fair game, *Colloq* chump, *Chiefly US and Canadian* fall guy; *Slang* °sucker, °sap, boob, °pushover, pigeon, °mark, *Brit* °mug, *Chiefly US and Canadian* patsy **2** cat's-paw, °pawn, °tool, °puppet, *Slang* stooge —*v.* **3** °deceive, °fool, °outwit, °cheat, °trick, °take in, °defraud, humbug, °hoax, °swindle, °hoodwink, bilk, gull, cozen, delude, °mislead, snooker, °victimize, *Colloq* bamboozle, flimflam, put one over on, pull a fast one on; *Slang* con, °rip off, rook, °take, *US and Canadian* snow, do a snow job on

duplicate *adj.* **1** °identical; °twin, °matching —*n.* **2** (exact *or* carbon) copy, photocopy, machine copy, °double, clone, °(perfect) match, °facsimile, °twin, °reproduction, °replica, replication, look-alike, *Trademark* Xerox (copy), *Slang* (dead) ringer —*v.* **3** °copy, photocopy, clone, °match, replicate, °imitate, °reproduce, °double, *Trademark* Xerox; °repeat, °equal

durable *adj.* °enduring, long-lasting, °stable, wear-resistant, heavy-duty, hard-wearing, long-wearing, °lasting, °persistent, °indestructible, °substantial, °sturdy, °tough, °stout, °strong, °firm, °sound, °fixed, °fast, °permanent, dependable, °reliable

duress *n.* **1** coercion, °threat, °pressure, constraint, compulsion; °force, °power **2** confinement, °imprisonment, incarceration, °captivity, °restraint, *Literary* durance

dusk *n.* °twilight, sundown, nightfall, °evening, sunset, °dark, eventide

dusky *adj.* **1** °dark, °black, ebony, sable, jet-black; °swarthy, swart, dark-complected, dark-complexioned **2** °shadowy, °shady, °dim, °dark, unilluminated, unlit, °murky, subfusc, subfuscous, °gloomy, °obscure

dutiful *adj.* °obedient, compliant, °willing, °obliging, filial, °faithful, °conscientious, °reliable, °responsible, °diligent, °attentive, punctilious, °respectful, °polite, °considerate, deferential, °submissive, °yielding, acquiescent, malleable, °flexible, pliant, °accommodating, *Formal, archaic* duteous

duty *n.* **1** °responsibility, °obligation, °burden, onus, devoir, °office, °work, °task, °assignment, °job, °stint, chore, °occupation, °calling, °function, °role, °part, °bit, °charge **2** °respect, °deference, °loyalty, fealty, fidelity, faithfulness, allegiance **3** °tax, excise, °tariff, impost, levy, °customs

dwarf *v.* °overshadow, °dominate, °diminish, °minimize

dwell *v.* **1** reside, °abide, °live, °lodge, °stay, °remain, °rest, *Formal* °domicile **2** ***dwell on or upon.*** harp on, °persist in, °emphasize, °stress, focus on, linger *or* tarry over, °elaborate (on); °labor

dwelling *n.* °abode, habitation, dwelling-place, °house, °domicile, °lodging, °quarters, °home, °residence, homestead

dwindle *v.* °diminish, °decrease, °shrink, lessen, °wane, °fade, °contract, condense, °reduce, °peter out, °waste away, die out *or* down *or* away, °ebb, °decline, °subside, °taper off, shrivel (up *or* away)

dying *adj.* expiring; °sinking, slipping away, °going, °failing, fading (fast), at death's door, on one's deathbed, with one foot in the grave, *in extremis;* °moribund

dynamic *adj.* dynamical, °vigorous, °active, °forceful, °energetic, °potent, °powerful, high-powered, °lively, spry, °vital, °electric, °spirited, zealous, °eager, °emphatic

dynamism *n.* °energy, °vigor, °pep, °vitality, liveliness, °spirit, spiritedness, forcefulness, °power, °drive, °initiative, °enterprise, *Colloq* get-up-and-go, zip, °push

dynasty *n.* °line, °family, °heritage, °house

E

eager *adj.* avid, zealous, °ardent, °earnest, °keen, °enthusiastic, °hot, °hungry, °fervent, fervid, °passionate, °spirited, inspirited, °energetic, energized, vehement, °animated, °excited, vitalized, stimulated; °desirous, yearning, desiring, craving, °wanting, °longing, itchy, °impatient; °anxious; *Colloq* °dying, *Slang US* hot to trot

eagerness *n.* **1** avidity, zeal, earnestness, keenness, °enthusiasm, °fervor, °hunger, vehemence, °animation, °vitality, °appetite, °zest, °relish, °spirit, spiritedness, °gusto, °verve, °dash, élan, vim, °vigor, °energy, *Colloq* get-up-and-go, zip, °go **2** °desire, °longing, wishing, yearning

eagle-eyed *adj.* °sharp-eyed, sharp-sighted, keen-eyed, keen-sighted, lynx-eyed, hawk-eyed; °perceptive, perspicacious, discerning, °sharp, watchful, °alert

ear *n.* **1** °attention, °heed, °notice, °regard, °consideration **2** °sensitivity, °appreciation, °taste, °discrimination

early *adv.* **1** beforehand, °ahead (of time), °prematurely **2** anciently, initially, °originally, at *or* near the start *or* beginning **3** betimes, at cockcrow *or* cock's crow, at (the crack *or* break of) dawn, at daybreak *—adj.* **4** untimely, °premature; °inopportune, °inappropriate **5** °initial, °beginning, °original, °first, °pioneer, advanced **6** primeval, °primitive, primordial, °ancient, °old, °prehistoric, antediluvian, °original; °antique, °antiquated

earn *v.* **1** °merit, °deserve, be worthy of, be entitled to, °win, °warrant, °rate, qualify for, have a claim *or* right to **2** °make, °pocket, °gross, °net, °clear, °realize, °receive, °get, °procure, °collect, °reap, °bring in, take home; °draw, *Colloq US* °pull down

earnest *adj.* **1** °serious, °solemn, °grave, °sober, °intense, °steady, °resolute, resolved, °firm, °determined, assiduous, °sincere, dedicated, committed, °devoted, °thoughtful **2** zealous, °ardent, °diligent, assiduous, °industrious, hard-working, °devoted, °eager, °conscientious, °keen, °fervent, fervid, °enthusiastic, °passionate **3** ***earnest money.*** °deposit, down payment, binder, handsel, °guarantee, °security, °pledge *—n.* **4** ***in earnest.*** °serious, °sincere

earnings *n. pl.* wages, °salary, °income, compensation, °pay, °stipend, emolument, °proceeds, °return, °revenue, °yield, takings, *Slang* °take

earth *n.* **1** °globe, mother earth, planet, °world, blue planet, terra **2** °soil, °dirt, loam, sod, clay, °turf, °ground, °mold

earthly *adj.* **1** °terrestrial, terrene, telluric **2** °worldly, mundane, °material, °materialistic, °physical, nonspiritual, °sensual, °carnal, fleshly, corporeal, °base, °natural **3** °human, °temporal, °secular, °profane, °mortal, °physical, nonspiritual, °material **4** conceivable, imaginable, °feasible, °possible

earthy *adj.* ribald, °bawdy, °unrefined, °coarse, °crude, °shameless, °wanton, °uninhibited, °abandoned, °vulgar, °lusty, °rough, °dirty, °indecent, °obscene

ease *n.* **1** °comfort, °repose, well-being, °relaxation, °leisure, °rest, contentment, calmness, tranquillity, °serenity, peacefulness, °peace, peace and quiet **2** easiness, °simplicity, °facility, effortlessness, adeptness **3** affluence, °wealth, °prosperity, °luxury, opulence, °abundance, °plenty **4** naturalness, informality, unaffectedness, ingenuousness, casualness, artlessness, insouciance, nonchalance, aplomb; unconcern *—v.* **5** °comfort, °relax, °calm, °tranquilize, quieten, °still, pacify, soothe, disburden **6** lessen, °diminish, abate, °mitigate, °reduce, °decrease, allay, alleviate, assuage, mollify, appease, palliate, °quiet, °relieve **7** °maneuver, °manipulate, inch, °guide, °steer, °slip **8** °facilitate, °expedite, °simplify, °smooth, °further, °clear, °assist, °aid, °advance, °forward, °help

easily *adv.* **1** smoothly, effortlessly, °readily, °simply, °handily, without a hitch, °hands down, without even trying, comfortably, with no *or* without difficulty, *Colloq* easy as pie **2** °by far, beyond *or* without (a *or* the shadow of) (a) doubt, °without question, indisputably, indubitably, °undoubtedly, doubtless(ly), unquestionably, °clearly, far and away, °definitely, definitively, conclusively, certainly, °surely, undeniably, °obviously, patently **3** °probably, most *or* very likely, °well, almost certainly

easy *adj.* **1** °simple, °effortless, °plain, °clear, straightforward, hands-down, uncomplicated, °elementary, °foolproof; easy as pie, easy as ABC, easy as falling off a log, easy as 1, 2, 3, easy as can be **2** °carefree, °easy-going, °casual, °lenient, undemanding, °relaxed, °quiet, °serene, °restful, °tranquil, °peaceful, untroubled, undisturbed, unoppressive, °gentle, °mild, °calm, °comfortable, °cozy, °unhurried, leisurely **3** °light, °lenient, undemanding, °mild, °flexible, °indulgent, °tolerant **4** °tractable, pliant, docile, compliant, °submissive, acquiescent, amenable, °accommodating, °soft, °suggestible, credulous, °trusting, °weak, °easy-going **5** unstrained, °gentle, °moderate, °unhurried, leisurely, °even, °steady, undemanding, °comfortable, unexacting **6** affable, °friendly, °amiable, °amicable, °agreeable, °outgoing, °informal, unceremonious, down-to-earth, unreserved, relaxing, °natural, °relaxed, °easy-going *—adv.* **7** effortlessly; calmly, unexcitedly, temperately, peacefully, tranquilly, serenely, nonchalantly, casually

easy-going *adj.* °relaxed, °casual, °mellow, °carefree, undemanding, °easy, even-tempered, forbearing, °lenient, °tolerant,

°permissive, overtolerant, overpermissive, °lax, °weak, *Colloq* °wishy-washy, laid-back

eat *v.* °dine, lunch, breakfast, sup, break bread, °snack, have a bite; °consume, °devour, take (in) nourishment, *Colloq* put *or* pack away, *Slang* nosh, put *or* tie on the nosebag *or US and Canadian* feedbag

eavesdrop *v.* listen in, °tap, overhear, °snoop; °spy, °pry

ebb *v.* **1** °recede, flow back, °subside, °go out, °go down; fall back *or* away, °retreat, retrocede, °retire **2** °decline, °flag, °decay, °wane, °diminish, °decrease, °drop, slacken, °fade (away), °drain (away), °dwindle, °peter out, °waste (away), °deteriorate —*n.* **3** low tide, low water, ebb tide, low point **4** °decline, °decay, °decrease, diminution, °wane, °drop, slackening (off), dwindling, lessening, deterioration, degeneration

ebullient *adj.* bubbling, overflowing, °effervescent, °excited, °effusive, exhilarated, °elated, °buoyant, °exuberant, °enthusiastic, zestful

eccentric *adj.* **1** unconventional, °unusual, uncommon, idiosyncratic, anomalous, °unorthodox, °out of the ordinary, °irregular, atypical, °incongruous, errant, aberrant, °exceptional, °individual, °singular, °unique; °abnormal, °odd, °peculiar, °strange, °curious, °bizarre, °outlandish, °queer, °quaint, quirky, °weird, °offbeat, *Colloq* far-out, °kinky, °cranky —*n.* **2** °original, °individualist, °nonconformist, queer fellow, odd fish, *Colloq* °character, °card, °freak, °(nut) case, °crank, oddball, weirdo *or* weirdie, *US* loner

eccentricity *n.* **1** unconventionality, unusualness, uncommonness, irregularity, nonconformity, individuality, individualism, °singularity, uniqueness, strangeness, oddness, bizarreness, distinctiveness, capriciousness, weirdness **2** idiosyncrasy, °quirk, °peculiarity, °mannerism, crotchet, aberration, anomaly, °oddity, °curiosity, caprice

echo *n.* **1** reverberation, °repercussion, °repetition, iteration, reiteration **2** °imitation, °copy, replica *or* replication, duplication, °reproduction, simulation, °facsimile; °reflection, mirror image, °repetition —*v.* **3** °resound, reverberate, °ring **4** °imitate, ape, °parrot, °mimic, °copy, °duplicate, °reproduce, simulate, °repeat, emulate, °mirror, °reflect

eclipse *v.* **1** °conceal, °hide, °blot out, °obscure, °block, °veil, °shroud, °cover, darken **2** °overshadow, °obscure, °surpass, °top, outshine —*n.* **3** concealment, covering, hiding, blocking, blockage, occultation, obscuring, obscuration, darkening, shading, dimming **4** °decline, downturn, °slump; °recession

economic *adj.* **1** °financial, °fiscal, pecuniary, °monetary, budgetary; commercial, °mercantile, °trade **2** °profitable, cost-effective, money-making, remunerative, °productive; °solvent

economical *adj.* **1** cost-effective, money-saving, °thrifty, unwasteful; °cheap, °inexpensive, °reasonable; °economic **2** °provident, °thrifty, °sparing, economizing, °prudent, °conservative, °frugal; parsimonious, °penurious, stingy, °cheap, °miserly, niggardly, °tight, closefisted, tightfisted, °mean, penny-pinching, scrimping

economize *v.* °save, °cut back, °husband, retrench; tighten one's belt, cut corners *or* costs, scrimp, skimp, °pinch pennies

economy *n.* **1** °thrift, husbandry, thriftiness, °conservation, conservatism, °saving, °restraint, °control, frugality **2** °brevity, briefness, succinctness, terseness, conciseness, concision, compactness, °restraint, curtness

ecstasy *n.* **1** °delight, °joy, °rapture, °bliss, °transport, nympholepsy *or* nympholepsia, °happiness, gladness, elation, °pleasure, °enjoyment, °gratification; heaven on earth **2** exaltation, °frenzy, °thrill, elation, °paroxysm, °excitement

ecstatic *adj.* exhilarated, thrilled, °exultant, blissful, euphoric, °rapturous, enraptured, nympholeptic, °enchanted, transported, °rhapsodic, °excited, °elated, °delighted, °joyful, °gleeful, °overjoyed, °happy, °glad, °beside oneself, °delirious, orgasmic, *Colloq* on cloud nine, *Brit* over the moon, in the seventh heaven, cock-a-hoop, *US* in seventh heaven, flying

eddy *n.* **1** °swirl, whirl, vortex, gurgitation; °whirlpool, maelstrom, Charybdis; dust devil, °whirlwind, °twister, tornado, cyclone, typhoon, °hurricane; waterspout —*v.* **2** °swirl, whirl, °turn, °spin

edge *n.* **1** °brink, °verge, °border, °side, °rim, lip, °brim; °fringe, °margin, °boundary, °bound, °limit, bourn, °perimeter, °periphery **2** acuteness, sharpness, keenness **3** harshness, sharpness, acrimony, pungency, °force, °urgency, effectiveness, incisiveness, causticity, °virulence, vehemence **4** °advantage, head start, °superiority, °lead, °upper hand **5** *on edge.* on tenterhooks, °nervous, °touchy, °sensitive, °prickly, itchy, °tense, irascible, crabbed, °irritable, °peevish, apprehensive, with one's heart in one's mouth, edgy, °anxious, °ill at ease, °restive, °restless, fidgety, *Colloq* uptight, like a cat on a hot tin roof —*v.* **6** inch, °move, °sidle, °crawl, °creep, °steal, worm, °work (one's way)

edible *adj.* eatable, esculent, palatable, good *or* fit (to eat), °wholesome, *Rare* comestible

edification *n.* enlightenment, °improvement, uplifting, enlightening, °guidance, °education, °information, °tuition, teaching, °schooling, °instruction

edit *v.* **1** redact, copy-edit, rewrite, rephrase, °modify, °alter, °adapt, °change, °revise, °correct, emend, °style, restyle, °polish, °touch up **2** Often, *edit out.* blue-pencil, °cut (out), °delete, censor, °erase, bleep, blip; bowdlerize, expurgate, °clean up **3** °cut, condense, compress, °shorten, crop, °reduce **4** °prepare, °compile, °assemble, °select, °arrange, °organize, °order, reorganize, reorder

edition *n.* °number, °issue, printing, print run; °copy; °version

editor *n.* rewrite man *or* woman, rewriter, copy editor, redactor, reviser; °writer, columnist, °journalist, editorial writer, *Brit* leader writer; editor in chief, managing editor, senior editor; compiler, °collector

editorial *n. Brit* °leader, leading article; op-ed article, think piece, opinion piece, position statement; °essay, article, column

educate *v.* °teach, °train, °instruct, edify, °tutor, °school, °inform, °enlighten, °indoctrinate, inculcate, °coach, °drill, °prepare, °ready, °rear, °bring up, °cultivate, °develop, °civilize

educated *adj.* **1** °cultivated, cultured, erudite, well-read, °lettered, °literary, °scholarly, °learned; (well-)informed, °knowledgeable, °enlightened **2** °refined, °polished, °cultivated, civilized; discerning, °critical, °sensitive

education *n.* **1** teaching, °schooling, training, °instruction, °tuition, tutelage, °edification, tutoring, cultivation, °upbringing, indoctrination, drilling **2** °learning, °lore, °knowledge, °information, erudition **3** °lesson, °course (of study)

educational *adj.* **1** °academic, scholastic, pedagogical, instructional **2** °informative, °instructive, enlightening, edifying, eye-opening, revelatory, educative

eerie *adj.* °frightening, °weird, °strange, uncanny, °ghostly, °spectral, °dreadful, °unearthly, °frightful, *Literary and Scots* eldritch, *Scots* °mysterious, *Colloq* °scary, creepy, spooky

effect *n.* **1** °result, consequence, °outcome, conclusion; °upshot, aftermath, °impact **2** effectiveness, efficacy, °force, °power, °capacity, potency, °influence, °impression, °impact, *Colloq* clout, °punch **3** °significance, °meaning, signification, purport, °sense, °essence, °drift, °implication, °import, °tenor, °purpose, °intent, °intention, °object, °objective **4** °impact, °impression, °form, °sensation **5** *in effect.* effectively, °virtually, for (all) practical purposes, °so to speak, more or less; °actually, in (point of) fact, °really, essentially, basically, °at bottom, °in truth, °truly, °to all intents and purposes, at the end of the day, any way you look at it **6** *take effect.* become operative *or* operational, come into force, begin *or* start to work *or* function *or* operate —*v.* **7** °bring about, °cause, make happen *or* take place, °effectuate, °achieve, °accomplish, °secure, °obtain, °make, °execute, °carry out, °produce, °create

effective *adj.* **1** °effectual, °efficacious, °productive; °capable, °useful, °serviceable, °competent, °operative, °able, °functional, °efficient **2** °impressive, °remarkable, °noticeable, °conspicuous, °outstanding, °striking, °powerful, compelling, °moving, °telling, °effectual **3** °operative, operational, °in operation, functioning, °real, °actual, °essential, °basic, °true

effects *n. pl.* belongings, °(personal) property, °gear, °possessions, °stuff, °things, °paraphernalia, chattels, °goods, *Colloq* °junk, crap, *Brit* clobber, *Taboo slang US* shit

effectual *adj.* **1** °effective, °efficacious, °efficient, °functional, °productive, °useful, °telling, °influential, °powerful, °forcible, °forceful; °capable, °adequate **2** °effective, °in force, °legal, °lawful, binding, °sound, valid

effectuate *v.* °bring about, °effect, °carry out, °implement, °accomplish, do, °execute, °realize, °achieve; °cause, make happen

effeminate *adj.* unmanly, womanish, womanly, sissyish, °weak, campy; °gay, °homosexual; *Slang US* limp-wristed, faggy, faggoty, *Brit* °bent, poncy

effervescent *adj.* **1** bubbling, fizzy, carbonated, sparkling, fizzing, gassy; foaming, foamy, frothing, frothy, °bubbly **2** bubbling, °bubbly, high-spirited, °vivacious, °ebullient, °lively, °exuberant, °buoyant, °animated, exhilarated, °excited, °enthusiastic, °irrepressible

efficacious *adj.* °effective, °effectual, °productive, °competent, °successful, °efficient, °useful, °serviceable; °capable

efficiency *n.* **1** effectiveness, efficacy, competence, °capability, adeptness, °proficiency, expertness, °expertise, know-how, °experience, °skill, skillfulness, °dexterity, adroitness **2** productivity, effectiveness, efficaciousness

efficient *adj.* unwasteful, °economic, °thrifty; °effective, °efficacious, °effectual, °competent, °productive, °proficient, °operative

effort *n.* **1** °exertion, striving, °struggle, °strain, °labor, °pains, °energy, toil, °application, °trouble, travail, °work, *Colloq* elbow grease **2** °attempt, °endeavor, °essay, °try, °venture, *Colloq* °stab, °crack **3** °achievement, °accomplishment, °creation, °feat, °deed, attainment, °exploit

effortless *adj.* easy (as pie *or* as A, B, C, *or* as 1, 2, 3), °simple, °painless, °smooth, trouble-free, uncomplicated

effrontery *n.* °impertinence, °impudence, audacity, °nerve, °presumption, presumptuousness, brazenness, boldness, insolence, temerity, brashness, rashness, °arrogance, °front, °indiscretion, *Archaic* frowardness, *Colloq* °gall, °brass, °nerve, cheek, lip, °mouth, *Slang Brit* °side

effusive *adj.* °demonstrative, gushing, (over)enthusiastic, unrestrained, unreserved, unchecked, °expansive, °emotional, °exuberant, °rhapsodic, °ebullient, °lavish, °voluble, °profuse; fulsome

egoistic *adj.* egoistical, self-centered, egocentric, narcissistic, self-seeking, self-absorbed, °selfish, self-serving, °self-indulgent, °self-important, solipsistic

egotistical *adj.* egotistic, °conceited, °proud, overweening, bragging, °boastful, boasting, swelled-headed *or* swellheaded *or* swollen-headed, °vain, vainglorious, self-worshiping, self-admiring, vaunting, crowing

eject *v.* **1** force *or* drive out, °expel, oust

°remove, °get rid of, °evict, *Colloq* throw *or* kick *or* boot out, send to the showers **2** °expel, °emit, throw up *or* out, °spew (forth), °discharge, °spout, disgorge, vomit (up *or* forth), send out *or* forth; °ooze, exude, extravasate **3** °discharge, °dismiss, cashier, drum out, °lay off, declare *or* make redundant, *Colloq* °fire, °sack, boot out, ax, give the sack *or* boot *or* ax, give (someone) his marching orders *or US also* walking papers, send packing

ejection *n.* **1** °expulsion, casting out *or* up, disgorgement, vomiting forth, throwing out *or* up, °discharge, emission, disgorging **2** °exile, °expulsion, banishment, deportation, ouster, °removal; °eviction, dispossession **3** °dismissal, °discharge, congé, cashiering, layoff, *Colloq* firing, sacking, *Slang* °the sack, the boot, the ax, the (old) heave-ho, *US* the bounce

elaborate *adj.* **1** °detailed, °painstaking, °meticulous, punctilious, °comprehensive, °thorough, °complete, °exhaustive, °intricate, °involved, °minute, °precise, °exact **2** °complicated, complex, convoluted, °ornate, °fancy, Byzantine, °laborious, °labored, °extravagant, °showy; ornamented, decorated, baroque, rococo, °busy, °fussy, gingerbread —*v.* **3** °ornament, °decorate, °complicate, °embellish, garnish, adorn **4** °enlarge, expand (upon *or* on), expatiate, °develop, °cultivate, °flesh out, °enhance, °refine, °enrich, °improve, °better, ameliorate, emend, °polish

elaboration *n.* **1** enhancement, °refinement, enrichment, °improvement, amelioration, melioration, betterment; °embellishment, adornment, garnish, garnishment, °decoration, overdecoration, gingerbread, *Slang* bells and whistles **2** enlargement, °development, amplification, °expansion

elapse *v.* °pass (by), °go (by), slip by *or* away, °pass away, slide by, glide by, °transpire

elastic *adj.* **1** °flexible, stretchable, stretchy, °stretch, bendable, °pliable, springy, °plastic, extensile, extensible, expansible, expandable, contractile, resilient, bouncy, compressible **2** adjustable, °adaptable, °accommodating, °flexible

elasticity *n.* **1** °flexibility, °resilience, rubberiness, plasticity, ductility, springiness, stretchability, stretchiness, °stretch, suppleness, pliancy, *Colloq* °give **2** °flexibility, adjustability, adaptability, °tolerance, suppleness

elated *adj.* exhilarated, uplifted, °elevated, °gleeful, °joyful, jubilant, joyous, °exultant, °ecstatic, blissful, °happy, °delighted, euphoric, °overjoyed, °excited, thrilled, transported, pleased (as Punch), °on top of the world, on cloud nine, *Colloq* tickled, tickled pink, *Brit* chuffed, over the moon, in the seventh heaven, *US* in seventh heaven

elder *adj.* **1** older, °senior **2** °venerable, respected, °preeminent, °eminent; °experienced, °veteran —*n.* **3** °senior, °superior; patriarch, elder statesman, dean, doyen *or* doyenne

elderly *adj.* **1** °old, past middle age, oldish, advanced in years *or* age, of advanced age, along in years, °gray, aging *or* ageing, °aged, °venerable; hoary, °ancient, senescent, °decrepit, superannuated; °senile, anile; *Colloq* over the hill, past it, long in the tooth, having one foot in the grave, old-fogyish *or* old-fogeyish —*n.* **2** ***the elderly.*** the retired, the old, senior citizens, golden agers, *Chiefly Brit* pensioners, old age pensioners, *Brit* OAP's, *Colloq* old-timers, (old) geezers, (old) fogies *or* fogeys, *Brit* wrinklies

elect *v.* **1** °choose, °select, °pick, °vote (for), °determine, °designate —*adj.* **2** chosen, elected, selected, picked out **3** °select, °choice, °first-rate, first-class

election *n.* °poll, °vote, referendum, °plebiscite; °selection, °choice, choosing, nomination, designation, °appointment; voting, electing

electioneer *v.* °campaign, °canvass, °support, °back, °promote

electric *adj.* charged, °tense, energized, °stimulating, °exciting, °thrilling, galvanizing, electrifying, °moving, °stirring

electricity *n.* °excitement, °verve, °energy, °tension, tenseness, fervency, °intensity, °ardor; vibrations

electrify *v.* **1** °startle, °shock, °stun, °jolt, °stagger, °astound, °jar, °astonish, °amaze **2** °excite, galvanize, °animate, °move, °rouse, °stir, °stimulate, °vitalize, °fire, °thrill, °arouse

elegance *n.* **1** °refinement, °grace, tastefulness, good taste, gentility, °polish, courtliness, °culture, politeness, politesse, °propriety, °dignity **2** °luxury, °grandeur, luxuriousness, sumptuousness, exquisiteness, °splendor, °beauty

elegant *adj.* **1** °tasteful, °exquisite, °handsome, °beautiful, °comely, °dapper, °smart, well-turned-out; °graceful, °choice, °superior, °fine, °select, °refined, °delicate, discerning, artistic; °dignified, °genteel, °sophisticated, °cultivated, °polished, urbane, Chesterfieldian, °suave, soigné(e), °debonair, courtly, to the manner born, °well-bred, well-born, highborn **2** artistic, °stylish, modish, à la mode, °chic, °fashionable, *Colloq* in, with it **3** °luxurious, °sumptuous, °grand, °opulent, °plush, *Colloq* °posh, swank, °swanky, ritzy, °fancy **4** apt, °clever, °ingenious, °neat

element *n.* **1** component, constituent, °ingredient, °essential, °fundamental, °part, °unit, °piece, °segment, °feature, °factor, °detail, °particular **2** °environment, °atmosphere, °situation, °locale, °territory, °sphere, °habitat, °medium, °domain **3** ***elements.*** **(a)** (adverse *or* unfavorable) weather, climatic conditions **(b)** °rudiments, basics, fundamentals, foundations, essentials, °principles

elemental *adj.* °basic, °fundamental, primal, °original, primordial, °primitive
elementary *adj.* **1** °simple, °rudimentary, °easy, straightforward, uncomplicated, °clear, understandable, °plain **2** °basic, °fundamental, °primary, °introductory, °initial, °beginning; °elemental
elevated *adj.* **1** raised, upraised, uplifted, lifted (up) **2** uplifted, °noble, °lofty, °high, °grand, °exalted, °dignified, °eminent, °pre-eminent, ennobled, °prominent, °notable, °illustrious, °distinguished, °imposing, °impressive, °sublime **3** °elated, °cheerful, °happy, exhilarated, °animated, °joyful, °glad
elevation *n.* **1** altitude, °height **2** °swelling, °lump, wen, eminence, °prominence; °hill, °height, °rise **3** advancement, °promotion, uplifting, enhancement, °advance **4** °grandeur, nobleness, loftiness, exaltation, sublimity, °distinction, °dignity, °refinement, cultivation
elfin *adj.* **1** elvish, elfish, elflike, impish, puckish, °frolicsome, spritelike, °arch, °playful, °mischievous, °tricky **2** °small, °wee, °diminutive, °tiny, °little, °dainty, Lilliputian
elicit *v.* °draw out, °call forth, °evoke, bring out *or* forth, °bring to light, °extract, wring, wrest, °wrench
eligible *adj.* **1** °fit, °worthy, °qualified, °proper, °suitable, °appropriate, °fitting **2** °single, °unmarried, unwed, °available
eliminate *v.* **1** °remove, °exclude, °rule out, °reject, °drop, °leave out, °omit **2** take out *or* away, °omit, °get rid of, °dispose of, °expel, °knock out **3** °erase, eradicate, expunge, °obliterate, °strike (out), cross out *or* off, °cut (out), excise, °delete, °throw out, °edit (out), blue-pencil, °cancel **4** °kill, °murder, assassinate, slay, °terminate, °exterminate, °dispose of, liquidate, °finish off, annihilate, °stamp out, °destroy, *Slang* °bump off, °polish off, *US* °rub out, °take for a ride, °bury, ice, °waste
elite *n.* **1** élite, °gentry, aristocracy, aristocrats, °elect, upper class, °nobility, privileged class, blue bloods, *crème de la crème*, *haut monde*, jet set, jet-setters, *US* Four Hundred, F.F.V., First Families of Virginia, *Colloq* °upper crust, beautiful people, *Brit* nobs —*adj.* **2** aristocratic, °elect, °upper-class, °privileged, blue-blooded, °noble, °exclusive, °choice, °best, °top
elixir *n.* **1** panacea, cure-all, nostrum, wonder drug, miracle drug, sovereign remedy **2** °essence, °potion, °extract, tincture, compound, °mixture **3** °pith, °core, °kernel, heart, °essence, °quintessence, °principle, °extract, °base, °basis, °soul
eloquent *adj.* **1** °expressive, articulate, silver-tongued, °fluent, well-spoken, °effective, °persuasive, convincing, cogent, °trenchant, °incisive, °graphic, °vivid, °striking, facile, °smooth, °glib, oratorical, °rhetorical **2** °suggestive, °meaningful, °pregnant
elsewhere *adv.* somewhere else, to another place; in another place, °abroad, °absent, away
elude *v.* **1** °evade, °escape, °avoid, °dodge, slip away from, *Colloq* °duck, give the slip, °shake off **2** °evade, °escape; baffle, °puzzle, °confuse, °bewilder, confound; °frustrate, °stump, °thwart
elusive *adj.* **1** °evasive, °slippery, °tricky, °shifty **2** °evasive, evanescent, °fleeting, °fugitive, transitory, indefinable, elusory, °intangible, impalpable
emaciated *adj.* emaciate, atrophied, shriveled, °wizened, shrunken, °haggard, °gaunt, °drawn, pinched, bony, skeletal, cadaverous, withered, wasted, consumptive, phthisic, anorexic *or* anorectic, wasting (away), °scrawny, °skinny, °thin, °lean, °spare, undernourished, underfed, °starved, half-starved
emanate *v.* **1** °issue, °come (out), °emerge, °proceed, °flow, °ooze, exude; °radiate **2** °radiate, give off *or* out, send out *or* forth, disseminate, °discharge, °put out, °emit; °exhale, °ooze, exude
emancipate *v.* °release, set free, °liberate, enfranchise, manumit, °loose, °let loose, let go, set free, disenthrall, unfetter, unchain, unshackle; °deliver
embargo *n.* **1** °restraint, °block, blockage, °bar, °ban, stoppage, cessation, proscription, °prohibition, interdiction, °check, °restriction, °barrier; °hindrance, °impediment —*v.* **2** °restrain, °block, °bar, °ban, °stop, °cease, proscribe, °prohibit, interdict, °check, °restrict, °hold back, °prevent; °hinder, °impede, °retard, °hold up
embark *v.* **1** °board, go aboard; entrain; enplane **2** Often, ***embark on.*** °commence, °begin, °enter (upon), °initiate, °launch, °start, °go into, °set about, take up *or* on, °engage in, °assume, °tackle
embarrass *v.* disconcert, °discomfit, chagrin, abash, °shame, °mortify, °humble, °humiliate, discountenance, discompose, °fluster, °upset, °distress, °disgrace, *Colloq* °show up
embarrassed *adj.* **1** °ashamed, °shamefaced, blushing, °disconcerted, discomfited, chagrined, abashed, shamed, mortified, humiliated, discountenanced, discomposed, flustered, distressed, red-faced, uncomfortable, °self-conscious, °sheepish, red in the face; humbled, disgraced **2** °in debt, in the red, °straitened, °insolvent, *Colloq* °short, °hard up, °broke, *Brit* skint
embarrassing *adj.* °awkward, humiliating, mortifying, shaming, °shameful, uncomfortable, discomfiting, °disconcerting, °touchy, distressing, worrying
embarrassment *n.* **1** bashfulness, awkwardness, clumsiness, discomposure, abashment, uneasiness, °discomfort, self-consciousness, mortification, chagrin **2** °difficulty, °mess, °predicament, °dilemma, °problem, °trouble, *Colloq* hot water, pickle, °fix, °scrape, °bind **3** °excess, °superfluity, superabundance, overabundance, *embarras de richesse*, *embarras de choix*, oversupply, °surplus, °profusion

embellish *v.* 1 °beautify, °improve, titivate *or* tittivate, °dress (up), trick out *or* up, °enhance, °elaborate, °enrich, embroider, gild, furbish (up), garnish, °decorate, adorn, °ornament, deck, bedeck, °trim, caparison, rubricate, varnish; gild refined gold, paint the lily, *Misquote* gild the lily 2 °elaborate, °exaggerate, °overdo, embroider, °enhance, °dress up

embellishment *n.* 1 °decoration, ornamentation, °ornament, °elaboration, adornment, embroidery 2 °exaggeration, enhancement, tinsel, garnish, gilding, °frill

embers *n. pl.* live coals; cinders, ashes; °remains, remnants

embezzle *v.* °misappropriate, peculate, misapply, °misuse, °steal, make off *or* away with, filch, °pilfer, purloin, *Law* defalcate; *Colloq* have one's hand in the till

embezzlement *n.* misappropriation, peculation, misapplication, °misuse, misusing, abstraction, °stealing, °theft, thievery, larceny, filching, purloining, pilferage, pilfering, *Law* defalcation

embittered *adj.* °bitter, °resentful, °sour, soured, °caustic, acrimonious, acid, envenomed; °angry, choleric, °rancorous

emblem *n.* badge, insigne, °symbol, °representation, °device, °seal, °crest, °token, °sign; trademark, logotype *or* logo

emblematic *adj.* emblematical, symbolic(al), °representative, representational

embodiment *n.* 1 incarnation, °realization, concretization, °manifestation, °expression, personification, materialization, actualization, reification, substantiation 2 consolidation, °collection, unification, incorporation, °inclusion, integration, °combination, concentration, systematization, °organization, codification, °synthesis, °epitome

embody *v.* 1 concretize, °realize, °manifest, °express, °personify, °materialize, reify, actualize, externalize, incarnate 2 °exemplify, °typify, °represent, °symbolize, °stand for 3 consolidate, °collect, °unite, °unify, °incorporate, °include, °integrate, °combine, °concentrate, systematize, °organize, comprise, codify, epitomize, synthesize

embrace *v.* 1 °hug, °clasp, °grasp, °hold, enfold, °cuddle, cleave together, *Archaic* °clip 2 °adopt, espouse, take up *or* in, avail oneself of, °use, make use of, °employ, °accept, °receive, °welcome 3 °include, comprise, °embody, °incorporate, °comprehend, encompass —*n.* 4 °hug, °squeeze, °clutch, *Slang* °clinch

emerge *v.* 1 °appear, °come out, come forth, °come up, °rise; °arise, °surface, come into view *or* notice, °come to light, be revealed, crop up, °turn out, °develop, become known, become apparent, °transpire, °happen, evolve 2 °issue, °emanate, come forth, °proceed

emergence *n.* °rise, surfacing, °appearance; °development, materialization, °manifestation

emergency *n.* °crisis, exigency, °danger, °predicament, °difficulty, °pinch

emigrant *n.* emigre *or* émigré, expatriate, displaced person, DP, °refugee, boat person; colonist, °settler

emigrate *v.* °migrate, °move, relocate, resettle; °leave, °quit, °depart, °forsake

eminent *adj.* 1 °distinguished, esteemed, °exalted, respected, revered, honored, °dignified, °notable, °noteworthy, °important, °noted, °outstanding, °prominent, °preeminent, °conspicuous, °superior, °great, °illustrious, °famous, °renowned, °well-known, °celebrated 2 °conspicuous, °outstanding, °marked

eminently *adv.* °very, °exceedingly, °extremely, exceptionally, remarkably, singularly, °notably, signally

emit *v.* °discharge, °eject, °expel, °emanate, send out *or* forth, pour out *or* forth, give off *or* out, °issue, °vent, °radiate; °exhale; exude, °ooze

emotion *n.* °feeling, °passion, °sentiment, °sensation

emotional *adj.* 1 °passionate, °impassioned, °ardent, °enthusiastic, °heated, zealous, °heartfelt, °excited, °fervent, fervid 2 °tense, °nervous, °excitable, highly strung, high-strung, °temperamental, °volatile, °hotheaded, °demonstrative 3 °sensitive, °warm, °sentimental, °tender, °moving, °poignant, °stirring, emotive, affective, °touching 4 °frantic, °agitated, irrational, °hysterical, °wild, ranting

emphasis *n.* °importance, °stress, °significance, °prominence, °attention, °weight, °gravity, °force, °moment, °preeminence, °priority, underscoring, underlining, *Technical* paralipsis

emphasize *v.* °stress, accentuate, °accent, underscore, °point up, underline, call *or* draw attention to, °mark, highlight, °play up, °spotlight, °feature

emphatic *adj.* °firm, uncompromising, °determined, °decided, °resolute, dogged; °earnest, °definite, unequivocal, unambiguous, °distinct, °dogmatic, °categorical, °peremptory, °explicit, °incisive, °insistent, affirmative, °positive, °sure, °certain, unmistakable *or* unmistakeable, °specific, °definitive, °direct; °forceful, °vigorous, °energetic, °assertive, °intense; °express, °pronounced, °strong

empirical *adj.* empiric, experiential, °practical, observed, pragmatic, °experimental

employ *v.* 1 °hire, °engage, °enlist, °recruit, °enroll, °sign (up), °take on, °retain, commission 2 °use, make use of, utilize, °apply 3 °occupy, °take (up), °engage, °involve

employee *n.* °worker, staff member, wage earner; °hand

employer *n.* 1 °proprietor, °owner, °patron, °manager, °director, °chief, °head, *Colloq* °boss, *Brit* gaffer, governor, guv'nor, guv 2 °company, °firm, corporation, °business, °establishment, °organization, *Colloq* °outfit

employment *n.* 1 °occupation, °job, °trade, °work, °business, °profession, °vocation,

°calling, livelihood, °pursuit, métier, °skill, °craft, *Colloq* °line, *Slang* °racket **2** °hire, hiring, °engagement, °engaging, employing, taking on, retaining, enlistment, enlisting **3** °use, utilization, °application, °operation, implementation

emptiness *n.* **1** voidness, hollowness, vacantness, °vacancy, vacuity, blankness, bareness, barrenness, °desolation, desertedness, vacuum, °void **2** senselessness, meaninglessness, pointlessness, aimlessness, purposelessness, futility, uselessness, worthlessness, hollowness **3** vacuity, vacuousness, vacantness, blankness, expressionlessness, emotionlessness

empty *adj.* **1** °void, unfilled, °hollow, °bare, °barren, °vacant, unfurnished, °unadorned, undecorated; emptied, drained, °spent, °exhausted **2** °vacant, unoccupied, °uninhabited, untenanted **3** °deserted, °desolate, °uninhabited, °wild, °waste, °bare, °barren; forsaken **4** trivial, °insincere, °hypocritical, °hollow, °cheap, °worthless, valueless, °meaningless, °insignificant, °insubstantial, unsatisfying, °idle **5** °vacant, °blank, deadpan, expressionless, poker-faced; vacuous, fatuous, °stupid, °foolish, °inane **6** °blank, °clean, °new, °unused, °clear **7** ***empty of.*** devoid of, lacking (in), °wanting, in want of, deficient in, °destitute of, without, sans —*v.* **8** °clear, °remove, take out *or* away, °put out, cast *or* throw out, °eject; °vacate, °evacuate; °dump, °drain, °exhaust, pour out, °void, °discharge, °unload

enable *v.* **1** °qualify, °authorize, °entitle, °permit, °allow, °sanction, °approve, empower, °license, commission, °entrust, depute, °delegate, °assign, °charter, franchise **2** capacitate, °facilitate, °expedite, °help, °aid, °assist **3** °permit, °allow, °approve, assent to, °go along with, °agree to, give the go-ahead *or* green light, *Colloq* okay *or* O.K.

enact *v.* **1** °pass, legislate, °ratify; ordain, °decree, °rule, °command, °order, °authorize **2** °act (out), °represent, °play, °portray, depict, °perform, appear as

enchant *v.* **1** °bewitch, cast a spell on, ensorcell *or* ensorcel, spellbind, °hypnotize, mesmerize, voodoo, *Brit* °magic, *US* hex, *Colloq* hoodoo **2** °charm, °fascinate, °beguile, °captivate, enthrall, °enrapture, °attract, allure, °delight, °entrance

enchanted *adj.* pleased, °delighted, °happy, thrilled, *French* enchanté(e)

enchanting *adj.* beguiling, bewitching, entrancing, °spellbinding, charming, fascinating, captivating, intriguing, °enthralling, alluring, °delightful, hypnotic, °attractive, appealing, winsome, °ravishing, °seductive

enchantment *n.* **1** witchcraft, °sorcery, °magic, wizardry, thaumaturgy, conjuration *or* conjury; °spell, °charm, °jinx, *US* hex **2** °charm, beguilement, allure, °fascination, °rapture, mesmerism, °bliss

encircle *v.* °surround, gird, °circle, °enclose, °ring, encompass, compass, confine, hem *or* hold in; wreathe

enclose *v.* **1** inclose, confine, °shut in, close *or* hem in, °surround, °pen, °encircle, encompass, °bound, °envelop, hedge in, wall in, immure, fence in *or* off, *US and Canadian* corral **2** °insert, °include, °contain; °wrap

enclosure *n.* **1** °fold, °pen, cote, °run, sty, yard, farmyard, barnyard, courtyard, quadrangle *or* quad, °square, °compound, *Brit* °close, *US and Canadian* corral **2** °fence, °wall, °rail, railing, °barrier, hedge, barricade, °boundary

encounter *v.* **1** °meet, come upon, run into *or* across, °happen upon, chance upon, °hit upon, °light upon, °stumble upon, *Colloq* °bump into **2** °face, °experience, °meet with, contend with, be faced with, come into contact with, wrestle with **3** come into conflict with, contend with, assail, cross swords (with), °grapple with, °engage, joust with, do battle with, confront, clash with, °join, °meet —*n.* **4** °meeting **5** confrontation, °brush, °quarrel, °disagreement, °dispute, altercation, °engagement, °action, °battle, °fight, °clash, °conflict, °skirmish, °contest, °competition, duel, contention, °struggle, °war, *Colloq* dust-up, °scrap, °run-in, set-to

encourage *v.* **1** hearten, embolden, °reassure, °buoy (up), °stimulate, °animate, °support, inspirit, °inspire, °cheer (up), urge *or* spur on *or* onward(s), °incite, *Colloq* egg on, °pep up **2** °promote, °advance, °aid, °support, °help, °assist, °abet, °foster, °forward, °boost, *Colloq* give a shot in the arm

encouragement *n.* **1** heartening, reassuring, reassurance, buoying up, °stimulating, stimulation, stimulus, animating, °animation, supporting, °support, promoting, °promotion, inspiring, °inspiration, cheering, urging, °spur, spurring, exhorting, exhortation, prodding, urging, innervation, inciting, °incitement **2** °boost, stimulus, °help, °aid, °support, *Colloq* pep talk

encroach *v.* Often, ***encroach on or upon.*** intrude, trespass, °infringe, invade, make inroads

encumber *v.* **1** °burden, °weigh down, load (up *or* down), °overload, overburden, °strain, °oppress, saddle, °tax, overtax **2** °hamper, °impede, °hinder, °handicap, °inconvenience, °trammel, °retard, °slow down

encumbrance *n.* °weight, °burden, onus, °cross (to bear), albatross, millstone, °handicap, °impediment, °hindrance, °obstacle, °obstruction, °liability, °disadvantage, °drag

encyclopedic *adj.* encyclopaedic, °comprehensive, °inclusive, °broad, °extensive, °universal, °thorough, °exhaustive, wide-ranging, °complete

end *n.* **1** °extremity, °extreme, °extent, °bound, °boundary, °tip, °limit, terminus **2** °close, °termination, conclusion, cessation, °expiration, °finish, °completion, finale, ending, windup; denouement *or* dénouement **3** °aim, °purpose, °intention, °intent, °objective, °object, °goal, °point, °reason, raison d'être, °destination, °motive, motivation, °aspiration

4 consequence, °result, °outcome, °effect, °upshot 5 °destruction, °death, °ruin, extermination, annihilation, °termination, conclusion 6 *at loose ends or Brit at a loose end.* °unsettled, unoccupied, °unemployed, uncommitted, undecided, °indecisive, ambivalent, vacillating, °purposeless, °aimless, adrift, drifting, betwixt and between, neither here nor there 7 *on end.* (a) °upright, °erect, °standing (b) continuously, uninterruptedly, unceasingly, incessantly, consecutively 8 *the end.* (a) the worst, the last straw, the final blow, *Colloq* °the limit, too much (b) the best, the greatest —*v.* 9 °terminate, conclude, bring to an end, °stop, °halt, °cease, wind up *or* down, °settle, put an end to, °discontinue, °break off, °cut off, °close, °finish, culminate, end up, *Brit* put paid to; °die (out), °expire, °climax, °peter out, vanish 10 °kill, put to death, annihilate, °exterminate, °terminate, °extinguish; °destroy, °ruin 11 °surpass, °outdo, outclass, outshine, °outstrip, °supersede

endanger *v.* imperil, °threaten, °jeopardize, °risk, put at risk, °hazard, °expose (to danger), put in jeopardy, tempt fate

endangered *adj.* imperiled, threatened, near extinction

endearing *adj.* °attractive, °engaging, likable *or* likeable, appealing, winsome, captivating, °winning

endeavor *v.* 1 °try, °attempt, °strive, make an effort, do one's best, °struggle, °exert oneself, °undertake; °aim, °aspire; *Colloq* take a stab at, have a go *or* crack *or* whack *or* shot at —*n.* 2 °effort, °pains, °attempt, °try, striving, °struggle, °venture, °enterprise, *Colloq* °stab, °crack, whack, °shot

endless *adj.* 1 °limitless, °unlimited, °boundless, unbounded, °infinite, °immeasurable, °eternal, unending 2 ceaseless, uninterrupted, incessant, unceasing, unending, °constant, °perpetual, interminable, unremitting, °nonstop, °continuous, °continual, °everlasting

endorse *v.* 1 indorse, °approve, °sanction, °authorize, °advocate, °support, °back, °subscribe to, °sustain, °confirm, countenance, put one's stamp *or* seal (of approval) on, set one's seal (of approval) to, give (something) one's imprimatur, *Colloq* okay *or* O.K. 2 countersign

endorsement *n.* 1 indorsement, °approval, affirmation, °sanction, authorization, confirmation, ratification, °support, °backing, approbation, seal *or* stamp of approval, imprimatur, *Colloq* okay *or* O.K. 2 countersignature

endowment *n.* 1 °grant, (financial) °aid, °subsidy, subvention, °allowance, °allotment, contribution, °donation, °gift, °present, °award; °bequest, °inheritance, dowry 2 °gift, °presentation, bestowal, °award, awarding, °settlement 3 *endowments.* qualities, talents, gifts, °abilities, aptitudes, capabilities, capacities, °qualifications, strengths; attributes, properties, characteristics

endurance *n.* 1 °stamina, staying power, °perseverance, °persistence, °resolution, °fortitude, °tenacity, °patience, °tolerance, *Colloq US* stick-to-itiveness 2 lasting quality, durability, longevity, lifetime, continuation

endure *v.* 1 °last, °persist, °stay, °remain, °abide, °prevail, °survive, °continue, °hold, °live (on), *Colloq* go the distance 2 °stand, °abide, °tolerate, °face, °survive, °withstand, °bear, °weather, °take (it), °suffer, °stomach, °undergo, °hold out (against), *Colloq* hang in (there), stick *or* sweat (it *or* something) out 3 °suffer, °undergo, °bear, °face, °stand, °put up with, °stomach, °take

enduring *adj.* °lasting, long-lasting, °durable, °abiding, continuing, long-standing, persisting, °persistent, °remaining, °steady, °steadfast; °eternal, °immortal, °permanent

enemy *n.* foe, °antagonist, °adversary, °opponent, °rival, °competitor, °contestant, contender; the opposition, the other side

energetic *adj.* °lively, °active, °vigorous, invigorated, °dynamic, °animated, °spirited, °untiring, °tireless, indefatigable, °sprightly, spry, °vital, high-powered, °brisk, vibrant, zesty, zestful, *Colloq* °hot, peppy, full of pep, full of get-up-and-go, zippy, on one's toes, zingy, full of beans

energize *v.* °enliven, liven up, °stimulate °animate, invigorate, °activate, actuate °move, °motivate, galvanize, °electrify, °inspire, inspirit, °pep up, waken, °rouse, °stir, °arouse, °excite, egg on, °urge

energy *n.* °vitality, forcefulness, vivacity, liveliness, °vigor, °animation, °spirit, °force, °dynamism, °drive, °verve, °dash, élan, °intensity, °power, °determination, puissance, °strength, °might, *Colloq* °pep, vim and vigor, *US* stick-to-itiveness, get-up-and-go, zip, zing

enervate *v.* °weaken, °tire, °strain, enfeeble, debilitate, °fatigue, °exhaust, °drain, °sap, °wear out, devitalize, °break, °defeat

enforce *v.* 1 insist upon *or* on, °stress, °require, °impose, °support, put into effect, °apply, °administer, °carry out, °inflict, bring to bear, °implement, °prosecute, °discharge; °reinforce; *Colloq* crack *or* clamp down 2 °force, compel, pressure *or Brit* pressurize, °press, coerce, lay stress upon *or* on, impose upon *or* on, impress upon *or* on, insist upon *or* on, °demand, °require; °intimidate, °browbeat, °bully, °railroad; *Colloq* °lean on, twist (someone's) arm

engage *v.* 1 °employ, °hire, enrol *or US also* enroll, °enlist, °retain, °sign (up), contract with *or* for, indenture; °rent, °book, °reserve, °secure, bespeak 2 °occupy, engross, °busy, absorb, °involve, °tie up, preoccupy, °employ 3 °pledge, °undertake, °bargain, °agree, covenant, °promise, °guarantee, °contract 4 °attract, °hold, °capture, °catch, °draw 5 join (in) combat *or* battle with, °meet, °encounter, °fight, °combat, °attack, °battle, clash with, °grapple with 6 *engage in.* °participate (in), °partake in, take part (in), °enter (into), °undertake, °embark on

engaged *adj.* 1 betrothed, affianced, plighted, pledged, promised; °spoken for 2 °busy, occupied, tied up, °involved, employed, °absorbed, °preoccupied, wrapped up

engagement *n.* 1 °appointment, °meeting, °date, rendezvous, °arrangement, commitment 2 betrothal 3 °agreement, °bargain, °obligation, °promise, °pledge, covenant, °contract 4 °job, °position, °post, commission, booking; °employment, °work; *Colloq* °spot, *Slang* (of a musician) gig 5 °fight, °battle, °conflict, °encounter, °combat

engaging *adj.* charming, °pleasant, °attractive, winsome, °winning, appealing, °agreeable, °delightful, °pleasing, likable *or* likeable, °friendly, °open

engine *n.* motor, °machine, °mechanism, appliance, °apparatus; locomotive

engineer *n.* 1 °designer, originator, inventor, contriver, architect, planner, °mastermind 2 (engine) driver, conductor, °operator 3 mechanic, technician, repairman —*v.* 4 °devise, °plan, °develop, °originate, contrive, °invent, °mastermind, °construct, °build, °make 5 °manipulate, °scheme, °plot, machinate, °intrigue, connive, conspire, °maneuver, °rig, °set up, °organize, °arrange, °put over, *Colloq* finagle, °wangle, °swing

engrave *v.* 1 °cut, °carve, °chisel, inscribe; °etch 2 °impress, °stamp, °set, °lodge, °fix, embed, imprint, ingrain

engraving *n.* 1 intaglio, cameo, etching, drypoint, woodcut, linocut, wood *or* steel engraving, anaglyph, block *or US also* cut 2 °print, °impression, etching, drypoint

enhance *v.* °improve, °better, augment, °boost, °raise, elevate, °lift, °heighten, °exalt, °enlarge, °swell, °magnify, °increase, °add to, °amplify, °intensify, °enrich, °embellish, °complement, °reinforce, °strengthen

enigma *n.* °puzzle, conundrum, °mystery, °riddle, poser, °problem

enjoy *v.* 1 °delight in, °appreciate, °like, take *or* derive pleasure *or* satisfaction in *or* from, °relish (in), °fancy, °take to, *Slang* °dig, get a kick *or* lift *or* charge out of, get high on, °get off on 2 benefit *or* profit from, take advantage of, °use, utilize, make use of, use to advantage, °have, °possess 3 ***enjoy oneself.*** have a good time, °make merry, *Colloq* have a ball *or* the time of one's life

enjoyment *n.* 1 °pleasure, °delight, °joy, °gratification, °satisfaction, °relish, °zest, °delectation, °recreation, °entertainment, °diversion, °amusement 2 °use, utilization, °exercise, °possession; °benefit, °advantage

enlarge *v.* 1 °increase, °expand, °magnify, °amplify, °extend, °swell, dilate, °spread, wax, °widen, broaden, °lengthen, elongate, °stretch, distend; °add to, °supplement, augment; °inflate; *Colloq* °blow up 2 ***enlarge on or upon.*** °expand on, expatiate on, °amplify, expound; °detail, °elaborate (on)

enlighten *v.* °inform, edify, °instruct, °teach, °tutor, °educate, °coach, apprise, make aware, °advise, °counsel

enlightened *adj.* °well-informed, °informed, °educated, °aware, °knowledgeable, literate, °rational, °reasonable, °sensible, commonsense, common-sensical, broad-minded, open-minded, °liberal; °cultivated, civilized °sophisticated, *Colloq* in the know

enlist *v.* 1 °enroll, °register, °join (up), volunteer, sign up *or* on; °engage, °recruit, °induct, °muster, conscript, °impress, °call up, *US* °draft 2 °employ, °hire, °engage, °retain, make available, °secure, °obtain, °get, °procure, °gather, drum up, °mobilize *Colloq* °organize

enliven *v.* 1 invigorate, inspirit, °animate, °pep up, °stimulate, °energize, vivify, °vitalize, °quicken, exhilarate, °arouse, °rouse, °awaken, °wake up, °spark (off), °kindle, enkindle, °fire (up), °inspire 2 °brighten, °cheer (up), °buoy (up), °gladden, uplift

enormity *n.* outrageousness, °outrage, atrociousness, °atrocity, wickedness, heinousness, flagitiousness, horribleness, °horror, °barbarity, savagery, monstrousness, horridness, °evil, viciousness

enormous *adj.* °huge, °immense, °gigantic, elephantine, gargantuan, mammoth, titanic, °colossal, tremendous, °vast, °massive, stupendous, Brobdingnagian, °gross, °monstrous, °prodigious

enormousness *n.* immensity, hugeness

enough *adj.* 1 °sufficient, °adequate, °ample —*n.* 2 sufficiency, adequacy, ample supply, °plenty —*adv.* 3 sufficiently, adequately, reasonably, satisfactorily, tolerably, passably

enquire *v.* 1 °inquire, °ask, °question, °query 2 See **inquire.**

enrage *v.* °anger, °infuriate, °madden, incense, °provoke, °inflame, make (someone's) blood boil, *Colloq* get (someone's) back *or* Irish *or* hackles *or* dander up, make (someone) see red, wave a red flag before (someone), make (someone's) blood boil, *US* burn (someone) up, *Slang US* tick (someone) off, *Taboo* piss (someone) off, *Brit* put (someone's) monkey up, *US* tee (someone) off

enrapture *v.* °enchant, °entrance, °transport, °thrill, °bewitch, spellbind, °fascinate, °charm, enthrall, °captivate, °beguile, °delight

enrich *v.* 1 endow, °enhance, °improve, upgrade, °better, ameliorate, °refine, °add to 2 °ornament, adorn, °decorate, °embellish; °beautify, °grace

enroll *v.* 1 °enlist, °register, sign up *or* on (for), °join; volunteer; °recruit; *Colloq* join up 2 °record, °register, °chronicle, °put down, °list, °note, inscribed, catalog

ensemble *n.* 1 °outfit, °costume, clothing, °clothes, attire, °apparel, garb, °garments, coordinates, *Colloq* get-up 2 °band, °combination, orchestra, °group; chorus, choir; *Colloq* combo 3 assemblage, composite, aggregate, °collection, °set, °whole, °entirety, °totality; agglomeration, conglomeration

enslave *v.* °subjugate, yoke, fetter, enchain

°shackle, °trammel, °dominate; °bind, indenture, *Archaic* enthrall

ensure *v.* **1** insure, °assure, make sure *or* certain, °confirm, °certify, °guarantee; °secure, °effect **2** insure, °protect, make safe, °safeguard, °guard, °secure

entail *v.* °involve, °require, °call for, necessitate, °demand, °occasion, °give rise to, °impose; lead to, °cause

entangle *v.* **1** °tangle, ensnarl, °snarl, enmesh, °catch (up), entrap, °snag, °foul, °implicate, °knot (up), °twist; °impede; °involve, embroil **2** °confuse, °mix (up), °twist, °snarl, ensnarl, ensnare, °hamper, °complicate, confound, °bewilder, °perplex, °embarrass

enter *v.* **1** go *or* come (in *or* into), °pass (into) **2** °penetrate, °pierce, °stick (into), °stab (into), °puncture; invade, infiltrate **3** °insert, inscribe, °write, set *or* write *or* put down, °note, °record, take *or* jot down, °register; log, °document, °minute **4** enter on *or* upon, °begin, °start, °commence, °undertake, set out on, °take up **5** °enroll, °enlist, sign on *or* up, °join, become a member of **6** present, °offer, proffer, °tender, °submit **7** °file, °register, °record, °submit **8** ***enter into.*** engage *or* participate in, °sign, be (a) party to, cosign, countersign

enterprise *n.* **1** °undertaking, °project, °venture, °adventure, °effort, °program, °plan, °scheme **2** boldness, °daring, °courage, mettle, adventurousness, audacity, °enthusiasm, zeal, °energy, °spirit, °drive, °vigor, °ambition, °initiative, °push, °eagerness, °determination, °resolve, purposefulness, °purpose; aggressiveness; *Colloq* get-up-and-go, zip, °pep, °gumption, °guts, *US* starch **3** °business, °operation, °firm, °company, °concern, °establishment

enterprising *adj.* °resourceful, °venturesome, °adventurous, °daring, °courageous, °bold, °brave, mettlesome, °audacious, °enthusiastic, °eager, °keen, zealous, °energetic, °spirited, °vigorous, °ambitious, °determined, resolved, °resolute, °earnest, °purposeful, purposive, goal-oriented; °aggressive, hard-working, indefatigable, °tireless, °diligent, assiduous, °industrious, persevering; *Colloq* °pushy, °go-ahead

entertain *v.* **1** °amuse, °divert; °delight, please; °occupy **2** °receive, °accommodate, °treat, be host (to), cater (for *or* to); have *or* see people *or* guests *or* visitors *or* company; *Colloq* °host **3** °contemplate, °consider, °have, °hold, °harbor, °foster, °tolerate, °allow, °maintain, °sustain, °support

entertaining *adj.* amusing, diverting, °delightful, enjoyable, °pleasant, °fun, °pleasing, °pleasurable, °interesting, °engaging; °funny, °comic, °humorous, °witty

entertainment *n.* **1** °amusement, °diversion, °distraction, °pastime, °recreation, °sport, °play, °fun, °pleasure, °enjoyment, °relaxation, °relief **2** °performance, °presentation, °diversion, °amusement, divertissement, °exhibition, °pageant, °spectacle, °show, °production, spectacular, °extravaganza

enthralling *adj.* captivating, entrancing, °spellbinding, °enchanting, bewitching, beguiling, fascinating, gripping, °absorbing, intriguing, hypnotizing, mesmerizing, °riveting

enthusiasm *n.* **1** °eagerness, keenness, earnestness, °fervor, avidity, zeal, °excitement, °passion, °ardor, °interest, °relish, °devotion, devotedness, °gusto, °exuberance, °zest; °fanaticism, °mania, °rage **2** °rage, °passion, °craze; °hobby, °interest, °pastime, °diversion, °amusement; *Colloq* °fad

enthusiast *n.* °fan, °devotee, aficionado, °lover, °admirer, °zealot, °addict, °fanatic, promoter, °supporter, °champion, °follower, °disciple, adherent, *US* booster, *Colloq* teeny-bopper, °bug, °hound, buff, °fiend, *Slang* nut, °freak, groupie, *US* °head

enthusiastic *adj.* °eager, °keen, °fervent, fervid, °hearty, °ardent, avid, °energetic, °vigorous, °devoted, °earnest, °passionate, °spirited, °exuberant, zealous, fanatic(al), °unqualified, unstinting, °irrepressible

entice *v.* °lure, allure, °tempt, °attract, °draw, °seduce, °coax, °persuade, °prevail on, °beguile, °cajole, blandish, °wheedle; °decoy, °lead on, inveigle, *Colloq* sweet-talk, soft-soap, *Slang* suck in

enticement *n.* **1** °temptation, allurement, beguilement, seduction, °cajolery, wheedling, blandishment, coaxing, °persuasion **2** °lure, bait, °decoy, °trap, °inducement, °attraction, °temptation, *Colloq* °come-on, sof soap

entire *adj.* **1** °complete, °whole, °total, °full, °undivided, °absolute, °thorough, unre served, unrestricted, undiminished, unconditional, °express, unexceptional, unmixed, unalloyed **2** °intact, °whole, °sound, unbroken, undamaged, unimpaired, inviolate, without a scratch, °unscathed, in one piece **3** °continuous, °full, °whole, °complete, uninterrupted

entirely *adv.* **1** °completely, °wholly, °altogether, fully, °totally, °utterly, unreservedly, unqualifiedly, unexceptionally, in every respect, in all respects, °thoroughly, to a T, *in toto*, exhaustively, all-out, from head to toe *or* foot, (right) down to the ground, from A to Z, °lock, stock and barrel, °root and branch, without exception *or* reservation **2** solely, exclusively, °only, unambiguously, unequivocally; °positively, °definitely, °clearly

entirety *n.* **1** completeness, °unity, °totality, wholeness, fullness, °integrity, °perfection **2** °whole, sum total, °everything, all

entitle *v.* **1** °allow, °permit, °qualify, make eligible, °authorize, °fit; enfranchise, °license, empower **2** °name, °title, °call, °label, °nickname, dub, °designate, °term; °christen, baptize

entity *n.* **1** °thing, °object, being, °existence, °quantity, article, °individual, °organism **2** °essence, real nature, quiddity, °quintessence, *Metaphysics* ens

entrance[1] *n.* **1** °(right of) entry, access, °admission, °admittance, entrée, introduction **2** °entry, entryway, access, door, °gate, °passage, °way (in); ingress **3** °arrival, °appearance; coming, °entry, coming *or* going in **4** °beginning, °start, commencement

entrance[2] *v.* °enchant, °enrapture, °fascinate, °bewitch, spellbind, °transport, °delight, °charm, °captivate, enthrall, °overpower, mesmerize, °hypnotize

entrenched *adj.* °rooted, deep-rooted, embedded, °fixed, (firmly) planted, established, °set, deep-seated, unshakable *or* unshakeable, ineradicable, °ingrained

entrust *v.* intrust, °trust, °charge, °assign, °delegate, confide

entry *n.* **1** access, °entrance, entrée, °admittance, °admission **2** access, °entrance, entryway, door, inlet, °passage, way in **3** °entrance, °arrival, coming *or* going in **4** °record, °item, °memorandum, °note, °account, listing; registration; *Colloq* memo **5** °competitor, °contestant, °player, entrant, °participant, °candidate; °rival, °adversary, °opponent

entwine *v.* intwine, interlace, °braid, interweave, intertwine, °weave, °knit, plait, °twist, °coil, °twine, °splice; °entangle, °tangle

enumerate *v.* **1** °list, °name, °itemize, °specify, °detail, °spell out, catalogue, tick off, take stock of, cite, °quote, °recite, °recount, °relate, °narrate, *US* °check off **2** °count, °calculate, °compute, °reckon, °tally, °add, °number

enunciate *v.* **1** articulate, °pronounce, utter, °voice, °say, °speak, vocalize, °express, °deliver, °present, *Formal* enounce **2** °state, °proclaim, °declare, promulgate, °announce, °broadcast, °pronounce, °propound

envelop *v.* **1** °wrap, °enclose, enfold, enwrap, °cover, engulf, °swathe, °shroud, enshroud, swaddle **2** °shroud, enshroud, °cover, °conceal, °hide, °screen, °shield, °obscure, °veil, °cloak

enviable *adj.* °desirable, wanted, desired, sought-after, covetable, °in demand

envious *adj.* °jealous, covetous, °resentful, begrudging, green-eyed, °green (with envy), °desirous

environment *n.* surroundings, environs, °atmosphere, ecosystem, °conditions, °habitat, °circumstances, °medium, °milieu; °territory, °locale, °setting, *mise en scène*, °situation

environmentalist *n.* ecologist, conservationist, naturalist, preservationist, nature lover, green *or* Green

envisage *v.* **1** visualize, °contemplate, °imagine, °picture, °conceive (of), °fancy, think *or* dream *or* conjure up, *Chiefly US* °envision **2** °foresee, °see, °predict, °forecast, °anticipate

envision *v.* °envisage, visualize, °imagine, conceive of, °foresee, °anticipate, °predict, °forecast, °prophesy

envoy *n.* °delegate, legate, °ambassador, diplomat, °minister, (papal) nuncio, attaché; °representative, emissary, °agent; *Formal* envoy extraordinary, minister plenipotentiary

envy *n.* **1** jealousy, enviousness, °resentment **2** covetousness, °desire, °longing —*v.* **3** covet, °begrudge, °resent

epicure *n.* °gourmet, connoisseur, °aesthete, °epicurean, °sybarite, hedonist, gastronome, bon viveur, *bon vivant*, Lucullus; gourmand

epicurean *adj.* **1** °sensual, sybaritic, °luxurious, °voluptuous, °carnal, °self-indulgent, pleasure-seeking, pleasure-oriented, hedonistic, °gluttonous, intemperate, overindulgent, crapulent *or* crapulous, swinish, porcine, piggish, °immoderate, orgiastic, libidinous, °wild, unrestrained, unconfined, °dissolute, dissipated, Bacchanalian, saturnalian **2** Lucullan, °gourmet —*n.* **3** °epicure

epidemic *adj.* **1** widespread, °universal, °prevalent, °prevailing, °rampant, °general, wide-ranging, pandemic —*n.* **2** °plague, °pestilence, °scourge, °rash, °growth, upsurge, outbreak, °spread

epigram *n.* **1** °witticism, bon mot, °quip, mot, turn of phrase, *jeu d'esprit*, Atticism; °pun, double entendre, *jeu de mots*, play on words, equivoque; paronomasia **2** °proverb, aphorism, °maxim, °saw, saying, adage, apophthegm *or* apothegm

epigrammatic *adj.* pithy, °terse, laconic, °concise, °succinct, compendious, piquant, °pungent, °trenchant, sententious, °witty, °pointed, °proverbial, aphoristic, apophthegmatic *or* apothegmatic, *Colloq* °snappy, punchy

episode *n.* **1** °event, °incident, °occurrence, °happening, °experience, °adventure, °affair, °matter **2** chapter, °scene, installment, °part

epitome *n.* **1** °essence, °quintessence, °embodiment, personification, archetype, exemplar, °(typical) example, °model, °prototype **2** °summary, °abstract, condensation, °synopsis, °digest, compendium, °abridgment, °abbreviation, conspectus, °résumé, contraction; °outline, °précis, syllabus

equable *adj.* **1** even-tempered, easygoing, °serene, °calm, placid, composed, °cool, imperturbable, °collected, unruffled, °tranquil, °peaceful, °levelheaded, *Colloq* unflappable **2** °uniform, unvarying, unvaried, °consistent, °stable, °steady, °regular, °even, unchanging, °invariable, °constant

equal *adj.* **1** °identical, the same (as), interchangeable, one and the same, coequal, selfsame; °like, °alike, tantamount, °similar (to), °equivalent, commensurate **2** °uniform, °regular, corresponding, °correspondent, congruent, congruous, (evenly) balanced, (evenly) matched, °matching; °equivalent, °even; commensurate, comparable, proportionate, (evenly) proportioned, °harmonious, °symmetrical; *Colloq* fifty-fifty, *Brit* level pegging, *US* even-steven **3** ***equal to.*** up to, °capable of, fit(ted) *or* suited *or* suitable for, adequate for, *Archaic or literary* sufficient unto —*n.* **4** °peer, °colleague, °fellow, °brother, °mate, counterpart, °equivalent, alter ego, compeer —*v.* **5** °match, °meet, °even, °correspond (to), °square (with), °tally (with), °tie (with), °parallel, come up to; °rival

equality *n.* **1** °parity, sameness, °identity, coequality, °uniformity **2** similarity, °likeness, °resemblance, equivalence, correspondence, conformity, congruence, similitude, analogy, comparability, °comparison, °coincidence **3** impartiality, fairness, °justice; egalitarianism

equalize *v.* regularize, °even up, °square, °balance, equate, °match, °standardize, °(make) equal

equip *v.* °furnish, °provide, °supply, °stock, °outfit, fit (out *or* up), rig (out *or* up), accouter *or* accoutre, array, attire, °dress, deck (out), caparison, °clothe, *Chiefly Brit* kit out *or* up

equipment *n.* °gear, °apparatus, furnishings, accouterments *or* accoutrements, appurtenances, °paraphernalia, °kit, materiel *or* matériel, °tackle, °outfit, °trappings, °tack, equipage, *Colloq Brit* clobber

equitable *adj.* °fair, evenhanded, °just, °impartial, °objective, unbiased, °unprejudiced, °square, fair-minded, open-minded, °disinterested, °dispassionate, °neutral, °tolerant, unbigoted, °reasonable, °judicious, °ethical, °principled, °moral, °proper, right-minded, *Colloq* fair and square

equity *n.* fairness, impartiality, evenhandedness, °justice, fair play, °objectivity, disinterest, fair-mindedness, equitableness, openmindedness, disinterestedness, neutrality, °tolerance, judiciousness, rightmindedness, high-mindedness

equivalent *adj.* **1** tantamount, commensurate, °alike, °similar, °close, comparable, corresponding, interchangeable, °equal, °synonymous, of a piece *or* a kind —*n.* **2** °match, °equal, °peer, counterpart, °twin

equivocal *adj.* **1** °evasive, misleading, °roundabout, hedging, °suspicious, duplicitous, °questionable, °oblique, circumlocutory, ambagious, ambivalent, amphibolic *or* amphibolous, *Colloq* waffling, °wishy-washy **2** °ambiguous, °vague, °hazy, °indefinite, unclear, °indistinct, enigmatic(al), °puzzling, °perplexing, indeterminate, °uncertain, *Colloq* waffling

equivocate *v.* °evade, °mislead, hedge, °deceive, °quibble, °dodge, weasel out (of), double-talk, °fence, °sidestep, skirt, °avoid, tergiversate, prevaricate, *Colloq* °waffle, beat about *or* around the bush, °pussyfoot

era *n.* °age, °period, time(s), day(s), epoch, °stage; °generation, °cycle, °date

erase *v.* **1** expunge, rub *or* scratch *or* blot *or* wipe out, °delete, °cancel, efface, °scratch, cross *or* strike out *or* off, °obliterate **2** °abolish, °destroy, °obliterate, °remove, °eliminate, °(get) rid of, eradicate, efface

erect *adj.* **1** °upright, °standing, upstanding, °straight, vertical, °perpendicular, °plumb —*v.* **2** °build, °construct, °put up, °raise; °pitch **3** °establish, °found, °set up, °form, °institute, °organize, °create

erode *v.* wear (down *or* away), eat away, °grind down, abrade, gnaw away (at), °consume, corrode, °wash away; °deteriorate, °destroy, deplete, °reduce, °diminish

erosion *n.* °wear (and tear), wearing (down *or* away), wasting away, washing *or* grinding *or* rubbing away, corroding, corrosion, abrading, abrasion, eating *or* gnawing away, chafing, fraying, weathering, attrition

erotic *adj.* **1** °sensual, °stimulating, °suggestive, titillating, °risqué, °bawdy, ribald, °seductive, °voluptuous, °lustful, *Colloq* °sexy **2** amatory, °venereal, amorous, Anacreontic **3** erogenous, °naughty, °carnal, arousing, °rousing, aphrodisiac, libidinous, lubricious *or* lubricous, °prurient, °lascivious, °lewd, concupiscent, salacious, °obscene, °pornographic, °dirty, °filthy, °nasty, *Colloq* °blue

err *v.* **1** be wrong, be in error, be mistaken, be inaccurate, be incorrect, be in the wrong, °go wrong, go astray, make a mistake, °miscalculate, °(make a) blunder, °bungle, °botch, °fumble, muff, make a mess of, make a faux pas, °mess up, *US* bobble; *Colloq* goof (up), °slip (up), drop a clanger, °foul up, *Brit* drop a brick, °blot one's copybook, *Slang* °screw up, *Brit* boob, *Taboo slang* fuck up **2** °misbehave, °sin, °transgress, trespass, °lapse, °fall, do wrong

errand *n.* **1** °trip, °journey **2** °mission, °charge, °assignment, commission, °task, °duty

erratic *adj.* **1** °irregular, unpredictable, °inconsistent, °unreliable, °capricious, °changeable, °variable; wayward, °unstable, aberrant, °flighty **2** °peculiar, °abnormal, wayward, °odd, °eccentric, °outlandish, °strange, °unusual, °unorthodox, °extraordinary, °queer, °quaint, °bizarre, °weird, unconventional **3** wandering, °meandering, directionless, planetary, °aimless, °haphazard, °discursive, errant, divagatory

erroneous *adj.* °wrong, °mistaken, °incorrect, °inaccurate, °inexact, °imprecise, °amiss, awry, °false, °faulty, misleading, °flawed, botched, bungled, °unsound, °invalid, °untrue, fallacious, °spurious, °counterfeit, *Colloq* off the mark, off course, *Brit* off beam, *US* off the beam

error *n.* **1** °mistake, inaccuracy, °fault, °flaw, °blunder, °slip, gaffe; °misprint, typographical error, erratum, °solecism; *Brit* °literal, *Colloq* slip-up, goof, clanger, °fluff, boo-boo, °howler, *Brit* bloomer, *Slang* foul-up, boner, *Brit* boob **2** °sin, °transgression, trespass, °offense, °indiscretion, wrongdoing, misconduct, iniquity, °evil, wickedness, flagitiousness **3** *in error.* **(a)** °wrong, °mistaken, °incorrect, °at fault **(b)** mistakenly, incorrectly, by mistake, erroneously

erupt *v.* **1** °eject, °discharge, °expel, °emit, burst forth *or* out, °blow up, °explode, spew forth *or* out, °break out, °spout, vomit (up *or* forth), throw up *or* off, spit out *or* up, belch (forth), °gush **2** °appear, °come out, °break out

eruption *n.* **1** outbreak, °outburst, °discharge, °expulsion, emission, bursting forth, °explosion, spouting, vomiting (up *or* forth), belching forth **2** outbreak, °rash

escape *v.* **1** °get away, break out *or* free, °bolt, °flee, °fly, run away *or* off, elope, decamp, abscond, steal *or* slip off *or* away, °take to one's heels, take French leave, °disappear, vanish, *Brit* levant, *Colloq* °take off, °clear out, cut and run, duck out, make oneself scarce, do a disappearing act, *Brit* do a moonlight flit, *US* vamoose, hightail it, skedaddle, *US and Canadian* °skip (town), fly the coop, °cut out; *Slang* vamoose, *Brit* do a bunk, °bugger off, mizzle off, *US and Canadian* scram, °blow, lam out, take it on the lam, take a (runout) powder, *Chiefly Australian* shoot through **2** °evade, °elude, °avoid, °dodge **3** °drain, °leak, °issue, seep, °discharge, °emanate **4** °elude, °evade, baffle, °stump, °mystify, °puzzle, be forgotten by, be beyond (someone) —*n.* **5** °flight, °getaway, departure, decampment, °bolt, jailbreak, prisonbreak, *Colloq* °break, breakout **6** °distraction, °relief, °diversion, °recreation **7** leakage, leaking, seepage, seeping, drainage, draining, °leak, °discharge, °outpouring, outflow, effluence, efflux, effluxion

escort *n.* **1** °guard, convoy, bodyguard, °protection, °guardian, °protector, chaperon, cortege *or* cortège, °retinue, entourage, safe-conduct, usher, °companion **2** °guide, °attendant, conductor, °leader, cicerone **3** °companion; °date, boyfriend, beau —*v.* **4** °accompany, °shepherd, °squire, usher, °conduct, °guide, °attend **5** °guard, convoy, °protect, watch over

especially *adv.* **1** °particularly, °specially, specifically, exceptionally, conspicuously, singularly, remarkably, extraordinarily, unusually, uncommonly, peculiarly, outstandingly, uniquely, °notably, strikingly, noticeably, markedly, signally **2** °chiefly, °mainly, predominantly, °primarily, °principally, °first, firstly, first of all, °above all

essay *n.* **1** article, °composition, °paper, °theme, °piece; °thesis, dissertation, disquisition, °tract **2** °attempt, °effort, °try, °endeavor, °venture; *Colloq* °shot, °go —*v.* **3** °try, °attempt, °endeavor, °strive, make an effort, °undertake, °venture, °tackle, °test, °go about, *Colloq* take a crack *or* whack *or* stab at, *Slang* have a go at, give (it *or* something) a shot, have a go *or* bash (at)

essence *n.* **1** °quintessence, quiddity, °(essential) nature, °substance, °spirit, being, °heart, °core, °pith, °kernel, marrow, °soul, °significance, °(active) principle, crux, cornerstone, foundation stone, *Colloq* bottom line **2** °extract, °concentrate, distillate, °elixir, tincture **3** ***in essence.*** essentially, basically, fundamentally, °materially, °substantially, °at bottom, in the final analysis, *au fond*; °in effect, °virtually **4** ***of the essence.*** °essential, °critical, °crucial, °vital, °indispensable, requisite, °important

essential *adj.* **1** °indispensable, °necessary, requisite, required, °important, °imperative, °vital, °material, quintessential **2** °fundamental, °basic, °intrinsic, °elemental, °elementary, °principal, °primary, °key, °main, °leading, °chief

establish *v.* **1** °found, °create, °institute, °set up, °start, °begin, °inaugurate, °organize, °form, constitute; °decree, °enact, ordain, °introduce **2** °secure, °settle, °fix, entrench, install *or* instal, °seat, ensconce; °lodge, °locate; °station **3** °prove, °confirm, °certify, °verify, affirm, °determine, °authenticate, °demonstrate, °show, °substantiate, corroborate, validate, °support, °back (up)

establishment *n.* **1** °foundation, founding, °formation, °organization, construction, °creation, °origin, origination, °institution, inauguration, setting up **2** °business, °concern, °firm, °company, °enterprise, °institution, °organization; °office; °shop, °store, °market **3** ***the Establishment.*** the system, the government, the authorities, the administration, the power structure, the ruling class, the (established) order, the conservatives, the powers that be; the Church

estate *n.* **1** °property, holdings, °domain, demesne, °land, landed estate, manor, mansion **2** °property, holdings, °assets, °capital, °resources, °wealth, °fortune; °belongings, °possessions, chattels **3** estate of the realm, °class, °caste, °order, °standing, °position, °(social) status, °state, °station, °place, °situation, °stratum, °level, °rank

esteem *v.* **1** °respect, value, °treasure, °prize, °cherish, hold dear, °appreciate, °admire, °look up to, regard highly, °venerate, °revere, °reverence, °honor, defer to; °like, °love, °adore **2** °consider, °judge, deem °view, °regard, °hold, °estimate, °account °believe, °think, °rate, °rank, °reckon, °evaluate —*n.* **3** °estimation, °(high) regard, °respect, °(high) opinion, °favor, °admiration, °appreciation, °approval, approbation

estimable *adj.* esteemed, °respectable, respected, °admirable, admired, valuable, valued, creditable, °worthy, °meritorious, °reputable, honored, °honorable, °laudable, °praiseworthy, commendable, °excellent, °good

estimate *v.* **1** °approximate, °gauge, °determine, °judge, °guess; assess, appraise, value, °evaluate, °reckon, °calculate, °work out, *Colloq* guesstimate *or* guestimate **2** °consider, °think, °believe, °guess, conjecture, °judge —*n.* **3** approximation, °gauge, °guess, conjecture, assessment, appraisal, °evaluation, °reckoning, °calculation, *Colloq* guesstimate *or* guestimate **4** °estimation, °belief, °opinion, °judgment, °thinking, °feeling, °sentiment, °sense, °(point of) view, °viewpoint

estimation *n.* **1** °opinion, °judgment, °view, °(way of) thinking, °mind **2** °esteem, °regard, °respect, °admiration **3** °estimate, approximation, °guess, °gauge

estranged *adj.* alienated, divided, separated, °withdrawn, disaffected, driven apart, dissociated, disassociated
etch *v.* **1** °engrave, incise, °carve, inscribe, °grave, °cut, °score, °scratch, corrode, eat into **2** °impress, imprint, °engrave, ingrain
eternal *adj.* **1** °everlasting, °timeless, °infinite, °endless, °immortal, °limitless **2** unending, °endless, ceaseless, unceasing, incessant, °perpetual, °constant, °continuous, interminable, uninterrupted, °nonstop, unremitting, °persistent, °relentless; °continual, °recurrent **3** unchanged, unchanging, immutable, °invariable, unvarying, unalterable, °permanent, °fixed, °constant, °everlasting, °enduring, °lasting, undiminished, unfaltering, unwavering
eternity *n.* endlessness, everlastingness, unendingness, boundlessness, °perpetuity, timelessness, infinity
ethical *adj.* °moral, °upright, °righteous, °right, °just, °principled, °correct, °honest, °proper, °open, °decent, °fair, °good, °virtuous, straightforward, high-minded, °noble
etiquette *n.* °code (of behavior), °form, °convention, °ceremony, formalities, °protocol, rules, custom(s), °decorum, °propriety, politesse, politeness, °courtesy, °(good) manners, °civility, seemliness
eulogize *v.* °praise, °extol, °laud, °applaud, °compliment, sound *or* sing the praises of, acclaim; °appreciate, °honor; °flatter
eulogy *n.* °praise, commendation, acclaim, acclamation, °tribute, °compliment, °applause, °homage, plaudits, encomium, accolade, paean, panegyric
euphemism *n.* amelioration, mollification, mitigation, cushioning, *Technical* paradiastole
evacuate *v.* **1** °empty, °clear (out), °exhaust, °drain, deplete, °purge, °get rid of, °void, °discharge, °vent; °divest, °deprive **2** °vacate, °desert, °leave, °depart (from), withdraw *or* retire (from), °go away (from), °quit, °relinquish, °abandon, decamp (from), move *or* pull out (of *or* from) **3** relocate, °move
evade *v.* **1** °avoid, °elude, °dodge, °sidestep, °escape (from); °get away (from), °get out of, °duck, circumvent, °shirk, *Colloq chiefly US and Canadian* weasel out (of) **2** °quibble, °equivocate, tergiversate, °maneuver, hedge, °shuffle, fudge, °fence, parry, *Colloq* °waffle, *Slang* cop out
evaluate *v.* **1** value, appraise, assess **2** °judge, °rank, °rate, °gauge, °estimate, °approximate, °calculate, °reckon, °compute, °figure, quantify, °determine, ascertain
evaluation *n.* **1** appraisal, valuation, assessment **2** °estimate, °estimation, approximation, rating, °opinion, ranking, °judgment, °reckoning, figuring, °calculation, computation, °determination
evaporate *v.* **1** vaporize; boil off *or* out; dehydrate, desiccate; *Technical* °sublime **2** °disappear, °disperse, °dissipate, vanish, evanesce, evanish, dispel; °fade (away), °melt away, °dissolve
evaporation *n.* **1** vaporization, drying (up *or* out), dehydration, desiccation, exsiccation, parching, searing **2** disappearance, dispersion, dispelling, °dissipation, evanescence, dematerialization, °dissolution, fading (away), melting (away)
evasion *n.* **1** °escape, avoidance, shirking, dodging **2** °subterfuge, °deception, °deceit, chicane *or* chicanery, °artifice, cunning, °trickery, sophistry, °excuse, dodging, prevarication, °lying, fudging, evasiveness, quibbling, equivocation, double-talk
evasive *adj.* °devious, °indirect, equivocating, °equivocal, misleading, °oblique, °ambiguous, sophistical, casuistic, °shifty, dissembling, cunning, °tricky, °deceitful, *Colloq* cagey, jesuitical
eve *n.* **1** evening *or* day *or* night before, time *or* period before; vigil **2** °verge, °threshold, °brink
even *adj.* **1** °smooth, °flat, °plane, °level, °regular, °uniform, °flush, °straight, °true **2** Sometimes, ***even with.*** level *or* uniform (with), coextensive (with), °flush (with), parallel (with *or* to) **3** °steady, °regular, °consistent, °constant, °uniform, unvaried, unvarying, °methodical, unchanging, °set, °equable, °stable, °measured, metrical, rhythmical, °orderly, ordered, °monotonous, unbroken, uninterrupted **4** even-tempered, °calm, °equable, composed, placid, °serene, °peaceful, °cool, °tranquil, unruffled, imperturbable, undisturbed, °impassive, °steady, °temperate, equanimous, °self-possessed, °sober, °staid, °sedate, sober-sided **5** balanced, °equal, the same, °identical, coequal, °level, °drawn, on a par, tied, neck and neck; °equivalent, *Colloq* fifty-fifty, *Brit* level pegging, *US* even-steven **6** °square, quits, °equal **7** °fair (and square), °square, °impartial, °disinterested, °neutral, °just, even-handed, °equitable, straightforward, °on the level, °honest, °upright, unbiased, °unprejudiced **8** °exact, °precise, °round, rounded off *or* out *or* up *or* down **9** ***get even (with).*** °repay, revenge oneself (on), even *or* settle accounts *or* the score (with), °requite, °reciprocate, °retaliate, be revenged *—adv.* **10** °still, °yet; all the (more), °indeed, (more) than ever **11** Sometimes, ***even with or though.*** °notwithstanding, °despite, °in spite of, disregarding **12** ***even so.*** °nevertheless, °nonetheless, °still, °yet, °notwithstanding, °all the same, in spite of that, despite that —*v.* **13** Usually, ***even up or out.*** °smooth, °flatten, °level, °equalize; align **14** ***even out or up.*** °equalize, °balance (out), °settle; °compensate
evening *n.* nightfall, eventide, °dusk, sunset, sundown, p.m., *Literary* gloaming
event *n.* **1** °occurrence, °happening, °incident, °episode, °occasion, °circumstance, °affair, °experience **2** °issue, °outcome, consequence, °result, conclusion, °upshot, °end, °effect **3** ***at all events or in any event.*** come what may, °in any case, °at any rate, °regardless, anyhow, anyway **4** ***in the***

event. in the reality *or* actuality, as it *or* things turned out, at the time, when it happened

eventful *adj.* °busy, °full, °active, °lively, °exciting, °interesting; °important, °significant, °signal, consequential, °notable, °noteworthy, °momentous, °memorable

eventual *adj.* **1** °ultimate, °final, °last, concluding, resulting **2** °due, expected, anticipated, °inevitable, °likely, consequent, resulting, resultant, foreordained, preordained, °unavoidable, °destined, predestined, °unavoidable, ineluctable, °probable

eventuality *n.* °circumstance, contingency, °event, °occurrence, °happening, °case; °likelihood, °chance, °possibility, °probability

eventually *adv.* °ultimately, °finally, °at last, in the end *or* long run, at the end of the day, °sooner or later, when all is said and done, in the final analysis, in due course, in (the course of) time, after all

ever *adv.* **1** at all, (at) any time, at any point *or* period, on any occasion, °in any case, by any chance **2** °always, °forever, °yet, °still, °even, at all times, in all cases, eternally, perpetually, endlessly, everlastingly, constantly, continuously, continually, forever and a day, till the end of time, till the cows come home, till Doomsday; °all the time

everlasting *adj.* °eternal, °deathless, undying, °immortal, °infinite, °timeless; never-ending, °perpetual, °constant, °continual, °continuous, °permanent, unceasing, incessant, interminable, °endless

everyday *adj.* **1** °daily, day-to-day, quotidian, °diurnal; circadian **2** commonplace, °common, °ordinary, °customary, °regular, °habitual, °routine, °usual, °run-of-the-mill, unexceptional, °accustomed, °conventional, °familiar **3** °prosaic, mundane, °dull, unimaginative, unexciting, °mediocre, °inferior

everyone *pron.* everybody, all (and sundry), one and all, each and every one *or* person, the whole world, everybody under the sun, every Tom, Dick, and Harry

everything *pron.* all, all things, the aggregate, the (whole *or* entire) lot, the total, the entirety, *Colloq* the whole kit and caboodle, the whole shooting match, *Chiefly US and Canadian* the whole shebang

everywhere *adv.* in all places, in *or* to each *or* every place *or* part, in every nook and cranny, high and low, °far and wide, near and far; ubiquitously, °universally, globally; °throughout

evict *v.* oust, dislodge, °turn out (of house and home), °expel, °eject, °remove, °dispossess, °put out, *Law* disseize, *Colloq* toss *or* throw *or* kick *or* boot out, *Brit* turf out

eviction *n.* ouster, dispossession, dislodgment, °expulsion, °ejection, °removal, *Law* disseizin, *Colloq* the boot

evidence *n.* **1** °proof, ground(s), fact(s), °data, °basis, °support, verification, attestation, affirmation, confirmation, validation, corroboration, substantiation, documentation, certification **2** °testimony, °statement, deposition, affidavit, averment, °assertion **3** °indication, °sign, °mark, °token, °manifestation, °demonstration, °hint, °suggestion, °clue, °trace, smoking gun —*v.* **4** °demonstrate, °show, °display, °manifest, °signify, °exhibit, °reveal, °denote, °attest, °prove, evince, °testify, °(bear) witness

evident *adj.* °clear, °obvious, °plain, °apparent, °manifest, °patent, palpable, °conspicuous, clear-cut, °express, unmistakable, °incontrovertible, understandable, comprehensible, recognizable, °perceptible, perceivable, °discernible, °noticeable

evidently *adv.* **1** °clearly, °obviously, plainly, °manifestly, palpably, °apparently, patently, indubitably, °undoubtedly, doubtless(ly), without a doubt, indisputably, incontestably, incontrovertibly, undeniably, unquestionably, °surely, certainly, to be sure **2** °apparently, °outwardly, °seemingly, it would seem, so it seems, as far as one can see *or* tell, to all appearances, °ostensibly

evil *adj.* **1** °bad, °awful, °wrong, °immoral, °wicked, °sinful, nefarious, iniquitous, °base, °corrupt, °vile, accursed, °damnable, °villainous, heinous, °infamous, flagitious, °foul, °nasty, °abominable, °atrocious, °horrible, horrid, °ghastly, °grisly, °dreadful, depraved, °vicious, malevolent, maleficent, malefic, black-hearted, °evil-minded **2** treacherous, °traitorous, °perfidious, insidious, °unscrupulous, unprincipled, °dishonest, °dishonorable, °crooked, °criminal, felonious, knavish, °sinister, underhand(ed), °dirty, °corrupt **3** °harmful, °destructive, °hurtful, °injurious, °mischievous, °detrimental, °ruinous, deleterious, °disastrous, catastrophic, pernicious, noxious, °malignant, malign, °virulent, toxic, °poisonous, °deadly, °lethal **4** °unfortunate, unlucky, °ominous, °inauspicious, dire, unpropitious, °calamitous, infelicitous, woeful **5** °bad, °offensive, °disgusting, °repulsive, °awful, °nasty, mephitic, noxious, °foul, pestilential, °putrid, °vile; °disagreeable, unpleasant —*n.* **6** badness, °sin, °vice, wickedness, iniquity, turpitude, immorality, °profligacy, depravity, degeneracy, corruption, °degradation, devilry *or* deviltry, villainy, nefariousness, viciousness, vileness, heinousness, flagitiousness, baseness, foulness **7** °harm, °hurt, °injury, °mischief, °damage, °ruin, °calamity, °misfortune, °catastrophe, °destruction, °disaster, cataclysm; °ill, °misery, °suffering, °pain, °sorrow, °woe, °agony, °anguish

evil-minded *adj.* **1** dirty(-minded), smutty, °obscene, depraved, °lewd, °lascivious, °lecherous, salacious, licentious, °filthy, °nasty; foulmouthed **2** °wicked, °sinful, flagitious, °vicious, °hateful, malicious, °spiteful, malevolent, °evil, °bad

evoke *v.* °summon (up), call up *or* forth, °elicit, conjure up, invoke, °recall, reawake(n), (a)wake, wake(n), (a)rouse, °raise

evolution *n.* °development, °advance, °growth, °progress, °progression, phylogeny, evolvement, developing, growing, evolving, °formation, maturation, °production

exact *adj.* **1** °precise, °accurate, °correct, °faithful, °true, °faultless, °identical, °literal, °perfect, consummate **2** °careful, °meticulous, °strict, rigorous, °accurate, °exacting, °severe, °fastidious, °scrupulous, °thorough, °painstaking, °rigid, punctilious —*v.* **3** °demand, °extort, °require, °enforce, insist on *or* upon, °extract, °impose, wrest, compel, enjoin, °call for, °requisition, °claim

exacting *adj.* °demanding, rigorous, °difficult, °rigid, °stern, °hard, °tough, °severe, °harsh, °burdensome, taxing, stringent, °imperative, unsparing, °oppressive, °tyrannical

exactly *adv.* **1** accurately, °precisely, strictly, °perfectly, correctly, unerringly, faultlessly, faithfully, scrupulously, °literally, °to the letter, word for word, °verbatim, closely; methodically, systematically **2** °definitely, °absolutely, °positively, undeniably, °surely, certainly, unequivocally, °completely, in every respect, in all respects, °particularly, specifically, explicitly, °just, °quite, °expressly, °precisely, accurately, °truly, *Colloq Brit* bang on

exaggerate *v.* °overstate, °magnify, °inflate, overdraw, embroider, °embellish, °elaborate, °enlarge, °stretch, °romance, overemphasize, overstress, overplay, °overdo, °exalt, hyperbolize, °paint, *Colloq* lay it on thick, °play up, °pile it on

exaggeration *n.* overstatement, °magnification, inflation, embroidery, °embellishment, °elaboration, enlargement, °stretch, romanticization, °extravagance, overemphasis, °excess, exaltation, enhancement, hyperbole; empty talk, °bombast, bragging, boasting, boastfulness, magniloquence, *Literary* gasconade, rodomontade, *Colloq* fish story, puffery, *Slang* bull(shit), °hot air

exalt *v.* **1** elevate, raise *or* lift (up *or* on high), upraise, uplift, upgrade, °boost, °promote, °advance **2** °praise, °honor, °extol, °glorify, °idolize, °dignify, ennoble, °revere, °reverence, °venerate, pay homage *or* tribute to, °celebrate; lionize **3** °stimulate, °excite, °animate, (a)rouse, °fire, °inspire, °electrify, °awaken, °spur, °stir (up), inspirit

exalted *adj.* **1** °elevated, °lofty, °high, °eminent, °notable, °noted, °prominent, °famous, famed, °celebrated, °distinguished, °dignified, honored, °prestigious, °glorified, °sublime, °grand **2** °elevated, °noble, °lofty, °superior, uplifting, heightened, high-flown; exaggerated, °pretentious, overblown, °inflated **3** °elated, °excited, °exultant, °ecstatic, jubilant, °overjoyed, °joyful, °rapturous, transported, blissful, °happy, joyous, in seventh heaven, uplifted, *Colloq* on cloud nine, *Brit* over the moon

examination *n.* **1** °investigation, °scrutiny, °study, °analysis, inspection, inquiry *or* enquiry, °probe, °search, °exploration, °research, °survey, going-over, checkup, check(out), appraisal, assessment **2** testing, °test, °quiz, exam **3** °interrogation, inquisition, inquiry *or* enquiry, catechism, cross-examination, *Colloq* third degree, grill(ing)

examine *v.* **1** °investigate, °scrutinize, °study, °peruse, °scan, °pore over, °analyze, °sift, °inspect, inquire *or* enquire into, go over *or* through *or* into, look over *or* into, °probe, °search, °explore, °research, °survey, °check up on, °check (out), appraise, assess, °weigh, *Brit* °vet, *Slang* °case **2** °test; interrogate, °quiz, catechize, cross-examine, °question, °sound out, *Colloq* grill, °pump

example *n.* **1** °instance, °case, °sample, °specimen, °illustration **2** °model, °prototype, °standard, archetype, exemplar, °pattern, benchmark, °norm, criterion **3** °warning, admonition, °lesson **4** ***for example.*** °for instance, as a case in point, as an illustration *or* example, by way of illustration, to illustrate, e.g., *exempli gratia*

exasperate *v.* **1** °anger, °infuriate, °enrage, incense, °madden, rile, drive mad; embitter; °inflame; *Colloq* drive crazy, °drive up the wall **2** °irritate, °irk, °annoy, °bother, °harass, pique, °gall, nettle, °rankle, °provoke, vex, °pester, °torment, °plague; hector, badger, *Colloq* °bug, needle, peeve, °get, get under (someone's) skin, rub the wrong way, °aggravate, *Brit* rub up the wrong way, *Slang* get (someone's) goat, piss (someone) off

excavate *v.* **1** dig (out *or* up), hollow *or* gouge (out), °scoop out, burrow *or* cut (out) **2** °unearth, uncover, °expose, °clear, °lay bare, °dig up, disinter, °bring up, exhume

excavation *n.* °cavity, °hole, °pit, crater, °cut, ditch, trench, trough, °burrow, °hollow, °shaft, °tunnel; °mine, °quarry

exceed *v.* **1** °surpass, °top, °excel, be superior to, go beyond, °beat, °overwhelm, °better, outdistance, °pass, °overtake, °outstrip, outrank, outrun, °outdo, outpace, °transcend, outshine, outreach, °overshadow, °eclipse **2** °overstep, go beyond, overextend

exceeding *adj.* °great, °huge, °enormous, °extraordinary, °excessive, °exceptional, °surpassing

exceedingly *adv.* °very, °extremely, °especially, exceptionally, considerably, incomparably, immeasurably, extraordinarily, remarkably; excessively, greatly, hugely, enormously

excel *v.* °surpass, be superior (to), °dominate, °top, °exceed, go beyond, °beat, °outstrip, outrank, °outdo, outpace, outshine, °overshadow, °eclipse; °shine, be preeminent

excellence *n.* °superiority, °merit, °(high) quality, goodness, fineness, greatness, °prominence, eminence, °preeminence, °distinction, value, °worth, °supremacy

excellent *adj.* °superb, °outstanding, °exceptional, °superior, °matchless, °peerless, unequaled, without equal, °nonpareil, °supreme, °superlative, °sterling, °capital, first-class, °first-rate, °prime, °choice, °select, °distinguished, °noteworthy, °notable, °worthy, the best, tiptop, °admirable, °splendid, °remarkable, °marvelous, °extraordinary, *Colloq* A-1 *or* A-one, °great, smashing, °super, °terrific, °fantastic, *Brit* °magic, *Dialectal* °champion, *Old-fashioned* top-hole, °ripping, tickety-boo, *US* A number 1, °major, *Australian* bonzer, *Slang* °cool, ripsnorting

except *prep.* **1** Sometimes ***except for.*** excepting, °save, but, excluding, °exclusive of, °barring, °bar, with the exception of, omitting, not counting, °apart from, but for, other than, °saving —*conj.* **2** ***except that.*** except *or* but (for the fact) that, but, save that —*v.* **3** °exclude, °omit, °leave out, °excuse

exception *n.* **1** °exclusion, °omission **2** debarment, blockage, lockout, shutout **3** departure, anomaly, irregularity, special case; °oddity, °freak, °rarity, °peculiarity, °quirk **4** ***take exception (to).*** make *or* raise (an) objection (to *or* against), °object (to), demur (at), °find fault (with), take offense *or* umbrage (at), be offended (at); °(call into) question, °cavil, °quibble, °challenge, °oppose, °disagree (with)

exceptionable *adj.* objectionable, °disputable, °questionable, criticizable, °unacceptable, °unsatisfactory

exceptional *adj.* **1** °special, °unusual, especial, °out of the ordinary, °extraordinary, uncommon, °rare, °singular; °strange, °irregular, aberrant, °odd, °peculiar, anomalous **2** °gifted, °talented, °superior, °outstanding, above average, °excellent, °prodigious, °extraordinary **3** handicapped, below average, °deficient, *Brit* ESN (= 'educationally subnormal')

excerpt *n.* **1** °extract, °selection, °quotation, citation, °passage, pericope —*v.* **2** °extract, °select, °quote, cite, cull (out), °pick (out), °take

excess *n.* **1** °surplus, overabundance, overflow, superabundance, nimiety, °superfluity, °surfeit, plethora, °glut, redundancy, oversufficiency, supererogation, °leftover; overkill **2** Often, ***excesses.*** debauchery, °extravagance, immoderation, °prodigality, overindulgence, intemperance, °dissipation, dissoluteness —*adj.* **3** °surplus, °extra, °superfluous, °excessive, °leftover, °residual, °remaining

excessive *adj.* **1** °immoderate, °inordinate, °disproportionate, °extravagant, °exorbitant, °superfluous, °excess, undue, °enormous, °extreme, °unreasonable, °unwarranted, unjustifiable, °outrageous, °unconscionable **2** overdone, fulsome, cloying, nauseating, °disgusting

exchange *v.* **1** °trade, barter, °switch, °change, interchange, °reciprocate, °return, *Colloq* swap *or* swop —*n.* **2** °trade, barter, °change, °traffic, °commerce, dealing, °truck, °transfer, interchange, reciprocity, reciprocation, °switch, quid pro quo, tit for tat, *Colloq* swap *or* swop **3** altercation, °argument, °quarrel, °disagreement, unpleasantness **4** °market, stock market, stock exchange, securities exchange, the Market, the Board, the Big Board, the Exchange, the Bourse, Wall Street, *US* the Street

excitable *adj.* °volatile, °jumpy, apprehensive, °nervous, °restive, °restless, fidgety, edgy, °touchy, highly strung, high-strung, mercurial, °emotional, °quick-tempered, °testy, hot-blooded, °feverish, °hysterical, *US* on a short string

excite *v.* **1** (a)rouse, °spur (on), °stir (up), °move, °animate, °enliven, °activate, °motivate, invigorate, °energize, °stimulate, °cause, °provoke, °prod, °agitate, °incite, °quicken, °urge, (a)wake, (a)waken, °call forth, °summon (up), °elicit, °inspire, inspirit, °rally, galvanize, °electrify, °foment, °fire (up), °inflame, °kindle, ignite, °initiate, instigate, °generate, °occasion, °begin, °start, °bring about, °effect, set in motion, *Colloq* get going, °spark, °wind up, get (someone) (all) steamed up, hop up, *US* kick-start, light a fire under **2** °agitate, °disturb, °perturb, °stir up, discompose, °fluster, °ruffle, °upset, disconcert **3** °thrill, °stir up, titillate, °work up, °arouse, °inflame

excited *adj.* **1** (a)roused, stirred (up), stimulated, °agitated, °disturbed, perturbed, °upset, worked up, wrought up, wound up, keyed up, °overwrought, discomposed, °disconcerted, discomfited, °nervous, edgy, °on edge, uneasy, flustered, ruffled, fidgety, °frantic, frenetic, aflame, °feverish, frenzied, °hysterical, °beside oneself, *Colloq* itchy, (all) hot and bothered, °high, on a high, off the deep end, °out of one's mind **2** °ardent, zealous, °impassioned, °passionate, °eager, energized, °energetic, °active, °brisk, °animated, °lively, °spirited, fervid, °fervent, vehement, stimulated, °enthusiastic, galvanized, electrified, intoxicated, *Colloq* turned on

excitement *n.* **1** restlessness, disquiet, disquietude, °tension, °agitation, °unrest, malaise, °discomfort, jumpiness, nervousness, freneticness, excitation **2** perturbation, °upset, °action, ado, °activity, °ferment, °furor, turmoil, °tumult, to-do, °stir, commotion, hubbub, brouhaha, °fuss, hurly-burly, *Colloq* fireworks **3** °animation, °eagerness, °enthusiasm, exhilaration, ebullience

exciting *adj.* **1** °stimulating, °intoxicating, heady, °thrilling, °stirring, °moving, inspiring, °rousing, °exhilarating, electrifying, galvanizing, energizing, °invigorating; °overwhelming, °overpowering, astounding, astonishing, °amazing, mind-boggling, *Colloq* far-out, rip-roaring, mind-blowing **2** °seductive, °sensuous, °voluptuous, °ravishing, captivating, charming, °tempting, enticing, alluring, °provocative, titillating, *Colloq* °sexy

exclaim *v.* call *or* cry (out), °proclaim, vociferate, utter, °declare, ejaculate, °shout, °yell,

°bawl, °bellow, burst out (with), °blurt out, *Colloq* holler

exclamation *n.* °outcry, °call, °cry, utterance, ejaculation, °interjection, vociferation, °shout, °yell, °bellow, *Colloq* holler

exclude *v.* **1** Often, ***exclude from.*** keep out *or* away, lock *or* shut out, °ban, °bar, debar, °prohibit, interdict, °forbid, proscribe, °deny, °refuse, disallow **2** °eliminate, °leave out, °reject, °omit, °except, °preclude, °repudiate, count out **3** °eject, °evict, °expel, oust, °get rid of, °remove, °throw out, *Colloq* toss out, *Slang* °bounce

exclusion *n.* **1** lockout, shutout, °ban, °bar, °prohibition, interdiction, forbiddance, °denial, °refusal, disallowance, proscription **2** elimination, °rejection, °omission, repudiation, °exception, preclusion **3** °ejection, °eviction, °expulsion, ouster, °removal, riddance

exclusive *adj.* **1** °incompatible, inimical; unshared, °unique, °absolute, restricted, °limited **2** °chic, clannish, °choice, °upper-class, aristocratic, closed, restricted, restrictive, °private, °snobbish, °fashionable, °elegant, °stylish, °select, *Colloq* °trendy, *Slang* classy **3** °only, °single, °one, °sole, °singular, °unique **4** Usually, ***exclusive of.*** excluding, excepting, °except for, omitting, ignoring, leaving aside, °apart from, (de)barring, not counting, eliminating

excruciating *adj.* tormenting, torturing, torturous, °agonizing, °painful, racking, °intense, °extreme, °unbearable, unendurable, °severe, °acute, °exquisite, °harrowing, distressful, distressing, °piercing, °insufferable

excursion *n.* **1** °trip, °tour, °outing, airing, °expedition, voyage, °cruise, °journey, junket, jaunt; °ramble, °stroll, °walk, hike, trek, °drive, °ride, °sail **2** °detour, deviation, side trip, °diversion, °digression, excursus

excuse *v.* **1** °forgive, °pardon, °overlook, absolve, °clear, exonerate, acquit, exculpate, °pass over, °disregard, wink at, °ignore, be blind to, look the other way, pay no attention *or* heed (to), find *or* prove innocent (of) **2** °release, let go *or* off, °liberate, °free, °relieve, °exempt, absolve; °dismiss, *Colloq* let off the hook **3** condone, °allow, °permit, °defend, apologize for, °justify, °warrant, °explain, °vindicate, °rationalize, °mitigate, extenuate, palliate —*n.* **4** apology, °explanation, °story, °reason, justification, °defense, °plea, vindication, condonation, rationalization, extenuation, mitigation, palliation; °basis, °grounds, °foundation, °cause **5** °forgiveness, °remission, °pardon, °indulgence, °reprieve, clearing, exculpation, absolution, exoneration, acquittal, °disregard, heedlessness, vindication, °clearance, acquittance **6** °evasion, °subterfuge, °pretense, °pretext, °makeshift, °escape, °loophole, way out, *Colloq* °alibi, °stall, *Slang* cop-out

execute *v.* **1** °accomplish, do, carry out *or* off *or* through, °perform, °discharge, dispatch *or* despatch, bring about *or* off, °implement, °engineer, °cause, *Colloq* °pull off, °put over, *Slang US* °swing, °cut, °hack (out) **2** °complete, °finish, °deliver; °achieve, consummate, °fulfill, °effect, °effectuate; °sign, °seal, validate, countersign **3** put to death, send to the gallows *or* gas chamber *or* electric chair; °kill, put to the sword, °butcher; liquidate, assassinate, °murder, °remove, slay, *Slang* °bump off, rub *or* wipe out, snuff (out), °knock off, *US* °waste, ice

execution *n.* **1** °accomplishment, °performance, carrying out, doing, °discharge, dispatch *or* despatch, implementation, prosecution, °realization, enactment **2** °completion, °fulfillment, °consummation, °achievement, attainment, implementation, bringing about, °administration, pursuance **3** °killing, capital punishment; assassination, °murder, °removal, liquidation, slaying **4** °skill, °art, mastery, °technique, °style, °manner, °mode, °touch, °approach, °delivery, °rendering, °rendition, °production

executive *n.* **1** chairman (of the board), °director, managing director, chief executive, president, °chief (executive officer), CEO, °manager, °head, °leader, °principal, administrator, °official; °supervisor, °foreman, °superintendent, °overseer, °boss, °master, *Colloq* Mr. Big, (chief *or* head) honcho, number one, kingpin, *Slang* top banana, big cheese, numero uno, top dog **2** °administration, °management, directorship, directorate, °government, °leadership, supervision —*adj.* **3** administrative, managerial, °supervisory, °official, governing, governmental, gubernatorial, regulatory

exemplary *adj.* **1** illustrative, °typical, °characteristic, °representative, archetypal; paradigmatic **2** °model, °meritorious, °outstanding, °noteworthy, °admirable, commendable, °praiseworthy, °excellent, °superior **3** cautionary, admonitory, °warning, monitory

exemplify *v.* **1** °illustrate, °typify, °represent, epitomize, °instance; °embody, °personify **2** °demonstrate, °display, °show, °exhibit, °model, depict

exempt *v.* **1** Often, ***exempt from.*** free *or* liberate *or* release from, excuse *or* relieve from, spare from, °let off, absolve, °except, *Colloq* let off the hook —*adj.* **2** exempted, °free, liberated, released, excused, relieved, spared, °let off, excepted, °immune, *Colloq* °off the hook

exemption *n.* °exception, °immunity, °freedom, °release, impunity, dispensation, °exclusion

exercise *v.* **1** °employ, °use, °apply, practice, bring to bear, put to use *or* effect; °discharge, °exert, °wield, °execute; utilize, °effect **2** °work out, limber up, warm up, °train, °drill **3** °harass, °annoy, °irritate, vex, harry, °distress, °worry, °concern, °burden, °try, °trouble, °perturb, °disturb, °agitate, make nervous, *Colloq* drive crazy, °drive up the wall —*n.* **4** °activity, workout, working out, warm-up, calisthenics, aerobics, isometrics, gymnastics; training, °drill, drilling **5** °action, °application, °practice, °performance, °discharge, °use, utilization, °employment, °execution, °operation

exert *v.* **1** °exercise, °use, utilize, put to use *or* work *or* effect, °employ, °wield, bring to bear, bring into play, °expend **2** ***exert oneself.*** °attempt, °try, °endeavor, make an effort, apply oneself, °strive, do one's best, °work, °strain, °struggle, toil, °push, °drive (oneself), go all out, give one's all, *Colloq* knock oneself out, cudgel one's brains, beat one's brains out, do one's damnedest, *Slang* bust a gut

exertion *n.* °action, °effort, striving, °strain, °work, °struggle, toil, °drive, °push, diligence, °industry, assiduity, assiduousness, sedulousness, sedulity, *Colloq US* stick-to-itiveness

exhalation *n.* **1** °expiration, exhaling, °breath, respiration, suspiration **2** °vapor, °breath, °air, °puff, whiff, °exhaust, emission, steam, °mist, gas, °fog, °fume, emanation, effluvium, °evaporation

exhale *v.* °breathe (out), °blow, °puff, °huff, °gasp, °evaporate, °pass off, °discharge, °emit, °emanate, °issue (forth), respire, suspire, give forth, blow off, °eject, °expel, exsufflate

exhaust *v.* **1** °use (up), °expend, °consume, °finish, deplete, °spend, °dissipate, °run through, squander, °waste, °fritter away, *Slang* °blow **2** °tire (out), °fatigue, °weary, °wear out, °enervate, °fag, overtire, °sap, °strain, °tax, °weaken, °prostrate, debilitate, disable, *Colloq* frazzle **3** °empty, °drain, °evacuate, °void, clean *or* clear out **4** °overdo, °overwork, treat thoroughly, deplete, °drain, °empty **5** °empty (out), drain (off *or* out), °vent, °issue, °escape, °discharge, °run out —*n.* **6** emanation, effluent, emission, °fumes, gas

exhausted *adj.* **1** °(dead) tired, °fatigued, °weary, wearied, worn-out, enervated, debilitated, overtired, °weak, weakened, °prostrate, fagged *or* played *or* burnt out, °spent, all in, out on one's feet, *Colloq* dog-tired, °dead (on one's feet), wiped out, drained, knocked out, done in, frazzled, *Slang* °(dead) beat, *Brit* knackered, *US and Canadian* pooped **2** °empty, emptied, °bare; depleted, consumed, done, gone, at an end, finished **3** °spent, worn-out, depleted, °impoverished, °poor, °infertile, °barren

exhausting *adj.* **1** tiring, fatiguing, wearying, enervating, wearing, debilitating **2** °arduous, °laborious, backbreaking, °strenuous, °hard, grueling, crippling, °difficult, °burdensome, onerous

exhaustion *n.* **1** emptying, drawing out *or* forth, °discharge, draining, evacuation, voiding, depletion, consumption, finish(ing) **2** tiredness, °fatigue, enervation, debilitation, weariness, lassitude

exhaustive *adj.* °complete, °comprehensive, (all-)inclusive, °thorough, all-encompassing, °encyclopedic, °extensive, thoroughgoing, far-reaching, °sweeping, full-scale, in-depth, maximal, °maximum, *Colloq* all-out

exhibit *v.* **1** °show, °display, °present, °offer, °expose; °show off, °parade, brandish, °flaunt; °demonstrate, °reveal, °betray, °manifest, °exemplify, evince, °evidence, °disclose, °express —*n.* **2** See **exhibition,** below.

exhibition *n.* °exposition, °fair, show(ing), °display, °demonstration, °presentation, °offering, *US* °exhibit, *Colloq* expo, demo

exhilarating *adj.* **1** °invigorating, °bracing, °stimulating, vivifying, enlivening, rejuvenating, °refreshing; vitalizing, fortifying, restorative, °tonic **2** cheering, uplifting, gladdening, elating, inspiriting, heartening, comforting, reassuring; °happy, °good, °delightful

exile *n.* **1** expatriation, banishment, °expulsion, deportation, transportation; °separation **2** expatriate, emigre *or* émigré(e), °emigrant, °outcast, deportee, pariah, displaced person, DP; °alien, °foreigner, °outsider —*v.* **3** deport, °expel, °alienate, °banish, expatriate, oust, °eject, °displace, °transport, drive *or* run *or* cast out, °outlaw, °exclude, oust, °evict, °bar, °ban; extradite; °maroon

exist *v.* **1** be, °continue, °prevail, °endure, °abide; °live, °breathe **2** °survive, subsist, eke out a living *or* an existence, stay alive, get by *or* along **3** °occur, °happen, be found, be present, °remain, °persist; °obtain, °prevail

existence *n.* **1** being, °presence, actuality, °fact **2** °life, living; continuance, continuation, °persistence, °permanence, duration, °endurance **3** °entity, being, °creature; ens, quiddity, °essence

exit *n.* **1** way out, egress, door, °gate; °outlet, °vent **2** departure, leave-taking, withdrawal, leaving, °retreat, retirement; °flight, exodus, evacuation, °escape —*v.* **3** go (out *or* away), °(take one's) leave, °depart, take *or* make one's departure, °retire, °(beat a) retreat, bid adieu, °withdraw, °run, °(take a) walk, °walk out (on), °quit, °escape, °take to one's heels, show a clean pair of heels, vanish, °disappear, *Colloq* °take off, skedaddle, °kiss goodbye, *US* °cut out; *Slang* °beat it, *US and Canadian* take it on the lam, lam (on) out of *or* from, take a (runout) powder

exorbitant *adj.* °extraordinary, °excessive, °extravagant, °outrageous, °immoderate, extortionate, °extreme, °unreasonable, °inordinate, °disproportionate, °unconscionable, °preposterous, undue, °unwarranted, unjustifiable, unjustified

exotic *adj.* **1** °foreign, °alien, nonnative, imported **2** °strange, °unfamiliar, °unusual, °bizarre, °odd, °peculiar, °unique, °singular, °extraordinary, °remarkable, °out of the ordinary, °different, °outlandish, °weird, °crazy **3** striptease, belly, go-go, topless, °bottomless, °nude

expand *v.* **1** °enlarge, °spread (out), °extend, °increase, open (out *or* up), °swell, °inflate, distend; °unfold **2** °prolong,

°lengthen, °stretch, dilate **3** °increase, °extend, °amplify, °magnify, broaden, °widen, augment, °heighten, °develop **4** Often, ***expand on.*** °detail, °enlarge on, °embellish, °develop, °amplify, expatiate on *or* upon, °elaborate (on); °flesh out

expanse *n.* °stretch, °extent, °area, °space, °range, °sweep, °reach, length and breadth, °spread

expansion *n.* **1** °increase, augmentation, °development, enlargement, °extension, burgeoning *or* bourgeoning, °flourishing, °growth, °spread **2** dilatation *or* dilation, stretching, distension *or* distention, inflation, °swelling

expansive *adj.* **1** expansible *or* expandable, inflatable, dilatable, extensible *or* extendible *or* extendable; extending, expanding, enlarging, spreading, opening *or* stretching (out) **2** °effusive, °open, °free, °easy, °genial, °amiable, °friendly, °warm, affable, °sociable, °outgoing, communicative, °outspoken, extrovert(ed) *or* extravert(ed), °talkative, loquacious, garrulous, °frank, unreserved **3** °broad, °extensive, far-reaching, wide-ranging; °comprehensive, widespread, all-embracing, (all-)inclusive

expect *v.* **1** °anticipate, look forward *or* ahead to, have *or* keep in view, await, °envisage, watch *or* look for, wait for, °contemplate, °foresee, *US* °envision **2** °assume, °presume, °suppose, °imagine, °believe, °think, °trust, °surmise, conjecture; °foresee, *US and Canadian* °guess **3** °look for, °want, °require, °wish, °need, °demand, reckon on *or* upon, hope for, calculate *or* count on *or* upon

expectant *adj.* °expecting, (a)waiting, °ready, °eager, apprehensive, °anxious, with bated breath, °hopeful, looking, watchful, anticipating

expectation *n.* **1** °anticipation, °confidence, hopefulness, watchfulness, apprehension, apprehensiveness, expectancy, °suspense **2** °hope, assumption, °presumption, °surmise, °supposition, °belief, conjecture, *US and Canadian* °guess **3** °demand, °requirement, °wish, °desire, °want, insistence, °reliance **4** °prospects, °outlook

expecting *adj.* °pregnant, gravid, with child, in a family way, *enceinte, Brit* in the family way, *US* in a family way, *Colloq* in the club, *Brit* preggers, *Slang US* with a bun in the oven

expedient *adj.* **1** °suitable, °appropriate, °fitting, °fit, °befitting, °proper, apropos, °right, °correct, °meet, °pertinent, °applicable, °practical, pragmatic, °worthwhile, °politic **2** °advantageous, °beneficial, °advisable, °desirable, recommended, °useful, °practical, utilitarian, °prudent, °wise, °propitious, °opportune, °helpful, °effective —*n.* **3** °device, °resource, °means, °measure, contrivance, °resort, °recourse

expedite *v.* **1** °hasten, °rush, °hurry, speed *or* step up, accelerate; dispatch *or* despatch **2** °advance, °facilitate, °promote, °forward, °ease, °enable

expedition *n.* **1** °exploration, °journey, voyage, field trip, °trip, °tour, °excursion; °enterprise, °undertaking, °mission, °quest **2** °speed, promptness, celerity, alacrity, dispatch *or* despatch, °haste, °rapidity, swiftness, quickness

expeditious *adj.* °ready, °quick, °rapid, °swift, °fast, °brisk, °speedy, °fleet, °efficient, °diligent

expel *v.* **1** °eject, dislodge, throw *or* cast out, drive *or* force out, °evict, put *or* push out, °remove, run (someone) off *or* out, °displace, °dispossess, show the door, °suspend, °dismiss, let go, *Colloq* °fire, *Brit* °sack, turf out **2** °banish, deport, °exile, expatriate, °outlaw, °maroon; proscribe, °ban, °bar, debar, °dismiss, °exclude, blackball, drum out, cashier, °discharge, oust, *Brit* °send down

expend *v.* **1** °pay out, °spend, disburse, °use, °employ, *Slang* lay *or* dish out, fork *or* shell out **2** °use up, °consume, °exhaust, deplete, °finish (off), °dissipate, °sap, °drain

expendable *adj.* °dispensable, °disposable, °nonessential, inessential *or* unessential, °unnecessary, replaceable; unimportant, °insignificant

expenditure *n.* °outlay, outgoings, disbursement, spending, °payment, °expense, °cost; °price, °charge, °fee

expense *n.* **1** Often, ***expenses.*** °payment, costs, °outlay, outgoings, disbursement, °expenditure, spending, out-of-pocket (expenses); °cost, °price, °charge, °fee, °rate **2** °detriment, °sacrifice, °cost, °loss, °impairment, °ruin, °destruction

expensive *adj.* costly, °dear, high-priced, up-market, valuable, °precious, °priceless, °extravagant; overpriced

experience *n.* **1** °knowledge, °contact, involvement, °practice, °familiarity, °acquaintance, °exposure; participation, °observation **2** °incident, °event, °happening, °affair, °episode, °occurrence, °circumstance, °adventure, °encounter; °trial, °test, °ordeal **3** common sense, °wisdom, sagacity, °knowledge, know-how, savoir-faire, savoir-vivre, °sophistication, °skill, °judgment, *Slang* savvy —*v.* **4** °undergo, live *or* go through, °suffer, °endure, °sustain, °face, °encounter, °meet (with), °feel, °sense, °taste, °sample, be familiar with, °know

experienced *adj.* **1** °adept, skilled, °skillful, °accomplished, °practiced, °proficient, °knowledgeable, °knowing, °wise, °sage, sagacious, °shrewd, °prepared, (well-) informed, trained, (well-)versed, °expert, °master, masterly, °qualified, °professional, °competent, °efficient, °capable, *au fait*; *Slang* on the ball, *US* savvy **2** °mature, °seasoned, °sophisticated, battle-scarred, °veteran; *Slang* in the know, *US* savvy

experiment *n.* **1** °test, °trial, °investigation, inquiry *or* enquiry, °examination, experimentation, °research, °proof **2** °procedure, °policy —*v.* **3** ***experiment on*** *or* ***with.***

°test, °try, °examine, °investigate, °research, °probe

experimental *adj.* **1** °hypothetical, °theoretical, °tentative, °speculative, conjectural, exploratory **2** °empirical, experiential

expert *n.* **1** °authority, °professional, °specialist, °scholar, °master, connoisseur, pundit, *Colloq* wizard, whiz, pro, ace, *Brit* °dab hand, boffin, *Slang US* maven *or* mavin —*adj.* **2** °skillful, skilled, trained, °knowledgeable, °learned, °experienced, °practiced, °qualified, °adept, °proficient, °accomplished, *au fait,* adroit, °dexterous, °polished, finished, °masterful, masterly, °first-rate, °excellent, °superb, wonderful, °superior, champion(ship), A-1 *or* A-one, °virtuoso, *Colloq* topnotch, *Brit* whizzo, wizard, *US* crackerjack, °crack

expertise *n.* expertness, °skill, °knowledge, know-how, °judgment, mastery; °dexterity, adroitness, *Slang* savvy

expiration *n.* expiry, °finish, °(coming to an) end, °termination, running out, ending, conclusion, concluding, °close, closing, discontinuance, discontinuation

expire *v.* **1** °cease, °(come to an) end, °close, °finish, °terminate, °run out, conclude, °discontinue **2** °die, breathe one's last, decease, °perish, °pass away **3** °exhale, breathe out, °expel

explain *v.* **1** °interpret, °define, explicate, °detail, delineate, make plain, °simplify, °spell out, °resolve, °get across, °clarify, °clear up, elucidate, °illustrate, expound, °describe, °disclose, °unfold, unravel, untangle **2** Also, ***explain away.*** °justify, °account for, °excuse, °rationalize, °legitimate, legitimatize, extenuate, palliate

explanation *n.* **1** °interpretation, °definition, explication, delineation, simplification, °resolution, clarification, elucidation, °description, °illustration, °exposition, °account, disclosure; exegesis, commentary, °criticism, °analysis **2** °excuse, rationalization, justification, vindication **3** °cause, °motive, °reason, °key, signification, °solution

explanatory *adj.* explanative, elucidative, revelatory, interpretive *or* interpretative, expository, descriptive; °critical, exegetic(al)

expletive *adj.* **1** °wordy, verbose, prolix, °repetitious, °redundant, tautological, iterative, reiterative, pleonastic; °unnecessary, unneeded, °needless, unessential, °nonessential, °gratuitous, °superfluous —*n.* **2** °oath, swearword, °curse, curse word, obscenity, epithet, *Colloq* cuss word, dirty word, four-letter word **3** filler, padding, redundancy, °tautology, pleonasm

explicit *adj.* **1** °specific, °categorical, (crystal-)clear, °definite, well-defined, °distinct, unambiguous, °precise, °exact, unequivocal, °express, stated, °plain, °manifest, unmistakable, °positive, °absolute, °final, °peremptory, °unqualified, unconditional **2** °open, °outspoken, unreserved, unrestrained, °candid, °frank, °direct, °forthright, straightforward, °definite

explode *v.* **1** °blow up, °burst, °blast, fly apart, °go off, °erupt, fulminate; °set off, detonate **2** °reject, °discredit, refute, °repudiate, °disprove, debunk, belie, give the lie to, *Slang* pick holes in, poke *or* shoot full of holes **3** lose one's temper, °rant, °rave, °rage, °storm, throw a tantrum, *Colloq* get into a tizzy, blow one's top, °fly off the handle, go through *or* hit the roof, hit the ceiling; *Slang* lose one's cool, go up the wall, *US* blow one's stack *or* cool, °flip (one's lid), freak out

exploit *n.* **1** °achievement, °deed, °feat, attainment, °accomplishment —*v.* **2** °use, take advantage of, °manipulate, make capital out of, °profit from, utilize, turn to account, °maneuver, °work

exploration *n.* °examination, °investigation, °search, °probe, inquiry *or* enquiry, °study, °research, °analysis, °review, °scrutiny, inspection, °survey, °reconnaissance, °observation; °expedition

explore *v.* **1** °survey, °tour, °travel, °reconnoiter, °traverse **2** °investigate, °scrutinize, °examine, inquire *or* enquire into, °inspect, °probe, °search, °research, °look into, °study, °analyze, °review, °observe

explosion *n.* **1** °blast, bang, °report, °burst, °boom, °clap, °crack, °eruption, °crash, °outburst, fulmination; detonation **2** °outburst, outbreak, °paroxysm, °upheaval, flare-up, °eruption, °burst, °fit, °spasm, °tantrum, *Colloq Brit* paddy *or* paddy-whack, wax **3** °increase, burgeoning *or* bourgeoning, °expansion, welling-up, mushrooming

explosive *adj.* **1** °volatile, °sensitive, °delicate, °tense, °anxious, °fraught, touch-and-go, °touchy, °inflammable, (highly) charged, °unstable, °uncertain, °unsound, °shaky, °hazardous, chancy, unpredictable, °precarious, °dangerous, °perilous, °critical, °nasty, °ugly, *Colloq* °dicey, iffy —*n.* **2** dynamite, TNT, gunpowder, gelignite, °plastic, plastique

expose *v.* **1** °(lay) bare, °reveal, uncover, °show, °exhibit, °present, °display, °disclose; divulge, °unveil, unmask, °discover, °air, ventilate, °let out, °leak, °betray, °bring to light, °make known **2** °risk, imperil, °endanger, °jeopardize, °hazard **3** ***expose to.*** °subject to, introduce to, °acquaint with, bring into contact with

exposition *n.* **1** °exhibition, show(ing), °presentation, °display, °demonstration, *US* °exhibit, *Colloq* expo **2** °description, °declaration, °statement, °explanation, explication, clarification, °interpretation, exegesis **3** °paper, °theme, article, °essay, °thesis, dissertation, treatise, disquisition, °study, critique, commentary

exposure *n.* **1** baring, uncovering, laying open, unveiling, disclosure, disclosing, unmasking, revealing, °revelation, exposé, airing, °publication, publishing, communicating, communication, leaking, °leak, divulging **2** °jeopardy, °risk, °hazard, endangerment, vulnerability, imperilment; °danger, °peril **3** °familiarity, °knowledge, °acquaintance, °experience, °contact, conversancy **4** °aspect, °view, °outlook, °orientation, frontage; °setting, °location, °direction

express *v.* **1** articulate, verbalize, °phrase, utter, °voice, °state, °word, °put (into words), set *or* put forth, put *or* get across, °communicate, depict, °portray; °say, °speak, °tell **2** °show, °indicate, °demonstrate, °manifest, °exhibit, evince, °evidence, °reveal, °expose, °disclose, divulge, °make known, °intimate, betoken, °signify, °embody, depict, °designate, °denote, convey **3** °symbolize, °represent, °signify, °stand for, °denote, °designate **4** press *or* squeeze *or* wring *or* force out, °expel, °extract —*adj.* **5** °explicit, °clear, °plain, unambiguous, unmistakable, °unqualified, °outright, °definite, °out-and-out, °downright, straightforward, °categorical, °direct, °specific, well-defined, °distinct, °precise, °accurate, °exact, °positive **6** °specific, °special, °particular, clearcut; °true **7** °quick, °speedy, °swift, °fast, °rapid, °prompt, °immediate; °direct, °nonstop

expression *n.* **1** verbalization, airing, °representation, °declaration, utterance, °assertion, enunciation, asseveration, °pronouncement, communication, voicing, °announcement **2** °representation, °manifestation, °sign, °token, °symbol, °show, °demonstration, °indication, °evidence **3** °look, mien, °air, °appearance, °face, °aspect, countenance **4** °tone, °note, nuance, °intonation, °accent, °touch, shading, loudness, softness; expressiveness, °emotion, °feeling, °sensitivity, °passion, °spirit, °depth, °ardor, °intensity, pathos **5** °word, °term, °phrase, °idiom, turn of phrase, locution, saying **6** °wording, phrasing, phraseology, °language, °style, °diction, °usage, °speech, °delivery

expressive *adj.* **1** indicative, °suggestive, allusive, °eloquent, revealing, °meaningful, °significant, denotative **2** °pointed, pithy, °explicit **3** °striking, °vivid, °telling, °pregnant, °loaded, °forceful, °moving, °emotional, °poignant, °provocative, thought-provoking

expressly *adv.* **1** distinctly, °definitely, categorically, explicitly, °absolutely, °positively, °directly, unambiguously, unequivocally, unmistakably, plainly, pointedly, °exactly, °clearly **2** purposely, °especially, purposefully, °particularly, specifically, °specially; °on purpose

expulsion *n.* expelling, °ejection, °eviction, repudiation, ouster, °removal, °dismissal, °discharge; *Colloq* (the old) heave-ho, *Brit* °(the) boot, °(the) sack, sacking, *US* °(the) bounce

exquisite *adj.* **1** °delicate, °fine, °elegant, °graceful, °excellent, °choice, well-crafted, well-made, well-executed, °refined, °elaborate **2** °ingenious, °detailed, recherché, °rare, °subtle, °deep, abstruse; °far-fetched **3** °beautiful, °perfect, °lovely, °attractive, °handsome, °comely, good-looking; °smart, °chic, °elegant, °striking **4** °acute, °sharp, °keen, °excruciating, °agonizing, °intense; °elaborate **5** °superb, °superior, °peerless, °matchless, °incomparable, unequaled, °rare, °precious, °choice, consummate, °outstanding, °superlative, °excellent, °select, °flawless, °perfect, wonderful, °splendid, °marvelous

extemporaneous *adj.* unstudied, °unpremeditated, extempore, extemporary, impromptu, improvised, °spontaneous, unrehearsed, extemporized, °unprepared, unplanned, unscripted, °offhand, ad-lib, *Colloq* off the cuff

extend *v.* **1** stretch *or* spread (out), outstretch, outspread, °open (out), unroll, °unfold; °reach, °range; °carry on, °draw out, °continue, °develop **2** °lengthen, elongate, °widen, °continue; broaden, °enlarge, °add to, augment; °increase, °stretch (out), °supplement **3** °last, °stretch, °continue, go *or* carry on; °perpetuate, drag on *or* out, keep up *or* on, °prolong **4** °offer, proffer, °give, °present, °hold out, stretch forth, °tender; °bestow; °grant, °impart, °confer, °accord, °advance

extension *n.* **1** stretching, °expansion, °increase, enlargement, augmentation, °development, amplification, broadening, widening, lengthening, °spread, spreading **2** °range, extensiveness, °scope, °extent, °magnitude, °gauge, compass, °sweep, °reach, °size, °volume, dimension(s), °proportions, °capacity, °span; °breadth, °width, °height, °length, °spread, °stretch **3** addendum, °addition, annex, wing, adjunct, ell, appendage; appendix, °supplement

extensive *adj.* **1** °broad, °wide, °expansive, far-reaching, far-ranging, wide-ranging, far-flung, °sweeping, widespread, °comprehensive, all-embracing; °national, nationwide, °international, intercontinental, cosmopolitan, worldwide, °global, °universal, °vast; cosmic; °catholic **2** °large, °big, °great, °huge, °substantial, °considerable, sizable, °immense, °enormous, °vast, °gigantic, °massive; °voluminous, °spacious, commodious, capacious

extent *n.* **1** °magnitude, dimensions, compass, °size, °range, °scale, °sweep, °scope, °expanse, immensity, °enormousness, capaciousness, spaciousness, °space, amplitude **2** °limit, °bounds, limitation, lengths; °range, °scope **3** °area, °region, °tract, °territory, compass

extenuating *adj.* °mitigating, lessening, tempering, palliating, moderating, diminishing, qualifying

exterior *adj.* **1** outer, °outside, °external, °outward, °superficial, °surface **2** °external, °extrinsic, °extraneous, °foreign, °alien, °exotic, °outside —*n.* **3** °outside, °surface, covering, coating, °facing, °face, °front, °skin, °shell, façade

exterminate *v.* °destroy, °root out, eradicate, extirpate, annihilate, °eliminate, weed out, °get rid of, °wipe out, °obliterate, put an end to, °terminate, liquidate, °massacre, °murder, °kill (off), °butcher, °slaughter, *Slang* °bump off, *US* °rub out, °waste

external *adj.* **1** outer, °outside, °outward, °exterior **2** °outside, °exterior, °extrinsic, °extraneous, °alien, °foreign, °exotic **3** °apparent, °visible, °perceptible, °superficial, °surface

extinct *adj.* **1** °defunct, °dead, died out, gone, departed, vanished **2** dated, outmoded, °old-fashioned, °antiquated, °obsolete, archaic, out-of-date, antediluvian, °ancient, old hat, °passé, *démodé* **3** °out, extinguished, quenched, burnt *or* put *or* snuffed out; °inactive, °dormant

extinguish *v.* **1** put *or* snuff *or* blow out, °quench; turn off *or* out **2** °kill (off), annihilate, °destroy, °obliterate, °abolish, °exterminate, °eliminate, do away with, nullify, eradicate, °remove, °banish, wipe *or* blot out **3** °obscure, °eclipse, °dim, °outdo, put in the shade, °overshadow, adumbrate, *Colloq* °show up

extol *v.* °exalt, elevate, uplift, °glorify, °praise, °laud, °applaud, commend, acclaim, °cheer, °celebrate, pay tribute *or* homage to, sing the praises of, °make much of, °honor, °congratulate, °compliment

extort *v.* °exact, °extract, °blackmail, °bully, coerce, °force, wring, wrest, *Colloq* °milk, bleed, put the arm on (someone)

extra *adj.* **1** additional, added, °auxiliary, accessory *or* accessary, °supplementary, supplemental, °further, ancillary, °subsidiary, collateral, adventitious **2** left-over, °excess, °spare, °surplus, °unused, °superfluous, supernumerary, °reserve —*n.* **3** °addition, addendum, accessory *or* accessary, appurtenance, °supplement, °bonus, °premium, dividend **4** °supplement, *US* markup, surcharge, *Slang US and Canadian* kicker **5** supernumerary, walk-on, *Colloq* °super, spear carrier —*adv.* **6** uncommonly, unusually, exceptionally, unexpectedly, extraordinarily, remarkably, °notably, surprisingly, amazingly, °very, °particularly, °especially, °extremely, strikingly **7** additionally, again, more, °in addition

extract *v.* **1** draw *or* pull (out), °remove, °withdraw, pluck *or* take out, draw forth, °extricate **2** °draw, °derive, °deduce, °develop, glean, °extricate, distill, °get, °obtain **3** °wrench, wring, wrest, °extort, °draw (forth), °evoke, °elicit, °extricate, winkle out, worm (out), prise (out), °force (out) **4** °copy, °quote, cite, °abstract, °select, °choose, glean, cull —*n.* **5** °concentrate, distillate, °essence, distillation, °quintessence, concentration, °extraction, decoction **6** °excerpt, °abstract, °quotation, citation, clipping, °cutting, °passage, °selection

extraction *n.* **1** °removal, extrication, withdrawal, uprooting, eradication, extirpation, deracination **2** °extract, °concentrate, distillate, °essence, distillation, °quintessence, concentration, decoction, °separation, °derivation **3** °origin, °birth, ancestry, descent, °lineage, °derivation, blood, °parentage, °breed, °strain, °race, °stock, °pedigree

extraneous *adj.* **1** unessential, °nonessential, inessential, °peripheral, °superfluous, °unnecessary, unneeded, °extra, added, additional, adventitious, supernumerary, °incidental, °needless **2** not pertinent, °impertinent, °inapplicable, inapt, unapt, unfitting, °inappropriate, °unrelated, °irrelevant, inapposite, unconnected, °remote, °alien, °foreign, °exotic, °strange, °outlandish, °external, °extrinsic, °out of place, off the mark *or* point *or* subject, beside the point *or* mark

extraordinary *adj.* **1** °unusual, uncommon, °remarkable, °exceptional, °particular, °outstanding, °special, °rare, °unique, °singular, °signal, °unheard-of, °curious, °peculiar, °odd, °bizarre, °queer, °strange, °abnormal, unprecedented, °unparalleled **2** °amazing, surprising, astonishing, astounding, °remarkable, °notable, °noteworthy, °marvelous, °fantastic, °incredible, °unbelievable, °impressive, °fabulous, °miraculous, °unparalleled, *Colloq* °super, smashing, °lovely, °gorgeous, far-out, °unreal

extravagance *n.* **1** wastefulness, °waste, lavishness, °profligacy, °prodigality, squandering, °dissipation, improvidence, exorbitance, recklessness, overspending, °excess **2** immoderation, immoderateness, excessiveness, outrageousness, unrestraint, superfluity, superfluousness, oversufficiency, preposterousness, unreasonableness, irrationality, °absurdity; capriciousness, whim, °fantasy, flightiness

extravagant *adj.* **1** °wasteful, °lavish, °profligate, °prodigal, °improvident, °reckless, °excessive, °spendthrift, °profuse, °extreme, °immoderate **2** unrestrained, uncontained, °wild, °outrageous, °preposterous, °immoderate, °ridiculous, °foolish, °fanciful, °unreasonable, °absurd, °impractical; undeserved, unjustified, unjustifiable **3** °expensive, costly, extortionate, °unreasonable, overpriced, °exorbitant, °high; °dear; *Colloq* °steep **4** °gaudy, °garish, °ostentatious, °showy, °ornate, °flashy, °loud, °flamboyant; exaggerated, high-sounding

extravaganza *n.* spectacular, °spectacle, °pageant, °production, °show, °exposition

extreme *adj.* **1** °unusual, uncommon, °exceptional, °outstanding, °notable, °noteworthy, °abnormal, °different, °extraordinary, °remarkable **2** °immoderate, °excessive, °severe, °intense, °acute, °maximum, worst **3** outermost, endmost, farthest, °ultimate, utmost, uttermost, remotest, °last, far-off, °faraway, °distant, °very **4** °rigid, °stern, °severe, °strict, °conservative, °hidebound, °stiff, stringent, restrictive, constrictive, uncompromising, Draconian, °harsh, °drastic **5** unconventional, °radical, °outrageous, °wild, °weird, °bizarre, °queer, °offbeat,

°exotic, °eccentric, °different, *outré*, *Slang* far-out, °way-out, *US and Canadian* kooky **6** beyond the pale *or* limits *or* bounds, °extravagant, °inordinate, °excessive, °disproportionate, °outrageous —*n.* **7** Often, ***extremes.*** limit(s), °bounds, utmost, °maximum, *Colloq* °swing **8** Often, ***go to extremes.*** limit(s), °bounds, °maximum, °acme, °zenith, °pinnacle, °summit, °height, apex, apogee, °peak, °extremity; °depth, nadir **9** ***in the extreme.*** °extremely, °very, exceptionally, °exceedingly, extraordinarily, unusually

extremely *adv.* °very, °exceedingly, outrageously, extraordinarily, unusually, uncommonly, exceptionally, damned, hellishly, to the nth degree, *Colloq Brit* bloody, *US* darned

extremity *n.* **1** °end, °termination, °limit, °edge, °boundary, °bound, °border, °margin; °periphery; °frontier **2** ***extremities.*** fingers, fingertips, toes; °hands, feet; arms, legs, limbs; paws, trotters, hooves, wings **3** °extreme, utmost, °maximum, limit(s), °bounds

extricate *v.* unravel, disentangle, untangle, °disengage, °(set) free, °turn loose, °release, °liberate, °rescue, °save, °deliver

extrinsic *adj.* °external, °extraneous, °irrelevant, °exterior, °unrelated, °outside; outer, °outward

exuberance *n.* **1** cheerfulness, °joy, joyfulness, ebullience, effervescence, exhilaration, buoyancy, °animation, °spirit, spiritedness, sprightliness, liveliness, °vitality, vivacity, °enthusiasm, °excitement, zeal, °zest, °energy, °vigor **2** °abundance, lavishness, effusiveness, flamboyance, copiousness, superabundance, °superfluity, °excess, °profusion, °prodigality, bounteousness, bountifulness

exuberant *adj.* **1** °cheerful, °joyful, °ebullient, °effervescent, °buoyant, °animated, °spirited, spry, °sprightly, °lively, °vivacious, °enthusiastic, zealous, °energetic, °vigorous **2** °happy, °glad, °delighted, °overjoyed, °joyful, °ecstatic, *Brit* in the seventh heaven, *US* in seventh heaven, *Colloq* on cloud nine

exult *v.* °rejoice, °revel, °glory (in), jump for joy, °delight, °celebrate, °make merry

exultant *adj.* °delighted, jubilant, °overjoyed, °elated, °joyful, °gleeful, °glad, °ecstatic, °exuberant, in seventh heaven, cock-a-hoop, *Colloq* on cloud nine, *Brit* over the moon

eye *n.* **1** eyeball, °orb, *Colloq* optic **2** °vision, (eye)sight, visual acuity, °perception **3** discernment, °perception, °taste, °judgment, °discrimination, percipience, perspicacity, °appreciation, °sensitivity; °knowledge, °recognition, comprehension **4** °liking, °affection, fondness, °partiality, °appreciation; lustfulness **5** °ogle, °leer, °look, wink, glad eye, sidelong glance **6** °view, °respect, °regard, °aim, °intention, °purpose, °design, °plan, °idea, °notion **7** °attention, °regard, °look, °scrutiny, °view, °examination, °observation; supervision **8** °guard, °lookout, °watch, vigil —*v.* **9** °examine, °scrutinize, °look at, °regard **10** °behold, gaze *or* look *or* peer at *or* upon, °contemplate, °study, °regard, °view, °inspect; °watch, °observe

eyewitness *n.* °witness, °observer, °spectator, viewer, watcher; °bystander, °onlooker, passerby

F

fabric *n.* **1** °cloth, textile, °material, °stuff **2** construction, constitution, °core, °heart, °foundation, °structure, framework, °organization, configuration, makeup

fabricate *v.* **1** °erect, °build, °construct, °frame, °raise, put *or* set up, °assemble, °fashion, °form, °make, °manufacture, °produce **2** °invent, °create, °originate, °make up, °manufacture, concoct, °think up, °imagine, °hatch, °devise, °design **3** °forge, °falsify, °counterfeit, °fake, feign, °manufacture; trump up, *Colloq* cook up, *Brit* cook

fabrication *n.* **1** construction, °assembly, assemblage, making, fashioning, °production, °manufacture, putting together, °building, erection, °formation, formulation, structuring, constructing, °organization, forming, framing, architecture **2** °invention, °creation, origination, make-up, °manufacture, hatching, concoction, contrivance, °design **3** °falsehood, °lie, °fib, prevarication, °story, °tale, untruth, fiction, °yarn, fable; falsification, °forgery, °fake, °sham, *Colloq* cock-and-bull story, *Brit* fairy story, fairy tale

fabulous *adj.* **1** fabled, mythic(al), °celebrated, °legendary, storied, °fictitious, °fictional, °unreal, °fanciful, °imaginary, storybook, fairytale **2** °fantastic, °marvelous, °incredible, °unbelievable, °inconceivable, wonderful, astounding, astonishing, °amazing, wondrous, °extraordinary, °miraculous, °phenomenal **3** °superb, °marvelous, °terrific, °wonderful, *Colloq* °great, °super, smashing, °thumping, °whopping, thundering, rattling, howling, *US* °neat, °keen, *Slang* fab, °hot, far-out, °cool, *Old-fashioned* fantabulous, in the groove, groovy, ace, *Brit* °magic, *US and Canadian* copacetic

face *n.* **1** visage, countenance, physiognomy, °features, lineaments, *Slang* °mug, mush, kisser, °pan, puss, *Brit* phiz, phizog, dial, clock **2** °look, °appearance, °aspect, °expression, mien **3** °mask, °veneer, façade, °front, °camouflage, °pretense, °disguise,

°(false) impression, °semblance, °masquerade **4** °dignity, °image, °self-respect, °standing, °reputation, repute, °name, °honor, °status **5** boldness, °daring, audacity, °effrontery, °impudence, °impertinence, °presumption, brashness, *Colloq* °gall, °brass, °nerve, cheek, °guts, gutsiness, *Brit* brass neck, *Slang US* balls **6** °surface, °exterior, °front, °outside, °cover, °facing, façade, °skin **7** right side, obverse, °front; dial **8** ***face to face.*** confronting, °facing, °opposite, *en face,* vis-à-vis, °tête-à-tête, à deux, eye to eye, head to head, *Colloq* eyeball to eyeball **9** ***in the face of.*** in defiance of, °notwithstanding, °despite, °in spite of, confronting, in opposition to **10** ***make a face.*** grimace, change one's expression, *Brit* girn, *Rare* murgeon **11** ***on the face of it.*** to all *or* outward appearances, °seemingly, °apparently, superficially, °evidently **12** ***show one's face.*** put in *or* make an appearance, °appear, °arrive, be seen, °turn up, *Colloq* °show up **13** ***to one's face.*** °directly, brazenly, eye to eye, °face to face, candidly, °openly, frankly —*v.* **14** confront, °brave, °meet (with), °encounter, °experience, deal *or* cope with, come *or* go up against; appear before **15** give (out) *or* front on *or* onto, front toward, °overlook, look out on *or* over; be opposite **16** °coat, °surface, °cover, clad, °dress, sheathe, overlay, °finish; °veneer **17** ***face down.*** confront, °intimidate, cow, °subdue, °overawe, °browbeat **18** ***face up to.*** **(a)** °admit, °accept, °acknowledge, °allow, °confess **(b)** confront, deal *or* cope with, come *or* go up against, °brave, come to terms with; brazen through *or* out, bite (on) the bullet, grasp the nettle

facilitate *v.* °ease, °expedite, °smooth, °further, °promote, °advance; °assist, °aid, °help

facility *n.* **1** °ease, smoothness, °fluency, effortlessness, °readiness, easiness, °skill, skillfulness, deftness, °dexterity, adroitness, °ability, °aptitude, °expertise, expertness, °proficiency, mastery, masterfulness, masterliness, °efficiency; quickness, alacrity, celerity, swiftness, °speed **2** Often, ***facilities.*** **(a)** °plant, °system, building(s), °structure, complex **(b)** convenience(s), °privy, °equipment, °lavatory, °toilet, powder room, *Nautical* °head, *Brit* water closet, WC, loo, *US and Canadian* rest room, men's room, ladies' room, *Colloq Brit* gents, ladies, *Slang Brit* °bog, karzy, *US and Canadian* john

facing *n.* façade, °front, cladding, °surface, overlay, °skin; coating

facsimile *n.* °copy, °reproduction, °print, carbon (copy), °replica, °duplicate, photocopy, fax, *Trademark* Xerox (copy), Photostat, *Colloq US* °dupe

fact *n.* **1** °reality, actuality, °truth, °certainty **2** °accomplishment, *fait accompli,* fact of life; °occurrence, °event, °happening, °incident, °episode, °experience, °act, °deed **3** Often, ***facts.*** °data, °information, particular(s), detail(s), point(s), item(s), factor(s), *Colloq* °lowdown, (inside) info, the score, *Brit* the gen, *US and Canadian* the poop **4** ***in fact.*** °indeed, to be sure, as a matter of (actual) fact, °in truth, °truly, truthfully, °actually, °really, °in reality, in point of (actual) fact, factually

faction *n.* **1** °group, °cabal, bloc, cadre, °camp, splinter group, °circle, camarilla, °clique, °set, coterie, °lobby, pressure group, junta *or* junto, °ring, °gang, *Brit* ginger group, *Colloq* °crowd **2** °dissension, °intrigue, °strife, °sedition, disharmony, °discord, °disagreement, quarreling, contention, °controversy, infighting, °rupture, °split, °rift, °schism, °clash

factious *adj.* contentious, disputatious, litigious, refractory, divisive, conflicting, °discordant, °argumentative, °at odds, at loggerheads, °quarrelsome, °seditious, °mutinous, °rebellious

factitious *adj.* fake(d), °bogus, °false, °mock, falsified, °artificial, °insincere, °unreal, °synthetic, fabricated, engineered, manufactured, °spurious, °counterfeit, °sham, simulated, °imitation, unauthentic, set *or* got up, rigged, *Colloq* phoney *or US also* phony

factor *n.* **1** constituent, °ingredient, °element, °part, °particular, °piece, component, catalyst; °circumstance, °consideration, °aspect, °fact, °influence, determinant, °cause **2** °agent, °representative, °proxy, middleman, °intermediary, °deputy, °go-between **3** banker, °financier, °backer, moneylender, lender

factory *n.* °works, °mill, °plant

factual *adj.* **1** °actual, °real, °true, °authentic, verifiable, °realistic, true-to-life, °genuine, valid, °bona fide **2** °accurate, °correct, °true, °faithful, °precise, unbiased, undistorted, °unvarnished, unexaggerated, °objective, °unprejudiced, straightforward

faculty *n.* **1** °ability, °capacity, °skill, °aptitude, °potential, °talent, °flair, °knack, °gift, °genius; °dexterity, adroitness, cleverness, °capability **2** °school, °department, °discipline **3** °staff, personnel, members, *Brit* dons **4** °power, authorization, dispensation, °sanction, °license, °prerogative, °privilege, °right, °permission, °liberty

fad *n.* °craze, °mania, °rage, °fashion, °trend, °fancy, °vogue

fade *v.* **1** (grow) dim *or* pale, grow faint, cloud (over), °dull; °bleach, whiten, etiolate, °wash out, blanch *or* blench, discolor **2** °droop, wither, °decline, die out *or* away, °perish, °ebb, °flag, °wane, °wilt, °waste away, °sag, °diminish, °dwindle, languish, °deteriorate, °decay, °shrivel, peter out *or* away

fag *v.* **1** Often, ***fag out.*** °exhaust, °weary, °tire (out), °fatigue, °wear out, °jade, *Colloq Brit* knacker, *US* poop —*n.* **2** *Brit* °bore, °nuisance, °drag, chore, °pain **3** *Brit* °servant, °menial, °flunky, drudge, lackey, underling **4** See **homosexual 1,** below. **5** cigarette, smoke, *Colloq* °butt, cig(gy), weed, coffin nail, cancer stick, *Old-fashioned* gasper

fail *v.* **1** not succeed, be unsuccessful, °miss, °miscarry, °misfire, °fall short (of), °fall flat, °fall through, falter, be (found) lacking *or* wanting, be defective, be deficient, be *or* prove inadequate, come to grief *or* naught *or* nothing, °go wrong, abort, meet with disaster, °founder, run aground, *Colloq* °flop, °fizzle (out), go up in smoke, *US* °strike out, *US, Canadian, and New Zealand* flunk **2** °let down, °disappoint, °forsake, °desert, °abandon, °neglect, °ignore, °slight **3** °decline, °peter out, °dwindle, °diminish, °wane, °deteriorate, °weaken, °decay, fade *or* die (out *or* away), °disappear, °flag, °ebb, °sink, languish, °give out; gutter, °go out **4** go bankrupt, go out of business, °go under, go into receivership, become insolvent, close up shop, close up *or* down, cease operation(s), *Brit* °go to the wall, *US* file for Chapter 11, *Colloq* °fold (up), go bust *or* broke, *US* drown in red ink

failing *n.* **1** °weakness, °shortcoming, °foible, °flaw, °fault, °defect, weak spot, blind spot, °blemish, °imperfection —*prep.* **2** lacking, °wanting, in default of, without, sans, in the absence of

failure *n.* **1** °failing, °default, nonperformance, remissness; °neglect, °omission, dereliction, deficiency **2** °breakdown, °collapse, discontinuance, °miscarriage, °loss; °decline, °decay, deterioration **3** °loser, nonstarter, misfire, °incompetent, also-ran, nonentity, *Colloq* °flop, °fizzle, damp squib, °dud, lemon, °washout, dead duck, *US* lead balloon **4** bankruptcy, °ruin, insolvency, °downfall, °crash, *Colloq* folding

faint *adj.* **1** °dim, °dull, °pale, faded, °indistinct, °vague, °hazy, °imperceptible, indiscernible, unclear, blurred, blurry, muzzy, wavering, faltering, ill-defined, °weak, °feeble, flickering, °subdued; °low, °soft, °slight, hushed, muffled, muted, °inaudible, stifled **2** °dizzy, lightheaded, unsteady, vertiginous, °giddy, *Colloq* woozy —*v.* **3** black out, °pass out, lose consciousness, swoon, °drop, °collapse, *Colloq* keel over —*n.* **4** loss of consciousness, blackout, unconsciousness, °collapse, swoon, *Medical* syncope

fainthearted *adj.* **1** °cowardly, timorous, °afraid, frightened, °scared, °faint, lily-livered, white-livered, pusillanimous; °timid, °shy, diffident; *Colloq* yellow(-bellied), chicken-hearted, chicken-livered, chicken **2** °irresolute, °weak, °ineffectual, °feeble, °puny, feckless

fair[1] *adj.* **1** °impartial, evenhanded, °disinterested, °equitable, °just, °unprejudiced, unbiased, °objective, *Colloq* °square **2** °honest, °aboveboard, °honorable, °lawful, °trustworthy, °legitimate, °proper, °upright, straightforward **3** °light, blond(e), fair-haired, flaxen-haired, tow-headed, tow-haired; light-complexioned, peaches-and-cream, °rosy; unblemished, °clear, °spotless, °immaculate **4** °satisfactory, °adequate, °respectable, pretty good, °tolerable, °passable, all right, °average, °decent, middling, °reasonable, *comme ci, comme ça*, not bad; °mediocre, °indifferent, *Colloq* °so-so, OK *or* okay **5** °favorable, °clear, °sunny, °fine, °dry, °bright, cloudless, °pleasant, halcyon, °benign **6** unobstructed, °open, °clear, °free **7** °attractive, good-looking, °handsome, °comely, °pretty, °beautiful, pulchritudinous, °lovely, beauteous **8** °civil, °courteous, °polite, °gracious, °agreeable

fair[2] *n.* °fête, °festival, kermis *or* kirmess, °exhibition, °exposition, °show; °market, bazaar, mart, *US* °exhibit

fairly *adv.* **1** °quite, °rather, °pretty, °somewhat, tolerably, adequately, sufficiently, passably, °moderately, *Colloq* °sort of, kind of **2** equitably, impartially, justly, °properly, °honestly, objectively **3** °absolutely, °totally, °utterly, °completely, °positively, °really, °actually, veritably, °virtually

fairyland *n.* dreamland, wonderland, never-never land, happy valley, °paradise, cloudland, enchanted forest, Cloud-cuckoo-land, Nephelococcygia, Shangri-La

faith *n.* **1** °belief, credence, °confidence, °conviction, °trust, °certainty, certitude, °assurance, assuredness, sureness, °reliance, dependence **2** °belief, °religion, °creed, °persuasion, dogma, teaching, °doctrine, °denomination, °sect **3** °duty, allegiance, °obligation, °promise, faithfulness, °loyalty, fidelity, °devotion, consecration, °dedication, fealty, °obedience

faithful *adj.* **1** °true, °loyal, °devoted, °steadfast, dedicated, °attached, unswerving, °firm, °staunch, unwavering, °constant **2** °close, °exact, °accurate, °true, °correct, °precise, °perfect, valid; °literal **3** °conscientious, °dutiful, °scrupulous, °careful, °meticulous, °thorough, punctilious, finicky *or* finical, °detailed, °fastidious, rigorous, °rigid, °severe, °particular **4** °reliable, dependable, trusted, °trustworthy, trusty, °honest, °true, °truthful, °righteous, °right, °moral, °virtuous, °upright, veracious

faithless *adj.* **1** °skeptical, doubting, °unbelieving, disbelieving, agnostic, atheistic, freethinking **2** unfaithful, °disloyal, treacherous, °traitorous, °perfidious, shifting, °shifty, °fickle, °inconstant, untrustworthy, °unreliable, °false, °hypocritical, °insincere, °dishonest, °crooked, °unscrupulous, conscienceless, recreant

fake *v.* **1** °falsify, °doctor, °alter, °modify, °counterfeit, °fabricate, °manufacture, °forge **2** °pretend, make a pretense of, dissemble, feign, °sham, °make believe, simulate, °affect —*n.* **3** °hoax, °counterfeit, °sham, °forgery, °imitation, *Colloq* phoney *or US also* phony **4** faker, °impostor, charlatan, °fraud, hoaxer, mountebank, °cheat, humbug, °quack, °pretender, *Colloq* phoney *or US also* phony —*adj.* **5** °false, °counterfeit, forged, °sham, °fraudulent, °imitation, pinchbeck, °bogus, °spurious, °factitious, *Colloq* phoney *or US also* phony

fall *v.* **1** °descend, °sink, °subside, °settle, drop *or* come (down), °plummet, °plunge, °dive, (take a) nose dive; cascade **2** °tumble, °trip, °stumble, °slump, °collapse, keel over, °topple, °crumple **3** °diminish, °(become) lower, °sink, °decline, fall *or* drop off, °drop, °decrease, °dwindle, °subside, come *or* go down **4** °slope, fall away, °decline **5** °succumb, °surrender, °yield, give up *or* in, °capitulate, be defeated *or* conquered, be captured, be taken (captive *or* prisoner), be overthrown, come *or* go to ruin, be destroyed, be lost **6** °die, °perish, drop dead, be slain *or* killed **7** ***fall apart.*** °disintegrate, °crumble, °collapse, fall *or* come *or* go to pieces, °break up, be destroyed; break apart, °fragment, °shatter **8** ***fall back.*** °retreat, °retire, °withdraw, °draw back; °recede **9** ***fall back on or upon.*** have recourse to, rely *or* depend on *or* upon, return to, count on *or* upon, °resort to, call on *or* upon, make use of, °use, °employ **10** ***fall behind.*** drop back, °trail, °lag; be in arrears **11** ***fall down.*** **(a)** °collapse, °drop **(b)** °fail, be (found) wanting *or* lacking, be unsuccessful, be *or* prove inadequate *or* disappointing **12** ***fall flat.*** °collapse, °fail, *Colloq* °flop, *US* °bomb (out), lay an egg, go over like a lead balloon **13** ***fall for.*** **(a)** fall in love with, be infatuated with **(b)** be fooled *or* duped *or* taken in *or* deceived by, °accept, °swallow, succumb to, *Slang* be a sucker for, *US and Canadian* be a patsy for **14** ***fall in.*** °cave in, °collapse, sink inward **15** ***fall in with.*** °join, °associate with, become associated *or* allied with, befriend; cooperate with, °go along with, concur with, °support, °accept **16** ***fall off.*** °diminish, °decrease, °decline, °deteriorate **17** ***fall on or upon.*** °attack, °assault, assail, °set upon **18** ***fall out.*** °disagree, °differ, °quarrel, °clash, squabble, wrangle, °dispute, °fight **19** ***fall short.*** prove *or* (turn out to) be inadequate *or* insufficient *or* deficient *or* lacking *or* wanting *or* disappointing, °miss, °fail, °disappoint **20** ***fall through.*** °fail, come to nothing *or* naught, °miscarry, °die, *Colloq* °fizzle (out), °flop **21** ***fall to.*** °start, °begin, °commence, set *or* go about, get under way, °undertake, °tackle, °take on; get moving, °attack, *Colloq* get the show on the road, get cracking, *US* get a wiggle on, move it —*n.* **22** °drop, descent, °dive, nose dive, °plunge, °tumble, dropping, falling **23** *Chiefly US and Canadian* autumn **24** °decline, °decay, °collapse, °downfall, °failure, °destruction, °ruin, deterioration, °eclipse **25** Usually, ***falls.*** cascade, cataract, °waterfall; rapids **26** depreciation, °sinking, diminution, °decrease, °decline, °lapse, downturn, downswing, °drop, drop-off, lowering, abatement, °slump, °collapse **27** °slope, declivity, descent, °decline, °drop, downhill, *Chiefly US and Canadian* °downgrade **28** °surrender, capitulation, °submission, °taking, °seizure, °capture, °overthrow, °defeat, °conquest, °downfall

fallacy *n.* °misconception, miscalculation, misjudgment, °mistake, °error, *non sequitur,* °solecism, °delusion; paralogism; sophism

false *adj.* **1** °untrue, unfactual, untruthful, °wrong, °amiss, °mistaken, °erroneous, °incorrect, °inaccurate, °inexact, °imprecise, °faulty, °flawed, °invalid, °unsound, °unreal, °imaginary, °fictitious, °spurious **2** °untrue, untruthful, °lying, misleading, fallacious, fabricated, made-up, concocted, mendacious, untrustworthy, °fraudulent, meretricious, °deceptive, °deceitful, treacherous, *Colloq* phoney *or US also* phony **3** °counterfeit, °imitation, simulated, °sham, forged, °fraudulent, °fake, °artificial, °synthetic, manufactured, °unnatural, °spurious, °bogus, ersatz, °factitious, °mock, pseudo, *Colloq* phoney *or US also* phony **4** °sham, feigned, °affected, °insincere, faked, manufactured, counterfeit(ed) **5** illogical, fallacious, °unsound, °invalid, °flawed, °faulty

falsehood *n.* °lie, °fib, prevarication, untruth, °fabrication, °misstatement, fiction, °(fairy) tale, °story, distortion, *Colloq* cock-and-bull story, *Slang Brit* load of codswallop

falsify *v.* °fake, °alter, °distort, misstate, °misrepresent, °twist, *Colloq* fudge, trump up, *Brit* cook

falsity *n.* untruthfulness, mendaciousness, fraudulence, deceptiveness, °deceit, deceitfulness, dishonesty, spuriousness, speciousness, casuistry, °hypocrisy, insincerity, falseness

fame *n.* °renown, repute, °reputation, °celebrity, illustriousness, °superiority, °preeminence, stardom, °prominence, eminence, °glory, °name, °notoriety, acclaim

familiar *adj.* **1** °well-known, °common, commonplace, °everyday, °ordinary, °current **2** °frequent, °usual, °customary, °habitual, °routine, °traditional **3** °friendly, affable, °close, °intimate, °sociable, °social, °free, free-and-easy, °relaxed; overfriendly, overfree, overfamiliar, °bold, °forward, °insolent, °impudent, °presumptuous, presuming, °disrespectful, unreserved, unrestrained; °informal, °casual, °cordial, unceremonious; *Colloq* °chummy, *Slang US and Canadian* buddy-buddy, palsy-walsy **4** ***familiar with.*** aware *or* conscious *or* cognizant of, knowledgeable about *or* of *or* in, conversant *or* acquainted with, no stranger to, on speaking terms with, up on *or* in, (well) versed in, informed of *or* about, °privy to, in the know about, *au courant, au fait*

familiarity *n.* **1** °knowledge, acquaintance(ship), °grasp, °understanding, comprehension, °cognizance, awareness, conversance, °experience **2** friendliness, affability, sociability, neighborliness, °fellowship, intimacy, intimateness, closeness, openness, naturalness, °ease, informality, unceremoniousness **3** boldness, presumptuousness, overfamiliarity, °presumption, °impudence, insolence, °impertinence, °impropriety

familiarize *v.* Usually, ***familiarize with.***

accustom (to), make familiar *or* acquaint (with), °initiate (in), inform (about *or* on), enlighten (about *or* as to), °teach (about), educate *or* instruct *or* tutor (in)

family *n.* **1** °(kith and) kin, kinsmen, °kindred, kinfolk *or Brit* kinsfolk, next of kin, relatives, °relations, household, °people, °one's own flesh and blood, one's nearest and dearest, ménage, *Colloq* folks **2** children, °offspring, °progeny, °issue, °brood, *Colloq* kids **3** ancestors, forebears, forefathers, progenitors; ancestry, °parentage, descent, °extraction, °derivation, °lineage, °pedigree, genealogy, family tree, °house, °line, bloodline, °dynasty; blood, °stock, °strain **4** °group, °set, °division, subdivision, classification, °type, °kind, °class, °genre, °order, species, genus

famine *n.* starvation; °shortage, °dearth, °scarcity, deficiency, paucity, exiguity, barrenness, °lack

famished *adj.* starving, °starved, °voracious, °ravenous, ravening, craving, °hungry

famous *adj.* °renowned, °celebrated, °popular, famed, °well-known, °noted, °eminent, °preeminent, °conspicuous, °prominent, °illustrious, °notable, acclaimed, °venerable, °legendary, °distinguished, °praiseworthy, honored, lionized

famously *adv.* excellently, °(very) well, superbly, marvelously, splendidly, capitally, spectacularly, superlatively

fan *n.* °admirer, °enthusiast, adherent, °devotee, aficionado, °follower, °supporter, °lover, °zealot, *Colloq* buff, °fiend, °hound, °bug, °addict, nut, *US* booster, *Slang* junkie, °freak, groupie

fanatic *n.* °maniac, extremist, °zealot, *Colloq* °fiend, nut, *Slang* °freak

fanatical *adj.* °fanatic, °extreme, distracted, °maniacal, °mad, °rabid, zealous, frenzied, °feverish, °burning, °frantic, frenetic, °obsessive, °fervent, °compulsive, monomaniacal, fervid, perfervid, °passionate, °enthusiastic, °agog, °immoderate, °excessive

fanaticism *n.* **1** °devotion, °dedication, devotedness; infatuation, °enthusiasm, °fervor, zeal, obsessiveness, franticness, °frenzy, hysteria **2** monomania, single-mindedness, °mania, °madness, extremism, °intolerance, °bigotry, °bias, °partiality, °prejudice, narrow-mindedness, close-mindedness

fancied *adj.* °imaginary, °unreal, °fanciful, imagined, °illusory, make-believe, °mythical, fairy-tale

fanciful *adj.* **1** °whimsical, °capricious, °impulsive, °inconstant, °fickle, °changeable, °variable **2** °extravagant, chimerical, °fantastic, °fabulous, °mythical, fairy-tale, °imaginative, °fancied, make-believe, °unreal, °illusory, imagined, °visionary, °imaginary **3** °curious, °odd, °peculiar, °bizarre, °unusual, °original

fancy *adj.* **1** °ornate, decorative, decorated, °ornamental, ornamented, °elaborate, embellished, embroidered, °fanciful, °extravagant, rococo, baroque, gingerbread, Byzantine, °complicated, °intricate, complex **2** °illusory, °capricious, °fanciful, °extravagant, °fantastic, °far-fetched, delusive, °whimsical, °visionary, °unrealistic, °grandiose **3** deluxe, °luxury, °luxurious, °choice, °select, °prime, °special, °elegant, °superior, °quality, °high-class; °posh **4** °high, °exorbitant, °inflated, °outrageous —*n.* **5** °imagination, °creation, °conception, inventiveness, creativeness, creativity **6** °imagination, °fantasy, °hallucination, °delusion, °illusion, unreality, make-believe, °dream, °daydream, pipe dream, mirage, phantasm, °phantom, figment (of the imagination), °impression **7** °liking, °inclination, fondness, °taste, °penchant, °attraction, °preference, °partiality, predilection, yearning, craving, hankering, °wish, °desire, °longing **8** °idea, whim, caprice, whimsy, °urge, impulse, °notion, vagary, °quirk, crotchet, °peculiarity —*v.* **9** °imagine, °conceive, °picture, visualize, °envisage, think *or* make up, conjure up, *US* °envision, *Colloq* dream up **10** °think, °imagine, °understand, °believe, °suspect, °guess, conjecture, °presume, °surmise, °assume, °take it, °suppose, °infer, °reckon **11** °like, be attracted to, take (a liking) to, °desire, °want, crave, long *or* pine for, have a yen *or* craving for, have an eye for, wish for, hunger for *or* after, °favor, °prefer, lust for *or* after

fanfare *n.* **1** °flourish, fanfaron, fanfaronade, (trumpet) blast *or* blare **2** hullabaloo, hubbub, brouhaha, commotion, °stir, ado, °show, °fuss, *Colloq* to-do, ballyhoo

fantasize *v.* °dream, °imagine, °daydream, °muse, °mull (over), build castles in the air *or* in Spain, °speculate, °envisage, stargaze; hallucinate, *US* °envision

fantastic *adj.* **1** °fanciful, °strange, °weird, °peculiar, °odd, °eccentric, °queer, °bizarre, °quaint, °outlandish, °exotic, °extravagant, °grotesque, °nightmarish, °alien, °remarkable **2** °imaginary, °illusory, illusive, °unreal, °visionary, °fanciful, °unrealistic, imagined, irrational **3** °unbelievable, °incredible, °preposterous, °extraordinary, °implausible, °absurd, °unlikely **4** °marvelous, spectacular, °splendid, wonderful, tremendous, °overwhelming, *Colloq* °great, °fabulous, °terrific

fantasy *n.* **1** °imagination, °fancy, creativity, inventiveness, °originality **2** °vision, °hallucination, °illusion, mirage, °delusion, chimera, °dream, °daydream, °(flight of) fancy, pipe dream **3** make-believe, °invention, °fabrication, fiction, °masquerade, fable, concoction, °pretense

far *adv.* **1** afar, far away *or* off, a good *or* great *or* long way *or* distance off *or* away **2** (very) much, considerably, decidedly, incomparably **3** *by far.* (very) much, considerably, decidedly, incomparably, (im)measurably, by a long shot, far and away, °clearly, plainly, °obviously, doubtless(ly), indubitably, °undoubtedly, °definitely, beyond (the shadow of a) doubt, without a doubt,

Colloq Brit by a long chalk **4** ***far and wide.*** °everywhere, near and far *or* far and near, extensively, °widely, high and low; here, there, and everywhere **5** ***far gone.*** **(a)** beyond *or* past help, advanced, deteriorated, worn-out, °dilapidated, near the end **(b)** °drunk, besotted, *Slang* °loaded, pissed, paralytic, paralyzed **6** ***go far.*** **(a)** °progress, °advance, °succeed, °go places, °get ahead, °rise (in the world), make a name for oneself, become successful, set the world on fire, *Brit* set the Thames on fire, *US* cut a swath **(b)** °help, °aid, °contribute, play a part **7** ***go too far.*** go overboard *or* over the top, not know when to stop, °go to extremes; °exceed, °overdo, °overstep, °transcend, go beyond **8** ***so far.*** **(a)** thus far, (up) to *or* till *or* until now *or* the present *or* this point, to date, to this point in time **(b)** to a certain extent *or* limit *or* point —*adj.* **9** (more) remote *or* distant, far-away, far-off; °extreme, farther, farthest

faraway *adj.* **1** °distant, °remote, far-off, °outlying, far-flung **2** °dreamy, °detached, °absent, °absent-minded, abstracted

farcical *adj.* °ludicrous, laughable, risible, °funny, °nonsensical, °ridiculous, °silly, °preposterous, °absurd, °foolish; comical, °humorous, droll, amusing

fare *n.* **1** °passenger, °traveler **2** °charge, °price, °cost **3** °food, °diet, victuals, meals, viands, eatables, °provisions —*v.* **4** do, make one's way, °manage, get on *or* along, °make out, °survive

farewell *n.* **1** adieu, °goodbye **2** departure, leave-taking, congé, °parting, *Colloq* sendoff —*interj.* **3** Adieu!, Goodbye!, So long!, Godspeed!, Adios!, Hasta luego!, Hasta la vista!, Auf Wiedersehen!, Ciao!, Sayonara!, Aloha!, Vaya con Dios!, *Colloq Brit* God bless!, *Old-fashioned* Toodle-oo!, Pip! Pip!, Ta-ta!, *US old-fashioned* See you later (Alligator)!, Don't take any wooden nickels!

far-fetched *adj.* °strained, stretched, °improbable, °implausible, °unlikely, °doubtful, dubious, °questionable, °forced, unconvincing, °unrealistic, °fantastic, °preposterous, hard to believe, °unbelievable, °incredible, *Colloq* hard to swallow, °fishy

farm *n.* **1** farmstead, farmhouse, grange, homestead, holding; °land, farmland, acreage, arable; *Brit* steading, smallholding, °allotment, *Scots* farm-toun, croft **2** ***buy the farm.*** °die, be killed —*v.* **3** °cultivate, work the land, till the soil **4** ***farm out.*** °contract, subcontract, °lease, °delegate, °let (out)

farmer *n.* husbandman, agriculturist, agronomist, yeoman, *Brit* smallholder, *US dialectal* granger

farming *n.* agriculture, agronomy, husbandry, agribusiness, cultivation

farsighted *adj.* **1** farseeing, foresighted, prescient, °provident, °prudent, °shrewd, °perceptive, discerning, insightful, °wise, sagacious, °acute, °sharp, °astute, °sensible, °imaginative **2** long-sighted, hyperopic *or* hypermetropic, presbyopic

fascinate *v.* °bewitch, °enchant, cast a spell on *or* over, ensorcell, spellbind, hold spellbound, put *or* have under a spell, °charm, °captivate, °intrigue, °beguile, °hypnotize, mesmerize, °transfix, °entrance, engross, enthrall, °enrapture, absorb, allure, °attract

fascination *n.* °enchantment, °sorcery, °magic, attractiveness, °attraction, °draw, °pull, °(animal) magnetism, °charm, allure, captivation, °influence, witchcraft, entrancement

fashion *n.* **1** °style, °mode, °vogue, °trend, °look, °taste **2** the fad, °mania, the craze, the rage, the latest (thing), *le dernier cri*, *Colloq Brit* the go **3** °manner, °mode, °way, °approach, °attitude **4** ***in fashion.*** See **fashionable,** below. —*v.* **5** °make, °model, °style, °shape, °form, °frame, °mold, °create, °construct, °forge, °work, °manufacture

fashionable *adj.* °in fashion, °chic, à la mode, modish, °stylish, °smart, in vogue, °up-to-the-minute, up-to-date, *Colloq* °trendy, in, with it, *Colloq Brit* all the go

fast[1] *adj.* **1** °quick, °swift, °fleet, °speedy, °brisk; °brief, °hurried, °hasty, high-speed, accelerated, °expeditious, °rapid, °express **2** °loose, °profligate, °wild, °extravagant, dissipated, intemperate, °irresponsible, sybaritic, °self-indulgent, °dissolute, unrestrained, indecorous, °rakish, licentious, °promiscuous, °immoral, °wanton, °lecherous, °lustful **3** °firm, fastened, secure(d), °fixed, tied, °bound, connected, °attached **4** °firm, °fixed, settled, °stable, °solid, °immovable, unshakable *or* unshakeable, °tight **5** °firm, °stable, °steadfast, °staunch, unwavering, °constant, °lasting, °close, °loyal, °devoted, °faithful, °permanent —*adv.* **6** °quickly, °swiftly, °rapidly, speedily, briskly, presto, °hastily, hurriedly, with all speed *or* haste, expeditiously, apace, °posthaste, like a flash, in the blink of an eye, in a wink, before one can *or* could say "Jack Robinson," in no time (at all), *Colloq* like a bat out of hell, °like a shot, PDQ *or* P.D.Q. (= 'pretty damn(ed) quick'), *Brit* like the clappers (of hell), *US and Canadian* quick like a bunny *or* rabbit, lickety-split **7** °firmly, fixedly, immovably, solidly, unshakably *or* unshakeably, °tightly, securely, soundly **8** closely, °close to, °immediately, °near, (close) on, °right **9** loosely, wildly, recklessly, intemperately, irresponsibly, fecklessly, extravagantly, sybaritically, self-indulgently, dissolutely, unrestrainedly, indecorously, rakishly, licentiously, promiscuously, immorally, wantonly, lecherously, lustfully

fast[2] *v.* **1** abstain, go hungry, deny oneself, °diet, starve (oneself) —*n.* **2** abstention, abstinence, fasting, °self-denial, °diet; hunger strike

fasten *v.* **1** °attach, °tie, °bind, °bond, °stick, affix, °anchor, °fix, °lock, °hook (up), °secure, °join, °connect, °link, °fuse, °cement, °clamp **2** °fix, rivet, °focus, °concentrate, °direct, °aim, °point

fastening *n.* fastener, °catch, °clasp, latch, °lock, °tie, °bond

fastidious *adj.* °squeamish, °delicate, overnice, °fussy, °meticulous, °finicky, finical, pernickety *or US also* persnickety, °particular, °difficult, °critical, hypercritical, supercritical, overprecise, punctilious, *Colloq* nit-picking, picky

fat *adj.* **1** °obese, °stout, overweight, °heavy, °plump, °rotund, corpulent, portly, °well-fed, °chubby, podgy *or chiefly US* pudgy, roly-poly, tubby, °bulky, fleshy, paunchy, potbellied, overfed, °flabby, elephantine, *Colloq* broad in the beam, °beamy, beefy, *Slang US* five-by-five **2** °oily, oleaginous, unctuous, °greasy, fatty, pinguid, sebaceous, adipose **3** °rich, °wealthy, °prosperous, affluent, well-to-do, °well-off, *Colloq* well-heeled, °loaded **4** °profitable, lucrative, °fruitful, remunerative, *Slang* cushy *—n.* **5** °obesity, corpulence, stoutness, overweight, heaviness, plumpness, rotundity, portliness, chubbiness, podginess *or chiefly US* pudginess, tubbiness, fleshiness, paunchiness, flabbiness **6** °riches, °wealth, °prosperity, fertility, °yield, °abundance, °plenty, plenteousness

fatal *adj.* **1** °fateful, °deadly, °murderous, °lethal, °mortal, toxic, °terminal, °final; baneful, °poisonous **2** °destructive, °fateful, °ruinous, °calamitous, °dreadful, °disastrous, °devastating, cataclysmic, catastrophic, °harmful, °mischievous, damaging **3** °fateful, °fated, °destined, predestined, decreed, ordained, foreordained, preordained, °predetermined, °inevitable, °unavoidable, °necessary, °essential, inescapable, ineluctable

fatality *n.* **1** °catastrophe, °disaster, °calamity, cataclysm **2** °death, °casualty

fate *n.* **1** °fortune, °lot, °luck, °chance, °life, °destiny, God's will, °providence, °doom, karma, kismet, toss *or* throw of the dice, *Colloq US and Canadian* the breaks, the way the cookie crumbles, the way the ball bounces **2** °doom, °destruction, °downfall, °undoing, °ruin, °disaster, °collapse, °death, nemesis, °end, °finish **3** °end, °outcome, °future, °destination, °disposition

fated *adj.* **1** °destined, predestined, °predetermined, decreed, °doomed, °fateful, ordained, foreordained, preordained, °decided **2** °sure, °certain, °doomed, damned, cursed **3** °fatal, °fateful, °unavoidable, inescapable, °inevitable, ineluctable

fateful *adj.* **1** °significant, °momentous, °ominous, °major, consequential, °important, °critical, °crucial, decisive, °weighty, °portentous, earthshaking, °pivotal **2** °deadly, °lethal, °fatal, °destructive, °ruinous, °disastrous, catastrophic, cataclysmic

father *n.* **1** sire, paterfamilias, *Colloq* dad, daddy, pa, papa, °pop, poppa, old man, °old boy, *Brit* governor, pater **2** forebear, °ancestor, forefather, °progenitor, primogenitor **3** °creator, °founder, originator, inventor, °author, architect, framer, initiator **4** °priest, confessor, curé, abbé, °minister, °pastor, °shepherd, parson, °clergyman, chaplain, *Colloq* padre, *Military slang* sky pilot *—v.* **5** sire, beget, °get, engender, procreate, °generate **6** °originate, °establish, °found, °invent, °author, °frame, °initiate, °institute, °create

fatherland *n.* motherland, native land, mother country, homeland, °(old) country, birthplace

fatherly *adj.* °paternal, °kindly, °kind, °warm, °friendly, °affectionate, °protective, °amiable, °benevolent, well-meaning, °benign, caring, °sympathetic, °indulgent, °understanding; parental

fathom *v.* °probe, °sound, °plumb, °penetrate, °search (out), °investigate, °measure, °gauge, °determine, ascertain, °work out, get to the bottom of, delve into, °understand, °grasp, °divine

fatigue *n.* **1** weariness, tiredness, °weakness, °exhaustion, lassitude, listlessness, °lethargy, languor, °sluggishness, enervation *—v.* **2** °weary, °tire, °weaken, °exhaust, °drain, °enervate, *Colloq* °fag (out)

fatigued *adj.* °weary, wearied, °tired, overtired, dead tired, °weak, weakened, °exhausted, °listless, °lethargic, languorous, sluggish, enervated, °strained, wasted, *Colloq* whacked (out), knocked out, °dead, °beat, dead beat, all in, *Brit* knackered, jiggered, buggered, *US and Canadian* pooped, bushed

fatness *n.* °obesity, stoutness, corpulence, *embonpoint*, portliness, plumpness, chubbiness, rotundity, podginess *or chiefly US* pudginess

fault *n.* **1** °imperfection, °flaw, °defect, °blemish, deficiency, °shortcoming, °failing, °weakness; °frailty, °foible, °peccadillo **2** °mistake, °error, °blunder, °lapse, °failure, °offense, °oversight, slip(-up), °indiscretion, gaffe, gaucherie, faux pas, *Slang* boner, °howler, goof, boo-boo, *Brit* boob **3** °responsibility, °liability, culpability; °blame, °accountability, answerability **4** °sin, °transgression, trespass, °misdeed, °offense, misdemeanor, °vice, °indiscretion, misconduct, °misbehavior **5** ***at fault.*** to blame, blamable, blameworthy, in the wrong, °responsible, answerable, °accountable, °liable, culpable, °guilty **6** ***find fault.*** °criticize, censure, take exception (to), °carp (at), °cavil (at), °pick at, °pick on, pick apart, pick holes in, °niggle, °fuss, *Colloq* nitpick, °knock **7** ***to a fault.*** excessively, °extremely, to an extreme, °in the extreme, unreasonably, °exceedingly, °unduly, disproportionately, immoderately, irrationally, *US* °overly *—v.* **8** find fault with, censure, °blame, °criticize, call to account, impugn, call into question, hold (someone) responsible *or* accountable *or* to blame, lay at (someone's) door, °accuse

faultfinding *n.* **1** °criticism, censure, carping, caviling, captiousness, hypercriticism, quibbling, fussiness, hair-splitting, pettifogging, *Colloq* nitpicking, pickiness *—adj.* **2** °critical, censorious, carping, caviling, captious, hypercritical, °fussy, hair-splitting, pettifogging, °niggling, contentious, °querulous, quibbling, *Colloq* nitpicking, picky

faultless *adj.* °perfect, °flawless, °immaculate, °ideal, °exemplary, °correct, °accurate, °foolproof, °irreproachable, unimpeachable, *Colloq Brit* bang on, spot on

faulty *adj.* °defective, °unsound, °imperfect, °flawed, impaired, °out of order, malfunctioning, °broken, °bad; damaged; *Slang* °on the blink, *Chiefly US* on the fritz

favor *n.* **1** goodwill, °approval, °support, approbation **2** °courtesy, good *or* kind deed, °good turn, °kindness, °gesture, *beau geste*; °service **3** °favoritism, °partiality, °prejudice, °bias, °preference, °patronage **4** °grace, °esteem, °consideration, °view, °regard, °opinion, °account, (good *or* bad) books; °disposition, °taste, predisposition **5** ***in favor (of).*** °for, pro, on the side of, in support (of), °at the back of, °backing, behind, on *or US and Canadian* in behalf (of), in back of —*v.* **6** °approve, °prefer, °like, have a liking *or* preference for, be partial to, °advocate, espouse, °back, °endorse, °support, °champion, °recommend, incline to *or* towards, °side with, take the side *or* part of, °go for, opt for, °fancy, °select, °choose, °elect, °single out, °sponsor, °adopt, °go in for **7** °pamper, °coddle, °baby, °protect, °indulge, be partial to **8** °advance, °forward, °promote, °facilitate, °expedite, °help, °benefit, °assist, °aid, °encourage, °accommodate, smile upon **9** °resemble, look like, °take after

favorable *adj.* **1** °advantageous, °promising, auspicious, °fair, °beneficial, °suitable, °fitting, °appropriate, encouraging, facilitative, °helpful, °helping, °supportive, supporting, °convenient, °useful, °opportune, °propitious, °accommodating, accommodative; facultative **2** °good, °promising, °positive, encouraging, reassuring, affirmative, well-disposed, °sympathetic; commendatory, °laudatory, °enthusiastic, °eager, °ardent, zealous

favorably *adv.* **1** graciously, indulgently, sympathetically, genially, °positively, agreeably, enthusiastically, with favor **2** advantageously, affirmatively, °positively, in favorable terms

favored *adj.* **1** preferred, chosen, °choice, selected, °popular, °favorite, °pet **2** advantaged, °privileged, blessed, °prosperous, °wealthy, °rich, affluent, °well-off

favorite *n.* **1** °choice, °pick, °preference, preferred, esteemed, °darling, °pet, °ideal, apple of (someone's) eye, *Colloq Brit* blue-eyed *or* white-haired *or* white-headed boy *or* girl, flavor of the month, *US* fair-haired boy *or* girl —*adj.* **2** °beloved, chosen, picked, selected, preferred, best-liked, most-liked, °favored, °choice, °pet, °ideal

favoritism *n.* °partiality, °bias, predisposition, prepossession, °prejudice, °bent, partisanship, nepotism, preferment; °preference, °leaning, °inclination, proclivity

fear *n.* **1** °dread, °terror, °fright, °panic, °horror, °alarm, trepidation, apprehension, fearfulness, apprehensiveness, °dismay, consternation, hesitation, qualms, diffidence, timidity, cravenness, °cowardice, second thoughts **2** awe, °respect, °reverence, °veneration **3** °horror, °specter, nightmare, bogey *or* bogy, °phobia, bugbear, *bête noire,* misgiving(s), foreboding(s) **4** °solicitude, °anxiety, angst, foreboding(s), °distress, misgiving(s), °concern, apprehension, °worry, uneasiness, unease —*v.* **5** be afraid *or* scared *or* fearful *or* frightened (of), °dread, quail *or* tremble *or* quake at, shudder at, °shrink from, °quiver **6** °revere, °respect, °venerate, be *or* stand in awe of **7** °expect, °anticipate, °imagine, °suspect, °foresee

fearful *adj.* **1** °afraid, °scared, frightened, terrified, alarmed, °panic-stricken, terror-stricken **2** °hesitant, °timid, timorous, °shy, diffident, unwilling, intimidated, °jumpy, °nervous, edgy, panicky, °anxious, apprehensive, °cowardly, pusillanimous, *Colloq* yellow, jittery **3** °awful, dire, °dreadful, °frightful, °frightening, °terrifying, °terrible, appalling, °ghastly, °atrocious, °horrible, horrifying, horrendous, horrific, °hideous, °gruesome, °grisly, °grim, baleful, °monstrous, unspeakable, °loathsome, heinous, °repugnant, °repulsive, °revolting, °disgusting, nauseating, °nauseous

fearfully *adv.* **1** hesitantly, timidly, timorously, shyly, diffidently, unwillingly, nervously, edgily, anxiously, apprehensively **2** °very, °awfully, °terribly, °extremely, °exceedingly, °frightfully, tremendously

fearless *adj.* °brave, °bold, °intrepid, valorous, °dauntless, °courageous, valiant, plucky, °daring, °audacious, °heroic, °venturesome, °gallant, °chivalrous

fearsome *adj.* °dreadful, °awesome, appalling, °formidable, daunting, °frightening, °frightful, awe-inspiring, °menacing, °terrible, °terrifying, intimidating

feasibility *n.* practicability, workability, applicability, viability, practicality

feasible *adj.* °practicable, workable, doable, °applicable, °viable, °practical, °possible, realizable, achievable, attainable, °sensible, usable, °realistic

feast *n.* **1** °banquet, (lavish) dinner, (sumptuous) repast, (Lucullan *or* Epicurean) treat, *Colloq* °spread, *Brit* beanfeast; *Slang* blow-out, *Brit* beano **2** °observance, °celebration, °rite, °ritual, solemnization, commemoration, memorialization, anniversary, birthday, jubilee, feast day, °festival, °fête, holy day, °holiday, red-letter day, °occasion, °event, °gala **3** °treat, °delight, °pleasure, °gratification —*v.* **4** °dine, wine (and dine), fare well *or* sumptuously, (over)indulge, °gorge (oneself), gormandize, eat one's fill **5** °entertain, °feed, wine and dine, °treat, °regale **6** °delight, °gratify, please, °cheer, °gladden

feat *n.* °exploit, °deed, °act, attainment, °achievement, °accomplishment, tour de force

feature *n.* **1** °characteristic, °attribute, °trait, °mark, °hallmark, earmark, °property, °character, °quality, °aspect, facet, °peculiarity, °quirk, idiosyncrasy **2** °(main) attraction, °draw, special attraction, high point *or* spot, best *or* memorable part; main film; *US and Canadian* drawing card; column, °piece, article, °item **3** ***features.*** °face, visage, physiognomy, countenance, looks, *Slang* °mug, kisser, chips and plaice *—v.* **4** °present, °promote, °publicize, advertise, highlight, °spotlight, put into the limelight, °star, °stress, °emphasize, call attention to, °play up, °puff up, *Colloq* headline, hype **5** be, °act, °perform, take *or* have a role *or* part, °participate, be involved *or* drawn in

federation *n.* °combination, confederacy, confederation, °amalgamation, coalition, °league, °alliance, °union, °association, *Bund,* °society

fee *n.* **1** °charge, °price, °cost, °fare, °bill, °tariff, °toll, *Colloq* damage(s) **2** °pay, °payment, emolument, compensation, recompense, °honorarium, °remuneration, °rate, wage(s), °stipend, °salary

feeble *adj.* **1** °weak, °infirm, °frail, °puny, °slight, feckless; debilitated, enervated, °decrepit, enfeebled, °exhausted, weakened; effete, °delicate, °fragile, °powerless, °impotent, impuissant, languid, spiritless, °sickly, ailing, °unsound, °faint, °dizzy; *Colloq* woozy, *Brit* wonky **2** °flimsy, °weak, °ineffectual, °ineffective, namby-pamby, half-baked, °lame, unconvincing, °shoddy, °thin, °insubstantial, °poor, °unsatisfactory, °insufficient, °inadequate, unavailing, °meager, °paltry, °insignificant, *Colloq* °wishy-washy, *Brit* °wet **3** °weak, °obscure, °dim, °imperceptible, °faint, °distant, °indistinct, unclear

feebleminded *adj.* °stupid, dull(-witted), witless, moronic, idiotic, imbecilic, °simple, °slow (on the uptake), slow-witted, weak-minded, dimwitted, addlepated, °half-witted, °deficient, subnormal, mentally defective, retarded, attocerebral, *Brit* ESN (= 'educationally subnormal'), *Colloq* °dumb, °thick, °soft in the head, bone-headed, empty-headed, °vacant, *Brit* gormless, *US* °exceptional

feed *v.* **1** °provision, cater *or* provide (for), victual, purvey, °provender, °supply, °maintain, nurture, °nourish, °board, °support, °sustain, wine and dine **2** °eat, °devour, graze, °pasture **3** ***feed on or upon.*** subsist *or* survive *or* depend *or* thrive on *or* upon, be nourished *or* gratified *or* supported by *—n.* **4** fodder, forage, pasturage, silage, °food, °provender

feel *v.* **1** °touch, °see, °note, °sense, °perceive, °experience, °determine; °handle, °manipulate, °finger **2** °stroke, °caress, °pet, °fondle **3** °sense, be conscious of, °perceive, be aware *or* sensible of, °experience **4** °sense, °believe, °think, °perceive, °judge, °consider, deem, °know, discern, intuit, *Colloq* get *or* have the impression, have a hunch, °guess, have a (funny) feeling, feel in one's bones **5** °undergo, °sense, °suffer, °bear, °endure, °withstand, °stand, °abide, °brook, °tolerate, °go through **6** °seem, °appear, strike one, give the impression, have a *or* the feeling **7** seem to be, be, regard *or* characterize oneself as, take oneself to be **8** ***feel for.*** sympathize *or* empathize with, commiserate with, bleed for, be sorry for, °pity, have compassion for **9** ***feel like.*** incline *or* lean to *or* towards, °prefer, °fancy, °want, °desire, crave *—n.* **10** °texture, °surface, °sensation, °touch, °finish **11** °feeling, °air, °atmosphere, °climate, ambiance *or* ambience, °sense, °note, °tone, °quality

feeler *n.* **1** antenna, tentacle, palp, sensor **2** °overture, °hint, °suggestion, foretaste, °probe, tester, sensor

feeling *n.* **1** °(sense of) touch, °sensitivity, °sense, °perception, °sensation, °sensibility **2** °intuition, °idea, °notion, °inkling, °suspicion, °belief, °hunch, theory, °sense; °premonition, °hint, presentiment, sense of foreboding, °sensation, °impression, °opinion, °view; °instinct, consciousness, awareness **3** °regard, °sympathy, empathy, °identification, compassion, tenderness, °appreciation, °concern, °understanding, °sensitivity, °sensibility **4** °ardor, °warmth, °passion, fervency, °fervor, ardency, °intensity, °heat, °sentiment, °emotion, vehemence **5** ***feelings.*** emotions, °sensitivity, sympathies, °sensibilities, susceptibilities **6** °feel, °mood, °atmosphere, °climate, °sense, °air, ambiance *or* ambience *—adj.* **7** sentient, °sensitive, °tender, tenderhearted, compassionate, °sympathetic

feint *n.* °distraction, mock attack, °bluff, °dodge, °maneuver, false move, °pretense, °ruse, ploy, °subterfuge, °deception, °tactic, °stratagem, gambit, °artifice

fell *v.* cut *or* knock *or* strike down, °floor, °prostrate, °level, hew (down), °flatten, °demolish, °mow (down); °kill

fellow *n.* **1** °man, °boy, °person, °individual, gentleman, °one, *Colloq* °guy, °chap, °customer, kid, *Brit* bloke, *Slang* geezer, gink, *US old-fashioned* gazabo **2** °colleague, °associate, °comrade, °companion, °ally, °peer, compeer **3** °mate, °match, counterpart, °partner, °complement, concomitant, °accessory **4** boyfriend, °man, °sweetheart, °love, young man; °lover, °paramour, *Formal* °suitor, *Old-fashioned* beau, *Archaic* swain, *Slang* °guy *—adj.* **5** associate(d), affiliate(d), allied, °auxiliary, °related

fellowship *n.* **1** °companionship, camaraderie, comradeship, amity, °brotherhood, fraternization, togetherness, °association, °friendship, amity, companionability, sociability, intimacy **2** °society, °club, °association, °alliance, guild, °league, °union, sisterhood, sorority, °brotherhood, °fraternity, congregation, °circle, community, °order, °organization, consortium, partnership; °lodge, °clan, °company, coterie, °set, °clique, coalition, bloc, cartel, °trust **3** friendliness, clubbiness, sociability, intimacy, amicability, affability, kindliness, cordiality, °familiarity, °affinity, °belonging, congeniality, °warmth, °hospitality

felon *n.* °criminal, °outlaw, lawbreaker, °offender, °culprit, °miscreant, malefactor, wrongdoer

feminine *adj.* **1** female, womanlike, womanly, °ladylike, °submissive, deferential, amenable, °gentle, docile, °tender, °soft, °delicate **2** °effeminate, womanish, unmanly, unmasculine, sissyish, sissified, effete, °affected

fence *n.* **1** °barrier, °enclosure, barricade, confine, °wall, °rampart; railing(s), palisade **2** ***on the fence.*** undecided, °indecisive, vacillating, uncommitted, °uncertain, °irresolute; °impartial, °neutral, °nonpartisan, unbiased, °unprejudiced, unaligned, °nonaligned, °independent —*v.* **3** °enclose, °encircle, °surround, circumscribe, °bound, coop, °restrict, hedge, confine, °fortify, °protect, °separate **4** parry, °avoid, °fend off, °sidestep, °dodge, °evade, hedge, stonewall, °equivocate, palter, tergiversate, vacillate, °shilly-shally, °quibble, °cavil, beat about *or* around the bush, °qualify, prevaricate, *Colloq Brit* °waffle

fend *v.* **1** ***fend for oneself.*** get *or* scrape along (on one's own), °make out, °get by, °make do, °shift for oneself, take care of *or* provide for *or* support oneself **2** ***fend off.*** °discourage, parry, keep *or* hold at bay, °resist, °repel, stave *or* ward *or* fight off, °deflect, °turn aside, avert, °divert

ferment *v.* **1** °boil, effervesce, °seethe, °bubble, °foam, °froth, °brew; °rise, °raise, °work, leaven **2** °excite, °stir up, °incite, instigate, °agitate, °foment, °inflame, °rouse, °provoke

ferocious *adj.* °fierce, °savage, °cruel, °vicious, feral, °fell, °brutal, bestial, °merciless, °ruthless, pitiless, °inhuman, barbaric, barbarous, °violent, °destructive, °murderous, °bloodthirsty, °sanguinary, °predatory, °fiendish, diabolical, °devilish, hellish, °monstrous

fertile *adj.* °fruitful, °prolific, fecund, °productive, bounteous, °profuse, °abundant, copious, fructuous, plenteous, generative, teeming, °rich, °luxuriant

fertilize *v.* **1** °impregnate, inseminate, pollinate, fecundate, fructify **2** manure, mulch, °feed, °nourish, °enrich, °dress, compost

fervent *adj.* **1** fervid, °fiery, °burning, °glowing, °hot, °intense, °passionate, °impassioned, °ardent, °hot-headed, °inflamed, fanatic(al), °excited, °frantic, frenzied **2** °eager, °earnest, °enthusiastic, zealous, °animated, °intense, °heartfelt, °emotional **3** °ecstatic, transported, °rapturous, °rapt, enrapt, enraptured, captivated

fervor *n.* fervency, °ardor, °warmth, °passion, vehemence, °glow, °intensity, zeal, °eagerness, earnestness, °enthusiasm, °animation, °gusto, ebullience, °spirit, °verve

fester *v.* **1** ulcerate, suppurate, °run, °ooze, °putrefy, putresce, necrose, °mortify, °rot, °decay, °decompose **2** °rankle, °smolder, °gall, °chafe, °inflame

festival *n.* **1** °holiday, holy day, °fête, °feast, commemoration, anniversary **2** °celebration, °fête, °festivities, carnival, °entertainment, red-letter day, gala day, anniversary, birthday

festivity *n.* **1** rejoicing, °gaiety, °mirth, jubilation, conviviality, joyfulness, °merriment, °revelry, merrymaking, °glee, jollity, jollification, felicity, *Colloq Brit* mafficking **2** ***festivities.*** celebration(s), °festival, °party, fun and games, °entertainment, °amusement, °hilarity, boisterousness, frivolity

fetch *v.* **1** °get, go after *or* for, °bring (back), °retrieve, °deliver, °obtain, carry *or* convey (back) **2** °summon, bring *or* draw forth, °call, °elicit **3** sell for, °bring (in), °go for, °yield, °earn, °make, °cost, °realize —*n.* **4** °reach, °stretch, °range, °span, °extent

fetching *adj.* °attractive, alluring, °taking, winsome, °winning, °cute, °enchanting, charming, captivating, intriguing

fête *n.* **1** °festival, °entertainment, °reception, levee, °gala, rejoicing, °celebration, °party, °festivities, °get-together, °social, °amusement, °revel, °fair, ball, °frolic, °spree, °jamboree, carnival, °event, °occasion, *Colloq* blowout, shindig, bash, do, bust, *Slang US and Canadian* wingding, °blast —*v.* **2** °entertain, °feast, roll *or* bring out the red carpet for, wine and dine, °celebrate, °honor, lionize, fuss over, kill the fatted calf for

fetish *n.* **1** °charm, °amulet, °talisman, totem, *Rare* periapt **2** °obsession, compulsion, °fixation, °mania, *idée fixe*

feud *n.* **1** °dispute, °conflict, °vendetta, °hostility, °strife, enmity, °animosity, hatred, °antagonism, °rivalry, °ill will, bad blood, hard feelings, contention, °discord, °grudge, °dissension, °disagreement, °argument, °quarrel, bickering, squabble, falling-out, estrangement —*v.* **2** °dispute, °quarrel, °bicker, °disagree, °conflict, °row, °fight, °fall out, °clash, be at odds, be at daggers drawn

feverish *adj.* °inflamed, flushed, °burning, °fiery, °hot, °ardent, °fervent, hot-blooded, °passionate, frenzied, °frantic, °excited, frenetic, zealous; *Pathology* febrile, pyretic, pyrexic

few *adj.* **1** hardly *or* scarcely any, not many, °insufficient; infrequent, °occasional —*n.* **2** °handful, some, °scattering —*pron.* **3** (only) one or two, not many

fiancé *n.* fiancée, betrothed, wife- *or* bride- *or* husband-to-be, intended

fiasco *n.* °failure, °disaster, °muddle, °mess, abortion, °botch, *Colloq* °fizzle, °flop

fib *n.* **1** °falsehood, (little) white lie, untruth, prevarication, °fabrication, °invention, misrepresentation, °story, °(fairy) tale, fiction; °lie; *Colloq* tall story, *US* tall tale, cock-and-bull story, whopper —*v.* **2** prevaricate, °misrepresent, fudge, °falsify, misspeak, palter; °lie; *Colloq* °waffle

fiber *n.* **1** filament, °thread, strand, fibril, tendril **2** °texture, °structure, °material, °fabric **3** °essence, °character, °nature,

°mold, °composition, constitution, °substance, °quality, °stripe, °cast, °makeup

fickle *adj.* °flighty, °capricious, °frivolous, unpredictable, °moody, °giddy, °fanciful, °whimsical, °fitful, mercurial, °volatile, °unstable, °changeable, mutable, °inconstant, changeful, unsteady, unsteadfast, °indecisive, undecided, vacillating *or rarely* vacillant, unsure, °uncertain, °irresolute, wavering, °erratic, °unreliable, undependable, °irresponsible, untrustworthy, °faithless, unfaithful, °disloyal, *Colloq* °wishy-washy

fictional *adj.* °unreal, °imaginary, invented, made-up, °mythical, °fanciful; °legendary, °fabulous

fictitious *adj.* **1** imagined, °imaginary, °nonexistent, °unreal, made-up, invented, fabricated, °mythical, °fancied, °fanciful, fictive, °untrue, apocryphal **2** °false, °counterfeit, °bogus, °artificial, °spurious; °assumed, improvised, made-up, invented, make-believe, °imaginary, *Colloq* phoney *or US also* phony

fiddle *v.* **1** Often, ***fiddle with.*** °meddle (with), °tamper (with), °interfere (with), °alter, °falsify, °fix; °cheat, °swindle, flimflam; *Colloq* finagle, *Brit* cook **2** Often, ***fiddle with or about or around.*** toy *or* trifle *or* fidget (with), twiddle *or* play *or* tinker (with), fool *or* fuss (with), *Colloq* mess *or* muck (about *or* around) (with), frivol (away), monkey (around) (with) —*n.* **3** violin, viola, viol, cello, violoncello, °kit

fiddlesticks *interj.* Nonsense!, Rubbish!, *Colloq* Fiddle-de-dee!, Balderdash!, Stuff and Nonsense!, Poppycock!, Pish and tush!, Tommyrot!, Hogwash!, Eyewash!, Baloney!, Bilgewater!, Moonshine!, Humbug!, Bosh!, Fiddle-faddle!, Bull!, Rot!, *Brit* Codswallop!, *Taboo Slang* Bullshit!, Balls!, Crap!, Horseshit!, *Brit* Bollocks! *or* Ballocks!

fidget *v.* **1** °squirm, twitch, °shuffle, °wriggle, wiggle, °fiddle, °fuss; °fret, °chafe —*n.* **2** cat on hot bricks, *US* cat on a hot tin roof, *Colloq* fuss-pot, fussbudget, *US* nervous Nellie **3** ***the fidgets.*** restlessness, fidgetiness, dither, uneasiness, the jitters, nervousness, itchiness, *Colloq* heebie-jeebies, jimjams, ants in one's pants

field *n.* **1** °ground, °land, arable, °pasture, grassland, °meadow, °green, °lawn, °common, clearing, °tract, °area, acreage, *Literary* greensward, lea, sward; *Archaic* mead **2** battlefield, battleground, airfield; °(cricket) pitch, football *or* hockey *or* soccer field, *American football* gridiron **3** °competition, competitors, players, entrants, contestants, participants, candidates, °possibilities, applicants **4** °area, °domain, °realm, °department, °territory, °province, °sphere, °scope, °division, °interest, °line, métier, °discipline, bailiwick, °specialty, specialization, °expertise, °forte, °strength —*v.* **5** °catch, °stop, °return, °retrieve, °pick up **6** °answer, reply to, °respond to, °handle, °manipulate, °deal with, react to, °cope with

fiend *n.* **1** See **devil.** **2** °addict, °maniac, °fanatic; °fan, aficionado, °enthusiast, °devotee, °hound, °follower, *Colloq* buff, nut, *Slang* °freak

fiendish *adj.* °cruel, °savage, °inhuman, °monstrous, °ghoulish, °malignant, malevolent, malicious, °wicked, °evil, °bad, black-hearted, °satanic, °devilish, Mephistophelian, demonic, demoniac(al), diabolic(al), cacodemonic, hellish, °infernal

fierce *adj.* **1** °ferocious, °savage, °wild, °truculent, brutish, feral, bestial, tigerish, °brutal, °cruel, °fell, °murderous, °bloodthirsty, °sanguinary, °homicidal, barbaric, barbarous, °inhuman, °dangerous **2** intractable, °angry, °furious, °hostile, °aggressive, vehement, frenzied, °stormy, °violent, turbulent, °wild, °tempestuous, °tumultuous, raging, °merciless, uncontrollable **3** °severe, °awful, °dreadful, °intense, °keen, dire, °bitter, °biting, racking

fiercely *adv.* °very, °extremely, °exceedingly, vehemently, intensely, impetuously, violently, furiously, ferociously, viciously, savagely

fiery *adj.* **1** °burning, °flaming, blazing, °hot, red-hot, white-hot, overheated; afire, °on fire, in flames, °ablaze **2** °glowing, red, °incandescent, °brilliant, °luminous, °glaring, gleaming, °radiant; aglow, afire **3** °ardent, °eager, °spirited, °passionate, °excited, °excitable, peppery, irascible, °touchy, °irritable, edgy, °hot-headed, °fierce

fight *v.* **1** contend (with), °battle, °conflict (with), °encounter, °war (against), °engage, °clash, °feud (with), °combat, bear *or* take up arms (against), °brawl, struggle *or* strive (with *or* against), cross swords (with), °close (with), come to *or* exchange blows (with), go to *or* wage war (with *or* against), joust (with), grapple *or* wrestle (with), °skirmish (with), tussle *or* scuffle (with *or* against); °box, °spar; *Old-fashioned* °broil **2** °dispute, °question, confront, °contest, °oppose, °contradict, °defy, confute, °protest, °resist, rail *or* struggle against, °withstand, refute, oppugn, make *or* take a stand against, contravene, confound **3** rise up, make *or* take a stand, °struggle, take up arms **4** °argue, °dispute, °bicker, °quarrel, wrangle, squabble, spat, °tiff, °fall out (over), have words, °disagree, °row, altercate, °debate **5** ***fight off.*** °repel, °repulse **6** ***fight shy of.*** °avoid, keep *or* remain aloof from *or* of, keep away from —*n.* **7** °battle, °conflict, °bout, duel, °(single) combat, monomachy, one-on-one, °action, warfare, °clash, °hostilities, °war, °match, °struggle, °engagement, °meeting, °encounter, °contest, fighting, °brawl, donnybrook, affray, °fray, °fracas, °disturbance, °riot, °row, melee *or* mêlée, tussle, scuffle, °scrimmage, °skirmish, °brush, *Colloq* free-for-all, set-to, °scrap, *Brit* scrum, bovver, *Slang US* rumble, *Old-fashioned* °broil **8** altercation, °argument, °quarrel, °feud, °dispute, °run-in, °disagreement, °dissension, dissidence, dissent, °difference (of opinion), squabble, bickering, spat, °misunderstanding, °row, °discord, *Colloq* ruckus **9** pugnacity, mettle, militancy, belligerence, truculence, °spirit, °pluck, zeal, °enthusiasm, °zest

figure *n.* **1** °physique, °build, °shape, °form, configuration, conformation, °build, °body, °outline, °silhouette; °cut, °cast; *Slang* bod, chassis **2** °appearance, °image, °likeness, °representation, °semblance **3** °person, °individual, °human (being) **4** °statue, effigy, °sculpture, bust, °mold, °cast, °image, °representation, °idol, icon **5** °picture, °illustration, diagram, °drawing, sketch, °plate **6** °personality, °celebrity, °somebody, °leader, °personage, °worthy, °notable, °individual, °presence, °force, °character **7** °number, numeral, cipher, digit; °character, °symbol, °device, °sign; °design, °pattern, °motif, °emblem —*v.* **8** Often, ***figure up.*** °calculate, °compute, °reckon, °work out; °count, °enumerate, numerate, °total, tot up, °tally, °sum **9** °picture, °imagine, °think, °take, °reckon, °consider, °calculate, °judge, °believe; °assume, °presume, °suppose; °accept, °acknowledge, °concede **10** °act, °participate, take *or* play a part *or* role, °appear, °feature, have a place; be included *or* mentioned, be featured *or* conspicuous **11** ***figure on or upon.*** **(a)** rely *or* depend on *or* upon, count on *or* upon, trust in, put faith in **(b)** plan on *or* upon, take into consideration *or* account, °consider, make allowance for **12** ***figure out.*** **(a)** °calculate, °reckon, °compute, °work out **(b)** °decipher, °translate, °understand, °interpret, °solve, °grasp, °get, °fathom, °see, °perceive, *Colloq* °dig, make head(s) or tail(s) of, get through one's head, get the hang *or* drift of, °catch on (to), get a fix on, *Brit* °twig, suss out

figurehead *n.* °puppet, °dummy, marionette, °mouthpiece, *Brit* man of straw, *US and Canadian* straw man, *Colloq* front man, *Chiefly US* °front

file *n.* **1** °document, documentation, dossier, °case, °data, folder, portfolio, °information **2** °line, °queue, column, °row, °rank —*v.* **3** classify, °organize, systematize, °categorize, alphabetize, chronologize, °order, °arrange, pigeonhole, interfile, put *or* place in order, °register, °record, °enter **4** °submit, send in, °complete, fill in *or US and Canadian also* fill out, °enter **5** °walk, °march, troop, °parade

fill *v.* **1** °crowd, °stuff, °cram, °jam, °load, °burden, °pack, °squeeze **2** °top (off), °top up, °fill up, make full; °inflate, °swell, °stretch, °blow up, distend, °expand **3** Sometimes, ***fill up.*** °supply, °provide, °furnish **4** °meet, °satisfy, °fulfill, °answer **5** °satisfy, °satiate, bloat, sate, °gorge, °stuff; °stock **6** °abound in, overflow, be abundant *or* plentiful in **7** °close, °stop (up), °block, °stuff, °plug, caulk, °seal **8** °occupy, °take over, °discharge, °carry out, do, °execute **9** ***fill in.*** **(a)** *US and Canadian also* °fill out, °make out, °complete, °answer **(b)** take the place, °stand in, °substitute **(c)** °inform, °tell, °advise, °notify, bring up to date, °share, let in on **10** ***fill out.*** **(a)** °swell, °expand, °grow, distend, °stretch; fatten, °increase **(b)** *US* fill in. See **9(a).** —*n.* **11** ***one's fill.*** °plenty, °enough; °surfeit, sufficiency

filling *n.* filler, stuffing, padding, wadding; °contents, components, *Colloq* innards

film *n.* **1** coating, °skin, °coat, membrane, °peel, integument, layer, overlay, covering, °cover, °sheet, dusting, °veil, *Technical* pellicle **2** motion picture, °movie, °picture; videotape; *Colloq* flick, pic; video **3** °veil, °screen, murkiness, °blur, smoke screen, haze, °mist, haziness, mistiness, cloud, °vapor, °fog, steam —*v.* **4** Usually, ***film over.*** °coat, °cover, °dim, °obscure, °fade (away), °veil, °screen, °blur, blear, °mist (over), cloud (over), °glaze (over) **5** °photograph, °shoot, °take, (video)tape

filmy *adj.* **1** gauzy, gossamer(-like), °sheer, °delicate, diaphanous, °transparent, translucent, °flimsy, °light, cobwebby, °insubstantial, °see-through, peekaboo **2** °murky, blurry, cloudy, °hazy, °misty, bleary, blurred, °dim, clouded, beclouded, milky, °pearly, °opalescent

filter *n.* **1** sieve, colander, °riddle, °screen, strainer, gauze, °cloth, cheesecloth, membrane —*v.* **2** Sometimes, ***filter out.*** °strain, °screen, °sift, winnow, °clarify, °refine, °purify, °clean; °separate, weed out, °exclude, °eliminate **3** leach, °percolate, °drip, seep, dribble, °trickle, °drain, run *or* pass through, °ooze

filth *n.* **1** sewage *or* sewerage, °dirt, slime, °muck, °sludge, sullage, effluent, °pollution, °trash, °rubbish, °garbage, °refuse, ordure, °(night) soil, excrement, feces, excreta, manure, droppings, guano, °dung, foul matter, filthiness, offal, leavings, carrion, °decay, putrescence, putrefaction, *Slang* crud, *Brit* gunge, *US* grunge, *Taboo slang* shit **2** corruption, vileness, baseness, foulness, rottenness, debasement, defilement, °taint, °pollution, adulteration, °perversion, °degradation, °taint; sullying, besmirchment **3** indecency, obscenity, smut, °pornography, corruption, nastiness, °vulgarity, grossness

filthy *adj.* **1** defiled, polluted, tainted, °foul, °nasty, °dirty, unclean, °vile, °putrid, °rotten, fetid *or* foetid, maggoty, flyblown, purulent, feculent, fecal, scummy, °slimy, mucky, *Slang* cruddy, *Brit* gungy, *US* grungy **2** °dirty, °unwashed, begrimed, squalid, °sordid, °shabby, soiled, °low, stained, grimy, °bedraggled, °unkempt, slovenly, °sloppy, °mean, °scurvy, °disgusting, °miserable, °wretched, *Slang Brit* gungy, *US* grungy **3** °immoral, taboo *or* tabu, °indecent, °impure, °obscene, smutty, °pornographic, X-rated, depraved, °corrupt, °dirty, °lewd, °lascivious, licentious, °gross, °offensive, °coarse, °bawdy, ribald, °blue, °suggestive, foul-mouthed, dirty-minded, filthy-minded

final *adj.* **1** ending, concluding, terminating,

finishing, closing, °last, °terminal, °ultimate, °end **2** conclusive, decisive, unalterable, °irreversible, °irrevocable, °incontrovertible, irrefutable, °indisputable, unchangeable, immutable, °definitive; settled, °fixed, °absolute, °certain, °sure

finality *n.* conclusiveness, decisiveness, unalterability, irreversibility, irrevocableness, incontrovertibility, irrefutability, indisputability, unchangeability, immutability, definitiveness, °certainty, certitude, sureness, fixedness

finalize *v.* conclude, °settle, °complete, °decide, *Colloq* °wrap up, °clinch, sew up

finally *adv.* **1** at (long) last, lastly, °eventually, in the end, °ultimately, °at length, when all is said and done, °in the long run, at the end of the day, at the last moment **2** conclusively, °once and for all, decisively, irrevocably, in fine, °completely, inexorably, °absolutely, definitively, °definitely, for good, °forever, for all time

finance *n.* **1** resource(s), banking, accounting, economics, °money (management), °business, °commerce, (financial) affairs, investment **2** ***finances.*** °capital, °money, °cash, °funds, °resources, °assets, holdings, °wealth, wherewithal *—v.* **3** °fund, subvene, invest in, °back, capitalize, °underwrite, °subsidize, °pay for, *Colloq US* bankroll

financial *adj.* °monetary, pecuniary, °fiscal, °economic

financier *n.* capitalist, banker, plutocrat, investor, °backer, *US* moneyman, *Colloq* angel

find *v.* **1** °discover, °come across, happen *or* come on *or* upon, hit upon *or* on, chance *or* stumble on *or* upon; °encounter, °bump into **2** Often, ***find out.*** uncover, °discover, °unearth, lay one's hand(s) on, °turn up, come up with, °reveal, °bring to light, light upon *or* on, °catch sight of, °see, espy, descry, °detect, °learn, °spot, °locate, °track down; °identify, become aware of, °determine, ascertain, °put one's finger on, °point to, *Colloq* °tumble to, *Brit* °twig; *Slang* °finger, rumble, *Brit* suss out **3** °discover, °perceive, °see, °understand, °notice, °mark, °remark, °note, °distinguish, discern; °realize **4** °consider, °think, °regard, °view, feel *or* discover to be **5** °get, °obtain, °procure, °secure, °acquire, °win, °gain; °experience **6** °recover, °locate, °get back; repossess, °recoup **7** °summon (up), °call up, °command, °gather (up), °muster (up), °rouse, °arouse, °awaken **8** °set aside, °allot, °assign, °manage, °get **9** °judge, decide *or* determine to be, °pronounce, °declare *—n.* **10** °discovery, °catch, °bargain, °deal; °boon, °windfall

finding *n.* **1** °discovery, °find **2** °judgment, °decree, verdict, °decision, °determination, °pronouncement, °declaration, conclusion

fine[1] *adj.* **1** °superior, °excellent, °superb, °magnificent, °supreme, °marvelous, °exceptional, °splendid, °exquisite, °elegant, first-class, °first-rate, °prime, °choice, °select, top-grade, high-grade, top-drawer, °quality, °admirable, °great, °good, °satisfactory, *Colloq* °out of this world, °great, OK *or* okay, peachy, °keen, *Brit* tickety-boo, *US* °neat, *Australian* bonzer, *Slang* °swell, °cool, *Brit old-fashioned* °ripping, *Dialectal* °champion **2** °sunny, °fair, °bright, °clear, cloudless, balmy, °pleasant, °dry, °nice **3** enjoyable, °satisfying, °entertaining, amusing, °good, °interesting, °pleasant, °nice **4** °accomplished, °skillful, consummate, outstanding, masterly, °brilliant, °virtuoso **5** °delicate, °subtle, °exquisite, well-made, °dainty, °elegant; °superior, °excellent, °outstanding **6** °delicate, °dainty, °thin, gossamer, diaphanous, gauzy, °sheer, °slender, °frail, °flimsy, filamentous, threadlike **7** powdered, powdery, pulverized, comminuted, crushed, fine-grained **8** °sharp, °keen, keen-edged, razor-sharp, °pointed, °acute **9** °subtle, °delicate, °refined, °acute, °keen, °discriminating, °critical, °precise, °nice, °hairsplitting **10** good-looking, °handsome, °attractive, °striking, °beautiful, °pretty, °lovely, °seemly, °fair, °comely, *Colloq US* °cute, *Scots* °bonny **11** °meritorious, °worthy, commendable, °admirable, °excellent, °superb, °splendid, °good, *Colloq* °great **12** °healthy, °well, healthful, °robust, all right, *Colloq* OK *or* O.K. *or* okay **13** °close

fine[2] *n.* **1** °penalty, °charge, °fee, mulct, °forfeit, amercement; forfeiture *—v.* **2** °penalize, °charge, mulct, amerce

finery *n.* decoration(s), ornaments, °trappings, trinkets, frippery, showy dress, *Colloq* best bib and tucker, Sunday best, Sunday clothes, °gear, glad rags

finesse *n.* **1** artfulness, °subtlety, cunning, craftiness, cleverness, °strategy, shrewdness, °skill, °style, °dash, élan, °panache, °knack, skillfulness, °talent, adroitness, expertness, °expertise, adeptness, °proficiency, °ability, °facility **2** °trick, °artifice, °stratagem, °wile, °ruse, °scheme, °machination, °intrigue, °device, °expedient, °maneuver, °deception, °deceit **3** °tact, °diplomacy, °discretion, °grace, °taste, °delicacy, °polish, °refinement, °elegance *—v.* **4** °maneuver, °manipulate, °bluff, °trick, delude, °deceive, °fool, °outwit, °hoodwink, *Colloq* finagle, *Slang* con

finger *n.* **1** digit **2** ***have a finger in.*** be *or* become *or* get involved in, figure in, have a hand in, °influence, interfere in, tamper *or* meddle *or* tinker *or* monkey with **3** ***keep one's fingers crossed.*** hope *or* pray for the best, touch *or esp. US* knock wood **4** ***lay or put a finger on.*** °(so much as) touch, °strike, °hit, °punch **5** ***lay or put one's finger on.*** **(a)** °recall, °remember, °recollect, bring *or* call to mind, °think of, °pin down **(b)** °locate, °find, °discover, °unearth, lay *or* put one's hands on, °track down, get hold of, °come by, °acquire; °buy, °purchase **(c)** °indicate, °identify, °point to, °pin down, *Colloq* zero (in) on **6** ***(not) lift or raise (even) a (little) finger.*** make an attempt *or* effort, °offer, make a move, °contribute, do one's part, do anything *or* something **7** ***pull or get one's finger out.*** get on with it, stop delaying *or* procrastinating, *Colloq* get cracking **8** ***put the finger on.*** °accuse, inform on *or* against, tell *or* tattle on, °betray, °bear witness, *Slang* snitch *or* squeal on, peach on **9** ***slip through one's fingers.*** °elude, °escape, °get away, vanish, °disappear **10** ***twist or wrap around one's little finger.*** °control, °dominate, °lord it over, have under control, °manipulate, °maneuver, wield power *or* authority over, have under one's thumb, have the upper hand over, be master of, °influence, make subservient —*v.* **11** °touch, °handle, °feel; toy *or* play *or* fiddle with **12** °identify, °point out, °put the finger on

finicky *adj.* **1** finical, °fussy, °fastidious, °critical, °difficult, °meticulous, hard to please, (over)delicate, (over)dainty, (over)particular, overnice, overprecise, niminy-piminy, punctilious, (over)scrupulous, *Colloq* pernickety *or US also* persnickety, °choosy, nitpicking, picky **2** °fussy, °elaborate, °detailed, °fine, °delicate

finish *v.* **1** °stop, conclude, °end, °cease **2** °complete, °accomplish, °perfect, °achieve, °carry out, °fulfill, consummate, °clinch, write "finis" to, *Colloq* °wrap up **3** Sometimes, ***finish off.*** °dispose of, dispatch *or* despatch, °exhaust, °consume, eat *or* drink (up), °use (up), °devour, °drain, *Colloq* °polish off **4** Sometimes, ***finish off.*** °kill, °exterminate, annihilate, °destroy, °get rid of, °dispose of, dispatch *or* despatch, put an end to, administer *or* deliver *or* give the coup de grâce, bring down, °overcome, °beat, °defeat, °conquer, °best, worst, *Colloq* °polish off, °terminate, *Slang* °bump off, °rub out, *US* °waste, ice **5** Sometimes, ***finish up.*** conclude, °close, °terminate, °wind up, °end, *Colloq* °knock off **6** Sometimes, ***finish up.*** end up, °settle **7** Sometimes, ***finish off.*** °perfect, put the final touches on, °polish, put a finish on **8** ***finish with.*** °release, let go, have *or* be done with, °let loose, set free —*n.* **9** conclusion, °termination, °end, °close, closing, °completion, culmination, ending, finale, *Colloq* winding-up, *US* windup **10** °death, °killing, annihilation, extermination, °downfall, °destruction, °defeat **11** °polish, °surface, °texture

finite *adj.* °limited, bounded, °bound, restricted, delimited, numerable, countable

fire *n.* **1** flame(s), °blaze; conflagration, °holocaust, inferno **2** °feeling, °passion, °ardor, ardency, °fervor, fervency, °intensity, °vigor, °spirit, °energy, vim, vivacity, °sparkle, °animation, liveliness, °verve, °pep, élan, éclat, °dash, °vitality, °eagerness, °enthusiasm, fever, feverishness **3** firing, fusillade, °volley, barrage, bombardment, salvo, cannonade, shelling, broadside, °flak **4** ***hang fire.*** °delay, be delayed, be in abeyance, be suspended, be shelved, be put off, be postponed, be up in the air, *Colloq* be put on hold, be (put) on the back burner **5** ***on fire.*** afire, °burning, blazing, alight, aflame, °flaming; °ardent, °passionate, °fervent, fervid, hot-blooded, °intense, aroused, stirred, stimulated, °enthusiastic, fired up, °eager, inspired, °excited **6** ***play with fire.*** undertake a risk *or* hazard *or* peril, run a risk, risk (something *or* everything), imperil *or* endanger (something), tempt fate, live dangerously **7** ***set fire to.*** See **8,** below. —*v.* **8** **(a)** °set fire to, set afire, set on fire, ignite, set alight, °kindle, °spark (off), put to the torch, °burn, *Slang US* torch **(b)** Sometimes, ***fire up.*** inflame, impassion, °incite, °excite, °provoke, °foment, °whip up, °arouse, °rouse, °work up, fire up, enkindle, light a fire under, °stimulate, inspirit, °motivate, °move, °stir, °animate, °inspire, °awaken, °energize, °vitalize, vivify **9** °discharge, °shoot, let go (with), °launch, °propel, °throw, catapult, °hurl **10** detonate, °set off, ignite, °set fire to, °light, °let off **11** °discharge, °dismiss, oust, let go, cashier, give (someone) notice, *Brit* make *or* declare redundant, *Colloq Brit* ask for *or* get (someone's) cards, *US* give (someone) a pink slip; *Slang* °bounce, give (someone) the bounce, ax, give (someone) the ax, show (someone) the door, can, give (someone) the (old) heave-ho, give (someone) his *or* her (*Brit*) marching *or* (*US*) walking papers, *Brit* °sack, give (someone) the sack, boot (someone) out, give (someone) the boot

firm *adj.* **1** °compact, °solid, °dense, compressed, condensed, concentrated, °rigid, °stiff, °hard, unyielding, °inflexible, inelastic **2** °stable, °fixed, °fast, °secure, °steady, °solid, stationary, anchored, moored, unmovable, °immovable **3** °steady, °strong, °sturdy, °tight, unwavering, unshakable *or* unshakeable, unswerving **4** °resolute, °determined, dogged, °definite, resolved, °positive, decisive, °decided, set on *or* upon, °steadfast, °constant, unflinching, °staunch, unshaken, unshakable *or* unshakeable, °immovable, °inflexible, °rigid, unwavering, undeviating, unchanging, unchangeable, °obstinate, obdurate, °stubborn, °strict, unyielding, unbending, unalterable —*v.* **5** Often, ***firm up.*** consolidate, °establish, °settle (down), °solidify, °resolve, °determine, °set up —*n.* **6** °company, °organization, corporation, limited company, public limited company, plc, partnership, proprietorship, °business, °enterprise, °concern, °house, conglomerate, multinational (company), cartel, *Colloq* °outfit; *Jargon US* CIA, Central Intelligence Agency

firmament *n.* °heaven, the heavens, °sky, the skies, arch *or* vault of heaven, *Literary* welkin, empyrean

firmly *adv.* **1** solidly, strongly, securely, °tightly, rigidly, °fast, immovably **2** resolutely, steadfastly, determinedly, staunchly, unwaveringly, decisively, unhesitatingly, constantly

first *adj.* **1** °foremost, °leading, °chief, °head, °premier, °prime, °primary, °principal, °preeminent **2** earliest, °original, °senior, oldest; °initial, °beginning, °maiden, °opening **3** °fundamental, °elementary, °basic, °primary, °cardinal, °key, °essential *—adv.* **4** °before, °in front, earliest, beforehand, °ahead, sooner, °foremost **5** in the first place, firstly, before all *or* anything else, initially, at the outset *or* beginning, to begin *or* start with, from the start, *Colloq* first off *—n.* **6** °beginning, °start, inception, commencement, °outset, *Colloq* word "go" **7** first place, blue ribbon, gold (medal), °triumph, °victory; °win **8** ***at first.*** initially, in the beginning, at the start *or* outset, *Colloq* from the word "go"

first-rate *adj.* first-class, high-grade, °prime, °excellent, °superior, °superb, °great, °remarkable, °admirable, °fine, °exceptional, °outstanding, °extraordinary, °unparalleled, °matchless, unsurpassed, *Colloq* A-1 *or* A-one, topnotch, tiptop, °crack, °top, ace, *Brit* whiz-bang *or* whizz-bang, wizard

fiscal *adj.* °financial, °economic, budgetary, pecuniary, °monetary

fishy *adj.* **1** dubious, °doubtful, °questionable, °unlikely, °far-fetched, °suspicious, not kosher, °peculiar, °odd, °queer, °strange, °suspect, °improbable, °implausible, *Colloq* °shady, °funny **2** piscine, fishlike, piscatory, piscatorial

fit[1] *adj.* **1** °fitting, °appropriate, °fitted, °suitable, suited, adapted, apt, °meet, apropos, °applicable; °befitting, °becoming, °convenient, °proper, °right, °correct, °fitting **2** °prepared, °ready, °able, °capable, °qualified, °worthy, °right, °adequate **3** °healthy, °well, °hale, °hearty, °stalwart, °vigorous, °strong, °sturdy, °robust, strapping, able-bodied, in good shape *or* trim *or* condition, in fine fettle **4** °ready, °angry, troubled, °upset, °inclined, °disposed, ready *or* likely *or* about to *—v.* **5** befit, °suit, °become, be suited to, be suitable *or* appropriate for, °answer, °satisfy **6** °join, °conform, °go (together), °match, °correspond, dovetail, °tally **7** °adjust, °modify, °change, °adapt, °alter, °accommodate, °shape, °fashion **8** °equip, °supply, °furnish, °provide, °outfit, fit out *or* up, °install, °rig out, gear up

fit[2] *n.* **1** °attack, °seizure, convulsion, °spasm, °spell, °paroxysm, °bout, °throe **2** °outburst, outbreak, °paroxysm, °spell, °period **3** °tantrum; °eruption, °explosion **4** ***by fits and starts.*** sporadically, °occasionally, fitfully, spasmodically, intermittently, erratically, haphazardly, °now and then, irregularly, unsystematically; unreliably

fitful *adj.* °irregular, °sporadic, °intermittent, °occasional, °periodic, °erratic, °spasmodic, °haphazard, unsystematic, °changeable, °unstable, °capricious, varying, fluctuating, °variable, uneven

fitness *n.* **1** aptness, appropriateness, suitability, suitableness, competence, pertinence, seemliness; eligibility, adequacy, qualification(s) **2** °health, healthiness, (good) (physical) condition, °vigor, well-being, °(good) shape, (fine) fettle, °tone, wholesomeness, salubriousness *or* salubrity

fitted *adj.* custom-made, °tailor-made; tailored, bespoke

fitting *adj.* **1** °fit, °befitting, °suitable, °appropriate, °meet, °becoming, °proper, *comme il faut,* °seemly, apt, apropos, apposite, germane, °relevant *—n.* **2** ***fittings.*** fitments, attachments, accessories, °elements, pieces, parts, units, fixtures; appointments, extras, installations, furnishings, °trappings, °furniture, °equipment, accoutrements, °paraphernalia, trimmings

fix *v.* **1** affix, °pin, °fasten, make fast, °attach, °secure, °stick, °connect, °link, °tie, °couple, °clasp, °clamp, rivet, °cement, °weld, °fuse **2** °establish, °set, °settle, °agree to, °determine, °organize, stabilize, °firm up, °solidify, °decide, conclude, °arrive at, °define, °specify, °resolve, °arrange, °install, °institute **3** °repair, °mend, °fix up, °remedy, °rectify, °correct, emend, °adjust, °patch (up), °regulate, put *or* set to rights, °doctor, °straighten out **4** °hold, °fasten, °focus, °direct, °level, rivet, °concentrate, °freeze; fixate **5** °hold, rivet, spellbind, mesmerize, °hypnotize, °fascinate, °freeze, immobilize **6** °concentrate, °focus **7** °harden, congeal, °thicken, °set, consolidate, °solidify, rigidify, become rigid, °stiffen, °freeze **8** °establish, °set, °settle, °organize, °install, °situate, °locate, °position, °place **9** °impose, °assign, allocate, °attribute, ascribe, °specify, °pin, °attach, °fasten, °establish **10** °settle, °set, stabilize, °freeze, °solidify; conventionalize **11** °bribe, suborn, °buy (off), °corrupt, °influence, °manipulate, *Colloq* grease (someone's) palm **12** °arrange, prearrange, predetermine, °set up, contrive, *Colloq* °fiddle, °pull strings, °rig **13** desexualize, desex, °alter, °cut; castrate, emasculate, °see to, eunuchize, geld, caponize; spay, oophorectimize, ovariectomize **14** retaliate against, wreak vengeance on, hit *or* strike *or* get back at, °get even with, even the score with, make reprisal against, avenge oneself against, take revenge *or* retribution on *or* against, °repay, °pay back, *Colloq* settle (someone's) hash, cook (someone's) goose, sort (someone) out **15** ***fix on or upon.*** decide (on *or* upon), °set, agree (on *or* upon), °choose, °select, °settle (on), °determine, °finalize **16** ***fix up.*** **(a)** °furnish, °supply, °provide, °accommodate, °set up, *Brit* °lay on **(b)** (re)decorate, °furnish, °renovate, °restore, furbish, °refurbish; straighten out *or* up, °organize, do up, °set up **(c)** °clear up, °resolve, °reconcile, °sort out, °settle **(d)** °repair, °patch (up) *—n.* **17** °dilemma, °predicament, °difficulty, corner, double bind, catch-22, °quandary, °mess, °(bad) situation, strait(s), *Colloq* pickle, °jam, °hole, (tight *or* tough) spot, °pinch, *US* °bind **18** °arrangement, prearrangement, °fiddle; bribery, subornation; *Slang chiefly US and Canadian* °setup

fixation *n.* °mania, °obsession, compulsion,

fixed idea, *idée fixe,* °fetish, monomania, preoccupation, infatuation, *Colloq* hang-up, °thing, °kick

fixed *adj.* 1 fastened, °attached, anchored, °set, secure(d), °firm, °stable, settled, °immovable, immobile, stationary, °rigid, °rooted, °solid; immobilized, stuck 2 established, °secure, unalterable, °steadfast, °set, °firm, unchangeable, unchanging, °persistent, unfluctuating, unflagging, unwavering, °inflexible, undeviating, unflinching, unblinking, °rigid, °rooted, immutable, °definite, °resolute, resolved, °determined, °intent; °obstinate, °stubborn 3 settled, resolved, agreed, °regular, °habitual, °decided, arranged, prearranged, °definite, established 4 arranged, prearranged, set-up, framed; °crooked, °dishonest, °bent, *Colloq* rigged, °put-up

fixture *n.* 1 °meet, °meeting, °event, °match, °occasion, °occurrence 2 appliance, accessory *or* accessary, °fitting, °equipment, °apparatus, °device, °instrument, °tool, °gadget, contrivance, appendage, fitment

fizz *v.* 1 °bubble, effervesce, °sparkle, °froth, °fizzle; °hiss, sputter, sizzle —*n.* 2 effervescence, °sparkle, carbonation, bubbling, °froth, °fizzle, fizziness 3 °hiss, hissing, sibilance 4 *US* soda, soda water, club soda, seltzer, *Dialect* °plain; soft drink, °tonic 5 champagne, *Colloq Brit* champers

fizzle *v.* 1 °fizz 2 Often, ***fizzle out.*** die (out *or* away), fizz out, °expire, °peter out, come to nothing *or* naught, °fail, °fall through, °miscarry, abort, °come to grief, °misfire, °collapse, °cave in —*n.* 3 failure, misfire, *Colloq* damp squib, washout, flop, dud

flabby *adj.* 1 °limp, °loose, °lax, flaccid, °slack, floppy, sagging, drooping, baggy, °pendulous, quaggy, °soft 2 °weak, °spineless, °feeble, °impotent, °ineffective, °ineffectual

flag[1] *n.* 1 °banner, ensign, °standard, °pennant, banneret, pennon, °streamer, bunting, jack, gonfalon, vexillum —*v.* 2 Often, ***flag down.*** °warn, °signal, °hail, °inform, °stop 3 °mark, °tag, °label, °tab, °identify, *Brit* tick (off), *US and Canadian* °check (off)

flag[2] *v.* 1 °droop, °sag, °dangle, hang down, swag, festoon 2 °weaken, languish, falter, °fail, °dwindle, °fade, °deteriorate, °waste away, °degenerate, °die, °decline, °diminish, °decrease, lessen, abate, °peter out, °taper off, °let up, °ease (up), °subside, °slump, °fall off, °wane, °ebb, °sink, °lag

flagrant *adj.* °blatant, °brazen, °bold, °barefaced, °audacious, arrant, °glaring, °outrageous, °shocking, °shameless, °scandalous, °atrocious, °infamous, °notorious, °defiant, egregious, °obvious, °conspicuous, °open, °complete, °out-and-out, utter, flagitious, °monstrous, heinous, °cruel, °villainous, treacherous, nefarious, °awful, °gross, °rank, °inconsiderate, °scornful, °contemptuous; reprehensible; °contemptible

flair *n.* 1 °talent, °ability, °aptitude, °feel, °knack, °genius, °skill, °mind, °gift, °faculty, propensity, °bent, proclivity, °facility 2 °chic, °panache, °dash, élan, éclat, °style, stylishness, °glamour, °verve, °sparkle, °vitality, °elegance, °taste, *Colloq* savvy, pizzazz *or* pizazz, *Old-fashioned* oomph

flak *n.* flack, °criticism, °disapproval, censure, °abuse, °blame, °aspersion, complaint(s), disapprobation, condemnation, *Colloq* brickbats

flake *n.* 1 snowflake; °scale, °chip, °bit, °piece, °scrap, °particle, tuft, °flock, scurf, °fragment, shaving, °sliver; wafer, lamina, *Technical* squama —*v.* 2 Often, ***flake off.*** °scale, °chip, °fragment; *Technical* desquamate, exfoliate 3 ***flake out.*** (a) °collapse, go to *or* fall asleep, drop off (to sleep), °pass out, keel over (b) become flaky, act crazy

flamboyant *adj.* 1 °elaborate, ornamented, °ornate, decorated, embellished, baroque, rococo, florid 2 °extravagant, °ostentatious, °showy, °gaudy, °flashy, °dazzling, °brilliant, °splendid, °dashing, °rakish, °swashbuckling, °jaunty; °high, °wide, handsome

flame *n.* 1 °fire, °blaze; conflagration 2 °passion, °fervor, °ardor, °intensity, °warmth, °fire, zeal, feverishness, °enthusiasm, °eagerness 3 boyfriend, girlfriend, °lover, heartthrob, °sweetheart, beau —*v.* 4 °burn, °blaze, °glow, °flare

flaming *adj.* °obvious, °conspicuous, °blatant, °flagrant, egregious, °extravagant, *Slang* bloody, bleeding, blasted, damned, blooming

flammable *adj.* °inflammable, combustible, burnable

flank *n.* 1 °side, °quarter; loin, haunch —*v.* 2 °edge, °border, °line 3 skirt, outmaneuver, outflank, °circle, go (a)round

flannel *n.* 1 °flattery, humbug, °nonsense, blarney, °rubbish, prevarication, *Colloq* eyewash, hogwash, baloney *or* boloney, soft soap, weasel words, sweet talk, bull, crap, *Brit* °waffle, cock, *US* bushwa; *Taboo slang* bullshit, horseshit, (load of) shit, *Brit* codswallop, bollocks *or* ballocks —*v.* 2 °flatter, hedge, °mislead, pull the wool over (someone's) eyes, *Colloq* soft-soap, sweet-talk, *Taboo slang* bullshit, horseshit, shit

flap *v.* 1 °slap, slat, °beat, flail, °wave, °wag, waggle, °flutter, thresh, thrash, °oscillate, °vibrate —*n.* 2 flapping, °beat, °wave, °wag, waggle, °flutter, oscillation 3 °fold, °fly, lappet, °lap, °tail, °tab 4 °upset, °agitation, to-do, ado, commotion, °panic, °flurry, °fuss, °distress, *Colloq* °state, tizzy, °sweat, *Brit* kerfuffle 5 °quarrel, °argument, °dispute

flare *v.* 1 Often, ***flare up.*** blaze *or* flame (up), °flash, °erupt, °break out; °dazzle, °flicker, glimmer, °shimmer, °flutter 2 Often, ***flare out.*** spread (out *or* outwards), °widen, broaden, °expand, °increase, °enlarge, °bulge, °swell 3 Often, ***flare up.*** °anger, lose one's temper, °chafe, °seethe, °fume, °rage, throw a tantrum, become incensed *or* angry; °blow up, burst forth,

°erupt, °explode; *Colloq* get one's back up, get one's Irish *or* dander up, see red, get worked up, °fly off the handle, lose one's cool, go out of *or* lose control, get hot under the collar, blow one's top —*n.* **4** °blaze, °flame, °burst, °outburst, °flash, °glare, °dazzle, incandescence, °brilliance, luminosity **5** °beacon, °light, °signal, torch, flambeau, °link **6** °spread, broadening, widening, °expansion, °swelling, °bulge, °increase, enlargement

flash *n.* **1** °blaze, °flame, °flare, °burst, °dazzle, °spark, °sparkle, coruscation, fulguration, °glitter, °twinkle, °twinkling, °flicker, flickering, scintilla, scintillation, glint, °shimmer, glimmer, °gleam, °beam, °ray, °shaft **2** (sudden *or* momentary) display, °stroke, °show, °manifestation, °outburst, outbreak, °sign, °indication, °exhibition; °touch, °hint, °suggestion **3** °moment, °(split) second, °instant, °twinkling (of an eye), trice, °minute, *Colloq* two shakes (of a lamb's tail), jiffy, °shake, before one can *or* could say Jack Robinson —*v.* **4** °burn, °blaze, °flame, °flare, °burst (out), °dazzle, °spark, °sparkle, coruscate, fulgurate, °glitter, °twinkle, °flicker, scintillate, °shimmer, glimmer, °gleam, °beam, °glare, °shine **5** °race, °speed, °dash, °streak, flick, °tear, °rush, °hurry, °hasten, °fly, zoom, °shoot, °bolt, whistle; °run, sprint, dart, scuttle, scamper, *Colloq* scoot, skedaddle, °take off, whizz *or* whiz —*adj.* **6** °dazzling, °showy, °ostentatious, °smart, °chic, *Colloq* °swish, classy, ritzy, snazzy **7** See **flashy, 1.**

flashy *adj.* **1** °flash, °gaudy, °flamboyant, °glaring, fulgurous, °showy, °ostentatious, °loud, °garish, °vulgar, °cheap, meretricious, °pretentious, °tawdry, °tasteless, *Colloq* °tacky, *Slang* jazzy, *US* glitzy **2** °superficial, cosmetic, °skin-deep, °surface, °shallow, °glib, °slick, facile, °insubstantial, °thin

flat *adj.* **1** °level, °horizontal, °even, °smooth, °plane, unbroken, uninterrupted **2** °prostrate, °prone, °supine, °lying (down), stretched out, °recumbent, outstretched, reclining, spread-eagle(d), °spread out, outspread **3** collapsed, leveled, overthrown, laid low **4** °downright, °outright, °unqualified, unreserved, unconditional, °absolute, °categorical, °explicit, °definite, °firm, °positive, °out-and-out, unequivocal, °peremptory, unambiguous, unmistakable, °direct, °complete, °total **5** featureless, °monotonous, °dull, °dead, uninteresting, unexciting, °vapid, °bland, °empty, two-dimensional, insipid, °boring, °tiresome, °lifeless, spiritless, °lackluster, °prosaic, °stale, °tired, °dry, jejune **6** deflated, collapsed, punctured, ruptured, blown out **7** unchangeable, unchanging, °invariable, unvaried, unvarying, °standard, °fixed, unmodified, unmodifiable, *Colloq US* cookie-cutter **8** °dead, insipid, °stale, °tasteless, flavorless, °unpalatable; decarbonated, noneffervescent **9** °exact, °precise **10** °definite, °certain, °sure, °irrevocable **11** °dull, °slow, sluggish, °inactive, depressed **12** °dull, mat *or* matt *or* matte, unshiny, nongloss(y), nonreflective, nonglare, unpolished **13** lacking perspective, two-dimensional, °lifeless, °unrealistic —*n.* **14** Often, ***flats.*** **(a)** *US* low shoes, loafers, sandals, *Colloq* flatties **(b)** lowland(s), plain(s), tundra, steppe(s), prairie(s), savannah, heath, °moor, pampas; mudflat(s); shallow(s), shoal, strand; °marsh, °bog, fen, °swamp **15** apartment, room(s), °suite (of rooms), *Chiefly US and Canadian* garden apartment, maisonette, penthouse, studio (apartment), walk-up, duplex, triplex, *Brit* bed-sitter, bedsit, *Colloq Brit* digs —*adv.* **16** °absolutely, °completely, categorically, °utterly, °wholly, uncompromisingly, irrevocably, °positively, °definitely, °directly; °exactly, °precisely, flatly **17** ***flat out.*** **(a)** at maximum *or* top *or* full *or* breakneck speed, speedily, °quickly, apace, °on the run, °rapidly, °swiftly, at full speed *or* gallop, °posthaste, hell-for-leather, like a bat out of hell, °like a shot, like (greased) lightning, like the wind **(b)** flatly, unhesitatingly, °directly, °at once, °immediately, forthwith, without delay; plainly, °openly, baldly, brazenly, brashly

flatten *v.* **1** level *or* even (off *or* out); °smooth (out), press *or* iron (out), °roll **2** knock down *or* over, °knock out, °floor, °prostrate **3** °raze, tear down, °demolish, °level

flatter *v.* **1** butter up, °play up to, °compliment, °praise, fawn (on *or* upon), toady to, truckle to, court, curry favor with, *Colloq* °flannel, soft-soap, °oil; *Slang* shine *or* suck up to, bootlick, *Taboo* kiss (someone's) *Brit* arse *or US* ass, brown-nose **2** °enhance, °complement, °suit, show to advantage **3** °cajole, °wheedle, °coax, inveigle, °beguile, sweet-talk

flatterer *n.* toady, sycophant, fawner, wheedler, time-server, courtier, back-scratcher, sponge, °parasite, leech, °hanger-on, sweet-talker, backslapper, truckler, lickspittle, *Colloq* °yes man; *Slang* bootlicker, *Taboo* brown-noser, *Brit* arse-kisser, arse-licker, bumsucker, *US* ass-kisser, ass-licker

flattering *adj.* **1** °complimentary, °becoming, °kind, enhancing **2** adulatory, °laudatory, gratifying, fulsome, honeyed, sugary, fawning, °ingratiating, unctuous, °slimy, *Chiefly Brit* smarmy

flattery *n.* adulation, °cajolery, blandishment, sweet talk, beguilement, wheedling, gloze, *Colloq* soft soap, *Slang* bootlicking, *Taboo* brown-nosing, *Brit* arse-kissing, arse-licking, bumsucking, *US* ass-kissing, ass-licking

flaunt *v.* °display, °show (off), °parade, °flourish, °exhibit, °sport, disport, °spotlight

flavor *n.* **1** °taste, °savor, °tang, piquancy, °zest; tastiness, savoriness; °essence, °extract, °seasoning, flavoring, °spice; °aroma, °odor, °scent; *Rare* sapor **2** °character, °spirit, °nature, °quality, °property, °mark,

°stamp, °essence, °characteristic, °style, °taste, °feel, °feeling, ambiance *or* ambience, °sense, tinge, °aroma, °air, °atmosphere, °hint, °suggestion, °touch, soupçon —*v.* **3** °season, °spice

flaw *n.* **1** °fault, °defect, °imperfection, °error, °mistake, °blemish, °blot, °stain, °taint, °(black) mark, °damage, disfigurement, °failing, °weakness, weak spot; °loophole **2** °crack, °break, °breach, °chink, °chip, °fracture, °rupture, fissure, cleft, °split, °slit, °cut, °gash, °rent, °rift, °tear, °rip, °puncture, °hole, perforation —*v.* **3** °damage, °harm, °spoil, °ruin, °mark, °weaken, disfigure **4** °discredit, °stigmatize, °damage, °hurt, °harm; °taint, °mar, °stain, °blot

flawed *adj.* damaged, harmed, marred, weakened, tainted, stained, tarnished, °defective, °imperfect, °unsound, °faulty

flawless *adj.* **1** °perfect, °pristine, °pure, uncorrupted, °chaste, virgin, °intact, °whole, °clean, °immaculate, unsullied, unspoiled *or* unspoilt, unsoiled, °impeccable, unblemished, °faultless, undamaged, unimpaired, °spotless, °untarnished **2** undeniable, unassailable, unimpeachable, °unquestionable, irrefutable, °foolproof, °sound, °demonstrable

flecked *adj.* spotted, dappled, pied, (be)speckled, (be)sprinkled, dotted, °marked, stippled, dusted, specked, spattered, freckled

flee *v.* **1** °quit, run away *or* off, °escape, °get away, °fly, °take flight, °bolt, °go (away), decamp, abscond, seek safety, °avoid, °make off, make an exit, make (good) one's escape, make a (clean) getaway, beat a (hasty) retreat, °take to one's heels, show a clean pair of heels, °turn tail, make tracks, make a run for it, cut and run, vanish, °disappear, *Brit* levant, *Colloq* °take off, scoot, make oneself scarce, °beat it, °clear out, fly the coop, skedaddle, scram, *Brit* scarper, *Australian and New Zealand* shoot through, *US and Canadian* take a (runout) powder, °skip (town), °cut out, hightail it, *Old-fashioned* skiddoo; *Slang* °split, *Brit* °bugger off, do a moonlight flit, do a bunk, *US and Canadian* vamoose, lam out, take it on the lam, °blow, bail out **2** °avoid, °evade, °shun, escape from, eschew

fleece *v.* °cheat, overcharge, °swindle, bilk, °defraud, °victimize, °plunder, °strip, °milk, °rob, *Colloq* °take, flimflam, gyp, diddle, bleed, take for a ride *or* to the cleaners, *Slang* °rip off, °chisel, °pluck, rook, °clip, °soak

fleet[1] *n.* armada, flotilla, °navy, naval (task) force, task force, squadron, convoy, °division

fleet[2] *adj.* °swift, °rapid, °fast, °speedy, °quick, °nimble, °expeditious, °agile

fleeting *adj.* transitory, °fugitive, °transient, °temporary, °passing, ephemeral, fugacious, evanescent, °momentary, °short-lived, °fly-by-night, °short, °brief

flesh *n.* **1** °meat; °tissue, muscle **2** °body, corporeality, °flesh and blood, human nature, physicality; mortality **3** ***flesh and blood.*** °real, °physical, corporeal, °human, °natural **4** ***in the flesh.*** °personally, °in person, °really, physically, bodily, °alive, living, in life **5** ***one's (own) flesh and blood.*** °kin, kinfolk *or Brit* kinsfolk, °family, °stock, blood, kith and kin, relatives, °relations —*v.* **6** ***flesh out.*** °substantiate, fill (in *or* out), give *or* lend substance *or* dimension to, °incorporate, °embody, °color

flex *n.* **1** wire, °lead, °cord, °cable, °extension —*v.* **2** °bend, °give, °stretch, curve **3** °exercise, °tense, °tighten, °contract

flexibility *n.* **1** pliability, pliancy *or* pliantness, °elasticity, resilience *or* resiliency, suppleness, flexibleness, bendability, limberness, °stretch, °give, °spring, springiness, ductility **2** conformability *or* conformableness, adaptability, versatility, adjustability *or* adjustableness, compliance *or* compliancy, manageability, tractability *or* tractableness, malleability, °obedience, submissiveness, docility, agreeableness, conformity

flexible *adj.* **1** °pliable, pliant, °elastic, resilient, °supple, bendable, limber, lithe, stretchy, stretchable, springy, extensible *or* extensile, ductile, flexile, tensile, °yielding, °willowy **2** modifiable, °adaptable, conformable, compliant, malleable, °obedient, °tractable, °manageable, cooperative, amenable, persuadable *or* persuasible **3** °easy, facile, °submissive, complaisant, docile

flicker *v.* **1** °twinkle, °blink, waver, glimmer, glint, °sparkle, °shimmer, °flare, gutter **2** °flap, °flutter, °quiver, °twitter, °fluctuate, °oscillate, °shake, °tremble, °vibrate —*n.* **3** glimmer, glint, glimmering, °sparkle, °spark, °twinkle, °twinkling, °gleam, °flare, °glare **4** °hint, °suggestion, °trace, glimmer, °vestige, scintilla, °spark

flight[1] *n.* **1** flying, soaring, winging, °excursion **2** (air) voyage *or* journey *or* trip **3** airplane, airliner, °plane, aircraft **4** °flock, °swarm, cloud, covey (of grouse *or* partridge), bevy (of quail), skein (of geese), exaltation (of larks) **5** feather

flight[2] *n.* **1** °escape, °retreat, departure, °exit, exodus, °getaway, fleeing, bolting, *Slang* °split **2** ***put to flight.*** chase *or* drive (off *or* away), °disperse, send off *or* away, send packing, °dismiss, °rout, °stampede **3** ***take flight.*** °flee, go *or* run away *or* off, abscond, °desert, °depart, °(beat a) retreat, °exit, °bolt, decamp, °withdraw, °take to one's heels, show a clean pair of heels, *Colloq* light out, shove off, *Brit* scarper, *US* take a (runout) powder, take it on the lam, lam out; *Slang* °split, *Brit* do a bunk, do a moonlight flit, °bugger off

flighty *adj.* **1** °fickle, °frivolous, °inconstant, °capricious, °fanciful, °changeable, °variable, mercurial, skittish, °volatile, °unstable, unsteady, °giddy, °wild **2** °irresponsible, lightheaded, rattlebrained, °silly, °harebrained, °dizzy, °crazy, °mad, °reckless,

°thoughtless, *Colloq* nutty, screwy, dotty, dippy

flimsy *adj.* **1** °slight, °frail, °weak, insubstantial *or* unsubstantial, °feeble, °makeshift, °fragile, frangible, breakable, °rickety, °ramshackle, °dilapidated, jerry-built, gimcrack, °slight, °delicate **2** °slight, trivial, °paltry, °feeble, unconvincing, °weak, °makeshift, °implausible, °unbelievable, °unsatisfactory, insubstantial *or* unsubstantial, °poor, °inadequate **3** °sheer, °light, gauzy, °transparent, °thin, °filmy, diaphanous, gossamer, °delicate

flinch *v.* wince, °draw back, °withdraw, cower, °cringe, °recoil, °start, quail, blench, °shrink (from), shy (away) (from), °dodge, °duck, *Colloq* bat an eye

fling *v.* **1** °toss, °pitch, °throw, °cast, °hurl, °heave, °sling, °propel, °fire, °let fly, °send, *Colloq* °lob, chuck —*n.* **2** °indulgence, debauch, binge, °spree, °party, *Colloq* blow-off **3** °gamble, °risk, °venture, °attempt, °try, °go, °shot, *Colloq* °crack, whirl, bash

flip *v.* **1** °toss, flick, °snap, °flop, °turn, °twist, °spin **2** °anger, become angry *or* furious, go mad, go crazy, go berserk, *US also* flip out, *Colloq* go off the deep end, lose one's cool, *Slang* flip one's lid *or Brit* top, °freak, *US* freak out, lose it

flippancy *n.* **1** frivolousness, facetiousness, °levity, lightheartedness, frivolity, jocularity, offhandedness, unseriousness **2** °disrespect, disrespectfulness, °impudence, °impertinence, irreverence, sauciness, rudeness, discourtesy, brazenness, brashness, pertness, insolence, *Colloq* cheek, cheekiness, lip, °mouth, *Slang Brit* °side

flippant *adj.* **1** °frivolous, facetious, lighthearted, jocular, offhand(ed), unserious, °shallow, °thoughtless, °superficial; °supercilious, belittling, °scornful, dismissive **2** °disrespectful, °impudent, °impertinent, °irreverent, saucy, °rude, °pert, °discourteous, °brazen, °brash, °insolent, *Colloq* °cheeky, °flip

flirt *v.* **1** coquette, play *or* act the coquette, °tease, °tantalize, °toy, °lead on, dally, philander, *Colloq Brit* °chat up; *Slang US* come on to **2** ***flirt with.*** trifle *or* toy *or* play *or* tinker with, °contemplate, °consider, °entertain, give a thought to, think about *or* of, *Colloq Brit* try on —*n.* **3** coquette, °tease, vamp, hussy, playgirl, minx; °philanderer, °playboy, *Slang* lady-killer, *Old-fashioned* wolf, sheik, masher, lounge lizard, *Taboo slang* cockteaser, prickteaser

flirtatious *adj.* coquettish, vampish, °seductive, flirty, °coy, philandering, °provocative, enticing, alluring, amorous, come-hither

flit *v.* °move, °go, °fly, °flee, dart, °skip, °skim, flick, °hop, °whisk, °flutter, °flash

float *v.* **1** °hover, °poise, bob, °waft, be suspended, °hang; °sail, °drift, °glide, swim **2** °launch, °establish, °set up, °organize, °found, °initiate, get going *or* moving **3** °negotiate, °arrange, °transact, bring *or* carry off, °get, °effect, consummate, *Colloq* °pull off, °swing —*n.* **4** raft, *Brit* °platform **5** °buoy; pontoon **6** (parade) exhibit *or* display

flock *n.* **1** °body, °company, °group, °band, °pack, °bunch, troop, °set, °collection, °assembly, convoy, °gathering, congregation, °crowd, °mass, °mob, °throng, °gang, multitude, °number, °quantity, °host, horde, °swarm, drove; °herd, °flight, troupe, °fleet, °school; bevy —*v.* **2** °assemble, °meet, °collect, °gather, come *or* go together, congregate, °crowd, °mass, °mob, °throng, °pour, °flood, °swarm, °herd (together), °band together, °go; *Colloq* gang up

flog *v.* **1** °whip, °lash, horsewhip, strap, flagellate, flay, °scourge, thrash, thresh, °beat; °chastise, °castigate, °punish **2** °sell; °promote, °publicize

flood *n.* **1** inundation, deluge, overflow(ing), debacle **2** °torrent, cataract, freshet, overflow, °stream, °spate **3** °abundance, deluge, overflowing, °surge, °outpouring, °torrent, tide, tidal wave, °stream, °rush, °flow, °glut, °surfeit, °satiety, °profusion, overabundance, superabundance, nimiety, plethora, °excess, °surplus, °superfluity —*v.* **4** inundate, °submerge, overflow, °swamp, °immerse, deluge, pour over, °drown **5** °overwhelm, °glut, oversupply, °saturate, °choke **6** °sweep, °flow, °swarm, °surge, °rush, °crowd, °pour **7** °permeate, °fill, engulf, °cover, pour into *or* throughout *or* over

floor *n.* **1** flooring, parquet, boarding, planking, *Nautical or colloq* deck **2** °story, °level; deck **3** °minimum, °bottom, °base, lower limit, lowest (level) —*v.* **4** knock over *or* down, bowl over, °prostrate, °fell, °overthrow, bring down, °(make) fall; °beat, °defeat, °conquer, °destroy, °rout, °overwhelm, °crush, °whip, trounce, thrash, drub, °best, worst **5** °stump, °bewilder, baffle, dumfound *or* dumbfound, °confuse, confound, disconcert, °nonplus, °perplex, °puzzle, °astound, °astonish, °amaze, °surprise, °shock

flop *v.* **1** °collapse, °drop (down), °fall (down), °tumble, °topple, plump down, plop down, flounce down **2** °flap, °wave, °swing **3** °fail, °fall flat, come to naught *or* nothing, °founder, *Colloq* °fold, *US* °bomb —*n.* **4** °failure, °fiasco, °disaster, nonstarter, debacle, *US* °fizzle, *Colloq* °dud, °washout, clanger, *US* lead balloon, °bomb; *Slang* lemon, *Brit* cock-up, damp squib

flounce *n.* **1** °frill, furbelow, peplum, °ruffle, °ornament, valance, trimming —*v.* **2** °fling, °toss, °bounce, °twist, °strut, °parade, °march, °storm, °stamp, *US* sashay

flounder *v.* °grope, °blunder, °stumble, °tumble, °struggle, °stagger, plunge about

flourish *v.* **1** °prosper, °thrive, °grow, °develop, °luxuriate, bloom, blossom, °flower, bear fruit, fructify, °boom, burgeon *or* bourgeon, °mature, °ripen, °increase, °succeed, °get ahead, do *or* fare well, °make good; go up *or* rise in the world; *Slang* go great guns **2** °wave, °wield, brandish, °wag, °swing, °twirl, °flaunt, vaunt, °swagger, °swish,

°shake —*n*. 3 °decoration, °embellishment, floridness, floweriness, ornamentation, °elaboration, adornment, °frill, embroidery, curlicue, furbelow 4 °fanfare, °display, °show, showiness, °dash, gesturing, °wave

flourishing *adj*. °luxuriant, °lush, thriving, prospering, blooming, blossoming, °fruitful, flowering, burgeoning *or* bourgeoning, °successful, °prosperous, booming, growing, increasing

flout *v*. °deride, °scorn, disdain, contemn, °spurn, decry, °denounce, misprize, °blaspheme, °depreciate, °degrade, abase, °belittle, °minimize, deprecate, °disparage, denigrate, °mock, °jeer, °guy, °ridicule, °scoff, °sneer, gibe *or* jibe (at), °taunt, °twit, °insult, affront, *Archaic* fleer; *Colloq* °put down, °chaff, °rag, °knock

flow *v*. 1 °stream, °pour, °run, °rush, °course, °surge, °move, °go, °proceed, °progress, °drift; °gush, °glide, purl, °roll, °ripple, °trickle, °gurgle, °bubble; °swirl, whirl, °circulate 2 °rush, °gush, °surge, °well (forth), °stream, °spring, °issue, °spout, °spurt, squirt, °spew, °flood, cascade, °fall, °rain; °brim, overflow, °spill, °teem 3 °issue, °originate, °come, °emanate, °rise, °begin 4 °spread, overspread, °cover —*n*. 5 °rush, °gush, °surge; °current, °course, °stream, °run, °movement, °drift 6 °abundance, superabundance, °flood, plethora, °excess, overflow(ing), deluge, tide, °supply; °plenty

flower *n*. 1 blossom, bloom, floret *or* floweret, bud, *Technical* efflorescence 2 cream, °best, °pick, elite *or* élite, crème de la crème, finest, choicest —*v*. 3 blossom, bloom, bud, burgeon *or* bourgeon, °come out, °open, °unfold, *Technical* effloresce

flowery *adj*. florid, °ornate, °fancy, elaborate(d), decorated, ornamented, °overwrought, embellished, rococo, baroque, arabesque, euphuistic, Gongoristic, Ossianic, grandiloquent, °bombastic, °inflated, °pompous, °affected, °artificial, high-flown, °showy

fluctuate *v*. °vary, °change, °alternate, °seesaw, °swing, vacillate, undulate, waver, °oscillate, °shift

fluctuation *n*. Sometimes, ***fluctuations***. variation(s), change(s), alternation(s), vacillation(s), swing(s), wavering(s), oscillation(s), undulation(s), ups and downs, instability, unsteadiness, °inconstancy

fluency *n*. articulateness, eloquence, °control, °command, °ease, °grace, effortlessness, °facility, felicity, smoothness, °polish, slickness, glibness, volubility

fluent *adj*. articulate, °eloquent, well-spoken, felicitous, °graceful, facile, °easy, °natural, °effortless, °ready, °smooth, °polished, flowing, °voluble, °glib, °slick; °expressive

fluff *n*. 1 down, fuzz, feather(s), thistledown, floss, lint, dust, dustball, fuzzball 2 ***bit of fluff***. poppet, °girl (friend), °mistress, *Slang* bit of all right, (bit of) crumpet, (bit of) skirt *or* stuff, *Old-fashioned Brit* popsy 3 °blunder, °error, °slip, °mistake, *Colloq* °howler, *Brit* bloomer, *US and Canadian* blooper —*v*. 4 °muddle, °spoil, °ruin, make a mess of, °bungle, °botch, *Colloq* °foul up, °screw up, °mess up, *US* snafu, *Slang Brit* cock up, *US* ball up, *Taboo* fuck up 5 ***fluff up***. °puff up, shake out *or* up, aerate

fluffy *adj*. 1 °soft, downy, puffy, whipped up, °light, airy, feathery, wispy 2 °frivolous, °superficial, trivial, unimportant, airy, °thin, lightweight, °light, °insubstantial, gossamer, *Brit* airy-fairy

fluid *n*. 1 °liquid, °solution, °liquor, ichor; gas, °vapor —*adj*. 2 °liquid, flowing, °running, runny, °watery, aqueous 3 °changeable, mutable, °flexible, adjustable, °variable, pliant, unformed, formless, unfixed, unstatic *or* nonstatic, °plastic, °protean, mercurial, °mobile, °unstable, shifting, °uncertain, °indefinite, °unsettled

fluke *n*. lucky *or* successful stroke, stroke of (good) luck, lucky *or* big break, °(happy) accident, quirk *or* twist of fate, °windfall, fortuity, serendipity

flummox *v*. °confuse, baffle, °perplex, °bewilder, confound, throw into confusion, °stymie, °stump, °puzzle, °mystify, fox, °deceive, °hoodwink, °nonplus

flunky *n*. 1 °servant, retainer, lackey, footman, °menial, minion, hireling, underling, °subordinate, °inferior; °slave; *Colloq* dogsbody, *Slang US and Canadian* gofer 2 toady, °hanger-on, yesman, jackal, doormat, stooge, lick-spittle, sycophant, *Colloq US and Canadian* apple-polisher, *Taboo* brown-noser

flurry *n*. 1 °activity, commotion, ado, to-do, °fuss, °upset, hubbub, pother, °stir, °excitement, °disturbance, °agitation, °tumult, whirl, °furor, bustle, °hurry, °hustle, °flutter, °fluster; °burst, °outburst; *Colloq* tizzy —*v*. 2 °confuse, °bewilder, °agitate, °put out, °disturb, °excite, °fluster, disconcert, °upset, °perturb, unsettle, °shake (up), *Colloq* °rattle

flush[1] *v*. 1 °blush, redden, crimson, °glow, °burn, °color (up) 2 Often, ***flush out***. °rinse, wash (out *or* away), douse, douche, hose down, °flood, °drench, °clean out, °cleanse, °purge, °discharge, °empty 3 °animate, °stir, °inflame, impassion, °quicken, °arouse, °excite, elate, °encourage, °cheer, °delight, °thrill, °gladden —*n*. 4 °blush, redness, bloom, rosiness, °color, blood, °glow, °radiance 5 °flood, deluge, drenching, °soaking, overflow, inundation, °rush, °gush, °surge, °stream, °flow 6 °thrill, °excitement, °passion, quickening, arousal, °stir, °stirring, °animation, elation, euphoria, °delight, °encouragement, °thrill, tingle

flush[2] *adj*. 1 (on the same) plane *or* level (with), °even, °smooth, °flat, °square, °true, °continuous; adjacent, next to 2 °full, overflowing, °replete, °abundant 3 °solvent, well-supplied, °comfortable; well-to-do, °well-off, well-found, °wealthy, °rich, °prosperous, affluent, moneyed, *Colloq* well-heeled, on Easy Street, °in the money, *US* in the chips; *Slang* °loaded, rolling (in money *or* it) —*adv*. 4

even(ly), square(ly), levelly, °plumb, °directly

fluster *v.* **1** °agitate, °stir (up), discompose, °discomfit, °discomfort, disconcert, °shake (up), °upset, disquiet, discommode, °bother, put out *or* off, °disturb, °perturb, °flurry, °flutter, make nervous, °throw off, °distract, °confuse, baffle, confound, °puzzle, °perplex, befuddle, °bewilder, °daze, °dazzle, *Colloq* °rattle, °throw, hassle, faze, *US* discombobulate —*n.* **2** °agitation, °upset, °discomfort, disquiet, °bother, °disturbance, commotion, perturbation, dither, °flurry, °flutter, nervousness, °distraction, °confusion, bafflement, befuddlement, °perplexity, bewilderment

flutter *v.* **1** °flap, °flop, °fluctuate, vacillate, °wave, waver, °oscillate **2** °flit, °flicker, flitter, °hover, °dance; °fuss **3** °tremble, °shake, °quiver, dither, °jump, °vibrate, twitch —*n.* **4** fluttering, flapping, flopping, °fluctuation, fluctuating, vacillation, vacillating, °wave, waving, oscillation, oscillating, trembling, °quiver, quivering **5** See **fluster, 2.**

flux *n.* instability, °change, °mutation, modification, °fluctuation, °unrest, °swing, °swinging, wavering, °movement, °motion, oscillation, °indecision, indecisiveness

fly *v.* **1** take wing, °take flight, take to the air, wing, °soar, °sail, °hover; °flutter, °flit, °flap **2** Also, ***fly away or off.*** °take flight, °depart, °leave, °flee, decamp, °bolt, run away *or* off, °escape, make (good) one's escape, °take to one's heels, show a clean pair of heels, rush *or* nip off *or* out *or* away, °(make a) run (for it), go *or* get away *or* off, abscond, make a getaway, cut and run, beat a (hasty) retreat, °take off, scoot, *Colloq* light out, °beat it, clear out *or* off, skedaddle, scram, *US* °cut out, hightail (it), take it on the lam, take a (runout) powder, lam out, take to the hills, take to the woods; *Slang Brit* scarper, °bugger off, *US* vamoose, °blow **3** °hasten, °hurry, °rush, °run, °race, °dash, sprint, °tear, scamper, scoot, *Colloq* make tracks **4** °pass (by), °elapse, °go (by), °expire, run its course, slip *or* slide by *or* away **5** aviate, °pilot; jet **6** ***fly in the face of.*** °flout, °defy, go against, contemn, °scorn, scoff at, °oppose, go *or* run counter to, °counter, °counteract, countervail, countermine, °contradict, contravene, °thumb one's nose at, *Colloq Brit* cock a snook at **7** ***fly off the handle.*** fly into a rage *or* fury *or* temper *or* passion, lose one's temper, have a fit *or* tantrum, be fit to be tied, go berserk, go crazy *or* mad, °explode, *Colloq* lose *or* blow one's cool, blow one's top, hit *or* go through the roof, *US* hit the ceiling, °blow one's stack, get worked up (over); *Slang* blow a fuse *or* a gasket, have a hemorrhage, flip one's lid *or Brit* one's top **8** ***let fly.*** **(a)** °throw, °toss, °cast, °hurl, °fling, °heave, °pitch, °lob, °sling, chuck, °shoot, °fire (off), let rip, °discharge, °launch, °propel, let go *or* off **(b)** let go with, let (someone) have it, °lash out, vent one's spleen, lose one's temper, burst out *or* forth, burst into, *Colloq* pull no punches, tear into —*n.* **9** Often, *Brit* ***flies.*** °flap, fly front, *US* zipper, *Brit* zip **10** ***fly in the ointment.*** °hitch, °snag, °impediment, °obstacle, °obstruction, °problem, °difficulty, °drawback, detraction, °rub, °hindrance, bugbear, bogey, bugaboo, *Offensive* nigger in the woodpile

fly-by-night *adj.* **1** °temporary, °short-lived, transitory, °fugitive, ephemeral, °transient, °fleeting, °passing, °brief, impermanent, here today, gone tomorrow **2** °unreliable, untrustworthy, °disreputable, °irresponsible, dubious, °questionable; °shifty, °dishonest, °sharp, °crooked, *Colloq* °shady, *Brit* cowboy

foam *n.* **1** °bubbles, °froth, spume, °lather, suds; effervescence, °sparkle, carbonation, °fizz —*v.* **2** °bubble, °froth, spume, °lather, suds up, soap up

focal *adj.* °central, focused, concentrated, convergent, centered, centralized

focus *n.* **1** °center, concentration, focal point, °heart, °core, °target, convergence, °hub, nave; cynosure **2** ***in focus.*** °clear, °distinct, well- *or* sharply defined **3** ***out of focus.*** unclear, °indistinct, blurred, blurry, °fuzzy, °woolly —*v.* **4** °concentrate, °center, °converge, °meet, pinpoint, °spotlight; bring into focus; *Colloq* zero in

fog *n.* **1** °mist, haze, smog, °vapor, cloud, *Colloq* pea-souper **2** °trance, °daze, °stupor, brown study, confused state; coma —*v.* **3** °dim, °obscure, cloud, bedim, becloud, °blind, °stifle **4** Usually, ***befog.*** °bewilder, °mystify, °perplex, °confuse, °muddle, °puzzle, °nonplus **5** Also, ***fog up or over.*** mist over *or* up, cloud up *or* over, °shroud

fogy *n.* Usually, ***old fogy or fogey.*** fogey, °conservative, °relic, *Colloq* fuddy-duddy, fossil, °antique, °stick-in-the-mud, back number, °square

foible *n.* °weakness, °imperfection, °weak point, °fault, °frailty, °shortcoming, °flaw, °defect, °failing, °blemish, °infirmity; °peculiarity, idiosyncrasy, °quirk, crotchet, °eccentricity, preoccupation, °kink, *Colloq* hang-up, °bug

foil[1] *v.* °thwart, °offset, °defeat, baffle, balk, parry, °frustrate, °counter, °check, °impede, °hamper, °outwit, circumvent, checkmate, °daunt, disconcert, °discomfit, °disappoint, pull the rug out from under (someone), cut the ground from under (someone's) feet, nullify, °nip in the bud, countervail (against), *Brit* put a spoke in (someone's) wheel, *Colloq* clip (someone's) wings, cut (someone) down to size, spoil (someone's) game, *Chiefly US and Canadian* faze

foil[2] *n.* layer, lamina, lamination, °sheet, membrane, °film, coating, °flake, °scale, wafer

foist *v.* palm *or* pass off, °impose, °unload, °put (off), °push (off), *Colloq* °lay (off), *Brit* fob off

fold *v.* **1** °bend, °ply, double (over *or* up), °overlap, crease, pleat, °gather, crimp **2** °enclose, °envelop, enfold, °wrap, enwrap, °clasp, °clip, °embrace, °hug, °gather **3** °give way, °collapse, °fail, close (up *or* down), °shut down, go out of business, go bankrupt, *Colloq* °go under, go broke, go bust, *Brit* °go to the wall —*n.* **4** crease, °wrinkle, crinkle, °pucker, pleat, °gather, crimp, °overlap, °lap

folk *n.* °people, °tribe, °(ethnic) group, °clan, °race; °society, °nation, °(general) public, °populace, °population, citizenry

follow *v.* **1** go *or* come after *or* next; go *or* walk *or* tread *or* move behind, bring up the rear, *Colloq* string *or* tag along **2** adhere to, cleave to, °support, °believe in, °accept, °adopt, conform to, comply with, °obey, be guided by, be modeled after *or* on, °observe, °heed, °mind, °go along with, °reflect, °mirror, °echo, °imitate, °copy, °mimic, ape **3** °attend, °accompany, °escort, go (along) with; °serve **4** °chase, °pursue, dog, °hunt (down), °stalk, °run down, °track, °trail, °tail, °trace, °shadow **5** °succeed, °supersede, step into the shoes of, take the place of, °replace, °supplant **6** °practice, °pursue, °engage in, °carry on, occupy oneself with, apply *or* dedicate *or* devote oneself to, °cultivate **7** °result from, ensue, °issue, °flow, °arise, °develop **8** °understand, °fathom, °comprehend, °get, °grasp, °see, °catch, °appreciate, °take in, keep up with, *Colloq* °dig **9** °watch, be a fan *or* aficionado of, °pursue, take an interest in, keep up with, keep abreast of, cheer *or* root for, °admire **10** *follow through* (*on*). persist *or* persevere, °continue, °perform, conclude, °realize, consummate, °pursue, °carry out, °see through, °make good, °discharge, adhere to, °keep **11** *follow up* (*on*). **(a)** °pursue, go after, °track, °investigate, °check (out), check up (on), °inquire, make inquiries, °look into **(b)** °pursue, °prosecute, °reinforce, consolidate, °support, °buttress, augment, °bolster, °ensure

follower *n.* **1** °disciple, adherent, °student, °pupil, °apprentice, protégé(e) **2** °attendant, °henchman, °servant, retainer, bodyguard, myrmidon **3** °supporter, °devotee, °fan, aficionado, promoter, °enthusiast, booster, °advocate, °proponent, *US* rooter, *Colloq* groupie

follow-through *n.* °perseverance, diligence, °persistence, steadfastness, °endurance, °stamina, indefatigableness, sedulousness, sedulity, pursuance, °tenacity, °resolve, °determination, *Colloq US* stick-to-itiveness

follow-up *n.* °reinforcement, °support, backup, bolstering; consolidation

folly *n.* **1** foolishness, °nonsense, °absurdity, daftness, silliness, preposterousness, absurdness, senselessness, fatuousness, fatuity, rashness, °stupidity, asininity, inanity, nonsensicality, nonsensicalness, idiocy, imbecility, irrationality, °lunacy, °insanity, °madness, craziness, °eccentricity, weak-mindedness, feeblemindedness, simple-mindedness, muddle-headedness, thick-headedness, stolidity, stolidness, obtuseness, brainlessness, *Colloq* dumbness, dopiness, nuttiness, *US and Canadian* kookiness **2** °absurdity, °mistake, °blunder, °error, faux pas, gaffe, *Colloq* goof, °fluff

foment *v.* °rouse, stir *or* whip up, °awaken, waken, °provoke, °incite, instigate, °initiate, °prompt, °start, °motivate, °inspire, °work up, °inflame, fan the flames (of), °kindle, galvanize, °rally, °excite, °stimulate, °encourage, °promote, °foster, °forward, °further, °advance, °cultivate, sow the seeds of, °spur, goad, egg on, °urge

fond *adj.* **1** °tender, loving, °affectionate, °warm, adoring, caring **2** °foolish, °bootless, °empty, °vain, naive *or* naïve *or* naïf **3** *fond of.* °partial to, °(having a) liking (for), soft on *or* about, affectionate towards, °attached to, having a fancy *or* taste for, fancying, predisposed *or* inclined to *or* towards; addicted to, *Colloq* hooked on

fondle *v.* °caress, °stroke, °pet, °pat, °touch, °cuddle, °snuggle; °handle, °touch

fondly *adv.* affectionately, lovingly, tenderly, °warmly, adoringly, caressingly

food *n.* °nourishment, nutriment, aliment, °sustenance, °subsistence; foodstuffs, edibles, eatables, viands, bread, victuals, °rations, °provisions, comestibles, *Brit* commons, *Colloq* grub, eats, chow, *Brit* °scoff, prog

fool *n.* **1** simpleton, ninny, ninnyhammer, nincompoop, ass, jackass, dunce, °dolt, °half-wit, numskull *or* numbskull, blockhead, bonehead, pinhead, °silly, featherbrain, loon, goose, booby, jay, goon, mooncalf, idiot, ignoramus, dimwit, nitwit, halfwit, imbecile, moron, °clod, clodpole, clod poll, clodpate, oaf, *Psychology* retardate, *Scots* gomeril, *Colloq* birdbrain, dumbbell, fathead, chump, schmuck, °twit, knucklehead, chucklehead, nit, twerp *or* twirp, *Brit* pillock, *US and Canadian* °jerk, °retard; *Slang* °sap, °dope, *Brit* git, *Australian* boofhead **2** (court) jester, °clown, °comic, comedian *or* comedienne, entertainer, °zany, buffoon, merry-andrew, *farceur,* °joker, jokester, droll, Punch, Punchinello, pierrot, harlequin **3** °butt, °dupe, gull, °victim, cat's-paw, *Colloq* chump, °greenhorn, °(easy) mark, *US* fall guy; *Slang* pigeon, °sucker, stooge, *Brit* °mug —*v.* **4** °trick, °deceive, °take in, °swindle, °defraud, °hoax, °cheat, °fleece, cozen, °hoodwink, °bluff, °dupe, gull, humbug, delude, °mislead, make a fool of; pull the wool over (someone's) eyes, have (someone) on, pull (someone's) leg, °tease, °twit, *Archaic* chouse; *Colloq* kid, con, snow, do a snow job on, bamboozle, put one *or* something over on, pull something *or* a fast one on, *Brit* °twist, *Chiefly US and Canadian* josh; *Slang* °pluck, *Brit* nobble **5** °joke, jest, °banter, °tease, °twit, feign, °fake, °pretend, °make believe, *Colloq* kid **6** *fool with or around or about* (*with*). play (around *or* about) (with), toy *or* trifle (with), mess *or* fiddle (around *or* about) (with), monkey (around *or* about) with, °meddle (with), tamper with, fribble (with) **7** ***fool around or about.*** **(a)** play *or* mess around *or* about, gambol, °frolic, romp, °cavort **(b)** waste *or* fritter away *or* squander *or* kill time, fribble, loiter, °dawdle, °idle, putter *or Brit* potter (about *or* around), lark *or* muck about *or* around, *Colloq* footle

foolhardy *adj.* °rash, °imprudent, °impetuous, °reckless, °brash, °venturesome, °bold, °cheeky, °daring, °audacious, temerarious, °adventurous, °daredevil, incautious, °hotheaded, °careless, °heedless, devil-may-care, °hasty, °thoughtless, °unthinking, °irresponsible, °wild, madcap, *Colloq US and Canadian* nervy, *Slang* gutsy

foolish *adj.* **1** °senseless, incautious, °imprudent, impolitic, °indiscreet, unwise, injudicious, ill-considered, °ill-advised, °misguided, °shortsighted, °impetuous, headlong, °rash, °brash, °reckless, °hasty, °heedless, °unwary, °foolhardy, °thoughtless, °mindless **2** °nonsensical, °stupid, asinine, °inane, °silly, fatuous, fatuitous, dimwitted, °scatterbrained, °harebrained, °crazy, °mad, °insane, demented, irrational, °erratic, °unstable, crackbrained, featherbrained, birdbrained, simple-minded, lightheaded, muddle-headed, numskulled *or* numbskulled, addlepated, rattlebrained, bemused, °confused, °feebleminded, moronic, idiotic, imbecilic, °half-witted, dull-witted, slow-witted, witless, brainless, empty-headed, blockheaded, boneheaded, thickheaded, °obtuse, °stolid, *Colloq* °dumb, balmy *or Brit* barmy, loony, nuts, nutty, batty, dopey *or* dopy, °soft (in the head), °dim, °thick, dippy, dotty, °dizzy, *Brit* potty, °daft, *Slang* cuckoo, goofy, screwy, wacky **3** °preposterous, °ridiculous, °absurd, irrational, illogical, °unreasonable, °ludicrous, °wild

foolproof *adj.* °safe, °certain, °sure, °trustworthy, dependable, °reliable, °infallible, unfailing, guaranteed, warranted, *Colloq* surefire

footing *n.* **1** °foundation, °basis, °base, ground(s) **2** °standing, °status, °level, °condition, °position, °terms, °state, °rank **3** foothold, toehold; °balance, °stability

footstep *n.* **1** °step, footfall, tread **2** Usually, ***footsteps.*** footprint(s), °track, °trail, °trace, spoor, footmark(s); °tradition, °example, way of life

for *prep.* **1** representing, championing; °in favor of, *Brit* on *or US and Canadian also* in behalf of, on the side of, in support of, in the service of, as a service to, for the benefit of, pro **2** in search *or* quest of, seeking, looking for *or* after, after, with a view *or* an eye to **3** °instead of, in place of, representing, as a replacement for, *Brit* on *or US and Canadian* in behalf of; in return *or* exchange for, in compensation *or* recompense *or* payment *or* repayment for, in requital for **4** for the treatment of, as a remedy for, against; for the purpose *or* object of **5** for the sake of, *Brit* on *or US and Canadian also* in behalf of, in the interest of **6** in the direction of, to, °toward, into **7** to save, in the interest *or* benefit of, for the sake *or* benefit of, conducive to; because of, on account of, °by reason of **8** to go to, destined for **9** suitable *or* suited for, fit *or* fitted *or* fitting for, appropriate for, proper for **10** for the duration of; °over (the extent of), during, in the course of, °throughout, °through **11** °despite, °in spite of, °notwithstanding, allowing for **12** ***as for.*** °regarding, in regard to, as regards, respecting, °concerning, as far as (something *or* someone) is concerned —*conj.* **13** because, since, as, inasmuch as, seeing that, owing *or* due to the fact that

forbid *v.* °prohibit, °ban, °hinder, °stop, °exclude, debar, °preclude, °prevent; °outlaw, interdict, disallow, proscribe, °taboo; °veto

forbidding *adj.* **1** °repellent, °repulsive, °offensive, odious, °abhorrent **2** °hostile, unfriendly, °stern, °harsh, °menacing, °threatening, °ominous, °dangerous, °bad, °nasty, °ugly, unpleasant

force *n.* **1** °power, °might, °energy, °strength, potency, °vigor, °intensity, °violence, °impact; °dynamism, °pressure **2** coercion, °pressure, constraint, °duress, compulsion, arm-twisting **3** troops, soldiers, army **4** °weight, persuasiveness, °persistence, cogency, effectiveness, efficacy, °strength, validity, °significance, value **5** °meaning, °import, °significance **6** ***in force.*** °in effect, °effective, °in operation, °operative, valid, binding, °current —*v.* **7** °make, °oblige, °require, compel, coerce, °exact, constrain, °enforce, impel, °intimidate, pressure *or Brit also* pressurize, °press, dragoon, twist (someone's) arm, *Colloq* bulldoze, °put the squeeze on (someone) **8** °push, °drive, °thrust, °propel; prise *or* prize, °break, °wrench, °crack, jemmy, *US* °pry **9** °exact, °extort, °extract, wrest, wring, °drag

forced *adj.* °artificial, °unnatural, contrived, °stilted, °calculated, °studied, °labored, °strained, °stiff, °false, feigned, fake(d), °mannered, °affected, °self-conscious, *Colloq* phoney *or US also* phony

forceful *adj.* **1** °vigorous, °energetic, compelling, °dynamic, °intense, °potent, °strong, °mighty, °powerful, °aggressive, °weighty, °effective, convincing, °persuasive **2** °effective, °efficacious, cogent, °logical, °impressive, °telling, convincing, °persuasive, °strong, °mighty, °forcible, °powerful, compelling, °irresistible; pithy, meaty

forcible *adj.* **1** See **forceful, 2.** **2** °drastic, °forceful, °violent, °aggressive, coercive, °severe, stringent

foreboding *n.* **1** apprehension, apprehensiveness, °feeling, °sense, °misgiving, °dread, °suspicion, °intuition, °anxiety, °fear **2** °premonition, augury, °prophecy, °prediction, prognostication, °warning, foretoken, foreshadowing, presentiment, °omen, °sign, portent, intimation, forewarning, presage, advance word

°consistently, persistently, interminably, perpetually

forecast *v.* **1** °predict, foretell, °prophesy, °prognosticate, °foresee, augur, presage, vaticinate, °anticipate; forewarn, °calculate —*n.* **2** °prediction, °prophecy, °prognosis, prognostication, °foresight, augury, vaticination, °anticipation; forewarning, °calculation

foregoing *adj.* °preceding, °above, °former, °previous, °precedent, °prior, antecedent; earlier, °preliminary, anterior; aforementioned, aforesaid

foregone *adj.* Usually in ***foregone conclusion.*** °assumed, established, preestablished, °predetermined, °fixed, °inevitable, °set, accepted, °cut and dried

foreign *adj.* **1** °alien, imported, nonnative; °overseas, °distant, tramontane, transalpine, transatlantic, transpacific **2** °strange, °outlandish, °exotic, °unfamiliar, °peculiar, °odd, °curious **3** °unknown, °unfamiliar, °strange, °inappropriate, °unrelated, unconnected, unassimilable, °remote, °extrinsic, °extraneous

foreigner *n.* °alien, nonnative, °immigrant, °newcomer, new arrival, °outsider, outlander, °stranger

foreman *n.* °superintendent, °manager, °boss, °supervisor, °overseer, *Brit* shopwalker, *US* floorwalker, *Colloq* °super, *Brit* gaffer, *US* straw boss

foremost *adj.* **1** °first, °primary, °prime, °leading, °preeminent, °supreme; °prominent, °notable, °noteworthy, °noted, °chief, °paramount, °main, °best, °superior —*adv.* **2** °first, firstly, °primarily, in (the) first place, before anything else

forerunner *n.* **1** °predecessor, °precursor, foregoer; forebear, °ancestor, forefather, °progenitor; herald, °harbinger, °envoy **2** °omen, portent, foretoken, °premonition, °sign, augury, °token

foresee *v.* presage, foretell, °envisage, °picture, °forecast, °predict, °prophesy, augur, *US* °envision

foreshadow *v.* presage, foretoken, portend, augur, °indicate, °prophesy, °predict, °bode, °signal, °signify, betoken

foresight *n.* **1** °providence, °prudence, °care, farsightedness, watchfulness, °caution, °precaution, longsightedness, perspicacity, °wisdom, sagacity, °insight, circumspection **2** prevision, °perception, °prospect, °vision, foreknowledge, prescience; °expectation

forestall *v.* °anticipate, °prevent, °obstruct, °hinder, obviate, °thwart, °preclude, °frustrate, avert, ward *or* stave *or* fend off, °intercept, parry, °stop, °delay

forethought *n.* premeditation, planning, plotting, farsightedness, long-sightedness

forever *adv.* **1** °always, for good, °ever, (for) evermore, forevermore, eternally, everlastingly, for ever and a day, undyingly, for eternity, till Doomsday, till the end of time, *Colloq* till the cows come home, till hell freezes over **2** constantly, continually, continuously, °all the time, unceasingly, incessantly, without cease *or* surcease, endlessly, °consistently, persistently, interminably, perpetually

foreword *n.* °preface, prologue, prelude, prolegomenon, °preamble, *Literary* proem; introduction

forfeit *n.* **1** °penalty, °fine, °fee, °charge, °damages, forfeiture, sequestration, amercement, mulct —*v.* **2** °lose, °yield (up), give up *or* over, °relinquish, °surrender, be stripped *or* deprived of, °forgo, °renounce, °waive —*adj.* **3** surrendered, °lost, yielded, relinquished, forgone, waived, renounced

forge *v.* **1** °make, °construct, °fashion, °fabricate, °manufacture, °shape, °mold, °cast, hammer out **2** °create, °invent, °conceive (of), °coin, °devise, °think up, °frame **3** °counterfeit, °copy, °reproduce, °imitate, °falsify, °fake, *Slang US* hang paper

forgery *n.* **1** counterfeiting, falsification, °fraud, fraudulence **2** °counterfeit, °fake, °sham, °imitation, *Colloq* phoney *or US also* phony

forget *v.* **1** fail *or* cease to remember *or* recall *or* think of, °lose, draw a blank **2** °leave (behind), omit *or* neglect (doing *or* taking) **3** °ignore, dismiss from (one's) mind *or* thoughts, °disregard, °overlook, consign to oblivion

forgetful *adj.* amnesiac; °absent-minded, distracted, abstracted, °inattentive, °preoccupied, neglectful, negligent, °careless, °lax, °dreamy, dreaming, in dreamland, in the clouds, in cloud-cuckoo-land *or* cloudland *or* Nephelococcygia, °remote, distrait(e), *Colloq* not turned on, turned off, out of it

forgive *v.* **1** °pardon, °excuse, °allow, make allowance(s) for, °indulge, condone, °vindicate; °overlook, °ignore, °disregard, pay no attention to, °pass over, *US* slough over **2** °clear, acquit, absolve, exculpate, exonerate; °spare; *Colloq* °let off **3** °cancel, °waive, °abolish, °void, nullify, °erase, °delete; *Colloq* °let off (the hook)

forgiveness *n.* **1** °pardon, °reprieve, absolution, °remission, acquittal, acquittance, amnesty, °allowance, vindication, exculpation, exoneration, *Archaic* shrift **2** °mercy, mercifulness, compassion, °grace, leniency, clemency, °indulgence, °tolerance

forgiving *adj.* °tolerant, °lenient, °sparing, forbearing, °merciful, compassionate, conciliatory, magnanimous, humane, soft-hearted, clement

forgo *v.* **1** °give up, °renounce, forswear, °forsake, °abandon, do *or* go without, °sacrifice, °eliminate, °omit, leave out *or* alone, °cede, °waive; °avoid, °shun, eschew, abstain from, °turn down, °pass up, °deny (oneself) **2** °resign, °give up, °yield, °surrender, °relinquish, °cede, °waive, °renounce, forswear, °abdicate, °abandon

forlorn *adj.* **1** °miserable, °wretched, °desolate, °woebegone, °lost, °pitiable, °pitiful, °pathetic, woeful, cheerless, °joyless, °unhappy, depressed, °sad, °desolate, disconsolate, °gloomy, lugubrious, °glum, °despondent, °dismal, °dejected, dispirited, low-spirited, comfortless, down, °melancholy, dolorous,

°sorrowful, °mournful, °inconsolable **2** °abandoned, forsaken, °deserted, neglected, shunned, °outcast, °alone, °lonely, °lonesome, friendless, bereft

form *n.* **1** °shape, configuration, conformation, °order, °organization, °arrangement, °formation, construction, °structure, °construct, °frame, °cut, °cast, °mold, °pattern, °appearance; °manifestation **2** °figure, °body, °build, °shape, °physique, anatomy; °silhouette, °aspect, °look, °appearance, °profile, contour; °carriage, °bearing, °attitude, °pose, *Slang US* bod, build **3** °type, °kind, °variety, °sort, °breed, species, genus, °genre, °character, °make, °brand, °color, °tone, °tint, °texture, °fabric, °material, feather, °description, °manner, °way, °nature, °style, °stamp, °manifestation **4** °blank; °model, °format, °frame, framework, °course, °procedure, °order, regimen, °method, °system, °ritual, °formula, rule(s), °practice, °technique, °way, °means, °approach, °mode, °fashion, °manner, °style **5** °condition, °state, °shape, °trim, fettle **6** °decorum, °behavior, deportment, °formality, °ceremony, °convention, °etiquette, °manners, °conduct, °custom, °protocol, °propriety, °ritual —*v.* **7** °make, °fabricate, °forge, °shape, °mold, °fashion, °produce, °turn out, °manufacture, °construct, °assemble, put together, °set up, °put up, °build, °erect, elevate, °raise; °organize, codify; °develop **8** °create, °originate, °devise, °invent, °compose, °formulate, give form *or* shape, °coin, concoct, °conceive, contrive, dream up, °imagine, visualize, °envisage, *US* °envision **9** °make up, constitute, be made up of, comprise, °be composed of; serve as **10** °acquire, °develop, °cultivate, °contract; °get **11** °develop, °grow, °arise, °appear, °materialize, °show up, take shape *or* form, °accumulate

formal *adj.* **1** °standard, °conventional, °customary, established, prescribed, °regular, °normal, °correct, °proper; °strict, formulaic, °inflexible, punctilious, °exacting, unchanging, °methodical, °orderly, °systematic, °set, pro forma, °ritual, ritualistic, °ceremonial, °proper, °official, °routine, °fixed, °rigid, °stiff, °stilted, °stately, starched, unbending, °solemn; confining, °straitened, °limited; *Colloq* °straight, °square **2** °explicit, °express, °definite, spelled-out, formalized, authorized, °official, °solemn, °legal, °lawful **3** prim, °ceremonious, °dignified, °stuffy, °strait-laced, °stiff, °precise, °exact

formality *n.* **1** Often, *the formalities.* °form, °convention, conventionality, °practice, °procedure, °custom, wont, °observance, °protocol, °ceremony, °rite, °ritual **2** strictness, punctilio, exactness, °precision, correctness, rigidity, stiffness, inflexibility **3** °etiquette, politesse, °decorum, punctilio, conformity, °propriety

format *n.* **1** °appearance, look(s), °aspect, layout, °plan, °design, °style, °form, dimension(s), °shape, °size **2** °composition, content(s), °makeup, constitution, °arrangement, °plan, °organization, °order, °setup

formation *n.* **1** °development, °appearance, materialization, °shape, °accumulation, °generation, °creation, crystallization, forming, genesis, °production **2** °establishment, °institution, °creation, founding, °setup, organizing, °organization, °development, °composition **3** array, °display, °pattern, °arrangement, °structure, grouping, °organization, configuration, °disposition

former *adj.* **1** °previous, earlier, °prior, ex-, one-time, °preceding, erstwhile, °late, °latest, °last, °recent, *ci-devant*, quondam, *Archaic* whilom **2** °old, °past, °bygone; °ancient, (pre)historic, departed, antediluvian

formerly *adv.* °once, °before, °previously, hitherto, long ago, °at one time, in the old days, once upon a time, in days gone by, in days *or* time past, time was, back then, when the world was young(er), *Colloq* way back *or US also* way back when

formidable *adj.* **1** alarming, appalling, °dreadful, °frightful, °awesome, awe-inspiring, °menacing, horrifying, °frightening, intimidating, daunting, petrifying, °terrifying **2** °terrific, °fantastic, °unbelievable, °incredible, °impressive, °prodigious, mind-boggling, °awesome, *Colloq* mind-blowing, freaky **3** °arduous, °indomitable, °overwhelming, staggering, °powerful, °mighty, °difficult, challenging, °burdensome, onerous

formula *n.* °recipe, rubric, formulary; rule(s), °prescription, °directions, °instructions, blueprint, °method, °technique, °means, °way, °pattern, °procedure, modus operandi, *Colloq US* MO (='modus operandi')

formulate *v.* **1** systematize, codify, °define, °specify, articulate, particularize, °denote **2** °devise, °originate, °create, think up *or* of, dream up, °conceive, concoct, °invent, °improvise, *Colloq* cook up **3** °develop, °forge, evolve, °work out, °design, map out, °block out, °draw up

forsake *v.* **1** °abandon, °desert, °quit, °leave, °flee, °depart, °vacate **2** °abandon, °desert, °leave, °jilt, °reject, °throw over, jettison, °cast off **3** °give up, °yield, °renounce, °repudiate, °relinquish, °forgo, forswear, °surrender, °resign, °abdicate, °recant, °deny, have *or* be done with, °turn one's back on

forte *n.* °talent, strong point, °gift, °specialty, °strength, °aptitude, °genius, *Colloq* long suit

forthcoming *adj.* **1** approaching, nearing, °impending, °imminent, coming, °(close) at hand, upcoming; near *or* close (by), (near *or* close) at hand, in the offing, on the horizon, *Colloq Brit* on the cards, *US* °in the cards **2** awaited, expected, anticipated, looked-for, watched-for, °prospective, foreseen **3** °outgoing, °friendly, °amiable, affable, °sociable, °accessible, °expansive, chatty, °talkative, communicative, °informative, °open, °free, revealing, unreserved

forthright *adj.* straightforward, °direct, °blunt, °candid, °frank, °aboveboard, unambiguous, unequivocal, °open, °outspoken, °uninhibited, unreserved, unconstrained, unrestrained

fortify *v.* **1** °strengthen, °reinforce, shore up, °buttress, °brace, °bolster, °secure **2** °cheer, °encourage, hearten, °buoy, invigorate, °energize, embolden, °reassure, °brace **3** °supplement, °enhance, °enrich, °boost, augment

fortitude *n.* °strength, mettle, °backbone, °courage, °nerve, °resolution, resoluteness, °perseverance, °endurance, °tenacity, pertinacity, °grit, °determination, willpower, *Colloq* °guts

fortunate *adj.* **1** °lucky, in luck, fortuitous, blessed **2** °favored, °advantageous, °propitious, auspicious, °providential, °favorable, °opportune, °timely, °well-timed

fortune *n.* **1** °position, °worth, °means, °assets, holdings, °wealth, °property, °estate, °possessions; °riches, affluence, opulence, °treasure, °money, °prosperity **2** °luck, °chance, fortuity; °lot, °fate, kismet, °destiny, karma; °future; *US* happenstance **3** Usually, ***fortunes.*** circumstance(s), experience(s), adventures, expectation(s), °lot

fortuneteller *n.* °oracle, soothsayer, °prophet, diviner, augur, °seer, clairvoyant, prognosticator, sibyl, haruspex, crystal gazer, tealeaf-reader, palmist, palm-reader, stargazer; futurologist

forward *adj.* **1** °advance, °leading, °foremost, °front, °head, °first **2** °bold, °pert, °impudent, °brash, °insolent, °impertinent, °disrespectful, °brazen, °audacious, °rash, unashamed, °unabashed, saucy, °flippant, °presumptuous, °cheeky, *Colloq* °flip, °fresh, °pushy **3** (well-)advanced, (well-)developed, °progressive, °precocious, forward-looking —*adv.* **4** forwards, °ahead, °onward, along; clockwise, deasil **5** up, °out, forth, to the fore, into consideration, into view, into the open, to the surface, onto the table —*v.* **6** °advance, °further, °promote, °back, °foster, °support, °aid, °assist, °help; °patronize, °encourage, °nourish, nurse along **7** dispatch *or* despatch, °send, °ship, °deliver, °transmit, °express, °post, °mail, consign, °remit; send on **8** °speed (up), accelerate, °advance, °hasten, °expedite, °hurry, °quicken, °step up

foster *v.* **1** °promote, °encourage, °stimulate, °further, °forward, °advance, °cultivate, nurture, °nourish, °support, °back, °assist, °help, °aid, succor, °patronize **2** °bring up, °rear, °raise, °take care of, °maintain, °care for

foul *adj.* **1** °offensive, °loathsome, °disgusting, °obnoxious, °revolting, °repulsive, °repellent, °repugnant, sickening, °nauseous, nauseating, °nasty, °beastly, *Archaic* fulsome **2** °filthy, unclean, °nasty, polluted, °putrid, putrescent, putrefactive *or* putrefacient, defiled, soiled, spoiled, °rotten, decayed, decomposed, °rancid, soured, turned, tainted, °moldy, °impure, adulterated, contaminated, °stale, °bad, *Brit* °off **3** °smelly, °stinking, noisome, fetid *or* foetid, °rank, evil-smelling, foulsmelling, malodorous, °musty, mephitic, graveolent **4** °wicked, °vile, °bad, °base, °abominable, °low, °sordid, iniquitous, °evil, flagitious, °atrocious, °monstrous, nefarious, °sinful, °immoral, amoral, °vicious, °villainous, °scandalous, °infamous, °dishonorable, °shameful, °disgraceful, ignominious; detestable **5** °dirty, °obscene, °filthy, °profane, scatological, °gross, smutty, foulmouthed, °blue, licentious, salacious, °lewd, °indecent, °improper, °coarse, uncouth, °vulgar, °rude, °scurrilous, °rough, indelicate, °immodest, °risqué, °off-color, °suggestive, °bawdy, ribald, Rabelaisian, Fescennine, *US* °raw, *Slang* raunchy **6** °abusive, °offensive, affronting, insulting, disparaging, maligning, thersitical, calumnious *or* calumniatory, aspersive, °slanderous, defamatory, libelous, denigrating, °derogatory, deprecatory *or* deprecative, depreciatory *or* depreciative, denunciatory *or* denunciative, °derisory, derisive, °scornful, belittling, fulminous, objurgatory *or* objurgative, °vituperative, invective **7** °dishonest, unfair, unjust, unsportsmanlike, °dishonorable, °fraudulent, underhand(ed), double-dealing, °two-faced, °corrupt, °venal, °dirty, treacherous, °perfidious, °traitorous, °unscrupulous, *Colloq* °crooked, °shady, *Slang, chiefly Brit* bent **8** °nasty, °dangerous, °rough, °disagreeable, unfavorable, °sloppy, °stormy, adverse; °windy, blustery; snowy, sleety, °wet, rainy **9** obstructed, blocked, choked, stopped(-up), plugged (-up), clogged(-up) **10** tangled, entangled, caught, ensnared, enmeshed, snarled **11** °illegal, prohibited, forbidden, interdicted, not fair; °dirty —*v.* **12** °dirty, °pollute, °sully, befoul, defile, °soil, °contaminate, °adulterate, °taint **13** °tangle, °entangle, °catch, °snare, ensnare, enmesh, °snag, °snarl, °jam, °twist **14** °disgrace, °dishonor, °sully, °taint, besmirch, defile, °soil, °stain, °smear, °tarnish, °blacken, denigrate, °debase, °degrade, abase, demean, °disparage, defame, derogate, asperse, devaluate, °depreciate, °vitiate, °belittle, °discredit, bring *or* call into disrepute **15** °obstruct, °block, °choke, stop *or* plug *or* clog (up) **16** ***foul up.*** **(a)** See **14,** above. **(b)** mismanage, °mishandle, °botch, °bungle, make a mess (of), °mess up, °spoil, °ruin, *Colloq* muff, *Brit* throw a spanner into (the works), *US* throw a monkey wrench into (the machinery); *Slang* °muck up, goof (up), °blow, °screw up, louse up, *Chiefly Brit* °bugger (up), *US and Canadian* snafu —*n.* **17** °violation, °infringement, infraction, illegality —*adv.* **18** °afoul, in conflict, °in trouble, in violation

foul play *n.* treachery, °chicanery, °perfidy, perfidiousness, duplicity, double-dealing, °deception, guile, °crime, sharp practice, skulduggery, dirty work *or* business, dirty trick(s); °murder, homicide, manslaughter; *Colloq* °hanky-panky

found *v.* **1** °establish, °originate, °institute, °set up, °organize, °inaugurate, °start, °initiate, °create, °bring about, °develop **2** °base, °ground, °establish, °set, °build; °rest

foundation *n.* **1** °basis, °base, substructure, understructure, underpinning, °bottom, foot, basement, °cellar **2** °basis, °base, °fundamental, (underlying *or* fundamental) principle, °grounds, °groundwork, °rationale, raison d'être, °purpose **3** founding, °establishment, instituting, °institution, °creation, origination, setting up, organizing, °organization, inauguration, °endowment

founder[1] *n.* originator, °creator, °progenitor, °author, framer, °father, architect, °designer, builder, initiator, establisher, institutor

founder[2] *v.* **1** °sink, go down *or* under, go to Davy Jones's locker, be wrecked *or* destroyed **2** °fail, °miscarry, °collapse, come to nothing *or* naught, °fall through, abort, falter, °break down, °come to grief, °die **3** °trip, °stumble, °stagger, °lurch, °fall, topple (over *or* down), °collapse; go lame

foundling *n.* orphan, waif; °stray, °outcast

fountain *n.* **1** fount, °spring, font, jet, °spout, °spray, °well, wellspring, wellhead, fountainhead **2** fount, °source, °origin, genesis

foxy *adj.* **1** °clever, °sly, cunning, °wily, °crafty, °tricky, guileful, °shifty, °devious, °slippery, °smooth, °slick, °artful, °resourceful, °ingenious, °calculating, °designing, plotting, °scheming, °disingenuous, °knowing, °shrewd, °sharp, °astute, °wise; foxlike, vulpine; *Colloq* cagey *or* cagy **2** °attractive, alluring, °seductive, vampish, *Colloq* °sexy

fracas *n.* **1** °trouble, °disturbance, commotion, °rumpus, °fuss, hubbub, °pandemonium, hullabaloo, °uproar, °disorder, °scramble, scuffle, °brawl, °roughhouse, rough-and-tumble, turmoil, °tumult, free-for-all, °riot, °fray, brouhaha, melee *or* mêlée, *Law* affray; *Brit* scrum, *US* brannigan; *Colloq* ruckus, punch-up, *Slang Brit* bovver **2** °argument, °disagreement, °quarrel, °dispute, °discord, wrangle, altercation, squabble, spat, °tiff, °fight, °row, tussle, donnybrook, °brawl, *Colloq* barney, °scrap

fracture *n.* **1** °break, breakage, breaking **2** °break, °crack, °split, °rupture, °breach, °separation, cleavage, °division, °rift —*v.* **3** °break, °rupture, °crack, °split, °breach, °separate, °cleave

fragile *adj.* °frail, breakable, °brittle, frangible, °delicate, °dainty, °thin, °light, °slight, °weak, °feeble, °infirm, °decrepit; °tenuous, °shaky, °flimsy, °rickety, unsubstantial *or* insubstantial

fragment *n.* **1** °piece, °portion, °part, °chip, shard *or* sherd, °splinter, °sliver, °scrap, °bit, °speck, snippet, °morsel, °crumb, °particle, °remnant, °shred, °snatch **2** *fragments.* smithereens; debris, *Literary disjecta membra* —*v.* **3** °shatter, °splinter, break *or* split (up), °explode, °disintegrate, come *or* go to pieces, °come apart

fragmentary *adj.* °disconnected, °piecemeal, °incomplete, scattered, °disjointed, °incoherent, °sketchy

fragrance *n.* fragrancy, °scent, °aroma, °smell, °odor, redolence, °perfume, °bouquet, balm

fragrant *adj.* °aromatic, odorous, °redolent, perfumed, balmy, odoriferous, ambrosial, sweet-scented, sweet-smelling

frail *adj.* **1** See **fragile. 2** ailing, unwell, °ill, °sick, °sickly, °poorly, °thin, °skinny, °slight, °puny, °scrawny, wasting *or* fading away, languishing, °infirm, °feeble; °crippled, consumptive, phthisic

frailty *n.* **1** °weakness, °infirmity, delicate condition, feebleness, fragility, °delicacy **2** susceptibility, °liability, suggestibility, impressionability, vulnerability; fallibility, °foible, °flaw, °defect, °imperfection, °fault

frame *n.* **1** framework, °shell, °form, skeleton, °support, chassis, framing, °structure, °fabric, scaffolding, construction **2** °border, casing, case mounting, °mount, °edge, edging; °setting **3** °system, °form, °pattern, °scheme, schema, °plan, °order, °organization, framework, °structure, °construct, construction, °arrangement, blueprint, °design, layout, °composition, °context, °makeup, configuration **4** °physique, °build, bone structure, °body, skeleton, °figure **5** *frame of mind.* °mood, °humor, °state, °condition, °attitude, °bent, °disposition —*v.* **6** °construct, °build, put together, °assemble, °set up, °put up, °erect, °raise, elevate **7** °make, °fashion, °form, °mold, °carve out, °forge, °originate, °create, °devise, °compose, °formulate, put together, °conceive, °draw up, °draft, °shape, °block out, give form *or* shape to; contrive **8** °enclose, °box (in); °set off **9** °set up, °incriminate (fraudulently), °trap, entrap

frank *adj.* **1** °open, °free, °candid, °direct, °outspoken, unreserved, °uninhibited, °honest, °sincere, °genuine, °truthful, plain-spoken, °forthright, °downright, °explicit, unrestrained, unchecked, unconstrained, unrestricted, °unabashed **2** °candid, naive *or* naïve, guileless, °artless, °ingenuous, °innocent, °(open and) aboveboard, on the up and up, *Colloq* upfront, °on the level

frantic *adj.* frenzied, °excited, frenetic, °nervous, °overwrought, °excitable, wrought-up, distracted, °distraught, °beside oneself, °hysterical, °wild, °berserk, °mad, running amok *or* amuck; °upset, °agitated, perturbed, at one's wit's end, °disconcerted, °confused; °hectic; *Colloq* in a state, in a tizzy, up the wall, in a dither, °out of one's mind, *Chiefly US and Canadian* discombobulated

fraternal *adj.* °brotherly, °platonic, °friendly, comradely, °idealistic, °intellectual

fraternity *n.* **1** community, °brotherhood, °crowd, °set, °clique, coterie, °circle, °society, *US* °club **2** brotherliness, °kinship, °fellowship, camaraderie, sodality, comradeship, °friendship, °companionship, relatedness, closeness, °association, affiliation, °solidarity, °unity, esprit de corps, clannishness **3** °company, guild, °clan, °league, °club, °union, °society, °association

fraternize *v.* consort (with), °associate (with), °socialize (with), go (around *or* round) with *or* together, spend time with *or* together, keep company (with), hobnob with, °mingle (with), °mix (with), take up with *or* together, keep up (with), °fall in with, rub shoulders (with), *Colloq* hang out (with *or* together), hang about *or* around with *or* together

fraud *n.* **1** °deception, °trickery, cheating, sharp practice, °chicanery, °deceit, swindling, double-dealing, duplicity, °artifice, °craft, guile, humbug, humbuggery, treachery, *Colloq* monkey business, funny business, °hanky-panky **2** °trick, °hoax, °swindle, °deception, °cheat, °wile, °stratagem, °dodge, bilk, °ruse, °sham, °fake, °subterfuge, *Colloq* flimflam, *Slang* gyp, °rip-off, scam **3** deceiver, trickster, cheat(er), °impostor, °swindler, charlatan, humbug, sharper, shark, bilk(er), °quack, mountebank, fake(r), °pretender, bluff(er), confidence man, inveigler, defrauder; °scoundrel, °rogue, *Archaic* knave; *Colloq* con man *or* artist, phoney *or US also* phony, flimflam artist, flimflammer, *US and Canadian* four-flusher; *Slang US* barracuda

fraudulent *n.* **1** °fake, °counterfeit, forged, °false, falsified, °spurious, °imitation, °sham, pinchbeck, *Colloq* phoney *or US also* phony **2** °deceitful, °dishonest, °criminal, °deceptive, °tricky, °artful, °crafty, double-dealing, duplicitous, °shifty, guileful, °sharp, *Colloq* °shady, °crooked, °bent

fraught *adj.* **1** Usually, ***fraught with.*** filled *or* charged *or* packed with, loaded with, teeming *or* replete *or* overflowing with, oversupplied with, abounding *or* abundant in, attended *or* accompanied by **2** °tense, °taut, stressful, °trying, °anxious, distressing, distressful, upsetting, °nerve-racking, °fretful, °strained, °traumatic

fray[1] *n.* °disturbance, °skirmish, °fight, °battle, °brawl, tussle, scuffle, °fracas, melee *or* mêlée, donnybrook, wrangle, °rumpus, °row, °quarrel, °dispute, altercation, *Law* affray, *Colloq* ruckus, punch-up

fray[2] *v.* °shred, wear (thin *or* threadbare), °wear out, °rub, abrade, °chafe, ravel, unravel, frazzle

freak *n.* **1** °monstrosity, °monster, mutant, deformity **2** anomaly, °rarity, °abnormality, irregularity, °oddity, °curiosity, rara avis, rare bird, *Brit* one-off, *Colloq* one-shot **3** whim, caprice, vagary, crotchet, °quirk, °eccentricity, °fancy, idiosyncrasy, °peculiarity **4** °enthusiast, °fan, °devotee, aficionado; °fanatic, °addict; *Colloq* buff, °fiend, nut —*adj.* **5** freakish, freaky, °abnormal, anomalous, °extraordinary, °unique, °rare, atypical, °unusual, °odd, °queer, °strange, °exceptional, °bizarre, °weird, °unparalleled, °unforeseen, unexpected, unpredicted, unpredictable, *Brit* one-off, *Colloq* one-shot

free *adj.* **1** °at liberty, unfettered, unchained, unshackled, unconfined, untrammeled, unencumbered, unrestrained, unrestricted, unconstrained, °uncontrolled, freeborn, °independent, self-governing, self-governed, self-ruling, autonomous, °democratic, °sovereign **2** liberated, °at large, let go, °let off, emancipated, delivered, manumitted, set free, unshackled, unfettered, released, freed, °loose, °out, *Colloq* sprung, on the loose **3** unoccupied, unengaged, °at liberty, not busy, °available, °accessible; °unused, °vacant, °empty, °spare, °extra, °uninhabited, untenanted **4** cost-free, free of charge, °complimentary, gratis, for nothing, without cost (or obligation), unencumbered, *Colloq* for free, °on the house **5** °unattached, unfastened, untied, °loose **6** unasked-for, °unsolicited, °gratuitous, unbidden, °voluntary, °spontaneous, unconditioned, unconditional **7** °generous, °lavish, °open, °liberal, munificent, unstinting, °bountiful, openhanded, unsparing; °charitable **8** °relaxed, °casual, °informal, free-and-easy, °easy, °natural, unceremonious, *Colloq* laid-back **9** °open, °aboveboard, °honest, °direct, °outspoken, °uninhibited, unconstrained, unrestrained, °relaxed **10** unhindered, °unimpeded, unencumbered, unhampered, unobstructed, allowed, permitted, °able, °clear, unrestricted, unregulated **11** ***free of.*** °rid of, exempt(ed) from, relieved of, safe from, not liable *or* subject to, immune from, unaffected by, °above, without, untouched by —*adv.* **12** °freely, °openly, °at will, unrestrictedly, °loose; loosely **13** gratis, at no cost, free of charge, without charge —*v.* **14** set free, set at liberty, enfranchise, °release, let go, °liberate, °let out, °let loose, unloose, unchain, unfetter, uncage; °emancipate, disenthrall, manumit; °pardon, parole, furlough **15** °disengage, untie, unbind, °loose, unfasten, °undo, unshackle, unlock, °open, °release, disentangle, °loosen, °detach, °extricate **16** °relieve, °rid, unburden, disburden, disencumber, unbosom; °rescue, °redeem

freedom *n.* **1** °liberty, °independence, °self-government, self-determination, self-direction, autonomy **2** °release, deliverance, °liberation, emancipation, manumission **3** °exemption, °immunity, deliverance, °liberation, °relief **4** °range, latitude, °scope, °play, deregulation, noninterference, °discretion, °margin, free hand; °facility, °ease, °license, °permission, °right, °privilege, °authority, authorization, °power, °carte blanche **5** free time, °leisure, spare time **6** °candor, °honesty, openness, frankness, candidness, unrestraint, unconstraint, naturalness **7** boldness, overfamiliarity, audacity, audaciousness, forwardness, brazenness, °brass, °impertinence, °impudence, °disrespect, °arrogance, °presumption, presumptuousness, °nerve, °gall

freely *adv.* **1** candidly, frankly, °openly, unreservedly, without reserve, unrestrainedly, without restraint, unconstrainedly, without constraint, unceremoniously, plainly **2** °willingly, spontaneously, °readily, °voluntarily, on (one's) own, independently, of (one's) own accord, of (one's) own volition *or* free will **3** unrestrainedly, unrestrictedly, without restriction, without let or hindrance, without interference **4** liberally, lavishly, unreservedly, generously, unstintingly, openhandedly, ungrudgingly, munificently, °amply, plentifully, abundantly **5** °readily, °easily, smoothly, cleanly, unobstructedly

freeze *v.* **1** °chill, °refrigerate, ice, deep-freeze, flash-freeze, frost **2** °solidify, congeal, °harden, °stiffen, ice up *or* over **3** °fix, immobilize, °paralyze, stop (dead (in one's tracks)), °stay, °pin, °transfix, Gorgonize; become fixed, stand (stock-)still *or* motionless; °peg, °stick, °set **4** ***freeze out.*** °exclude, debar, °ban, °reject, °ostracize; °eject, drive away *or* out, °expel, force out —*n.* **5** frost, *Brit* freeze-up, *US* ice-up, deepfreeze **6** °fix, immobilization

freezing *adj.* °frigid, °icy, arctic, frosty, boreal, hyperboreal, numbing, Siberian, °polar, glacial, ice-cold, °wintry, bone-chilling, °bitter, °biting, bitter(ly) cold, perishing, °cold, °chill, tooth-chattering; chilled to the bone, frozen, shivering, *Archaic* frore

freight *n.* **1** °transport, transportation, °carriage, conveyance, shipping, shipment, freightage, °delivery **2** °goods, °cargo, tonnage, freightage; °load, boatload, shipload, lorryload, °haul, consignment, payload

frenzy *n.* **1** °excitement, °agitation, °fury, fever, °furor, °passion, turmoil, °transport **2** °distraction, °paroxysm, °seizure, °outburst, °bout, °fit

frequent *adj.* **1** °recurrent, recurring, °habitual, °regular, °familiar, °everyday, °customary, °usual, °ordinary, °normal, °common, repeated, iterative, reiterative, °persistent, continuing, °continual, °constant; °many, numerous, countless, innumerable —*v.* **2** °haunt, °patronize, °visit, °resort to, go to *or* attend regularly, *Colloq* hang out *or* around at

frequently *adv.* **1** °often, regularly, continually, °repeatedly, over and over (again), again and again, °a lot, many times, many a time, time after time, time and (time) again, *Archaic* oftentimes, ofttimes **2** °often, habitually, customarily, regularly, °usually, °ordinarily, °generally, commonly, every so often, many a time, as often as not, *Archaic* oftentimes, ofttimes

fresh *adj.* **1** °new, today's, °brand-new; °(most) recent, late(st) **2** °new, °modern, up-to-date, °novel, °original, newfangled, °unusual, unconventional, °different, °alternative, °unorthodox **3** °raw, °inexperienced, untested, °unsophisticated, °green, °untried, °unfledged, °immature, untrained, naive *or* naïve, °callow, (still) wet behind the ears, *Brit* still in nappies; *US* still in diapers **4** additional, °new, °further, renewed, °extra, °supplementary **5** °alert, refreshed, °vigorous, °energetic, invigorated, spry, °lively, full of vim and vigor, fresh as a daisy, °keen, °bright, °brisk, °active, *Colloq* bright-eyed and bushy-tailed **6** °wholesome, °healthy, °well, refreshed, °glowing, °fair, °rosy, ruddy, blooming, °flourishing **7** °moderate, °brisk, °strong; °cool, °clean, °pure, °clear, unpolluted **8** °bold, °impudent, °impertinent, °brazen, °brassy, °forward, °disrespectful, saucy, °pert, °cheeky, °presumptuous, °insolent, °rude, *Colloq* smart-aleck *or* smart-alecky, *US* sassy, °flip

freshen *v.* **1** °strengthen, °increase, blow harder **2** Sometimes, ***freshen up.*** invigorate, °revive, °refresh, °enliven, (re)vitalize, °stimulate, titivate *or* tittivate, °rouse, liven up **3** ventilate, air out, deodorize, °purify **4** °strengthen, °spike, °lace, °fortify

fret *v.* **1** °worry, be concerned, agonize, lose sleep, be upset *or* distressed *or* anxious *or* disturbed, °grieve, °brood, whine, °fuss, °complain, *Colloq* °stew, tear one's hair **2** °worry, °concern, °distress, vex, °annoy, °irritate, °torment, °provoke, *US* °rankle

fretful *adj.* °irritable, vexed, ill-tempered, bad-tempered, °peevish, edgy, °cross, °petulant, °testy, °touchy, tetchy, splenetic, irascible, choleric, crabby, fractious, °short-tempered, grumpy, sulky, °moody, °fault-finding, carping, °querulous, whining, complaining, captious, ill-natured, °disagreeable, °impatient, °snappish, °waspish, °short, °abrupt, °curt, *US and Canadian* °cranky

friction *n.* **1** abrasion, rubbing, abrading, chafing, fretting, attrition, scraping, °grating, °erosion **2** °disagreement, °discord, °conflict, contention, °dispute, °dissension, disharmony, °controversy, dissent, bickering, °argument, wrangling, ill feeling, °ill will, bad blood, °animosity, °rivalry, °hostility, °antagonism, °strife

friend *n.* **1** °(boon) companion, °partner, °comrade, crony, °familiar, confidant(e), °intimate, Achates, alter ego, °ally, compeer; °acquaintance, °playmate, pen pal *or Brit also* pen friend; *Colloq* °chum, °pal, *Brit* cocker, *Chiefly Brit and Australian and New Zealand* °mate, *Australian* cobber, *US and Canadian* (bosom) buddy, *SW US* compadre; *Slang Brit* (old) china **2** °ally, °associate, °fellow, confederate, °colleague, coworker, confrère, compatriot, consociate, *US* °cohort **3** roommate, bunkmate, flatmate, soul mate, bedfellow, °lover, °sweetheart, °escort; °girl, °woman, girl friend, concubine, °mistress, *Old-fashioned* doxy; °man, boyfriend, *Old-fashioned* beau; *Colloq US* alternative other, POSSLQ (= 'Person of the Opposite Sex Sharing Living Quarters'), roomie; *Slang* °baby, moll, sugar daddy, *US* °squeeze, °twist, *Chiefly Brit* bird **4** °benefactor, benefactress, °patron, °supporter, °advocate, adherent, °backer, °financier, Maecenas; angel, investor

friendly *adj.* **1** °amicable, congenial, °sociable, companionable, comradely, convivial, °familiar, well-disposed, °close, on good terms, simpatico, °comfortable, °at home, °neighborly, clubby, °fraternal, °brotherly, sisterly, *Colloq* °chummy, pally, °thick, *Brit* matey, *US* palsy-walsy, buddy-buddy **2** °amiable, °affectionate, loving, °demonstrative, °cordial, warmhearted, °warm, °genial, °agreeable, °good-natured, °pleasant, °kind, °kindly, kindhearted, °agreeable, affable, approachable, °accessible, unreserved, °open, *Brit* clubbable

friendship *n.* **1** amity, congeniality, sociability, companionability, comradeship, °fellowship, conviviality, °familiarity, closeness, neighborliness, °harmony, clubbiness, °fraternity, °brotherhood, sisterhood, °alliance **2** friendliness, amiability, amicability, °esteem, °warmth, °devotion, °affection, fondness, °attachment, °(deep) regard, °rapport, intimacy, °love

fright *n.* **1** °fear, °alarm, °terror, °dread, °horror, °panic, trepidation, °dismay, consternation, apprehension, *Colloq* (blue) funk **2** °scare, °shock **3** °specter, °monster, eyesore, *Colloq* °sight, °mess

frighten *v.* °terrify, °scare, °alarm, °panic, °startle, °shock, °petrify, °horrify, °dismay, °appall, °unnerve, °distress, °daunt, cow, °intimidate, *Colloq* scare out of one's wits, make one's hair stand on end, scare the (living) daylights out of, scare stiff, *Brit* °put the wind up (someone), put the frighteners on (someone)

frightening *adj.* °terrifying, alarming, °startling, °shocking, petrifying, horrifying, dismaying, appalling, unnerving, dire, distressing, daunting, intimidating, °formidable, °frightful, °fearful, hair-raising, °harrowing, °dreadful, *Colloq* °scary, spooky

frightful *adj.* **1** See **frightening. 2** °awful, °dreadful, °terrible, °disagreeable, °atrocious, °abhorrent, °loathsome, °grisly, °ghastly, °lurid, °macabre, °horrible, horrifying, horrid, horrendous, °nasty, °hideous, °vile, unspeakable, nauseating, °nauseous, °repugnant, °repulsive, °shocking, °revolting, °abominable, °offensive, °ugly

frightfully *adv.* °awfully, °very, °extremely; amazingly, surprisingly

frigid *adj.* **1** °cold, arctic, frosty, frozen, glacial, °icy, hyperboreal, °polar, bone-chilling, boreal, Siberian, °freezing, °wintry, °chilly, °chill, *Archaic* frore **2** °cold, °cool, °coldhearted, °forbidding, austere, unemotional, unfeeling, °stiff, °rigid, prim, °strait-laced, °stony, °callous, °steely, obdurate, °thick-skinned, impervious, °inaccessible, °remote, °unapproachable, unfriendly, °standoffish, °haughty, °aloof, °reserved **3** °unapproachable, unresponsive, °impassive, °passive, °indifferent, °cold; °impotent

frill *n.* **1** trimming, °decoration, °ornament, furbelow, °flounce, °ruffle **2** ornamentation, frippery, falderal *or* falderol *or* folderol, frou-frou, showiness, °ostentation, °embellishment, °luxury, trimming, °extra, °addition, °superfluity, °gewgaw, °(bit of) paraphernalia, *Colloq US* foofaraw, bells and whistles, *Slang* jazz

fringe *n.* **1** trimming, °edge, edging, °border, °frill, °flounce, °ruffle, purfle, purfling, ruff, ruche *or* rouche, rickrack *or* ricrac, °ornament, °decoration, furbelow **2** °border, °perimeter, °edge, °boundary, °bounds, °periphery, °limits, °margin, °outskirts, march(es); *Technical* fimbria —*v.* **3** °edge, °border, °trim, °surround

frisk *v.* **1** °caper, gambol, °cavort, °frolic, °skip, °trip, romp, curvet, °leap, °dance, °prance, °play, rollick **2** °search, °inspect, °examine, °check (out), °go over

frisky *adj.* °lively, °frolicsome, rollicking, °playful, °active, °animated, (high-)spirited, coltish

fritter *v.* ***fritter away.*** squander, °waste, °idle away, misspend, °dissipate

frivolous *adj.* **1** °trifling, °inconsequential, unimportant, trivial, nugatory, °insignificant, °minor, °petty, °paltry, °niggling, °peripheral, °superficial, °worthless, *Colloq* °small-time, *Brit* twopenny *or* tuppenny, two-a-penny, *US* two-bit, penny-ante, nitty-gritty **2** °scatterbrained, birdbrained, °silly, featherbrained, °irresponsible, °flippant, °casual, °flighty, °giddy, °foolish, °childish, °puerile; airy, °light, °slight, *Brit* airy-fairy, *Colloq* °flip

frolic *n.* **1** °merriment, merrymaking, °gaiety, °sport, °fun (and games), high jinks, jollity, °mirth, jollification, °festivity, °celebration, °revelry, °play, horseplay, *Colloq* skylarking, partying **2** romp, °party, °spree, °revel, gambol, °caper, gambado, antic; escapade, °prank —*v.* **3** °frisk, °cavort, °caper, skylark, gambol, rollick, romp, cut capers, curvet, °play, °skip, °sport, have fun, *Colloq* °party, make whoopee, horse around *or* about

frolicsome *adj.* °playful, °merry, °frisky, °sportive, °gay, °lively, °sprightly, °animated, °spirited, coltish

front *n.* **1** °face, façade, °facing, forepart, anterior; obverse **2** frontage, forefront **3** °beginning, °head, fore, vanguard, forefront, van **4** °bearing, demeanor, mien, °air, °face, countenance, façade, °mask, °expression, °show, °appearance, °aspect, °look, °exterior **5** °disguise, °cover, °guise, °mask, cover-up, °show, °pretext, façade **6** °movement, °organization, °league, bloc, °party, °group, °faction, wing **7** haughtiness, overconfidence, °effrontery **8** ***in front.*** °first, °leading, °ahead, to the fore, in the forefront, in the vanguard *or* van, °in advance, in the lead, °before; °winning **9** ***up front.*** **(a)** See **8,** above. **(b)** °open, straightforward, °honest, °direct, °forthright, °frank, °candid —*adj.* **10** °first, °advance, °foremost, °leading, °head; °main —*v.* **11** °overlook, °face, look out on *or* toward, be opposite **12** ***front for.*** act for, °represent; °substitute for, °replace

frontier *n.* front line; °border, °boundary, bound(s), marches, (far) reaches, limit(s), °pale, extreme(s), bourn

froth *n.* **1** °foam, spume, suds, °lather, °bubbles; °head **2** trivia, °rubbish, °nonsense, twaddle, °babble, °gibberish, °drivel, *Colloq* °hot air, gas, °gab, piffle *—v.* **3** °foam, spume, °bubble, °fizz, effervesce, aerate **4** °foam, salivate; °lather

frown *v.* **1** °scowl, glower, °glare, knit one's brows, grimace, give a dirty look, *Brit* lour *or* lower, *US* °lower **2** ***frown on or upon.*** °disapprove (of), (look on *or* regard *or* view with) disfavor, discountenance, look down on *or* upon, look askance at, not take kindly to, not think much of, look disapprovingly upon, *Colloq* take a dim view of, be turned off by *—n.* **3** °scowl, glower, °glare, grimace, dirty look, *Brit* lour *or Brit* lower, *US* °lower

frugal *adj.* **1** °thrifty, °sparing, economic(al), °careful, °prudent, °provident, °saving, °conservative, conservational, °moderate **2** parsimonious, °penurious, penny-pinching, cheeseparing, °mean, °miserly, stingy, niggardly, tight(-fisted), close(fisted), hand-to-mouth **3** °meager, °paltry, °poor, skimpy, scant(y), °small, °negligible, piddling

fruit *n.* Often, ***fruits.*** product(s), result(s), revenue(s), outgrowth, °outcome, consequence(s), return(s), advantage(s), benefit(s), profit(s), emolument, °payment, °income, compensation, recompense, desert(s)

fruitful *adj.* **1** °productive, °fertile, °prolific, fecund; fructiferous, frugiferous, fructuous **2** °effective, °worthwhile, well-spent, °profitable, °successful, °useful, °rewarding, °advantageous, °beneficial, °productive, °fertile **3** °plentiful, °abundant, bounteous, °bountiful, °prolific, plenteous, copious, °luxurious, °rich, °flourishing

fruition *n.* °realization, °fulfillment, °consummation, °achievement, °success, materialization, °maturity, ripeness, maturation, °completion; °perfection

fruitless *adj.* °barren, unfruitful, unproductive, °worthless, °bootless, °futile, °pointless, °useless, °vain, °idle, unavailing, °ineffectual, °ineffective, °unprofitable, for naught, to no avail, °unsuccessful, unrewarding, abortive

frustrate *v.* **1** °thwart, °foil, °stymie, °block, baffle, °check, balk *or* baulk, °disappoint, °discourage, °forestall, °prevent, °stop, °halt, °cripple, °hinder, °hamper, °impede, hamstring, °defeat, °counteract, °neutralize, nullify, °counter, °fight off, °repel, °repulse **2** °discourage, °disappoint, °upset, °exasperate

fuel *n.* **1** tinder, combustible, kindling; fossil *or* nuclear fuel **2** ammunition, °encouragement, stimulus, °incitement, °provocation **3** °nourishment, nutriment, °sustenance, °food, nutrition *—v.* **4** °nourish, °feed, °sustain; °stimulate, °encourage, °incite, °provoke, °inflame, exacerbate, °excite

fugitive *n.* **1** °runaway, escapee, °deserter, °refugee, *Archaic* runagate *—adj.* **2** fleeing, escaped, running away, °runaway **3** °fleeting, °passing, °brief, °short-lived, transitory, °transient, ephemeral, evanescent, °momentary, °volatile, fugacious

fulfill *v.* **1** °bring about, °achieve, °accomplish, bring *or* carry to completion, °carry out, °complete, consummate, °discharge, live up to, °abide by, °observe, °realize, °effect, bring *or* carry off, °carry through, °keep, °satisfy, do, °perform, °execute, °effectuate, °achieve **2** °answer, °satisfy, °meet, °implement, look *or* see to, conform to *or* with, comply with, °obey

fulfillment *n.* °completion, °consummation, °performance, carrying out *or* through, °discharge, °realization, implementation, °execution, °accomplishment, compliance, conformity *or* conformance, making good, °meeting, °satisfaction, answering, °achievement

full *adj.* **1** filled, °replete, brimming, brimful, °packed, jampacked, °congested, °loaded, bursting, chockablock, chock-full *or* choke-full *or* chuck-full, jammed, crammed, °solid, well-supplied, crowded, stuffed; gorged, saturated, sated, satiated **2** °complete, °thorough, °detailed, °comprehensive, °total, (all-)inclusive, °broad, °extensive, all-encompassing, °exhaustive, plenary **3** °complete, °entire, °whole **4** utmost, greatest, °maximum, highest, °top; °extreme **5** °wide, °ample, °generous, °broad, copious, loose (-fitting) **6** occupied, engrossed, °absorbed, immersed, °preoccupied, obsessed, consumed, °engaged, °concerned **7** filled *or* rounded out, round(ish), well-rounded, °plump; °robust, °shapely, well-shaped, curvaceous, °buxom, busty, °voluptuous, full-bodied, well-proportioned, well-built, *Slang* stacked, *Brit* well-stacked, *US* zaftig, built **8** unrestricted, nonrestricted, unconditional, °unqualified **9** °sentimental, °emotional, overflowing **10** unobscured, unshaded, undimmed, °open, °broad, °bright, shining, °brilliant, °dazzling, °glaring, °intense, blazing, blinding; °harsh, °vivid, revealing **11** °powerful, °resonant, °rich, °deep, °loud **12** °complete, °whole, °entire; °comprehensive, uncut, °unabridged, °intact, unshortened, unbowdlerized, uncensored *—adv.* **13** fully, °completely, °entirely, °wholly, °thoroughly, °altogether **14** squarely, °directly, °right, °precisely, °exactly, bang, *Colloq* °slap, smack **15** °very, °perfectly, °exceedingly, °quite, *Slang* damned *—n.* **16** °maximum, greatest degree, fullest **17** ***in full.*** °completely, fully, °entirely, °wholly, °thoroughly, in its entirety, °totally, *in toto* **18** ***to the full or fullest.*** °completely, fully, °quite, °thoroughly, to the utmost, to the greatest *or* fullest extent; a great deal, greatly, hugely, enormously

fumble *v.* **1** °grope, °feel, °stumble **2** °mishandle, °drop, muff, °bungle, °botch, *Colloq US* bobble, flub

fume *v.* **1** °seethe, °smolder, °chafe, °boil, °rage, °storm, °rant, °flare up, °bluster, lose one's temper, °explode, *Colloq* get steamed (up) (over *or* about), lose one's cool, flip one's lid, °flip (out), °fly off the handle, hit the roof, raise the roof, blow one's top *or* stack, get hot under the collar, blow a gasket, go off the deep end **2** smoke —*n.* **3** Usually, ***fumes.*** smoke, °vapor, effluvium, gas, °exhalation, °exhaust; °smell, °odor, °aroma, °fragrance, °stench, stink, miasma; °pollution, smog

fumigate *v.* °disinfect, °cleanse, °purify, sanitize, °sterilize, decontaminate

fun *n.* **1** °merriment, merrymaking, °gaiety, °glee, jollity, °mirth, °cheer, high spirits, °delight, °frolic, °festivity, high jinks; °amusement, °diversion, °sport, °enjoyment, °recreation, °entertainment, °pastime, °joy, °pleasure, *Colloq* (making) whoopee **2** tomfoolery, horseplay, joking, playfulness, clowning, pranks, °sport, jesting, jocularity, °nonsense, fooling around *or* about, *Colloq* skylarking **3** ***in or for fun.*** jokingly, teasingly, in jest, facetiously, with tongue in cheek, playfully, as a lark, for a joke *or* gag; not seriously **4** ***Like fun!*** Under no circumstances!, No way!, *Colloq* Like hell!, *US* No way, Jose! **5** ***make fun of.*** °poke fun at, °tease, °deride, °(hold up to) ridicule, scoff at, °lampoon, °parody, °satirize, make sport *or* game of, °taunt, °gibe, °rag, *Colloq* kid, rib, *Brit* °send up

function *n.* **1** °purpose, °aim, °use, role *or* rôle, raison d'être, °responsibility, °mission, °charge, °concern, °business, °province, °duty, °job, °occupation, °work, °office, °task, chore, °assignment, commission, °activity **2** °reception, °gathering, °affair, °party, dinner, °banquet, °gala, °ceremony, °formality, °rite, °ritual; °occasion, °event —*v.* **3** °act, °operate, °perform, °behave, °work, °go, °run **4** °serve, take the role *or* rôle of, act the part of, act as, work as

functional *adj.* **1** utilitarian, °useful, °serviceable, °practical, °practicable, functioning, working; °essential, °important, °effective **2** working, operating, operational, °running, °going

functionary *n.* °official, commissioner, bureaucrat, officeholder, °officer

fund *n.* **1** °supply, °stock, °reserve, °store, °pool, °cache, reservoir, repository, °mine **2** Often, ***funds.*** °money, °(hard) cash, ready money, °assets, °means, °wealth, °resources, wherewithal, °savings, °capital, nest egg, °endowment, *Colloq* °loot, lucre, pelf, °green, bread, dough, *Brit* °ready, °readies, lolly, *US* bucks, °scratch —*v.* **3** °finance, °back, capitalize, °stake, °support, °pay for, endow, °grant, °subsidize

fundamental *adj.* **1** °basic, °rudimentary, °elementary, °primary, °main, °prime, °first, °principal, underlying, °cardinal, °central, °essential, quintessential, constitutional, °inherent, °intrinsic, °important, °crucial, °critical, °organic, °vital —*n.* **2** °principle, °law, °rule, axiom, °essential, °element, sine qua non, cornerstone, °keystone

funeral *n.* obsequies, exequies; °burial, interment, sepulture, entombment, inhumation; cremation

funereal *adj.* °grave, °solemn, °sad, °unhappy, morose, °somber, °mournful, °doleful, °sorrowful, °melancholy, °gloomy, lugubrious, °dismal, °grievous, depressing, °dreary, woeful, °dark, sepulchral

funny *adj.* **1** comical, °humorous, °comic, °ludicrous, laughable, °ridiculous, risible, waggish, sidesplitting, °hilarious, °uproarious, jocular, jocose, °merry, droll, facetious, °witty, °farcical, slapstick, °zany; amusing, °entertaining, diverting, *Colloq* °hysterical **2** °peculiar, °odd, °unusual, °curious, °strange, °mysterious, mystifying, °puzzling, °queer, °weird, °bizarre, °remarkable, unconventional, °eccentric, *Slang* off the wall

furious *adj.* **1** °angry, enraged, raging, infuriated, fuming, incensed, irate, maddened, °mad, boiling, wrathful, provoked, °beside oneself, up in arms, in high dudgeon, on the warpath, foaming at the mouth, *Literary* wroth, *Colloq* steaming, livid, in a tizzy, *Slang* up the wall **2** °fierce, °wild, °violent, °savage, °intense, unrestrained, °frantic, frenzied

furnish *v.* **1** °supply, °provide, °afford, °equip, °outfit, fit (out *or* up), rig (out *or* up), °provision, °give, stock up, *Colloq Brit* kit out *or* up **2** °decorate, °equip

furniture *n.* **1** furnishings, household (goods); movables, chattels, °paraphernalia, °effects, °possessions, °belongings, *Colloq* °gear, °things, °stuff, *Slang* shit **2** °fittings, fitments, °equipment, fixtures, °apparatus, °devices, °tackle, °tack, °trappings, °gear, accoutrements *or US also* accouterments, accessories, appliances, *Colloq Brit* clobber

furor *n.* **1** °uproar, °outburst, °tumult, commotion, turmoil, brouhaha, ado, hurly-burly, to-do, hubbub, °stir, °fuss, °disturbance, °excitement **2** °rage, °craze, °mania, °vogue, °enthusiasm, °obsession, °fad

furrow *n.* **1** °groove, °channel, °rut, trench, °track, ditch, gutter, trough, fosse, fissure, sulcus, sulcation, flute, °score, °cut, °gash, °scratch, °line; °wrinkle, crease, corrugation, crow's-feet, *Technical* sulcus —*v.* **2** °groove, °channel, flute, °score, °cut, °gash, °scratch; °plow, harrow **3** °wrinkle, crease, corrugate, °knit, °pucker, crinkle

further *adj.* **1** more, additional, another, other, °new, supplemental, °supplementary, °accessory, °auxiliary, °extra, °spare, °fresh **2** farther, more distant *or* remote —*adv.* **3** furthermore, °besides, °moreover, too, also, additionally, °in addition, over and above, beyond, °above, what is more, °to boot, °yet, then (again), again **4** farther, at *or* to a greater distance *or* depth —*v.* **5** °advance, °promote, °favor, push *or* urge onward(s) *or* forward(s), °forward, °foster, °back, °patronize, °support, °help, °assist, °aid

furtherance *n.* °promotion, advancement, °pursuit, °backing, boosting, °boost, fostering, championing, championship, advocating, advocacy, °patronage, °support, °help, °aid, °assistance, succor

furtive *adj.* **1** °secret, °private, °secretive, clandestine, °surreptitious, °stealthy, underhand(ed), covert, °hidden, conspiratorial, skulking, °deceitful, under-the-table, under-the-counter, huggermugger, *Colloq* °sneaky **2** °sly, °foxy, cunning, °crafty, °wily, °shifty, untrustworthy, *Colloq* °sneaky

fury *n.* **1** °anger, °rage, wrath, °indignation, ire, choler, °rancor **2** impetuosity, ferocity, savagery, vehemence, fierceness, tempestuousness, turbulence, °violence **3** virago, °shrew, spitfire, hellcat, termagant, vixen, she-devil, °hag, °witch, °bitch, *Archaic* beldam

fuse *v.* °blend, °merge, °unite, °combine, °compound, °mix, commingle, coalesce, flow *or* come together, consolidate, °amalgamate; °melt

fuss *n.* **1** °bother, pother, dither, °fluster, °flurry, °fret, commotion, ado, bustle, to-do, °excitement, furor *or Brit* furore, °unrest, °(deal of) trouble, disquiet, °upset, °stir, °uproar, °disturbance, °stir, hubbub, °agitation, brouhaha, *Colloq* hoo-ha, °flap, stink, *Brit* kerfuffle, *Slang US* hoopla —*v.* **2** make a fuss, rush about *or* around, °flutter, *Colloq* kick up a fuss

fussy *adj.* **1** °particular, °finicky, finical, °dainty, °discriminating, °difficult, °fastidious, °exacting, °demanding, *Colloq* picky, °choosy, nit-picking, pernickety *or US also* persnickety **2** °fancy, °elaborate, overdecorated, gingerbread, rococo, °ornate, °detailed, Byzantine

futile *adj.* °unsuccessful, unavailing, °useless, °unprofitable, °vain, abortive, profitless, °bootless, °worthless, °empty, °sterile, °barren, unproductive, °impotent, °ineffective, °ineffectual

future *n.* **1** days *or* time to come; tomorrow —*adj.* **2** coming, tomorrow's, later, °prospective, following, unborn, °subsequent, expected, approaching; to be, to come

fuzzy *adj.* **1** °woolly, downy, linty, fleecy, furry, °fluffy, frizzy, flossy, flocculent, floccose, floccus; feathery **2** °dim, °faint, °hazy, foggy, °misty, blurred, blurry, °indistinct, unclear, °vague, °shadowy, °indefinite, °obscure, ill-defined, °woolly, distorted

G

gab *v.* **1** °jabber, gabble, °chatter, gibber, blather *or* blether, prate, °prattle, °blab, °gossip, *Colloq Brit* natter, witter, *Slang* jaw, yak, *US* run (off) at the mouth —*n.* **2** °chatter, chitchat, °prattle, gibber-jabber, °jabber, °gossip, blarney, blather *or* blether, tittle-tattle; cackle, °moonshine, °nonsense, °drivel, twaddle, °rubbish, gobbledegook *or* gobbledygook, °mumbo jumbo, poppycock, bunk *or* bunkum, balderdash, stuff and nonsense, hogwash, eyewash, *Colloq* piffle, flummery, °rot, bull, codswallop, *Slang* crap, °garbage, *Chiefly Brit* tosh, *Brit* (a load of old) cobbler's, *Taboo slang US* bullshit, horseshit, *Brit* shit, balls

gad *v.* Usually, ***gad about or around.*** gallivant, °run around, flit about, traipse

gadget *n.* contrivance, °device, appliance, °creation, °invention, °machine, °tool, utensil, °implement, °instrument, °mechanism, °apparatus, *Colloq* °contraption, widget, thingumabob *or* thingamabob *or* thingumbob, thingamajig *or* thingumajig *or* thingummy, whatchamacallit, whatitsname, *Brit* doodah, *US* hickey, doodad, doohickey, whosis, whatsis, dingus, *Chiefly US and Canadian* gizmo *or* gismo

gag[1] *v.* **1** °silence, °stifle, °still, °muffle, °stop (up), muzzle, °quiet, °curb, °suppress, °repress, °restrain, throttle, strangle, °check, °inhibit, °discourage **2** retch, °choke, °heave; gasp for air, struggle for breath; *US* keck —*n.* **3** °restraint, °curb, muzzle, °check

gag[2] *n.* **1** °joke, °witticism, jest, °quip, °pun, °gibe, *Colloq* °wisecrack, *Slang* °crack **2** practical joke, °hoax, °prank, °trick, *Colloq* fast one

gaiety *n.* **1** cheerfulness, exhilaration, elation, °glee, *joie de vivre,* buoyancy, lightheartedness, blitheness, °happiness, felicity, °pleasure, °delight, °joy, joyfulness, joyousness, exultation, °merriment, °mirth, mirthfulness, jubilation, good *or* high spirits, sprightliness, liveliness, joviality, jollity, °hilarity **2** Often, ***gaieties.*** merrymaking, °festivity, °festivities, °celebration, °revelry, revels, rejoicing, conviviality, *Old-fashioned Brit* mafficking **3** colorfulness, brightness, gaudiness, garishness, °brilliance, cheeriness

gaily *adv.* **1** showily, gaudily, brightly, splendidly, brilliantly, colorfully, flashily, flamboyantly, garishly **2** °happily, cheerfully, cheerily, gleefully, joyously, joyfully, jubilantly, merrily, blithely, lightheartedly, airily, jauntily, insouciantly

gain *v.* **1** °get, °obtain, °acquire, °procure, attain, °achieve, °secure, °earn, °win, °capture, °bag, °net, °harvest, °reap, °garner, glean, °collect, °gather, °come by, °pick up **2** °make, °get, °profit, gain ground, °earn, °benefit, °realize, °clear, °bring in, °produce, °yield **3** °improve, °recuperate, °progress,

°rally, get better, °advance, gain ground **4** catch up (to *or* on *or* with), °approach, get nearer (to), °overtake, close with, close in (on), narrow the gap, gain ground **5** leave behind, outdistance, draw *or* pull away (from), widen the gap, get *or* go *or* move farther ahead, get farther away (from), increase the lead **6** °reach, °arrive at, °get to, °come to **7** °increase, move ahead, °improve, °advance, °progress, gain ground —*n.* **8** °profit, °advantage, °margin, °yield, °return, °revenue, °income, dividend, °benefit, emolument, °payment, °pay, °money; °proceeds, °earnings, winnings; *Colloq chiefly US* °take, payout, °payoff **9** °increase, °increment, °improvement, °rise, °addition, enhancement, °elevation, augmentation, upward *or* forward movement, °advance, °progress **10** °acquisition, °achievement, attainment

gainful *adj.* °advantageous, °profitable, °productive, °fruitful, °beneficial, °useful, valuable, °worthwhile, °rewarding, remunerative, lucrative, moneymaking

gala *n.* **1** °fête, °festival, °festivity, °feast, °celebration, °event, red-letter day, °holiday, holy day, carnival, °occasion, °happening, °event, °pageant, °party, ball; field day —*adj.* **2** °merry, festive, °joyful, joyous, °gleeful, jovial, °gay, celebratory, °jolly, convivial, °happy, °cheerful, cheery

gale *n.* **1** windstorm, strong wind, (big *or* hard) blow, °blast, turbulence, °storm, °tempest **2** °outburst, °burst, °explosion, °eruption; °peal, °roar, °scream, °shout, °howl, °shriek

gall[1] *n.* **1** °bitterness, acerbity, acrimony, harshness, vitriol, asperity, bile, spleen, causticness *or* causticity, °bite, mordacity *or* mordaciousness, sharpness, rancidness *or* rancidity; °venom, °poison, °rancor **2** °impudence, insolence, °impertinence, audacity, brashness, brazenness, sauciness, °effrontery, temerity, overconfidence, °front, *Colloq* °brass, °nerve, °guts, cheek, lip, crust, °sauce, *US and Canadian* chutzpah, moxie; *Taboo slang* balls

gall[2] *n.* **1** °sore (spot), abrasion, °scrape, graze, °scratch, °chafe **2** irritation, °annoyance, °nuisance, °bother, exasperation, vexation, *Colloq* aggravation —*v.* **3** °irritate, °chafe, abrade, °fret, °scrape, °rub, °grate, °scratch **4** °irritate, °annoy, °bother, vex, °irk, °exasperate, °harass, harry, °plague, °provoke, goad, °nag, °pester, hector, badger, nettle, needle, °ruffle, °fret, °anger, °enrage, °inflame, °infuriate, incense, °arouse, *US* °rankle

gallant *adj.* **1** °brave, °courageous, °bold, valiant, °daring, °dauntless, °intrepid, plucky, °fearless, valorous, unafraid, undaunted, °manly, manful, plucky, mettlesome, stouthearted, lionhearted, °heroic, °dashing, (high-)spirited **2** °chivalrous, courtly, °courteous, °polite, °attentive, gentlemanly, °noble, °gracious, °considerate, °thoughtful, °well-bred, mannerly **3** °dignified, °elegant, °imposing, °grand, °noble, °glorious, °fine, °splendid, °majestic, °stately, °magnificent —*n.* **4** °champion, °hero, knight, cavalier, paladin **5** °lover, Romeo, °sweetheart, °beloved, °paramour, boyfriend, beau, °escort, °suitor, °admirer, *Literary* swain

gallows *n.* gibbet

galore *adv.* in abundance, in large quantity *or* numbers *or* amounts, in excess, °everywhere, aplenty, in profusion

gamble *v.* **1** °risk, °venture, °hazard, °bet, wager, °stake, °chance, °speculate; °play, °game, *Brit* punt **2** ***gamble on.*** °back, bet *or* wager on, stake *or* put money on, take a chance *or* flier on, try one's luck *or* fortune on, lay *or* place *or* make a wager *or* bet on; °count on, °rely on —*n.* **3** °chance, °risk, °venture; uncertainty, °speculation, *Colloq US* crapshoot **4** °bet, wager, °stake, *Brit* punt

game *n.* **1** °amusement, °pastime, °diversion, °distraction, °recreation, °play; °sport **2** °contest, °competition, meeting *or US also* meet, tournament *or also* tourney, °match, °encounter, °engagement, °event, °round; regatta **3** °scheme, °plan, °plot, °design, °stratagem, °strategy, °tactic, °artifice, °trick, device(s), ploy **4** °occupation, °line (of work), °job, °position, °field, °business, °trade, °profession, *Slang* °racket **5** °quarry, °prey; °victim, °target **6** ***play games.*** dissemble, °dissimulate, be deceitful *or* underhand, °misrepresent, °pretend, practice deceit *or* deception, °fake, feign —*adj.* **7** °ready, °willing, °prepared; plucky *or* spirited *or* daring *or* adventurous enough **8** plucky, °spirited, high-spirited, °daring, devil-may-care, °adventurous, unflinching, °courageous, °brave, °bold, °heroic, *Colloq* nervy, gutsy —*v.* **9** °gamble

gamut *n.* °range, °scale, spectrum, compass, °spread, °sweep, °field, series

gang *n.* **1** °group, °band, °crowd, °company, °pack, °mob, °ring **2** °clique, °set, coterie, °circle, °party, °company, °team, troupe —*v.* **3** ***gang up (on or against).*** conspire *or* plot against, combine *or* unite *or* unify *or* join (against), league *or* ally *or* club *or* band (against), join forces (against), °overwhelm

gangster *n.* °criminal, gang member, °racketeer, mafioso, °soldier, hooligan, gunman, °thug, mugger, °robber, °tough, ruffian, desperado, brigand, bandit, *Brit* skinhead, *Australian and New Zealand* larrikin, *Chiefly US and Canadian* °hoodlum, gunslinger, *Colloq* crook; *Slang* hood, hit man, *US* gunsel, torpedo, mobster, goon

gap *n.* **1** °opening, °space, °aperture, °distance, °hole, °void, °gulf, °cavity, °break, °breach, °crevice, °chink, °crack, °split, °division, cleft, °rift, °rip, °tear, °rent; °interruption, °interval, lacuna, hiatus, discontinuity, disruption; °lull, °pause, °rest, °recess, °halt, °stop, °suspension, °delay, °wait, °intermission, °respite **2** °difference, divergence, °disparity, °disagreement, inconsistency, °discrepancy; °division, °distinction

gape *v.* **1** °stare, °gawk, goggle, *Slang* °rubberneck, *Brit* gawp *or* gaup **2** yawn, open wide, °part; °split

garbage *n.* °rubbish, °refuse, °waste, °muck, offal, sweepings, °swill, °filth, slops, dross, °scraps, °junk, °litter, debris, detritus, *Chiefly US and Canadian* °trash, *Slang* crap

garble *v.* **1** °warp, °distort, °twist, °corrupt, °adulterate, °slant, °color, °mangle, °mutilate, °pervert, °doctor, °falsify, °misrepresent, belie, misstate, misquote, misreport, mistranslate, misrender; °misunderstand, misconstrue, misread **2** °confuse, °mix up, °jumble, °mumble, °mutter

garish *adj.* °gaudy, °flashy, °glaring, °cheap, °tawdry, florid, raffish, °vulgar, °harsh, °loud, meretricious, brummagem, °showy, °crude, °tasteless, *Colloq* °flash, *Slang US* glitzy

garland *n.* **1** wreath, festoon, °crown, chaplet, circlet —*v.* **2** wreathe, festoon, °crown, °decorate, °coil, °spiral, °encircle, °ring, °circle

garments *n. pl.* garb, °clothes, clothing, raiment, °dress, attire, °apparel, °costume, °outfit, °habit, vestments, habiliment; °wardrobe; °uniform, livery; *Colloq* duds, °rig, togs, *Slang* °rags, threads, °gear

garner *v.* °gather, °collect, °accumulate, °assemble, °amass, °store (up), °stock (up), °husband, lay in *or* up *or* down *or* by, heap *or* pile up, put away *or* by, °stow (away), °cache, °store, °save, °reserve

gash *n.* **1** °cut, °slash, °wound, °score, cleft, °incision, laceration, °slit, °groove, °split —*v.* **2** °cut, °slash, °wound, °score, °cleave, incise, °lacerate, °slit, °groove, °split

gasp *v.* **1** °pant, gulp for air, fight for air *or* breath; catch one's breath, snort, °huff, °puff —*n.* **2** snort, °puff, °blow, °gulp, wheeze

gate *n.* **1** gateway, °barrier, doorway, door, access, °entrance, °exit, °passage, °opening **2** admissions, °attendance, °crowd, audience, assemblage

gather *v.* **1** °collect, °assemble, °accumulate, °amass, °muster, heap *or* pile (up), °garner, °pick, °harvest, glean, get *or* bring together, stockpile, °stock **2** °collect, °assemble, convene, °meet, °huddle, forgather *or* foregather, get *or* come together, congregate, °turn out, flock *or* herd (together), °group, °cluster, °throng, °crowd, °swarm, °rally **3** °purse, shirr, °pucker, tuck, °ruffle, pleat, draw *or* pull together, °contract, constrict **4** °draw, conclude, °infer, °assume, °deduce, °understand, °learn, °hear, be led to believe **5** °increase, °grow, °enlarge, °expand, °extend, wax, °heighten, °deepen, °intensify, °build, °rise

gathering *n.* °assembly, convocation, °convention, congress, assemblage, °meeting, °get-together, °turnout, conclave, °rally, aggregation

gaudy *adj.* °garish, °flashy, °glaring, °tawdry, °loud, °cheap, florid, °showy, °ostentatious, raffish, °vulgar, °crude, °tasteless, brummagem, meretricious, tinselly, gimcrack, °shoddy, trashy, *Brit* tatty, *US and Canadian* honky-tonk, *Colloq US* °tacky, chintzy

gauge *v.* **1** °measure, °determine, °weigh, °calculate, °compute, °reckon, °figure, *US technical also* gage **2** °judge, °evaluate, appraise, assess, °rate, °estimate, °guess, *US technical also* gage —*n.* **3** °standard, °yardstick, criterion, benchmark, °basis, °measure, °norm, °model, °example, °pattern, °rule, °touchstone, °test, °guide, guideline, *US* litmus test, *Technical also* gage **4** °scope, °capacity, °amount, °extent, °measure, °size, dimension(s), °magnitude, °degree, °limit

gaunt *adj.* **1** °emaciated, °scrawny, °rawboned, bony, angular, °haggard, skeletal, wasted, starved-looking, cadaverous, scraggy, spindly, °meager, hollow-cheeked, °spare, °skinny, lank(y), pinched, °thin, underweight **2** °dreary, °dismal, °bleak, °bare, °barren, °deserted, °desolate, °harsh, °hostile, unfriendly, inimical, °stern, °forbidding, °stark, °grim, °forlorn

gawk *n.* **1** oaf, lout, bumpkin, °clod, °boor, churl, °dolt, dunderhead *or* dunderpate, ninny, gormless ninnyhammer, ignoramus, °fool, simpleton, ass, bungler, bumbler, *Colloq* clodhopper, lummox, *Slang chiefly US old-fashioned* galoot *or* galloot, °lug —*v.* **2** °stare, goggle, °gape, *Colloq* °rubberneck, *Slang Brit* gawp *or* gaup

gay *adj.* **1** See **homosexual, 1,** below. **2** °happy, °blithe, jovial, lighthearted, °carefree, debonair *or Brit also* debonnaire, °cheerful, °gleeful, °bright, °joyful, joyous, jubilant, high-spirited, °merry, °lively, °vivacious, °buoyant, °effervescent, °bubbly, bubbling, sparkling, *US* chipper **3** °garish, °gaudy, °flashy, °bright, °brilliant, °vivid, many-colored —*n.* **4** See **homosexual, 2,** below.

gaze *v.* **1** look at *or* on *or* upon *or* over, °view, °regard, °contemplate, °stare; °wonder, °gape —*n.* **2** fixed *or* steady *or* intent look, °stare, °look

gear *n.* **1** °cog, cogwheel; gearbox, °mechanism, machinery; °works **2** °equipment, °apparatus, appliances, implements, tools, °tackle, utensils, supplies, material(s), accessories, accouterments *or* accoutrements, appurtenances, °paraphernalia, panoply, °outfit, °trappings, fixtures, materiel *or* matériel **3** clothing, °apparel, attire, °clothes, °garments, °habit, habiliments, vestments, raiment, °regalia, °uniform, livery, *Colloq* duds, togs, *Brit* clobber **4** °belongings, °things, °stuff, °effects, °kit, chattels, °goods, impedimenta, (bag and) baggage, accouterments *or* accoutrements, *Colloq* °junk, *Slang* shit —*v.* **5** °adjust, °adapt, °fit, °suit, °tailor, °accommodate

gem *n.* **1** gemstone, °jewel, stone, precious *or* semiprecious stone **2** °ideal, °quintessence, perfect example; °pearl (of great price), °marvel, °flower, °elite, cream, *crème* *de la crème,* °pick, °nonpareil, °treasure, °prize, °masterpiece, *chef d'oeuvre*

general *adj.* **1** °common, °prevailing, accepted, °popular, °public, communal, community, widespread, shared, °extensive, °prevalent, °universal, worldwide, °global; °comprehensive, °inclusive, (all-)inclusive, nonexclusive, °overall, unrestricted **2** °ordinary, °common, °normal, °customary, °habitual, °regular, °usual, °run-of-the-mill, °everyday, °familiar, °accustomed; nonspecialized, unspecialized, nonspecific, unspecific **3** °mixed, assorted, °miscellaneous, heterogeneous, °encyclopedic, diversified, extended, °broad, °comprehensive, (all-)inclusive, nonexclusive, °overall, blanket, across-the-board, °sweeping, °panoramic, °catholic, composite, combined, blended, °hybrid, °mongrel **4** °vague, °indefinite, °broad, ill-defined, °loose, °inexact, °imprecise, undetailed, nonspecific, unspecific, generalized, °overall; °approximate

generality *n.* **1** generalization, abstraction, °abstract, vague *or* loose *or* sweeping *or* indefinite statement, imprecise *or* vague notion **2** Often, ***generalities.*** principle(s), law(s), abstraction(s), generalization(s), universality *or* universalities

generally *adv.* **1** °usually, commonly, °ordinarily, in general, customarily, habitually, conventionally, normally, typically, °on average, °as a rule, by and large, °for the most part, mostly, °mainly, °on the whole, predominantly **2** superficially, nonspecifically, unspecifically, °roughly, broadly, in a general way, loosely, °approximately, °largely, °in the main, °mainly, °principally

generate *v.* **1** °produce, °create, °originate, °make, °manufacture **2** °spawn, °father, sire, bring into being, procreate, °breed, beget, engender, °propagate **3** °produce, °create, °give rise to, °inspire, °whip up, °cause, °initiate **4** °produce, °create, °invent, °coin, °make up, °fabricate, °fashion, °devise, °develop, °form, °forge, °mold, contrive, °construct, put together

generation *n.* **1** °production, °reproduction, propagation, procreation, begetting, fathering, siring **2** time(s), day(s), °age, °period, °era, epoch **3** origination, °creation, genesis, inception, °initiation, °start, °beginning, °institution, °establishment, °formation, formulation **4** crop; °age (group); contemporaries

generous *adj.* **1** bounteous, °bountiful, magnanimous, °charitable, eleemosynary, °philanthropic, °lavish, openhanded, °free, °liberal, unstinting, ungrudging, beneficent, °benevolent, bighearted, munificent **2** magnanimous, °benevolent, °charitable, °unselfish, °humanitarian, humane, °kindly, °noble, high-minded, °lofty, °good, °disinterested, °unprejudiced **3** °plentiful, °full, °lavish, overflowing, °abundant, bounteous, °handsome, copious, °ample

genial *adj.* affable, °amiable, °cordial, °warm, °friendly, congenial, °agreeable, °good-natured, good-humored, °neighborly, well-disposed, °sociable, °kindly, °kind, °hospitable, easygoing, °relaxed, °pleasant, °nice, °cheerful, cheery, convivial

genitals *n. pl.* genitalia, sexual *or* reproductive organs, sex organs, organs of procreation *or* generation, °private parts, °privates

genius *n.* **1** °mastermind, °master, °virtuoso, °intellect; maestro, °expert, °adept; *Colloq* °brain, Einstein **2** °intelligence, °brilliance, °wit, °ingenuity, brains, °ability, °aptitude **3** °talent, °gift, °knack, °faculty, °flair, °aptitude, °forte, °capacity, °ability, °capability

genre *n.* °kind, °sort, °type, °class, °style, °brand, °character, °category, genus, species, °variety, °fashion

genteel *adj.* **1** overpolite, °unnatural, °pretentious, °affected, °mannered, putting on airs, pompous, overdone, *Colloq* °posh, la-di-da *or* lah-di-dah, phoney *or US also* phony, *Brit* county **2** courtly, °polite, °civil, well-mannered, °well-bred, °courteous, mannerly, °gracious, °proper, °respectable, °decorous, °ladylike, gentlemanly, °chivalrous, cavalier, °debonair, °suave, patrician, °high-class, °upper-class, aristocratic, thoroughbred, blue-blooded, °noble, °royal, *Colloq* classy, tony, upper-crust, *US* silk-stocking **3** °refined, °polished, °sophisticated, debonair *or Brit also* debonnaire, °suave, urbane, cosmopolitan, °cultivated, cultured, °elegant, *Colloq* ritzy

gentle *adj.* **1** °kind, °kindly, °mild, °tender, °benign, °moderate, °easy, °quiet, °calm, °still, °temperate, unruffled, untroubled, undisturbed, °tranquil, °restful, °peaceful, pacific, placid, °smooth, °lenient, °patient, °indulgent, °soothing, °thoughtful, °gracious, compassionate, humane, tenderhearted, °merciful; °soft, °light, balmy **2** °tame, °tractable, docile, °manageable, controllable; °broken **3** °gradual, °easy, °moderate

gentry *n.* ladies and gentlemen, °elite, aristocracy, landed gentry, gentlefolk, upper class(es) *or* strata, cream, *crème de la crème*; landowners, *Brit* squirearchy, *Colloq* °upper crust

genuine *adj.* **1** °authentic, °real, °bona fide, °veritable, °legitimate, °true, °original, °proper, not counterfeit *or* fake; pukka *or* pucka **2** °candid, °frank, °open, °sincere, °earnest, °honest, unfeigned

germ *n.* **1** microorganism, °microbe, bacterium, virus, *Colloq* °bug **2** °source, °origin, fount, embryo, °seed, °root, rudiment, °beginning, °start, °base, °basis

gesture *n.* **1** °movement, °motion, gesticulation, °signal, °indication, °action, *Colloq US* high sign **2** °formality, °move; gambit, ploy; °token, °indication, °symbol —*v.* **3** °motion, gesticulate, °signal, °sign, °indicate, *Colloq US* give (someone) the high sign

get *v.* **1** °obtain, °secure, °acquire, come by *or* into (the) possession of, °procure, °pick up; °collect; °buy, °purchase, °book, °retain, °hire, °engage, °rent, °lease; accede to, °inherit, fall heir to, °succeed to **2** °receive; be given, °come by **3** °earn, °receive, °realize, °make, °take, °gross, °clear, °net, °pocket, be paid; °win, *Colloq* take home, °pull down **4** °fetch, go (to *or* and) get, go for *or* after, °pick up; °bring (back), °retrieve **5** °catch, °contract, °have, °suffer from, °come down with, fall ill *or* sick with, be afflicted with, become infected with, °acquire **6** °become, °fall **7** °become, °turn, °grow **8** °capture, °seize, °arrest, °take, apprehend, °grab, °pick up, °lay hold of, °bag, *Colloq* collar, °nab, °pinch **9** °manage, °arrange, °come, °succeed; contrive, fix it, °maneuver, °manipulate, *Colloq* °wangle **10** °reach, °arrive (at), °come, °go, °travel, °journey **11** °catch, °take, °enter, °make, come *or* go by, travel *or* journey by **12** °reach, get in touch with, °communicate with, get onto *or* through to, *Colloq* °contact **13** °receive, °pick up, tune in to *or* on, listen to *or* watch **14** °persuade, °prevail upon, °coax, °induce, °influence, °cajole, °wheedle, talk (someone) into, °sway, bring (someone) round, °make, °cause **15** °put, °place, °set, °fit, °maneuver, °manipulate, wiggle, °wriggle **16** °affect, °stir, °move, °touch, °arouse, °stimulate, °excite, have an impact *or* effect on, make an impression on, °impress, leave a mark on, °get to, *Colloq* turn (someone) on **17** °get at, °irritate, °annoy, vex, °irk, nettle, pique, °provoke, °anger, °exasperate, °bother, °perturb, rile, *Colloq* °bug, get (someone's) goat, rub (someone) (up) the wrong way, *Sometimes nonstandard* °aggravate **18** baffle, °confuse, confound, °puzzle, °perplex, °bewilder **19** °understand, °appreciate, °fathom, °see, °grasp, apprehend, °perceive, °follow, °comprehend, °take in, °work out, make head(s) or tail(s) of **20** °catch, °hear **21** °derive, °learn, glean, absorb, °take in **22** °have, °place, °put, °fix, pinpoint **23** °get even with, °revenge oneself on, take vengeance on, pay (someone) back, settle *or* even the score with, °get back at **24** °strike, °hit, °punch, smack; °shoot; °hurt, °harm, °damage, °injure; *Slang* sock, slug **25** ***get about.*** See **29,** below. **26** ***get across.*** get *or* put over, °put across, °get through, °communicate, make clear, °impart **27** ***get ahead.*** °succeed, °prosper, be *or* become successful, do well, °flourish, °thrive, °make good, °progress, rise (up) in the world, *Colloq* °go places **28** ***get along.*** **(a)** be friendly *or* compatible (with), °associate (with), °agree (with), be agreeable, °get on (with), *Colloq* hit it off (with) **(b)** °manage, °cope, °shift, °fare, °survive, make both ends meet, keep the wolf from the door, keep one's head above water, °get on, *Colloq* °get by, °make out, °make do **(c)** °leave, °depart, go *or* move away, get going, °get on, go along, °proceed **(d)** °progress, °proceed, °get on, °advance, move ahead *or* along *or* on **(e)** °get on, °age, get *or* become *or* grow older, °advance **29** ***get around or about or round.*** **(a)** °spread, become known, °leak (out), °circulate, be bruited about *or* around, be noised abroad, go about *or* around **(b)** be socially active, °socialize, go *or* get out; runaround *or* about, gad about **30** ***get around or round.*** **(a)** °cajole, °wheedle, °flatter, °persuade, °coax, °win over **(b)** °bypass, circumvent, skirt, °avoid, °evade, °elude, °outsmart, °outwit, outmaneuver, outflank, steal a march on, *Colloq* give (someone) the runaround **(c)** get *or* come to, °reach, °arrive at (finally), find time for **31** ***get at.*** **(a)** gain access to, access, °reach, put *or* lay one's hands on, °get to **(b)** °intend, °mean, °suggest, °hint (at), °insinuate, °imply, have in mind *or* view, °contemplate **(c)** °tease, °taunt, °criticize, find fault with, °carp, °nag, °pick on, *US* °get to. See also **17,** above. **(d)** °get to, °influence, °intimidate, °corrupt, °bribe, °undermine, °subvert, suborn **(e)** °learn, °find out, ascertain, °determine **32** ***get away.*** **(a)** °escape, °leave, break out *or* away, °flee, °depart, make good one's escape, elude one's captors, break free, °disappear **(b)** °escape, take a holiday *or US also* vacation, get *or* take a rest *or* respite **(c)** °start, get *or* take off **33** ***get back.*** **(a)** °return, come *or* go back **(b)** reacquire, °recover, regain, °retrieve, °recoup, repossess **34** ***get back at.*** See **23,** above. **35** ***get behind.*** °back, °support, °promote, °finance, °fund, °push, *Colloq* °plug, hype **36** ***get by.*** See **28 (b),** above. **37** ***get down.*** **(a)** dismount, alight, °descend, come *or* go down, climb *or* step down, °get off **(b)** °write (down), °note (down), °record, make a note of **(c)** °depress, dispirit, °sadden, dishearten, °discourage, deject **(d)** °swallow, °eat **38** ***get down to.*** concentrate *or* focus on, turn attention to, °attend to **39** ***get in.*** **(a)** °enter, get into *or* on *or* onto, °embark, entrain, emplane *or* enplane, get *or* go aboard **(b)** °enter, °arrive, °return, come *or* go in **(c)** fit *or* squeeze in, °insert, °slip in, °include **(d)** °arrive, °come in, °land **40** ***get into.*** **(a)** °put on, don, dress in, get dressed in **(b)** °go into, °discuss, become involved in, °pursue, °treat, °describe, delineate, °detail, °follow up on, °penetrate **(c)** be into, be *or* become involved in, °take up, °pursue; °enjoy, °like, become enthusiastic about, *Slang* °get off on, get *or* become high on **(d)** See **39 (a),** above. **41** ***get off.*** **(a)** alight, °disembark, get down from, °get out of, dismount, °descend (from), climb *or* step down off *or* from, deplane, detrain **(b)** °leave, °depart, °go (off), set out *or* off **(c)** °remove, °take off, °shed, doff **(d)** cause to be set *or* go free, be *or* cause to be acquitted *or* liberated *or* released **42** ***get off on.*** See **40 (c),** above. **43** ***get on.*** **(a)** See **28,** above. **(b)** See **39 (a),** above. **(c)** grow *or* become late **44** ***get onto.*** **(a)** See **12,** above. **(b)** See **48 (b),** below. **(c)** °discover, learn about, become aware of, find out about, *Colloq Brit* °twig, *US* cotton (on) to **45** ***get out (of).*** **(a)** °leave, °depart, go out *or* away, be off, °retire **(b)** °escape, extricate oneself; be released **(c)** °extract, °draw, wrest, °force, drag *or* pry out, wring *or* get from **(d)** °gain, °profit **(e)** °avoid, °evade, °sidestep, °escape **(f)** See **29 (b),** above. **46** ***get over.*** **(a)** surmount, °cross, °climb, °pass, °traverse **(b)** recover *or* recuperate from, °survive **(c)** °finish, °complete, bring to an end **(d)** See **26,** above. **47** ***get round.*** See **29, 30,** above. **48** ***get through.*** **(a)** (help to) succeed *or* complete **(b)** °reach, °contact **(c)** °finish, conclude **(d)** °communicate (with) **49** ***get*** **(*to*). (a)** °arrive at, °come to; °near, °approach **(b)** See **31 (a), (c), (d),** above. **50** ***get together.*** **(a)** °gather, °accumulate, °collect, °assemble **(b)** °assemble, convene, °gather, °meet, congregate, °socialize **(c)** arrive at *or* reach an agreement *or* settlement, °come to terms, come to an understanding **51** ***get up.*** **(a)** °arise, °awaken, °wake (up) **(b)** °stand (up) **(c)** °mount, °climb (up), ascend **(d)** °create, °devise, °organize, °arrange, °prepare **(e)** °dress, °clothe, °apparel, °outfit, attire, °turn out, deck out, °rig out, °dress up, fit out *or* up **(f)** °study, °learn, *US* get up on **52** ***get up to.*** become *or* be involved in, be up to

getaway *n.* °escape, °flight, °retreat

get-together *n.* °gathering; °meeting, °conference, °convention

getup *n.* **1** °costume, °outfit; °rig **2** °format, layout, °arrangement, °structure, °look, °style

gewgaw *n.* trinket, °bauble, gimcrack, °trifle, knickknack *or Brit also* nicknack, bagatelle, kickshaw, °toy, °novelty, bijou, °vanity; bric-a-brac *or* bric-à-brac

ghastly *adj.* **1** °dreadful, °awful, °terrible, °terrifying, °frightful, °hideous, °horrible, horrendous, horrid, horrifying, °grim, °grisly, °loathsome, °gruesome, °ugly, °repellent, °repulsive, °shocking, appalling, *Colloq* °gross, °scary **2** °grim, cadaverous, °haggard, ashen, °wan, °pale, pallid, pasty (-faced), °drawn, livid, °ghostly, °spectral, °macabre **3** °awful, °bad, °terrible, °ill, ailing, °sick

ghost *n.* **1** apparition, °phantom, °specter, phantasm, °shade, °spirit, wraith, poltergeist, banshee, doubleganger, doppelgänger, ghoul, manes, *No. Eng. dialect* boggart; °hallucination, °illusion, °vision; *Colloq* spook **2** °hint, °suggestion, °shadow, °trace, scintilla, glimmer

ghostly *adj.* **1** °spectral, ghostlike, wraithlike, phantasmal, °phantom, °eerie, °unreal, °unnatural, °supernatural, preternatural, °unearthly, °sinister, °strange, uncanny, °weird, *Colloq* spooky, °scary, creepy **2** See **ghastly, 2,** above.

ghoulish *adj.* **1** °devilish, demonic, °satanic, diabolic(al), °fiendish, demoniac(al), cacodemonic, Mephistophelian; °infernal, hellish, malign **2** °macabre, °grisly, °morbid, °gruesome, °disgusting, °monstrous, °abominable, °hideous, horrendous, °horrible, horrifying, horrid, °brutal, barbaric, °savage, °ruthless, pitiless, °merciless, °cruel, °vicious, feral, °inhuman, °bloodthirsty, °ferocious, *Colloq* °sick

giant *n.* **1** °superhuman, titan, colossus, Goliath; giantess, Amazon, °ogre; behemoth, °monster, leviathan, mammoth —*adj.* **2** See **gigantic,** below.

gibberish *n.* °drivel, tripe, °nonsense, °rubbish, gibber, °prattle, twaddle, gabble, °jabber, balderdash, jibber-jabber, blather *or* blether, jabberwocky, gobbledygook *or* gobbledegook, °mumbo jumbo, rodomontade, Gongorism, cackle, °chatter, °patter, °jargon, °babble, claptrap, poppycock, *Colloq* tripe, codswallop, bunk, piffle, *US* °garbage, horsefeathers; *Slang* crap, *Brit* (a load of old) cobblers, *Taboo slang* balls, *US* bull(shit), crock (of shit)

gibe *v.* **1** jibe (at), °jeer (at), °scoff (at), °flout, °mock, °deride, °make fun of, °poke fun at, °ridicule, °twit, °taunt, °sneer (at), °chaff, °tease, °rag, °heckle, *No. Eng. dialect* gird, *Colloq* kid, rib, *US and Canadian* razz —*n.* **2** jibe, °jeer, °taunt, °sneer, °dig, cutting remark, °thrust, °chaff, °raillery, scoffing, °derision, °ridicule, °mockery, *Rare* mycterism, *Slang* °crack, °wisecrack

giddy *adj.* **1** °dizzy, °faint, unsteady, lightheaded, vertiginous, reeling, *Colloq* woozy **2** °silly, °frivolous, °scatterbrained, °flighty, °capricious, °irresponsible, °erratic, °fickle, °volatile, °impulsive, °reckless, °whimsical

gift *n.* **1** °present, °donation, °favor, °grant, largess *or* largesse, °bounty, benefaction, °offering, °honorarium, contribution, giveaway, °premium, °bonus, °prize; alms, handout, °dole, °charity, °benefit; °tip, gratuity, baksheesh *or* backsheesh, *pourboire,* cumshaw **2** °talent, °ability, °aptitude, °genius, °flair, °knack, °facility, °forte, °strength, strong point, °bent, °capability, °capacity, °power

gifted *adj.* °talented, °able, skilled, °capable, °skillful, °outstanding, °excellent, °superior, °superb, °brilliant, °expert, °master, °masterful, masterly, °virtuoso, first-class, °first-rate, top-drawer, top-flight, °good, *Colloq* topnotch, ace, crackerjack, °crack

gigantic *adj.* °big, °large, °huge, °enormous, °massive, °giant, °colossal, °immense, mammoth, tremendous, stupendous, °towering, staggering, °vast, titanic, gargantuan, elephantine, cyclopean, herculean, Brobdingnagian; kingsize, extra-large, *Colloq* °jumbo, walloping, °whopping, °thumping, thundering, strapping, super-duper, *US* humongous

giggle *v.* **1** °titter, °snicker, snigger, °chuckle, °laugh, chortle, cackle, °twitter —*n.* **2** °titter, °snicker, snigger, °chuckle, °laugh, chortle, cackle, °twitter **3** °joke, °prank, °laugh

gimmick *n.* **1** °device, °strategy, °stratagem, ploy, °trick, °ruse, °wile, °subterfuge, °maneuver, °artifice, °deception, °trap, °snare, *US* °hook, *Colloq* °dodge **2** °device, contrivance, °gadget, °invention, *Colloq* °contraption, widget, thingumbob *or* thingumabob *or* thingamabob, thingamajig *or* thingumajig *or* thingummy, whatchamacallit, whatitsname, *Brit* doodah, *US* doohickey, doodad, hickey, whosis, whatsis, dingus, Rube Goldberg, *Chiefly US and Canadian* gizmo *or* gismo

gingerly *adv.* **1** warily, cautiously, charily, carefully, delicately, °fastidious, daintily, squeamishly, tentatively, nervously, cannily, circumspectly, guardedly, watchfully, timidly, timorously, shyly *—adj.* **2** °wary, °cautious, chary, °careful, °fastidious, °delicate, °dainty, °squeamish, °tentative, °nervous, canny, circumspect, °guarded, watchful, °timid, timorous, °shy

girl *n.* **1** female, °woman, °lass, (young) lady, °miss, mademoiselle, wench, *Fräulein,* °maid, °maiden, damsel, demoiselle, *Irish* colleen, *Australian and New Zealand* sheila, *Colloq* chick, filly, gal, *Slang* bird, °frail, skirt, °piece, mouse, *Brit* crumpet, bit of skirt *or* stuff, *Old-fashioned Brit* popsy, *US* dame, °broad, (bit of) San Quentin quail *or* jailbait **2** girlfriend, °sweetheart; betrothed, fiancée; °mistress, °lover, °friend, live-in lover, inamorata, °tally, *US* POSSLQ (= 'Person of the Opposite Sex Sharing Living Quarters'), *Colloq Brit* popsy, *Slang* moll, *US* °twist, °squeeze

girth *n.* **1** circumference, °perimeter, ambit, °periphery, °circuit **2** °belt, girdle, °border, cincture, waistband, cestus, cummerbund, *Archaic* °zone, *US and Canadian* cinch

gist *n.* °essence, °core, °heart, °substance, °point, °theme, °quintessence, °pith, °meat, marrow, °focus, °nub, °significance, (main *or* basic) idea; °direction, °drift

give *v.* **1** °present, °deliver, °pass (over), turn *or* hand over, °confer, °vouchsafe, °provide, °supply, °furnish, °bestow, °donate, °accord, °afford, °award, °hand out, °contribute, °distribute, °grant, °allow, °transfer, °make over, °entrust **2** °exchange, °pay, °transfer, °trade, barter, swap *or* swop **3** °impart, °pass on, °communicate, °transmit, °send, convey, °express **4** afflict with, °cause, °occasion **5** °sacrifice, °devote, °dedicate, °yield (up), °surrender, °give up, °cede, °concede, consign, apply (oneself) to **6** °present, °offer; °announce, °introduce **7** °present, °announce, °offer, °recite, °sing, °act, °perform, °read, °put on **8** utter, °emit, °give out (with), °issue **9** °yield, °relax, °give way, °fail, °collapse, °buckle, °break down, fall *or* come apart **10** °cause, °lead, °induce, °persuade, °make, °prompt, °move, °dispose **11** °cede, °relinquish, °concede, °allow, °surrender, °yield **12** ***give away.*** **(a)** See **1,** above. **(b)** °reveal, °betray, °let out, divulge, °disclose, °expose, °inform on, uncover, °leak, °let slip; let the cat out of the bag; *Colloq* blow the whistle on, *Slang* rat on, *US* fink on **13** ***give in.*** °yield, °submit, °give up, give ground, back away (from), back off, °capitulate, °surrender, admit defeat **14** ***give off.*** °give out, °emit, exude, °exhale, °discharge, send *or* throw out, °release, smell of **15** ***give out.*** **(a)** See **14,** above. **(b)** °distribute, °hand out, °give, °deal (out), pass out *or* around, disseminate, °dispense, °allot, apportion, allocate, °assign, °distribute, °issue, mete *or* hand out, °ration (out), °dole (out), °pay, *Colloq* dish *or* fork out, °shell out **(c)** °publish, °announce, °make known, °broadcast, °impart, °issue, °make public, °reveal **(d)** become exhausted, be reduced *or* depleted, °fail, °run out **(e)** See **8,** above. **16** ***give over.*** °assign, °resign, °hand over, °surrender, °relinquish, pass over, °give up; °entrust **17** ***give up.*** **(a)** °abandon, °stop, °cease, °quit, °leave off, °forgo, °forsake, °renounce, desist from, °swear off, abstain from; °reject; *Colloq* °cut out, chuck **(b)** °surrender, °capitulate, °yield, °cede, °concede, °give in (to defeat), throw in the towel *or* sponge; °despair **(c)** See **4,** above. **(d)** See **13,** above. **(e)** See **16,** above. *—n.* **18** °slack, °play, °leeway, °excess; °flexibility, °stretch

give-and-take *n.* compromise, °cooperation, reciprocity, interaction, fair exchange, teamwork, joint effort, synergy

given *adj.* **1** stated, accepted, agreed (-upon), delineated, confirmed, °noted, affirmed, specified, settled, °set, (pre)-arranged, preordained, foreordained **2** presupposed, °assumed, °understood, postulated, premised, conceded, acknowledged, allowed **3** °prone, °accustomed, dedicated, addicted, °inclined, °disposed *—n.* **4** assumption, donnée; °fact, °certainty, °reality, actuality, °gospel, the truth

glad *adj.* **1** °happy, pleased, contented, gratified, satisfied; °delighted, thrilled, °joyful, °overjoyed, tickled, *Colloq* tickled pink *or* to death, pleased as punch, *Slang Brit* chuffed **2** °(ready and) willing, °happy, °keen, °eager, (well-)disposed, °inclined, °ready

gladden *v.* °cheer, °enliven, °brighten, °delight, hearten, exhilarate, elate, °buoy (up), °animate

gladly *adv.* cheerfully, °happily, °readily, °willingly, with pleasure

glamorous *adj.* **1** alluring, fascinating, charming, °attractive, °magnetic, captivating, °enthralling, °desirable, appealing, °enchanting, entrancing, intriguing, beguiling, bewitching, magical **2** °chic, °smart, °stylish, °fashionable, *Colloq* °trendy

glamour *n.* allure, °fascination, °charm, attractiveness, °brilliance, °glitter, °attraction, °magnetism, charisma, captivation, desirability, °appeal, °enchantment, bewitchment, witchcraft, °sorcery, °magic

glance *v.* **1** glimpse, °peek, °peep, °scan, °look, *Colloq Brit* have a shufty *or* shufti at, take a dekko at **2** °reflect, glint, °glisten, °shimmer, °twinkle, °gleam, °flicker, glimmer, °sparkle, scintillate, °glitter, °flash **3** °bounce (off), °reflect, ricochet, °rebound, carom *—n.* **4** glimpse, °peek, °peep, °look, *coup d'oeil*, *Colloq* gander, *Brit* shufty *or* shufti, dekko **5** °gleam, glint, glimmer,

°shimmer, °twinkle, °sparkle, scintillation, °glitter, °flicker, °flash

glare *n.* **1** °dazzle, °brilliance, brightness, °splendor, resplendence, °radiance, effulgence, °luster, °shine, °flame, °flare, °blaze **2** °frown, dirty *or* nasty *or* black look, °scowl, °stare, glower, lower *or Brit also* lour **3** garishness, gaudiness, floridity *or* floridness, flashiness, tawdriness, showiness, °ostentation, meretriciousness —*v.* **4** °frown, give a dirty *or* nasty *or* black look, °scowl, °stare, glower, lower *or Brit also* lour, look daggers (at)

glaring *adj.* **1** °blatant, °flagrant, egregious, °conspicuous, °obtrusive, °prominent, °evident, °obvious, °manifest, °patent, °overt, °clear, °visible, unconcealed, °outrageous, °gross, flagitious, °atrocious, heinous, °shameless, °disgraceful, °shocking, °scandalous **2** °garish, °dazzling, °brilliant, blinding, blazing, °vivid, °harsh, °strong

glass *n.* **1** glassware, crystal **2** °mirror, looking glass **3** window, °pane, windowpane, plate glass **4** tumbler, drinking glass, beaker, goblet **5** barometer **6** lens, magnifying glass, °telescope, spyglass, microscope **7** ***glasses.*** °spectacles, eyeglasses, lorgnon, lorgnette, opera glasses, binoculars, field glasses, bifocals, trifocals, goggles, sunglasses, *Colloq* specs

glassy *adj.* **1** shining, °shiny, gleaming, °smooth, °slippery, °slick, °glossy, °icy, mirrorlike **2** °fixed, staring, trancelike, hypnotic, °vacant, °empty, expressionless, °blank, °void, vacuous, dazed, °dull, glazed, °cold, °lifeless

glaze *v.* **1** varnish, lacquer, shellac, enamel, °coat, °cover; °polish, burnish, °shine, °gloss —*n.* **2** varnish, lacquer, shellac, enamel, coating, covering; °polish, °shine, °gloss, °luster, patina

gleam *n.* **1** °light, glimmer, glint, °glow, °flicker, °shine, °shimmer, °glitter, °twinkle, °spark, °flare, °glare, °flash; °beam, °ray, °shaft **2** °hint, °suggestion, °indication, °vestige, °trace, scintilla, °inkling, glimmer, °ray, °spark, °flicker **3** °look, glint —*v.* **4** glimmer, glint, °shimmer, °shine, °twinkle, °glitter, °glisten, °beam, °sparkle

glee *n.* °delight, °exuberance, cheerfulness, high *or* good spirits, °cheer, exhilaration, elation, exultation, °joy, °happiness, °rapture, gladness, felicity, °pleasure, joyfulness, °merriment, jubilation, joyousness, joviality, jollity, °gaiety, mirthfulness; °enjoyment, °satisfaction, *Schadenfreude*

gleeful *adj.* °happy, °merry, °joyful, °delighted, °exuberant, °ecstatic, °cheerful, in high *or* good spirits, exhilarated, °elated, °exultant, °rapturous, °overjoyed, pleased, jubilant, joyous, jovial, °jolly, °gay, mirthful

glib *adj.* °ready, °fluent, °smooth, °slick, facile, smooth-spoken, smooth-tongued, smooth-talking, fast-talking, °fluid, °easy, unctuous, °suave, °nonchalant, °superficial

glide *v.* °slide, °slip, °coast, skate, °soar, °float, °sail, glissade, °stream, °flow

glisten *v.* °shine, °reflect, glint, glimmer, °gleam, °sparkle, °glitter, wink, °blink; °glow, °twinkle

glitter *v.* **1** See **glisten,** above. —*n.* **2** See **gleam, 1,** above. **3** See **glamour,** above. **4** showiness, gaudiness, garishness, °flash, flashiness, °ostentation, floridity *or* floridness, °spectacle, °pageantry, °splendor, refulgence, °brilliance, *Colloq* pizazz, razzle-dazzle, razzmatazz, *Slang US* glitz

gloat *v.* Often, ***gloat over.*** exult (in), °glory (in), °relish (in), °revel (in), crow (over *or* about), °delight (in)

global *adj.* worldwide, °international, °broad, °extensive, wide-ranging, far-reaching, °epidemic, pandemic, °universal

globe *n.* **1** °earth, °world, planet, Terra **2** °sphere, ball, °orb; globule

gloom *n.* **1** shadowiness, gloominess, °shade, °shadow, murkiness, murk, dimness, °dusk, dullness, °dark, darkness, cloudiness, blackness, °obscurity **2** despondency, °depression, °sadness, dejection, downheartedness, °melancholy, °woe, °sorrow, moroseness, °desolation, low spirits, blues, doldrums, °despair, dolor, °misery, *Colloq* dumps

gloomy *adj.* **1** °shadowy, shaded, °shady, °murky, °dim, °dusky, °dull, °dark, cloudy, °overcast, °obscure, °black, inky, *Literary* Stygian **2** depressed, °melancholy, °sad, °dejected, morose, °glum, lugubrious, °unhappy, cheerless, °dismal, °moody, down, downcast, °desolate, °doleful, °sorrowful, crestfallen, chapfallen, °downhearted, °forlorn, °despondent, °miserable, °joyless, dispirited, despairing, °dreary, °sullen, °blue, distressed, °down in the mouth, in the doldrums, saturnine, *Colloq* (down) in the dumps **3** depressing, cheerless, °dreary, °dismal, dispiriting, °sad, disheartening

glorified *adj.* **1** overrated, °pretentious, overdone, high-flown, high-sounding, °affected, °pompous, °exalted, *Colloq* jumped-up **2** °sham, °pretend, °imitation, °counterfeit, °fake, °substitute, ersatz, *Colloq* phoney *or US also* phony

glorify *v.* **1** elevate, °exalt, °raise (up), upgrade, °promote, °advance, °boost, °enhance, °dignify, ennoble, °immortalize **2** canonize, deify, °idolize, °revere, °venerate, °sanctify, °worship, pay tribute *or* homage to, ennoble, °idealize, apotheosize, °eulogize, panegyrize, °adore, °honor, °look up to, °celebrate, °extol, °praise, °laud, commend, °hail, lionize, °applaud, acclaim

glorious *adj.* **1** °illustrious, famed, °famous, °renowned, °celebrated, °distinguished, honored, °eminent, °excellent **2** °outstanding, °splendid, °magnificent, °marvelous, wonderful, spectacular, °fabulous, °dazzling **3** enjoyable, °delightful, °fine, °great, °excellent, °pleasurable, °superb, *Colloq* °heavenly **4** °beautiful, °splendid, °brilliant, °gorgeous, resplendent, °admirable, °superior, °excellent, °estimable

glory *n.* **1** °honor, °fame, repute, °reputation, exaltation, °celebrity, °renown, eminence, °distinction, illustriousness, °prestige, °dignity, immortality **2** °honor, °veneration, °reverence, °homage, °gratitude, glorification, exaltation, °worship, adoration, °praise, laudation, thanksgiving; benediction, °blessing **3** °splendor, °pomp, magnificence, °grandeur, °beauty, °brilliance, °radiance, effulgence, refulgence, °excellence, °pageantry, °nobility, °triumph, greatness **4** aureole, nimbus, °halo; °crown, circlet, corona —*v.* **5** °revel, °relish, °delight, °exult, pride oneself, crow, °rejoice, °gloat; °show off, °boast

gloss[1] *n.* **1** °sheen, °luster, °polish, °glow, °glaze, °shine, °gleam, burnish, brightness **2** °show, façade, °mask, °front, °surface, °veneer, °disguise, °camouflage, false appearance, °semblance —*v.* **3** °glaze, °polish, burnish, °shine **4** Usually, ***gloss over.*** °veil, °cover up, °smooth over, °conceal, °hide, °disguise, °camouflage, °mask, *Colloq* °whitewash

gloss[2] *n.* **1** °explanation, °interpretation, exegesis, explication, °definition, elucidation, °comment, commentary, annotation, critique, °criticism, °analysis, footnote; °translation —*v.* **2** comment on *or* upon, °explain, °interpret, explicate, °define, elucidate, annotate, °criticize, °analyze, °review, *US* critique; °translate **3** See **gloss**[1], **4,** above.

glossary *n.* °gloss, (specialized *or* special-subject) °dictionary, wordbook, word list

glossy *adj.* **1** shining, °shiny, °smooth, °polished, glazed, °lustrous, burnished, °smooth, °sleek, waxed, °glassy, glistening **2** °slick, °specious, °put-on, °artificial, meretricious, contrived, °pretended, simulated, feigned, °insincere, pseudo, °false, °unreal; °bogus, °counterfeit, °fraudulent, °imitation, *Colloq* phoney *or US also* phony

glow *n.* **1** luminosity, phosphorescence, incandescence, °light, lambency, °luster **2** °light, brightness, °gleam, luminousness, °brilliance, °radiance, resplendence, °splendor, effulgence **3** °flush, °blush, redness, ruddiness, °burning, °excitement, °warmth, °fervor, fervency, °enthusiasm, feverishness, °thrill, *Colloq* °rush —*v.* **4** °shine, °radiate, incandesce, phosphoresce, glimmer, °gleam, °light up **5** °heat, overheat, °burn; ablate **6** °flush, bloom, °color, °blush **7** °blush, °flush, redden, °color, turn red *or* scarlet

glowing *adj.* **1** aglow, °incandescent, °burning, lambent, °luminous, candent; smoldering **2** °rich, °warm, vibrant, °bright, °brilliant **3** °laudatory, °complimentary, °enthusiastic, eulogistic, °rhapsodic, °favorable, encomiastic, panegyrical

glue *n.* **1** °cement, adhesive, mucilage, gum, paste —*v.* **2** °cement, paste, °stick, affix, °fix, °seal

glum *adj.* °gloomy, °sullen, morose, dispirited, °woebegone, °dismal, °sad, sulky, °dour, °moody, °sour, crestfallen, °doleful, down, °low, °pessimistic, lugubrious, saturnine

glut *n.* **1** °excess, °surplus, overabundance, superabundance, °surfeit, oversupply, overflow, °superfluity, nimiety **2** saturation, glutting, satiation —*v.* **3** oversupply, °flood, °saturate, °swamp, inundate, deluge, °overload, overstock, °clog, °stuff, °gorge **4** °satiate, sate, °choke, °cram, °overload, overfeed, °gorge, °surfeit, °pall, cloy, °jade, °sicken, °weary

glutton *n.* trencherman, gormandizer, gourmand *or* gormand, overeater, hog, pig, *grangousier, Colloq* greedy-guts, *Slang Brit* gannet, *US* chowhound

gluttonous *adj.* °voracious, gormandizing, edacious, °greedy, °ravenous, insatiable, esurient, piggish, °hoggish, swinish

gluttony *n.* overeating, gormandizing, gormandism, °greed, hoggishness, piggishness, °rapacity, voraciousness, greediness, voracity, insatiability, edacity, crapulence, crapulousness, intemperance, immoderation, *Archaic* gulosity

gnarled *adj.* twisted, knotty, °lumpy, °bumpy, knotted, °bent, °crooked, distorted, contorted, warped; arthritic

gnaw *v.* **1** °chew, nibble, °eat, °bite, champ **2** °erode, eat away, corrode, wear down *or* away, °fret, °consume, °devour **3** °fret, °irritate, harry, hector, °pester, °worry, °bother, °plague, °trouble, °torment, torture, °distress, badger, °harass, °haunt, °nag, vex, °gall, nettle, °irk, peeve, °annoy

go *v.* **1** move (ahead *or* forward *or* onward), °proceed, °advance, °pass, °make headway, °travel, voyage, °set off, °tour, trek, wend, °stir, budge **2** °leave, °depart, °go out, move (out *or* away), decamp, °make off, °withdraw, °repair, °retire, °retreat, *Colloq* °take off **3** °function, °operate, °work, °run, °perform **4** °lead, open to, give access to, communicate to *or* with, connect with *or* to **5** °lead, °communicate with, °run **6** °fit, °belong (together), agree *or* conform (with each other), harmonize, °blend, °match, be appropriate *or* suitable (for *or* to), complement each other **7** °become **8** °fit, °extend, °reach, °span, °stretch **9** be disposed of *or* discarded *or* thrown away, be dismissed, be got rid of *or* abolished, be given up, be cast *or* set *or* put aside, be done with **10** °disappear (without a trace), vanish (into thin air), °evaporate **11** °pass, °elapse, slip *or* tick away, °fly **12** °fail, °fade, °decline, °flag, °weaken, °degenerate, °wear out, °give (out); °give way, °collapse, fall *or* come *or* go to pieces, °disintegrate, °crack **13** °die, °expire, be gone, meet one's maker, pass on *or* away, shuffle off this mortal coil, go to one's reward, go to the happy hunting ground, go to that great cricket pitch in the sky, *Slang* kick the bucket, snuff it **14** °sound, °pronounce, °enunciate, articulate, °say, utter **15** °survive, °last (out), °endure, °live, °continue **16** be used up *or* consumed *or* finished **17** go to the toilet *or* the lavatory *or* the bathroom, move (one's) bowels, °urinate, °defecate, *Slang* pee, take a leak *or* a crap, *Chiefly Brit* go to the loo, *Chiefly US* go to the john, *Taboo slang* (take a) piss *or* shit **18** ***go about.*** °approach, °tackle, °set about, °undertake, °begin, °start **19** ***go ahead.*** °proceed, °continue, move *or* go forward, °advance, progress, °go on **20** ***go along (with).*** **(a)** °escort, °accompany **(b)** °agree (to), concur (with), acquiesce (to), assent (to), °support **21** ***go around or about or Brit usually round (with).*** **(a)** move *or* go around, °circulate **(b)** °revolve, °rotate, °spin, whirl, °twirl **(c)** °socialize (with), frequent *or* seek the company of, spend time with, °associate with, *Colloq* hang around *or* about (with), °hang out (with) **(d)** wander *or* move around *or* about **(e)** °suffice, be sufficient *or* adequate *or* enough, °satisfy **22** ***go at.*** °attack, °assault, assail **23** ***go away.*** °go (off), °leave, °depart, °withdraw, °exit; °retreat, °recede, decamp **24** ***go back (to).*** **(a)** °return (to); °revert (to), change back (to) **(b)** °originate (in), begin *or* start (with), date back (to) **25** ***go back on.*** °renege (on), °break, °retract, °repudiate, °forsake **26** ***go by.*** **(a)** °pass (by), go past, move by; °elapse **(b)** rely *or* count *or* depend *or* bank on, put faith in (to), be guided by, judge from **27** ***go down.*** **(a)** °sink, °go under, °founder, °submerge **(b)** °decrease, °decline, °drop, °sink **(c)** °fall, be defeated *or* beaten, suffer defeat, °lose, °collapse **(d)** be remembered *or* memorialized *or* recalled *or* commemorated *or* recorded **(e)** find favor *or* acceptance *or* approval, be accepted **28** ***go for.*** **(a)** °fetch, °obtain, °get **(b)** apply *or* relate to, °concern, °involve **(c)** °fancy, °favor, °like, °admire, be attracted to, °prefer, °choose, *Slang* °dig **(d)** °attack, °assault, assail, °set upon **(e)** set one's sights on, aim for, focus attention *or* effort(s) on **29** ***go in for.*** **(a)** °go into, °enter, enroll in, °start, °begin, °embark on, °pursue, °take up, °embrace, espouse, °undertake, °follow, °adopt, *US* go out for **(b)** °like, °fancy, °favor, °practice, do, °engage in **30** ***go into.*** **(a)** See **29 (a),** above. **(b)** delve into, °examine, °pursue, °investigate, °analyze, °probe, °scrutinize, °inquire into, °study **(c)** °touch on, °discuss, °mention **31** ***go off.*** **(a)** °go out, cease to function **(b)** °explode, °blow up, detonate, °erupt; °fire, be discharged **(c)** °occur, °happen, °take place **(d)** °depart, °leave, °go (away), °set out, °exit, decamp, °quit **(e)** °deteriorate, °rot, molder, go stale, go bad, °spoil, °sour, °turn **(f)** Usually, ***go off into.*** break into *or* out in, start off into **32** ***go on.*** **(a)** °continue, °proceed, °keep on, °carry on; °persist, °last, °endure, °persevere **(b)** °happen, °occur, °take place, °come about, *Colloq* °come off **(c)** come on, begin *or* resume functioning **(d)** °enter, make an entrance **(e)** gabble, °chatter, drone on, *Brit* natter, *Colloq Brit* witter (on), rabbit on **(f)** rely *or* depend on, °use **33** ***go out.*** **(a)** fade *or* die (out), °expire, cease functioning, °go off, be extinguished **(b)** °depart, °leave, °exit **(c)** °socialize, °associate; court, °go together, *Brit* °walk out, *US* °date **34** ***go over.*** **(a)** °review, skim (through *or* over), °go through, °scan, °look at, °read, °study; °inspect, °examine, °scrutinize, °investigate **(b)** be received **(c)** °clean, tidy *or* neaten (up) **(d)** °rehearse, °repeat, °reiterate, °review, °go through; retrace **35** ***go through.*** **(a)** °experience, °suffer, °undergo, °bear, °take, °stand, °tolerate, °put up with, °brook, °submit to, °endure, live through, °brave **(b)** be accepted *or* approved, °pass (muster) **(c)** See **34 (a),** above. **36** ***go together.*** **(a)** harmonize, °accord, °agree, °fit, °go, suit each other, °belong (with each other) **(b)** See **33 (c),** above. **37** ***go under.*** **(a)** See **27 (a),** above. **(b)** °fail, go bankrupt, *Slang* go belly-up **38** ***go up.*** **(a)** °rise, °increase **(b)** °explode, °blow up **39** ***go with.*** **(a)** go together with, harmonize with, blend with, be suitable *or* suited for, fit (in) with, accord *or* agree with **(b)** socialize with, °associate with, °accompany, court, *Brit* walk out with, *US* °date **40** ***go without.*** do *or* manage *or* get by without, °lack, be deprived of, °need; abstain from, survive *or* live *or* continue without —*n.* **41** °chance, °turn, °opportunity, °try, °attempt, *Colloq* whack, °crack, whirl, °shot, °stab

go-ahead *n.* **1** °permission, °approval, °leave, authorization, °sanction, *Colloq* °say-so, okay *or* OK, green light, *US* the nod —*adj.* **2** °ambitious, °enterprising, °progressive, forward-looking, °resourceful

goal *n.* °object, °aim, °purpose, °end, °objective, °target, °ambition, °ideal, °aspiration

gob *n.* chunk, °piece, °blob, °lump, gobbet, °morsel, °fragment, °bite

gobbledegook *n.* **1** gobbledygook, °jargon, °nonsense, °gibberish, °moonshine, °rubbish, tommyrot, °mumbo jumbo, humbug, balderdash, eyewash, hogwash, poppycock, °drivel, *Colloq* bunk, °rot, °garbage, bosh, pish and tush, piffle, bilge (water), codswallop, *Slang* crap, malarkey *or* malarky, bull, *Brit* (load of old) cobblers, *Taboo slang US* bullshit **2** gobbledygook, equivocation, double-talk, °deception, deceptiveness, vagueness, quibbling, circumlocution, obscurantism, obfuscation, ambagiousness, shiftiness

go-between *n.* °intermediary, °agent, middleman, °medium, °mediator, °negotiator, °messenger, internuncio, °liaison; intercessor, interceder

goblin *n.* elf, gnome, hobgoblin, °imp, kobold, leprechaun, °demon, brownie, pixie, nix *or* nixie

god *n.* °deity, demigod, demiurge, divinity, °spirit, °immortal, °genius, °power, tutelary, numen

godless *adj.* **1** °wicked, °evil, iniquitous, °sinful, unrighteous, unholy, hellish; °impious, °blasphemous, °profane, °sacrilegious,

°ungodly **2** atheistic, nullifidian, agnostic, °unbelieving, °skeptical

godlike *adj.* **1** °divine, °godly, °sacred, °holy, °saintly, angelic, °seraphic, blest, blessed, sainted **2** °heavenly, °celestial, blissful, °rapturous, °ecstatic, beatific, ethereal

godly *adj.* °religious, °pious, °devout, God-fearing, °good, °righteous, °holy, °virtuous, °moral, °pure, °saintly, reverent, pietistic, °devoted, °faithful

godsend *n.* °gift, °blessing, benediction, °boon, °windfall, bonanza, stroke of (good) fortune, piece *or* bit of (good) luck

goggle-eyed *adj.* °agog, awe-struck, wide-eyed, °thunderstruck, agape, open-mouthed, gawking, staring, dumfounded *or* dumbfounded, astonished, astounded, amazed, stupefied, dazed, surprised

going *adj.* **1** thriving, °successful, succeeding, °prosperous, °wealthy, affluent, booming, prospering, °flourishing, growing **2** °current, °present, °contemporary, °active, °effective, accepted, °prevailing, °prevalent, °universal, °common, °usual, °customary **3** ***going on.*** approaching, nearing, °nearly, °almost, not quite

golden *adj.* **1** yellow, yellowish, gold, blond *or* blonde, flaxen, aureate; tow(-haired) **2** gold, auriferous; gilded, gilt, aureate; *Technical* auric, aurous **3** °bright, shining, °brilliant, °sunny, gleaming, °lustrous, °shiny, glittering, °dazzling, resplendent, °radiant, °glowing, sparkling **4** °happy, blissful, °delightful, °joyful, °glorious, joyous, °exuberant **5** °flourishing, halcyon, °prosperous, thriving, °favorable, °excellent, °outstanding, °productive, °fertile, blessed, blest, °good, °successful, palmy **6** °gifted, °talented, °favored, °special, °exceptional, °favorite, cherished, °pet, *Brit* blue-eyed, white-headed, white-haired, *US* fair-haired **7** °advantageous, °propitious, auspicious, °promising, °rosy, °opportune, °optimistic, °favorable

good *adj.* **1** °agreeable, °satisfactory, commendable, °acceptable, °fair, °adequate, admissible, °tolerable, all right, °passable, *Colloq* okay *or* OK **2** °admirable, °outstanding, °first-rate, first-class, °fine, °superb, °superior, tiptop, °extraordinary, °exemplary, °choice, °excellent, °capital, °marvelous, wonderful, °splendid, °sterling, *Colloq* super (-duper), °great, smashing, cracking, °fantastic, °terrific, °unbelievable, groovy, °fabulous, fab, °serious, A-1 *or* A-one, *Old-fashioned Brit* tickety-boo, *US* fab, fantabulous, °bad, °major, *Brit* °brilliant, brill, ace, °crucial, *North England* °champion, *Chiefly US* A-OK **3** °correct, °proper, °decorous, °orderly, °right, °seemly, °fit, °fitting, °suitable, °meet, °appropriate, allowable, °permissible, admissible, °passable, °satisfactory, °tolerable **4** °obedient, well-behaved, °proper, well-mannered **5** °moral, high-minded, °righteous, °noble, °wholesome, °chaste, °pure, °honorable, °ethical, upstanding, °upright, °virtuous, °worthy, °lofty, °elevated, °saintly, angelic, °godly, °godlike **6** °kind, °benevolent, beneficent, °gracious, °gentle, °kindly, °nice, °considerate, °friendly, °solicitous, goodhearted, °sympathetic, °benign, °charitable, humane, kindhearted, well-disposed **7** °fresh, °unspoiled, °edible, consumable, palatable **8** °genuine, valid, °legitimate, °authentic, °honest, °proper, °reliable, °secure, dependable, °safe, creditable, °sound, °solid, °substantial, well-founded, °trustworthy, °honest, °actual, °real; credible, believable, convincing, compelling, cogent **9** °honorable, esteemed, respected, °respectable, °well-thought-of, °reputable, established, °solid **10** well-proportioned, °shapely, °attractive **11** °thorough, °complete, °penetrating, °careful **12** °gifted, °talented, °competent, °capable, °skillful, °clever, °accomplished, °proficient, °adept, adroit, skilled **13** °advantageous, °propitious, °opportune, °beneficial, °profitable, °favorable; °safe, °secure, °reliable, °sound, °sensible **14** °healthy, salubrious, salutary, °beneficial, °wholesome **15** °best, °company, Sunday, special-occasion, most luxurious **16** °ample, °sufficient, °adequate, °considerable, °full, °extensive, sizable, °large, °substantial **17** approving, °complimentary, °flattering, °positive, °favorable, °enthusiastic, °laudatory, eulogistic, encomiastic **18** °great, °considerable, sizable, °substantial, °fair —*n.* **19** °benefit, °advantage, °profit, °use, °usefulness, °gain, °worth, avail **20** goodness, °morality, °virtue, °merit, righteousness, °right, °rectitude, °worth, °probity, virtuousness, °integrity, °nobility, high-mindedness, honorableness, °honesty **21** ***goods.*** **(a)** °possessions, °(personal) property, chattels, °things, °gear, °belongings, °effects, °paraphernalia, movables, °stuff **(b)** °merchandise, commodities, °wares, °stock, °produce, tangibles, °assets **(c)** *US and Canadian* (incriminating) evidence *or* proof *or* information *or* documentation *or* facts *or* data **(d)** °fabric, °cloth, textile, °material, yard *or* piece goods

goodbye *interj.* Good-bye! *or* Goodby!, Farewell!, *Hawaiian* Aloha!; *Italian* Arrivederci!, Ciao!; *German* Auf Wiedersehen!; *French* Au revoir!, Adieu!; *Japanese* Sayonara!; *Spanish* ¡Adios!, ¡Hasta la vista!, ¡Hasta luego!; *Latin* Vale!; *Colloq* Bye! *or* 'Bye!, Bye-bye!, Toodle-oo!, So long!, *Brit* Tata!, Cheerio!, Cheers!, Cheery pip!, Toodle pip!, *Old-fashioned* Pip! Pip!, *US* See you later (Alligator)!

good-for-nothing *adj.* **1** °worthless, °useless —*n.* **2** ne'er-do-well, °wastrel, waster, °idler, °loafer, layabout, lazybones, slugabed, sluggard, black sheep, *Colloq US* goldbrick, goof-off

goodly *adj.* °considerable, sizable, °substantial, °ample, °great, °large, °significant, consequential

good-natured *adj.* good-humored, °friendly, °agreeable, °genial, °gracious, good-hearted, °pleasant, °mellow, easygoing, °considerate, °nice, °kind, °kindly, kindhearted, tenderhearted, °charitable, °tolerant, °generous, °courteous, °cordial, °warm, warmhearted, °amiable, °amicable, cooperative

goody-goody *adj.* °smug, °sanctimonious, °self-righteous, °priggish, prim, holier-than-thou, Pecksniffian, °hypocritical

gooey *adj.* **1** gluey, °sticky, °tacky, glutinous, mucilaginous, gummy **2** °sweet, sugary, saccharine, °sentimental, unctuous, cloying, syrupy, mawkish, °maudlin, *Colloq* °mushy, slushy, °sloppy

gore[1] *n.* blood, °carnage, butchery, °slaughter, °bloodshed

gore[2] *v.* °pierce, °stab, °poke, horn, °penetrate, °puncture, spear, °gouge, °spit, °stick, °impale, disembowel

gorge *n.* **1** °ravine, °canyon, defile, °pass, chasm, fissure, °crevasse, gully *or* gulley, wadi *or* wady, °gap, *Brit* gill *or* ghyll, *US and Canadian* °notch **2** °vomit, vomitus —*v.* **3** °fill, °stuff, °glut, °cram; °gulp, gobble (down), °devour, °bolt (down), wolf (down), gormandize, °swallow

gorgeous *adj.* **1** resplendent, °splendid, °magnificent, °glorious, °exquisite, °sumptuous, °dazzling, °grand, °beautiful, splendrous, breathtaking, °radiant, refulgent, °brilliant, °showy, colorful, *Colloq* splendiferous **2** °great, °terrific, °fantastic, wonderful, °marvelous, °glorious, spectacular, °superb, °excellent, *Colloq* fantabulous, marvy, smashing, °super, °nifty, °neat, °swell

gory *adj.* bloody, °sanguinary, bloodsoaked, bloodstained; °gruesome, °grisly, horrific, bloodcurdling

gospel *n.* °truth, °fact, °certainty

gossip *n.* **1** °chat, °conversation, °talk, chitchat, small talk, °palaver; tittle-tattle, °prattle; *Scot* clishmaclaver; gup; *Colloq Brit* natter, chinwag **2** °rumor, °scandal, hearsay, °information, *on dit*, °word, *Colloq* °grapevine, (inside) info, tittle-tattle, *Slang* °dope, *Chiefly US* scuttlebutt, *US and Canadian* poop **3** rumor mill, rumormonger, scandalmonger, gossipmonger, newsmonger, °busybody, tattletale, quidnunc, blabber, blatherskite, telltale, °talebearer, flibbertigibbet, *Colloq* bigmouth, chatterbox, °blabbermouth, Nosy Parker —*v.* **4** Sometimes, ***gossip about.*** bruit, °tattle, °rumor, °whisper, blether *or US* blather, gabble, *Colloq* °blab, *Brit* natter, *Slang* jaw

gouge *v.* **1** °chisel, °gash, incise, °scratch, °groove, °dig; scoop *or* hollow (out) **2** °extort, °extract, bilk, °defraud, wrest, °wrench, °squeeze, °blackmail, *Colloq* °milk, bleed, °skin, °fleece, °cheat, °swindle —*n.* **3** °groove, °furrow, °scratch, °gash, °hollow; trench, ditch

gourmet *n.* °epicure, connoisseur, Lucullus, gastronome, *gourmand, bon vivant*, bon viveur

govern *v.* **1** °rule, °control, °direct, °reign, hold sway (over), °lead, °conduct, °guide, °manage, °regulate, °run, °supervise, superintend, °oversee, °steer, captain, °pilot, °command, °head (up), °look after, sit on the throne, wield the scepter, wear the crown, run the show, be in power, be in charge (of), exercise *or* wield power *or* control (over), have *or* hold the whip hand, *Colloq* wear the pants, be in the saddle *or* driver's seat **2** °control, °check, °bridle, °curb, °master, °subdue, °restrain, °contain, °hold in, °suppress, °repress

government *n.* **1** °rule, °command, °authority, °regulation, °control, °management, °direction, °administration, °sway, superintendence, supervision, °oversight, °guidance, °domination **2** °administration, °ministry, °regime

grab *v.* **1** °snatch, lay *or* catch hold of, fasten upon, °grasp, °seize; °catch, °grip, °clutch; *Colloq* latch on to, get one's hands *or* fingers on, °nab, *US* °snag **2** °appropriate, expropriate, °seize, commandeer, °take over, usurp, arrogate **3** °arrest, °capture, °catch, *Colloq* °nab, °pinch, collar —*n.* **4** °snatch, °clutch; °grasp, °grip

grace *n.* **1** °elegance, gracefulness, suppleness, °finesse, °refinement, °ease, °polish, °poise **2** tastefulness, °(good) taste, cultivation, suavity *or* suaveness, °culture, °savoir-faire, discernment, °discrimination, °(good) manners, politeness, °breeding, °consideration, decency, °etiquette, °tact, °propriety, °decorum, mannerliness **3** °indulgence, °forgiveness, °mercy, mercifulness, leniency, compassion, clemency, °charity, goodwill, goodness **4** °kindness, °favor, kindliness, °benevolence, generosity, goodness, graciousness, becomingness, seemliness; °excellence, °virtue, strength of character, considerateness **5** °blessing, thanksgiving, °prayer, benediction —*v.* **6** adorn, °embellish, °set off, °decorate, °ornament, °beautify, °enhance, garnish **7** °dignify, °enhance, °distinguish, °enrich, °honor, °favor

graceful *adj.* **1** °fluid, flowing, °supple, lissom *or* lissome, lithe, facile, °smooth, °nimble, °agile, deft **2** °tactful, well-mannered, °polite, °courteous, mannerly, °refined, °tasteful, °elegant, courtly, urbane, °polished, °suave

gracious *adj.* °kind, °courteous, °polite, well-mannered, °kindly, °benevolent, beneficent, °indulgent, kindhearted, warmhearted, °cordial, °warm, °friendly, °sociable, °good-natured, °amiable, affable, °benign, °accommodating, °obliging, °agreeable, °considerate

grade *n.* **1** °degree, °position, °rank, °status, °stage, °standing, °station, gradation, echelon, °class, °level, °category, °condition, °state, °estate, °situation, rung **2** rating, °mark, °score **3** °class, °form, year **4** °hill, °slope, °rise, gradient, acclivity, declivity, °incline, °decline, ascent, descent, upgrade, °downgrade **5** ***make the grade.*** °pass, measure up, °succeed, °qualify, *Colloq US* °make it, *Slang US and Canadian and New Zealand* hack *or* cut it —*v.* **6** classify, °class, °order, °organize, °rank, °sort, °size, °group,

°categorize, °rate **7** °mark, °rate, °correct, °evaluate

gradual *adj.* °easy, °gentle, °even, °moderate, °slow, °piecemeal, inchmeal, °regular, °steady

gradually *adv.* slowly, evenly, °piecemeal, inchmeal, drop by drop, °step by step, bit by bit, little by little, piece by piece, *gradatim*

graduate *n.* **1** bachelor, postgraduate, *US* alumnus (*pl.* alumni) *or* alumna (*pl.* alumnae) —*v.* **2** gradate, °mark, °calibrate, °grade, °scale

graft[1] *n.* **1** bud, scion, °shoot, °splice, implantation *or* implant, °transplant —*v.* **2** °implant, °splice, °insert, °join

graft[2] *n.* corruption, jobbery; bribery, extortion, *Colloq* payola, °kickback

grain *n.* **1** °seed, °kernel, stone, pip, °pit **2** cereal, corn, grist **3** °particle, °bit, °fragment, °crumb, °speck, granule, °morsel, mote, molecule, atom, fleck, iota, ounce, °scrap, °trace, scintilla, °hint, °suggestion, whit, °jot (or tittle), °dab, soupçon, °taste, *Colloq US and Canadian* smidgen *or* smidgin **4** °texture, °pattern, °fiber, °weave, °nap

grand *adj.* **1** °large, °great, °huge, °immense, °enormous, °impressive, °imposing, °splendid, °fine, °majestic, °stately, °lofty, °monumental, °lavish, °magnificent, °opulent, °luxurious, °palatial, °sumptuous, *Colloq* °posh **2** °dignified, °distinguished, august, respected, °eminent, °preeminent, °outstanding, °celebrated, °illustrious, °renowned, °notable, °legendary, °exalted, revered, °venerable, °immortal **3** °flamboyant, overdone, histrionic, °ostentatious, °pretentious, °grandiose, lordly **4** °complete, °total, °sum, °comprehensive, (all-)inclusive; bottom-line **5** °marvelous, wonderful, °outstanding, first-class, °first-rate, °splendid, °excellent, °superb, °admirable, *Colloq* °great, marvy, smashing, °terrific, °fantastic, °fabulous, fantabulous, °super **6** °principal, °chief, °main, °head, °leading, °foremost, highest

grandeur *n.* **1** °splendor, magnificence, majesty, sublimity, luxuriousness, °pomp **2** °nobility, augustness, nobleness, eminence, majesty

grandiose *adj.* **1** °pretentious, °ostentatious, °showy, °flamboyant, °bombastic, histrionic, °extravagant, °pompous, fustian, high-flown, high-flying, overambitious, overdone, overdramatic, °melodramatic, Ossianic, °inflated, °affected, florid, °flashy, *Colloq* highfalutin *or* hifalutin, °flash **2** °imposing, °impressive, °ambitious, °grand, °monumental, °magnificent, °lofty

grant *v.* **1** °give, °confer, °bestow, °present, °award, °offer; °supply, °furnish, °distribute, °donate; allocate, °assign **2** °concede, accede (to), °cede, °give (up), °agree (to), °consent (to), °allow, °permit, °admit; °let —*n.* **3** °gift, °present, °endowment, °bequest, subvention, °subsidy, °award, grant-in-aid, °donation, contribution, concession, °allowance

granular *adj.* grainy, granulated, particulate, comminuted, gravelly, sandy, °gritty

grapevine *n.* rumor mill, jungle telegraph, grapevine telegraph; °rumor, °gossip

graphic *adj.* **1** °vivid, °distinct, well-defined, °detailed, °explicit, °particular, °clear, lucid, °plain, °manifest, crystal-clear, unmistakable *or* unmistakeable, unambiguous, °accurate, °precise, well-drawn, °photographic, descriptive, °telling, °picturesque, °pictorial, °realistic, °lifelike, true-to-life, *Colloq* °gory **2** written, °drawn, diagrammatic, delineated, °visible

grapple *v.* **1** °grasp, °grab, °grip, °seize, °clasp, °catch, °wrestle; °hold, °clutch, °snatch **2** *grapple with.* °come to grips with, °cope with, contend with, °deal with, struggle with, °tackle, °face, °take on

grasp *v.* **1** °grip, °grab, °seize, °clasp, °clutch, °snatch, °hold, take *or* lay *or* catch hold of, *Colloq* °nab **2** °understand, °comprehend, °appreciate, °catch (on), °get, get the drift *or* point of, °follow, °see, °realize, apprehend, °learn, *Colloq* make heads or tails of, *Slang* °dig —*n.* **3** °hold, °grip, °clutches, °clasp, °embrace, °lock **4** °possession, °control, °power, mastery, °sovereignty, suzerainty, °hold **5** °understanding, comprehension, apprehension, awareness, °perception, °sense

grasping *adj.* °greedy, °avaricious, acquisitive, °rapacious, °mean, °miserly, stingy, °penurious, parsimonious, niggardly, °tight, tightfisted, penny-pinching, closefisted, °mercenary

grate *v.* **1** °shred, °rasp, °scrape, °rub, triturate **2** °scrape, °rasp, °rub, °grind, °scratch, screech, stridulate **3** Often, *grate on or upon.* °annoy, vex, °irk, °irritate, °pester, set one's teeth on edge, °jar, °fret, °chafe, rub one (up) the wrong way, go against the grain, *Colloq* get on one's nerves

grateful *adj.* °thankful, appreciative

gratification *n.* °satisfaction, °fulfillment, °enjoyment, °pleasure, °delight, compensation, recompense, °reward, °return, °requital

gratify *v.* please, °satisfy, °fulfill, °delight, °compensate, recompense, °reward, °requite, °cheer, °gladden, °favor

grating *adj.* **1** jarring, °strident, °raucous, °harsh, °discordant, dissonant, unharmonious, °offensive, irritating, °irksome, annoying, vexatious, galling **2** grinding, °gritty, squeaky, jangling, screeching, creaking, °shrill, °piercing, squawking, croaking, rasping —*n.* **3** °grate, grid, reticle *or* reticule, grille, lattice, trellis, °screen, °network, reticulation

gratitude *n.* thankfulness, °appreciation, gratefulness; °thanks, °return, compensation, thanksgiving

gratuitous *adj.* **1** gratis, °free, °complimentary, °spontaneous **2** unasked-for, unrequested, unsought-for, °wanton, unprovoked, °unsolicited, unlooked-for, uncalled-for, °unwelcome, unjustified, °unwarranted, baseless, °groundless, °needless, °unfounded, ungrounded, unjustifiable, irrational

grave[1] *n.* °crypt, °sepulcher, °tomb, vault, mausoleum, last *or* final resting place, eternal rest

grave[2] *adj.* **1** °serious, °somber, °solemn, °earnest, unsmiling, °staid, °sedate, °sober, °dour, °gloomy, °grim, grim-faced, grim-visaged, *Brit* po-faced **2** °serious, °critical, °vital, °dangerous, matter of life and death, °crucial, °urgent, °weighty, °important, °pressing, °pivotal, °perilous

graveyard *n.* burial ground, churchyard, cemetery, God's acre, necropolis, potter's field, *Western US* boot hill, *Rare* golgotha, *Slang* boneyard

gravity *n.* **1** gravitation; °attraction **2** seriousness, acuteness, immediacy, °importance, °significance, °weight, °magnitude, °severity, °urgency, exigency, momentousness, weightiness **3** °solemnity, °dignity, somberness, staidness, sedateness, °sobriety, gravitas, soberness, °reserve; gloominess, grimness

gray *adj.* **1** grey, ashen, °leaden, °colorless, °pale, pallid, °wan, livid, °pearly, griseous, smoky, sooty, bloodless **2** grey, °gloomy, °dismal, °dull, depressing, °glum, °dreary, °somber, °drab, cheerless, °dark, °murky, foggy, °misty, cloudy, °overcast, °sunless **3** grey, °aged, °elderly, hoary, °old, °venerable, °ancient **4** grey, °mature, °wise, °experienced

greasy *adj.* **1** °oily, sebaceous, fatty, °fat, buttery, lardy, soapy, oleaginous, pinguid, butyraceous, saponaceous, waxy **2** unctuous, °oily, °slippery, slithery, °smooth, °glib, fawning, °slick, toadying, sycophantic, *Slang Brit* smarmy

great *adj.* **1** °big, °large, °huge, °immense, °enormous, °gigantic, °giant, °grand, °extensive, °prodigious, °colossal, °massive, °vast, tremendous; °spacious, capacious, mammoth, gargantuan, °monstrous, titanic, cyclopean, Brobdingnagian **2** °large, °huge, °immense, °enormous, °gigantic, °prodigious, °vast, tremendous, °abundant, countless **3** °extreme, °considerable, °marked, °pronounced, °inordinate, °extraordinary, °significant; °excess, °excessive **4** °critical, °important, °crucial, °momentous, °significant, °serious, °weighty, consequential **5** °important, °prominent, °major, °eminent, °celebrated, °distinguished, °famous, famed, °renowned, °notable, °noteworthy, °illustrious, °outstanding, °well-known, °weighty, °influential, *Rare* eximious **6** °talented, °gifted, °excellent, °outstanding, °exceptional, °major, °superlative, °superior, °leading, °best, °incomparable, °matchless, °peerless, °skillful, artistic, °brilliant, °first-rate, °remarkable, °top, °accomplished **7** °lofty, °elevated, °exalted, °noble, high-minded, °grand **8** °talented, skilled, °skillful, adroit, °clever, °adept, °able, °proficient, °expert **9** °keen, zealous, °eager, °active, °enthusiastic, °devoted, °ardent, °passionate **10** °close, °devoted, dedicated, °fast, °faithful, °true, °loyal, °intimate, loving **11** °terrible, °bad, °awful, unforgivable, horrendous, heinous, °grievous, horrific, °horrible, °terrific, °huge, °colossal, °enormous, °gigantic, °significant, °cardinal, egregious, °basic, °profound, °flagrant, °glaring, arrant, consummate, °out-and-out **12** spectacular, °marvelous, °outstanding, °excellent, °superb, °grand, wonderful, °fine, *Colloq* °fantastic, °terrific, stupendous, marvy, smashing, fantabulous, *Old-fashioned Brit* tickety-boo

greed *n.* **1** greediness, °avarice, avariciousness, covetousness, acquisitiveness, cupidity, avidity, craving, yearning **2** meanness, stinginess, miserliness, selfishness, niggardliness, penuriousness, parsimony, closefistedness, penny-pinching, tightfistedness **3** °gluttony, voraciousness, edacity, esurience, voracity, overeating, gormandizing, ravenousness, insatiableness

greedy *adj.* **1** °ravenous, °voracious, °gluttonous, piggish, °hoggish, swinish, cormorant, edacious, esurient, insatiable, °unquenchable **2** °avaricious, acquisitive, covetous, °grasping, craving; °materialistic, money-hungry **3** stingy, °miserly, °mean, °selfish, niggardly, parsimonious, °penurious, penny-pinching, °mercenary, close-fisted, tightfisted, °close, *Colloq* °near, °tight, *Brit* mingy

green *adj.* **1** verdant, grassy, °fresh, °leafy; °rural, country-like **2** °immature, unripe, unripened; naive *or* naïve *or* naïf, °callow, untested, untrained, unversed, °inexperienced, °new, °raw, unseasoned, °unsophisticated, °gullible, °amateur, unskilled, unskillful, amateurish, nonprofessional, inexpert, *Colloq* wet behind the ears **3** environmental, conservationist —*n.* **4** °lawn, sward, °common, grassland **5** °environmentalist, conservationist, preservationist

greenhorn *n.* °newcomer, beginner, °novice, tyro, neophyte, °novice, °initiate, °learner, tenderfoot, *Colloq* rookie

greet *v.* **1** °welcome, °receive, usher in, °meet **2** °hail, accost, °address, °salute

greeting *n.* **1** salutation, °hail, hello, °welcome, °reception **2** greeting card, °card, °message, °note **3** ***greetings.*** °regards, °respects, best *or* good wishes, devoirs, °compliments

grief *n.* **1** °anguish, °suffering, °agony, °misery, wretchedness, °pain, °hurt, °sadness, °sorrow, dejection, °depression, despondency, °melancholy, unhappiness, °woe, °torment, °desolation, heartbreak, °remorse, °regret, ruth, heartache **2** °distress, °trouble, °difficulty, tribulation, °trial, °burden, °load, onus, °ordeal, travail, °affliction, °worry, °bitterness, °curse; adversity, °misfortune, evil days, bad *or* ill fortune *or* luck, °calamity, °disaster, °catastrophe, trauma **3** ***come to grief.*** °fail, go to rack and ruin, meet with disaster, °miscarry, fall *or* come apart, *Colloq* come unstuck

grievance *adj.* 1 °wrong, °ill, °injustice, °disservice, unfairness, °injury, °damage, °harm, °outrage, affront, °indignity, °hardship; °calamity 2 °complaint, °objection, °charge, plaint, °allegation, °grudge, *Colloq* °gripe, bone to pick, *Brit* crow to pluck, *Slang* beef

grieve *v.* 1 °mourn, °bemoan, °lament, °regret, rue, deplore, °bewail, mope, eat one's heart out 2 °weep, °cry, °mourn, °moan, °keen, °suffer, °sorrow; shed tears, °complain

grievous *adj.* 1 °severe, °heavy, °painful, °grave, °serious, distressing, °harmful; damaging, °hurtful, °acute, wounding 2 egregious, °awful, °flagrant, °terrible, °outrageous, heinous, °dreadful, °atrocious, °monstrous, appalling, °shocking, °deplorable, °calamitous, °lamentable, intolerable, °shameful, °unbearable

grim *adj.* 1 °stern, °severe, unrelenting, °resolute, uncompromising, unyielding, °inflexible, adamant, °stony, iron, unbending, °firm, intractable, unflinching, unmoving, °unmoved, °implacable, inexorable, °determined, °steadfast, °(dead) set, °fixed, °decided, °obstinate, headstrong, °stubborn, obdurate, dogged, unwavering 2 °forbidding, °formidable, °harsh, °ferocious, °fierce, °cruel, °savage, °merciless, °heartless, °ruthless, pitiless, °vicious, °brutal, brutish, feral, °inhuman, °fiendish, °violent, °bloodthirsty, °murderous, °homicidal, °fell 3 dire, °dreadful, °ghastly, °awful, °frightful, °frightening, °sinister, °hideous, horrid, horrific, °horrible, horrendous, °terrible, °terrifying, °terrific, °harrowing, °dread, alarming, appalling, °grotesque, °gruesome, °eerie, °macabre, flagitious, heinous, °evil, °wicked, iniquitous, °atrocious, °monstrous 4 stern-visaged, austere, °dour, disapproving, frowning, °grave, saturnine, °solemn, °somber, humorless, °forbidding, °severe, °strait-laced, uncompromising, puritanical, prim, °prudish, °gruff, °bluff, curmudgeonly, *Brit* po-faced

grime *n.* °dirt, °filth, soot, °mud, °muck, slime, scum

grind *v.* 1 °pound, °powder, °pulverize, abrade, °crush, granulate, °mill, °grate, °rasp, °crumble, kibble, mash, triturate, bray, comminute 2 °sharpen, °whet; °file, °smooth, °polish 3 gnash, °grit, °grate 4 Also, ***grind away.*** °labor, toil, °slave (away); °study, lucubrate, burn the midnight oil, *Colloq* °cram, *Brit* swot 5 ***grind down.*** wear down *or* away, °crush, °oppress, °subdue, °suppress, °tyrannize, °persecute, maltreat, °ill-treat, harry, °harass, °hound, hector, °plague, badger 6 ***grind out.*** °produce, °generate, crank out, churn out, °turn out —*n.* 7 toil, °labor, °drudgery, travail, °exertion, °task, chore

grip *n.* 1 °hold, °grasp, °clutch, handgrip, °clasp, handclasp 2 °control, °command, °hold, mastery; °authority, °influence, °power, °rule, °domination, °sovereignty, °tenure, °dominion, suzerainty, °custody 3 °grasp, °understanding, apprehension, comprehension, °sense, °sensitivity, °feel, °feeling, awareness, °perception, °view, *Slang US* °handle 4 handgrip, valise, (traveling *or* overnight) bag, °case, satchel, °suitcase, *Brit* holdall, *US and Canadian* carryall 5 ***come or get to grips with.*** °tackle, confront, °approach, °handle, °meet (head on), °undertake, grapple *or* contend with, cope *or* deal with, °face —*v.* 6 °grasp, °clutch, °clasp, °hold, °seize 7 engross, °engage, °hold, °fascinate, enthrall, °entrance, absorb, mesmerize, °hypnotize, spellbind, rivet

gripe *v.* 1 °complain, °moan, grumble, whimper, whine, bleat, °nag, °cavil, °carp, grouse, *Colloq* beef, *Brit* whinge, *Slang* °bitch, bellyache —*n.* 2 °complaint, °grievance, °objection, °protest; complaining, moaning, grumbling, whimpering, whining, °nagging, caviling, carping, grousing, *Colloq* beef, *Brit* whinging, *Slang* bitching, bellyaching 3 Usually, ***gripes.*** cramp, °twinge, °pang, °pain, °ache, colic, °distress, *Colloq* bellyache

grisly *adj.* °gruesome, °gory, °abhorrent, °abominable, °awful, appalling, °hideous, °shocking, °nasty, °dreadful, °repulsive, °repellent, °repugnant, °disgusting, sickening, nauseating, horrific, horrid, horrendous, horrifying, °terrible, °terrifying, °terrific

grit *n.* °courage, courageousness, valor, °bravery, °fortitude, °resolution, resoluteness, °resolve, toughness, mettle, °pluck, °spirit, °backbone, °nerve, gameness, intrepidity *or* intrepidness, dauntlessness, °tenacity, °determination, firmness, hardiness, hardihood, staunchness, stalwartness, doughtiness, fearlessness, *Colloq* °guts, gutsiness, °spunk, spunkiness, starch, *Brit* °bottle, *US and Canadian* chutzpah, moxie, stick-to-itiveness

gritty *adj.* 1 sandy, gravelly, °granular, grainy, °rough, abrasive, rasping, arenose 2 °courageous, valorous, °brave, °resolute, °tough, mettlesome, plucky, °spirited, °game, °intrepid, °dauntless, °tenacious, °determined, °persistent, °firm, °hardy, °staunch, °stalwart, doughty, °fearless, *Colloq* gutsy, spunky

groan *v.* 1 °moan, °sigh, °murmur, wail, whimper, whine 2 °complain, grumble, grouse, °object, °protest, *Colloq* °gripe, beef, yammer, *Brit* whinge, *Slang* °bitch —*n.* 3 °moan, °sigh, °murmur, wail, whimper, whine 4 °complaint, grumble, grousing, muttering, *Colloq* °gripe, griping, beef, yammering, *Slang* bitching

groggy *adj.* unsteady, °shaky, wobbly, weak-kneed, °weak, staggering, stupefied, dazed, stunned, reeling, punch-drunk, °numb, numbed, benumbed, °faint, in a trance *or* stupor, muddled, addled, °confused, bewildered, confounded, puzzled, baffled, befuddled, *Colloq* dopey, punchy, woozy, *Brit* muzzy

groom *n.* 1 stableboy, stableman, *Brit* stable lad, *Archaic* ostler *or* hostler, equerry 2 bridegroom —*v.* 3 °spruce up, °dress, tidy *or* neaten up, smarten up, titivate *or* tittivate, °preen, °primp, °refresh 4 °fit, °train, °prepare, °coach, °tutor, °brief, °drill, °prime, (get *or* make) ready, °adapt, °shape

groove *n.* °slot, °cut, °channel, °furrow, °gouge, trough; flute, °scratch, striation *or* stria, rifling, °rifle, *Architecture* glyph, *Technical* sulcus

grope *v.* °feel, °fumble, fish, °probe

gross *adj.* 1 °fat, °obese, corpulent, overweight, °big, °large, °bulky, °great, °heavy, °ponderous, °massive, cumbersome, °unwieldy 2 °total, aggregate, °entire, pretax, (all-)inclusive, °overall, °whole 3 °coarse, °vulgar, °crude, °unsophisticated, uncultured, uncultivated, °earthy, crass, indelicate, °indecent, °inappropriate, °unseemly, °improper, °unrefined, °bawdy, ribald, Rabelaisian, °raw, °rude, °offensive, °obscene, °lewd, °dirty, smutty, °pornographic, °filthy 4 °outrageous, °flagrant, °obvious, °plain, °glaring, °shameful, °blatant, °monstrous, heinous, °manifest, °evident 5 °disgusting, °repulsive, °repellent, °revolting, nauseating —*v.* 6 °earn, bring *or* take in, °make —*n.* 7 °(overall) total, °take, intake, takings, °receipts, °gate

grotesque *adj.* 1 distorted, °bizarre, freakish, twisted, °misshapen, malformed, °deformed, °gruesome, °gnarled 2 °absurd, °incongruous, °weird, °odd, °fantastic, °strange, °queer, °peculiar, °curious, °outlandish, °offbeat, °abnormal, aberrant, anomalous, °ludicrous, °ridiculous, °preposterous

ground *n.* 1 °earth, °soil, °turf, sod, °dirt, loam, clay; °land, °terrain 2 °territory, °area, °range, °scope, compass 3 Often, ***grounds.*** °basis, °foundation, °base, °reason, °footing, justification, °rationale, °argument, °cause, °motive, °excuse 4 ***grounds.*** °sediment, °dregs, lees, °deposit, settlings, *Brit* grouts —*v.* 5 °base, °establish, °organize, °found; °settle, °set 6 °instruct, °teach, °train, °coach, °tutor, °inform, °prepare, °initiate

groundless *adj.* baseless, without foundation, °unsound, °unfounded, unsupported, unjustified, unjustifiable, °unwarranted, uncalled-for, °gratuitous, unreasoned, °unreasonable, °speculative, suppositional, °hypothetical, °tenuous, °flimsy, °illusory, °imaginary, chimerical

groundwork *n.* °basis, spadework, preparation(s), °base, °foundation, underpinning(s), cornerstone

group *n.* 1 °assembly, assemblage, °gathering, congregation, °company, °number, °alliance, °union, °association, °organization, °league, °society, coterie, °clique, °set, °band, °circle, °club, °party, °body, °faction, °crowd, °team, °corps, guild, troupe, °unit, troop, °platoon, °squad, °gang 2 °batch, aggregation, °set, grouping, °collection, assemblage, °bunch, °accumulation, conglomeration, agglomeration, °assortment, series; °pile, °heap, °bundle —*v.* 3 classify, °class, °sort, °bracket, °organize, °order, °rank, assort, °categorize, catalog 4 °collect, °assemble, °arrange, °place, °dispose, °gather, °organize, bring *or* put together, °set apart

groveling *adj.* °obsequious, fawning, toadying, toadeating, sycophantish, subservient, slavish, °servile, °submissive, kowtowing, cringing, cowering, truckling, sniveling, scraping, tugging the forelock, abject, crawling, °base, °low, °mean, °sordid, *Colloq* bootlicking, *US* apple-polishing; *Slang* brownnosing, *Brit* arse-kissing, arse-licking, *US* ass-kissing, ass-licking

grow *v.* 1 °flourish, °develop, °increase, become larger *or* greater, °enlarge, wax, °swell, °expand, broaden, °thicken, °spread, °lengthen, multiply, burgeon *or* bourgeon, °thrive, °luxuriate, °prosper, °mature, °ripen, bloom, °flower, blossom, fructify, bear *or* yield fruit 2 °develop, evolve, °arise, °issue, °stem, °spring (up), °originate 3 °plant, °cultivate, °breed, nurture, °raise, °propagate, °produce; °sow 4 °become, °get 5 ***grow on.*** get *or* become accepted by, come *or* begin to be liked by, to gain *or* increase in interest *or* attraction to, become more pleasing to 6 ***grow up.*** °mature, reach *or* attain maturity *or* adulthood, come of age, reach one's majority

growth *n.* 1 °development, °evolution, evolvement, cultivation, nurturing, °increase, °expansion, broadening, °extension, enlargement, °spread, °proliferation, flowering 2 vegetation, crop 3 °advance, advancement, °success, °improvement, °expansion, °rise, °progress 4 wen, excrescence, wart, °lump, °tumor, °swelling, intumescence

grudge *n.* 1 °bitterness, °resentment, °rancor, °ill will, hard feelings, °spite, °grievance, pique, °dislike, °aversion, antipathy, animus, °animosity, enmity, °venom, malice, malevolence, hatred —*v.* 2 °begrudge, °resent, °envy, °mind, covet

gruesome *adj.* °ghastly, °repugnant, °horrible, horrid, horrific, horrendous, °grisly, °hideous, °revolting, °repellent, °repulsive, °loathsome, °grim, °grotesque, °macabre, °abominable, °frightful, °frightening, °fearsome, °shocking, °terrible, °awful

gruff *adj.* 1 °surly, crusty, grumpy, curmudgeonly, °cantankerous, °sour, °peevish, churlish, °rude, uncivil, bearish, °testy, °querulous, °irritable, °cross, °petulant, crabbed, irascible, °sullen, sulky, °bluff, °abrupt, °curt, °blunt, °brusque, °short, °short-tempered, ill-humored, ill-natured, bad-tempered, stinging, °cutting, °biting, acerbic, acrimonious, acid, °caustic, *Colloq* grouchy, crotchety 2 throaty, °deep, °rough, guttural, rasping, °low, °husky, hoarse, harsh(-sounding)

guarantee *n.* 1 guaranty, °warranty, °assurance, °pledge, °bond, °obligation, °promise;

°word (of honor), °oath, °undertaking *—v.* **2** guaranty, °warranty, °assure, °ensure, °pledge, °promise, °undertake, stand behind, vouch for, °certify, make sure *or* certain, swear to, attest to

guard *v.* **1** °protect, °shield, °safeguard, (keep *or* stand) watch (over), °defend, convoy, °escort, °police, °look after, °tend, °mind **2** °control, °mind *—n.* **3** °sentinel, °watchman, sentry, security guard, custodian, °guardian, °protector, °picket, °watch, bodyguard; evzone, Bashibazouk; *Brit* warder, wardress, *Slang* °screw, *Brit* °minder **4** °protection, convoy, °escort, °patrol **5** °defense, °protection, °safety, °safeguard, °security, °shield

guarded *adj.* °careful, °cautious, heedful, °prudent, circumspect, °wary, °noncommittal, restrained, °mindful, °suspicious, leery *or Brit also* leary, apprehensive; loath *or* loth, °reticent, °reluctant, *Colloq* cagey

guardian *n.* °protector, defender, paladin, °champion; trustee, custodian, °keeper, preserver

guerrilla *n.* guerilla, partisan *or* partizan, resistance *or* freedom *or* underground fighter, °irregular; insurgent, saboteur, °terrorist; *US history* Jayhawker, *French history* Maquis

guess *v.* **1** conjecture, °estimate, hypothesize, °speculate, postulate, *Slang* guesstimate **2** °think, °suppose, conclude, °assume, °believe, daresay, °surmise, °judge, deem, °reckon, °imagine, °fancy, °feel, °suspect, °divine *—n.* **3** conjecture, °estimate, °hypothesis, °speculation, °surmise, assumption, °judgment, °feeling, °suspicion, °supposition, postulate, theory; guesswork; *Colloq* shot in the dark, *Slang* guesstimate

guest *n.* °visitor, °company, caller; °patron, °customer, lodger, boarder, roomer

guidance *n.* **1** °leadership, °direction, °management, °government, °conduct, °control, °regulation, °charge, handling, °rule, °auspices **2** °counsel, °advice, counseling, advisement, °instruction, teaching

guide *v.* **1** °lead, show *or* lead the way, °conduct, °shepherd, °direct, usher, °steer, orient *or Brit* orientate **2** °steer, °pilot, °maneuver, °navigate, °direct **3** °counsel, °advise, °influence, °sway; °supervise, °oversee, °handle, °manage, superintend, °direct, °control, °regulate, °govern **4** °instruct, °teach, °tutor, °train *—n.* **5** °leader, conductor, °director, cicerone, chaperon, mentor, °counsel, °counselor, adviser *or* advisor, guru, °master **6** °model, criterion, exemplar, °standard, °ideal, °example, °inspiration **7** °beacon, °light, °signal, guiding light, °landmark, lodestar, °sign, marker **8** handbook, °manual, enchiridion, °vade mecum, guidebook, Baedeker

guilt *n.* **1** culpability, guiltiness, criminality, °blame, °responsibility, blameworthiness; °crime, sinfulness, feloniousness, wrongdoing, misconduct **2** °remorse, self-reproach, °regret, °sorrow, contrition, repentance, °shame, contriteness, self-condemnation, bad conscience

guilty *adj.* **1** °responsible, culpable, answerable, blameworthy, °at fault, °delinquent, °wrong; offending, reprehensible **2** °remorseful, contrite, °regretful, °sorry, °apologetic, °repentant, °sorrowful, conscience-stricken, rueful, °penitent; °ashamed, °shamefaced, °sheepish, °embarrassed, red-faced

guise *n.* **1** °appearance, °aspect, °semblance, °look, °image, °likeness, mien; °air, °behavior, °conduct, deportment, comportment, °bearing, demeanor **2** °semblance, °disguise, façade, °front, °pretense

gulf *n.* **1** bay, bight, cove, inlet, °sound, loch *or* sea loch, firth *or* frith, fjord, *Irish* lough, *Brit* °creek **2** chasm, °deep, °depth, °abyss, abysm, °void, °space, °opening, °rift, °breach, °gap, °separation, °split

gullible *adj.* °innocent, °green, °simple, credulous, °unsophisticated, naive *or* naïve *or* naïf, °unsuspecting, °unwary, unsuspicious, wide-eyed, born yesterday, °inexperienced, °immature

gully *n.* gulley, °channel, riverbed, watercourse, °gorge, °ravine, °canyon, °notch, °cut, °pass, defile, °valley, °corridor, wadi, *Brit* gill *or* ghyll, *Western US* arroyo, *US and Canadian* gulch

gulp *v.* **1** °bolt, gobble, wolf (down), °devour, °gorge, °swallow, throw down, toss off, quaff, guzzle, °swill, *Colloq* knock back, swig, *US* chug-a-lug **2** °swallow, °suppress, °stifle, °choke (back), °smother, strangle *—n.* **3** °mouthful, °swallow, °draft, °swill, *Colloq* swig

gumption *n.* **1** resourcefulness, shrewdness, cleverness, °(mother) wit, °(common) sense, astuteness, °judgment, *Colloq* horse sense, brains, *Slang Brit* nous **2** °backbone, °grit, °pluck, mettle, °enterprise, °initiative, °courage, °spirit, gameness, °nerve, °daring, °vigor, °energy, boldness, audacity, °stamina, *Colloq* °spunk, °guts, get-up-and-go, *US* moxie, *Slang Brit* °bottle, *Taboo slang* balls

gurgle *v.* **1** °bubble, burble, °babble, °ripple, °splash, plash, °lap, °murmur, purl *—n.* **2** °babble, burble, bubbling, babbling, burbling, °splash, gurgling, splashing, plashing, murmuring, purl, purling

gush *v.* **1** cascade, °rush, °flood, °stream, °spurt, jet, °spout, °burst; °run, °flow **2** bubble over, overflow, be ebullient *or* effusive *or* effervescent, effervesce, °make much of, fuss over, °prattle, °chatter, °babble, °jabber, blather *or* blether, *Colloq Brit* natter, witter *—n.* **3** cascade, °rush, °flood, °flow, °stream, °spurt, jet, °spout, °burst, °torrent **4** °exuberance, effusion, bubbling over, °outburst

gushy *adj.* gushing, fulsome, cloying, mawkish, °excessive, °effusive, overdone, (over)sentimental, (over)enthusiastic, *Colloq* °sloppy, slushy

gust *n.* **1** °puff, °blow, °wind, °breeze, °blast *—v.* **2** °puff, °blow, °blast, °surge, °increase

gusto *n.* °enthusiasm, °relish, °zest, °appetite, zeal, zealousness, avidity, °eagerness, °enjoyment, °appreciation, °pleasure, °delight, °satisfaction

gut *n.* **1** Often, ***guts.*** °bowels, intestines, entrails, viscera, °stomach, offal, vitals, vital parts, (of a fish) gurry, *Brit* (of a deer) gralloch, *Colloq* °insides, innards *or* inwards **2** °stomach, abdomen, belly; beer belly, bay window, corporation **3** ***guts.*** **(a)** °backbone, °bravery, boldness, audacity, °pluck, °courage, °determination, °daring, °spirit, °grit, mettle, °gumption, °nerve, intestinal fortitude, *Colloq* °spunk, gutsiness, *Slang Brit* °bottle, *Taboo* balls **(b)** °integrity, willpower, °stamina, °endurance, forcefulness, °dynamism —*v.* **4** disembowel, eviscerate, °draw, °dress, °clean **5** °ransack, °pillage, °plunder, °sack, despoil, °strip, °ravage, °loot, °rifle, *Rare* depredate; °clean out, °devastate, °empty —*adj.* **6** °basic, °heartfelt, °instinctive, instinctual, intuitive, visceral, deep-seated, °emotional

guttersnipe *n.* waif, street arab, (street) urchin, °ragamuffin, brat, gamin, °rogue, *Colloq Brit rare* mudlark

guy *n.* **1** °man, °lad, °youth, °boy, °fellow, °person, *Colloq* °chap, geezer, *Brit* bloke, *Slang* gink, cat, °customer, *US* °dude, *Old-fashioned* gazabo *or* gazebo —*v.* **2** °mock, °ridicule, °make fun of, °caricature, °satirize, °poke fun at, °lampoon, *Colloq* rib, °take off, *Brit* °send up

gyrate *v.* °rotate, °spin, °revolve, turn (round *or* about), whirl, °twirl, °swirl, °pirouette; °swivel

H

habit *n.* **1** °custom, °routine, °practice, °convention, °policy, °pattern, °usage, °mode, °rule, wont, praxis **2** °tendency, °disposition, °manner, °practice, °way, °custom, °inclination, °bent, predisposition, second nature, °frame of mind, °attitude, °penchant, propensity, proclivity; addiction, compulsion **3** attire, clothing, °dress, °apparel, °clothes, garb, °costume, °garments, vestments, °uniform, raiment, livery, °regalia, habiliment(s), *Colloq* °gear

habitable *adj.* livable, inhabitable

habitat *n.* °abode, °home, °haunt, °domain, °range, °territory, bailiwick, °realm, °terrain, °element, °environment, surroundings, *Colloq* stamping ground

habitual *adj.* **1** settled, °fixed, °customary, °usual, °conventional, °accustomed, °set, °rooted, established, °traditional, °standard, °routine, °ritual, °regular, °normal, wonted, °common, °ordinary, °natural **2** inveterate, established, °chronic, confirmed, hardened, °ingrained, °frequent, °persistent, °constant, °continual, °perpetual

habitué *n.* frequenter, °patron, regular customer, *Colloq* °regular

hack[1] *v.* **1** °chop, hew, °lacerate, °gash, °slash, °cut; °mangle, °butcher, °mutilate, °ruin, °destroy, smash, °batter, °damage, °deface **2** bark, cough —*n.* **3** °cut, °gash, °slash, °chop

hack[2] *n.* **1** drudge, penny-a-liner, scribbler, Grubstreet writer **2** plodder, drudge, toiler, °menial, °flunky, lackey, °slave, *Brit* °fag, *Slang* °grind, *Brit* swot **3** saddle horse, riding horse, hackney, *Archaic* palfrey —*adj.* **4** hackneyed, trite, °banal, overdone, commonplace, °routine, stereotyped, °stock, °tired, °tedious, °mediocre, overworked, °stale, unoriginal, °run-of-the-mill, °humdrum, moth-eaten, °moldy, *Colloq* old hat

hag *n.* crone, °fury, °witch, ogress, gorgon, harpy, fishwife, harridan, °shrew, virago, termagant, vixen, hellcat, maenad *or* menad, Xanthippe, *Archaic* beldam; dog, °beast, °monster; *Colloq* battle-ax, *Slang* °bitch, °bag, *US* two-bagger

haggard *adj.* °gaunt, °drawn, wasted, °emaciated, hollow-eyed, hollow-cheeked, °scrawny, scraggy, °ghastly, cadaverous, °run-down, wearied, °weary, careworn, °spent, played-out, °exhausted, toilworn, °worn, shrunken, withered

haggle *v.* wrangle, °bargain, higgle, °bicker, chaffer, palter, °dispute, squabble, °quibble, °negotiate; barter, °deal; *Colloq US* °dicker

hail[1] *v.* **1** °greet, accost, °address, °signal, °call **2** °cheer, °salute, °applaud, °approve, °glorify, °praise, °laud, °honor, acclaim, °congratulate, felicitate, °acknowledge

hail[2] *v.* **1** rain *or* beat *or* shower (down) on, °bombard, °pelt, °volley, barrage —*n.* **2** °volley, °storm, °shower, °torrent, bombardment, barrage

hair *n.* **1** tresses, locks, mane, curls, ringlets; braids, plaits **2** hairsbreadth, whisker, °trifle, fraction, skin of one's teeth

hairdo *n.* coiffure, hairstyle, °cut, coif

hairless *adj.* bald, bald-headed, bald-pated, glabrous, calvous

hairsplitting *adj.* quibbling, (over)fussy, hypercritical, °petty, captious, carping, °faultfinding, °finicky, (over)nice, °fastidious, caviling, °niggling, *Colloq* nit-picking

hairy *adj.* **1** hirsute, °shaggy, downy, fleecy, °fluffy, °woolly, lanate *or* lanose, lanuginous *or* lanuginose, bristly, setaceous, setal, hispid, comate *or* comose, fringy, crinite, trichoid, strigose *or* strigous, strigillose; whiskered, bewhiskered, bearded, barbate, unshaven **2** °tricky, °dangerous, °perilous, °risky, °uncertain, °precarious, °hazardous, °frightening, worrying, °nerve-racking, *Colloq* °scary **3** tangled, °intricate, knotty, complex, °complicated, °difficult, °problematic, °confused, confusing

hale *adj.* °healthy, °hearty, °fit (as a fiddle), °sound, able-bodied, °hardy, °wholesome, °robust, °flourishing, in good *or* fine fettle, °in the pink

halfhearted *adj.* °indifferent, uncaring, unconcerned, °lukewarm, uninterested, °dispassionate, °cool, °unenthusiastic, half-baked, °nonchalant, °phlegmatic, °lackadaisical, insouciant

half-wit *n.* dunce, °fool, idiot, simpleton, ninny, ass, ninnyhammer, moron, imbecile, °dolt, dunderhead *or* dunderpate, rattlebrain, nincompoop, dullard, *Colloq* numskull *or* numbskull, nitwit, dimwit, birdbrain, *Brit* nit, °twit

half-witted *adj.* °stupid, °foolish, °silly, °simple, °inane, asinine, moronic, imbecilic, doltish, rattlebrained, °feebleminded, attocerebral, cretinous, °thick, ***non compos mentis,*** dimwitted, weak-minded, *Colloq* °dumb, *Brit* dotty, barmy (in the crumpet)

hall *n.* **1** °corridor, hallway, passageway, °passage; foyer, °entry, entryway, °lobby, vestibule **2** auditorium, assembly *or* meeting *or* convention hall, °theater, amphitheater, hired hall; lecture room *or* hall, classroom

hallmark *n.* **1** authentication, verification, seal *or* stamp (of authenticity *or* approval), °mark, °device, °sign, °symbol; plate mark; assay mark **2** °feature, °stamp, °mark, earmark, trademark, °characteristic, °identification

hallow *v.* **1** consecrate, °bless, °sanctify, °dedicate, °honor, enshrine, °glorify **2** °venerate, °worship, °revere, °reverence, °respect, °honor, pay homage *or* respect *or* honor to, °exalt

hallucination *n.* °fantasy, mirage, °daydream, °illusion, °delusion, °vision, °dream, aberration, chimera, phantasm, °phantom, figment of the imagination, apparition, °specter, °ghost; paresthesia

halo *n.* nimbus, °aura, aureole *or* aureola, corona, °radiance, *Painting* vesica, mandorla; °ring, disk *or* disc, °circle, annulation, annulus

halt *n.* **1** °stop, °standstill, °end, °termination, °close, stoppage, cessation *—v.* **2** °stop, °quit, °end, °terminate, °cease, °check, °curb, °stem, °discontinue, desist, bring *or* come *or* draw to an end *or* close, put an end *or* stop to, conclude, shut *or* close down *or* up

halting *adj.* °hesitant, hesitating, wavering, shifting, uneven, faltering, stumbling, °faulty, unsteady, °awkward, stammering, stuttering

hamper[1] *v.* °slow, balk *or* baulk, °delay, °hold up, °retard, °inhibit, °encumber, °hinder, °obstruct, °block, °impede, °prevent, interfere with, °frustrate, °restrict, °curb, °limit, °handicap, °restrain, °trammel, °bar, barricade, °shackle, °clog, °curtail, lessen, °reduce, °diminish

hamper[2] *n.* basket, pannier, creel, *Brit* punnet; hanaper, *Dialectal* skep

hand *n.* **1** *Slang* mitt, paw, *US* lunch-hook **2** °help, °aid, °assistance, helping hand, °relief, °boost; leg up **3** °influence, °agency, participation, involvement, °part, °share **4** °(manual) laborer, °worker, workman, °man, °help, °employee **5** °pointer, °indicator, °index **6** °(round of) applause, °ovation, °clap **7** handwriting, °penmanship, °script; calligraphy **8** Often, ***hands.*** °control, °hold, °grasp, °possession, °custody, °clutches, keeping, °power, disposal, °jurisdiction, °authority, supervision, °management, guardianship, °care **9** ***at hand.*** °nearby, °close, °near, °close by, °handy, °(readily) available, to *or* on hand, at one's fingertips, °convenient, within (arm's) reach, °accessible, °present; approaching, °imminent, around the corner **10** ***hand in glove.*** °hand in hand, in league, together, in collusion, collusively, connivingly, conspiringly, intimately, closely, jointly, *Colloq* in cahoots **11** ***hand in hand.*** together, °side by side, °hand in glove **12** ***hand over fist.*** °quickly, speedily, °rapidly, °swiftly, steadily, °like mad **13** ***hands down.*** °easily, °readily, effortlessly *—v.* **14** °give, °pass, °deliver, present to *or* with **15** ***hand down or on or over.*** **(a)** °bequeath, °will, °pass on; °transfer, °turn over **(b)** See **18 (a),** below. **16** ***hand in.*** °submit, °give in, °tender, proffer, °offer **17** ***hand out.*** °distribute, disseminate, pass out *or* round *or* around, °give out, °deal (out), mete *or* dole out, °dispense; disburse **18** ***hand over.*** **(a)** °deliver, °submit, °yield, °give up, °surrender, °turn over; °transfer **(b)** See **15 (a),** above.

handcuffs *n. pl.* manacles, °shackles, *Colloq* cuffs, bracelets, *Slang Brit* darbies

handful *n.* **1** °few, °couple, sprinkling, small number; fistful **2** (behavior *or* disciplinary) problem, °bother, mischief-maker, °troublemaker, °nuisance

handicap *n.* **1** °hindrance, °restraint, °encumbrance, °restriction, limitation, °impediment, °barrier, °bar, °obstacle, °(stumbling) block, constraint, °check, °curb, °trammel, °disability, °disadvantage *—v.* **2** °hinder, °hamper, °restrain, °encumber, °restrict, °limit, °impede, °bar, °block, °check, °curb, °trammel, disable, °disadvantage

handily *adv.* **1** °readily, °easily, effortlessly, without strain, comfortably, with both hands tied (behind one's back) **2** skillfully, capably, deftly, cleverly, dexterously, adroitly, expertly, proficiently, masterfully

handle *n.* **1** °grip, hilt, handgrip, haft, helve *—v.* **2** °feel, °touch, °finger, °hold; °caress, °fondle, °pat **3** °manage, °run, °operate, °direct, °administer, °supervise, °oversee, °control, °command, °guide **4** °steer, °control, °manage, °cope with, °maneuver, °manipulate **5** deal *or* trade *or* traffic in, °(buy and) sell, °market **6** °treat, °control, °deal with,

°cope with **7** °treat, °employ, °use, utilize; °deal with, °wield, °tackle, °manipulate

handsome *adj.* **1** good-looking, fine-looking, °attractive, °fair, °comely **2** °generous, sizable, °large, °big, °substantial, °considerable, °good, °goodly, °ample, °abundant

handy *adj.* **1** °nearby, °accessible, °available, at *or* on *or* to hand, °close (by), °convenient, at one's fingertips, within (easy) reach, °(at the) ready **2** usable, °serviceable, maneuverable, °clever, °useful, °helpful, °practical **3** deft, °clever, °dexterous, adroit, °adept, skilled, °skillful, °proficient, °expert

hang *v.* **1** °suspend, °depend, °dangle; be poised *or* suspended, °hover, °swing **2** gibbet, send to the gallows, lynch, °execute, °kill, *Colloq* °string up, °stretch **3** °drape, °fall **4** ***hang about or around.*** **(a)** loiter, °wait, °linger, dally, °idle, °tarry, *Colloq* °hang out **(b)** Also, ***hang about or around (with).*** frequent, °haunt, °visit, spend time at; °associate with, socialize with, hobnob with, rub elbows with, consort with, fraternize with, mix *or* mingle with, *Colloq* °hang out (with) **5** ***hang back (from).*** be reluctant, °recoil (from), °shrink (from), °hesitate, falter, stay away (from) **6** ***hang fire.*** be delayed, remain unsettled *or* unfinished, be in suspense *or* abeyance; °stall, °hold up, °delay **7** ***hang on.*** **(a)** Also, ***hang on to.*** hold on (to), °cling (to), °clutch, °grip, °grasp, °grab **(b)** °wait, °stay, °stop **(c)** °wait, °persist, °remain, °carry on, °persevere, °go on, °hold out, °endure, hold the phone, *Colloq US* hang in there **(d)** Also, ***hang onto or upon.*** listen carefully *or* attentively, give one's undivided attention, be rapt **(e)** depend *or* rely (on), be dependent *or* contingent (on), be subject (to), be conditioned *or* conditional (on) **8** ***hang one's head.*** be ashamed *or* humiliated *or* abashed *or* humbled *or* embarrassed **9** ***hang out.*** See **4 (a)**, above. **10** ***hang over.*** be put off *or* postponed *or* delayed **11** ***hang together.*** **(a)** °unite, be united, be as one, °stick together, join forces, °cooperate, act in concert *or* harmony **(b)** make sense, be logical, be consistent, °correspond, °match (up), cohere, be coherent **12** ***hang up.*** break the connection, °disconnect, °cut off, put down the receiver

hanger-on *n.* °follower, dependent, leech, °parasite, toady, sycophant, °yes man, *Colloq* scrounger, *US* freeloader, *Slang* groupie, sponger *or* sponge

hangman *n.* executioner, *Archaic Brit* Jack Ketch

hanker *v.* Usually, ***hanker after or for.*** yearn for, long for, thirst after *or* for, hunger after *or* for, itch for, pine for, lust after *or* for, covet, crave, have a hankering for, °want, °desire, °fancy, *Colloq* have a yen for

hanky-panky *n.* °mischief, °trickery, double-dealing, legerdemain, °deception, duplicity, °chicanery, naughtiness, foolishness, tomfoolery, *Colloq* funny business, jiggery-pokery, monkey business, shenanigans, goings-on, antics

haphazard *adj.* **1** °random, °arbitrary, °chance, fortuitous, aleatory, °accidental, °unforeseen, unlooked-for, unexpected, adventitious, serendipitous **2** °casual, °offhand, hit-or-miss, unsystematic, slapdash, °slipshod, °careless, disorganized, °disorderly

happen *v.* **1** °occur, °take place, °come about, °go on, °come to pass, °develop; betide, °chance, °prove, °materialize, *Colloq* °transpire, °come off, *Slang* cook **2** befall, °become of **3** ***happen on or upon.*** come upon, chance *or* hit on *or* upon, stumble on *or* upon, °find, °turn up, °encounter, °meet with

happening *n.* °event, °incident, °occurrence, °occasion, taking place, °circumstance, °chance, °episode, °phenomenon

happily *adv.* **1** fortunately, luckily, propitiously, providentially, opportunely **2** joyfully, joyously, delightedly, gleefully, cheerily, cheerfully, °gaily, merrily, blithely; enthusiastically, heartily **3** °gladly, with pleasure, agreeably, contentedly, °willingly, peaceably

happiness *n.* °pleasure, °delight, felicity, °enjoyment, °joy, joyousness, joyfulness, jubilation, cheerfulness, cheeriness, °cheer, blithesomeness, gladness, lightheartedness, exhilaration, elation, °exuberance, high spirits, °glee, °ecstasy

happy *adj.* **1** pleased, °delighted, °glad, joyous, °joyful, °overjoyed, jubilant, °cheerful, cheery, °blithe, blithesome, °glad, lighthearted, contented, exhilarated, °exultant, °elated, °exuberant, thrilled, °gleeful, euphoric, °ecstatic, satisfied, gratified, *Colloq* °on top of the world, on cloud nine, pleased as Punch, tickled pink, *Brit* in the seventh heaven, over the moon, *US* in seventh heaven **2** °lucky, fortuitous, °propitious, °fortunate, auspicious, °advantageous, °beneficial, °favorable, felicitous, °opportune, °timely, °well-timed, apt, °appropriate

harangue *n.* **1** diatribe, °tirade, °oration, peroration, declamation, philippic, screed, exhortation, vituperation, rodomontade, °speech, °address, *Colloq* spiel *—v.* **2** declaim, °hold forth, °preach, °lecture, sermonize, pontificate, °vituperate, rant and rave

harass *v.* badger, harry, hector, °trouble, °torment, °bother, °exasperate, °hound, °plague, °persecute, vex, °annoy, °irritate, °pester, °worry, °beset, bait, °nag, pick on *or* at, °tease, torture, *Brit* chivy *or* chivvy *or* chevy, *Slang* give (someone) a hard time

harbinger *n.* °forerunner, herald, °precursor, °omen, foretoken, °sign, portent, augury

harbor *n.* **1** °port, (safe) haven, anchorage, mooring *—v.* **2** °shelter, keep safe, °protect, °shield, °guard, °safeguard, °conceal, °hide **3** °cherish, °foster, nurture, °nurse, °keep, °retain, °maintain, °hold, cling to

hard *adj.* **1** °rigid, °stiff, °solid, °inflexible, °firm, °dense, condensed, compressed,

°close, solidified, hardened; °stony, rocklike, °concrete, °petrified, granite(like), flinty, °steely; °tough, °rugged, leathery, °callous; unyielding, adamant(ine), impenetrable, obdurate, impervious, °impregnable **2** °difficult, °laborious, °arduous, backbreaking, °burdensome, onerous, fatiguing, tiring, °exhausting, wearying, °strenuous, °tough, °toilsome **3** °difficult, °perplexing, knotty, °puzzling, baffling, enigmatic, °intricate, °complicated, complex, tangled, °involved, °thorny, °incomprehensible, inscrutable, unsolvable, insoluble, *Colloq* °tough **4** °stern, °cold, °callous, intractable, °exacting, °strict, °demanding, hardhearted, stonyhearted, °severe, °tyrannical, °despotic, °dictatorial, magisterial, °oppressive, °cruel, °ruthless, pitiless, °merciless, °savage, °brutal, brutish, °inhuman, °heartless, °harsh, °unkind, °implacable, °unsympathetic, °dispassionate, uncompassionate, unfeeling, obdurate, indurate; unsentimental, insensitive, °thick-skinned, °tough, hard-boiled, °stony, hard-bitten, unfeeling, unsparing **5** °bad, °difficult, °grievous, °calamitous, wracking, °disastrous, °dark, °grim, distressing, °devastating, °agonizing, °painful, unpleasant, °severe, austere, *Colloq* °tough, °rough **6** °cool, unemotional, °calculating, uncompromising, °methodical, °critical, °systematic, °practical, pragmatic, businesslike, °realistic, °penetrating, searching, hardheaded, *Colloq* °tough, hard-nosed **7** sedulous, assiduous, °devoted, °conscientious, °industrious, indefatigable, °untiring, °persistent, dogged, °intent, °eager, zealous, °ardent, °energetic, °keen, avid **8** °cold, °bare, °plain, °straight, straightforward, °blunt, °unvarnished, °unquestionable, verifiable, °real, °indisputable, undeniable, incontestable, °incontrovertible, °strict, inescapable, ineluctable, °unavoidable, unalterable, immutable **9** °angry, °bitter, acrimonious, °hostile, antagonistic, °harsh, unpleasant, unfriendly **10** spirituous, °alcoholic, °strong **11** addictive, habit-forming **12** °sharp, well-defined, °clear, °distinct, °stark, °definite *—adv.* **13** °vigorously, forcefully, forcibly, energetically, mightily, arduously, laboriously, strenuously, earnestly, actively, dynamically, eagerly, intensely, ardently, heartily, zealously, °intently, spiritedly, diligently, assiduously, sedulously, studiously, determinedly, steadfastly, conscientiously, industriously, devotedly, urgently, persistently, untiringly, indefatigably, perseveringly, unfalteringly, relentlessly, doggedly **14** violently, °deeply, intensely, °badly, distressingly, °painfully, °severely, agonizingly **15** °intently, carefully, earnestly **16** harshly, °severely, °badly, °ill **17** ***hard up.*** °poor, °indigent, poverty-stricken, °impoverished, penniless, impecunious, bankrupt, *Colloq* in the red, °broke, bust(ed), °on one's uppers, *Slang Brit* skint

harden *v.* **1** °set, °solidify, °stiffen, °freeze **2** °intensify, °strengthen, °brace, °fortify, toughen, °reinforce, °stiffen

hardly *adv.* °scarcely, °barely, °only, °just, only just; not quite, °by no means; °seldom, °rarely

hardship *n.* °want, °privation, deprivation, °suffering, °misery, °distress, °affliction, adversity, austerity, °misfortune, unhappiness, ill fortune, bad luck, °difficulty, °trouble

hardware *n.* **1** tools, metal goods, *Brit* ironmongery **2** °(computer) equipment, components, °devices, machinery; arms, munitions, armament(s), materiel

hardy *adj.* **1** °robust, °sturdy, °strong, °rugged, °tough, °durable, °sound, °stalwart, °stout, °vigorous, able-bodied, red-blooded, °fit, °hale, °healthy, *Colloq* °husky **2** °bold, °courageous, °daring, valorous, valiant, °brave, °manly, °intrepid, °fearless, °heroic, plucky

harebrained *adj.* **1** °rash, °foolhardy, °wild, madcap, °reckless, °heedless, °improvident, °visionary, °fanciful, airy, *Colloq* crackpot **2** °foolish, °silly, °inane, asinine, °flighty, witless, brainless, °mindless, °giddy, °frivolous, °scatterbrained

harm *n.* **1** °injury, °damage, °mischief, °hurt, °abuse, °misfortune **2** °evil, wrongdoing, wickedness, iniquity, °wrong, badness *—v.* **3** °hurt, °damage, °injure, °abuse, maltreat, °wound

harmful *adj.* °dangerous, pernicious, deleterious, °destructive, damaging, °bad, °detrimental, °injurious; °unhealthy, noxious, baleful, toxic, °poisonous, °venomous, *Archaic* baneful

harmless *adj.* °benign, innocuous, °inoffensive, °gentle, °mild, °innocent, °safe; nontoxic, nonpoisonous, nonvenomous

harmonious *adj.* °agreeable, compatible, congruous, consonant, in accord, congenial, complementary, °sympathetic, concordant, *Colloq* simpatico

harmony *n.* **1** °agreement, °accord, concord, compatibility, °rapport, unanimity, °unity **2** consonance, congruity, °balance, orderliness, closeness, togetherness, consistency, °fitness, parallelism **3** melodiousness, euphony, tunefulness

harrowing *adj.* distressing, vexing, alarming, unnerving, °frightening, °terrifying, horrifying, °horrible, torturous, chilling, °heart-rending, °nerve-racking, °traumatic, °agonizing, °painful; °disturbing, upsetting, worrying, worrisome, °disconcerting, daunting, dismaying, disquieting

harsh *adj.* **1** °rough, °coarse, bristly, °scratchy, °hairy, °crude; hoarse, °grating, °raucous, rasping, °husky, guttural; clashing, inharmonious *or* unharmonious, °discordant, atonal, dissonant, cacophonous, °strident, °shrill, grinding, °sour; °bitter, acrid **2** °stern, austere, °bleak, °dour, °unkind, unfeeling, comfortless, uncompassionate, unfriendly, °grim, °hard, °Spartan, stringent, overexacting, Draconian, °tyrannical, °stark, °severe, °cruel, °abusive, °punishing, °punitive, °brutal, brutish, °inhuman, °merciless, °ruthless, pitiless **3** unpleasant, °disagreeable, °impolite, °discourteous, uncivil, °rude, °nasty, °curt, °abrupt, °brusque, °bluff, °gruff, curmudgeonly, choleric, splenetic, °surly, °sullen, irascible, °short-tempered, °petulant, °peevish, °waspish, grouchy, °bilious, °cross, acrimonious, °sarcastic, acerbic

harvest *n.* **1** crop, °yield, °produce, °output, °fruit; °vintage —*v.* **2** °reap, °gather, °pick, glean, °collect **3** °earn, °make, °take in, °collect, °garner, °get, °receive, °obtain, °procure, °net

hash *n.* **1** °mixture, °confusion, hotchpotch *or US and Canadian* hodgepodge, °potpourri, gallimaufry, farrago, °mishmash, °jumble, °mess, °shambles, olla podrida, mélange, °medley **2** °fiasco, °disaster, °botch, °mess, *Slang Brit* balls-up, *US* snafu —*v.* **3** Often, ***hash up.*** °mangle, mess *or* mix up, make a hash *or* mess *or* jumble of, °muddle, °bungle, °botch, °mishandle, mismanage, °ruin, °spoil, °butcher, *Colloq* foul *or* louse up, °screw up, muff, *Brit* °bugger up

haste *n.* **1** swiftness, °rapidity, quickness, °speed, °velocity, °expedition, °urgency, dispatch *or* despatch, alacrity, celerity, briskness **2** °hurry, °rush, rashness, hastiness, °hustle, bustle, impetuousness *or* impetuosity, recklessness, precipitancy

hasten *v.* **1** °hurry, °rush, make haste, °fly, °run, sprint, °race, °bolt, °dash, °scurry, scamper, scuttle, °speed **2** °hurry (up), °speed (up), dispatch *or* despatch, °send, °move, °quicken, accelerate, °expedite, °rush, impel, °urge

hastily *adv.* **1** °quickly, speedily, °swiftly, °rapidly, °at once, °immediately, °instantaneously, °promptly, without delay, right away, straightaway, °posthaste, hurriedly, °directly, °suddenly, in haste, precipitately, °on the spur of the moment, in a flash *or* wink, before one can *or* could say "Jack Robinson," *Colloq* pronto, °like a shot, like greased lightning, *US* lickety-split, *Slang* pdq *or* PDQ (= 'pretty damn(ed) quick') **2** impetuously, impulsively, rashly, recklessly, unthinkingly, thoughtlessly, heedlessly, incautiously

hasty *adj.* **1** °quick, °speedy, °swift, °rapid, °fast, °brisk, °prompt, °immediate, instantaneous **2** °careless, °rash, °precipitate, °impetuous, °impulsive, °reckless, °thoughtless, °unthinking, incautious, °heedless, ill-considered, °inconsiderate **3** °quick, °speedy, °cursory, °superficial, °fleeting, °passing, slapdash, °perfunctory, °momentary, °brief **4** °irritable, °quick-tempered, irascible, °testy, °passionate, °impatient, hot-tempered, °petulant, °waspish, °volatile, contentious, choleric, splenetic, bearish, °short-tempered, *US, Canadian, and Irish* cranky

hatch *v.* **1** °breed, °brood, °incubate, °bring forth **2** °devise, contrive, concoct, °design, °formulate, °originate, °invent, dream up, *Colloq* cook up

hate *v.* **1** °loathe, °abhor, °detest, have an aversion to, be averse to, abominate, °dislike, execrate, °despise, °scorn **2** be loath, be reluctant *or* unwilling *or* disinclined; °resist, shrink *or* flinch from, °dislike —*n.* **3** hatred, abhorrence, °loathing, odium, °animosity, animus, antipathy, °aversion, °hostility, °antagonism, malice, enmity, detestation

hateful *adj.* **1** °loathsome, detestable, °abhorrent, horrid, °horrible, °abominable, odious, execrable, °despicable, °scurvy, °obnoxious, heinous, °foul, °contemptible, °repugnant, °repulsive, °repellent, °revolting, °vile **2** °malignant, malefic, malevolent, malicious, °evil, °mean, °spiteful, °contemptuous

haughty *adj.* °arrogant, °proud, °superior, °self-important, °smug, self-satisfied, complacent, °pretentious, °conceited, °egotistical, °snobbish, °overbearing, °lofty, °presumptuous, overweening, patronizing, °supercilious, °vain, °condescending, °contemptuous, belittling, derisive, °disdainful, °scornful, *Colloq* highfalutin *or* hifalutin, °hoity-toity, stuck-up, swellheaded *or* swelled-headed *or* swollen-headed, high and mighty, on one's high horse, snooty, la-di-da *or* lah-di-dah *or* la-de-da, *Slang* snotty, °uppish, uppity

haul *v.* **1** °drag, °pull, °tug, °tow, °trail, °lug, °heave, °draw **2** °cart, °transport, °carry, convey, °truck, °move —*n.* **3** °pull, °tug, °drag, °draw; °heave; °attraction **4** °catch, °take, °yield, °harvest, °bag

haunt *v.* **1** °visit, °frequent, hang about *or* around, spend time at, *US* habituate **2** °beset, °obsess, °plague, °torment, °trouble, °possess, °prey on —*n.* **3** gathering place, meeting place, stamping ground, *Colloq* hangout

have *v.* **1** °possess, own, °keep; °maintain **2** °receive, °take, °accept, °get, °obtain, °acquire, °procure, °secure **3** °entertain, be struck by **4** °possess, °bear, °contain, °include, comprise **5** suffer with *or* from, be suffering with *or* from, be experiencing, be undergoing, be enduring, be subjected to **6** °arrange, °organize, °set up, °prepare; °hold **7** °partake of, participate in, °experience, °enjoy; °eat; °drink **8** give birth to, °bear, °deliver, °bring into the world; beget, sire, °father **9** °make, °demand; °force, °oblige, °cause, °induce, °press, °require, compel **10** ***had better or best.*** ought to, °must, should **11** ***had rather or sooner.*** prefer to, would rather *or* sooner **12** ***have on.*** **(a)** be wearing, be dressed *or* clothed *or* attired in **(b)** be committed to, have planned, have in the offing, have on the agenda **(c)** °trick, °tease, °deceive, pull (someone's) leg, play a joke on, °fool

havoc *n.* **1** °ruin, devastation, °destruction, °desolation, rack *or* wrack and ruin, despoliation, spoliation, °damage **2** °confusion, °chaos, °upset, °disorder, °mayhem, °shambles, disruption

hazard *n.* **1** °peril, °danger, °risk, endangerment, °threat, °jeopardy **2** °chance, °gamble, uncertainty, °luck, °fortune —*v.* **3** °venture, °dare; °gamble, °risk, °jeopardize, °endanger, °threaten, imperil, °stake

hazardous *adj.* unsafe, °risky, °perilous, fraught with danger, °questionable, °shaky, °dangerous, °precarious, °uncertain, unpredictable, °ticklish, °tricky, *Dialect* °parlous, *Colloq chiefly Brit* °dicey, dicky *or* dickey, *Slang* °hairy

hazy *adj.* **1** °misty, foggy, smoggy, cloudy, °overcast **2** °indistinct, blurred, blurry, °dull, °dim, °faint, °nebulous, °vague, unclear, °fuzzy, °indefinite, muddled

head *n.* **1** skull, pate, cranium, *Colloq* dome, *Slang* coco(nut), belfry, noggin, bean, nut, rocker, noodle, gourd, *Brit* conk, crumpet, noddle, °loaf **2** °chief, °leader, administrator, chief executive officer, CEO, °(managing) director, MD, president, chairman, chairwoman, chairlady, chairperson, °chair, °employer, °principal, °superintendent, °supervisor, governor, prime minister, headmaster, headmistress, *Colloq* °boss, head man, the man, *Brit* guv'nor, guv, *US* (chief) honcho; *Slang* big cheese, *US* Mr. Big **3** °front, vanguard, forefront, van, forepart **4** °aptitude, °intellect, °intelligence, °talent, °perception, perceptiveness, °mentality, °faculty, °flair, °genius, °brain, °mind, °wit, *Colloq* brains, gray matter **5** °crisis, apex, (critical *or* turning) point, °peak, °crest, °(fever) pitch, °climax, culmination, conclusion, crescendo **6** °source, °origin, fount, font, fountainhead, wellspring **7** °top, first place, leading position, °leadership, forefront **8** ***head over heels.*** °completely, °entirely, °deeply, °utterly, °wholly, fully, *Colloq* °madly, wildly —*adj.* **9** °first, °chief, °main, °principal, °leading, °premier, °foremost, °prime, °preeminent, °cardinal, °paramount, °supreme, °superior, °senior —*v.* **10** °go, °move, °proceed, °turn, °steer, °aim, °point, head for, make a beeline for **11** head up, be in *or* take charge (of), °direct, °supervise, °oversee, °control, °govern, °run, °(take the) lead, °guide, °manage, °command, °rule, °administer, °conduct **12** °lead, °precede, °top **13** ***head off.*** **(a)** °intercept, °divert; °cut off, °stop, °block **(b)** °stop, °forestall, °prevent, °inhibit, avert, ward *or* fend off

headache *n.* **1** migraine, *Technical* cephalalgia **2** °worry, °bother, vexation, °inconvenience, °nuisance, °annoyance, °problem, °difficulty, °trouble, bane, *Colloq* °pain (in the neck), *Slang* pain in the *Brit* arse *or US* ass

headway *n.* **1** °progress, forward motion, °improvement **2** ***make headway.*** °advance, °progress, move forward, °go, °gain (ground), get *or* go ahead, °proceed, get going

heal *v.* **1** °cure, °repair, °renew, revitalize, °rejuvenate, °restore; °mend, °recuperate, °recover, °improve **2** °reconcile, °settle, °patch up, put *or* set straight *or* right, °remedy, °repair, °mend

health *n.* **1** °condition, °fitness, °trim, fettle, °form, constitution **2** healthiness, haleness, healthfulness, robustness, °vigor, vigorousness, salubrity, salubriousness, well-being, °strength

healthy *adj.* **1** °well, °fit, °trim, in good *or* fine fettle *or* shape, in good health, °robust, °hale (and hearty), °sturdy, °strong, °vigorous, thriving, °flourishing, *Colloq* °in the pink **2** °wholesome, healthful, salubrious, salutary, °beneficial, nourishing, °nutritious, °tonic, °bracing

heap *n.* **1** °collection, °pile, °mound, °stack, °accumulation, aggregation, agglomeration, congeries, conglomeration, °hoard, °mass, °store, °mountain, stockpile, °supply, *Colloq US and Canadian* stash **2** Often, ***heaps.*** °abundance, plethora, superabundance, lot(s), °plenty, °great deal, °scores, peck, °sea, *Colloq* lashings, load(s), °piles, ton(s), raft(s), pots, oodles, scad(s), *US and Canadian* slew —*v.* **3** °collect, °gather, °harvest, °reap, glean, °garner, °pile (up), °accumulate, cumulate, aggregate, °amass, stockpile, °save (up), bank, lay by *or* up *or* in, °set aside, *Colloq* stash (away) **4** °shower, °load, °bestow, °give, °provide, °burden

hear *v.* **1** °perceive, °understand, °listen (to), °attend (to), pay attention (to), °catch, °heed, heark *or* hearken (to) *or US also* harken (to) **2** °understand, °learn, °discover, °find out, °gather, °get wind of, °pick up, ascertain, be told *or* advised *or* informed **3** ***hear of.*** °entertain, °consider; °approve (of), °sanction, condone, agree *or* consent *or* assent to

heart *n.* **1** *Colloq* ticker, °pump **2** °stomach, °nerve, °courage, °bravery, mettle, °will, boldness, °pluck, °resolution, °determination; callousness, insensitivity, heartlessness; *Colloq* °guts, °spunk **3** °(basic) nature, °core, °center, °focus, °hub, °middle, marrow, °pith, °essence, °quintessence, °nucleus, °nub, crux, basics, fundamentals, *Colloq* nitty-gritty **4** °sincerity, sentiment(s), feeling(s), °spirit, °verve, °enthusiasm **5** °humanity, humanitarianism, °sympathy, °understanding, °kindness, kindliness, compassion, empathy, goodness, °consideration, °concern, °soul, tenderness, magnanimity, generosity, °sensitivity, °sensibility, °sentiment, °pity, °(brotherly) love, °affection

heartbroken *adj.* °brokenhearted, °downhearted, dispirited, °unhappy, °miserable, grief-stricken, °upset, °dejected, heartsick, crestfallen, °despondent, depressed, disconsolate, distressed, °woebegone, °doleful, °sorrowful, °mournful, morose, disheartened, °disappointed, crushed

heartfelt *adj.* °sincere, °honest, °genuine, unfeigned, °earnest, °serious, °wholehearted, °deep, °profound, dedicated, °devoted, °ardent, committed, °fervent, fervid, °hearty, °passionate

heartless *adj.* °cruel, hardhearted, °callous, unconcerned, °inhuman, inhumane, °unkind, unfeeling, °unsympathetic, °brutal,

°cold, °merciless, pitiless, °ruthless, °cold-blooded

heart-rending *adj.* °agonizing, distressing, °excruciating, °bitter, °painful, heartbreaking, °harrowing, °piteous, °tragic, depressing, °poignant

heartwarming *adj.* **1** °moving, °touching, warming, affecting, uplifting, inspiriting, cheering, encouraging **2** °satisfying, gratifying, °pleasing, comforting, °pleasurable, °rewarding

hearty *adj.* **1** °genial, °warm, kindhearted, °affectionate, °amiable, °amicable, °friendly, affable, °cordial, °open, convivial **2** °genuine, unfeigned, °authentic, °sincere, °heartfelt, °warm, °wholehearted, °honest, °earnest, °devout, °stalwart, °stout **3** °enthusiastic, °vigorous, °energetic, °eager, zealous, °exuberant, °robust, °active, °animated, °strong **4** °abundant, °ample, °substantial, °solid, sizable, °satisfying, °square; nourishing, °invigorating, strengthening **5** °healthy, °hale, °vigorous, °robust, °strong, °sound

heat *n.* **1** °warmth, warmness, hotness, fever, fieriness, torridity *or* torridness **2** °passion, °ardor, °fervor, fervidness, °intensity °fury, zeal, zealousness, earnestness, vehemence, °eagerness, °enthusiasm, °excitement, tenseness, °tension, °stress, °agitation, arousal, impetuosity, stimulation, exhilaration —*v.* **3** °warm (up); °boil **4** Often, ***heat up.*** °excite, °intensify, impassion, °inflame, °kindle, ignite, °quicken, inspirit, °rouse, awaken *or* waken, °stir, °animate, °stimulate, °warm (up), °activate, *Colloq Brit* hot up

heated *adj.* °impassioned, °excited, intensified, aroused, quickened, stimulated, °inflamed, vehement, °fiery, frenzied, °frantic, frenetic, °passionate, °fervent, fervid, °ardent, °intense, °furious, °stormy, °tempestuous, °violent; °angry, °bitter

heathen *n.* **1** unbeliever, °infidel, °pagan, idolater *or* idolatress, polytheist, atheist, nullifidian, °skeptic, agnostic, heretic —*adj.* **2** °infidel, °pagan, atheist(ic), °godless, nullifidian, °skeptic(al), doubting, agnostic, °heretical, irreligious **3** °savage, °barbarian, barbaric, °uncivilized, °primitive, unenlightened, uncultured, Philistine; polytheistic, pantheistic

heave *v.* **1** °raise, °lift, °hoist, °haul, °pull, °draw, °tug; °move **2** °throw, °toss, °hurl, °fling, °cast, °sling, °pitch, °let fly, °send, °launch, *Colloq* °peg, chuck **3** °breathe, utter, °sigh, °groan, °moan, °gasp **4** °gag, retch, °vomit, be sick, °regurgitate, disgorge, *Colloq* °throw up, *Slang* puke, lose one's lunch, return one's dinner, *US* upchuck, spiff one's biscuits

heaven *n.* **1** °paradise, °bliss, hereafter, nirvana, Abraham's bosom, Elysian Fields *or* Elysium, Valhalla, Zion, happy hunting ground, Avalon, Isles of the Blessed, the Blessed *or* Fortunate *or* Happy Isles *or* Islands **2** ***heavens.*** °sky, °firmament, *Literary* welkin, empyrean **3** °happiness, °bliss, °joy, °rapture, °ecstasy, °paradise, contentment, seventh heaven, Eden, °utopia, heaven on earth

heavenly *adj.* **1** °divine, angelic, °seraphic, °celestial, °holy, °immortal, blessed, beatific, beatified, °spiritual, °saintly; supernal, °unearthly, otherworldly, ultramundane, extramundane, extraterrestrial **2** °delightful, wonderful, °marvelous, °sublime, paradisiac(al) *or* paradisaic(al), °glorious, °splendid, °superb, °exquisite, °perfect, °ideal, °excellent, °fantastic, °rapturous, entrancing, blissful, *Colloq* °gorgeous, °divine, smashing, °great

heavy *adj.* **1** °weighty, °ponderous, °massive, *Literary* massy; °compact, °dense **2** °abundant, overflowing, °excessive, copious, °profuse, °prodigious, °ample, unmanageable **3** °serious, °grave, °important, °crucial, °critical, °acute **4** °burdensome, onerous, °oppressive, °weighty, °unbearable, °severe, °grievous, distressful, °sore, intolerable, insupportable *or* unsupportable, °awful **5** °sad, °sorrowful, distressing, °grievous, upsetting, depressing, °gloomy, °somber, °melancholy **6** °unhappy, °miserable, depressed, °melancholy, grieving, °sad, °dejected, °downhearted, disconsolate, downcast, °despondent, °gloomy, heavy-hearted, morose, crestfallen, cheerless **7** °ponderous, °tedious, °monotonous, °boring, uninteresting, °leaden, °dull, °prosaic, °dry, dry as dust, °stodgy, °staid, °stuffy, stifling, stultifying **8** °thick, °coarse, °broad, °blunt, °clumsy, °ungraceful **9** °gloomy, cloudy, °overcast, °bleak, °dismal, °dreary, °leaden, °gray, °dark, lowering *or chiefly Brit* louring, °threatening **10** °intense, concentrated, °severe, °forceful, °violent, °torrential **11** overweight, °fat, °obese, °stout, °chubby, °plump, corpulent, portly, paunchy, tubby, *Brit* podgy *or US* pudgy, *Colloq* beer-bellied **12** °weighty, °difficult, complex, °recondite, arcane, °deep, °profound, esoteric, °incomprehensible, impenetrable, unfathomable **13** burdened, laden, encumbered, °loaded, overloaded, weighed down

heavy-handed *adj.* **1** °awkward, °clumsy, °inept, maladroit, unskillful, °ungraceful, graceless, bungling **2** autocratic, imperious, magisterial, °overbearing, °despotic, °dictatorial, °tyrannical, °oppressive, °domineering, ironhanded, °harsh, °severe

heckle *v.* badger, °pester, °annoy, °irritate, °bother, nettle, bait, °harass, harry, °plague, hector, °taunt, °jeer, *Colloq* hassle, °bug, *Brit, Australian, and New Zealand* barrack

hectic *adj.* °feverish, °excited, °agitated, °busy, bustling, rushed, hyperactive, overactive, frenzied, °frantic, °chaotic, °wild, °mad, frenetic, °riotous

heed *v.* **1** pay attention to, °attend, (take *or* make) note (of), listen to, °mark, °consider, °bear in mind; °take, °follow, °obey, °mind, °respect, °accept, °abide by —*n.* **2** °attention, °notice, °ear, °mind, °respect, °consideration, °thought

heedless *adj.* °inattentive, uncaring, unmindful, neglectful, unobservant, °regardless; °oblivious, °deaf, °blind

heel[1] *n.* **1** °end, butt *or* tail *or* fag (end), °stump, °remainder, °remnant, °rind, crust **2** cad, °scoundrel, swine, °rogue, scamp, °philanderer, *Old-fashioned* worm, knave, *Chiefly Brit* blackguard, *Colloq Brit* rotter, *Old-fashioned* bounder, *Slang* bastard, *Brit* sod **3** ***down at the heel.*** °poor, °destitute, °impoverished, down-and-out, on (one's) uppers, in straitened circumstances; °shabby, °seedy, °dowdy, out at the elbows, °rundown, slovenly, *Brit* out at elbows, down at heel, *US* out at the elbows, *Colloq* °broke, strapped **4** ***take to (one's) heels.*** °take flight, °flee, °escape, run off *or* away, show a clean pair of heels, *Colloq* °split, *Brit* do a moonlight flit, *US* take a (runout) powder, fly the coop, *Australian and New Zealand* shoot through —*v.* **5** dog, °follow (closely), °shadow, °chase, °pursue

heel[2] *v.* °list, °lean (over), °tilt, °tip, °incline

hefty *adj.* **1** °big, °large, °bulky, cumbersome, °awkward, °unwieldy, °clumsy, °substantial, °massive **2** °brawny, °strong, °powerful, °burly, °muscular, strapping, °rugged, °robust, *Colloq* °husky, beefy **3** °substantial, °considerable, sizable, °impressive, °enormous, °huge, *Colloq* thumping *or Brit* socking great

height *n.* **1** altitude, °elevation, °level; tallness **2** °acme, °crest, °pinnacle, °top, °zenith, apogee, °peak, apex, °maximum, high point, °summit, °climax, culmination, °extreme **3** Often, ***heights.*** °elevation, °mound, °hill, eminence, °prominence, °mountain, °peak, °crag, °summit; tor, °cliff, °bluff, promontory, escarpment, scarp, headland, *Northern Brit* °fell

heighten *v.* **1** °raise, elevate, °build up, °increase, °lift (up), upraise **2** °intensify, °deepen, °strengthen, °reinforce, °amplify, °magnify, °increase, °enhance, augment, °add to, °supplement

heir *n.* heiress, beneficiary, inheritor, legatee, successor

hell *n.* **1** Erebus, Hades, Acheron, Tartarus, Gehenna, Tophet, Abaddon, Pandemonium, Dis, Sheol, Avernus, °underworld, infernal regions, °abyss, abode of the damned, inferno, hellfire, lower world, nether regions, bottomless pit, other place **2** °chaos, °misery, °torment, °agony, torture, °ordeal, nightmare, °trial **3** °anguish, °pain, °agony, °torment, torture, °misery, °suffering, °affliction **4** °criticism, censure; scolding, castigation, °reprimand, upbraiding

helm *n.* **1** tiller, °wheel, rudder, steering gear *or* apparatus **2** directorship, presidency, chairmanship, °leadership, °control, °rule, °command, *Colloq* driver's seat, saddle

help *v.* **1** °aid, °assist, lend a hand, °support, °serve; succor **2** °relieve, alleviate, °mitigate, °improve, °facilitate, °ease, °better, °remedy, °cure **3** °stop, °refrain from,

°avoid, eschew, °resist, °keep from, forbear, °escape **4** °assist, °serve, °advise, °inform **5** ***help oneself.*** °appropriate, °take, arrogate, commandeer, expropriate; °steal, purloin, usurp, plagiarize, °pirate, *Colloq* °pinch, °lift, *Brit* °nick, *US* °boost —*n.* **6** °aid, °support, succor, °assistance **7** employee(s), worker(s), °staff, helper(s), hand(s), assistant(s), laborer(s), domestic(s), servant(s), *Brit* °daily (help) **8** °supporter, °aide, °assistant, helper **9** °relief, °remedy, °cure, balm

helpful *adj.* °useful, °serviceable, °practical, pragmatic, utilitarian, °beneficial, valuable, °profitable, °advantageous, °constructive, °productive; °supportive, reassuring, °sympathetic, °considerate, caring, °accommodating, °kind, cooperative, °neighborly, °friendly, °benevolent

helping *n.* serving, °portion, °ration, plateful, *Brit* °help, *Colloq* dollop

helpless *adj.* **1** dependent, °vulnerable, °weak, °feeble, °infirm, °lame, °crippled, °disabled **2** °confused, baffled, mystified, bewildered, perplexed, at sea, confounded, muddled, nonplussed **3** weakened, °weak, debilitated, °faint, enfeebled, °feeble, worn-out, °spent, °exhausted, °prostrate, enervated **4** °worthless, °incapable, °incompetent, °useless, unavailing, °inefficient, °inept, unfit, °unqualified

helter-skelter *adj.* **1** °disorderly, disorganized, °confused, muddled, °haphazard, °careless, jumbled, °random, °topsy-turvy, *Colloq* higgledy-piggledy —*adv.* **2** confusedly, °pell-mell, in all directions, recklessly, unsystematically, chaotically, erratically, aimlessly, *US* every which way, *Colloq* higgledy-piggledy

hence *adv.* **1** °therefore, °consequently, °thus, °accordingly, ergo, as a result, for that *or* this reason **2** away from here *or* from this place **3** from now, in the future

henceforth *adv.* hereafter, henceforward *or* henceforwards, from now on, *Colloq US* from here on out

henchman *n.* (fellow) mobster *or* gangster *or* hoodlum, bodyguard, myrmidon, right-hand man, °associate, °attendant, °follower, °supporter, confidant, crony, *Colloq* sidekick, hooligan, *Brit* °minder, *US* buddy, °cohort; *Slang* °heavy, *US* torpedo, gunsel, goon

henpeck *v.* °nag, °harass, hector, °pester, °torment, °bully, °carp, °cavil

herd *n.* **1** °group, °pack, °bunch, °cluster, °flock, °crowd, multitude, °host, horde, °throng, °mass, °swarm, °press, °crush; assemblage, °collection **2** common herd, °rabble, °hoi polloi, great unwashed, °riffraff, masses —*v.* **3** °gather, congregate, °flock, °assemble, °collect **4** °round up, °gather (together), °shepherd, °drive, *Western US and Canadian* wrangle, corral

hereditary *adj.* **1** heritable, inheritable, transmissible, transferable, inherited, genetic, congenital, °inborn, innate; atavistic

2 °traditional, handed down, inherited, bequeathed, willed; ancestral

heretical *adj.* °unorthodox, heterodox, °impious, freethinking, heretic, apostate *or* apostatical, iconoclastic, °schismatic, °skeptic, agnostic, atheist(ic), idolatrous, °heathen, °pagan, °infidel, °godless

heritage *n.* **1** °estate, °inheritance, legacy, patrimony, birthright **2** °tradition

hermetic *adj.* hermetical, airtight, sealed; impervious

hermit *n.* °recluse, eremite, anchorite *or* anchoret *or* anchoress, °solitary, stylite

hero *n.* **1** °heroine, °champion, exemplar, °star, superstar, °idol, °ideal, man of the hour, luminary, °notable, °celebrity; knight, paladin, warrior **2** °protagonist, (male) lead *or* star, leading man *or* actor, °principal

heroic *adj.* **1** °brave, °courageous, °bold, valiant, valorous, undaunted, °dauntless, stouthearted, °noble, °intrepid, °gallant, °chivalrous, °daring, plucky, °audacious, °fearless, °manly, virile, manful **2** °noble, altruistic, magnanimous, °generous, upstanding, °honorable, °virtuous, °staunch, °steadfast, °stalwart, °determined **3** °desperate, °drastic, °extreme **4** °grand, larger than life, exaggerated, magniloquent, °grandiose, °extravagant; °giant, °gigantic, °enormous, °huge, titanic, °colossal, stupendous **5** mythological, epic, Homeric, °legendary, °classical, °fabulous, wonderful, °miraculous **6** °majestic, °lofty, °elevated, °grand, august, °towering, °eminent, °distinguished, °prominent

heroine *n.* °(female) lead, leading actress *or* lady, prima donna *or* ballerina, *première danseuse*, diva

hesitant *adj.* **1** hesitating, undecided, °uncertain, °unsettled, °irresolute, vacillating, shilly-shallying, dithering, fluctuating, wavering, °unresolved, ambivalent, in *or* of two minds, °indefinite, *Brit* havering **2** °halting, stammering, stuttering, faltering

hesitate *v.* **1** °delay, hold *or* hang back, °pause, dillydally, °wait, temporize, think twice, balk, boggle at, °shrink from, demur, °scruple, *Brit* haver, jib, *Colloq* °stall **2** °fumble, °equivocate, tergiversate, °fluctuate, °alternate, waver, dither, vacillate, °shilly-shally **3** °stammer, stutter, falter, sputter, splutter, °stumble, hem and haw

hidden *adj.* concealed, °secret, obscure(d), °occult, °veiled, °cryptic, °recondite, arcane, covert, esoteric, unseen, °private

hide[1] *v.* **1** °conceal, °secrete, °cache, squirrel away; go underground, take cover, °lie low, go into hiding, °lurk, go to ground, drop out of sight, hibernate, latibulize, *Colloq* hide out, hole up, °lie low, *Brit* lie doggo **2** °conceal, °cover, °mask, °camouflage, °disguise, °veil, °shroud, °screen, °cover up, keep secret **3** °eclipse, °blot out, °obscure, °block **4** °suppress, °hush (up), °repress, °silence, keep quiet *or* secret

hide[2] *n.* **1** °pelt, °skin, °fell, leather, fur, °fleece —*v.* **2** °flog, °whip, °lash, flail, °beat, thrash

hideaway *n.* °refuge, °retreat, °sanctuary, hide-out, hiding place, °lair, (safe) haven, *Colloq* °hole, hidey-hole

hidebound *adj.* °strait-laced, °conventional, ultraconventional, °conservative, °reactionary, °rigid, °set (in one's ways), °narrow-minded, close-minded, °inflexible, intractable, uncompromising, restricted, °cramped, °bigoted, °intolerant

hideous *adj.* **1** °grotesque, °ugly, °repulsive, °revolting, °repellent, °monstrous, °beastly, gorgonian, °unsightly, °ghastly, °disgusting, °grisly, nauseating, °nauseous, sickening, °gruesome **2** °foul, °abhorrent, heinous, horrifying, appalling, °outrageous, °abominable, °vile, °shocking, °loathsome, °contemptible, °hateful, odious, °atrocious, horrific, °beastly, °damnable, execrable

high *adj.* **1** °tall, °lofty, °elevated, °towering **2** °extreme, °excessive, °extraordinary, °exorbitant, °outrageous, *Colloq* °steep, °stiff **3** costly, °dear, °expensive, high-priced **4** °great, °huge, °enormous, °considerable, °strong; °violent, turbulent **5** °exalted, °elevated, °lofty, °superior, °high-class **6** consequential, °important, °grave, °serious, °weighty, °momentous, heinous; °capital **7** high-pitched, high-frequency, squeaky, °acute, treble, soprano; °shrill, °strident, °sharp, °penetrating, °piercing, ear-splitting **8** °cheerful, °exuberant, °elated, °boisterous, exhilarated, °hilarious, °merry, °excited **9** euphoric, intoxicated, inebriated, °drunk, drugged, *Colloq* °loaded, tipsy, turned on, on a trip, *Slang* stoned, spaced out, *Brit* squiffy, *US* spacy, squiffed **10** gamy, tainted, °aged, °ripe, *Slang Brit* pongy **11** °chief, °leading, °important, °principal, °foremost **12** °elaborate, °luxurious, °grand, °extravagant, °lavish, °rich, °prodigal, sybaritic **13** °considerable, °favorable, °great —*adv.* **14** far up; great in extent —*n.* **15** °peak, °record, °height, °maximum, °acme, apex **16** intoxication, altered consciousness **17** anticyclone

highbrow *n.* **1** °scholar, °intellectual, savant, °sage, °mastermind, °genius; °aesthete, connoisseur, *Colloq* egghead, °brain —*adj.* **2** °scholarly, °intellectual, °learned, erudite, °deep, bookish, cultured, °sophisticated, °cultivated, °aesthetic, *Colloq* brainy

high-class *adj.* **1** °first-rate, °superior, °better, top-drawer, *Colloq* tops, tip-top, A-1 *or* A-one, °super, °great **2** aristocratic, °upper-class, °elite, °select, °exclusive; upper-crust, °fancy, *Brit* county, *US and Canadian* tony, *Slang* classy

highly *adv.* **1** greatly, much, tremendously, °well, enthusiastically, °warmly, immensely, hugely **2** °very, °extremely, °quite, exceptionally, extraordinarily, incomparably, decidedly **3** °favorably, °well, enthusiastically, approvingly, °warmly, praisefully **4** °well, influentially, powerfully, strongly, authoritatively, effectively, importantly

hilarious *adj.* °funny, sidesplitting, °humorous, comical, amusing, °entertaining, mirthful; °merry, °gay, °jolly, jovial, °cheerful, cheery, joyous, °joyful, rollicking, °uproarious; *Colloq* °hysterical

hilarity *n.* °laughter, °gaiety, joviality, jollity, °merriment, °mirth, °exuberance, °glee, boisterousness, cheerfulness, joyfulness, jubilation, elation, °revelry, conviviality, high spirits, vivacity, exhilaration

hill *n.* **1** °elevation, °rise, highland, °mound, °prominence, promontory, eminence, °knoll, hillock, hummock, °height, foothill, tor, °mount, upland, downs *or* downland, *Scots* brae, *Northern Brit* °fell, *Western Brit* tump, *US and Canadian* butte **2** °heap, °pile, °mound, °stack; °mountain **3** °slope, incline *or* decline, acclivity *or* declivity, gradient *or esp. US* °grade, upgrade *or* °downgrade

hinder *v.* **1** °hamper, °delay, °interrupt, °impede, interfere with, °foil, °thwart, °frustrate, °forestall, °bar, °stymie, °check, balk *or* baulk, °encumber, °obstruct, °handicap, set *or* keep *or* put *or* hold back, °defer, °retard, °restrain, °slow, °postpone **2** °stop, °prevent, °check, °preclude, °arrest; °discourage, °deter, °inhibit, obviate

hindrance *n.* **1** °obstruction, °impediment, °snag, °check, °barrier, °obstacle, °restraint, °drawback, °hitch, °stumbling block, °deterrent, °encumbrance **2** °prevention, °curb, limitation

hint *n.* **1** °suggestion, °clue, °implication, °inkling, °indication, °tip, tip-off, intimation, allusion, °innuendo, insinuation; °pointer, °help, °advice **2** °trace, °suggestion, °touch, °taste, °breath, °dash, soupçon, whiff, undertone, tinge, °whisper —*v.* **3** °suggest, °imply, °indicate, °tip (off), °intimate, allude, °insinuate, °mention, °clue, °cue, °signal, °refer, advert

hip *adj.* °informed, °aware, °knowledgeable, °knowing, °perceptive, °alert, in *or* up on, onto, *Colloq* °wise (to), with it, °cool, *Old-fashioned* hep

hippie *n.* bohemian, *Old-fashioned* dropout, beatnik, °beat, longhair, flower child *or* person, hipster

hire *v.* **1** °engage, °employ, °take on, °appoint, °enlist, °sign on **2** °rent, °lease, °engage, °charter **3** ***hire out.*** °rent (out), °lease (out), °let (out), °charter (out) —*n.* **4** °rent, °lease, °charter, letting **5** °(hire) charge, °cost, °fee, °price, °rate, °rent, rental

hiss *n.* **1** hissing, sibilance **2** catcall, °jeer, boo, hoot, *Slang* raspberry, *US* Bronx cheer —*v.* **3** boo, hoot, °jeer, °deride, °mock, °taunt, decry, °disparage

historic *adj.* °momentous, °important, °noteworthy, °significant, red-letter, °notable, °celebrated, °distinguished, °prominent, °great, consequential, °signal, unforgettable, °memorable

historical *adj.* °factual, °true, verifiable, °reliable, °real, °authentic, recorded, documented

history *n.* **1** °account, °story, record, °description, depiction, portrayal, °representation, °telling, retelling, °recital, °narration, °narrative, °relation, retailing **2** °news, °summary, recapitulation, °report, °intelligence, °information **3** °past, °background, °life; experiences, adventures, °story, biography **4** record, °experience, °information, biography, CV *or* curriculum vitae, *US* °résumé **5** °chronicle, annals, °record, °account **6** ancient history, the past, yesterday, the (good old) days, days of yore, olden days, yesteryear, antiquity **7** dead letter, yesterday's news, old hat

hit *v.* **1** °strike, cuff, smack, °knock, whack, bash, bang, thump, thwack, °punch, buffet, °slap, swat, bludgeon, °club, smite; °spank, thrash, °beat, pummel, °batter, °flog, °scourge, birch, cane, °lash, °belabor, flagellate, °whip, horsewhip, cudgel, *Archaic* fustigate; *Colloq* °belt, wallop, clobber, clout, sock, °clip, °crown, bop, conk, paste, °lambaste, °zap **2** °strike, bat, swat, °knock, °drive, °propel **3** °strike, collide *or* impact with, run *or* smash *or* crash into, bump *or* bang into **4** °affect, °touch, °stir, °move, °wound, °hurt, strike *or* hit home, make *or* leave an impression *or* a mark on, °(make an) impact (on) **5** °dawn on, enter one's mind, °occur to, °strike **6** °reach, attain, °arrive at, °gain, °achieve **7** °experience, °encounter, °meet (with) **8** Also, ***hit up.*** importune, °beseech, °petition, °beg, implore, entreat, °ask for **9** ***hit on or upon.*** **(a)** come *or* happen *or* chance *or* light on *or* upon, °discover, °find, uncover, °unearth, stumble *or* blunder on *or* upon, °arrive at **(b)** °devise, think of *or* up, °invent, dream up, come up with, °work out, °see, °perceive, °detect, discern, °find —*n.* **10** °impact, °collision; °blow, °punch, °knock, °strike, swat, °shot, smack, °bump, bang, *Colloq* whack, thwack, conk, bop, sock **11** °success, °triumph, coup, °winner, °sensation, *Colloq* smash (hit), sellout **12** °kick, °jolt, °thrill, *Slang* °charge, *US* °rush, bang

hitch *v.* **1** °connect, °couple, °fasten, °attach, °join, harness, °tie, °unite, °hook (up), °link, °fix **2** Often, ***hitch up.*** °raise, °pull up, hike (up), °tug (up), °hoist, °yank, °jerk, *Brit* hoick **3** hitchhike, thumb a lift *or* ride, *Colloq US* bum a ride —*n.* **4** °snag, °catch, °difficulty, °trouble, °problem, °mishap, °handicap, entanglement, °interference, °impediment, °hindrance, °obstruction, °obstacle

hoard *n.* **1** °supply, °stock, °store, stockpile, °reserve, °fund, reservoir, °accumulation, °collection, °cache —*v.* **2** °amass, °collect, °accumulate, °pile (up), °assemble, °gather, °put away, stockpile, °store, °reserve, °set aside, °save (up), squirrel away, lay in *or* away *or* aside *or* up, *Colloq* stash away

hoax *n.* **1** °deception, °fraud, °swindle, °trick, flam *or* flimflam, imposture, °cheat, humbug, mare's nest, *Slang* con (game), gyp, scam, °game, *US* snow job —*v.* **2** °deceive, °defraud, °swindle, °trick, °fool, °dupe, °take in, cozen, °hoodwink, gull, °bluff, *Slang* con, gyp, bamboozle

hobble *v.* **1** °limp, falter, dodder, °totter, °stagger, °reel, °weave, °stumble, °shuffle, shamble **2** °shackle, fetter, °restrain, °restrict, °hamper, °hinder, °impede, °trammel —*n.* **3** °limp, °shuffle, shamble, claudication, °stagger

hobby *n.* °pastime, avocation, sideline, °recreation, °diversion, °relaxation

hobnob *v.* °associate, °fraternize, °socialize, consort, °mingle, rub elbows *or* shoulders, °mix, hang about *or* around, keep company

hocus-pocus *n.* **1** °trickery, °chicanery, °deceit, °deception, °artifice, °cheat, duplicity, °mischief, °hoax, humbug, °trick, °swindle, °pretense, *Colloq* con (game), jiggery-pokery, flimflam, °hanky-panky **2** °mumbo jumbo, abracadabra, incantation, °nonsense, rigamarole *or* rigmarole, °gibberish, *Colloq* gobbledygook **3** sleight of hand, legerdemain, prestidigitation, °magic, conjuring, jugglery

hodgepodge *n.* °miscellany, °mixture, gallimaufry, °jumble, farrago, mélange, °mishmash, °mess, °tangle, °medley, °hash, conglomeration, agglomeration, olio, olla podrida, °potpourri, ragbag, °welter, *Chiefly Brit* hotchpotch, *Colloq* omnium-gatherum, mixed bag

hoggish *adj.* piggish, °greedy, °avaricious, insatiable, °gluttonous, °voracious, edacious, acquisitive, °possessive, self-seeking, °selfish

hoi polloi *n.* °riffraff, °rabble, °mob, common herd, proletariat, °populace, common people, °crowd, masses, multitude, °rank and file, plebeians, multitude, bourgeoisie, man in the street, *Brit* admass, man on the Clapham omnibus, *US* John Q. Public, *Colloq* great unwashed, proles, plebs, *US* silent majority

hoist *v.* **1** °lift (up), elevate, °raise, °heave, uplift, winch —*n.* **2** crane, °lift, elevator, davit, winch, °tackle

hoity-toity *adj.* °haughty, °arrogant, overweening, °snobbish, °disdainful, °supercilious, °conceited, °lofty, °superior, °self-important, *Colloq* high and mighty, stuck-up, snooty, uppity *or chiefly Brit* uppish, *Brit* toffee-nosed, *Slang* snotty

hold *v.* **1** °grasp, °grip, °clasp, °seize, °clutch, °keep; °carry, *Colloq* hang onto **2** °hug, °embrace, °clasp, cradle, clench, °clutch, enfold **3** °maintain, °keep, °put **4** °maintain, °keep, °sustain, absorb, °occupy, °engage, °involve, engross, °monopolize **5** confine, °restrain, detain, °contain, coop up **6** °imprison, detain, confine, place into custody, put behind bars, °jail **7** °believe, deem, °judge, °consider, °regard, look on *or* upon, °maintain, °think, °esteem, °take, °assume **8** °accommodate, °support, °carry **9** °contain, °include, comprise **10** °call, convene, °assemble, convoke; °run, °conduct, °engage in, participate in, °have, °carry on, preside over, officiate at **11** °apply, hold good, be in effect *or* in force, stand *or* hold up, hold *or* prove *or* be true, be the case, °function, °operate, be *or* remain *or* prove valid *or* relevant *or* applicable *or* operative, *Colloq* hold water, °wash **12** °have, °possess **13** remain *or* keep (fast), °stay, °stick **14** ***hold back.*** **(a)** °restrain, °repress, °suppress, °curb, °inhibit, °control, °check, keep back, °hinder **(b)** °withhold, °reserve, °deny, keep back, °refuse **15** ***hold down.*** **(a)** °control, °restrain, °check; °reduce, °diminish **(b)** °keep, °maintain, °manage **16** ***hold forth.*** **(a)** Often, ***hold forth on or upon.*** lecture (on), declaim, °harangue, preach (on *or* about), orate, sermonize (on), discourse (on), speechify (on *or* about), expatiate *or* expand on *or* upon, *Colloq* °go on (about), *Brit* rabbit *or* natter *or* witter on (about) **(b)** °hold out, °offer, proffer, °tender, °submit, °advance, °propose, °propound, °hold out, °extend **17** ***hold in.*** **(a)** °control, °curb, °check, °hold back, °restrain, °contain **(b)** °conceal, °hide, °suppress **18** ***hold off.*** **(a)** °delay, °defer, °put off, °refrain from, °postpone, °avoid **(b)** °repel, keep off, °repulse, °fend off, °rebuff, °resist, °withstand **19** ***hold on.*** **(a)** °grip, °grasp, °hold, °clutch, °cling **(b)** °keep, °maintain, °cling, °hang on, °retain **(c)** °stop, °wait, °hold off, *Colloq* °hang on **20** ***hold out.*** **(a)** °last, °carry on, °persist, °persevere, °continue, °hang on, stand firm *or chiefly US* pat, °endure **(b)** °offer, proffer, °extend, °hold forth, °present **21** ***hold over.*** **(a)** °postpone, °delay, °defer, °put off, °hold off, °suspend **(b)** °continue, °retain, °extend, °prolong **22** ***hold up.*** **(a)** °rob, °waylay, *Colloq* °mug, °stick up; knock off *or US* over **(b)** °delay, °impede, °hinder, slow (down *or* up), °set back, detain **(c)** °last, °survive, °fare, °bear up, °endure **(d)** °present, °show, °exhibit, °display **23** ***hold with.*** °support, °sustain, agree to *or* with, °favor, countenance, °approve (of), °subscribe to, condone, concur with —*n.* **24** °grasp, °grip, °clasp, °clutch **25** foothold, toehold, °purchase **26** °power, dominance, mastery, °control, ascendancy, °authority, °influence, leverage, °sway, *Colloq* °pull, clout

holdup *n.* **1** °(armed) robbery, *Colloq* stickup, mugging, *US* heist **2** °delay, °setback, °hitch, °snag, °interruption, lacuna, °gap, hiatus, °break, stoppage

hole *n.* **1** °cavity, °pit, °hollow, °excavation, °burrow, crater, cavern, °cave, °recess, °niche, °nook, °pocket, °depression, °indentation, dent, °impression **2** °opening, °aperture, orifice, perforation, °puncture, °slit, °slot, °breach, °rip, °tear, °rent, °break, °crack, fissure **3** hole in the wall, °shack, °hut, shanty, °slum, °hovel; *Slang* °dump, °dive, °joint **4** °cell, °prison, °dungeon, donjon, °keep, °jail, oubliette, brig, °cage **5** °difficulty, °trouble, °dilemma, °predicament, °situation, °fix, corner, *Colloq* °(tight) spot, hot water, °scrape, °box, °bind, pickle, catch-22, °mess, °muddle **6** °flaw, °shortcoming, inconsistency, °fault, °error, °mistake, °fallacy, °discrepancy, °loophole —*v.* 7 °puncture, °pierce, °perforate

holiday *n.* 1 time off, °break, °recess, °respite, °leave (of absence), furlough, sabbatical, *Chiefly US* vacation 2 °festival, °feast, °celebration, °fête; °gala, °fair, red-letter day, °event

hollow *adj.* 1 °vacant, °empty, °void, unfilled 2 °sunken, concave, indented, dented, recessed, depressed 3 °hungry, °ravenous, °starved, °empty, °famished 4 °insincere, °false, °hypocritical, °sham, °artificial, °counterfeit, feigned, °fraudulent, °spurious, °deceitful, mendacious, °deceptive, cynical 5 °empty, °futile, costly, Pyrrhic, °worthless, °vain, unavailing, °bootless, °fruitless, profitless, °unprofitable, valueless, °ineffective, °pointless, °senseless, °meaningless 6 muffled, °dull, °flat, °low, sepulchral, toneless —*n.* 7 °hole, °cavity, cavern, crater, basin, °depression, °excavation, °pit, trough, °furrow, °indentation, dent, °impression; °valley, dale, dell, glen, °dip —*v.* 8 °excavate, dig (out *or* up), °gouge, °scoop, °furrow, dredge

holocaust *n.* 1 conflagration, firestorm, inferno, °fire; °destruction, devastation 2 genocide, mass murder, °massacre, blood bath, pogrom, butchery, °carnage, annihilation, extinction, extermination, eradication, elimination

holy *adj.* 1 °sacred, °religious, consecrated, sanctified, blessed, hallowed, venerated, °divine, °heavenly, supernal, °celestial 2 °godly, °godlike, °saintly, saintlike, °pious, °devout, reverent, reverential, °faithful, God-fearing, °chaste, °pure, unsullied, °clean, sinless, °spotless, °immaculate, undefiled, uncorrupted, untainted

homage *n.* °obeisance, °respect, °deference, °honor, °esteem, °admiration; °loyalty, allegiance, fidelity, °tribute

home *n.* 1 dwelling place, °residence, °domicile, °abode, °dwelling, °house, °(living) quarters, habitation, lodging(s), *Brit* accommodation *or US* accommodations, *Colloq* °place, *Chiefly Brit* digs, diggings 2 °(home) base, residency, °territory, °haunt, home ground, bailiwick, *Colloq* stamping ground 3 hospice, °retreat, nursing home, old folks' *or* people's home, retirement community, almshouse, poorhouse, °refuge, haven, °institution, °shelter, rest home, *US* snug harbor 4 ***at home.*** (a) °comfortable, at ease, °relaxed, °cozy, composed, °tranquil, placid, °peaceful, °serene, untroubled (b) in, °accessible, °available, welcoming 5 ***at home with** or **in.*** comfortable with, conversant with, knowledgeable in *or* about, °familiar with, well-versed in, competent in, expert in, proficient in, skilled in, up on, current in, adept in, adroit in, qualified in, (well-) informed in *or* on *or* about —*adj.* 6 °domestic, °native, °national, °internal 7 °domestic, household 8 °family, °domestic —*adv.* 9 homeward(s) 10 to the heart *or* core, to the quick; effectively, tellingly, °profoundly, °deeply, stingingly, cuttingly, harshly, °severely, *Colloq* where it hurts, where one lives 11 ***bring** or **drive home.*** °stress, °emphasize, °impress upon, make clear

homeless *adj.* 1 dispossessed, °outcast, exiled, °vagabond, °derelict, °unsettled; unhoused —*n.* 2 ***the homeless.*** knights of the road, vagrants, vagabonds, tramps, *US* bums, hoboes

homely *adj.* 1 homy *or chiefly US* homey, homelike, unpretentious, °modest, unassuming, °simple, °unaffected, °informal, °plain, °natural, °everyday, °unsophisticated, °homespun, commonplace, °ordinary, °familiar, °friendly, °amiable, °neighborly, affable, congenial, *Colloq chiefly US* folksy 2 homy *or chiefly US* homey, homelike, °warm, °cozy, °snug, °domestic, °comfortable, °easy, °serene, °peaceful, °restful, °tranquil 3 °ugly, °plain, uncomely, unattractive, unlovely, ill-favored

homesick *adj.* nostalgic, °longing, pining, °lonely, °lonesome; °wistful, °reminiscent

homespun *adj.* °rustic, °plain, °simple, °unrefined, unpolished, °unsophisticated, down-to-earth, °coarse, °rough, °rude, °crude, inelegant, °amateur, amateurish, nonprofessional, °unprofessional; handmade

homicidal *adj.* °murderous, °lethal, °deadly, death-dealing, °mortal, blood-thirsty, °sanguinary, °ferocious, °maniacal, °berserk, amuck *or* amok, °mad, °insane

homogeneous *adj.* °uniform, °consistent, unvarying, °identical, °constant; °similar, comparable, °alike, °akin

homosexual *n.* 1 °gay, homophile; lesbian, tribade, sapphist; *All the following are offensive and derogatory* °pervert, invert, *Slang* °queer, fairy, pansy, nancy, nance, °queen, drag queen, homo; butch, (bull) dyke; *Brit* poof, poofter, ginger (beer), *US* °fruit, auntie, °fag, faggot —*adj.* 2 °(of either sex) gay, homoerotic, homophile; (of a female) lesbian, tribadic, sapphic; °(of a male) effeminate; *All the following are offensive and derogatory* °perverted, inverted, *Colloq chiefly Brit* °bent, *Slang* °queer, °camp, campy, °kinky, *Chiefly US* fruity, limp-wristed, faggy, °swish, swishy

honest *adj.* 1 °trustworthy, °truthful, veracious, trusty, °honorable, creditable, °decent, law-abiding, uncorrupted, uncorrupt, incorruptible, °ethical, °moral, °virtuous, °principled, °upright, high-minded, dependable, °reliable, °reputable, on the up and up 2 °aboveboard, °straight, °square, square-dealing, °fair, °just, on the up and up, straightforward, °proper, °genuine, °bona fide, °real, °authentic, *Colloq* °on the level, *US* square-shooting 3 °candid, °frank, °open, °plain, straightforward, °forthright, °direct, °sincere, °ingenuous, °explicit, °uninhibited, unreserved, unrestrained, unconstrained, °aboveboard, plain-spoken, unambiguous, unequivocal, *Colloq* °up front 4

°fair, °just, °equitable, °legitimate, valid, °rightful, °sound, °proper

honestly *adv.* **1** truthfully, honorably, creditably, decently, ethically, morally, uprightly, dependably, reliably, in good faith, justly, °fairly, equitably, evenhandedly, disinterestedly, objectively, impartially **2** candidly, frankly, °openly, straightforwardly, forthrightly, °sincerely, °truly, ingenuously, unreservedly, °aboveboard, unambiguously, unequivocally, plainly, °simply, °straight (out), °to one's face, in plain words *or* English, bluntly

honesty *n.* **1** trustworthiness, uprightness, °rectitude, °probity, °integrity, °virtue, virtuousness, °honor **2** truthfulness, veracity, °candor, openness, frankness, forthrightness, directness, straightforwardness, outspokenness, °sincerity, guilelessness, ingenuousness, bluntness **3** fairness, °equity, equitableness, evenhandedness, °objectivity, impartiality, disinterestedness, justness, °justice

honor *n.* **1** °integrity, °honesty, fairness, justness, °probity, uprightness, decency, goodness, righteousness, °rectitude, °justice, °morality, °principles, virtuousness, °virtue **2** °respect, °esteem, °reverence, °veneration, approbation, °deference, °admiration, °homage, °regard, accolade, °praise, °kudos, °fame, glory, °celebrity, °distinction, °prestige, illustriousness **3** °privilege, °distinction, °pleasure, °joy, °delight; °credit, °blessing **4** virginity, °chastity, °virtue, °purity, innocence —*v.* **5** °respect, °esteem, °revere, °venerate, adulate, °adore, °worship, °approve, °prize, value, defer to, °admire, pay homage to **6** °praise, °laud, °glorify, °celebrate, °eulogize, °salute, °hail, acclaim, ennoble, °dignify, °exalt **7** °keep, °maintain, °carry out, live up to, °discharge, °fulfill, °observe, °meet **8** °pay, °redeem, °accept, °clear, °cash

honorable *adj.* **1** °upright, upstanding, °trustworthy, trusty, °honest, °just, °fair, °moral, °principled, uncorrupt, uncorrupted, incorruptible, high-minded, °noble, °virtuous **2** °right, °correct, °proper, °fitting, °appropriate, °virtuous, °ethical, °worthy, °respectable, °reputable, °decent, °square **3** °fair (and square), °impartial, °equitable, °just, °honest, unbiased, °unprejudiced, nonprejudicial, evenhanded, °straight, °disinterested, guileless, °ingenuous, °artless, °open, °sincere, °aboveboard, on the up and up, undeceiving, undeceitful, *Colloq* °up front, °on the level **4** °distinguished, °prestigious, °eminent, °notable, °noteworthy, °noted, °illustrious, °famous, famed, honored, °exalted, respected, °celebrated, °renowned, acclaimed, °well-thought-of

honorarium *n.* °(token) fee, compensation, recompense, °pay, °payment, °remuneration, emolument

honorary *adj.* °nominal, °titular, in name *or* title only, ex officio

hoodlum *n.* °gangster, °thug, °racketeer, mobster, desperado, °terrorist, ruffian, °tough, °rowdy, knave, *Colloq* hooligan, baddie *or* baddy, crook, *US* plug-ugly, *Slang* goon, *Brit* yob, yobbo, *US* °mug, bad actor, roughneck, hood, gunsel, hit man, torpedo, *French* apache, *Australian* larrikin

hoodwink *v.* °fool, °trick, °deceive, delude, °dupe, gull, °hoax, °defraud, °mislead, humbug, °outwit, *Colloq* bamboozle, pull the wool over (someone's) eyes, pull a fast one (on someone), lead (someone) up *or* down the garden path, put one over on (someone), throw dust in (someone's) eyes, take (someone) for a ride, string (someone) along, *Slang* rook, con, suck in, *US* sucker in, snow

hook *n.* **1** hanger, °peg, holder; fastener, °catch, °clasp, °clip, °pin **2** °snare, °trap; fishhook **3** ***by hook or by crook.*** °somehow (or other), someway, come what may, by fair means or foul, (by) one way or another **4** ***hook, line, and sinker.*** °completely, °entirely, all the way, through and through, °thoroughly, °entirely, °totally, °utterly, °wholly **5** ***off the hook.*** °(set) free, °(in the) clear, out of it; out of trouble, acquitted, exonerated, cleared, °let off, vindicated, °off —*v.* **6** °catch, °trap, entrap, °snare, ensnare; °grab, °capture, collar, °nab, °seize; *Chiefly US and Canadian* °snag, *Colloq* °pinch **7** °steal, °pilfer, filch, palm, shoplift, °rob, *Slang* snitch, °rip off, *Euphemistic* °liberate, °remove, °borrow, °appropriate, *Brit* °nick, *Chiefly Brit* °pinch

hop *v.* **1** °jump, °leap, °bound, °spring, vault; °skip, °caper, gambol, °dance **2** take a (short) trip *or* voyage, °travel, °come, °go, °proceed; °fly —*n.* **3** °jump, °leap, °bound, °spring, vault; °skip, °caper, °dance **4** (short) trip *or* flight *or* journey *or* voyage

hope *n.* **1** °desire, °wish, °expectation, yearning, hankering, craving, °longing, °fancy; °ambition, (day)dream **2** °prospect, °promise, °expectation, expectancy, °confidence, °anticipation, assumption, °security, °faith, °conviction, °belief, °trust —*v.* **3** °aspire, count *or* rely on *or* upon, °anticipate, °contemplate, °foresee, °look forward to, °expect, await, °wait **4** °trust; °wish, °want, °desire; *Dialect* °expect

hopeful *adj.* **1** °expectant, anticipating, °optimistic, °sanguine, °confident, assured **2** °promising, °bright, °rosy, reassuring, heartening, encouraging, auspicious, °propitious, inspiriting

hopefully *adv.* **1** expectantly, optimistically, sanguinely, confidently **2** with (any) luck, if things go well, all being well, it is hoped, expectedly

hopeless *adj.* **1** °desperate, beyond hope *or* saving, irreparable, beyond repair, irremediable, °lost, gone, °irretrievable; °incurable, °terminal, °deadly, °fatal, °lethal **2** °bad, °poor, °incompetent, °inferior, °inadequate, °inept, °unqualified, unfit, unskillful, °deficient **3** despairing, °despondent, °forlorn, °woebegone, disconsolate, °inconsolable, depressed, °dejected, °melancholy, downcast, °gloomy, °miserable, discouraged, °wretched, lugubrious, °funereal, °sorrowful, °sad, °unhappy **4** °futile, °vain, °bootless, unavailing, °impossible, °impracticable, unworkable, °pointless, °worthless, °useless

horizon *n.* °view, purview, °range, °scope, vista, compass, °perspective, °prospect, ken, field of vision, limit(s)

horizontal *adj.* °level, °flat, °plane; °prone, °supine

horrible *adj.* **1** °awful, horrendous, horrid, horrifying, horrific, °terrible, °terrifying, °dreadful, °abominable, °abhorrent, appalling, °frightening, °frightful, °ghastly, °grim, °grisly, °ghoulish, °gruesome, °loathsome, °hideous, °repulsive, °revolting, °disgusting, sickening, nauseating, °nauseous, °harrowing, bloodcurdling, °macabre, unspeakable, °shocking **2** °awful, °nasty, unpleasant, °disagreeable, horrid, °terrible, °dreadful, °obnoxious, °offensive, °atrocious, °monstrous, °contemptible, detestable, °despicable, *Colloq Brit* °beastly

horrify *v.* **1** °terrify, °frighten, °scare, °alarm, °intimidate, °panic, scare *or* frighten to death, °petrify, *Colloq* scare *or* frighten the living daylights out of, scare stiff, make (someone's) hair stand on end, make (someone's *or* the) blood run cold, curl (someone's) hair, scare the pants off **2** °shock, °startle, °upset, °put off, °outrage, °dismay, °appall, °distress, discountenance, disconcert

horror *n.* **1** fear and loathing, repugnance, °terror, °dread, hatred, °revulsion, detestation, abhorrence, °distaste, °dislike; °aversion, antipathy, °hostility, °animosity, animus, °rancor; odium, execration **2** °fear, °dismay, °distress, °dread, °fright, °alarm, °upset, perturbation, °panic, °terror, fear and trembling, trepidation, °anxiety, angst, apprehension, uneasiness, queasiness, nervousness, awe

hors d'oeuvre *n.* appetizer, apéritif, antipasto, smorgasbord *or* smörgåsbord, °relish; *Chiefly Brit* starter; *Archaic* warner

hospitable *adj.* **1** welcoming, °gracious, °courteous, °genial, °friendly, °agreeable, °amicable, °cordial, °warm, congenial, °sociable, °generous **2** open-minded, °receptive, amenable, approachable, °tolerant

hospital *n.* medical center, health center, °infirmary, clinic, polyclinic, dispensary, sick bay; asylum, sanatorium, nursing home, convalescent home *or* facility, *US* °sanitarium

hospitality *n.* graciousness, °courtesy, courteousness, friendliness, amicability, cordiality, °warmth, congeniality, sociability, generosity

host[1] *n.* **1** hostess, innkeeper, hotelier, hotelkeeper, hotelman, landlord *or* landlady, manager *or* manageress, proprietor *or* proprietress, *Brit* publican **2** entertainer, master *or* mistress of ceremonies, emcee, MC, °announcer, *Brit* presenter, compere, *US* tummler —*v.* **3** °entertain, act *or* play the host *or* hostess, °have

host[2] *n.* army, °swarm, °crowd, horde, multitude, °throng, °mob, °pack, °herd, troop, legion, °body, °assembly, assemblage, drove

hostage *n.* °pledge, °security, surety, °pawn, °captive, °prisoner, gage

hostile *adj.* **1** °opposed, antagonistic, °contrary, against, anti, adverse; °averse, °loath **2** unfriendly, inimical, °unsympathetic, °cold, °inhospitable; unfavorable **3** warring, °belligerent, bellicose, °warlike, combative, °militant, °aggressive

hostility *n.* **1** °antagonism, °opposition, enmity, °animosity, antipathy, animus, °ill will, malevolence, malice, °aversion, unfriendliness **2** ***hostilities.*** °war, warfare, fighting, °combat, °action, state of war, °bloodshed

hot *adj.* **1** °fiery, white hot, redhot, piping hot, °burning, blistering, °scorching, roasting, frying, sizzling, searing, boiling, scalding, steaming, simmering, °torrid, °sweltering, °sultry, °heated **2** °spicy, peppery, °sharp, piquant, °pungent, °biting, acrid **3** °intense, °fervent, zealous, °ardent, °enthusiastic, °passionate, fervid, vehement, °excited, °animated; °impetuous, °fiery, °fierce, °inflamed, °sharp, °violent **4** °eager, °keen, avid, °anxious, °burning; °intense, °fervent, zealous, °ardent, °enthusiastic, °passionate, fervid, vehement, °excited, °animated, °earnest, *Slang US* gung ho **5** °recent, °fresh, °new, °latest, °brand-new **6** °popular, sought-after, commercial, saleable, marketable **7** °lustful, °lecherous, libidinous, lubricous *or* lubricious, °sensual, concupiscent, °prurient, licentious, oversexed, sex-crazed, sex-mad, *Archaic* lickerish, horn-mad, *Slang* horny, *Chiefly Brit* °randy, *US* °hard up **8** °intense, °vivid, °striking, °bright, °brilliant, °dazzling, °loud **9** electrified, °live, charged, powered **10** °dangerous, °precarious, °risky, °sensitive, °delicate, °unstable, °touchy, unpredictable

hot air *n.* blather *or* blether, bunkum, verbiage, °talk, °wind, pretentiousness, pomposity, °bombast, grandiloquence, magniloquence, flatulence, gasconade, rodomontade, *Colloq* claptrap, bosh, gas, guff

hotbed *n.* breeding ground, fertile source

hotel *n.* hostelry, inn, °lodging, caravanserai; motel, motor hotel, bed and breakfast *or* B & B, guest house, °pension, *Australian and New Zealand* °pub, *US* tourist house

hotheaded *adj.* °impetuous, headlong, hot-tempered, °quick-tempered, °volatile, °rash, °hasty, °wild, °foolhardy, °reckless, °precipitate, °thoughtless, °heedless, madcap, °daredevil, devil-may-care

hothouse *n.* **1** °hotbed, greenhouse, glasshouse, conservatory —*adj.* **2** °dainty, °delicate, °sensitive, °fragile, °frail, pampered, overprotected, sheltered, shielded, spoiled, coddled, babied

hotly *adv.* intensively, energetically, doggedly, persistently, zealously, fervently, fervidly, ardently, °warmly, enthusiastically

hound *v.* °bully, °browbeat, °persecute, °nag, °harass, °annoy, °pester, harry, badger

house *n.* **1** °residence, °dwelling, dwelling place, °home, °abode, household, homestead, °domicile, lodging(s), °quarters, °building, edifice **2** °family, °line, °lineage, °dynasty, °clan, ancestry, °strain, °race, blood, descendants, forebears **3** legislature, legislative body, congress, °parliament, °assembly, °council, °diet **4** °establishment, °firm, °concern, °company, °business, °organization, °enterprise, °undertaking, *Colloq* °outfit **5** auditorium, °theater, concert hall **6** house of ill repute *or* ill fame *or* prostitution, °brothel, whorehouse, bagnio, bordello, *Archaic* bawdyhouse, *Colloq* sporting house, crib, *Slang US* cathouse **7** ***on the house.*** °free, gratis, for nothing, as a gift —*v.* **8** °shelter, °accommodate, °domicile, °lodge, °quarter, °put up, °take in, °board, billet, °harbor **9** °contain, °accommodate, °quarter

housing *n.* **1** homes, houses, lodging(s), °quarters, °accommodations, habitation, °dwelling; °shelter, °protection **2** °case, casing, °cover, covering, °enclosure, container, °box, °shield

hovel *n.* °hole, °shack, shanty, (pig)sty, pigpen, coop, crib, °hut, *Colloq US* °dump

hover *v.* **1** °drift, °poise, °float, °hang, be *or* hang suspended, hang in the air **2** °linger, loiter, °wait, hang about *or* around

however *adv.* **1** °notwithstanding, °regardless, °nevertheless, °nonetheless, °despite (that), °in spite of (that), °still, but, °though, °yet, °even so, be that as it may, come what may, no matter what; °at any rate, anyway, anyhow, on the other hand, in all events, °in any event, °in any case, after all **2** to whatever manner *or* extent *or* degree, howsoever, no matter how, in any way *or* manner *or* respect, anyhow, how, in whatever way *or* manner —*conj.* **3** how, how on earth, how in the world, in what way *or* manner **4** no matter how, regardless how, putting *or* setting aside how, notwithstanding how

howl *v.* **1** yowl, °cry, wail, ululate, bay; °shout, °yell, °bellow, °scream, °roar, *Colloq* holler —*n.* **2** yowl, yowling, ululation, ululating, wail, wailing, yelp, yelping, °cry; °shout, °yell, °bellow, °scream, °roar, *Colloq* holler

howler *n.* °blunder, °mistake, °error, gaffe; malapropism, Irish bull; *Brit* bloomer, *US* clinker, *Colloq Brit* clanger, *US* boner

hub *n.* °center, °focus, focal point, °pivot, °heart, °core, °nucleus, nave

huddle *n.* **1** °cluster, °group, °bunch, °clump, °pack, °herd, °crowd, °throng, °mass **2** °meeting, °conference, °discussion, consultation —*v.* **3** °cluster, °gather, crowd *or* press together, throng *or* flock together, °nestle, jam *or* cram together, squeeze together **4** °meet, °discuss, °confer, °consult

hue *n.* °color, °tint, °shade, tinge, °tone, °cast, tincture, *Technical* chroma

huff *n.* **1** *in a huff.* piqued, peeved, °testy, irritated, angered, vexed, annoyed, in high dudgeon, provoked, exasperated, °petulant, in a pet, *Colloq* (all) het up —*v.* **2** °puff, °blow, °bluster

hug *v.* **1** °embrace, °clasp, °squeeze, °cuddle, °snuggle, *Archaic or literary* °clip **2** follow closely, cling to, stay *or* keep near *or* close to —*n.* **3** °embrace, °clasp, °squeeze, *Colloq* °clinch

huge *adj.* °large, °great, °enormous, °gigantic, °giant, °immense, °massive, tremendous, gargantuan, °prodigious, mammoth, °colossal, °monumental, Brobdingnagian, titanic, stupendous, elephantine, leviathan, °mountainous, °vast, *Colloq* °jumbo, °whopping

hulk *n.* **1** shipwreck, °wreck, °derelict, °shell, skeleton **2** oaf, °clod, lout, ox, *Slang US* galoot *or* galloot, klutz

hulking *adj.* °clumsy, °awkward, ungainly, lubberly, oafish, loutish; °unwieldy, cumbersome, °bulky, °ponderous, °massive, °ungraceful, inelegant

hull *n.* **1** framework, skeleton, °frame, °structure, °body **2** °shell, pod, °case, husk, °skin, °peel, °rind, *US* shuck —*v.* **3** °shell, °peel, °skin, husk, *US* shuck

hum *v.* **1** °buzz, drone, thrum, °murmur, whirr, purr, °vibrate, *Technical* bombinate *or* bombilate **2** bustle, °stir, be active, move briskly, *Colloq* tick (over) **3** intone —*n.* **4** °buzz, buzzing, drone, droning, thrum, thrumming, °murmur, murmuring, murmuration, whirr, whirring, purr, purring, vibration

human *adj.* **1** °mortal, anthropoid, hominoid, android; hominid; *Possibly offensive* manlike **2** °sensitive, °defenseless, °weak, fallible, °vulnerable **3** °kind, °kindly, kindhearted, °considerate, °charitable, compassionate, °merciful, °benign, benignant, °tender, °gentle, °forgiving, °lenient, °benevolent, beneficent, °generous, magnanimous, °humanitarian, °understanding, °accommodating, °sympathetic, °good-natured, humane, °sensitive —*n.* **4** human being, °person, °individual, °woman, °man, °child, °mortal, °one, °soul, someone, °somebody

humanitarian *adj.* **1** See **human, 3.** —*n.* **2** Good Samaritan, °benefactor, benefactress, °philanthropist, altruist

humanity *n.* **1** human race, °people, °society, humankind, Homo sapiens; the public, °the masses, community; *Possibly offensive* °man, mankind **2** humanness, human nature, mortality **3** °kindness, kindliness, kindheartedness, °consideration, helpfulness, charitableness, openheartedness, warmheartedness, goodwill, °benevolence, compassion, mercifulness, °mercy, benignity, tenderness, °warmth, gentleness, leniency *or* lenience *or* lenity, beneficence, generosity, unselfishness, magnanimity, °understanding, °sympathy, °sensitivity

humble *adj.* **1** °modest, °reserved, unpretentious, unostentatious, self-effacing, unassuming, unpresuming **2** °submissive, °meek, °servile, °obsequious, deferential,

°mild, °respectful, subservient, °subdued **3** °lowly, °low, °inferior, °mean, ignoble, °ordinary, °plebeian, °common, °simple, °obscure, unprepossessing, unimportant, °undistinguished, °insignificant; lowborn, °base, baseborn *—v.* **4** °chasten, bring *or* pull down, °subdue, abase, °debase, demean, °lower, °degrade, °downgrade, °reduce, make (someone) eat humble pie, lose face, °shame, °humiliate, °crush, °break, °mortify, chagrin, *Colloq* °put down, take (someone) down a peg *or* notch

humdrum *adj.* °dull, °boring, °tedious, °tiresome, wearisome, °monotonous, unvaried, unvarying, °routine, undiversified, unchanging, °repetitious, uneventful, unexciting, uninteresting, °prosaic, mundane, °ordinary, commonplace, °common, °banal, °dry, insipid, jejune

humid *adj.* °damp, °moist, °muggy, °clammy, °sticky, °steamy, soggy, °sultry, °wet

humiliate *v.* See **humble, 4.**

humiliation *n.* °disgrace, °shame, mortification, °dishonor, ignominy, °indignity, °discredit, loss of face, obloquy, abasement, depreciation, detraction, °degradation, derogation, belittlement, disparagement, shaming, °embarrassment, humbling

humility *n.* modesty, meekness, self-effacement, shyness, diffidence, timidity, timorousness, meekness, bashfulness, mildness, unpretentiousness, submissiveness, °servility, self-abasement, lowliness

humor *n.* **1** funniness, comedy, °wit, facetiousness, ludicrousness, drollery, jocoseness *or* jocosity, jocularity, waggishness, °raillery, °banter **2** comedy, farce, jokes, jests, witticisms, °wit, *Slang* wisecracks, gags **3** °mood, °frame of mind, °temper; spirit(s); °disposition, °nature, temperament *—v.* **4** soothe, °gratify, placate, please, mollify, °indulge, appease, °pamper, cosset, °coddle, mollycoddle, °jolly, °baby, °spoil

humorous *adj.* °funny, comical, facetious, laughable, risible, °ludicrous, °farcical, sidesplitting, °hilarious, °merry; droll, °whimsical, amusing, °witty, waggish, jocular, jocose, °playful, °pleasant, *Colloq* °hysterical

hump *n.* **1** °bulge, °lump, °bump, protuberance, °protrusion, °projection, °knob, node, °mass, °hunch, enlargement, °swelling, °growth, excrescence, tumefaction, tumescence; °mound, barrow, °tell, hummock, hillock, tumulus, *Brit dialect* tump *—v.* **2** °hunch, °arch, curve, crook, °bend **3** °drag, °lug, °haul, °carry, °heave

hunch *n.* **1** °(intuitive) guess, °intuition, °feeling, °impression, °suspicion, °premonition, presentiment **2** See **hump, 1.** *—v.* **3** See **hump, 2.**

hunger *n.* **1** hungriness, °emptiness, °appetite, ravenousness, voraciousness, voracity; °famine, starvation **2** yearning, °desire, craving, °itch, °thirst, °longing, hankering, °mania, cupidity, *Formal* cacoëthes, *Colloq* yen *—v.* **3** Usually, ***hunger for or after.*** crave, °yearn, °desire, °thirst, °want, °hanker, *Colloq* yen, have a yen

hungry *adj.* **1** °famished, °starved, starving, °ravenous, °voracious, °empty, °hollow, *Colloq chiefly Brit* peckish **2** craving, covetous, °eager, avid, °greedy, °keen, yearning, °desirous, °longing, hungering, thirsting, starving, °dying, *Colloq* hankering **3** acquisitive, °greedy, °thirsty, insatiable, °deprived

hunt *v.* **1** °chase, °pursue, dog, °hound, °stalk, °trail, °track (down), °trace; °course **2** Also, ***hunt for or up or out or through.*** °seek (out), °search (for), go in search of *or* for, look (high and low) for, °quest after, go in quest of, °scour, °ransack, °investigate, pry into, go over *or* through with a fine-tooth comb, °examine, °explore, *Colloq US* °check out *—n.* **3** °chase, °pursuit, tracking (down), stalking, hunting; °course **4** °search, °quest

hunter *n.* huntsman, huntswoman, stalker, tracker, Nimrod, Orion; huntress

hurdle *n.* **1** °barrier, °obstacle, °impediment, °hindrance, °obstruction, °bar, °handicap, °restraint, °snag, °(stumbling) block, °check, °difficulty, °complication, °interference *—v.* **2** °leap (over), vault (over), °jump (over)

hurl *v.* °throw, °toss, °shy, °sling, °fling, °pitch, °cast, °send, °fire, °heave, °propel, °let fly, *Colloq* chuck

hurricane *n.* cyclone, tornado, typhoon, °whirlwind, °twister, windstorm, °storm, °gale, °blow

hurried *adj.* **1** °hasty, °feverish, °frantic, °hectic, °breakneck, frenetic, °impetuous, rushed, °precipitate, °swift, °quick, °speedy; °brief, °short **2** °superficial, °cursory, °offhand, °perfunctory, slapdash

hurry *v.* **1** °rush, °hasten, make haste, °speed, °race, °dash, °hustle, °scurry, °tear, °fly, °run, °shoot, scoot, scamper, scuttle, hotfoot (it), *Colloq* °shake a leg, get cracking, °get a move on, go hell for leather, skedaddle, °step on it, step on the gas, *Chiefly US* hightail (it), go like greased lightning, get a wiggle on **2** °speed up, accelerate, °hasten, °rush, °push, °press, °expedite; °urge, egg *—n.* **3** °haste, °rush, °urgency, °eagerness; °agitation, disquiet, °upset, dither, °fuss, bustle, ado, to-do, °furor, commotion, turmoil, °stir, pother; *Colloq* °stew, °sweat

hurt *v.* **1** °harm, °injure, °wound; °damage, °impair, °mar, °spoil, °vitiate, °ruin **2** °ache, °smart, °pain, °pinch, °sting, °burn, °torment, °gripe **3** °distress, °grieve, °affect, °afflict, aggrieve, °depress, °upset, °disappoint, °pain, cut to the quick, affront, °offend **4** °injure, °maim, °wound, °cripple, °lame, disable, °incapacitate, °damage, °mutilate, °mangle *—n.* **5** °harm, °injury, °damage, °detriment, °disadvantage **6** °ache, °pain, °pang, °distress, °discomfort, °suffering, °torment, torture, °agony; °anguish, °misery, °woe, dolor, °sadness, °depression

—*adj.* 7 injured, wronged, pained, rueful, grieved, °unhappy, aggrieved, °sad, °wretched, °woebegone, °sorrowful, °mournful, depressed, °dejected, °dismal, °gloomy, °melancholy **8** damaged, °defective, impaired, marred, °broken, °worn, °dilapidated, shopworn, scratched, bruised, scarred

hurtful *adj.* **1** °harmful, °injurious, °detrimental, pernicious, °prejudicial, disadvantageous, damaging, deleterious, °destructive, noisome, noxious, baneful, °mischievous **2** °nasty, °cruel, °cutting, malicious, °mean, °unkind, wounding, °spiteful

hurtle *v.* °rush (headlong), °tear, °shoot, °race, °speed; °plunge

husband *n.* **1** °mate, spouse, °groom, bridegroom, °partner, *Colloq* old man, hubby —*v.* **2** save, °keep, °retain, °hoard, °conserve, °preserve, °store; budget, °economize (on), °manage

hush *interj.* **1** Shush!, Quiet!, Be *or* Keep quiet *or* silent *or* still!, Hold your tongue!, Mum's the word!, *Slang* Shut up!, Clam up!, Shut your trap!, Button your lip!, Shut your gob!, *Brit* Belt up!, *US* Hush up!, Shut your face!, *US dialect* Hush your mouth! —*v.* **2** shush, °silence, °still, °quiet **3** °suppress, °mute, °soften, soft-pedal, °whisper **4** Usually, ***hush up.*** °suppress, °repress, °quash, °cover up, °hide, °conceal, keep quiet, *Colloq* °squelch **5** soothe, allay, °calm, °quiet, mollify, pacify, placate, °tranquilize —*n.* **6** °silence, °quiet, stillness, °peace, tranquillity

husky *adj.* **1** °brawny, strapping, °sturdy, °burly, well-built, °robust, °hefty, °rugged, °powerful, °strong, °stout, thickset, °muscular, °tough, *Colloq* beefy **2** hoarse, °gruff, °dry, °harsh, rasping, °rough, °raucous

hustle *v.* **1** °rush, °push, °hurry, °hasten, °run, °dash, scamper, scuttle, °scurry, sprint **2** shove, °push, °drive, °force, °hasten, °expedite, °press **3** shove, °crowd, °push, jostle, elbow, °thrust, °force **4** °push, °eject, °force, coerce, °drive, *Colloq* °bounce —*n.* **5** pushing, jostling, buffeting, jarring, elbowing, shoving, nudging **6** °activity, °action, °stir, °movement

hut *n.* °cabin, °shack, shanty, °shed, lean-to, °shelter, cote, *Literary* °cot, *Australian* gunyah

hybrid *n.* °mixture, crossbreed, half-breed, °mongrel, °cross, composite, °combination, °compound

hygienic *adj.* °clean, °sanitary, °sterile, disinfected, germ-free, aseptic, °pure

hypnotize *v.* °fascinate, mesmerize, °entrance, cast a spell over *or* on, °captivate, °enchant, °charm, spellbind, °bewitch, °enrapture, ensorcell, °transport

hypocrisy *n.* °deceit, deceitfulness, duplicity, double-dealing, °deception, °chicanery, guile, quackery, charlatanism *or* charlatanry, falseness, fakery, °pretense, pretentiousness, °lying, mendacity, pharisaism *or* phariseeism, Tartuffery, insincerity, °dissimulation, two-facedness, double standard(s), sanctimony, sanctimoniousness, *Colloq* phoneyness *or US also* phoniness

hypocrite *n.* deceiver, double-dealer, °quack, charlatan, impostor *or* imposter, mountebank, confidence man *or* trickster, faker, °pretender, °liar, °pharisee, whited sepulcher, Tartuffe, flimflammer, *Colloq* phoney *or US also* phony, con man, flimflam man *or* artist, two-face

hypocritical *adj.* °deceptive, °deceitful, deceiving, °insincere, dissembling, feigning, dissimulating, double-dealing, °false, °fake, faking, °two-faced, pretending, °pretentious, °lying, mendacious, pharisaic(al), °sanctimonious, °dishonest, underhand, treacherous, °perfidious, untrustworthy

hypothesis *n.* theory, °theorem, postulate, premise *or* premiss, °proposition, assumption, °supposition, °speculation

hypothetical *adj.* °assumed, °supposed, conjectural, conjectured, hypothesized, putative, surmised, °assumed, presumed, suspected, imagined, guessed, °speculative, speculated, °theoretical, suppositional, suppositious *or* supposititious

hysterical *adj.* **1** °raving, °mad, °beside oneself, crazed, irrational, distracted, °rabid, °frantic, frenzied, °wild, °berserk, °uncontrolled, uncontrollable, unrestrained, unrestrainable **2** °hilarious, sidesplitting, °uproarious, °farcical, comical, °funny

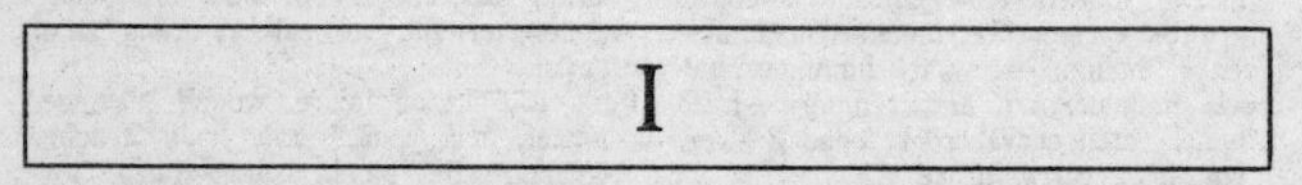

I

icing *n.* **1** frosting, °glaze, coating **2** °bonus, °(fringe) benefit, °reward, (extra) added attraction, °extra, dividend

icy *adj.* **1** ice-cold, °frigid, arctic, °bitter, glacial, °freezing, frozen, °chill, hyperborean *or* hyperboreal, °polar, Siberian, °wintry, °raw, °cold, chilling, °chilly **2** °cool, °chill, °chilly, °frigid, °distant, °aloof, °remote, °freezing, ice-cold, unemotional, unimpassioned, °stony, °steely, °callous, flinty, °formal, °reserved, °forbidding, unfriendly, °hostile

idea *n.* **1** concept, °conception, °construct, °thought, °notion, °plan, °design, °scheme, °suggestion, °recommendation **2** °notion, °fancy, °impression, °picture, °(mental) image, concept, °conception, °perception, °understanding, awareness, apprehension, °inkling, °suspicion, °hint, °suggestion, approximation, °clue, intimation, °guess, °estimate, °estimation, °impression **3** °belief, °opinion, °sentiment, °feeling, teaching(s), °doctrine, °tenet, °principle, °philosophy, °view, °viewpoint, °outlook, °notion, °conviction, °position, °stance **4** °aim, °goal, °purpose, °objective, °object, °end, °point, °reason, raison d'être **5** °hypothesis, theory, °notion, °dream, fantasy *or* phantasy

ideal *n.* **1** °model, °paragon, °standard, criterion, paradigm, exemplar, °pattern, °example, °epitome **2** °acme, °(standard of) perfection, °nonpareil **3** ***ideals.*** °principles, °morals, standards *—adj.* **4** °perfect, °excellent, °supreme, consummate, °complete, °model, °idyllic **5** conceptual, imagined, °imaginary, °unreal, °visionary, °idealistic, °fictitious, Utopian, notional, mythical *or* mythic, °fantasy, °dream, °romantic, chimeric(al), °illusory, °fanciful, °fancied

idealistic *adj.* °visionary, °romantic, romanticized, °optimistic, starry-eyed, °quixotic, Panglossian, °impractical, °unrealistic

idealize *v.* °exalt, elevate, °glorify, °worship, ennoble, deify, apotheosize, °put on a pedestal, romanticize

ideally *adv.* **1** under *or* in the best of circumstances, at best, in a perfect world, all things being equal **2** theoretically, in theory, °in principle **3** °perfectly

identical *adj.* **1** °same, °twin, °duplicate, °indistinguishable, interchangeable; selfsame **2** °similar, °matching, °like, °alike, comparable, °equal, °equivalent, corresponding

identification *n.* **1** °connection, °recognition, distinguishing, °indication, °perception, detection, °selection, naming, labeling, pinpointing, designation, characterization, °denomination; authentication, verification, °establishment, certification, substantiation, corroboration, *Colloq* fingering **2** classification, classifying, cataloging, categorization, categorizing, pigeonholing **3** ID, ID card, identity card, badge, credentials **4** °connection, °association, affiliation, empathy, °sympathy, °rapport, °relationship

identify *v.* **1** classify, °categorize, catalog, pigeonhole, °sort (out), °specify, pinpoint, home (in) on, °name, °label, °tag, °recognize, °place, °mark, pinpoint, °single out, °point out, *Colloq* °put one's finger on **2** °connect, °associate, °relate, °ally **3** °diagnose, °specify, °name, °recognize **4** Usually, ***identify with.*** empathize (with), °sympathize (with), °relate (to), *Colloq* °dig

identity *n.* **1** sameness, oneness, unanimity, indistinguishability, °agreement, °accord, congruence **2** °personality, individuality, distinctiveness, uniqueness, particularity, °singularity

ideology *n.* belief(s), convictions, tenets, credo, °philosophy, °principles, °creed, dogma, teachings, °doctrine

idiom *n.* **1** °language, °tongue, °speech, °vernacular, °dialect, argot, patois, °jargon, °cant, idiolect, °parlance, *façon de parler*, phraseology **2** °expression, °(set) phrase, phrasing, locution, °cliché

idle *adj.* **1** °unused, °inactive, unoccupied, nonoperative, stationary **2** °unemployed, °out of work, °redundant, jobless, workless, *Colloq* °at leisure, °at liberty, between assignments, resting, *US* on the beach **3** °indolent, °lazy, °listless, °lethargic, loafing, °slothful, °shiftless, °lackadaisical, loitering, fainéant **4** °bootless, °fruitless, unproductive, abortive, unfruitful, °pointless, °vain, °trifling, trivial, °shallow, nugatory, °superficial, °insignificant, °meaningless, °senseless, unimportant, °frivolous, °worthless, °useless, otiose, unavailing, °futile *—v.* **5** Often, ***idle away.*** °waste, °fritter away, while away, °kill **6** laze (about), loiter, kill time, °loaf, loll, °lounge, take it easy, putter *or Brit* potter about, mess about, fool away, fool around *or* about, *Colloq Brit* °muck about, °bugger about, *US* lallygag *or* lollygag, goof off *or* around, *Military slang US* goldbrick

idleness *n.* **1** °inactivity, inaction, °lethargy, °torpor, °indolence, laziness, °sluggishness, °sloth, slothfulness, shiftlessness, °inertia, lassitude, °torpor, *flânerie, dolce far niente*; unemployment, *Colloq US* lallygagging *or* lollygagging, *Military slang US* goldbricking **2** shirking, malingering, dawdling, loafing, time-wasting, lazing, *Colloq* dillydallying, shilly-shallying, *Brit* skiving

idler *n.* °loafer, layabout, °slacker, shirker, sluggard, lazybones, slugabed, °laggard, dawdler, clock-watcher, drone, °slouch, ne'er-do-well, fainéant, *Colloq* lounge lizard, *Military slang US* goldbrick *or* goldbricker

idly *adv.* **1** unproductively, lazily, indolently **2** offhandedly, unconsciously, mechanically, thoughtlessly, unthinkingly, obliviously, insensibly, indifferently

idol *n.* **1** °(graven) image, icon *or* ikon, effigy, °fetish, tiki, °symbol **2** hero *or* heroine, superstar, °celebrity, luminary, matinee idol, °favorite, °pet, °darling

idolize *v.* °adore, °admire, adulate, °worship, °revere, °reverence, °venerate, °put on a pedestal, °exalt, °glorify, deify, lionize, °look up to, apotheosize

idyllic *adj.* Arcadian, paradisaic(al) *or* paradisiac(al), °heavenly, Edenic, halcyon, °ideal, idealized, °pastoral, °rustic, bucolic, °picturesque, charming, °unspoiled, °peaceful, pacific

ignorance *n.* unfamiliarity, unawareness, unconsciousness, benightedness, unenlightenment, °inexperience, greenness

ignorant *adj.* **1** unknowing, °uninformed, untaught, °uneducated, unschooled, unread, unlearned, unlettered, °illiterate **2** °unaware, °unfamiliar, °unconscious, °benighted, unenlightened, unwitting, in the dark, °oblivious, *Formal* nescient **3** °inexperienced, °green, °naive, °innocent, °unsophisticated **4** uncouth, °ill-mannered, °discourteous, °impolite, uncivil, °boorish

ignore *v.* **1** °disregard, °overlook, pass over *or* by, turn a blind eye to, be blind to, °turn one's back on, turn a deaf ear to, wink at, brush off *or* aside **2** snub, give (someone) the cold shoulder, °reject, send to Coventry, °turn one's back on, *Colloq* give (someone) the brushoff *or* go-by, °cut, turn one's nose up at

ill *adj.* **1** ailing, °unsound, °sick, °indisposed, °infirm, °unhealthy, °diseased, afflicted, in bad health, °sickly, unwell, not well, out of commission; invalided, valetudinarian; *Colloq* °under the weather, in a bad way, °poorly, not up to snuff, °out of sorts, on the sick list, off one's feed, *Slang Brit* dicky, °seedy **2** °bad, °wicked, °sinful, °evil, iniquitous, °immoral, depraved, °vicious, °vile, °wrong, °corrupt **3** °hostile, unfriendly, antagonistic, °belligerent, malevolent, malicious, ill-wishing, unkind(ly), °harsh, °cruel **4** °harmful, °hurtful, °injurious, °detrimental, damaging, pernicious, °dangerous, adverse, deleterious, baleful, °bad, unfavorable, °destructive, °disastrous, catastrophic, °ruinous, cataclysmic **5** °bad, °miserable, °wretched, °disastrous, unfavorable, unpropitious, °untoward, °disturbing, °unfortunate, unlucky, °inauspicious, °ominous, °unpromising, °sinister, °unwholesome **6** ***ill at ease.*** uncomfortable, discomfited, uneasy, edgy, °on edge, fidgety, °nervous, °anxious, °disturbed, distressed, troubled, °awkward, unsure, °uncertain —*n.* **7** °evil, °abuse **8** °harm, °damage, °injury, °hurt, °mischief, °trouble, °misfortune, °misery, °affliction, °pain, °distress, °woe, woefulness, °discomfort, unpleasantness, °disaster, °catastrophe, cataclysm, °calamity, adversity, °damage, °suffering, °ruin, °destruction **9** °injustice, inequity, °wrong, °evil, °sin, °transgression, °abuse, °mistreatment, maltreatment —*adv.* **10** °badly, adversely, unfavorably, °poorly, inauspiciously, unfortunately, unluckily **11** °badly, adversely, unfavorably, critically, harshly, unkindly **12** unkindly, harshly, unfairly, unjustly, improperly, °badly, wrongly, wrongfully, unsatisfactorily, °poorly, malevolently, maliciously **13** °scarcely, °hardly, °by no means, in no way

ill-advised *adj.* **1** inadvisable, ill-judged, injudicious, ill-considered, °misguided, unwise, °imprudent, °inappropriate, unpropitious, inexpedient, impolitic, wrongheaded, °thoughtless; °indiscreet **2** °hasty, °rash, °reckless, °impetuous, °foolhardy, incautious, °shortsighted, °improvident

illegal *adj.* °unlawful, °illegitimate, °criminal, felonious, outlawed, prohibited, interdicted, forbidden, proscribed, wrongful, °unauthorized, ***verboten***, °illicit, *Law* actionable

illegible *adj.* unreadable, unintelligible, indecipherable *or* undecipherable, °incomprehensible

illegitimate *adj.* **1** See **illegal. 2** bastard, °natural, fatherless, born out of wedlock, born on the wrong side of the blanket, misbegotten **3** °irregular, °improper, °incorrect, nonstandard, °invalid, °unauthorized, °spurious

ill-founded *adj.* °groundless, baseless, without foundation, unsupported, unsubstantiated, °empty, unjustified, unproven, uncorroborated, °unsound, °erroneous

illicit *adj.* **1** See **illegal. 2** °wrong, °improper, underhand(ed), °secret, furtive, clandestine, backdoor, *Colloq US* °sneaky

illiterate *adj.* unlettered, analphabetic; unschooled, untaught, °uneducated, °ignorant, °benighted, unenlightened

ill-mannered *adj.* °rude, °discourteous, °impolite, ill-bred, uncivil, °disrespectful, uncourtly, ungallant, °ungracious, indecorous, ungentlemanly, unladylike, °impudent, °insolent, insulting, °impertinent, °brazen

illness *n.* sickness, °disease, °disorder, °affliction, °ailment, malady, °complaint, °infirmity, °disability, indisposition, °affection, *Colloq* °bug

ill-treat *v.* °mistreat, maltreat, °abuse, °misuse, °harm, °hurt, °injure, °persecute, °mishandle

illuminate *v.* **1** °light (up), °brighten, °lighten, throw *or* cast *or* shed light on *or* upon **2** °clarify, throw *or* cast *or* shed light on *or* upon, °enlighten, °clear up, elucidate, °explain, explicate, °reveal **3** rubricate, °decorate, adorn, °embellish, °ornament

illumination *n.* **1** lighting, °light, brightness, °radiance, luminosity, incandescence, fluorescence, phosphorescence **2** enlightenment, °insight, °information, °learning, °revelation, °edification, °instruction, awareness, °understanding, clarification

illusion *n.* **1** °deception, °delusion, °fancy, °misconception, misapprehension, °fallacy, °error, °mistake, mistaken *or* false impression **2** °fantasy, °daydream, °hallucination, phantasm, °phantom, chimera, phantasmagoria, mirage, aberration, °vision, °specter, figment of the imagination, will o' the wisp, ignis fatuus

illusory *adj.* illusive, °imaginary, °fictional, °unreal, °untrue, fallacious, °false, °mistaken, imagined, °fanciful, °fancied, hallucinatory, °deceptive, misleading, °apparent

illustrate *v.* **1** °instance, °exemplify, °demonstrate **2** °picture, °illuminate, grangerize; °decorate, °embellish, emblazon, °ornament, adorn

illustration *n.* **1** °example, °case (in point), °instance, °sample, °specimen, exemplar, *Colloq* °for instance **2** °picture, depiction, °representation, °figure

illustrious *adj.* °distinguished, °famous, °noted, °renowned, famed, °eminent, °well-known, °prominent, °important, °notable, respected, esteemed, °venerable, honored, acclaimed, °celebrated, °great

ill will *n.* °dislike, °animosity, hatred, °hate, °loathing, abhorrence, detestation, malevolence, malice, °hostility, enmity, animus, antipathy, °aversion, °rancor, acrimony, °spite, °venom, vitriol, acerbity

image *n.* **1** °likeness, °representation, °picture, °sculpture, °statue, effigy, °figure, °portrait, simulacrum; icon *or* ikon, °idol, graven image, °fetish, tiki **2** °epitome, °duplicate, °copy, counterpart, °facsimile, °replica, °double, °twin, doppelgänger, clone, *Colloq* spit and image *or* spitting image, (dead) ringer **3** °impression, concept, °conception, °perception, °idea, °notion, mental picture **4** °epitome, °representative, °model, °(typical) example, °essence, archetype, °embodiment, incarnation, personification, materialization, reification, corporealization **5** °figure (of speech), trope, °metaphor, allusion, simile, °symbol **6** °form, °appearance, °likeness, °guise, °semblance, °aspect, °mold, °cast

imagery *n.* figurativeness, allusion, symbolism

imaginary *adj.* °fictitious, °fanciful, °fancied, chimerical, imagined, fictive, illusory *or* illusive, °visionary, made-up, °unreal, °untrue, mythical *or* mythic, notional, °abstract; °legendary, mythological

imagination *n.* **1** mind's eye, °fancy; creativity, inventiveness, °ingenuity, °insight, °inspiration, °vision, imaginativeness, creative power(s) **2** °thought, °thinking, (mental) acuity, °intelligence, °wit

imaginative *adj.* **1** °creative, °original, °clever, °ingenious, inventive, innovative, inspired, inspiring, °enterprising, °resourceful **2** °fanciful, °fantastic, °visionary, poetic(al), °whimsical, contrived, °fictitious, °fictional

imagine *v.* **1** °think of, °contemplate, °picture, °envisage, °consider, °ponder, °meditate on, °envision, visualize, °conceive (of), conceptualize, °create, °think up, concoct, °devise, *Colloq* dream up, cook up **2** °suppose, °guess, conjecture, °assume, °presume, °take it, °infer, take (it) for granted, take it as given, °think, °fancy, °believe, °gather, °surmise, °suspect, °judge, deem

imitate *v.* **1** °mimic, °copy, ape, °parrot, °monkey, emulate, impersonate, do an impression of; °echo, simulate **2** °copy, °mimic, °mock, °parody, °satirize, °burlesque, °caricature, travesty, *Colloq* spoof, °take off, *Brit* °send up

imitation *n.* **1** copying, mimicking, mimicry, aping, parroting, emulating, emulation, impersonating, impersonation, °impression **2** impersonation, °parody, satirization, °burlesque, °caricature, °mockery, travesty, *Colloq* °takeoff, *Brit* sendup **3** °copy, °fake, °counterfeit, °forgery **4** °copy, °replica, replication, °reproduction, simulation, °facsimile, °duplicate, duplication, simulacrum —*adj.* **5** °fake, °synthetic, °artificial, simulated, °sham, ersatz, °mock, °factitious, °reproduction, man-made, *Colloq* phoney *or US also* phony

immaculate *adj.* **1** °spotless, stainless, unblemished, °pure, °clean, °untarnished, unsullied, unsoiled, snow-white, spick-and-span *or* spic-and-span, °dapper, °spruce; °tidy, °neat **2** °pure, °chaste, °innocent, virginal, °virtuous, vestal, °pristine, undefiled, untainted, °unspoiled, unblemished, stainless, unadulterated **3** °faultless, °flawless, °perfect, errorless, °impeccable

immaterial *adj.* **1** unimportant, °inconsequential, nugatory, trivial, °trifling, °petty, °slight, °insignificant, °flimsy, °light, unessential, °nonessential, of little account *or* value **2** airy, incorporeal, °disembodied, ethereal, ephemeral, evanescent, unsubstantial

immature *adj.* **1** °premature, °undeveloped, unripe, °rudimentary, half-grown, unformed, °unfledged, fledgling, unfinished, °young, °new, °fresh, °incomplete **2** °green, °callow, °unsophisticated, °naive, jejune, °inexperienced, babyish, °childish, °childlike, °puerile, °juvenile, °raw, *Colloq* wet behind the ears

immeasurable *adj.* °vast, °infinite, °immense, °huge, °great, °limitless, °boundless, °endless, interminable, unbounded, °unlimited, measureless, °inestimable, unfathomable; innumerable, °numberless, uncountable, uncounted, incalculable

immediate *adj.* **1** instantaneous, °instant, °abrupt, °sudden, °swift; °spontaneous, °instinctive, triggered, °unhesitating, °unthinking, °automatic, reflex, knee-jerk **2** °direct, nearest, next, closest, adjacent, proximate; °nearby **3** existing, °present, °current, °actual, °pressing, °urgent

immediately *adv.* **1** °at once, instantly, °instantaneously, °promptly, right away, right now, without delay, unhesitatingly, without hesitation, forthwith, this instant, °directly, in a wink, in a second, in a minute, ***tout de suite,*** instanter, *Chiefly Brit* straightaway *or* straight away, *Colloq* pronto, in a jiffy, in two shakes of a lamb's tail, before one can *or* could say "Jack Robinson," at the drop of a hat **2** °directly, closely, intimately —*conj.* **3** when, as soon as, the moment (that), *Brit* °directly

immense *adj.* °enormous, °gigantic, °extensive, °vast, °huge, °massive, °voluminous, tremendous, staggering, stupendous, mammoth, °colossal, °giant, titanic, cyclopean, °jumbo, elephantine, Brobdingnagian, *Slang US* humongous

immerse *v.* **1** °plunge, °sink, °submerge, °dip, dunk, °duck, inundate **2** °plunge, °sink, °submerge, °bury, absorb, engross, °engage, °occupy, °involve

immigrant *n.* °newcomer, °arrival, °settler, *Australian* °migrant; °alien, °foreigner, outlander, °outsider

imminent *adj.* °impending, looming, °threatening, °menacing, °at hand, nigh, °immediate, close (by *or* at hand), (forth)coming, drawing near *or* close *or* nigh, °momentary

immoderate *adj.* °excessive, °extreme, °exorbitant, °unreasonable, °inordinate, °extravagant, intemperate; °outrageous, °preposterous, exaggerated, unrestrained, undue

immodest *adj.* **1** °indecent, °shameless, °shameful, indecorous, titillating, revealing; indelicate, °improper, °wanton, °loose, unrestrained, °provocative, °obscene, °lewd, smutty, °dirty, °lascivious, °bawdy, °coarse, *Colloq* °sexy **2** °brazen, °forward, °bold, °impudent, °impertinent, °brash, °arrogant, °insolent, °presumptuous, °disrespectful, *Colloq* °fresh, °cheeky

immoral *adj.* **1** °corrupt, °bad, °wicked, °evil, iniquitous, °sinful, °impure, unethical, unprincipled, °abandoned, °base, °wrong, °vile, depraved, °dissolute, °degenerate, °reprobate, unregenerate, nefarious, flagitious, °villainous, treacherous, °unscrupulous, °dishonest **2** °immodest, debauched, °indecent, °wanton, °libertine, °lecherous, °lustful, libidinous, °carnal, concupiscent, salacious, licentious, °lascivious, °lewd, °obscene, °pornographic, °dirty, smutty, °filthy

immortal *adj.* **1** undying, °eternal, °deathless, °everlasting, imperishable, sempiternal, never-ending, °endless, ceaseless, °perpetual, °timeless, °constant, °permanent, °indestructible **2** °divine, °heavenly, °godlike **3** remembered, °celebrated, unfading, °famous, °renowned, °classic, lauded, praised, honored, °timeless —*n.* **4** Olympian, god *or* goddess; hero *or* heroine, °legend, °genius, °great

immortalize *v.* °celebrate, °honor, °glorify, °memorialize, °commemorate, apotheosize, canonize, beatify, °exalt, ennoble, °extol

immovable *adj.* **1** unmovable, °fixed, °fast, °rooted, °set, immobile, stationary, motionless, °stable, riveted, anchored, frozen **2** immutable, unchangeable, unalterable, settled, °set, unmovable, °fixed, °inflexible; unshakable *or* unshakeable, unswerving, °firm, °determined, °steadfast, °staunch, °rigid, dogged, obdurate, unyielding, unwavering, °resolute, unflinching, adamant(ine), °stony, unbending, °impassive, emotionless, °unmoved

immune *adj.* inoculated, vaccinated; °exempt, °safe, protected, insusceptible *or* unsusceptible, invulnerable, untouched, °unaffected

immunity *n.* **1** °exemption, nonliability, invulnerability, °protection, °excuse, °release, °exclusion, °privilege, °freedom, °indemnity, amnesty, exoneration, absolution **2** insusceptibility *or* unsusceptibility, °protection, inoculation, vaccination

imp *n.* devil(kin), °demon, sprite, evil spirit, hobgoblin, °goblin, elf, pixie *or* pixy, leprechaun, puck, brownie, fairy; scamp, urchin, gamin, °rogue, °rascal, mischief-maker, brat

impact *n.* **1** °collision, °contact, °striking, °crash, smash, °bump, colliding, crashing, smashing, bumping **2** °effect, °impression, °influence, °import, °meaning, °bearing, °force, °thrust, °weight, °burden, °brunt, repercussions, results, consequences —*v.* **3** °strike, °hit, °collide with **4** °affect, °modify, °change

impair *v.* °weaken, °cripple, °damage, °harm, °mar, °injure, °spoil, °ruin

impairment *n.* lessening, weakening, °damage, °harm, °injury, °flaw, °imperfection, reduction, vitiation, deterioration, °decrease, diminution, enfeeblement, debilitation, undermining, worsening, marring

impale *v.* spear, °stab, °pierce, skewer, °spit, °stick, °transfix, °spike

impart *v.* **1** °give, °cede, °lend, °bestow, convey, °confer, °grant, °afford, °accord, °contribute **2** °communicate, °tell, °relate, °transmit, °reveal, divulge, °disclose, °pass on, °intimate, confide

impartial *adj.* °fair, °just, evenhanded, °disinterested, °neutral, °unprejudiced, unbiased, °objective, °equitable

impasse *n.* °deadlock, dead end, °stalemate, standoff, °block, blockage, *Colloq* blind alley

impassioned *adj.* °passionate, inspired, °spirited, °stirring, °fervent, °emotional, fervid, °ardent, °heated, °warm, °rousing, aroused, vehement, zealous, °eager, °earnest, °enthusiastic, °vigorous, °animated, °fiery, °inflamed, °glowing

impassive *adj.* °cool, apathetic, °calm, °serene, composed, °unmoved, °cold, °cold-blooded, °reserved, imperturbable, unimpressionable, unruffled, controlled, contained, °phlegmatic, °lackadaisical, °stoical, unemotional, °taciturn, unfeeling, °stolid, emotionless, uncaring, °indifferent, undisturbed, °callous, °unsympathetic, °stony, °dispassionate, °detached, °nonchalant, unconcerned, insouciant, °remote

impatient *adj.* **1** uneasy, °nervous, fidgety, °agitated, °restless, °restive, unquiet, °eager, °fretful, °agog, chafing, °impetuous, athirst, *Slang* itchy, *US* antsy **2** °irritable, irascible, °testy, °short-tempered, °querulous, °waspish, °brusque, °curt, °short, hot-tempered, °snappish, °indignant, °demanding

impeach *v.* **1** °charge, °accuse, arraign, °indict, °incriminate, °implicate, inculpate, °blame, censure **2** °(call into) question, °challenge, °attack, °disparage, °discredit, impugn, deprecate, °belittle, asperse, cast aspersions on, declaim, °slander, malign, °vilify

impeccable *adj.* °faultless, °flawless, °perfect, °ideal, °pure, °correct, °proper, °spotless, °immaculate, unblemished, unimpeachable, °blameless

impede *v.* °bar, °obstruct, °block, °thwart, °check, °hinder, °hamper, °slow, °retard, °restrain, °brake, °hold up, °delay, °foil, confound, °inhibit, °curb, °spike, °stop

impediment *n.* °bar, °barrier, °obstruction, °block, °check, °hindrance, °encumbrance, °restraint, °holdup, °hitch, °snag, °restriction, °stricture, bottleneck, °delay, hang-up, °inhibition, °curb

impending *adj.* °imminent, approaching, (close *or* near) at hand, °close, nearing, °forthcoming, brewing, to come, in view, °in prospect, in store, in the offing, on the horizon, in the air; looming, °threatening, °menacing; *Colloq Brit* on the cards, *US* °in the cards

imperative *adj.* **1** °mandatory, compulsory, °necessary, required, requisite, demanded, °obligatory, °indispensable, °essential, °crucial, °vital, °urgent, °pressing, exigent **2** imperious, commanding, °authoritarian, °overbearing, °peremptory, autocratic, °domineering, magisterial, lordly, °arbitrary, °dictatorial, °dogmatic, °tyrannical, °despotic, *Colloq* °bossy

imperceptible *adj.* **1** °invisible, indiscernible, °indistinguishable, undetectable, °obscure, °vague, ill-defined; °inaudible **2** °indistinct, unclear, unnoticeable, °slight, °subtle, inconsiderable, inappreciable, °minute, °tiny, °slight, minuscule, infinitesimal, microscopic

imperfect *adj.* °wanting, unfinished, °undeveloped, °incomplete, °deficient, °defective, °faulty, °flawed, patchy

imperfection *n.* °flaw, °failing, °fault, °error, °defect, °blemish, °damage; inadequacy, insufficiency, deficiency, °frailty, °weakness, °foible, °shortcoming, °peccadillo, shortfall, fallibility, °infirmity

imperial *adj.* **1** kingly, kinglike, queenly, queenlike, °princely, princelike, °regal, °royal, °sovereign **2** °majestic, °royal, °regal, °lofty, °exalted, °supreme, august, °noble, °superior, °imposing, °splendid, °magnificent, °grand, °excellent

impermeable *adj.* impenetrable, impassable, impervious, closed, sealed, °hermetic

impersonal *adj.* **1** °detached, °objective, °disinterested, °fair, °equitable, °dispassionate, °unprejudiced, unbiased **2** °formal, °stiff, °strait-laced, °wooden, °rigid, prim, °stuffy, °cool, °detached, unfriendly, °cold, °mechanical

impertinence *n.* insolence, boldness, brazenness, °impudence, °presumption, presumptuousness, brashness, sauciness, pertness, °incivility, forwardness, impoliteness, discourtesy, °disrespect, audacity, rudeness, °effrontery, *Colloq* cheek, °brass, brassiness, °nerve, °gall, *Slang* chutzpah

impertinent *adj.* °presumptuous, °insolent, °bold, °brazen, °impudent, °brash, saucy, °pert, uncivil, °forward, °impolite, °discourteous, °disrespectful, °audacious, °rude, *Colloq* °cheeky, °fresh, °brassy, *US* nervy

impetuous *adj.* °spontaneous, °unpremeditated, °impulsive, unplanned, °hasty, °abrupt, °precipitate, °quick, °unthinking, unreasoned, °offhand, °rash, °reckless, spur-of-the-moment, unreflective, headlong

impetus *n.* °drive, stimulus, °push, impulse, goad, °thrust, °energy, °momentum, stimulation, °incentive, motivation, °encouragement, °inspiration

impious *adj.* irreligious, °irreverent, °ungodly, °sacrilegious, °blasphemous, °profane, unholy, °wicked, °sinful, iniquitous

implacable *adj.* unappeasable, unmollifiable, unpacifiable, unforgiving, intractable, uncompromising, °inflexible, inexorable, unyielding, unrelenting, °ruthless, °cruel, pitiless, °merciless, °hard, °rigid, °unsympathetic, uncompassionate

implant *v.* **1** °introduce, °instill, °insinuate, °inject; °indoctrinate, inculcate, °teach, °impress, imprint **2** °graft, °root, embed, inlay —*n.* **3** °graft, scion, ingraft; °insert

implausible *adj.* °improbable, °unlikely, °doubtful, dubious, °questionable, °unbelievable, °incredible, °far-fetched, unconvincing, °debatable, °unreasonable

implement *n.* **1** utensil, °tool, °instrument, °apparatus, °device, appliance, contrivance, °mechanism, °(piece of) equipment, *Colloq* °gadget, °contraption —*v.* **2** °carry out, °execute, °accomplish, °perform, °achieve, °(put into) effect, °bring about, °cause, °fulfill, °realize

implicate *v.* **1** °involve, °include, °associate, embroil, ensnare, entrap, enmesh, °entangle **2** °incriminate, inculpate, °connect, °involve, °associate, °suspect, °concern

implication *n.* **1** involvement, °connection, °inclusion, °association, entanglement **2** °suggestion, °hint, insinuation, °innuendo, intimation **3** °significance, purport, °drift, °meaning, denotation, conclusion, °inference, °import, connotation, °sense, °burden, °substance, °essence, °pith

implicit *adj.* **1** implied, °indirect, inferable, °understood, unspoken, undeclared, °tacit, °inherent, inferential, latent **2** °absolute, unquestioning, unquestioned, °unqualified, °total, °sheer, °complete, °unmitigated, unalloyed, °undiluted, °unlimited, unconditional, unreserved, utter, °full, °wholehearted

imply *v.* **1** °suggest, °hint (at), °intimate, °insinuate **2** connote, allude to, °refer to, advert to, °signify, °signal, betoken, °denote, °indicate, °mean, °express; °involve, °include, °evidence, °assume, °presume, °entail

impolite *adj.* °discourteous, °ill-mannered, uncivil, °rude, °ungracious, ungentlemanly, unladylike, °pert, °disrespectful, saucy, °boorish, churlish, °crude, indecorous, indelicate, °unrefined, ill-bred, °vulgar, °coarse

imponderable *adj.* unmeasurable, °inestimable, °inconceivable, °incomprehensible, °subtle

import *v.* **1** °introduce, °bring in **2** convey, °mean, °signify, °denote, °imply, betoken —*n.* **3** °meaning, °sense, denotation, signification, °gist, °drift, °thrust, °intention, °implication, purport, connotation, °suggestion, allusion, intimation **4** °importance, °significance, °weight, consequence, °moment, °substance

importance *n.* **1** °significance, consequence, °import, value, °worth, °weight, °account, °concern, °moment, °substance, °matter **2** eminence, °distinction, °esteem, °standing, °status, °position, °rank, °prominence, °preeminence, °prestige, °power, °influence, °note

important *adj.* **1** °significant, consequential, °critical, °material, °vital, °urgent, °portentous, °weighty, °grave, °substantial, °momentous, °signal **2** °leading, °prominent, °notable, °noted, °noteworthy, °worthy, °eminent, °distinguished, respected, high-ranking, top-level, high-level, °superior, °outstanding, °foremost, °conspicuous, °impressive **3** °influential, °effective, well-connected, °powerful, °formidable, °mighty, °impressive

impose *v.* **1** °inflict, °force, °foist **2** °interrupt, °interfere, °intrude, interpose, °insinuate **3** levy, °place, °put, °exact **4** ***impose on or upon.*** **(a)** saddle, °burden **(b)** °exploit, take advantage (of), °misuse

imposing *adj.* °grand, °magnificent, °impressive, °stately, august, °majestic, °effective, commanding

imposition *n.* **1** inflicting, infliction; applying, °application, enforcing, enforcement, levy, levying, promulgating, promulgation, introducing, introduction, placing, °placement, laying on **2** °burden, onus, °weight; intrusion, °misuse

impossible *adj.* **1** °hopeless, °impracticable, °inconceivable, unimaginable, °unthinkable, unattainable, unsuitable, °out of the question, unachievable, unrealizable, unworkable, unresolvable, unsolvable **2** °absurd, °ludicrous, °preposterous, °ridiculous, illogical, unworkable, °outrageous, °farcical, °outlandish, °crazy, °weird

impostor *n.* imposter, impersonator, °pretender, deceiver, °cheat, °fraud, °swindler, trickster, confidence man, shark, charlatan, mountebank, °hypocrite, *Colloq* con man, phoney *or US also* phony, tricky Dick, flimflam man, *US* fourflusher

impotence *n.* **1** °weakness, powerlessness, helplessness, °frailty, feebleness, enervation, debilitation **2** impotency, inadequacy, inefficacy, ineffectualness, ineffectiveness, ineptness, °incompetence **3** sterility, infertility

impotent *adj.* **1** °weak, °powerless, °helpless, °frail, °feeble, enervated, debilitated, °infirm **2** °inadequate, °ineffective, °ineffectual, °inept, °incompetent **3** °sterile, °barren, °infertile, infecund

impoverished *adj.* **1** °destitute, °poor, poverty-stricken, °penurious, beggared, °needy, necessitous, impecunious, in sore *or* bad straits, °straitened, in distress, badly off, bankrupt, °insolvent, ruined, *Colloq* (dead *or* flat *or* stony) broke, bad off, pinched, up against it, °on one's uppers, °short, *US* strapped, wiped out, *Slang Brit* skint **2** stripped, °barren, °desolate, wasted, °empty, depleted, denuded, drained, °exhausted

impracticable *adj.* **1** unworkable, infeasible *or* unfeasible, °impossible, unattainable, unachievable **2** unsuitable, unfit, unusable, °useless, °inapplicable

impractical *adj.* **1** °visionary, starry-eyed, °unrealistic, °romantic, °quixotic, °wild **2** °useless, °ineffective, °ineffectual, unworkable, unavailing, °impracticable

imprecise *adj.* °inexact, °inaccurate, °wrong, inexplicit, °indefinite, ill-defined, °indistinct, °vague, °hazy, cloudy, blurred, °fuzzy, °woolly, °ambiguous

impregnable *adj.* invulnerable, impenetrable, inviolable, unconquerable, °invincible, °unbeatable, °indomitable, °secure, °safe, °mighty, well-fortified

impregnate *v.* **1** °fertilize, inseminate, fecundate, make pregnant **2** imbue, °suffuse, °permeate, °penetrate, pervade, infuse, °saturate, °drench, °soak, °steep, °fill

impress *v.* **1** °affect, °touch, °move, °reach, °stir, °strike, °sway, °influence, °persuade, *Colloq* °grab, get under one's skin **2** °print, imprint, °stamp, °mark, °engrave, emboss **3** Often, ***impress on or upon.*** °stress, °emphasize, °urge, °bring home (to)

impression *n.* **1** °sensation, °feeling, °sense, °suspicion, awareness, consciousness, °idea, °belief, °fancy, °notion **2** °impact, °effect, °influence **3** dent, °indentation, °depression, °hollow, °mark; °stamp, °impress, °brand **4** printing, °issue, °print, °copy, °run **5** impersonation, °imitation; °parody, °satire, *Colloq* °takeoff, *Brit* sendup

impressionable *adj.* °suggestible, °susceptible, persuadable *or* persuasible, impressible, °receptive, °responsive

impressive *adj.* evocative, °moving, affecting, °stimulating, °exciting, °stirring, °powerful, °provocative, arousing, awe-inspiring, °awesome, °imposing, °formidable, °portentous, redoubtable

imprison *v.* incarcerate, confine, detain, remand, °jail, °lock up, intern, °shut up, put behind bars, put in *or* throw into irons, °put away, *Colloq Brit* °send down, *US* °send up (the river)

imprisonment *n.* incarceration, confinement, °detention, remand, °custody, *Literary* durance (vile)

improbable *adj.* °doubtful, dubious, °unlikely, °questionable, °unrealistic, °far-fetched, °remote, °implausible, °unthinkable, hard to believe *or* imagine, °inconceivable, °unbelievable, °fanciful, °incredible, °ridiculous, °ludicrous, °absurd, °crazy, °mad, °insane, °wild, °weird, °peculiar, °strange; °impossible; *Colloq* °fishy

improper *adj.* **1** °wrong, °mistaken, °erroneous, °false, °incorrect, °inaccurate, °inexact, °imprecise, °amiss, °faulty, °untrue, °irregular, °abnormal **2** unfit, unsuitable, °inappropriate, inapt, °inapplicable, infelicitous, °incongruous, unsuited, °unseemly, unbefitting, unfitting, uncalled-for, inapposite, malapropos, out of keeping, °out of place, °incompatible, °inopportune **3** indecorous, °indecent, indelicate, °immodest, °unseemly, °untoward, °unbecoming, °impolite, °suggestive, °risqué, °off-color, °obscene, °corrupt, °immoral, °sinful, °wicked, °lewd, °lascivious

impropriety *n.* **1** improperness, erroneousness, incorrectness, °falsity, falseness, inaccuracy, inaccurateness, inexactitude, inexactness, imprecision, impreciseness, irregularity, °abnormality **2** unfitness, unsuitableness, inappropriateness, inaptness, inapplicability, infelicity, infelicitousness, incongruity, incongruousness, unseemliness, incompatibility, inopportuneness **3** indecorousness, bad *or* poor taste, indecency, °indelicacy, immodesty, unseemliness, suggestiveness, immorality, sinfulness, wickedness, lewdness, lasciviousness **4** °slip, °blunder, °mistake, °error, gaffe, gaucherie, faux pas

improve *v.* **1** °better, ameliorate, upgrade, uplift, °amend, °enhance, °fix up, °reform, °redeem, °rehabilitate, redress, °repair, °correct, °rectify, put *or* set right, emend; °modernize, update, °refurbish, recondition, °renovate, °repair, °overhaul, remodel **2** °develop, °increase, °advance, °promote, °further, °benefit; °look up, °recover, °pick up, *Colloq* give a new lease of *or US* on life, take a turn for the better, *US* take a new lease on life **3** °convalesce, °recuperate, °recover, get better, °mend, °rally, °(make) progress, gain (strength *or* ground), °revive

improvement *n.* **1** betterment, amelioration; °reform, rehabilitation, upgrading, enhancement, °repair **2** °recovery, °rise, °increase, °gain, °advance, upswing, °progress; recuperation, convalescence **3** °advance, change for the better

improvident *adj.* **1** °shortsighted, °imprudent, °wasteful, °profligate, °prodigal, °spendthrift, °extravagant, °lavish, °profuse, happy-go-lucky, penny-wise and pound-foolish, uneconomic(al), thriftless **2** incautious, °unwary, °rash, °reckless, °impulsive, °impetuous, headlong, °heedless, °careless, °unthinking, unthoughtful, unmindful

improvise *n.* **1** ad-lib, extemporize, *Colloq* play (it) by ear, fake it, wing it **2** °invent, concoct, °devise, contrive, jury-rig; °make do

imprudent *adj.* °indiscreet, °impulsive, °rash, °reckless, °hasty, incautious, °impetuous, °improvident, °careless, °heedless, °foolhardy, °irresponsible, injudicious, ill-judged, °thoughtless, ill-considered, °ill-advised, inadvisable, unwise, inexpedient, °foolish, °mad, °crazy, °insane, °inane, °silly, °perverse, °wrong, wrongheaded

impudence *n.* °impertinence, °effrontery, insolence, °disrespect, °presumption, presumptuousness, audacity, shamelessness, pertness, sauciness, boldness, brazenness, °incivility, rudeness, impoliteness, *Colloq* lip, °gall, guff, °sauce, °mouth, *Brit* backchat, °side, *US* back talk, *Slang* chutzpah

impudent *adj.* °shameless, °impertinent, °insolent, °disrespectful, °forward, °presumptuous, °audacious, °pert, saucy, °bold, °brazen, °cocky, cocksure, °arrogant, uncivil, °ill-mannered, °rude, °impolite, *Colloq* °fresh, °brassy, °cheeky

impulsive *n.* °impetuous, °emotional, unpredictable, °unpremeditated, unplanned, spur-of-the-moment, °extemporaneous, unconsidered, °offhand, °instinctive, °involuntary, °spontaneous, °quick, °sudden, °precipitate, °immediate, °snap, °rash, headlong, °reckless, devil-may-care, °foolhardy, madcap, °wild

impure *adj.* **1** °dirty, soiled, unclean, sullied, tainted, polluted, defiled, °foul, °filthy, feculent, infected, scummy, °putrid, putrescent, °rotten **2** °mixed, alloyed, contaminated, adulterated, debased, °unrefined **3** unclean, unhallowed, forbidden, disallowed, *Judaism* tref **4** °unchaste, °immoral, °sinful, °wicked, °evil, °vile, unvirtuous, unvirginal, corrupted, defiled, debased, vitiated, °degenerate, depraved, °loose, °wanton, °lustful, °promiscuous, libidinous, °dissolute, licentious, °obscene, °prurient, °dirty, °filthy, lubricous *or* lubricious, salacious, °lascivious, °lewd, °lecherous

impurity *n.* **1** °pollution, contamination, defilement, adulteration, dirtiness, uncleanness, foulness **2** Often, ***impurities.*** °dirt, contaminant, pollutant, °pollution, smut, °filth, foreign matter *or* body **3** unchastity, immorality, sinfulness, wickedness, °evil, vileness, corruption, degeneration, depravity, looseness, wantonness, °lust, lustfulness, promiscuity, promiscuousness, libidinousness, dissoluteness, licentiousness, obscenity, prurience, dirtiness, filthiness, lubricity, salaciousness, lasciviousness, lewdness, lecherousness

imputation *n.* °charge, indictment, °accusation, °allegation, °challenge, censure, °blame, reproach, °slur, °aspersion, °attribution, ascription, insinuation, °implication, °innuendo

impute *v.* ascribe, °assign, °attribute, °credit, °charge, put *or* set down to; °insinuate, °imply, °suggest, hint at

inability *n.* incapacity, incapability, °incompetence, unfitness, ineptness, °ineptitude, unqualifiedness, °impotence

inaccessible *adj.* **1** unavailable, unobtainable, unattainable, unreachable, °unapproachable **2** impenetrable, impassable, °out-of-the-way

inaccurate *adj.* °wrong, °incorrect, °erroneous, °mistaken, °inexact, °imprecise, °faulty, °flawed, °imperfect, °amiss, awry, °false, fallacious, illogical, °unsound, *Colloq* off the mark, off the beam, °cold, *Chiefly US* all wet, *US* (way) off base, *Slang* cockeyed, full of hot air

inactive *adj.* **1** °passive, placid, °quiet, °tranquil, quiescent, °serene, °peaceful, pacific, resting, unmoving, motionless, immobile, immobilized, °still, °inert, °lifeless, °inanimate, sluggish, °listless, °lethargic, °lackadaisical, languid, °indolent, °lazy, °torpid, somnolent, °idle, °slothful, °supine **2** nonfunctioning, inoperative, °dormant; unoccupied, °idle, °unemployed, jobless, °out of work, out of a job

inactivity *n.* **1** passiveness *or* passivity, placidity *or* placidness, °quiet, tranquillity, °serenity, °peace, peacefulness; motionlessness, immobility, stillness, °inertia, inertness, lifelessness, °sluggishness, listlessness, °lethargy, languidness, °indolence, laziness, °torpor, somnolence, °idleness, slothfulness, °sloth **2** inaction, quiescence;

hibernation, estivation *or esp. Brit* aestivation

inadequate *adj.* **1** °insufficient, °deficient, not enough, too little, °scarce, °meager, °scanty, skimpy, °sparse, °(in) short (supply); °unsatisfactory, °imperfect, °incomplete, °defective, unsuitable, °disappointing, °flawed, °faulty **2** ***inadequate to.*** unsuited to *or* for, unfit for, unqualified for, not up to, unequal to, °unworthy of, inapt for, inept for, °incapable of

inadmissible *adj.* disallowed, unallowable, unallowed, forbidden, °unacceptable, prohibited, unsuitable, unsuited, °unqualified, °inappropriate, °inapplicable, °improper, objectionable, °exceptionable, °incorrect, °wrong

inadvertent *adj.* **1** unintentional, unintended, °unpremeditated, °accidental, °unthinking, unwitting, °chance; °unconscious, unplanned, unstudied, undesigned, uncalculated **2** °careless, °inattentive, negligent, °heedless, unobservant

inalienable *adj.* untransferable, intransferable, °absolute, °inherent, unconsignable, sacrosanct, inviolable, nonnegotiable, unnegotiable, unchallengeable, *Law* imprescriptible, entailed, indefeasible

inane *adj.* °silly, asinine, °vapid, °vacant, vacuous, °absurd, fatuous, °foolish, °senseless, °nonsensical, °unreasonable, °preposterous, °ludicrous, °ridiculous, laughable, risible, °mad, lunatic, °crazy, °stupid, °dumb, idiotic, moronic, imbecilic, *Colloq* nutty, nuts, °daft, daffy, screwy, batty, dippy, wacky, cuckoo, loony, goofy, *Brit* bonkers, dotty

inanimate *adj.* °lifeless, motionless, immobile, unmoving, °inactive, °inert, °still, spiritless, soulless, °cold, °dead, °defunct

inapplicable *adj.* °inappropriate, unsuitable, unsuited, inapt, °irrelevant, °unrelated, unconnected, inapposite, beside the point *or* question, °extraneous, off the mark, *Colloq US* off base

inappropriate *adj.* °improper, unfitting, unfit, unsuitable, unsuited, unbefitting, °incompatible, malapropos, ungermane, inapt, inapposite, out of keeping, °incongruous, infelicitous, °inopportune, untimely, °irrelevant, °inapplicable

inarticulate *adj.* **1** °disjointed, unconnected, °incoherent, °incomprehensible, jumbled, unintelligible, unclear, illogical, °discursive, °rambling, scrambled, °wild, irrational, muddled, mixed-up, °confused, digressive **2** mumbled, garbled, blurred, muffled, muttered, faltering, °halting, °indistinct, unclear, unintelligible **3** °speechless, °tongue-tied, °(struck) dumb, °mute, voiceless

inattentive *n.* unobservant, °heedless, °careless, negligent, neglectful, °indifferent, uncaring, apathetic, °slack, °remiss, unconcerned, °detached, unmindful, distracted, distrait(e), °absent-minded, abstracted, in a brown study, daydreaming, oscitant, woolgathering, musing, °oblivious, (with one's head) in the clouds, in a world of one's own

inaudible *adj.* unheard, °imperceptible, °indistinct, °low, °faint, muted, °quiet, °soft, muffled, stifled

inaugurate *v.* **1** °initiate, °begin, °commence, enter upon, °start, °introduce, usher in, °institute, °launch, °originate, °set up, get under way, get going **2** °install, °induct, °invest, °establish, instate

inauspicious *adj.* °unpromising, unlucky, °unfortunate, unfavorable, unpropitious, °untoward, ill-starred, °ominous, ill-omened, ill-fated, °portentous, °menacing, °doomed, °sinister, °dark, °gloomy, cloudy, clouded, °black

inborn *adj.* innate, congenital, °inherent, inherited, °hereditary, inbred, °natural, °native, constitutional, deep-seated, deep-rooted, °ingrained, instinctive *or* instinctual, *Technical* connate

incandescent *adj.* °glowing, red-hot, white-hot, alight, aflame, °flaming, °burning, °fiery, candent, flaring

incapable *adj.* **1** Often, ***incapable of.*** °unable (to), °powerless (to), °incompetent (of), unfit (to), °unqualified (to), °impotent (to), unequal to, not up to **2** ***incapable of.*** insusceptible to, °resistant to, impervious to, ill-disposed to, disinclined to, not open to

incapacitate *v.* disable, °cripple, °paralyze, °lame, °wound, °maim, °impair, °weaken, enfeeble, °enervate, °exhaust, devitalize; immobilize, inactivate, deactivate, put out of action, indispose

incentive *n.* °incitement, °impetus, °encouragement, goad, °prod, °provocation, °spur, impulse, °enticement, °lure, °inducement, stimulus, motivation, *Colloq* carrot

incidence *n.* frequency, °rate, °degree, °extent, °occurrence, °prevalence; °quantity, °amount, °number

incident *n.* **1** °event, °occasion, °occurrence, °proceeding, °circumstance, °fact, °happening, °experience, °episode **2** °disturbance, °scene, °affair, °upset, commotion, °fracas, °skirmish, set-to, *Colloq* to-do, do

incidental *adj.* **1** °casual, °chance, fortuitous, aleatory, °random, °haphazard, serendipitous, unpredictable, °accidental, adventitious, unplanned, unlooked-for, *Colloq* fluky **2** °subordinate, °secondary, ancillary, °minor, lesser, °nonessential, unimportant, trivial, °negligible, °inconsequential, °insignificant, °petty, °trifling, °paltry

incidentally *adv.* **1** °by the way, by the bye, apropos (of), parenthetically **2** casually, as luck would have it, accidentally, °by chance, perchance

incision *n.* °cut, °gash, °slit, °slash

incisive *adj.* **1** °keen, °sharp, °acute, °piercing, perspicacious, °perceptive, percipient, °penetrating, °trenchant, canny, °shrewd **2** °sarcastic, °biting, mordant, °cutting, °caustic, °sardonic, ironic(al), °sharp, acid, °tart, acrid, acrimonious, °bitter, acerbic, cynical, stinging, °critical

incite *v.* °stimulate, °inspire, °prompt,

°move, °stir, stir *or* whip *or* work up, bestir, °excite, °fire, exhort, °agitate, °foment, °inflame, °provoke, °rally, goad, °spur, °prick, °prod, °drive, °push, egg on, °encourage, °urge, °influence, °wake, waken, °awaken, °rouse, °arouse

incitement *n.* **1** stimulation, instigating, spurring, urging, influencing, awakening, wakening, arousing, prodding, prompting, °stirring, °whipping, °exciting, firing, exhorting, agitating, fomenting, inflaming, firing, provoking, rallying, goading, pricking, needling **2** stimulus, °incentive, °inducement, °enticement, °temptation, impulse, motivation, °influence, instigation, °provocation, °inspiration, °persuasion, exhortation, °agitation, fomentation, °inflammation, arousal, °encouragement, °excitement

incivility *n.* rudeness, boorishness, coarseness, discourtesy, uncourtliness, unmannerliness, indecorum, indecorousness, discourteousness, impoliteness, tactlessness, ungentlemanliness, bad breeding, ill breeding, bad manners, °misbehavior

inclement *adj.* °extreme, intemperate, °severe, °harsh, rigorous; °stormy, °violent, rainy, squally, blustery, °raw, °bad, °tempestuous

inclination *n.* **1** °bow, bowing, °bend, bending, °nod, °nodding, °tilt, tilting **2** °slope, °slant, °angle, °bend, °incline, °tilt **3** °disposition, predisposition, °tendency, °bent, °bias, °leaning, °preference, °turn, °cast, proclivity, propensity, °attitude, proneness, susceptibility, predilection, °partiality, °affection, °taste, °liking, °desire, velleity **4** °desire, °longing, craving, °appetite, °taste, °stomach, °sympathy, predilection, °penchant, °fancy, °eagerness, °enthusiasm, zeal, °fervor, °ardor

incline *v.* **1** °tend, °lean, °bend, °bow, °slant, °tilt, °angle, bank, °slope, ascend, °rise, °descend **2** °dispose, °influence, °persuade, predispose, °make, °lead, °prejudice, °bias **3** °tend, °lean, gravitate, show favor *or* preference, be attracted to, be biased *or* prejudiced, have a mind; be disposed *or* predisposed, °lean, °tend —*n.* **4** °slope, °pitch, °grade, gradient, °slant, °ramp, °hill, °dip, descent, declivity, °rise, ascent, acclivity

inclined *adj.* **1** tending, °disposed, predisposed, °prone, °willing, °keen, °eager, *Colloq* of a mind **2** °likely, apt, °liable, minded, °prone **3** sloping, slanting, °leaning, bending, tilting, gravitating, °bearing, verging

include *v.* **1** °incorporate, °embody, comprise, °embrace, °cover, encompass, °take in, subsume, °comprehend, °contain **2** classify, °categorize, °group, °file, °list, catalog, °tabulate, °register **3** °involve, °count, °number, allow for

inclusion *n.* incorporation, involvement, counting, numbering, grouping, classification

inclusive *adj.* **1** °comprehensive, °general, all-encompassing, °wide, °broad, °extensive, °full, °umbrella, blanket, across-the-board, all-in-one, unified **2** ***inclusive of.*** including, embracing, comprising, taking in, covering, incorporating, embodying

incognito *adj.* **1** °unknown, disguised, concealed, °unidentified, in disguise, unrecognizable, unrecognized —*adv.* **2** unrecognizably, in disguise, °secretly, °on the sly, under cover, clandestinely

incoherent *adj.* °confused, garbled, mixed up, disordered, jumbled, muddled, scrambled, °rambling, illogical, irrational, °wild, unstructured, disjoined, °disconnected, °disjointed, °loose, unconnected, uncoordinated, unintelligible, °inarticulate

incombustible *adj.* °nonflammable, noninflammable, fireproof, noncombustible; flameproof

income *n.* °return, revenue(s), °receipts, °proceeds, profit(s), gain(s), takings

incoming *adj.* **1** arriving, entering **2** °new, entering

incomparable *adj.* beyond compare, unequaled, °matchless, °peerless, inimitable, °unparalleled, unrivaled, °nonpareil, °transcendent, °surpassing, °supreme, °superior, °superlative, unsurpassed, unsurpassable

incompatible *adj.* °mismatched, unsuited, °discordant, clashing, jarring, °inconsistent, °contradictory, conflicting, uncongenial, irreconcilable, °incongruous; antithetic, °opposed, °opposite, °contrary, antipathetic, antagonistic, °hostile

incompetence *n.* °inability, incapacity, inadequacy, insufficiency, deficiency, °ineptitude, inefficiency, uselessness, faultiness

incompetent *adj.* °unqualified, unfit, °unable, °incapable, unskilled, unskillful, °inept, maladroit, inexpert, °awkward, floundering, °clumsy, bungling, gauche, °useless, °inadequate, °insufficient, °ineffective, °ineffectual, °inefficient

incomplete *adj.* unfinished, °undone, °imperfect, °undeveloped, °deficient, °defective, unaccomplished, °partial, °sketchy, °crude, °rough, °fragmentary, fragmented, °piecemeal

incomprehensible *adj.* unintelligible, unfathomable, impenetrable, °deep, abstruse, arcane, °recondite, indecipherable, undecipherable, inscrutable, °cryptic, °obscure, °opaque, °dark, °occult, °perplexing, °mysterious, mystifying, enigmatic, °puzzling, over (someone's) head, baffling, unimaginable, °inconceivable

inconceivable *adj.* °incredible, °unbelievable, °unthinkable, unimaginable, °incomprehensible, °unheard-of, undreamt-of, unthought-of, °impossible, °overwhelming, staggering, *Colloq* mind-boggling

inconclusive *adj.* °indecisive, °unresolved, °indefinite, °unsettled, °open, indeterminate, °in limbo, *Colloq* up in the air

incongruous *adj.* °inconsistent, inharmonious, disharmonious, °discordant, dissonant, disconsonant, °incoherent, °incompatible, incongruent, conflicting, °unbecoming, °unseemly, unsuited, unsuitable, unapt, °inappropriate, misallied, unfitting, unfit, °improper, malapropos, unmeet, °absurd, discrepant, disparate, °different, °divergent, disagreeing, °contrary, °contradictory, °paradoxical, out of step, out of keeping, out of line

inconsequential *adj.* unimportant, °insignificant, trivial, °trifling, nugatory, inconsiderable, inappreciable, °negligible, °minor, °paltry, °petty, °immaterial, °slight, lightweight, °worthless, *Colloq* piddling

inconsiderate *adj.* °thoughtless, unthoughtful, °unthinking, unconcerned, uncaring, unmindful, °heedless, unheeding, insensitive, °unsympathetic, °tactless, °intolerant, °rude, °ungracious

inconsistent *adj.* **1** See **incongruous. 2** °irregular, °capricious, °fickle, °erratic, °inconstant, uneven, unpredictable, °unreliable, undependable, °unstable, unsteady, °changeable, °variable

inconsolable *adj.* disconsolate, brokenhearted, °heartbroken, °desolate, °forlorn, despairing, °miserable, °wretched, griefstricken

inconspicuous *adj.* unnoticeable, °unnoticed, °unobtrusive, unostentatious, °insignificant, °indefinite, °indistinguishable, °undistinguished; °modest, unassuming, °discreet

inconstancy *n.* changeableness, fickleness, irregularity, mutability, variability, unsteadiness, unsteadfastness, capriciousness, volatility, mercurialness *or* mercuriality, inconsistency, unreliability; faithlessness, unfaithfulness

inconstant *adj.* °changeable, mutable, °fickle, °capricious, mercurial, °volatile, vacillating, unsteady, unsteadfast, °irresolute, °unreliable, undependable, fluctuating, wavering, °erratic, °inconsistent, °flighty, °unstable, °unsettled, °fitful, °vague, °indefinite, °variable, °moody

incontinent *adj.* **1** unrestrained, unconstrained, unrestricted, °uncontrolled, uncontrollable, ungoverned, °ungovernable, unbridled, uncurbed **2** °lecherous, libidinous, °lascivious, °libertine, °lustful, °lewd, debauched, °wanton, °dissolute, °loose, lubricous *or* lubricious, salacious, °profligate, °obscene, °dirty, °filthy **3** self-soiling, bedwetting, *Medical* enuretic

incontrovertible *adj.* irrefutable, °indisputable, indubitable, undeniable, incontestable, °unquestionable, °sure, °certain, °definite, °definitive, established, °absolute, °positive

inconvenience *n.* **1** °disadvantage, °discomfort, °pain, °trouble, °bother, °annoyance, °nuisance, awkwardness, °disturbance, disruption, °burden, °drawback, °hindrance, °impediment, °difficulty, °upset **2** cumbersomeness, unwieldiness, burdensomeness, onerousness, troublesomeness, disadvantageousness, awkwardness, inappropriateness, untimeliness —*v.* **3** discommode, °trouble, incommode, °disturb, °disrupt, °upset, °put out, °bother, °annoy, °irritate, °irk

inconvenient *adj.* cumbersome, °unwieldy, °burdensome, onerous, °troublesome, bothersome, annoying, irritating, °irksome, °unsettling, °disturbing, upsetting, disrupting, disadvantageous, °awkward, °inappropriate; inexpedient, °inopportune, untimely, ill-timed

incorporate *v.* °embody, °include, °combine, comprise, °embrace, °integrate, consolidate, °unite, °amalgamate, assimilate, coalesce, °unify; °merge, °mix, °blend

incorrect *adj.* °wrong, °mistaken, °inaccurate, °untrue, °imprecise, °inexact, °erroneous, fallacious, °specious; °improper, °false, °faulty

incorrigible *adj.* °bad, °naughty, °villainous, °wicked, °sinful, °hopeless; intractable, unchangeable, unalterable, °habitual, inveterate, °incurable, °stubborn, hardened, obdurate, °inflexible, uncontrollable

incorrupt *adj.* **1** °moral, °upright, °righteous, °pure, upstanding, °honorable, °good, °virtuous, °honest, straightforward, °straight, unimpeachable, incorruptible, undefiled, °impeccable, °spotless, °immaculate, °faultless, °flawless **2** error-free, °correct, uncorrupted

increase *v.* **1** °grow, °swell, °enlarge, dilate, wax, °expand, °extend, distend, °inflate, augment, snowball, °enhance, °heighten, °raise, °develop, multiply, burgeon *or* bourgeon, °flourish, °proliferate, °spread, broaden, °widen, °lengthen, *Colloq* jack up **2** °prolong, °advance, °further, °improve, °better, °strengthen —*n.* **3** °growth, enlargement, °expansion, °extension, augmentation, enhancement, °development, multiplication, °proliferation, °spread **4** °addition, °increment, escalation, inflation, °gain, °rise, °boost **5** ***on the increase.*** waxing, developing, growing, expanding, increasing, escalating, on the rise, proliferating, spreading

incredible *adj.* **1** °unbelievable, beyond belief, °inconceivable, unimaginable, °unthinkable, °improbable, °implausible, °far-fetched, °absurd, °preposterous, °ridiculous, °unlikely, °impossible, °unrealistic, °unreal, °fictitious, mythic(al) **2** °extraordinary, astounding, astonishing, °amazing, wonderful, awe-inspiring, °awesome, tremendous, °marvelous, °prodigious, *Colloq* far-out, *US* humongous

incredulous *adj.* disbelieving, °unbelieving, dubious, °doubtful, °skeptical, mistrustful, °distrustful, °suspicious

increment *n.* °increase, °addition, °gain, accrual *or chiefly Brit* accrument, augmentation

incriminate *v.* °accuse, °charge, °blame, °implicate, inculpate, °indict, °impeach, °involve, °entangle, *Colloq* point the finger at, *Chiefly US* °put the finger on, *Slang US* °finger

incubate *v.* °hatch, °brood; °nurse, nurture, °develop

incumbent *adj.* **1** °obligatory, °necessary,

required, °mandatory, compulsory, binding, °demanding, commanding, prescribed **2** officeholding —*n.* **3** officeholder, °official, °occupant

incur *v.* bring upon *or* on (oneself), °draw, °attract, °arouse, °provoke, invite, expose (oneself) to, lay (oneself) open to

incurable *adj.* **1** irremediable, °terminal, inoperable, °fatal, °hopeless **2** °hopeless, inveterate, °habitual, °incorrigible, dyed-in-the-wool, unflagging, °relentless, irredeemable; irreparable, unrectifiable

indebted *adj.* obligated, owing, °obliged, °beholden, °bound, °liable, °responsible

indecent *adj.* **1** indecorous, indelicate, °immodest, °improper, °unbecoming, unsuitable, unfit, °inappropriate; in bad taste **2** °unseemly, °shameless, °shameful, °offensive, °outrageous, °repellent, °repulsive, °distasteful, °ill-mannered, °rude, °suggestive, °coarse, °risqué, °vulgar, °blue, °obscene, °gross, °rank, °prurient, °dirty, °foul, °filthy, °pornographic, ithyphallic, scatological, salacious, °lascivious, licentious, °lewd, lubricous *or* lubricious, smutty, °vile, °degenerate, debauched

indecision *n.* hesitation, wavering, indecisiveness, vacillation, irresolution, uncertainty, ambivalence, shilly-shally *or* shilly-shallying, °fluctuation, tergiversation

indecisive *adj.* **1** hesitating, °hesitant, wavering, °doubtful, vacillating, undecided, °irresolute, °uncertain, °of two minds, ambivalent, shilly-shallying, °wishy-washy, namby-pamby, fluctuating, tergiversating **2** °indefinite, indeterminate, undecided, °inconclusive, °open, °unsettled, °moot, °doubtful

indeed *adv.* **1** certainly, °surely, to be sure, doubtless(ly), °undoubtedly, undeniably, °definitely, °positively, °absolutely, °exactly, just so, °actually, °truly, truthfully, °seriously, (all) joking aside, in (point of) fact, °of course, °really, °in reality, to be realistic, °naturally, upon my word, on my honor, on my oath, *Brit* °rather, *Colloq* no kidding **2** what is more, °still, not to say, as a matter of fact, if the truth be known, to say the least —*interj.* **3** Is that so!, You don't say!, Really!, By George!, By Jove!, (Upon) my word!, My goodness!, Goodness!, Gracious!, Mercy!, Good Lord!, Good heavens!, My stars!, Fancy that!, Imagine (that)!, Well, I'll be (damned)!, *Colloq Brit* Blimey!, Cor!, Crikey!

indefinite *adj.* **1** °uncertain, undetermined, undefined, °imprecise, °inexact, inexplicit, unspecified, °unsettled, unfixed, unspecific, nonspecific, °vague, °general, indeterminate, undecided, sub judice **2** °vague, unclear, °obscure, °confused, confusing, °puzzling, baffling, °cryptic, bewildering, mystifying, °equivocal, °ambiguous, unspecific, nonspecific, inexplicit, °inexact, °imprecise **3** ill-defined, undefined, blurred, blurry, °hazy, °indistinct, °obscure, °dim, °fuzzy, unrecognizable, °indistinguishable **4** °unlimited, °unknown, uncounted, uncountable, undefinable, indeterminate, indeterminable, unbounded, °boundless, °immeasurable, incalculable, °limitless, °endless, °infinite **5** °hesitant, °vague, shilly-shallying, vacillating, °indecisive, undecided, °inconstant, wavering, unsure, °uncertain, *Colloq* °wishy-washy

indelible *adj.* ineradicable *or* uneradicable *or* noneradicable, inerasable *or* unerasable *or* nonerasable, ineffaceable, inexpungible, °indestructible, uncancelable *or* noncancelable, °enduring, °permanent, °lasting, °fixed, °ingrained, inextirpable

indelicacy *n.* coarseness, crudeness, roughness, °vulgarity, boorishness, churlishness, offensiveness, rudeness, immodesty, indecency, shamelessness; °incivility, indecorum, inelegance, uncourtliness, unmannerliness, impoliteness, unrefinement, unseemliness, tastelessness, bad *or* poor taste, grossness

indemnity *n.* **1** compensation, repayment, reimbursement, °remuneration, recompense, °consideration, °restitution, reparation(s), redress, indemnification, °return, quid pro quo, °restoration, °award, °reward, °payment, disbursement, °amends, °requital, °atonement, °reckoning, quittance **2** °insurance, °protection, °security, °safety, °guarantee, °assurance, underwriting, °warrant, °endorsement, certification; °exemption, impunity, °privilege

indentation *n.* °notch, dent, °nick, °cut, °score, °mark, °depression, °impression, °hollow, dimple, °pit; *Typography* indention

independence *n.* **1** °freedom, °liberty, autonomy, °sovereignty, self-rule, home rule, self-determination, °self-government, self-direction, autarchy **2** °confidence, °self-confidence, self-sufficiency, self-reliance, self-assurance

independent *adj.* **1** °free, self-governing, autonomous, °sovereign **2** unrestrained, unrestricted, unfettered, untrammeled, unregulated, °uncontrolled, separate(d), unconnected, °disconnected, °unrelated, °distinct **3** self-reliant, °self-sufficient, self-assured, (self-)confident, °bold, individualistic, °competent **4** °voluntary, °nonpartisan, °spontaneous, °unsolicited, unbidden, °unprejudiced, unbiased, °nonaligned, unaligned, °disinterested, °neutral **5** °unlimited, unrestricted, affluent, °self-sufficient; unearned **6** unallied, unaffiliated, uncommitted, individualistic, undecided **7** °outside, °external, unaffiliated, nonaffiliated, unconnected, °disinterested **8** ***independent of.*** °irrespective of, disregarding, °notwithstanding, ignoring, excluding; °exclusive of, °except for, °barring, °apart from, °besides, beyond, *US* aside from —*n.* **9** °individual, °nonconformist, maverick, *Colloq* loner

indestructible *adj.* °durable, long-lasting, °everlasting, °eternal, °endless, °perennial, °permanent, °fixed, unchanging, °changeless, unchangeable, °indelible, ineradicable, inextirpable, immutable, unalterable, °constant, undying, nonperishable, imperishable; unbreakable, nonbreakable, shatterproof

index *n.* **1** °guide, directory, °list, listing, table of contents, catalogue, °key, °thesaurus **2** °mark, °sign, °clue, °token, °hint, °pointer, °indicator, °indication, °guide **3** index finger, forefinger, first finger; °pointer, marker, needle, *Chiefly Brit typography* °hand, *Chiefly US typography* fist **4** °ratio, °measure, °formula, °factor

indicate *v.* **1** °point out, °point to, °mark, °specify, °designate, °indicate; call *or* direct attention to, °show **2** °imply, °suggest, betoken, °manifest, °signify, bespeak, °reveal, evince, °evidence, °denote **3** °suggest, °hint, °imply, °intimate; °say, °express, °state, °disclose, °tell, °make known, make clear, °register, °show, °display, °exhibit **4** °call for, °require, °demand, °need, °recommend

indication *n.* **1** °sign, °signal, °token, °suggestion, °hint, intimation, °inkling, °clue, °implication, °symptom **2** reading, °measure, °degree **3** °omen, portent, forewarning, °warning, augury, foreshadowing, foretoken **4** ***indications.*** °evidence, °data, clues, signs

indicative of *adj.* signifying, indicating, indicatory of, suggesting, °suggestive of, hinting (at), symptomatic of, denotative of, characteristic of, typical of, typifying

indicator *n.* °pointer, needle; °gauge, meter, °display

indict *v.* Often, ***indict for.*** charge (with), accuse (of *or* with), arraign (for), incriminate (in *or* for), inculpate (in *or* for), cite (for *or* with), °denounce (for), blame (for *or* with); °summon, summons, subpoena

indifference *n.* **1** unconcern, apathy, listlessness, disinterest, coolness, nonchalance, insouciance, aloofness, °detachment, °disregard, inattention, pococuranteism *or* pococurantism, coldness, phlegm, stolidity, callousness, insensibility, impassiveness *or* impassivity **2** unimportance, insignificance, irrelevance, unconcern, inconsequence, °triviality **3** dispassion, disinterestedness, impartiality, neutrality, °objectivity, fairness, equitableness, evenhandedness

indifferent *adj.* **1** unconcerned, apathetic, uncaring, °listless, °disinterested, uninterested, °cool, °nonchalant, °lukewarm, °lackadaisical, laodicean, °dispassionate, insouciant, °aloof, °detached, °distant, removed, °inattentive, pococurante, °cold, °phlegmatic, °stolid, °callous, unemotional, uncompassionate, insensitive, unfeeling, °inconsiderate, °unsympathetic, °insensible, °impassive **2** °impartial, °neutral, °just, evenhanded, °objective, °fair, °equitable, unbiased, °unprejudiced, °nonpartisan, nondiscriminatory, °dispassionate, °disinterested **3** °neutral, °average, °mediocre, °fair, °undistinguished, uninspired, lightweight, °passable, middling, °ordinary, commonplace, °everyday, °so-so, not bad; °poor, °inferior, not very *or* particularly *or* especially good, *Slang Brit* naff **4** unimportant, °insignificant, trivial, °trifling, nugatory, °immaterial, °inconsequential, °minor, inappreciable, °slight, neither here nor there

indigenous *adj.* **1** °native, °local, autochthonous, endemic, °natural, °aboriginal, °original **2** innate, °inborn, inbred, °inherent

indigent *adj.* °needy, °poor, °destitute, poverty-stricken, in want, penniless, °impoverished, °penurious, impecunious, necessitous, *Colloq* (dead *or* flat *or* stony) broke, °hard up, °short, °on one's uppers, *Brit* skint, *US* strapped

indigestion *n.* dyspepsia, upset stomach, stomach distress; stomach ache, gastralgia

indignant *adj.* provoked, exasperated, °disgruntled, piqued, irked, irritated, annoyed, vexed, °angry, °furious, irate, angered, enraged, incensed, wrathful, in high dudgeon, in a temper, in a rage, in a pet, *Literary* wroth, *Colloq* peeved, riled, °in a huff, huffy, miffed, °mad, livid, °sore, *US* teed-off, *Slang* pissed off

indignation *n.* °anger, °fury, °rage, wrath, exasperation, irritation, °annoyance, vexation, °resentment, *Literary* ire, choler

indignity *n.* °insult, affront, °outrage, °injury, °offense, °humiliation, °disrespect, °slight, °dishonor, snub, obloquy, contumely, °scorn, reproach, °abuse, discourtesy, °aspersion, *Colloq* °slap (in the face)

indirect *adj.* **1** °roundabout, circuitous, circumambient, °devious, °tortuous, zigzag, winding, °rambling, roving, wandering, °erratic, °meandering, ambagious, °crooked, °oblique, twisted, twisting; circumlocutory, periphrastic **2** °secondary, °incidental, ancillary, collateral, °accidental, °side, °subordinate, °subsidiary, °accessory, additional, adscititious, adventitious

indiscreet *adj.* °imprudent, °tactless, incautious, impolitic, undiplomatic, °improvident, injudicious, °ill-advised, ill-judged, ill-considered, °rash, °reckless, °audacious, °bold, temerarious, °impulsive, °hasty, °impetuous, °thoughtless, insensitive, °heedless, °careless, °unthinking, °mindless, unwise, naive *or* naïve, °foolish, °foolhardy

indiscretion *n.* **1** imprudence, tactlessness, improvidence, injudiciousness, rashness, recklessness, audacity, boldness, temerity, impulsiveness, hastiness, °haste, impetuousness, impetuosity, thoughtlessness, insensitivity, heedlessness, carelessness, naiveté *or* naïveté *or* naivety, foolishness, foolhardiness, °folly **2** °blunder, °error, °mistake, °slip, °lapse, °misstep, gaffe, faux pas, °peccadillo, *Colloq* boner, *Brit* bloomer

indiscriminate *adj.* **1** undiscriminating, unselective, unparticular, uncritical, undiscerning, °careless, °promiscuous, °random **2** °confused, °haphazard, unorganized, °chaotic, disorganized, jumbled, disordered, disarranged, scrambled, mixed-up, °casual, °random, unsystematic, unsystematized, uncoordinated, unmethodical, wholesale, °erratic, *Colloq* higgledy-piggledy

indispensable *adj.* **1** °crucial, °vital, °essential, °urgent, °imperative, °necessary, needed, needful, required, requisite, demanded, °in demand, called for, °of the essence, °important, compelling **2** °key, °unavoidable, inescapable, ineluctable, compulsory, °mandatory, sine qua non, °obligatory

indisposed *adj.* **1** °ill, ailing, unwell, °sick, °sickly, °unsound, °unhealthy, in bad health, valetudinarian, out of commission, *Colloq* on the sick list, °(doing) poorly, laid up, in a bad way, not up to snuff, off one's feed *or Brit also* grub, °under the weather **2** °averse, °disinclined, °loath, unwilling, °reluctant, °resistant, °hesitant

indisputable *adj.* °unquestionable, °incontrovertible, incontestable, irrefutable, undeniable, indubitable, beyond doubt, °sure, °certain, °positive, °definite, °definitive, °absolute, °fixed

indistinct *adj.* **1** °faint, °dim, °obscure, °vague, blurred, blurry, °filmy, °hazy, °misty, bleary, °shadowy, °fuzzy, foggy, °murky, °muddy, unclear, indiscernible, °illegible, muffled, unintelligible, °indistinguishable, indeterminate, °confused, °indefinite **2** °indistinguishable, °ambiguous, not distinct, °equivocal, inseparable, ill-defined, undefined, °nebulous, °vague, °confused

indistinguishable *adj.* **1** Often, ***indistinguishable from.*** undifferentiated (from), °identical (to), °alike, like two peas in a pod, °twin, inseparable **2** indiscernible, °imperceptible, °indefinite, unclear, °indistinct

individual *adj.* **1** °single, °sole, °particular, °separate, °distinct, °discrete, °solitary, lone **2** °singular, °special, °specific, idiosyncratic, own, °characteristic, °distinctive, individualistic, °unique, °peculiar, °personal, °proper; unitary —*n.* **3** °person, °human (being), °(living) soul, °mortal; °one, °party

individualist *n.* °independent, freethinker, °nonconformist, maverick, loner, lone wolf

individually *adv.* one at a time, °singly, one by one, °separately, severally, °apart

indoctrinate *v.* °train, °teach, °instruct, °school, °discipline, °drill, brainwash, propagandize; inculcate, imbue, °instill, °implant

indolence *n.* laziness, slothfulness, °sloth, °sluggishness, °idleness, °lethargy, shiftlessness, languor, languidness, lassitude, listlessness, °torpor, torpidity, °inertia, inaction, °inactivity, faineance, *dolce far niente,* oscitancy

indolent *adj.* °lazy, °slothful, sluggish, °idle, °lethargic, °shiftless, languorous, languid, °torpid, °inert, °inactive, °stagnant, fainéant, °listless

indomitable *adj.* °resolute, resolved, °determined, °steadfast, °staunch, °persistent, unstoppable, °irrepressible, indefatigable, °untiring, °tireless, unflagging, unyielding, unswerving, unwavering, unflinching, undaunted, °dauntless, °fearless, unafraid, °intrepid, °brave, °courageous, plucky, mettlesome; unconquerable, °unbeatable, °invincible

induce *v.* **1** °lead, °persuade, °influence, prevail on *or* upon, °sway, °move, °convince, °get, °talk into, °prompt, °incite, instigate, actuate, °motivate, impel, °encourage, °inspire, °stimulate, °nudge, °push, °press, °urge, °prod, goad, °spur, egg on, °coax, °cajole, °lure, °entice, inveigle, °seduce **2** °cause, bring about *or* on, °produce, °give rise to, engender, °create, °generate, lead to; °effect, °occasion, set in motion

inducement *n.* °attraction, °lure, °incentive, stimulus, °enticement, bait, °encouragement, °incitement, °provocation, °spur, °premium, °consideration, °reward, *Colloq* carrot, *Chiefly US* °come-on

induct *v.* **1** install *or* instal, °inaugurate, °invest, instate, °establish, swear in **2** °call up, °enlist, conscript, °enroll, °register, *US* °draft

indulge *v.* **1** Often, ***indulge in.*** °yield (to), °succumb (to), °favor, °gratify, °humor, °oblige (with), °comply (with), °minister to, °cater to, °pander to, °treat (to), °pamper (with) **2** °coddle, °baby, °pamper, cosset, mollycoddle, °spoil

indulgence *n.* **1** °tolerance, sufferance, °understanding, °patience, goodwill, °allowance, forbearance; acceptance, overlooking **2** self-indulgence, °luxury, °extravagance, °profligacy, self-gratification, self-satisfaction **3** °treat, °luxury, °extravagance

indulgent *adj.* °tolerant, °permissive, °patient, °understanding, forbearing, °lenient, easygoing, °relaxed, °liberal, °lax, °kind, °kindly, well-disposed, °agreeable

industrious *adj.* sedulous, assiduous, hardworking, °diligent, °intense, °conscientious, °energetic, °dynamic, °aggressive, °vigorous, °untiring, °tireless, indefatigable, unflagging, °persistent, pertinacious, dogged, °tenacious, *US* hustling

industry *n.* **1** °production, °manufacture, °trade, °commerce, °business **2** diligence, assiduity, sedulousness, °energy, °exertion, °effort, °application, °perseverance, °persistence, °work, °labor, toil **3** industriousness, °energy, °activity, °vigor, °hustle, bustle, °dynamism, °enterprise, earnestness, °determination

ineffable *adj.* **1** unutterable, unspeakable, °unmentionable, °taboo **2** °inexpressible, indefinable *or* undefinable, indescribable *or* undescribable, beyond description, beyond words

ineffective *adj.* **1** unproductive, unfruitful, °bootless, °idle, °vain, °useless, °ineffectual, °inefficacious, inoperative, nonfunctioning, °inadequate, °insufficient, °worthless **2** °inefficient, °incompetent, °incapable, unskilled, unskillful, °inept, unfit, unproficient

ineffectual *adj.* **1** °unsuccessful, unavailing, °futile, °bootless, °sterile, °barren, °fruitless, unproductive, °ineffective, °inefficacious, inoperative **2** °weak, °feeble, effete, °impotent, °tame, °lame, °powerless, °inefficient, °incompetent, °inadequate

inefficacious *adj.* See **ineffectual** and **ineffective.**

inefficient *adj.* **1** °ineffective, °incompetent, °incapable, °unqualified, inexpert, unskilled, unskillful, unfit, °inept, °ineffectual, °deficient **2** uneconomic(al), °wasteful, disorganized, °slipshod

ineligible *adj.* °unqualified, °unacceptable, unfit, unsuited, unsuitable, °inappropriate, °improper

inept *adj.* **1** °clumsy, °awkward, bungling, maladroit, ungainly, bumbling, gauche, inexpert, unskilled, unskillful, °incompetent, °inefficient **2** °inappropriate, inapt, °unseemly, °improper, unfitting, unfit, unsuitable, impolitic, undiplomatic, injudicious, °imprudent, °indiscreet, ill-considered, ill-judged, °ill-advised, unadvised, unadvisable *or* inadvised, °misguided, inexpedient, °out of place, unwise

ineptitude *n.* **1** ineptness, clumsiness, awkwardness, maladroitness, ungainliness, gaucherie, °incompetence, inefficiency, unfitness, unsuitableness **2** inappropriateness, inaptness, °absurdity, unsuitability, unseemliness

inequality *n.* **1** °disparity, °difference, °discrepancy, unevenness, nonconformity, incongruence, incongruity, inconsistency, °dissimilarity, imbalance **2** °bias, °prejudice, °partiality, unfairness, °injustice, inequity

inert *adj.* **1** °inactive, unreactive, unresponsive, °neutral **2** motionless, immobile, °inanimate, °lifeless, °still, °quiet, quiescent, stationary, °static **3** sluggish, °slow, °torpid, °dull, °inactive, °idle, °indolent, °lazy, °slothful, °leaden, °slack, °passive, °supine, °dormant, otiose, °listless, languid *or* languorous

inertia *n.* inertness, °inactivity, °sloth, °sluggishness, °torpor, dullness, °idleness, °indolence, laziness, slothfulness, passivity, apathy, lassitude, dormancy, listlessness, languor, immobility, motionlessness

inestimable *adj.* **1** incalculable, °immeasurable, measureless, °untold, incomputable; °priceless, °invaluable, °precious **2** countless, innumerable, °vast, °immense, °prodigious, °boundless, unfathomable, °infinite, incalculable, °immeasurable, measureless, °untold, incomputable

inevitable *adj.* °unavoidable, inescapable, ineluctable, unpreventable, °certain, °sure, °destined, °fated, assured, inexorable, °irrevocable, unchangeable, °absolute, ordained, decreed, °authoritative, incontestable

inexact *adj.* °imprecise, °inaccurate, °erroneous, °incorrect, °wrong, °false, °faulty, °indefinite, fallacious, °fuzzy, muddled

inexcusable *adj.* unjustifiable, unjustified, indefensible, unpardonable, unforgivable, intolerable, inexpiable

inexhaustible *adj.* **1** °limitless, °boundless, °unlimited, unbounded, unrestricted, °endless, measureless, indeterminate, °infinite, incalculable **2** °untiring, °tireless, indefatigable, unflagging, unfailing, unfaltering, unwearying, unwearied

inexpensive *adj.* °cheap, °economical, low-priced, low-cost, °reasonable, budget (-priced)

inexperience *n.* immaturity, innocence, naiveté *or* naïveté *or* naivety, greenness, callowness, unsophistication

inexperienced *adj.* °immature, °innocent, naive *or* naïve *or* naïf, °green, °callow, °unsophisticated, unworldly, °unfledged, °raw, uninitiated, untrained, unschooled, °uninformed, unseasoned, *Colloq* (still) wet behind the ears, born yesterday

inexplicable *adj.* unexplainable, °unaccountable, unintelligible, inscrutable, °puzzling, enigmatic, mystifying, °perplexing, confounding, baffling, bewildering, °incomprehensible

inexpressible *adj.* unutterable, °ineffable, unspeakable, indescribable, indefinable

inextinguishable *adj.* °unquenchable, °irrepressible, unsuppressible; °enduring, undying, imperishable, °eternal, °everlasting

inextricably *adv.* inescapably, ineluctably, unavoidably, irretrievably, °completely, inseparably, indissolubly, °totally, complicatedly, intricately

infallible *adj.* **1** unerring, °faultless, °flawless, °perfect, oracular, unmistaken **2** unfailing, dependable, °sure, °secure, °certain, °reliable, °foolproof

infamous *adj.* **1** °notorious, °disreputable, ill-famed, stigmatized, °scandalous, discreditable, °dishonorable, ignominious **2** °bad, °awful, °wicked, °evil, iniquitous, °villainous, heinous, °vile, °abominable, °outrageous, execrable, °abhorrent, opprobrious, °despicable, °loathsome, detestable, odious, °foul, °scurvy, °rotten, °atrocious, flagitious, °revolting, °monstrous, egregious, °base, °low, °shameful, °disgraceful

infamy *n.* **1** °notoriety, ill repute, ill fame, disrepute, °shame, ignominy, obloquy, °disgrace, °dishonor, °stigma, °discredit **2** wickedness, °evil, iniquity, villainy, heinousness, vileness, abomination, °outrage, abhorrence, opprobrium, loathsomeness, detestation, hatred, odium, °atrocity, °revulsion, °monstrosity, egregiousness, °shame, shamefulness, °disgrace, disgracefulness

infancy *n.* **1** babyhood, early childhood **2** beginning(s), inception, early *or* initial stage(s), commencement, °start, °emergence, °dawn, °rise

infantile *adj.* °childish, °immature, °puerile, babyish, °juvenile

infatuated *adj.* fascinated, beguiled, °enchanted, bewitched, spellbound, °charmed, ensorcelled, enraptured, °possessed, hypnotized, mesmerized, captivated, besotted, taken with, obsessed, °smitten, enamored, °fond

infectious *adj.* contagious, °catching, communicable, transmissible

infer *v.* °deduce, °derive, °draw, conclude,

°understand, °gather, °surmise, °guess, °assume

inference *n.* °deduction, conclusion, °understanding, °surmise, assumption, °presumption

inferior *adj.* **1** °lower, nether; *Typography* subscript **2** lesser, °lower, °subordinate, °secondary, °junior, °minor, unimportant, °insignificant, °lowly, subservient, °humble, °servile **3** °poor, °bad, low-quality, °mediocre, °indifferent, °imperfect, °defective, second-rate, second-class, substandard, low-grade, °shoddy, gimcrack, *Colloq* grotty, junky, crummy *or* crumby, °lousy, *Slang* crappy, *Brit* naff —*n.* **4** °subordinate, underling, °junior, °menial, lackey, flunky *or* flunkey, dogsbody, cat's-paw, doormat, stooge, °yes man, lickspittle, bootlicker

inferiority *n.* **1** unimportance, insignificance, lowliness **2** inadequacy, deficiency, insignificance, unimportance, worthlessness **3** shoddiness, °imperfection, mediocrity

infernal *adj.* **1** hellish, °underworld, nether, Hadean **2** °devilish, diabolic(al), demonic(al), demoniac(al), °fiendish, °satanic, Mephistophelian; °damnable, damned, execrable, malicious, malevolent, maleficent, °wicked, °evil, iniquitous, flagitious, °villainous, heinous, dire, °sinister, °dreadful

infertile *adj.* °sterile, °barren, infecund, unproductive, unfruitful, °nonproductive

infest *v.* invade, °plague, °beset, °overrun, overspread, °flood, swarm over, inundate, pervade, °permeate, °penetrate, infiltrate

infidel *n.* unbeliever, °heathen, disbeliever, heretic, °pagan, agnostic, atheist, nullifidian, freethinker

infidelity *n.* **1** unfaithfulness, faithlessness, treachery, traitorousness, disloyalty, °perfidy, falseness, apostasy, heresy **2** adultery, cuckoldry; °affair, °liaison, amour, *Colloq* cheating

infinite *adj.* **1** °boundless, °vast, °limitless, °unlimited, illimitable, °endless, interminable, indeterminable, indeterminate, °inestimable, astronomical, °numberless, multitudinous, uncountable, uncounted, innumerable, incalculable, °inexhaustible, °immense, °enormous, °immeasurable, measureless, °bottomless, unfathomable **2** °eternal, °everlasting, °perpetual, °endless, unending, °inexhaustible, undying, never-ending

infirm *adj.* **1** °ill, °indisposed, debilitated, °frail, °fragile, °weak, °feeble, weakened, ailing, °decrepit, enfeebled, °failing, wasted, on the decline, °sick, °sickly, unwell, °lame, °crippled **2** °shaky, °flimsy, wobbly, wobbling, °doddering, °unstable, faltering, vacillating, wavering, unsteady, unsteadfast, °inconstant, °changeable, °irresolute

infirmary *n.* clinic, °hospital, sick bay, first-aid station; dispensary, *Brit* nursing home, surgery

infirmity *n.* **1** °weakness, feebleness, frailness, °frailty, debility, °decrepitude, sickliness **2** sickness, °ailment, °disease, malady, °affliction, °disorder, °defect, °complaint

inflame *v.* **1** °arouse, °incite, °touch off, ignite, enkindle, °provoke, °rouse, °excite, impassion, °foment, incense, °agitate, °stir (up), °fire (up), °heat, °anger, °enrage, °madden, °infuriate, whip *or* lash up, °work up, rile, °exasperate, °stimulate, °animate, °move, °motivate, °urge, °prod, goad, °spur (on), °rally, °drive **2** °aggravate, °intensify, °deepen, °heighten, °fan, exacerbate, °increase, augment, °fuel

inflamed *adj.* irritated, °sore, °angry, chafing, chafed, red, °swollen, °heated, °hot, fevered, °feverish, infected, septic

inflammable *adj.* burnable, combustible, °flammable

inflammation *n.* irritation, redness, °swelling, °sore, infection

inflammatory *adj.* incendiary, °fiery, inflaming, °explosive, °rousing, °provocative, °rabid, rabble-rousing, °passionate, °fervent, fervid, °frantic, frenzied, fomenting, demagogic, insurgent, °riotous, °mutinous, °seditious, °rebellious, °revolutionary, °traitorous, treacherous

inflate *v.* **1** °blow up, balloon, °expand, dilate, °enlarge, °swell, °pump up, puff up *or* out, distend **2** °boost, °increase **3** °exaggerate, °amplify, °magnify, °blow up

inflated *adj.* **1** exaggerated, °conceited, overblown, °grandiose, puffed-up, overstated, magnified, amplified, overdrawn, °smug, egotistic, °immodest, °cocky, °vain, °self-important, *Colloq Brit* swelled-headed, *US* swellheaded **2** grandiloquent, °bombastic, orotund, high-flown, °pompous, °pretentious, °extravagant, magniloquent

inflexible *adj.* unbending, °stiff, °rigid, °firm, rigorous, unyielding, adamant(ine), °severe, Rhadamanthine, inelastic, °hard (and fast), determined, °fixed, obdurate, °immovable, intractable, unvaried, unvarying, °invariable, unchangeable, immutable, °obstinate, °stubborn, pigheaded, mulish, dyed-in-the-wool, headstrong, refractory, °steely, °stony, °resolute, resolved, unadaptable, unaccommodating, uncompliant, uncompromising, unshakable *or* unshakeable

inflict *v.* °impose, °apply, °visit, °administer, levy, force on *or* upon; °trouble, °afflict

influence *n.* **1** °power, °pressure, °weight, °sway, °impact, °force, °effect, leverage, potency; °hold, °control, mastery, ascendancy, *Colloq* °pull, clout **2** °connections, °favor, °favoritism, *Colloq* °pull —*v.* **3** °affect, °move, °change, °modify, °alter, °bias, °sway, °persuade, °induce, °work on, °impress (upon), play *or* act upon *or* on, °incline; bring pressure to bear on *or* upon, °move, °motivate, °manipulate, *Brit* pressurize, *US* °pressure, *Colloq* pull strings *or US also* wires

influential *adj.* °powerful, °weighty, °strong, °forceful, °effective, °effectual, °efficacious, °instrumental, °telling, °significant,

°persuasive, °dominant, °leading, guiding, °authoritative, °predominant, °important, °substantial, °prestigious, °significant, controlling

inform *v.* **1** °tell, apprise, °advise, °communicate, °enlighten, °notify, °acquaint, °brief; °impart, °disclose, divulge, °reveal, °report, *Colloq* °tip (off) **2** Usually, ***inform against or on.*** °betray, °give away, °incriminate, °implicate, °identify, °tattle (on), *Colloq* °tell (on), °blab (on), rat (on), *US* blow the whistle (on); *Slang* peach (on), snitch (on), squeal (on), °put the finger on, °sing, °name names, *Brit* nark (on), grass (on), split on, blow the gaff, *US* °finger

informal *adj.* **1** unceremonious, °casual, °natural, unstilted, °familiar, °ordinary, °everyday, °unaffected, unassuming, unpretentious, °simple, °relaxed, °free, free and easy, *Brit* common or garden, *US* garden-variety **2** °unofficial, unconventional, unconstrained, °casual, °everyday, °simple **3** °vernacular, colloquial, °simple, °unaffected, °ordinary, unpretentious, °everyday

information *n.* °knowledge, °data, °facts, °intelligence, °message, °word, °advice, °news, tidings, °report, communication, *Colloq* info, °lowdown, *Slang* °dirt, °(inside) dope, *Brit* gen, bumf, *US* poop

informative *adj.* communicative, °instructive, °educational, edifying, revealing, illuminating

informed *adj.* **1** °intelligent, °knowledgeable, °enlightened, °educated, °learned, cultured, °cultivated **2** °alert (to), °aware (of), advised, in touch, *au fait,* briefed, conversant (with), (well-)versed, up (on), up-to-date, *Colloq* in the know, °wise

informer *n.* °traitor, betrayer, tattletale, taleteller, informant, *Slang* stool pigeon, snitch, squealer, weasel, *Brit* grass, nark, *Chiefly US* rat, *US* stoolie, canary, shoofly

infrequently *adv.* °rarely, °seldom, sporadically, °occasionally, °now and then, irregularly, exceptionally

infringe *v.* **1** °violate, contravene, °break, °disobey, °transgress, °overstep **2** ***infringe on or upon.*** intrude on, impinge on, trespass on, encroach on, invade

infringement *n.* °violation, °breach, contravention, infraction, disobedience, infraction, °noncompliance, breaking, °transgression

infuriate *v.* °enrage, °anger, °madden, incense, make (someone's) blood boil, °provoke, °inflame, work *or* stir *or* fire up, rile, °arouse, vex, pique, °gall, °annoy, °irritate, °bother, °chafe, °agitate, °irk, nettle, °exasperate, raise (someone's) hackles, make (someone's) hackles rise, *Brit* have *or* get (someone's) blood up, *Colloq* miff, °bug, peeve, get under (someone's) skin, get *or Brit also* put (someone's) back up, make (someone) see red, *Chiefly US* get (someone's) Irish *or* dander up, *US* burn up, *Slang* piss (someone) off

ingenious *adj.* °clever, °skillful, skilled, °shrewd, cunning, °crafty, canny, °dexterous, adroit, °acute, °sharp, °keen, °resourceful, °adept, apt, °smart, °gifted, °bright, °brilliant, °talented, deft, °handy, inventive, Daedalian, °creative, °imaginative, °original, *Colloq* °neat, °keen, *US* crackerjack, *Slang* on the ball

ingenuity *n.* ingeniousness, °genius, °brilliance, cleverness, °skill, shrewdness, cunning, °craft, °art, °knack, °flair, °dexterity, dexterousness, adroitness, acuteness, sharpness, keenness, resourcefulness, adeptness, aptness, smartness, canniness, °gift, °talent, °ability, °capability, °faculty, deftness, handiness, inventiveness, creativity, creativeness, °imagination, imaginativeness, °originality

ingenuous *adj.* **1** naive *or* naïve, °simple, °innocent, °unsophisticated, °childlike, °suggestible, °artless, °sincere, °genuine, °trusting, guileless, °natural, °straight, uncomplicated, °(fair and) square, °honest, °fair, °just, °open, undeceitful, °unaffected, undeceptive, undissembling, unfeigning, °(open and) aboveboard, *Colloq* °on the level **2** °frank, °candid, °open, °trustworthy, °honorable, °forthright, °direct, straightforward, foursquare, °honest, °outspoken, °blunt, °bluff, °bold, unreserved, °free, °uninhibited, °unabashed

ingrained *adj.* engrained, deep-rooted, °fixed, inveterate, deep-seated, °fundamental, °basic, °essential, °inherent, °inborn, innate, inbred, inherited, °hereditary, °organic, °intrinsic, °native, °natural

ingratiating *adj.* fawning, °groveling, sycophantic, toadying, toadeating, °servile, °obsequious, °flattering, °timeserving, wheedling, cajoling, unctuous, °oily, buttery, sweet-talking, sugary, saccharine, *US* blandiloquent, *Colloq* bootlicking, °slimy, *Brit* smarmy, *US* apple-polishing, *Slang US* brown-nosing

ingratitude *n.* unthankfulness, ungratefulness, thanklessness, unappreciativeness, nonrecognition

ingredient *n.* constituent, °element, °part, component, °factor; (*plural*) makings

inhabit *v.* dwell in, reside in, live in, abide in, °occupy, °settle; locate in, °populate, °people; colonize

inhabitant *n.* °resident, dweller, °denizen, °citizen, °tenant, °occupant, occupier

inhale *v.* breathe in, °inspire, draw *or* suck in

inherent *adj.* °intrinsic, indwelling, °essential, °basic, innate, connate, ingrained *or* engrained, °native, congenital, inherited, °hereditary, °inborn, inbred, °indigenous, immanent, built-in

inherit *v.* come into, fall *or* be *or* become heir to, be bequeathed, °succeed to, be left, °receive, °acquire, *Colloq* °come by

inheritance *n.* patrimony, °heritage, legacy, °bequest, birthright; °property

inhibit *v.* °discourage, °repress, °frustrate,

°hold back, °bridle, °curb, °control, °govern, °hinder, °restrain, °impede, °obstruct, interfere with, °check, °prevent, °bar, °stop

inhibited *adj.* °reticent, restrained, repressed, °reserved, °self-conscious, °shy, abashed, °embarrassed, *Colloq* uptight

inhibition *n.* self-consciousness, °restraint, constraint, °impediment, °hindrance, °bar, °barrier, °defense, defense mechanism, blockage, °interference, °check, °curb, °stricture

inhospitable *adj.* **1** unwelcoming, unreceptive, °uninviting, unsociable, °unsocial, °aloof, °cold, °cool, °standoffish, unfriendly, inimical, antisocial, °hostile, xenophobic **2** unfavorable, °forbidding, °hostile, °barren, °desert, °uninviting, uninhabitable

inhuman *adj.* **1** inhumane, °merciless, °cruel, pitiless, °ruthless, °heartless, °severe, °unsympathetic, unfeeling, °unkind, unkindly, uncompassionate, °coldblooded, °vicious, stonyhearted, hardhearted, °callous, insensitive, barbaric, barbarous, °savage **2** °animal, bestial, °brutal, brutish, °fiendish, diabolical, demonic

initial *adj.* **1** °original, °primary, °first; °prime, °beginning, incipient, inaugural, °opening, °introductory, commencing —*v.* **2** °sign, °approve, °endorse —*n.* **3** monogram

initiate *v.* **1** °begin, °commence, enter upon *or* on, °originate, °introduce, set in motion, °start, °give rise to, get under way, °launch, get *or* set going, trigger, °set off, actuate, °activate, instigate, °institute, °inaugurate **2** °admit, °accept, °introduce **3** °teach, °instruct, °train, °tutor, °drill, °coach —*n.* **4** °novice, beginner, new boy *or* girl, °greenhorn, rookie, neophyte, tyro *or* tiro, °newcomer, tenderfoot, fledgling, °apprentice, °(raw) recruit, abecedarian, novitiate, catechumen, *Brit* fresher *or US only* freshman, *Australian* new chum

initiation *n.* **1** °beginning, commencement, inauguration, origination, °debut, introduction, inception, °establishment **2** °admittance, °admission, °entrance, induction, enrollment, instatement, investiture, ordination, °installation; °ceremony, °rite, °ritual

initiative *n.* **1** first move *or* step, °lead, opening move **2** °enterprise, aggressiveness, °drive, °ambition, ambitiousness, resourcefulness, °leadership, °dynamism, °energy, °vigor, °hustle, élan, *Colloq* get-up-and-go, °pep, °snap, zip, zing

inject *v.* **1** °introduce, °insert, drive *or* force (in), °shoot (in), intromit; inoculate **2** °introduce, °insert, imbue, °instill, °bring in, interject, throw in

injunction *n.* **1** °prohibition, interdict, interdiction, °restriction, °restraint, *US Law* restraining order **2** °order, mandate, directive, °command, °direction, °instruction, ruling, °dictate, exhortation; °warning, admonition

injure *v.* **1** °harm, °wound, °hurt, °damage, °impair **2** °wrong, °offend, °abuse, °hurt, °wound, °outrage, °slight, °insult, affront, °mistreat, °misuse, °ill-treat, maltreat

injurious *adj.* **1** damaging, °harmful, °hurtful, °bad, deleterious, unfavorable, °detrimental, °unhealthy, insalubrious, pernicious, °destructive; adverse, °ruinous **2** °abusive, insulting, °scornful, °slanderous, libelous, defamatory, °scandalous, °scurrilous, °harsh, calumnious, disparaging, °derogatory, deprecatory, °contemptuous, denigrating, °offensive

injury *n.* °damage, °hurt, °harm, °wound, °impairment; °wrong, °abuse, maltreatment, °mistreatment, °mischief, °offense, °outrage; °mayhem

injustice *n.* **1** unfairness, °favoritism, °discrimination, °bias, °inequality, °partiality, partisanship, °prejudice, °bigotry, onesidedness, unjustness, inequity **2** °wrong, °injury

inkling *n.* °hint, °suggestion, glimmering, °suspicion, °whisper, intimation, °indication, soupçon, °clue, °notion, (faintest *or* foggiest) idea, °tip, tip-off

inmate *n.* °prisoner, °convict, °captive, jailbird, *Slang Brit* °lag; °patient, °case; °inhabitant, °occupant, °resident

innocent *adj.* **1** not guilty, guiltless, °blameless, °honest, °(in the) clear, unimpeachable, above suspicion, above reproach, °faultless **2** °pure, sinless, °virtuous, °chaste, virgin(al), undefiled, untainted, unstained, unsullied, °pristine, °incorrupt, uncorrupted, °immaculate, °spotless, unblemished, unpolluted **3** °harmless, well-intentioned, °safe, innocuous, °inoffensive, unobjectionable **4** naive *or* naïve *or* naïf, °unsuspecting, unsuspicious, °ingenuous, °unsophisticated, °trusting, trustful, °gullible, credulous, °green, °inexperienced, °childlike, unworldly, guileless, °artless, °simple, °open, unartificial, °sincere —*n.* **5** infant, babe (in arms *or* in the wood(s)), °child; ingénue, °novice, beginner, °newcomer, *Colloq* °greenhorn

innovation *n.* **1** °novelty; °invention **2** modernization, °alteration

innuendo *n.* insinuation, °imputation, °suggestion, °hint, intimation, °implication, allusion, °overtone; °reference, animadversion

inoffensive *adj.* °harmless, unobjectionable, innocuous, unoffending, °neutral, °retiring, °mild, °tame

inopportune *adj.* °inappropriate, malapropos, ill-timed, untimely, °inconvenient, unsuited, unsuitable, °out of place, unpropitious, unfavorable, °inauspicious, ill-chosen, °unseasonable, °unseemly, °untoward, °unfortunate

inordinate *adj.* **1** °immoderate, unrestrained, intemperate, °excessive, °disproportionate, °extravagant, overdone, °extreme, °exorbitant, °outrageous, °preposterous, °unconscionable, °unreasonable, undue, uncalled-for, °unwarranted **2** °irregular, °disorderly, disordered, °uncontrolled,

°unlimited, unregulated, unsystematic, °erratic, °haphazard

inquire *v.* **1** Usually, ***inquire into.*** °search, °investigate, °probe, °examine, °research, °look into, °inspect, °study, °explore, °survey, °scrutinize **2** See **enquire.**

inquiry *n.* **1** enquiry, °investigation, °probe, °examination, °research, °search, inspection, °study, °exploration, °survey, °scrutiny, inquest; questioning, querying, °interrogation, cross-examination, inquisition **2** enquiry, °question, °query, °interrogation

inquisitive *adj.* **1** inquiring, °curious, probing, questioning, °interested, investigative, searching, exploring, analytical **2** prying, °intrusive, *Colloq* snooping, snoopy, nosy *or* nosey

inroad *n.* **1** incursion, °raid, °attack, °invasion, °penetration, foray, encroachment, forced entry, intrusion **2** Often, ***inroads.*** advance(s), °progress, breakthrough

insane *adj.* **1** °mad, demented, °psychotic, schizophrenic, schizoid, ***non compos mentis,*** manic, °maniacal, lunatic, °deranged, °unbalanced, psychoneurotic, °neurotic, °eccentric, °crazy, of unsound mind, crazed, unhinged, out of one's mind *or* head, mad as a hatter *or* a March hare, quirky, *Colloq* round the bend *or* twist, off one's rocker *or* chump, loopy, loony, certifiable, °mental, screwy, dotty, cuckoo, not all there, not have all one's marbles, off the wall, out of it, *Brit* potty, *Slang* °daft, nutty (as a fruitcake), nuts, spaced out, spacy, batty, have bats in one's belfry, not right upstairs, balmy, crackers, have a screw loose, schizo, *Brit* barmy (in the crumpet), bonkers, *US* bugs, bughouse, loco, crazy as a bedbug, (gone) off the deep end, kooky, °kinky, out to lunch **2** °stupid, °dumb, °dull, °silly, asinine, °ridiculous, idiotic, irrational, °absurd, fatuous, °ludicrous, °foolish, °nonsensical, °irresponsible, °reckless, °wild, imbecilic, moronic, °feebleminded, °harebrained, addlepated, °scatterbrained, thimble-witted, attocerebral, *Brit* gormless, *Colloq* nutty, screwy, °crazy

insanity *n.* **1** °madness, °lunacy, mental illness *or* disorder, dementia (praecox), psychosis, schizophrenia, (mental) derangement, °mania; psychoneurosis, neurosis **2** °folly, foolishness, °stupidity, idiocy, imbecility, °lunacy, °absurdity, fatuity, fatuousness, °nonsense, senselessness, irresponsibility, irrationality, inanity

insecure *adj.* **1** °uncertain, °afraid, unsure, unconfident, °nervous, °worried, °anxious, °disconcerted, apprehensive, uncomfortable, °shaky, °jumpy, unnerved, °fearful **2** unsafe, °dangerous, unprotected, °vulnerable, °unguarded, °defenseless, undefended, exposed, °open **3** °unstable, °shaky, wobbly, °precarious, °infirm, °weak, °flimsy, °frail, °rickety, unsubstantial, °rocky, °unsound, unsteady, °unreliable, °uncertain

insensible *adj.* **1** insensate, °unconscious, insentient, °numb, benumbed, °senseless, °torpid, anesthetized, *Colloq* °out, out of it **2** Often, ***insensible to or of.*** insensitive, °callous, °indifferent, impervious, °impassive, apathetic, °cool, unsusceptible; °unaffected, °unmoved, untouched; unaware, °deaf, °inconsiderate; hardhearted, °thick-skinned, unfeeling, emotionless, °dispassionate, °thoughtless, *Colloq* cloth-eared

insert *v.* **1** °introduce, place *or* put *or* stick in, intercalate; interpolate, interject, interpose *—n.* **2** insertion, °addition, addendum, °supplement, °advertisement, broadside, °brochure, tip-in, handbill, °circular, *Colloq Brit* advert, *US* ad, flier *or* flyer; outsert, wraparound *or* wrapround

inside *n.* **1** °interior, °center, °core, °middle, °heart; °contents; lining, °backing **2** Usually, ***insides.*** °bowels, entrails, viscera, gut(s), °stomach, *Colloq* innards **3** ***inside out.*** everted, reversed; backwards *—adj.* **4** °favored, °advantageous, °favorable, advantaged, °privileged, preferred, °preferential, °propitious, °exclusive; °internal, °private, °secret, °confidential, °privy, clandestine **5** °internal, °interior; arranged, prearranged *—adv.* **6** fundamentally, basically, °at bottom, °by nature **7** in prison, in jail, imprisoned, incarcerated, *Slang Brit* in quod, *US* up the river *—prep.* **8** within, *US* inside of

insight *n.* °perception, percipience, °sensitivity, perspicacity, perceptiveness, perspicaciousness, discernment, acuteness, acuity, acumen, sharpness, °understanding, °judgment, comprehension, °vision

insignificant *adj.* °paltry, °trifling, °petty, inconsiderable, °inconsequential, trivial, unimportant, °nonessential, °minor, °negligible, nugatory, unessential, °niggling, °puny, °insubstantial, unsubstantial, *Colloq* piddling

insincere *adj.* °hypocritical, °dishonest, dissembling, °deceptive, °disingenuous, °deceitful, untruthful, °false, °artificial, ungenuine, treacherous, °perfidious, °faithless, double-dealing, duplicitous, °two-faced, Janus-faced, °lying, mendacious, °sly, Machiavellian, cunning, °crafty, °slick, °foxy, vulpine, °wily, °artful, °evasive, °shifty, time-serving, unctuous, °slimy, °slippery, °tricky, underhanded, °crooked, *Colloq* phoney *or US also* phony

insinuate *v.* **1** °impute, °suggest, °hint, °intimate, °imply, °whisper, °indicate; convey, °signify **2** °insert (oneself), °inject (oneself), worm *or* work *or* inveigle *or* maneuver (oneself *or* one's way); infiltrate, °intrude **3** °inject, infuse, °instill, °introduce

insist *v.* **1** °demand, °require, °call for, °command, importune, °urge, exhort, °argue, remonstrate, expostulate **2** assert, °state, °declare, °emphasize, °stress, °maintain, °persist, °hold, °dwell on, °vow, avow, aver, asseverate

insistent *adj.* °firm, dogged, °emphatic, °persistent, °tenacious, °resolute, °determined, °assertive, uncompromising, unfaltering, unwavering, persevering, perseverant, unrelenting, inexorable, °stubborn,

°obstinate, unyielding, compelling, °urgent, importunate

insolent *adj.* °impertinent, °impudent, °pert, saucy, °bold, °presumptuous, °brazen, °brash, °disrespectful, insulting, °contemptuous, °offensive, °rude, °crude, uncivil, °insubordinate, *Colloq* °fresh, °brassy, °cheeky, *Slang Brit* smart-arsed *or US* smart-ass(ed), °wise

insolvent *adj.* bankrupt, ruined, in receivership, penniless, °impoverished, °destitute, *US* in Chapter 11, *Colloq* °broke, wiped out, in the red, °on the rocks, (gone) bust, gone to the wall, *Brit* in Queer street, skint

inspect *v.* °examine, °scrutinize, °study, °scan, °survey, °vet, check (up (on) *or* out), °investigate, °pore over; °peruse

inspiration *n.* **1** awakening, arousal, stimulus, °revelation, impulse, °feeling, afflatus, enlightenment, °insight, °spur, °incitement, °incentive; °spirit, °energy, élan, °passion, °ardor, zeal, °enthusiasm, °vigor, °gusto, ebullience, °sparkle **2** °influence, stimulus, stimulation, °encouragement, °provocation, °suggestion, °guide, °education

inspire *v.* **1** °animate, °activate, actuate, °stimulate, invigorate, °stir, °move, waken, °awaken, °arouse, °rouse, instigate, °prompt, °rally, °energize, °enliven, °vitalize, vivify, galvanize, inspirit, °excite, °spark (off), °quicken, °kindle, °fire, °provoke **2** °encourage, °strengthen, °support, °reinforce, °buoy (up), uplift, °boost, affirm, °confirm, °fortify, °buttress

install *v.* **1** instal, °invest, instate, °initiate, °establish, °inaugurate, °induct, °institute; °place, °put, °position, °introduce, °settle **2** instal, °fit, °set up, °connect, °fix (in place)

installation *n.* **1** investiture, instatement, °initiation, °establishment, inauguration, induction, °institution, °placement, introduction, solemnization, swearing-in, consecration, *Ecclesiastical* ordination; crowning, coronation **2** °fitting, °placement, °connection, positioning **3** °base, °post, °station, depot, °camp, °establishment

instance *n.* **1** °case (in point), °example, exemplar, °illustration, °precedent, exemplification, °occurrence, °event **2** ***for instance.*** °for example, as an example, °say, e.g.; °in the event, as it happens *or* happened

instant *n.* **1** °moment, °point, °second, °time **2** °moment, °second, °minute, °flash, °twinkling (of an eye), trice, *Colloq* jiffy —*adj.* **3** instantaneous, °immediate, on-the-spot, overnight **4** °urgent, crying, °pressing, °earnest, °imperative, °critical, exigent; split-second, °direct **5** °ready-made, ready-mixed, °prepared, ready-to-serve, precooked

instantaneously *adv.* instantly, °immediately, °at once, °(right) now, °directly, forthwith, °promptly, this minute *or* second *or* instant, without delay, *tout de suite,* instanter, *Brit* straightaway *or US* right away; *Colloq* pronto, *US* momentarily

instead *adv.* **1** as an alternative *or* a substitute **2** ***instead of.*** alternatively, preferably, in preference to, in place of, in lieu of, rather than, as a substitute for; as contrasted with, as opposed to

instill *v.* imbue, inculcate, infuse, ingrain *or* engrain, °implant; °insinuate, °impart

instinct *n.* °intuition, °feel, °feeling, empathy, °sensitivity, °tendency, propensity, °leaning, °bent, °skill, °talent, °faculty, sixth sense, °knack, predisposition, °capacity, °aptitude; °subconscious

instinctive *adj.* **1** instinctual, intuitive, °natural, innate, °native, °inborn, inbred, congenital, constitutional, reflex, visceral, intestinal, °intrinsic, intuitional, °subconscious, *Colloq* °gut **2** °immediate, °involuntary, irrational, °mechanical, °automatic, °spontaneous

institute *n.* **1** °society, °organization, °association, °league, °alliance, guild **2** See **institution, 2.** —*v.* **3** °establish, °found, °launch, °organize **4** °inaugurate, °introduce, °initiate, °set up, °start, °begin, °originate, °commence, °pioneer

institution *n.* **1** establishing, °establishment, forming, °formation, origination, founding, °foundation, °installation, introduction, °creation, °organization **2** °establishment, °institute, academy, °foundation, university, college, °school **3** °hospital, medical center, sanitarium *or Brit* sanatorium, °home, asylum **4** °custom, °tradition, °habit, °practice, °routine, °rule, °order (of the day), °code (of practice); °doctrine, dogma

instruct *v.* **1** °teach, °train, °tutor, °drill, °educate, °coach, °inform, °guide, edify, °prepare, °indoctrinate, inculcate **2** °direct, °order, °bid, °require, °tell, enjoin, °command, importune, °charge

instruction *n.* **1** Often, ***instructions.*** °order, °direction, °brief, briefing, directive, guideline, °advice, °recommendation, °rule; °information; *Colloq* °drill **2** teaching, °education, °schooling, training, °drill, drilling, °tuition, °guidance, indoctrination, °preparation, lessons, classes, coaching, tutelage; tutorial

instructive *adj.* °informative, informational, informatory, °educational, instructional, °helpful, revealing, edifying, enlightening, illuminating

instructor *n.* °teacher, trainer, °tutor, °coach, mentor, adviser *or* advisor, educator, pedagogue, scholastic, academe, academician, °doctor, docent, lecturer, professor, *Brit* °master, °mistress, don, preceptor

instrument *n.* **1** °implement, °tool, °device, °apparatus, utensil, appliance, contrivance, °mechanism, °gadget, *Colloq* °contraption, thingumabob, thingumajig, thingummy, thingy, whatsit, whatitsname, whatnot, what-d'you-call-it, *Brit* gubbins, *US and Canadian* gizmo *or* gismo **2** °agency, °means, °way, °factor, °mechanism, instrumentality, wherewithal, (prime) mover, catalyst, °agent **3**

°contract, °(legal) document, °(written) agreement, °pact, °compact, °paper

instrumental *adj.* °helpful, °useful, utilitarian, contributory, of service, °supportive, supporting, °advantageous, catalytic, conducive, °beneficial, valuable, °significant, °important; °accessory, ancillary

insubordinate *adj.* °disobedient, °rebellious, °defiant, refractory, °mutinous, insurgent, insurrectional, insurrectionist, °revolutionary, °seditious, incompliant *or* uncompliant, uncooperative, °recalcitrant, contumacious, fractious, °unruly, °perverse, °contrary, °obstreperous, *Colloq Brit* stroppy

insubstantial *adj.* **1** unsubstantial, °insignificant, °meager, diaphanous, °small, °flimsy, °frail, °weak, °feeble, °paltry, °puny, °slight, °thin, °tenuous, °fragile, °light, gossamer, wispy, wisplike, °fine **2** °illusory, °unreal, illusive, °imaginary, imagined, °fanciful, °fancied, °visionary, °immaterial, °intangible, impalpable, incorporeal, airy, ethereal, °spiritual, chimerical, °phantom, phantasmal, phantasmagorical, hallucinatory, °fantastic; °false

insufferable *adj.* °unbearable, insupportable *or* unsupportable, intolerable, unendurable, °impossible

insufficient *adj.* °inadequate, °deficient, °unsatisfactory, °meager, °scanty, scant, °scarce; too little, not enough

insulate *v.* **1** °detach, °separate, °isolate, °segregate, °shelter, °preserve, set *or* keep apart, sequester, sequestrate, quarantine **2** °lag, °protect, °shield, °cushion, °wrap, °cover

insult *v.* **1** °offend, affront, °slight, °outrage; °abuse, °dishonor, defame, °injure; asperse, °slander, °libel —*n.* **2** °offense, affront, °indignity, °slight, °outrage, barb, °dig, °slur, °dishonor, °abuse, defamation, discourtesy; °aspersion, °slander, °libel; *Colloq* °slap (in the face), °put-down

insurance *n.* °assurance, surety, °indemnity, indemnification, guarantee *or* guaranty, °warranty, °bond, °security, °protection, °cover

intact *adj.* °whole, °entire, °perfect, °complete, °integral, °sound, unbroken, °solid, (all) in one piece, °undivided, uncut, together, untouched, unreduced, undiminished, unimpaired, inviolate, unblemished, °unscathed, uninjured, unharmed, undamaged, unsullied, undefiled, untainted

intangible *adj.* impalpable, unperceivable, °imperceptible, incorporeal, unsubstantial, °insubstantial, °imponderable, °immaterial, ethereal, vaporous, airy, evanescent, °vague, °obscure, °dim, °imprecise, °indefinite, °shadowy, °fleeting, °elusive

integral *adj.* **1** °basic, °elementary, °elemental, °fundamental, °essential, °intrinsic **2** See **intact.**

integrate *v.* °combine, °unite, °blend, bring *or* put together, °assemble, °merge, °amalgamate, °join, °knit, °mesh, consolidate, coalesce, °fuse; *US* desegregate

integrity *n.* **1** °honesty, °probity, veracity, uprightness, °honor, °rectitude, °principle, °morality, goodness, trustworthiness, decency, °virtue, incorruptibility, righteousness **2** wholeness, °entirety, °unity, togetherness, soundness, completeness, coherence, oneness, °totality

intellect *n.* **1** rationality, °reason, reasonableness, °(common) sense, °understanding, °judgment, cleverness, °intelligence, °mind, *Colloq* brains **2** See **intellectual, 3.**

intellectual *adj.* **1** °mental, cerebral **2** °thoughtful, thought-provoking, °highbrow, °academic, bookish, °scholarly, *Colloq* brainy —*n.* **3** °thinker, °intellect, °highbrow, °mastermind, °genius, *Colloq* °brain, egghead **4** °scholar, academician, professor, savant, °sage, wise man, guru, polymath, pundit, °authority

intelligence *n.* **1** °intellect, °understanding, °aptitude, °capacity, brainpower, cleverness, astuteness, quickness, alertness, keenness, brightness, shrewdness, °wit, mother wit, °(common) sense, °insight, perspicacity, °perception, discernment, °discretion, percipience, perspicaciousness, °wisdom, sagacity, *Colloq* brains, savvy, gray matter, *Slang Brit* nous **2** °information, °knowledge, °word, °data, °facts, °advice, °news, tidings, findings, *Colloq* °dope, °lowdown, info, *Brit* gen, *US* °inside, poop

intelligent *adj.* °bright, °smart, °clever, discerning, perspicacious, °perceptive, percipient, °understanding, °rational, apt, °astute, °quick, °quick-witted, °keen, °sharp, °alert, °shrewd, canny, insightful, °gifted, °sensible, °wise, °sage, sagacious, °enlightened, °knowing, °aware, °knowledgeable, erudite, *au fait, Colloq* brainy, *Chiefly US* savvy

intelligentsia *n. pl.* intellectuals, literati, savants, illuminati, masterminds, highbrows, *Colloq* brains, eggheads, brains trust

intelligible *adj.* understandable, comprehensible, fathomable, decipherable, °legible, °clear, °plain, lucid, unambiguous

intend *v.* °mean, have in mind *or* in view, °propose, °contemplate, °design, °plan, °aim, °purpose, °resolve, °determine

intense *adj.* **1** °extreme, °excessive, °severe, °strong, °great, °fierce, °harsh, °acute, °powerful, °profound, °deep **2** °eager, °enthusiastic, °keen, °earnest, °sincere, °heartfelt, °deep, °passionate, °impassioned, °ardent, zealous, °animated, °burning, consuming, °fervent, fervid, perfervid, vehement, °frantic, °fanatical, frenzied **3** highly strung *or Chiefly US* high-strung, °emotional, °temperamental, °tense, °touchy, °testy, °volatile, °hysterical, °hot-headed, °feverish, °nervous, (high-)spirited, °impetuous, °impulsive, *Colloq* uptight

intensify *v.* °concentrate, °focus, °sharpen, °whet, °strengthen, °reinforce, °heighten, escalate, °deepen, °quicken, °emphasize, °magnify, °increase, augment, °double, redouble, °heat up, *Colloq* °step up, *Brit* hot up

intensity *n.* concentration, °focus, °strength, forcefulness, °force, °power; °vigor, °energy, vehemence, °fervor, zeal, °ardor, °passion, °sincerity

intensive *adj.* concentrated, focused, intensified, °comprehensive, °exhaustive, thorough(going), all-out

intent *n.* **1** °intention, °aim, °goal, °target, °purpose, °object, °objective, °end, °design, °plan, °idea **2** °inclination, °tendency, °desire, intending **3** ***to all intents and purposes.*** °virtually, °practically, for all practical purposes, (almost) as good as, (almost) the same as, more or less, °in effect —*adj.* **4** concentrated, focused, °fixed, °steady, °intense, °determined, °earnest, engrossed, °absorbed, °rapt, °steadfast, °resolute, °attentive **5** °bent, °set, °resolute, committed, °decided, °firm, °keen; resolved, °eager, °determined, zealous, avid, °enthusiastic

intention *n.* °aim, °purpose, °intent, °design, °goal, °end, °object, °objective, °target, °ambition

intentional *adj.* °deliberate, intended, °premeditated, meant, °willful, designed, planned, °preconceived, °studied, considered, contrived; °purposeful, °on purpose

intently *adv.* closely, attentively, concentratedly, earnestly, fixedly, unflinchingly, determinedly, °searchingly, steadily, steadfastly, continuously, assiduously, doggedly, unremittingly, eagerly, keenly, studiously

intercept *v.* °interrupt, °deflect, °stop, °arrest, °check, °interfere (with), °head off, °block, °impede, °cut off, °seize, °grab, °catch, °trap

intercourse *n.* **1** °commerce, °traffic, °trade, °dealings, °exchange, communication, °contact, interaction **2** sexual intercourse, coitus, coition, sexual congress *or* union, mating, copulation, sexual relations, carnal knowledge, making love, lovemaking, intimacy, sexual connection, *Colloq* °sex

interest *n.* **1** °attention, attentiveness, °concern, °regard, °curiosity, °scrutiny, °notice, °engagement **2** °concern, °significance, °importance, °weight, °moment, °note, consequence **3** Often, ***interests.*** °profit, °advantage, °benefit, °good, avail, °worth, value, °consideration, °behalf, behoof **4** °share, °portion, °stake, investment, °piece, °cut, °percentage, participation, involvement **5** Often, ***interests.*** °business, °concern, °affair, °property; °hobby, °pastime, °diversion, avocation, °amusement, °entertainment, °pursuit, °relaxation, °occupation **6** (lending) fee *or* charge, °percentage, °rate, *Slang US* vigorish —*v.* **7** °engage, absorb, engross, °attract, °draw, °catch, °capture, °captivate, °hold, °fascinate, °intrigue, °excite, °incite, °provoke, °arouse, °affect, °quicken, infect, °animate, °kindle, °fire **8** °influence, °induce, °persuade, °move, °tempt, °involve, °enroll, °enlist, °dispose, °incline, °prevail upon, °talk into, °concern

interested *adj.* **1** Also, ***interested in.*** °engaged, °absorbed, engrossed, °drawn (to), attracted (by), °involved (in), °curious (about), fascinated (by), °keen (on), stimulated (by), °responsive (to), °concerned (about) **2** °concerned, °involved, nonobjective, °partial, °biased, °prejudiced, °prejudicial, °partisan, predisposed

interesting *adj.* °absorbing, °engaging, gripping, °riveting, engrossing, °attractive, compelling, intriguing, °provocative, °stimulating, °exciting, °inviting, fascinating, °enchanting, °spellbinding, captivating

interfere *v.* **1** °meddle, °intrude, °butt in, °intervene, intercede, interpose, °interrupt, *Colloq* horn in, put *or* stick in one's oar *or* one's oar in, poke one's nose in, *US* kibitz **2** °hinder, °impede, °hamper, °block, °obstruct, °encumber, °slow, °retard, °handicap, °set back, get in the way of, °frustrate, °conflict, °inhibit, °trammel, °subvert, °sabotage

interference *n.* **1** meddling, intrusion, intruding, intervention, interceding, intercession **2** °hindrance, °impediment, °block, °obstruction, °encumbrance, impedance, °difficulty, °snag, °hitch, °handicap, °setback; frustration, °inhibition, °conflict, °opposition

interior *adj.* **1** °inside, °internal, inner, inward **2** °internal, °domestic, °civil, °national, °local, °home **3** inner, °private, °intimate, °personal, °individual, °secret, °hidden, °veiled **4** upland, inland, upcountry, landlocked —*n.* **5** °inside **6** °heart, °center, °middle, °core, °depths **7** uplands, upcountry, heartland, hinterland

interjection *n.* °exclamation, ejaculation, °cry, interpolation, utterance

interlude *n.* °interval, entr'acte, °intermission, °pause, °stop, stoppage, °respite, °interruption, °break, hiatus, lacuna, °gap, °halt, °wait, breathing space, °recess, °rest, °spell, °lull, *Colloq* °letup

intermediary *n.* °go-between, middleman, °agent, °representative, °broker, °intermediate, third party, °mediator, arbitrator, arbiter, referee, °umpire, °judge

intermediate *adj.* **1** °middle, in-between, medial, midway, halfway, transitional, intervening, °intermediary **2** See **intermediary.**

intermission *n.* See **interlude.**

intermittent *adj.* °irregular, discontinuous, °disconnected, °sporadic, °occasional, °random, °spasmodic, °fitful, °broken, °periodic, alternating, cyclic(al), rhythmic(al), pulsating, seasonal, on-and-off, on-again-off-again, stop-and-go, stop-go

internal *adj.* See **interior, 1, 2, 3.**

international *adj.* supranational, °global, worldwide, °universal, intercontinental, cosmopolitan, ecumenic(al) *or* oecumenic(al); °foreign

interpret *v.* **1** °explain, explicate, °clear up, °clarify, elucidate, °illuminate, throw *or* shed light on, °simplify, °decipher, decode, °define, °spell out, make sense (out) of, °translate, °paraphrase **2** °understand, construe,

°take (to mean), °read, figure *or* work out, °sort out, unravel

interpretation *n.* **1** °explanation, clarification, elucidation, simplification, decipherment, °solution, working out, unraveling, sorting out, decoding, °definition, °illustration, °translation, paraphrasing **2** °analysis, diagnosis, °examination, exegesis, explication, reading, construal, °inference, °understanding

interrogation *n.* questioning, °examination, cross-examination, inquisition, °investigation, *Colloq* third degree, grilling

interrupt *v.* **1** °break in, °cut in, intrude in, °butt in, interfere in, °punctuate, °disturb, *Colloq* barge in, °chime in, horn in **2** °discontinue, °break off, °cut off, °cut short, interfere with, °disrupt, °suspend, °hold up, °halt, °stop, °end, °terminate, °cease

interruption *n.* **1** °break, intrusion, °disturbance, °interference, disruption **2** °break, °gap, °interval, lacuna, hiatus, °respite, °rest, °pause, pausing, °intermission, stopping, °stop, °suspension, cessation, °cease, ceasing, surcease, hesitation, *Prosody* caesura, *Colloq* °letup

interval *n.* **1** °intermission, °interlude, entr'acte, °break, °pause; °recess, °rest (period), °period, °time, °wait, °spell, °delay, °lapse **2** °meanwhile, °meantime, interim **3** °gap, °opening, °space, °hole, °void, lacuna, °distance, interstice, *Architecture* intercolumniation

intervene *v.* **1** °interfere, °intrude, °break in, °interrupt, intercede, °meddle, interpose, °butt in, *Colloq* poke one's nose in, horn in, put in one's oar, °step in **2** come *or* go (between), °pass, °elapse

interview *n.* **1** °meeting, °(press) conference, °discussion, °conversation, °talk, question period, audience **2** °evaluation, appraisal, vetting, assessment —*v.* **3** °question, °examine, interrogate, °sound out, talk with *or* to **4** appraise, °evaluate, °check (out), °vet

intimate[1] *adj.* **1** °close, °personal, °warm, °affectionate, loving, °dear, °bosom, cherished, °familiar, *intime* **2** °secret, °confidential, °private, °personal, °privy, °hidden, *intime*; °detailed, °penetrating, °deep, °profound, °thorough, °exhaustive **3** °sexual; °carnal **4** °cozy, °informal, °snug, °friendly, °warm, °comfortable; *intime, à deux,* °tête-à-tête, *Colloq* comfy —*n.* **5** °friend, °associate, °comrade, crony, °familiar, confidant(e), °(constant) companion, Achates, alter ego, °colleague, confrère, *Colloq* sidekick, °chum, °pal, *Brit and Australian* °mate, *US* buddy, *Slang Brit* china (plate), mucker

intimate[2] *v.* °hint, °imply, °suggest, °insinuate, °indicate, °refer to, allude to, °communicate, °make known, give (someone) to understand, °warn, °caution, *Colloq* °tip (off)

intimidate *v.* °frighten, °scare, °alarm, cow, °daunt, °dismay, abash, °appall, awe, °overawe, °browbeat, °menace, °threaten, °terrify, °petrify, terrorize, °tyrannize; *Slang* have *or* get (someone) by the short and curlies

intolerance *n.* °bias, °prejudice, °bigotry, °discrimination, °partiality, illiberality, dogmatism, narrow-mindedness; racism, racialism, sexism, classism, ageism, xenophobia

intolerant *adj.* **1** °unsympathetic, unforbearing, unindulgent, °impatient, °inconsiderate, °inhospitable, uncharitable **2** °biased, °prejudiced, °bigoted, discriminatory, °partial, illiberal, °narrow-minded, °parochial, °provincial, °jaundiced, warped, twisted, °one-sided, °opinionated, close-minded; racist, racialist, sexist, classist, ageist, xenophobic

intonation *n.* °accent, accentuation, speech *or* sound pattern, °delivery, modulation, articulation, °pronunciation, vocalization, °pitch, °tone, inflection

intoxicate *v.* **1** inebriate, make drunk, addle, stupefy, °muddle, befuddle **2** °stimulate, °excite, °overwhelm, elate, exhilarate, °animate, °enliven, invigorate, inspirit, °thrill, galvanize, °electrify, make one's head spin, °take one's breath away, infatuate, °entrance, °enchant, °enrapture, °fascinate, °bewitch, cast a spell on, ensorcell

intoxicating *adj.* **1** °alcoholic, spirituous, inebriant **2** °exhilarating, °invigorating, °thrilling, °exciting, heady, °stimulating, electrifying, entrancing, fascinating

intrepid *adj.* °fearless, °brave, °bold, °daring, °dauntless, undaunted, °steadfast, °resolute, °courageous, unafraid, plucky, °gallant, valiant, valorous, doughty, °audacious, °heroic, °manly, manful, °dashing, °adventurous, °venturesome, stouthearted, lionhearted, °game

intricate *adj.* **1** °involved, °complicated, convoluted, entangled, tangled, knotty, complex, twisted, winding, °tortuous, sinuous, anfractuous, °labyrinthine, °elaborate, Byzantine, °fancy, °ornate, rococo, Daedalian *or* Daedalean *or* Daedalic, *Literary* daedal *or* dedal **2** °perplexing, °puzzling, mystifying, enigmatic

intrigue *v.* **1** °fascinate, °beguile, °captivate, °attract, absorb, °charm, pique, °interest, titillate, arouse *or* excite the curiosity (of) **2** conspire, °plot, connive, °scheme, °maneuver —*n.* **3** °conspiracy, °plot, °scheme, °maneuver, collusion, °stratagem, °trickery, °chicanery, double-dealing, guile, °subterfuge, °artifice, °machination, °deception **4** °affair, °liaison, amour, °romance, °affaire, *affaire d'amour, affaire de coeur,* intimacy; adultery

intrinsic *adj.* °inherent, °basic, °fundamental, °essential, °proper, °elemental, °organic, °natural, °native, inbred, congenital, inherited, °hereditary, innate, °inborn, immanent, indwelling, underlying, constitutional; °real, °true, °actual, °genuine

introduce *v.* **1** °acquaint, °present, °make known **2** bring in *or* up, °advance, °present, °broach, put *or* set forth, °put forward, °suggest, °offer, °propose, °mention **3** °announce, °present **4** °start, °begin, °originate, °launch, °establish, °set up, °pioneer, °initiate, usher in, °institute, bring out *or* in, °set up, °organize **5** °insert, °add, interpose, °inject, °put in, interpolate

introductory *adj.* **1** °opening, °prefatory, °preliminary, °preparatory, °beginning, inaugural, °initial **2** °primary, °basic, °fundamental, °elementary, °first, °rudimentary

intrude *v.* °interfere, °break in, °interrupt, °intervene, push in, interpose, °butt in, °infringe, °encroach, °obtrude, *Colloq* horn in, barge in

intruder *n.* **1** interloper, gate-crasher, uninvited guest, unwelcome visitor; trespasser, encroacher, invader, infiltrator, squatter; °burglar, °thief **2** meddler, °busybody, *Colloq* snoop(er), Nosy Parker, *US* kibitzer, buttinsky

intrusive *adj.* intruding, interfering, meddlesome, invasive, meddling, prying, °inquisitive, °obtrusive, importunate, °officious, °presumptuous, °forward; °unwelcome, uncalled-for, unwanted, unsought, *Colloq* °nosy, °pushy, snoopy

intuition *n.* °instinct, °insight, °hunch, sixth sense, presentiment, °premonition, °foreboding; °perception, perceptiveness, percipience, perspicacity, common sense, mother wit

invalid[1] *adj.* **1** ailing, °sick, °sickly, °ill, °infirm, valetudinarian, °disabled —*n.* **2** °patient, valetudinarian, °victim, sufferer, °incurable, °cripple, *Chiefly US and Canadian* shut-in

invalid[2] *adj.* °void, null (and void), nullified, annulled, repudiated, °untrue, °false, °faulty, °erroneous, °wrong, °spurious; °incorrect, °imperfect, impaired, °unsound, °untenable, °ineffective

invaluable *adj.* °priceless, valuable, °precious, of inestimable *or* incalculable value; irreplaceable, irredeemable; costly, °expensive, high-priced, °dear

invariable *adj.* **1** unchanging, °changeless, unvarying, invariant, unwavering, °constant, °steady, °stable, °regular; °fixed, °fast, °set, °rigid, °uniform, unfailing, unexceptional **2** immutable, unchangeable, unalterable, unmodifiable **3** °permanent, °fixed, °enduring, °abiding, °eternal, unaltered, unvarying, unchanged, unvaried, unmodified

invasion *n.* **1** incursion, °raid, foray, intrusion, °inroad, encroachment, trespass, infiltration; °infringement, infraction, °transgression, °violation **2** °attack, °assault, onslaught, °aggression, °offensive, °drive, storming, blitzkrieg

invent *v.* **1** °create, °devise, contrive, °originate, °think up, dream up, °conceive, concoct, °make up, °imagine, °formulate, °improvise, °design, °hit upon; °coin **2** °fabricate, °make up, concoct, *Colloq* cook up

invention *n.* **1** °creation, origination, contriving, devising, °conception, contrivance, introduction, °development **2** °creation, contrivance, °device, °gadget, *Colloq* °contraption, *US* gizmo **3** fiction, figment, °story, °fantasy, °fabrication, °tale, fable, °yarn, °fib, tall story *or* tale, falsification, °fake, °sham, °falsehood, °lie, prevarication

invest *v.* **1** °venture, °lay out, °put in, °sink **2** °devote, °allot, °spend, °contribute, °supply, °provide **3** °install, °inaugurate, °induct, °initiate, instate, °establish, ordain, swear in, °seat

investigate *v.* enquire *or* inquire into, °examine, °study, °consider, °explore, °probe, °look into, °research, °scrutinize, °analyze, °sift (through), winnow

investigation *n.* enquiry *or* inquiry, °examination, °study, °review, °exploration, °quest, °search, °probe, °research, discovery procedure, °scrutiny, °analysis, inquest, inquisition, °interrogation, questioning

invigorating *adj.* °stimulating, °bracing, rejuvenating, °tonic, vitalizing, restorative, energizing, vivifying, enlivening, °exhilarating; °fresh, healthful, °healthy, salubrious, salutary

invincible *adj.* **1** unconquerable, °unbeatable, °indomitable, insuperable, undefeated, unstoppable **2** °impregnable, invulnerable, impenetrable, °indestructible, unassailable

invisible *adj.* **1** unseeable, °imperceptible, undetectable, imperceivable; unseen **2** concealed, °hidden, disguised, camouflaged, masked, covered, unperceived, °veiled, indiscernible

invitation *n.* **1** summons, °request, °call, °bidding, *Colloq* invite **2** °attraction, °inducement, allure, allurement, °enticement, °temptation, °magnetism, bait, °lure, °draw, °pull

inviting *adj.* alluring, °tempting, enticing, °attractive, beckoning, appealing, captivating, °engaging, intriguing, °irresistible, winsome, beguiling, bewitching, entrancing, fascinating, tantalizing, °seductive

involuntary *adj.* °unconscious, unintentional, °unthinking, °impulsive, °spontaneous, °unpremeditated, °instinctive, instinctual, unwitting; °automatic, reflex, °mechanical, conditioned, °uncontrolled, uncontrollable

involve *v.* **1** °include, °contain, comprise, °cover, °embrace, °incorporate, encompass, °take in, subsume, °embody, °comprehend, number among, count in **2** °imply, °entail, °suggest, °mean, betoken, °require, necessitate, °presuppose **3** Often, ***involve in or with.*** °implicate, °concern, °affect, °touch, °entangle, °draw in; °incriminate, inculpate; °associate with, connect with, catch (up) in

involved *adj.* **1** implicated, °concerned, °affected, °interested, °active **2** tangled, °complicated, complex, twisted, snarled, convoluted, °confused, confusing, °intricate, °tortuous, °elaborate, knotty, Byzantine, °labyrinthine **3** ***involved with.*** associated with, entangled with, embroiled with, enmeshed with, *Colloq* °mixed up with

irk *v.* °irritate, °annoy, vex, °pester, °provoke, °chafe, nettle, °exasperate, *Colloq* needle, miff, °aggravate, °bug, peeve, rub (someone) the wrong way, °put out
irksome *adj.* irritating, annoying, vexing, vexatious, chafing, nettling, exasperating, bothersome, °troublesome, °burdensome, °tiresome, °tedious, °boring, wearisome, uninteresting, *Colloq* aggravating, pestiferous
irregular *adj.* **1** uneven, °bumpy, °lumpy, °coarse, °rough, unequal, unsymmetrical, asymmetric(al), °pitted, potholed, °jagged, craggy, °lopsided **2** °sporadic, uneven, °random, °erratic, unequal, °fitful, °haphazard, unsystematic, unsystematized, °disorderly, °uncertain, unmethodical; °occasional, °casual **3** °extraordinary, °unusual, °eccentric, °abnormal, anomalous, aberrant, °unnatural, °peculiar, °queer, °odd, °weird, °bizarre, °strange, °singular, nonconforming, °nonconformist, °exceptional, unconventional, °offbeat, uncommon, freakish, *Colloq* freaky
irrelevant *adj.* °inappropriate, °inapplicable, °impertinent, °unrelated, °alien, inapposite, malapropos, °beside the point, inapt, nongermane, unconnected, °extraneous, neither here nor there, °out of place, °gratuitous, uncalled-for, *Colloq* °out of the blue, off the beam, *Slang* off the wall
irrepressible *adj.* unrestrainable, irrestrainable, uncontainable, uncontrollable, unmanageable, insuppressible *or* unsuppressible, unstoppable, °ebullient, °buoyant, °effervescent, bubbling, °boisterous
irreproachable *adj.* °blameless, unimpeachable, beyond reproach, unreprovable, °faultless, °innocent, above suspicion, °impeccable, inculpable, °honest, °pure
irresistible *adj.* **1** °irrepressible, unconquerable, °indomitable, °overpowering, °unbearable, °overwhelming, °overriding, unmanageable, °ungovernable, uncontrollable **2** unstoppable, inexorable, °relentless, °unavoidable, ineluctable, inescapable
irresolute *adj.* vacillating, wavering, faltering, °indecisive, infirm of purpose, in *or US only* of two minds, undecided, °hesitant, hesitating, shifting, changing, °erratic, °uncertain, unsure, undetermined, °unresolved, °halfhearted, *Colloq* °wishy-washy
irrespective of *prep.* °regardless of, °notwithstanding, °despite, °apart from, °in spite of, without regard to, ignoring, discounting
irresponsible *adj.* °careless, °reckless, devil-may-care, unanswerable, °unaccountable, nonliable, °rash, °unruly, °wild; °unreliable, undependable, untrustworthy, °weak, feckless, °ineffectual
irretrievable *adj.* **1** nonretrievable, unretrievable, unrecoverable, irrecoverable, unsalvageable, unsavable, °lost, irreclaimable **2** irreparable, irremediable, uncorrectable, unrectifiable, irredeemable, °irreversible, °irrevocable
irreverent *adj.* **1** °blasphemous, °impious, °profane, °sacrilegious, unholy, °ungodly, irreligious **2** °disrespectful, insulting, °insolent, °rude, °discourteous, uncivil, derisive, °impudent, °impertinent, saucy, °flippant, mocking, tongue-in-cheek, *Colloq* °flip, °cheeky
irreversible *adj.* unreversible, nonreversible, °irrevocable, unchangeable, unalterable, °permanent, °fixed, °final, unrepealable, irredeemable, °irretrievable
irrevocable *adj.* °irreversible, unchangeable, immutable, °changeless, °fixed, unalterable, settled, unrecallable, °irretrievable, irrepealable, undoable; irreparable, °permanent, °enduring, °everlasting
irritable *adj.* °impatient, °excitable, °testy, °touchy, °quarrelsome, grouchy, °fretful, °peevish, °cross, crabby, crusty, °short-tempered, °petulant, °prickly, irascible, °moody, °temperamental, °gruff, °cantankerous, curmudgeonly, dyspeptic, bad-tempered, ill-tempered, ill-humored, snappy *or* snappish, grumpy *or Brit also* grumpish, *Colloq* crotchety, *US and Canadian and Irish* °cranky
irritate *v.* °annoy, vex, nettle, °pester, °provoke, °bother, °anger, °enrage, °chafe, pique, °exasperate, °ruffle, hector, °harass, harry, °nag, °plague, °worry, °fret, °fluster, °trouble, pick at *or* on, *Colloq* needle, get under (someone's) skin, get in (someone's) hair, hassle, peeve, get on (someone's) nerves, drive (someone) up the wall, get (someone's) hackles up, get (someone's) back up, drive (someone) crazy *or* mad, *Brit* rub (someone) up the wrong way, get up (someone's) nose, *US* rub (someone) the wrong way, burn (someone) up
island *n.* isle, islet, ait, cay, °key; atoll; archipelago; *Brit dialect* eyot, holm
isolate *v.* °separate, °segregate, sequester, cloister, °detach, °cut off, send to Coventry, °ostracize, °maroon, °exclude, °shut out, °bar, debar, °banish, deport, °transport, °exile, °reject, °eject, °throw out, °expel, °shun, °spurn, °avoid, °ignore, snub; quarantine; *Colloq* °cut, send (someone) to Siberia, give (someone) the cold shoulder
isolated *adj.* **1** lone, °solitary, °single, °singular, °unique, anomalous, °separate, °special, °particular, °individual, °exceptional, °unrelated **2** °alone, separated, segregated, °secluded, sequestered, cloistered, unconnected, °detached, °(set) apart, removed, °cut off, excluded; °forlorn, °lonely, hermitic(al), eremitic(al), anchoretic(al), troglodytic(al), monastic **3** °secluded, °remote, °out-of-the-way, off-the-beaten-track, unfrequented, °lonely; °secret, °hidden
issue *n.* **1** outflow, °outgoing, °exit, egress, issuance, emanation, efflux, debouchment, °emergence, °outlet **2** °outcome, conclusion, consequence, culmination, °result, °end, °effect, °consummation, °event, °climax, *Colloq* °payoff **3** °point, °topic, °subject, °matter, °affair, °problem, °question **4** Usually, ***major issue.*** (major *or* big) problem

or difficulty, °controversy, °fight, °dispute, *cause célèbre* **5** printing, °edition, °version; °copy, °number **6** °publication, promulgation, issuance, issuing, °distribution, °delivery, dissemination, broadcasting, °proclamation, °circulation **7** °offspring, child *or* children, descendant(s), °progeny, °young, scion(s), son(s), daughter(s) **8** ***at issue.*** in contention, in dispute, °unresolved, °unsettled, °uncertain, up in the air, to be decided **9** ***take issue.*** °disagree, °argue, contend, °dispute, °oppose, take exception *—v.* **10** °proclaim, promulgate, °declare, °publish, °put out, put *or* set forth, °announce, °circulate, °distribute, °release, °deliver, °broadcast, disseminate, get out **11** °emerge, come *or* go forth, °exit, °emanate, °discharge, °stream, °flow, °pour; °appear, °originate, °spring, °stem, °arise

itch *v.* **1** °tickle, tingle, °prickle **2** °desire, crave, °hanker, °hunger, °thirst, °yearn, pine, °wish, °want, °die *—n.* **3** °tickle, tickling, tingle, tingling, °prickle, prickling, irritation **4** °desire, craving, hankering, °hunger, °thirst, yearning, °longing, *Colloq* yen

item *n.* **1** °detail, article, °point, °particular, °matter, °thing, °element, component, °ingredient **2** °piece, °mention, °notice, °note, °memorandum, memo, filler, jotting

itemize *v.* °enumerate, °list, °specify, particularize, °detail, °document, °number, °record, °count, °tabulate

J

jab *v.* **1** °stab, °thrust, °poke, °dig, °prod; °plunge; °nudge; °tap **2** °punch, °hit, °strike, °belt, smack, °rap, whack, thwack, cuff, thump, wallop; elbow; *Colloq* °clip, sock, slug, biff *—n.* **3** °stab, °thrust, °poke, °dig, °prod, °nudge **4** °punch, °belt, smack, °rap, whack, thwack, cuff, thump, wallop, *Colloq* °clip, sock, slug, biff

jabber *v.* **1** blether *or US only* blather, °chatter, °babble, gibber, gabble, prate, °prattle, °patter, °drivel, °rattle, *Brit* natter, *Scots* yatter, *Colloq* °gab, gas, °yap, witter *—n.* **2** See **jargon, 2.**

jade *n.* **1** °nag, °hack, *Slang Brit* °screw, *US* °plug **2** °shrew, harridan, °nag, °hag, °drab, °witch, crone, hussy, minx, vixen, virago, termagant, beldam, slut, °slattern, trull, trollop, baggage, °tart, *Slang* battle-ax, °broad, °bitch, old bag, floozy *or* floozie *or* floosie

jaded *adj.* **1** °exhausted, °weary, °tired, dead tired, bone-tired, bone-weary, dog-tired, °fatigued, enervated, °spent, *Colloq* °(dead) beat, °dead, bushed, fagged, *US and Canadian* pooped **2** sated, satiated, cloyed, °surfeited, glutted, gorged, fed up, sick (and tired) of, slaked; °dull, bored

jag *n.* °spree, °carouse, °orgy, °bout, *Colloq* binge, *US and Canadian* toot

jagged *adj.* °rough, uneven, °notched, sawtooth, °ragged, toothed, spiked, indented, denticulate, °serrated, chipped

jail *n.* **1** °prison, lockup, reformatory, *Brit* borstal, *Brit also* gaol, *US* penitentiary, °reform school, *Nautical* brig, *Slang* cooler, clink, can, °jug, °stir, slammer, *Brit* °nick, quod, choky *or* chokey, *US* calaboose, big house, °pen, coop, hoosegow, pokey *—v.* **2** °imprison, °lock up, incarcerate, detain, confine, *Brit* °send down, *Brit also* gaol, *US* °send up (the river)

jailer *n.* turnkey, °guard, *Brit* warder, governor, *Brit also* gaoler, *US* warden, *Slang* °screw

jam *v.* **1** °cram, °force, °push, °wedge, °stuff, °press, °ram, °squeeze, shove, °pack, °crowd **2** °block, °obstruct, congest, °fill up, °clog, °plug, °stop up **3** °slam, °activate, actuate *—n.* **4** °obstruction, blockage, blocking, °block, congestion, °tie-up, bottleneck, stoppage **5** °crush, °squeeze, °crowd, °mob, °swarm, multitude, °throng, °mass, horde, °pack, °press **6** °trouble, °difficulty, °predicament, °quandary, °dilemma, *Colloq* °bind, °fix, °hole, pickle, hot water, °(tight) spot, °scrape

jamboree *n.* °gathering, °get-together, °party, °celebration, °fête, °festival, °festivity, carnival, °frolic, °revelry, °spree, °carouse, jubilee, revels, charivari *or US and Canadian also* shivaree

jangle *v.* **1** clatter, °clash, °rattle, clang, clank, °crash, °ring, °jingle **2** °jar, °upset, °irritate *—n.* **3** jangling, clatter, °clash, °rattle, jarring, clang, clanging, clank, clanking, °crash, clangor, °noise, °din, °racket, clamor, dissonance, cacophony, reverberation, *Literary* stridor

jar[1] *n.* crock; °receptacle, °vessel, container, urn, °pot, vase; °jug, pitcher, ewer, flagon, carafe, °bottle, amphora

jar[2] *v.* **1** °shake, °agitate, °disturb, °stir, °shock, °jolt, jounce, °bounce, °jog, °jerk, °jiggle, joggle **2** °disagree, °conflict, °clash, °bicker, °quarrel, wrangle, °oppose, °discord **3** °disturb, °upset, disconcert, unsettle, disquiet, °bother, °trouble, vex, °gall, °offend, °take aback, °irritate, °grate, °irk, nettle, °annoy *—n.* **4** °shock, °start, °jolt, °surprise

jargon *n.* **1** °cant, argot, °parlance, °idiom, °vernacular, slang; patois, creole, °dialect, pidgin; *Colloq* °lingo **2** blether *or US also* blather, °chatter, °babble, °gibberish, °jabber, gabble, gobbledygook, °prattle, °patter, °drivel, cackle, jabberwocky, twaddle, °(stuff and) nonsense, °rubbish, codswallop, balderdash, bunk, humbug, °palaver, *bavardage, Colloq* rot, °garbage, hogwash, bosh, piffle, flapdoodle, chitchat, °gab, claptrap, *Slang* bull, crap

jaundiced *adj.* **1** colored, tainted, distorted, twisted, °prejudiced, °opinionated, °biased, °preconceived, untrustworthy, °bigoted, °partial, unfair, °perverted; °dishonest, °corrupt **2** splenetic, cynical, °bitter, °envious, °resentful, °jealous, °hostile, °spiteful, unfriendly, disapproving, °critical, unfavorable, disparaging, denigrating

jaunty *adj.* **1** °spirited, °lively, high-spirited, °buoyant, °brisk, °frisky, °sprightly, °free (and easy), °blithe, jovial, °happy, jubilant, °jolly, °merry, °cheerful, °gay **2** °chic, °smart, °stylish, °dashing, °debonair, °elegant, colorful, °spruce, °flashy, °flash, °showy, °flamboyant, *Colloq* °sporty, natty

jealous *adj.* **1** °resentful, °bitter, grudging, °envious, covetous, green with envy, green-eyed **2** °distrustful, distrusting, mistrustful, mistrusting, °suspicious; °anxious, °insecure, threatened, imperiled, °vulnerable

jealously *adv.* watchfully, carefully, guardedly, protectively, warily, vigilantly, scrupulously, zealously, eagerly, attentively, anxiously, suspiciously

jeer *v.* **1** Often, ***jeer at.*** °mock, laugh *or* scoff *or* sneer (at), °flout, °deride, °ridicule, °make fun of, °thumb one's nose at, gibe *or* jibe, °chaff, decry, °twit, °taunt, *Colloq* °rag, bullyrag, roast, *Brit* cock a snook at, *Brit and Australian* barrack, *Slang* °knock —*n.* **2** °taunt, gibe *or* jibe, °aspersion, hoot, °hiss, boo, catcall; °derision, °ridicule, obloquy

jell *v.* **1** °set, congeal, °solidify, °harden, °coagulate, °thicken, °stiffen, gelatinize **2** °(take) form, take shape, crystallize, °materialize, come together, be set

jeopardize *v.* °endanger, imperil, °threaten, °menace, °risk, °hazard, °venture

jeopardy *n.* Usually, *in* (sometimes *at*) ***jeopardy.*** danger, °peril; °threat, °menace, °risk, °hazard, °chance, uncertainty, vulnerability, °exposure, °liability

jerk *v.* **1** °yank, °wrench, °pluck, °nip, °tug, °twist, °tweak **2** twitch, °lurch, °jolt, °jump, °start, jig, °jiggle, °wriggle, wiggle —*n.* **3** °yank, °pull, °wrench, °tug, °twist, °tweak **4** °lurch, °jolt, °start, °bump **5** idiot, °fool, moron, imbecile, *Slang US* °dope, °creep, yoyo, nerd, dweeb

jewel *n.* **1** °gem, gemstone, °brilliant, °ornament, bijou, *Colloq* °rock, sparkler **2** °treasure, °marvel, °find, °godsend, °gem, °pearl, °prize, °boon, *Colloq* °catch

jewelry *n.* gems, precious stones, jewels, ornaments, °finery, bijouterie

jiggle *v.* **1** °jog, joggle, jig, °shake, °agitate, wiggle, °wriggle, °jerk —*n.* **2** °jog, joggle, jig, °shake, wiggle, °jerk

jilt *v.* °throw over, °reject, °dismiss, °drop, °discard, °desert, break (up) with, °forsake, °abandon, *Colloq* ditch, °dump, brush off *or* give (someone) the brushoff, *Chiefly US and Canadian* give (someone) his *or* her walking papers

jingle *v.* **1** tinkle, °ring, tintinnabulate, clink, °chink, °chime —*n.* **2** tinkle, tinkling, °ring, ringing, tintinnabulation, clink, clinking, °chink, chinking, °chime, chiming **3** °tune, ditty, °melody, °song, °rhyme, verse, doggerel

jingoism *n.* chauvinism, flag waving, superpatriotism, nationalism; hawkishness, warmongering, belligerence, bellicosity

jinx *n.* **1** °(evil) spell, °curse, evil eye, malediction, voodoo, *US and Canadian* hex **2** nemesis, Jonah —*v.* **3** °curse, °bewitch, °damn, °doom, °sabotage, °condemn, *US and Canadian* hex

jitters *n. pl.* shakes, fidgets, °nerves, uneasiness, queasiness, nervousness, skittishness, restlessness, apprehension, apprehensiveness, *Slang* heebie-jeebies, willies, *US* whim-whams

job *n.* **1** °work, °employment, °position, berth, livelihood; °career, °occupation, °calling, °vocation, °appointment, °pursuit, °field, °trade, °craft, °profession, métier, °area **2** °assignment, °responsibility, °concern, chore, °task, °undertaking, °function, °duty, °role, °mission, °province, contribution, °charge **3** °task, °undertaking, °procedure, °proceeding, °affair, °operation, °project, °activity, °business, °matter, chore **4** °problem, °difficulty, °burden, °nuisance, °bother; toil, °grind, °drudgery; *Colloq* °headache, °pain (in the neck), hassle, *Slang* pain in the *Brit* arse *or US* ass **5** °crime, felony; °robbery, burglary, *Slang US and Canadian* °caper —*v.* **6** Often, ***job out.*** °let out, °assign, apportion, °allot, share out, °contract, °hire, °employ, subcontract, °farm out, consign, commission

jog *v.* **1** °trot, lope, dogtrot, °run **2** °jar, °prod, °nudge, °arouse, °stir, °stimulate, °prompt, °activate, °shake **3** °bounce, °shake, °jolt, joggle, jounce, °jerk

join *v.* **1** °unite, °connect, °couple, °link, °marry, yoke, °combine, fasten *or* tie *or* glue *or* weld *or* solder (together), °unify **2** ally *or* league with, associate (oneself) with, team up with, throw (one's lot) in with, °enlist (in), sign (up) (with), °enroll (in), °enter **3** go *or* be with, °associate with, °accompany, attach (oneself) to, participate with **4** border (on *or* upon), °meet, °touch, abut, °butt, adjoin, be adjacent (to), extend to, °verge on, °coincide (with), juxtapose, be contiguous *or* conterminous (with), be coextensive (with)

joint *n.* **1** °seam, °union, °juncture, °connection, °junction, intersection **2** *Slang* °dive, °dump, *US and Canadian* honky-tonk **3** roast —*adj.* **4** shared, °mutual, combined, collective, cooperative, °common, communal, collaborative

jointed *v.* articulated, segmented, sectioned, sectionalized, hinged

joke *n.* **1** jest, °witticism, °quip, bon mot, °laugh, wordplay, °pun, °story, anecdote, *Colloq* °gag, °wisecrack, one-liner, °crack **2** laughingstock, °butt, °(fair) game, buffoon **3** farce, °mockery, °absurdity, travesty, °caricature *—v.* **4** jest, °quip, °pun, °frolic, °wisecrack, °tease, °taunt, °banter, °chaff, °fool, *Colloq* kid, *US* crack wise

joker *n.* **1** jokester, °comedian, comedienne, funnyman, humorist, jester, °comic, °clown, °wag, °wit, punster, droll, °zany, merry-andrew, buffoon, trickster, prankster, *Colloq* °card, gagster, gagman, kidder **2** °catch, °hitch, °snag, °drawback, °trap, °twist, °pitfall, fine *or* small print, *Colloq* catch-22, no-win situation, *Taboo* nigger in the woodpile

jolly *adj.* **1** °merry, °cheerful, °frolicsome, °gay, jovial, °joyful, °sportive, convivial, jocund, jocose, jocular, °frisky, coltish, °playful, festive, jubilant, cheery, °exuberant, high-spirited, °animated *—v.* **2** Often, ***jolly along.*** °humor, appease, °deceive, °string along, °fool, °hoax

jolt *v.* **1** °jar, °shake (up), jostle, °bump, °bounce, °jerk **2** °butt, °strike, °hit, °push, °nudge, elbow, °knock, °jab **3** °shock, °astonish, °astound, °amaze, °surprise, °startle, °stun, dumbfound *or* dumfound, stupefy, strike dumb, °daze, °shake (up) *—n.* **4** °lurch, °jar, °jerk, °bump, °jump, °bounce, °start **5** °blow, °shock, °surprise, bolt from the blue, °bombshell

jot *v.* **1** Usually, ***jot down.*** make a note of, write *or* note (down), put *or* set *or* take down, °record *—n.* **2** °scrap, °grain, °(wee) bit, °speck, mite, iota, whit, °particle, tittle, *Colloq* slightest, *US and Canadian* tad, smidgen *or* smidgin

journal *n.* **1** °periodical, °magazine, gazette, newspaper, °paper, newsletter, °review, tabloid; °daily, weekly, monthly, fortnightly, °quarterly, annual **2** °diary, °chronicle, dossier, °record, °register, log, logbook, minute book, °minutes, documentation, album, °scrapbook, °memoir, almanac, annal, °history, yearbook, record book; °roll, catalog, °list

journalist *n.* °reporter, newspaperman, newspaperwoman, °correspondent, newsman, newswoman, member of the fourth estate, gentleman *or* lady of the press, stringer; columnist; °hack; newscaster, anchorman, anchorwoman, °anchor, anchorperson, commentator, broadcaster, *Brit* pressman, paragraphist; newsreader, *Colloq* °scribe, newsmonger, *US and Canadian* legman, newshawk, newshound, newshen

journey *n.* **1** °trip, voyage, °excursion, °tour, °travel, °outing, °expedition, junket, °cruise, jaunt, °pilgrimage, peregrination, odyssey, trek **2** °way, °passage, °passing, °transit, °transition, °progress, °course, °trip, °route, °career *—v.* **3** °travel, °tour, voyage, go (abroad *or* overseas), make *or* take a trip, make *or* wend one's way, make a pilgrimage, peregrinate, trek, rove, °range, °wander, °roam, °cruise, °gad (about), gallivant *or* galivant *or* galavant

joy *n.* **1** °pleasure, °gratification, °satisfaction, °happiness, contentment, °enjoyment, gladness, °delight, felicity, elation, exaltation, °ecstasy, °bliss, exhilaration, exultation, °rapture **2** °gaiety, cheerfulness, °cheer, °glee, buoyancy, joviality, jollity, jocundity, joyfulness, joyousness, jubilation, °merriment, lightheartedness, blithesomeness **3** °delight, °pleasure, °treat, °blessing, °gratification, °satisfaction, °prize

joyful *adj.* **1** °cheerful, °happy, °buoyant, °gleeful, °merry, jovial, °jolly, jocund, joyous, jubilant, °gay, lighthearted, °blithe, blithesome, °sunny **2** °glad, pleased, gratified, °delighted, °happy, °elated, °ecstatic, exhilarated, °exultant, °overjoyed, jubilant, in heaven, *Brit* in the seventh heaven, *US* in seventh heaven, *Colloq* on cloud nine, tickled (pink), *Brit* over the moon

joyless *adj.* **1** °sad, °unhappy, °miserable, depressed, °dejected, °mournful, °downhearted, downcast, down, °despondent, dispirited, °melancholy, heavy-hearted, cheerless, °doleful, grief-stricken, disheartened, saddened, crestfallen, °wretched, disconsolate, °inconsolable, morose, heartsick, °sorrowful, woeful, °woebegone **2** °gloomy, depressing, dispiriting, disheartening, °dreary, lugubrious, cheerless, °dismal, °bleak, °inhospitable, °desolate, °grim, austere, °severe

judge *n.* **1** °justice, magistrate, jurist, *Isle of Man* deemster *or* dempster, *Slang Brit* beak **2** arbitrator, arbiter, °umpire, referee, adjudicator, judicator, °mediator, °moderator **3** connoisseur, °expert, °authority, arbiter, appraiser, evaluator, reviewer, critic, ***arbiter elegantiarum*** or ***elegantiae*** *—v.* **4** adjudicate, adjudge, arbitrate, °decide, °find, conclude, °settle, °determine, °decree, pass judgment, deem, °rule, pronounce *or* pass sentence **5** assess, °evaluate, appraise, °estimate, °rate, value, °weigh, °measure, °review, °consider, °size up, °appreciate **6** referee, °umpire, mediate, °moderate, arbitrate **7** °believe, °suspect, °think, °consider, °suppose, °guess, conjecture, °surmise, conclude, °infer

judgment *n.* **1** judgement, °discretion, discernment, °discrimination, judiciousness, °prudence, °wisdom, °wit, sagacity, perspicacity, clearheadedness, °perception, perspicuousness, percipience, acumen, °intelligence, °(good) sense, common sense, levelheadedness, °understanding, shrewdness **2** judgement, °decision, ruling, verdict, conclusion, °determination, °opinion, adjudication, °finding, °decree, °order; °outcome, °result, °upshot **3** judgement, °criticism, censure, °disapproval, °reproof, condemnation **4** judgement, °opinion, °view, °belief, °(way of) thinking, °mind, °perception; °sentiment **5** judgement, °evaluation, valuation, appraisal, °estimation, assessment

judicial *adj.* **1** °legal, judiciary, judicatory, juridic(al); °official, forensic **2** °critical, analytical, °discriminating, distinguishing, discerning, °keen, °sharp, °perceptive, percipient, perspicacious, differentiating, discriminatory, discriminative, °judicious **3** judgelike, magisterial, °impartial, °fair

judicious *adj.* °sensible, common-sensical, °sound, °sober, °intelligent, °aware, °enlightened, °wise, °sage, sapient, °thoughtful, °reasonable, °rational, °sane, °logical, discerning, °discriminating, discriminative, °astute, °perceptive, percipient, perspicacious, °well-advised, (well-)informed, °prudent, °discreet, °tactful, °diplomatic, °politic, °careful, considered, circumspect

jug *n.* pitcher, ewer, urn, carafe, °bottle, flask, decanter, °jar

juggle *v.* °manipulate, tamper with, °falsify, °fix, °rig, °distort, misstate, °misrepresent, °alter, °arrange, *Colloq* °doctor, cook

juice *n.* **1** °extract, °liquid, °fluid **2** °essence, °pith, °extract, °vigor, °force, °vitality, °spirit, °strength, °power

juicy *adj.* **1** °succulent, °moist, °lush **2** °interesting, °sensational, °lurid, colorful, °vivid, °exciting, °stirring, °thrilling, intriguing, fascinating, °provocative, °suggestive, °racy, °spicy, °risqué

jumble *v.* **1** °disorder, °mix (up), °mingle, °confuse, confound, °muddle, °shuffle, disarrange, disorganize, °tangle, °entangle —*n.* **2** °muddle, °tangle, °medley, °mess; °disorder, °confusion, disarray, °chaos, °clutter

jumbo *adj.* °huge, °gigantic, °enormous, elephantine, °immense, oversized, king-sized, *Colloq US* humongous

jump *v.* **1** °leap, °bound, °spring, °pounce, °hurdle, vault, °hop, °skip; °caper, °cavort, gambol **2** °start, °jerk, wince, °flinch, °recoil **3** Sometimes, ***jump over.*** °skip (over), °omit, pass over *or* by, °bypass, °avoid, °leave out, °ignore, °disregard, °overlook, °gloss over **4** °pass, °move, °leap, °skip **5** °advance, °increase, °rise, °gain, °surge, escalate **6** ***jump at.*** °accept, °grab, °snatch, swoop up, °leap at, °pounce on **7** ***jump on.*** °attack, swoop down on; °reprimand, °rebuke —*n.* **8** °leap, °bound, °spring, °pounce, °hurdle, vault, °hop, °skip **9** °rise, °increase, °boost, hike, °advance, °gain, °surge, escalation, upsurge, °increment, °elevation **10** barricade, °obstacle, °hurdle, °fence, °rail, °obstruction **11** °start, °jerk, °spasm, twitch, °recoil, °lurch, °jolt **12** °break, °gap, hiatus, lacuna, °space, °hole, °breach, °rift, °interruption

jumpy *adj.* °nervous, °agitated, °anxious, jittery, fidgety, °restless, edgy, °on edge, °tense, °shaky, skittish, °fretful, uneasy, °queasy, °restive, panicky

junction *n.* °juncture, °union, °combination, joining, conjunction, °meeting, linking, °connection, conjoining, intersection, confluence; crossroads, interchange

juncture *n.* **1** See **junction. 2** °point, °time, °moment, °stage, °period

junior *adj.* °secondary, lesser, °lower, °minor, °subordinate, °inferior; younger

junk *n.* **1** °rubbish, °waste, °refuse, °litter, debris, °scrap; *US* °garbage, °trash —*v.* **2** *Colloq* °discard, °throw away, °scrap, °cast aside, jettison, *US* °trash

junta *n.* junto, °cabal, °clique, °faction, °gang, coterie, °band, °set, camarilla

jurisdiction *n.* °authority, °power, °prerogative, °dominion, °sovereignty, °say, °control, °rule, ascendancy, hegemony, °influence; °province, °district, °area, bailiwick, compass, °realm, °sphere (of influence), °reach, °clutches, °range, °orbit

just *adj.* **1** °fair, °equitable, °impartial, unbiased, °unprejudiced, °reasonable, fair-minded, evenhanded, °neutral, °objective **2** °upright, °righteous, right-minded, °honorable, °honest, °ethical, °moral, °principled, °straight, °decent, °good, upstanding, °virtuous, °lawful **3** justified, justifiable, well-founded, well-grounded, °legitimate, valid, °reasonable, °rightful, (well-)deserved, °due, °fitting, °proper; condign —*adv.* **4** °only, °merely, nothing but, solely, °simply, at best, at most, no more than **5** °exactly, °precisely, °perfectly; °barely, only just, °hardly, °scarcely, by a hair's breadth, *Colloq* by the skin of one's teeth **6** (only *or* just) now, a moment ago, (very) recently, °lately

justice *n.* **1** fairness, impartiality, °objectivity, objectiveness, °equity, equitableness, fair-mindedness, justness, evenhandedness, neutrality, fair play **2** the law, the police; °punishment, °prison, °imprisonment, incarceration, °detention **3** °law, °right, °morality, lawfulness, rightfulness, legitimacy, judiciousness **4** See **judge, 1.**

justify *v.* °vindicate, °legitimate, legitimatize *or* legitimize, legalize, °rationalize, °substantiate, °defend, °support, °uphold, °sustain, validate, °warrant, °confirm; °excuse, °explain, absolve, acquit, exculpate

jut *v.* °extend, °overhang, °project, °protrude, °stick out, beetle

juvenile *adj.* **1** °young, youthful, underage, °minor, teenage(d), °immature, °adolescent, °childish, °infantile, babyish, °puerile, °unsophisticated —*n.* **2** °youth, °boy, °girl, °adolescent, °minor, *Law* infant

K

keen[1] *adj.* **1** °enthusiastic, avid, zealous, °devoted, °ardent, °fervent, fervid, °earnest, °impassioned, °passionate, °intense, °active; °agog, °eager, itching, °anxious **2** °sharp, sharpened, razor-sharp, razorlike, knife-edged; °trenchant, °incisive, °cutting, rapierlike, °pointed, mordant, acid, vitriolic, acerbic, astringent, °biting, acrid, acrimonious, stinging, °scorching, °caustic, searing, °withering, °virulent, °pungent, °sarcastic,

°sardonic **3** °painful, °bitter, °acute, °poignant, °fierce, °grievous, °severe, distressing, distressful, °strong, °deep, °profound, °intense, °extreme, °heartfelt **4** °vivid, °detailed, °specific, unmistaken, unmistakable *or* unmistakeable, °distinct **5** °sharp, °acute, °sensitive, °penetrating, °discriminating, °fine **6** °intelligent, °sharp, °acute, °perceptive, perspicacious, percipient, °sensitive, discerning, °astute, °smart, °bright, °discriminating, discriminative, quick(-witted), °shrewd, °clever, canny, cunning, °crafty, °wise **7** ***keen on or about.*** °fond of, enamored of, devoted to, °interested in

keen[2] *v.* **1** °weep, wail, °moan, °lament, °mourn, °grieve; °bewail, °bemoan —*n.* **2** dirge, elegy, knell, °lament, °lamentation, requiem, monody, threnody, thanatopsis, epicedium, *Scots and Irish* coronach

keep *v.* **1** °retain, °hold, hang on to, °preserve, °conserve, °have, °save, °maintain, °control **2** °hold, °have, take care *or* charge of, °mind, °tend, °care for, °look after, °guard, keep an eye on, watch over, °protect, °safeguard; °maintain, °feed, °nourish, victual, °board, nurture, °provide for, °provision **3** °accumulate, °save (up), °amass, °hoard (up), °husband, °retain, °preserve, put *or* stow away **4** °maintain, °store, °preserve **5** Often, ***keep on or at.*** °continue, °carry on, °persist (in), °persevere (in); °prolong, °sustain **6** keep to, °abide by, °follow, °obey, °mind, adhere to, °attend to, pay attention to, °heed, °regard, °observe, °respect, °acknowledge, defer to, accede (to), °agree (to) **7** °stay, °remain **8** °support, °finance, °provide for, °subsidize, °maintain **9** confine, detain; °imprison, incarcerate, jail *or Brit also* gaol **10** °celebrate, °observe, solemnize, °memorialize, °commemorate **11** °last, be preserved, °survive, °stand up, stay fresh **12** °harbor, °maintain, °safeguard, keep dark **13** ***keep from.*** °prevent, keep *or* hold back, °restrain, °(hold in) check, °restrict, °prohibit, °forbid, °inhibit, disallow, °block, °obstruct, °deny, °curb, °deter, °discourage **14** ***keep in.*** **(a)** keep *or* hold back, °repress, °suppress, °stifle, °smother, muzzle, °bottle up, °withhold, °conceal, °hide, °shroud, °mask, °camouflage **(b)** confine, shut in *or* up, coop up, detain; fence in —*n.* **15** °upkeep, °maintenance, °support, room and board, °subsistence, °food, °sustenance, living **16** donjon, °tower, °dungeon

keeper *n.* custodian, °guardian, °guard, warden, caretaker; warder, °nurse, °attendant, *Brit* °minder

keepsake *n.* °memento, souvenir, °token, °reminder, °remembrance, °relic

keg *n.* cask, barrel, °butt, hogshead, tun, puncheon

kernel *n.* **1** °grain, °seed, pip, stone; nut, °meat, *US* nutmeat **2** °center, °core, °nucleus, °heart, °essence, °quintessence, °substance, °gist, °pith, °nub, quiddity

key *n.* **1** latchkey, skeleton key, passkey, opener **2** °clue, °cue, °guide, °indication, °indicator, °explanation **3** °pitch, °tone, °timbre, °level, tonality, frequency **4** °legend, °explanation, °description, explication, clarification, °translation **5** °mood, °tenor, °tone, °humor, °style —*adj.* **6** °important, °essential, °vital, °necessary, °crucial, °critical, °main, °pivotal

keystone *n.* °necessity, crux, linchpin, °basis, °principle, °foundation, cornerstone

kick *v.* **1** °boot, punt **2** °recoil, °backlash, °rebound —*n.* **3** punt, drop-kick **4** °recoil, °backlash, °rebound

kickback *n.* °rebate, refund, °share, compensation, commission, °percentage, °reward; °bribe, °payoff, *Colloq chiefly US* payola, *US* plugola

kidnap *v.* °abduct, °capture, °seize, °carry off, *Slang* °snatch

kill *v.* **1** °execute, slay, °murder, assassinate, do away with, put to death, cause the death of, liquidate, dispatch *or* despatch, take (someone's) life, °finish (off), put an end to, write "finis" to, °silence, kill off, administer the *coup de grâce*, °eliminate, put (someone) out of (his *or* her) misery, °exterminate, °extinguish, °obliterate, eradicate, °destroy, annihilate, °massacre, °slaughter, decimate, °butcher, °(of animals) put down, put to sleep, *Slang* do in, bump *or* knock off, °hit, °polish off, snuff (out), °take for a ride, *US* °waste, °rub out, ice, fit with concrete overshoes *or* a wooden kimono **2** °destroy, °ruin, °devastate, °ravage, wreak *or* work havoc on, kill off **3** °muffle, °neutralize, °deaden, °damp, °silence, nullify, °dull, absorb, °smother, °stifle, °suppress, °still **4** °exhaust, °tire (out), °fatigue, °weary, *Colloq* °fag (out) **5** °hurt, °pain, °torment, torture **6** °quash, °suppress, °defeat, °veto, °cancel **7** °consume, °use up, °spend, while away, °occupy, °fill, °pass, °idle —*n.* **8** °game, °prey; °quarry **9** °death, °killing, °end, °finish, deathblow, *coup de grâce*; °termination, denouement *or* dénouement, conclusion

killer *n.* **1** °murderer, assassin, slayer, °cutthroat, °butcher, exterminator, Bluebeard, (Jack the) ripper, *Slang US* torpedo, hit man, triggerman, gunsel, hooligan, gunfighter, iceman, hatchet man **2** *Slang old-fashioned* bee's knees, *US* humdinger, doozy, killer-diller (from Manila), lollapalooza *or* lallapalooza, lulu, daisy, dilly

killing *n.* **1** °murder, °carnage, butchery, °execution, °slaughter, °bloodshed, °death, °massacre, genocide, liquidation, mass murder *or* destruction, decimation, extermination, blood bath, manslaughter; slaying, homicide, °fatality **2** coup, bonanza, °success, °windfall, stroke of luck, °gain, °profit, *Colloq Brit* °bomb —*adj.* **3** °devastating, °ruinous, °destructive, °punishing, °exhausting, debilitating, fatiguing, tiring, enervating, °difficult, °arduous

killjoy *n.* °spoilsport, damper, dampener, grouch, grump, malcontent, pessimist, cynic, prophet of doom, Cassandra, *Colloq* wet blanket, sourpuss, *US* party pooper, gloomy Gus, picklepuss

kin *n.* 1 °family, relative(s), relation(s), °kindred, *US and Canadian* kinfolk *or Brit* kinsfolk, kinsman, kinswoman, °stock, °clan, blood relation(s), blood relative(s) *—adj.* 2 °related, °akin (to), °kindred, consanguineous, consanguine, cognate, agnate

kind[1] *adj.* °friendly, °kindly, °nice, congenial, affable, approachable, °amiable, °obliging, °accommodating, °amicable, well-disposed, °courteous, °good, °good-natured, °benevolent, well-meaning, well-wishing, °thoughtful, well-intentioned, °generous, bighearted, °humanitarian, °charitable, °philanthropic, °gentle, °understanding, °sympathetic, °considerate, °lenient, °tolerant, °indulgent, compassionate, kindhearted, °gracious, °warm, warmhearted, °cordial, tenderhearted, °affectionate

kind[2] *n.* 1 °sort, °type, °variety, °style, °genre, species, °class, °breed; °brand, °make 2 °nature, °character, °manner, °description, °sort, °persuasion, °stripe, feather, kidney

kindle *v.* ignite, °light, set alight, °set fire to, set afire, °inflame, °fire, °foment, °incite, instigate, °provoke, °prompt, °prick, goad, °spur, °whip up, °stir (up), °work up, °excite, °agitate, °shake up, °jolt, °arouse, °rouse, (a)waken, °inspire, inspirit, °stimulate, °animate, °enliven, °energize, innervate, galvanize

kindly *adj.* 1 See **kind**[1], above. *—adv.* 2 cordially, graciously, obligingly, amiably, amicably, politely, genially, courteously, thoughtfully, considerately, hospitably, agreeably, pleasantly 3 please, be so kind as to, be good enough to

kindness *n.* 1 friendliness, kindheartedness, warmheartedness, graciousness, goodness, goodnaturedness, goodheartedness, goodwill, °benevolence, benignity, humaneness, °humanity, decency, tenderness, gentleness, kindliness, °charity, charitableness, generosity, °philanthropy, beneficence, compassion, °sympathy, °understanding, thoughtfulness, °consideration, cordiality, °hospitality, °warmth, geniality, °indulgence, °tolerance, °patience 2 °favor, good deed *or* turn, °service, act of kindness; generosity, °assistance, °aid

kindred *adj.* 1 °close, associated, °united, allied, analogous, °like, °similar, °matching, °parallel, °common, °related; °akin 2 °related, consanguineous, consanguine, cognate, agnate *—n.* 3 See **kin, 1,** above.

king *n.* prince, crowned head, majesty, °sovereign, °monarch, ruler, regent, emperor, *Colloq Brit* °royal

kingdom *n.* 1 °realm, empire, °sovereignty, principality, °monarchy 2 °field, °area, °domain, °province, °sphere (of influence), °territory, bailiwick, *Colloq* °turf

kink *n.* 1 °twist, crimp, °tangle, °knot, °wrinkle, curl, °coil, curlicue, crinkle 2 °pang, °twinge, °stab, °spasm, cramp, stitch, °tweak, crick 3 °difficulty, °complication, °flaw, °hitch, °snag, °defect, °imperfection, distortion, deformity 4 crotchet, °quirk, whim, caprice, °fancy, vagary, °eccentricity, idiosyncrasy

kinky *adj.* 1 °outlandish, °peculiar, °odd, °queer, quirky, °bizarre, crotchety, °eccentric, °strange, idiosyncratic, °different, °offbeat, °unorthodox, °capricious, °irregular, °erratic, unconventional, °unique, freakish, °weird, °fantastic, °whimsical 2 °perverted, °unnatural, °deviant, °degenerate, warped, °abnormal, depraved 3 °crisp, frizzy, frizzed, frizzled, curly, crimped, °wiry; knotted, tangled, twisted

kinship *n.* 1 consanguinity, °(blood) relationship, (family) ties, (common) descent, °lineage, °flesh and blood 2 °connection, correspondence, parallelism, °relationship, similarity, °association, °agreement, °alliance; °affinity

kiss *v.* 1 osculate, peck, *Colloq* smack, smooch, neck, *Old-fashioned* spoon, canoodle 2 °touch, °brush, graze 3 ***kiss goodbye.*** bid adieu, say farewell to, °give up, °relinquish, °abandon, °forsake, °desert, °renounce, °repudiate, °forget (about), °dismiss, °disregard, °ignore *—n.* 4 osculation, peck, *Colloq* smack, smooch, *US and Canadian* buss, *Slang Brit* smacker

kit *n.* °apparatus, °gear, °equipment, °paraphernalia, appurtenances, °rig, accoutrements *or US also* accouterments, °tackle, °trappings, supplies, furnishings; instruments, tools, utensils, implements

kitchen *n.* kitchenette *or Brit also* kitchenet, cookhouse; scullery, pantry, larder; *Nautical* galley, *Brit* caboose

kittenish *adj.* °coy, °seductive, °flirtatious, coquettish, °sportive, °playful

kitty *n.* °pot, °pool, °collection

knack *n.* °genius, °intuition, °gift, °talent, °facility, °skill, °aptitude, °bent; °ability, °flair, °dexterity, °capacity, adroitness, °proficiency, skillfulness

knife *n.* 1 °blade *—v.* 2 °stab, °pierce, °slash, °cut, °wound

knit *v.* 1 join *or* fasten *or* weave (together), interweave, interlace, interconnect, intertwine, °link, °bind, °unite, tie (up *or* together), consolidate, °combine, °compact 2 °grow (together), °heal, °mend, °join 3 °furrow, °contract, °wrinkle, °knot, crease

knob *n.* °boss, stud, protuberance, °projection, °protrusion, °handle

knock *v.* 1 °strike, °hit, °rap, thwack, whack, thump, bang, °tap 2 *Colloq* °criticize, deprecate, carp *or* cavil at, °disparage, °put down, °run down 3 ***knock around or about.*** **(a)** °wander, °roam, °ramble, rove, °travel, gad about **(b)** °associate with, consort with **(c)** °discuss, °debate, °talk over, *Colloq* kick around **(d)** °beat (up), maltreat, °mistreat, maul, °manhandle, °batter, °abuse, °hit, °strike 4 ***knock down.*** **(a)** °raze, °demolish, °destroy, °level, °wreck, lay in ruins, throw *or* pull down **(b)** °fell, °floor, °cut down **5** ***knock off.*** **(a)** *Colloq* stop work(ing), °quit, go home, clock off *or* out, °terminate, °lock up, °close down **(b)** °steal, °pilfer, thieve, °rob, *Colloq* °lift, *Brit* °pinch, *Slang US* knock over, *Brit* °nick **(c)** See **kill, 1,** above. **(d)** make quick *or* short work of, °complete, °finish, bring to an end, *Colloq* °polish off **(e)** °copy, °imitate **6** ***knock out.*** **(a)** knock *or* render unconscious, °floor, °prostrate, trounce, °whip, *Slang* °flatten, K.O. *or* kayo **(b)** °overwhelm, °overcome, °daze, °stagger, °astound, °astonish, °bewilder, °stun, *Colloq* bowl over, blow (someone's) mind, *Slang Brit* knock for six **7** ***knock up.*** **(a)** knock *or* put together, °improvise **(b)** °arouse, (a)waken, °wake up **(c)** *Slang* °impregnate, get with child, make pregnant —*n.* **8** °blow, °rap, °tap, thump, pounding, hammering **9** °blow, °punch, °jab, smack, thwack, whack, °right, °left, cuff, *Colloq* clout, bop, biff, conk **10** °slap (in the face), censure, °criticism, condemnation, °slur, °insult

knockoff *n.* °imitation, °copy, simulation, °replica, °facsimile, duplication

knockout *n.* **1** *coup de grâce, Slang* K.O., kayo **2** °success, °sensation, °triumph, *Colloq* °hit, °winner, smash, smash-hit, stunner

knoll *n.* hillock, hummock, °mound, barrow, °hill, °elevation, °rise

knot *n.* **1** °snarl, gnarl, °tangle; °tie, °bond **2** °collection, assemblage, aggregation, congregation, °crowd, °cluster, °bunch, °gathering, °company, °band, °gang, °crowd, °throng —*v.* **3** °fasten, °tie, °bind, °secure, °lash, °tether, affix, °fix, °attach

know *v.* **1** °understand, °comprehend, be familiar with, °grasp, be acquainted with, be versed *or* skilled in **2** °recognize, °identify, °recall, °remember, °recollect **3** be sure *or* certain *or* positive **4** °distinguish, °separate, discern, °differentiate, °recognize, °identify **5** be aware *or* conscious *or* cognizant of, be informed *or* advised of, have knowledge of

knowing *adj.* **1** conspiratorial *or* conspiratory, °secret, °private; °significant, °meaningful, °eloquent, °expressive; °shrewd, canny, °artful, °sly, °wily, °crafty **2** °wise, °clever, °shrewd, (well-)informed, °knowledgeable, °aware, °expert, °qualified, °astute, °perceptive, °intelligent, sagacious

knowledge *n.* **1** °knowing, awareness, apprehension, cognition, °grasp, °understanding, discernment, consciousness, °conception, °insight **2** °facts, °information, °data, °intelligence **3** acquaintance(ship), °familiarity, °appreciation, conversance, °expertise, °experience, adeptness, °proficiency **4** °schooling, °education, °scholarship, °instruction, °learning, erudition

knowledgeable *adj.* **1** °aware, *au fait, au courant,* °up to date, (well-)informed, (well-) acquainted, cognizant, °familiar, °enlightened, °expert, °knowing, *Colloq* in the know **2** well-educated, erudite, °learned, cultured, well-read, °intelligent, °sophisticated, °worldly, °wise, °sage, sagacious

kowtow *v.* Often, ***kowtow to.*** genuflect (before), salaam (to), °prostrate oneself (before), bow (down) (to *or* before), pay court to, scrape before, cringe before, fawn (before), grovel (before), toady ((up) to), °pander to, truckle ((up) to), dance attendance on, *Colloq* butter up, *Slang* suck up to, °play up to, shine up to, *Taboo slang US* brownnose

kudos *n.* °praise, acclaim, °glory, °fame, °renown, °honor, plaudits, °applause, laudation, acclamation, accolade

L

label *n.* **1** °identification, identifier, ID, °mark, marker, earmark, °tag, ticket, sticker, °stamp, imprint, °hallmark, °brand, *Brit* docket **2** °name, °denomination, designation, appellation, °nickname, epithet, sobriquet, classification, characterization, °description **3** trademark, trade name, °brand, logo, °mark —*v.* **4** °identify (as), °mark, °tag, earmark, ticket, °stamp, °hallmark, imprint, °brand, *Brit* docket **5** °name, denominate, °designate, °call, °term, dub, classify, °categorize, pigeonhole, °class, °characterize, °describe, °portray, °identify, *Colloq US* °peg

labor *n.* **1** toil, °(hard) work, travail, °exertion, °effort, laboriousness, °strain, °drudgery, °pains, °industry, °slavery, donkeywork, *Colloq* °sweat, °grind, elbow grease, *Brit* swot **2** employees, workers, wage earners, laborers **3** °effort, °task, °job, chore, °undertaking **4** travail, childbirth, parturition, labor pains, contractions, °delivery —*v.* **5** °work, toil, travail, drudge, °strain, °strive, °struggle, °slave, *Colloq* °sweat, °grind, *Brit* °peg away (at), swot **6** °dwell on, °overdo, overemphasize, harp on, overstress, °strain, *Colloq* °belabor **7** ***labor under.*** be burdened *or* troubled *or* distressed by, be deluded *or* deceived by, be disadvantaged by, °suffer, °endure

labored *adj.* **1** °strained, °forced, °difficult, °hard, °laborious, °heavy **2** overdone, °excessive, °overwrought, °ornate, °elaborate, overworked, overembellished, contrived, °affected, °artificial, °unnatural

laborer *n.* °worker, workman, °hand, blue-collar worker, working man, manual worker, drudge, *Colloq Brit* navvy

laborious *adj.* **1** °arduous, °burdensome, onerous, °strenuous, grueling, backbreaking, herculean, °exhausting, taxing, tiring, fatiguing, wearying, wearisome, °toilsome, °difficult, °tough, °hard, uphill, °stiff **2** °painstaking, °detailed, °careful, °thorough, °diligent, °scrupulous, °exhaustive, °steady, °steadfast, °relentless, unrelenting, dogged, assiduous, sedulous, persevering, °persistent, °untiring, °tireless, indefatigable, unremitting **3** °industrious, hard-working, dogged, °determined, unwavering, °obstinate, °stubborn, unflagging, obdurate **4** °labored, °strained, °forced, °ponderous, overworked

labyrinthine *adj.* labyrinthian, mazelike, mazy, °tortuous, sinuous, winding, convoluted, °complicated, confusing, °perplexing, °puzzling, enigmatic, baffling, confounding, complex, Daedalian, daedal, °intricate, Byzantine, twisted, °gnarled, snarled, tangled, knotted, knotty, Gordian

lace *n.* **1** lacework, tatting, openwork, filigree, °mesh, °web, webbing, °net, netting, °network **2** shoelace, shoestring, bootlace, °cord, °string, thong, °tie, lacing —*v.* **3** °thread, °weave, °string, °twine, interweave, intertwine **4** °spike, °fortify, °strengthen **5** ***lace into.*** **(a)** °attack, °assault, °beat, assail, thrash, °belabor, fall on *or* upon, °set upon, pounce on *or* upon, °lay into, *Colloq* °light into **(b)** °berate, °scold, revile, °attack, °upbraid, °castigate, rant *or* rave at

lacerate *v.* °gash, °cut, °slash, °tear, °rip, °claw, °mangle; °wound, °rend, °hurt

lack *n.* **1** °want, deficiency, °dearth, °absence, °scarcity, °shortage, °need, insufficiency, paucity, °deficit, inadequacy —*v.* **2** °want, °need, °require, be deficient in, be *or* fall short of, be without

lackadaisical *adj.* **1** °lethargic, languorous, languid, °listless, °lazy, sluggish, spiritless, °idle, °indolent, °inactive, °slothful, fainéant **2** °unenthusiastic, °dull, apathetic, insouciant, uncaring, unconcerned, °indifferent, °blasé, °cold, °cool, °lukewarm, °tepid, unexcited, °phlegmatic, unemotional, unexcitable, uninterested, unimpressed, uninspired, °unmoved, pococurante

lackluster *adj.* °drab, °dull, lusterless, °flat, °dingy, °colorless, °dismal, °dreary, unexciting, °boring, °prosaic, °tiresome, °tedious, wearisome, uninteresting, two-dimensional, insipid, °vapid, °bland, unimaginative, °thick, °slow, °dense, *Colloq* °wishy-washy, blah

lad *n.* °boy, young man, °fellow, schoolboy, °youth, °juvenile, youngster, hobbledehoy, °stripling, (street) urchin, (street) arab, gamin, *Colloq* °guy, (little) shaver, kid, *US* °sprout

ladylike *adj.* °well-bred, well-born, aristocratic, °noble; °refined, °respectable, cultured, °polished, °elegant, mannerly, °gracious, °genteel, °courteous, °polite, courtly, °dignified, °proper, °correct, °decorous

lag *v.* **1** °fall behind, °linger, loiter, °delay, °straggle, °trail, hang back, dally, °dawdle, inch *or* poke along **2** °diminish, °decrease, slacken, abate, slow (down *or* up), °flag, °wane, °ebb, falter, °fail, °let up, fall (off *or* away), °ease (up), °lighten

laggard *n.* straggler, °idler, dawdler, loiterer, °slouch, sluggard, °loafer, snail, loller, *Colloq Brit* slowcoach, *US* slowpoke

lair *n.* **1** den, °burrow, °hole, °nest, °tunnel, °cave, °hollow, covert **2** hide-out, °hideaway, °retreat, hiding place, °refuge, asylum, °sanctuary, *Colloq* hidey-hole

laissez faire *n.* laisser faire, laissez-faireism, free enterprise, nonintervention, noninterference, °freedom, free trade, individualism, *laissez* or *laisser aller*, deregulation, decontrol, laxness

lambaste *v.* **1** °beat, °whip, °scourge, °flog, °lash, maul, horsewhip, cane, birch, thrash, bludgeon, trounce, drub, pummel, °batter, °belabor, cudgel **2** censure, °rebuke, °scold, °reprimand, chide, admonish, °reprove, °upbraid, °berate, °scold, revile, °attack, °castigate, flay, *Colloq* °dress down, get on (someone's) back, rake *or* haul over the coals, *US* °call down, *Slang* chew *or* bawl out

lame *adj.* **1** °crippled, °disabled, handicapped, hobbled, limping, incapacitated, impaired, °halting, °halt, spavined, *Colloq US* gimpy **2** °feeble, °weak, °flimsy, °thin, unconvincing, unpersuasive, °awkward, °clumsy, °poor, °ineffective, *Colloq* half-baked

lament *v.* **1** °mourn, °bemoan, °bewail, wail, °weep (over), grieve (for *or* over), °keen (over), sorrow (for *or* over) —*n.* **2** °lamentation, moaning, °mourning; °keen, dirge, elegy, knell, requiem, monody, threnody, thanatopsis, epicedium, *Scots and Irish* coronach

lamentable *adj.* °deplorable, °wretched, °miserable, °terrible, distressing, °awful, °regrettable, °pitiful, °despicable, intolerable, °unfortunate

lamentation *n.* °mourning, grieving, moaning, weeping, wailing, crying, sobbing, lamenting

lampoon *n.* **1** °burlesque, °caricature, °satire, °parody, pasquinade *or* pasquil, squib, *Colloq* °takeoff, *Brit* sendup —*v.* **2** °burlesque, °caricature, °satirize, °parody, pasquinade *or* pasquil, °mock, °ridicule, squib, *US* skewer, *Colloq* °take off, put *or* run down, *Brit* °send up

lance *n.* **1** spear, pike, javelin, assegai; lancet —*v.* **2** °pierce, °stab, °puncture, °prick, incise, °open, °slit

land *n.* **1** °earth, °(solid) ground, terra firma **2** °dirt, °earth, °soil, °turf, sod, loam, °mold **3** °property, °grounds, real property *or* realty *or US and Canadian also* real estate, acreage; °estate **4** °fatherland, motherland, °nation, °country, homeland, native land —*v.* **5** °arrive, alight, °light, touch *or* come *or* go down, splash down, settle on *or* upon, °come to rest, berth, °dock, °disembark, debark, go ashore, deplane, dismount **6** °catch, °capture, take captive, *Colloq* °bag **7** °get, °secure, °obtain, °win, °acquire

landing *n.* **1** touchdown, alighting, splashdown, docking **2** disembarkation, deplaning, °arrival **3** landing place, °dock, °pier, jetty, wharf, quay

landlady *n.* **1** proprietor *or* proprietress, lady of the house, °mistress, manager *or Brit* manageress, hostess **2** See **landlord, 2,** below.

landlord *n.* **1** °host, publican, °proprietor, innkeeper, hotelier, °manager, restaurateur, Boniface **2** °landlady, landowner, householder, °(property) owner, lessor, *Brit* freeholder

landmark *n.* **1** °feature, °guide, guidepost; °identification **2** turning point, watershed, milestone, °monument *—attributive* **3** °critical, °crucial, °pivotal, °important, °historic, °significant, precedent-setting, °momentous, °notable, °noteworthy, °major

landscape *n.* °prospect, °view, °scene, °aspect, vista, countryside

language *n.* **1** °speech, °tongue, °idiom, °parlance, °dialect, idiolect, patois, °jargon, °cant, argot, °vernacular, *Colloq* °lingo **2** communication, °intercourse, interaction **3** °jargon, lingua franca, vocabulary, °terminology, °vernacular, *Colloq* °lingo **4** °wording, °words, phrasing, phraseology, °style, °diction

lanky *adj.* °thin, loose-jointed, lank, °lean, °gaunt, gangling, rangy, long-legged

lap[1] *v.* **1** Often, ***lap up.*** lick up, °tongue; °sip, °drink **2** °wash, °splash, °ripple, plash, purl **3** ***lap up.*** **(a)** °consume, °drink, °eat **(b)** °accept, °believe, °credit, °fall for, *Colloq* °swallow (whole), °buy

lap[2] *n.* **1** °circuit, °orbit, ambit, °circle, °tour, °trip, °revolution **2** °flap, °fold, lappet, °projection, lapel, °overlap *—v.* **3** °overlap, °fold, enfold, °envelop, °wrap

lapse *n.* **1** °slip, °error, °mistake, °fault, °failing, °oversight, °blunder, °shortcoming, °omission, *Formal* lapsus, *Colloq* slip-up, °fluff, goof **2** °gap, °break, °interval, °intermission, °interruption, °pause, lacuna, hiatus, *Prosody* caesura, *Colloq* °holdup **3** °decline, lowering, °fall, deterioration, °drop, diminution, descent *—v.* **4** °decline, °lower, °fall, °drop, °diminish, °sink, °slip, °slump, °subside, °deteriorate **5** °run out, °expire, be discontinued, become void, °terminate, °end, °cease, °stop **6** °pass, °elapse, °go by, °slip away

large *adj.* **1** °big, °great, °broad, °stout, °heavy, thickset, chunky, °stocky, heavyset, °brawny, °husky, °sturdy, °hefty, °muscular, strapping, °burly, °solid, °weighty, corpulent, °fat, °obese, rotund, portly, adipose, °beamy, overweight **2** °big, °generous, °bountiful, °charitable, eleemosynary, °philanthropic, openhanded, magnanimous, munificent, °unselfish, bighearted, largehearted, °substantial, °considerable, °ample, beneficent, °liberal; °goodly, °kind, °good; *Colloq* °tidy **3** °big, °huge, °ample, °enormous, °gigantic, °immense, °colossal, °monumental, °massive, mammoth, Brobdingnagian, gargantuan, elephantine, °monstrous, staggering, sizable *or* sizeable, °substantial, °wide, °broad, capacious, °extensive, *Colloq* °jumbo, *US* humongous, ginormous *—adv.* **4** °big, prominently, overwhelmingly, imposingly, °eminently, °preeminently *—n.* **5** ***at large.*** **(a)** °free, unfettered, °at liberty, on the loose, unconfined, unrestrained **(b)** °generally, °mainly, in general, °chiefly, as a whole, in a body, °altogether, °in the main

largely *adv.* °chiefly, °mainly, °as a rule, by and large, °generally, in general, to a great extent, mostly, in great part, in great measure, °in the main, °on the whole, pretty much, essentially, °at bottom, basically, fundamentally

largess *n.* largesse, gifts, alms, grants, bonuses, °endowments, presents, contributions, donations, handouts; °support, subvention, °aid, °subsidy, °charity, °philanthropy, generosity, munificence, °bounty, liberality, openhandedness

lark *n.* **1** °frolic, °spree, escapade, °caper, °fling, romp, °adventure, °revel, jape, °game, antic, horse play, shenanigans, °mischief, °prank, practical joke *—v.* **2** Often, ***lark about.*** °frolic, °caper, romp, °revel, °play, °sport, °cavort, gambol, *Colloq* skylark

lascivious *adj.* **1** °lustful, °randy, °lecherous, licentious, °lewd, °prurient, salacious, libidinous, °erotic, °sensual, lubricious *or* lubricous, ruttish, goatish, hircine, satyrlike, °wanton, Cyprian, debauched, *Slang* horny, °hot **2** °pornographic, °obscene, °blue, °lurid, °indecent, smutty, °dirty, Fescennine, °filthy, °vile, ribald, °bawdy, °gross, °coarse, °offensive

lash[1] *n.* **1** °whip, °scourge, cat-o'-nine-tails, cat, quirt, knout, bullwhip, thong; rope's end **2** °stroke, °blow, °strike, °slash, °cut *—v.* **3** °flog, °beat, thrash, °switch, °whip, °scourge, horsewhip, °lambaste, flail, smite, thwack, *Colloq* whack **4** ***lash out.*** °attack, flay, °lambaste, °belabor, °punish; °criticize, °berate, °scold

lash[2] *v.* °fasten, °tie, °bind, °secure, °rope, °fix, strap, make fast

lass *n.* °girl, young woman, °miss, mademoiselle, schoolgirl, *Old-fashioned* °maiden, °maid, damsel, demoiselle; *Scots* lassie, *Irish* colleen

lasso *n.* **1** lariat, °rope, *Southwestern US* reata *or* riata *—v.* **2** °rope

last[1] *adj.* **1** hindmost, rearmost, aftermost; °final **2** °latest, newest, most recent *or* up-to-date **3** °final, concluding, °terminal, °ultimate, terminating **4** °definitive, conclusive, decisive, closing *—adv.* **5** behind, at *or* in the end, in *or* at the rear, after *—n.* **6** °end, °termination, °finish **7** ***at last.*** °finally, °eventually, °ultimately, °at length

last[2] *v.* **1** °continue, °endure, °survive, °keep on, °persist, °remain, °stay, °abide, °carry on, °hold out, *Colloq* go the distance **2** °wear, °stand up, °endure, °survive

last[3] *n.* °mold, matrix, °form, °model, °pattern

lasting *adj.* °permanent, °enduring, °durable, °everlasting, long-term, undying, °eternal

late *adj.* **1** °tardy, delayed, °overdue, behindhand, dilatory, unpunctual; °belated, *US* past due **2** °recent, °last, °new, °fresh, °current, up-to-date **3** deceased, departed, °dead; °former, °past, ex-, °recent, °previous, °preceding, °old. See also **5,** below. **4** *of late.* See **5,** below. *—adv.* **5** recently, °lately, °previously, °formerly, °once, heretofore, in recent *or* former time(s), °of late, latterly. See also **3,** above. **6** till *or* at an advanced hour *or* time **7** tardily, unpunctually, belatedly **8** recently, °lately

lately *adv.* See **late, 5,** above.

latest *adj.* **1** See **last**[1], **2,** above. **2** °fashionable, °current, °modern, °up-to-the-minute, *Colloq* in *—n.* **3** most recent *or* up-to-date *or* modern development *or* news *or* example

lather *n.* **1** suds, °froth, °foam **2** °sweat; dither, °fuss, pother, °flutter, *Colloq* tizzy, °state, °flap *—v.* **3** soap (up); °foam, °froth **4** thrash, °beat, °belabor, maul, drub, °flog, whack, pummel, buffet, °whip, flail, °lash

laud *v.* °praise, commend, °celebrate, sing *or* speak *or* sound the praises of, °honor, acclaim, °extol, °glorify, °promote, °advance, °recommend, °exalt

laudable *adj.* °praiseworthy, °meritorious, creditable, °admirable, °outstanding, °excellent, °noteworthy, °notable, commendable, °estimable, creditable

laudatory *adj.* laudative, praiseful, eulogistic, panegyric(al), encomiastic(al), °complimentary, °favorable

laugh *v.* **1** °titter, °giggle, snigger, °snicker, °chuckle, chortle, guffaw, split one's sides, *Colloq* break *or* crack up, roll on the floor, go into hysterics, roar with laughter, hoot **2** Often, ***laugh at.*** **(a)** °deride, °ridicule, °mock (at), °jeer (at), make a mockery of, poke fun (at), make fun *or* sport (of), make an ass *or* a fool (out) of, °tease, °taunt, pull (someone's) leg, °satirize, pasquinade *or* pasquil, °parody, °lampoon, jest (at), °joke (about), °scoff (at), °scorn, *Colloq Brit* take the mickey out of, *US* roast **(b)** laugh away *or* off, °spurn, °dismiss, °brush aside, °minimize, shrug off, °reject, °ignore, °disregard, °deny, °belittle, *Colloq* pooh-pooh *—n.* **3** °titter, °giggle, snigger, °snicker, °chuckle, chortle, guffaw, horse laugh

laughter *n.* laughing, tittering, giggling, sniggering, snickering, chuckling, chortling, guffawing

launch *v.* **1** °start (off), set in motion, set *or* get going, °begin, embark upon *or* on, °initiate, °inaugurate **2** °originate, °establish, °organize, °set up, °found, °open, °start **3** °shoot, °fire, °discharge, °hurl, °throw, °sling, °pitch, °fling, catapult, °send, dispatch *or* despatch **4** °float, set afloat *—n.* **5** inauguration, °start, °initiation, °opening **6** °boat, skiff, °tender, motorboat, runabout, gig, dinghy

launder *v.* **1** °wash, °clean, °scrub, °cleanse **2** legitimize, legitimatize, °legitimate, legalize

laurels *n. pl.* honor(s), distinction(s), °fame, awards, tributes, rewards, acclaim, acclamation, °glory, °renown, °celebrity, °popularity, °reputation; successes, accomplishments

lavatory *n.* water closet, °toilet, bathroom, gents' (room), ladies' (room), men's (room), restroom, °privy, *Chiefly military* or *institutional* latrine; *Nautical* °head; *Chiefly Brit* WC *or* wc, *Brit* (public) convenience, *US* °equipment, outhouse; *Colloq* (little) boys' *or* girls' room, powder room, *Brit* loo, lav, *US* can; *Slang Brit* °bog

lavish *adj.* **1** °profuse, °abundant, °liberal, copious, °plentiful, °prolific, °opulent **2** °generous, °liberal, openhanded, unstinting, °bountiful, unsparing, °unselfish, °effusive, °free **3** °extravagant, °wasteful, exaggerated, °prodigal, °improvident, °excessive, °unreasonable, °immoderate, °profligate, uncurbed, unrestrained, intemperate *—v.* **4** squander, °waste, °throw away, °dissipate, °spend, °expend, °sink **5** °shower, °bestow, °thrust, °heap, °pour

law *n.* **1** °rule, °regulation, ordinance, statute, °act, enactment, bylaw, °measure, edict, °decree, °order, directive, °injunction, °command, commandment, canon, mandate, ukase **2** corpus juris, °(legal) code, constitution, rules and regulations, °charter, *Law* °equity **3** °principle, °proposition, theory, °theorem, °formula, axiom, °deduction, corollary, postulate, conclusion, °inference

lawful *adj.* **1** °legal, licit, °legitimate, de jure, constitutional, °just, °rightful, valid, °proper **2** °permissible, allowable, justifiable, authorized, allowed, permitted

lawless *adj.* **1** anarchic(al), anarchistic, °chaotic, °unruly, unregulated **2** °illegal, °illicit, °unlawful, °criminal, felonious, larcenous, °dishonest, °corrupt, °venal, *Colloq* °crooked **3** °villainous, nefarious, °wicked, °sinful, flagitious, iniquitous, treacherous

lawn *n.* sward, greensward, °turf, sod, °green

lawyer *n.* °counsel, °advocate, member of the bar, legal practitioner, *Brit* solicitor, barrister, Queen's *or* King's counsel, bencher, *US* attorney(-at-law), counselor(-at-law), *Derogatory* shyster, ambulance-chaser, pettifogger, *Slang US* °mouthpiece

lax *adj.* **1** °loose, °slack, °casual, °slipshod, easygoing, °careless, negligent, °permissive, °weak, °indulgent, °flexible, °relaxed **2** °imprecise, undefined, °indefinite, nonspecific, unspecific, °vague, °shapeless, amorphous, °general, °broad, °inexact, hit-or-miss, °careless, °untidy, *Colloq* °sloppy

lay[1] *v.* **1** °place, °put (down), °set (down), °position, °deposit; °spread **2** °set, °arrange **3** Often, ***lay down.*** °establish, °build, °construct **4** °stake, °bet, wager, °gamble, °hazard, °risk **5** °destroy, °suppress, exorcise **6** °present, °offer, °submit, set *or* put forth, °advance, bring *or* put forward, °set out **7** °charge, °impute, °direct, °lodge, °prefer,

°aim, °attribute, ascribe **8** copulate (with), °couple (with), have (sexual) intercourse (with), °sleep (with), °lie (with), bed, go to bed (with), °mate (with), have sex (with), go all the way (with), °service, *Slang* °screw, shack up (with), *Brit* roger, *Taboo* fuck. **9** ***lay bare.*** °expose, °reveal, uncover, °disclose, divulge, °bring to light, °show, °unveil, lift the veil from **10** ***lay down.*** °stipulate, °require, °demand, insist on, °dictate **11** ***lay hold of.*** °seize, °grab, °snatch, °nab, catch *or* get hold of, °get **12** ***lay in.*** See **19 (a),** below. **13** ***lay into.*** °attack, °assault, °set about, assail, °lambaste, °belabor **14** ***lay it on.*** °exaggerate, °overstate, embroider **15** ***lay low.*** See **18 (c),** below. **16** ***lay off.*** **(a)** °suspend; °dismiss, °discharge, °fire, let go, cashier, drum out of the corps, *Colloq* °(give the) sack, (give the) ax, kick out, °(give the) boot, boot out, give (someone) his *or* her walking papers **(b)** °let up, °quit (it), °stop (it), °cease, desist, °leave off, leave alone, *Colloq* knock (it) off, cut (it) out, °come off (it) **17** ***lay on.*** **(a)** °provide, °cater (for), °supply **(b)** °impose, °charge, assess; °demand, °require **18** ***lay out.*** **(a)** °design, °plan, °outline, sketch, °arrange, °set up **(b)** °advance, disburse, °spend, °expend, °pay, °give, °contribute, *Colloq* °shell out, ante up, kick in with, fork out **(c)** °lay low, °floor, °prostrate, knock down *or* out, strike *or* cut down, °flatten, °fell, *Colloq* knock for six, kayo *or* K.O. **19** ***lay up.*** **(a)** °lay in, °amass, °accumulate, °save (up), °hoard, °preserve, °store, °keep, °put away, °put by **(b)** hospitalize, °incapacitate, disable, confine to bed, keep indoors

lay [2] *adj.* **1** °secular, nonclerical, laic, nonecclesiastical **2** °amateur, nonprofessional, nonspecialist

lay [3] *n.* ballad, °song, °air, °refrain, °strain, °melody; °poem, ode, °lyric, °rhyme, ballade

lazy *adj.* **1** °indolent, °slothful, dilatory, °idle, °shiftless, °inactive, °listless, fainéant, otiose, °slack, °lax, °lethargic **2** °slow, languid, °easy, easygoing, sluggish, slow-moving, languorous

lead *v.* **1** °conduct, °escort, usher, °guide, show the way, °pilot, °steer **2** °cause, °influence, °prompt, °bring, °incline, °induce, °persuade, °move, °dispose, °convince **3** °head (up), °direct, °govern, °command, °supervise, superintend, °preside (over), take the lead, take *or* assume command (of), °manage, captain, *Colloq* °skipper **4** come *or* be *or* go first, °excel, °surpass, °exceed, °precede, be ahead (of), °outstrip, °distance, outrun, °outdo **5** °live, °experience, °spend, °pass; while away **6** be conducive to, °create, engender, °cause, °contribute to, °result in, bring on *or* about, °produce **7** ***lead astray.*** °lead on, °mislead, misguide, °misdirect, °deceive; °fool, °decoy, °hoodwink, *Colloq* bamboozle **8** ***lead off.*** start (off *or* in *or* out *or* up), °begin, °commence, get going *or* moving, get under way, °initiate, °inaugurate, *Colloq* kick off **9** ***lead on.*** **(a)** See **7,** above. **(b)** °lure, °entice, °seduce, °beguile, inveigle, °tempt **10** ***lead up to.*** **(a)** prepare *or* pave *or* clear (the way), do the groundwork *or* spadework, °precede **(b)** °approach, °broach, °bring up, °present, °introduce, work up *or* round *or* around to, get (up) to —*n.* **11** °front, vanguard, van, lead *or* leading position *or* place, advance *or* advanced position *or* place **12** °advantage, °edge, °advance, °supremacy, °margin, °priority, primacy, °preeminence **13** °direction, °guidance, °leadership, °precedent, °example, °model, exemplar, °pattern, °standard **14** °tip, °clue, °hint, °suggestion, °cue, intimation; °prospect, °possibility, °potential; *Colloq* tip-off **15** leash, °tether, °restraint, °cord, °chain **16** °protagonist, hero *or* heroine, leading *or* starring role *or* part, leading *or* lead actor *or* actress, leading lady *or* man, male *or* female lead, °principal; prima donna, diva, prima ballerina, *première danseuse, premier danseur* **17** wire, °cable, *Brit* °flex —*adj.* **18** °leading, °foremost, °first; °main, °chief, °principal, °premier, °paramount

leaden *adj.* **1** °heavy, onerous, °ponderous, °dense, °burdensome **2** °heavy, °dull, numbing, °oppressive **3** °gray, °dull, °dingy, °gloomy, glowering, lowering, °dreary, °dismal, °oppressive, °dark, °sullen, °somber **4** °inert, °lifeless, °listless, sluggish, °inanimate, °inactive, °lethargic, languid, languorous, °torpid, spiritless, °stagnant, °static, °dormant, soporific, °sleepy

leader *n.* **1** °chief, °head, commander, ruler, °superior, °director, chairman, chairwoman, chairlady, chairperson, chieftain, captain, commandant, °principal, *Colloq* °boss, bossman, kingpin, big cheese, number one, numero uno, *Brit* gaffer, *Chiefly US* Mr. Big, *Slang US* the man **2** bandmaster, °director, *US and Canadian* conductor, bandleader, concertmaster

leadership *n.* °direction, °guidance, °management, directorship, °administration, supervision, °command, °regulation, °control, °operation, °influence, °initiative; governorship, superintendence, °running

leading *adj.* **1** °important, °influential, °chief, °prime, °cardinal, °foremost, °paramount, °primary **2** °best, °outstanding, °preeminent, greatest, °supreme, °peerless, °matchless, unequaled, unrivaled, unsurpassed

leaflet *n.* folder, °circular, °brochure, handbill, °bill, booklet, °advertisement, *US and Canadian* throwaway, flier *or* flyer, *Colloq Brit* advert

leafy *adj.* °green, verdant, bosky, woody, °shady, shaded, arborescent

league *n.* **1** confederation, °association, °alliance, °combination, coalition, °federation, confederacy, guild, °society, °fraternity, °union, °band, °fellowship, °club **2** ***in league (with).*** allied (with), °united (with), associated (with), leagued (with), federated (with), collaborating (with), conspiring (with), in collusion (with), *Colloq* in cahoots (with) —*v.* **3** °ally, °unite, °associate, °band, °combine, °collaborate, °join (forces), conspire, collude

leak *n.* **1** leakage, leaking, °discharge, °trickle, °escape, seepage, seeping, oozing, exudation **2** °hole, fissure, °crack, °chink, °crevice, °aperture, °opening, °puncture, °cut, °break, °split, °gash, °rent, °tear, °gap, °flaw **3** disclosure, °revelation —*v.* **4** °escape, °discharge, °spill, °trickle, °drip, seep, °ooze, exude, extravasate **5** °disclose, divulge, °let slip, °release, °give away (the game), make known *or* public, let (something *or* it) be known, *Colloq* °spill the beans (about); let the cat out of the bag **6** ***leak out.*** °transpire, become known, °come out, be revealed

lean[1] *adj.* **1** °thin, °slim, °slender, rangy, °spare, °wiry, °lanky, lank, °skinny, angular, bony, °rawboned, °gaunt, gangling, gangly, °spare, °meager, skeletal, scraggy, °scrawny, °haggard, °emaciated, pinched, wasted, shrunken, macilent **2** unfruitful, unproductive, °barren, °infertile, °poor, °meager, °scanty, °bare, arid, °sparse, °impoverished **3** °impoverished, °destitute, °needy, poverty-stricken, °penurious, °indigent, necessitous, °hard, °bad, °difficult

lean[2] *v.* **1** rest (against *or* on *or* upon), be held up *or* supported by **2** °incline, °slant, °tilt, °bend, °tip **3** Often, ***lean toward(s).*** °favor, gravitate toward(s), tend toward(s), be disposed toward(s), °prefer, show a preference for, incline toward(s), be *or* lean on the side of, be biased toward(s), be (prejudiced) in favor of **4** ***lean on.*** **(a)** °rely on, °depend on, °count on, believe *or* trust in, pin one's hopes *or* faith on *or* upon **(b)** °pressure, bring pressure to bear on, °intimidate, °threaten, cow, terrorize, °terrify, °scare, °frighten, °warn, °menace, °endanger, imperil, *Brit* pressurize

leaning *n.* °bent, °inclination, °bias, °prejudice, °favoritism, °partiality, predilection, °liking, °taste, °preference, °penchant, °sympathy, °tendency, tendentiousness

leap *n.* **1** °spring, °bound, °jump, vault (into); °hurdle, °clear, hop over, skip over, °negotiate **2** °jump, °cavort, gambol, °dance, °frisk, °caper, °frolic, romp, °prance, curvet **3** °jump, °rush, °hasten, form hastily, accept (prematurely *or* without question) **4** ***leap at.*** °jump at, °accept, be eager for, move quickly, °take —*n.* **5** °spring, °bound, °jump, vault, °hurdle, °hop, °skip **6** °jump, °increase, (up)surge, °rise, upswing, °growth, escalation **7** ***by leaps and bounds.*** °rapidly, °quickly, °swiftly, speedily

learn *v.* **1** Often, ***learn of.*** °find out, °discover, °hear (of), chance *or* hit upon, °understand, °gather, have revealed to one; °determine, ascertain, uncover **2** be taught, be instructed in, °master, become proficient (in), acquire knowledge (of) **3** °understand, see the light, get the picture, *Colloq* °catch on, get the idea, get it, *Brit* °twig **4** °memorize, commit to memory, learn by heart

learned *adj.* (well-)informed, erudite, °knowledgeable, ***au fait,*** cultured, °intellectual, °highbrow, (well-)educated, °scholarly, °academic, scholastic, °lettered, °experienced, skilled, practiced, °accomplished, °expert, literate, well-read, (well-)versed, (well-)trained, (well-)grounded

learner *n.* °student, °pupil, °scholar, trainee, °apprentice, °novice, tyro, abecedarian, beginner, °initiate, neophyte

learning *n.* °knowledge, erudition, °culture, °scholarship, °lore, °information, °wisdom

lease *n.* **1** rental agreement *or* contract, sublease, sublet —*v.* **2** °rent (out), °let (out), sublet (out), sublease (out), °charter (out), °hire (out)

leave[1] *v.* **1** go (away *or* off), °depart, °set off, be off, get away *or* off, °retire, °retreat, °withdraw, decamp, °(make an) exit, °run, be gone, bid (someone *or* something) goodbye, say goodbye *or* adieu (to), take (one's) leave (of), °quit, °desert, °pull out, °check out, °fly, *Colloq* push *or* shove off, °take off, skedaddle, °flit, °disappear, do a disappearing act, °pull up stakes, up-anchor, *Slang* °beat it, scram, vamoose, °split, *Brit* beetle off, do a bunk, do a moonlight flit, hop it, *Taboo slang Brit* °bugger off **2** go *or* run off, deviate from **3** °forget, °mislay, °lose **4** °abandon, °desert, take leave of, °wash one's hands of, °turn one's back on; °quit, resign from, °give up, °renounce, °drop (out of) **5** °make, °render, cause to be *or* become *or* remain **6** °bequeath, °will, °hand down, °devise, demise, °transfer **7** °entrust, °commit, °assign, °cede, °relinquish, give over *or* up, consign, °resign **8** cause *or* allow to remain, have as a remainder, °yield, °give **9** ***leave off.*** °stop, °cease, desist, forbear, °give up, °refrain from, °discontinue, abstain (from), °renounce **10** ***leave out.*** °omit, °disregard, °ignore, °neglect; count out, °reject, °exclude, °eliminate, °bar, °except

leave[2] *n.* **1** °permission, authorization, °consent, °freedom, °liberty, °license, °sanction, dispensation **2** furlough, leave of absence, time off, sabbatical, °recess, °holiday, vacation **3** departure

lecherous *adj.* °lewd, °lascivious, salacious, libidinous, °sensual, lubricious *or* lubricous, °lustful, concupiscent, licentious, °prurient, dirty-minded, filthy-minded, °carnal, goatish, hircine, °randy, °libertine, °wanton, °profligate, depraved, °degenerate, °decadent, °dissolute, *Slang* horny

lecture *n.* **1** °speech, °address, °talk, discourse, disquisition, treatise, dissertation, °paper, °lesson, °instruction, °sermon, declamation, °harangue, diatribe, philippic, screed **2** °reproof, °reprimand, °rebuke, °criticism, censure, reproach, scolding, upbraiding, chiding, berating, °tongue-lashing, remonstration, *Colloq* dressing-down, telling-off, *Slang Brit* wigging, *US and Canadian* chewing-out —*v.* **3** make *or* deliver *or* give a speech *or* address *or* talk, discourse:

sermonize, °hold forth, moralize, pontificate, orate, °preach, declaim, expound, go on about, °harangue **4** °reprove, °reprimand, °rebuke, reproach, °scold, °upbraid, °berate, chide, tongue-lash, remonstrate with, rail at, fulminate against; admonish, °warn; *Colloq* °dress down, °tell off, send (someone) off with a flea in (his *or* her) ear, *Slang Brit* wig, *US and Canadian* °chew out

ledge *n.* shelf, °projection, °step, mantel *or* mantle, mantelpiece *or* mantlepiece, °overhang, sill

leer *v.* **1** °ogle, °eye —*n.* **2** °ogle, the eye, *Colloq* once-over, *Slang* glad eye

leery *adj.* °suspicious, °skeptical, dubious, °doubtful, doubting, °distrustful, °wary, °cautious, chary, °careful

leeway *n.* °space, elbowroom, °room, °play, °scope, °slack, latitude, wide berth; °freedom

left *adj.* **1** left-hand, sinistral, *Nautical* °port, (formerly) larboard, *Heraldry* °sinister **2** leftist, left-wing, °progressive, °liberal, socialist(ic), °pink; °radical, communist(ic), red —*n.* **3** left side *or* hand *or* fist, *Nautical* °port, portside, (formerly) larboard

left-handed *adj.* **1** °clumsy, °awkward, gauche, fumbling, maladroit, cack-handed **2** insulting, disparaging, derisive, uncomplimentary, insulting, °paradoxical, °ambiguous, °questionable, dubious, °doubtful

leftover *n.* **1** Usually, ***leftovers.*** remainder(s), remnant(s), °rest, °residue, residuum, °balance, °surplus, °excess, °superfluity, overage; scrap(s), leavings, crumbs, °odds and ends, debris *or* débris, °refuse, °waste, °rubbish, rubble, detritus, *Archaic* orts —*adj.* **2** °remaining, °residual, °extra, °excess, °unused, uneaten

leg *n.* **1** limb, °member, *Colloq* °pin, °peg, °stump, *Slang* gam **2** °support, °brace, °prop, °upright, °standard, column, °pillar **3** °part, °portion, °segment, °stretch, °stage, °section, °length, °lap **4** ***a leg up.*** °boost, °assistance, °push, °help, helping hand, °advance, °support, *US and Canadian* °assist **5** ***leg it.*** °run, °hurry, °hasten, °scurry, *Colloq* scoot, skedaddle **6** ***not a leg to stand on.*** °defenseless, unsupported, insupportable *or* unsupportable, indefensible, unjustifiable, °untenable, °invalid **7** ***on one's or its last legs.*** °decrepit, °failing, °exhausted, °dying, worn-out, °run-down, falling apart *or* to pieces, broken-down, the worse for wear; °dilapidated, °rickety, °shabby, °ramshackle, crumbling, tumbledown **8** ***pull (someone's) leg.*** °tease, °mock, °jeer at, °taunt, °gibe, °make fun of, °chaff, °guy, °fool, °deceive, *Chiefly Brit* °twit, *Colloq* rib, kid, °rag **9** ***shake a leg.*** **(a)** °hurry (up), °hasten, °rush, *Colloq* get going *or* moving *or* cracking, look alive *or* lively **(b)** °dance, trip the light fantastic (toe), *Slang* hoof it, *US* cut a rug **10** ***stretch one's legs.*** (take *or* go for a) walk, °(take some) exercise

legal *adj.* **1** °lawful, licit, statutory, °acceptable, °permissible, permitted, admissible, authorized **2** °legitimate, °proper, °right, °rightful, °sound, constitutional, authorized, *Slang* legit **3** °judicial, juridical, judiciary, forensic

legalistic *adj.* narrow(-minded), disputatious, contentious, litigious, °literal, °strict, °niggling, °hairsplitting, caviling, quibbling, jesuitical, pettifogging, °nice, °fine, °subtle, *Colloq* nitpicking

legend *n.* **1** epic, °saga, °myth, °story, °(folk) tale, °romance, °narrative, fable, °tradition, fiction, *Scandinavian* edda **2** °celebrity, °phenomenon, °tradition, °wonder, luminary, °personage, °somebody **3** °key, table of symbols, °code, explanatory note **4** °motto, °slogan, inscription, caption, °title

legendary *adj.* **1** fabled, storied, °traditional; °heroic, epic, mythic **2** °fanciful, °imaginary, °fabulous, °mythical, °romantic, °fictional **3** °famous, °celebrated, °noted, famed, °well-known, °renowned, °illustrious, °immortal, °prominent, °eminent, °great, acclaimed, °noteworthy

legible *adj.* °readable, decipherable, °clear, understandable, °plain, °distinct

legitimate *adj.* **1** valid, °proper, °right, °rightful, authorized, °legal, °genuine, °real, °true, °authentic **2** °lawful, licit, °legal, by law, de jure, statutory **3** common-sensical, °sensible, °reasonable, °proper, °correct, °acceptable, valid, °logical, justifiable, °just, °fair —*v.* **4** legitimize, legitimatize, legalize, °authorize, °sanction, °warrant, validate, °certify

leisure *n.* **1** spare *or* free time, °time (off), °liberty, °freedom, °opportunity **2** °holiday, vacation, °respite, °relief, °rest, °recreation, °relaxation, °ease, breathing space, °quiet, tranquillity, °repose, *US military* rest and recreation, R and R **3** ***at leisure.*** **(a)** unoccupied, °inactive, retired, resting, °free, on holiday *or chiefly US and Canadian* vacation; °at liberty, °available, °unemployed **(b)** Often, ***at one's leisure.*** °at one's convenience, °when convenient, °unhurriedly, °in one's own time —*adj.* **4** recreational **5** °free, unoccupied, nonworking, unencumbered, °idle, °holiday, vacation

leisured *adj.* °wealthy, °rich, affluent, °prosperous, moneyed *or* monied, well-to-do

lend *v.* **1** make a loan of, °loan, °advance **2** °impart, °furnish, °bestow, °give, °confer, °contribute, °add **3** ***lend itself to.*** °suit, °fit, be fitted *or* appropriate *or* suitable (to *or* for), be applicable *or* adaptable (to *or* for)

length *n.* **1** °extent, °measure, °span, °reach, °size, °magnitude, dimension, °measurement **2** duration, °stretch, °term, °period, °space **3** ***at full length.*** fully, °completely, to the fullest extent **4** ***at length.*** **(a)** °finally, at (long) last, °eventually, after a (long) time *or* while, °ultimately; °in the long run **(b)** for a long time, interminably, for ages **(c)** °in depth, °thoroughly, °completely, exhaustively, extensively, to the fullest *or* greatest extent, °in detail

lengthen *v.* make longer, °extend, elongate;

°stretch, drag out, °draw out, °prolong, protract, °expand, °continue
lengthy *adj.* °long, overlong, long-drawn (-out), °protracted; °endless, interminable, prolonged, long-winded, °wordy, prolix, verbose, garrulous, °talkative, loquacious, °boring, °dull, °tedious
lenient *adj.* °gentle, °kind, °kindly, °easy, °sparing, °merciful, °tender, humane, tenderhearted, kindhearted, °indulgent, °permissive, °forgiving, easygoing, °tolerant, °patient, compassionate, forbearing, °understanding, magnanimous, °generous, °charitable
lesson *n.* **1** °exercise, °drill, reading, °lecture, °recitation; °assignment, homework, °task **2** °class, °session; °instruction, teaching, tutoring, °schooling; °practice **3** °example, exemplar, °model, °guide, °maxim, °paragon, °message, °deterrent, discouragement; °warning, admonition; °moral, °precept **4** °punishment, chastisement, chastening, castigation, scolding, chiding, °rebuke, °reprimand, °reproof
let[1] *v.* **1** °allow (to), °permit (to), °sanction (to), give permission *or* leave (to), °authorize (to), °license (to), °suffer (to) **2** °cause (to), arrange for, °enable (to) **3** Sometimes, ***let out.*** °rent (out), °hire (out), °lease (out), °charter (out); °contract (out), subcontract (out), °farm (out), °job (out) **4** ***let down.*** °disappoint, °fail, °frustrate; disenchant, dissatisfy, °disillusion **5** ***let in.*** °admit, allow in; °include, °take in, °receive, °welcome, °induct, °install **6** ***let off.*** **(a)** °pardon, °forgive, °excuse, °release, °discharge, let go **(b)** exonerate, absolve, °clear, acquit, °vindicate, *Slang* let off the hook **(c)** detonate, °explode, °discharge, °fire, °set off **(d)** °emit, give out *or* off, °release, throw off *or* out, °let loose, exude **7** ***let on.*** **(a)** °confess, °admit, °disclose, divulge, °reveal, °expose, let it be known, °let out, °say, °tell, °give away, °let slip, °betray; °leak **(b)** feign, °affect, °pretend, °fake, °(put on an) act, simulate, dissemble, °dissimulate **8** ***let out.*** **(a)** See **7 (a),** above. **(b)** °(let) loose, °liberate, °(set) free, °release, let go, °discharge **(c)** °emit, °give vent to, °produce **(d)** °end, °stop, °break up, °finish, °close, °terminate **9** ***let up.*** °decrease, abate, °ease (up), slacken, °diminish, lessen, °mitigate, °subside, °moderate **10** ***let up on.*** ease up on, slack off on
let[2] *n.* °hindrance, °impediment, °obstruction, °obstacle
letdown *n.* °disappointment, disillusionment, disenchantment
lethal *adj.* °deadly, °fatal, °mortal
lethargic *adj.* **1** lethargical, sluggish, °slow, °dull, °heavy, °lazy, °indolent, °phlegmatic, °slothful, °idle, languid, languorous, °listless, fainéant, °inactive, °torpid, stuporous, comatose; °indifferent, apathetic **2** °weary, °tired, fagged out, °fatigued, enervated, °weak, °exhausted, °drowsy, °sleepy, somnolent
lethargy *n.* **1** °sluggishness, °sloth, dullness, heaviness, laziness, °indolence, phlegm, °idleness, languidness, languor, listlessness, ***dolce far niente,*** °inactivity, °inertia, °torpor, °stupor; °indifference, apathy **2** weariness, tiredness, °fatigue, °weakness, °exhaustion, drowsiness, sleepiness, somnolence
letter *n.* **1** °character, °symbol, °sign **2** °missive, epistle, communication, °note, °line, °message, dispatch *or* despatch; correspondence **3** ***letters.*** °literature, the humanities, belles-lettres, the classics; erudition, °culture, the world of letters, °learning, °scholarship **4** ***to the letter.*** °precisely, °literally, °exactly, accurately, strictly, *sic,* °thus, letter-for-letter, ***literatim,*** word-for-word, °verbatim —*v.* **5** inscribe, °write, °spell (out)
lettered *adj.* literate, °literary, (well-) educated, erudite, °scholarly, °learned, °well-informed, °enlightened, °knowledgeable, (well-)versed, well-read, cultured, °cultivated
letup *n.* °cease, °stop, stopping, ceasing, cessation, surcease, °break, °interruption, °pause, °intermission, °suspension, time out *or* off; moderation, lessening, abatement, diminution, °relief, hesitation, °respite, °relaxation
level *adj.* **1** °even, °smooth, °plane, °uniform, °plain, °flat, °flush, °straight, °true **2** °horizontal; °prone, °supine **3** °uniform, °constant, °steady, °consistent, °invariable, unvarying, unalterable, unchanging, unfluctuating; °very **4** °parallel, °even, °equal, °equivalent, °consistent **5** up (on), informed (about *or* on), up to date (on *or* with), ***au fait*** (with), ***au courant*** (with) **6** °even, tied, °equal, neck and neck **7** See **levelheaded,** below. —*v.* **8** level off, °even, °smooth (out), °flatten (out) **9** °destroy, °demolish, °raze, °lay waste, °devastate, °knock down, tear down, °pull down, °wreck, bulldoze **10** °aim, °point, draw a bead, °direct, °train, °focus **11** ***level with.*** be *or* play fair with, be honest *or* straight with, be open *or* frank *or* straightforward with, *Colloq* be up front with —*n.* **12** °plane, °horizontal, °elevation, °height; altitude **13** °floor, °story **14** °plane, °position, °status, °standing, °rank, °stage **15** ***on the level.*** °straight, straightforward, °honest, °direct, °sincere, °square, °open, °aboveboard, *Colloq* °up front, on the up and up, *US* straight-shooting
levelheaded *adj.* (well-)balanced, °sensible, °sane, °reasonable, common-sensical, °level, unruffled, undisturbed, unperturbed, imperturbable, even-tempered, composed, °calm, °cool, °collected, °tranquil, °serene, unflappable, °poised, °relaxed, °self-possessed
levity *n.* lightheartedness, lightness, frivolity, frivolousness, °flippancy, trivialization, °triviality, facetiousness
lewd *adj.* °lascivious, salacious, °lecherous, °lustful, licentious, °carnal, goatish, hircine, satyric(al), ruttish, concupiscent, libidinous, lubricious *or* lubricous, °indecent, °offensive, °wild, debauched, °obscene, smutty, °crude, °dirty, °foul, °filthy, °rude, °porno-

graphic, °prurient, °gross, °dissolute, Fescennine, °bawdy, ribald, °scurrilous, °raw, °blue, °erotic, °suggestive, °unchaste, unvirtuous, *Colloq* °randy, *Slang* °hot, horny

liability *n.* **1** answerability, °responsibility, °burden, onus, °accountability **2** °obligation, °debt, indebtedness, arrear(s), debit **3** °disadvantage, °drawback, °hindrance, °impediment, °encumbrance, °snag, °hitch, °barrier, °obstacle, °obstruction, °burden, onus **4** °exposure, susceptibility, vulnerability

liable *adj.* **1** °likely, apt, °prone, °inclined, °disposed **2** answerable, °responsible, °accountable, obligated, blamable, blameworthy, *Law* actionable **3** exposed, °susceptible, °vulnerable, °open, °subject

liaison *n.* **1** °connection, communication, contact, linkage, affiliation, °relationship, °relations **2** °contact, °intermediary, °link, °tie, °medium, °go-between, °agent **3** °(love) affair, amour, °relationship, *affaire d'amour, affaire de coeur,* °intrigue, °romance, entanglement, flirtation

liar *n.* fabricator, prevaricator, perjurer, falsifier, teller of tales, false witness, Ananias, Baron von Münchhausen, *Colloq* fibber

libel *n.* **1** defamation, vilification, denigration, denunciation, deprecation, depreciation, belittlement, disparagement, derogation, °disgrace, ill repute, °dishonor, obloquy, °shame, °humiliation, mortification **2** °slander, calumny, °lie, °falsehood, prevarication, untruth, misrepresentation, °aspersion, °innuendo, insinuation, °slur, °smear, °blot, °stain, smirch, °stigma —*v.* **3** defame, °vilify, denigrate, °denounce, deprecate, °depreciate, °belittle, °disparage, derogate, °disgrace, °dishonor, °shame, °humiliate, °mortify **4** °slander, calumniate, lie about, °misrepresent, asperse, °insinuate, °slur, °smear, malign, °stain, °blacken, °discredit, besmirch, °stigmatize, traduce, °vilify, *Rare* vilipend, *Colloq chiefly US* bad-mouth

liberal *adj.* **1** °generous, °bountiful, °free, openhearted, °open, openhanded, bounteous, °charitable, °philanthropic, munificent, magnanimous, °big, bighearted, unstinting, °unselfish, unsparing; °lavish, °abundant, °ample, °large, °handsome, °plentiful, copious **2** °progressive, libertarian, reformist, humanistic, °left (of center), latitudinarian, °nonpartisan, unaligned *or* nonaligned, individualistic **3** °free, not literal, °flexible, °lenient, °loose, °broad, °open, °disinterested, °impartial, °dispassionate, °fair, broadminded, openminded, °unprejudiced, unbigoted, unjaundiced, unopinionated, °tolerant —*n.* **4** °progressive, libertarian, reformer, progressivist, latitudinarian, °independent, freethinker, leftist, left-winger

liberalize *v.* **1** broaden, °widen, °extend, °expand, °stretch, °enlarge **2** °loosen, °ease, slacken, °relax, °modify, °change, °moderate, °soften

liberate *v.* **1** °(set) free, °release, set at liberty, disenthrall, °emancipate, manumit, °deliver, enfranchise, °(let) loose, let go, °let out, °let off **2** °steal, °pilfer, purloin, °take, °appropriate

liberation *n.* freeing, liberating, deliverance, emancipation, enfranchisement, enfranchising, °delivery, °rescue, rescuing, °release, releasing, loosing, unfettering, unshackling, unchaining

libertine *n.* **1** lecher, °reprobate, °profligate, °rake, rakehell, °roué, debaucher, womanizer, °seducer, fornicator, adulterer, debauchee, whoremonger, °philanderer, Don Juan, Lothario, Casanova, *Colloq* wolf, lady-killer, (old) goat, dirty old man —*adj.* **2** licentious, °lecherous, °reprobate, °profligate, °rakish, rakehell, philandering, °dissolute, °immoral, °degenerate, depraved, debauched, °decadent, °dirty, °filthy, amoral, °wanton, °lewd, °lascivious, °prurient, lubricious *or* lubricous, salacious, Paphian, libidinous, ruttish, goatish, hircine, satyric(al), °carnal, bestial, *Colloq* °randy, *Slang* horny

liberty *n.* **1** °freedom, °independence, self-determination, autonomy, self-rule, °self-government, self-direction, °sovereignty **2** °right, °freedom, franchise, °carte blanche, °privilege, °prerogative, °license, °leave, °permission, authorization **3** °freedom, °license, °initiative, °exemption, °exception, °privilege **4** ***at liberty.*** °free, °uninhibited, unfettered, unconstrained, unrestricted, unrestrained, liberated **5** ***take a liberty or the liberty or, often, liberties.*** be unrestrained *or* presumptuous *or* bold *or* uninhibited *or* overfamiliar *or* forward *or* aggressive *or* impudent *or* impertinent *or* audacious *or* improper; display *or* exercise boldness *or* impropriety *or* presumption *or* presumptuousness *or* indecorum *or* unseemliness *or* boldness *or* arrogance

license *n.* **1** °leave, °permission, °liberty, authorization, °authority, entitlement, dispensation, °right, °carte blanche, °freedom, latitude, free choice, °privilege, °charter **2** °permit, certificate, credential(s), paper(s) **3** °disregard, deviation, departure, nonconformity, °noncompliance, divergence —*v.* **4** °authorize, °allow, °permit, °certify, °sanction, °approve, commission **5** °certify, °document, accredit, °entitle, validate, °enable, empower

lie[1] *v.* **1** prevaricate, °fabricate, °misrepresent, °invent, commit perjury, perjure *or* forswear oneself, *Colloq* °fib —*n.* **2** °falsehood, untruth, falsification, misrepresentation, fiction, °invention, prevarication, °fib, °fabrication, *Colloq* °story, cock-and-bull story, °(tall) tale, whopper, *US* fish story, fishtale

lie[2] *v.* **1** °recline, stretch out, be prostrate *or* recumbent *or* prone *or* supine **2** °rest, °repose; can be found, be, be situated **3** °rest, °repose, be, reside, °dwell, °abide, °remain, °belong **4** °press, °burden, °weigh, °rest, be **5** ***lie low.*** °hide, remain concealed *or* in hiding, keep out of sight, *Colloq Brit* lie doggo —*n.* **6** ***lie of the land.*** °state,

°status, °condition, °situation, °atmosphere, °mood, °spirit, °temper, °character

life *n.* **1** °existence, °entity, being; sentience, viability **2** °existence, survival, living, °subsistence, °sustenance **3** °existence, living, way of life, life style **4** °existence, lifetime, °time; duration **5** °person, °mortal, °human (being), °individual, °soul **6** biography, autobiography, memoir(s), °(life) story **7** °soul, °spirit, spark of life, vital spark, moving spirit, life force, *élan vital*; lifeblood; °animation, °vitality, liveliness, sprightliness, vivacity, °sparkle, °dazzle, °dash, élan, °vigor, °verve, °zest, °flavor, pungency, freshness, effervescence, *brio*, °flair, vim, °energy, °exuberance, °enthusiasm, *Colloq* °pep, zing, get-up-and-go **8** °obsession, preoccupation, °passion, °fixation, compulsion **9** °bounce, °resilience, °spring, °elasticity

lifeless *adj.* **1** °dead **2** °unconscious, °inanimate, insensate, °inert, unmoving, °dead, °insensible **3** °dull, °boring, °tiresome, °heavy, °lackluster, °torpid, °tedious, °flat, °stale, uninteresting, °colorless, uninspiring, °vapid, °wooden **4** °barren, °desert, °desolate, °bare, °sterile, °bleak, °empty, °uninhabited, unoccupied, °dreary, °waste

lifelike *adj.* °authentic, °realistic, °natural, true-to-life, °real, °faithful, °graphic, °vivid

lift *v.* **1** °raise, elevate; °hoist, °heave (up) **2** Often, ***lift up.*** °exalt, °raise, elevate, uplift, °boost, upgrade, °promote, °advance; °improve, ameliorate, °better, °dignify, °enhance, ennoble, enshrine, deify, °immortalize **3** °discontinue, °end, °terminate, °stop **4** °withdraw, °cancel, °confiscate, take away, rescind, °void, annul **5** °rise, °disappear, °dissipate, vanish **6** °steal, °appropriate, °pilfer, °pocket, thieve, °take, purloin; plagiarize, °copy, *Colloq* °pinch, crib, °liberate, *Slang Brit* °nick, *Old-fashioned* half-inch —*n.* **7** °ride **8** °encouragement, °boost, stimulus, °inducement, °inspiration, reassurance, cheering up, *Colloq* °shot in the arm

light[1] *n.* **1** °illumination, brightness, °daylight, lamplight, candlelight, firelight, gaslight, torchlight, starlight, moonlight, sunlight; gegenschein, counterglow **2** lamp, light bulb, torch, °beacon, lantern, candle, °flare, headlight *or* headlamp, streetlight *or* streetlamp, *US and Canadian* flashlight **3** °radiance, °radiation, luminescence, °glare, °gleam, °glow, °reflection, luminosity, °shine, °sparkle, scintillation, incandescence, phosphorescence, fluorescence **4** daybreak, °dawn, sunrise, *US* sunup **5** clarification, enlightenment, °insight, °understanding, elucidation, simplification, °explanation **6** window, windowpane **7** °match, lighter, °spill, °taper, °fire, °flame, ignition **8** highlight **9** ***bring to light.*** °reveal, °unearth, °find, uncover, °unveil, °discover, °expose, °disclose, °make known **10** ***come to light.*** be revealed, be unearthed, be uncovered, be unveiled, be discovered, be exposed, be disclosed, °appear, °come out, °turn up, °transpire, °develop, evolve, °emerge **11** *US* ***in light of*** *or Brit* ***in the light of.*** °considering, °in view of, in consideration of, taking into account, keeping *or* bearing in mind **12** ***shed*** *or* ***throw*** **(*some*** *or* ***a little*) *light on.*** °explain, elucidate, °simplify, °clarify —*adj.* **13** (well-)illuminated, °bright, alight, (well-)lit, (well-)lighted, shining, °luminous, effulgent, °brilliant, beaming, °incandescent, phosphorescent, fluorescent **14** °pale, light-hued —*v.* **15** ignite, set alight, set *or* put a match to, °kindle; °burn, °touch off, °set fire to, °fire **16** °illuminate, °light up, °lighten, °brighten **17** °turn on, switch on, °put on **18** ***light up.*** °lighten, °brighten, cheer up, liven up

light[2] *adj.* **1** lightweight, °portable **2** underweight, °skinny, °slight **3** °faint, °dim, °obscure, °indistinct, unclear, faded, °imperceptible **4** °faint, °gentle, °mild, °slight, °delicate, °insignificant **5** °dainty, °graceful, °delicate, °gentle, °slight **6** not weighty, °frivolous, unimportant, °insignificant, °inconsequential, inconsiderable, trivial, °trifling, evanescent, unsubstantial, °slight, °superficial **7** °nimble, °agile, °active, °swift, spry, lithe, °sprightly, lightsome, light-footed, limber, lissom *or* lissome **8** simple-minded, lightheaded, °scatterbrained, rattle-brained, bird-brained, featherbrained, °hare-brained, °flighty, °giddy, °dizzy, °silly, °inane, °foolish, °frivolous, empty-headed, °vacant, vacuous, °shallow, °superficial **9** °cheerful, °happy, °gay, °sunny, °merry, lighthearted, happy-go-lucky, easygoing, °joyful, jovial, °jolly **10** °easy, not burdensome, endurable, °bearable, °tolerable, °supportable, undemanding, °effortless, untaxing, °moderate **11** amusing, °entertaining, °witty, diverting **12** ***make light of.*** °dismiss, °write off, shrug off; °trivialize; °ridicule —*v.* **13** alight, °land, come *or* go down, °descend, °settle; deplane, disembark *or* debark, detrain, dismount **14** ***light into.*** °attack, assail, °lambaste, °assault, pounce *or* fall on *or* upon, °beat, °belabor; °abuse, tongue-lash, °harangue, °upbraid, °scold, °berate, *Colloq* °lace into; *Slang* clobber **15** ***light on*** *or* ***upon.*** chance *or* happen *or* stumble *or* hit on *or* upon, °come across, °encounter, °find, meet up with

lighten[1] *v.* **1** °illuminate, °brighten, °light up **2** °cheer (up), °brighten, °gladden, °shine; °smile

lighten[2] *v.* disencumber, disburden, °relieve, alleviate, °reduce, lessen, °mitigate

likable *adj.* likeable, °genial, °amiable, congenial, °pleasant, simpatico, °agreeable, °pleasing, °attractive, appealing, °nice, °friendly, °winning, charming, °engaging, °good-natured, winsome

like[1] *adv.* **1** °similar (to), °akin (to), allied (to), parallel (to *or* with), comparable (to *or* with), °equivalent (to), °equal (to), °identical (to), cognate (with), analogous (to), corresponding (to), °correspondent (to), °close (to), homologous (to *or* with), of a piece (with), (much) the same (as), along the same lines (as), not unlike 2 in the mood for, disposed to —*adv.* 3 as if, as though —*prep.* 4 similar to, identical to *or* with 5 in the same way as, in the manner of, similarly to 6 such as, °for example, °for instance, e.g., that is (to say), i.e., in other words, °namely, to wit, viz. —*n.* 7 °match, °equal, °peer, °fellow, opposite number, counterpart, °twin 8 same *or* similar kind *or* sort *or* ilk *or* type *or* kidney *or* breed *or* mold *or* cast *or* strain

like[2] *v.* 1 be fond of, °approve of, °appreciate, be partial to, have a fondness *or* liking for, have a weakness for, °take to, °delight in, take pleasure in, derive *or* get pleasure from, find agreeable *or* congenial, feel attracted to, be *or* feel favorably impressed by, °relish, °love, °adore, adulate, *Colloq* °take a shine to, *Slang* °go for, °dig, get a kick out of, *US* °get off on, groove on, get a bang *or* a charge out of 2 Usually, ***would or should like.*** °prefer, °want, °wish, °ask —*n.* 3 Usually, ***likes.*** °preference, °partiality, predilection, °liking

likelihood *n.* °probability, strong *or* distinct possibility, good chance

likely *adj.* 1 °probable, °liable, expected 2 °probable, conceivable, °reasonable, credible, °plausible, °tenable 3 °fitting, °able, °suitable, °probable, °seemly, °meet, °right, °proper, °qualified, °acceptable, °appropriate, apposite; °favorite, odds-on, °favored, °promising 4 disposed to, apt to, inclined to, liable to —*adv.* 5 °probably, °undoubtedly, indubitably, no doubt, in all probability, *Colloq* like as not

liken *v.* °compare, equate, °match, juxtapose

likeness *n.* 1 similarity, °resemblance, correspondence, analogy, °agreement, parallelism 2 °copy, °replica, °facsimile, °duplicate, °reproduction, °model, °representation, °portrait, painting, °picture, °drawing, °photograph, °sculpture, °statue, statuette, °image, simulacrum, icon *or* ikon 3 °appearance, °face, °figure, °image

likewise *adv.* 1 similarly, in the same *or* like manner *or* way 2 as well, too, also, furthermore, °further, °besides, °in addition, °moreover, °to boot

liking *n.* 1 °affinity, fondness, °affection, °love, °partiality, °bias, °preference, °bent, predilection, predisposition, °inclination, °appreciation, °penchant; °eye, °appetite, soft spot, °weakness 2 °taste, °pleasure, °fancy, °preference

limbo *n.* ***in limbo.*** up in the air, consigned to oblivion, °in abeyance, suspended, hanging (fire), neither here nor there, *Colloq* on hold, treading water, holding one's breath, *US* in a holding pattern, on the shelf, on the back burner

limit *n.* 1 Sometimes, ***limits.*** °extent, bound(s), °end, limitation, °check, °curb, °restriction, °restraint 2 Often, ***limits.*** °border, °edge, °end, °extent, °boundary, bound(s), (boundary *or* border *or* partition) line, °frontier, °perimeter, °periphery 3 Often, ***limits.*** °area, °territory, confines, °zone, °region, °quarter, °district, precinct(s) 4 ***the limit.*** (a) °the end, the last straw, the straw that broke the camel's back, all (that) one can take, °enough, too much, *Colloq* it (b) °outrage, °joke, °surprise, *Colloq* °caution —*v.* 5 °check, °curb, °bridle, °restrict, °restrain, hold in check 6 °restrict, confine, delimit, °narrow, °focus, °guide, °channel 7 °set, °define, °determine, °fix

limited *adj.* 1 circumscribed, restricted, °fixed, °predetermined; °small, °little, reduced, °minimal 2 °narrow, restricted, restrictive, °meager

limitless *adj.* unrestricted, unrestrained, unconfined, unbounded, °boundless, °extensive, °vast, °immense, °enormous, °unlimited, illimitable; interminable, unceasing, incessant, undefined, °immeasurable, innumerable, °numberless, countless, myriad, unending, °perpetual, °everlasting, °eternal

limp[1] *v.* 1 °hobble, °stagger, °totter, dodder, falter —*n.* 2 °hobble, hobbling, °stagger, staggering, °totter, tottering, dodder, °doddering, falter, faltering, claudication, *Slang US* gimp

limp[2] *adj.* 1 flaccid, °flabby, °lax, °slack, °soft, drooping, °relaxed, unstarched, unstiffened, °soft, °flexible, °pliable, floppy, °loose 2 °exhausted, °tired, °fatigued, worn-out, °spent, enervated, wasted, debilitated, °weak, °feeble, °frail 3 °weak, °feeble, °ineffective, °ineffectual, °flimsy, half-hearted, °lukewarm, °spineless, thewless, namby-pamby, *Colloq* wishy-washy, *Slang* gutless

line[1] *n.* 1 °mark, pencilmark, penmark, °rule, °score; °stroke, underline, underscore; diagonal, °slash, virgule, shilling mark, solidus, separatrix, °oblique 2 °strip, °belt, °stripe, °band, °border, °edge, edging 3 °wrinkle, crease, crinkle, °furrow, crow's-foot 4 °border, borderline, °frontier, °limit, °boundary; demarcation, °threshold 5 °outline, °silhouette, contour, °figure, °profile 6 °row, °rank, column, °file, °string, °chain, concatenation, °train, °parade, cortege *or* cortège, cordon, °retinue, °procession, °succession, *Brit* °queue, *Colloq Brit* crocodile, tailback 7 °field, °area, °activity, °forte, °specialty, specialization, °business, °profession, °occupation, °(line of) work, °job, °vocation, °pursuit, °trade, °calling, °employment, *Colloq* °racket, °game 8 °note, °word, °card, postcard, °letter, *US* postal card 9 °course, °direction, °path, °way, °route, °road, °track, °procedure, °tack, °policy, °strategy, tactic(s), °approach, °plan 10 °information, °data, °word, °lead, °clue, °hint 11 °cord, °string, °thread, °twine, °yarn, strand, filament, °rope, °cable, hawser 12 °track, railway *or US and Canadian also* railroad 13 °telephone, wire, °cable 14 °front (line), vanguard, °formation 15 ancestry, descent, °stock, °lineage, °succession, °family, °parentage, °extraction, °heritage, genealogy

16 °assortment, °stock, °merchandise, offerings, °goods, °brand, °make, °type, °kind, °variety 17 Often, ***lines.*** °part, °role, °speech, °script, °words, *Theater US* °sides 18 °story, °(sales) pitch, blarney, *Colloq* spiel, song and dance, *Slang* con 19 ***in or into line.*** **(a)** aligned, in alignment, °true, °straight, in a row, °plumb **(b)** in agreement, in accord, in accordance, in conformity, in step, in harmony, *US* lined up **(c)** Usually, ***into line.*** under *or* in control 20 ***in line for.*** ready for, short-listed for, on the short list for, up for, being considered for, under consideration for, a candidate for, in the running for —*v.* 21 °rule, inscribe, °score, underline, underscore 22 °edge, °border, °fringe 23 ***line up.*** **(a)** °organize, °prepare, °ready, °assemble, °set up, put *or* set in place, °develop, °formulate, °arrange (for), °coordinate **(b)** arrange for, °secure, °get (hold of), °obtain, contract for; uncover, °dig up, °acquire, °engage, °hire, °sign (up), contract with, °hire, °employ **(c)** form a line *or* file, get in *or* into line, form ranks *or* columns, *Military* °fall in, *Brit* queue up **(d)** align, array, °straighten, °order

line[2] *v.* 1 interline, °cover, °face; ceil 2 ***line one's pockets.*** accept bribes, °graft, *US* °sell out, *Colloq US* be on the take

lineage *n.* 1 °extraction, ancestry, family tree, °pedigree, descent, °stock, bloodline, °parentage, genealogy 2 forebears, forefathers, foremothers, °family, °people, °clan; descendants, °succession, °progeny, °offspring

linen *n.* Often, ***linens.*** bedclothes, bedding, bed linen(s), sheets and pillowcases; table linen(s), napery, tablecloths and napkins; bath linen(s), towels and washcloths

linger *v.* 1 Sometimes, ***linger on.*** °stay (behind), °remain, °tarry, loiter, °persist, °hang on, °endure, °persevere, °survive, *Colloq* hang *or* stick about *or* around 2 °pause, °dawdle, dally, °lag, °idle 3 Often, ***linger on or over.*** °dwell on, °elaborate, harp on, °labor 4 °procrastinate, dither, °shilly-shally, temporize

lingering *adj.* 1 °long, °persistent, °protracted, °remaining 2 °slow, long-drawn-out, °gradual

lingo *n.* °jargon, argot, °cant, patois, pidgin, creole, °parlance, °vernacular, °dialect, °idiom, °language, °talk, °speech; gobbledygook, °gibberish, °mumbo jumbo

link *n.* 1 °tie, °bond, coupling, connector, vinculum; °element, constituent, component 2 °connection, °tie-up, °tie-in, °relation, °relationship, °association, affiliation, interdependence —*v.* 3 Often, ***link up.*** °couple, °join, °fasten (together), °unite; concatenate 4 °connect, tie (up *or* in *or* together), °associate, °relate, °identify with

liquid *n.* 1 °fluid, °liquor, °juice, °solution —*adj.* 2 °fluid, flowing, °running, runny, °fluent, liquefied, °watery, molten, melted 3 °bright, shining, °brilliant, °clear, °transparent, translucent, limpid 4 convertible; °solvent, °profitable

liquor *n.* 1 °spirits, °alcohol, °(strong) drink, intoxicants, John Barleycorn, schnapps, *US and Irish* whiskey *or Brit* whisky, demon rum, °moonshine, *US* white lightning, white mule; *Colloq* °booze, pick-me-up, hard stuff, firewater, °juice, mother's ruin (= 'gin'), *US* Kickapoo mountain joy juice; *Slang* rotgut, *Chiefly US and Canadian* hooch *or* hootch, *US* °sauce, red-eye, mountain dew 2 °liquid, °fluid, °extract, °broth, °stock, distillate, °concentrate, infusion

list[1] *n.* 1 listing, roster, °roll, rota, catalog, directory, °register, °index, °record, °schedule, °muster, slate, beadroll, laundry list, shopping list, inventory, °file, tabulation; bibliography, *liber veritatis, catalogue raisonné* —*v.* 2 catalog, °register, °index, °record, °note, °itemize, °enumerate, °schedule, °tabulate, °chronicle, °book, °enter, °enroll

list[2] *v.* 1 °lean (over), °tilt, °slant, °heel (over), °tip, °careen, °cant, °incline —*n.* 2 °lean, °tilt, °slant, °heel, °tip, °cant, °slope, °inclination

listen *v.* 1 °hear, pay attention (to), °attend, lend an ear (to), prick up one's ears, keep one's ears open, *Archaic* heark *or US also* hark (to), hearken *or also* harken (to) 2 °obey, °heed, °mind, pay attention (to), do as one is told

listless *adj.* sluggish, °lethargic, °weary, °weak, enervated, °spent, languid, °lifeless, °heavy, °phlegmatic, unemotional, °impassive; °unenthusiastic, °indifferent, apathetic, unconcerned, °lukewarm, °tepid, °cool, uncaring, insouciant; pococurante, laodicean

litany *n.* 1 °prayer, invocation, °supplication, °petition 2 °recitation, °recital, enumeration, listing, °list, cataloging, catalog, inventorying, inventory

literal *adj.* 1 word-for-word, °verbatim, line-for-line, letter-for-letter, *literatim*, °exact, °precise, °faithful, °strict 2 denotative, etymological, semantic, °dictionary, lexical, °basic, °essential, °pure, °simple, simplistic, °real, °objective, °true, °genuine, °bona fide, °unvarnished, unadulterated, unembellished, simple-minded, uncomplicated, unbiased, °unprejudiced, *Colloq* honest-to-goodness, honest-to-God 3 °prosaic, °matter-of-fact, °colorless, °dull, down-to-earth, literal-minded, unimaginative, °humdrum, °boring, °tedious

literally *adv.* 1 word for word, °verbatim, line for line, letter for letter, *literatim*, faithfully, strictly, °exactly, °precisely, closely; °thus, *sic* 2 °actually, °truly, °in fact, °really

literary *adj.* 1 erudite, well-read, cultured, °learned, bookish, °scholarly, °lettered, °cultivated, °refined, °educated; literate 2 written, °formal, °scholarly, °pedantic, °learned, °academic, scholastic, schoolmarmish

literature *n.* 1 writing(s), °letters, belles-lettres, creative writing(s) 2 °information, °facts, °data, publicity; °propaganda; brochures, pamphlets, handouts, handbills, leaflets, circulars

litigant *n.* litigator, °party, plaintiff, appellant, °suitor, petitioner, suer, defendant, appellee, accused

litigation *n.* lawsuit, °suit, °action, °case, legal remedy

litter *n.* **1** °rubbish, debris, °refuse, °fragments, °odds and ends, *US and Canadian* °trash, *Colloq* °junk **2** °brood, °issue, °offspring, °young **3** stretcher, palanquin *or* palankeen, sedan chair —*v.* **4** °clutter, °strew, °scatter

little *adj.* **1** °small, °short, °slight, °tiny, °minute, °diminutive, °miniature, mini, °baby, doll-sized, °undersized, °dwarf, midget, pygmy, °elfin, °toy, bantam, °petite, °wee, infinitesimal, minuscule, Lilliputian, teeny, teeny-weeny, teensy-weensy, itty-bitty, itsy-bitsy, microscopic **2** °young, °small, youthful **3** °small, °sparse, skimpy, °meager, scant, °insufficient, °inadequate, not enough, °scanty, barely *or* hardly any **4** °short, °brief **5** °trifling, trivial, °small, °minor, °petty, °paltry, °insignificant, inconsiderable, unimportant, °inconsequential, °negligible **6** small (-minded), °petty, picayune, °mean, ungenerous, illiberal, °cheap, narrow(-minded), unimaginative, °shallow —*adv.* **7** °seldom, °rarely, hardly ever, °scarcely **8** (but *or* only) slightly, °barely, °hardly, °scarcely, no, not any, not much **9** °scarcely, °hardly —*n.* **10** °bit, °dab, dollop, °particle, spoonful, °taste, thimbleful, °speck, °spot, °scrap, °crumb, °particle, *Colloq* smidgen

live *adj.* **1** living, breathing, °animate, °viable, existent; °material, °physical, °tangible, °real, °actual, palpable **2** °energetic, °lively, °spirited, °vigorous, °active, °dynamic, °busy; °current, °contemporary **3** °burning, °glowing, °flaming, alight, red-hot, white-hot **4** °loaded, °explosive, unexploded, combustible **5** charged, electrified —*v.* **6** °breathe, °exist; °function **7** °survive, °persist, °last, °persevere, °endure; °spend, °continue, live out, °complete, °end, conclude, °finish **8** reside, °dwell, be; °abide, °stay, °remain, °lodge, °room **9** subsist, °get along, °survive, °fare

lively *adj.* **1** full of life, °vigorous, °energetic, °vivacious, °spirited, °brisk, spry, °active, °animated, °frisky, °sprightly, °agile, °nimble, °perky, chirpy, bouncy, °buoyant, °gay, cheery, °cheerful, *Colloq* chipper, full of pep, peppy **2** °strong, °intense, °vivid, °keen, °pointed, °eager, °energetic, °active **3** °active, °busy, bustling, °stirring, °eventful, swarming, teeming; astir, °alive **4** °vivid, °bright, °gay, °cheerful, °glowing, °brilliant, °gorgeous, °rich

liven *v.* **1** Often, ***liven up.*** brighten, °cheer, °enliven, °perk up **2** invigorate, °stimulate, °energize, inspirit, °activate, °animate, °fire, °stir (up), put (some) life into, °enliven, °perk up, *Colloq* °pep up

load *n.* **1** °weight, °burden; onus, °pressure, °encumbrance, millstone, °cross, albatross, °responsibility, °care, °anxiety, °worry, °trouble **2** shipment, consignment, °cargo, °weight —*v.* **3** °pack, °pile, °stack, °heap, °fill, lade, °stuff, °cram, °jam, °squeeze **4** Often, ***load down.*** °weigh down, °burden, °encumber, saddle with, °overwhelm

loaded *adj.* **1** overloaded, overwhelmed, burdened, laden, weighted (down), filled (up), chock-full, chockablock, stuffed, jammed, °packed, crowded, brimming, brimful, crammed **2** charged, primed, °ready **3** charged, °tricky, manipulative, insidious, °prejudiced, °prejudicial, °trap, °devious **4** °rich, °wealthy, affluent, moneyed, well-to-do, well-off, *Colloq* °flush, well-heeled, *US* in the chips, *Slang* rolling in it **5** °drunk

loaf[1] *n.* **1** °brick, °cake, °block, chunk; °lump, cube **2** °head, °sense, brains, *Colloq* noggin, noodle, °block, bean, *Brit* noddle, *Slang Brit* chump

loaf[2] *v.* **1** lounge (about *or* around), loiter, °idle, laze, lie about *or* around, take it easy, vegetate, watch the grass grow, *Colloq US* lallygag *or* lollygag, *Slang Brit* skive, *Military* scrimshank, *US* goof off, *US military* goldbrick, *Taboo US* fuck off, fuck the dog **2** ***loaf away.*** °waste, °fritter away, °idle away

loafer *n.* °idler, layabout, °wastrel, shirker, *flâneur,* ne'er-do-well, °tramp, vagrant, *Old-fashioned* lounge lizard, slugabed, *Colloq* lazybones, *Brit* drone, *US* °bum, (ski *or* tennis *or* surf) bum, *Slang Brit* skiver, *Military* scrimshanker, *US military* goldbrick(er), *Taboo US* fuck-off

loan *n.* **1** °advance, °allowance, °credit, °accommodation —*v.* **2** °lend, °advance, °allow, °credit

loath *adj.* loth, unwilling, °reluctant, °averse, °disinclined, °indisposed

loathe *v.* °detest, °hate, °despise, °abhor, abominate, execrate, shrink *or* recoil from, shudder at

loathing *n.* hatred, abhorrence, °aversion, °hate, odium, detestation, antipathy, repugnance, °horror, °revulsion

loathsome *adj.* detestable, °abhorrent, odious, °hateful, °disgusting, execrable, °abominable, °despicable, °contemptible, noisome, °offensive, °horrible, °repulsive, °repugnant, nauseating, sickening, °revolting, °nasty, °vile

lob *v.* **1** loft, °toss, °pitch, °shy, °heave, °fling, chuck, °hurl, °throw —*n.* **2** °toss, °throw, °bowl, °pitch, °hit, *US* °fly

lobby *n.* **1** foyer, entrance hall, vestibule, °entry, *US* entryway; reception (room *or* area), waiting room, °corridor, °hall, hallway **2** special-interest group, pressure group, lobbyist —*v.* **3** °(bring) pressure (to bear), °(exert) influence, °persuade, pull strings *or* wires, put one's weight behind, °sway, °press, °push, °promote, °urge, *Brit* pressurize

local *adj.* **1** °neighborhood, °neighboring, °nearby, °close by; °adjoining **2** °provincial, regional, °district, °state, county, shire, °municipal, °city, °town, village, °neighborhood;

restricted, °limited, °specific, °particular, °peculiar —*n.* **3** °resident, °native, townsman, townswoman, townsperson **4** neighborhood pub
locale *n.* °site, °location, °spot, °place, °setting, venue, °neighborhood, °situation, locality
locate *v.* **1** °situate, °place, °site, °position, °set (up), °fix, pinpoint, °establish, °settle, °base **2** °find, °come across, °discover, °unearth, lay *or* put *or* get one's hand(s) *or* finger(s) on, chance *or* hit upon, °turn up, °track down
location *n.* **1** °site, °place, °locale, °spot, °setting, °situation, °position **2** °finding, °discovery, laying *or* putting *or* getting one's hand(s) *or* finger(s) on, unearthing, turning up, tracking down
lock[1] *n.* **1** padlock, hasp, °bolt, latch, °bar, °hook, °clasp, °catch **2** °hold; °control, °power, °sway, °authority, °command, supervision —*v.* **3** Often, ***lock up.*** padlock, °bolt, latch, °bar, °secure, °seal **4** °clasp, °entangle, °engage, °join, °entwine, °close; °clutch, °grasp, °grapple **5** ***lock away.*** See **9,** below. **6** ***lock in.*** **(a)** °secure, °retain, °fix, °plant, °implant, stabilize **(b)** °commit, °oblige, constrain, °bind **(c)** lock up *or* away, confine, °restrain, coop up **7** ***lock on.*** fix on *or* upon, °track, °follow, °pursue, °keep track of **8** ***lock out.*** °exclude, °shut out, close out, keep out, °bar, debar **9** ***lock up or away.*** confine, jail *or Brit also* gaol, °imprison, coop up, incarcerate, detain, impound, put behind bars, °restrict, °cage
lock[2] *n.* tress, curl, ringlet
lodge *n.* **1** hunting lodge, °cabin, chalet, °cottage, °house; gatehouse, °shelter, °hut **2** °branch, chapter —*v.* **3** reside, °live, °dwell, °abide, °stay, °stop, °room, occupy rooms **4** °accommodate, °board, °put up, billet, °quarter, °house, °take in; °shelter, °harbor **5** °stick, °wedge, °catch, °deposit, become stuck *or* wedged *or* fixed *or* caught *or* deposited, embed itself, become embedded **6** °register, °enter, °record, °submit, bring forward, set forth *or* out, °file
lodging *n.* Often, ***lodgings.*** accommodation(s), °shelter, °quarters, °rooms, apartment, °housing, °house, °dwelling, dwelling place, °residence
lofty *adj.* **1** °tall, °high, °elevated, °towering, soaring **2** °exalted, °majestic, °imposing, °grand, °magnificent, °noble, °regal, °imperial, blue-blooded, thoroughbred, aristocratic, magisterial, august, °stately, °venerable, °distinguished, °dignified, °elevated, °eminent, °celebrated, honored, °honorable, respected, °renowned, °famous, °prominent, °illustrious, °notable, °leading, °preeminent, °sublime, °immortal **3** °elevated, °honorable, °superior, °exalted, °noble **4** °grand, °grandiose, °haughty, °arrogant, °disdainful, °condescending, °contemptuous, °scornful, °supercilious, contumelious, patronizing, °superior, overweening, vainglorious, °pompous, °snobbish, *Colloq* high and mighty, snooty, uppity, *Brit* °uppish, *Slang* snotty, *Brit* toffee-nosed
logic *n.* **1** °reasoning, °deduction, dialectics, ratiocination, inferential *or* scientific reasoning **2** (good *or* common) sense, sound judgment, °wisdom, °presence of mind **3** reasonableness, °intelligence, judiciousness, practicality, rationality
logical *adj.* **1** syllogistic(al), inferential, deductive, inductive **2** °reasonable, °plausible, °sensible, °sound, valid, °intelligent, °judicious, °practical, °rational, °wise, °proper **3** well-organized, °sound, °coherent, °consistent, °sensible, °rational, °reasonable, well-reasoned, well-thought-out
lonely *adj.* **1** °single, °solitary, °sole, lone, °one; °unaccompanied, °alone **2** °desolate, °uninhabited, °deserted, °barren **3** friendless, °lonesome, °abandoned, °outcast, forsaken; °solo, hermitlike, eremitic(al), °reclusive, °secluded, °retiring, °withdrawn, °unsocial
lonesome *adj.* **1** °alone, forsaken, friendless, rejected, °unpopular, °unwelcome, °outcast, °deserted, °abandoned, °estranged **2** See **lonely, 2.**
long[1] *adj.* **1** °extensive, extended, elongate(d), °large, °great, °big **2** °lengthy, prolonged, °protracted; °extensive, extended, °sustained
long[2] *v.* °wish, crave, °want, °yearn, °desire, °hunger, °fancy, covet, dream of, °hanker, eat one's heart out
longing *n.* craving, °wish, yearning, °hunger, °fancy, °desire, hankering, *Colloq* yen
look *v.* **1** Usually, ***look at.*** °see, °observe, °consider, °contemplate, °regard, °view, °survey, °inspect, °scrutinize, °study, °scan; pay attention, °attend, °notice, °watch, °witness; *Literary* °behold, *Slang US* eyeball **2** °seem (to be), °appear (to be) **3** °face, °front (on), °overlook, look out on **4** ***look after.*** °care for, °take care of, be responsible for, °attend, °mind, °watch, °serve, °wait on, °nurse, °protect **5** ***look down on or upon or US at.*** disdain, °despise, contemn, °scorn, °disparage, derogate, °spurn, °sneer, misprize, *Colloq* turn one's nose up at, look down one's nose at **6** ***look for.*** **(a)** °seek, °demand, °require **(b)** °hunt for, forage for, °search for **(c)** °expect, °hope, °anticipate, °count on, °reckon on **7** ***look forward to.*** **(a)** °anticipate, await, wait for **(b)** °expect, count *or* rely on *or* upon **8** ***look into.*** °examine, °study, °investigate, °inspect, delve into, °dig into, °probe, °scrutinize, °explore, °go into, °research, °check (out), °check into **9** ***look out.*** be careful, be alert, be vigilant, be on the qui vive, be watchful, watch out, °beware, pay attention, be on guard **10** ***look over.*** °look at, °examine, °read, °scan, °study, check (out *or* over), *Slang US* eyeball **11** ***look up.*** **(a)** °seek, °search for, °hunt for, try to find, track *or* run down **(b)** get in touch with, (tele)-phone, °ring (up), °visit, °call on, °call up, look *or* drop in on, go to see **(c)** °improve,

get better, °pick up, show improvement, °progress, °gain, make headway *or* progress **12** ***look up to.*** °admire, regard highly, °respect, °esteem, °honor, °revere, °extol, °worship, °idolize, °venerate **—*n.* 13** °gaze, °glance **14** looks, °appearance, °aspect, °bearing, °manner, °air, demeanor; °expression, countenance, °face, mien

lookalike *n.* °twin, °double, exact *or* perfect likeness *or* match, clone, *Colloq* spit and image *or* spitting image; doppelgänger; *Slang* (dead) ringer

lookout *n.* **1** °guard, sentry, °sentinel, °watchman **2** °alert, qui vive; °guard, °watch **3** °responsibility, °worry, °concern, °problem, °difficulty, *Colloq* °headache

loom *v.* **1** °appear, °emerge, take shape *or* form, °materialize, °surface, °arise **2** °menace, impend, °threaten, °overshadow, °tower, °dominate, hang *or* hover over **3** ***loom large.*** °dominate, °predominate, play a big *or* an important role *or* part

loop *n.* **1** hoop, noose, °ring, °circle, °bow, °eye, eyelet, °coil, whorl, *Nautical* °bend **—*v.* 2** °twist, °coil, °wind, °tie, °circle, curl, °entwine, °turn, °ring, *Nautical* °bend

loophole *n.* °outlet, way out, means of escape, °escape, °subterfuge, °pretext, °evasion, °quibble, *Colloq* °dodge

loose *adj.* **1** °unattached, unconnected, °disconnected, °detached, °free, unsecured, unfastened, °movable **2** unconfined, untied, unfettered, released, freed, unshackled, unchained; °free, °at liberty, °at large, on the loose, untrammeled **3** unconfining, free-flowing, flowing, baggy, °slack, hanging **4** disordered, disorganized, unbound, untied, messy; strewn *or* spread *or* tossed *or* thrown about *or* around, scattered (about *or* around), in disorder, in disarray, dispersed **5** °rambling, °disconnected, unstructured, unconnected, discontinuous, nonspecific, unspecific, °indefinite, °imprecise, °inexact, °inaccurate, °free, °broad, °rough, °offhand, °casual, °careless, °untidy, °sloppy, slapdash, °general, °vague **6** °lax, °relaxed, negligent, °careless, °sloppy **7** °wanton, °dissolute, debauched, °immoral, °promiscuous, °abandoned, °fast, °libertine, °profligate, licentious, °lewd, °perverted, °corrupt **—*adv.* 8** ***break loose.*** °escape, °flee **9** ***hang or stay loose.*** °relax, stay *or* keep calm *or* cool, cool off *or* down, sit back, take it easy **10** ***let or set or turn loose.*** °discharge, let go (with); °emit, °give out (with), °fire **—*v.* 11** let go, °(set) free, °release, let *or* set *or* turn loose; °liberate, °deliver **12** untie, °undo, unfasten, let go, °disengage, °relax, °ease, °loosen, slacken; °cast off **13** let go, °let fly, °fire, °discharge, °shoot, unleash, °deliver

loosen *v.* **1** °loose; °undo, unfasten, unhook, unbutton, unlace, untie, unbind, unbuckle; unscrew **2** °weaken, °detach, °separate, °sever, break *or* cut (apart)

loot *n.* **1** °booty, °spoils, °plunder, °prize, °haul, *Slang* swag, boodle **—*v.* 2** °plunder, °sack, °ransack, °rob, °pillage, despoil, °raid, °ravage, maraud, *Rare* depredate

lop *v.* Often, ***lop off.*** chop off, °trim, °top, °head, crop, °prune, °dock, °clip, snip off, shear off, °cut off, °pare, °shorten, hack off, amputate

lopsided *adj.* **1** uneven, askew, °one-sided, awry, unsymmetrical, asymmetrical, unequal, °crooked, °unbalanced, °irregular, *Colloq* cockeyed **2** uneven, unequal, °one-sided, °biased, °disproportionate, unfair, warped, twisted

lord *n.* **1** °master, °monarch, ruler, °sovereign **2** °noble, nobleman, °peer, aristocrat; earl, duke, °count, viscount, baron **3** ***The or Our Lord.*** God, the Almighty, God Almighty, the Creator, the Supreme Being, Christ, Jesus, Jehovah **—*v.* 4** ***lord it over.*** domineer, °swagger, be overbearing, *Colloq* °boss (around), act big, pull rank

lore *n.* **1** folklore, beliefs, °culture, tradition(s), °mythology, myths, mythos, ethos, teaching(s), °doctrine, °wisdom **2** °knowledge, °learning, erudition

lose *v.* **1** °mislay, misplace, °displace, °part with; suffer the loss of, be deprived of **2** °forfeit, °yield **3** °give up, °yield, °capitulate, admit defeat, °succumb, bow to, be defeated *or* conquered, suffer defeat, be beaten *or* overcome *or* worsted *or* bested, *Colloq* lose out **4** °waste, °let slip, squander, °dissipate, fritter *or* trifle away, °run out of; °consume, °use (up), °expend, °spend **5** °elude, °evade, °escape, throw *or* shake off, give the slip

loser *n.* also-ran, °misfit, °failure, °fiasco, nonstarter, *Colloq* °flop, °dud, °washout, bummer, lead balloon, lemon, born loser, *Brit* damp squib, *Brit and Australian* no-hoper, *US* clinker, nebbish, schlemiel *or* schlemihl *or* shlemiel, schlimazel *or* shlimazel *or* shlimazl, schnook, sad sack

loss *n.* **1** deprivation, bereavement, °privation, °denial, °sacrifice, forfeiture, disappearance **2** diminution, °erosion, reduction, impoverishment, depletion, shrinkage **3** °disadvantage, °detriment, °harm, °impairment, °injury, °damage **4** °waste, wastage, wasting, squandering **5** °defeat, °setback, °disadvantage, °disappointment, °failure, °downfall, °collapse, °breakdown, °ruin; drubbing, trouncing **6** Often, ***losses.*** debit(s), °liability (liabilities), negative cash flow **7** Often, ***losses.*** °death, °dying, °passing, demise, °destruction, extermination, extinction, annihilation

lost *adj.* **1** gone, departed, vanished, strayed; missing, mislaid, misplaced, irrecoverable **2** wasted, °misspent, gone by the board, squandered, °down the drain, °spent, °exhausted, *Colloq* out of the window **3** °confused, baffled, perplexed, puzzled, mystified, bewildered, confounded, adrift, °helpless, disoriented, at sea, astray **4** forgotten, °bygone, °extinct, °past, °obsolete, vanished, buried **5** °dead, °extinct, departed, fallen, °late **6** destroyed, demolished, devastated, ruined, wrecked, irreparable, unsalvageable, irreclaimable, irremediable **7**

damned, cursed, accursed, °abandoned, °corrupt, fallen, °wanton, °unchaste, °dissolute **8** °hopeless, °distraught, distracted, °desperate, °frantic, frenzied

lot *n.* **1** °collection, °batch, consignment, °assortment, °group, °portion, °set, °quantity, grouping, apportionment **2** °luck, °fortune, °destiny, °fate, kismet, °plight, °doom, °end **3** °lottery, °drawing, °raffle, drawing lots *or* straws **4** °share, °portion, °division, °interest, °part, °allotment, °assignment, apportionment, °ration, °allowance **5** ***a lot or lots.*** **(a)** a good *or* great deal **(b)** much, loads *or* a load, mountains *or* a mountain, tons *or* a ton, barrels *or* a barrel, stacks *or* a stack, piles *or* a pile, heaps *or* a heap, masses *or* a mass, °oceans, *Colloq* oodles, scads, *US* gobs **(c)** °many, myriad, numerous, countless, reams, infinite *or* an infinity, quantities *or* a quantity, enormous numbers *or* an enormous number, *Colloq* oodles, scads, loads, tons, masses **6** ***the lot.*** °everything, *Colloq* the whole kit and caboodle, all

lotion *n.* cream, liniment, balm, °salve, °ointment, embrocation, unguent, pomade

lottery *n.* °raffle, sweepstake, °drawing, °pool, *Brit* tombola

loud *adj.* **1** deafening, earsplitting, booming, blaring, stentorian, thundering, °thunderous, sonorous, °noisy, clamorous, °piercing, fortissimo **2** °tawdry, °garish, °flashy, °gaudy, °tasteless, °extravagant, °showy, °ostentatious, *Colloq* splashy, snazzy, jazzy

lounge *v.* **1** °idle, °loaf, laze, loll, languish, vegetate **—*n.*** **2** °lobby, foyer, waiting room, °reception (room), vestibule **3** cocktail lounge, *Brit* (lounge *or* saloon) bar **4** sofa, °couch, divan, studio couch, daybed, settee, °settle, love seat, chaise longue; causeuse, °tête-à-tête, °serpentine; *US and Canadian* davenport

lour *v.* See **lower** [2], below.

lousy *adj.* **1** °awful, °terrible, °mean, °contemptible, °low, °base, °hateful, detestable, °despicable, °vile, °wretched, °miserable, °scurvy, °dirty, °vicious, *Colloq* °rotten **2** °bad, °poor, °awful, °terrible, °inferior; low-quality, °shoddy, °shabby, °miserable, second-rate, °wretched **3** pedicular, pediculous, *Brit* lice-infested, lice-ridden, *US* louse-infested, louse-ridden **4** ***lousy with.*** alive with, overloaded with, swarming with, teeming with, *Colloq* crawling with, knee-deep in

lovable *adj.* loveable, °adorable, °darling, °dear, cherished, °likable, °attractive, °engaging, °cute, °fetching, °taking, alluring, °endearing, appealing, winsome, °sweet, °tender, cuddly, °affectionate, charming, °enchanting

love *n.* **1** °warmth, °affection, °attachment, fondness, tenderness, °devotion, °attraction, °friendship, amity, °regard, °admiration, °fancy, adoration, adulation, °ardor, °passion, °fervor, °rapture, infatuation **2** °liking, °delight, °enjoyment, °pleasure, fondness, °attraction, predilection, °bent, °leaning, proclivity, °inclination, °disposition, °weakness, °partiality, °preference, °taste, °relish, °passion **3** °darling, °beloved, °sweetheart, sweetie, °sweet, honey, dear one, dearest, angel, turtledove, truelove, light of one's life, °lover, °paramour, °mate, intended, betrothed; girlfriend, inamorata, ladylove, young lady, fiancée; boyfriend, beau, inamorato, °suitor, swain, young man, °fiancé, *Archaic* leman, °tally, *US* POSSLQ (= 'Person of the Opposite Sex Sharing Living Quarters'), *Colloq* °girl, °woman, °guy, °man **4** °sympathy, tenderness, °concern, °charity, °care, °solicitude, °affinity, °rapport, °harmony, °brotherhood, sisterhood, fellow feeling **5** ***love affair.*** **(a)** amour, °liaison, °affair, °romance, °relationship, *affaire de coeur, affaire d'amour,* °intrigue **(b)** °passion, °mania, *Colloq* °thing **6** ***make love (to) or (with).*** °embrace, °cuddle, °caress, °fondle, have sexual intercourse, °take, *Archaic* °know, *Colloq* neck, °pet, canoodle, °romance, have sex, make the beast with two backs, *US and Canadian* °make out; *Taboo slang* °screw, fuck, °hump, bang, *Brit* roger, bonk **—*v.*** **7** °cherish, °admire, °adore, be in love with, lose one's heart to, °worship, °idolize, dote on, °treasure, be infatuated with, think the world of, adulate, hold dear, °like, *Colloq* be hung up on, be crazy *or* nuts *or* wild *or* mad about, have a crush on **8** °delight in, take pleasure in, derive pleasure *or* enjoyment from, °relish, be partial to, have a passion *or* preference *or* taste for, be attracted to, be captivated by, be fond of, °like, °enjoy, °appreciate, value, *Colloq* get a kick from *or* out of, be wild about, be thrilled by, *US* get a bang *or* charge from *or* out of

love letter *n.* billet-doux, *Archaic* mash note

lovely *adj.* **1** good-looking, °pretty, °handsome, °attractive, °comely, °fair, °fetching, °engaging, captivating, alluring, enticing, bewitching, °ravishing, °gorgeous, °beautiful, beauteous, pulchritudinous **2** °satisfying, °satisfactory, °agreeable, enjoyable, gratifying, °nice, °pleasing, °pleasant, °pleasurable, °engaging, °delightful

lover *n.* See **love, 3,** above.

low[1] *adj.* **1** °short, squat, °little, °small, stubby, stumpy, °stunted; low-lying **2** °inadequate, °insufficient, °deficient, down, °short, °sparse, °scanty, scant, °limited **3** °coarse, °unrefined, indelicate, °improper, °naughty, °risqué, °indecent, °unseemly, °vulgar, °crude, °common, °rude, °offensive, °gross, ill-bred, °lewd, °obscene, ribald, °bawdy, °scurrilous, smutty, °pornographic, °dirty **4** °weak, °frail, °feeble, debilitated, enervated, °sickly, °unhealthy, °infirm, °shaky, °decrepit, °ill, °sick **5** °ineffectual, °ineffective, °weak **6** °miserable, °dismal, °wretched, °abysmal, °sorry, abject, °destitute **7** °humble, °poor, lowborn, °lowly, °base, °inferior, baseborn, °plebeian, proletariat, ignoble **8** °unhappy, depressed, °dejected, °sad, °gloomy, °melancholy, °miserable, °despondent, disconsolate, °blue, downcast, down, °glum, °wretched, morose, crestfallen, °brokenhearted, °heartbroken, °tearful, lachrymose, °sorrowful, °mournful, heavy-hearted **9** °inferior, second-rate, °poor, °bad, not up to par, °worthless, °shoddy, °shabby, °mediocre, substandard **10** °inferior, °lower, lesser, °small, smaller **11** low-cut, décolleté, revealing, *Colloq US* low and behold in the front and vie de Bohème in the back **12** °base, °vile, abject, °contemptible, °despicable, °mean, °menial, °servile, ignoble, degraded, °vulgar, °foul, dastardly, depraved, °nasty, °sordid **13** °quiet, hushed, °soft, °subdued, °gentle, muted, muffled, stifled, °indistinct, whispered, murmured, murmurous **14** unfavorable, °critical, adverse

low[2] *v.* moo, °bellow; °bawl

lowdown *n.* °information, °intelligence, °data, the facts, inside story, *Colloq* info, °dope, °dirt, *Brit* bumf

lower[1] *v.* **1** °drop, °reduce, °decrease, °mark down, °discount, lessen, °diminish, °downgrade, °cut, °slash **2** let *or* move *or* bring *or* put down, °drop **3** cut *or* lop off, cut *or* take down, °reduce, °diminish, crop, °trim **4** abase, °debase, °degrade, °discredit, °shame, °disgrace, demean, °belittle, °humble, °humiliate; °stoop, °deign, °condescend **5** °turn down, quieten, °moderate, °modulate, °soften, tone *or* tune down *—adj.* **6** farther down **7** earlier **8** ***lowercase.*** °small, minuscule

lower[2] *v.* **1** °lour, darken, °threaten, °menace, °loom **2** °lour, °frown, °scowl, glower; °sulk, °pout, mope

lowly *adj.* See **low**[1]**, 7,** above.

loyal *adj.* °faithful, °true, dependable, °devoted, °trustworthy, trusty, °steady, °steadfast, °staunch, trusted, °reliable, °stable, unswerving, unwavering, dedicated, °constant, °patriotic

loyalty *n.* faithfulness, fidelity, dependability, devotedness, °devotion, allegiance, patriotism, trustworthiness, steadfastness, staunchness, firmness, °resolution, °resolve, reliability, °stability, °dedication, constancy

luck *n.* **1** °fortune, °chance, °destiny, °fate, °accident, fortuity, serendipity; °fluke, stroke of luck, *US* happenstance **2** good fortune, °(good) break **3** chance(s), success rate, fortune(s)

lucky *adj.* **1** °fortunate, blessed, °favored, °charmed **2** °providential, °timely, °opportune, °propitious, °favorable, auspicious, °advantageous, °convenient, fortuitous

ludicrous *adj.* °ridiculous, laughable, °absurd, °farcical, °nonsensical, °preposterous, °incongruous, asinine, °foolish, °silly, °zany, °crazy, comical, risible; °funny, facetious, droll, waggish, jocular, °witty, jocose

lug *v.* °drag, °tug, °tow, °haul, °heave; °carry, tote, °transport

luggage *n.* baggage, bags, °gear, impedimenta, °paraphernalia, °things, °belongings

lukewarm *adj.* **1** °tepid, room temperature, °warm **2** °cool, °indifferent, °halfhearted, °chill, °chilly, °phlegmatic, unresponsive, °unenthusiastic, °nonchalant, °lackadaisical, apathetic, insouciant, laodicean, °unmoved, *US* half-baked, *Colloq* laid-back

lull *n.* **1** °pause, °respite, °interlude, °intermission, °interval, °break, hiatus, °interruption, °stop, °halt, °lapse, °delay, *Literary* caesura, *Colloq* °letup **2** °quiet, quiescence, °hush, °calm, calmness, stillness, °silence, °peace, peacefulness, tranquillity *—v.* **3** soothe, °calm, °quiet, °hush, pacify, mollify, °tranquilize

lumber *n.* **1** °odds and ends, °junk, °clutter, °jumble, rejects, white elephants; °rubbish, °litter, *Chiefly US* °trash **2** °timber, wood, beams, planks, boards

luminous *adj.* **1** °shiny, shining, °bright, °brilliant, lighted (up), lit (up), illuminated, °radiant, alight, resplendent, °lustrous, gleaming, shimmering, glistening, sparkling, °dazzling, refulgent, effulgent **2** °glowing, aglow, luminescent, °incandescent, phosphorescent, fluorescent **3** °clear, lucid, perspicuous, percipient, perspicacious, °penetrating, discerning, °perceptive, cleareyed, clearheaded, °keen, °acute, °sharp, °explicit, °incisive, °specific, °express; understandable, °intelligible

lump[1] *n.* **1** °mass, °piece, °gob, gobbet, °clod, chunk, clot, °wad, °clump, hunk, nugget; cube, °wedge, °cake **2** °bump, °growth, °swelling, protuberance, °protrusion, °prominence, °bulge, excrescence, tumescence, nodule, °knob; wen, cyst, °boil, carbuncle, blister, wart, corn *—v.* **3** Often, ***lump together.*** °combine, °join, consolidate, °collect, °bunch, °group, °unite, °mass, aggregate, °blend, °mix, throw *or* put together

lump[2] *v.* Usually, ***lump it.*** allow, °tolerate, °suffer, °put up with, °bear, °stand, °brook, °endure

lumpy *adj.* chunky, °bumpy, uneven, °granular, grainy

lunacy *n.* **1** °madness, °insanity, dementia, craziness, derangement, psychosis, °mania **2** °folly, foolishness, bad *or* poor judgment, illogicality, illogic, senselessness, ridiculousness, irrationality, foolhardiness, °stupidity

lunge *n.* **1** °thrust, °jab, °strike **2** °dive, °plunge, °rush, °leap, °jump, °spring, °pounce *—v.* **3** °dive, °plunge, °charge, °pounce, °dash, °bound, °jump; °thrust, °stab, °strike, °hit, °jab, °cut

lurch[1] *n.* ***leave in the lurch.*** °desert, °abandon, °forsake; °drop, °jilt

lurch[2] *n.* **1** °stagger, °sway, °pitch; °list, °tilt, °toss *—v.* **2** °stagger, °sway, °stumble; °roll, °tilt, veer, °pitch, °list, °heel, °wallow

lure *v.* **1** °tempt, °attract, °induce, °coax, inveigle, °seduce, °draw in, °entice, °lead on, °decoy, °charm, °persuade, allure, °catch *—n.* **2** bait, °decoy, °attraction, °temptation, °inducement, magnet, siren song, °charm, *US* drawing card, *Slang* °come-on

lurid *adj.* **1** °sensational, °vivid, °shocking,

°startling, °graphic, °melodramatic **2** °ghastly, horrid, horrifying, horrendous, °gory, °grisly, °gruesome, °macabre, °revolting, °disgusting, appalling, °frightful, °terrible, °awful **3** °pale, ashen, sallow, °wan, pallid, °ghastly, baleful **4** °glaring, °fiery, °flaming, °burning, aglow, °glowing, glowering

lurk *v.* skulk, °slink, °prowl, °steal, °sneak, °hide, °(lie in) wait, °lie low

luscious *adj.* delectable, °delicious, mouthwatering, °tasty, toothsome, °savory, appetizing, °rich, °sweet, °epicurean, ambrosial, palatable, °pleasant; °succulent, °juicy, *Colloq* scrumptious, °yummy

lush *adj.* **1** °luxuriant, °thick, °lavish, °flourishing, verdant, °green, °dense, °overgrown, °exuberant **2** °juicy, °succulent, mouthwatering, °fresh, °moist, °ripe **3** °palatial, °extravagant, °elaborate, °luxurious, °opulent, °sumptuous, *Colloq* ritzy, °plush

lust *n.* **1** sensuality, libido, libidinousness, sexuality, lustfulness, concupiscence, sexual appetite, *Slang* horniness **2** °desire, °drive, °energy, voracity, avidity, avidness, °ambition, ravenousness *—v.* **3** ***lust after.*** °desire, crave, hunger *or* thirst *or* hanker for *or* after, ache for

luster *n.* **1** °sheen, °gleam, °glow, °gloss, luminosity, luminousness, °radiance **2** °glory, °renown, °brilliance, °celebrity, °honor, °distinction, °fame, illustriousness

lustful *adj.* libidinous, °carnal, concupiscent, licentious, °lewd, °prurient, °lascivious, salacious, *Colloq* horny, °randy

lustrous *adj.* °glossy, °shiny, shined, °polished, burnished

lusty *adj.* **1** °vigorous, °healthy, °strong, °energetic, °robust, hale and hearty, °lively; °buxom **2** °vigorous, °substantial, °strong, °husky, °powerful

luxuriant *adj.* **1** °abundant, °profuse, copious, °lush, °rich, bounteous, overflowing, °full, °luxurious **2** °lavish, °full, °rank, °prolific, thriving, rife, °exuberant, °lush, abounding, plenteous, °abundant, superabundant, °dense, °fruitful, teeming **3** °ornate, °elaborate, decorated, °fancy, rococo, baroque, °flowery, frilly, florid, overdone, °flamboyant, °showy, °ostentatious, °gaudy, °garish, *Colloq* °flashy

luxuriate *v.* **1** Often, ***luxuriate in.*** °wallow in, swim in, bask in, °indulge in, °delight in, °relish, °revel in, °enjoy oneself, °savor, °appreciate, °like, °love **2** live in luxury *or* comfort, be in the lap of luxury, have a good *or* great *or* marvelous time, take it easy, °enjoy oneself, live the life of Riley, live off the fat of the land, *Colloq* have the time of one's life, have a ball, *US* live high off the hog

luxurious *adj.* **1** °opulent, °sumptuous, °grand, °extravagant, °lavish, °magnificent, °splendid, deluxe, °fancy; °epicurean, °gourmet; *Colloq* °swanky, swank, ritzy, °plush, °posh **2** °self-indulgent, °voluptuous, voluptuary, sybaritic, hedonistic, pampered

luxury *n.* **1** opulence, °splendor, sumptuousness, °grandeur, °extravagance, magnificence, richness, luxuriousness **2** °indulgence, self-indulgence, hedonism, sybaritism, voluptuousness **3** °security, °confidence; °gratification, °satisfaction, °enjoyment, °pleasure, °delight, °comfort **4** °frill, °extravagance, °extra, °indulgence, °nonessential, °expendable, °treat

lying *n.* **1** prevarication, fibbing, mendacity, mendaciousness, falsification, untruthfulness, °perjury; dishonesty, °deceit, duplicity *—adj.* **2** untruthful, °false, mendacious, °hypocritical, °dishonest, °deceitful, °deceptive, duplicitous, treacherous, °perfidious

lyric *adj.* **1** melodic, songlike, °musical, °melodious, °lyrical **2** °personal, °subjective, °individual, idiosyncratic; °sentimental, °rhapsodic **3** °sweet, dulcet, °graceful, silvery, lilting, mellifluous, °mellow, °light *—n.* **4** ***lyrics.*** libretto, °book, °words

lyrical *adj.* **1** See **lyric, 1,** above. **2** °enthusiastic, °ecstatic, encomiastic, °rapturous, °rhapsodic, °effusive, °impassioned, °emotional, °ebullient, °exuberant, panegyrical

M

macabre *adj.* °grim, °ghastly, °grisly, °gory, °gruesome, °grotesque, °ghoulish, °fiendish, °dread, °eerie, °fearsome, °frightful, °frightening, °terrifying, °terrible, °dreadful, dire, °morbid; deathly, °deadly, deathlike, °ghostly, cadaverous

machiavellian *adj.* °deceitful, cunning, °shrewd, °crafty, °wily, °foxy, °scheming, °tricky, °perfidious, nefarious, treacherous, °sneaky

machination *n.* plotting, °scheming, intriguing, maneuvering, °designing, manipulating; °plot, °scheme, °intrigue, °maneuver, °design, °stratagem, °ruse, °trick, °trickery, °artifice, dirty trick(s), °wile, manipulation, ploy, tactic(s), °move, gambit

machine *n.* **1** °mechanism, °device, °apparatus, contrivance, appliance, °instrument, °implement, °tool, utensil, °gadget, *Colloq* °contraption, *US and Canadian* gizmo *or* gismo **2** °engine, motor, prime mover, °vehicle; °car, automobile, motorcar, *US* auto **3** °organization, °system, °ring, °gang, °cabal, °clique, °party, °faction *—v.* **4** °shape, °make, °manufacture

machismo *n.* masculine pride *or* arrogance, manliness, virility, masculinity, °grit, *Colloq* °guts, *Slang* balls

macho *adj.* °manly, masculine, virile, °proud, °arrogant

mad *adj.* **1** °insane, °deranged, °crazy, crazed, demented, lunatic, unhinged, °delirious, out of one's mind *or* head, °psychotic, °maniacal, °(mentally) unbalanced, mentally ill, of unsound mind, ***non compos mentis***, *Chiefly Brit* daft, *Colloq* out of one's head, touched (in the head), screwy, cuckoo, °mental, balmy, certifiable, having a screw loose, dotty, cracked, mad as a March hare, mad as a hatter, not all there, off the wall, stark raving mad, *US* nutty as a fruitcake, *Chiefly Brit* potty; *Slang* nuts, loony, goofy, loopy, crackers, batty, off one's rocker *or* trolley, out of one's tree, bananas, *US* out to lunch, bughouse, bugs, crazy as a bedbug *or* a coot, loco, wacky, out of one's tree, meshuga, *Brit* round the bend *or* twist, twisted, off one's chump, barmy, bonkers **2** °foolish, °silly, °childish, °immature, °puerile, °wild, °nonsensical, °foolhardy, madcap, °heedless, °senseless, °absurd, °imprudent, unwise, °indiscreet, °rash, °ill-advised, ill-considered, °reckless, °extravagant, irrational, fatuous **3** °wild, °ferocious; °rabid **4** °furious, °angry, infuriated, incensed, enraged, irate, fuming, °berserk, irritated, provoked, wrathful, exasperated, *Literary* wroth **5** ***like mad.*** °madly, feverishly, in a frenzy, frenziedly, desperately, excitedly, violently, wildly, hysterically, furiously; enthusiastically, fervently, ardently; *Colloq* like crazy **6** ***mad (about or for).*** °crazy, °infatuated, °ardent, °enthusiastic, °eager, avid, zealous, °passionate, °fervent, fervid, °keen, °fanatical, °wild, *Colloq* hooked, *Brit* dotty, *Slang* nuts

madden *v.* **1** °infuriate, °anger, °enrage, incense, °provoke, °inflame, excite (someone) to (a) frenzy *or* rage, make (someone's) blood boil, raise (someone's) hackles, make (someone) see red, get (someone's) back up, drive (someone) crazy, *Literary* raise (someone's) ire, *Colloq* drive (someone) up the wall, *Brit* drive (someone) round the bend *or* twist, *US* tick (someone) off, burn (someone) up, tee (someone) off, °bug **2** °irk, vex, pique, °exasperate, °irritate **3** bait, badger, °torment, °plague, bedevil, *US* rile, hassle

madly *adv.* **1** insanely, hysterically, dementedly, wildly, distractedly, frenziedly **2** foolishly, stupidly, inanely, ridiculously, ludicrously, idiotically, absurdly, irrationally, senselessly **3** furiously, wildly, ferociously, °fiercely, energetically, desperately, °like mad, vehemently, feverishly, excitedly, fanatically, violently, impetuously **4** excessively, °extremely, desperately, intensely, passionately, wildly, ardently, fervently, fervidly, °exceedingly

madman *n.* madwoman; lunatic, psychopath, °psychotic, °maniac, *Colloq* crackpot, psycho, loony, screwball, *US* kook, *Slang* nut, nutcase, *Brit* nutter

madness *n.* **1** °insanity, °lunacy, °mania, dementia, psychosis, mental illness **2** craziness, °lunacy, °folly, foolishness, °nonsense, senselessness, ridiculousness, pointlessness, illogicality, illogic, illogicalness, impracticality, preposterousness, futility

magazine *n.* **1** °periodical, °journal, °publication **2** arsenal, ammunition *or* munitions dump, armory

magic *n.* **1** witchcraft, °sorcery, wizardry, black magic, necromancy, black art, voodoo, obeahism, devilry *or* deviltry, diabolism, demonolatry, occultism; sortilege, theurgy, white magic; °spell **2** legerdemain, conjuring, prestidigitation, sleight of hand, °illusion, °hocus-pocus, °trickery **3** °enchantment, allure, allurement, °charm, bewitchment, °spell, witchery, witchcraft, wizardry, °glamour, °fascination, °magnetism, ensorcellment —*adj.* **4** magical, °miraculous **5** necromantic, °occult, mystic, shamanistic, theurgical **6** magical, °enchanting, entrancing, bewitching, fascinating, hypnotic, mesmerizing, °spellbinding, charming, °magnetic, ensorcelling

magician *n.* **1** conjuror *or* conjurer, illusionist, wizard, °sorcerer, sorceress, magus, necromancer, enchanter, enchantress, Merlin, Houdini, Circe, °witch, warlock; thaumaturge, theurgist **2** °marvel, miracle worker, °virtuoso, wizard, °genius, °master, *Colloq* whiz

magnetic *adj.* °attractive, attracting, °engaging, captivating, °enthralling, °seductive, alluring, entrancing, bewitching, beguiling, °arresting, °spellbinding, °irresistible, charismatic, °winning, winsome, °inviting

magnetism *n.* °attraction, °draw, °appeal, allure, °magic, °lure, attractiveness, °charm, °pull, seductiveness, irresistibility, drawing power, charisma, ***duende***, likableness, sex appeal

magnification *n.* enlargement, amplification; buildup, strengthening, enhancement, aggrandizement, raising, °elevation, °increase, °expansion, heightening, glorification, ennoblement

magnificent *adj.* °great, °excellent, °splendid, °superior, °superb, °marvelous, °glorious, °grand, °fine, °impressive, °imposing, awe-inspiring, °brilliant, commanding, august, °noble, °majestic, °regal, °distinguished, °elegant, °exalted, °sublime, °outstanding; °sumptuous, resplendent, °rich, °opulent, °luxurious, °lavish

magnify *v.* **1** °enlarge, °expand, °amplify, °inflate, °increase, augment, °exaggerate, °heighten, °build up, °boost, °dramatize, °aggravate, °worsen, exacerbate; °overstate, *Colloq* °blow up, make a mountain out of a molehill **2** °enlarge, °blow up

magnitude *n.* **1** greatness, °size, °extent, bigness, immensity, °enormousness, dimensions **2** °importance, °significance, consequence, °note

maid *n.* **1** °girl, °maiden, °lass, °miss, nymphet, nymph, wench, damsel, mademoiselle, demoiselle, *Scots* lassie; virgin, ***virgo***

intacta 2 housemaid, maidservant, °domestic, chambermaid, lady's maid, *Literary or archaic* abigail, *Brit* °daily, *Archaic colloq Brit* tweeny 3 *old maid.* spinster, bachelor girl

maiden *n.* 1 See **maid, 1,** above. —*adj.* 2 virgin, virginal, undefiled, °intact, °chaste, (*virgo*) *intacta*; °unmarried, unwed 3 inaugural, °first, °initial, *Colloq US* shakedown

mail *n.* 1 °post, correspondence; °letters —*v.* 2 °post, °send, dispatch *or* despatch

maim *v.* °cripple, °mutilate, °lame, disable, °incapacitate, °wound, wing, °impair, hamstring, put out of action *or* commission; °injure, °harm, °damage

main *adj.* 1 °chief, °primary, °prime, °(most) important, °principal, °cardinal, °paramount, °first, °foremost, °leading, °preeminent, °predominant, predominating, °dominant, ranking, °major; °outstanding 2 largest, biggest, greatest, strongest 3 °necessary, °essential, °basic, °particular, °fundamental, °critical, °crucial, °vital 4 °sheer, °brute, utter, °pure, °out-and-out, °absolute, °mere, °plain —*n.* 5 °pipe, duct, °channel, °line, °pipeline, water *or* gas main, *Brit* °(electric) cable, mains, °power (supply), conduit 6 °strength, °power, °might, °effort, °energy, °vigor 7 *in the main.* See **mainly,** below.

mainly *adv.* °in the main, °chiefly, °principally, predominantly, °generally, °above all, °on the whole, in general, mostly, most of all, effectively, essentially, °at bottom, first and foremost, °for the most part, °largely, by and large, °primarily, °as a rule, °usually, all in all, on balance, for all practical purposes, °in the long run

mainstay *n.* main *or* chief *or* principal support, °anchor (to windward), sheet anchor, °bulwark, °buttress, linchpin, main *or* greatest strength

maintain *v.* 1 °continue, °preserve, °persevere in, keep going, °persist in, °keep (up), °carry on, °retain, °perpetuate, °prolong, °sustain, °uphold 2 °look after, °take care of, °care for, °preserve, °(keep in) service, keep up, keep in repair; nurture, °support 3 °hold, °state, °say, °declare, °claim, assert, °allege, °testify, contend, aver, avow, °announce, °proclaim, °vouchsafe, °profess, °insist (on), affirm 4 °defend, °stand by, °keep, fight for; take up the cudgels for, make a case for, °advocate, °champion, take *or* make a stand for, °plead for, °back (up), °support, °vindicate, °justify, *Colloq* go to bat for

maintenance *n.* 1 °upkeep, °care, °preservation, °conservation, °support, sustention, sustentation 2 continuation, continuance, perpetuation, prolongation, °persistence, maintaining 3 °upkeep, livelihood, °subsistence, °support, °allowance, living, °sustenance, °stipend, subvention, contribution, alimony, °keep

majestic *adj.* 1 °regal, °dignified, °grand, °imperial, °royal, °noble, lordly, °lofty, °elevated, °exalted, °glorious, °magnificent, °monumental, °impressive, °striking, °imposing, °awesome, °splendid, °marvelous, kingly, queenly, °princely 2 °pompous, °supercilious, °disdainful, °superior, °arrogant, °haughty, magisterial, imperious, °grandiose, °affected

major *adj.* 1 larger, greater, bigger, °main, °chief, °important 2 °vital, °important, °critical, °crucial, °principal, °foremost, °paramount, °primary, °prime, °main, °big, biggest, °preeminent, °notable, °noteworthy, °significant, °outstanding, °dominant, dominating; °serious, °grave, worst

majority *n.* 1 °bulk, °preponderance, °mass, more than half, the better *or* best part, the greater part *or* number, lion's share 2 adulthood, °maturity, seniority, womanhood, °manhood

make *v.* 1 °build, °assemble, °construct, °erect, put together, °set up, °fashion, °form, °mold, °shape, °frame, °create, °originate, °fabricate, °manufacture, °produce, °put out, °forge, contrive, °devise 2 °cause, compel, °force, impel, coerce, °provoke, °urge, exhort, °press, °pressure, °require, °command, °order, °induce, °persuade, °prevail upon, insist upon, °oblige, *Brit* pressurize 3 °bring about, °occasion, °cause, °give rise to 4 make out *or* up, °draw (up), °create, °write, °sign, °frame 5 °produce, °cause, °create, °generate 6 °enact, °pass, °frame, °establish, °institute 7 °earn, °return, °reap, °garner, °take in, °get, °procure, °gather, °clear, °realize, °gross, °net, °pocket, °acquire, °obtain, °receive; °win, °gain, *Slang US* °pull down 8 °amount to, constitute, °represent, add up to, °total, °come to 9 °change, °turn, °alter, °modify, °transform, °convert; transmute, mutate, metamorphose 10 °become, be, change *or* turn *or* grow into, perform as 11 serve as *or* for, be suitable for, be, prove to be, turn out to be, °turn into, °become 12 °fetch, °realize, °bring, °earn, °return 13 °score, °earn, °secure 14 °reach, °arrive at, attain, °get (to), °win, °achieve, °accomplish; °come in, *Brit* be placed, *US* °place 15 °prepare, °arrange, rearrange, °tidy (up), °neaten (up) 16 °record, °arrange, °fix, decide (on *or* upon), °agree (to) 17 °prepare, °fix, cook 18 °deliver, °present 19 °traverse, °cover, do, °travel, °navigate 20 do, °go, travel *or* move at, °move 21 °judge, °think, °calculate, °estimate, °reckon, °gauge, °suppose 22 °establish, °set up, °organize 23 °appoint, °name, °select, °choose, °elect, °vote (in as), °designate, °authorize, commission, °delegate, depute, deputize, °assign, °sanction, °approve, affirm, °certify, °confirm 24 °seduce, make it with 25 *make as if or as though.* °pretend, feign, act as if *or* as though, °affect, make a show *or* pretense of, give the impression of 26 *make away.* run off *or* away, °flee, °fly, °make off, abscond, °take to one's heels, decamp, beat a (hasty) retreat, *Colloq* run for it, make a run for it, °beat it, °clear out, cut and run, skedaddle, °take off, °cut out, °skip (town), make tracks, *US* fly the coop,

Slang scram, vamoose, *US* hightail it, take a (runout) powder **27** ***make away with.*** °steal, °rob, filch, °pilfer, purloin, walk away *or* off with, *Colloq* °borrow, °liberate, *Slang* °pinch, °hook, °swipe, °rip off, °lift, *US* °boost **28** ***make believe.*** °pretend, °fancy, playact, °dream, °fantasize, °imagine, act as if **29** ***make do.*** get by *or* along, °cope, scrape by *or* along, °manage, °muddle through, °survive, *Colloq* °make out **30** ***make for.*** **(a)** head for *or* toward(s), aim for, steer (a course) for, proceed toward(s), be bound for **(b)** °assault, °attack, °set upon, °charge, °rush (at), °pounce upon, fall upon *or* on, °go for, lunge at, °storm, assail **(c)** °promote, °contribute to, be conducive to, °favor, °facilitate **31** ***make good.*** **(a)** °make up (for), °pay (for), compensate for, recompense (for), °repay, °offset, make restitution for, °settle, °square, °rectify, put to rights, set right, °remedy, °correct, °restore **(b)** °succeed, °prosper, °flourish, °thrive, *Colloq* °make it **(c)** °fulfill, °carry out, *Colloq* °deliver (the goods) **32** ***make it.*** **(a)** °succeed, °prosper, °triumph, °win, °make good, *Colloq* °make the grade **(b)** °arrive, °get (somewhere), °show up, °appear, °turn up **33** ***make known.*** °tell of, °impart, °disclose, °reveal, divulge, °mention, °communicate, °announce, °declare, promulgate, °publish, °let slip, *Colloq* °tip off **34** ***make much of.*** **(a)** °exaggerate, °overstate, °color, hyperbolize, *Colloq* make a big deal of, °blow up **(b)** °coddle, cosset, °baby, °pamper, dote on, °flatter, toady (up) to, °cajole, °humor, °indulge, *Colloq* butter up **35** ***make off.*** See **make, 26,** above. **36** ***make off with.*** See **make, 27,** above. **37** ***make out.*** **(a)** °see, discern, descry, espy, °detect, °discover, °distinguish, °perceive **(b)** °complete, °fill in, *Brit* °fill up, *US and Canadian* °fill out **(c)** °draw (up), write (out *or* down), °record, *Colloq US* °cut **(d)** °understand, °fathom, °comprehend, °figure out, °perceive, °follow, °grasp, °see, °decipher, °read **(e)** °suggest, °imply, °hint, °insinuate, °indicate, °impute, °intimate, make to appear, °pretend, make as if *or* as though, °represent; °present, °show, °demonstrate, °establish **(f)** °get on, °survive, °manage, °fare, °thrive, °succeed **38** ***make over.*** **(a)** do over, remodel, redecorate, °alter **(b)** °transfer, °hand over, °sign over, convey, °assign, °turn over **39** ***make up.*** **(a)** °complete, °fill out, °finish (out), °flesh out **(b)** °compose, °form, constitute, be comprised of **(c)** °hatch, °invent, concoct, °devise, °create, °construct, dream up, °originate, °coin, °compose, *Colloq* cook up **(d)** be reconciled, make peace, settle amicably, °come to terms, bury the hatchet **(e)** °construct, °build **40** ***make up for.*** °compensate, redress, °make good, °atone, °make amends **41** ***make way.*** move aside, clear the way, allow to pass, make room *or* space —*n.* **42** °kind, °brand, °style, °sort, °type, °mark **43** ***on the make.*** °aggressive, °assertive, °go-ahead, °enterprising, °vigorous, °energetic, *Colloq* °pushy

makeshift *adj.* **1** °temporary, °stopgap, °expedient, °emergency, °temporary, jury-rigged, improvised, °tentative, °standby, slapdash —*n.* **2** °stopgap, °expedient, improvisation, °substitute

makeup *n.* **1** cosmetics, *maquillage,* greasepaint, *Colloq* war paint **2** constitution, °character, °cast, °disposition, °personality **3** constitution, °arrangement, construction, °composition, °format, configuration, °build, °form

male *adj.* masculine, man's; virile, °manly, manful; *Archaic* spear

malignant *adj.* **1** °virulent, pernicious, °deadly, °fatal, toxic, °poisonous, °harmful, life-threatening **2** malign, malevolent, °evil, malicious, pernicious, °vicious, invidious, °spiteful, °bitter, °hateful, °venomous

man *n.* **1** gentleman, °male, °fellow, *Colloq* °guy, °chap, *Brit* bloke, °squire, *Slang* gink, geezer, *US* gazabo **2** °people, human beings, mankind, mortals, Homo sapiens, °humanity, humankind, the human race **3** valet, manservant, gentleman's gentleman, °servant, retainer, houseboy, houseman —*v.* **4** °staff, °people, °crew; °cover

manacle *n.* **1** ***manacles.*** °shackles, fetters, °handcuffs, gyves, chains, irons, *Colloq* cuffs, *Slang* bracelets, *Brit* darbies —*v.* **2** °shackle, fetter, handcuff, °restrain, put *or* throw *or* clap in irons, °chain, *Colloq US* cuff **3** confine, °inhibit, °restrain, °curb, °check, °control, °hamper

manage *v.* **1** °handle, °administer, °run, °supervise, °look after, watch over, °direct, °head, °oversee, superintend, °direct, preside over, be in charge (of), °take care of, °control; °rule (over), °govern, °regulate **2** °handle, cope *or* deal with, °control, °govern, °manipulate **3** °conduct, °carry on, °carry out, °bring off, °control, °undertake, °take care of, °look after, °handle **4** °succeed, °function, °make do, °make it, °shift (for oneself), get along *or* by *or* on, °make out, °muddle through, °survive

manageable *adj.* controllable; °tractable, compliant, amenable, docile, tamable, °tame, trainable, teachable, manipulable, °submissive

management *n.* **1** managing, °control, supervision, manipulation, handling, °direction, directing, directorship, °administration, °government, °conduct, governance, °operation, °running, superintendence, °command, °guidance, stewardship **2** °administration, executive(s), bosses, directors, °board (of directors), directorate, *Colloq* °(top) brass

manager *n.* °supervisor, °superintendent, °director, °executive, °head, °proprietor, °overseer, °foreman, forewoman, administrator, *Chiefly Brit* manageress, *US* straw boss, *Colloq* °boss, °chief

mandatory *adj.* compulsory, °obligatory,

requisite, required; °essential, commanded, demanded, °necessary, needed

maneuver *n.* 1 °move, °stratagem, °tactic, °trick, gambit, ploy, °subterfuge, °ruse, °dodge, °artifice, °device, °wile, *démarche*; °strategy, °plan, °plot, °scheme, °intrigue, °machination 2 °exercise, °operation, °drill, war game, °operation, kriegspiel, training —*v.* 3 °manipulate, contrive, °plot, °scheme, machinate, °intrigue, °trick, °devise, °engineer, °finesse, °manage, *Colloq* finagle, °wangle 4 °manipulate, °operate, °run, °drive, °guide, °navigate, jockey

mangle *v.* °destroy, °mutilate, °butcher, deform, disfigure, °spoil, °mar, °ruin, °wreck; °cut, °hack, °lacerate, °chop (up), °crush, °damage, °cripple, °maim

mangy *adj.* scruffy, °dirty, °sleazy, °wretched, °miserable, °repulsive, °sorry, squalid, slovenly, °unkempt, °filthy, °dingy, °seedy, °poor, °shabby, °mean, °low, ignominious, °base, abject, odious, °disreputable, moth-eaten, °contemptible, °despicable, °nasty, °scurvy

manhandle *v.* maul, paw, °rough up, °batter, °beat (up), pummel, °abuse, °mistreat, maltreat, °ill-treat, trounce, °belabor, *Slang* knock about *or* around, clobber

man-hater *n.* °misanthrope, misanthropist

manhood *n.* 1 masculinity, manliness, manfulness, virility, *Colloq* °machismo 2 °bravery, °pluck, boldness, °determination, °resolution, °fortitude, °grit, °spirit, °force, *US* intestinal fortitude, *Colloq* °guts

mania *n.* 1 °rage, °craze, °passion, °obsession, compulsion, °urge, °fascination, preoccupation, °furor, yearning, craving, °desire, cacoëthes, *Colloq* °fad, yen 2 °madness, °lunacy, °insanity, dementia, derangement, hysteria, *Technical* manic disorder

maniac *n.* 1 °madman, madwoman, lunatic, psychopath, °psychotic, *Colloq* crackpot, *Slang* nut, *Brit* nutter, loony, *US* kook 2 °fanatic, °fan, °enthusiast, °zealot, *Slang* °freak, °fiend

maniacal *adj.* 1 manic, °maniac, °insane, lunatic, °mad, demented, °deranged, °hysterical, mentally ill, of unsound mind, ***non compos mentis***, °psychotic 2 °hysterical, °berserk, °wild, °crazy, *Slang* loony

manifest *adj.* 1 °apparent, °clear, °evident, °obvious, °plain, °patent, °blatant, °conspicuous, unmistakable *or* unmistakeable, °discernible, recognizable, comprehensible, °distinct, palpable, °definite, °explicit, unambiguous, °unquestionable, indubitable, °indisputable —*v.* 2 °show, °demonstrate, °exhibit, evince, °reveal, °disclose, °display, °betray; °express, °declare 3 °prove, corroborate, °substantiate, °attest

manifestation *n.* °display, °exhibition, °demonstration, °show, disclosure, °appearance, °exposure, °presentation, °sign, °indication, °mark, °expression, °example, °instance; °declaration, avowal, °publication, °announcement

manifestly *adv.* °evidently, °clearly, °obviously, plainly, °apparently, patently, unmistakably *or* unmistakeably, palpably, unquestionably, indubitably, °undoubtedly, indisputably

manifold *adj.* °diverse, diversified, multifarious, °varied, °various, assorted, multiplex, °miscellaneous, °sundry, many-sided, many different, *Literary* °divers; °many, numerous, multitudinous

manipulate *v.* 1 °manage, °handle, °control, °maneuver, orchestrate, choreograph, °influence, °use, °exploit, °play on, utilize 2 °handle, °control, °operate, °direct, °work, °use, °employ, °negotiate 3 °rig, °falsify, °juggle, tamper with, °doctor, *Colloq* cook, *chiefly Brit* °fiddle

manly *adj.* manful, virile, °courageous, °bold, °brave, °intrepid, valorous, valiant, °dauntless, °fearless, plucky, °daring, °venturesome, stouthearted, °resolute, °stable, °steadfast, unflinching, unwavering, unshrinking, °chivalrous, °gallant, °noble, °heroic; masculine, °male, *Colloq* °macho, red-blooded

manner *n.* 1 °way, °mode, °style, °technique, °procedure, °method, °fashion; °means, °approach 2 °air, °behavior, mien, demeanor, °bearing, deportment, comportment, °conduct, °attitude, °aspect 3 ***manners.*** °etiquette, °decorum, °(good) form, politeness, proprieties, °protocol, politesse, °civility, °ceremony, social code, social graces, formalities, niceties, amenities, social conventions; °behavior, °conduct

mannered *adj.* °artificial, contrived, °stilted, °stiff, °affected, °insincere, °pompous, °pretentious, posed, °unnatural, °hypocritical, *Colloq* phoney *or US also* phony, pseudo, highfalutin *or* hifalutin *or* hifaluting, la-di-da *or* lah-di-dah *or* la-de-da, °hoity-toity, on one's high horse, high-hat, uppity *or Brit* uppish

mannerism *n.* °quirk, °peculiarity, idiosyncrasy, °trait, °characteristic, °habit

mantle *n.* 1 °cloak, °cape, °wrap, shawl, pelisse, pelerine 2 covering, °cover, °sheet, °veil, blanket, °screen, °cloak, °shroud, °pall, canopy, curtain —*v.* 3 °cover, °clothe, °envelop, °surround, °encircle, °shroud, °veil, °screen, °obscure, °cloak, °conceal, °hide, °mask, °wrap, °disguise

manual *n.* handbook, °vade mecum, enchiridion; °directions, °instructions, °guide

manufacture *v.* 1 °make, (mass-)produce, °construct, °build, °assemble, °fabricate, put together, °turn out, °create, °originate 2 concoct, °create, contrive, °invent, °make up, °fabricate, °think up, *US and Canadian* create out of *or* from whole cloth, *Colloq* cook up —*n.* 3 making, (mass-)production, construction, °building, °assembly, °fabrication, turning *or* putting out, putting together, °creation, origination

manufacturer *n.* maker, °producer, industrialist, fabricator

many *adj.* 1 numerous, multitudinous, myriad, °profuse, innumerable, °numberless, uncountable **2** °diverse, multifarious, °varied, °various, assorted, °sundry, *Literary* °divers —*pron., n.* **3** horde(s), crowd(s), lot(s), swarm(s), throng(s), mass(es), °profusion, multitude(s), °abundance, °plenty, shoal(s), flock(s), drove(s), torrent(s), flood(s), number(s), score(s), hundred(s), (thousand(s), etc.); *Colloq* ton(s), scads

mar *v.* **1** °damage, °ruin, °mutilate, °deface, °spoil, °scar, disfigure **2** °damage, °wreck, °ruin, °impair, °harm, °hurt, °blight, °blot, °taint, °stain, °tarnish

march *v.* **1** °parade, °step, stride, °strut, tread, °pace, °walk —*n.* **2** °parade, °procession, °demonstration, cortege *or* cortège, °walk **3** °walk, trek, slog, hike

margin *n.* **1** °edge, °border, °perimeter, °periphery; °rim, lip, °side, °brink, °verge **2** limit(s), bound(s), °boundary (line), °border, °frontier, °line, partition line **3** °allowance, °play, °leeway, latitude, °scope, °freedom, °room, °space; compass

marginal *adj.* **1** borderline, °minimal, °small, °slight, °negligible, °insignificant, °tiny, infinitesimal **2** borderline, on the edge, °disputable, °questionable, °doubtful, dubious

marine *adj.* **1** maritime, °nautical, naval, °seafaring, seagoing, oceangoing, °sea **2** maritime, °sea, °oceanic, aquatic, saltwater, pelagic, thalassic

mark *n.* **1** °spot, °stain, °blemish, °smear, smudge, °trace, °impression, dent, °nick, °scratch, pockmark *or* pock, °streak, °line, *Brit* splodge, *US* splotch **2** °sign, °symbol, insigne, °emblem, °device, °hallmark, earmark, fingerprint, badge, °characteristic, °token, °brand, °stamp, °label, °identification, °indication, °feature, °attribute, °trait, °quality, °property **3** °standard, criterion, °norm, °yardstick, °level, °measure **4** rating, °grade, grading **5** °influence, °impression, °effect **6** °target, °goal, °objective, °aim, °purpose, °end, °object **7** marker, °indicator, °guide, signpost, °landmark **8** consequence, °importance, °note, noteworthiness, notability, °distinction, eminence, °dignity, °prestige, °standing, °account **9** ***make one's mark.*** °succeed, °get ahead, °triumph, distinguish oneself, attain distinction, bring honor upon oneself, acquit oneself, bring credit to oneself, have an effect, *Colloq* make it big, °make the grade —*v.* **10** Sometimes, ***mark up.*** °spot, °stain, °blemish, °smear, smudge, °streak, dent, °trace, pockmark, °nick, °scratch, °cut, °chip, °pit, °bruise **11** °signify, °specify, °indicate, °designate, °identify, tick, °label **12** pay attention to, °attend (to), pay heed to, °note, °notice, take notice of, °watch, °see, °look at, °observe; °respect, °mind, °heed, °obey **13** °brand, °stamp, °identify, °characterize, °distinguish **14** °correct; °grade, °evaluate, assess, appraise **15** ***mark down.*** **(a)** °write (down), °record, °register, make (a) note of, °note (down) **(b)** °decrease, °reduce, devalue, devaluate, °cut, °slash, °discount **16** ***mark up.*** **(a)** See **10,** above. **(b)** °increase, °raise, hike, up

marked *adj.* °noticeable, °conspicuous, °decided, °pronounced, °considerable, °remarkable, °significant, °signal, unmistakable *or* unmistakeable, °prominent, °obvious, °patent, °evident, °apparent

market *n.* **1** marketplace, °exchange, stock exchange **2** °shop, °store, bazaar, supermarket, *Chiefly US* superstore **3** °demand, customer base, °call —*v.* **4** °sell, °merchandise, retail, vend, °peddle, hawk, make available, °furnish; °trade (in), buy and sell, deal in

maroon *v.* °abandon, °cast away, °desert, strand, °forsake; °isolate, seclude

marriage *n.* **1** matrimony, wedlock **2** nuptials, °wedding **3** °association, °alliance, confederation, °federation, affiliation, °connection, coupling, °union, °merger, °amalgamation, integration, *Colloq* hookup

marry *v.* **1** °wed, join in matrimony *or* wedlock, become man and wife, *Colloq* get hitched *or* spliced, tie the knot **2** °match (up), go *or* fit together, °fit; °unite, °unify, °bond, °weld, °fuse, put together, °couple, °join, °link; °league, affiliate, °ally, °amalgamate, °combine

marsh *n.* °swamp, °bog, fen, slough, quagmire

martial *adj.* **1** °warlike, °belligerent, bellicose, °pugnacious, °militant **2** °military, soldierly, °courageous, °brave, valorous, valiant, °stalwart, °staunch, stouthearted

marvel *v.* **1** °wonder (at), °gape (at), be awed *or* amazed (by), be agog *or* astonished (at), —*n.* **2** °wonder, miracle, °phenomenon

marvelous *adj.* wonderful, astonishing, °amazing, astounding, surprising, °remarkable, °extraordinary, °phenomenal, °glorious, °splendid, °superb, °excellent, spectacular, breathtaking, °miraculous, °unbelievable, °incredible, °sensational, mind-boggling, °unparalleled, *Colloq* °terrific, °great, °fantastic, °fabulous, smashing, °crazy, far-out, *Slang* °wild, groovy, °super, °out of this world, fantabulous, *Brit* spot *or* bang on, *US* marvy

mask *n.* **1** false face, domino **2** °disguise, °guise, °camouflage, °show, °semblance, °pretense, °cover, coverup, false colors, false flag, concealment, °cloak, façade, °veil —*v.* **3** °disguise, °camouflage, °cover (up), °conceal, °hide, °obscure, °veil, °screen, °shroud

masquerade *n.* **1** masked ball, masquerade ball, costume party, *ballo in maschera*, bal masqué **2** °disguise, °deception, °pose, °dissimulation, °bluff, °subterfuge, false show, outward show, fakery, imposture, play-acting, false front, cover-up, °camouflage, *Colloq* °act, °front, *Slang* °put-on —*v.* **3** Usually, ***masquerade as.*** °pretend (to be), pass oneself off (as), impersonate, simulate, °pose (as), °imitate, °mimic

mass *n.* **1** °pile, °heap, °mountain, °load, °stack, °mound, °bunch, °bundle, °lot,

°batch, °quantity, °hoard, °store, °collection, °accumulation, aggregation, agglomeration, congeries, °assortment, °miscellany, assemblage, conglomeration **2** °abundance, °quantity, °profusion, °volume, multitude, horde, °host, °mob, °crowd, °throng, drove(s), herd(s), swarm(s), legion(s), score(s), number(s), *Colloq* bunch(es), ton(s), °mountain, °piles, bags, barrels, oodles, lots, °oceans, loads, scads, *US* °mess, slew(s), motherlode *or facetious* motherload **3** °block, concretion, chunk, °lump, hunk, nugget **4** °majority, best *or* better *or* greater part, °bulk, °body, °preponderance, almost all, lion's share **5** dimension, °size, °magnitude, °bulk, bigness, massiveness, °enormousness, immensity **6** ***the masses.*** the common people, the (common) herd, the proletariat, the plebeians, °hoi polloi, the lower class(es), the man *or* woman in the street, *Brit* the man *or* woman on the Clapham omnibus, A. N. Other, *US* John Q. Public, John *or* Jane Doe, Richard Roe *—v.* **7** °amass, pile *or* heap up, °gather **8** aggregate, °accumulate, °collect, °assemble, congregate, °meet, get *or* come together, °gather, forgather *or* foregather, °throng, convene, flock together, °rally, °group, °cluster, marshal, °muster, °mobilize

massacre *n.* **1** °slaughter, slaughtering, °carnage, annihilation, annihilating, blood bath, °killing, °execution, extermination, exterminating, butchery, butchering, °(mass) murder, murdering, slaying, liquidation, pogrom, genocide *—v.* **2** °slaughter, annihilate, °kill, °execute, °exterminate, °butcher, °murder, slay, liquidate, °destroy, °eliminate, °obliterate, eradicate, put to the sword, decimate, *Colloq* °mow down, *Slang* °bump off

massage *n.* **1** rubdown, °rub, manipulation, kneading *—v.* **2** rub down, °manipulate, knead, palpate **3** °manipulate, °handle, °maneuver, *Colloq* finagle, *Brit* °fiddle

massive *adj.* °big, °large, oversized, °huge, °bulky, °enormous, °hulking, °immense, °gigantic, °towering, mammoth, °colossal, titanic, °vast, tremendous, °prodigious, °mountainous, gargantuan, Brobdingnagian, cyclopean, elephantine, °jumbo, stupendous, °mighty, °weighty, °ponderous, *Literary* massy, *Colloq* walloping, °whopping, °monster, *Brit* whacking (great), *US* ginormous, humongous

master *n.* **1** °owner, °head, °chief, °leader, chieftain, commander, °lord, governor, °director, controller, °employer, °manager, °overseer, °supervisor, °superintendent, taskmaster, slave driver, °principal, °sovereign, °monarch, ruler, *Colloq* lord high muck-a-muck, Pooh-Bah, kingpin, big fish, °boss, °skipper, *Brit* gaffer, *US* kingfish, the man, big fish, big boss, bossman; *Slang US* big cheese, big wheel, Mr. Big, chief *or* head honcho **2** °expert, °authority, °genius, craftsman, °adept, maestro, °mastermind, past master, old hand, °virtuoso, ace, °professional, *Colloq* pro, wizard, *Chiefly Brit* °dab hand, *US* crackerjack; *Slang US* maven *or* mavin **3** °teacher, °tutor, °instructor, °guide, °leader, guru, swami *—adj.* **4** °adept, °ingenious, °expert, °masterful, masterly, °skillful, skilled, °proficient **5** °overall, controlling, °principal, °main, °prime, °basic, °chief **6** °main, biggest, °principal, owner's *—v.* **7** °learn, °grasp, become expert in, know inside out and backwards, °know, °understand **8** °control, °overcome, °repress, °suppress, °subdue, °bridle, °check, °quell, get the better of, *Colloq* get a grip on

masterful *adj.* **1** masterly, °adept, °expert, °excellent, °superior, °superb, adroit, °exquisite, °superlative, °supreme, consummate, °accomplished, °peerless, °matchless, °first-rate, °proficient, °dexterous, deft, °skillful, skilled, *Colloq* °crack **2** °authoritarian, °dictatorial, °tyrannical, °despotic, °arbitrary, °domineering, imperious, °overbearing, °arrogant, dominating, autocratic, highhanded, magisterial, overweening, °self-willed, *Colloq* °bossy

mastermind *v.* **1** °plan, °devise, °conceive, °think up, °engineer, °design, °generate, °create, °manage, °organize, °develop, work up *or* out *—n.* **2** planner, contriver, conceiver, °creator, architect, °genius, °mind, °intellect, *Colloq* brain(s)

masterpiece *n.* masterwork, ***magnum opus***, ***chef d'oeuvre***, tour de force, °jewel, work of art, work of genius, ***pièce de résistance***

match *n.* **1** °equal, °equivalent, °peer, °fellow, °mate; °parallel, °replica, °copy, °double, °twin, °lookalike, °facsimile, counterpart **2** °contest, °competition, °game, °meet, tourney, °tournament, °bout, duel, °rivalry, °trial **3** °marriage, betrothal, °alliance, °combination, °compact, °contract, partnership, °union, affiliation **4** °prospect, °candidate *—v.* **5** match up, °join, °marry, °unite, °link, °combine, put together, pair up *or* off, juxtapose, conjoin **6** °equal, be equivalent (to), °resemble, °compare (with), °tie, measure up (to), °compete (with), °vie (with), °rival **7** °fit, °go with, °suit, °accord, °agree, harmonize, °go (together), °coordinate, °blend, °correspond

matching *adj.* **1** corresponding, homologous, comparable, °equivalent, complementary **2** analogous, °like, corresponding, °identical

matchless *adj.* °unique, °original, °peerless, unequaled, without equal, inimitable, unmatched, °incomparable, °unparalleled, beyond compare

mate *n.* **1** °companion, °associate, °colleague, °fellow, °chap, co-worker, °comrade, crony, °ally, °friend, alter ego, *Colloq* °chum, °pal, *US* buddy, °cohort, *Slang Brit* cully, china **2** spouse, °partner, helpmeet, helpmate, consort, husband *or* wife, better half, *Colloq* hubby, old man *or* lady *or* woman, lord and master, *US* bride, *Slang Brit* trouble and strife (= 'wife') **3** °fellow, °twin, counterpart, °parallel, one of a pair *—v.* **4** °pair (up), °match (up), °marry, °wed, °join, °unite, °couple, °link (up) **5** °breed, °couple, copulate, °pair (up) **6** °match (up), °fit (together), synchronize, °join

material *n.* **1** °substance, °matter, °stuff, °fabric **2** °cloth, °fabric, textile, °stuff **3** constituents, °elements, components **4** °information, °data, °facts, statistics, figures, documents, documentation, °papers, °notes, °resources, °means, °research, °apparatus, supplies *—adj.* **5** °physical, °tangible, °concrete, °solid, °real, substantive, °substantial, palpable, corporeal, bodily **6** consequential, °important, °significant, °serious, °substantial **7** °worldly, °earthly, mundane, °temporal, nonspiritual, °secular, °lay, °materialistic

materialistic *adj.* °expedient, money-oriented, possession-oriented, °greedy, *Slang* yuppie

materialize *v.* **1** °appear, °turn up, become visible, become manifest, be revealed, take shape *or* form, °form, °emerge **2** °happen, °come to pass, °take place, °occur, become manifest *or* real, be realized, become an actuality, be actualized

materially *adv.* °substantially, palpably, significantly, °seriously, essentially, basically, considerably, greatly, much, °in the long run, °at bottom

maternal *adj.* motherly, °warm, nurturing, caring, °understanding, °affectionate, °tender, °kind, °kindly, °devoted, °fond, doting; maternalistic

maternity *n.* **1** motherhood, parenthood, pregnancy **2** parenthood, motherhood

mathematical *adj.* arithmetical; °precise, °exact, rigorous

matrimonial *adj.* marital, °marriage, °wedding, conjugal, °nuptial; married, °wedded, connubial

matter *n.* **1** °material, °substance, °stuff, sum and substance **2** °situation, °issue, °question, °affair, °business, °subject, °topic, °condition, °thing, °fact, °concern; °occurrence, °episode, °incident, °event, °occasion, °proceeding **3** °problem, °difficulty, °trouble, °complication, °worry, °upset, °dilemma, °quandary, °enigma, °puzzle **4** °content, essentials, °pith, °context, °theme, °argument, purport, °implication; signification, °meaning, meaningfulness, °import, °importance, °significance, °moment, °weight, consequence **5** °amount, °sum, °quantity, °question *—v.* **6** be important *or* of importance, °count, be of consequence, make a difference, mean something

matter-of-fact *adj.* straightforward, °direct, °forthright, °sober, °factual, unimaginative, unartistic, °prosaic, unpoetic, °dry, dry-as-dust, °dull, °boring, °tiresome, °flat, mundane, °lifeless, featureless, °unvarnished, °colorless, unembellished, °unadorned

mature *adj.* **1** °adult, grown (up), full-grown, fully grown, of age, fully fledged, full-fledged, fully developed, matured, °experienced, °knowledgeable, °sophisticated **2** °ripe, °ready, ripened, °mellow, °aged, °seasoned **3** °complete, matured, °perfect, perfected, °polished, °refined, °ready, fully developed, consummated *—v.* **4** °grow up, °age, °develop, come of age; *Brit* be one's age, *US* act one's age **5** °ripen, °mellow, °age, °season; maturate **6** °develop, °perfect, °refine, °polish, maturate, bring to fruition

maturity *n.* **1** adulthood, °majority, full growth *or* development **2** ripeness, °readiness, mellowness; maturation **3** °readiness, °perfection, °completion, fullness, °consummation, operability, applicability; maturation

maudlin *adj.* °sentimental, (over)emotional, mawkish, °romantic; °tearful, lachrymose, weepy, teary(-eyed); *Colloq* °mushy, slushy, *Brit* soppy, *US* soupy

maxim *n.* saying, °proverb, axiom, aphorism, adage, °byword, °saw, apophthegm *or* apothegm, °epigram, °motto, °slogan; mot, °witticism; °cliché, °truism

maximize *n.* **1** °increase, broaden, °improve, °magnify, augment, °add to, °expand, °build up, °enlarge **2** °inflate, overplay, °overdo, °overstate, °exaggerate, oversell, °make much of, overstress, (over) color, °enhance, embroider (on), °embellish, °elaborate, °magnify

maximum *n.* **1** most, utmost, uttermost, greatest, °peak, °extreme, °extremity, °pinnacle, °top, highest, °(upper) limit **2** °zenith, °pinnacle, °peak, °limit, apex, °acme, apogee, °climax, °crest, high(est) point, °top, °summit *—adj.* **3** maximal, greatest, most, utmost, uttermost, °superlative, °supreme, °paramount, °extreme, highest, °top, topmost, climactic, crowning

maybe *adv.* °perhaps, °possibly, *Literary* perchance, *Archaic* or *dialectal* mayhap, *Archaic* peradventure

mayhem *n.* maihem, °violence, °havoc, °destruction, °disorder, devastation, °chaos; °fracas, commotion, °confusion

maze *n.* labyrinth, complex, intricacy, twistings and turnings, convolutions

meadow *n.* °field, meadowland, °pasture, pastureland, *Literary or archaic* lea, mead

meager *adj.* **1** °scanty, scant, °poor, °paltry, °inadequate, skimpy, scrimpy, °sparse, °spare, °insufficient, °bare, °puny, piddling, °trifling, °pathetic, exiguous, *Colloq* °measly **2** °spare, °skinny, °scrawny, bony, °emaciated, °gaunt, °thin, °lean, bare-boned, (half-)starved, underfed, undernourished, starving **3** °spare, °plain, bare-boned, °unadorned, unembellished, unelaborate, unelaborated, °simple, simplified, oversimplified, °bare, °inadequate, °deficient, undetailed, °indefinite, nonspecific, °general, °broad, °loose, °vague **4** unfruitful, °infertile, °barren, °deficient, °poor, unproductive

meal *n.* **1** °food, repast, victuals, °nourishment, °spread, collation, refection; dinner, supper, breakfast, lunch, luncheon, *Brit* tea **2** ***make a meal of.*** °overdo, overplay, go overboard, go *or* carry to extremes, carry *or* go too far, do to excess

mealy-mouthed *adj.* °mincing, °reticent, °reluctant, °hesitant, °equivocal, equivocating, °ambiguous, °indirect, unwilling to call a spade a spade, euphemistic, °roundabout, °vague, circumlocutory, periphrastic, °hypocritical, °deceitful, °artful, °slick, °oily, unctuous

mean [1] *v.* **1** °intend, °design, °purpose, °plan, °aim, have in mind, °contemplate, have in view; °want, °wish, °expect, °hope; be motivated by, have as justification **2** °denote, °signify, °indicate, °note, °specify, °designate, °represent, betoken, °signal, °carry, convey, °drive at, °refer to, allude to, °communicate, °express, °bring out, get over *or* across; °imply, °suggest, connote, °intimate, °hint (at) **3** portend, °show, foretell, °foreshadow, °promise, presage, augur, herald **4** carry *or* have the weight *or* significance *or* importance of

mean [2] *adj.* **1** stingy, °miserly, °tight, °close, °cheap, parsimonious, °penurious, stinting, niggardly, penny-pinching, tightfisted, close-fisted, °mercenary, uncharitable, ungenerous, mean-spirited, unaccommodating, °small, °petty, *Colloq* °near, money-grubbing, °measly, *Brit* mingy **2** °lowly, °low, °base, °inferior, abject, °menial, °servile, degraded, °degenerate, undignified, ignoble, °plebeian, proletarian, °modest, °humble, °common **3** °disgraceful, °run-down, °poor, °sorry, °miserable, scruffy, °seedy, °scurvy, °shabby, squalid, °wretched, °vile, °mangy, °sordid, °contemptible, °dismal, °dreary, °abysmal **4** °unkind, malicious, °cruel, unaccommodating, disobliging **5** °cantankerous, churlish, °nasty, °hostile, ill-tempered, bad-tempered, °sour, unpleasant **6** °excellent, wonderful, °marvelous, °great, °exceptional, °effective, °skillful, skilled, *Colloq* far-out, *Slang US* bad

mean [3] *n.* **1** °average, °middle, °norm, °(happy) medium **2** ***by all means.*** **(a)** °absolutely, °definitely, certainly, °surely, assuredly, °of course, °positively **(b)** °in any event, °at all events, no matter what, without fail, at any cost, °in any case **3** ***by means of.*** by dint of, via, °through, °by way of, with the help *or* aid of, employing, using, utilizing **4** ***means.*** **(a)** °instrument, °agency, °method, °process, °technique, °mode, °manner, way(s), °approach, °course, °procedure, avenue, °medium, °vehicle **(b)** °resources, °funds, °money, wherewithal, °capital, °finances, °backing, °support **(c)** °substance, °wealth, °property, °position, financial stability **5** ***by no means.*** by no manner of means, in no way, not at all, definitely *or* absolutely not, on no account, not conceivably, not in one's wildest dreams *or* fantasies, not by any stretch of the imagination, *Colloq* no way, *US* no way José *—adj.* **6** °middle, °center, °intermediate, medial, °medium, median, °average, middling

meander *v.* **1** °wander, °ramble, zigzag, °snake, °wind, °twist, °turn; °stroll, amble, rove, *Colloq* mosey, *Brit* swan around *or* about *—n.* **2** Often, ***meanders.*** meandering(s), turn(s), turning(s), twist(s), twisting(s), winding(s), curve(s), curving(s), loop(s), looping(s), bend(s), coil(s), zigzag(s), convolutions; tortuosities, flexuosities, anfractuosities

meandering *adj.* wandering, °roundabout, circuitous, sinuous, °tortuous, winding, °serpentine, °indirect, flexuous, curvy, °crooked, convoluted, °labyrinthine, mazy, anfractuous

meaning *n.* **1** °sense, °import, °content, signification, denotation, °message, °substance, °gist **2** purport, °implication, °drift, °spirit, connotation, °significance, °intention **3** °interpretation, °explanation

meaningful *adj.* **1** °significant, °important, consequential, °serious, °sober, °deep, °substantial, pithy, substantive, °telling, °weighty, valid, °relevant **2** °suggestive, °pregnant, telltale, °pointed, sententious, °significant, °expressive, °eloquent

meaningless *adj.* **1** °empty, °hollow, vacuous, unsubstantial, °absurd, °silly, °foolish, fatuous, asinine, °ridiculous, °preposterous, °nonsensical **2** °ineffective, °ineffectual, °inefficacious, °bootless, unavailing, to no avail, trivial, nugatory, °trifling, °puny, °paltry, °worthless, not worth anything *or* a straw *or* a rap, valueless, °inconsequential, unimportant, of no moment, °insubstantial, °vain, °pointless, °senseless, °purposeless, undirected, °irrelevant, °insignificant

means *n.* See **mean** [3], **4,** above.

meantime *n., adv. See* **meanwhile,** below.

meanwhile *n.* **1** interim, °meantime, °interval *—adv.* **2** in the meanwhile, °meantime, in the meantime, in the interim, for the moment, °temporarily, for now, °for the time being, during the interval, in the intervening time

measly *adj.* °sparse, scant, °scanty, °meager, °paltry, °pathetic, skimpy, °puny, piddling, °miserly, niggardly, °miserable, beggarly, stingy, *Colloq Brit* mingy

measure *n.* **1** °amount, °quantity, °magnitude, amplitude, °size, °bulk, °mass, °extent, °reach, dimension, °scope, °proportions, °range, °spread; °capacity, °volume; °width, °length, °breadth, °height; °weight **2** °scale, gauge *or Technical* gage, °yardstick, °rule, *US* litmus test **3** °system, °standard, criterion, °rule, °method; barometer, Richter scale **4** assessment, °evaluation, valuation, appraisal, value, gauge *or* gage, °rank, rating, °measurement, °stamp, °estimation **5** °quota, °allotment, °ration, °share, °amount, °degree, °proportion, °quantity, °allowance; °portion, °part **6** Often, ***measures.*** step(s), °procedure, °proceeding, °action, °course (of action), °plan, °method, °means, avenue, tactic(s), °way, °direction, °approach, °technique **7** °bill, °resolution, legislation, °act, statute, °law; °plan, °proposal **8** °bound, °limit, °end, °extreme, °extent, limitation, moderation, °control, constraint, °restraint **9** °beat, °rhythm, °cadence, meter, °time;

°melody, °tune, °bar, °theme, °motif **10** ***for good measure.*** °to boot, °in addition, additionally, as a dividend, into the bargain, °besides, as *or* for a bonus, °moreover, furthermore —*v.* **11** °rank, °rate, gauge *or* gage, meter, °weigh, °calculate, °reckon, °compute, °calibrate, °determine, ascertain, figure out *or* up, assess, appraise, °estimate, °evaluate, °judge, value; °survey, °find out **12** °proportion, °pace, °adapt, °gauge, °relate, °tailor, °fit, °adjust, °regulate, °control **13** ***measure off*** *or* ***out.*** mark off *or* out, °limit, delimit, °fix, pace off *or* out, °lay off **14** ***measure out.*** mete out, dole out, °ration (out), °parcel out, apportion, °allot, share out, °assign, allocate; °give out, deal out, °distribute, °issue, °pass out, °hand out, °dispense, °disperse, spread around *or* about **15** ***measure up (to).*** **(a)** °meet, °equal, °fulfill, °match, °reach, attain **(b)** °qualify (for), be suitable (for), be equal to, be fit *or* fitted for, be adequate (to), be up to, *Colloq* °make the grade, come up to scratch, be up to snuff, *US* cut the mustard

measured *adj.* **1** °slow, regulated, °unhurried, leisurely, °stately, °majestic, °dignified, °sedate, °solemn **2** °careful, °cautious, °prudent, °calculated, °studied, considered, °deliberate, °systematic, °sober, °intentional, planned, regulated, °premeditated, well-thought-out, reasoned **3** rhythmic(al), °regular, cadenced, °steady, °uniform, °even, °monotonous **4** °precise, regulated, °exact, °predetermined, modulated, quantified; clockwork

measurement *n.* **1** measuring, °reckoning, gauging *or* gaging, ascertainment, °determination, assessment, °estimation, appraisal, °evaluation, valuation, °judgment, °calculation, computation, mensuration, commensuration; metage **2** dimension, °extent, °size, °amount, °magnitude, amplitude; °length, °breadth, °height, °width, °depth; °area; °volume, °capacity; °weight, tonnage; °(elapsed) time, °period; (square *or* cubic) footage, (square) yardage, mileage, acreage

meat *n.* **1** °flesh; °food, °nourishment, °sustenance, viands, victuals, nutriment, °provisions, °provender, comestibles, edibles, eatables, *Colloq* eats, chow, grub **2** °pith, °core, °heart, marrow, °kernel, vital part, °essence, °gist, °substance, basics, essentials, crux

mechanical *adj.* **1** °automatic, automated, machine-driven; machine-made **2** °automatic, reflex, °involuntary, °instinctive, °routine, °habitual, °unconscious, °perfunctory, machinelike, robotlike **3** °impersonal, °distant, °cold, °matter-of-fact, unfeeling, °insensible, ritualistic, °lifeless, spiritless, °dead, °inanimate, unanimated, unemotional, unartistic, mechanistic, °colorless, uninspired, businesslike

mechanism *n.* **1** °device, appliance, contrivance, °apparatus, °instrument, °machine **2** machinery, workings, °works, °structure, °system, °organization, °arrangement **3** °way, °means, °method, °procedure, °approach, °technique, °medium, °process, °agency **4** materialism, mechanicalism, physicalism, logical positivism, identity theory, monism

meddle *v.* °interfere, °intrude, °butt in, °pry, °intervene, interlope, °tamper, °snoop, *Rare* intermeddle, *Colloq* stick *or* poke one's nose in, have a *or* one's finger in the pie, kibitz

mediator *n.* arbitrator, arbiter, referee, °umpire, °judge, °negotiator, °intermediary, °go-between, middleman, °moderator, °liaison, intercessor, interceder, conciliator, appeaser, °peacemaker

medicinal *adj.* healing, remedial, °therapeutic, curative, restorative, sanative; medical, iatric(al), *Medicine* roborant, analeptic, alexipharmic

medicine *n.* medication, medicament, °remedy, °drug, pharmaceutical, °prescription, *Archaic* physic; nostrum, panacea, cure-all

mediocre *adj.* middling, °indifferent, °ordinary, commonplace, °average, °medium, °everyday, °run-of-the-mill, °pedestrian, °undistinguished, uninspired, unimaginative, unexceptional, °tolerable, °fair, not (that *or* too) good, not bad, second-rate, third-rate, °inferior, °poor, *Brit* common-or-garden variety, *US* garden-variety, *Colloq* °so-so, fair to middling, nothing to brag *or* to write home about, no great shakes

meditate *v.* **1** °reflect, °think, °muse, °ponder, °study, ruminate, cogitate, °contemplate, cerebrate, be lost in thought, be in a brown study **2** Often, ***meditate on*** *or* ***upon.*** °consider, °contemplate, mull over, reflect on *or* upon, ponder on *or* over, °chew over, °plan, °scheme, °devise, °design, °conceive, °frame, °think up, have in mind

meditative *adj.* °thoughtful, °pensive, contemplative, °reflective, °studious, cogitative, excogitative, abstracted, °rapt, engrossed, lost *or* deep in thought, ruminative, brooding

medium *adj.* **1** °average, °middle, mid, medial, median, °normal, °standard, °usual, °everyday, °ordinary; mid-sized **2** See **mediocre,** above. —*n.* **3** °average, °middle, midpoint, compromise, °center, °mean, °norm, mediocrity **4** °atmosphere, °environment, ambiance *or* ambience, °milieu **5** °means, °method, °mode, °approach, instrumentality, °device, °mechanism, intermediation, °technique, contrivance, °agency, °expedient, °way, °course, °route, °road, avenue, °channel, conveyance, °vehicle

medley *n.* °mixture, °assortment, °combination, °miscellany, mélange, °collection, conglomeration, agglomeration, hotchpotch *or* *US and Canadian also* hodgepodge, olio, °blend, gallimaufry, omnium-gatherum, °pastiche, °potpourri, salmagundi, olla podrida, °mishmash, °jumble, °mess, farrago, °stew, goulash, *Colloq* mixed bag

meek *adj.* **1** °modest, °humble, °submissive, unassuming, unambitious, unpretentious,

°mild, °bland, °patient, deferential, °shy, °retiring, °lowly **2** °tame, °timid, °weak, docile, compliant, °submissive, °yielding, acquiescent, unaggressive, nonmilitant, °tractable, °manageable, °subdued, repressed, spiritless, suppressed, °broken, *Colloq* wimpish

meet[1] *v.* **1** °encounter, °come across, chance on *or* upon, happen on *or* upon, stumble on *or* into, °see, *Colloq* run across *or* into, °bump into **2** Often, ***meet with.*** rendezvous (with), °get together (with); convene, °assemble, °gather, °collect, forgather *or* foregather, congregate **3** make the acquaintance of, be introduced to, first encounter, °come across, °find **4** °link up, °join, come together, °unite, adjoin, abut, °touch, intersect **5** °answer, °deal with, °handle, °satisfy, °fulfill, °take care of, °dispose of, °heed, °observe, °carry out; °gratify, °pay, °settle, °defray, liquidate **6** ***meet with.*** °encounter, be met by, °experience; °undergo, °endure, °suffer, °have, °go through —*n.* **7** °competition, °contest, °meeting, °match, tourney, °tournament; °muster, °rally

meet[2] *adj.* °fitting, °suitable, °appropriate, °proper, °fit, congruous

meeting *n.* **1** °appointment, °engagement, rendezvous, °encounter, assignation, tryst, *Slang US* °meet **2** °assembly, °convention, °conference, °gathering, congress, conclave, °session, congregation, convocation, *US* caucus, *Colloq* °get-together **3** convergence, converging, confluence, joining, °union, °junction, conjunction, intersection **4** See **meet, 7,** above.

melancholy *adj.* **1** °sad, morose, depressed, unhappy, °dejected, °despondent, °blue, °downhearted, °glum, °gloomy, woeful, °woebegone, lugubrious, disconsolate, downcast, dispirited, low-spirited, cheerless, crestfallen, chapfallen, °forlorn, °heartbroken, °mournful, °sorrowful, °miserable, °dismal, *Colloq* °down in the mouth, (down) in the dumps, °low —*n.* **2** °sadness, °sorrow, °misery, °woe, °gloom, unhappiness, blues, moroseness, °depression, dejection, dejectedness, despondence, despondency, downheartedness, glumness, gloominess, woefulness, lugubriousness, disconsolateness, dispiritedness, cheerlessness, mournfulness, sorrowfulness, miserableness, dolor, °anguish

mellow *adj.* **1** °soft, °juicy, °luscious, °delicious, °rich, °sweet, flavorful, full-flavored, °ready, °ripe, °mature, ripened, °aged **2** °musical, °melodious, °full, °pure, °rich, °sweet, dulcet, mellifluous, euphonious, vibrant **3** °soft, softened, °subtle, muted, pastel **4** easygoing, °genial, °gentle, °good-natured, °easy, °cordial, °friendly, °warm, °amiable, °agreeable, °pleasant, °cheerful, °happy, jovial, felicitous; °suave, mellowed out, *Colloq* °cool —*v.* **5** °mature, °ripen, °age, °season, °sweeten, °develop, °improve (with age), °soften

melodious *adj.* sweet(-sounding), dulcet, °tuneful, euphonious, °harmonious, melodic, °lyrical, °musical, mellifluous, mellisonant, silvery, °golden

melodramatic *adj.* °sensational, sensationalistic, °dramatic, stagy, °theatrical, emotionalistic, (over)sentimental, (over) sentimentalized, overdrawn, overworked, °overwrought, overdone, exaggerated, histrionic, blood-and-thunder, *Colloq* hammy, *US* schmaltzy, hokey

melody *n.* **1** °song, °tune, °air, °strain, °measure, °theme, °refrain **2** tunefulness, melodiousness, euphoniousness, euphony, °harmony, musicality, sweetness

melt *v.* **1** °soften, °thaw, liquefy, °fuse, °dissolve, liquidize, deliquesce **2** °soften, °thaw, mollify, assuage, °touch, °move, °disarm, °mellow **3** Usually, ***melt into.*** °blend, °fade, °merge, °disappear, °dissolve, °shrink **4** ***melt away.*** °disappear, °dissolve, vanish, °evaporate, °go away, °fade, °pass, °decline, °decrease, °shrink, °dwindle, °diminish

member *n.* °colleague, °associate, °fellow

memento *n.* **1** souvenir, °keepsake, °remembrance, °relic, °trophy, °token **2** ***mementos.*** memorabilia

memoir *n.* **1** °account, °report, reportage, °narrative, °essay, dissertation, disquisition, °paper, °journal, °record, biography, °life **2** ***memoirs.*** autobiography, reminiscences, recollections, memories, °diary, confessions, °letters, life story; annals, °history, account(s), record(s), °chronology

memorable *adj.* unforgettable, catchy, never-to-be-forgotten, °noteworthy, °notable, °remarkable, °significant, °important, °worthy, °momentous, °eventful, °historic, °illustrious, °celebrated, °great

memorandum *n.* °note, °record, °minute, °reminder, °message, *Brit* chit *or* chitty, *Colloq* memo

memorial *adj.* **1** commemorative —*n.* **2** °monument, marker, °plaque, cenotaph, °statue, °memento, °remembrance, °reminder, souvenir

memorialize *v.* °honor, °commemorate, pay homage *or* respect *or* tribute to, °remember, °eulogize, °celebrate, °mark

memorize *v.* learn by heart *or* rote, commit to memory, learn word for word, °retain; °remember

memory *n.* **1** °recall, °recollection, retention **2** °recollection, °reminiscence, °thought **3** °remembrance, °honor, °homage, °respect, °tribute, °celebration

menace *v.* **1** °threaten, °intimidate, °daunt, terrorize, °terrify, cow, °bully, °frighten, °scare, °alarm; bare one's teeth —*n.* **2** °threat, °danger, °peril, °hazard, °risk **3** intimidation, °scare, °threat, °warning, commination

menacing *adj.* °threatening, looming, °impending, °ominous, °frightening, °terrifying, intimidating, minacious, minatory *or* minatorial, lowering *or Brit also* louring; °dangerous, °perilous, °hazardous, °risky, chancy

mend *v.* **1** °repair, °fix, °patch (up), °rectify,

°correct, °remedy, °restore, °rehabilitate; °heal **2** °correct, °improve, °better, ameliorate, °reform, °revise, °rectify, set *or* put right, emend **3** °heal, °improve, °recover, °convalesce, °recuperate, get better —*n.* **4** °repair, °patch **5** ***on the mend.*** recovering, recuperating, convalescing, convalescent, improving

menial *adj.* **1** °lowly, °servile, °humble, subservient, °base, °low, °mean, slavish, demeaning, °degrading, ignoble; °routine, unskilled **2** °servile, fawning, °groveling, toadying, sycophantic, °obsequious, cringing, °timeserving, °flattering, sniveling, *Colloq* bootlicking, *Slang taboo* brown-nosing —*n.* **3** lackey, flunky *or* flunkey, serf, °slave, underling, minion, *Brit* °fag, *Colloq Brit* dogsbody, skivvy, *US* gofer **4** toady, sycophant, °yes man, lickspittle, leech, °parasite, timeserver, *Colloq* bootlicker, *Slang taboo* brown-nose(r)

mental *adj.* **1** °intellectual, cognitive, cerebral, perceptual, °rational, conceptual, °theoretical, noetic, °abstract **2** lunatic, °mad, °crazy, °psychotic, demented, mentally ill, °unstable, °unbalanced, °deranged, °disturbed, °daft, certifiable, *Slang* off one's rocker, nutty, batty, balmy, loony, screwy, bonkers, crackers, nuts, bananas, *US* loco, *Brit* barmy

mentality *n.* **1** °intelligence, °brain, °capacity, °intellect, °wit, °sense, °judgment, acuity, acumen, I.Q., rationality, °understanding **2** °inclination, °attitude, °bent, mind-set, °disposition, °frame of mind, temperament, °outlook, °view

mention *v.* **1** speak *or* write about, °refer to, allude to, touch on *or* upon, make mention (of), bring up *or* in, °introduce, °broach, call *or* direct attention to, °note, °name, cite, °acknowledge; °point out, °indicate, °make known, adduce, °report, °quote **2** divulge, °reveal, °intimate, °disclose, °impart, °suggest, advert (to), °hint (at), °imply, °insinuate —*n.* **3** °reference, allusion, °note, naming, citation, mentioning, *Colloq* cite **4** °recognition, °tribute, °acknowledgment, °kudos, °praise **5** °announcement, °reference, referral, °remark

mercantile *adj.* commercial, °business, °trade, marketing, °market

mercenary *adj.* **1** money-oriented, °grasping, °greedy, acquisitive, covetous, °predatory, °avaricious, °venal, *Colloq* money-grubbing **2** °venal, bribable, °corrupt, bought, *Colloq US* on the take —*n.* **3** hireling, legionnaire, soldier of fortune

merchandise *n.* **1** °goods, commodities, products, °stock, °staples, °produce —*v.* **2** °trade, deal in, traffic in, °market, °distribute, retail, °(buy and) sell, °promote, advertise

merchant *n.* **1** °dealer, retailer, °seller, shopkeeper, store owner, °trader, tradesman *or* tradeswoman, vendor **2** °peddler, hawker; (traveling) salesman, °(sales) representative, commercial traveler, huckster, door-to-door salesman, *US old-fashioned* drummer, *Colloq* (sales) rep **3** distributor, wholesaler, jobber, °broker, °agent, forwarder; businessman, merchant prince, °mogul, °tycoon, magnate, industrialist, *US* baron

merciful *adj.* compassionate, °sympathetic, °forgiving, °kind, °kindly, clement, kind-hearted, forbearing, °sparing, °lenient, °tender, humane, °liberal, °mild, tenderhearted, °softhearted, °gracious, °generous, magnanimous, benignant, beneficent, °charitable, °thoughtful, °considerate, °indulgent, °big

merciless *adj.* °cruel, pitiless, °ruthless, °heartless, °unmerciful, inhumane, °inhuman, °brutal, °savage, barbarous, barbaric, °barbarian, °crude, °rude, °rough, °harsh, °tough, °callous, °hard, hardhearted, illiberal, °tyrannical, stonyhearted, °cold, °severe, unsparing, insensitive, °indifferent, °unsympathetic, unforgiving, °ungracious, malevolent, °thoughtless, uncharitable, °inconsiderate, °unmoved, unbending, °inflexible, °relentless, unrelenting, inexorable

mercy *n.* compassion, °pity, forbearance, °quarter, °tolerance, °sympathy, °favor, °forgiveness, °kindness, kindliness, leniency, tenderness, °humanity, humaneness, liberality, kindheartedness, tenderheartedness, softheartedness, graciousness, generosity, magnanimity, benignity, beneficence, °charity, thoughtfulness, °consideration, °indulgence

mere *adj.* °bare, °basic, scant, °stark, °sheer; °absolute, unmixed, °only, °just, nothing but, °pure (and simple), °unmitigated, °undiluted

merely *adv.* **1** °only, °simply; basically, purely, essentially, fundamentally, °at bottom **2** °only, no more than; °barely, °scarcely, °simply, solely, °entirely

merge *v.* °combine, coalesce, °unite, °join, °amalgamate, consolidate, °pool, °blend, °mix, °mingle, commingle, °fuse

merger *n.* °combination, coalescence, °union, merging, °amalgamation, consolidation, coalition, pooling, blending, mixing, mingling, commingling, fusing, fusion

merit *n.* **1** °worth, worthiness, value, °excellence, °quality, °virtue, °good, goodness **2** Often, ***merits.*** °assets, strong point, °advantage, rights and wrongs —*v.* **3** °earn, °deserve, °warrant, °rate, have a right *or* claim to, be entitled to, be qualified for, be worthy of

meritorious *adj.* °honorable, °laudable, °praiseworthy, commendable, creditable, °admirable, °estimable, °excellent, °exemplary, °outstanding

merriment *n.* jollity, joviality, merrymaking, °revelry, °gaiety, high *or* good spirits, °mirth, mirthfulness, joyfulness, felicity, jubilation, °festivity, exhilaration, buoyancy, °exuberance, °cheer, cheerfulness, °glee, °fun, °hilarity, °enjoyment, °happiness, blithefulness, blithesomeness, frolicking

merry *adj.* **1** °cheerful, °happy, °gay, cheery, °jolly, jovial, in high *or* good spirits, mirthful,

°joyful, joyous, °hilarious, jubilant, rejoicing, festive, °exhilarating, °exuberant, °vivacious, convivial, °buoyant, °gleeful, °blithe, blithesome, °carefree, lighthearted, °delighted **2** ***make merry.*** °revel, °celebrate, °carouse, °frolic

mesh *n.* **1** meshwork, °network, netting, °net, °web, webbing, lattice, latticework, °screen, screening, interlacing, lacework, grid, °grate, °grating, grater, sieve, strainer, trellis, trelliswork, decussation, *Technical* rete, reticle *or* reticule *or* graticule, reticulation, plexus, plexure, reticulum; interstice **2** Often, ***meshes.*** °grip, °clutches, °grasp, toils, °web, °trap, entanglement, °tangle, complex, °complexity, intricacy *—v.* **3** °catch, °entangle, enmesh, °grab, °trap, entrap, °snare, ensnare, °involve **4** °engage, °fit (together), dovetail, °knit, enmesh, °match, interlock

mess *n.* **1** °chaos, °disorder, disarray, disorganization, °shambles, °muddle, disarrangement, °clutter, hotchpotch *or US also* hodgepodge, °litter, °tangle, dog's breakfast *or* lunch *or* dinner, mare's nest, °jumble, °confusion, °mishmash; untidiness **2** concoction, °mixture, °medley, °miscellany, °hash, gallimaufry, farrago, olio, olla podrida, °potpourri, smorgasbord *or* smörgåsbord, kedgeree **3** °predicament, °difficulty, °plight, °pinch, °trouble, °dilemma, °quandary, imbroglio, *Colloq* foul-up, °stew, °fix, hot water, (pretty *or* fine) kettle of fish, pickle, °jam, *Slang* screw-up, *Brit* balls-up, can of worms, *US* snafu *—v.* **4** ***mess about or around (with).*** **(a)** potter, °fool (around), dally, busy oneself, fiddle about *or* around, °play **(b)** philander, °trifle, °toy, °flirt, °seduce, sleep around, °fool around, °run around **5** ***mess up.*** **(a)** disarrange, disarray, dishevel, °tousle, *Colloq US* muss (up) **(b)** °ruin, °destroy, make a shambles of, °wreck, °bungle, °botch, °foul up, *Colloq* make a hash of, *Slang* °muck up **(c)** °dirty, °clutter up, make untidy, turn upside down, pull to pieces, °upset **6** ***mess with.*** interfere in *or* with, °intervene, meddle with *or* in, intrude in, butt in *or* into, tinker with, tamper with, get involved in *or* with

message *n.* **1** communication, °bulletin, °report, communiqué, °news, dispatch *or* despatch, °information, °word, °intelligence, tidings; °note, °missive, °letter, °memorandum **2** °speech, °address, °presentation, °statement, °declaration **3** °idea, °point, °import, °meaning, °essence, °implication

messenger *n.* °envoy, emissary, legate, nuncio, °intermediary, °go-between; °page, errand boy *or* °girl, messenger boy *or* girl, courier, °runner, dispatch rider, Pheidippides, Mercury, Hermes; herald, °harbinger; *Colloq US* gofer

Messiah *n.* deliverer, liberator, emancipator, savior *or* saviour, rescuer

metaphor *n.* °figure (of speech), allusion, analogy, analogue, °reference, °image, trope, °symbol; simile, parabole; metonymy, symbolism, °imagery

metaphoric *adj.* metaphorical, nonliteral, allusive, analogic(al), analogous, figurative, °symbolic, referential, parabolic(al), metonymic, metonymous, tropological

mete *v.* Usually, ***mete out.*** deal (out), apportion, °distribute, °dole (out), °allot, °assign, allocate, °parcel out, °share (out), °ration (out), °measure out, °dispense, °hand out, °give out, °pass out, *Colloq* dish out

meteoric *adj.* **1** °brief, °short-lived, °temporary, transitory, °transient, ephemeral, evanescent, impermanent, °fleeting, °momentary, °swift, overnight **2** °brilliant, °dazzling, flashing, spectacular, °sensational

method *n.* **1** °way, °means, °procedure, °approach, °route, avenue, °road, °mode, °manner, °technique, °process, °routine, modus operandi; °plan, °scheme, °program, °course, °practice, °pattern, °system, methodology; *Colloq US* MO (= 'modus operandi') **2** °arrangement, °order, °system, °structure, °organization, °design, °pattern, orderliness, neatness, °regularity, °discipline

methodical *adj.* organized, ordered, °systematic, structured, businesslike, °orderly, °neat, °tidy, °regular, °routine, balanced, disciplined, °painstaking, °meticulous, °deliberate, paced, °laborious, plodding, °labored

meticulous *adj.* °careful, °precise, °accurate, °exact, °fastidious, °scrupulous, °thorough, °particular, °painstaking, punctilious, °fussy, °finicky, °demanding, °strict, °critical, °exacting, °perfectionist

metropolis *n.* °capital, °(capital) city; metropolitan area, urban sprawl, megalopolis, °municipality

microbe *n.* microorganism, microzoon, °germ; bacterium, virus, *Colloq* °bug

midday *n.* °noon, noontime, twelve (o'clock) noon, *US* high noon

middle *adj.* **1** °central, °center, halfway, mid, midway, °mean, medial, *Technical* mesial *—n.* **2** °center, midpoint, °midst, halfway point; °heart, bull's-eye **3** midriff, waist, midsection, °stomach

midst *n.* °middle, °center, midpoint, halfway point

midwife *n.* accoucheur *or* accoucheuse

might *n.* **1** °strength, °power, °energy, °force, muscle, potency, *Literary* puissance **2** °influence, °authority, °weight, °sway, °dominion, ascendancy, °superiority, mightiness, °capability, °capacity, °power, °effect, effectiveness, *Colloq* clout

mighty *adj.* **1** °powerful, °strong, °potent, °influential, °dominant, °predominant, ascendant, °weighty, doughty, °authoritarian, autocratic, °indomitable **2** °strong, °muscular, °powerful, °robust, strapping, °sturdy, °brawny, °burly, well-built, able-bodied, °hardy, *Colloq* °husky, °hefty **3** °big, °large, °huge, °grand, °great, °enormous, °gigantic, tremendous, °towering, °monumental, °prodigious, °massive, °bulky *—adv.* **4** °very, °extremely

migrant *n.* 1 wanderer, °rover, °drifter, gypsy, nomad, itinerant, °transient, migrator, wayfarer, bird of passage, peregrinator, °traveler; vagrant; *Colloq US* wetback —*adj.* 2 °transient, migratory, itinerant, peripatetic, drifting, nomadic, °traveling, gypsy, floating; vagrant

migrate *v.* 1 °go, °move, °travel, °settle, resettle, relocate, move house; °emigrate, immigrate, expatriate 2 °wander, °roam, voyage, rove, °drift, °range

mild *adj.* 1 placid, °peaceful, °calm, °tranquil, °bland, °mellow, °inoffensive, °gentle, °serene, °good-natured, affable, °amiable, °kind, °kindly, °equable, easygoing, °temperate, nonviolent, conciliatory, °indulgent, °merciful, °forgiving, compassionate, °lenient, forbearing, °peaceable, pacific, °passive, °submissive, °yielding, °tractable, °meek, unassuming, °modest, °quiet, °subdued 2 clement, balmy, °warm, °fair, °pleasant, °temperate, placid, °moderate 3 °bland, °soothing, lenitive, mollifying, demulcent, emollient, °gentle, calming, softening

milieu *n.* °environment, °climate, surroundings, environs, °background, ambiance *or* ambience, °sphere, °setting, °context, °atmosphere, °medium, °element, °precincts

militant *adj.* 1 °aggressive, combative, °pugnacious, °belligerent, °hostile, contentious, antagonistic, °offensive, °truculent, °fierce, °ferocious, °warlike, bellicose, °martial, jingoistic, hawkish 2 warring, fighting, combatant, combating, embattled; °at war, up in arms —*n.* 3 fighter, °aggressor, combatant, °belligerent, warrior, °soldier

military *adj.* 1 °martial, soldierly, naval, army, fighting, °service —*n.* 2 (armed) services *or* forces, army, °navy, air force, military establishment, soldiery

militate *v.* 1 Usually, ***militate against.*** °discourage, work *or* go *or* operate against, °foil, °counter, countervail, °cancel (out), °reduce (possibility of), °prevent, °hinder, °resist, °oppose 2 Usually, ***militate for or in favor of.*** be on the side of, °favor, °further, °promote, °help, °aid

milk *v.* °drain, bleed, °extract, °tap, °exploit, wring, draw off *or* out, °withdraw

milksop *n.* sissy *or Brit also* cissy, °coward, °weakling, namby-pamby, mollycoddle, crybaby, nancy (boy), dastard, poltroon, caitiff, (little) Lord Fauntleroy, poltroon, *Archaic* caitiff, *US* milquetoast, mama's boy, *Colloq* chinless wonder, *Brit* mother's *or* mummy's boy, *US* mama's boy, pantywaist, *Slang* pansy

mill *n.* 1 grinder, quern, crusher, °roller 2 °plant, °factory, °works, workshop, °shop, foundry 3 ***been through the mill.*** °experienced, °knowledgeable, °sophisticated, toughened, hardened, °seasoned, battle-scarred, *Colloq* been through the wringer, in the know 4 ***run-of-the-mill.*** °average, unexceptional, °ordinary, °common, unremarkable, °everyday, °basic, °simple, *Brit* common-or-garden variety, *US* garden-variety —*v.* 5 °grind, °crush, comminute, °powder, °pulverize, °grate, granulate, °pound, triturate, masticate, bray; °crunch, mince 6 ***mill about or around.*** °meander, °wander, °walk, °stroll, amble, move about *or* around, °crowd, °throng, °swarm

mimic *v.* 1 °imitate, ape, °copy, simulate, °mirror, °echo 2 °reproduce, °duplicate, °copy 3 °mock, °ridicule, °satirize, °caricature, °parody, °make fun of, °lampoon, impersonate, *Colloq* °take off —*n.* 4 impersonator, imitator, impressionist, caricaturist, parodist, *Colloq* copycat —*adj.* 5 imitative, °imitation, °mock, simulated, mimetic, °sham, make-believe, pretend(ed); °fake, °counterfeit, feigned

mincing *adj.* °effeminate, °dainty, °delicate, niminy-piminy, foppish, dandyish, overdainty, °affected, °put-on, °pretentious, °precious, *Brit* twee, *Colloq* la-di-da *or* lah-di-dah *or* la-de-da

mind *n.* 1 °intelligence, °intellect, °wit, wits, °mentality, °brain, brains, brainpower, °sense, sagacity, °wisdom, °perception, percipience, °reason, astuteness, °insight, shrewdness, sapience, *Colloq* gray matter 2 °memory, °recollection; °remembrance 3 °aptitude, °head, °perception, °capacity, °brain 4 °intellect, °intellectual, °sage, °genius, °thinker, *Colloq* °brain 5 °intention, °disposition, °temper, temperament, °humor, °fancy, °tendency, °bent, °inclination, °bias, °persuasion 6 °opinion, °sentiment, °attitude, °(point of) view, °feeling, °judgment, °belief, °viewpoint, °position 7 °feeling, °position, °will, °wish, °desire, plan(s) 8 °attention, °thoughts, concentration, °thinking 9 ***bear or keep in mind.*** °remember, do not forget *or* overlook, °recall, °retain, be aware *or* cognizant *or* mindful of, °consider 10 ***give someone a piece of one's mind.*** °castigate, °scold, °rebuke, °reprimand, rail at, °reprove, reproach, °chastise, °upbraid, °berate, read (someone) the riot act, *Colloq* °tell off, °dress down, haul *or* rake over the coals, skin alive, *US* °bawl out; *Slang* give someone hell, *US* °chew out 11 ***know one's (own) mind.*** be decided *or* resolved, be firm *or* resolute, be sure *or* certain *or* positive, be (self-)assured *or* (self-)confident, be in touch with oneself 12 ***make up one's (own) mind.*** °decide, °choose, conclude, form an opinion; °determine, °consider, °weigh, °judge, deem 13 ***of or in two minds.*** vacillating, undecided, ambivalent, °uncertain, shilly-shallying, unsure, wavering 14 ***out of one's mind.*** °insane, °mad, °crazy —*v.* 15 object to, °resent, take offense at, be offended by, °dislike, be troubled *or* annoyed by, °care, have an objection to, disapprove of, be bothered *or* affronted by 16 °heed, °attend to, pay attention to, °obey, listen to, make *or* take note of, °mark, °note 17 °watch, be careful of, take care with, be cautious of 18 watch over, °take care of, °care for, °look after, °sit with, babysit, °guard, keep an eye on *or* out for, have *or* take charge of, °attend **19** ***never mind.*** °ignore, °disregard, °forget, pay no attention to, do not think twice about, do not give a second thought to, erase *or* obliterate *or* cancel from the mind, slough off

minder *n.* **1** (baby) sitter, nanny, °nurse, governess, *Chiefly Brit* child minder **2** bodyguard, °escort, °protector

mindful *adj.* Often, ***mindful of.*** aware, °alert, attentive to, °alive, °conscious, heedful, °conscientious, watchful, °vigilant, on the qui vive, on the lookout, circumspect, °cautious

mindless *adj.* **1** °stupid, asinine, °thick, thickheaded, °obtuse, idiotic, imbecilic, moronic, °thoughtless, witless, °senseless, brainless, °feebleminded, fatuous, addlebrained, addlepated, featherbrained, *Colloq Brit* gormless **2** °inattentive, °unthinking, °thoughtless, °unaware

mine *n.* **1** °pit, °excavation, lode, °vein; colliery, coalfield **2** °source, motherlode, °vein, °store, °storehouse, °supply, °deposit, depository *or* depositary, repository, °reserve, °hoard, treasure trove, reservoir, wellspring; °abundance, °fund, gold mine, °wealth, °treasury —*v.* **3** °excavate, °dig, °quarry, °extract, scoop out *or* up, °remove, °unearth; °derive, °extract, °draw **4** °ransack, °search, °rake through, °scour, °scan, °read, °survey, look through, °probe

mingle *v.* **1** °mix, °blend, intermingle, commingle, intermix, °combine, °amalgamate, °merge, °compound, °marry, °join, °unite **2** °mix, °socialize, °associate, °join, °circulate, °fraternize, °hobnob, consort, °go, spend time, *Colloq* hang about *or* around *or* out, rub shoulders, *Brit* pal up, *US* pal around

miniature *adj.* °small, small-scale, °little, °tiny, °diminutive, °minute, °wee, minuscule, mini, microscopic, micro, midget, °dwarf, bantam, °baby, pygmy, °pocket, Lilliputian, *US* vest-pocket, *Colloq* °minimal

minimal *adj.* least, smallest, minutest, littlest, tiniest, slightest; °minimum, °nominal, °token

minimize *v.* **1** °reduce, °shrink, lessen, °diminish, °prune, °abbreviate, °pare (down), °cut (down), °curtail, °abridge, °shorten, °decrease, minify **2** °belittle, de-emphasize, downplay, °play down, make little *or* light of, °disparage, decry, deprecate, °depreciate, misprize, devalue, devaluate, undervalue, underrate, °underestimate, *US* °talk down

minimum *n.* **1** least, lowest, nadir —*adj.* **2** °minimal, °nominal, reduced, minutest, littlest, least, slightest, lowest

minister *n.* **1** cleric, °clergyman, clergywoman, ecclesiastic, °pastor, vicar, °priest, °father, reverend, churchman, °divine, parson, °preacher, man *or* woman of the cloth, evangelist, °missionary, dean, curate, curé, abbé, chaplain, *Colloq* padre, *Slang US military* sky pilot, Holy Joe **2** °envoy, °delegate, legate, diplomat, °ambassador, emissary, plenipotentiary, minister plenipotentiary, envoy extraordinary, minister resident, consul, °agent, chargé d'affaires, *Brit* cabinet officer *or* member —*v.* **3** Usually, ***minister to.*** attend (to *or* on *or* upon), °wait on, °care for, °look after, °see to, °accommodate; °serve, °supply, °aid, °help, °assist, °support

ministry *n.* **1** priesthood, sacred calling, the church, the pulpit, °the cloth; °religion, holy orders **2** clergy, clergymen *or* clergywomen, clericals, °the cloth, church elders *or* elders of the church **3** °department, °office, °bureau, °agency

minor *adj.* **1** lesser, smaller, °secondary, °subordinate, °subsidiary **2** °insignificant, °obscure, °inconsequential, unimportant, °trifling, trivial, °negligible, inconsiderable, °slight, °petty, °paltry, °small, *Colloq* °small-time, one-horse, *Brit* two-a-penny, *US* minor-league, bush-league, penny-ante, two-bit, picayune —*n.* **3** °child, youngster, °youth, °stripling, °teenager, °adolescent, schoolboy, schoolgirl, °boy, °girl, °lad, laddie, °lass, lassie, *Law* °ward, infant

minstrel *n.* bard, troubadour, balladeer, jongleur, skald *or* scald, minnesinger, Meistersinger

mint *n.* **1** °(small) fortune, °lot, king's ransom, millions, billions, *Colloq* °bundle, °pile, °heap, wad(s), °packet, pot(s), loads, ton, *Slang Brit* °bomb, *US* (big) bucks —*v.* **2** °make, °coin, °produce, °earn

minute[1] *n.* **1** °instant, °second, split second, °flash, °moment, before one can *or* could say "Jack Robinson," before you can say "knife," blink *or* wink *or* twinkling of an eye, *coup d'oeil*, trice, *Colloq* one sec, two secs, bat of an eye, °shake, jiffy, tick, *Brit* half a mo, two shakes (of a lamb's tail) **2** ***minutes.*** log, °record, °journal, °transcript, °notes, °summary, °résumé, °proceedings, °transactions, °memorandum **3** ***up-to-the-minute.*** °latest, newest, °modern, up-to-date, °trendy, °fashionable, °smart, all the rage, in vogue, °stylish, °in style, °in fashion, à la mode, *Colloq* in, with it, hep *or* hip, °hot, °cool, *US* °now —*v.* **4** °record, °transcribe, °take down, °write down, °note, make (a) note of, °document, log

minute[2] *adj.* **1** °small, °little, °tiny, tiniest, minuscule, °miniature, °wee, infinitesimal, microscopic, micro, °diminutive, mini, °baby, pint-sized, bantam, Lilliputian, *Colloq* teeny, teensy(-weensy), itty-bitty, eensy-weensy, itsy-bitsy **2** unimportant, °petty, °insignificant, least, °slight, °mere, °meager, °trifling, trivial, °minor, °small, °little, *Colloq* piddling, *US* picayune

miraculous *adj.* °marvelous, wonderful, wondrous, °incredible, °unbelievable, °inexplicable, unexplainable, °extraordinary, spectacular, °amazing, astounding, astonishing, mind-boggling, °remarkable, °phenomenal, °fantastic, °fabulous; magical, °supernatural, preternatural, °superhuman, *Colloq* °out of this world, *Slang* far-out, °crazy

mire *n.* **1** °swamp, °bog, fen, °marsh, quagmire, °morass, slough, *Brit dialect* sump **2**

°mud, °ooze, °muck, slime, °dirt —*v.* **3** enmire, °bog down, become entangled *or* tangled, become enmeshed *or* meshed, become involved **4** °dirty, °soil, begrime, °muddy, befoul, besmirch, °sully, °tarnish, °smear, °blacken, defile, smudge

mirror *n.* **1** looking glass, °glass, speculum, reflector **2** °reflection, °reproduction, °picture, °representation, replication, °(mirror) image —*v.* **3** °reflect, °reproduce, °represent, depict, °repeat, °echo, send back

mirth *n.* °merriment, merrymaking, jollity, °gaiety, °fun, °laughter, °amusement, °frolic, frolicking, joviality, joyousness, °revelry, rejoicing, °glee, high spirits, mirthfulness, °hilarity, buoyancy, *Formal* jocundity

misalliance *n.* mésalliance, mismarriage, mismatch, mismatchment, bad match, mismating

misanthrope *n.* misanthropist, mankind-hater; °man-hater, woman-hater, misogynist; loner, °hermit, °recluse, anchorite *or* anchoret, *Colloq* lone wolf

misanthropic *adj.* man-hating; antisocial, °unsocial, unfriendly, egocentric, °egoistic

misappropriate *v.* **1** °embezzle, °steal, filch, expropriate, °pocket, *Formal* peculate, defalcate **2** misapply, °misuse, °pervert, misemploy

misbehave *v.* °disobey, behave badly *or* improperly, be bad *or* naughty *or* mischievous, *Colloq* °carry on, act up, *Slang* raise hell, raise Cain

misbehavior *n.* naughtiness, badness, misconduct, misdemeanor(s), disorderliness, disobedience, delinquency, disorderly conduct, °rowdyism

miscalculate *v.* misjudge, °err, misevaluate, misestimate, misreckon, miscompute, miscount, misappreciate, misread; °underestimate, undervalue, underrate; overestimate, overvalue, °overrate

miscarriage *n.* °failure, abortion, °collapse, °breakdown, °failing, mismanagement, nonfulfillment, °defeat, nonsuccess, frustration

miscarry *v.* abort, °fail, °fall through, °break down, °go wrong, °founder, come to nothing *or* naught *or* nought, go awry, °come to grief, go amiss, °misfire, go up *or* end up in smoke, °perish, °die

miscellaneous *adj.* °varied, heterogeneous, °diverse, °mixed, diversified, °divers, motley, °sundry, assorted, °various, varying, multifarious, multiform, many-sided, multiplex, °manifold

miscellany *n.* °mixture, °assortment, °variety, °medley, °diversity, mixed bag, job lot, ragbag, mélange, °potpourri, gallimaufry, motley, hotchpotch *or US also* hodgepodge, salmagundi, olio, olla podrida, smorgasbord *or* smörgåsbord, °odds and ends, omnium-gatherum, °hash, °mess, *Brit* lucky dip, °jumble, *US* grab bag

mischief *n.* **1** °misbehavior, naughtiness, impishness, elfishness *or* elvishness, roguishness, rascality, devilry *or* deviltry, mischievousness, playfulness, devilment, badness, *Colloq* monkey business, shenanigans, *Brit* monkey tricks *or US* monkeyshines **2** °harm, °injury, °damage, °detriment, °trouble, °hurt, °wrong, °difficulty, disruption, °destruction, °misfortune, °evil

mischievous *adj.* **1** °naughty, impish, roguish, rascally, °devilish, elfish *or* elvish, puckish, scampish, °frolicsome, °playful, °sportive **2** °harmful, °injurious, °hurtful, damaging, pernicious, °detrimental, °destructive, deleterious, °dangerous, °spiteful, malicious, °vicious, malign, baleful, baneful, noxious, °wicked, °evil, °bad

misconceive *v.* °misunderstand, misconstrue, misjudge, °mistake, misapprehend, °misinterpret, misread, get *or* have the wrong idea, get *or* have (hold of) the wrong end of the stick

misconception *n.* false *or* wrong notion *or* idea, °misunderstanding, misconstruction, misconstrual, misjudgment, miscalculation, misapprehension, mistaken belief, °error, °mistake, °delusion

miscreant *n.* **1** °villain, °wretch, mischief-maker, scamp, °rascal, °criminal, evildoer, °felon, malefactor, °rogue, °reprobate, °scoundrel, wrongdoer, °good-for-nothing, ne'er-do-well, blackguard, hooligan, ruffian, °hoodlum, °thug, °rowdy, *Archaic* knave, caitiff, varlet, rapscallion, *Colloq* crook, roughneck, scallywag *or* scallawag *or* scalawag, *Slang* hood, *Brit* °mug, °rough, *Australian* larrikin, *US* baddie *or* baddy, bad actor —*adj.* **2** °villainous, °wretched, °mischievous, rascally, °criminal, felonious, °corrupt, malefic, malevolent, °evil, depraved, °base, nefarious, iniquitous, °vicious, unprincipled, ne'er-do-well, °reprobate, scoundrelly, °wicked

misdeed *n.* Often, ***misdeeds.*** offense, °crime, felony, wrongdoing, misdoing, °transgression, misdemeanor, °fault, misconduct, °sin, trespass, °wrong, °peccadillo

misdirect *v.* misguide, misadvise; misaddress

miser *n.* skinflint, hoarder, niggard, penny-pincher, pinchpenny, cheeseparer, Scrooge, *Colloq* cheapskate, *US* tightwad

miserable *adj.* **1** °wretched, °unhappy, depressed, woeful, °woebegone, °sad, °dejected, °forlorn, disconsolate, °despondent, °heartbroken, °sorrowful, °brokenhearted, °mournful, °desolate, °desperate, despairing, °downhearted, °melancholy, °glum, low-spirited, °gloomy, °dismal, lachrymose, °tearful, *Colloq Brit* °cut up **2** unpleasant, °inclement, °inconvenient, °untoward, °bad, unfavorable, °awful, °terrible, adverse, *Colloq* °rotten, °lousy **3** °inadequate, °unworthy, °poor, °deplorable, °contemptible, °bad, °despicable, °sorry, °pitiful, °pathetic, °lamentable, *Colloq* °rotten, °lousy **4** squalid, °wretched, °bad, abject, °deplorable, °shabby, °mean, °vile, °shameful, °scurvy, °awful, °disgraceful, °contemptible

miserly *adj.* stingy, °penurious, niggardly, pennypinching, parsimonious, °mean,

°cheap, cheeseparing, °tight, tightfisted, °close, closefisted, °mercenary, °avaricious, °greedy, covetous, *Colloq* money-grubbing, *Brit* mingy, *US* chintzy

misery *n.* **1** unhappiness, °distress, °discomfort, wretchedness, °woe, °sadness, °melancholy, °sorrow, dolor, heartache, °grief, °anguish, °anxiety, angst, °depression, °despair, °desperation, °desolation, despondency, °gloom **2** squalor, °poverty, destitution, °privation, indigence, penury, wretchedness, sordidness **3** °hardship, °suffering, °calamity, °disaster, °curse, °misfortune, °ordeal, °woe, °trouble, °catastrophe, °trial, tribulation, adversity, °burden, °affliction **4** °spoilsport, damper, °killjoy, dampener, Job's comforter, grouch, grump, malcontent, pessimist, cynic, prophet of doom, Cassandra, *Colloq* wet blanket, sourpuss, *US* party pooper, gloomy Gus, picklepuss

misfire *v.* **1** °fail, abort, °miscarry, °go wrong, °fizzle (out), °fall through, *Colloq* °flop, come a cropper, *Brit* go phut, *US* go pfft *or* phht —*n.* **2** °miscarriage, °failure, °fizzle, °dud, *Colloq* abort, °flop

misfit *n.* oner, °eccentric, °individual, °nonconformist, maverick, square peg in a round hole

misfortune *n.* **1** bad luck, ill luck, ill fortune, hard luck, infelicity, adversity, °loss **2** °accident, misadventure, °mishap, °calamity, °catastrophe, mischance, °disaster, contretemps, °tragedy, °blow, °shock; °reverse, stroke of bad luck, *Colloq* bad news

misgiving *n.* apprehension, °mistrust, °worry, °concern, °anxiety, °qualm, °scruple, disquiet, hesitation, °doubt, °question, uncertainty, °suspicion, unease, uneasiness, °discomfort; °dread, °premonition, °foreboding, *Colloq* funny feeling

misguided *adj.* misled, °wrong, misdirected, °foolish, °unreasonable, °erroneous, °mistaken, misplaced, °imprudent, unwise, impolitic, °ill-advised, fallacious, uncalled-for, laboring under a misapprehension, °wide of the mark, *Colloq* °off (the mark), barking up the wrong tree

mishandle *v.* **1** °abuse, °mistreat, maltreat, °ill-treat, °beat (up), brutalize, maul, °molest, °injure, °hurt, °harm, handle *or* treat roughly, °manhandle, *Colloq* knock about *or* around **2** mismanage, °bungle, °botch, misconduct, °mangle, °mess up, °muddle, °wreck, °ruin, °destroy, *Colloq* muff, make a mess *or* hash of, *Slang* °screw up, °bugger up, *Taboo* fuck up

mishap *n.* See **misfortune, 2,** above.

mishmash *n.* °mess, °medley, °hash, gallimaufry, farrago, °potpourri, °jumble, °pastiche, °mixture, salmagundi, hotchpotch *or* *US also* hodgepodge, °tangle, omnium-gatherum, mélange, olio, olla podrida, goulash, °stew

misinform *v.* misguide, °mislead, misadvise, °misdirect, delude, °deceive, °dupe, °defraud, °fool, gull, °lead astray, throw someone off the scent, *Colloq* con, slip *or* put something over on someone, pull a fast one on someone, *US* give (someone) a bum steer, throw someone a curve

misinformation *n.* disinformation, misintelligence; red herring, false trail, false scent

misinterpret *v.* °misunderstand, °mistake, misconstrue, °misconceive, misread, misjudge, misapprehend, *Slang* °screw up, °bugger up

mislay *v.* misplace, °lose, mislocate; misfile

mislead *v.* °misinform, °lead astray, misguide, °misdirect, throw off the scent *or* track, pull the wool over someone's eyes, °fool, °outwit, °bluff, °hoodwink, °trick, humbug, bamboozle, °deceive, °dupe, gull, cozen, *Colloq* con, °take in, lead up the garden path, flimflam, slip *or* put *or* pass one over on, *Slang* °take, *US* give someone a bum steer

mismatched *adj.* mismated, ill-matched, ill-mated, °incompatible, unfit, °inappropriate, unsuited, unsuitable, °incongruous, misallied, disparate, uncongenial, °inconsistent, inharmonious, °discordant

misprint *n.* °error, °mistake, erratum, typographical error, printer's *or* printing error, *Brit* °literal, *Colloq* typo

misrepresent *v.* °distort, °twist, °pervert, °garble, misstate, °mangle, °falsify, belie, °disguise, °color

miss[1] *v.* **1** °skip, °forgo, °absent oneself from, be absent from, fail to keep; °avoid, °evade, °escape, °dodge, *Colloq* °pass up **2** long for, yearn for, pine for, feel nostalgia for, be nostalgic for *or* about, °want, °need, wish for **3** °misunderstand, °misinterpret, misconstrue, misapprehend, fail to understand *or* perceive, °mistake **4** Sometimes, ***miss out (on).*** °pass up, °omit, °leave out, °slip up (on), °overlook, °let slip (by), let pass, °pass over, °disregard, °ignore —*n.* **5** °omission, °oversight, °slip, °failure, °mistake, °error, °blunder, *Colloq* slip-up

miss[2] *n.* Ms., °girl, °lass, lassie, °maid, °maiden, young lady, young woman, schoolgirl, mademoiselle, nymphet, °teenager, virgin, spinster, °old maid, *Brit* bachelor girl, *Irish English* colleen, *Literary* nymph, *Archaic* demoiselle, damsel, *Colloq old-fashioned* gal, *US* coed, Valley girl, bachelorette, *Slang* teeny-bopper, groupie, *Chiefly Brit* bird, *Old-fashioned US* bobby-soxer

misshapen *adj.* distorted, twisted, contorted, °crooked, °deformed, °crippled, malformed, °grotesque, awry, warped, °gnarled, ill-proportioned, ill-made, °monstrous, *Technical* acromegalic

missile *n.* °projectile, brickbat; guided missile, ballistic missile

mission *n.* **1** °task, °duty, °function, °purpose, °job, °office, °work, °assignment, °errand, °charge, °business, commission, °undertaking, °pursuit, °activity, °aim, °objective **2** °calling, °occupation, °vocation, °trade, °line (of work), °profession, métier **3** delegation, legation, deputation, commission, °committee, °group, °ministry

missionary *n.* evangelist, °preacher, °minister, proselytizer

missive *n.* °letter, communication, °message, °dispatch, °note, °line, postcard, °card, epistle

misspent *adj.* wasted, squandered, °idle, dissipated, thrown away, profitless, °prodigal

misstatement *n.* **1** falsification, misreport, misquotation, miscitation, distortion, misrepresentation, misconstruction, misinterpretation, °perversion, °lie, °falsehood, untruth, °fabrication **2** °solecism, °error, °mistake, gaffe, faux pas, °slip of the tongue, *lapsus linguae,* °blunder, *Slang* °howler, *Brit* bloomer, *US and Canadian* blooper

misstep *n.* **1** false step, °blunder, °mistake, °error, bad *or* wrong *or* false move, °trip, °stumble, °slip **2** °indiscretion, °mistake, °lapse, faux pas, °oversight, °error, gaffe, *Colloq* slip-up, *Slang* °howler, *Brit* bloomer, *US and Canadian* blooper, goof

mist *n.* **1** °fog, haze, smog, (low-hanging) cloud, °vapor; drizzle, *Brit dialect* mizzle —*v.* **2** Usually, ***mist up or over.*** cloud (up *or* over), becloud, °fog, °befog, °dim, °blur, °film, steam up

mistake *n.* **1** °misconception, misapprehension, °error, °fault, miscalculation, misjudgment, °blunder, °botch, °fumble, bad move, °misstep, °slip, erratum, gaffe, faux pas, *Colloq* boo-boo, clanger, muff, °howler, *Brit* boob, bloomer, *US* blooper, goof, goof-up, flub **2** °indiscretion, °misstep, false step, wrong move —*v.* **3** °misunderstand, °misinterpret, misjudge, misconstrue, take the wrong way, get wrong, misread, misapprehend **4** ***mistake for.*** °mix up with, misidentify as, confuse with, take for

mistaken *adj.* **1** (all *or* completely) wrong, °amiss, °incorrect, °in error, °wide of the mark, in the wrong, °inaccurate, °out of order, *Colloq* barking up the wrong tree, °off, (way) off the beam, on the wrong track, *US* full of hot air, *Slang* full of it (= *Taboo* 'full of shit'), *US* all wet **2** °erroneous, °faulty, °false, fallacious, misinformed, °incorrect, °wrong, °inaccurate, °flawed, warped, distorted, twisted, °misguided, *Slang* cockeyed

mistreat *v.* °abuse, maltreat, ill-use, °ill-treat, °misuse, °damage, °manhandle, °harm; °hurt, °injure, °molest, maul, °rough up, brutalize

mistreatment *n.* °abuse, maltreatment, ill use, ill treatment, brutalization, °misuse; manhandling, molestation, mauling, roughing-up, rough handling, battery, °assault

mistress *n.* **1** °lover, girlfriend, live-in lover, kept woman, concubine, inamorata, °paramour, *Literary* odalisque, *Archaic* doxy, *Colloq US* alternative other, POSSLQ (Person of the Opposite Sex Sharing Living Quarters) **2** schoolmistress, instructress, governess; headmistress

mistrust *v.* **1** °suspect, °distrust, be suspicious of, °doubt, be *or* feel wary *or* suspicious *or* doubtful of *or* about, have (one's) doubts about, °question, have reservations; °beware; *Slang* be *or* feel leery of *or* about —*n.* **2** °suspicion, °distrust, °doubt, °skepticism, wariness, °reservation, chariness, misgiving(s), uncertainty, unsureness, apprehension, apprehensiveness

misty *adj.* cloudy, foggy, °hazy, °murky; °fuzzy, °dim, blurred, blurry, unclear, °indistinct, °vague, °dark, °opaque, °shadowy, °obscure, unintelligible

misunderstand *v.* °misconceive, misconstrue, °misinterpret, misapprehend, get (it *or* it all) wrong, get the wrong idea (about), misread, misjudge, °miscalculate, miss the point (of)

misunderstanding *n.* **1** °misconception, misconstruction, misinterpretation, misapprehension, misreading, misjudgment, miscalculation, wrong idea, wrong *or* false impression, *malentendu,* mistaking, *Technical* parasynesis **2** °disagreement, °discord, °dispute, °argument, °difference, °dissension, °controversy, °quarrel, °rift, *Colloq* falling-out

misuse *n.* **1** misapplication, misusage, misappropriation, misemployment, diverting, °diversion, perverting, °perversion **2** misusage, °abuse, corruption, °solecism, malapropism, barbarism, catachresis, ungrammaticality, infelicity **3** See **mistreatment,** above. —*v.* **4** °abuse, misapply, misemploy, °misappropriate; °pervert **5** See **mistreat,** above.

mitigate *v.* °moderate, °temper, °reduce, abate, lessen, °decrease, °relieve, °ease, ease up (on), °relax, alleviate, °remit, assuage, allay, °let up (on), slacken, °slacken up (on), °tone down, °lighten, appease, palliate, mollify, °calm, °tranquilize, soothe, placate, quiet *or chiefly Brit* quieten, °still, °soften, °dull, °blunt, take the edge off, *US* lighten up (on)

mitigating *adj.* °extenuating, justifying, excusatory, palliating, vindicating, qualifying

mix *v.* **1** °mingle, °combine, intermingle, °blend, °incorporate, put together, °merge, °unite, °alloy, commingle, °amalgamate, coalesce **2** °socialize, °fraternize, consort, °hobnob, go round *or* around *or* about (together), °get together, keep company, °join (with), °associate (with), *Colloq* hang out *or* about *or* around (with) **3** ***mix in.*** °add, stir in, °combine, fold in **4** ***mix up.*** **(a)** See **mix, 1,** above. **(b)** °confuse, confound, °bewilder, °muddle, °perplex, °puzzle, °fluster, °upset; addle, °disturb; *Colloq US and Canadian* discombobulate **(c)** °snarl, ensnarl, °tangle, °entangle, °scramble, °jumble **(d)** °confuse, interchange, °exchange **5** ***mix up in.*** °involve, °implicate, °include, °connect, draw *or* drag into **6** ***mix up with.*** °confuse, °mistake, misidentify, confound; interchange, °exchange —*n.* **7** °mixture, °blend, °compound; °amalgam, °combination, °alloy, °assortment, °distribution

mixed *adj.* **1** °hybrid, halfbred, °mongrel,

interbred, crossbred; °impure, tainted, adulterated **2** °confused, muddled; °varied, °various, °diverse; conflicting, °contradictory, °opposing, clashing, °opposite **3** ***mixed up in or with.*** °involved, connected, associated

mixture *n.* **1** °assortment, °amalgam, °amalgamation, °medley, °combination, mingling, intermingling, composite, °blend, °jumble, °mix, °miscellany, mélange, °mess, °mishmash, hotchpotch *or US also* hodgepodge, gallimaufry, farrago, olio, olla podrida, °hash, °potpourri, ragout, goulash, omniumgatherum, salmagundi **2** mixing, °amalgamation, amalgamating, combining, mingling, intermingling, °combination, °blend, blending, °association, associating, °compound, compounding, °synthesis, interweaving, merging, °merger, fusion, fusing, °alloy, alloying

mix-up *n.* °confusion, °mess, °muddle, hotchpotch *or US also* hodgepodge, °tangle, °jumble, *Colloq* °botch, °mishmash, foul-up, *Slang US* screw-up, snafu, *Taboo slang Brit* balls-up

moan *n.* **1** °complaint, °lament, °lamentation, °groan, wail, moaning, °grievance —*v.* **2** °complain, °lament, °groan, wail, °bewail, grumble, °bemoan, deplore, whine, whimper, *Colloq* grouse, °gripe, beef, °bitch, *Brit* whinge **3** °sigh, °mourn, °weep, °sorrow, °cry, wail, °keen, °grieve, °sob, °snivel, °bawl, mewl, pule, ululate

mob *n.* **1** horde, °host, °press, °throng, °crowd, °pack, °herd, °swarm, °crush, °jam, multitude, °mass, °body, assemblage, °collection, °group **2** °rabble, °riffraff, proletariat, °populace, °the masses, great unwashed, °hoi polloi, *canaille,* bourgeoisie, lower classes, scum (of the earth), dregs of society —*v.* **3** °crowd (around), jostle, °throng, °surround, °beset, clamor over, swoop down on

mobbed *adj.* crowded, °packed, thronged, °congested, teeming, swarming, °full, filled

mobile *adj.* **1** °movable, nonstationary, unstationary, unfixed, °traveling, °portable, transportable **2** motorized, °mechanical, transportable, °movable **3** °expressive, °sensitive, °animated, °plastic, °flexible, *US* facile **4** °agile, °versatile, °nimble, °quick, °alert, °active, °responsive **5** ambulatory, ambulant

mobilize *v.* °assemble, marshal, conscript, °enroll, °enlist, °organize, °muster, levy, °rally, °activate, °call up, °prepare, °ready, *US* °draft

mock *v.* **1** °deride, °ridicule, °make fun of, °tease, °taunt, °tantalize, °jeer (at), gibe *or* jibe (at), °thumb one's nose at, °chaff, °laugh at, °poke fun at, °make sport of, °guy, °scorn, °flout, °abuse, °defy, °scoff (at), °sneer (at), disdain, °disparage, decry, *Archaic* fleer (at), *Colloq* °rag, rib, kid, put (someone) on, *Brit* take the mickey out of, cock a snook at **2** ape, °mimic, °imitate, °caricature, °lampoon, °satirize, °parody, °burlesque, travesty, *Colloq* spoof, °take off, *Brit* °send up —*adj.* **3** °substitute, °artificial, simulated, °fake, °synthetic, °imitation, °false, forged, ersatz, °sham, feigned, °counterfeit, °fraudulent, °bogus, make-believe, °pretend, *Colloq* phoney *or US also* phony, pseudo

mockery *n.* **1** °ridicule, °derision, disdain, taunting, disparagement, °abuse, °scorn, °contempt, contumely, decrial **2** °semblance, °imitation, impersonation; °caricature, °parody, °burlesque, travesty, °lampoon, °satire, pasquinade, farce; °miscarriage; *Colloq* spoof, °takeoff, *Brit* sendup **3** °disappointment, °joke, °laugh, °absurdity

mode[1] *n.* **1** °way, °manner, °method, °approach, °form, °course, °fashion, °procedure, °technique, °system, °wise, modus operandi, methodology, standard operating procedure, SOP **2** °status, °condition, °state, configuration, °setup

mode[2] *n.* °fashion, °style, °look, °vogue; °trend, °rage, °craze, *Colloq* °fad

model *n.* **1** °representation, °replica, mock-up, maquette, scale model, working model, °miniature, °dummy, °image, °likeness, °facsimile, °copy **2** °original, °mold, archetype, °prototype, °pattern, °paragon, °ideal, exemplar, °example, °standard **3** °ideal, °paragon, exemplar, °epitome, *beau idéal,* cream, *crème de la crème, ne plus ultra,* °nonpareil, nonesuch *or* nonsuch **4** °subject, sitter, poser **5** mannequin; °dummy **6** °design, °kind, °type, °style, °version; °variety, °sort, °form, °fashion, configuration; °brand, °mark —*v.* **7** °fashion, °mold, °shape, °form, sculpt, °carve (out), °make, °fabricate, °produce **8** pose in, °display, °show (off), °wear, *Colloq* °sport **9** ***model after or on.*** °imitate, °copy, pattern on *or* after, emulate, °follow —*adj.* **10** °copy, °imitation, °facsimile, °representative, °miniature **11** °ideal, °exemplary, °perfect, archetypal, unequaled, consummate, inimitable

moderate *adj.* **1** °temperate, °calm, °reasonable, °cool, °judicious, °rational, balanced, unexcessive, °modest, °sober, °sensible, common-sensical, controlled, °deliberate, °steady **2** °center, middle-of-the-road, nonradical, nonreactionary **3** °fair, middling, °average, °ordinary, °medium, °middle, °modest, °mediocre, unexceptional, *Colloq* fair to middling —*n.* **4** middle-of-the-roader, nonradical, nonreactionary, centrist —*v.* **5** abate, °calm, mollify, soothe, °ease, °relax, alleviate, °mitigate, °soften, °dull, °blunt, °cushion, °relieve, °reduce, lessen, °remit, slacken, °diminish, °decrease, defuse, °temper, *Colloq* °let up (on) **6** mediate, arbitrate, referee, °judge, °chair, °supervise, °preside (over), °coordinate, °run, °regulate, °manage, °direct

moderately *adv.* °somewhat, °rather, °quite, °fairly, °pretty, comparatively, °slightly, passably, more or less; to some extent, °within reason, to a certain extent, °to a degree, to some degree, in some measure, in moderation, within limits; temperately; *Colloq* °sort of, kind of

moderator *n.* °mediator, arbiter, arbitrator, °judge, referee, °umpire; *Chiefly US* °chair, chairperson, chairman, chairwoman, chairlady, presiding officer, president, coordinator, °(discussion) leader; anchorman, anchorwoman, anchorperson; master of ceremonies, toastmaster, *Brit* compere, *Colloq* emcee, MC

modern *adj.* up-to-date, °current, °contemporary, today's, °new, °fresh, °novel, °brand-new, °up-to-the-minute, present-day, °latest, new-fashioned, newfangled; à la mode, modish, in vogue, °fashionable, °in fashion, °stylish, °in style, °chic, *Chiefly Brit* flavor of the month, *Slang* °trendy, in, with it, mod, °hip, °hot

modernize *v.* °renovate, streamline, redo, redecorate, °refurbish, refurnish, update, do over, °rejuvenate, °refresh, °revamp, redesign, remodel, refashion, remake

modest *adj.* **1** unassuming, unpresuming, °humble, unpretentious, °unobtrusive, °reserved, retiring, diffident, °shy, °bashful, demure, °coy, shamefaced, self-effacing, °self-conscious, °reticent, °reluctant, °timid, °meek, timorous, *Rare* verecund **2** °humble, °simple, °plain, °ordinary, unpretentious, °homely, °lowly, unexceptional, unostentatious; °inconspicuous, °unobtrusive **3** °moderate, °limited, °understated, unimportunate, unexaggerated, °reasonable, °sensible, constrained, restricted, restrained

modicum *n.* °bit, °trifle, °jot, tittle, atom, scintilla, °spark, °particle, iota, °speck, °grain, whit, °scrap, °shred, snippet, °sliver, °fragment, °splinter, °morsel, °crumb, ounce, dram, °drop, °dash, °spot, °touch, tinge, °hint, °suggestion, *Colloq* smidgen

modify *v.* **1** °adjust, °adapt, °change, °transform, °alter, °revise, °amend, redo, remake, remold, reshape, reconstruct, °reform, °revamp, refashion, remodel, rework, °reword, reorient, reorganize **2** °reduce, °decrease, °diminish, lessen, °moderate, °temper, °soften, °lower, abate, °tone down, °modulate; °qualify, °limit, °restrict

modulate *v.* °adjust, °regulate, °set, °tune, °balance, °temper, °moderate, °modify; °lower, tune *or* tone *or* turn down, °soften

mogul *n.* magnate, °tycoon, baron, mandarin, *Colloq* big shot, big gun, big cheese, Pooh-Bah, °bigwig, big wheel, big (White) Chief, Big Daddy, hotshot, VIP, big noise, nabob, *Slang US* Mr. Big

moist *adj.* **1** °damp, wettish, dampish, dewy, dank, °humid, °clammy, °muggy, °steamy, °misty, foggy **2** °damp, °wet, rainy, drizzly, soggy, moisture-laden **3** °tearful, teary, °misty, lachrymose

mold[1] *n.* **1** °form, °cast, matrix, °die; template *or* templet, °pattern, °form **2** °form, °shape, °pattern, °format, °structure, °build, construction, °design, °arrangement, °organization, configuration, °kind, °brand, °make, °line, °type, °stamp, °cut **3** °character, °nature, °stamp, °type, °kind, kidney, ilk, °sort —*v.* **4** °shape, °form, °make, °work, °fashion, configure, sculpture *or* sculpt, °model, knead, °construct, °carve, °cut **5** °forge, °cast, °stamp, die cast **6** °influence, °shape, °form, °affect, °make, °control, °direct, °guide, °lead

mold[2] *n.* mildew, fungus, °blight, smut

mold[3] *n.* °soil, °earth, loam, topsoil, °dirt, humus

moldy *adj.* °aged, °ancient, outdated, °old-fashioned, antediluvian, °unused, °stale, decayed, decaying, carious, mildewed, moldering, °musty; spoilt *or* spoiled, °rotten, rotting, °putrid, putrescent, putrefying, °rancid, °rank, decomposed, decomposing, mucid

molest *v.* **1** °annoy, °irritate, vex, °disturb, °pester, badger, needle, °provoke, nettle, °tease, °harass, harry, °worry, hector, °irk, °bother, °gall, °chafe, roil, °torment, °plague, beleaguer **2** accost, meddle with, interfere with, °annoy, °abuse, °bother, °attack, °ill-treat, maltreat, °manhandle; paw

moment *n.* **1** °instant, °second, °minute, half a second, two seconds, °flash, °twinkling, blink *or* wink of an eye, twinkling of an eye, trice, *Colloq* jiffy, °shake, two shakes (of a lamb's tail), before one can *or* could say "Jack Robinson," before you can say "knife," *Brit* mo, half a mo, tick **2** °instant, °time, °second, °minute, hour, °point (in time), °juncture, °stage **3** °importance, °weight, consequence, °significance, °import, °gravity, seriousness, °prominence, °concern, °note, °interest, °consideration

momentary *adj.* °fleeting, °temporary, ephemeral, evanescent, impermanent, °fugitive, °passing, transitory, °brief, °short-lived, °quick, °short, °hasty

momentous *adj.* °important, °weighty, consequential, °significant, °grave, °serious, decisive, °crucial, °critical, °vital, °pivotal, °portentous, charged, laden, °fraught, of concern

momentum *n.* °energy, °force, °drive, °strength, °impetus, °power, °inertia, impulse, °thrust, °push

monarch *n.* **1** ruler, °sovereign, potentate, crowned head; °queen, °king, empress, emperor, tsar *or* czar **2** ruler, °sovereign, °chief, °lord, °master, °owner, *Colloq* °boss

monarchy *n.* **1** °kingdom, empire, °domain, °dominion, principality; °state, °nation, °country **2** monocracy, autocracy, absolutism, royalism, monarchism, °sovereignty, totalitarianism, authoritarianism; °despotism, °tyranny

monastery *n.* abbey, cloister, priory, friary, charterhouse, hospice, *Buddhism* vihara, *Hinduism* ashram, *Tibetan Buddhism* lamasery

monetary *adj.* pecuniary, °cash, °money, °fiscal, °financial, °capital; numismatic, *Technical* nummular, nummary

money *n.* **1** currency, legal tender, medium of exchange, specie, °(hard) cash, ready money, banknotes, paper money, *Brit* °notes, *US* bills, coin(s), °change, small change, *Derogatory* (filthy) lucre, pelf, *Colloq* shekels, *US* folding money, cold (hard) cash, *US and Canadian and Australian* shinplasters, *Brit* lolly; *Slang* °loot, dough, bread, spondulix *or* spondulicks, boodle, readies *or* (the) ready, moolah, *US* °(long) green, greenbacks, mazuma, wampum, simoleons, bucks, °scratch, gelt, kale, cabbage, lettuce, spinach, *Old-fashioned* jack, *Brit* rhino, Bugs Bunny **2** °resources, °wealth, °fortune, °funds, °capital, wherewithal, affluence, °means, °(liquid) assets, °riches; *Slang* °bundle **3** °gain, °profit, °net, *Colloq* °take, °percentage, *Slang* °rake-off **4** ***in the money.*** °rich, °wealthy, affluent, moneyed *or* monied, °well-off, well-to-do, °prosperous, *Colloq* °flush, in clover, in *or* on Easy Street, *Slang* °loaded, well-heeled, rolling in it *or* in money *or* in dough, filthy rich, stinking rich, °fat

mongrel *n.* cur, mutt, crossbreed, mixed breed, °hybrid, halfbreed, *Technical* bigener; lurcher

monitor *n.* **1** watchdog, °supervisor, °sentinel, °guard, °guardian, custodian; *Brit* invigilator, prefect, *Rare* prepositor *or* prepostor; *US* proctor **2** °(television) screen, cathode ray tube screen, CRT, °display, *Chiefly Brit* visual display unit, VDU *—v.* **3** °watch, °oversee, °observe, check (out *or* up on), audit, °supervise, superintend, °scan, °examine, °study, °follow, keep an eye on, °survey, °keep track of, °track, °trace, °record, *Brit* °vet

monk *n.* °brother, °religious, cenobite, monastic, *Loosely* friar

monkey *n.* **1** simian, ape, primate, *Colloq* °monk **2** °fool, ass, laughingstock, °butt, °victim, °target, °(fair) game, *Colloq* goat, *Slang* °sucker **3** °imp, °devil, mischief-maker, °rascal, scamp, rapscallion *—v.* **4** °mimic, mime, °imitate, impersonate, °copy, ape, °duplicate **5** Usually, ***monkey around or about (with).*** °fool around (with), °play (with), fiddle (about *or* around) with, meddle (with *or* in), interfere (with *or* in), mess (about *or* around) (with), °tinker (with), °tamper (with), *Colloq US* screw around (with)

monograph *n.* treatise, dissertation, disquisition, °essay, °paper

monolithic *adj.* °massive, °huge, °enormous, °monumental, °imposing, °colossal, °gigantic, °giant; featureless, °uniform, undifferentiated, characterless; °rigid, impenetrable, invulnerable, unbending, °inflexible, °solid, °stolid, intractable, °immovable

monopolize *v.* corner (the market in), °control, °dominate, own, *Slang* hog

monotonous *adj.* °boring, °tedious, °dull, °tiresome, °humdrum, sleep-inducing, soporific, wearisome, wearying, tiring, monotonic, °repetitious, °prosaic, °banal, °dry, dry-as-dust, uninteresting, °dreary, °colorless, unexciting, °run-of-the-mill, °ordinary, commonplace, °routine, uneventful, °everyday, °mechanical, banausic, *Colloq* ho-hum

monster *n.* **1** °beast, °fiend, °ogre, °giant, dragon, °brute, °demon, troll, bogeyman **2** °monstrosity, (living) abortion, mutant, °mutation, °freak, deformity, *lusus naturae*, eyesore, °horror, miscreation, missing link *—adj.* **3** See **monstrous, 3,** below.

monstrosity *n.* **1** See **monster, 2,** above. **2** monstrousness, heinousness, horribleness, horridness, hideousness, awfulness, nightmarishness, dreadfulness, frightfulness, °horror, hellishness, ghoulishness, fiendishness, °barbarity

monstrous *adj.* **1** °awful, °horrible, horrid, horrific, horrendous, horrifying, °hideous, °ugly, °nightmarish, °dreadful, heinous, °grisly, °gruesome, °disgusting, °nauseous, nauseating, °repulsive, °repellent, °revolting, °frightful, °grotesque, hellish, °ghoulish, freakish, °fiendish, barbaric, barbarous, °savage, °inhuman, °merciless, °ruthless, °brutal, brutish, °beastly **2** °outrageous, °shocking, °scandalous, °atrocious, appalling, °wicked, °villainous, °evil, °vile, insensitive, °cruel, °base, debased, °shameful, °shameless, °infamous, °disgraceful, nefarious, egregious, °foul, °vicious, flagitious, °loathsome, depraved **3** °gigantic, °giant, °huge, °vast, °enormous, °colossal, °monster, gargantuan, °jumbo, °immense, tremendous, titanic, °prodigious, °massive, °towering, elephantine, mammoth

monument *n.* **1** marker, cairn, °memorial, °tablet, shrine, commemoration; °sepulcher, gravestone, °tombstone, headstone, °tomb, mausoleum, cenotaph **2** °testimony, °testimonial, testament, °token, °witness, °record, °evidence, °example, exemplar

monumental *adj.* **1** staggering, awe-inspiring, °outstanding, °prominent, stupendous, °vast, °awesome, epoch-making, °historic, history-making, °memorable, °lasting, °permanent, unforgettable, °significant, °notable, °noteworthy, °impressive, °marvelous, °prodigious, wonderful, wondrous, spectacular, °magnificent, °grand, °striking, °glorious, °enduring, °classic **2** °massive, °huge, °gigantic, °enormous, °prodigious, °colossal, °immense, °vast, tremendous **3** commemorative, °memorial **4** egregious, catastrophic, °calamitous, °huge, °enormous, °awful, abject, °terrible, unforgivable, °unbelievable, °monstrous, *Colloq* °whopping

mood *n.* **1** °humor, °attitude, °inclination, °disposition, °nature, °temper, °frame of mind, °spirit, °atmosphere, °sense, °feeling **2** ***in the mood.*** °ready, °willing, °eager, °keen, (well-)disposed, °inclined, °sympathetic, minded

moody *adj.* **1** °sullen, °melancholy, °blue, °sad, °unhappy, °dejected, depressed, crestfallen, downcast, °despondent, chapfallen, in the doldrums, °downhearted, °gloomy, °glum, moping, mopy, mopish, sulky, sulking, morose, brooding, broody, heavy-hearted, °dour, cheerless, °dismal, °desolate, disconsolate, lugubrious, disheartened, saturnine, *Colloq* °down in the mouth, (down) in the dumps, °out of sorts, *US* off (one's) feed **2** °testy, crotchety, °short-tempered, °abrupt, °short, °curt, °impatient, crabby, crusty, huffy, huffish, crabbed, °cantankerous, curmudgeonly, ill-humored, ill-tempered, °cranky, °petulant, °waspish, °temperamental, °snappish, °snappy, °irritable, °peevish, °touchy, piqued; in a (fit of) pique, in high dudgeon **3** °fickle, °volatile, °capricious, mercurial, °unstable, °fitful, °flighty, unsteady, °changeable, °erratic, uneven, °inconstant, undependable, °unreliable, unpredictable

moonshine *n.* **1** moonlight, moonbeams **2** °(stuff and) nonsense, °rubbish, tarradiddle, humbug, °drivel, twaddle, balderdash, blather *or* blether, *Colloq* °hot air, claptrap, pack of lies, con, bosh, gas, eyewash, hogwash, bunk, guff, piffle, hokum, °rot, malarkey, bilge (water), tripe, (the old) song and dance, °line, *Brit* tommyrot, *US* applesauce, razzmatazz, jive, *Slang* crap, bull, hooey, *Brit* tosh, *US* °garbage, BS, *Taboo slang* horseshit, bullshit **3** poteen, *Colloq chiefly US and Canadian* hooch *or* hootch, white lightning, white mule, home brew, bootleg, *US* Kickapoo (Mountain) Joy Juice

moor[1] *n.* heath, moorland, wasteland, *Northern English and Scots* °fell

moor[2] *v.* °secure, °tie up, make fast, °dock, berth, °(drop) anchor; °fix

moot *adj.* **1** °debatable, arguable, undecided, undetermined, °controversial, °doubtful, °disputable, open to debate, °at issue, °indefinite, problematic(al), °questionable, open (to question *or* to discussion), confutable, confuted, contestable, contested, °unsettled, °unresolved, up in the air, unconcluded *—v.* **2** bring up *or* forward, °introduce, °broach, °put forward, proffer, °posit, °propound, °advance, °submit, °suggest

moral *adj.* **1** °ethical; °right, °good, °pure, °honest, °proper, °upright, °honorable, °decent, moralistic, °respectable, high-minded, °virtuous, upstanding, °righteous, °principled, °scrupulous, incorruptible, °noble, °just **2** °ethical, moralizing, moralistic *—n.* **3** °lesson, homily, teaching, °point, °message; aphorism, °maxim, °precept, apophthegm *or* apothegm, adage, °saw, °proverb, °epigram, °motto, °slogan **4** ***morals.*** °behavior, °conduct, mores, °belief, habit(s), custom(s), practice(s), principle(s), scruples, ethics, °ideals, standards; °probity, °morality, °rectitude, °integrity

morale *n.* °dedication, spirit(s), °unity, esprit de corps, °disposition, °attitude, °confidence, °self-confidence, °self-esteem

morality *n.* **1** ethics, °morals, ethicalness, moralness, principle(s), mores, °integrity, °propriety, standards, °ideals; °honesty, °right, rightness, righteousness, °rectitude, °justice, fair play, fairness, decency, uprightness, °integrity **2** °behavior, °conduct, habit(s), custom(s)

morass *n.* **1** °bog, °marsh, °swamp, fen, quagmire, slough, marshland, moorland **2** entanglement, °confusion, °muddle, °mess, quagmire, °tangle, quicksand

moratorium *n.* °halt, hiatus, °suspension, °stay, °respite, °freeze, °delay, waiting period, °postponement

morbid *adj.* **1** °unhealthy, °unwholesome, disordered, °unsound, °sick, pathological, pathogenic **2** °grim, °ghoulish, °macabre, °monstrous, °ghastly, °grotesque, °grisly, °gruesome **3** °gloomy, lugubrious, °glum, morose, °somber, °blue, °sad, °melancholy, °despondent, depressed, °dejected, downcast

moreover *adv.* furthermore, °further, °besides, not only that, more than that, what is more; °to boot, into the bargain, °in addition, additionally, as well, too

moribund *adj.* **1** °dying, *in extremis,* at death's door, °failing, fading, with one foot in the grave, half dead, breathing one's last, expiring, °on one's last legs, on one's deathbed **2** ending, declining, °obsolescent, °weak, on the way out, waning, °on the wane, dying out; stagnating, °stagnant

morning *n.* **1** forenoon, (the) a.m., °dawn, daybreak, sunrise, *Literary* morn, *Archaic* cockcrow, dayspring, morrow, *Chiefly US* sunup *—adj.* **2** matutinal, matinal, a.m., forenoon

morsel *n.* **1** °mouthful, °bite, gobbet, spoonful, forkful, °chew, °taste, °sample, nibble, °bit, °drop, dollop, soupçon **2** °bit, °crumb, °fragment, °scrap, °sliver, °splinter, shard *or* sherd, °shred, °remnant, °particle, atom, °speck, whit, fraction, °grain, granule, °pinch, °piece, *Colloq* smidgen

mortal *adj.* **1** °human; transitory, °temporal, °transient, ephemeral **2** °physical, bodily, corporeal, corporal, fleshly, °earthly, °worldly, perishable **3** °deadly, °fatal, °lethal, °terminal, °destructive, °disastrous **4** °relentless, °implacable, unrelenting, °bitter, sworn, °deadly, unremitting, unappeasable, unceasing **5** abject, °extreme, °awful, °great, °enormous, °intense, °terrible, °inordinate, dire *—n.* **6** °human (being), °man, °woman, °person, °soul, °individual, °creature, earthling

mortify *v.* **1** °humiliate, °shame, °humble, °embarrass, abash, chagrin, °rebuff, °crush, °discomfit, deflate, bring down, °degrade, °downgrade, °reduce, °chasten, °subdue, °suppress, make someone eat humble pie, teach someone his *or* her place, *Colloq* °put down **2** °punish, °castigate, °discipline, °control, °subdue, °subjugate **3** gangrene, °fester, necrose, °putrefy, °rot, °decompose, °decay, putresce

mother *n.* **1** dam, materfamilias, °(female) parent, *Old-fashioned or formal or jocular* mater, *Formal* progenitrix; matriarch, *Colloq* ma, old lady, old woman, *Brit* mummy, °mum, *US* mom, mommy, mama, mamma, maw, mammy, mam **2** °source, °origin, genesis **3** nourisher, nurturer, °nurse *—adj.*

4 °native, °natural, innate —*v.* 5 nurture, °nourish, °nurse, °care for, °look after, °protect, °shelter, watch over, °take care of 6 °pamper, °baby, °coddle, °spoil, °indulge, fuss over, overprotect

motif *n.* °theme, °idea, °topic, °subject, concept, leitmotif; °pattern, °figure, °refrain, °device, °ornament, °decoration, °element, °convention

motion *n.* 1 °movement, °moving, °change, °shift, shifting, °action, °going, °traveling, °travel, °progress, °passage, °transit; °activity, commotion, °stir, °agitation, turmoil, turbulence 2 mobility, movability, motility 3 gait, °bearing, °carriage, tread, °walk, °step 4 °gesture, gesticulation, °signal, °sign 5 °proposal, °suggestion, °proposition, °recommendation, °offering, °submission —*v.* 6 °gesture, gesticulate, °beckon, °signal, °sign, °wave

motivate *v.* °prompt, °activate, °move, °inspire, °incite, °induce, actuate, °stimulate, °provoke, °influence, °encourage, °occasion, °bring about, °cause; °excite, egg (on), °urge, °prod, °spur, galvanize, goad, °rouse, °arouse, °stir (up), °wheedle, °coax, °persuade, °cajole, °tempt, °push, impel, °drive, instigate

motive *n.* 1 °inducement, °incentive, motivation, stimulus, motivating force, stimulation, °incitement, °influence, °cause, °reason, °rationale, °grounds; °attraction, °lure, °enticement, goad, °spur, °urge, °prod 2 °purpose, °aim, °intention, °intent, °object, °objective, °goal, °end, *arrière pensée*; °ambition, °desire; *Colloq* °angle —*adj.* 3 driving, impelling, propelling, propulsive, °moving, kinetic, activating, °operative

mottled *adj.* dappled, brindled, marbled, streaked, splodgy *or US* splotchy, blotched, blotchy, freckled, spotted, °spotty, patchy, °speckled, flecked, sprinkled, spattered, splashed, streaky, stippled, pied, piebald; multicolored, °variegated, parti-colored, *Colloq* splodged *or US* splotched

motto *n.* °maxim, °proverb, saying, adage, °saw, aphorism, apophthegm *or* apothegm, gnome, °slogan, °byword, catchword, battle cry, °guide, °moral, °principle, °rule, °precept

mound *n.* 1 hillock, °rise, hummock, °hill, °hump, bank, °elevation, °plateau, °knoll, °knob, °swell, dune, °slope, tor, *Chiefly W US* mesa, *Chiefly W US and Canadian* butte 2 °heap, °pile, °stack, *Archaeology* tumulus, °tell, barrow, (kitchen) midden

mount[1] *n.* See **mountain, 1,** below.

mount[2] *v.* 1 °climb (up), °go up, ascend, °scale, clamber up, make one's way up 2 °rise (up), °arise, °soar, °fly (up), rocket (upward(s)) 3 climb *or* get *or* clamber up on, bestride, straddle, bestraddle 4 °(put on) display, °(put on) exhibit, put on exhibition, °present, install *or* instal, °stage, °prepare, °ready, °put on, put in place, °set up; °arrange, °coordinate, °compose, °organize, set in motion, °launch 5 °frame, mat *or* matt, °set off 6 °increase, wax, °rise, escalate, °intensify, °swell, °expand, °grow, mount up, multiply, °pile up, °build up, °accumulate —*n.* 7 °setting, mounting, °support; °backing, °background, °set, °arrangement, backdrop, °scene 8 horse, steed, charger, palfrey

mountain *n.* 1 °height, °elevation, °mount, eminence, °prominence, °peak, alp, tor, °summit, *No. Eng. and Scots* °fell, *Scots and Irish Eng.* ben 2 °heap, °pile, °stack, °mound, °accumulation, °abundance, °mass, *Colloq* ton(s), °heaps, °piles, stacks

mountainous *adj.* 1 craggy, alpine, Himalayan 2 °huge, °towering, °high, °steep, °enormous, °immense, °formidable, °mighty, °monumental, °prodigious, staggering

mourn *v.* °grieve (over), °lament, °sorrow (over), °bemoan, °bewail, °keen, weep for *or* over, °regret, rue, deplore

mournful *adj.* 1 °sad, °sorrowful, °dismal, °melancholy, °blue, afflicted, °doleful, dolorous, grief-stricken, rueful, °forlorn, °woebegone, °somber, lugubrious, °funereal, °joyless, dispirited, cheerless, °unhappy, °downhearted, heavy-hearted, disconsolate, °heartbroken, °inconsolable, °despondent, °desolate, despairing, heartsick, °overcome, °prostrate 2 °deplorable, °sorrowful, °grievous, distressing, upsetting, °tragic, saddening, disheartening, depressing, °lamentable, catastrophic, °calamitous, °disastrous

mourning *n.* 1 °grief, °lament, grieving, °lamentation, sorrowing, keening, weeping, wailing 2 bereavement, °loss, °anguish, °sorrow, °misery, °grief, °sadness, °woe, woefulness, °melancholy, heartache, despondency, °despair, °desolation 3 °black, widow's weeds, sackcloth and ashes

mousy *adj.* 1 mousey, mouse-colored, °dun, °gray, grayish-brown, brownish-gray, brownish, brown, °dull, lusterless, °lackluster, °drab, °flat, °plain, °colorless 2 °timid, cowering, timorous, °shy, self-effacing, diffident

mouth *n.* 1 lips; maw, jaws, oral cavity, *Technical* stoma, *Slang* °trap, kisser, muzzle, °gob, chops, °yap, *US* bazoo 2 °opening, °aperture, doorway, door, gateway, °gate, access, °entrance, inlet, °entry, entryway, way in, entrée; °passage, passageway, °way, orifice; °exit, way out, °vent, °outlet, outfall, *Technical* debouchment *or* debouchure, debouch *or* débouché, embouchure 3 bragging, boasting, braggadocio, empty *or* idle talk, °bombast, rodomontade, fustian, *Slang* claptrap, °hot air, gas 4 °disrespect, °impudence, insolence, sauciness, rudeness, °impertinence, pertness, boldness, audacity, presumptuousness, brashness, °flippancy, *Colloq* lip, cheek, backchat, °sauce, freshness, *US* sass, back talk 5 grimace, °pout, *moue*, °face 6 ***down in or at the mouth.*** °dejected, °despondent, °sad, °sorrowful, °unhappy, °melancholy, °blue, crestfallen, dispirited, disheartened, downcast, *Colloq* (down) in the dumps, broken up —*v.* 7

utter, °say, °speak, °pronounce, °announce, °enunciate, articulate, °voice, °sound, °express, vocalize; declaim, orate

mouthful *n.* °morsel, °bite, spoonful, forkful, °lump, chunk, °gob, hunk

mouthpiece *n.* **1** embouchure; °bit **2** spokesman, spokeswoman, spokesperson, °agent, °representative, intermediator, °mediator, °delegate **3** °lawyer, attorney, *Slang US* shyster

movable *adj.* moveable, floating, °variable, °changeable, unfixed; °portable, transportable, transferable

move *v.* **1** °shift, °stir, budge, make a move, °go; °proceed, °advance, °progress **2** move house, move out, °remove, move away, relocate, decamp, °depart, change residence, °emigrate, go *or* make off, °transfer, *Colloq* °take off (for), °pull up stakes, *Brit* up sticks, *Slang US* °split (for) **3** °shake (up), °disturb, °stir (up), °agitate, °affect, °touch **4** °affect, °touch, °stir, °shake up, °agitate, °hit (hard), °upset, °strike, smite, °disturb, °ruffle, disquiet, have an (*or* a profound) effect (on), make a (deep) impression (on) **5** °provoke, °arouse, °excite, °stir up, °lead, °rouse, °stimulate **6** °arouse, °rouse, °provoke, actuate, °lead, °prompt, °spur, °motivate, °influence, impel, °prod, °remind, °inspire, °make **7** °propose, put forward *or* forth, °forward, °advance, °submit, °suggest, °advocate, °propound —*n.* **8** °change, changeover, relocation, °transfer, °shift, °removal **9** °maneuver, °device, °trick, °caper, °dodge, ploy, °stratagem, °artifice, °ruse, °action, °act, °deed, *Colloq* °gimmick **10** °turn, °time, °opportunity **11** °gesture, gesticulation, °action, °motion, °stirring **12** ***get a move on.*** **(a)** get moving, °begin, °start, °commence, get going, get under way, get started, stir *or* bestir oneself, *Colloq* get *or* start the ball rolling, get the show on the road, °break the ice, get cracking, step on it *or* the gas **(b)** °hurry, °hasten, make haste, °rush, °run **13** ***on the move.*** **(a)** °traveling, in transit, on the way, on one's way, on the road, on the go, °moving **(b)** on the go, working, °on the run, °busy, occupied **(c)** °proceeding, progressing, advancing, moving ahead, succeeding, on the go

movement *n.* **1** repositioning, °move, °motion, relocation, °moving, migration, °shift, °transfer, °flow, displacement **2** °action, °activity, °move, °moving, °stir, °stirring **3** °gesture, gesticulation, °move, °flicker, °sign, °signal; °maneuver, change of attitude *or* position **4** °mechanism, °works, workings, moving parts, machinery, °action, gears, *Colloq* innards **5** °campaign, °crusade, °drive; °front, °faction, °party, °group, wing **6** °change, °activity, °action, °shift, advance *or* decline, increase *or* decrease, upward *or* downward movement, °stirring; °development, °progress **7** °drift, °trend, °tendency, °course, °swing

movie *n.* **1** motion picture, °film, moving picture, °silent (picture), talking picture, *Colloq* talkie, flick **2** Usually, ***movies.*** picture show, cinema, flicks, *Colloq* big *or* large screen, silver screen

moving *adj.* **1** °touching, °poignant, emotive, affecting, °stirring, °heart-rending, °emotional, °telling, °effective, °impressive, °striking, compelling; °pathetic, °exciting, °thrilling, inspiring, inspirational, impelling, °persuasive **2** °active, °mobile, unfixed, unstationary, motile, °going, operating, working, in motion, °on the move

mow *v.* **1** °cut (down), scythe, °trim, shear **2** ***mow down.*** annihilate, °kill, °massacre, °butcher, °slaughter, °exterminate, liquidate, eradicate, °wipe out, °cut down, cut to pieces, °destroy, decimate

muck *n.* **1** ordure, manure, °dung, excrement, feces, droppings; guano **2** °dirt, °filth, bilge, slime, °sludge, °ooze, scum, sewage, °mire, °mud, feculence, *Colloq* gunge, gunk, *US* grunge —*v.* **3** ***muck about.*** °fool around, waste time, °idle, loiter, mess around *or* about **4** ***muck up.*** °ruin, °wreck, °destroy, make a mess of, °botch, °mess up, °bungle, *Colloq* °screw up, *Slang* °bugger up, make a muck of

mud *n.* °muck, °ooze, slime, °mire, clay, °sludge, °silt, °dirt, *US and Canadian* gumbo *or* gombo

muddle *v.* **1** °bewilder, °confuse, confound, °mystify, baffle, °mix up, disorient, befuddle, °perplex, °bemuse, °puzzle, °befog **2** °confuse, °mix up, °jumble, °scramble, °entangle, °tangle, °mess up, °disorder, disarrange, disorganize, °bungle, mismanage, *Colloq* muff **3** ***muddle through.*** °(barely) manage, °cope, °make it, scrape through *or* along, contrive, °make do, °get by, °get along —*n.* **4** °mess, °confusion, °mix-up, °jumble, °tangle, °disorder, hotchpotch *or US also* hodgepodge, °mishmash, °chaos, °disaster, *Colloq* °stew, *Slang US* screwup, snafu, *Taboo slang Brit* balls-up

muddy *adj.* **1** fouled, befouled, muddied, mud-spattered, °dirty, grubby, grimy, soiled, mud-caked, °slimy, mucky, miry; oozy, squelchy, squashy, boggy, fenny, marshy, swampy; *Formal* feculent; *Colloq* squishy, squushy **2** °confused, unclear, °vague, °obscure, °dull, °dim, °fuzzy, muddled, addled, mixed-up **3** °drab, °subdued, blurred, °dingy, °flat, °murky, mat, °washed-out —*v.* **4** °obscure, °dull, °dim, °confuse, °mix up, °befog, cloud **5** °dirty, °soil, begrime, smirch, besmirch, °spatter, bespatter

muffle *v.* **1** Often, ***muffle up.*** °wrap, °swathe, swaddle, °cloak, °envelop, °cover (up), enfold, °shroud, enshroud, °conceal, °protect **2** °deaden, °silence, °suppress, °stifle, °subdue, °damp, °dampen, °mute, °hush, °quiet, °tone down, °still

muffler *n.* scarf, boa; shawl, °wrap

mug *n.* **1** °jug, tankard, stein, toby (jug), °pot, beaker, cup **2** °face, visage, °features, countenance, *Slang* puss, kisser, mush, *Brit* clock, dial, *Archaic* phiz *or* phizog, *US* °pan **3** °fool, °duffer, simpleton, °dupe, gull, °innocent, *Colloq* chump, °mark, soft *or* easy touch, *Brit* muggins, *Slang* °sucker —*v.* **4** make a face *or* faces, grimace **5** °attack, °set upon, °rob, °assault; garrote, throttle **6** ***mug up (on).*** °study, *Formal* lucubrate, *Colloq* °cram, burn the midnight oil, °get up (on), *Brit* swot, bone up (on)

muggy *adj.* °humid, °damp, °sticky, °sultry, °oppressive, °clammy, °steamy, °close, °stuffy, °moist, soggy

mull *v.* Usually, ***mull over.*** ponder, °consider, °study, think (over *or* about), cogitate (on *or* over *or* about), con, °evaluate, °turn over, °weigh, deliberate (on *or* over), °reflect (on), °muse (on), °review, °examine, °contemplate, °meditate (on), °chew over, ruminate (on *or* over)

mum *adj.* **1** °silent, °mute, close-mouthed, °quiet, °tight-lipped —*n.* **2** ***Mum's the word.*** Don't tell a soul, Keep silent, Keep secret, Keep quiet, Keep (something) to oneself, Keep (something) under one's hat, Say nothing, Tell no one, Play dumb, *Brit* Keep schtum

mumble *v.* °murmur, °mutter, say inarticulately, utter indistinctly, swallow one's words

mumbo jumbo *n.* **1** °gibberish, °nonsense, °rubbish, gobbledegook *or* gobbledygook, °drivel, humbug, bunkum, double-talk, rigmarole *or* rigamarole, jabberwocky, blather *or* blether, poppycock, *Colloq* eyewash, °rot, tommyrot, hogwash, bilge, bosh, bull, malarkey *or* malarky, claptrap, piffle, *US* hooey, °moonshine, bunk, *Slang* bull, crap, *Brit* tosh, *Taboo slang* bullshit **2** °spell, incantation, °chant, °formula, °charm, abracadabra, °hocus-pocus, °rite, °ritual, conjuration, °magic

munch *v.* °chew, °crunch, masticate, champ, chomp, scrunch

municipal *adj.* civic, °civil, metropolitan, urban, °city, °town, village, borough, parish, *Brit* °council

municipality *n.* °city, °metropolis, °town, village, borough, °district, township; suburb, exurb

murder *n.* **1** homicide, manslaughter, regicide, patricide, matricide, parricide, fratricide, sororicide, uxoricide, infanticide; °killing, slaying, assassination **2** °slaughter, butchery, genocide, °massacre, liquidation, decimation, extermination, eradication, wiping out, murdering, slaying, °killing, °bloodshed, °carnage —*v.* **3** °kill, slay, assassinate, put to death, end the life of, put away *or* down, °put out of one's misery, °wipe out, °destroy, °butcher, °massacre, liquidate, °exterminate, eradicate, annihilate, °extinguish, °slaughter, °lay low, *Slang* °eliminate, °bump off, °knock off, do in, °polish off, blow away, *US* °rub out, °waste, ice, °take for a ride, fit with a concrete overcoat *or* with concrete overshoes, snuff (out) **4** °spoil, °ruin, °mar, °destroy, °wreck, °kill, °mangle, °butcher, °mutilate

murderer *n.* murderess, °killer, slayer, assassin, homicide, °cutthroat, liquidater, executioner, °butcher, *Slang* hit man

murderous *adj.* **1** °fatal, °lethal, °deadly, deathly, °mortal, °destructive, °devastating, °sanguinary, bloody, °brutal, °savage, °bloodthirsty, barbarous, °fell, °cruel, °inhuman **2** °killing, °strenuous, stressful, °difficult, °arduous, °exhausting, °punishing, hellish, °harrowing, rigorous, intolerable, °unbearable

murky *adj.* °dark, °gloomy, °threatening, °dim, clouded, cloudy, °overcast, °gray, °dismal, °dreary, °bleak, °somber, °grim, °funereal, °shady, °shadowy

murmur *n.* **1** °undercurrent, undertone, background noise *or* sound, rumble, rumbling, °mumble, mumbling, drone, droning, °buzz, buzzing, murmuration, murmuring, °hum, humming, whispering, *Formal* susurration *or* susurrus **2** muttering, complaining, °complaint, grumble, grumbling, *Colloq* grousing, grouse —*v.* **3** °mumble, °mutter, °whisper **4** °complain, grumble, °mutter, °moan, °lament, wail, *Colloq* grouse

muscular *adj.* °sinewy, °brawny, °burly, °powerful, powerfully built, strapping, °rugged, °husky, °robust, athletic, °sturdy, well-muscled, broad-shouldered

muse *v.* cogitate, °meditate, °reflect, °contemplate, ruminate, think over, °think about, °consider, °chew over, °deliberate, °revolve, °weigh, °evaluate, °study, mull over, °brood (over), °ponder; be absorbed (in thought), be in a brown study, °dream, °daydream, be in a trance *or* reverie

mushy *adj.* **1** °soft, pulpy, doughy, squidgy, spongy; swampy, boggy, miry; *Colloq* squishy, squushy, squashy **2** mawkish, °maudlin, °sentimental, °romantic, saccharine, sugary, syrupy, *Colloq* corny, °sloppy, °gooey, slushy, *Brit* °wet, *Slang* schmaltzy

musical *adj.* °tuneful, melodic, °harmonious, lilting, °lyrical, °melodious, mellifluous, dulcet, euphonious

must *v.* **1** ought (to), should, have to, be obliged *or* obligated to, be compelled *or* forced to, be required to —*n.* **2** °necessity, requisite, °requirement, °obligation, sine qua non, °essential

muster *v.* **1** call *or* come together, °assemble, convoke, convene, °collect, °mobilize, °rally, °round up, °gather, marshal, °summon (up) —*n.* **2** °rally, °assembly, assemblage, convocation, °meet, °meeting, °convention, congress, °roundup, °turnout, °gathering, congregation, aggregation, aggregate **3** ***pass muster.*** come up to scratch, °make the grade, measure up, be acceptable, *Colloq* come *or* be up to snuff

musty *adj.* **1** °moldy, °damp, mildewed, mildewy, °sour, °rancid, spoiled, decayed, °rotten, °putrid, fetid *or* foetid, fusty, °stale **2** °stale, °old-fashioned, °antiquated, antediluvian, °ancient, out-of-date, °bygone, °passé, old hat, °obsolete, archaic, °tired, hoary, worn-out, trite, clichéd, stereotypical

mutation *n.* **1** °change, changing, °alteration, altering, modification, modifying, °transformation, transforming, metamorphosis, metamorphosing, transmutation, transmuting, transfiguration, transfiguring, °evolution, evolving, °variation, varying **2** °variant, °variation, deviation, °deviant, mutant, anomaly, departure

mute *adj.* **1** °silent, °dumb, °speechless, voiceless, wordless, °tight-lipped, °taciturn, °tacit, °reserved, °quiet, *Colloq* °mum **2** unspoken, unsaid, °tacit, °silent —*v.* **3** °deaden, °silence, °muffle, °stifle, °dampen, °damp, °subdue, °suppress, quiet *or Brit also* quieten, °hush, soft-pedal, °turn down, °tone down

mutilate *v.* **1** °maim, disfigure, °mangle, °cripple, °lame, °butcher, disable; dismember, amputate, hack off, °cut off, lop off, tear off, °rip off **2** °spoil, °mar, °ruin, °damage, °deface, vandalize, °destroy

mutinous *adj.* **1** °rebellious, °revolutionary, °subversive, °seditious, insurgent, insurrectionary **2** °recalcitrant, refractory, contumacious, °obstinate, °defiant, °insubordinate, °disobedient, °unruly, unmanageable, °ungovernable, uncontrollable

mutiny *n.* **1** °revolt, rebellion, °revolution, °subversion, subversiveness, insurgency, insurgence, insurrection, °uprising —*v.* **2** °rebel, rise up (against), °strike, °revolt; °disobey, °subvert, °agitate (against)

mutter *v.* **1** °mumble, °murmur, grunt **2** grumble, °complain, *Colloq* grouch, grouse, *Brit* chunter

mutual *adj.* **1** °reciprocal, reciprocated, requited, interactive, complementary **2** °common, communal, °joint, shared

mysterious *adj.* **1** °puzzling, enigmatic, baffling, insoluble, unsolvable, bewildering, confounding, confusing, °perplexing, mystifying, °weird, °bizarre, °strange, uncanny, °curious **2** °cryptic, arcane, °secret, inscrutable, covert, °hidden, furtive, unclear, °dark, concealed, °occult, °inexplicable, °incomprehensible, mystic(al), °unknown, unfathomable, °recondite, abstruse

mystery *n.* **1** °puzzle, °enigma, conundrum, °riddle, °question **2** °obscurity, °secrecy, indefiniteness, vagueness, nebulousness, °ambiguity, ambiguousness, inscrutability, inscrutableness **3** detective story *or* novel, °murder (story), *Colloq* whodunit

mystical *adj.* **1** allegorical, symbolic(al), mystic, cabalistic, arcane, unrevealed, °secret, °occult, °supernatural, esoteric, otherworldly, preternatural, °cryptic, concealed, °hidden, clandestine, °private, °veiled, °ineffable, °mysterious **2** See **mysterious, 2,** above.

mystify *v.* °fool, °hoax, humbug, °confuse, confound, °mix up, °bewilder, °stump, °puzzle, baffle, *Colloq* bamboozle, °stump, °flummox, *Slang* °beat

mystique *n.* °mystery, °magic, charisma, °aura, inscrutability, supernaturalism, preternaturalism, strangeness

myth *n.* **1** °legend, fable, allegory, °parable, °tradition, °saga, epic, °(folk) tale, °story, mythos; °history **2** fable, °lie, °(tall) tale, °fib, prevarication, fiction, untruth, °falsehood, °fabrication, cock-and-bull story, *Colloq* whopper

mythical *adj.* **1** mythic, mythological, fabled, °legendary, °traditional, folkloric, storied, °romantic, fairy-tale, storybook; allegorical, °symbolic, parabolic(al) **2** mythic, °fanciful, °imaginary, °fictitious, make-believe, made-up, chimerical, °untrue

mythology *n.* (body of) myths, folklore, °tradition, °lore, stories, mythos

N

nab *v.* °catch, °capture, °arrest, put *or* place under arrest, °seize, apprehend, °pick up, °bring in, take into custody, *Colloq* °pinch, collar, °run in, °nail, *Brit* °nick

nag[1] *v.* **1** Sometimes, ***nag at.*** °annoy, °irritate, °irk, °pester, °criticize, °ride, °scold, °carp (at), °upbraid, badger, °harass, harry, vex, °henpeck, °torment, hector, °pick at, goad, °pick on, find fault with, °berate, nettle, °bully, °provoke, °plague, °worry, °bother, *Brit* chivy *or* chivvy *or* chevy, *Colloq* needle —*n.* **2** °scold, harpy, °pest, °shrew, virago, termagant, fishwife

nag[2] *n.* °jade, Rosinante; horse, °hack, pony, dobbin, racehorse, thoroughbred, *Slang* gee-gee, *US* hayburner, °plug, bangtail

nagging *adj.* distressing, °chronic, °continuous, °continual, °persistent, unrelenting, °relentless, recurring

nail *n.* **1** fastener, °fastening, °spike, °pin **2** fingernail, toenail, °claw, talon **3** ***bite one's nails.*** °worry, agonize, °fret, lose sleep (over), °chafe, °suffer, *Colloq* stew (over *or* about) **4** ***hard or tough as nails.*** **(a)** °tough, °vigorous, °hardy **(b)** °cold, unsentimental, °unsympathetic, unfeeling **5** ***hit the nail on the head.*** be accurate, be correct, be precise, be right, put (one's) finger on it **6** ***on the nail.*** °immediately, °at once, *Brit* °straightaway, *US* right away, °promptly, without delay, on the spot, *Colloq US* on the barrelhead —*v.* **7** °attach, °secure, °join, °pin, °tack, clinch *or* clench; °fasten, °fix, °focus, rivet, °glue **8** See **nab,** above. **9** °hit, °strike; °punch; °shoot **10** ***nail down.***

°settle, °secure, °resolve, °complete, conclude, make final; °finalize

naive *adj.* naïve *or* naïf, °ingenuous, °innocent, credulous, °childlike, born yesterday, °unaffected, °unsophisticated, °inexperienced, °green, unworldly, °unsuspecting, unenlightened, unsuspicious, °trusting, trustful, °gullible, °artless, guileless, °simple, simplistic, simple-minded, unpretentious, unpretending, °candid, °natural

naiveté *n.* naïveté *or* naivety *or* naïvety, ingenuousness, innocence, credulity, credulousness, °inexperience, °(blind) trust, gullibility, artlessness, callowness, guilelessness, °simplicity, unpretentiousness, °candor, naturalness, frankness, openness, °sincerity

naked *adj.* **1** stark-naked, unclothed, undraped, °bare, exposed, stripped, undressed, unclad, uncovered, bared, °nude, in the nude, *Colloq* in the altogether, in one's birthday suit, in the buff, °in the raw, ***au naturel***, in a state of nature, *Brit* starkers, in the nuddy **2** unaided, unassisted **3** °plain, °unadorned, unembellished, °stark, °overt, °patent, °obvious, °conspicuous, °manifest, °sheer, °undisguised, °unvarnished, °unmitigated, °evident, palpable, unconcealed, in plain sight *or* view, °blatant, °barefaced, undeniable, °glaring, °flagrant, unmistakable *or* unmistakeable, unalloyed, unmixed, °blunt, unadulterated, °pure **4** unsheathed, unprotected, °bare, exposed

name *n.* **1** designation, °label, appellation, °term, °tag, °style, *Colloq* moniker *or* monicker, °handle **2** °reputation; repute, °honor, °esteem, °(high) regard, °respect, °rank, °standing, rating, °preeminence, °superiority, eminence, notability, °prominence, °prestige, °favor, °distinction, °renown, °fame, °popularity, °celebrity **3** °personage, °somebody, °celebrity, °star, superstar, °hero, VIP, °dignitary, luminary, *Colloq* big shot, °bigwig, big cheese, big name *—v.* **4** °label, °tag, °style, °entitle; °call, dub, °christen, baptize **5** °choose, °elect, °select, °delegate, °nominate, °designate, °appoint; °identify, denominate, pinpoint, °specify **6** ***name names.*** °identify, °specify, °mention, cite

nameless *adj.* **1** unnamed, innominate, °unidentified, anonymous, pseudonymous, °incognito, °unknown, °unheard-of, °unsung **2** °inexpressible, indefinable, unidentifiable, unspecified, unspecifiable **3** °ineffable, unutterable, unspeakable, °unmentionable, °abominable, °horrible, indescribable, °repulsive

namely *adv.* specifically, to wit, that is (to say), *id est*, i.e., ***videlicet***, viz., ***scilicet***, sc.; °for example, °for instance, ***exempli gratia***, e.g. *or* eg *or* eg.

nap [1] *v.* **1** °doze, °nod (off), catnap, *Colloq* catch forty winks, drop off (to sleep), get some shuteye, snooze, zizz, *US* catch a few Z's *—adv.* **2** ***napping.*** °unawares, off guard, unexpectedly, in an unguarded moment *—n.* **3** °doze, catnap, siesta, *Colloq* forty winks, shuteye, snooze, zizz, *Brit* lie-down

nap [2] *n.* °pile, °fiber, °texture, °weave, down, shag

narcotic *adj.* **1** soporific, stuporific, hypnotic, °sedative, somnolent, sleep-inducing, opiate, dulling, numbing, anesthetic, stupefacient, stupefying, stupefactive, tranquilizing, Lethean *—n.* **2** °drug, soporific, stuporific, hypnotic, °sedative, opiate, anesthetic, stupefacient, °tranquilizer

narrate *v.* °relate, °tell, °recount, °report, give an account (of), °recite, °rehearse, °repeat, °review, °unfold, °chronicle, °describe, °detail, °reveal, retail

narration *n.* **1** °telling, relating, unfolding, recounting, chronicling, recording, describing; °report, °recital, °recitation, °rehearsal, °relation, °chronicle, °description, portrayal, detailing, °revelation, °story, °tale, °narrative **2** reading, voice-over

narrative *n.* **1** °story, °tale, °chronicle, °description, °revelation, portrayal, °account, °report, °record, °history, °recital, °statement *—adj.* **2** story-telling, chronicling, anecdotal

narrator *n.* °reporter, storyteller, °raconteur, taleteller, teller of tales, anecdotist *or* anecdotalist, relator, annalist, chronicler, describer, °author; voice-over

narrow *adj.* **1** constricted, °slender, °slim, °thin, restricted, °straitened, attenuated, narrowed; narrowing, tapering **2** confined, confining, °limited, °cramped, °close, °meager, pinched, °tight, incommodious **3** °strict, °careful, °close, °precise, °exact, °exacting, °demanding, °finicky, finical, °sharp, °meticulous, °scrupulous, °fussy, °rigid, searching, °critical **4** restricted, °limited, circumscribed, proscribed, denotative **5** See **narrow-minded,** below. **6** °close, hairsbreadth, °lucky **7** stingy, niggardly, parsimonious, °miserly, °tight, °sparing, tightfisted, °mean, mercenary, *Brit* mingy, *Dialectal* °near, *Colloq* °close *—v.* **8** constrict, °limit, °qualify, °reduce, lessen, °diminish, °decrease **9** °limit, °restrict, °focus, confine, °concentrate, narrow down *—n.* **10** ***narrows.*** strait(s), °channel, °passage

narrowly *adv.* **1** °barely, °(only) just, °scarcely, °hardly, by a hair's breadth; by the skin of one's teeth, *Colloq* by a whisker **2** closely, carefully, meticulously, scrupulously, °searchingly, critically

narrow-minded *adj.* °bigoted, °prejudiced, illiberal, °narrow, °biased, °opinionated, °one-sided, °intolerant, nonobjective, °conservative, °reactionary, °parochial, ultraconservative, stiff-necked, °conventional, °hidebound, fundamentalist, literal-minded, narrow-spirited, mean-minded, mean-spirited, °petty, pettifogging, °small-minded, puritanical, unprogressive, °old-fashioned, old-fogyish, °strait-laced, *Colloq* °stuffy, *US* close-minded, °square, screed-bound, rednecked

nasty *adj.* **1** °foul, °filthy, °dirty, unclean,

°offensive, °disgusting, nauseating, °revolting, °horrible, °loathsome, °repugnant, °repellent, °vile, odious, °obnoxious, objectionable, °nauseous, sickening, vomit-provoking, fetid *or* foetid, noisome, mephitic, °rank, malodorous, °rancid, noxious **2** unpleasant, °disagreeable, °unsavory, °painful, objectionable, annoying, °untoward, °awkward, °difficult, °bad, °serious **3** °obscene, °dirty, °pornographic, °blue, smutty, °lewd, °vulgar, °sordid, °indecent, licentious, °gross, °coarse, °crude, °rude, ribald, °bawdy, °risqué, °off-color, °suggestive, *Colloq* X-rated, raunchy **4** unpleasant, °disagreeable, °ugly, bad-tempered, °vicious, currish, °surly, °abusive, °spiteful, irascible, ill-natured, ill-tempered, °cruel, °inconsiderate, °rude, churlish, °obnoxious, crotchety, curmudgeonly, °cantankerous, crabbed, °cranky, *US and Canadian* °mean **5** °bad, °severe, °acute, °painful, °serious; °dangerous, °critical

nation *n.* °country, °state, °land, political entity, polity, °domain, °realm

national *adj.* **1** nationwide, countrywide, °state, governmental, °civil; °public, °popular, *US* federal **2** °nationalistic, nationalist, °patriotic, jingoistic, chauvinistic —*n.* **3** °citizen, °subject, °inhabitant, °resident; °native

nationalistic *adj.* nationalist, °patriotic, jingoist(ic), chauvinist(ic), xenophobic, isolationist

nationality *n.* **1** citizenship **2** °race, °nation, ethnic group, ethnos, °clan, °tribe; °strain, °stock, °pedigree, °heritage, °roots, °extraction, bloodline, °breed

native *adj.* **1** innate, natal, °inborn, °natural, °inherent, congenital, indwelling, inherited, °hereditary, in the blood, °intrinsic, constitutional **2** °domestic, °local, homegrown; °indigenous, autochthonous, °aboriginal **3** °basic, °first, °best, °original, °exclusive **4** °national, ethnic, °clan, tribal **5** °aboriginal, °provincial, °local **6** born; by birth —*n.* **7** aborigine, indigene, autochthon; °national, °citizen, °resident, °inhabitant

natural *adj.* **1** °ordinary, °common, commonplace, °normal, °standard, °regular, °usual, °customary, unexceptional, °routine, °habitual, °typical, °everyday; °reasonable, °logical, °sensible, accepted **2** °normal, °ordinary, °regular, expected; °spontaneous **3** °simple, °basic, °fundamental, °real, unartificial, °genuine, unembellished, °unadorned, unpretentious **4** unstudied, unconstrained, °candid, °frank, °spontaneous, °unaffected, °easy, °honest, °straight, straightforward, °artless, guileless, °impulsive, °unpremeditated, °unaffected, °ingenuous, °unsophisticated, unsophistic(al) **5** See **native, 1,** above **6** °true, °real, °genuine, °actual, °authentic, °bona fide **7** °lifelike, true-to-life, °realistic **8** °illegitimate, bastard **9** °consistent, consonant, consequent, °logical, °reasonable, °fitting, °appropriate, °proper, expected, not incongruous, understandable **10** °organic, organically grown, nonchemical, °health —*n.* **11** °genius, artist, °talent **12** *Archaic* idiot, imbecile, simpleton, °fool, °half-wit

naturally *adv.* **1** °(as a matter) of course, °needless to say, to be sure, certainly, °surely, not unexpectedly, as expected *or* anticipated, °obviously, °clearly, logically, °consequently, as a consequence *or* result **2** normally, °by nature, by character, °really, °actually, genuinely; inherently, instinctively, innately, congenitally **3** unaffectedly, unpretentiously, °easily, candidly, °openly, °simply, plainly, °honestly, straightforwardly, uncomplicatedly

nature *n.* **1** °quality, properties, °features, °character, °personality, °makeup, °essence, constitution, °identity, attributes, °disposition, temperament, complexion **2** °universe, cosmos, °world, °creation, °environment **3** scenery, countryside, wildness, primitiveness, °simplicity **4** °kind, °variety, °description, °sort, °class, °category, °type, °genre, species; °stamp, °cast, °mold, feather, kidney, °color, °stripe **5** ***by nature.*** See **naturally, 2,** above.

naught *n.* nought, °nothing, °nil, °zero, aught *or* ought; °ruin, °destruction, °disaster, °collapse, °failure

naughty *adj.* **1** °mischievous, impish, puckish, roguish, scampish, °devilish; °frolicsome, °playful **2** °disobedient, refractory, °insubordinate, °bad, °perverse, °wicked, fractious, °unruly, wayward, unmanageable, °ungovernable, °undisciplined, °defiant, °obstreperous **3** °improper, °offensive, °vulgar, °indecent, °immoral, °risqué, °off-color, ribald, °bawdy, °blue, °pornographic, smutty, °lewd, °obscene, °dirty, *Colloq* X-rated, raunchy

nauseate *v.* °sicken, °disgust, °repel, °revolt, °offend

nauseated *adj.* sickened, °disgusted, repelled, revolted, offended, °sick (to one's stomach), °queasy, °squeamish; seasick, carsick, airsick

nauseous *adj.* nauseating, °loathsome, sickening, °disgusting, °repellent, vomit-provoking, °offensive, °revolting, °repugnant, °repulsive, °abhorrent, °nasty, °foul, unpleasant, stomach-turning, *Technical* emetic

nautical *adj.* maritime, °marine, °seafaring, seagoing; naval; boating, yachting, sailing; navigational

navel *n.* *Technical* umbilicus, omphalos, *Colloq* bellybutton

navigable *adj.* **1** °passable, traversable, negotiable, unblocked, unobstructed, °clear **2** maneuverable, sailable, controllable, steerable, yare

navigate *v.* **1** °sail, voyage, °cruise, °journey; °cross, °traverse **2** °maneuver, °handle, °sail, °guide, °pilot, °steer, °direct, °skipper, captain, *Nautical* con

navigation *n.* pilotage, helmsmanship, seamanship, steersmanship, steering, sailing

navigator *n.* °pilot, helmsman, seaman, tillerman, wheelman, steersman, °skipper

navy *n.* °fleet, flotilla, naval force(s), armada, *Literary* argosy

naysayer *n.* denier, refuser, disdainer, rejecter *or* rejector; prophet of doom, pessimist, °skeptic, dissenter, defeatist

near *adv.* **1** close (by *or* at hand), not far (off *or* away), °nearby, nigh, in *or* into the vicinity *or* neighborhood, within (easy) reach **2** °close to, next to **3** °nearly, °almost, just about, well-nigh, close to being; not quite, °virtually *—adj.* **4** °close, °imminent, °immediate, °impending, looming, coming, approaching, °forthcoming; in the offing, °at hand **5** near by, °close, adjacent, next-door, close-by, °adjoining, abutting, °neighboring, contiguous **6** stingy, °mean, niggardly, °miserly, parsimonious, °penurious, °cheap, penny-pinching, cheeseparing, °selfish, °close, tightfisted, closefisted **7** °close, °intimate, connected, °related, °attached **8** °close, °narrow, hairsbreadth *—prep.* **9** °close to, in the vicinity *or* neighborhood of, next to, adjacent to, within reach of, within a mile of; a stone's throw from, not far (away) from *—v.* **10** °approach, draw near *or* nigh, come close *or* closer, °verge on, approximate on, lean toward(s)

nearby *adv.* **1** °close by, close at hand, not far off *or* away, in the vicinity *or* neighborhood, within (easy) reach, °about, °around *—adj.* **2** °close, within reach, °handy, °accessible, at *or* to hand, adjacent

nearly *adv.* **1** °almost, not quite, °about, °approximately, all but, just about, °virtually, well-nigh, °practically, as good as, more or less; °around, approaching, nearing, °barely, °hardly, °scarcely, °close to **2** closely, identically, °exactly, °precisely

nearsighted *adj.* **1** myopic, °shortsighted **2** *Chiefly US* °shortsighted, °narrow-minded, blinkered, °narrow, close-minded, illiberal, °unthinking, °heedless, insular, °partial, °one-sided, °parochial, °unsophisticated, unimaginative, °biased, unobjective, °opinionated, °dogmatic, °prejudiced, °intolerant, °bigoted

neat *adj.* **1** °tidy, °orderly, °clean, uncluttered, °trim, °spruce, natty, °fastidious, spick-and-span, °shipshape (and Bristol fashion), organized, well-organized, well-ordered, °systematic, *Brit dialect* trig, *Colloq* neat as a pin, *Brit* dinky **2** °straight, unadulterated, unmixed, °undiluted, uncut, unblended, °pure; °on the rocks **3** unembellished, °unadorned, unornamented, °simple, °elegant, °graceful, °smart, uncomplicated, °regular, °precise, copperplate; calligraphic **4** deft, adroit, °clever, °efficient, °ingenious, °expert, °practiced, °skillful, °dexterous **5** °fine, wonderful, °marvelous, °great, °splendid, °excellent, °exceptional, °capital, °grand, first-class, *Colloq* °cool, smashing, °keen, °nifty, topnotch, A-1 *or* A-one, *Brit* top-hole, *Chiefly US* A-OK, *Slang* °swell, far-out, °boss, *Brit* topping, *US and Canadian* spiffy

neaten *v.* Often, ***neaten up.*** tidy (up), straighten (up *or* out), °clean (up), °spruce up, °(put in) order, *Brit dialect* trig

nebulous *adj.* °vague, °hazy, clouded, unclear, °obscure, °indistinct, °fuzzy, °muddy, ill-defined, °shapeless, amorphous, blurred, indeterminate, °murky, °opaque, turbid, °dim, foggy, °faint, °pale

necessarily *adv.* inevitably, unavoidably, inescapably, axiomatically, inexorably, ineluctably, irresistibly, incontrovertibly, automatically, °naturally, °(as a matter) of course, as a result, certainly, °surely, to be sure, like it or not, °willy-nilly, perforce, of necessity, by definition

necessary *adj.* **1** °indispensable, °essential, required, needed, compulsory, requisite, °vital, demanded, °imperative, °obligatory, needful, °of the essence, °important, of the utmost importance, top priority, high priority, °urgent, exigent, compelling, life-and-death *or* life-or-death **2** °inevitable, °unavoidable, inescapable, ineluctable **3** °sure, °certain, °predetermined, predestined, °fated, inexorable; resulting, resultant *—n.* **4** See **necessity, 1,** below.

necessity *n.* **1** °requirement, °essential, °necessary, requisite, °need, °prerequisite, °basic, °fundamental, sine qua non, desideratum, constraint **2** indispensability, unavoidability, needfulness, inexorability **3** °poverty, °want, indigence, °need, destitution, penury, °straits, °difficulty, °difficulties, pauperism, neediness **4** °urgency, °emergency, °crisis, °misfortune, exigency, °pinch, °extreme, matter of life and death

need *v.* **1** °require, °demand, °want, be in want of, °call for, have need of *or* for; °lack, °miss, have occasion for *—n.* **2** °necessity, °requirement; °call, °demand, constraint **3** °essential, °necessary, requisite, °prerequisite, °necessity, °basic, °fundamental, sine qua non, desideratum **4** °distress, °difficulty, °trouble, (dire *or* desperate) straits, °stress, °emergency, exigency, °extremity, neediness, needfulness; °poverty, penury, impecuniousness, destitution, °privation, deprivation, indigence, beggary **5** °want, °lack, °dearth, °shortage, paucity, °scarcity, insufficiency, desideratum

needless *adj.* **1** °unnecessary, °nonessential, unessential, unneeded, unwanted, °useless, uncalled-for, °gratuitous, °superfluous, °redundant, °excess, °excessive, tautological, °dispensable, °expendable, supererogatory, *de trop,* pleonastic **2** ***needless to say.*** °naturally, °(as a matter) of course, °obviously, it goes without saying

needy *adj.* °poor, °indigent, poverty-stricken, °destitute, °impoverished, penniless, impecunious, necessitous, underprivileged, °deprived, disadvantaged, below the poverty level, in dire straits, in *or* on the way to the poorhouse, in reduced circumstances, °down-and-out, °insolvent, *Colloq* °on one's uppers, flat *or* stony broke, °hard up, strapped, pinched, on the breadline, up against it, *Brit* on the dole, *US* dead broke, on welfare, on relief

negative *adj.* **1** °contradictory, anti, °contrary, dissenting, dissentious, disputing, disputatious, °argumentative, adversarial, adversative, antagonistic, antipathetic, adverse, *US* °adversary **2** °pessimistic, °unenthusiastic, °cool, °cold, uninterested, unresponsive **3** nullifying, annulling, neutralizing, voiding, canceling **4** negating, refusing, denying, gainsaying, °opposing **5** ***in the negative.*** negatively, "No"

neglect *v.* **1** °disregard, °ignore, °slight, pay no attention to, be inattentive to, °overlook, °pass by, °spurn, °rebuff, °scorn, disdain, contemn, *Colloq* cold-shoulder **2** °fail (in), °omit; °disregard, let slide *or* pass, be remiss (about *or* in *or* regarding), °abandon, lose sight of, °forget, °shirk —*n.* **3** °disregard, °disrespect, inattention, °indifference, slighting, unconcern, °oversight, heedlessness, neglectfulness, carelessness, inadvertence **4** °negligence, laxity, laxness, slackness, neglectfulness, passivity, passiveness, °inactivity, inaction, dereliction, °default, °failure, °failing, remissness

negligence *n.* inattention, inattentiveness, °indifference, carelessness, unconcern, dereliction, °failure, °failing, heedlessness, laxity, laxness, °disregard, °oversight, °omission, inadvertence, °neglect, remissness, forgetfulness, oscitancy *or* oscitance

negligible *adj.* °insignificant, °minor, unimportant, °trifling, trivial, °inconsequential, piddling, inappreciable, °small, °slight, °paltry, nugatory, °worthless, °petty, °niggling, not worth mentioning *or* talking about

negotiate *v.* **1** °deal, °bargain, °dicker, °haggle, chaffer, palter; °discuss, °debate, mediate, °consult, °parley, °speak, °talk, °transact, °come to terms **2** °arrange (for), °organize, orchestrate, °conduct, °handle, °maneuver, °manage, °engineer, °work out, °settle, °get, °obtain, bring off *or* about, °carry off, °accomplish, do, °execute, °effect, °complete, conclude, *Colloq* °pull off **3** °maneuver, °clear, get through *or* past *or* round *or* over, °pass, °cross, *Colloq* make (it (through *or* past *or* around *or* over))

negotiation *n.* **1** °discussion, mediation, arbitration, bargaining, °parley, parleying, °talk, coming to terms **2** °deal, °bargain, °transaction, °agreement, °arrangement, °understanding, °determination, °decision, °settlement; °contract, °pact, °compact, covenant, concordat, °treaty

negotiator *n.* arbitrator, arbiter, °mediator, °moderator, diplomat, °ambassador, °go-between, middleman, intercessor, interceder, intervener, °agent, °broker

neighborhood *n.* **1** locality, °area, °region, °vicinity, vicinage, environs, °quarter, °district, precinct(s), purlieus, °locale; surroundings, confines **2** ***in the neighborhood of.*** °approximately, °about, °around, °nearly, °practically, °close to, °almost, more or less, *Colloq* in the ballpark of, in the region of, *Brit* getting on for, not far off, *US* within an eyelash of, *Slang* as near as dammit to

neighboring *adj.* °nearby, °near, °around, adjacent (to), °surrounding, °adjoining, contiguous (to), °touching, bordering (on), next (to), nearest

neighborly *adj.* °friendly, °cordial, °warm, °amiable, °agreeable, affable, companionable, well-disposed, °kindly, °kind, well-wishing, °genial, °sociable, °social, °harmonious, °considerate, °thoughtful, °helpful, °gracious, °courteous, °civil

neologism *n.* neoterism, coinage, neology, nonce word; °blend, portmanteau word

nerve *n.* **1** °courage, coolness, boldness, °bravery, intrepidity, °determination, valor, °daring, fearlessness, dauntlessness, °pluck, mettle, °spirit, °fortitude, °will, °tenacity, steadfastness, staunchness, firmness, doughtiness, resoluteness, *Colloq* °guts, °grit, °gumption, °spunk, *US* sand, *Brit* °bottle, *US* moxie, *Taboo slang* balls **2** °effrontery, brazenness, °gall, °impertinence, °brass, °impudence, insolence, audacity, brashness, °presumption, presumptuousness, temerity, *Colloq* cheek, °sauce, chutzpah, *Slang* crust **3** ***get on someone's nerves.*** °annoy, °irritate, °upset **4** ***nerves.*** °tension, nervousness, hysteria, °anxiety, fretfulness, °stress, °worry, apprehension, °fright, *Colloq* the jitters, *Slang* the willies, the heebie-jeebies, *US* the whim-whams

nerve-racking *adj.* nerve-wracking, °harrowing, °agonizing, distressing, °trying, vexing, vexatious, °troublesome, worrisome, °irksome, irritating

nervous *adj.* **1** highly strung, °excitable, °sensitive, °tense, °agitated, wrought up, worked up, °upset, flustered, ruffled, °disturbed, perturbed, distressed, °worried, °anxious, troubled, °concerned, disquieted, edgy, °on edge, on tenterhooks, fidgety, °fretful, uneasy, apprehensive, frightened, °fearful, °shaky, °scared, skittish, *US* on a tightrope, *Colloq* °jumpy, jittery, flappable, in a stew, in a dither, in a sweat, in a tizzy, in a flap, uptight, *Brit* nervy, *US* on pins and needles, *Slang* strung out **2** °difficult, °tense, °critical

nest *n.* **1** roost, °perch, eyrie *or US also* aerie, den, °lair **2** snuggery, °retreat, °refuge, °haunt, °hideaway, hide-out; °resort

nestle *v.* °cuddle (up), °snuggle (up), °huddle, curl up, nuzzle (up)

net[1] *n.* **1** °network, netting, °mesh, meshwork, °web, webbing, openwork, lattice, latticework, trellis, trelliswork, lacework, reticulum, reticle, rete, plexus, grid, gridwork, grille, °grate, °grating, fretwork; sieve, °screen, strainer, sifter —*v.* **2** °catch, °capture, °trap, entrap, °snare, ensnare, °bag

net[2] *n.* **1** nett, °(net) profit, °gain, °earnings, return(s), *Colloq US* °take —*adj.* **2** °clear, after deductions, after taxes, take-home, °final, bottom-line **3** °final, °end, closing, concluding, conclusive, °effective, °ultimate

—*v.* **4** °make, °realize, °clear, take home, °bring in, °earn, °pocket, °take in, °get

network *n.* **1** See **net**[1], **1,** above. **2** °system, °arrangement, °structure, °organization, complex, grid, crisscross, °web, plexus; °maze, labyrinth, jungle, °tangle

neurotic *adj.* psychoneurotic, °unstable, °disturbed, °confused, irrational, disordered, maladjusted, °distraught, °overwrought, °anxious, °nervous, °obsessive, °deviant, °abnormal

neuter *adj.* **1** asexual, sexless, epicene —*v.* **2** desex *or* desexualize, °doctor; castrate, emasculate, geld, capon *or* caponize, eunuchize; spay, ovariectomize, oophorectomize; *Colloq* °fix, °cut, *US* °alter

neutral *adj.* **1** nonbelligerent, noncombatant, unaligned, °nonaligned, unaffiliated, uninvolved, unallied, nonallied, °nonpartisan, °impartial, °disinterested, °indifferent, °dispassionate, unbiased, uncommitted, °noncommittal, °aloof, °withdrawn, °detached, °remote, removed **2** °dull, °drab, °colorless, achromatic, toneless, indeterminate, °washed-out, °pale, °indefinite, °indistinct, °indistinguishable, indeterminate, °vague, °drab, beige, ecru

neutralize *v.* °void, annul, °cancel (out), nullify, invalidate, negate, °delete, °undo, make *or* render ineffective, counterbalance, °counteract, °offset, °equalize, °even, °square, compensate for, °make up for

never *adv.* **1** at no time, not ever, not at any time, on no occasion, under no circumstances *or* condition(s), on no account, not at all, *Colloq* not in a million years, not till hell freezes over **2** in no way, not in any way, not in the least, not in any degree, not under any condition; (*postpositive*) not

nevertheless *adv.* °still, °notwithstanding, °yet, in spite of that, despite that, °nonetheless, °regardless, be that as it may, for all that, °even so, but, °however, just *or* all the same, everything considered, °at any rate, anyway, °in any case, °in any event, °at all events, *Literary* withal

new *adj.* **1** °novel, °original, °unique, °unusual, °different, °fresh, °creative, °imaginative, °brand-new **2** °latest, °late, °modern, °contemporary, modish, °stylish, °fashionable, °chic, °recent, advanced, up-to-date, °brand-new, late-model, *Colloq* °trendy, *Slang* mod, °hip **3** °fresh, °further, additional, supplemental, °supplementary **4** °unfamiliar, °unknown, °strange, °different; °unique, unheard of **5** revitalized, reborn, renewed, rejuvenated, changed, altered, redone, restored, redesigned, remodeled **6** °inexperienced, °green, °fresh, °callow, °unfledged, budding, °immature, unripe, untrained **7** °late, °young, °recent **8** °uncharted, unexplored, untrodden, °unknown, °experimental

newcomer *n.* **1** °alien, °immigrant, °foreigner, outlander, °stranger, °settler, colonist, °outsider **2** beginner, °amateur, °novice, proselyte, neophyte, tiro *or* tyro, °initiate, trainee, °learner, fledgling *or Brit also* fledgeling, *US* freshman, *Colloq* °greenhorn

news *n.* **1** tidings, °word, °information, °advice, °intelligence; °rumor, °talk, °gossip, hearsay, °dirt, °scandal, exposé, *Colloq* info, °lowdown, °scoop, *US* scuttlebutt, *Slang* °dope **2** dispatch *or* despatch, °report, °account, °story, communication, °bulletin, communiqué, °announcement, °information, °message, °word, °statement, °(press) release, °(news) flash **3** newscast, news broadcast *or* telecast, news program **4** °(good) copy, front-page news, °(hot) item

nice *adj.* **1** °pleasant, °agreeable, °amiable, °amicable, °friendly, °cordial, °warm, °gracious, warmhearted, °kind, °kindly, °outgoing, charming, °genial, °delightful, °courteous, °polite, °refined, gentlemanly, °ladylike, winsome, °likable, °attractive **2** °good, °satisfactory, commendable, °worthy, °worthwhile **3** °good, °fine, °superb, °superior, °attentive, °sharp, °acute, °keen, °careful, °exact, °exacting, rigorous; °precise, °accurate, unerring, °scrupulous, °meticulous, punctilious, °discriminating, discriminative, °perceptive, °delicate, °fastidious, °flawless, °faultless, °subtle, °strict, °close, °small, °slight, °minute, complex, °complicated, °intricate **4** °delicate, °subtle, °sensitive, °exquisite, hair-splitting, overnice, °fine, °critical, °ticklish, °dangerous, °precarious, °perilous, *Colloq* °hairy **5** °trim, well-turned-out, °tidy, °neat, °fine **6** ***nice and ...*** pleasantly, delightfully, pleasingly, agreeably, enjoyably, gratifyingly, satisfyingly, comfortably

niche *n.* **1** °recess, °hollow, alcove, °nook **2** °place, °position, *Colloq* °slot, pigeonhole

nick *n.* **1** °cut, °notch, °chip, °gouge, °gash, °scratch, dent, °indentation, °flaw, °mark, °blemish, °defect —*v.* **2** °cut, °notch, °chip, °gouge, °gash, °scratch, dent

nickname *n.* **1** pet name, sobriquet, epithet, agnomen, *Colloq* moniker *or* monicker, °handle **2** °diminutive, shortening

nifty *adj.* **1** °smart, °stylish, modish, °chic, °spruce **2** °healthy, in good form, spry, °energetic, °agile, °quick **3** °excellent, °neat, °great, °splendid, °fine, °clever, °skillful, apt, °suitable **4** °satisfactory, °satisfying, °good, °profitable, °substantial, °considerable

niggle *v.* °find fault, °nag, °carp, °fuss, °cavil, °criticize; °complain, *Colloq* grouse, *Slang* °bitch, *US* kvetch

niggling *adj.* **1** irritating, worrying, worrisome, °irksome, vexing, vexatious, annoying, °troublesome **2** °petty, nugatory, °trifling, trivial, °fussy, °insignificant, unimportant, °inconsequential, °frivolous, *Colloq* piddling, nit-picking, *US and Canadian* picayune

night *n.* **1** (Stygian *or* Cimmerian) °dark *or* darkness *or* blackness *or* °gloom; nighttime, shades of night, *Formal* tenebrosity *or* tenebrousness *or* tenebriousness **2** nightfall, gloaming, °twilight, °dusk, eventide, °evening, evensong, edge of night, sunset, sundown, end of day, vespers **3** ***night and day.*** °all the time, continually, incessantly, unceasingly, continuously, unendingly, endlessly, round-the-clock, ceaselessly, °nonstop

nightly *adj.* **1** every night, each night, each and every night, night after night **2** nighttime, nocturnal, bedtime *—adv.* **3** every night, each night, nights, after dark, after sunset; nocturnally

nightmarish *adj.* °frightening, °terrifying, alarming, horrific, °horrible, °dreadful, °awful, °ghastly, dismaying, °agonizing, worrisome, exasperating, frustrating, Kafkaesque, *Colloq* creepy, °scary

nil *n.* °nothing, °zero, °nought, ought *or* aught, *Tennis, table tennis, etc.* love, *Brit cricket* °duck, *US* goose egg, *Slang US* zip, zilch

nimble *adj.* **1** °agile, °lively, °active, °light, lithe, limber, spry, °sprightly, °brisk, °smart, °energetic, °rapid, °quick, °swift, adroit, deft, °dexterous; nimble-fingered; nimble-footed **2** °agile, °alert, °acute, nimble-witted, °quick-witted, ready-witted, °intelligent, °keen, °sharp; °smart, °brilliant, sparkling, °scintillating, coruscating

nip[1] *v.* **1** °bite, nibble; °pinch, °snip, °clip, °cut, °snap, °tweak, twitch, °trim, °lop, crop, shear; °grip, °squeeze **2** ***nip in the bud.*** °stop, °arrest, °check, °thwart, °frustrate, °stymie, °forestall; °quash, °squelch, °suppress, °extinguish, °put down *—n.* **3** °bite, nibble, °morsel, °pinch, °snip **4** °chill, coldness, iciness, sharpness, °tang, °bite

nip[2] *n.* °taste, °drop, °sip, *soupçon,* °portion, °swallow, °gulp, °mouthful, °finger, draft *or Brit* draught, °peg, °tot, *Scots* dram, *Colloq* snort, °shot

nobility *n.* **1** nobleness, °dignity, °grandeur, illustriousness, greatness, °glory, °influence, °authority, °leadership, °distinction, °probity, °integrity, °excellence, goodness, °character, °rectitude, righteousness, ethics, °honesty, honorableness, decency, justness, high-mindedness, magnanimity, °prestige, loftiness, primacy, °significance **2** °rank, °position, °class, °birth, blue blood **3** ***the nobility.*** the gentry, the elite, the aristocracy, *Colloq* the upper crust, the ruling class(es), °the Establishment, *US* the Four Hundred

noble *n.* **1** nobleman, noblewoman, aristocrat, patrician, °lord, lady, °peer; gentleman, gentlewoman, *Colloq* blue blood *—adj.* **2** highborn, °high-class, upperclass, aristocratic, titled, high-ranking, lordly, patrician, *Colloq* blueblood(ed) **3** °dignified, °eminent, °distinguished, august, °grand, °lofty, °elevated, °illustrious, °prestigious, °preeminent, °noted, honored, esteemed, °celebrated, °renowned, acclaimed, respected, venerated **4** °upright, °righteous, °honorable, °honest, °virtuous, incorruptible, °chivalrous, °staunch, °steadfast, °true, °loyal, °faithful, °trustworthy, °principled, °moral, °good, °decent, self-sacrificing, magnanimous, °generous **5** °splendid, °magnificent, °imposing, °impressive, °stately, °exquisite, °sublime, °grand, °striking, °stunning, °superb, °admirable, °elegant, °rich, °sumptuous, °luxurious

nobody *pron.* **1** no one, not anyone, no person *—n.* **2** nonentity, °unknown, °zero, cipher, *Colloq* °nothing

nod *v.* **1** °greet, °acknowledge, °recognize **2** say yes; °consent, assent, °agree, concur, acquiesce **3** °doze (off), °nap, drowse, drop off, fall asleep **4** °slip (up), °err, make a mistake, be mistaken *or* wrong; be careless *or* negligent *or* lax *or* inattentive *—n.* **5** °signal, °sign, °cue, °indication, °gesture **6** °approval; °consent, acquiescence, concurrence, assent, °agreement, *Colloq* OK *or* O.K. *or* o.k. *or* okay

nodding *adj.* °casual, °slight, °superficial, °distant; °incomplete

noise *n.* **1** °sound, clamor, °crash, °clap, °clash, clangor, °din, °thunder, thundering, rumble, rumbling, °outcry, hubbub, °uproar, hullabaloo, °racket, charivari *or US and Canadian also* shivaree, °rattle, caterwauling, °rumpus, °blare, °blast, blasting, bawling, babel; commotion, °bedlam, °fracas, °tumult, °pandemonium, turmoil; discordance, dissonance, cacophony; *Archaic* alarms *or* alarums and excursions, *Colloq* ruckus, ruction, ballyhoo **2** °sound, °disturbance *—v.* **3** Often, ***noise about*** *or* ***around.*** °circulate, °spread, °rumor, bruit (about)

noiseless *adj.* muted, °quiet, °soft, hushed, muffled, deadened, dampened, damped; °silent, °mute, °still, °inaudible, soundless

noisy *adj.* °loud, deafening, earsplitting, jarring, °grating, °harsh, °piercing, °shrill, °discordant, unmusical, dissonant, cacophonous *or* cacophonic, resounding, clarion, clamorous, clangorous, °thunderous, °uproarious, blaring, blasting, °obstreperous, vociferous, °boisterous, °tumultuous, °riotous

nominal *adj.* **1** °titular, in name only, °formal, °pretended, °so-called, °self-styled, *soi-disant,* °professed, purported, °supposed, would-be, representational, represented, supposititious *or* suppositious; proposed, propositional; °puppet **2** °insignificant, trivial, °trifling, °minor, minuscule, °tiny, °small, °insubstantial, °minimal, inconsiderable, °token

nominate *v.* °choose, °select, °name, °appoint, °designate, °suggest, °offer, °submit, °recommend, °propose, °present, put up *or* forward; °forward; *Formal* °put forth

nominee *n.* °candidate, officeseeker, designee, selectee, appointee, assignee

nonaligned *adj.* uncommitted, nonallied, nonaffiliated, unaligned, unaffiliated, unallied; °neutral, °impartial

nonbeliever *n.* unbeliever, disbeliever, cynic, doubting Thomas, doubter, °skeptic, freethinker, agnostic, atheist, nullifidian; °infidel, °heathen, °pagan

nonchalant *adj.* °cool, unexcited, unexcitable, unperturbed, imperturbable, undisturbed, untroubled, unflappable, unruffled,

°dispassionate, unemotional, °detached, °distant, unconcerned, °indifferent, pococurante, insouciant, uninterested, °aloof, °blasé, °offhand, °calm, °collected, composed, easygoing, free and easy, happy-go-lucky, °casual, °relaxed, at ease; °unenthusiastic, apathetic; *Colloq* laid-back, together

noncommittal *adj.* °wary, °cautious, °careful, °gingerly, °guarded, °(playing it) safe, circumspect, watchful, °prudent, canny, °tentative, on guard, °reserved, °cool; precautionary *or* precautional, precautious; *Colloq* playing it cool, playing it safe, playing it *or* one's cards close to the chest

noncompletion *n.* nonfulfillment, unfulfillment, nonperformance, incompleteness, deficiency

noncompliance *n.* disobedience, nonconformity, nonobservance, °disregard, disregarding, °failure, noncooperation, uncooperativeness, unresponsiveness, °rejection, °refusal, °denial

nonconformist *n.* **1** nonconformer, °renegade, maverick, °rebel, °radical, °individualist, heretic, dissenter, °dissident, iconoclast, loner, °exception, anomaly —*adj.* **2** nonconforming, °renegade, maverick, °rebellious, °radical, individualist(ic), °heretical, dissentient, °dissident, iconoclastic

nondescript *adj.* indescribable, unclassifiable, unclassified, °ordinary, common-or-garden variety, °common, commonplace, unremarkable, °colorless, °drab, °everyday, °bland, uninteresting, insipid, characterless, undistinctive, unexceptional

none *pron.* no one, not anyone, °nobody, no person; not one; not any; °nil

nonessential *adj.* **1** nonvital, unessential, unneeded, °unnecessary, °needless, °inconsequential, °insignificant, unimportant, °superfluous, °dispensable, °expendable, °gratuitous, uncalled-for, °extraneous, °peripheral, °extra, *de trop,* adventitious, additional, supplemental, adscititious, °redundant, °accessory, °subordinate, °secondary, °subsidiary —*n.* **2** unessential, inessential, nonentity, cipher, °zero, °nobody; °extra, supernumerary, spear carrier, *Colloq* °nothing, *Slang US* nebbish

nonetheless *adv.* See **nevertheless,** above.

nonevent *n.* anticlimax, *Colloq* nonstarter, lead balloon, °dud, *Brit* damp squib

nonexistent *adj.* °unreal, °imaginary, imagined, °fictional, fictive, °fanciful, °fancied, °mythical, °fabulous, fabled, °illusory, chimerical, delusive

nonflammable *adj.* noncombustible, °incombustible, noninflammable, unburnable; fire-retardant

no-nonsense *adj.* °serious, unfrivolous, businesslike, °practical, nontrivial, untrivial

nonpareil *n.* °paragon, °model, °standard, *ne plus ultra,* exemplar, °ideal, *Literary* nonesuch, *Colloq* oner, one in a million, *Brit* one-off

nonpartisan *adj.* **1** nonpartizan, °nonaligned, unaligned, unaffiliated, °independent, noncommitted, uncommitted, °neutral, uninvolved, °free, °(sitting) on the fence **2** °impartial, evenhanded, °fair, °just, °objective, unbiased, °unprejudiced, °equitable, °dispassionate, °disinterested —*n.* **3** °independent, °neutral, mugwump

nonplus *v.* confound, °perplex, °puzzle, °confuse, °dismay, baffle, °stop, °check, °stun, °shock, dumbfound *or* dumfound, °take aback, °astonish, °astound, *US* faze, *Colloq* bring up short, °flummox, °stump

nonproductive *adj.* **1** unproductive, °barren, °sterile, °infertile, unfertile, unfruitful, infecund **2** °ineffectual, °bootless, °ineffective, °impractical, unavailing, °pointless, °useless, °worthless, °wasteful, time-consuming, time-wasting

nonsense *n.* **1** °rubbish, °drivel, °gibberish, gobbledegook *or* gobbledygook, twaddle, °trash, °babble, balderdash, °moonshine, °bombast, fustian, rodomontade, puffery, flummery, blather *or* blether, bunkum, poppycock, stuff and nonsense, double-talk, °jargon, °mumbo jumbo, jabberwocky, cackle, gas, °palaver, *Colloq* bunk, piffle, °rot, bosh, eyewash, hogwash, malarkey *or* malarky, bilge (water), baloney *or* boloney, claptrap, °hot air, *Brit* tosh, *Old-fashioned Brit* gammon, °waffle, *US* applesauce, horsefeathers, °garbage, bushwa; *Slang* crap, tripe, bull, hooey, double Dutch, *Brit* (a load of old) cobbler's, *Taboo slang* bullshit, horseshit **2** °mischief, clowning, antics, capering, horseplay, pranks, tricks, jokes, silliness, foolishness, inanity, frivolity, tomfoolery, joking, jesting, waggishness, buffoonery, shenanigans, *Colloq* monkeybusiness, *Brit* monkey tricks, *US* monkeyshines

nonsensical *adj.* °senseless, °meaningless, °absurd, °ridiculous, °ludicrous, laughable, °preposterous, irrational, warped, askew, °crazy, °mad, °silly, °foolish, °harebrained, asinine, idiotic, moronic, imbecilic, °stupid, °dumb, *Colloq* nutty, screwy, cockeyed, °fool, screwball, *Slang* loony

nonstop *adj.* **1** uninterrupted, °continuous, unbroken, °direct **2** unending, °endless, interminable, unceasing, ceaseless, °continual, °continuous, uninterrupted, unbroken, °persistent, °relentless, °constant, unremitting, °steady, round-the-clock, °ongoing, continuing, °unhesitating, unfaltering, °tireless; °regular, °habitual —*adv.* **3** unendingly, endlessly, interminably, unceasingly, ceaselessly, continually, continuously, uninterruptedly, persistently, relentlessly, constantly, unremittingly, steadily, round-the-clock, day-in and day-out, tirelessly; regularly, habitually

nook *n.* **1** °cranny, °recess, °niche, alcove, corner, °cavity, °crevice, °crack, °opening **2** °retreat, hide-out, °hideaway, °nest; inglenook

noon *n.* twelve o'clock (noon), °midday, 1200 hours, noontime, high noon, *Archaic* noontide; noonday

norm *n.* 1 °usual, °average, °mean, °normal 2 °model, °standard, °type, °pattern, criterion, °rule, °measure, °gauge, °yardstick, bench mark

normal *adj.* 1 °standard, °regular, °average, °conventional, °usual, °run-of-the-mill, °ordinary, °routine, °universal, °general, °common, °customary, °natural, °typical, conformist, °orthodox; °healthy 2 °sane, °stable, °rational, °reasonable, well-adjusted

normalize *v.* regularize, °standardize, °regulate, °control; °conform

nosy *adj.* nosey, °curious, °inquisitive, prying, meddlesome, °spying, peeping, eavesdropping, *Colloq* snooping, snoopy

notable *adj.* 1 °noteworthy, °noted, °famous, famed, °well-known, °renowned, °illustrious, °important, °prominent, °eminent, °outstanding, °great, °distinguished, °celebrated, acclaimed 2 °remarkable, °different, °distinctive, °singular, °unusual, uncommon, °preeminent, °peerless, °matchless, unmatched, unequaled, °unparalleled, °extraordinary, °conspicuous, °outstanding, °memorable, unforgettable, °striking —*n.* 3 °dignitary, °personage, °worthy, VIP; °celebrity, luminary, *Colloq* °(big) name, big shot

notably *adv.* 1 °particularly, °especially, markedly, noticeably, signally, distinctly, remarkably, unusually, uncommonly, outstandingly, conspicuously, °clearly, °obviously, °evidently, °manifestly, specifically, distinctly, curiously, oddly, uniquely, strangely, strikingly, shockingly, surprisingly, stunningly 2 meaningfully, significantly, importantly, prominently

notation *n.* 1 °note, °memorandum, jotting, °record, °reminder, minute(s), °abstract, *Colloq* memo 2 symbols, signs, °code, characters, symbolism

notch *n.* 1 °nick, °cut, dent, °indentation, °groove, cleft, °score, °mark, °gouge, °gash 2 °step, °grade, °level, rung, °peg, °degree, °stage, gradation —*v.* 3 °nick, °cut, dent, indent, °groove, °score, °mark, °gash, °gouge 4 ***notch up.*** °gain, °win, °accomplish, °achieve, °score, °register, °mark (up)

notched *adj.* serrate(d), saw-tooth(ed), crenelate(d), crenate, serriform, pinked, scalloped, zigzag, toothed, dentate, denticulate(d), dentiform

note *n.* 1 See **notation, 1,** above. 2 °message, °letter, communication, (piece of) correspondence, °memorandum, epistle, postcard *or* (postal) card, fan letter, °love letter, billet-doux, bread-and-butter letter, °word, °line, thank-you note, *Colloq* memo, *US old-fashioned* mash note 3 °comment, commentary, °remark, °observation, °explanation, annotation, footnote, side note, marginalia (*pl.*), °gloss, critique, °criticism, *Literary* scholium, exegesis, eisegesis, *Technical* shoulder note 4 banknote, °money, °bill, currency, treasury note; promissory note, demand note, bill of exchange, letter of credit, °(bank) draft, note of hand; *Colloq* folding money 5 °theme, °characteristic, °motif, °element, °quality, °mood, °tone, °tenor 6 °signal, °cue, intimation, °hint, °inkling, °suspicion, °clue, °suggestion, °idea, °tip, *Slang* tip-off 7 °heed, °attention, °notice, °regard, °respect, °thought, *Colloq US* °mind 8 °mark, consequence, °substance, °importance, °moment, °weight, °distinction, °merit, °prestige, (high) rank *or* standing, eminence, °prominence, repute, °reputation, °renown 9 °tone, °sound; °key 10 ***notes.*** jottings, impressions, record(s), °report, (thumbnail) sketch, °(rough) draft, °outline, °synopsis —*v.* 11 °notice, °observe, °perceive, °see, °mark, °think about, give thought to, °consider, °contemplate, °study, pay attention to, °attend to; °look into, °investigate, °check out 12 °record, °register, °write down, put *or* set down, put on record, °jot down, put in writing, °chronicle 13 call attention to, remark on *or* about, °mention, °report, °touch on, comment on *or* about

noted *adj.* respected, °eminent, °distinguished, °illustrious, esteemed, acclaimed; °well-known, °famous, famed, °prominent, °celebrated, °notable, °popular; °notorious

noteworthy *adj.* °notable, of note, °exceptional, °extraordinary, out-of-the-ordinary, °unusual, °rare, uncommon, °singular, °unique, °different

nothing *n.* 1 °nought, nothing at all *or* whatsoever, no thing, not anything, *Taboo slang Brit* bugger-all, (sweet) fanny adams *or* f.a. *or* FA, SFA, fuck-all 2 cipher, °zero, °nobody, nonentity 3 °trifle, bagatelle, *Colloq* peanuts

notice *v.* 1 °note, take *or* make note (of), take notice (of), pay *or* give attention to, °attend (to), °heed, take heed (of), give heed to, °mark, °remark, °mind, °observe, °perceive, °see 2 °mind, °observe, °perceive, discern, °see, °detect, °make out, °identify, °recognize, *Colloq* °spot —*n.* 3 °attention, awareness, consciousness, °perception, °observation, °cognizance 4 °regard, °consideration, °respect, °observation, °attention, °note, °heed 5 notification, °announcement, °information, °advice; °warning, °bulletin, °poster, intimation 6 °criticism, critique, °review, °comment, commentary 7 ***give notice.*** °warn, admonish, °notify, °announce, °advise, °inform

noticeable *adj.* 1 °discernible, perceivable, °observable, °perceptible, recognizable, distinguishable, °visible, palpable, °manifest, °distinct, °evident, °clear, clear-cut, °conspicuous, °obvious; °patent, unmistakable *or* unmistakeable, °undisguised, unconcealed 2 °noteworthy, °notable, °significant, °signal, °remarkable, °important, °singular, °exceptional, °pronounced, °distinct, especial, °considerable, °major

notify *v.* 1 °inform, °tell, °advise, °alert, apprise, °warn 2 °announce, °publish, °declare, °proclaim, give notice of; °intimate, °hint

notion *n.* 1 °idea, °thought, concept, °conception, °image, °impression, general idea, °(mental) picture, °inkling 2 °fancy, whim, crotchet, whimsy, caprice, impulse, °inclination, vagary, °conceit, °quirk, °kink

notoriety *n.* notoriousness, disrepute, °dishonor, °disgrace, °infamy, °shame, °discredit, °scandal, °stain, °blot, obloquy, ignominy, opprobrium

notorious *adj.* 1 °disreputable, °dishonorable, °disgraceful, °infamous, °shameful, shaming, °embarrassing, discreditable, °scandalous, °naughty, °flagrant, ignominious, opprobrious 2 °celebrated, °renowned, °famous, °well-known, fabled, °legendary, °memorable

notwithstanding *adv.* 1 °nevertheless, °nonetheless, despite that, in spite of that, °yet, anyway —*prep.* 2 °despite, °in spite of, °regardless of, °in the face of, against —*conj.* 3 although, °though, °even though, despite the fact that

nought See **naught.**

nourish *v.* 1 °feed, °sustain, °support, °maintain, °keep, °provide for, °care for, °take care of, °look after, nurture, °nurse 2 °foster, °cherish, °nurse, °maintain, °harbor, °keep, nurture, °sustain 3 °strengthen, °fortify, °encourage, °promote, °stimulate, °cultivate, °help, °advance, °aid

nourishment *n.* °food, °sustenance, nutriment, nutrition, victuals

novel *adj.* 1 °new, °unusual, °unfamiliar, unconventional, °fresh, °different, °original, °creative; untested, °untried —*n.* 2 °story, °tale, °narrative, °romance; novella, novelette, bestseller, *Colloq* blockbuster

novelty *n.* 1 °originality, newness, uniqueness, freshness, innovativeness 2 °gimmick, gimcrack, °trifle, °gewgaw, °bauble, knickknack, °toy, trinket, °ornament, °plaything, brummagem, kickshaw

novice *n.* beginner, neophyte, °newcomer, proselyte, tiro *or* tyro, novitiate *or* noviciate, °learner, °amateur, °initiate, °apprentice, trainee, probationer, fledgling *or Brit also* fledgeling, *US* freshman, *Colloq* °greenhorn, rookie

now *adv.* 1 °at present, just now, right now, at the present time *or* moment, at this (very) moment *or* minute *or* second *or* instant 2 these days, °nowadays, today, in these times, at the moment, in this day and age, under *or* in the present circumstances *or* conditions, in the present climate, things being what they are, contemporarily, any more, any longer; °for the time being, for the nonce 3 °at once, °immediately, right away, without delay, instantly, °promptly, *Chiefly law* instanter, *Chiefly Brit* °straightaway 4 ***now and then*** *or* ***again.*** °occasionally, from time to time, °at times, °on occasion, °sometimes, sporadically, °once in a while, every now and then *or* again, randomly, intermittently; °infrequently, °seldom, °rarely, once in a blue moon —*adj.* 5 °contemporary, up-to-date, °modern, °stylish, °fashionable, °trendy, *Colloq* in, with it

nowadays *adv.* See **now, 2,** above.

nub *n.* 1 °projection, protuberance, °knob, °boss, °lump, °bump, knop, °protrusion, °bulge, node, °knot; excrescence, °swelling, tumescence 2 °essence, °core, °heart, °nucleus, crux, °point, °gist, °pith, °kernel, °meat, °(sum and) substance, main issue, gravamen

nuclear *adj.* atomic

nucleus *n.* °core, °heart, °center, °kernel, °pith, °focus, °nub

nude *adj.* unclothed, undressed, uncovered, ***au naturel,*** °bare, °naked, in the nude, stark-naked, undraped, without a stitch (on), *Colloq* in the buff, in the altogether, in one's birthday suit, mother naked, *Brit* starkers, *Brit and Australian* in the nuddy

nudge *v.* 1 °jog, °poke, elbow, °jab, °dig, °bump, °prompt, shove; °prod, °push, *US* °encourage —*n.* 2 °jog, °poke, elbow, °jab, °dig, °bump, shove; °prod, °push, °encouragement

nuisance *n.* 1 °annoyance, °inconvenience, °trial, °ordeal, °burden, irritation, irritant, thorn in the flesh *or* side, °difficulty, °bother, *US* bur under the saddle, *Colloq* pain (in the neck *or* rear), °headache, hassle, *Slang* pain in the *US* ass *or Brit* arse, *US and Canadian* pain in the butt 2 °bore, °pest, °nag, °tease, tormentor

numb *adj.* 1 numbed, benumbed, °insensible, insensate, °dead, deadened, without feeling, sensationless, °senseless; asleep —*v.* 2 benumb, anesthetize, °drug, °deaden, °dull, °freeze, °paralyze, immobilize, °stun

number *n.* 1 numeral, integer, °figure, digit 2 °few, °handful, °crowd, slew, °gang, °bunch, °party, bevy, covey, troop, °company, °platoon, °swarm, horde, multitude, °mob, °host, army, °mass, hundred, thousand, million, billion; °several, °many, numbers, legions, *US and Canadian* slew(s) *or* slue(s), *Colloq* loads, tons 3 °issue; °edition, °copy —*v.* 4 °count, °enumerate, °compute, °calculate, °tally, °figure (up), °add (up), °include, °total, °tot (up), °reckon, °sum (up)

numberless *adj.* uncountable, uncounted, countless, innumerable, incalculable, °immeasurable, numerous, °untold, myriad, °infinite

nuptial *adj.* °bridal, °matrimonial, °wedding, spousal, °wedded, marital; connubial, conjugal, *Literary* hymeneal

nurse *n.* 1 angel of mercy, Florence Nightingale, *Brit* sister —*v.* 2 °care for, °look after, °tend, °attend, °minister to, °treat; nurture, °foster, °coddle, °baby, °pamper, °cherish, °preserve, keep alive, °cultivate, °develop 3 wet-nurse, suckle, breast-feed, °nourish 4 °preserve, °harbor, keep alive, nurture, °foster

nutritious *adj.* healthful, °healthy, nutritive, °wholesome, life-giving, °beneficial, salutary, nourishing, alimentary, nutrimental

O

oar *n.* **1** °paddle, scull **2** oarsman, oarswoman, bencher, sculler, rower, paddler

oasis *n.* **1** fertile patch, watering hole **2** haven, °refuge, °(safe) harbor, °sanctuary, °retreat, asylum, °resort, °sanctum

oath *n.* **1** °vow, avowal, °pledge, °promise, °word (of honor), °plight, guarantee *or* guaranty, warrant *or* warranty, °(sworn) statement, *Archaic* troth **2** °curse, °profanity, blasphemous language *or* expression *or* word, imprecation, malediction, swearword, °expletive, four-letter word, obscenity, dirty word

obedience *n.* compliance, dutifulness, °observance, °respect, respectfulness, tractability, conformity *or* conformance, °yielding, conformability, adaptability, °agreement, agreeability, agreeableness, acquiescence, submissiveness, °submission, subservience, docility, passiveness, passivity

obedient *adj.* compliant, °dutiful, duteous, °observant, °respectful, °tractable, °yielding, conformable, °adaptable, °agreeable, amenable, acquiescent, °submissive, subservient, docile, °passive, °timid, biddable, pliant

obeisance *n.* °deference, °respect, respectfulness, °homage, °submission, °reverence, °honor

obese *adj.* °fat, overweight, °stout, fleshy, °gross, corpulent, °heavy, °plump, portly, tubby, pudgy, °chubby, paunchy, °rotund, potbellied, *Rare* abdominous

obesity *n.* corpulence, plumpness, tubbiness, chubbiness, grossness, *embonpoint*, rotundity, portliness, paunchiness, °size, °bulk, °weight, avoirdupois

obey *v.* **1** °comply (with), °agree (to), °consent (to), °submit (to), °abide (by), °observe, °respect, adhere to, °follow, conform (to *or* with), acquiesce (to *or* in), °mind, °accept, °heed, defer to, °yield (to), knuckle under (to), °give way (to), °surrender (to), °succumb (to), °give in (to), truckle to, bow to, bend to, take *or* accept orders from **2** °discharge, °execute, °effect, °carry out, °fulfill, °meet, °satisfy, do, °perform; °serve, °act

obituary *n.* necrology, death notice, °eulogy, necrologue, *Colloq* obit

object *n.* **1** °thing, °tangible, °item; °reality, °entity, °fact, °phenomenon **2** °focus, °target, °butt, °aim, °destination, °quarry, °goal **3** °purpose, °end, °intention, °objective, °reason, °intent, °idea, °goal —*v.* **4** protest (to *or* against), °interfere (with), raise objections (to), °argue (against), °oppose, be against, take exception (to), °disapprove (of), draw the line (at), °complain (about), remonstrate (over *or* about), take a stand (against), °refuse

objection *n.* °protest, °opposition, °exception, °argument, °challenge, °interference, demur *or* demurral *or* demurrer, °question, °doubt, °disapproval, °complaint, remonstration, remonstrance, °stand, °refusal, °dislike, antipathy

objective *adj.* **1** °fair, °impartial, °just, °judicious, °equitable, °neutral, °disinterested, °dispassionate, openhanded, open-minded, °detached, unbiased, °unprejudiced, unbigoted, evenhanded, uncolored, unjaundiced —*n.* **2** °target, °goal, °object, °aim, °purpose, °end (in view), °intent, °intention, °design, °aspiration, °ambition, °hope

objectivity *n.* impartiality, fairness, fairmindedness, equitableness, equitability, evenhandedness, neutrality, disinterest, °detachment, °indifference, dispassion

obligate *n.* °oblige, °pledge, °commit, °bind; °require, compel, constrain, °force

obligation *n.* **1** °responsibility, °duty, °charge, °burden, onus; °accountability, °liability, °trust; °demand, °requirement, compulsion, *Literary* devoir **2** constraint, °requirement, °contract, °promise, °pledge, °bond, °agreement, covenant **3** °debt, °liability

obligatory *adj.* required, demanded, °necessary, requisite, compulsory, °mandatory; °incumbent; °indispensable, °essential

oblige *v.* **1** °accommodate, °indulge, °favor, serve, please, °cater to, °gratify **2** °make, °require, °demand, °force, compel, coerce, °bind, °obligate

obliged *adj.* **1** °thankful, °grateful, appreciative, °beholden, °indebted, obligated **2** °bound, required, compelled, °forced, made, obligated

obliging *adj.* °accommodating, °willing, °indulgent, °gracious, °courteous, °civil, °considerate, °polite, °agreeable, amenable, °kind, °kindly, °helpful, °friendly, °amiable, °neighborly, °supportive

oblique *adj.* **1** slanting, slanted, sloping, aslant, °inclined, diagonal, inclining, angled, angling, canted, canting, banked, banking, cambered, °crooked, askew, °divergent, diverging, tilted, atilt, tilting **2** awry, °devious, °roundabout, °indirect, circuitous, circumlocutionary, °evasive, °sly, °sidelong, °offhand, °surreptitious, furtive, implied, clandestine, underhand(ed), °deceitful, °devious, °deceptive, °false

obliterate *v.* **1** °erase, expunge, °rub out, efface, eradicate, °wipe out, °delete, dele, strike off *or* out, °strike from, °rule out, °eliminate, °write off **2** annihilate, °destroy, °kill, °exterminate, °wipe out, °eliminate, °blot out, eradicate, extirpate

oblivion *n.* **1** blankness, blackness, darkness, °obscurity, nothingness, nihility, anonymity, extinction, nonexistence, °void, °limbo **2** unawareness, obliviousness, forgetfulness, heedlessness, °disregard, unconsciousness, insensibility

oblivious *adj.* °unaware, °unconscious, unmindful, disregardful, °insensible, insensitive, °distant, unconcerned, °detached, removed, unfeeling, abstracted, °absent-minded, °forgetful, Lethean

obnoxious *adj.* °revolting, °repulsive, °repugnant, °disgusting, °offensive, objectionable, fulsome, noisome, °vile, °repellent, °nauseous, nauseating, sickening, °foul, noxious, mephitic, °unsavory, execrable, °abominable, °abhorrent, °loathsome, detestable, °hateful, odious, °scurvy, °base, °obscene, °despicable, °awful, °terrible, °unpalatable, °distasteful, unlikable, unpleasant, °nasty, *Colloq chiefly Brit* °beastly

obscene *adj.* **1** inelegant, °improper, °rude, °impure, °unchaste, °shameless, °shameful, °indecent, °immodest, °off-color, indecorous, indelicate, °risqué, °vulgar, °immoral, °degenerate, amoral, °dissolute, °broad, °suggestive, °erotic, °sensual, ribald, debauched, °wanton, °loose, °libertine, °bawdy, °blue, scabrous, °coarse, °dirty, °filthy, smutty, °pornographic, libidinous, °lewd, licentious, °lecherous, °lustful, goatish, °carnal, ruttish, °lascivious, °filthy, salacious, °prurient, °disgusting, °offensive, °repulsive, °foul, °abominable, °vile, °loathsome, °gross, foul-mouthed, °scurrilous, scatological, *Literary* Cyprian, Paphian, Fescennine, thersitical **2** °evil, °wicked, heinous, °atrocious, °awful, °outrageous, °repulsive, °shocking, °repellent, °obnoxious, off-putting, objectionable, °beastly, intolerable, °insufferable, °unpalatable, °distasteful, °nauseous, nauseating, sickening, execrable, °despicable, °nasty

obscure *adj.* **1** °dark, unlit, °gloomy, °somber, °dismal, °murky, °dusky, °black, Cimmerian, tenebrous, °dim, °faint, blurred, °veiled, °shadowy, subfusc, subfuscous, umbral, °shady, °hazy, foggy, befogged, clouded, °nebulous, °overcast, cloudy **2** unclear, °uncertain, °ambiguous, °vague, °hazy, °doubtful, dubious, °equivocal, °indefinite, °indistinct, °fuzzy, blurred, °confused, confusing, delphic, °puzzling, enigmatic, °perplexing, baffling, mystifying, °mysterious, °cryptic, °incomprehensible, °unfamiliar, °foreign, °strange **3** °secret, concealed, °hidden, °remote, °out-of-the-way, °inconspicuous, unnoticeable, °secluded, °unnoticed **4** °unknown, °unheard-of, anonymous, unnamed, °insignificant, unimportant, °inconsequential, °humble, °lowly, °mean, inglorious, °inconspicuous, °undistinguished, °unnoticed, °unsung, °minor, little-known **5** abstruse, arcane, °recondite, esoteric, °intricate, complex, °occult, out-of-the-ordinary, °unfamiliar, *Colloq* far-out —*v.* **6** °cover, °conceal, °hide, °veil, °shroud, °cloak, °mask, °screen, °disguise, °keep from **7** °dim, bedim, cloud, becloud, °dull, °shroud, °shade, adumbrate, °overshadow, darken, obfuscate, °block, °eclipse

obscurity *n.* **1** dimness, darkness, °gloom, murk, murkiness, duskiness, °dusk, blackness, faintness, blurriness, °shade, °shadow, haze, °fog, cloudiness, nebulousness **2** abstruseness, ambiguousness, intricacy, °complexity, unintelligibility; °mystery, arcanum, °secret, esoterica (*pl.*) **3** insignificance, unimportance, ingloriousness, inconspicuousness, anonymity, namelessness, °limbo

obsequious *adj.* °low, cringing, toadying, toadyish, sycophantic(al), sycophantish, unctuous, truckling, °groveling, crawling, fawning, deferential, °ingratiating, °menial, °flattering, °servile, slavish, subservient, °submissive, abject, °mealy-mouthed, °slimy, *Colloq* boot-licking, *Chiefly Brit* smarmy, *Taboo slang* brown-nosing, *Brit* arse-kissing, arse-licking, *US* ass-licking, ass-kissing

observable *adj.* °perceptible, perceivable, °noticeable, °discernible, recognizable, detectable, °visible, °apparent, °distinct, °evident, °manifest, °plain, °obvious, °clear, °explicit, °transparent, °patent, °tangible, unmistakable *or* unmistakeable

observance *n.* **1** °observation, observing, °obedience, obeying, compliance, complying, conformity, conforming, adherence, adhering, keeping, accordance, °regard, °recognition, recognizing, °respect, respecting, °heed, heeding, °attention **2** °ceremony, °celebration, °ceremonial, °practice, °rite, °ritual, °service, °performance, °form, °custom, °convention, °tradition, °formality, °usage, °habit, wont, °institution **3** °observation, °examination, inspection, °scrutiny, looking, watching

observant *adj.* **1** watchful, °alert, °attentive, °vigilant, on the lookout, on the qui vive, on guard, wide-awake, regardful, °mindful, °aware, °keen, keen-eyed, °sharp-eyed, °eagle-eyed, °perceptive, °sharp, °shrewd **2** Usually, ***observant of.*** °obedient (to), compliant (with), °respectful (of), heedful (of), attentive (to *or* of), conformist (to), adherent (to)

observation *n.* **1** watching, °examination, °scrutiny, inspection, viewing, °survey, °surveillance; °notice, °discovery, °attention, awareness **2** °comment, °remark, °note, °reflection, °opinion, °sentiment, °point of view, °impression, °feeling, commentary, °criticism; utterance, °word, °announcement, °pronouncement, °proclamation, °declaration

observe *v.* **1** °obey, °abide by, comply with, be heedful of, °attend to, conform to, °regard, °keep, °follow, adhere to, °respect, pay attention to **2** °watch, °look at, °examine, °monitor, °scrutinize, °study, °regard, °view, °inspect, °pore over, °contemplate, °consider, *Colloq* check (out *or* up on), check over, °size up, *Slang* °case **3** °see, °mark, °notice, °look, °perceive **4** Sometimes, ***observe on or upon.*** comment (on *or* upon), remark (on *or* upon), °mention, °say, °note, °refer (to), make reference to, animadvert on *or* upon *or* to; °state, °declare **5** °celebrate, °keep, solemnize, °respect, keep holy, °mark, °commemorate, °memorialize, °remember, °recognize

observer *n.* °witness, °eyewitness, °spectator, viewer, °onlooker, beholder, watcher, looker-on; nonparticipant

obsess *v.* °haunt, °harass, °plague, bedevil, °torment, °take over, preoccupy, °dominate, °control, °grip, °possess, °hold

obsession *n.* fixed idea, *idée fixe*, °fixation, °conviction, preoccupation, prepossession, °passion, °mania, °phobia, *Colloq* hang-up, °thing

obsessive *adj.* haunting, harassing, tormenting, dominating, controlling, possessing, all-encompassing, °passionate, unshakable *or* unshakeable

obsolescent *adj.* fading, waning, °on the wane, declining, °dying, on the way out, on the decline, going *or* passing out of use *or* fashion *or* style

obsolete *adj.* °out of date, out of fashion, out-dated, °passé, °out, °dead, outmoded, °old, °antiquated, antediluvian, °ancient, superannuated, dated, archaic, °old-fashioned, *démodé*; °unused, °disused, discarded, superseded, °extinct, *Colloq* old hat

obstacle *n.* °impediment, °hindrance, °obstruction, °hurdle, °hitch, °catch, °snag, °stumbling block, °barrier, °bar, °check

obstinacy *n.* obstinateness, stubbornness, doggedness, °tenacity, persistence *or* persistency, mulishness, pigheadedness, willfulness, contrariness, perverseness, perversity, cantankerousness, recalcitrance, uncooperativeness, rebelliousness, contumacy, contumaciousness, refractoriness, intractability, intransigence, pertinacity, pertinaciousness, obduracy, fixedness, stolidity, inflexibility, firmness, *Archaic* frowardness, *Colloq Brit* bloody-mindedness

obstinate *adj.* °stubborn, dogged, °tenacious, °persistent, mulish, °perverse, headstrong, pigheaded, °single-minded, °willful, strong-willed, °self-willed, °contrary, °recalcitrant, uncooperative, °rebellious, contumacious, refractory, intransigent, pertinacious, obdurate, °fixed, °inflexible, °stony, adamant, °set, unmoving, °immovable, inexorable, intractable, unchangeable, °resolute, °steadfast, unyielding, persevering, °stiff, °rigid, °hard, *Archaic* froward, *Colloq Brit* bloody-minded

obstreperous *adj.* vociferous, clamorous, °noisy, °loud, °raucous, °riotous, °uproarious, °tumultuous, °boisterous, °rowdy, rumbustious, °tempestuous, °unruly, °disorderly, unmanageable, uncontrollable, °uncontrolled, unrestrained, irrepressible, out of control, °undisciplined, roisterous, °wild, turbulent, *Colloq* rambunctious, *Brit* mafficking

obstruct *v.* **1** °block, °bar, °check, °prevent, °stop (up), °arrest, °halt, °clog, make impassable; bring to a standstill **2** °hamper, °slow, °impede, interfere with, °retard, °hinder, °interrupt, °delay, °stay, °stall **3** °preclude, °prevent, debar, °block, °prohibit, °forbid, °stop, stand in the way of

obstruction *n.* **1** °obstacle, °barrier, °bar, °check, °stumbling block, °hindrance, °impediment, °hurdle, °hitch, °snag, °catch, bottleneck, limitation, constraint, °restriction **2** checking, stopping, cessation, proscription, °forbidding, forbiddance; hindering, impeding, limiting, °halting, slowing

obtain *v.* **1** °get, °procure, °acquire, °come by, come into (the) possession of, °secure, get hold of *or* one's hands on, °grasp, °capture, °take possession of, °seize; °buy, °purchase **2** °earn, °gain **3** °prevail, be in force, be in vogue, °exist, subsist, have (a) place, be prevalent, be established, be customary, °apply, be relevant, °relate

obtrude *v.* thrust (oneself) forward *or* forth, °intrude, °impose (oneself), °force (oneself)

obtrusive *adj.* interfering, °intrusive, meddling, °officious, meddlesome, importunate, °forward, °presumptuous, °forceful, *Colloq* °pushy

obtuse *adj.* **1** rounded, unpointed, °blunt **2** °dull, insensitive, unfeeling, imperceptive, °thick-skinned, °stolid, °thick, °dense, doltish, cloddish, thickheaded, dull-witted, dimwitted, slow-witted, (mentally) retarded, boneheaded, lumpish, loutish, oafish, °simple, simple-minded

obvious *adj.* °clear, °plain, °apparent, °patent, °perceptible, °evident, °self-evident, °barefaced, clear-cut, °manifest, palpable, (much) in evidence, °conspicuous, °open, °visible, °overt, ostensible, °pronounced, °prominent, °glaring, undeniable, unconcealed, unhidden, unsubtle, °distinct, °simple, bald, bald-faced, straightforward, °direct, self-explanatory, °indisputable, unmistakable *or* unmistakeable

obviously *adv.* °clearly, plainly, °apparently, patently, °evidently, °simply, certainly, °of course, undeniable, unmistakably *or* unmistakeably, indubitably, doubtless(ly)

occasion *n.* **1** °time, °moment, °circumstance, °incident, °occurrence, °opportunity, °chance, °opening, °advantage **2** °reason, °cause, °call, justification, ground(s), °warrant, °provocation, prompting, impulse, stimulus, °incitement, °inducement **3** °event, °function, °happening, °affair, °observance, commemoration, °ceremony, °celebration, °gala, °party **4** ***on occasion.*** See **occasionally,** below. *—v.* **5** °give rise to, °bring about, °cause, °bring on, °effect, °prompt, °provoke, °evoke, °call forth, °elicit, °call up, °induce, impel, °create, °generate, engender, °produce, °make (for)

occasional *adj.* **1** °intermittent, °irregular, °periodic, °random, °sporadic, infrequent, °casual, °incidental **2** additional, °extra, °spare, °supplementary, °incidental, °auxiliary, °accessory **3** °special, °particular, °ceremonial, °ritual

occasionally *adv.* °sometimes, °on occasion, °(every) now and then, from time to time, °at times, °(every) now and again, °once in a while, every so often, periodically, intermittently, sporadically, irregularly, off and on

occult *adj.* 1 °secret, °dark, concealed, °private, °privy, °hidden, °obscure, °veiled, obscured, shrouded, °vague, abstruse, °shadowy, °mystical, °mysterious, cabalistic, esoteric, °recondite, arcane 2 magical, °mystical, alchemic(al), unexplained, unexplainable, °inexplicable, °puzzling, baffling, °perplexing, mystifying, °mysterious, °incomprehensible, inscrutable, indecipherable, impenetrable, unfathomable, transcendental, °supernatural, preternatural, mystic —*n.* 3 Usually, ***the occult.*** the supernatural, the unknown, the black arts; arcana, cabbala *or* cabala *or* kabbala *or* kabala; cabbalism, occultism, °sorcery, witchcraft, black magic

occupant *n.* °resident, °inhabitant, occupier, °tenant, lessee, leaseholder, renter, °owner, householder, indweller, dweller, °denizen, lodger, roomer, boarder; addressee; °incumbent

occupation *n.* 1 °job, °position, °post, °situation, °appointment, °employment, °vocation, °line (of work), °career, °field, °calling, °trade, métier, °craft, °skill, °profession, °business, °work 2 °possession, °tenure, occupancy, °rule, °control, suzerainty, subjugation, °subjection, °oppression, °bondage 3 °conquest, °seizure, appropriation, takeover

occupy *v.* 1 °capture, °seize, °take possession of, °conquer, invade, °take over, °overrun, garrison, °dominate, °hold 2 live *or* reside *or* dwell in, °tenant, be established *or* ensconced *or* situated in, establish *or* ensconce *or* situate oneself in, °inhabit, be settled in *or* into, settle in *or* into, take up residence in, make one's home in, move in *or* into; be located in 3 °engage, °busy, absorb, °monopolize, °hold, take up *or* over, °catch, °grab, °seize, °grip; °divert, °amuse, °entertain, °distract, °beguile, preoccupy, hold (someone's) attention, °interest, engross, °involve 4 fill (in *or* up), °take up, °cover, extend over, °consume, °use (up), *Colloq* eat up

occur *v.* 1 °happen, °take place, °arise, °come about, befall, °come to pass, °chance, °appear, °surface, °materialize, °develop, become manifest, manifest itself, *Colloq* °transpire, crop up, °come off, °turn up 2 ***occur to.*** °dawn on, °strike, °hit, °come to, suggest itself to, cross (someone's) mind, enter (someone's) head, be brought to (someone's) attention

occurrence *n.* 1 °happening, °event, °incident, °phenomenon, °affair, °matter, °experience 2 °existence, °instance, °manifestation, materialization, °appearance, °development 3 frequency, °incidence, °rate; °likelihood, °chance

ocean *n.* 1 °(deep blue) sea, °(bounding) main, high seas, °the deep, Davy Jones's locker, the depths, *Colloq* the briny, °the drink 2 Often, ***oceans.*** °flood, °abundance, multitude, °profusion, plethora, *Colloq* scads, loads, tons, lots, oodles, gobs, zillions

oceanic *adj.* °marine, pelagic, thalassic; saltwater, deep-water, aquatic, maritime, °sea, °ocean

odd *adj.* 1 °strange, °peculiar, °unusual, uncommon, °different, unexpected, °unfamiliar, °extraordinary, °remarkable, atypical, untypical, °exotic, °out of the ordinary, °unparalleled, unconventional, °exceptional, °unique, °singular, °individual, anomalous, idiosyncratic, °rare, °deviant, °outlandish, uncanny, °queer, °curious, °bizarre, °weird, °eccentric, °funny, °quaint, °fantastic, °freak, °abnormal, freakish, *Colloq* °offbeat, screwy, °kinky, freaky, *Slang Brit* °bent, rum, *US and Canadian* kooky *or* kookie 2 °occasional, °casual, part-time, °irregular, °random, °sporadic, discontinuous, °disconnected, °various, °varied, °miscellaneous, °sundry, °incidental 3 °leftover, °surplus, °remaining, °unused, °spare, °superfluous, °extra 4 uneven, unmatched, unpaired

oddity *n.* 1 °peculiarity, strangeness, unnaturalness, curiousness, incongruity, incongruousness, °eccentricity, outlandishness, extraordinariness, unconventionality, bizarreness, weirdness, queerness, oddness, unusualness, individuality, °singularity, distinctiveness, anomalousness, anomaly, *Colloq* kinkiness, *US and Canadian* kookiness 2 °peculiarity, °curiosity, °rarity, °freak, °original, °phenomenon, °character, °eccentric, °nonconformist, fish out of water, odd bird, rara avis, °misfit, square peg in a round hole, maverick, *Colloq* °card, °crank, weirdie *or* weirdo, oner, *Brit* odd fish, *US and Canadian* kook, oddball, screwball 3 °peculiarity, irregularity, anomaly, idiosyncrasy, °eccentricity, deviation, °quirk, °mannerism, °twist, °kink, crotchet

odds *n. pl.* 1 °chances, °likelihood, °probability 2 °edge, °advantage, °lead, °superiority 3 °difference, °inequality, °disparity, unevenness, °discrepancy, °dissimilarity, °distinction 4 ***at odds.*** °at variance, at loggerheads, at daggers drawn, at sixes and sevens, at cross purposes, at each other's throats, in disagreement, °in opposition, on bad terms, not in keeping, out of line, inharmonious, conflicting, clashing, disagreeing, differing 5 ***odds and ends.*** oddments, °fragments, debris, leftovers, leavings, remnants, bits (and pieces), particles, shreds, snippets, °scraps, °rubbish, °litter, *Colloq Brit* odds and sods

odor *n.* 1 °smell, °scent, °aroma, °bouquet, °fragrance, °perfume, redolence; °stench, stink, fetor *or* foetor 2 °air, °breath, °hint, °suggestion, °atmosphere, °spirit, °quality, °flavor, °savor, °aura, °tone

off *adv.* 1 away, °out, °elsewhere 2 °distant, away, afar, far off —*adj.* 3 °incorrect, °wrong, °inaccurate, °in error, °mistaken, °misguided, misled, off the mark 4 °mad, °insane, °crazy, °eccentric, touched (in the head), *Colloq* dotty, dippy, nutty, potty 5 °remote, °distant, °improbable, °unlikely 6 off work, °at leisure, °idle, °free, °open 7 °sour, °moldy, °bad, °rotten, °rancid, turned,

°high **8** °bad, unpropitious, °disappointing, °unsatisfactory, disheartening, displeasing, °slack, °slow, substandard, °below par, below average, °quiet **9** canceled, postponed **10** situated, °fixed, supplied

offbeat *adj.* °strange, °eccentric, °bizarre, °weird, °peculiar, °odd, °queer, unconventional, °unorthodox, bohemian, idiosyncratic, °unusual, unexpected, °outré, °outlandish, °deviant, °novel, innovative, *Colloq* °kinky, °way-out, far-out, off the wall, freaky, °weirdo

off-color *adj.* **1** unwell, °ill, off form, °out of sorts, °queasy, °sick, °run down, °awful, °seedy, *Colloq* °under the weather, °poorly, *Slang* °lousy, °rotten **2** indelicate, °risqué, ribald, °bawdy, °indecent, °suggestive, °broad, indelicate, inelegant, °improper, °inappropriate, °unseemly, °blue

offend *v.* **1** hurt (someone's) feelings, affront, °insult, °slight, snub, °give offense, °hurt, °pain, displease, disgruntle, chagrin, °humiliate, °embarrass; pique, °fret, °gall, vex, °annoy, °irritate, nettle, needle, °rankle, °provoke, °ruffle, °outrage, rile, °anger, *Colloq* miff, put (someone's) back up, put (someone's) nose out of joint, tread *or* step on (someone's) toes, put (someone) out, °rattle **2** °disgust, °sicken, turn (someone's) stomach, °nauseate, °repel, °repulse, °revolt, *Colloq* turn (someone) off

offender *n.* °criminal, malefactor, lawbreaker, °outlaw, wrongdoer, °culprit, °miscreant, °transgressor, °sinner, evildoer, *Slang* crook

offense *n.* **1** °violation, °breach, °crime, felony, misdemeanor, infraction, °transgression, trespass, °wrong, wrongdoing, °sin, °peccadillo, °misdeed, °fault, °infringement, malefaction; dereliction, °lapse, °slip, °error **2** ***give offense.*** incur displeasure, create annoyance *or* irritation *or* resentment *or* pique, evoke indignation *or* anger; °slight, °injure, °hurt, °harm, °offend, °insult, °outrage, *Colloq* put (someone) down **3** ***take offense.*** take umbrage, feel displeasure *or* annoyance *or* resentment *or* pique *or* indignation, be angered *or* enraged

offensive *adj.* **1** antagonistic, °hostile, contentious, °quarrelsome, attacking, °aggressive, °threatening, °provocative, combative, °martial, °belligerent, °warlike, bellicose **2** insulting, °rude, °disrespectful, uncivil, °insolent, °discourteous, °impolite, unmannerly, °impertinent, °impudent, objectionable, displeasing **3** °disgusting, °unsavory, °unpalatable, nauseating, °nauseous, noisome, noxious, °obnoxious, °repugnant, °repulsive, °repellent, °revolting, °abominable, °foul, °loathsome, °vile, sickening, fetid *or* foetid, °rank, malodorous, mephitic, °putrid, putrescent, putrefying, °rancid, °rotten —*n.* **4** °attack, °offense **5** °attack, onslaught, °drive, °assault, °offense, °push

offer *v.* **1** proffer, °propose, °tender, °bid **2** make available, °present, °tender, put on the market, °sell, put up for sale, °put up, °furnish **3** proffer, °provide, °submit, put forward *or* forth, °advance, °tender, °extend, °make; °suggest **4** volunteer, present oneself, step *or* come forward —*n.* **5** °proposal, °bid, °tender, °offering **6** °proposal, °presentation, proffer, °proposition

offering *n.* °sacrifice, oblation, contribution, °donation, °gift, °present

offhand *adj.* **1** offhanded, °casual, °informal, °nonchalant, °cool, °distant, °aloof, easygoing, °blasé, unceremonious, °relaxed, °easy, °smooth, unconcerned, insouciant, lighthearted, uninterested, °superficial, °cursory, cavalier, °careless **2** °curt, °brusque, °abrupt, °perfunctory, °ungracious, °glib, °smooth **3** extempore, impromptu, °unpremeditated, unstudied, °extemporaneous, °informal, off the cuff, ad-lib —*adv.* **4** extempore, impromptu, extemporaneously, informally, off the cuff, ad-lib, °on the spur of the moment, at the drop of a hat **5** casually, informally, °incidentally, °by the way, offhandedly, by the bye, parenthetically, °in passing, ***en passant***, cursorily, superficially

office *n.* **1** °business, °organization, °department, °firm, °house, °establishment, °company, corporation **2** commission, °department, °branch; °section, °division **3** workplace, °offices; °room, °area **4** °duty, °obligation, °responsibility, °charge, commission, °service, °employment, °occupation, °position, °post, °appointment, °assignment, chore, °task, °job, °place, berth, °work, °role, °function, °purpose, °part, °bit, *Colloq* °thing, *Slang* shtick **5** ***offices.*** °indulgence, intermediation, °auspices, °support, advocacy, aegis, °help, °aid, intercession, mediation, °patronage, °favor, °backing, back-up

officer *n.* **1** °(public) official, °dignitary, officeholder, public servant, officebearer, (political) appointee, °(government) agent, bureaucrat, °functionary, commissioner, administrator, °manager, °director; apparatchik **2** policeman, policewoman, °police officer, officer of the law, °constable, *Old-fashioned* catchpole, *US* lawman, peace officer, G-man, T-Man, *Colloq* gendarme, *Slang* cop, copper, fuzz, *US* dick, narc, *Brit* Old Bill, tec

official *adj.* **1** authorized, °legitimate, °lawful, °legal, °authentic, °bona fide, °proper, °true, accredited, valid, documented, licensed, sanctioned, endorsed, certified, verified, recognized, accepted **2** °ceremonial, °formal, °solemn, ritualistic, °ceremonious, °pompous, °stiff, °proper, °seemly, °decorous —*n.* **3** See **officer, 1,** above.

officiate *v.* °preside, °direct, °manage, °chair, °conduct, °oversee, °head (up), °run, °lead, °supervise, superintend; °umpire, referee, °judge, adjudicate, °moderate, mediate

officious *adj.* °dictatorial, °intrusive, intruding, meddlesome, meddling, °obtrusive, °forward, °bold, interfering, °aggressive, °insistent, °persistent, °demanding, importunate

offset *v.* **1** °compensate, counterbalance, countervail, counterpoise, °counteract, °balance (out), °equalize, even (out *or* up), °square, °cancel (out), °neutralize, nullify, °make up (for), °atone (for), redress; recompense, °repay, make amends *or* restitution, °make good, °reimburse, indemnify —*n.* **2** compensation, counterbalance, counteraction, °check, equalizer, neutralizer

offshoot *n.* **1** °branch, °spur; °shoot, limb, bough, °twig, °stem, appendage, °sucker, °sprout, sprig, tendril, scion **2** °descendant, °relation, °relative, °kin, °kindred, °offspring, scion, °heir **3** outgrowth, °development, °branch, spinoff; by-product, °derivative

offspring *n.* (*Often used as plural.*) °child, °progeny, °issue, °seed, youngster, °brood, °young, successor, °heir

often *adv.* °frequently, regularly, much, many times, °usually, habitually, commonly; °ordinarily, again and again, over and over again, time after time, °repeatedly, time and (time) again, in many cases *or* instances, on numerous occasions, day in (and) day out, continually, *Literary* oftentimes, oft

ogle *v.* **1** °leer, °eye, make eyes at, *Colloq* give (someone) the glad eye, give (someone) the once-over, make sheep's eyes at **2** °gape, °gaze, goggle, °gawk, °stare, *Slang Brit* gawp *or* gaup —*n.* **3** °leer, °stare, °gape, goggle, oeillade, *Colloq* once-over, glad eye

ogre *n.* ogress, °monster, °giant, °fiend, °demon, troll, man-eater, bogey, bogeyman, bugbear, °specter, Minotaur, Cyclops, Gorgon, Caliban; °brute, sadist, °villain, cad, °scoundrel

oil *n.* **1** lubricant, grease, lubricator, unguent **2** °fuel —*v.* **3** lubricate, grease

oily *adj.* **1** °greasy, oleaginous, °fat, fatty, adipose, pinguid, sebaceous, soapy, saponaceous, buttery, butyraceous, lardaceous; °slippery, °slimy, slithery, °smooth, unctuous **2** °glib, °smooth, unctuous, °servile, °obsequious, sycophantic, °ingratiating, °flattering, °hypocritical; °suave, urbane, °sophisticated, *Colloq* smarmy

ointment *n.* unguent, balm, °salve, emollient, embrocation, demulcent, pomade, pomatum, petrolatum; °lotion, cream

OK *interj.* **1** O.K.!, Okay!, Fine!, Yes!, Definitely!, Agreed!, Very well!, All right! —*adj.* **2** °satisfactory, °acceptable, °correct, °suitable, all right, °fine, °good, °in order **3** °adequate, °mediocre, °fair, middling, °passable, °tolerable, *Colloq* °so-so, pretty good, not bad, not great **4** °well, °healthy; °sound, in good condition, in fine fettle, °fine, all right —*v.* **5** °approve, °sanction, °ratify, °authorize, °endorse, °support, °agree to, °allow, °consent to, *Colloq* give the go-ahead *or* green light to, give the thumbs-up *or* the nod to *or* on, rubber-stamp —*n.* **6** °approval, °sanction, ratification, authorization, °endorsement, °agreement, °support, °permission, °consent —*adv.* **7** all right, satisfactorily, °well (enough), adequately

old *adj.* **1** °elderly, aging, °aged, advanced in years *or* age, long-lived, past one's prime, °gray, full of years, getting on (in years), hoary, superannuated, *Colloq* over the hill, past it **2** °ancient, °antiquated, antediluvian, fossil, °prehistoric, Noachian, °obsolete, °antique, outdated, out-of-date, old-time, dated, archaic, °stale, outmoded, °passé, *Literary* Ogygian **3** °timeworn, decayed, °dilapidated, °ramshackle, disintegrated, crumbling, °shabby, worn-out, dusty, broken-down, tumbledown, °disused, °unused, °cast off, °cast aside **4** long-standing, °well-established, °enduring, °lasting, age-old, °time-honored **5** °former, olden, °bygone, °early, primordial, °primitive **6** °previous, °preceding, °prior, °former, quondam, erstwhile, one-time, ex- **7** °experienced, °veteran, °practiced, (well-)versed, °knowledgeable, °proficient, °accomplished, °adept, skilled, °expert, old-time **8** °dear, °beloved, loved, esteemed, valued, °precious, °well-known, °intimate, °close, °familiar

old-fashioned *adj.* °antiquated, °antique, °passé, outmoded, outdated, unfashionable, °stale, dated, out-of-date, °tired, old-time, °obsolete, °obsolescent, °dead, superseded, replaced, °disused, °out, oldfangled, old hat

omen *n.* portent, augury, °sign, °token, foretoken, °indication, °harbinger, forewarning, °premonition, foreshadowing, handwriting on the wall, prognostic, presage

ominous *adj.* **1** °foreboding, °threatening, °fateful, °dark, °black, °gloomy, lowering *or* louring, °menacing, °sinister; unpropitious, unfavorable, ill-omened, ill-starred, °unpromising, star-crossed, °inauspicious **2** minatory, °warning, admonitory, cautionary **3** °portentous, °prophetic, oracular, vaticinal, predictive, prognostic, augural, mantic, sibylline *or* sibyllic *or* sibylic, °meaningful, premonitory, foreshadowing, foretelling, foretokening, indicative

omission *n.* **1** noninclusion, omitting, leaving out *or* off, excluding, eliminating, dropping, skipping; °exclusion, °exception, deletion, elimination, excision **2** °failure, °default, °neglect, dereliction, °oversight, °shortcoming, °negligence

omit *v.* **1** °leave out, °exclude, °skip, °except, °pass over; °delete, °erase, °cancel, eradicate, °edit out, °strike (out), dele, °cut (out), °cross out, °obliterate **2** °neglect, °disregard, °fail, °forget, °overlook, °let slide, °ignore

once *adv.* **1** once upon a time, °formerly, (at) one time, on a former occasion, °previously, °before, in days gone by, in olden days, in the (good) old days, long ago, some time ago, years *or* ages *or* eons ago, in days of yore **2** one time, on one occasion, a single time **3** ***once and for all.*** °finally, °positively, °definitely, decidedly, conclusively, for good **4** ***once in a while.*** °occasionally, °(every) now and then, °now and again, °at times, °sometimes, periodically, from time to time, at intervals, sporadically —*conj.* **5** °(if) ever, as soon as, at any time —*n.* **6** ***at once.*** **(a)** °immediately, straightaway, right away, °directly, without delay, °promptly, instantly, °posthaste; in a wink, in the twinkling of an eye, in a minute *or* moment *or* second *or* split second, °in no time (at all), before one can turn around, before one can *or* could say "Jack Robinson," in a trice, *Colloq* in a jiffy, in two shakes of a lamb's tail **(b)** together, °at the same time, simultaneously, at a stroke, in the same instant, in the same breath, *Colloq* at one go, at a go, in one go

oncoming *adj.* **1** advancing, arriving, coming, nearing, approaching, onrushing, °imminent —*n.* **2** °onset, °beginning, nearing, °arrival, °advance, °approach

one *adj.* **1** °single, lone, °solitary, °individual, °sole, °only **2** unified, °united, inseparable, joined, °undivided, one and the same, °identical, °equal, at one, °harmonious, in unison, °whole, °entire, °complete **3** a particular, a certain, a given, a specific —*pron.* **4** a person, an individual, a man *or* a woman, everybody, °everyone, anybody, anyone; °people; *Possibly offensive* °man —*n.* **5** °joke, °story, anecdote, chestnut, one-liner; limerick, °rhyme, ditty, °song; bromide

one-sided *adj.* **1** °partial, °biased, °partisan, °prejudiced, °bigoted, unfair, unjust, inequitable, close-minded, °narrow-minded, °intolerant **2** °lopsided, °unbalanced, unequal, unequalized, uneven, °disproportionate, *Slang* cockeyed **3** unilateral, °independent, exclusionary, °exclusive

ongoing *adj.* **1** continuing, continued, °continuous, °continual, ceaseless, unbroken, uninterrupted, °constant, °perpetual, °nonstop, °relentless, °persistent, unending, °endless, interminable, °running **2** developing, evolving, growing, °successive, unfolding, progressing, °progressive

onlooker *n.* °spectator, °observer, looker-on, °eyewitness, °witness, watcher, viewer; °bystander, passerby

only *adj.* **1** °sole, °single, °solitary, lone, one and only, °exclusive —*adv.* **2** solely, °just, exclusively, °alone **3** °merely, °simply, °barely, at best, at worst, at most, °just, purely, not *or* no more than, not *or* no greater than —*conj.* **4** but, °however, on the other hand, on the contrary, contrariwise

onset *n.* **1** °attack, °assault, onrush, onslaught, °charge, °strike, °hit, °raid, storming, sally, sortie **2** °beginning, °start, °outset, °initiation, inauguration, commencement, inception, °dawn, °birth, °origin, genesis, °appearance, °debut

onward *adj.* **1** °forward, advancing, °progressive, progressing, moving onward *or* forward —*adv.* **2** onwards, forward(s), on, henceforward, °henceforth, °ahead, °in front, on, forth

ooze *n.* **1** slime, °muck, °mud, °mire, °silt, °sludge, °sediment, slush, *Colloq* goo, gunk, guck, *Slang US* glop, goop —*v.* **2** exude, °weep, seep, °secrete, bleed, °leak, °drain, °trickle; °emit, °discharge

opacity *n.* **1** opaqueness, darkness, murkiness, dimness, °obscurity, impermeability, impenetrability **2** °obscurity, density, impenetrability, unintelligibility, indefiniteness, vagueness, reconditeness, abstruseness, °ambiguity, equivocation, mystification **3** °stupidity, dullness, denseness, thickness, obtuseness

opalescent *adj.* opaline, iridescent, nacreous, °pearly, °lustrous

opaque *adj.* **1** °dark, °murky, °dim, turbid, °muddy, cloudy, °obscure, obscured, obfuscated, °black, °impermeable, impenetrable, clouded, nontransparent, untransparent, nontranslucent, °hazy, blurred, blurry, smoky **2** unclear, °vague, °indefinite, °obscure, unfathomable, unplumbable, baffling, mystifying, °ambiguous, °equivocal, impenetrable, °cryptic, enigmatic, °puzzling, °perplexing, °mysterious, °elusive, abstruse, arcane, °recondite **3** unintelligent, °dense, °thick, °dull, °obtuse, °stupid, dull-witted, °stolid, thickheaded, dunderheaded, dunderpated, °slow, doltish, °backward, cloddish

open *adj.* **1** ajar, gaping, agape, unfastened, unlocked, unbarred, unbolted, unlatched, unclosed **2** yawning, agape, uncovered, revealed, unsealed, exposed, °bare **3** unwrapped, unsealed, unfastened **4** °free, °accessible, °public, °available; obtainable; unrestricted, unobstructed, unencumbered, °unimpeded, unhindered, unhampered, unregulated, unconditional, °unqualified **5** unprotected, unenclosed, unsheltered, °bare; uncovered, exposed **6** °unsettled, unagreed, unsigned, unsealed, unclinched, unestablished, unconcluded, undecided, °pending **7** undecided, °unsettled, °unresolved, °debatable, arguable, °problematic, °moot, *US* up in the air **8** unscheduled, unbooked, unspoken-for, unreserved, uncommitted, °free, unpromised **9** °clear, unobstructed, wide-open, uncluttered, °roomy, °spacious, °extensive, °expansive; treeless, uncrowded, unfenced, unenclosed; ice-free, °navigable, unblocked, °passable **10** °available, unfilled, °vacant, untaken **11** °receptive, open-minded, °flexible, amenable, persuasible *or* persuadable, pliant, °willing, °responsive **12** exposed, °public, °well-known, widely known, unconcealed **13** °evident, °obvious, °conspicuous, °manifest, °clear, unconcealed, unequivocal, °plain, palpable, °apparent, °patent, °downright, °out-and-out, °blatant, °flagrant, °glaring, °brazen **14** °generous, °liberal, °charitable, unreserved, openhanded, munificent, magnanimous, bighearted, beneficent, bounteous, °unselfish, unstinting, °humanitarian, altruistic **15** unreserved, °candid, °frank, °outspoken, straightforward, °forthright, °direct, °honest, °sincere, guileless, °artless, °fair **16** °free, unrestrained, unconstrained, °uninhibited, unreserved, unrestricted **17** unfolded, extended, °spread (out), outstretched, outspread **18** °liable, °subject, °susceptible, exposed, °inclined, predisposed, °disposed **19** unprotected, undefended, unfortified, exposed —*v.* **20** °begin, °start, °initiate, °commence, get under way, °inaugurate, °launch, put in *or* into operation, °activate, get going, set in motion; °establish, °set up; *Colloq* get *or* start the ball rolling, get *or* put the show on the road, kick off **21** unlock, unbar, unlatch, unbolt, unfasten; uncover; uncork, unseal; °undo, untie, unwrap; °pull out **22** unblock, °clear, unobstruct, unclog, unstop **23** °disclose, °unveil, uncover, °expose, °display, °show, °exhibit, °reveal, divulge, °bring to light, °communicate, °bring out, unbosom, °explain, °present, °announce, °release, °publish, °air, °make known, advertise **24** °expand, °spread (out), stretch out, open up *or* out, unfurl, °extend **25** °present, °offer, °furnish, °provide, °afford, °yield, °reveal, uncover, °raise, °contribute, °introduce

opening *n.* **1** °break, °breach, °rent, °rift, cleft, °crack, °crevice, fissure, °cranny, °chink, °pit, °gap, °split, °slit, °slot, °aperture, °hole, orifice, °separation **2** °opportunity, °chance, °occasion, toehold, foothold, *Colloq* °break, toe *or* foot in the door, *Brit* look-in **3** °job, °position, °opportunity, °vacancy **4** °beginning, commencement, °start, °birth, °origin, °outset, °onset, inauguration, °launch, send-off, °initiation, °presentation, °debut; vernissage, *US* start-off, start-up

openly *adv.* **1** brazenly, brashly, flagrantly, unabashedly, unashamedly, unreservedly, boldly, audaciously, flauntingly **2** frankly, unreservedly, plainly, forthrightly, candidly, °directly, °outright, °freely, outspokenly

operable *adj.* workable, °practicable, °serviceable, usable, °functional, °fit, operational, in working order *or* condition

operate *v.* **1** °go, °run, °perform; °work, °function, °serve, °act **2** °manage, °run, °direct, °conduct, °control, °carry on, °ply, °manipulate, °handle; *US* °drive

operation *n.* **1** °function, functioning, working, °running, °performance, °action, °motion, °movement **2** manipulation, handling, °direction, °running, °control, °management, managing; maneuvering **3** °undertaking, °enterprise, °venture, °project, °affair, °deal, °procedure, °proceeding, °(day-to-day) business, °transaction **4** Often, ***operations.*** °action, °maneuver, °mission, °task, °campaign, °exercise **5** ***in or into operation.*** functioning, °operative, °in effect, °in force, operating, operational, °functional, °effective, °efficacious

operative *adj.* **1** See **operation, 5,** above. —*n.* **2** °worker, °hand, °employee; craftsman, craftswoman, artisan, mechanic, machinist **3** private detective, (private) investigator, *Colloq* private eye, °sleuth, *Brit* sleuthhound, *US* P.I., gumshoe, *Slang* (private) dick, *US* shamus, °eye **4** espionage *or* intelligence agent, counterespionage *or* counterintelligence agent, °spy, counterspy, undercover agent *or* man, (FBI *or* CIA) agent, *US* G-man, *Colloq US* company man, member of the firm

operator *n.* **1** (bus *or* taxi *or* train) driver; °worker, °operative, manipulator, practitioner **2** °director, administrator, °manager, °supervisor, °superintendent **3** machinator, faker, °fraud, manipulator, maneuverer, *Colloq* finagler, °wise guy, *Slang* smooth *or* slick operator, smoothie, wheeler-dealer, big shot, big-time operator, *Chiefly US and Canadian* big wheel

opinion *n.* **1** °belief, °judgment, °thought, °sentiment, °(point of) view, °viewpoint, °conviction, way of thinking, °perception, °idea, °impression, °notion, °conception, theory, *idée reçu*; °mind **2** °evaluation, °estimation, °estimate, appraisal, °appreciation, °impression

opinionated *adj.* **1** °stubborn, pigheaded, °obstinate, doctrinaire, °inflexible, °dogmatic, °single-minded, cocksure, obdurate, °dictatorial, dogged, mulish, bull-headed, °overbearing **2** °prejudiced, °biased, °bigoted, °one-sided, °jaundiced, colored, °partial, °partisan

opponent *n.* °antagonist, °adversary, disputant, °contestant, °competitor, contender, °rival, foe, °enemy; the opposition

opportune *adj.* **1** °favorable, °advantageous, auspicious, °good, felicitous, °happy, °propitious, °beneficial, °helpful, °fortunate, °lucky, °profitable **2** °timely, °well-timed, °seasonable, apt, °appropriate, germane, °pertinent, °convenient, °fitting, °suitable, °becoming

opportunistic *adj.* °expedient, °selfish, taking advantage, exploitive *or* exploitative, unprincipled, Machiavellian, opportunist

opportunity *n.* °chance, °occasion, °opening, °possibility, °moment, °time, *Slang* °break

oppose *v.* **1** °resist, °counter, °object (to), °defy, take a stand against, °withstand, °resist, °combat, °contest, °attack, counterattack, °fight, °grapple with, contend with *or* against **2** °check, °bar, °obstruct, °block, °hinder, °impede, °stop, °slow, °curb, °restrain, °inhibit, interfere with, °restrict, °prevent, obviate, °preclude, °thwart, °foil, °frustrate **3** °match, °offset, counterbalance, °contrast, pit *or* set against, play off (against), °set off

opposed *adj.* Often, ***opposed to.*** against, °in opposition (to), °opposing, in conflict (with), antipathetic, conflicting, °contrary (to), °at variance (with), antithetical (to), °hostile (to), inimical (to), °opposite (to), contrasting

opposing *adj.* °opposite, conflicting, °contrary, antithetical, antagonistic, antipathetic, °hostile, inimical, contrasting, °rival, °contradictory, °incompatible, irreconcilable, °dissident, discrepant

opposite *adj.* **1** °facing, vis-à-vis, *en face* **2** °opposing, conflicting, °contrary, contrasting, °contradictory, antithetical, differing, °different, °divergent, °diverse, antagonistic, °inconsistent, irreconcilable —*n.* 3 °reverse, °converse, °contrary, antithesis

opposition *n.* 1 °hostility, °antagonism, unfriendliness, °resistance, counteraction, °disapproval, °objection, °conflict, defiance, °contrast, antipathy, adversity, *Colloq* °flak 2 °competition, °opponent, °adversary, °competitor, °antagonist, °enemy, foe, °rival, other side 3 ***in opposition.*** competing, competitive, antagonistic, °hostile, conflicting, in conflict, antithetic(al), °opposed, at daggers drawn, in deadly embrace

oppress *v.* 1 °burden, °afflict, °trouble, °weigh down, °overload, °encumber, °wear (down), °press, °weary, overburden, °overwhelm, *Brit* pressurize, *US* °pressure 2 °crush, °repress, °put down, °suppress, °subjugate, °tyrannize (over), °subdue, °overpower, °enslave, °persecute, maltreat, °abuse, harry, °harass, trample underfoot, ride roughshod over

oppression *n.* °repression, °suppression, subjugation, °subjection, °tyranny, °despotism, enslavement, °persecution, maltreatment, °abuse, °torment, torture, °hardship, °injury, °pain, °anguish, °injustice

oppressive *adj.* 1 °burdensome, °overpowering, °overwhelming, onerous, °heavy, cumbersome, °exhausting, racking, °unbearable, intolerable, °agonizing, unendurable, °harsh, °brutal, °severe, °tyrannical, °repressive; dispiriting, depressing, disheartening, discouraging, °grievous, distressing, dolorous, °miserable, °harrowing, °wretched 2 suffocating, stifling, °stuffy, °close, airless, unventilated, uncomfortable

oppressor *n.* °bully, °tyrant, taskmaster, taskmistress, °despot, autocrat, persecutor, slave driver, °dictator, overlord, iron hand, °scourge, tormentor, torturer, intimidator

optimistic *adj.* °sanguine, °positive, °cheerful, °buoyant, °bright, °hopeful, °expectant, °confident, bullish, °idealistic, Pollyannaish

optimum *n.* 1 °best, finest, most favorable, °ideal, °perfection, °model, °paragon, exemplar —*adj.* 2 °best, finest, most favorable, °ideal, °perfect, choicest, optimal, °first-rate, first-class, °sterling, °prime, °capital, °excellent, °exceptional, °superlative, °extraordinary, °unique, °peerless, unequaled, unexcelled, unsurpassed

option *n.* 1 °choice, °selection, °alternative, °recourse, °opportunity, way out 2 °choice, °privilege, °election, °opportunity, °chance

optional *adj.* °voluntary, discretionary *or* discretional, elective, facultative, °free, °spontaneous, uncoerced, unforced, noncompulsory, uncompulsory, nonmandatory, unmandatory, nonrequisite, unrequisite

opulent *adj.* 1 °wealthy, affluent, °rich, °prosperous, well-to-do, °well-off, °comfortable, *Colloq* °flush, well-heeled, °loaded, rolling in it, made of money, in clover, on Easy Street, *Brit* on velvet, *US* in velvet, in the chips 2 °luxurious, °lavish, °sumptuous 3 °abundant, copious, °bountiful, °plentiful, °prolific, °profuse, plenteous

opus *n.* °work, °composition, °production, *oeuvre,* °creation; ***magnum opus***

oracle *n.* 1 °prophet, sibyl, °seer, soothsayer, augur, °fortuneteller, diviner, prognosticator, *US* reader (and adviser *or US* advisor), Cassandra, Nostradamus; °authority, guru, °mastermind, mentor, wizard 2 °prophecy, augury, °prediction, divination, °advice, prognostication, °answer, °message, divine utterance

oral *adj.* °spoken, said, °verbal, uttered, voiced, vocal, vocalized, enunciated, °pronounced, articulated, word-of-mouth, viva voce

oration *n.* °speech, °declaration, °address, °lecture, °recitation, discourse, monologue, declamation; valedictory, °eulogy, homily, panegyric; *Colloq* spiel

oratory *n.* public speaking, speechmaking, eloquence, °rhetoric, way with words, command of the language, °fluency, glibness, grandiloquence, magniloquence, declamation; elocution, °diction, enunciation, articulation, °address; *Colloq* gift of the gab

orb *n.* °sphere, ball, °globe

orbit *n.* 1 °circuit, °course, °path, °track, °revolution, °circle, °round, °cycle —*v.* 2 °revolve, go *or* turn around, °circle, °encircle

ordeal *n.* °trial, °test, tribulation(s), °hardship, °affliction, trouble(s), °suffering, °distress, °anguish, nightmare, °misery, °grief, °misfortune, adversity, °tragedy, °disaster

order *n.* 1 °organization, °arrangement, grouping, °disposition, °form, °structure, categorization, systematization *or* systemization, classification, codification, disposal, layout, array, °sequence, *Colloq* °setup 2 °organization, °uniformity, °regularity, °system, °pattern, °symmetry, °harmony, tidiness, orderliness, neatness 3 °category, °class, °caste, °level, °kind, °sort, °rank, °group, °scale, °importance, hierarchy, °position, °status, °degree, *Colloq* pecking order 4 °command, °direction, directive, °instruction, commandment, °dictate, mandate, edict, behest, °request, °demand, ukase, °decree, fiat, °proclamation, °pronouncement, pronunciamento; °rule, °regulation, °law, ordinance, statute, °requirement 5 °procedure, proceeding(s), °discipline, °conduct 6 °condition, °state (of affairs) 7 purchase order, °request, °requisition, commitment, commission, °instruction 8 °calm, °peace, peacefulness, tranquillity, °quiet, °serenity, law and order, °discipline, lawfulness 9 °brotherhood, °fraternity, sisterhood, sorority, °fellowship, sodality, °association, °organization, °society, guild, °sect, °company, community, °lodge, °body, knighthood 10 ***in order.*** **(a)** °neat, °clean, °tidy, °shipshape, °orderly, (well-)organized, °ready, °prepared, arranged **(b)** °fitting, °suitable, °appropriate, °correct, °right, apt, called for; required, demanded, needed 11 ***in order that.*** so (that), with the aim *or* purpose that, to the end that 12 ***in order to.*** to, for the purpose of **13** ***out of order.*** **(a)** disordered, nonsequential, out of sequence, nonalphabetical, disorganized, unorganized, in disorder **(b)** °unseemly, °out of place, °improper, uncalled-for, unsuitable, indecorous, *Colloq chiefly Brit* not cricket **(c)** out of commission, °broken, in disrepair, nonfunctioning, nonfunctional, not working, °broken down, inoperative, out of kilter *or Brit also* kelter, *Colloq* (gone) haywire, kaput, bust(ed), *US* out of whack, on the fritz, °shot; *Slang* °on the blink, *Brit* wonky, gone phut *—v.* **14** °direct, °command, °instruct, °charge, °tell, °bid, °require, enjoin; °demand, ordain; °force, °make **15** °requisition, °ask for, send (away) for, °call for, apply for, °reserve, °engage, commission, contract for; °purchase, °buy **16** °organize, systematize, °arrange, classify, °categorize, codify, °lay out, °sort (out), straighten (out *or* up)

orderly *adj.* **1** in (good) order, (well-)organized, °neat, °shipshape, °tidy, arranged, °methodical, °systematic, systematized *or* systemized, °harmonious, °symmetrical, °regular, °uniform **2** well-behaved, disciplined, °decorous, law-abiding, well-mannered, °peaceable, °tranquil, mannerly, °polite, °courteous, °civil, civilized, nonviolent *—n.* **3** °assistant, adjutant, °attendant, °messenger; °menial, °servant; nurse's aide; *Brit military* batman; *US* candy-striper; *Slang US and Canadian* gofer

ordinarily *adv.* °usually, normally, °as a rule, commonly, °generally, in general, customarily, routinely, typically, habitually, by and large, °for the most part

ordinary *adj.* **1** °usual, °normal, expected, °common, °general, °customary, °routine, °typical, °habitual, °accustomed, °traditional, °regular, °everyday, °familiar, °set, °humdrum **2** °common, °conventional, °modest, °plain, °simple, °prosaic, °homespun, commonplace, °run-of-the-mill, °everyday, °average, unpretentious, workaday, °mediocre, °fair, °passable, °so-so, °undistinguished, unexceptional, unremarkable, uninspired, °pedestrian, °bourgeois, °peasant, °provincial, °unrefined, *Colloq Brit* common-or-garden variety, *US* garden-variety *—n.* **3** °standard, °norm, °average, status quo, °convention, expected **4** ***out of the ordinary.*** °extraordinary, °unusual, uncommon, °strange, °unfamiliar, °different, unexpected, unconventional, °curious, °eccentric, °peculiar, °rare, °exceptional, °original, °singular, °unique, °odd, °bizarre, °weird, °offbeat, °outlandish, °striking, °quaint, °picturesque

organ *n.* **1** °device, °instrument, °implement, °tool; °member, °part, °element, °unit, component, °structure, *Technical* °process **2** °medium, °vehicle, °voice, °mouthpiece, forum, °publication, °paper, °magazine, newsletter, house organ, newspaper, annual, semiannual, °quarterly, monthly, fortnightly, weekly, hebdomadal, °daily, °journal, °periodical

organic *adj.* **1** living, °natural, biological, biotic, °animate, breathing **2** °basic, °elementary, °essential, innate, °inborn, °natural, °native, °ingrained, °primary, °fundamental, visceral, constitutional, °inherent, structural, °integral **3** organized, °systematic, °coherent, coordinated, integrated, structured, °methodical, °orderly, °consistent

organism *n.* living thing, °structure, °body; being, °creature

organization *n.* **1** organizing, structuring, assembling, °assembly, putting together, coordination, systematizing, systematization, classifying, classification, categorizing, categorization, codifying, codification **2** °structure, °pattern, configuration, °design, °plan, °scheme, °order, °system, °organism, °composition, °arrangement, constitution, °makeup, grouping, framework, °format, °form, °shape **3** °body, °system, °institution, °federation, confederacy, confederation, °society, °group, °league, coalition, conglomerate, °combine, consortium, °syndicate, °organism

organize *v.* **1** °structure, °coordinate, systematize, systemize, °order, °arrange, °sort (out), classify, °categorize, codify, catalogue, °group, °tabulate, pigeonhole, °standardize **2** °form, °found, °set up, °establish, °institute, °start, °begin, °create, °originate, °initiate, put together, °build, °develop, US pull together

orgy *n.* **1** bacchanalia, bacchanal, saturnalia, Dionysia, debauch, carousal, °carouse, °spree, °revel, °party, *Colloq* binge, °bender, °drunk, bust, *Slang* °jag, *US and Canadian* toot, °tear **2** overindulgence, °splurge, °spree, °fling, *Slang US* °bender

orient *n.* **1** east *—adj.* **2** *Literary* oriental, eastern *—v.* **3** °adjust, °adapt, acclimatize *or* acclimate, habituate, °accommodate, °condition, °accustom, °familiarize, feel one's way, assess, get one's bearings, *Colloq* orientate

orientation *n.* **1** °placement, °bearings, °attitude, alignment, °lie, placing, °situation, layout, °location, °position, positioning, °arrangement, °setup **2** introduction, training, °initiation, briefing, familiarization, assimilation, acclimatization, °preparation, °instruction

origin *n.* **1** °source, °derivation, °rise, fountainhead, °foundation, °basis, °base, wellspring, fount, provenance, *Chiefly US* provenience **2** °creation, genesis, °birth, birthplace, cradle, dawning, °dawn, origination, °start, °beginning, commencement, °outset, °launch, launching, inception, inauguration **3** Often, ***origins.*** °parentage, ancestry, °extraction, descent, °lineage, °pedigree, genealogy, °stock, °heritage

original *adj.* **1** °initial, °first, earliest, °primary, °beginning, starting, °basic **2** °native, °indigenous, autochthonous, °aboriginal, primordial, primeval, °primitive **3** °master, °actual, °primary, °authentic, °true, °genuine, °real, °basic; prototypic(al), archetypal,

°source **4** °creative, °novel, innovative, °unique, °imaginative, °unusual, inventive, °ingenious; first-hand, °fresh, underived, unprecedented —*n.* **5** °prototype, archetype, °source, °model, °pattern; °master **6** °eccentric, °nonconformist, °individualist, *Colloq* °case, °card, °character, *Brit* queer fish

originality *n.* creativeness, creativity, inventiveness, °ingenuity, innovativeness, °innovation, °novelty, newness, unorthodoxy, unconventionality, cleverness, °daring, resourcefulness, °independence, individuality, uniqueness, nonconformity

originally *adv.* in *or* at *or* from the beginning, (at) first, from the first, initially, to begin with, at *or* from the outset, at *or* from the start, in the first place *or* instance, *Colloq* from the word "go," from day one

originate *v.* **1** °create, °bring about, engender, give birth to, beget, °conceive, °initiate, °inaugurate, °start, °begin, °introduce, °launch, °found, °set up, °institute, °establish, °invent, °coin, °devise, °pioneer, °design, contrive, concoct, °mastermind, °compose, °organize, °formulate, °form, °generate, °produce, °develop, evolve **2** °arise, °rise, °begin, °start, °come, °spring, °stem, °flow, °issue, °emerge, °emanate, °proceed, °grow, °develop, evolve, °derive, °result

ornament *n.* **1** enhancement, °embellishment, adornment, °decoration, ornamentation, gingerbread, trimming, garnish, garnishment, °frill, embroidery, beautification, °accessory; frippery; knickknack, furbelow, °bauble, °gewgaw, *Slang US* tchotchke —*v.* **2** °decorate, °embellish, °enhance, adorn, °trim, garnish, embroider, °elaborate, °beautify, accessorize, deck (out), °dress up

ornamental *adj.* decorative, beautifying, adorning, garnishing, embellishing

ornate *adj.* °elaborate, florid, overdone, °labored, rococo, baroque, gingerbread, arabesque, °fancy, °lavish, °rich, °flowery, °busy, °fussy, frilly, °intricate; high-flown, euphuistic, Ossianic, °bombastic, °pompous, °pretentious, °affected, °grandiose, fulsome, highfalutin *or* hifalutin, grandiloquent, °flamboyant

orthodox *adj.* conformist, accepted, °authoritative, authorized, recognized, received, °official, °standard, °prevailing, °prevalent, °common, °regular, °popular, °ordinary, doctrinal, established, °traditional, traditionalist, °accustomed, °conventional, °customary, °conservative

oscillate *v.* °fluctuate, °vibrate, waver, °seesaw, °swing, °sway; vacillate, °equivocate, °shilly-shally, hem and haw, tergiversate

ostensibly *adv.* °outwardly, externally, superficially, patently, ostensively, demonstrably, °apparently, °evidently, °seemingly; °clearly, plainly, °manifestly, conspicuously, °obviously, patently, noticeably, prominently

ostentation *n.* °show, °display, °exhibition, exhibitionism, showing off, °pretension, pretentiousness, flaunting, flashiness, °flourish, flamboyance, °parade, window-dressing

ostentatious *adj.* °showy, °boastful, °braggart, vaunting, °vain, vainglorious, flaunting, °pretentious, °flamboyant, °theatrical, *Colloq* °flash

ostracize *v.* blackball, blacklist, °banish, °exile, °boycott, °isolate, °segregate, °exclude, excommunicate, snub, °shun, °avoid, *Chiefly Brit* send to Coventry, *Colloq* °cut, cold-shoulder, give (someone) the cold shoulder

otherwise *adv.* **1** if not, or else, under other circumstances, in another situation, on the other hand **2** differently, in another manner *or* way

out *adv.* **1** °outside, outdoors, in *or* into the open air **2** away (from), °abroad, °elsewhere, not (at) home, gone (from), gone away (from), °absent (from) **3** in *or* into the open, to *or* into public notice, for all to see, out of the closet **4** revealed, exposed, °visible, °discernible, °manifest, in sight, in view **5** °short, minus, missing, in default, out of pocket **6** °free, °at liberty, °at large, °loose, unconfined **7** °completely, °thoroughly, effectively, °entirely —*adj.* **8** °unconscious, °senseless, °insensible, *Colloq* out cold, out like a light **9** dated, outdated, outmoded, °passé, °old-fashioned, °antiquated, old hat, *démodé*, °obsolete, unfashionable **10** °outlying, °distant, far-off, °peripheral **11** °exhausted, gone, finished, ended; °over, completed **12** °inaccurate, °incorrect, °wrong, °at fault, °faulty, °off, °wide of the mark **13** °unacceptable, forbidden, prohibited, not allowed, *Colloq* not on **14** extinguished, unlit; °off, doused; inoperative, nonfunctioning, out of order *or* commission, unserviceable, °broken —*n.* **15** °alibi, °excuse, °escape, °loophole, °evasion

out-and-out *adj.* °complete, °unmitigated, unalloyed, °undiluted, °pure, utter, °perfect, consummate, °outright, °total, °downright, °unqualified, °thorough, thoroughgoing, through and through, dyed-in-the-wool

outburst *n.* outbreak, °eruption, °explosion, blowup, flare-up, fulmination; upsurge, °surge, °outpouring, welling (forth), upwelling, outflow(ing), °rush, °flood, effusion, effluence *or* efflux; °fit, access, °attack, °spasm, °paroxysm, °seizure, °tantrum

outcast *n.* pariah, °exile, °reject, *persona non grata*, leper, untouchable, expatriate, °refugee, displaced person, DP, evacuee

outcome *n.* °result, consequence, end (result *or* product), aftereffect, °effect, °upshot, °sequel, °development, outgrowth, aftermath, °wake, °follow-up, *Medicine* sequela (usually *pl.* sequelae), *Colloq* °payoff, bottom line

outcry *n.* °protest, protestation, decrial, °complaint, °indignation, °uproar, vociferation, clamor, clamoring, commotion, °outburst, °noise, hullabaloo, °howl, howling, hoot, hooting, boo, booing, °hiss, hissing

outdo *v.* °exceed, °surpass, °excel, °transcend, °beat, °outstrip, outshine, °top, °cap, trump, °overcome, °defeat, °outweigh

outdoor *adj.* °outside, out-of-door(s), alfresco, open-air

outfit *n.* **1** °gear, °rig, °equipment, equipage, °apparatus, accoutrements *or US also* accouterments, °paraphernalia, °trappings, °tackle, °tack, utensils **2** °clothes, °costume, °ensemble; attire, garb, clothing, °dress; *Colloq* get-up, togs **3** °firm, °concern, °business, °organization, °company, °(military) unit, corporation; °party, °set, °group; *Colloq* °setup —*v.* **4** fit (out *or* up), °equip, kit out, °provision, °stock, accoutre *or US also* accouter, rig (out *or* up), °supply, °furnish

outgoing *adj.* **1** departing, °retiring, ex-, °former, °past, emeritus, leaving, withdrawing **2** °genial, °friendly, °amiable, °cordial, °warm, °expansive, approachable, affable, °accessible, amenable, easygoing, °amicable, °sociable, congenial, extrovert, °familiar, °informal, communicative

outing *n.* jaunt, junket, °excursion, °trip, °expedition, °tour, °ride, *Colloq* °spin

outlandish *adj.* °unfamiliar, °strange, °odd, °queer, °offbeat, °peculiar, °curious, °exotic, °foreign, °alien, °unknown, °unheard-of, °different, °exceptional, °extraordinary, °quaint, °eccentric, °bizarre, °outré, °weird, °fantastic, °unusual, °singular, °unique; freakish, °grotesque, barbarous; *Colloq* far-out, camp(y), °kinky

outlast *v.* °survive, outlive; outwear; °weather

outlaw *n.* **1** °criminal, °gangster, °robber, desperado, bandit, highwayman, brigand, footpad, picaroon, °pirate, fugitive (from justice *or* the law), °renegade, *US* road agent —*v.* **2** °forbid, disallow, °ban, interdict, °bar, °exclude, °prohibit, proscribe

outlay *n.* °expense, °cost, °expenditure, spending, disbursement, °payment

outlet *n.* **1** way out, °exit, egress, °loophole, °relief, °escape, escape hatch, °vent, °opening, °release, safety valve, °discharge **2** retailer, °shop, °store, °market

outline *n.* **1** °profile, °silhouette, contour, °periphery, °boundary, footprint **2** °précis, °synopsis, °résumé, °summary, °digest, °abstract, conspectus, °survey, overview, °rundown, recapitulation, °review, (thumbnail) sketch, skeleton, °(overall) plan, layout, framework, °draft, °scenario —*v.* **3** °trace, °draft, sketch, °rough out, °profile, °block (out), °plan (out), °lay out, °define, delineate

outlook *n.* **1** °view, °position, °point of view, °viewpoint, °prospect, °perspective, °slant, °angle, °standpoint, °attitude, °opinion **2** °prospect, °forecast, expectation(s)

outlying *adj.* °distant, far-off, far-flung, outer, outermost, °out-of-the-way, °remote, °faraway, °peripheral, farthest

out-of-the-way *adj.* **1** untraveled, unfrequented, °isolated, °lonely, °outlying, °obscure, °hidden, °secluded, °inaccessible **2** °unusual, °odd, °peculiar, °extraordinary, °far-fetched, °remarkable, °outré, °exceptional, °outlandish, °strange, °rare, uncommon, °exotic, °unheard-of, unconventional, °queer, °weird, °bizarre

outpouring *n.* effusion, outflow, °flow, °outburst, °flood, deluge, °torrent, °spate, emanation, spouting, °spurt, gushing, efflux, effluence, outrush, tide, cascade, cataract, Niagara, *Technical* debouchment

output *n.* **1** °production, °result, °yield, crop, °harvest **2** productivity, °achievement, °efficiency —*v.* **3** °put out, °produce, °generate, °create, °manufacture, °yield, °achieve

outrage *n.* **1** °violence, °atrocity, inhumanity, barbarism, °enormity, °evil, °barbarity, savagery, brutality, malignity, malefaction, wrongdoing, evildoing, maltreatment, °abuse, cruelty, °injury, °harm, °damage **2** °resentment, affront, °bitterness, °indignation, °hurt, °shock, °anger, wrath, ire **3** °insult, °indignity, °slight —*v.* **4** °offend, °insult, affront, vex, displease, °distress, nettle, °chafe, °infuriate, °anger, °enrage, °madden, make one's blood boil, raise (someone's) hackles, rile **5** °violate, °desecrate, defile, °do violence to, °injure, °harm, °abuse, °damage **6** °rape, °violate, °ravage, °ravish, deflower, °attack

outrageous *adj.* **1** °excessive, °extravagant, °immoderate, °exorbitant, °enormous, °unreasonable, °preposterous, °shocking, °extreme, °unwarranted, exaggerated, °unconscionable, °inordinate, intolerable, °disgraceful, °shameful, °scandalous **2** °vicious, °cruel, heinous, °atrocious, barbaric, °inhuman, °abusive, °beastly, °horrible, horrid, horrendous, iniquitous, °villainous, °wicked, °evil, egregious, °flagrant, °grievous, °infamous, execrable, °abominable, °grisly, °hideous, °monstrous, °vile, °unthinkable, °foul, °awful, unspeakable, appalling, °offensive, °indecent **3** °indecent, °offensive, °immoral, °rude, indelicate, °obnoxious, °profane, °obscene, °dirty, °filthy, °lewd, salacious, °foul, smutty, scatological, °pornographic, objectionable, °repellent, °repulsive, nauseating, °nauseous, °nasty, °gross, °revolting, °shocking, °repugnant, °disgusting, fulsome, °perverted, depraved, °dissolute, °degenerate, dissipated, debauched, °profligate; °explicit, unrestrained; foulmouthed, thersitical, insulting; °unseemly, °inappropriate, indecorous, °improper, °naughty, appalling, °embarrassing; *Literary* Fescennine, *US* shy-making

outré *adj.* unconventional, °unusual, °extravagant, °bizarre, °weird, °strange, °odd, °peculiar, °grotesque, °outlandish, freakish, °out-of-the-way

outright *adj.* **1** °unqualified, °total, unreserved, unrestricted, °full, °complete, unconditional, unequivocal, °clear, °direct, °definite, unmistakable *or* unmistakeable **2** °undisguised, °unmitigated, utter, consummate, °pure, °out-and-out, all-out, °sheer, °absolute, °stark, bald, °thorough, arrant, thoroughgoing, through and through, °downright, °direct, °definite, unmistakable *or* unmistakeable *—adv.* **3** °directly, °at once, °immediately, °instantaneously, instantly, then and there *or* there and then, *Brit* °straightaway, *US* right away, on the spot, right off **4** °completely, °entirely, °exactly, °precisely, °totally, *in toto,* °utterly, baldly, starkly, consummately, purely, °thoroughly, °directly, unhesitatingly, °quite, °absolutely, explicitly, categorically, straightforwardly, plainly, °openly, forthrightly, unequivocally, unambiguously, candidly **5** unrestrictedly, unqualifiedly, unreservedly, unconditionally

outset *n.* °beginning, °start, inauguration, inception, °first, *Colloq* kickoff

outside *n.* **1** °exterior, °face, °facing, °shell, °skin, °case, casing, °surface, °front; façade **2** °aspect, °appearance, °look, demeanor, °face, °front, façade, mien, °mask, °disguise, false front, °pretense **3** °extreme, °limit, most, °maximum, utmost, °best, worst, longest **4** the world at large *—adj.* **5** °exterior, °external, out-of-door(s), °outdoor **6** °maximum, maximal, highest, °best, worst, greatest, most, largest, longest, farthest **7** °private, °home, °cottage, °secondary, °peripheral, °independent, freelance **8** °unlikely, °remote, °faint, *Colloq* °slim **9** °foreign, °alien, °outward; unconnected, excluded, uninvolved, disinvolved, °independent, °separate, °different *—adv.* **10** outdoors, out-of-doors

outsider *n.* nonmember, noninitiate, °foreigner, °alien, outlander, °stranger, °newcomer, °guest, °visitor, trespasser, interloper, °intruder, squatter, invader, *Colloq* gatecrasher

outskirts *n. pl.* periphery, °edge, environs, outer reaches, °vicinity, border(s), suburb(s), exurb(s), general area *or* neighborhood, purlieus, fringes, vicinage, faubourg(s)

outsmart *v.* °outwit, outfox, outthink, outmaneuver, outmanipulate, outplay, steal a march on, get the better *or* best of, °trick, °dupe, °hoodwink, °fool, °deceive, °hoax, gull, make a fool of; °swindle, °cheat, °defraud, cozen, *Colloq* put one over on, pull a fast one on, °take in, make a monkey (out) of, bamboozle, con, *Brit* nobble, *Slang* slip *or* put one *or* something over on (someone)

outspoken *adj.* °candid, °frank, °open, °free, °direct, unreserved, unreticent, straightforward, °forthright, °explicit, °specific, plain-spoken, plain-speaking, unequivocal, unceremonious, unambiguous, unsubtle, °uninhibited, unshrinking, °blunt, °bold, °brusque, °brash, undiplomatic, °tactless, °crude

outstanding *adj.* **1** °prominent, °eminent, °renowned, °famous, famed, unforgettable, °memorable, °celebrated, °distinguished, °special, °choice, °noteworthy, °notable, °noted, °important, °conspicuous, °exceptional, °excellent, °superior, first-class, °first-rate, °superb, °remarkable, °extraordinary, °marvelous, °sensational, *Colloq* smashing, °super **2** °unsettled, on-going, °unresolved, °unpaid, °due, owed *or* owing, receivable *or* payable; °remaining, °leftover

outstrip *v.* °overcome, °surpass, °outdo, outperform, outshine, outclass, °better, °beat, °transcend, °best, worst, °exceed, °excel, outdistance, °overtake, °top, °cap, put in the shade, °eclipse

outward *adj.* **1** °external, °exterior, outer, °outside, °outlying, °manifest, °obvious, °evident, °apparent, °visible, °observable; °superficial, °surface, °extrinsic, °skin-deep, °shallow, °pretended, °false, ostensible, °formal, °physical, bodily, fleshly, °carnal, mundane, °worldly, °secular, °temporal, °terrestrial, °material, nonspiritual *—adv.* **2** outwards, °outside, away, °out, without

outwardly *adv.* externally, °apparently, visibly, superficially, °ostensibly, °evidently, °seemingly, °on the surface, to all appearances, °to all intents and purposes

outweigh *v.* °overcome, outbalance, overbalance, overweigh, tip the scales, preponderate (over), °surpass, °prevail (over), override, take precedence (over), °compensate (for), °make up for

outwit *v.* See **outsmart,** above.

oval *adj.* egg-shaped, ovoid, ovate, oviform, obovoid, obovate; elliptical, ellipsoid(al)

ovation *n.* °applause, acclamation, acclaim, plaudits, cheers, cheering, clapping, laudation, °praise, °kudos, *Colloq* °(big) hand

over *prep.* **1** °above, on, upon, on top of, atop (of) **2** more than, greater than, upward(s) of, in excess of, °(over and) above, (over and) beyond; °exceeding **3** across, to *or* from *or* on the other side of; beyond **4** °for, during, in *or* over *or* during the course of, °through, °throughout **5** °(all) through, °throughout, °(all) about, all over *—adj.* **6** done (with), finished, terminated, concluded, ended, °past, settled, closed, at an end, over with *—adv.* **7** to, onto, °past, beyond, across **8** °remaining, as a remainder, as surplus, °outstanding **9** (once) again, once more, one more time **10** down, to the ground *or* floor

overall *adj.* °total, °complete, °comprehensive, (all-)inclusive, °whole, °entire, all-embracing, blanket

overawe *v.* °overwhelm, °intimidate, cow, °daunt, awe, °bully, hector, °browbeat, °dominate, domineer, °frighten, °scare, °terrify, disconcert, °discomfit, °upset, abash

overbearing *adj.* °repressive, °domineering, bullying, imperious, °officious, high and mighty, highhanded, overweening, magisterial, lordly, °authoritarian, °willful, °despotic, °dogmatic, autocratic, °tyrannical, °dictatorial, °peremptory, °arbitrary, °assertive, °arrogant, cavalier, °haughty, °superior, °supercilious, °pretentious, *Colloq* °bossy, °pushy, °hoity-toity, highfalutin *or* hifalutin, snooty, *Slang* snotty

overcast *adj.* cloudy, clouded, °sunless, moonless, starless, °murky, °gray, lowering *or* louring, °dull, °dark, darkened, °dreary,

°somber, °gloomy, °dismal, °threatening, °menacing

overcome *v.* **1** °beat, °defeat, °conquer, °overpower, °subdue, worst, °best, °triumph over, win (out) (over), °prevail (over), °overthrow, °overwhelm, vanquish, get the better *or* best of, °whip, drub, °rout, °break, °subjugate, °suppress, °crush, °master, *Colloq* lick —*adj.* **2** beaten, defeated, overwhelmed, °subdued, worsted, bested; °affected, °speechless, swept off one's feet, rendered helpless, overpowered, moved, influenced, at a loss (for words), *Colloq* bowled over

overconfident *adj.* **1** °brash, °arrogant, cocksure, °cocky, °brazen, hubristic *or* hybristic, swaggering, °audacious, °overbearing, vainglorious, *Colloq* °pushy **2** °heedless, °foolhardy, °thoughtless, °shortsighted, °hasty

overcritical *adj.* supercritical, hypercritical, captious, carping, °niggling, caviling, °querulous, °faultfinding, °finicky, °fussy, °hairsplitting, °difficult, °fastidious, °harsh, °severe, °demanding, °exacting, °small, °small-minded, *US and Canadian* picayune, *Colloq* picky, nit-picking, pernickety *or US also* persnickety

overcrowded *adj.* jammed, °packed, °congested, °populous, overpopulous, jam-packed, overpopulated; swarming, crawling, choked, packed to the gunwales

overdo *v.* **1** carry to excess, overindulge, be intemperate, go *or* carry to extremes, overact, °exaggerate, carry *or* go too far, overreach, not know when to stop, paint the lily (or gild refined gold), out-Herod Herod, *Colloq* go overboard, do to death, lay it on thick, lay it on with a trowel; go off the deep end **2** °overwork, do too much, overtax, °exhaust, °fatigue, °overload, overburden, *Colloq* bite off more than one can chew, burn the candle at both ends

overdue *adj.* °late, °tardy, behindhand, behind, unpunctual, °belated, *US* past due

overeat *v.* °gorge, binge, gormandize, stuff oneself, overindulge, guzzle, °feast, wolf down, overfeed, do the gavage, *Colloq* pack away, *Brit* pig, *US* pig out

overgrown *adj.* covered, °overrun, overspread, °luxuriant, weedy, °abundant

overhang *v.* **1** °jut (out), beetle, °bulge (out), project (out), °protrude, °stick out, °loom (out), °extend (out), hang (out) over **2** impend, °threaten, °menace, imperil, °loom —*n.* **3** °ledge, °projection, °bulge, °protrusion, °extension

overhaul *v.* **1** °overtake, °pass, gain on *or* upon, draw ahead of, catch up with, get ahead of, °outstrip, outdistance, leave behind, °lap **2** °renovate, °refurbish, recondition, rebuild, °restore, °repair, °service, °adjust, °patch (up), °mend, °fix (up) —*n.* **3** reconditioning, overhauling, refurbishing, rebuilding, renovation, servicing, °adjustment, mending, fixing (up)

overhead *adv.* **1** °(up) above, (up) in the air *or* sky, high up, on high, °aloft, skyward —*adj.* **2** °elevated, raised, °upper —*n.* **3** *Brit overheads, US overhead.* (basic *or* fixed) costs, operating cost(s), expense(s), °outlay, disbursement(s), running cost(s), expenditure(s), °maintenance, cost(s) of doing business

overjoyed *adj.* °delighted, °ecstatic, °elated, °happy, °rapturous, euphoric, jubilant, thrilled, transported, *Colloq* tickled pink, in seventh heaven, on cloud nine, *Brit* over the moon

overlap *v.* **1** °lap (over), overlie, overlay, shingle, *Technical* imbricate, strobilate **2** °coincide, °correspond, intersect —*n.* **3** °lap, °flap, overlay, fly (front) *or Brit* flies, imbrication

overload *v.* **1** °weigh down, °burden, overburden, °load (up), overtax, saddle with, °tax, °strain, °impede, °handicap, °oppress, °encumber, cumber, overcharge —*n.* **2** surcharge, overcharge, overburden, dead weight, °oppression, °handicap, °tax, °load, °encumbrance, °impediment, °hindrance

overlook *v.* **1** °miss, slip up on, °omit, °neglect, °slight, °disregard, fail to notice, °ignore, °pass over, °leave out, °forget, *Colloq* °pass up **2** °blink at, wink at, let go (by), let pass, let ride, turn a blind eye to, shut (one's) eyes to, pretend not to notice, take no notice of, °ignore, °disregard, °forgive, °pardon, °excuse, °permit, °allow, forget about, °write off, condone, make allowances (for), let bygones be bygones, °gloss over **3** front on (to), °face, give upon, command *or* afford a view of, look out on *or* over, have as a vista *or* view

overly *adv.* excessively, too, °exceedingly, immoderately, disproportionately, °unduly, inordinately, extraordinarily, °very, *Colloq* damned

overpower *v.* **1** °overcome, °overwhelm, °beat, vanquish, °conquer, °defeat, °crush, °put down, worst, °best, °prevail, °master, °quell, °subdue, °subjugate **2** °overcome, °overwhelm, dumbfound *or* dumfound, °daze, °stagger, °amaze, °stun, stupefy, °nonplus, °strike, *Colloq* °floor

overpowering *adj.* °overwhelming, °irresistible, °powerful, °telling, compelling, unendurable, °unbearable, °oppressive

overrate *v.* overvalue, make too much of, exaggerate the worth *or* value of, attach too much importance to, overprize, assess too highly

overreact *v.* °exaggerate, make much ado about nothing, make too much of (something), make a mountain out of a molehill, lose all *or* one's sense of proportion, blow (up) out of (all) proportion

overriding *adj.* °dominant, dominating, °predominant, predominating, compelling, °prevailing, °primary, °prime, most important, overruling, °overwhelming, °paramount, preponderant, °principal, °cardinal, °main, °chief

overrun *v.* invade, °defeat, °attack, °ravage, °destroy, °overwhelm, °conquer, harry, vandalize, °plunder, maraud, °scourge, despoil, °sack, °strip, °pillage, °storm, *Colloq* blitz

overseas *adv.* °abroad

oversee *v.* °direct, °manage, °watch (over), keep an eye on, °administer, superintend, °run, °supervise, °operate, °manipulate, °handle, °control

overseer *n.* °superintendent, °supervisor, °manager, °foreman, forewoman, °superior, *Colloq* °boss, °chief, °super, *Brit* gaffer, *US* straw boss, (head *or* chief) honcho

overshadow *v.* **1** °dominate, outshine, °eclipse, °dwarf, °diminish, °minimize, put in(to) *or* throw into *or* leave in the shade, steal the limelight from, tower over *or* above, °excel **2** °spoil, °blight, °ruin, °mar, take (all) the pleasure from, put a damper on, take the edge off, °impair, take the enjoyment out of

oversight *n.* **1** °omission, inadvertence, °neglect, laxity, laxness, °fault, °failure, dereliction, °error, °mistake, °blunder, carelessness, heedlessness **2** supervision, superintendence, °surveillance, °management, °direction, °guidance, °administration; °charge, °care, °custody, keeping, °hands, °protection, °auspices

overstate *v.* °exaggerate, °magnify, hyperbolize, embroider, overstress, °color, make (too) much of, overdraw, overemphasize, °stretch, °enlarge, °inflate, °blow up

overstep *v.* °exceed, °transcend, °surpass, go beyond

overt *adj.* °apparent, °evident, °plain, °clear, °obvious, °manifest, clear-cut, unconcealed, °patent, °open, °visible, °observable, °public

overtake *v.* **1** catch (up with *or* to), °reach, draw level *or* even with, °overhaul, gain on *or* upon, move by *or* past, °pass, leave behind, °outstrip, outdistance **2** come upon, °seize, °catch (unprepared), befall, °strike, °hit, °overwhelm

overthrow *v.* **1** °defeat, °beat, °rout, °conquer, °overpower, °master, bring down, depose, oust, °overwhelm, unseat, unhorse, °topple, °overturn, dethrone, thrash, worst, °best —*n.* **2** °defeat, °rout, °conquest, deposing, ousting, unseating, toppling, °overturn, overturning, °downfall, °end, °ruin, °fall, °collapse, °destruction, °suppression, quashing, crushing, subjugation, *US* ouster

overtone *n.* undertone, connotation, °hint, °suggestion, °innuendo, insinuation, intimation, °indication, °implication

overture *n.* Often, ***overtures.*** approach, °advance, °offer, °proposal, °proposition, °tender

overturn *v.* **1** °turn over, knock down *or* over, °tip over, °capsize, upend, °upset, °turn turtle, turn upside down, turn topsy-turvy, invert **2** bring down, °overthrow, °throw over, °upset, depose, unthrone, dethrone, unseat, oust, °eject —*n.* **3** overturning, °overthrow, unseating, ousting, toppling, °fall, °destruction, °ruin, °defeat, *US* ouster

overwhelm *v.* **1** °overpower, °overcome, overtax, °devastate, °stagger, °crush, °defeat, °destroy, °subdue, °suppress, °quash, °quell, °conquer, °beat, bring down, °prostrate, °weigh down, °oppress **2** inundate, °overcome, engulf, °submerge, °flood (over); deluge, °swamp, °bury, °immerse **3** °overcome, °stagger, °astound, °astonish, dumbfound *or* dumfound, °shock, °stun, °bewilder, °confuse, confound, °nonplus, °surprise, °take aback, *Colloq* bowl over, knock off one's feet *or* pins, blow one's mind, discombobulate, *Brit* knock for six

overwhelming *adj.* **1** °overpowering, uncontrollable, °irresistible, °devastating, unendurable, °unbearable, crushing, °burdensome, °formidable **2** °awesome, awe-inspiring, stupefying, astounding, astonishing, staggering, bewildering, mind-shattering, °prodigious, mind-boggling, *Colloq* mind-blowing

overwork *v.* **1** overexert, overstrain, overburden, °oppress, overtax, °overload, overuse **2** °slave (away), burn the midnight oil, lucubrate —*n.* **3** overexertion, overstrain, °strain

overwrought *adj.* **1** °tense, °nervous, jittery, °jumpy, fidgety, °touchy, in a dither *or* twitter, all atwitter, overexcited, °on edge, overstimulated, °frantic, frenetic, distracted, *Brit* strung up, *US* strung out, *Colloq* (all) worked up, edgy, in a tizzy, wound up, uptight **2** overworked, °ornate, °elaborate, baroque, rococo, florid, °flowery, °fussy, °ostentatious, °busy, °gaudy, °garish

owe *v.* **1** be in debt to, be indebted to, be beholden to **2** ***owing to.*** because of, on account of, °thanks to; °through, as a result of, resulting from, *Colloq* due to

owner *n.* possessor, holder; °proprietor, proprietress

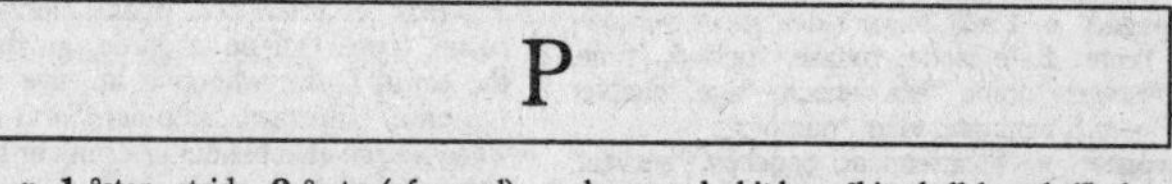

P

pace *n.* **1** °step, stride **2** °rate (of speed), °tempo, °speed, °velocity, *Colloq* °clip —*v.* **3** °walk, stride, tread; °traverse **4** °measure, gauge *or* gage, °judge, °rate, °estimate, °determine, °reckon, °figure, °compute

pack *n.* **1** °parcel, °package, °packet, °bundle, bale, backpack, knapsack, rucksack, haversack, kit-bag, °kit, duffel *or* duffle bag **2** °load, °lot, °bunch, multitude, °heap, °pile, °accumulation, °mass, amassment, °mess, barrel, peck **3** °group, °collection, °assembly, assemblage, congregation, °gathering, °crowd, °number, °throng, horde, °mass, °crew, °gang, °body, lots, loads, °band, °company, °party, °set, °flock, °herd, drove, °mob, °swarm, bevy, covey, °circle, coterie, °clique **4** deck —*v.* **5** Often, ***pack in*** *or* ***into.*** °package, bale, °bundle, °compact, °crowd, °cram, °jam, °fill, °stuff, °squeeze, °ram, °press, °wedge, tamp **6** ***pack it in.*** °stop, °cease, °end, °finish, °quit, °wind up, °terminate, °give up, call it a day, *Colloq* chuck **7** ***pack off.*** °dismiss, send off *or* away, bundle off *or* out, hustle off *or* out *or* away, °get rid of, drive off *or* away, order off *or* away *or* out, send (someone) about his (*or* her) business **8** ***pack up.*** **(a)** get *or* gather together, °put away, °store **(b)** °quit, °stop, °break down, °fail, °give out, °stall, °die, give up the ghost, *Colloq* conk out, have had it

package *n.* **1** °packet, °parcel, °box, container, °case, carton, °bundle **2** °combination, °unit, package deal —*v.* **3** °wrap, °pack, containerize, carton, °case, encase, °enclose, °include; °combine, °unite, coupled, °incorporate

packed *adj.* filled, °full, °loaded, crowded, stuffed, jammed, crammed, brimful, chockablock, chock-full, jampacked, overloaded, overflowing, loaded *or* filled to the gunwales, up to there, bursting, groaning, °swollen, °replete, *Colloq* wall-to-wall

packet *n.* **1** °package, °parcel, °pack, °batch **2** loads, lot(s), °great deal, °fortune, °mint, *Colloq* °bundle, pretty penny, pile(s), tidy sum, king's ransom, *Brit* °bomb

pact *n.* °agreement, °treaty, °bargain, °alliance, °contract, °compact, concord, covenant, concordat, entente, °understanding, °arrangement, °deal

pad *n.* **1** °cushion, pillow, °wad, wadding, stuffing, padding, °filling, filler **2** writing pad, note pad, memo pad, °block (of paper), jotter, *US* filler **3** °flat, apartment, room(s), °home, °place, °quarters, *Colloq* hangout, *Brit* digs *or* diggings, *Slang US* °flop —*v.* **4** °cushion, °wad, °stuff, °fill; upholster **5** Sometimes, ***pad out.*** °expand, °inflate, °stretch, dilate, °lengthen, protract, °extend, °blow up, °flesh out, °puff up, augment, °spin out, °amplify

paddle *n.* **1** °oar, °sweep, scull —*v.* **2** °row, scull, °oar **3** °wade **4** °spank, paddywhack *or* paddywack, thrash, °beat, °whip, °flog

pagan *n.* **1** °heathen, unbeliever, idolater, polytheist, °infidel, Gentile —*adj.* **2** °heathen, °infidel, idolatrous, polytheistic, heathenish, Gentile

page[1] *n.* **1** leaf, folio, °side, °sheet, verso *or* recto **2** °episode, °phase, °period, °time, °stage, °point, °era, epoch, °age, chapter —*v.* **3** paginate, folio, °number

page[2] *n.* **1** °attendant, pageboy, °servant, errand boy *or* girl, messenger (boy *or* girl), *Brit* foot-boy, *US* bellman, bellhop, *Offensive used of an adult* bellboy —*v.* **2** °announce, °summon (forth), send for *or* after, °call, bleep, beep, °call for, call out

pageant *n.* °spectacle, °display, °grandeur, °tableau, °show, °parade, °procession, °ceremony, °formality, °ritual, °event, °affair, °extravaganza, °presentation, °gala

pageantry *n.* °pomp, °ceremony, °display, magnificence, °extravagance, panorama, showiness, °show

pain *n.* **1** °hurt, °suffering, °discomfort, soreness, °ache, aching, °pang, °spasm, smarting, cramp **2** °anguish, °agony, °affliction, °distress, °grief, °woe, °suffering, °misery, travail, wretchedness, °despair, °torment, tribulation, °trial, torture, dolor, discomposure, °ordeal, disquiet **3** irritation, vexation, °annoyance, °bother, °nuisance, °pest, *Colloq* pain in the neck, °headache, °drag, °bore, *Taboo slang* pain in the *Brit* arse *or US* ass **4** ***pains.*** °effort, °trouble, °exertion, toil, °labor —*v.* **5** °hurt, °distress, °grieve, °wound, °injure; °trouble, °depress, °sadden, °sorrow, cut to the quick

painful *adj.* **1** hurting, °grievous, °hurtful, °sore, distressing, distressful, °excruciating, torturous, °agonizing, smarting, stinging, aching, achy, throbbing, °burning, °piercing, stabbing, °sharp, °tender, °sensitive, °raw, °bitter, *Formal* nociceptive **2** vexing, vexatious, annoying, harassing, irritating, °irksome, aggravating, galling, exasperating, unpleasant, afflictive, °harrowing, worrisome, worrying, troubling, disquieting, °disturbing, distressing **3** °painstaking, °laborious, °careful, rigorous, °arduous, assiduous, sedulous, °diligent, °earnest, °conscientious, °meticulous, °scrupulous, °detailed, °thorough, thoroughgoing, °exacting, °demanding

painfully *adv.* agonizingly, distressingly, disagreeably, unpleasantly, unfortunately, °sadly, woefully, lamentably, ruefully, unhappily

painkiller *n.* anodyne, analgesic, anesthetic, °sedative, palliative

painless *adj.* trouble-free, °easy, °simple, °comfortable, °effortless, *Colloq* easy as 1, 2, 3 *or* as ABC, easy as pie, a piece of cake, °pushover, child's play, *Slang* cinch, no sweat

painstaking *adj.* See **painful, 3,** above.

paint *n.* **1** °color, °tint, dye, coloring, pigment, °stain **2** coating, °coat, °surface; enamel **3** °makeup, cosmetics, *maquillage,* greasepaint, *Colloq* war paint, °face —*v.* **4** depict, °portray, °picture, °show, °represent, delineate, °render, °draw, limn, °characterize, °describe **5** °coat, °brush, °apply, °cover, daub **6** °color, °tint, dye, °stain, °decorate **7** ***paint the town red.*** °make merry, °carouse, °revel, go on a spree, go out on the town, *Colloq* whoop it up, live it up, (go on a) pub-crawl, °step out, *Slang* make whoopee, go on a bender *or* drunk *or* binge, booze it up

pair *n.* **1** °couple, twosome, two of a kind, set of two, matched set, duo, dyad, twins, °double, doublet; °brace, °span, yoke, °team, tandem —*v.* **2** °match (up), °mate, pair off *or* up, °team (up), put together, °partner, °twin, °double, °join, °unite, yoke; °wed,

°marry, join in wedlock *or* in holy matrimony

pal *n.* **1** °friend, consort, °comrade, alter ego, crony, °companion, amigo, °playmate, classmate, *Colloq* °chum, sidekick, °mate, *Chiefly US and Canadian* buddy —*v.* **2** ***pal (up) with or about or US around (with).*** °associate (with), be *or* become friendly *or* friends (with), be *or* get *or* become on friendly *or* intimate terms (with), go (around *or* about) with, °fraternize (with), consort (with), spend time together *or* with, keep company (with), *Colloq* hang out *or* about *or* around (with), knock about *or* around (with)

palace *n.* mansion, °castle, stately *or* palatial home *or* residence, manor (house), °(country) estate, chateau, *palazzo,* villa

palatial *adj.* °luxurious, deluxe, °magnificent, °splendid, °stately, °sumptuous, °opulent, °majestic, °magnificent, °grand, °elegant, palatine, *Slang* °posh, ritzy, °swanky, classy

palaver *n.* **1** °nuisance, °procedure, red tape, to-do, rigmarole *or* rigamarole, *Colloq* song and dance, °bother, °nonsense, °business, carry-on, °performance **2** °chatter, °babble, °jabber, (empty *or* small) talk, blather *or* blether, °gossip, prating, °prattle, prattling, palavering, *Brit* natter, nattering, *Scots* clishmaclaver, *Colloq* jawing, °hot air, *Colloq Brit* witter, wittering **3** °parley, °talk, °conference, °discussion, colloquy, °conversation, confabulation, °meeting, °get-together, round table, powwow, *Colloq* confab, °huddle, chinwag —*v.* **4** °chatter, °babble, °jabber, blather *or* blether, °gossip, °prattle, prate, chitchat, gabble, *Brit* natter, witter, *Colloq* jaw, chinwag, *US and Canadian* shoot the breeze, *Slang* yak, yackety-yak **5** °confer, °consult, °discuss, °parley, °talk, °converse, powwow, °meet, °get together, sit down (together), confabulate, °negotiate, *Colloq* confab, °huddle, chew the fat *or* the rag

pale[1] *adj.* **1** °colorless, °white, °wan, sallow, waxen, livid, ashen, ashy, pallid, bloodless, whitish, °pasty, °washed-out, anemic, blanched, wheyfaced, drained, °ghostly, °ghastly, peaky *or* peakish, °peaked, cadaverous **2** °faint, °light, °dim, °washed-out, pastel **3** °feeble, °weak, °flimsy, °meager, enfeebled, °ineffective, °ineffectual, °puny, °insignificant, °paltry, °lame, °poor, °inadequate, °halfhearted, °tame, spiritless, °empty, °sterile, °lifeless, uninspired, anemic, *Colloq* half-baked —*v.* **4** blanch, blench, °dim, whiten **5** °diminish, lessen, °fade (away), °decrease, abate

pale[2] *n.* **1** paling, palisade, °picket, °upright, °post, °stake **2** °boundary, limit(s), °restriction, °bounds, border(s), confines **3** ***beyond the pale.*** °improper, °irregular, °unseemly, unsuitable, °indecent, °unacceptable, °inadmissible, forbidden, anathema, disallowed, prohibited, *verboten,* interdicted; *US* °unusual, °bizarre, °peculiar, °outré, °weird, °abnormal, °strange

pall[1] *n.* **1** °shroud, covering, °mantle, °cloth, °veil **2** gloomy *or* melancholy *or* somber *or* grave *or* depressing air *or* mood *or* atmosphere; damper, cold water, *Colloq* wet blanket

pall[2] *v.* **1** Often, ***pall on or upon.*** °bore, °tire, °weary, °jade, °irk, °irritate, °sicken **2** sate, °satiate, cloy, °glut, °surfeit, °gorge

paltry *adj.* °trifling, trivial, °petty, °small, °insignificant, °worthless, °pitiful, °pathetic, °pitiable, °puny, °sorry, °wretched, °miserable, °inconsequential, inconsiderable, unimportant, °meager, °mean, beggarly, °base, °low, °contemptible, *Colloq* piddling, *Brit* twopenny, tuppenny, twopenny-halfpenny, mingy, *US* penny-ante, *Slang* Mickey Mouse

pamper *v.* °baby, °coddle, cosset, (over)indulge, °spoil, mollycoddle, °cater to, °pet, *Rare* cocker, *Irish* cosher

pamphlet *n.* booklet, °brochure, °tract, °essay, folder, °leaflet, °circular; handbill, °bill, °notice, °bulletin, °advertisement, handout, ad, *Brit* advert, *US* flier, throwaway

pan *n.* **1** saucepan, frying pan, skillet, °pot, casserole, *US* spider **2** °face, visage, mien, façade, *Slang* kisser, °mug, puss **3** °depression, °indentation, concavity, °cavity, °hollow, °pit, °hole, crater —*v.* **4** °wash, °separate, °sift **5** °criticize, censure, °find fault, °put down, °reject, flay, excoriate, *Brit* hammer, *Colloq* °knock, roast, slate, *Slang US* °trash, *Brit* °rubbish **6** ***pan out.*** °succeed, °thrive, °prosper, °flourish, fare well, °make it; °work out, °turn out, °result, °come out, °end (up), conclude, culminate, eventuate

panache *n.* °flourish, °dash, élan, éclat, °chic, °sophistication, °savoir-faire, °savoir-vivre, flamboyance, °verve, °style, cultivation, °(good) taste, °flair, smartness, boldness, self-assurance, °swagger, °vigor, liveliness, °spirit, brio, °gusto, °zest, °animation, °enthusiasm, °energy

pandemonium *n.* °bedlam, °chaos, turmoil, °disorder, °tumult, °frenzy, °uproar, °furor, °confusion

pander *v.* **1** Usually, ***pander to.*** °satisfy, °gratify, °humor, °indulge, °fulfill, bow to, yield to, truckle to, °cater to **2** °procure, °pimp, °solicit —*n.* **3** panderer, °pimp, °procurer, solicitor, whoremonger, white slaver, *Slang* flesh-peddler, *Brit* ponce, mack

pane *n.* panel, °sheet, °glass, windowpane, °light, °quarrel, bull's-eye

pang *n.* **1** °pain, °stab, °ache, °pinch, °twinge, stitch, °spasm **2** °qualm, hesitation, °scruple, °misgiving, °remorse, °regret, contrition, contriteness, self-reproach, mortification, °guilt, °anguish, °discomfort, malaise

panic *n.* **1** °terror, °alarm, °fear, °fright, °dread, °horror, °dismay, consternation, hysteria; °anxiety, apprehension, apprehensiveness, nervousness **2** source of merriment, °comedian, °clown, funnyman, jester, °comic, °wit, °wag, °zany, *farceur,* droll, *Colloq* °(laugh) riot, °scream —*v.* **3** be terrified *or* alarmed *or* fearful *or* frightened *or* terror-stricken *or* terror-struck, °dread, °fear, lose one's nerve; °frighten, °scare; *Colloq* °go to pieces, °fall apart, *Brit* lose one's bottle **4** °frighten, °scare, °alarm, °terrify, °unnerve

panic-stricken *adj.* panic-struck, terrified, alarmed, horrified, aghast, terror-stricken *or* terror-struck, panicky, frenzied, in a frenzy, °hysterical, beside oneself with fear *or* terror, °fearful, °afraid, °scared (stiff), °petrified, horror-struck *or* horror-stricken, frightened *or* scared out of one's wits, appalled, stunned, stupefied, perturbed, unnerved, °nervous, distressed, °upset, jittery, °jumpy, (all) worked up, *Colloq* in a cold sweat, in a flap, in a tizzy, *Slang taboo* scared shitless, shitting green

panoramic *adj.* °sweeping, commanding, °extensive, °comprehensive, °wide, °overall, °scenic, far-reaching, all-embracing, far-ranging, all-encompassing, °inclusive, bird's-eye, °general

pant *v.* **1** °gasp, °huff (and puff), °blow, °heave, breathe hard, wheeze **2** Usually, ***pant for or after.*** crave, °hanker after, hunger *or* thirst for *or* after, yearn for, ache for, °want, °desire, covet, wish for, long *or* pine *or* sigh for, have one's heart set on, die for, be dying for, *Colloq* have a yen for, give one's eyeteeth *or* right arm for

pants *n. pl.* **1** *In Britain* (men's) drawers, smallclothes, smalls, underpants, boxer shorts, trunks, undershorts, Y-fronts, briefs, *Colloq* smalls; (women's) knickers, camiknickers, panties, drawers, bloomers, pantalettes, °tights, pantyhose, undies **2** *In the US* trousers, slacks, breeches, (Oxford) bags, knickerbockers, flannels, °shorts, Bermuda shorts *or* Bermudas, pedal pushers, bellbottoms, pegtops, hiphuggers, (blue) jeans, dungarees, denims, *Trademark* Levis, *Scots* trews; *Scots and North England* breeks, *US* knickers, *Colloq* cut-offs

paper *n.* **1** newspaper, tabloid, °daily, weekly, °journal, gazette, °publication, °periodical, newsletter, °organ, *Colloq* °rag, °sheet **2** Often, ***papers.*** **(a)** document(s), °instrument, legal papers, °form, certificate, °deed, ownership papers; credential(s), °identification **(b)** docket, files, dossier, record(s), archive(s) **3** °stationery, letterhead, writing paper, letter paper, notepaper; foolscap; scrap *or US also* scratch paper; wrapping paper; gift-wrapping, gift-wrap; wallpaper **4** article, °composition, °essay, °assignment, °report, °thesis, °study, °tract, °analysis, critique, exegesis, treatise, dissertation, disquisition, manuscript, Ms. *or* ms., autograph, holograph, typescript, °script, °speech —*v.* **5** (hang) wallpaper, °line; °post, °distribute

par *adj.* **1** °standard, °normal, °average, expected —*n.* **2** °level, °rank, °standing, °scale, °standard **3** ***above par.*** above average, °superior, °outstanding, °excellent, °exceptional; °choice, °select, °prime **4** ***at par.*** °average, °level, °even, °equal, °equivalent, °standard; par value **5** ***below or under par.*** **(a)** below average, substandard, °inferior, second-rate, °mediocre, middling, not up to par, °poor, °inadequate, °unsatisfactory, °wanting, °bad, °wretched, °miserable, °awful, °terrible, *Colloq* °lousy, not up to snuff *or* scratch **(b)** °ill, °sickly, °unhealthy, unwell, not (very) well, not oneself, not in good *or* the best shape, in bad shape, *Brit* off form, off color; *Colloq* °under the weather, °poorly, not up to snuff **6** ***up to par.*** all right, °adequate, °average, °satisfactory, good enough, °passable, °acceptable, *Colloq* OK *or* O.K. *or* okay, up to scratch *or* snuff, fair to middling

parable *n.* allegory, fable, °lesson, morality tale

parade *n.* **1** °procession, °march, °train, °file, °promenade, cortège, column; entourage **2** °exhibition, °(ostentatious) display, °show, °spectacle, array, °pomp, °splash **3** °promenade, °walk, °(pedestrian) way, mall, esplanade —*v.* **4** °march, pass in review, °promenade, °walk, °file **5** °strut, °flaunt, °show (off), brandish, °wave, vaunt, °display, °air

paradise *n.* **1** °heaven, City of God, Zion, Elysium, Elysian Fields, happy hunting grounds, Abraham's bosom, heavenly kingdom, Promised Land, Celestial City, New Jerusalem, Avalon, Valhalla, Hesperides, Isles *or* Islands of the Blessed, seventh heaven **2** heaven on earth, (Garden of) Eden, (land of) Goshen, °utopia, Shangri-La, Land of Beulah **3** °bliss, °happiness, °rapture, °heaven, °delight, blessedness, °ecstasy, seventh heaven, °joy, dreamland, nirvana

paradox *n.* contradiction, self-contradiction, incongruity, inconsistency, °absurdity, °ambiguity, °enigma, °puzzle, °mystery, °quandary, °problem, °dilemma

paradoxical *adj.* °contradictory, self-contradictory, conflicting, oxymoronic, °impossible, °improbable, °incongruous, illogical, °inconsistent, °absurd, °ambiguous, confusing, °equivocal, enigmatic, °puzzling, baffling, °incomprehensible, bewildering, °perplexing, °mysterious, °problematic

paragon *n.* °epitome, archetype, °model, °prototype, °quintessence, °pattern, °standard, exemplar, °ideal, *beau idéal,* criterion

parallel *adj.* **1** °similar, corresponding, congruent, analogous, analogic(al), °correspondent, °like, °matching, homologous, °coordinate, °equivalent, coequal, °proportional, proportionate, *pari passu, mutatis mutandis,* in proportion, °uniform; contemporary *or* cotemporary, contemporaneous *or* cotemporaneous —*n.* **2** analogue, °match, homologue, °equivalent, °complement, counterpart, °equal, coequal **3** analogy, parallelism, equivalence, complementarity, °relationship, °kinship, correspondence, °resemblance, °likeness, similarity, °symmetry, °equality, coequality, °parity, correlation; °proportion, °balance, equiponderance, equipoise, counterbalance, °offset —*v.* **4** correspond to *or* with, °match, equate to *or* with, be likened to, correlate to *or* with, compare with *or* to, °imitate, °repeat, °echo, iterate, °reiterate, °duplicate, °follow, °agree with; keep pace with, °conform (to), °balance, °set off, °offset, even off *or* up, be accompanied by, coincide with, *Colloq* jibe with

paralyze *v.* **1** immobilize, inactivate, deactivate, °transfix; °halt, °stop **2** °deaden, °numb, °freeze, anesthetize, benumb, render insensible **3** disable, °cripple, °incapacitate, disenable

paramount *adj.* °preeminent, °chief, °supreme, °dominant, °main, °predominant, °cardinal, °first, °prime, °primary, °principal, °essential, °vital, requisite, °basic

paramour *n.* °lover, °love, inamorato *or* inamorata, amorist, °mistress, gigolo, concubine, *cicisbeo*, kept woman, *Colloq* °flame, sugar daddy, *US* POSSLQ (= 'Person of Opposite Sex Sharing Living Quarters'), *Slang* fancy man *or* woman

paraphernalia *n.* usually *pl.* equipment, °apparatus, accessories, °outfit, appliances, utensils, °gear, °rig, material(s), materiel, °things, °tackle, equipage, accouterments *or* accoutrements, °effects, chattels, °possessions, °belongings, appurtenances, °trappings, °property, baggage, impedimenta, supplies, °stuff, *Colloq* °junk, *Brit* °rubbish, clobber, *Slang* crap, *Taboo US* shit

paraphrase *n.* **1** rephrasing, rephrase, rewording, restatement, rewriting, rewrite, °rehash, °rendition, °rendering, °version, *Technical* paraphrasis —*v.* **2** rephrase, °reword, restate, rewrite, explicate, °explain

parasite *n.* leech, °hanger-on, *Colloq* freeloader, sponger *or* sponge, °bloodsucker, cadger, scrounger *or* scrounge, barnacle, jackal, hyena

parcel *n.* **1** °package, °packet, carton, °box, container, °case **2** °portion, °plot, plat, °lot, °piece, °section, °tract **3** °lot, °group, °batch, °collection, °pack, °bundle, °set —*v.* **4** Often, ***parcel out.*** apportion, °allot, °deal (out), °dole (out), °mete (out), °hand out, °distribute, °share (out), °divide, *Colloq* divvy (up)

parch *v.* dry (out *or* up), desiccate, dehydrate, exsiccate; °scorch, sear, °burn, bake; °shrivel (up), wither

pardon *n.* **1** °forgiveness, °forgiving, amnesty, °remission, °release, reprieval, absolution, °indulgence, °excuse, excusal, °allowance, overlooking, condonation, exoneration, exculpation —*v.* **2** °forgive, °remit, °release, °reprieve, absolve, °indulge, °allow, °overlook, °let off, °excuse, condone, exonerate, exculpate

pare *v.* **1** °trim, °peel, °skin, °shave (off), shuck; decorticate, excoriate **2** Often, ***pare down.*** °reduce, °diminish, °decrease, cut (back *or* down), °curtail, °slash (back), °lower, lessen

parent *n.* **1** father *or* mother, °progenitor, progenitrix, procreator, begetter, materfamilias *or* paterfamilias; foster parent, stepmother *or* stepfather, °guardian, *Colloq* old lady *or* old man, *Brit old-fashioned or facetious* mater *or* pater **2** °source, °origin, originator, wellspring, fountainhead, °root

parentage *n.* °lineage, ancestry, °line, °family, °extraction, descent, °origin, °pedigree, °stock, °birth, °strain, bloodline, °heritage, °roots

parenting *n.* (of children) rearing, °upbringing, raising, nurturing

parity *n.* **1** °equality, equivalence, consistency, °uniformity, °par, °likeness, similarity, analogy, congruity, similitude, conformity, congruence **2** °proportion, parallelism, analogy, °balance, correspondence

park *n.* **1** garden, green(s), common(s), °preserve, °reserve, greensward, parkland, woodland, °estate, *Chiefly Brit* °reservation **2** *Brit* car park, *US and Canadian and New Zealand* parking lot —*v.* **3** °leave, °put, °deposit, °store

parlance *n.* way *or* manner of talking *or* speaking, *façon de parler*, phrasing, phraseology, °speech, °wording, °language, °idiom, °dialect, °jargon, *Colloq* °lingo

parley *n.* **1** °conference, °discussion, °dialogue, °palaver, deliberation, °meeting, colloquy, colloquium, confabulation, powwow, talk(s), *Colloq* °huddle, confab —*v.* **2** °confer, °discuss, °palaver, °deliberate, °talk (over), °negotiate, °deal, *Colloq* °huddle

parliament *n.* **1** In Great Britain, ***Parliament.*** Houses of Parliament, House of Lords and House of Commons, Westminster, the House, Mother of Parliaments **2** legislature, °council, congress, °diet, °assembly, upper and lower house *or* chamber

parliamentary *adj.* °formal, ordered, °orderly, procedural, conforming, conformist, *US* according to *Roberts Rules of Order*

parlor *n.* living room, *Old-fashioned or Brit* drawing room, *Chiefly Brit* sitting room, °reception (room), °lounge

parlous *adj.* °perilous, °risky, °precarious, °uncertain, °dangerous, °hazardous, °difficult, °ticklish, °awkward, *Colloq* chancy, iffy, *Slang* °hairy

parochial *adj.* regional, °provincial, °narrow, °local, insular, °isolated, °limited, restricted, °narrow-minded, °petty, °shortsighted, °hidebound, °conservative, °conventional, illiberal, °bigoted, °prejudiced, °intolerant, °one-sided, °partial, °biased, °stubborn, °opinionated, °dogmatic, °rigid, °stiff, stiff-necked, °immovable, intractable, unchangeable, unchanging, close-minded, °unsophisticated, unworldly, uncultivated, uncultured

parody *n.* **1** °burlesque, °lampoon, °satire, °caricature, °mockery, mimicry, *Colloq* takeoff, spoof, *Brit* sendup **2** travesty, °mockery, feeble *or* poor imitation, distortion, °perversion, corruption, debasement —*v.* **3** °burlesque, °lampoon, °satirize, °caricature, °mock, °mimic, ape, °ridicule, °deride, °laugh at, °poke fun at, °guy, scoff at, sneer at, rib, °tease, °twit, roast, pillory, make a laughingstock (of), °make sport of, °make fun of, make a monkey of, *Archaic* fleer, *Colloq* °take off, spoof, kid, *Brit* °send up

paroxysm *n.* °fit, convulsion, °spasm, °throe, °seizure, °spell, °outburst, °eruption, °explosion, *Colloq* flare-up

parrot *n.* **1** imitator, °mimic, *Colloq* copycat —*v.* **2** °imitate, °mimic, ape, °copy, °echo, °repeat, °reiterate

part *n.* **1** °piece, °portion, °division, °allotment, °share, °percentage, participation, °interest; °parcel, °fragment, °scrap, shard; some **2** °portion, component, °factor, constituent, °element, °ingredient **3** °role, °function, °duty, °responsibility, °share; °say, °voice, °influence, participation, involvement, °business **4** °role, °character **5** °side, °interest, °cause, °behalf, °faction, °party **6** °neighborhood, °quarter, °section, °district, °region, °area, corner, °vicinity, vicinage, *Colloq* neck of the woods **7** °piece, °portion, °segment, °section; °department, °division, component, °unit **8** ***for the most part.*** mostly, °generally, °usually, °mainly, °in the main, by and large, °on the whole, °chiefly, °principally, essentially, for all practical purposes, °to all intents and purposes, in most cases *or* instances **9** ***in part.*** °partly, °partially, to some extent *or* degree, in some measure, °relatively, comparatively, °somewhat **10** ***on the part of (someone)*** *or* ***on (someone's*** *or* ***one's) part.*** °by, on *or US also* in behalf of, °(as) for, as regards, as far as (someone) is concerned, in the name of, for the sake of, in support of **11** ***take (a) part (in).*** °participate (in), °join (in), be (a) party to, play a part *or* role (in), be involved (in *or* with), associate oneself (with), have *or* take a hand in, °partake (of), °contribute (to) —*v.* **12** °separate, part company, °split up, go his *or* her (*or* their) separate way(s), °break up, say *or* bid goodbye (*or* adieu, etc.); °leave, °depart, go (away *or* off) **13** °separate, °divide, put *or* pull apart, put asunder **14** ***part with.*** °give up, °yield, °relinquish, °release, °sacrifice, °forgo, °renounce, °forsake, let go, °surrender —*adj.* **15** °partial, fractional, °limited

partake *v.* **1** Usually, ***partake in.*** °share (in), °participate (in), take (a) part (in), enter (in *or* into) **2** Usually, ***partake of.*** **(a)** °receive, °get, have a share *or* portion *or* part (of), °share **(b)** °evoke, °suggest, hint at, °intimate, °imply, possess *or* have the quality of

partial *adj.* **1** °incomplete, °fragmentary, not total *or* whole, °imperfect **2** °prejudiced, °biased, °partisan, °inclined, influenced, °one-sided, °jaundiced, unfair, discriminatory **3** ***partial to.*** °in favor of, predisposed to, °fond of, having a soft spot *or* weakness for, having a liking *or* taste *or* predilection for, having a fondness for, feeling an attraction *or* affinity to *or* toward(s), finding enjoyment in

partiality *n.* **1** °prejudice, °bias, °inclination, °favoritism, predilection, predisposition, °leaning, °preference **2** °preference, °taste, °relish, °liking, fondness, °appreciation, °fancy, °love, °eye, °weakness, soft spot, °penchant; fetish *or* fetich

partially *adv.* °partly, °in part, to some extent *or* degree, to a limited *or* a certain extent *or* degree, not totally *or* wholly *or* entirely, restrictedly, incompletely, in some measure, °relatively, comparatively, °moderately, (up) to a (given *or* certain) point, °somewhat

participant *n.* **1** participator, partaker, sharer, °party, contributor, prime mover —*adj.* **2** Usually, ***participant in*** *or* ***of.*** participating, partaking, sharing

participate *v.* Often, ***participate in.*** take part (in), °share (in), partake (in *or* of), °join (in), °engage (in), get *or* become involved (in), be *or* become associated (with), enter (in *or* into), °contribute (to)

particle *n.* atom, molecule, scintilla, °spark, mote, °suggestion, °hint, °suspicion, °gleam, °bit, °crumb, °jot, tittle, whit, mite, °speck, °dot, °spot, iota, °grain, °morsel, °shred, °sliver, °scrap, *Colloq* smidgen or smidgin

particular *adj.* **1** °certain, °specific, °special, °peculiar, °singular, °single, °isolated, °individual, °distinct, °discrete, °separate, °definite, °precise, °express **2** °marked, °special, especial, °exceptional, °remarkable, °noteworthy, °notable, °outstanding, °unusual **3** °detailed, itemized, item-by-item, °thorough, °minute, °precise, °exact, °exacting, °painstaking, °nice, rigorous, °close, blow-by-blow **4** °fussy, °meticulous, °finicky, finical, °fastidious, °discriminating, °selective, °demanding, hypercritical, °critical, *Colloq* pernickety *or US also* persnickety, °choosy, picky —*n.* **5** Usually, ***particulars.*** °detail, minutia, fine point, °item, °specific, °element, °fact, °circumstance, °information **6** ***in particular.*** °particularly, specifically, °precisely, °exactly, °especially, °specially; °particular, °specific, °special, °definite

particularly *adv.* **1** °especially, °specially, exceptionally, peculiarly, singularly, distinctively, uniquely, unusually, uncommonly, °notably, outstandingly, markedly, extraordinarily, °very, °extremely, strikingly, surprisingly, amazingly **2** °in particular, specifically, °especially, °principally, °mainly, exceptionally, °expressly, explicitly, °notably, markedly; °only, solely

parting *n.* **1** separating, splitting, dividing, breaking (up *or* apart), sundering, cleaving; °separation, °split, °division, breakup, °rift, °rupture **2** leave-taking, °farewell, saying goodbye, departure, leaving, °going (away), making one's adieus *or* adieux; valediction —*adj.* **3** closing, °final, concluding, °last, departing, valedictory; deathbed, °dying

partisan *n.* **1** partizan, °devotee, °follower, °supporter, adherent, °backer, °champion, °enthusiast, °fan, °zealot, °fanatic, *Chiefly US and Canadian* booster, *Colloq US* rooter **2**

guerrilla *or* guerilla, freedom fighter, underground *or* resistance fighter, °irregular —*adj.* **3** °one-sided, factional, °biased, tendentious, °sectarian, °opinionated, °partial, °bigoted, °prejudiced, °parochial, myopic, °shortsighted, °nearsighted, °narrow, °narrow-minded, °limited **4** guerrilla *or* guerilla, °freedom, °underground, °resistance, °irregular

partition *n.* **1** °separation, °division, splitting (up), split-up, partitionment, breakup, breaking up, segmenting, segmentation **2** °allotment, allotting, apportionment, apportioning, °distribution, distributing, meting out, doling out, rationing (out), sharing (out), dividing (up), giving *or* handing *or* passing out, parceling out, *Colloq* divvying up **3** (room) divider, °(dividing) wall, °barrier, °screen, separator **4** °compartment, °room, °chamber, °section, °part, °area, °division, subdivision, °cell, °stall, °booth —*v.* **5** °divide (up), °separate, °cut up, subdivide, °split (up) **6** Often, ***partition off.*** °divide, °separate, subdivide, °wall off, °screen (off), fence off

partly *adv.* See **partially,** above.

partner *n.* **1** sharer, partaker, °associate, °colleague, °participant, °accomplice, °accessory, confederate, °comrade, °ally, collaborator, °companion, teammate, °fellow, alter ego, °friend, *Colloq* °pal, sidekick, °mate, *US and Canadian* buddy, °cohort **2** wife *or* husband, spouse, °mate, helpmate, helpmeet, consort; °(live-in) lover, *US* significant other, POSSLQ (= 'Person of Opposite Sex Sharing Living Quarters') **3** °companion, fellow dancer

party *n.* **1** °(social) gathering, (cocktail *or* dinner) party, °celebration, fête *or* fete, °function, °reception, soirée, levee, °festivity, °festivities, °festival, °frolic, °spree, romp, carousal *or* carouse, saturnalia, bacchanalia, debauch, °orgy, *Colloq* °get-together, bash, bust, shindig *or* shindy, ball, at-home, do, *US* blowout, toot, *Brit* beanfeast, beano, knees-up, *Slang US* °hop, *Chiefly US and Canadian* wingding, bust-up, *Brit* rave *or* rave-up **2** °group, °company, °band, °body, °corps, °gang, °crew, °team, °squad, troop, °platoon, °detachment, °detail, cadre, °unit, *Colloq* °bunch, °outfit **3** °side, °interest, °faction, °league, °club, coalition, bloc, °division, °sect, °denomination, °clique, coterie, °set, °cabal, junta *or* junto, partisans, adherents, confederacy, confederation, °federation, *Chiefly US and Canadian* caucus **4** °participant, participator, confederate, °associate, °ally, °accomplice, °accessory, approver, ratifier, upholder, contributor, °supporter, °advocate, °backer, °aid, helper, seconder, promoter, °partisan, defender, exponent, °proponent, °champion **5** °individual, °person, °litigant, plaintiff, defendant, °side, °interest, signer, signatory, cosignatory, °participant, *US* cosigner

parvenu *n.* **1** parvenue, °upstart, arriviste, nouveau riche, °intruder, °adventurer, social climber —*adj.* **2** nouveau riche, °upstart, °intrusive

pass *v.* **1** Often, ***pass by.*** proceed *or* move past, go by *or* past **2** °proceed, move (onward(s)), °go (ahead), °progress, °extend, °lie, °run, °flow, °fly, °roll, °course, °stream, °drift, °sweep **3** let pass, let go (by), °overlook, °disregard, °ignore, pay no heed, °omit, °skip **4** °qualify (in), °pass muster (in), get *or* come through, °succeed **5** °spend, °devote, °use (up), °expend, °employ, °occupy, °fill, while away, °take (up); °dissipate, °waste, °fritter away, °kill **6** °surpass, °exceed, °outdo, °transcend, go beyond, overshoot, °outstrip, outrun, surmount, outdistance **7** °allow, °tolerate, °permit, °approve, °sanction, °accept, °authorize, °endorse, °carry, °agree to, °confirm **8** °give, hand round *or* along *or* over, °transfer, pass on *or* over, °deliver, convey, *Sports US* hand off, *Colloq* °toss, °throw, °reach **9** utter, °express, °issue, °declare, °pronounce, °deliver, °set forth, °offer **10** °go away, °disappear, vanish, °evaporate, fade away, °melt away, evanesce, °cease (to exist), °(come to an) end, °die out, go by the board, °terminate, *Literary* evanish, *Colloq* blow over **11** °go (by), °expire, °elapse; slip by *or* away, °fly; °crawl, °creep, °drag **12** °evacuate, °void, °eliminate, excrete, °defecate, °urinate **13** ***come to pass.*** befall, °happen, °occur, °take place, °come about, °arise, *Colloq* °come off **14** ***pass away.*** **(a)** °die, °expire, °perish, °succumb, breathe one's last, °pass on, go to one's reward, go to one's last resting place, (go to) meet one's maker, *Colloq* go west, give up the ghost, *Slang* croak, kick the bucket, *Chiefly US* bite the dust, turn up one's toes **(b)** vanish, °disappear, °go away, °stop, °cease, °end **15** ***pass by.*** See **1,** above **16** ***pass for or as.*** **(a)** be taken for, be mistaken for, be regarded as, be accepted as **(b)** impersonate, °imitate, °mimic, pass (oneself) off as, come *or* go as, be disguised as, disguise oneself as, assume the guise of, °masquerade as, °pose as, assume the role of, act the part of, act like, pretend to be, °play **17** ***pass off.*** °evaporate, °disappear, evanesce, be emitted **18** ***pass on.*** °proceed, °continue, °progress **(a)** °bequeath, hand down *or* on, °transfer, °make over, °will, °cede, °give **(b)** See **14, (a),** above. **19** ***pass (oneself) off as.*** See **16, (b),** above. **20** ***pass out.*** **(a)** °faint, °collapse, swoon, black out, °drop, *Colloq* conk out, keel over **(b)** °distribute, dole out, mete out, °deal (out), °hand out **21** ***pass over.*** See **3,** above **22** ***pass up.*** °reject, °decline, °refuse, °waive, °turn down, °dismiss, °spurn, °renounce; °deny (oneself), °skip, °give up, °forgo, let go (by), °abandon, forswear, °forsake, let pass, °ignore, pay no heed, °disregard, °omit —*n.* **23** defile, °gorge, col, cwm, °cut, °canyon, °notch, °gap, °gully, couloir; °passage, °opening, °way, °route, °road **24** authorization,

°permit, °license, °approval, safe-conduct, green light, °go-ahead; °permission, °freedom, °liberty, °authority, °clearance; *Colloq* OK *or* O.K. *or* okay **25** free pass, complimentary ticket, *Slang US* twofer, Annie Oakley **26** °state (of affairs), °condition, °situation, °stage, °juncture, °status, crux; °predicament, °crisis **27** °attempt, °trial, °try, °effort, °endeavor **28** (sexual *or* indecent) overture *or* advance(s), °proposition, indecent proposal **29** °maneuver, °approach; °passage, °flight, fly-by, °transit **30** °transfer, °toss, °throw, *US* hand-off

passable *adj.* **1** °satisfactory, °acceptable, °tolerable, all right, °adequate, admissible, allowable, °presentable, °average, °fair (enough), fair to middling, fairly good, middling, not bad, unexceptional, °sufficient, °indifferent, *Colloq* OK *or* O.K. *or* okay, °so-so **2** traversable, °navigable, °open, unobstructed, unblocked

passage *n.* **1** °movement, °moving, °going, °transition, °transit, traversal, °traverse, °progress, crossing, °passing **2** °extract, °excerpt, °selection, °section, °part, °portion, °text, paragraph, canto, stanza, verse, °line, °sentence, °phrase, citation, °quotation **3** °way, °route, avenue, °course, °channel; °road, thoroughfare **4** °corridor, °hall, passageway, hallway, vestibule, °lobby, foyer **5** °change, °mutation, °shift, conversion, °progression, °passing **6** °passing, °elapse, °progress, °progression, °flow, °march, °advance **7** voyage, °trip, °journey, °cruise, crossing, °sail, °run, °travel, °traveling; *Brit* accommodation *or US* accommodations, arrangement(s), °facilities **8** safe-conduct, °permission, °privilege, °liberty, °freedom, visa, authorization, °allowance **9** enactment, ratification, °sanction, °approval, acceptance, °passing, adoption, °endorsement, endorsing, legitimatization *or* legitimization, legalization, legislation, constitutionalization, ordainment **10** °traffic, trafficking, dealing, shipment, shipping, °commerce, °trade, °exchange, °transaction **11** °aperture, °hole, orifice, °opening; °entry, access, inlet; °exit, °outlet

passé *adj.* °old-fashioned, unfashionable, dated, out-of-date, °behind the times, outmoded, °obsolete, °obsolescent, °antiquated, archaic, démodé, °quaint, °antique, superseded, *Colloq* °out, not *or* no longer in, old hat, back number

passenger *n.* rider, °fare, °traveler, voyager, commuter

passing *adj.* **1** disappearing, vanishing, ephemeral, °brief, °going, fading (away), slipping away, °short-lived, expiring, °transient, transitory, °temporary, °momentary, °fleeting, transitional, impermanent **2** °hasty, °superficial, °cursory, °casual, °quick, °fleeting, °brief, °summary, °abrupt, dismissive; glancing **3** ***in passing.*** °by the way, °incidentally, by the by, parenthetically, *en passant* —*n.* **4** °death, °dying, demise, °end, °loss, expiry, °expiration, dying out, extinction, disappearance, vanishment

passion *n.* **1** Often, ***passions.*** °ardor, ardency, °eagerness, °intensity, °fervor, fervency, fervidness, zeal, zealousness, avidity, avidness, °zest, zestfulness, vivacity, vivaciousness, °gusto, °verve, °emotion, °feeling, °animation, °spirit, spiritedness, °vigor, °enthusiasm, °eagerness; °zealotry, °fanaticism, feverishness **2** °fit, °outburst, °frenzy, °paroxysm, °seizure, °spasm, convulsion, °eruption, °whirlwind, °tempest, °storm, °ferment, °fury, furor *or Brit* furore **3** infatuation, °mania, °obsession, °craze, craving, °lust, °(unquenchable) thirst, °(insatiable) hunger, °itch, yearning, °longing, °desire, concupiscence, °love, °affection, °enthusiasm, compulsion, fondness, predilection, keenness, °fancy, °fascination, °partiality, °liking, °interest, °weakness, *Colloq* yen **4** °love, heart's desire, °beloved, °idol, hero *or* heroine, °obsession, *Colloq* heartthrob, dreamgirl *or* dreamboy **5** Usually, ***Passion.*** °pain, °suffering, °agony, martyrdom

passionate *adj.* **1** °ardent, °eager, °intense, fervid, zealous, avid, °earnest, zestful, °feverish, fanatic(al), vehement, °impassioned, °emotional, °animated, °spirited, °enthusiastic, °vigorous, invigorated, °energetic **2** aroused, °lustful, °lecherous, °erotic, °sexual, amorous, °sensual, *Colloq* °hot **3** °quick-tempered, irascible, °hot-headed, °fiery, °testy, huffy *or* huffish, °peevish, °cranky, peppery, choleric, °touchy, blious, °snappish, °volatile, °cross, °temperamental, °irritable, °quarrelsome, °pugnacious, °argumentative, contentious, °belligerent, *Rare* atrabilious *or* atrabiliar

passive *adj.* **1** °inactive, nonaggressive, °inert, motionless, unresponsive, °quiet, °calm, °tranquil, °serene, placid, °still, °idle, unmoving, °unmoved, °impassive, untouched, °cool, °indifferent, °phlegmatic, uninterested, uninvolved, °dispassionate, apathetic, °lifeless, °listless, quiescent, unperturbed, °unaffected, imperturbable, unshaken, *Colloq* laid-back, out of it **2** °submissive, repressed, deferential, °yielding, compliant, complaisant, °receptive, °flexible, malleable, °pliable, °tractable, docile, °subdued, °sheepish, ovine, lamblike, cowlike, bovine, °tame, °gentle, °meek, °patient, unresisting, unassertive, forbearing, °tolerant, resigned, long-suffering, *Colloq US* excuse-me-for-living **3** unexpressed, °tacit, unrevealed, undisclosed, °implicit, unasserted

password *n.* watchword, °shibboleth, open sesame, countersign

past *adj.* **1** °over, done, finished, (over and) done with, gone (and forgotten), dead (and buried *or* gone), °defunct **2** °late, °former, one-time, °sometime, °previous, °prior, erstwhile, quondam, whilom; °last, °recent —*adv.* **3** on, °(close) by, °nearby **4** ago, °before, heretofore, since —*n.* **5** °history, °background, °life, lifetime, °existence, °career, lifestyle, biography **6** days *or* years *or* times gone by, days of yore, old times, olden times *or* days, former times, (good) old days, days of old, days beyond recall

pastiche *n.* °mixture, °medley, °blend, °compound, composite, °patchwork, olla podrida, °potpourri, motley, °miscellany, omnium-gatherum, mélange, gallimaufry, farrago, °mishmash, hotchpotch *or US also* hodgepodge, °tangle, *Colloq* °mess

pastime *n.* °hobby, avocation, °recreation, °diversion, °distraction, °amusement, °entertainment, °fun, °play, leisure-time activity, °relaxation, °leisure, °sport, divertissement

pastor *n.* vicar, °clergyman, clergywoman, parson, °minister, churchman, churchwoman, rector, canon, reverend, °father, °divine, ecclesiastic, °priest, bishop

pastoral *adj.* **1** bucolic, °idyllic, Edenic, °innocent, °simple, °tranquil, °serene, °quiet, °restful, °peaceful, °peaceable, placid, pacific, °harmonious, °simple, uncomplicated, *Literary* Arcadian, georgic **2** °country, °rural, °rustic, °provincial, °farming, agricultural, agrarian; °humble **3** °clerical, ministerial, ecclesiastic(al), church(ly) *—n.* **4** idyll, eclogue, georgic

pasture *n.* °meadow, meadowland, pastureland, grassland, grass, lea, °range; pasturage

pasty *adj.* °wan, pallid, pasty-faced, sallow, °pale, pale-faced, wheyfaced, °sickly, anemic

pat[1] *v.* **1** °tap, °touch, °dab, °pet, °stroke, °caress **2** ***pat on the back.*** °congratulate, commend, °praise, °compliment, °encourage, °reassure *—n.* **3** °tap, °touch, °dab, °stroke, °caress **4** °(small) piece, °lump, °cake, °portion; patty **5** ***pat on the back.*** commendation, °praise, °compliment, °flattery, °encouragement, °credit, reassurance, °approval, °endorsement, °recognition; honeyed words

pat[2] *adv.* **1** °perfectly, °exactly, °precisely, faultlessly, flawlessly, just so *or* right, *Brit* off pat **2** aptly, suitably, appositely, °readily, °appropriately, fittingly, relevantly *—adj.* **3** apt, °suitable, apposite, °ready, °appropriate, °fitting, °relevant

patch *n.* **1** °piece, °scrap, °reinforcement; °shred, °snip, snippet, °tatter; °pad **2** °area, °section, °segment, plat, °plot, °lot, °tract, °ground, °parcel, °field **3** °responsibility, °area, bailiwick, °territory; °(line of) country, line of work **4** °period, °interval, °spell, °stage, °episode, °time; °experience *—v.* **5** patch up *or* over, °mend, °repair, vamp, °revamp, darn, °sew (up), °reinforce, °cover **6** Often, ***patch up.*** °fix (up), °doctor, jury-rig, °improvise, knock together *or* up **7** ***patch up.*** °settle, set right *or* straight, °straighten out, °reconcile, °resolve, °heal; come *or* bring to terms, bury the hatchet, kiss and make up, call a truce

patchwork *n.* pastiche *or* pasticcio, °mixture, °confusion, hotchpotch *or US also* hodgepodge, gallimaufry, olio, olla podrida, °mishmash, °jumble, mélange, °medley, °hash, *US* crazy quilt, *Colloq* mixed bag

patent *n.* **1** certificate of invention, letters patent, trade name, trademark, copyright, *US* service mark; °license, °permit, °charter, franchise, °grant; °control *—adj.* **2** °obvious, °clear, °transparent, °manifest, °apparent, °plain, °evident, °self-evident, unmistakeable *or* unmistakable, unequivocal, °explicit, palpable, °tangible, °physical, °conspicuous, °flagrant, °blatant, °prominent

paternal *adj.* **1** °fatherly, °kindly, °indulgent, °solicitous, °fond, °concerned, °devoted, loving; patriarchal **2** patrilineal *or* patrilinear, patriclinous *or* patroclinous *or* patriclinal *or* patroclinal *or* patriclinic *or* patroclinic, patrilateral, patrimonial

paternity *n.* fatherhood, fathership; °parentage, descent, °heritage, °line, °lineage, °extraction, °family, °stock, °strain, blood, patrilineage

path *n.* **1** footpath, pathway, towpath, °track, °trail, °walk, walkway, *Brit* footway **2** °way, °course, °track, °route, °road; °orbit, °trajectory, °circuit **3** °course, °approach, °channel, °direction, °procedure, °process, °way, avenue, °means, °method, °technique, °strategy, °scheme, °plan, *Colloq US* game plan, °scenario

pathetic *adj.* **1** °moving, °stirring, affecting, affective, °touching, °emotional, emotive, °poignant, °tragic, °heart-rending, heartbreaking, °pitiful, °pitiable, °piteous, plaintive, plangent, °wretched, °miserable, °sorrowful, °grievous, °sad, °doleful, dolorous, °mournful, woeful, °lamentable **2** °meager, °paltry, °feeble, °inadequate, °poor, °petty, °puny, °sorry, piddling, *Colloq* °measly, *Slang* crummy

patience *n.* **1** °tolerance, forbearance, °restraint, toleration, sufferance, leniency, °submission, °resignation, °self-control, imperturbability, even temper, unflappability, composure, calmness, °serenity, equanimity **2** diligence, °tenacity, doggedness, indefatigability, °endurance, assiduity, °perseverance, constancy, °persistence, steadfastness, pertinacity, °determination, °resolve, °resolution, firmness, °stoicism, °fortitude, *Colloq US* stick-to-itiveness

patient *adj.* **1** resigned, °submissive, °stoical, long-suffering, compliant, acquiescent, °passive, °self-possessed, °philosophical, °serene, unaggressive **2** °diligent, dogged, °tenacious, °persistent, assiduous, sedulous, °steadfast, °staunch, perseverant, unwavering, unswerving, °constant, unfaltering, unfailing, °untiring, °tireless, indefatigable, pertinacious, °determined, resolved, °resolute, °firm, unyielding **3** forbearing, °tolerant, °forgiving, °lenient, °accommodating *—n.* **4** °invalid, sufferer, °case, valetudinarian

patriot *n.* nationalist, loyalist; flag waver, jingo, jingoist, chauvinist

patriotic *adj.* nationalist(ic), loyalist; flag-waving, jingoist(ic), chauvinist(ic)

patrol *n.* **1** °guard, sentry, °watch, °watchman, °sentinel, patrolman **2** °rounds, policing, patrolling, °beat; protecting, °protection, guarding, safeguarding, defending, watchfulness, °vigilance —*v.* 3 °police, °guard, °protect, °defend, watch over, walk a beat, make (the) rounds, stand *or* keep guard *or* watch (over), keep vigil

patron *n.* 1 patroness, °benefactor, benefactress, °philanthropist, Maecenas, °protector, °supporter, defender, °advocate, °champion, °guardian (angel), °sponsor, °backer, promoter, °sympathizer, °friend, *US* booster; friend at court; *Colloq* angel 2 °customer, °client, purchaser, °buyer, patronizer, °habitué, °regular, frequenter

patronage *n.* 1 sponsorship, °support, °backing, °promotion, °encouragement, boosting, °aid, °help, °sympathy, financing, °auspices, °protection, guardianship, aegis 2 °trade, °business, °custom, trading, °traffic 3 condescension, disdain, °scorn, °contempt, contumely, °superiority, patronizing, stooping, deigning, °humiliation 4 °favoritism, °partiality, °preference, °bias, nepotism, political patronage, granting of indulgences, *US* °spoils (system)

patronize *v.* 1 °look down on, °scorn, look down one's nose at, treat condescendingly, talk down to, treat as (an) inferior, disdain, demean, °put down, °humiliate, *Formal* contemn 2 bring trade to, deal *or* trade *or* do *or* transact business with, buy *or* purchase from, °frequent, shop at, be a customer *or* client of 3 °sponsor, °support, °back, °promote, °encourage, °boost, °aid, °assist, °help, °fund, contribute *or* subscribe to, °underwrite, °foster

patter[1] *v.* 1 tiptoe; °scurry, scuttle, °skip, °trip 2 °spatter, pitter-patter, °tap, pitapat; °beat, °pelt —*n.* 3 °spatter, spattering, pitapat, pitter-patter, tattoo, drum, thrum, °beat, beating, °tap, rat-a-tat, tap-tap-tap

patter[2] *n.* 1 °pitch, sales talk, spiel, °line 2 °chatter, °prattle, prate, babbling, °babble, gabble, gabbling, cackle, cackling, °palaver, °jabber, jabbering, chitchat, small talk, °gossip, blather *or* blether, gibberish *or* gibber, *Chiefly Brit* natter, nattering, *Scots* clishmaclaver, *Colloq* °gab, gabbing, *Slang* gas, °hot air, yackety-yak, yak —*v.* 3 °chatter, °prattle, prate, °babble, gabble, cackle, °palaver, °jabber, °rattle (on), chitchat, chaffer, °gossip, blather *or* blether, gibber, *Chiefly Brit* natter, witter (on), *Colloq* °gab, *Slang* gas, yackety-yak, yak, jibber-jabber

pattern *n.* 1 °model, °original, archetype, °prototype, exemplar, °paragon, °ideal, °standard, °yardstick, criterion, °gauge, °measure 2 °figure, °motif, °design, °device, °decoration, °ornament 3 °system, °order, °arrangement, °plan, °theme; °repetition, consistency, orderliness, °regularity, °sequence, °cycle 4 blueprint, diagram, °plan, layout, °design, °draft, °guide, template *or* templet, stencil, °mold, matrix 5 °sample, °example, °instance, °specimen, °representation 6 layout, configuration, °figure, °formation, °composition —*v.* 7 Often, ***pattern on.*** °model on, °imitate, °copy, °mimic, °duplicate, °follow, emulate, simulate 8 °decorate, °figure, °ornament

paunch *n.* belly, potbelly, *Colloq* corporation, *US* bay window, *Slang* beer belly

pauper *n.* have-not, °indigent, down-and-out(er), bankrupt, °insolvent; °beggar, mendicant; °tramp, hobo, vagrant, *US* °bum

pause *v.* 1 °hesitate, °interrupt, °delay, °hold up, °discontinue, °break, °wait, mark time, °suspend, intermit, falter, °rest —*n.* 2 hesitation, °interruption, °delay, °lull, °lapse, °moratorium, °holdup, °wait, °break, breather, breathing space, discontinuity, lacuna, hiatus, °abeyance, discontinuation, discontinuance, *Prosody* caesura, *Music* fermata, *Colloq* °letup

pave *v.* 1 macadamize, tarmac, asphalt, tile, °flag, °concrete, °cover, °surface 2 ***pave the way for or to.*** prepare *or* smooth the way for, open the door for, make easy *or* easier for; °facilitate, °ease

pawn[1] *v.* 1 °pledge, mortgage, hypothecate, °plight, °deposit, *Formal* pignorate, *Archaic* gage, *Colloq Brit* °pop, *Chiefly US and Canadian* hock 2 °venture, °stake, °risk, °gamble, °hazard, °chance, °jeopardize —*n.* 3 collateral, guaranty *or* guarantee, °pledge, surety, °security, °assurance, °bond, bail, °deposit

pawn[2] *n.* °tool, cat's-paw, °puppet, °instrument, °dummy, °dupe, *Colloq* stooge

pay *v.* 1 recompense, °compensate, remunerate, °reward, indemnify; °repay, refund, °reimburse; °pay off, °pay out, pay up, °satisfy, °clear, °remit, °discharge, liquidate, °settle, °honor, °meet 2 °reward, °benefit, recompense, °requite, °compensate 3 °extend, °bestow, °transmit, °pass on, °give, °deliver 4 °benefit, °profit, avail, (turn out to) be *or* prove profitable *or* worthwhile, yield a return, be advantageous, produce results, °pay off 5 Often, ***pay back.*** °repay, °retaliate, settle (accounts) (with), even the score *or* a score (with), °reciprocate, °requite, take *or* get revenge on, avenge oneself for *or* on, treat in kind, hit *or* strike *or* get back (at), settle *or* pay off (with), exact one's pound of flesh (from), make (someone) pay (for), °punish, °chastise, °castigate, *Brit* °pay out, *Colloq* get even (with) 6 °suffer (the consequences), °answer (for), °make amends (for), °atone (for), get one's (just) deserts, undergo punishment (for), be punished (for) 7 produce *or* make *or* generate *or* earn money, yield a return, °pay off 8 ***pay back.*** (a) recompense, °compensate, remunerate, °reward, indemnify; °repay, °pay off, refund, °reimburse (b) See 5, above. 9 ***pay for.*** See 6, above. 10 ***pay off.*** (a) See 4 *and* 7 *and* 8 (a), above. (b) °bribe, suborn, buy off, grease (someone's) palm, give (someone) a bribe *or* a rebate, *Colloq* give (someone) a kickback, slip (someone) something 11 ***pay out.*** (a) °distribute, deal out, °give out, °disperse, disburse (b) disburse, °expend, °spend, °contribute, *Colloq* °shell out, °lay out, *US and Canadian and Australian and New Zealand,* kick in with, *Slang* cough up, fork out *or* over *or* up **(c)** °release, °loosen, °let out, slack *or* slacken off (on) **(d)** See **5,** above **—*n.*** **12** °payment, compensation, recompense, °settlement, °return; °remuneration, °consideration, °reward, °money, °wages, °salary, °fee, °honorarium, °remittance, °stipend, °income, takings, take-home (pay), °gain, °profit, *Colloq US* °take

payable *adj.* °due, owed, owing, °outstanding, °unpaid, receivable, °mature

payment *n.* **1** See **pay, 12,** above. **2** °expenditure, disbursement, °distribution, °outlay, °fee, contribution, °charge, °expense, payout

payoff *n.* **1** See **pay, 12,** above. **2** °result, °outcome, °upshot, conclusion, windup, °settlement, final reckoning, *Colloq* punch line, °crunch, grand finale, *Slang US and Canadian* kicker **3** °bribe, °graft, °rebate; °ransom, blood money, *Colloq* °kickback, hush money, *Chiefly US* payola, *US* plugola

peace *n.* **1** °serenity, tranquillity, °calm, calmness, placidity *or* placidness, peace of mind, °quiet, peacefulness, peaceableness, stillness **2** °harmony, °accord, harmoniousness, concord, amity, peacefulness, peacetime; cease-fire, armistice, °truce

peaceable *adj.* **1** See **peaceful, 1,** below. **2** pacific, °inoffensive, dovish, peace-loving, °mild, nonviolent, nonbelligerent, unbelligerent, unwarlike, nonwarring, noncombative, °temperate, °agreeable, compatible, congenial, °genial, °friendly, °amiable, °amicable, °cordial, °civil

peaceful *adj.* **1** °peaceable, °serene, placid, °calm, °quiet, quiescent, °gentle, °restful, °tranquil, untroubled, undisturbed, unruffled **2** See **peaceable, 2,** above.

peacemaker *n.* conciliator, pacifier, reconciler, propitiator, placater, pacificator, °mediator, arbitrator, intermediator, °intermediary, diplomat, appeaser, interceder, °go-between, referee, °umpire, adjudicator; peacemonger

peak *n.* **1** °top, °pinnacle, °crest, °ridge, tor, mountaintop, °summit, °mountain, eminence, °elevation, °hill **2** °top, °tip, tiptop, apex, °acme, culmination, apogee, °zenith, high point, °crown, °extreme, utmost, uttermost, °perfection, ***ne plus ultra,*** °consummation, °climax **3** visor, °brim, *US* °bill, nib **—*v.*** **4** °rise, °crest, culminate, °(reach a) climax, °top (out)

peaked *adj.* pinched, °unhealthy, °sickly, ailing, °ill, unwell, °infirm, °unwholesome, °pale, pallid, °wan, waxen, anemic, °pasty, sallow, wheyfaced, ashen, °washed-out, drained, °emaciated, wasted, °gaunt, hollow-eyed, °haggard, °drawn, °weak, °feeble, *Brit* peaky *or* peakish

peal *n.* **1** ringing, °ring, carillon, °chime, chiming, °toll, tolling, clang, clangor, tintinnabulation, clamor, reverberation; knell; °clap, °crash, °roar, rumble, °thunder **—*v.*** **2** °ring, °toll, °chime, clang, tintinnabulate, reverberate, resonate, °resound; knell; °boom, °crash, °roar, °roll, rumble, °thunder

pearl *n.* °gem, °treasure, °prize, cream, °flower, °wonder, °nonpareil

pearly *adj.* nacreous, pearllike, perlaceous, °lustrous, mother-of-pearl

peasant *n.* °rustic, countryman, countrywoman, °farmer, °provincial, °(farm) worker, (country) bumpkin, bucolic; peon, fellah, muzhik *or* mouzhik *or* mujik; *Historical* esne, serf, *Archaic* swain, hind, churl, *Derogatory* yokel, hillbilly, bogtrotter, oaf, °lump, lout, °boor, churl, °clod, clodhopper; *Colloq US and Canadian* hick, galoot *or* galloot, *Derogatory* hayseed, rube, *Derogatory and offensive US* poor white (trash)

peccadillo *n.* °slip, °error, °lapse, °mistake, infraction, °violation, °misdeed, °shortcoming, °misstep, °blunder, faux pas, °indiscretion, gaffe, °botch, °stumble, °fault, petty sin, °(minor) transgression, trespass, *Colloq* slip-up, goof

peculiar *adj.* **1** °odd, °curious, °strange, °queer, °bizarre, °weird, °unusual, °abnormal, anomalous, aberrant, deviant *or* deviate, °eccentric, uncommon, °outlandish, °exceptional, °extraordinary, out-of-the-ordinary, °offbeat, °unorthodox, atypical, idiosyncratic, unconventional, °out-of-the-way, °quaint, °unique, °singular, one-of-a-kind, sui generis, °distinct, °distinguished, °special, °particular, quirky, °funny, freakish, *Slang* far-out, freaky, *Brit* rum **2** Usually, ***peculiar to.*** typical of, characteristic of, characterized by, natural to, symptomatic of, appropriate to *or* for, distinctive of, restricted to, °specific to, °indicative of, denotative of, limited to, individual to, personal to, special to, unique to; seen *or* observed (only) in, local to, native to, indigenous to **—*n.*** **3** *Typography* °arbitrary, °sort

peculiarity *n.* **1** idiosyncrasy, °oddity, °eccentricity, °abnormality, irregularity, °quirk, °kink, crotchet, caprice **2** °feature, °characteristic, °property, °quality, °trait, °attribute, earmark, °hallmark, °mark, particularity, °singularity, °specialty

pedantic *adj.* **1** didactic, doctrinaire, donnish, pedagogic, pedantical, preachy, professorial, bookish, °ostentatious, °pretentious, sententious, °pompous, °vain, °stuffy, °stilted, °stiff, °dry **2** °perfectionist, °scrupulous, overscrupulous, finicky *or* finical, °fussy, punctilious, °fastidious, °meticulous, °exact, choplogic, hair-splitting, quibbling, *Colloq* nit-picking

peddle *v.* °sell, hawk, °market, vend, huckster, *Colloq* °push, °flog

peddler *n.* hawker, (door-to-door) salesman *or* saleswoman *or* salesperson, vendor, huckster, °seller, colporteur, *US* drummer, *Chiefly Brit* pedlar, *Archaic* chapman, *Colloq* cheapjack

pedestal *n.* **1** °foundation, °base, °platform, °stand, substructure, mounting, °pier, foot, °support, *Technical* plinth, socle, dado **2** ***put or place or set on a pedestal.*** °glorify,

°exalt, °worship, deify, °revere, °idolize, °dignify, apotheosize, ennoble, elevate, °raise

pedestrian *n.* **1** walker, stroller, ambler, rambler, footslogger; itinerant, peripatetic —*adj.* **2** °boring, °dull, °banal, °tiresome, commonplace, mundane, °tedious, unimaginative, uninteresting, °monotonous, °run-of-the-mill, °humdrum, °stock, °prosaic, insipid, °dry, °flat, jejune, °colorless, °dreary, °pale, °ordinary, hackneyed, trite, (as) dull as ditchwater *or US also* dishwater, °vapid, °stale, uninspired, uninspiring, spiritless, °lifeless, °dead **3** walking, strolling, ambulatory, on foot, °rambling, peripatetic

pedigree *n.* (line of) descent, ancestry, genealogy, blood, bloodline, °line, °extraction, °lineage, °stock, °heritage, °family, °derivation, °birth, °parentage, °strain, °roots

peek *v.* **1** °peer, °peep, glimpse, °look, squint (at), squinny (at), *Scots* keek, *Colloq* take *or* have a gander (at), *Brit* take a dekko (at) —*n.* **2** °look, glimpse, °peep, °glance, *Scots* keek, *Colloq* gander, look-see

peel *v.* **1** Sometimes, ***peel off.*** °skin, °strip (off), °pare, flay, °flake off, descale, decorticate; shuck, °hull, bark, °scale; desquamate **2** °strip, undress, °disrobe; do a striptease **3** ***peel off.*** take off *or* doff, strip off —*n.* **4** °skin, °rind, coating, peeling

peep *v.* **1** °chirp, tweet, cheep, squeak, °twitter, °pipe, chirrup —*n.* **2** °chirp, tweet, cheep, squeak, °twitter, °pipe, chirrup, chirr *or* chirre *or* churr **3** °sound, °complaint, °outcry, °protest, protestation, grumble, °murmur

peer[1] *n.* **1** °noble, nobleman *or* noblewoman, lord *or* lady, aristocrat; duke *or* duchess, marquess *or* marchioness, earl *or* countess, viscount *or* viscountess, baron *or* baroness **2** °equal, coequal, compeer, °like, °match, confrere, °associate, °colleague

peer[2] *v.* **1** °peep, °peek, squint (at), squinny (at), °look, °examine; °spy **2** °appear, peep through *or* out, °break through, °show, become visible, °emerge

peerless *adj.* without equal, unequaled, °matchless, unmatched, unrivaled, °unique, °incomparable, beyond compare, °unparalleled, °nonpareil, inimitable, unexcelled, unsurpassed, °superior, °superb, °excellent, °supreme, °superlative, finest, °best, ***ne plus ultra***, °sovereign, consummate, °preeminent, °paramount

peevish *adj.* °irritable, °testy, °touchy, °fretful, ill-humored, °waspish, °petulant, crabbed, churlish, °querulous, °short-tempered, ill-natured, tetchy, °cross, bad-tempered, ill-tempered, °faultfinding, captious, carping, caviling, crusty, curmudgeonly, crotchety, °cantankerous, grumpy *or* grumpish, pettish, acrimonious, splenetic, *Colloq* °bilious, *US and Canadian and Irish* °cranky

peg *n.* **1** °pin, dowel, °rod, °stick, °bolt; thole *or* tholepin; clothes peg, °hook **2** ***take down a peg (or two).*** °humble, °diminish, °lower, °subdue, °suppress, °downgrade, °dishonor, °mortify, °humiliate, °put down, abase, °debase, devalue *or* devaluate —*v.* **3** °fasten, °secure, make fast, °fix, °attach, °pin **4** °fix, °attach, °pin, °set, °control, °limit, °restrict, confine, °freeze, °bind, °regulate, °govern **5** °toss, °throw, °shy, °flip, °sling, °cast **6** ***peg away*** *or US also* ***along.*** work (away) (at), °persevere (at), apply oneself (to), persist (in *or* at), go to *or* at (it), °keep at (it), stick to *or* with *or* at (it), stay with *or* at (it), carry on (with *or* at), *Colloq* plug away (at), beaver away (at), hammer *or* bang *or* peck away (at)

pell-mell *adv.* **1** °helter-skelter, slapdash, rashly, feverishly, incautiously, confusedly, chaotically, wildly, impulsively, recklessly, slapbang, impetuously, °hastily, hurriedly, precipitately, spontaneously —*adj.* **2** °helter-skelter, slapdash, °rash, °feverish, incautious, °confused, disordered, °disorderly, disorganized, °wild, °mad, °chaotic, °tumultuous, panicky, °impulsive, °reckless, °precipitate, °impetuous, °hasty, °hurried —*n.* **3** °confusion, °disorder, °chaos, °tumult, °pandemonium, turmoil, melee *or* mêlée, °furor, commotion, °bedlam, brouhaha, hubbub, °excitement

pelt[1] *v.* **1** °bombard, °shower, °bomb, °pepper, strafe, °batter, °shell, assail, °assault, °attack, *US* pummel *or* pommel, °belabor, °pound, *Old-fashioned* lay about, *Slang US* clobber, wallop, paste, work over **2** Often, ***pelt down.*** °beat, °dash, °pound, °hit; come down, °teem, °pour, *Colloq* rain cats and dogs, bucket down, *US* rain pitchforks **3** ***pelt along*** *or* ***over.*** °hurry, °rush, °run, °dash, °shoot, scoot, °scurry —*n.* **4** °stroke, °blow, whack, °hit, smack, °slap, thwack, bang, thump, *Colloq* wallop, °belt

pelt[2] *n.* °skin, °hide, °coat, fur, °fleece

pen[1] *n.* **1** writing instrument, fountain pen, ballpoint (pen), *Brit Trademark* Biro, *Old-fashioned* quill —*v.* **2** write (down *or* up *or* out), °jot down, °(make a) note (of), °draft, °draw up, °compose, put on paper, commit to paper, commit to writing, put in writing, scribble, °scrawl, °scratch, *Formal* indite

pen[2] *n.* **1** coop, °enclosure, hutch, (pig)sty, °pound, °fold, °stall, confine, *US and Canadian* corral —*v.* **2** Often, ***pen up.*** °enclose, confine, coop up, °shut up, impound, °round up, *US and Canadian* corral

penal *adj.* correctional, °punitive, disciplinary

penalize *v.* °punish, °discipline, mulct, amerce, °fine, °handicap, impose *or* invoke a penalty against, impose a penalty on, *Formal* amerce; °sentence

penalty *n.* °punishment, °discipline, °penance, °sentence; °forfeit, °fine, °handicap, °price, mulct, *Formal* amercement; °imprisonment, incarceration

penance *n.* **1** °punishment, °penalty, reparation, °amends, °atonement, self-punishment, self-mortification, °regret, repentance, contrition, °suffering, °penitence **2** ***do penance.*** °pay, °suffer, make amends *or* repara-

tion(s), °atone, wear sackcloth and ashes *or* a hair shirt
penchant *n.* °inclination, °bent, proclivity, °leaning, °bias, predisposition, predilection, °partiality, proneness, propensity, °tendency, °affinity, °liking, °preference, fondness, °taste
pendant *n.* °ornament, tassel, lavaliere, medallion, locket, necklace, rivière, eardrop, teardrop, °drop, *Old-fashioned* carcanet
pending *prep.* **1** awaiting, waiting (for), depending on, °till, until, 'til, till such time as; while, during —*adj.* **2** °unsettled, undetermined, undecided, unconfirmed, unfinished, °inconclusive, up in the air, hanging fire, in the balance, °in abeyance; °forthcoming, °imminent, °impending, in the offing, *Colloq US* in a holding pattern, on hold
pendulous *adj.* **1** pendent, hanging, drooping, sagging, dangling, suspended, pensile **2** °swinging, swaying, waving, undulating, undulatory, oscillating, oscillatory
penetrate *v.* **1** °enter, go *or* pass through *or* into, °pierce, °bore (into), °lance, spear, °probe, °stab, °puncture, °perforate, °drill **2** °permeate, °diffuse, °suffuse, pervade, filter *or* seep through, percolate through **3** °reach, °get to, °get at, °touch, °affect, °hit, °strike **4** °sink in, be absorbed, be understood, °register, come *or* get through, become clear, °come across, be realized, *Colloq* soak in, seep in **5** °understand, °sense, become aware *or* conscious of, °see (through), gain insight (in)to, discern, uncover, °discover, °find (out), °comprehend, °grasp, °work out, unravel, °fathom, °perceive, *Colloq* °get, °figure out, °dig, *Brit* suss out
penetrating *adj.* **1** °incisive, °trenchant, °keen, searching, °deep, °acute, °sharp, °perceptive, perspicuous, percipient, °quick, °discriminating, °intelligent, °sensitive, °clever, °smart, discerning **2** °piercing, °shrill, °strident, earsplitting, earshattering, °pervasive; °pungent, °harsh, °biting, mordant, °strong, stinging
penetration *n.* **1** °piercing, perforation, puncturing, °incision, °puncture, °penetrating; °inroad, °entry, °entrance **2** °insight, keenness, °perception, percipience, °intelligence, perspicacity, perspicuity, perspicaciousness, perceptiveness, acuteness, incisiveness, °sensitivity, sentience, °understanding, acuteness, discernment, °discrimination, cleverness, shrewdness, °wit, quick-wittedness
penitence *n.* °penance, contrition, °regret, repentance, regretfulness, °compunction, °remorse, °sorrow, sorrowfulness, ruefulness, °grief, °sadness, °shame, self-reproach
penitent *adj.* contrite, °regretful, °repentant, °remorseful, °sorrowful, °sorry, rueful, grief-stricken, °sad, °shamefaced, self-reproachful, °apologetic, conscience-stricken
penmanship *n.* calligraphy, °hand, fine Italian *or* Italic hand, handwriting, °script, °writing, longhand, chirography
pennant *n.* °flag, °banner, pennon, °streamer, banderole, gonfalon, ensign, °colors, °standard, labarum, *Chiefly nautical* jack, *Nautical and yachting* burgee, *Technical* vexillum
pension *n.* **1** °benefit, °allowance, annuity, °subsistence, superannuation, °allotment, old-age pension, *US* social security, *Colloq* golden handshake —*v.* **2** Usually, ***pension off.*** °(cause to) retire, superannuate; °dismiss; *Colloq* °shelve, put out to pasture
pensioner *n.* retiree, °veteran, °senior citizen, *Brit* OAP (= 'old age pensioner'), *US* golden ager, *Colloq Brit* wrinkly
pensive *adj.* °thoughtful, °meditative, musing, in a brown study, cogitative, contemplative, °reflective, °preoccupied, ruminative, °wistful, daydreaming, in a trance, in a reverie, brooding, °sober, °serious, °grave
pent-up *adj.* restrained, constrained, repressed, stifled, bottled-up, corked-up, held-in, checked, held-back, curbed, °inhibited, restricted
penurious *adj.* **1** stingy, °mean, penny-pinching, °miserly, °tight, tightfisted, close-fisted, cheeseparing, niggardly, °cheap, ungenerous, parsimonious, skinflinty, °thrifty, begrudging, grudging, Scroogelike, *Colloq* °near, *Brit* mingy, *US* chintzy **2** °poor, poverty-stricken, °destitute, °impoverished, penniless, °indigent, °needy, impecunious, necessitous, beggarly, bankrupt, *Colloq* (stony *or* flat) broke, °hard up
people *n. pl.* **1** persons, individuals, men and women, ladies and gentlemen, males and females, living souls; mortals; bodies **2** °relations, relatives, °kin, kinsmen, kinfolk, °family, kith and kin; ancestors, forebears **3** masses, °(general) public, °hoi polloi, consumers, multitude, °populace, common people, common man, commoners, subjects, citizenry, plebeians, grass roots, proletariat, °rank and file, the crowd, commonalty *or* commonality, ***mobile vulgus,*** bourgeoisie; man *or* woman in the street, everyman, everywoman, Mr. *or* Mrs. Average, *Brit* A. N. Other, Joe Bloggs, man *or* woman on the Clapham omnibus, *US* John Doe, Mary Doe, Richard Roe, John Q. Public; *Colloq and often derogatory* proles, °the rabble, ragtag and bobtail, silent majority, common herd, *Brit* plebs, admass —*n. sing.* **4** °race, community, °clan, °tribe, °folk, °nation, °population, °society —*v.* **5** °populate, colonize, °settle, °occupy
pep *n.* **1** °vigor, vim (and vigor), °spirit, °animation, vivacity, °energy, °verve, °zest, °fire, sprightliness, °life, effervescence, °sparkle, ebullience, °dash, °enthusiasm, *brio*, élan, *Colloq* zip, zing —*v.* **2** ***pep up.*** °stimulate, invigorate, °animate, °enliven, °vitalize, vivify, °energize, exhilarate, °quicken, °arouse, breathe (some) life into, °inspire, °activate, actuate, °fire, cheer up, *Colloq* buck up, °spark, work *or* fire up, *US* °wind up

pepper *v.* sprinkle, °scatter, °dot, speckle, fleck, bespeckle, °spatter, stipple, mottle

perceive *v.* **1** °see, °make out, discern, °catch sight of, glimpse, °spot, espy, apprehend, °take in, °notice, °note, °discover, descry, °observe, °mark, °remark, °identify, °distinguish, °detect **2** °appreciate, °grasp, °feel, °sense, apprehend, °understand, °gather, °comprehend, °deduce, °infer, °figure out, ascertain, °determine, conclude, °decipher, *Colloq* °dig, °catch on **3** Often, ***perceive of.*** °regard, °view, look on, °consider, °contemplate, °judge, deem, °believe, °think

percentage *n.* °share, °part, °portion, °proportion, °interest, °piece, *Colloq* °cut

perceptible *adj.* °discernible, detectable, °observable, perceivable, °noticeable, distinguishable, recognizable, °apparent, °evident, °notable, °obvious, °patent, °manifest, palpable, °plain, °clear, °prominent, unmistakable *or* unmistakeable

perception *n.* **1** °appreciation, °grasp, apprehension, °understanding, comprehension, °knowledge, °perspective, °view **2** °intuition, °insight, °instinct, °feel, °feeling, °sense, °impression, awareness, °idea, °notion, consciousness, °realization

perceptive *adj.* °astute, °alert, °attentive, °quick, °alive, °quick-witted, °intelligent, °acute, °sharp, °sensitive, °sensible, percipient, discerning, °observant, perspicacious; on the qui vive; *Colloq* on the ball

perch *n.* **1** roost, °rest, °seat; °spot, °location, °position, °place, °site, vantage point, °perspective —*v.* **2** roost, °rest, °sit, °nest; °place, °put, °set, °situate, °locate, °position, °site

percolate *v.* seep, °steep, °transfuse, leach, °drip, °drain, °strain, °filter, pervade, infuse, °ooze, transude, filtrate, °trickle, °permeate, °suffuse, °penetrate

perdition *n.* damnation, °hell, hellfire, °doom, °ruin, condemnation, °destruction, ruination, °downfall

peremptory *adj.* **1** commanding, °imperative, compelling, °obligatory, °mandatory, irrefutable, °incontrovertible, decretal **2** decisive, °final, preclusive, °arbitrary, °categorical, unequivocal, °dogmatic, unconditional, unreserved, °flat, °out-and-out, °outright, °unqualified, °unmitigated **3** imperious, °authoritative, °tyrannical, °despotic, °dictatorial, autocratic, °emphatic, °positive, °firm, °insistent, *Colloq* °bossy

perennial *adj.* **1** °durable, °lasting, continuing, °enduring, °constant, °stable, lifelong, °persistent, incessant, uninterrupted, °continual, °continuous, °chronic **2** °permanent, unfailing, never-failing, °endless, unending, ceaseless, unceasing, imperishable, undying, °perpetual, °everlasting, °timeless, °eternal, °immortal, *Literary* sempiternal

perfect *adj.* **1** °complete, °absolute, finished, (fully) realized, fulfilled, consummate, °pure, °entire, °whole, perfected, °best, °ideal **2** °sublime, °ideal, °superb, °supreme, °superlative, °best, °flawless, °faultless, °preeminent, °excellent, °exquisite, unexcelled, unrivaled, unequaled, unmatched, °matchless, °incomparable, °nonpareil, °peerless, inimitable **3** °blameless, °righteous, °holy, °faultless, °flawless, °spotless, °immaculate **4** °fitting, °appropriate, °(just) right, apt, °suitable, °correct, °proper, made-to-order, °best, *Brit* spot on **5** °precise, °exact, °accurate, °correct, unerring, °true, °authentic, °lifelike, right on, °excellent, °superlative, °superb, °reliable, *Brit* spot on **6** utter, °absolute, °complete, °mere, °thorough, °out-and-out, through and through; 24-karat, °categorical, °unqualified, unalloyed, °unmitigated **7** °expert, °proficient, °accomplished, °experienced, practiced, °skillful, skilled, °gifted, °talented, °adept, deft, adroit, °polished, °professional, masterly, °masterful —*v.* **8** °complete, °finish, °realize, °fulfill, consummate, °accomplish, °achieve, °effect, °execute, carry out *or* through, °bring (to perfection) **9** °rectify, °correct, emend, (put *or* set) right, °improve, °refine, °polish, °cultivate, °better, ameliorate

perfection *n.* **1** °purity, flawlessness, faultlessness, sublimity, °superiority, °excellence, °preeminence, transcendence **2** °completion, completeness, °achievement, °fulfillment, °realization, °consummation, °accomplishment, attainment **3** °ideal, °paragon, °model, archetype, °pattern, °mold, °standard, idealization, °essence, °quintessence, °acme, °pinnacle, °summit

perfectionist *n.* **1** °purist, pedant, precisian, precisionist, stickler, *Colloq* fuss-pot, *US* fussbudget —*adj.* **2** °meticulous, °precise, punctilious, °scrupulous, °exacting, °particular, °demanding, °fastidious, °fussy; °obsessive; *Colloq* picky, nit-picking

perfectly *adv.* **1** °completely, purely, °entirely, °absolutely, °utterly, °totally, °wholly, consummately, °thoroughly, °quite, °definitely, °positively, unambiguously, unequivocally, unmistakably *or* unmistakeably, explicitly, °truly, °very, °extremely, extraordinarily, remarkably **2** superbly, superlatively, flawlessly, faultlessly, impeccably, inimitably, incomparably, sublimely, exquisitely, marvelously, admirably, wonderfully **3** °exactly, °precisely, flawlessly, faultlessly, accurately, °literally, line for line, word for word, °verbatim, letter for letter, °to the letter, *literatim* **4** °very, °full, °quite, *Dialectal* °right, *Brit* °jolly, *Slang* damned, bloody

perfidious *adj.* treacherous, °deceitful, °traitorous, treasonous, treasonable, °disloyal, °faithless, °false, unfaithful, °untrue, insidious, °hypocritical, °two-faced, Janus-faced, °corrupt, °dishonest

perfidy *n.* perfidiousness, treachery, °deceit, traitorousness, treason, disloyalty, faithlessness, falseness, °falsity, unfaithfulness, °infidelity, insidiousness, °hypocrisy, °betrayal

perforate *v.* °riddle, °puncture, °pierce,

honeycomb, °drill, °bore, °punch; °enter, °penetrate, pass into

perform *v.* **1** °execute, °complete, bring off *or* about, °accomplish, °effect, °carry out, °discharge, °dispatch, °conduct, °carry on, do, °fulfill, *Colloq* °pull off, °knock off, °polish off **2** do, °act, °behave, °operate, °function, °run, °work, °go, °respond **3** °present, °stage, °produce, °put on, °mount, do; °act, depict, °take, °play, appear as

performance *n.* **1** °execution, °completion, bringing off *or* about, °accomplishment, effectuation, carrying out, °discharge, °dispatch, °conduct, carrying on, doing, °fulfillment **2** °show, °exhibition, °exhibit, °play, playing, °engagement, °act, °appearance, *Colloq* gig **3** playing, acting, °interpretation, °presentation, portrayal **4** °behavior, °conduct, deportment, demeanor **5** °scene, °show, °exhibition, °display

performer *n.* actor *or* actress, °thespian, trouper, °player, *Chiefly Brit* artiste

perfume *n.* **1** °essence, °extract, *parfum*, eau de Cologne, toilet water, °scent, °fragrance; °aroma, °odor, °smell, °bouquet, nose —*v.* **2** °scent

perfunctory *adj.* **1** °routine, °mechanical, °automatic, robotlike, °unthinking, businesslike, unspontaneous, °formal, dismissive, °inattentive, uninvolved, apathetic, °indifferent, unconcerned, removed, °distant, *dégagé*, °offhand, °heedless, uninterested, °hasty, °hurried, °superficial, °cursory, °fleeting, rushed **2** °careless, °slipshod, slovenly, negligent, °sketchy, °spotty

perhaps *adv.* °maybe, °possibly, it is possible that, conceivably, as the case may be, it may be, *Archaic or literary* perchance, peradventure, *Archaic or dialectal* mayhap

peril *n.* °danger, °threat, °risk, °jeopardy, °exposure, vulnerability, susceptibility, uncertainty, insecurity

perilous *adj.* °dangerous, °risky, °hazardous, °vulnerable, °susceptible, °uncertain, °insecure, unsafe, unsure

perimeter *n.* °boundary, °border, borderline, °margin, °periphery, °limit(s), °bounds, ambit, circumference, °edge, °verge, °fringe(s), *Archaic or literary* bourn *or* bourne

period *n.* **1** °interval, °time, °term, °span, duration, °spell, °space, °stretch; while; *Colloq chiefly Brit* °patch **2** °era, days, epoch, eon *or* aeon, °age, years **3** full stop

periodic *adj.* °periodical, °intermittent, °regular, °recurrent, °repetitive, iterative, cyclic(al), repeated; episodic, °sporadic, °occasional

periodical *n.* °magazine, °journal, °paper, °publication, newsletter, °organ, serial, weekly, fortnightly, semimonthly, monthly, bimonthly, °quarterly, semiannual, annual, yearbook, almanac, *Rare* hebdomadal *or* hebdomadary

peripheral *adj.* **1** °incidental, unimportant, °minor, °secondary, inessential *or* unessential, °nonessential, °unnecessary, °superficial, °tangential, °irrelevant, °beside the point **2** circumferential, °external, perimetric, °outside, outer

periphery *n.* **1** °perimeter, circumference, °border, °edge, °rim, °brim, ambit, °boundary, °bound, °margin **2** °surface, °edge, °superficies

perish *v.* °die, °expire, lose (one's) life, be killed, be lost, meet (one's) death, be destroyed

perjury *n.* °lying, mendacity, mendaciousness, forswearing, prevarication, bearing false witness

perk *n.* See **perquisite,** below.

perk up *v.* cheer up, become jaunty, °brighten, liven up, invigorate, smarten up, °quicken, (re)vitalize, °pep up, °revive, inspirit, *Colloq* buck up

perky *adj.* °lively, cheery, °cheerful, °jaunty, bouncy, °bright, invigorated, °vigorous, vitalized, peppy, °spirited, °sprightly, °frisky, °animated, °vivacious, °effervescent, °bubbly, °buoyant, °gay, *Colloq* bright-eyed and bushy-tailed, full of pep

permanence *n.* permanency, °stability, durability, fixedness, changelessness, lasting quality, longevity, °endurance, °persistence, dependability, reliability, survival

permanent *adj.* **1** °everlasting, °eternal, unending, °endless, °perpetual, unceasing, °constant, undying, imperishable, °indestructible, °stable, °abiding, long-lasting, °lasting, °enduring, °perennial, long-lived, °durable **2** unchanging, °invariable, °changeless, °fixed, unchangeable, immutable, unalterable, °stable, °persistent

permanently *adv.* °forever, for good, °once and for all, forevermore, °always, eternally, everlastingly; perpetually, constantly, incessantly, °nonstop, continuously, endlessly, ceaselessly, unendingly, interminably

permeate *v.* imbue, °diffuse, °penetrate, pervade, infiltrate, °enter, spread through(out), °saturate, seep through(out), percolate through, soak through

permissible *adj.* allowable, admissible, °acceptable, allowed, permitted, °tolerable, °legal, licit, °lawful, °legitimate, authorized, °proper, °(all) right; pardonable, excusable, °venial, *Colloq* O.K. *or* OK *or* okay, kosher, legit

permission *n.* °consent, assent, °leave, acquiescence, sufferance, °tolerance, laxity, leniency *or* lenience, °leave, °license, °sanction, acceptance, authorization, °approval, approbation, countenance, °allowance, °liberty, °indulgence, sufferance; franchise, enfranchisement

permissive *adj.* assenting, consenting, °indulgent, °lenient, latitudinarian, acquiescent, °lax, easygoing, °liberal, °tolerant, nonconstraining, nonrestrictive, libertarian

permit *v.* **1** Often, ***permit to.*** °allow, °agree (to), °consent (to), give permission *or* leave (to), °authorize, °sanction, °license, °tolerate, countenance, °suffer, °brook, °admit, °grant, °enable, empower, franchise, enfranchise; °let —*n.* 2 °license, °authority, authorization, franchise, °warrant; °pass, passport, visa

perpendicular *adj.* 1 °erect, °upright, vertical, °plumb, °straight (up-and-down) 2 Often, ***perpendicular to.*** at right angles (to), at ninety degrees (to)

perpetrate *v.* °commit, °execute, °perform, carry out *or* through, °effect, °effectuate, °accomplish, do, be responsible for, °practice, *Colloq* °pull (off)

perpetual *adj.* 1 °eternal, °infinite, °everlasting, never-ending, unending, °perennial, ageless, °timeless, long-lived, °permanent, unceasing, °lasting, °enduring, unvarying, unchanging, immutable, °invariable, undeviating, *Literary* sempiternal 2 °constant, uninterrupted, °continuous, unfailing, incessant, °persistent, unremitting, unending, °nonstop, °endless, °recurrent, °continual, °repetitive

perpetuate *v.* °continue, °maintain, °extend, keep (on *or* up), keep going, °preserve, °memorialize, °immortalize, eternalize

perpetuity *n.* °permanence, constancy, timelessness; °eternity

perplex *v.* °confuse, °bewilder, °puzzle, °mystify, °distract, baffle, befuddle, confound, °muddle, disconcert, °stump, °nonplus, °stymie, stupefy, °stun, °daze, dumbfound *or* dumfound, flabbergast, *Colloq* bamboozle, hornswoggle, *Chiefly US and Canadian* discombobulate, throw for a loop

perplexing *adj.* confusing, bewildering, °puzzling, mystifying, baffling, confounding, °disconcerting, stupefying, flabbergasting, enigmatic, °paradoxical, °incomprehensible, unfathomable, impenetrable, °recondite, arcane, °labyrinthine, complex, °complicated, Byzantine, °intricate, °involved, convoluted, twisted, knotty, Gordian

perplexity *n.* 1 °confusion, bewilderment, bafflement, °distress, °doubt, °difficulty 2 intricacy, °complexity, complicatedness, arcaneness, reconditeness, impenetrability, impenetrableness, involvement, unfathomability, °obscurity, °difficulty 3 °puzzle, °enigma, °mystery, °dilemma, °problem, °paradox, catch-22, °quandary, °predicament, °bind

perquisite *n.* °consideration, emolument, °bonus, °(fringe) benefit, °extra, dividend, gratuity, °tip, douceur, baksheesh, °token (of appreciation), *US* lagniappe *or* lagnappe, *Colloq* °perk

persecute *v.* 1 °oppress, °suppress, °subjugate, maltreat, °ill-treat, °abuse, °outrage, °molest, °victimize, °tyrannize, °afflict, °punish, martyr, °torment, torture 2 °bother, °annoy, °pester, °plague, hector, °bully, badger, harry, °harass, °irritate, °worry, vex, °trouble, importune, °hound

persecution *n.* 1 °oppression, °suppression, subjugation, maltreatment, ill-treatment, °abuse, °outrage, molestation, victimization, °tyranny, °affliction, °punishment, °torment, torture 2 °bother, °annoyance, hectoring, bullying, badgering, harrying, harassing, irritation, °worry, vexation, °trouble

perseverance *n.* °persistence, steadfastness, °determination, °resolution, °resolve, decisiveness, °decision, firmness, purposefulness, pertinacity, staying power, °stamina, sedulousness, assiduity, °grit, °pluck, tirelessness, indefatigableness, indefatigability, °patience, °endurance, diligence, °devotion, °tenacity, doggedness, stubbornness, inflexibility, °obstinacy, obstinateness, obdurateness, *Colloq* °guts, *US* stick-to-itiveness

persevere *v.* Often, ***persevere in or with or at.*** °persist, °resolve, °decide, °endure, °continue, carry on *or* through, keep at *or* on *or* up, be steadfast *or* staunch *or* constant, keep going, stand fast *or* firm, °see through, be *or* remain determined *or* resolved *or* resolute *or* stalwart *or* purposeful *or* uncompromising, be tenacious *or* persistent *or* constant *or* pertinacious *or* assiduous *or* sedulous, be tireless *or* untiring *or* indefatigable, show determination *or* pluck *or* grit, be plucky, be patient *or* diligent *or* stubborn *or* inflexible *or* adamant *or* obstinate *or* obdurate, show *or* exhibit *or* demonstrate patience *or* diligence *or* stubbornness *or* inflexibility *or* obstinacy *or* obduracy, remain dogged, pursue doggedly, be intransigent *or* intractable, cling to, stick to, °support, stop at nothing, °sustain, *Colloq* °stick with, stick (it) out

persist *v.* 1 Often, ***persist in or at.*** °persevere, be persistent, °insist (on), stand firm *or* fast, be steadfast *or* staunch, °strive, toil, °labor, work (hard) (at) 2 °remain, °continue, °endure, °carry on, keep up *or* on, °last, °linger, °stay

persistence *n.* °perseverance, °resolve, °determination, °resolution, steadfastness, °tenacity, constancy, assiduity, °stamina, tirelessness, indefatigability, indefatigableness, °pluck, °grit, °patience, diligence, pertinacity, doggedness, stubbornness, °obstinacy, obduracy

persistent *adj.* 1 persisting, persevering, °tenacious, °steadfast, °firm, °fast, °fixed, °staunch, °resolute, resolved, °determined, unfaltering, unswerving, undeviating, unflagging, °tireless, °untiring, indefatigable, dogged, unwavering, °stubborn, °obstinate, obdurate, °inflexible, °rigid 2 continuing, °constant, °continuous, °continual, unending, interminable, unremitting, unrelenting, °perpetual, incessant, unceasing, °nonstop

person *n.* 1 °individual, °human (being), being, man *or* woman *or* child, °(living) soul; °mortal 2 ***in person.*** physically, °personally, bodily, °actually, myself *or* yourself *or* himself *or* herself *or* ourselves *or* yourselves *or* themselves, *Colloq* °in the flesh

persona *n.* °face, °front, façade, °mask, °guise, °exterior, °role, °part, °character, °identity, self

personage *n.* °celebrity, luminary, °notable, VIP (= 'very important person'), °name,

°somebody, °personality, °star, superstar, magnate, °mogul, *Colloq* big shot, big wheel, hotshot, hot stuff, *Brit* big noise, *Theater US* headliner

personal *adj.* **1** °individual, °physical, bodily, °actual, °live; °in person, °in the flesh **2** °intimate, °exclusive, °private, °special, °particular **3** °intimate, °close, °dear, °bosom, °familiar, °special **4** °intimate, °individual; disparaging, slighting, °offensive, °derogatory, °critical, deprecating, belittling, adverse, unfriendly, insulting

personality *n.* **1** °character, °nature, temperament, °disposition, °makeup, °persona; °identity, °psyche **2** °celebrity, luminary, °star, superstar, °name, headliner, °somebody

personalized *adj.* monogrammed, initialed, individualized; signed

personally *adv.* **1** °in person, °alone, by oneself, on one's own, myself *or* yourself *or* himself *or* herself *or* ourselves *or* yourselves *or* themselves, *Colloq* °in the flesh **2** in one's own view *or* opinion, for one's part, for oneself, as far as one is concerned, from one's own viewpoint, from where one stands, as one sees it *or* things, as for oneself **3** as an individual, as a person, privately, °in private

personify *v.* **1** °embody, °typify, °exemplify, epitomize, be the embodiment of, °manifest, °represent, °stand for, °symbolize, *Archaic* impersonate, personate **2** humanize, personalize

perspective *n.* **1** °(point of) view, °viewpoint, °standpoint, °prospect, vantage point, °position, °angle, *Colloq* where one is coming from **2** °attitude, °position, °angle, °approach, °sentiment, °outlook, °lookout

perspiration *n.* °sweat, dampness, wetness; sweating; *Technical* sudor; diaphoresis

persuade *v.* **1** °urge, °induce, °prevail upon, °influence, exhort, importune, °dispose, °incline, °prompt, °sway, °press **2** bring round, °convince, °win over, talk *or* argue into, °convert

persuasion *n.* **1** °inducement, inducing, °influence, influencing, exhortation, exhorting, persuading **2** °opinion, °belief, °creed, °faith, set of beliefs, °religion, °(religious) conviction; °sect, °denomination, °faction, °school (of thought), affiliation

persuasive *adj.* convincing, °telling, °influential, °effective, °productive, °impressive, °efficacious, cogent, °weighty, compelling, °forceful, valid, °winning, °authoritative, °dynamic

pert *adj.* °forward, °brash, °brazen, °cheeky, °insolent, °impertinent, °flippant, saucy, °bold, °presumptuous, °impudent, °disrespectful, °audacious, °rude, °impolite, uncivil, °ill-mannered, unmannerly, *Archaic* malapert, *Colloq* °fresh, °flip, out of line, °brassy, big-mouthed, wise-guy, *Slang US* smart-ass(ed), wise-ass(ed), *Brit* smart-arsed

pertain *v.* Often, ***pertain to.*** concern, °refer to, °regard, have reference *or* relation (to), °apply (to), °relate (to), °include, °cover, °affect, appertain (to), be appropriate (to), be fitting (for), befit, °bear on, have bearing (on)

pertinent *adj.* pertaining, °appropriate, °fitting, °suitable, apt, °relevant, germane, apropos, apposite

perturb *v.* °upset, °disturb, °fluster, °ruffle, unsettle, disconcert, make uneasy, °discomfit, vex, °worry, °agitate, °shake up, °alarm, disquiet, °confuse, discompose, °unnerve, addle, disorganize

perusal *n.* reading, °scrutiny, °check, °examination, °study, inspection, scanning, °review

peruse *v.* °read, °study, °scan, °scrutinize, °examine, °inspect, °review, °browse, run one's eye over

pervasive *adj.* °penetrating, pervading, omnipresent, °general, inescapable, °prevalent, °universal, widespread, ubiquitous, permeating, permeative

perverse *adj.* **1** °wrong, wrongheaded, awry, °contrary, wayward, °incorrect, °irregular, unfair, °improper, °contradictory **2** °cantankerous, °testy, curmudgeonly, churlish, crusty, bad-tempered, °petulant, captious, °cross, cross-grained, °peevish, °waspish, °snappish, °bilious, splenetic, fractious, ill-tempered, °quarrelsome, irascible, °sullen, contentious, °touchy, °obstreperous, crabby, crabbed, °irritable, °surly, *Colloq* grouchy, *Brit* stroppy, *US and Canadian* °cranky **3** °stubborn, °self-willed, wrongheaded, intractable, °willful, obdurate, °obstinate, pigheaded, adamant(ine), °inflexible, unbending, refractory, unyielding

perversion *n.* **1** deviation, irregularity, misdirection, corruption, °subversion, distortion, twisting, falsification, misrepresentation, °diversion, sidetracking **2** unnatural act, deviation, deviance *or* deviancy, °abnormality, depravity, °vice, aberration, debauchery, *Colloq* kinkiness, *Brit* °kink

pervert *v.* **1** °deflect, °divert, °sidetrack, turn aside *or* away, °subvert, °misdirect, °distort, °twist, °abuse, °falsify, misapply, misconstrue, °misrepresent, °corrupt **2** °seduce, °lead astray, debauch, °degrade, °corrupt, °demoralize, °subvert **3** °deviant, °degenerate, debauchee, *US* °deviate, *Colloq* °weirdo

perverted *adj.* °deviant, °deviate, °abnormal, amoral, unmoral, °immoral, °bad, depraved, °unnatural, warped, twisted, °profligate, °dissolute, °delinquent, °degenerate, °evil, °wicked, malign, malicious, malefic, malevolent, °evil-minded, °sinful, iniquitous, °base, °foul, °corrupt, unprincipled

pessimistic *n.* °gloomy, °negative, despairing, °hopeless, °inauspicious, depressed, °despondent, °dejected, °melancholy, °downhearted, heavy-hearted, defeatist, °glum,

°sad, °blue, °unhappy, cheerless, °joyless, cynical, °bleak, °forlorn

pest *n.* °nuisance, °annoyance, °nag, irritant, °bother, gadfly, bane, °trial, heckler, vexation, °curse, thorn in one's flesh, *Colloq* °pain (in the neck), *Slang US (Yiddish)* nudge *or* noodge *or* nudzh, nudnik, *Taboo slang* pain in the *Brit* arse *or US and Canadian* ass

pester *v.* °annoy, °nag, °irritate, °irk, °bother, get at *or* to, badger, °plague, vex, °fret, hector, °harass, harry, °heckle, nettle, °chafe, peeve, pique, °provoke, °exasperate, bedevil, get *or* grate on (someone's) nerves, get under (someone's) skin, get in (someone's) hair, °try (someone's patience), °torment, °persecute, *Brit* chivvy, *Colloq* drive (someone) up the wall, needle, give (someone) the needle, hassle, °ride, give (someone) a hard *or* bad time, °bug

pestilence *n.* **1** °plague, °epidemic, pandemic, Black Death, *Rare* °pest **2** °scourge, °blight, °curse, cancer, canker, bane, °affliction

pet[1] *n.* **1** °darling, °favorite, °idol, apple of (someone's) eye, *Colloq Brit* blue-eyed boy, *US* fair-haired boy *—adj.* **2** °tame, trained, domesticated **3** °favorite, °favored, preferred, cherished, °special, °particular; indulged, prized, treasured, °precious, dearest, adored, °darling *—v.* **4** °caress, °fondle, °stroke, °pat; °cuddle, nuzzle, °nestle, °snuggle, *Colloq* neck, smooch *or Australian and New Zealand also* smoodge *or* smooge, *Chiefly US and Canadian* °make out **5** °humor, °pamper, °favor, °baby, °coddle, cosset, mollycoddle, cocker, °spoil, °indulge, °dote on

pet[2] *n.* (bad *or* ill) temper, pique, °sulk, °(bad) mood, °fume, *Colloq Brit* paddy *or* paddywhack *or* paddywack

peter out *v.* °diminish, °evaporate, °wane, come to nothing *or* naught *or US also* nought, °die out, °disappear, °fail, fade (out *or* away), °dwindle (into nothing), °run out, °give out, °flag, °melt away

petite *adj.* °delicate, °dainty, mignon, °diminutive, °small, °little, °slight, °tiny, small-boned, *Colloq Brit* dinky

petition *n.* **1** °request, °application, solicitation, °suit, entreaty, °supplication, °plea, °appeal *—v.* **2** °request, °ask, apply to, apply for, °solicit, °sue, °call upon, entreat, supplicate, °plead, appeal (to) *or* (for), °beseech, implore, importune, *Rare* obsecrate

petrified *adj.* **1** horrified, horror-stricken, terrified, terror-stricken, °panic-stricken, frightened, °afraid, paralyzed, numbed, benumbed, frozen **2** shocked, °speechless, dumbfounded *or* dumfounded, dumbstruck, stunned, °thunderstruck, astonished, astounded, confounded, stupefied, appalled, aghast, *Colloq* flabbergasted **3** ossified, fossilized

petrify *v.* **1** °frighten, °scare, °horrify, °terrify, °paralyze, °numb, benumb **2** °shock, dumbfound *or* dumfound, °stun, °astonish, °astound, °amaze, confound, disconcert, stupefy, °appall, *Colloq* flabbergast **3** ossify, fossilize, turn to stone

petty *adj.* **1** °insignificant, trivial, °paltry, °minor, °inferior, °niggling, °trifling, °negligible, °puny, inessential, °nonessential, °inconsequential, unimportant, °slight, nugatory, of no account, *US* dinky, *Colloq* piddling, °measly, no great shakes, no big deal, °small-time, *Brit* twopenny-halfpenny *or* tuppenny-ha'penny, *US and Canadian* picayune **2** °miserly, °mean, mingy, stingy, cheeseparing, grudging, °small-minded, °cheap, niggardly, parsimonious, °tight, tightfisted, °close, closefisted

petulant *adj.* °peevish, pettish, °impatient, ill-humored, °testy, °waspish, irascible, choleric, °cross, captious, ill-tempered, bad-tempered, splenetic, °moody, °sour, °bilious, crabby, crabbed, °irritable, huffish, huffy, °perverse, °snappish, crotchety, °cantankerous, curmudgeonly, grouchy, grumpy

phantom *n.* **1** apparition, °specter, °ghost, °spirit, phantasm, °shade, wraith, revenant, °vision, *Formal* eidolon, phantasma, *Colloq* spook **2** figment (of the imagination), °illusion, °delusion, chimera *or* chimaera, °hallucination, °fancy, mirage

pharisaic *adj.* pharisaical, °hypocritical, °insincere, °self-righteous, °pretentious, holier-than-thou, °sanctimonious, pietistic(al), formalistic, canting, unctuous, °oily, °slimy, *Literary* Tartuffian, Pecksniffian, *Colloq* °goody-goody, *Chiefly Brit* smarmy

pharisee *n.* °hypocrite, °pretender, dissembler, humbug, °fraud, whited sepulcher, pietist, formalist, canter, *Literary* Tartuffe, Pecksniff, *Colloq* phoney *or US also* phony

pharmacist *n.* pharmacologist, *Rather old-fashioned or formal* apothecary, *Brit* (pharmaceutical) chemist, *US and Canadian* °druggist, *Formal* posologist, *Colloq* pill pusher, *US* pill roller

pharmacy *n.* **1** dispensary, *Rather formal or old-fashioned* apothecary, *Brit* chemist's (shop), *US and Canadian* drugstore, druggist's **2** pharmaceutics, pharmacopoeia

phase *n.* **1** °stage, °period, °development, °step **2** °time, °moment, °juncture, °occasion **3** °state, °form, °shape, configuration, °aspect, °appearance, °look, °condition, °status **4** facet, °side, °angle, °viewpoint, °point of view, *Colloq* °slant *—v.* **5** ***phase in.*** °(gradually) introduce, usher in, °work in, °inject, °insert, °insinuate, °include, °incorporate **6** ***phase out.*** ease out *or* off, °taper off, °wind up, put a stop to, °(gradually) eliminate, °remove, °withdraw, °discontinue, °end

phenomenal *adj.* °outstanding, °remarkable, °exceptional, °extraordinary, °unusual, freakish, °rare, uncommon, °singular, °unorthodox, unprecedented, °unheard-of, °unparalleled, °unbelievable, °incredible, °marvelous, wonderful, °amazing, astonishing, astounding, staggering, °stunning, °prodigious, °miraculous, °fantastic, *Colloq* mind-boggling, mind-blowing

phenomenon *n.* **1** °event, °happening, °occurrence, °incident, °occasion, °experience, °fact **2** °wonder, °curiosity, °spectacle, °sight, °sensation, °marvel, °rarity, °exception, miracle, *Slang* stunner

philanderer *n.* °flirt, °gallant, °roué, °rake, Casanova, Lothario, Don Juan, Romeo, °lover, °playboy, gay dog, *Colloq* lady-killer, womanizer, *Old-fashioned* wolf, *Slang* stud

philanthropic *adj.* °charitable, eleemosynary, °generous, magnanimous, munificent, °benevolent, openhanded, ungrudging, unstinting, beneficent, °humanitarian, altruistic, humane

philanthropist *n.* contributor, °donor, benefactor *or* benefactress, patron *or* patroness, °sponsor, Maecenas, Good Samaritan, °humanitarian, altruist

philanthropy *n.* **1** generosity, °benevolence, °charity, °patronage, magnanimity, charitableness, public-spiritedness, bigheartedness, thoughtfulness, almsgiving, kindheartedness, beneficence, benignity, liberality, openhandedness **2** °donation, contribution, °largess, °aid, °grant, °assistance, °help

philistine *n.* **1** °boor, °barbarian, °yahoo, lowbrow, Boeotian, vulgarian, ignoramus, °bourgeois, *US* Babbitt —*adj.* **2** uncultured, uncultivated, °tasteless, commonplace, unenlightened, °unrefined, unread, unlettered, °uneducated, untutored, unlearned, anti-intellectual, °narrow-minded, °boorish, lowbrow, °dull, °prosaic, °boring, °bourgeois, crass, commercial, °materialistic

philosophical *adj.* **1** philosophic, °abstract, esoteric, °learned, °scholarly, erudite, °theoretical, °rational, °logical, °impractical **2** °detached, unconcerned, unemotional, unimpassioned, composed, °thoughtful, °reflective, °meditative, cogitative, contemplative, °judicious, °sober, °levelheaded, °realistic, °practical, pragmatic(al), down-to-earth, °cool, °calm, °serene, placid, °stoical, °patient, unruffled, coolheaded, °tranquil, unperturbed, even-tempered, °temperate, °moderate, °equable, equanimous, imperturbable

philosophy *n.* **1** metaphysics, epistemology, °logic, natural *or* moral *or* metaphysical philosophy, rationalism, °thinking, aesthetics **2** °viewpoint, °(point of) view, °outlook, °opinion, °attitude, °feeling, °sentiment, °idea, °notion, °ideology, (set of) beliefs *or* values, tenets, *Weltanschauung*, worldview **3** °stoicism, °sang-froid, °control, °self-control, °restraint, coolness, composure, calmness, °serenity, placidity, coolheadedness, equanimity, thoughtfulness, imperturbability, self-possession, aplomb, dispassion, °patience, °resignation

phlegmatic *adj.* **1** phlegmatical, stoic(al), unemotional, °unenthusiastic, unanimated, sluggish, apathetic, uninvolved, °lethargic, unfeeling, uncaring, °cold, unresponsive, °stolid, °unmoved, insensitive, °unaffected, °insensible, °indifferent, unconcerned, uninterested, °listless, °torpid, °indolent, °inactive, °passive, *Rare* hebetudinous **2** phlegmatical, °self-possessed, self-controlled, controlled, restrained, composed, °calm, °serene, °tranquil, placid, coolheaded, equanimous, °cool, undisturbed, unperturbed, unruffled, imperturbable, even-tempered, °philosophical, °temperate, °moderate

phobia *n.* °fear, °horror, °terror, °dread, hatred, detestation, abhorrence, °loathing, execration, °aversion, °revulsion, repugnance, °dislike, °distaste, antipathy; disquiet, nervousness, °qualm, °distrust, °suspicion, apprehension, °worry

phony *adj.* **1** phoney, °unreal, °fake, °synthetic, °artificial, °factitious, °false, °fraudulent, °imitation, °bogus, °spurious, °counterfeit, °mock, ersatz, paste, trumped-up; °sham, °pretended, °insincere, °hypocritical, dissimulating, °deceitful, °dishonest; *Colloq* pseudo *or Brit* pseud —*n.* **2** phoney, °fake, °fraud, °imitation, °counterfeit, °forgery, °hoax, °sham **3** phoney, trickster, faker, humbug, °impostor, °pretender, charlatan, mountebank, double-dealer, °counterfeiter, °quack, deceiver, *Colloq Brit* pseud, *Slang US* paperhanger

photograph *n.* **1** snapshot, °print, °picture, °slide, transparency; °negative, °positive, *Colloq* photo, °snap, °shot, pic (*pl.*, pix) —*v.* **2** take a picture (of), °shoot, °film, °take, *Colloq* °snap

photographer *n.* lensman, lenswoman, cameraman, camerawoman, cinematographer, *paparazzo* (*pl.*, *paparazzi*), *Old-fashioned* photographist

photographic *adj.* **1** °vivid, °natural, °realistic, °graphic, °accurate, °exact, °precise, °faithful, °detailed, °lifelike, true-to-life **2** cinematic, filmic, °pictorial

phrase *n.* **1** clause, noun phrase, verb phrase, prepositional phrase, adverbial phrase, adjectival phrase **2** °expression, word group, collocation, locution, °idiom, idiomatic expression, collocution, °proverb, °motto, °slogan, saying, catch phrase, adage, °maxim, axiom, °saw, colloquialism, °cliché, platitude, commonplace, *Colloq* chestnut **3** phraseology, phrasing, °wording, °language, °usage, way *or* manner of speaking, °diction, °parlance, *façon de parler, modus loquendi, modus scribendi*, speech habit, °style, choice of words, word choice, syntax, vocabulary —*v.* **4** °express, °term, °word, °put, °frame, °formulate, °couch, put into words, put *or* set forth, verbalize, articulate, °voice, utter, °say, °write; °describe, delineate

physical *adj.* bodily, corporeal, corporal, fleshly, incarnate, °carnal, °mortal, °earthly, °natural, somatic; °material, °tangible, palpable, °real, °actual, °true, °concrete, °manifest, °solid

physician *n.* °doctor, medical doctor, M.D., doctor of medicine, medical practitioner, general practitioner, G.P., medical man *or* woman, °specialist, diplomate, *Brit navy* surgeon, *Colloq* doc, medico, medic, *US* °man, *Slang* sawbones, bones

physique *n.* °build, °figure, °body, °frame, °shape, bodily structure, °form, *Slang* chassis, *US* bod, built

pick *v.* **1** Often, ***pick out.*** °select, °choose, cull, °sort out, hand-pick, °single out, opt for, fix *or* decide upon *or* on, °elect, settle upon *or* on, °screen (out), °sift (out) **2** °pluck, °gather, °collect, °harvest, bring *or* take in, °garner **3** °provoke, °foment, °incite, °start, °initiate, work *or* stir up **4** ***pick at.*** **(a)** °criticize, carp at, find fault with, cavil (at *or* about), quibble (at *or* about), °pick on, °nag (at), °niggle (at), °harass, °pester, °annoy, °irritate, °bother **(b)** nibble (at), peck at **5** ***pick off.*** °shoot (down), °kill **6** ***pick on.*** °bully, °ride, °intimidate, °abuse, °browbeat, badger, harry, hector, °harass, °tease, °taunt, needle, °torment **7** ***pick out.*** **(a)** See **1**, above. **(b)** discern, °distinguish, tell apart, °make out, °recognize, °separate, °discriminate **8** ***pick up.*** **(a)** °raise (up), °lift (up), heft, °hoist, °take up **(b)** °gather, °collect, glean, °take up **(c)** °tidy (up), °neaten, straighten up *or* out, °clean (up) **(d)** °acquire, °learn, become acquainted with; °master; *Colloq* get the hang of **(e)** °acquire, °find, °come by, get hold of, °obtain; °buy, °purchase, °get **(f)** °improve, get better, °gain, °make headway, °recover, °perk up, °rally, °recoup, °(make) progress, move ahead, °increase, *Colloq* make a comeback **(g)** accelerate, °speed up **(h)** °arrest, apprehend, take into custody, *Colloq* °pinch, collar, °nab, bust, °run in, °pull in, *Brit* °nick **(i)** °call for, give a lift *or* ride to, °collect, go for *or US also* after, go to get **(j)** °meet, introduce oneself to, strike up an acquaintance with, accost, make advances to **(k)** °catch, °come down with, °contract, °get —*n.* **9** °selection, °choice, °option, °preference **10** choicest, °best, *crème de la crème,* cream

picket *n.* **1** °stake, °pale, °post, °peg, stanchion, °upright, vertical, palisade, paling **2** demonstrator, protester, striker **3** picquet, °sentinel, °watchman, °guard, °observer, °patrol, vedette *or* vidette *or* vedette boat —*v.* **4** °enclose, °shut in, wall in, °fence (in), hem in, °box in **5** °protest, °demonstrate, blockade

picnic *n.* **1** garden party, *fête champêtre,* meal alfresco, barbecue, *US* clambake, *US and Canadian* cookout **2** child's play, *Colloq* °pushover, °snap, cinch, °piece of cake, walkover, *US and Canadian* °breeze, lead-pipe cinch **3** ***no picnic.*** °difficult, °arduous, torture, torturous, °agony, °agonizing, °painful, °disagreeable, discomfiting, °misfortune, *Colloq* °tough, tough luck, tough going, °rough, a pain in the neck, *US* tough sledding, *Taboo slang* pain in the *Brit* arse *or US* ass

pictorial *adj.* **1** °graphic, °picturesque, °vivid, °telling, °striking, °expressive, °plain, °explicit, °clear, lucid **2** illustrated

picture *n.* **1** °drawing, painting, °representation, °portrait, depiction, artwork, °illustration, sketch, °photograph **2** °image, (perfect *or* exact) likeness, °(carbon) copy, °double, °duplicate, °twin, °(exact) replica, look-alike, °facsimile, *Colloq* spitting image *or* spit and image, *Slang* (dead) ringer **3** °impression, °idea, °notion, °understanding, °image **4** °model, °prototype, °epitome, °essence, °embodiment, incarnation, personification, perfect example **5** ***put (someone) in or into the picture.*** inform *or* advise fully, *Colloq* fill (someone) in —*v.* **6** °envision, °envisage, visualize, °imagine, °fancy, conceive of, see in the mind's eye **7** depict, °draw, °portray, °paint, °represent, °show, °illustrate, °display

picturesque *adj.* **1** colorful, °interesting, intriguing, °unusual, °unique, °original, charming, °idyllic, °fetching, °attractive, °pretty, °lovely, °quaint, °delightful, °pleasing, °scenic **2** colorful, °graphic, °realistic, °vivid, °striking

piece *n.* **1** °bit, °morsel, °scrap, chunk, hunk, °sliver, °lump, °portion, °particle, °fragment, °shred, shard *or* sherd, °remnant, °quantity **2** °wedge, °slice, serving, °helping, °portion **3** °share, °portion, fraction, °part, °division, °segment, °section, °interest, holding, °percentage, °proportion **4** °(short) story, article, °essay, °report, °theme, °draft; °poem; music, °opus, °(musical) number, °composition, °arrangement, °tune, °melody, °song, °air, °jingle, ditty; °production, °play, °drama, sketch, °show **5** °man, °token, chessman, chesspiece, checker, *Brit* draughtsman **6** ***go to pieces.*** °fall apart, °disintegrate, °crumble, °shatter; be shattered, be upset, be disturbed, have a nervous breakdown, go out of *or* lose control, °break down, *Colloq* crack up **7** ***in pieces.*** smashed, destroyed, ruined, shattered, °broken, in smithereens **8** ***of a piece (with).*** °similar, similarly constituted, °alike, of the same sort *or* kind *or* type, °uniform, the same, part and parcel (of the same thing), °identical; in harmony, in agreement, °harmonious, in keeping **9** ***piece of cake.*** *Colloq* °snap, cinch, *US and Canadian* lead-pipe cinch, °breeze **10** ***piece of (one's) mind.*** *Colloq* scolding, °rebuke, °lecture, °reprimand, °tongue-lashing, chiding, rap over *or US* on the knuckles, *Colloq* °hell, what for, dressing-down, *US* bawling-out, chewing-out **11** ***piece of the action.*** °share, °portion, °interest, °stake, °percentage, holding, °quota **12** ***speak (one's) piece.*** have (one's) say, express (one's) opinion, say what is on (one's) mind; vent (one's) spleen, *Colloq* get a load off (one's) mind *or* chest —*v.* **13** ***piece together.*** °assemble, put together, °connect, °gather, °compose; °fix, °unite, °restore, °mend **14** ***pièce de résistance.*** —*n.* highlight, (special *or* main) feature *or* attraction, *spécialité* (*de la maison*), °masterpiece, *chef d'oeuvre*, °specialty

piecemeal *adv.* **1** piece by piece, little by little, inch by inch, bit by bit, inchmeal, °gradually, °by degrees, slowly, in bits and pieces, °by fits and starts, fitfully, intermittently, sporadically, disjointedly **2** into fragments *or* shreds *or* pieces —*adj.* **3** °fragmentary, bit by bit, inchmeal, °gradual, °disjointed, °sporadic

pier *n.* **1** wharf, landing (stage *or* place), jetty, quay, floating dock, *Technically inaccurate* °dock **2** °pile, piling, °post, °upright, column, °support, °buttress

pierce *v.* **1** °stab, °puncture, °penetrate, thrust *or* poke into, °lance, spear, °spit, run through *or* into, skewer, °impale, °fix, °transfix **2** bore into *or* through, °penetrate, °drill, °perforate, °riddle, punch through, °hole, tunnel into **3** °penetrate, °fathom, °see, °understand, °comprehend, °grasp, °discover, °realize **4** °affect (keenly), °touch, °move, °melt, °stir, °rouse, °pain, cut to the quick, °wound, °strike

piercing *adj.* **1** °strident, °shrill, °harsh, earsplitting, earshattering, high-pitched, screaming, shrieking, screeching, °loud, blaring **2** probing, searching, °penetrating, °sharp, °keen; °arresting, gripping, °spellbinding, °enthralling, fascinating, entrancing **3** °penetrating, °icy, frosty, °frigid, chilling, °freezing, °cold, numbing, °keen, °wintry, arctic, °raw, °bitter, °fierce, °biting, nipping, nippy **4** stabbing, shooting, °excruciating, °exquisite, °acute, °sharp, °severe, °agonizing, °fierce, °intense, °painful, racking

piety *n.* **1** °devotion, devotedness, °respect, °deference, °dedication, dutifulness, °loyalty, °affection **2** piousness, °reverence, °veneration, devoutness, holiness, godliness, pietism, devotedness, °devotion, °observance, religiousness, °grace, °sanctity

pile[1] *n.* **1** °heap, °mound, °stack, °accumulation, stockpile, °mass, °supply, °deposit, °collection, assemblage, °batch, °hoard, aggregation, congeries, conglomeration, °assortment, agglomeration, concentration, amassment **2** °money, °fortune, °wealth, holdings, *Colloq* °bundle, °loot, °mint, *Slang* °packet, tidy sum, *US* bankroll, °roll, °wad **3** Usually, ***piles.*** °abundance, overabundance, superabundance, °plenty, °great deal, °quantity, ocean(s), lot(s), stack(s), plethora, *Colloq* oodles, ton(s), bag(s), heap(s), bundle(s) **4** See **pier, 2,** above. —*v.* **5** Often, ***pile up.*** °stack (up), °heap (up), °mound, °accumulate, stockpile, °amass, °collect, °assemble, °hoard, aggregate, cumulate **6** ***pile in or into.*** °enter, get in *or* into, crowd in *or* into, pack in *or* into, flood in *or* into, jam in *or* into, crush in *or* into, *Colloq* jump in *or* into **7** ***pile it on.*** °exaggerate **8** ***pile on or onto.*** **(a)** get in *or* into *or* on *or* onto, crowd on *or* onto, jump on *or* onto **(b)** °attack, °assault, °jump on, °overwhelm **9** ***pile out.*** °leave, get out (of) *or* down (from), °exit **10** ***pile up.*** °accumulate, °amass, °collect

pile[2] *n.* °nap, shag, °plush; fuzz, bristles, °fleece

piles *n. pl.* hemorrhoids.

pileup *n.* **1** °(road) accident, smash, °crash, (multiple) (rear-end) collision, *Colloq* smash-up **2** °accumulation, °heap, °stack, °mass, *Colloq* °mountain

pilfer *v.* °steal, °rob, °plunder, thieve, filch, °embezzle, °misappropriate, purloin, °take, walk off with, palm, *Colloq* °appropriate, °pinch, °snatch, °grab, °lift, °borrow, *Brit* °nick, snaffle, *US* °boost, *Slang* °hook, snitch, °swipe, °rip off

pilgrim *n.* hajji *or* hadji *or* haji, *Medieval history* palmer; crusader

pilgrimage *n.* hajj *or* hadj, holy expedition, °crusade; °expedition, °journey, trek, voyage, °tour, °trip, °excursion

pill *n.* **1** °tablet, capsule, bolus, pellet, pilule; °medicine, medication, medicament, °drug, pharmaceutical, °remedy, °cure; cough drop, pastille, lozenge, troche **2** °nuisance, °bore, °pest, *Colloq* °pain (in the neck), °crank, °drag

pillage *v.* **1** °plunder, °raid, °ravage, °sack, despoil, °rob, °loot, °ransack, °rifle, maraud, depredate, °devastate, vandalize, °ruin, °demolish, °raze, °level, °strip —*n.* **2** °plunder, rapine, despoliation, looting, °robbery, °sack, sacking, ransacking, marauding, brigandage, piracy, freebooting, buccaneering, banditry, °depredation, devastation, vandalization, defilement, laying waste, °destruction, razing, demolition, leveling, °ruin, stripping **3** °plunder, °loot, °booty, °spoils

pillar *n.* **1** column, pilaster, °pile, piling, °pier, °upright, °post, °shaft, °prop; atlas, caryatid **2** °mainstay, °supporter, °worthy, upholder, °backbone, °(tower of) strength, °leader

pilot *n.* **1** aviator, aviatrix, flier, airman, airwoman, aeronaut, captain **2** steersman, helmsman, °navigator, *US* wheelman *or* wheelsman; °guide, °leader, cicerone, conductor —*v.* **3** °guide, °steer, °run, °direct, °shepherd, °control, °lead, °navigate, °drive; °fly

pimp *n.* **1** °procurer, panderer *or* pander, white slaver, whoremonger, *Slang US* hustler —*v.* **2** °procure, °pander, °solicit, *Slang US* °hustle

pimple *n.* pustule, papule, °boil, °swelling, °eruption, blackhead *or Technical* comedo, excrescence, *Brit* °spot, *Scots* plouk *or* plook, *US* whitehead, *Old-fashioned US* hickey

pin *n.* **1** °peg, dowel, °bolt, thole, tholepin, °spike, rivet; *Brit* drawing pin, *US* pushpin **2** °brooch, °clip; stickpin, tiepin, scarfpin, *US* tietack —*v.* **3** °attach, °fix, affix, °fasten, °secure, °tack; °hold, °staple, °clip **4** ***pin down.*** **(a)** °force, °make, compel, coerce, constrain, °press, *Brit* pressurize, *US* °pressure **(b)** °define, °specify, pinpoint, °name, °identify, °determine, put *or* lay one's finger on, home *or* zero in on, focus on **(c)** confine, °hold (down), °fix, immobilize, °tie down, constrain **5** ***pin on.*** °blame, hold responsible *or* accountable, point the finger at, °accuse; lay at (someone's) door, *Slang* °nail

pincers *n. pl.* pliers, nippers, tweezers

pinch *v.* **1** °squeeze, °nip, °tweak, °press, compress, °grip, °grasp **2** °squeeze, cramp, confine, °crush, °hurt **3** °steal, thieve, °rob, °take, shoplift, filch, °pilfer, purloin, *Colloq* °lift, *Brit* °nick, *US* °boost, *Slang* °swipe, °knock off **4** °arrest, apprehend, take into custody, *Colloq* °nab, °run in, collar, bust, *Brit* °nick **5** ***pinch pennies.*** scrimp, °save, skimp, °economize —*n.* **6** °squeeze, °nip, °tweak, °twinge **7** °touch, (tiny *or* wee) bit, soupçon, °jot, mite, °taste, *Colloq US* tad, smidgen *or* smidgin **8** °predicament, °emergency, °crisis, °difficulty, °dilemma, (ticklish *or* delicate) situation, °complication, *Colloq* pickle, °jam, °scrape, *Chiefly Brit* °crunch

pink[1] *n.* **1** ***in the pink.*** at one's best, °healthy, °hearty, in the best of health, in top form, in good shape, *Colloq US* up —*adj.* **2** °rosy, rose, rose-colored, pinkish, flesh-color(ed), salmon(-color(ed))

pink[2] *v.* serrate, °notch, scallop; °perforate, °puncture, °prick

pinnacle *n.* °top, °peak, apex, °acme, °summit, °zenith, °maximum, °climax, crowning point, °consummation, utmost, °extreme, °perfection; °tip, °cap, °crest, °crown

pioneer *n.* **1** pathfinder, frontiersman, frontierswoman, trailblazer, explorer, colonist, (early) settler; groundbreaker, °forerunner, °precursor, predecessor, innovator, °leader, trendsetter, pacemaker, pace-setter —*v.* **2** °create, °originate, °invent, °initiate, take the first step, °introduce, °institute, actuate, trigger, °set off, °inaugurate, °start, °begin, °launch, °establish, °found, °set up, °develop, lay the groundwork *or* foundation, set *or* put in motion, take the lead, lead *or* show the way, blaze the trail, be a prime mover, open up, break new ground, *Colloq* kick off, get the ball rolling

pious *adj.* **1** °devout, °religious, reverent, reverential, worshipful, °dutiful, God-fearing, °godly, °faithful, °holy, dedicated, °devoted, °spiritual, °moral, °good, °virtuous, right-minded, °saintly, °holy, angelic, °seraphic, Christ-like, God-like **2** °hypocritical, °sanctimonious, pietistic, °self-righteous, °pharisaic, °mealy-mouthed, °pretended, °fraudulent, °goody-goody, unctuous, °oily, *Colloq Brit* smarmy

pipe *n.* **1** °pipeline, tube, duct, hose, °line, °main, conduit, °passage, conveyor, °channel **2** briar, meerschaum, corncob, calabash, clay pipe, water pipe, hookah, narghile, chibouk *or* chibouque, peace pipe *or* pipe of peace *or* calumet, *Colloq* Irish briar, *Brit* hubble-bubble, *US* bong **3** panpipe, whistle, boatswain's pipe, tooter, horn, °wind, wind instrument, woodwind, °brass **4** tootle, tweet, skirl, warble, whistle, °peep, cheep **5** °transmit, °deliver, °channel, °conduct, convey, °supply **6** *US* °look at, °notice, °spot, °note, *Colloq* get a load of **7** ***pipe down.*** become quieter, quiet(en) down, make less noise, °hush (up), shush (up), °whisper, *Colloq* belt up, °shut up **8** ***pipe up.*** °speak (up), °say, raise one's voice, make oneself heard, °offer, volunteer

pipeline *n.* **1** °pipe, tube, duct, hose, °line, °main, conduit, °passage, conveyor, °channel **2** ***in the pipeline.*** on the way, °under way, in the offing, °ready, °imminent, coming, *Colloq* in the works, cooking, *US* °in work

pirate *n.* **1** buccaneer, sea rover, corsair, privateer, freebooter, sea robber, filibuster, *Archaic* picaroon **2** plagiarist, plagiarizer, infringer —*v.* **3** plagiarize, °infringe, °copy, °reproduce, °steal, °appropriate, poach, *Colloq* °lift, °pinch, crib

pirouette *n.* **1** °spin, whirl, °twirl, °turn, °revolution, pivoting —*v.* **2** °spin, whirl, °turn (round), °revolve, °pivot

pistol *n.* gun, handgun, °revolver, °automatic, *Slang* °rod, °piece, shooting iron, *Chiefly US* gat, *US* Saturday night special, heater, roscoe

piston *n.* plunger

pit[1] *n.* **1** °hole, °excavation, °shaft, °cavity, °mine, mineshaft, ditch, trench, trough **2** pothole, °hollow, °depression, dent, °indentation, dimple, pockmark **3** °abyss, chasm, °well, °crevasse, crater **4** ***the pits.*** °awful, °terrible, the worst, *Slang* °lousy —*v.* **5** dent, pockmark, °dig, °scar, hollow out, °gouge **6** Often, ***pit against.*** °match, °oppose, °set against; °contrast

pit[2] *n.* stone, °seed, pip

pitch[1] *v.* **1** °toss, °throw, °cast, °fling, °hurl, °heave, °sling, °fire, °launch, °shoot, °send, °let fly, *Cricket* °bowl, *Colloq* chuck, °peg, °lob, *Brit* bung **2** °erect, °raise, set *or* put up, °position, °fix, °place **3** °plunge, °fall (headlong), °dive, °drop, °plummet, (take a) nose dive **4** *Chiefly nautical* toss about, °lurch, °plunge, °flounder, go head over heels, go keel over truck, *US* pitchpole *or* pitchpoll **5** ***pitch in.*** °contribute, °cooperate, °help, °assist, *Colloq* °chip in **6** ***pitch into.*** **(a)** °attack, °lay into, assail, lash out at, °abuse, rail against, *Colloq* °lace into, tear into, jump down (someone's) throat, °jump on **(b)** °attack, °assault, °set upon, °belabor, *Colloq* °light into, sail into, tear into **7** ***pitch on or upon.*** °determine, °decide on, °select, °pick, °choose, opt for, °elect, °nominate, °name, *Colloq* °light on

pitch[2] *n.* tar, bitumen, asphalt

pitch-black *adj.* °black, °dark, ebon(y), stygian, inky (black), unlit, unlighted, pitch-dark, coal-black, jet-black; raven, sable

pitched *adj.* organized, planned, °deliberate, coordinated, arranged, systematized

piteous *adj.* °pitiable, °pathetic, °pitiful, plaintive, °miserable, °heart-rending, plangent, °poignant, distressing, °grievous, heartbreaking, °mournful, °sad, °doleful, dolorous, °tearful, °lamentable, °deplorable, °regrettable, rueful, woeful, °moving, °emotional

pitfall *n.* 1 °trap, °pit 2 °danger, °peril, °hazard, °catch, °difficulty, °snag

pith *n.* 1 °core, °heart, °kernel, °nucleus, crux, °gist, °focus, focal point, °essence, °meat, marrow, °nub, °point, °spirit, °substance, °quintessence 2 °weight, °burden, gravamen, °gravity, °force, °moment, °import, °importance, °significance, °substance, °depth, °matter

pitiable *adj.* See **piteous,** above.

pitiful *adj.* 1 See **piteous,** above. 2 °small, °little, °insignificant, °trifling, unimportant, beggarly, °sorry, °mean, °contemptible

pittance *n.* mite, shoestring, *Slang* peanuts, chickenfeed, small potatoes

pitted *adj.* eaten away, corroded, eroded, pockmarked, defaced, marred, pierced, perforated

pity *n.* 1 °sympathy, commiseration, °sorrow, condolence, compassion, tenderness, *Archaic* ruth 2 (crying *or* damned) shame, sad thing, °disgrace, °misfortune, °sin, °sacrilege, *Colloq* °crime —*v.* 3 °sympathize, °feel for, commiserate with, feel sorry for, feel *or* have compassion *or* tenderness for, bleed for, weep for

pivot *n.* 1 pintle, gudgeon, hinge, °swivel, °pin, kingpin, spindle, fulcrum 2 °center, °heart, focal point, °hub, nave, crux —*v.* 3 °rotate, °revolve, °turn, °spin, °twirl, whirl, °swivel 4 hinge, °depend, °hang, be contingent, revolve around, °rely

pivotal *adj.* °critical, °central, °focal, °crucial, °significant, °important, °essential, °vital, °pressing, °urgent, °radical

place *n.* 1 °location, °site, °position, °point, °spot, locus, °area, °locale, °scene, °setting 2 °locale, °area, °neighborhood, °vicinity, °district, °section, part of the country, °quarter, °region; °city, °town, village, hamlet 3 °status, °station, °standing, °grade, °rank, °position, °niche, °slot, °situation, °estate, °state, circumstance(s) 4 °function, °role, °part, °purpose, °duty, °obligation, °task, °responsibility, °charge, chore, °burden, °concern, °mission 5 °position, °job, °post, berth, °appointment, livelihood; °employment, °occupation, *Colloq* billet 6 °home, °house, °flat, apartment, room(s), °quarters, lodgings, *Rather formal* °residence, °domicile, °dwelling, °abode, *Colloq* digs *or* diggings, °pad 7 stead; lieu 8 °position, °situation, °circumstances, °condition 9 °seat, °chair, °position 10 ***go places.*** °succeed, become successful, °get ahead, °advance, °prosper, °thrive, °flourish, go up in the world, °make good, strike it rich, *Colloq* °arrive, make a splash, *US and Canadian* hit pay dirt, luck out 11 ***in place.*** **(a)** °fitting, °suitable, °appropriate, °right, °proper, °correct, good form **(b)** ***in situ,*** in (the right *or* proper *or* correct) position, °ready, all set, °set up, °in order, all right, *Colloq* OK *or* O.K. *or* okay 12 ***out of place.*** °awkward, uncomfortable, unsuitable, °inappropriate, °wrong, °improper, misplaced 13 ***put (someone) in his or her or their place.*** °humble, °mortify, bring down, °embarrass, °squelch, *Colloq* cut down to size, take down a peg (or two) 14 ***take place.*** °happen, °occur, °go on, °come about; °arise, *Colloq* °transpire —*v.* 15 °put (out), °position, °situate, °locate, °dispose, °arrange, °order, °set (out), °lay, °deposit; °station, °post, °spot, pinpoint, *Colloq* °stick, *Brit* bung 16 °class, classify, °sort, °order, °arrange, °rank, °group, °categorize, °bracket, °grade; °regard, °view, °see, °consider 17 °identify, °put one's finger on, °recall, °remember, °recognize; °associate 18 °put, °set, °assign, °give

placement *n.* 1 °arrangement, placing, °position, °distribution, array, °disposition, deployment, positioning, stationing, °organization, °order, ordering, °location, locating, arraying, emplacement, emplacing 2 °employment, °appointment, °engagement, hiring

plagiarism *n.* plagiarizing, plagiary, piracy, pirating, °theft, purloining, °stealing, copying, appropriating, appropriation, thievery, usurpation, infringing, °infringement, °imitation, *Euphemistic* borrowing, *Colloq* lifting, cribbing

plague *n.* 1 °scourge, °epidemic, °pestilence, °affliction, pandemic, °calamity, °curse, °evil, bane, °blight, °visitation 2 irritation, °annoyance, °nuisance, °pest, vexation, °bother, thorn in one's side *or* flesh, °torment, torture, *Colloq* °pain (in the neck), °headache, aggravation, *Slang* °drag, °bitch, hassle, *Taboo slang* pain in the *US* ass *or Brit* arse —*v.* 3 badger, harry, °hound, °pester, °annoy, vex, °irritate, °bother, °harass, °nag, nettle, needle, °exasperate, °gall, °annoy, °irk, °torment, torture, °anguish, °distress, *Brit* chivy *or* chivvy *or* chevy, *Colloq* °bug

plain *adj.* 1 °flat, °smooth, °even, featureless, °level, °plane 2 °clear, °evident, °simple, °distinct, crystal-clear, lucid, °vivid, °transparent, °apparent, °obvious, °patent, °self-evident, °manifest, °distinct, unmistakable *or* unmistakeable, unequivocal, unambiguous, understandable, °intelligible, °graphic, °direct, in black and white 3 °open, °honest, straightforward, °forthright, °direct, °frank, °candid, °blunt, °outspoken, °ingenuous, °sincere, guileless, °artless, unreserved 4 °simple, °unadorned, undecorated, unembellished, °basic, austere, °stark, unostentatious, °colorless, °drab, °bare, °unvarnished, °Spartan 5 °homely, unattractive, ordinary-looking, unlovely, °ugly —*n.* 6 prairie, grassland, °pasture, meadowland, veldt *or* veld, pampas, campo, llano, savanna *or* savannah, steppe, tundra, champaign *or* campagna; heath; °moor, moorland; °plateau, flatland; down, downland, *Literary* wold, *Literary or archaic* mead

plan *n.* 1 °design, layout, blueprint, °scheme, °method, °procedure, °system, °arrangement, °program, °project, °formula, °pattern, *Colloq* °script, °scenario 2 °drawing, sketch, °design, layout, blueprint, °chart, map, diagram, °representation —*v.* 3 lay out *or* down, °design, °arrange, °devise, °outline, °organize, °plot, map out, delineate, °develop 4 °intend, °expect, °envisage, °envision, °foresee, °aim, °contemplate, °propose

plane *n.* 1 flat *or* level (surface) 2 airplane, aircraft, airliner, jet (plane) —*adj.* 3 °flat, °even, °level, °smooth, °plain, °regular, unbroken, uninterrupted, °uniform, °horizontal —*v.* 4 °glide, °skim, skate, skid, °slip, °slide

plank *n.* °board, °timber, °slab

plant *n.* 1 °flower, vegetable, herb, bush, shrub, tree, vine, weed 2 °factory, °mill, °shop, °works, workshop, foundry 3 °equipment, machinery, °apparatus; °gear, fixtures 4 °spy, (undercover *or* secret) agent, °informer, informant —*v.* 5 bed (out), °sow, °seed, °set (out), °transplant 6 °implant, °establish, °root, °fix, ingrain, °lodge, °instill, °insinuate, °inject, °introduce, °impress, imprint 7 °place, °put, °position, °station, °assign, °situate 8 °hide, °secrete, °conceal

planter *n.* flowerpot, cachepot

plaque *n.* 1 °tablet, medallion, °plate, panel, marker, °slab, plaquette 2 badge, °brooch, °pin, °patch, medallion, medal, insignia *or* insigne 3 °prize, °honor, °award, °trophy

plaster *v.* °smear, daub, bedaub, °spread, °coat, °cover, overlay, superimpose

plastic *adj.* 1 moldable, shapable *or* shapeable, fictile, °soft, malleable, workable, ductile, °flexible, °soft, pliant, °supple, °pliable, clayey, waxy 2 °impressionable, °receptive, °open, persuadable *or* persuasible, °susceptible, °tractable, compliant, °responsive, °manageable, unformed, °inexperienced 3 °artificial, °synthetic, °imitation, °fake, °counterfeit, ersatz, paste, °bogus, meretricious, °sham; °cheap, pinchbeck, °shoddy; *Colloq* phoney *or US also* phony, crummy, *US* chintzy

plate *n.* 1 °platter, dish, *Archaic* trencher, charger 2 °course, serving, °portion, dish, °platter 3 layer, leaf, °sheet, °pane, panel, lamina, °slab 4 coating, °coat, plating, layer, lamination 5 °illustration, °picture, °print, *US* °cut —*v.* 6 °cover, °coat, overlay, °face, laminate

plateau *n.* 1 tableland, upland, highland, mesa 2 °level, °lull, °pause, leveling off

platform *n.* 1 °stand, dais, °stage, podium, °rostrum 2 °policy, party line, principle(s), tenet(s), °program, °plank

platonic *adj.* nonphysical, asexual, nonsexual, °celibate, °chaste, °dispassionate, °detached, °spiritual, °ideal, °intellectual

platoon *n.* °company, °squad, squadron, °group, °patrol, °team, cadre, °body, °formation, °unit, *Colloq* °outfit

platter *n.* serving dish, server, salver, tray, °plate, dish

plausible *adj.* 1 °likely, believable, °reasonable, credible, °tenable, conceivable, °thinkable, °probable, imaginable, admissible, °sound, °sensible, °rational, °logical, °acceptable, °trustworthy, °presentable 2 °specious, °deceptive, meretricious, misleading, °deceitful, casuistic, sophistical, jesuitical, °smooth, °empty

play *v.* 1 amuse oneself, °frolic, °frisk, °cavort, gambol, °caper, °sport, have fun, have a good time, °enjoy oneself, disport (oneself), °carouse 2 °participate (in), take part (in), °join (in), be occupied (in *or* with); °engage in, contend in, °take up, occupy oneself in *or* with, °undertake 3 °engage, contend with, compete with *or* against, °challenge, vie with, pit oneself against, °take on, °rival 4 °portray, depict, °perform, act *or* take the role *or* part of, °act 5 perform (upon *or* on); °put on 6 °operate 7 °gamble, °bet, wager, °stake, °place, °put 8 ***play along.*** **(a)** Often, ***play along with.*** cooperate, °participate, go along (with), do *or* play one's part, be a party to **(b)** °manipulate, °jolly along 9 ***play around.*** **(a)** °fool around, °tease, *Colloq* monkey about *or* around, horse around *or* about **(b)** dally, °flirt, be unfaithful; philander, womanize; *Colloq* °fool around, °run around, sleep around, play the field 10 ***play at.*** °pretend, °make believe, °fake, feign, simulate, °affect 11 ***play ball.*** °cooperate, °agree, work together, work hand in glove, °play along 12 ***play by ear.*** °improvise, extemporize, ad-lib, *Colloq* wing it 13 ***play down.*** °belittle, °minimize, °diminish, °disparage, °make light of, deprecate, decry, de-emphasize 14 ***play for time.*** °delay, °procrastinate, °stall (for time), temporize, °hesitate, *Colloq* °drag one's feet 15 ***play on or upon.*** °use, °misuse, °abuse, trade on, °exploit, take advantage of, °impose on 16 ***play the game.*** °behave, °conduct oneself, deport oneself, °act 17 ***play up.*** **(a)** °stress, °emphasize, underscore, underline, accentuate, call attention to, highlight, °spotlight, °dramatize, °build up **(b)** act up, °misbehave, give *or* cause trouble, malfunction, *Colloq* go on the blink *or US* fritz, *Brit* be wonky 18 ***play up to.*** curry favor with, °flatter, toady to, ingratiate oneself with, butter up, truckle to, court, *Colloq* soft-soap, suck up to, bootlick, *US* apple-polish, *Slang taboo* brown-nose 19 ***play with.*** **(a)** °toy with, °trifle with, treat cavalierly *or* lightly, °make light of, think nothing of, dally with, amuse oneself with **(b)** °consider, °think about, °toy with, not treat seriously **(c)** °mess with, °fiddle with, °toy with, fidget with —*n.* 20 °drama, stage play, °show, °piece, °production, °entertainment 21 °behavior, °actions, deportment, °conduct, demeanor 22 °amusement, frivolity, °entertainment, °recreation, °fun, °pleasure, °sport, merrymaking, °revelry, tomfoolery, *Colloq* horseplay, skylarking, monkey business, *Brit* monkey tricks *or US* monkeyshines **23** °move, °maneuver, °action **24** °flexibility, looseness, °freedom, °leeway, °margin, °room, °space, °movement, °motion, *Colloq* °give **25** °treatment, coverage, °attention

playboy *n.* man about town, °roué, °rake, debauchee, gay dog, womanizer, Don Juan, Casanova, Lothario, Romeo, *Colloq* wolf, lady-killer

player *n.* **1** °contestant, °participant, °competitor, contender; athlete, sportswoman, sportsman, *Colloq US* jock **2** actor *or* actress, °performer, entertainer, trouper, °thespian **3** gambler, bettor *or esp. Brit* better, gamester, speculator, *Brit* punter **4** musician, instrumentalist, °performer, °virtuoso

playful *adj.* **1** (high-)spirited, °cheerful, °frisky, °frolicsome, °kittenish, °sprightly, fun-loving, °sportive, coltish, °mischievous, puckish, impish, elfish, °devilish **2** joking, facetious, teasing, roguish, waggish, jesting, °humorous, tongue-in-cheek

playmate *n.* playfellow, °friend, °comrade, *Colloq* °pal, °chum, *US and Canadian* buddy

plaything *n.* **1** °toy, °game, knickknack *or* nicknack, °pastime **2** °tool, cat's-paw, °dupe, pigeon, °pawn, *Colloq US and Canadian* fall guy

playwright *n.* °dramatist, dramaturge *or* dramaturgist, scriptwriter, screenwriter, scenarist

plea *n.* **1** °request, entreaty, °appeal, °petition, °supplication, °suit, °cry, solicitation **2** °answer, °defense, °argument **3** °excuse, °reason, °explanation, justification; °pretext

plead *v.* **1** Often, ***plead for.*** °request, °appeal (for), °cry (for), °ask (for), °seek, °beg (for), °pray (for), supplicate (for) **2** Usually, ***plead with.*** °request (of), entreat, appeal to, °petition, °ask, apply to, implore, °beseech, °beg, importune, °solicit; °demand **3** assert, °say, aver, °allege, °argue, °maintain, °offer, °put forward, °declare, affirm, avow, °swear

pleasant *adj.* **1** °pleasing, °pleasurable, °nice, enjoyable, °satisfying, °good, °lovely, °attractive, °inviting, enjoyable, gratifying, °delightful, charming, °agreeable, °suitable, °fitting, °appropriate; °harmonious, euphonious, melodic, mellifluous; °delicious, delectable, palatable, °savory, toothsome **2** °friendly, affable, °amiable, °amicable, gregarious, companionable, °sociable, °engaging, °attractive, °winning, °open, approachable, °outgoing, welcoming, °hospitable, °agreeable, °gracious, charming, congenial, °genial, °nice, °likable, urbane, °cultivated, °genteel, °polite, °courteous, well-mannered, °suave, °debonair, °polished, °well-bred, cultured **3** °fair, °sunny, °clear, °bright, cloudless, balmy, °nice, °fine

please *v.* **1** °delight, °gratify, °satisfy, °suit, °humor, °content, °cheer, °gladden, °amuse, °divert, °interest, °entertain **2** °like, °prefer, °choose, °desire, °want, see fit, °wish, °will, °elect, opt

pleased *adj.* °happy, °delighted, °glad, gratified, satisfied, contented, thrilled; *Colloq* tickled pink, pleased as punch, on cloud nine, in seventh heaven, °on top of the world, walking on air, *Brit* over the moon, chuffed

pleasing *adj.* **1** See **pleasant, 1,** above. **2** See **pleasant, 2,** above.

pleasurable *adj.* See **pleasant, 1,** above.

pleasure *n.* **1** °enjoyment, °happiness, °delight, °joy, °satisfaction, °fulfillment, contentment, °gratification; °comfort, °recreation, °amusement, °entertainment, °diversion **2** °choice, °option, °desire, °wish, °preference, °fancy, °inclination, °discretion

plebeian *adj.* **1** proletarian, working-class, blue-collar, low-class, lower-class, °lowly, lowborn, °common, °mean, °humble, °inferior, peasantlike, *Colloq* non-U **2** °unrefined, °coarse, °vulgar, ignoble, lowbrow, unpolished, uncouth, crass, brutish, gauche, °provincial, °rustic, °popular, commonplace, °undistinguished —*n.* **3** proletarian, common man *or* woman, commoner, man *or* woman in the street, (any *or* every) Tom, Dick, or Harry, *Brit* man *or* woman on the Clapham omnibus, *Colloq* pleb, prole

plebiscite *n.* popular vote *or* ballot, referendum, °poll

pledge *n.* **1** °promise, °oath, °vow, °word (of honor), convenant, °assurance, guaranty, °guarantee, °warrant, °warranty **2** bail, surety, collateral, °security, °deposit, °earnest (money), °pawn, gage, °bond, guaranty, °guarantee **3** °toast, °tribute, °cheer, °health —*v.* **4** °swear, °vow, °promise, give one's word (of honor), °contract, °undertake, °agree, °vouch, °vouchsafe **5** °deposit, °pawn, mortgage, *Archaic* gage, *Colloq US and Canadian* hock **6** °toast, °drink (to), drink (someone's) health

plentiful *adj.* **1** °ample, °abundant, °profuse, copious, °lavish, plenteous, °bountiful, °generous, bounteous **2** °fertile, °fruitful, °productive, bumper, °luxuriant, thriving, °prolific

plenty *n.* **1** °abundance, more than enough, great deal, mass(es), quantity *or* quantities, multitude(s), number(s), load(s), °mess, °scores, *Colloq* lot(s), mountain(s), heap(s), stack(s), pile(s), load(s), ton(s), ocean(s), oodles, *US and Canadian* slew(s) **2** plentifulness, fertility, copiousness, °abundance, plenteousness, °wealth, °profusion, lavishness, °prodigality, plenitude, bountifulness

pliable *adj.* **1** °flexible, pliant, °elastic, °plastic, fictile, malleable, workable, bendable, bendy, ductile, flexuous, °supple; lithe, limber **2** °tractable, °adaptable, °flexible, pliant, compliant, persuadable *or* persuasible, °impressionable, °susceptible, °responsive, °receptive, docile, °manageable, °yielding

plight *n.* °condition, °state, °circumstances, °situation, °case; °difficulty, °predicament, °quandary, °dilemma, catch-22, °straits, °trouble, °extremity, *Colloq* °hole, °jam, pickle, °spot, °scrape, °fix, °bind, hot water, °mess, fine kettle of fish, fine state of affairs

plod *v.* **1** Often, ***plod along.*** trudge (along), °tramp, slog, °drag, tread, °lumber, °labor, *Colloq* stomp, galumph **2** Often, ***plod along or away.*** °labor, °work, drudge, toil, moil, °slave (away), grind (away *or* along), grub (on *or* along), plug (along *or* away), *Brit* peg away (at) *or* along

plot[1] *n.* **1** °scheme, °plan, °intrigue, °machination, °cabal; °conspiracy **2** °story (line), chain of events, °theme, °outline, °scenario, °thread, skeleton —*v.* **3** °scheme, °plan, °intrigue, machinate, °cabal, collude, conspire, °hatch, °devise, °design, °arrange, °organize, concoct, dream up, °conceive, *Colloq* cook up **4** °draw, °plan, diagram, °lay down, °outline, °calculate, °compute, °figure, °chart, map (out), °find, °determine, depict, °show

plot[2] *n.* °lot, plat, patch *or* parcel (of land), °tract, acreage, °area, *Brit* °allotment

plow *v.* **1** °till, °cultivate, °furrow, harrow, *Literary* delve, *Chiefly Brit* plough **2** °drive, °plunge, °push, bulldoze, °lunge, °dive, shove, °hurtle, °crash, *Chiefly Brit* plough

pluck *n.* **1** °courage, °spirit, °bravery, °grit, boldness, intrepidity, °backbone, mettle, °determination, gameness, °resolve, °resolution, steadfastness, hardiness, sturdiness, stoutheartedness, stoutness, °fortitude, °nerve, *Colloq* °guts, °spunk, *US* sand, *Slang Brit* °bottle, *US* moxie —*v.* **2** °pick, °remove, °withdraw, °draw out, °extract **3** °snatch, °grab, °yank, °jerk, °tear (away) **4** °tug (at), °pull (at), °catch (at), °clutch (at); vellicate

plug *n.* **1** °stopper, stopple, bung, cork **2** °chew, °twist, quid, °wad, pigtail, cavendish **3** publicity, °mention, °promotion, °recommendation, °puff, blurb, PR; °advertisement, *Colloq* advert, hype —*v.* **4** Often, ***plug up.*** °stop (up), close (up *or* off), seal (off *or* up), cork, °stopper, bung, °block, °jam, °stuff, °clog, °obstruct, dam (up) **5** °publicize, °mention, °promote, °push, advertise, °puff, commend, *Colloq* °boost, beat the drum for **6** See **plod, 2,** above.

plum *n.* °find, °catch, coup, °prize, °treasure; °bonus, cream

plumb *n.* **1** °weight, (plumb) bob, °plummet, °lead, sinker —*adj.* **2** vertical, °perpendicular, straight up and down —*adv.* **3** vertically, perpendicularly, straight up and down **4** °exactly, °precisely, °dead, °right, accurately, *Colloq* °slap, *Brit* bang, °spot —*v.* **5** °sound, °fathom, °measure, °probe, °explore, °gauge, delve, °penetrate

plummet *v.* See **plunge, 1,** below.

plump[1] *adj.* **1** °chubby, °stout, fleshy, °ample, full-bodied, portly, tubby, °rotund, squat, chunky, °buxom, corpulent, roly-poly, °fat, °obese, overweight, steatopygous, *Brit* podgy *or US* pudgy, *Colloq* busty, °beamy, hippy, beefy, well-upholstered —*v.* **2** puff up *or* out

plump[2] *v.* **1** °drop, °plummet, °fall, °plunge, °dive, °sink, °collapse, °flop **2** °deposit, set *or* put (down), plunk, plop **3** ***plump for.*** °support, °choose, °select, °back, °side with, campaign for —*n.* **4** °drop, plunk, °flop, thump, clunk, °clump, °thud, °bump —*adv.* **5** abruptly, °suddenly, °directly, unhesitatingly, °at once, unexpectedly, surprisingly, without warning, (all) of a sudden, plunk, bang —*adj.* **6** °direct, unequivocal, unmistakable *or* unmistakeable, unambiguous, °definite, °definitive, °blunt, °simple, °plain, °forthright, °downright, °straight, °matter-of-fact

plunder *v.* **1** °pillage, °loot, °rob, °ravage, °ransack, °rifle, despoil, °spoil, vandalize, °sack, °strip, maraud, °devastate, °desolate, °lay waste **2** prey on *or* upon, °pirate, °capture, °seize —*n.* **3** °pillage, looting, °robbery, °depredation, rapine, despoliation, spoliation, vandalization, °sack, vandalism, vandalizing, sacking **4** °booty, °loot, °spoils, prizes, *Slang* boodle

plunge *v.* **1** °descend, °drop, °plummet, °dive, °pitch, nose-dive, °fall (headlong) **2** °submerge, °sink, °immerse; engulf, °overwhelm —*n.* **3** °dive, nose dive, °fall, °pitch, °plummet, °drop, descent; submersion, immersion **4** °gamble, wager, °bet, °risk

plus *prep.* **1** and, added to, increased by, with the addition of, with an increment of, (coupled) with, together with —*adj.* **2** added, additional, °supplementary, °extra —*n.* **3** °addition, °bonus, °extra, °gain, °benefit, °asset, °advantage, °profit, °return

plush *adj.* °luxurious, °posh, costly, (de)-luxe, °palatial, °lavish, °rich, °opulent, °sumptuous, °regal, °elegant, *Colloq* ritzy, classy, *Old-fashioned* swank(y)

ply *n.* layer, leaf, thickness, °fold

pocket *n.* **1** °pouch, °sack, °bag, °receptacle, reticule, satchel **2** °cavity, °pit, °hollow, crater **3** °area, °island, °camp, °center, °cluster, concentration —*v.* **4** °take, °appropriate, °keep; filch, °embezzle, °steal, purloin, thieve, °pilfer, help oneself to, palm, *Colloq* walk off *or* away with, °pinch, °swipe, °rip off, °hook, °lift, snitch, *Brit* °nick, snaffle

poem *n.* verse, °lyric, rhyme *or Archaic* rime, °song, ode, rhapsody, °jingle, ditty

poet *n.* poetess, versifier, metrist, lyricist *or* lyrist, versemaker, sonneteer, elegist, bard, °minstrel; rhymester *or* rimester *or* rhymer *or* rimer, poetaster

poetic *adj.* **1** poetical, lyric(al), metrical, °musical, melodic; °idyllic, elegiac, georgic, °rhapsodic, epic, dithyrambic **2** artistic, °aesthetic, Parnassian, Hippocrenian, °melodious

poetry *n.* verse, versification, metrical composition, metrics, °rhyme, *Archaic* poesy

poignant *adj.* **1** distressing, upsetting, °agonizing, °grievous, °painful, woeful, °melancholy, °blue, °sad, °sorrowful, °tragic, °disastrous, heartrending, heartbreaking, °excruciating, °bitter, °pathetic, °pitiable, °piteous, °pitiful, °miserable, °moving, °touching **2** °keen, °acute, °intense, °incisive, °sharp, stinging, °pointed, °piercing, °penetrating, barbed, °cutting, °caustic, acid, acerbic, °bitter, °biting, mordant, °sarcastic, °sardonic, °severe **3** °sincere, °earnest, °heartfelt, °deep, °profound, °dramatic, deeply felt, °stirring, °moving, °touching, °emotional

point *n.* **1** °dot, °mark, °speck; °(full) stop, °period; decimal point **2** °tip, °peak, apex, °spike, °spur, prong, sharp end **3** °spot, °place, °stage, °position; °site, °station, °location, °locale **4** °time, °moment, °instant, °juncture **5** °focus, °essence, °meat, °pith, quiddity, °substance, °heart, °nucleus, crux, °nub, °core, °bottom, °details, *Colloq* °guts, nitty-gritty **6** °purpose, °intent, °intention, °aim, °goal, °object, °objective, °sense **7** °thrust, °drift, °theme, purport, °burden, °import, °implication, °significance, signification, °sense, °meaning; °application, applicability, relevancy, appropriateness **8** promontory, °projection, headland, °cape, peninsula **9** °brink, °verge **10** °detail, °particular, °item, °element, nicety, °aspect, facet, °matter, °issue, °subject, °question; specifics **11** °pointer, °hint, °suggestion, piece of advice, °tip **12** °thought, °idea, °consideration; °notion, °view, °plan, °tactic; something **13** °unit, °tally, °score **14** °attribute, °characteristic, °feature, °aspect, °trait, °quality, °side, °property **15** ***beside the point.*** °irrelevant, inapt, °inappropriate, malapropos, °incidental, °immaterial, unimportant, °pointless, °inconsequential **16** ***in point of.*** in reference to, °regarding, as regards, in the matter of, °concerning, with respect to **17** ***make a point of*** *or US also* ***make (it) a point to.*** make an effort (to), put *or* place emphasis on, go out of one's way (to); °emphasize, °single out, °stress **18** ***to the point.*** °relevant, °pertinent, °appropriate, °fitting, apropos, germane, apt, °applicable, apposite —*v.* **19** Often, ***point to.*** °indicate, call *or* direct attention **20** °direct, °level, °aim, °train **21** ***point out.*** **(a)** °designate, call *or* direct attention to, °show, °exhibit, °indicate, °identify **(b)** °say, °bring up, °mention, allude to, °emphasize, °stress, °point up, °single out; call attention to, °remind **22** ***point up.*** °emphasize, °stress, accentuate, underline, underscore, °accent, °spotlight

point-blank *adj.* **1** °direct, °straight, °blunt, °flat, straightforward, °abrupt, °categorical, °explicit, uncompromising, °unmitigated, unalloyed, °downright, °outright, °to the point, straight-from-the-shoulder, (open and) above-board, unreserved **2** °close, °short, °nearby —*adv.* **3** °directly, *Brit* °straightaway, *US* right away, bluntly, °flat, flatly, abruptly, categorically, unqualifiedly, explicitly, uncompromisingly, unmitigatedly, °outright, unreservedly, plainly, frankly, °openly, candidly **4** °directly, °straight

pointed *adj.* **1** needle-shaped, °sharp, °acute, barbed, °peaked, spiked, spiky, *Technical* acuminate, cuspidate, aciform, acicular, aciculiform, aculeous, apiculate, spiculate, serrate(d), acuminate, mucroniform, mucronulate, mucronate(d), muricate, hebetate **2** °incisive, °piercing, °cutting, °sharp, °pungent, °keen, °penetrating, °telling, °trenchant, °biting, unmistakable *or* unmistakeable

pointer *n.* **1** °indicator, °rod, °stick; °index, °sign, arrow, *Typography* fist **2** °tip, °advice, °hint, °suggestion, °recommendation, piece of advice

pointless *adj.* °purposeless, °aimless, °worthless, °ineffective, °meaningless, °ineffectual, °futile, unproductive, °fruitless, °bootless, °useless, °vain, °senseless, °absurd, °silly, °stupid, °inane, asinine, fatuous, °preposterous, °nonsensical, °ridiculous, °empty, °hollow

point of view *n.* **1** °viewpoint, °perspective, °approach, °position, °angle, °slant, °orientation, °outlook, °stance, °standpoint, vantage point **2** °opinion, °view, °belief, °(way of) thinking, °principle, °doctrine

poise *n.* **1** °balance, equilibrium, equipoise, equiponderance, °parity, °par **2** composure, °control, self-possession, aplomb, °assurance, °dignity, equanimity, °sang-froid, coolheadedness, imperturbability, °presence of mind, coolness, staidness, °reserve, sedateness, calmness, °serenity, tranquillity, *Colloq* °cool —*v.* **3** °balance, be balanced, °hover, °hang, °float; make *or* be *or* get ready, °prepare

poised *adj.* **1** composed, controlled, °self-possessed, unflappable, (self-)confident, (self-)assured, °dignified, coolheaded, imperturbable, unruffled, °cool, °staid, °reserved, °sedate, °calm, °serene, °tranquil, *Colloq* together **2** °ready, standing by, waiting, °prepared **3** teetering, hovering, tottering, wavering, suspended, trembling, wobbling, balanced

poison *n.* **1** toxin, °venom, bane; miasma, mephitis **2** virus, bane, cancer, canker, corrupt *or* evil influence, °pestilence, °plague, °blight —*v.* **3** defile, °adulterate, infect, °taint, °pollute; °contaminate, °debase, °pervert, °vitiate, °subvert, °warp, envenom **4** °murder, °kill, do away with, °destroy, dispatch *or* despatch

poisonous *adj.* **1** °lethal, °deadly, °fatal, °mortal, toxic, septic, °virulent, noxious *or rare* nocuous, °venomous, °malignant, pernicious, miasmic, mephitic **2** malicious, malevolent, °malignant, corruptive, °vicious, baleful, °evil, °foul, diabolic(al), defamatory, libelous, °slanderous, °dangerous, deleterious

poke *v.* **1** °jab, °stick, °prod, °dig, goad, °stab, °thrust, °push, elbow, °nudge, °jog, jostle, °butt, shove **2** °punch, °hit, °strike, °box, cuff, smite, smack **3** °pry, nose (about *or* around), stick one's nose into, °intrude, °dig, °probe, °investigate; °meddle, °interfere, °butt in, °tamper; *Colloq* °snoop **4** ***poke fun (at).*** °tease, °ridicule, °mock, °make fun of, °jeer (at), °chaff, °taunt, °twit,

°make sport of, needle, *Colloq* kid, rib, *Brit* °send up, take the mickey out of —*n.* 5 °jab, °prod, °dig, °stab, °thrust, °push, elbow, °finger, °nudge, °jog, jostle, °butt, shove 6 °punch, °hit, °box, °jab, cuff, smack, °blow

polar *adj.* 1 arctic, antarctic, °frigid, °icy, glacial, °freezing, frozen, numbing, Siberian, hibernal, hyperborean, brumal, °wintry 2 °opposite, °opposed, antithetical, °contrary, °contradictory, diametric, antipodal, antagonistic, °hostile

pole[1] *n.* °rod, °stick, °staff, °spar, °shaft, mast, °standard, °upright; flagpole, flagstaff, jackstaff; beanpole, hoppole

pole[2] *n.* 1 °extremity, °end, °limit, °extreme 2 ***from pole to pole.*** °everywhere, all over, °far and wide, high and low, leaving no stone unturned, throughout the world *or* the length and breadth of the land, *Colloq US* everyplace 3 ***poles apart.*** (very *or* completely) different, worlds apart, at opposite extremes, at opposite ends of the earth, °at odds, irreconcilable

police *n.* 1 constabulary, policemen, policewomen, police officers, *Colloq* boys in blue, the (long arm of the) law, the cops, the gendarmes, *Slang* the coppers, the fuzz, *US* the heat, *Brit* the (Old) Bill —*v.* 2 °patrol, °guard, °watch, °protect 3 °enforce, °regulate, °administer, °oversee, °control, °observe, °supervise, °monitor

police officer *n.* °officer, policeman, policewoman, °constable, *Brit* police constable, PC, WPC, *Chiefly US* peace officer, patrolman, patrolwoman, *Colloq* cop, gendarme, *Brit* bobby; *Slang* copper, fuzz, flatfoot, *Brit* rozzer, Old Bill, *Offensive and derogatory* pig, *US* bull, fuzzball, *Historical Brit* peeler

policy *n.* °approach, °procedure, °(game) plan, °design, °scheme, °program, °method, °system, °management, °conduct, °behavior, °strategy, tactic(s), principle(s), °protocol, °regulation, °rule, °custom, °way, °practice, ways and means, °action

polish *v.* 1 °shine, °brighten, burnish, buff, furbish, wax, °clean, °smooth, °rub, °gloss 2 Often, ***polish up.*** °refine, °improve, °perfect, °finish, °cultivate, ameliorate, °enhance; °correct, emend 3 ***polish off.*** **(a)** conclude, °end, °terminate, °finish **(b)** °kill, slay, °murder, dispatch *or* despatch, °destroy, °dispose of, do away with, liquidate, °eliminate, *Slang* °bump off, °rub out, do in, °take for a ride **(c)** °dispose of, °put away, °eat, °consume, wolf (down) 4 ***polish up.*** °study, °review, °learn, *Archaic* con, *Colloq* bone up (on), *Slang Brit* swot up (on) —*n.* 5 °gloss, °shine, °luster, °sheen, °glaze, smoothness, °brilliance, °sparkle, °gleam, °glow, brightness, °radiance 6 wax, °oil

polished *adj.* 1 °accomplished, °adept, °proficient, °expert, °fine, °outstanding, °skillful, °gifted, °masterful, masterly, °virtuoso, °excellent, °superior, °superb, °superlative; °flawless, °faultless, °perfect, °impeccable 2 °refined, °elegant, °cultivated, °graceful, °debonair, °sophisticated, urbane, soigné(e), courtly, °genteel, cultured, civilized, °well-bred, well-mannered, °polite

polite *adj.* 1 °civil, °respectful, well-mannered, mannerly, °courteous, deferential, °diplomatic, °tactful, °formal, °proper, °cordial 2 See **polished, 2,** above.

politic *adj.* 1 °ingenious, °shrewd, °crafty, canny, cunning, °designing, °scheming, °clever, °wily, °foxy, °tricky, °artful, Machiavellian, °evasive, °shifty, *Colloq* cagey 2 °tactful, °diplomatic, °discreet, °prudent, °judicious, °wise, °sage, sagacious, °sensible, °intelligent, percipient, °discriminating, °far-sighted, °expedient, °perceptive

political *adj.* 1 governmental, civic, °civil, °public, °state, °national, federal; administrative, bureaucratic 2 °partisan, °factious, factional

politician *n.* legislator, lawmaker, statesman, stateswoman; °minister, *Brit* Member of Parliament, MP, *US* public *or* civil servant, administrator, °official, bureaucrat, office-bearer, senator, congressman, congresswoman, °representative, assemblyman, assemblywoman, selectman; *Colloq US derogatory* politico, (political) boss *or* hack, machine politician, ward heeler, wirepuller

politics *n.* 1 public affairs, political science, civics, civil affairs, °government, statecraft, °diplomacy, statesmanship 2 maneuvering, manipulation, wirepulling, °machination

poll *n.* 1 voting, °vote, °returns, °tally, figures 2 opinion poll, °survey, °canvass, census, ballot, °count —*v.* 3 °sample, °survey, °question, °canvass, ballot, °ask, °interview; °count, °enumerate, °tally, °register, °record 4 °receive, °get, °win, °register, °tally

pollute *v.* 1 °contaminate, °adulterate, befoul, °foul, °soil, °spoil, °taint, °stain, °dirty, °sully, °blight, °poison 2 °corrupt, °desecrate, °profane, defile, °violate

pollution *n.* contamination, adulteration, corruption, polluting, fouling, befouling, soiling, spoiling, tainting, staining, dirtying, sullying, blighting, poisoning, vitiation

pomp *n.* °glory, °grandeur, magnificence, °splendor, °show, °extravaganza, °pageantry, °ceremony, °spectacle, °brilliance, ceremoniousness

pompous *adj.* 1 °vain, vainglorious, °proud, °arrogant, °pretentious, °ostentatious, °showy, °grandiose, °haughty, °overbearing, °conceited, °egotistical, °self-important, °boastful, °braggart, °inflated, °snobbish, magisterial, imperious, pontifical, °affected, exhibitionist, *Colloq* uppity, highfalutin *or* hifalutin, °hoity-toity, high-hat, *Slang* snooty, snotty 2 °bombastic, °flowery, grandiloquent, °pedantic, °stuffy, fustian, orotund, °ornate, embroidered, flatulent, °windy, turgid, °inflated, high-flown, euphuistic

ponder *v.* °consider, muse (over *or* on), brood (over *or* upon *or* on), mull over, °deliberate (over), meditate (upon *or* on), think (over *or* on *or* about), °weigh, ruminate (over), °chew over, cogitate, excogitate, reflect (on *or* over), °contemplate

ponderous *adj.* **1** °weighty, °unwieldy, °heavy, °massive, °huge, °big, °large, °awkward, °clumsy, cumbersome *or* cumbrous **2** °dull, °tedious, °labored, °laborious, °tiresome, turgid, °boring, °dreary, °pedestrian, °stilted, °windy, °inflated, long-winded, °wordy, verbose, prolix, elephantine, °pompous, grandiloquent, overdone

pool *n.* **1** pond, lake, tarn, °mere, lagoon; swimming pool, leisure pool, *Brit* paddling pool, *US* wading pool, *Formal* natatorium **2** °collection, fund(s), °purse, stakes, reserve(s), bank, *Colloq* °pot, jackpot, °kitty **3** °syndicate, °trust, °group, consortium, cartel, °combine —*v.* **4** °accumulate, °collect, °gather, °combine, °merge, consolidate, °amalgamate, °league, bring *or* come *or* band *or* get together, team (up) with

poor *adj.* **1** °needy, °destitute, °indigent, in want, in need, penniless, poverty-stricken, °impoverished, badly off, necessitous, poor as a church mouse, °straitened, pinched, in reduced circumstances, impecunious, financially embarrassed, °down-and-out, out of pocket, ruined, °insolvent, bankrupt, *Colloq* °broke, °hard up, °on one's uppers, °short, *US* wiped out, *Brit* in Queer street, *Slang Brit* skint **2** °low, °bad, skimpy, °meager, scant, °scanty, °inadequate, °deficient, °insufficient, °sparse **3** °barren, unproductive, unfruitful, °fruitless, °infertile, °sterile; depleted, °exhausted, °impoverished **4** °bad, °awful, °inadequate, °unsatisfactory, °unacceptable, bumbling, °inefficient, amateurish, °unprofessional, °inferior, second-rate, third-rate, low-grade, °shabby, °shoddy, °mediocre, °defective, °faulty, °flawed, substandard, °sorry, not up to par *or* snuff, °slipshod, below *or* under par, *Colloq* °rotten, °lousy **5** °insignificant, °slight, °paltry, °inconsequential, °mean, °modest, trivial, °trifling **6** °unfortunate, unlucky, °pathetic, luckless, °pitiful, °pitiable, ill-fated, °miserable, °wretched, ill-starred, star-crossed, jinxed, hapless **7** °bad, °ill

poorly *adv.* **1** °badly, inadequately, unsatisfactorily, incompetently, inexpertly, improperly, crudely, unprofessionally, amateurishly —*adj.* **2** unwell, °indisposed, ailing, °sick, °below par, *Colloq* °rotten, °under the weather

pop *v.* **1** °burst, °explode, bang, °go off **2** Often, ***pop in or out or by.*** °visit, °stop, °call, °appear, *Colloq* drop in, *Brit* nip in **3** °bulge, °protrude, °stick out, *US* bug out —*n.* **4** °explosion, bang, °report, °crack **5** soft drink, soda (water); cola, *Brit* fizzy drink, lemonade, *US* soda (pop)

populace *n.* °people, masses, commonalty, °(general) public, commoners, multitude, °hoi polloi, °crowd, °throng, °rabble, peasantry, proletariat, common folk, °rank and file, working class, bourgeoisie, °mob, *Contemptuous* great unwashed, °riffraff, °rabble, *canaille*, ragtag and bobtail

popular *adj.* **1** °favorite, °favored, in favor, accepted, well-received, approved, (well-) liked, °fashionable, °in fashion, °stylish, in vogue, °celebrated, °renowned, acclaimed, °famous, °in demand, sought-after, all the rage, *Colloq* °trendy, in, °hot **2** °conventional, °stock, commonplace, °public, °normal, °standard, °general, °universal, °average, °everyday, °ordinary, °routine, °common, °habitual, °prevalent, °current, °prevailing, °dominant, °predominant, predominating, °customary **3** °lay, nonprofessional, °amateur, understandable, °accessible, popularized, simplified

popularity *n.* °favor, acceptance, °approval, °esteem, °regard, repute, °reputation, °vogue, °trend, stylishness, °renown, acclaim, °fame, °celebrity, lionization, °(hero) worship, *Colloq* trendiness

popularly *adv.* commonly, °generally, °ordinarily, °usually, °universally, °widely, regularly, customarily, prevalently, habitually

populate *v.* colonize, °settle, °people, °occupy; °inhabit, dwell in, reside in, live in

population *n.* °people, °populace, inhabitants, residents, natives, denizens, citizenry, citizens, °folk

populous *adj.* crowded, (heavily) populated, peopled, teeming, thronged, crawling, swarming, jammed, jampacked, °packed

pore[1] *v.* ***pore over.*** °study, °examine, °scrutinize, °peruse, °read, °go over, *Colloq* con

pore[2] *n.* °opening, orifice, °hole, °aperture, °vent, perforation, *Technical* spiracle, stoma

pornographic *adj.* °obscene, °lewd, °offensive, °indecent, °prurient, smutty, °taboo, °blue, °dirty, salacious, licentious, °nasty, X-rated, *Colloq* porno, *US* raunchy

pornography *n.* obscenity, smut, °filth, °dirt, erotica, *Colloq* porn

porous *adj.* spongy, spongelike, permeable, pervious, penetrable

port *n.* °harbor, haven, seaport; mooring, anchorage; °refuge

portable *adj.* transportable, °manageable, carryable, °handy, °light, lightweight, °compact, °pocket, pocket-sized, °little, °small, *US* carry-on, vest-pocket, shirt-pocket

portentous *adj.* **1** °ominous, °threatening, °momentous, °sinister, °fateful, alarming, °menacing, °foreboding, ill-omened, °inauspicious, unfavorable, ill-starred, ill-fated, star-crossed, lowering *or* louring, °gloomy, °unpromising, unpropitious **2** °extraordinary, °amazing, astonishing, astounding, °prodigious, °awesome, awe-inspiring, °remarkable, °marvelous, °phenomenal, °fabulous, °fantastic, mind-boggling, wondrous, °miraculous

porter[1] *n.* **1** bearer, (baggage) carrier *or* attendant, *US Airports* skycap, *US Railways* redcap **2** cleaner, *Chiefly US and Canadian* janitor, °superintendent, *Colloq US* °super

porter[2] *n.* doorkeeper, °watchman, doorman, gatekeeper, concierge, caretaker, *US* tiler

portico *n.* porch, veranda *or* verandah, gallery, colonnade, galilee

portion *n.* 1 °segment, °part, °section, °division, subdivision, °parcel, °piece, hunk, chunk, °lump, °wedge, °slice, °sliver, fraction, °fragment, °bit, °morsel, °scrap 2 °share, °part, °allotment, °quota, °ration, apportionment, °allowance, allocation, °assignment, °percentage, °measure, °division, °quantity 3 °helping, serving; °ration, °plate, °platter —*v.* 4 Often, ***portion out.*** apportion, share out, allocate, °ration, °allot, °partition, °assign, consign, dole out, °deal (out), °parcel out, °distribute, °administer, °dispense, °disperse, °divide, °split up, °carve up, °cut up, °break up, °section, *Colloq* divvy up

portrait *n.* °picture, °likeness, °image, sketch, °rendering, vignette; °representation, °description, °profile, thumbnail sketch, portrayal, picturization, depiction; °account, °story, characterization, °study, °record, °file, dossier

portray *v.* 1 °represent, °picture, °show, depict, °paint, °render, °characterize, °describe, delineate 2 act *or* play (the part *or* role of), take the part *or* role of, °represent, °pose as, impersonate

pose *v.* 1 °sit, °model; °position, °place, °arrange, °set (up), °put 2 Usually, ***pose as.*** °portray, act *or* play (the part *or* role of), take the part *or* role of, °represent, impersonate, be disguised as, °masquerade as, pretend *or* profess to be, pass (oneself off) as, °pass for, °imitate, °mimic; attitudinize, °posture, put on airs, *Colloq* °show off 3 °set, °put, °ask, °submit, °broach, °posit, °advance, °present, predicate, postulate —*n.* 4 °position, °attitude, °posture, °stance 5 °affectation, °act, °pretense, attitudinizing, affectedness, °display, façade, °show, °ostentation

poseur *n.* posturer, exhibitionist, °pretender, °impostor, masquerader, attitudinizer; °fake, faker, dissembler, °fraud, *Colloq* °showoff, phony *or* phoney

posh *adj.* (de)luxe, °luxurious, °elegant, °sumptuous, °lavish, °opulent, °rich, °royal, °regal, °luxury, °grand, °fashionable, *Colloq* swank(y), classy, ritzy, *Slang* snazzy

posit *v.* postulate, hypothesize, °propound, put *or* set forth, °put forward, °advance, °propose, °pose, °offer, °submit, predicate

position *n.* 1 °posture, °attitude, °stance, °pose; °disposition, °arrangement, disposal 2 °site, °placement, °situation, °whereabouts, placing, emplacement, °location 3 °viewpoint, °point of view, °outlook, °attitude, °angle, °slant, °stance, °stand, °opinion, °inclination, °leaning, °bent, °sentiment, °feeling, way of thinking 4 °status, °condition, °state, °circumstances, °situation 5 °class, °caste, °place, °rank, °standing, °station, °status, °importance 6 °job, °occupation, °situation, °post, °office, °function, °appointment, °capacity, °place, °role, *Colloq* billet, berth, *Australian* possie *or* possy 7 °hypothesis, °thesis, °principle, contention, °assertion, predication, °belief, °proposition, postulate —*v.* 8 °put, °place, °situate, °site, °set, °fix, °settle, °dispose, °arrange 9 °place, °locate, °establish, °determine, °fix, localize

positive *adj.* 1 °sure, °certain, °definite, unequivocal, °categorical, °absolute, °unqualified, unambiguous, unmistakable *or* unmistakeable, clear-cut, °clear, °explicit, °express, decisive, °indisputable, indubitable, °unquestionable, unquestioned, incontestable, uncontested, undeniable, °reliable, °persuasive, convincing, irrefutable 2 °definitive, °emphatic, °decided, °forceful, °firm, °peremptory, °definite 3 °sure, °certain, °confident, convinced, satisfied 4 °beneficial, °favorable, °complimentary, °productive, °useful 5 °overconfident, °dogmatic, doctrinaire, pontifical, °opinionated, pigheaded, °stubborn, °obstinate, obdurate, °arbitrary, overweening, °arrogant, °assertive, °dictatorial, °despotic, imperious, *Rare* thetic(al) 6 °practical, °realistic, utilitarian, °productive, °functional, pragmatic(al), °realistic, °matter-of-fact, *Colloq* hard-nosed 7 encouraging, °supportive, °constructive, reassuring, °enthusiastic, °favorable, affirmative, yes, confirming 8 auspicious, °promising, °propitious, encouraging; °optimistic, °favorable, °cheerful, °confident; *Colloq* bullish, °upbeat 9 °complete, utter, °total, °perfect, °out-and-out, consummate, °unmitigated, °thorough, thoroughgoing; egregious, °glaring, °stark, °sheer, °outright, °unqualified, unequivocal, *Colloq* dyed-in-the-wool

positively *adv.* °definitely, °absolutely, unquestionably, certainly, (most) assuredly, undeniably, °undoubtedly, °surely, to be sure, emphatically, unmistakably *or* unmistakeably, unqualifiedly, categorically, indisputably, beyond *or* without (a *or* the shadow of) (a) doubt, indubitably, beyond question

possess *v.* 1 be possessed *or* in possession of, °have, own, °enjoy, be blessed *or* endowed with 2 °have, be born *or* gifted *or* endowed with, °contain, °embody, °embrace, °include 3 °dominate, °control, °govern, °consume, take control of, preoccupy, °obsess; °charm, °captivate, °enchant, cast a spell over, °bewitch, enthrall 4 ***be possessed with*** *or* ***of.*** °have, be held *or* influenced *or* dominated by, be imbued *or* inspired *or* permeated *or* affected with 5 ***possess oneself of.*** °acquire, °achieve, °get, °come by, °gain, come into, °win, °obtain, °procure, °secure, °take, °seize, take *or* gain possession of

possessed *adj.* obsessed, driven, controlled, dominated, ridden, bedeviled, consumed, haunted, pressed, maddened, crazed, demented, frenzied, *Colloq* eaten up

possession *n.* 1 ownership, °title, proprietorship, °control, °hold, °tenure, keeping, °care, °custody, guardianship, °protection 2 holding, °territory, °province, °dominion, colony, protectorate 3 ***possessions.*** °belongings, °property, °effects, chattels, °assets, worldly goods, °things 4 ***take or***

gain possession of. °seize, °capture, °take, °conquer, °occupy, °acquire, °win, °possess oneself of, °secure, °obtain; repossess

possessive *adj.* **1** °greedy, unyielding, °selfish, ungiving, ungenerous, stingy, niggardly, °materialistic, covetous, acquisitive **2** overprotective, controlling, °grasping, dominating, °domineering, °overbearing

possibility *n.* **1** °chance, °odds, °prospect, conceivability, °feasibility, plausibility, °likelihood, admissibility **2** Often, ***possibilities.*** °opportunity, potentiality, °potential, °capacity, °promise

possible *adj.* **1** °feasible, °plausible, imaginable, conceivable, °thinkable, credible, °tenable, °reasonable, admissible **2** realizable, °practicable, workable, °practical, doable, achievable, attainable, reachable, accomplishable, °viable, *Colloq* on

possibly *adv.* **1** °maybe, °perhaps, God willing, *Deo volente,* if possible, *Archaic or literary* perchance, mayhap, peradventure **2** in any way, under any circumstances, by any chance, by any means, at all, conceivably

post[1] *n.* **1** °pole, °stake, °upright, column, °pillar, °pale, °picket, °shaft, °standard, newel, °pier, pylon, °pile, piling, °strut, shore, stanchion, °leg, °prop, °stay, °support, °brace —*v.* **2** advertise, °announce, °proclaim, °publish, °circulate, °propagate, promulgate; put *or* pin *or* tack *or* stick *or* hang up, affix

post[2] *n.* **1** °assignment, °appointment, °position, °situation, °job, °place, °duty, °role, °function, °employment, °work, °task, chore —*v.* **2** °place, °put, °station, °assign, °appoint, °position, °situate, °set, °locate

post[3] *n.* **1** postal service, °mail; °delivery; °collection —*v.* **2** °send, dispatch *or* despatch, °transmit, *Chiefly US and Canadian* °mail **3** °record, °enter, °register, °list **4** ***keep (someone) posted.*** °inform, °advise, °brief, °notify, *Colloq* fill (someone) in on

poster *n.* placard, °notice, °bill, °advertisement, °announcement, broadside, broadsheet; °circular, flier

posterior *adj.* **1** hind, °rear, °back, after, °hinder, rearward, *Nautical* aft **2** later, after, latter, ensuing, following, succeeding, °subsequent —*n.* **3** °buttocks, °bottom, rump, °seat, *derrière, Colloq* behind, °rear, backside, °tail, hinie, °butt, °duff, *Slang Brit* °bum, *Taboo slang US* ass, *Brit* arse, *Yiddish* tokhes *or* tokus *or* tochis *or* tuchis

posterity *n.* descendants, successors, heirs, children, °offspring, °issue, °progeny

posthaste *adv.* °quickly, °at once, without delay, °immediately, °directly, °straightaway, right away, °promptly, speedily, °swiftly, instantly, before one can *or* could say "Jack Robinson," before you can say "knife," rapidly, at full tilt, in a wink, in a trice, in the twinkling of an eye, *Colloq* pronto, chop-chop, PDQ (= 'pretty damn(ed) quick'), *US and Canadian* lickety-split, like greased lightning

post-mortem *n.* **1** autopsy, necropsy **2** °review, °analysis, *Slang US* Monday morning quarterbacking

postpone *v.* °delay, adjourn, °defer, keep in abeyance, put off *or* aside, lay aside, °suspend, °shelve, put *or* keep on ice, temporize, dally, *Colloq* put on the back burner, *US* °table

postponement *n.* °delay, adjournment, °abeyance, °suspension, °stay, deferment, deferral, °moratorium

posture *n.* **1** °pose, °position, °attitude, °stance, °appearance, °carriage **2** °position, °condition, °situation, °state, °disposition; °arrangement, °organization, layout, array, °format **3** °attitude, °stance, °position, °feeling, °sentiment, °outlook, °(point of) view, °viewpoint, °orientation, °disposition, °frame of mind, °mood —*v.* **4** °pose, attitudinize, °affect, put on a show, do for effect, *Colloq* °show off

pot *n.* **1** °pan, saucepan, cauldron, cookpot, stewpot; kettle **2** jackpot, bank, °kitty **3** potbelly, °paunch, °gut, *Colloq* corporation, beer belly, spare tire, *US* bay window

potent *adj.* **1** °powerful, °strong; °mighty, °vigorous, °forceful, °formidable, °authoritative, °influential, *Literary* puissant **2** °effective, convincing, cogent, °persuasive, compelling, °efficacious, °telling, °sound, valid, °impressive

potential *adj.* **1** °possible, °likely, °implicit, implied, °imminent, developing, budding, embryonic, °dormant, °hidden, concealed, covert, latent, quiescent, °passive, °future, unrealized, °undeveloped —*n.* **2** °capacity, °capability, °possibility, °aptitude, potency, *Colloq* the (right) stuff, what it takes

potion *n.* °draft, °brew, beverage, °drink, philtre, potation, °elixir, °tonic, cup, °dose, concoction, decoction

potpourri *n.* °mixture, °medley, °miscellany, °assortment, olla podrida, smorgasbord *or* smårgøsbord, gallimaufry, salmagundi, °patchwork, °collection, hotchpotch *or US also* hodgepodge, melange *or* mélange, motley, pastiche *or* pasticcio, °mishmash, °jumble, °mess

pottery *n.* earthenware, ceramics, terra cotta, crockery, stoneware, porcelain, china, delftware

pouch *n.* °pocket, °sack, °bag, °purse, reticule, *Dialect* °poke

pounce *v.* **1** Often, ***pounce on or upon.*** spring (on *or* upon), leap (at *or* on), swoop down (on *or* upon), °fall upon, jump (at *or* on), °strike, take by surprise *or* unawares, °attack, °ambush, *Colloq* °mug —*n.* **2** °spring, °leap, °swoop, °jump

pound[1] *v.* **1** °beat, °batter, °pelt, hammer, pummel; thump, °belabor, thrash, bludgeon, cudgel, maul, °strike, *Colloq* lambaste *or* lambast, *Slang* paste, clobber, work over, give (someone) the works *or* a pasting **2** °crush, °powder, °pulverize, bray, comminute, triturate, mash, °pulp **3** °beat, throb, hammer, °pulse, °pulsate, palpitate **4**

pound into. °instill, din into, drill into, drub into, hammer into, beat into **5** *pound out.* °rid, °expel, °clear, °cleanse, °empty, °purge, beat out, hammer out **6** beat out; hammer out, °produce —*n.* **7** pounding, °beat, beating, thump, °thumping

pound[2] *n.* °enclosure, °pen, °compound, confine, yard

pour *v.* **1** °flow, °run, °gush, °rush, °flood, °stream, °course, °spout, °discharge, °spurt, °spew out, cascade **2** °empty, °discharge, °let out **3** °rain, °teem, *Colloq* come down in buckets *or* by the bucketful, bucket down, rain cats and dogs, *US* rain pitchforks **4** °stream, °swarm, °crowd, °throng, °teem, °emerge, sally forth, °issue (forth), °go (forth)

pout *v.* **1** mope, °brood, °sulk, make a *moue,* pull a long face, °frown, lour *or* lower, knit one's brows —*n.* **2** °frown, *moue,* long face

poverty *n.* **1** °want, penury, indigence, insolvency, destitution, pauperism, impecuniousness, neediness, beggary **2** °scarcity, scarceness, °want, °need, °lack, meagerness, insufficiency, °shortage, °dearth, paucity, inadequacy

powder *n.* **1** dust; talc **2** *take a (runout) powder.* °run away, abscond, °escape, vanish, °disappear, *Slang Brit* scarper, do a moonlight flit, *US* take it on the lam —*v.* **3** °pulverize, bray, °grind, °crush, °pound, granulate, triturate, comminute, levigate **4** sprinkle, besprinkle, dust, dredge, °cover, °coat

power *n.* **1** Sometimes, *powers.* °capacity, °capability, °ability, °potential, °faculty, competency *or* competence, potentiality, *Colloq* what it takes, *US* the (right) stuff, the goods **2** °control, dominance, °authority, mastery, °rule, °influence, °sway, °command, ascendancy, °sovereignty, °dominion, °weight, clout, *Colloq* °pull, *US* °drag **3** °control, °command, °authority **4** °strength, °might, °vigor, °energy, °force, mightiness, potency, forcefulness, °brawn, muscle, *Literary* puissance **5** °talent, °skill, °ability, °faculty, °gift, °aptitude, °genius, °knack **6** °authority, °license, °right, authorization, °privilege, °warrant, °prerogative **7** Often, *powers.* °activity, effectiveness, °effect, °ability, °capacity, active ingredient(s) **8** °energy, °momentum, °impetus, °drive, °force, °inertia **9** (mechanical *or* electrical *or* atomic) energy, °electricity, °fuel **10** *powers that be.* °government, °administration, °authorities, incumbents

powerful *adj.* **1** °potent, °strong, °mighty, °vigorous, °robust, °energetic, °sturdy, °stalwart, °tough, resilient, °dynamic **2** °influential, °strong, compelling, °forceful, °potent, °substantial, °weighty, °authoritative, °effective; °important, °impressive, °telling, °effectual, °formidable, °persuasive **3** °strong, °potent; °intense, °substantial, °great, °high

powerless *adj.* **1** °helpless, °incapable, °unable, unfit, °incompetent, °ineffectual, °ineffective **2** incapacitated, °helpless, °weak, °feeble, debilitated, °crippled, paralyzed, °disabled

practicable *adj.* doable, °feasible, workable, performable, achievable, attainable, accomplishable, °possible, °viable

practical *adj.* **1** pragmatic, °useful, usable *or* useable, °functional, °realistic, °reasonable, °sound, utilitarian, °applicable, °serviceable, °empirical, °efficient **2** °sensible, °reasonable, common-sense *or* common-sensical, °everyday, °ordinary, down-to-earth, °expedient, °matter-of-fact, mundane, businesslike, hardheaded, °judicious, *Colloq* hard-nosed **3** applied, °field, hands-on, °personal, °everyday

practically *adv.* **1** °almost, °(very) nearly, well-nigh, °virtually, °in effect, just about, essentially, fundamentally, °at bottom, basically, when all is said and done, at the end of the day, °to all intents and purposes **2** realistically, matter-of-factly, °clearly, °simply, reasonably, rationally, sensibly

practice *n.* **1** °custom, wont, °habit, °routine, °convention, °tradition, °rule, °procedure, °usage, °mode, °style, °way, modus operandi, technique *or* technic, *Formal* praxis, *Colloq* MO (= 'modus operandi') **2** °exercise, °discipline, °drill, practising, °repetition, °rehearsal, training, °preparation; workout, warm-up; °application, °study **3** °pursuit, °exercise, °work, °profession, °career, °vocation, °conduct; °business, °office **4** *in practice.* °practically, °actually, day-to-day, realistically, in real life **5** *out of practice.* °inexperienced, unpracticed, °unaccustomed, rusty —*v.* **6** °drill, °exercise, °work out, °train, °prepare, °rehearse, °run through, °repeat, °study, *Brit* practise **7** °carry on, make a practice of, °perform, do, °act, °carry out, put into practice, *Brit* practise

practiced *adj.* **1** °accomplished, °proficient, °expert, skilled, °experienced, °capable, °adept, °seasoned, °able, °qualified, °gifted, °talented, °skillful, °masterful, consummate, °superb, °superior, *Brit* practised **2** trained, rehearsed, °versed, °cultivated, schooled, finished, perfected, *Brit* practised

praise *n.* **1** acclaim, °approval, approbation, °applause, plaudits, °kudos, °endorsement, acclamation, °tribute, accolade, °compliments, commendation, encomium, °eulogy, panegyric, °ovation **2** °honor, glorification, adoration, exaltation, °devotion, °homage, °worship, °veneration, adulation, °reverence, °glory, hymn *or* song of praise, paean, hosanna —*v.* **3** acclaim, °approve, °laud, °applaud, °endorse, pay tribute to, °compliment, commend, °eulogize, °extol, °honor, sing the praises (of) **4** °worship, °revere, °reverence, °exalt, °glorify, °adore, pay homage to, °venerate, give thanks to, °hallow

praiseworthy *adj.* commendable, °laudable, °admirable, creditable, °worthy, °meritorious, °deserving, °exemplary

prance *v.* °caper, °dance, gambol, °skip, °cavort, romp, °leap, °frisk, °jump, °spring, °bound, *Dressage* curvet, capriole

prank *n.* °trick, °(practical) joke, °frolic, escapade, antic, °caper, °stunt, °lark, jest, jape, monkeytricks *or esp. US* monkeyshines, °mischief

prattle *v.* **1** prate, °babble, blather *or* blether, blither, gibber, °jabber, gibberjabber, °palaver, °tattle, twaddle, gabble, °chatter, °patter, °drivel, °twitter, °rattle on, °go on (and on), maunder, *Brit* natter, *Colloq* witter (on), gas, °gab, °spout, °gush, run (on) at the mouth, *US* run off at the mouth, *Slang* jaw, ya(c)k, ya(c)kety- ya(c)k, shoot off one's mouth —*n.* **2** prate, prating, °babble, babbling, blather *or* blether, blathering *or* blethering, gibber, gibbering, °jabber, jabbering, °palaver, palavering, °tattle, tattling, twaddle, °chatter, chattering, gabble, gabbling, °patter, °drivel, °twitter, twittering, rattling on, °going on, maundering, cackle, *US* gibber-jabbering, twattle, clack, *Colloq* gas, °gab, running off at the mouth, *Slang* jawing, ya(c)kety- ya(c)k **3** jabberwocky, gobbledygook *or* gobbledegook, °mumbo jumbo, °rubbish, balderdash, °(stuff and) nonsense, humbug, bunkum, tommyrot, °trash, °rot, foolishness, *Colloq* pish and tush, °hot air, flapdoodle, rigamarole *or* rigmarole, bunk, piffle, °moonshine, poppycock, claptrap, bull, hogwash, °swill, *Brit* tosh, fiddle-faddle, baloney, *Chiefly US* °garbage, horsefeathers, *Slang* crap, hooey, guff, *Taboo slang* bullshit, *US* crock (of shit)

pray *v.* **1** °beseech, °ask, call upon *or* on, entreat, implore, °request, appeal to, °plead (with), °beg (for), importune, °solicit, °petition, supplicate, *Rare* obsecrate **2** say one's prayers, offer a prayer

prayer *n.* **1** °petition, °supplication, °request, entreaty, °plea, °suit, °appeal, *Rare* obsecration **2** °devotion, praying, invocation, °(divine) service, *Literary* orison

preach *v.* **1** deliver a sermon, evangelize, spread the Word *or* the Gospel; catechize **2** moralize, sermonize, °advise, °counsel, admonish, °reprimand, °lecture, °harangue, pontificate; °urge, inculcate, °advocate

preacher *n.* °minister, evangelist, °clergyman, clergywoman, cleric, ecclesiastic, reverend, °divine, *Colloq* tubthumper

preamble *n.* introduction, °foreword, prologue, °preface, *Formal* proem, prolegomenon, exordium

precarious *adj.* °uncertain, °unreliable, unsure, °risky, °hazardous, unpredictable, °insecure, °unstable, unsteady, °unsettled, °shaky, °doubtful, dubious, °questionable, °tricky, °delicate, °ticklish, °sensitive, °slippery, touch-and-go, (hanging) in the balance, hanging by a thread, Damoclean, °perilous, treacherous, °dangerous, °difficult, °problematic, *Colloq* chancy, *Brit* °dodgy, °dicey, *US* iffy, *Slang* °hairy

precaution *n.* **1** °provision, preventive measure, safety measure, °safeguard, °insurance, °protection, °cover, °escape **2** °foresight, °prudence, °providence, °forethought, °caution, cautiousness, circumspection, °care, °attention, watchfulness, °vigilance, alertness, wariness, chariness, apprehension, farsightedness, °anticipation

precede *v.* come *or* go *or* proceed before *or* first, go ahead *or* in advance (of), °lead (the way), pave the way (for), herald, usher in, °introduce, antecede; °foreshadow, antedate, predate

precedence *n.* precedency, °priority, °preeminence, °superiority, °supremacy, °preference, °privilege, °prerogative, °importance, °rank, °position, primacy

precedent *n.* °prototype, °model, °example, exemplar, °pattern, paradigm, °yardstick, criterion, °standard, °lead

preceding *adj.* °foregoing, °former, °previous, °above, °prior, earlier, above-mentioned, aforementioned, above-stated, above-named

precept *n.* **1** °rule, °guide, °principle, unwritten law, canon, guideline, °dictate, °code, °injunction, °law, commandment, °instruction, directive, °prescription, mandate, °charge; statute, °regulation, edict, ukase, °decree, °order, fiat, ordinance **2** °maxim, °proverb, axiom, °motto, °slogan, saying, °byword, aphorism, apophthegm *or* apothegm

precinct *n.* **1** Usually, ***precincts.*** °area, °territory, °region, °province, environs, purlieus, °borders, °bounds, confines **2** °sphere, °neighborhood, °zone, sector, °section, °quarter, °district, °locale

precious *adj.* **1** °dear, dearest, costly, °expensive, high-priced, valuable, °invaluable, prized, °priceless, irreplaceable, *Colloq* °pricey **2** esteemed, °choice, cherished, °beloved, idolized, adored, loved, valued, prized, revered, venerated, °venerable, hallowed **3** °precise, °exquisite, overrefined, chichi, overnice, °studied, °artificial, effete, °affected, overdone, °pretentious, euphuistic, alembicated **4** °sweet, °sentimental, °quaint, °dainty, °cute, mignon, bijou, *Colloq Brit* twee, *Slang US* cutesy

precipice *n.* °cliff, escarpment, °bluff, °crag

precipitate *v.* **1** accelerate, °hasten, °speed (up), °advance, °hurry, °quicken, °expedite, bring on *or* about, trigger, °provoke, instigate, °incite, °facilitate, °further, °press, °push forward **2** °hurl, °fling, °cast, °launch, °project —*adj.* **3** headlong, °violent, °rapid, °swift, °quick, °speedy, °meteoric, °fast **4** °sudden, °abrupt, unannounced, unexpected, unanticipated **5** °rash, °impetuous, °hasty, °volatile, hotheaded, °careless, °reckless, incautious, injudicious, °foolhardy, °impulsive, unrestrained

precipitation *n.* showers, drizzle, °downpour, °rain, rainfall, snow, snowfall, °hail, sleet

precipitous *adj.* **1** °abrupt, °steep, °perpendicular, °sheer, °bluff, acclivitous, declivitous **2** See **precipitate, 5,** above.

précis *n.* °outline, °summary, °synopsis, *aperçu,* °résumé, conspectus, °survey, overview, °abstract, °abridgment, °digest, compendium, recapitulation; table of contents

precise *adj.* **1** °correct, °exact, °definite, well-defined, °explicit, word-for-word, °verbatim, °literal, letter-for-letter, *literatim*, °faithful, °specific, unambiguous, unequivocal, °strict, °authentic, °perfect, °true, veracious, °truthful, unerring, error-free, °accurate **2** °strict, °meticulous, °scrupulous, °careful, °conscientious, °exact, unconditional, rigorous, °rigid, puritanical, unbending, °inflexible, unyielding, °demanding, °severe, prim, °absolute **3** °fastidious, °particular, °finicky, finical, °fussy, °meticulous, °scrupulous, °careful, °conscientious, °nice, °exacting, °critical, °demanding **4** °exact, °very

precisely *adv.* **1** °exactly, °just, strictly, *Colloq* °on the nail, smack, °slap, on the nose, *Brit* bang on, spot on **2** °exactly, exactingly, correctly, rigorously, °absolutely, punctiliously, minutely, carefully, meticulously, scrupulously, conscientiously, strictly, rigidly, inflexibly; in all respects, in every way

precision *n.* **1** correctness, exactness, fidelity, faithfulness, exactitude, preciseness, °accuracy, °rigor, °perfection, flawlessness, faultlessness, literalism, unerringness **2** definiteness, °care, nicety, meticulousness, rigorousness, °rigor, fastidiousness, punctiliousness, scrupulousness, unambiguousness, nicety, strictness, explicitness

preclude *v.* obviate, °bar, °prevent, °stop, °exclude, °prohibit, °shut out, °forestall, °rule out, debar, °check, °block, °obstruct, avert, °avoid, °thwart, °frustrate, °impede, °inhibit, °hinder, interfere with

precocious *adj.* advanced, °mature, °bright, °gifted, °intelligent, °smart, °quick

preconceived *adj.* beforehand, predisposed, prejudged, °predetermined, °prejudiced, °biased, anticipatory

preconception *n.* predisposition, prejudgment, predetermination, °prejudice, °bias, °presumption, °presupposition, assumption, *idée fixe*, prepossession, preconceived notion *or* idea

precondition *n.* °prerequisite, °stipulation, °condition, °essential, °must, sine qua non, °imperative, °requirement, °proviso, °provision, °qualification, °necessity

precursor *n.* **1** °harbinger, herald, vanguard **2** See **predecessor, 1,** below.

predatory *adj.* **1** predacious *or* predaceous, carnivorous, preying, raptorial **2** °rapacious, °ravenous, plundering, robbing, pillaging, marauding, despoiling, looting, piratical, vulturine, °avaricious, °greedy, °voracious, larcenous, thieving, extortionate, usurious

predecessor *n.* **1** °forerunner, °predecessor, antecedent **2** forebear, forefather, °ancestor, antecedent

predestination *n.* °destiny, °future, °lot, °fortune, kismet, karma; °doom, °fate; foreordainment, foreordination

predetermined *adj.* **1** °fixed, prearranged, preestablished, °set (up), °foregone, preplanned, preset **2** °fated, °doomed, °destined, ordained, foreordained, *Colloq* °cut and dried, *Brit* on the cards, *US* °in the cards

predicament *n.* °dilemma, °quandary, °difficulty, °trial, °situation, °state, °condition, imbroglio, °emergency, °crisis, °impasse, *Colloq* pickle, °jam, °fix, °pinch, °scrape, °spot, °bind, corner, °hole, °mess, *US* °box

predict *v.* foretell, °prophesy, °forecast, °foresee, augur, °prognosticate, forewarn, presage, vaticinate; portend, °foreshadow, foretoken, forebode; °intimate, °hint, °suggest

predictable *adj.* foreseeable, foreseen, °probable, °likely, °liable, expected, anticipated, (reasonably) sure *or* certain, *Colloq Brit* on the cards, *US* °in the cards

prediction *n.* °forecast, °prophecy, augury, °prognosis; intimation, °hint, °suggestion

predominance *n.* predominancy, °superiority, °influence, dominance, °preeminence, °preponderance, ascendancy, °precedence, °power, °supremacy, °hold, °sway, hegemony, °leadership, mastery, °control, °dominion, °sovereignty, transcendence *or* transcendency, °authority, the upper hand, the whip hand, °advantage, the edge

predominant *adj.* °dominant, predominating, controlling, °sovereign, ruling, °preeminent, preponderant, ascendant, °superior, °supreme, °leading, °paramount, °main, °chief, °transcendent, °important, °telling, °influential, °primary, °prevailing, °prevalent

predominate *v.* Often, ***predominate over.*** dominate, °control, °rule, °reign, preponderate, °outweigh, °obtain, °prevail, °overshadow, get *or* have the upper hand, °lord it over, hold sway, overrule

preeminence *n.* **1** See **predominance,** above. **2** peerlessness, magnificence, °excellence, °distinction, eminence, inimitability, °superiority

preeminent *adj.* **1** See **predominant,** above. **2** °peerless, °excellent, °distinguished, °eminent, inimitable, °superb, unequaled, °matchless, °incomparable, °outstanding, °unique, unrivaled, unsurpassed, °supreme, °superior

preeminently *adv.* °primarily, °principally, °by far, far and away, °manifestly, °eminently, °notably, conspicuously, prominently, signally, uniquely, extraordinarily, °supremely, superbly, matchlessly, incomparably, outstandingly

preempt *v.* °appropriate, usurp, arrogate, °take over, °assume, °take possession of, °seize, °acquire, °take, °possess, expropriate

preen *v.* **1** °trim, °clean, plume, °groom **2** °primp, °dress up, titivate *or* tittivate, prettify, °beautify, prink, °spruce up, deck (out), *Colloq* doll up, *Brit* tart up

preface *n.* **1** introduction, °foreword, prologue, °preamble, *Formal* proem, prolegomenon, exordium —*v.* **2** °precede, °introduce, prefix, °begin, °open

prefatory *adj.* °opening, °introductory, °preliminary, °preparatory

prefer *v.* **1** °favor, like better, °fancy, lean *or* incline toward(s) *or* on the side of, be inclined, be partial to, °pick, °select, opt for, °choose, °single out, take a fancy to, °embrace, espouse, °approve, °esteem **2** °present, °offer, °propose, proffer, °advance, °submit, °tender, °put forward, °file, °lodge, °enter

preference *n.* **1** °favorite, °choice, °selection, °desire, °option, °pick **2** °partiality, proclivity, °prejudice, °favoritism, predilection, °liking, °fancy, predisposition, °bent, °inclination, °leaning

preferential *adj.* °advantageous, °biased, °prejudiced, °favorable, °privileged, °partial, °better, °favored, °superior

pregnant *adj.* **1** gravid, parturient, °expectant, (heavy) with child, *enceinte, Colloq* °expecting, in a family way, *Brit* preggers, *Slang* having a bun in the oven, *Brit* in the (pudding) club, °up the spout **2** charged, °fraught, °loaded, °weighty, °significant, °meaningful, °suggestive, °eloquent, °expressive, °pointed **3** °fruitful, teeming, °fertile, fecund, °rich, abounding, °replete, °productive

prehistoric *adj.* **1** primordial, primal, primeval, °primitive, earliest, °early, antediluvian, Noachian *or* Noachic, fossil, °ancient **2** °antiquated, outdated, °old-fashioned, °passé

prejudice *n.* **1** °partiality, °preconception, prejudgment, °bias, °leaning, °warp, °twist, preconceived notion, predisposition, predilection, jaundiced eye, jaundice **2** °bigotry, unfairness, °bias, partisanship, °favoritism, cronyism, °discrimination, °intolerance, °inequality; racism, racialism, apartheid, Jim Crowism, sexism, (male) chauvinism —*v.* **3** °bias, °influence, °warp, °twist, °distort, °slant; °color, jaundice, °poison

prejudiced *adj.* **1** unfair, °one-sided, °biased, °jaundiced, °opinionated, predisposed, °partial, °partisan, nonobjective, unobjective **2** °bigoted, °intolerant, °narrow-minded, closed-minded, °parochial, sexist, racist, chauvinistic

prejudicial *adj.* °injurious, damaging, °detrimental, °harmful, unfavorable, inimical, deleterious, disadvantageous, counterproductive, pernicious

preliminary *adj.* **1** °advance, °prior, °introductory, °beginning, °initial, °opening, °preparatory, °prefatory, °preceding, antecedent, forerunning; premonitory; *Formal and technical* prodromal *or* prodromic —*n.* **2** introduction, °beginning, °opening, °preparation, °groundwork, prelude, °precedence; °overture **3** ***prelims.*** Rarely, ***preliminaries.*** introduction, °preface, °foreword, °preamble, prologue, front matter, *Formal* proem, exordium, prolegomenon, prodromus, prodrome

premature *adj.* **1** °immature, °undeveloped, underdeveloped, °unfledged, untimely, unready, °early, unripe, °green **2** °hasty, untimely, ill-timed, too early, too soon, beforehand, °unseasonable, overhasty, °impulsive, °inopportune

prematurely *adv.* **1** untimely, too soon, too early **2** rashly, (over)hastily, at half cock, half-cocked

premeditated *adj.* planned, °conscious, °intentional, intended, °willful, °deliberate, °studied, purposive; contrived, preplanned, °calculated, °preconceived

premier *n.* **1** prime minister, PM, head of state, chief executive, president, chancellor —*adj.* **2** °first, °prime, °primary, °chief, °principal, °head, °main, °foremost, top-ranking, highest-ranking, ranking, °leading, °top, °preeminent

première *n.* **1** premiere, first night, °opening (night), °debut —*v.* **2** premiere, °open, °debut —*adj.* **3** premiere, °opening, °debut, °first, °original, °initial

premise *n.* **1** premiss, assumption, °proposition, postulate, °hypothesis, conjecture, °assertion, °supposition, °thesis, °presupposition, °proposal, °theorem, °surmise, °basis, °ground —*v.* **2** °assume, °propose, postulate, hypothesize, hypothecate, conjecture, °posit, assert, °suppose, °presuppose, °theorize, °surmise, put *or* set forth, predicate, °argue

premium *n.* **1** °bonus, °extra, dividend, °prize, °award, °reward, °perquisite **2** °incentive, °inducement, stimulus, °incitement, °lure, bait, °spur, goad, °reward, *Colloq* °come-on, *Slang US and Canadian* freebie **3** value, °importance, °regard, °stock, °store, °appreciation **4** ***at a premium.*** **(a)** °scarce, °rare, scant, °scanty, °sparse, hard to come by, °in short supply, *Colloq* scarce as hen's teeth, *Chiefly Brit* °thin on the ground **(b)** costly, °expensive, °dear, high-priced, *Colloq* °steep, °stiff

premonition *n.* °intuition, °foreboding, presentiment, forewarning, °suspicion, °feeling, °hunch, *Colloq* funny feeling, sneaking suspicion

preoccupied *adj.* **1** engrossed, lost in thought, °rapt, °thoughtful, °pensive, °absorbed, cogitating, cogitative, meditating, musing, reflecting, °reflective, contemplative, contemplating, pondering, brooding, ruminating, in a brown study **2** °vague, °offhand, °faraway, °absent-minded, abstracted, °oblivious, °unaware, wrapped up, immersed, °inattentive, distracted, distrait, *Colloq* turned off, *US* out of it

preparation *n.* **1** Often, ***preparations.*** **(a)** °groundwork, spadework, provision(s), °foundation, preparing, °measures, °proceedings **(b)** plans, °arrangements **2** °fitness, °readiness, readying, preparing, training, °education, teaching, °instruction, instructing, °tuition, briefing, grooming, *Colloq* gearing up, prep, *US* prepping **3** drawing up, drafting, planning, setting up, putting together, organizing, °organization, composing, making **4** °work, preparing, getting ready, °study, studying, practicing, °practice,

Colloq cramming, *Brit* swotting **5** °substance, °compound, concoction, °mixture, °product, °material, °stuff, °composition

preparatory *adj.* **1** preparative, °preliminary, °introductory, °prefatory, °opening **2** °elementary, °basic, °essential, °fundamental, °primary, °rudimentary **3** ***preparatory to.*** °before, in preparation for, °preceding

prepare *v.* **1** (get *or* make) ready, °prime, °arrange, °(put in) order, °organize, °provide for, make provision(s) for, lay the groundwork (for), °(make) fit, °fit (out), °equip, °outfit, °adapt **2** °train, (get *or* make) ready, °study, °practice, *Colloq* °cram, *Brit* swot, °get up **3** °train, °educate, °teach, (get *or* make) ready, °groom, °brief, °develop **4** cook (up), °make, do, *Colloq* °whip up, *US and Canadian* °fix **5** °manufacture, °fabricate, °produce, °make, °put out, °build, °construct, °assemble, put together, °turn out, °fashion, °forge, °mold **6** °brace, °strengthen, °steel, °fortify, °ready **7** °process, °produce, °make, °treat, °change, °modify, °transform

prepared *adj.* **1** °ready, °set, °advance, prearranged, planned **2** treated, processed, modified, changed **3** °willing, °disposed, predisposed, °able, °inclined, of a mind; °ready, °(all) set **4** oven-ready, microwave-ready, microwave-able, °instant, convenience, ready-to-eat, ready-to-serve, precooked, °ready-made

preparedness *n.* °vigilance, alertness, °readiness, °fitness

preponderance *n.* **1** °majority, greater part, °bulk, °mass, lion's share **2** °weight, °influence, weightiness, °superiority, °supremacy, °predominance, primacy, ascendancy, °sway, °strength, °force, °power, °advantage, °control, °authority, hegemony, °leadership, °rule

prepossessing *adj.* °attractive, appealing, °pleasing, °favorable, °engaging, charming, captivating, fascinating, winsome, °winning, °magnetic, alluring, bewitching, °taking, °fetching, °inviting, good-looking, °handsome, °lovely, °beautiful

preposterous *adj.* °absurd, °ridiculous, °ludicrous, laughable, risible, asinine, °foolish, °senseless, irrational, °nonsensical, fatuous, fatuitous, °mindless, °insane, °crazy, crack-brained, °mad, idiotic, moronic, imbecilic, °incredible, °unbelievable, °outrageous, °extravagant, °extraordinary, °extreme, °exorbitant, °outlandish, °outré, °weird, °bizarre, *Colloq* balmy, *Brit* barmy, *Slang* nutty, screwy, batty, dotty, wacky, loony, cuckoo, *US* wacko

prerequisite *adj.* **1** °essential, °necessary, requisite, °imperative, °indispensable, °obligatory, required, called for, demanded —*n.* **2** °precondition, °requirement, °qualification, requisite, °condition, sine qua non, °proviso, °provision, °necessity

prerogative *n.* °privilege, °right, °liberty, °power, °due, °advantage, °license, franchise, °claim, °sanction, °authority, authorization

prescribe *v.* ordain, °order, °direct, °dictate, °demand, °decree, °require, enjoin, °rule, °set (down), °stipulate, °command, °instruct, °define, °specify, °impose, °lay down, °exact, constrain

prescription *n.* **1** °formula, °recipe, °instruction, °direction **2** °remedy, medication, °medicine, °drug, °preparation, medicament

prescriptive *adj.* °dictatorial, constrictive, didactic, restrictive, °dogmatic, °authoritarian, °overbearing, autocratic, imperious

presence *n.* **1** °proximity, nearness, closeness, adjacency, °vicinity, *Formal* propinquity **2** °attendance, °company, °companionship, °society, °association, °existence, °manifestation, manifestness, being **3** °poise, self-assurance, °bearing, self-possession, °confidence, mien, °carriage, comportment, deportment, °air, °personality, °aspect, °aura, °appearance **4** °spirit, wraith, °specter, °shade **5** ***presence of mind.*** aplomb, °sophistication, coolness, coolheadedness, composure, imperturbability, phlegm, °sang-froid, self-possession, self-assurance, °calm, equanimity, levelheadedness, quick-wittedness, alertness, *Colloq* °cool

present[1] *adj.* **1** °current, °contemporary, present-day, existing, existent, up-to-date, *Colloq* °now **2** °nearby, nearest, °immediate, closest, adjacent, proximate, propinquitous; °close, °remaining; accounted for —*n.* **3** ***at present.*** (right *or* just) now, °for the time being, for the present, today, these days, *Nonstandard* °presently, *Colloq* at this point in time **4** ***the present.*** the time being, the moment, the hour, the nonce, this juncture, these days, our times; today, °(right) now, °nowadays; *Colloq* this point in time

present[2] *n.* **1** °gift **2** °donation, °offering, °bounty, °grant, largesse *or* largess, contribution, °endowment **3** °tip, gratuity, *pourboire*, baksheesh *or* backsheesh, °bonus; alms, handout, °dole, °aid, °allowance —*v.* **4** °introduce, °acquaint with, °make known **5** °offer, °give, °stage, °show, °exhibit, °put on (a show), °mount, °produce **6** °give (out), °award, °confer (on), °bestow (on), turn *or* hand over, °grant, °provide, °furnish; °dispense, °distribute, dole out, °pass out, deal out, mete out **7** °offer, bring (in *or* up), proffer, °tender, °introduce, °produce, °submit, set *or* put forth, °put forward, adduce; °register, °file, °record **8** °introduce, °announce, *Brit* compère *or* compere, *Colloq* emcee

presentable *adj.* **1** °fit, °fitting, °suitable, °acceptable, °satisfactory, °adequate, °passable, °tolerable, admissible, all right, allowable, up to par *or* standard *or* the mark, good enough, *Colloq* °up to scratch, OK *or* O.K. *or* okay, up to snuff **2** °decent, °proper, °polite, °decorous, °respectable, °well-bred, well-mannered, fit to be seen

presentation *n.* **1** giving, bestowal, °offering, proffering, presenting, °award, awarding, conferral, conferring, °delivery; °donation 2 °appearance, °image, °display, visual(s), °spectacle, °show, °performance, °demonstration, °production 3 °debut, °launch, introduction, unveiling, disclosure

presently *adv.* °soon, by and by, in a little while, °shortly, after a short time, in due course, after a while *or* a time, before long, in a moment *or* a minute *or* a while, *Archaic or literary* anon, *Colloq* in a jiffy, in two shakes (of a lamb's tail), *Nonstandard* °now, °at present

preservation *n.* 1 °upkeep, °maintenance, °care, °conservation 2 keeping, retention, retaining, perpetuation, perpetuating, continuation, °safekeeping, °security, safeguarding, °protection, protecting, °conservation

preserve *v.* 1 keep safe, °protect, °guard, °take care of, °care for, °safeguard, watch over, °shield, °shelter, °defend, °spare 2 °keep (up), °maintain, °conserve, °spare, °perpetuate; °continue, °support, °sustain, °save 3 °conserve, °put up, pickle, °cure, smoke, kipper, °salt, corn, marinate, can, °freeze, freeze-dry, °refrigerate, °dry, dehydrate, vacuum-pack; embalm, mummify —*n.* 4 Often, ***preserves.*** conserve(s), °jam, jelly, confiture, marmalade 5 °(game) reserve, °reservation, °sanctuary, *Brit* °park

preside *v.* °supervise, °run, °oversee, °direct, °operate, °lead, °head (up), °govern, °rule, °manage, °handle, °control, °chair, °administer, administrate, °regulate, °officiate

press *v.* 1 subject to *or* exert pressure *or* force, °force, °push, impel, °thrust, °bear (on), weigh on *or* upon, °jam, °cram, °crush; pressure *or Brit also* pressurize 2 °squeeze, compress, °depress, °push 3 °squeeze, °crush, compress, mash 4 iron, °smooth, °flatten, put through a mangle; steam 5 °clasp, °embrace, °hug, hold (close *or* tight(ly)), take in one's arms, throw one's arms about *or* around, cleave to, *Archaic* °clip 6 constrain, °urge, °force, °pressure, compel, °demand, °persuade, °induce, °prod, °provoke, importune, °beseech, °ask, °request, °beg, entreat 7 °crowd, °flock, °gather, °mill, °swarm, °throng, °seethe, °cluster, congregate, °meet, °converge, °huddle —*n.* 8 crowding, °gathering, thronging, converging, convergence, °crowd, °throng, °swarm, °cluster, °huddle, °pack, °herd, °host, multitude, horde, °mob, °crush 9 °urgency, °haste, °hurry, °hustle, bustle, °pressure, °stress 10 ***the press.*** (a) newspapers, the papers, Fleet Street, the fourth estate, the media, the wire *or* news services, broadcasting, °television, °radio (b) newspaper people, newspapermen *or* newspaperwomen, newsmen *or* newswomen, reporters, correspondents, ladies *or* gentlemen of the press, journalists, commentators, *paparazzi, Brit* leader writers, *US* editorial writers, *Colloq* newshounds, *Brit* journos

pressing *adj.* °urgent, compelling, °crucial, °pivotal, °burning, °grave, °serious, °major, °important, °vital, high-priority, °critical, °portentous, °momentous, °profound, °significant

pressure *n.* 1 °force, compression; °weight, °power, °strength 2 compression, °pressing, squeezing, compressing, °tension, °stress, crushing 3 °affliction, °oppression, °press, °weight, °burden, °load, albatross, °strain, °stress, °urgency, demands, exigency *or* exigencies, vexation, °distress, trouble(s), adversity, difficulty *or* difficulties, °straits, constraint(s), problem(s) 4 °influence, °power, °sway, constraint, insistence, coercion, intimidation, arm-twisting; °inducement, °persuasion, urging, °pressing —*v.* 5 °persuade, °influence; prevail upon *or* on, °press, °urge, °sway, °intimidate, bring pressure to bear (on), apply pressure (on *or* to), coerce, °force, compel, constrain, °require, °demand, °make, insist upon *or* on, *Brit* pressurize, *Colloq* twist (someone's) arm, °lean on, turn the heat on, *Slang* put the screws on *or* to

prestige *n.* °status, °reputation, °standing, °rank, stature, °importance, °significance, eminence, °esteem, °preeminence, °prominence, °predominance, primacy, °superiority, °supremacy, ascendancy, °distinction, °renown, °regard, °fame, °cachet, repute, °celebrity, °glamour, stardom

prestigious *adj.* °important, °significant, °eminent, °estimable, °imposing, °impressive, °preeminent, °prominent, °distinguished, august, °dignified, °renowned, °famous, famed, °well-known, °illustrious, acclaimed, respected, °celebrated, °noted, °notable, °noteworthy, °outstanding, °glorious, honored, °glamorous

presumably *adv.* °probably, in all likelihood, (very *or* most) likely, in all probability, °seemingly, doubtless(ly), indubitably, no doubt, °undoubtedly, unquestionably, without a doubt, °surely, certainly, °on the face of it, all things considered, all things being equal

presume *v.* 1 °assume, take for granted, °suppose, °surmise, °infer, °presuppose, °take it, °gather, °understand, °think, °believe, °imagine, °suspect, °fancy, conjecture, postulate, °posit, °theorize, °speculate, hypothesize, hypothecate, *US and Canadian* °guess 2 °dare, °take the liberty, be so presumptuous as, make (so) bold (as), have the audacity *or* effrontery, go so far as, °venture 3 Often, ***presume on or upon.*** encroach (on *or* upon), impose (on *or* upon), °take liberties (with), intrude (on *or* upon *or* into)

presumption *n.* 1 °arrogance, °pride, °effrontery, audacity, boldness, brazenness, °impudence, °impertinence, insolence, temerity, overconfidence, presumptuousness, forwardness, immodesty, *Colloq* pushiness, cheek, cheekiness, °nerve, °gall, chutzpah, °brass, *Brit* brass neck 2 assumption, °supposition, °presupposition, °preconception, premise *or* premiss, °surmise, °proposition, postulation; °probability, °likelihood, plausibility, °feasibility **3** assumption, °stand, °position, °inference, °feeling, °deduction, conclusion, °conviction, °bias, °guess, theory, °hypothesis, conjecture, °belief, °thought; °suspicion **4** ground(s), °reason, °basis, °evidence

presumptive *adj.* **1** °likely, °reasonable, °plausible, °tenable, believable, credible, conceivable, °acceptable, justifiable, °sensible, °rational, °sound **2** inferred, presumed, °assumed, °supposed, °understood, predicted, predicated

presumptuous *adj.* °arrogant, °proud, prideful, °audacious, °bold, °brazen, saucy, °impudent, °impertinent, °insolent, temerarious, °brash, °overconfident, overweening, °forward, presuming, °immodest, °egotistical, *Colloq* °pushy, °cheeky, too big for one's boots, *Brit* °uppish

presuppose *v.* See **presume, 1,** above.

presupposition *n.* See **presumption, 1, 2,** above.

pretend *v.* **1** feign, °profess, °represent, °allege, °make believe, °make out **2** °try, °attempt, °endeavor, °venture, °presume, °undertake **3** °make believe, act *or* play, play-act, °fake, feign, put on an act, dissemble, °sham, sail under false colors

pretended *adj.* °so-called, °alleged, asserted, °reputed, °professed, ostensible, purported, °imaginary, make-believe, °fictitious, °fictional, °sham, °false, °fake, feigned, °bogus, °counterfeit, °spurious, *Colloq* phoney *or US also* phony, pseudo, °pretend

pretender *n.* claimant, aspirant, °candidate, °suitor, °rival, seeker

pretense *n.* **1** °show, °display, °pretension, °ostentation, °airs, °front, façade, °appearance, make-believe, fiction, °hypocrisy, fakery, faking, feigning, humbuggery, humbug, °deception, °artifice, °pretext, posturing, pretentiousness, pretending, °camouflage, cover-up **2** °hoax, humbug, °artifice, °pretext, °sham, °show, °pose, façade, °front, cover-up, °cover, °cloak, °veil, °mask, °masquerade, °disguise, °guise, °deception, °ruse, °dodge, °blind, °fabrication, °invention, fiction, °story, fable, make-believe, fairy tale, figment, falsification, °impression **3** °excuse, °pretext, °pretension

pretension *n.* **1** Often, ***pretensions.*** claim(s), pretense(s), aspiration(s), ambitiousness, ambition(s) **2** °pretext, °pretense, pretentiousness, °ostentation, pretending, °affectation, °hypocrisy

pretentious *adj.* **1** °ostentatious, °showy, °superficial, °pompous, °arrogant, °bombastic, °inflated, high-flown, exaggerated, vainglorious, fastuous, °grandiose, grandiloquent, °extravagant, magniloquent **2** °snobbish, °lofty, °haughty, flaunting, *Colloq* high and mighty, highfalutin *or* hifalutin, °hoity-toity, high-hat, *Slang* snotty, *Brit* toffee-nosed

pretext *n.* **1** °pretense, °excuse, °camouflage, °guise, °disguise, °cover, °veil, °cloak, °color **2** °ruse, red herring, °cover (story), °rationale, °pretense, rationalization, °explanation

pretty *adj.* **1** °comely, °attractive, good-looking, nice-looking, appealing, °lovely, °cute, minion *or* mignon *or* mignonne, °graceful, °fair, °bonny, °fetching, charming, winsome, °beautiful, pulchritudinous, *Colloq* easy on the eye(s) **2** °tuneful, melodic, °melodious, dulcet, °musical, °lyrical, °harmonious, catchy, mellifluous, euphonious —*adv.* **3** °rather, °quite, °fairly, °moderately, reasonably, tolerably; °somewhat; °very, °extremely, unbelievably, incredibly

prevail *v.* **1** hold sway, °win (out), °predominate, °succeed, °triumph, gain *or* achieve a victory, prove superior, gain mastery *or* control **2** °predominate, be prevalent *or* widespread *or* current, preponderate, °dominate, be the order of the day **3** ***prevail on or upon.*** °persuade, °induce, °influence, °sway, °dispose; °incline, °win over, bring round, °convince

prevailing *adj.* **1** °dominant, °predominant, °prevalent, °main, °chief, °principal, common(est), °usual, °customary, °universal **2** °influential, °effective, °effectual, dominating, affecting, °powerful, °potent, °forceful, ruling, °telling, °main, °principal

prevalence *n.* **1** prevalency, frequency, commonness, currency, universality, ubiquitousness, ubiquity, pervasiveness, omnipresence, extensiveness; °predominance, °practice, acceptance, °popularity **2** °sway, °control, °rule, primacy, ascendancy, mastery, °predominance

prevalent *adj.* °universal, °catholic, °common, °frequent, °prevailing, °current, ubiquitous, °pervasive, omnipresent, °general, °usual, °customary, commonplace, °extensive, widespread, established, ascendant, °dominant, °predominant, governing, ruling

prevent *v.* °anticipate, °preclude, obviate, °forestall, avert, °avoid, °prohibit, °ban, °bar, °forbid, interdict, °taboo, enjoin, proscribe, °foil, °frustrate, °obstruct, debar, °intercept, °nip in the bud, abort, °thwart, °check, °block, ward *or* fend *or* stave off, baffle, balk *or* baulk, °(put a) stop (to), °arrest, °(bring to a) halt, °hinder, °impede, °curb, °restrain, °hamper, °inhibit, °delay, °retard, °slow, °mitigate, °control

prevention *n.* preventing, °anticipation, preclusion, obviation, forestalling, avoidance, avoiding, °prohibition, prohibiting, °ban, banning, °bar, °barring, forbiddance, °forbidding, interdiction, interdicting, °taboo, tabooing, enjoining, °injunction, proscription, proscribing, foiling, frustration, frustrating, °obstruction, obstructing, debarment, debarring, interception, intercepting, abortion, aborting, thwarting, checking, °check, blocking, °block, warding *or* fending *or* staving off, balk *or* baulk, balking *or* baulking, stopping, °arrest, °arresting, °halt, °halting, °hindrance, hindering, impedance, impeding, °curb, curbing, °restraint, restraining, hampering, °inhibition, inhibiting, °delay, delaying, retardation, retarding, slowing, mitigation, °mitigating, °control, controlling

preventive *adj.* **1** preventative, preventing, hindering, impeding, restraining, hampering, inhibitive *or* inhibitory, inhibiting, restrictive **2** preventative, prophylactic, precautionary, anticipatory *or* anticipative, °protective, counteractive —*n.* **3** preventative, °hindrance, °curb, °inhibition, °impediment, °block, °barrier, °obstacle, °obstruction **4** preventative, prophylactic, °protection, °shield, °safeguard, °prevention, countermeasure, counteractant, counteragent, inoculum *or* inoculant, vaccine, serum, °antidote, °remedy

preview *n.* advance showing, private showing; °opening, vernissage

previous *adj.* **1** °former, °prior, °past, earlier, one-time, °foregoing, °sometime, erstwhile, °preceding, *Literary* quondam, *Archaic* whilom **2** °prior, °former, °foregoing, °above, °preceding, *Formal* antecedent, anterior, aforementioned, above-mentioned, beforementioned, aforesaid, above-named **3** °premature, untimely, too soon *or* early **4** ***previous to.*** previously to, °before, °prior to, °preceding, anterior to, antecedent to

previously *adv.* °before, °once, °formerly, earlier, °at one time, then, beforehand, heretofore, theretofore, hitherto, thitherto, in the past, in days gone by, in days of old, in days *or* time past, in the old days, some time ago, a while ago, once upon a time, yesterday, *Literary* in days of yore, in olden days *or* times

prey *n.* **1** °quarry, °kill, °game, °objective, °target **2** °victim, °target, °objective; °dupe, *Colloq* °mark, *Slang* fall guy, °pushover, *Brit* °mug —*v.* **3** ***prey on or upon.*** **(a)** live off, feed on *or* upon, °eat, °consume, °devour, °kill, °destroy, °stalk, °pursue, °hunt, °seize **(b)** °victimize, go after, °exploit, °use, take advantage of, °intimidate, °bully, °cheat, °dupe, °swindle, gull, °trick, snooker, °defraud, °outwit, °outsmart, outfox, °hoodwink, *Literary* cozen, *Colloq* rook, bamboozle, flimflam **(c)** °oppress, weigh on *or* upon, °burden, °depress, °distress, °strain, vex, °worry

price *n.* **1** °charge, °cost, °expense, °expenditure, °outlay, °payment, °amount, °figure, °fee; °quotation, appraisal, value, valuation, °evaluation, °worth **2** °sacrifice, °toll, °penalty, °cost, consequence **3** °reward, °bounty, °premium, °prize, °payment, °bonus, °honorarium, *Literary* guerdon **4** ***without price.*** See **priceless, 1,** below. —*v.* **5** value, °evaluate, °rate, assay, assess, °cost (out)

priceless *adj.* **1** costly, °dear, °expensive, high-priced, valuable, °invaluable, °precious, °inestimable, incalculable; irreplaceable, °unique **2** °hilarious, °riotous, °(screamingly) funny, sidesplitting, °hysterical, droll, comical, amusing

pricey *adj.* pricy, °expensive, °dear, costly, °exorbitant, °outrageous, °excessive, extortionate, *Colloq* °steep, *Brit* over the odds

prick *n.* **1** °puncture, pinhole, pinprick; °hole, perforation **2** °sting, °pinch, °twinge, °prickle, tingle, °pain —*v.* **3** °puncture, °pierce, °stab, °jab, °punch, °perforate, °riddle; °lance **4** °stab, °sting, °hurt, °prickle, °pinch, °bite, °smart

prickle *n.* **1** °spine, °bristle, barb, °thorn, bur, needle, tine, °spike, °spur, prong **2** pricking, prickliness, °itch, itchiness, °sting, tingling, tingle —*v.* **3** tingle, °sting, °itch, °smart **4** °stick, °jab, °prick

prickly *adj.* **1** bristly, °thorny, brambly, spiny, barbed, briery, spinous, spiky, *Technical* setaceous, setose, acanthoid, aciculate, aculeate, muricate, spiculate **2** tingling, stinging, pricking, prickling, itchy, crawly, crawling **3** °touchy, °irritable, °petulant, °cantankerous, °testy, °waspish, bad-tempered, °peevish, fractious, °short-tempered, curmudgeonly, *Colloq* °cranky **4** nettlesome, °thorny, °ticklish, °touchy, °troublesome, °intricate, °complicated, complex, knotty, °hard, °difficult, contentious

pride *n.* **1** °honor, proudness, °self-esteem, °self-respect, ***amour-propre,*** °dignity **2** °conceit, egotism, self-importance, °vanity, hubris, °arrogance, overconfidence, overweeningness, self-admiration, self-love, self-importance, smugness, haughtiness, hauteur, °snobbery, snobbishness, *Colloq* uppitiness **3** °boast, °flower, °best, °prize, pride and joy, °treasure, °jewel, °gem —*v.* **4** Usually, ***pride oneself on.*** be proud of, take pride in, °delight in, °revel in, °celebrate, glory in

priest *n.* priestess, clergyman *or* clergywoman, ecclesiastic, cleric, churchman *or* churchwoman, reverend, vicar, °divine, man *or* woman of the cloth, man *or* woman of God, curate, confessor, °minister (of the gospel), servant of God, °father, °mother, holy man *or* woman, °preacher, °missionary, evangelist, abbé, abbot *or* abbess, *Colloq* padre

priestly *adj.* °clerical, ecclesiastic, °pastoral, hieratic, sacerdotal; ministerial, canonical, °missionary

prig *n.* (ultra)conservative, °prude, °purist, pedant, schoolmarm, °puritan, (Mrs.) Grundy, Grundyite, Grundyist, precisionist, precisian, conformist, formalist, *Colloq* stuffed shirt, °stick-in-the-mud, °goody-goody

priggish *adj.* (ultra)conservative, prim, demure, °prudish, °purist, puristic, °pedantic, schoolmarmish, °strait-laced, °hidebound, stiff-necked, puritanical, conformist, (Mrs.) Grundyish, punctilious, °formal, formalistic, °strict, °severe, °fastidious, °fussy, °particular; °precious, ***précieux*** or ***précieuse,*** niminy-piminy, overnice, *Colloq* °stick-in-the-mud, °goody-goody, °prissy, oldmaidish, stuffed-shirt, °stuffy, uptight, nitpicking, *Brit* twee

primarily *adv.* **1** °principally, °mainly,

°chiefly, °especially, °at bottom, °particularly, first of all, °preeminently, basically, essentially, fundamentally, °on the whole, °for the most part, mostly, predominantly *or* predominately, °generally **2** initially, °originally, from *or* at the start, °first (and foremost), in the first instance, *ab initio*

primary *adj.* **1** °first, °prime, °principal, °chief, °main, °leading, °preeminent, °cardinal, °fundamental, °basic, °essential, °predominant, °elementary, °elemental, underlying **2** earliest, °first, °original, °initial, °primitive, primeval, primordial, embryonic, germinal, °beginning, °ultimate **3** firsthand, °direct, °immediate **4** °elementary, °basic, °rudimentary, °fundamental **5** unmixed, unadulterated, °pure, °simple, °rudimentary, °fundamental, °principal

prime *adj.* **1** See **primary, 1,** above. **2** °best, °foremost, °chief; °first-rate, first-class, °choice, °select, °superior, °preeminent, °leading, ranking, °predominant, °unparalleled, °matchless, °peerless, °noteworthy, °outstanding, °admirable, °worthy, °exceptional, °excellent, °extraordinary **3** °original, °fundamental, °basic, °elemental, °elementary —*n.* **4** °youth, springtime; best years, heyday, °pinnacle, °acme, °peak, °zenith —*v.* **5** (make *or* get) ready, °prepare, °educate, °teach, °instruct, °coach, °train, °tutor, °drill **6** °inform, °advise, °notify, apprise, °brief

primitive *adj.* **1** °first, °original, °aboriginal, earliest, primordial, primal, primeval *or Brit also* primaeval, °pristine, °prehistoric; antediluvian, Noachian *or* Noachic, °old, °ancient **2** °crude, °rude, °unrefined, °raw, barbaric, uncultured, °barbarian, °coarse, °rough, °uncivilized, °savage, uncultivated, °unsophisticated, uncouth **3** °simple, °basic, simplistic, naive *or* naïve *or* naïf, °childlike, °unsophisticated, uncultivated, °unrefined, unpolished, °rough, untutored, untaught, untrained, unschooled, °undeveloped

primp *v.* °preen, prink, prettify, titivate *or* tittivate, plume, °dress up, °groom, *Colloq* doll up, get (all) dolled up, °spruce up, put on one's best bib and tucker, *Chiefly Brit* tart up, get (all) tarted up, *Slang* deck out, trick out *or* up, put on one's glad rags, *Brit* fig out, *US* gussy up, get (all) gussied up, dude up

princely *adj.* **1** °lavish, °bountiful, °generous, °liberal, °ample, °substantial, °huge, °enormous **2** °lavish, °magnificent, °splendid, °luxurious, °majestic, °royal, °regal, °sumptuous, °superb, *Colloq* ritzy, swank(y), °posh, °plush **3** °royal, °noble, °regal, °sovereign, of royal *or* noble blood *or* rank

principal *adj.* **1** °chief, °primary, °prime, °paramount, °main, °first, °foremost, ranking, °preeminent, °predominant, °dominant, °prevailing; °leading, starring **2** °important, °prominent, °leading, °key, °cardinal —*n.* **3** °owner, °proprietor, chairman, chairwoman, chairperson, °(managing) director, °head, president, °chief, chief executive officer, CEO, manager *or Brit* manageress, °superintendent, °supervisor, *Colloq* °boss, *US* (head *or* chief) honcho **4** dean, °director, *Chiefly Brit* headmaster, headmistress, °master, rector, (vice) chancellor **5** °(working) capital, capital funds, °resources, investment, °backing, (cash) reserve(s), °assets; °money **6** °star, °lead, °heroine, °hero, leading lady *or* man, leading role, main part; diva, *première danseuse, premier danseur,* prima donna, prima ballerina

principally *adv.* °chiefly, °mainly, °first (and foremost), °primarily, °above all, °in the main, mostly, °for the most part, °largely, predominantly, °on the whole, °at bottom, °in essence, essentially, basically, fundamentally; °especially, °particularly

principle *n.* **1** °truth, °given, °precept, °tenet, °fundamental, °grounds, °law, °rule, dictum, canon, °doctrine, teaching, dogma, °proposition, (basic) assumption, postulate, axiom, °maxim, °truism, °guide, °standard, criterion, °model **2** Often, ***principles.*** °philosophy, °code, °attitude, °(point of) view, °viewpoint, °sentiment, °belief, credo, °creed, °idea, °notion, ethic, sense of right and wrong **3** °(sense of) honor, uprightness, °honesty, °morality, °morals, °probity, °integrity, °conscience **4** ***in principle.*** on principle, in theory, theoretically, basically, fundamentally, °at bottom, °in essence, essentially, °ideally

principled *adj.* °moral, °righteous, right-minded, °virtuous, °noble, high-minded, °ethical, °honorable, °proper, °correct, °right, °just, °upright, °honest, °scrupulous

print *v.* **1** °impress, imprint, °stamp, °publish, °issue, °run off, °put out; °copy; °(pull a) proof —*n.* **2** °reproduction, °copy, °replica, °facsimile; °positive, °photograph, etching, (steel *or* wood) engraving, lithograph, woodcut, linocut, silk screen, rotogravure, *Trademark* Xerox; °picture, °illustration; *Colloq* photo, °cut, pic (*pl.* pix) **3** °text, printed matter, °type, °writing; °language, °wording, °(choice of) words, phrasing

prior *adj.* **1** °former, °previous, earlier, one-time, ex, erstwhile; °old, °last, °late, °latest, *Literary* quondam, whilom **2** ***prior to.*** °before, °previous to, previously to, °till, until °preceding

priority *n.* °precedence, precedency, primacy, °urgency, immediacy, °predominance, °preeminence, °preference, °rank, °superiority, °prerogative, °right, seniority, °importance, °weight, immediacy

prison *n.* jail *or Brit also* gaol, °dungeon, oubliette, lockup, penal institution, house of correction, correctional institution, reformatory, house of detention; confinement, °detention; *Old-fashioned* °reform school, *Military* guardhouse; *US* penitentiary, *US Military* brig; *Brit* remand center, detention center, remand home, community home, *Brit Military* glasshouse, *Brit formal* CHE (= 'community home with education on the premises'), *Brit old-fashioned* approved school, *Brit archaic* bridewell; *Slang* clink, can, cooler, °jug, °stir, *US* °pen, calaboose, slammer, hoosegow, *US old-fashioned* big house, *US and Canadian* pokey *or* poky, *Brit* quod, chokey *or* choky

prisoner *n.* °convict, trusty; internee, detainee; *Colloq* lifer, jailbird *or Brit also* gaolbird; *Slang* con, *Brit* °(old) lag, *Old-fashioned* ticket-of-leave man

prissy *adj.* °fussy, °precious, overnice, finicky *or* finical, °strait-laced, schoolmarmish, prim (and proper), °prudish, °squeamish, °fastidious, *Colloq* oldmaidish

pristine *adj.* **1** °original, primal, °basic, primeval *or Brit also* primaeval, °primitive, primordial, earliest, °first, °initial **2** uncorrupted, °pure, unsullied, undefiled, virginal, virgin, °chaste, untouched, °unspoiled, unpolluted, °untarnished, °spotless, °immaculate, °natural

privacy *n.* **1** °seclusion, retirement, °solitude, isolation, °retreat, sequestration, reclusiveness, reclusion, solitariness; monasticism **2** °secrecy, secretiveness, clandestineness, confidentiality, surreptitiousness, covertness, concealment

private *adj.* **1** °(top) secret, °confidential, undisclosed, °hidden, clandestine, concealed, covert, °surreptitious, °off the record, not for publication, °unofficial, *Colloq* hush-hush **2** °privileged, restrictive, restricted, °exclusive, °special, °reserved, °personal, °inaccessible, nonpublic; °hidden, °secluded, concealed, °secret, °sneaking **3** °personal, °individual, own, °intimate, °particular **4** °solitary, seclusive, °reclusive, °withdrawn, °retiring, °reticent, ungregarious, nongregarious, °unsocial, unsociable, antisocial, °reserved, uncommunicative, hermitic(al), hermitlike, eremitic(al); sequestered, °secluded, retired —*n.* **5** private soldier, infantryman, foot soldier, *US* enlisted man, *Colloq Brit* tommy, Tommy Atkins, squaddie, *US* GI (Joe), *Slang US* grunt **6** ***in private.*** °in secret, °secretly, privately, *sub rosa*, °personally, confidentially, behind closed doors, off camera, °off the record, *US* on the Q.T.; clandestinely, secretively, sneakily, sneakingly, surreptitiously, furtively, covertly, °on the sly **7** ***private parts or privates.*** °genitals, sexual *or* sex organs, genitalia

privation *n.* °need, neediness, °want, deprivation, °hardship, indigence, °necessity, °poverty, penury, destitution, strait(s), pauperism, beggary; °distress, °misery

privilege *n.* °benefit, °advantage, °right, °prerogative, concession, °allowance, °indulgence, °immunity, °exemption, dispensation, °freedom, °liberty, franchise, °permission, °consent, °leave, authorization, °sanction, °authority, °license, °carte blanche

privileged *adj.* **1** °favored, advantaged, indulged, entitled, elite *or* élite, °special, honored **2** protected, exempt(ed), °immune; licensed, empowered, admitted, permitted, sanctioned, authorized, enfranchised, chartered **3** °powerful, ruling; °wealthy, °rich **4** °confidential, °secret, °private, °privy, °inside, off the record, not for publication, restricted, *Colloq* hush-hush

privy *adj.* **1** See **privileged, 4,** above. **2** ***privy to.*** aware of, in on, on to *or* onto, sharing (in), cognizant of, apprised of, informed *or* advised about *or* of, informed on, knowledgeable about, *Colloq* in the know about, *Slang* hip to, °wise to, *Old-fashioned* hep to —*n.* **3** °lavatory, (outside *or* outdoor) toilet, latrine, water closet, WC, *US* outhouse, *Colloq chiefly Brit* loo, *Slang Brit* °bog, *US* crapper, *Taboo slang US* shithouse

prize[1] *n.* **1** °reward, °award, °trophy, °premium; °honor, accolade, *Literary* guerdon **2** winnings, jackpot, °purse, °receipts, °gain, °windfall, stakes, *Colloq* °haul, *Chiefly US* °take **3** °aim, °goal **4** °loot, °booty, spoil(s), °trophy, °plunder, pickings —*adj.* **5** °choice, °excellent, (prize-)winning, °best, °champion, °outstanding, °select, °superior, °superlative, °first-rate

prize[2] *v.* value, °treasure, °esteem, °cherish, °appreciate, rate highly, hold dear

probability *n.* °likelihood, likeliness, °odds, °expectation, chance(s), °(distinct) possibility, °presumption

probable *adj.* °(most) likely, apt, °(quite) possible, presumed, °plausible, undoubted, indubitable, °apparent, °unquestionable, °evident, ostensible, odds-on, °feasible, believable, credible

probably *adv.* °(very) likely, in all likelihood, in all probability, °undoubtedly, doubtlessly, indubitably, unquestionably, °presumably, °quite, all things considered, °to all intents and purposes, °possibly, °perhaps, *Colloq* as likely as not, °quite

probe *v.* **1** °explore, °examine, °scrutinize, °investigate, °search (into), °look into, °go into, °study, °dig into, delve into, poke about *or* around, *Colloq* poke into **2** °poke, °prod, °explore, °examine; °plumb, °dig —*n.* **3** °investigation, °examination, °exploration, °scrutiny, °search, °study, inquiry *or* enquiry, inquest

probity *n.* °integrity, uprightness, °honesty, °morality, °rectitude, °virtue, goodness, decency, righteousness, right-mindedness, °sincerity, trustworthiness, °honor, °equity, justness, °justice, fairness

problem *n.* **1** °difficulty, °trouble, °question, °dilemma, °quandary, °predicament, °complication, hornet's nest, imbroglio, °mess, °muddle, °stew, *Colloq* can of worms, fine kettle of fish, (pretty) pickle, *Brit* facer **2** °puzzle, conundrum, poser, °riddle, °question, °enigma, puzzler, *Colloq* mind-boggler, hard *or* tough nut to crack —*adj.* **3** °unruly, unmanageable, intractable, uncontrollable, °difficult, °ungovernable, refractory, °incorrigible, °obstreperous, °delinquent, maladjusted, °disturbed, emotionally upset

problematic *adj.* problematical, °difficult, °uncertain, °questionable, questioned, °doubtful, doubted, °debatable, °disputable, disputed, °unsettled, °moot, undecided, °controversial, °tricky, °touchy, °sensitive, *Colloq* °hairy, iffy

procedure *n.* °way, °conduct, °course, °action, course of action, °method, methodology, °mode, °form, °system, °approach, °strategy, °plan (of action), °scheme, modus operandi, °operation, °policy, ways and means; °routine, °tradition, °practice, °custom, wont, standard operating procedure, *Colloq* MO (= 'modus operandi'), SOP (= 'standard operating procedure'), *Chiefly Brit* °drill

proceed *v.* **1** Sometimes, ***proceed with.*** go *or* move (on *or* ahead *or* forward), °advance, °continue, °progress, °carry on, get *or* move along, get going *or* moving *or* under way, °start, °pass on, make progress *or* headway, push *or* press on *or* onward(s), forge ahead; °resume, °renew, go on with, °pick up (where one left off) **2** Often, ***proceed from or out of.*** °result from, °arise (from), °come (from), stem from, °spring from, °develop (from), issue (from *or* forth), derive from, be derived (from), descend from, °emerge (from), grow (from *or* out of), originate (in *or* from *or* with), °begin (with), start (with *or* from) *—n.* **3** ***proceeds.*** profit(s), °gain, °yield; °income, °receipts, return(s), °gate, box office, *US* °take

proceeding *n.* **1** °measure, °act, °(course of) action, °move, °step, °undertaking, °deed, °procedure, °process, °operation, °transaction, °maneuver, °feat, °accomplishment **2** ***proceedings.*** **(a)** °transactions, report(s), °minutes, record(s), annals, affairs, °dealings, °business, account(s), archives, *Formal* acta **(b)** events, goings-on, doings; celebration(s); performance(s)

process *n.* **1** °procedure, °proceeding, °operation, °system, °method, °approach, °technique; course of action **2** °activity, °function, °development *—v.* **3** °treat, °prepare, (make *or* get) ready, °change, °modify, °transform, °convert, °alter **4** °handle, °take care of, °organize, °deal with, °manage; °dispose of, °answer, °manipulate

procession *n.* **1** °parade, °march, cavalcade, motorcade, cortege *or* cortège, column, °line, °file, °train, marchpast **2** °succession, °cycle, °sequence, °string, °train, °chain, series, °course, °run, °progression, cavalcade

proclaim *v.* **1** °announce, advertise, °circulate, °declare, °broadcast, °pronounce, °make known, bruit (about), trumpet, °publish, promulgate, herald; °profess, °protest, °enunciate, articulate **2** °brand, accuse of being, stigmatize as, °pronounce, °rule, °decree, °characterize, °report

proclamation *n.* **1** °announcement, °advertisement, °declaration, °publication, promulgation, °statement, manifesto, pronunciamento, notification, °notice **2** proclaiming, announcing, advertising, declaring, broadcasting, publishing, promulgating, heralding, making known, bruiting about

procrastinate *v.* **1** temporize, act evasively, °play for time, dally, °delay, °stall; °postpone, °defer, put off *or* aside, °shelve, *US* °table **2** °hesitate, °pause, waver, vacillate, be undecided, °equivocate, tergiversate, °shilly-shally

procure *v.* **1** °obtain, °acquire, °get, °come by, °secure, get *or* lay one's hands on, get (a) hold of, °gain, °win, come into, °pick up, °find, °appropriate, °requisition; °buy, °purchase **2** °accomplish, °bring about, °effect, °cause, °produce

procurer *n.* pander *or* panderer, °pimp, white slaver, flesh-pedlar *or US also* flesh-peddler *or* flesh-pedler, *Archaic* whoremaster, bawd; madam, procuress

prod *v.* **1** °jab, °dig, °poke, °nudge, elbow **2** °spur, °urge, impel, egg on, °push, °thrust, °prompt, °rouse, °stir, °incite, °move, °motivate, actuate, °activate, °provoke, °encourage, °stimulate **3** °incite, goad, needle, °irritate, °irk, °annoy, °pester, °harass, hector, badger, °plague, °nag, °hound, carp at, °cavil; °henpeck *—n.* **4** °jab, °dig, °poke, °nudge, elbow, °push **5** goad, °spur; needle, rowel **6** stimulus, °push, °prompt, °reminder, °signal, °cue

prodigal *adj.* **1** °wasteful, °extravagant, °spendthrift, °lavish, °excessive, °profligate, squandering, °immoderate, intemperate, °wanton, °improvident, °reckless **2** °generous, °bountiful, copious, °profuse, bounteous, °lavish, °liberal, °luxuriant, °sumptuous, °abundant, abounding, °rich, °plentiful, plenteous, superabundant, thriving, swarming, teeming *—n.* **3** °wastrel, °spendthrift, °profligate, squanderer, waster, big spender

prodigality *n.* **1** wastefulness, °waste, °extravagance, °excess, excessiveness, immoderation, intemperateness, wantonness, recklessness, °profligacy, improvidence, °dissipation, squandering **2** lavishness, profuseness, °luxury, luxuriousness, luxuriance, °abundance, °plenty, °bounty, bountifulness, bounteousness, copiousness, °profusion, profuseness, sumptuousness, richness, plentifulness, plenteousness, superabundance, °exuberance

prodigious *adj.* **1** °vast, °immeasurable, °colossal, °enormous, °huge, °giant, °gigantic, °immense, mammoth, °monumental, tremendous, stupendous, titanic, Brobdingnagian, gargantuan, herculean, cyclopean, leviathan, °monstrous, °extensive, *Colloq US* ginormous, humongous **2** °amazing, astonishing, astounding, °startling, °extraordinary, °exceptional, °marvelous, wonderful, wondrous, °fabulous, °miraculous, °phenomenal, spectacular, °fantastic, °sensational, °unusual, staggering, °striking, dumbfounding *or* dumfounding, °remarkable, °noteworthy, °notable, *Colloq* flabbergasting, mind-boggling, mind-blowing

prodigy *n.* **1** (child *or* girl *or* boy) genius, wonderchild, *Wunderkind,* °mastermind, °talent, °intellect, intellectual *or* mental giant, wizard, °virtuoso, *Colloq* °brain, Einstein, whiz kid *or* whizz kid, whiz *or* whizz, walking dictionary *or* encyclopedia **2** °wonder, °marvel, °phenomenon, °sensation, miracle

produce *v.* **1** °make, °develop, °turn out, put *or* bring out, °manufacture, °fabricate, °generate, °create; °construct, °assemble, put together, °compose; °mold, °cast; extrude **2** °yield, °give rise to, °cause, °bring up, °bring forth, °spark, °initiate, °occasion, °bring about, °prompt, °evoke, °start, °create, °generate, beget, °originate **3** °generate, beget, °create, put out *or* forth, °breed, °propagate, °bear, give birth to, °hatch, °grow **4** bring forward *or* in *or* out, °introduce, °present, °offer, °show, °exhibit, °display, °stage, °put on, °mount **5** °disclose, °reveal, °bring to light, °show, °display, °draw **6** °supply, °furnish, °provide, °deliver, °distribute —*n.* **7** vegetables, °fruit, *Chiefly Brit* greengrocery

producer *n.* **1** maker, °manufacturer, fabricator, processor, °creator; grower, °farmer **2** °(in Britain) director, auteur, impresario, *régisseur*; (in US and Canada) entrepreneur, (business *or* financial) manager, organizer, impresario

product *n.* **1** °result, consequence, °output, °outcome, °issue, °effect, fallout, °yield, °upshot; spinoff, °offshoot, by-product **2** artifact, good(s), °produce, commodity, °output, °merchandise, °offering, °work

production *n.* **1** producing, °manufacture, manufacturing, making, °fabrication, °preparation, origination, °creation, °output, putting out, °development; °formation, forming, forging, shaping, molding, casting, °assembly, °building, construction **2** °product, °(end) result, °work, °effort, handiwork, °output, °opus, *oeuvre* **3** (in Britain) artistry, °direction, staging; (in US and Canada) °display, °presentation, *mise en scène,* °setting **4** °drama, °play, (stage *or* television *or* radio) show, °performance; °film, motion *or* moving picture, °movie

productive *adj.* **1** °fruitful, °fertile, °rich, fecund, °plentiful, plenteous, °abundant, °bountiful, bounteous, °prolific, °dynamic **2** °imaginative, °creative, inventive, °resourceful, generative, °ingenious, °fertile, °vigorous **3** °profitable, remunerative, °rewarding, valuable, °worthwhile

profane *adj.* **1** °irreverent, °sacrilegious, °blasphemous, idolatrous, irreligious, °infidel, °heathen, °unbelieving, disbelieving, °pagan, atheist(ic), °impious, °godless, °ungodly, °sinful, °wicked, iniquitous, °contemptuous, °disrespectful **2** unsanctified, unholy, unconsecrated, defiled, °impure, unclean, unhallowed, nonreligious, nonsacred, unsacred; °lay, nonclerical, °secular, °temporal; *Judaism* tref *or* treif *or* treifa, nonkosher **3** °bad, °dirty, °filthy, smutty, °foul, foulmouthed, °obscene, °vulgar, °coarse, uncouth, °low, °taboo, °blasphemous, °bawdy, ribald, °scurrilous, °off-color, °immodest, °improper, °naughty, °indecent, unprintable, °unmentionable, indecorous, indelicate, °common; °abusive, °vituperative, °venomous, thersitical, *Literary* Fescennine, *Colloq* °blue —*v.* **4** °debase, °contaminate, °pollute, °taint, °vitiate, °degrade, defile, °desecrate, °violate, °pervert, °corrupt

profanity *n.* blasphemy, obscenity, cursing, curse word(s), swearing, swear word(s), foul *or* bad *or* dirty *or* vulgar *or* coarse *or* filthy *or* smutty *or* taboo language, four-letter word(s), billingsgate

profess *v.* **1** assert, °claim, aver, asseverate, °state, affirm, °confirm, °confess, °declare, °say, °hold, °maintain, °present, °offer, proffer, °tender, °set forth, °put forward, °pronounce, enounce, °enunciate, °announce, utter, °vow, avow **2** °pretend, lay claim, make a pretense, purport, act as if, simulate

professed *adj.* **1** °pretended, ostensible, °apparent, °alleged, purported, °so-called, would-be, °self-styled, *soi-disant(e)* **2** confessed, avowed, sworn, admitted, acknowledged, confirmed, certified, declared

profession *n.* **1** °occupation, °calling, °work, °field, °vocation, °employment, métier, °trade, °business, °craft, °line, °sphere, specialty *or Brit* speciality, °job, °position, °post, °situation, *Slang* °racket **2** confession, affirmation, °statement, avowal, °assertion, asseveration, °declaration, °acknowledgment, °testimony, averment, °admission, °announcement

professional *adj.* **1** trained, °educated, °practiced, °veteran, °experienced, °seasoned, °able, skilled, °skillful, °gifted, °talented, °qualified, °knowledgeable, licensed, °official, °expert, °masterful, masterly, °master, °efficient, °adept, °proficient, °competent, °polished, finished **2** °excellent, °proficient, °efficient, °skillful, masterly, °thorough, °prompt, °conscientious, °authoritative, businesslike —*n.* **3** °master, °expert, maestro, °virtuoso, past master *or* mistress, °specialist, °authority, *Colloq* wizard, pro, whiz *or* whizz, *US* maven *or* mavin, *Brit* °dab hand

proficiency *n.* °facility, °skill, °talent, adeptness, °expertise, expertness, skillfulness, °aptitude, °capability, °ability, °dexterity, competence *or* competency, °ingenuity, °knack, °savoir-faire, *Colloq* know-how

proficient *adj.* °skillful, skilled, °talented, °adept, °gifted, °expert, °experienced, °practiced, *au fait,* °veteran, well-versed, (highly) trained, °professional, °qualified, °capable, °able, °accomplished, °dexterous, °competent, °knowledgeable, topnotch, °first-rate, *Colloq* ace, °crack, whiz-bang *or* whizz-bang, *Brit* wizard

profile *n.* **1** °outline, °silhouette, contour, side view **2** biography, (biographical *or* thumbnail *or* character) sketch, °life, °portrait, vignette **3** °analysis, °study, °survey, °examination; graph, diagram, °chart, °list, statistics —*v.* **4** °describe, °draw, sketch, limn

profit *n.* **1** Often, *profits.* gross *or* net profit, net *or Brit also* nett, return(s), °gain, °yield,

°revenue, °proceeds, bottom line, °surplus, °excess, *US* °take, *Slang* gravy, *US* vigorish **2** °advantage, avail, °good, °benefit, °welfare, °gain, value, °interest, °use, °usefulness, *Archaic or Literary* behoof *—v.* **3** °advance, °further, be of profit to, °benefit, °promote, °aid, °help, be advantageous *or* of advantage, °serve, avail, °improve **4** Often, ***profit from.*** take advantage of, °use, turn to advantage *or* account, °exploit, utilize, make (good) use of, make capital (out) of, capitalize on, °maximize, make the most of, *Slang* cash in on **5** °clear, °realize, °earn, °gain, *Colloq* make a killing, °clean up, °rake it in, make a bundle *or* a packet

profitable *adj.* **1** °beneficial, °productive, lucrative, °fruitful, (well-)paying, well-paid, °worthwhile, °effective, cost-effective, °gainful, remunerative, money-making, °rewarding **2** °beneficial, °helpful, °useful, utilitarian, valuable, °worthwhile, °advantageous, °productive, °rewarding

profiteer *n.* **1** °racketeer, exploiter, extortionist, black marketeer *—v.* **2** overcharge, °fleece, °exploit, °milk, make the most of; °extort; *US* °gouge

profligacy *n.* **1** debauchery, °vice, immorality, °sin, sinfulness, wickedness, °evil, °dissipation, dissoluteness, degeneracy, licentiousness, depravity, corruption, promiscuity, lechery, lasciviousness, lewdness, indecency, °perversion, carnality, libertinism, wantonness, unrestraint, eroticism, sybaritism, voluptuousness, sensuality **2** °prodigality, °extravagance, °excess, °waste, wastefulness, recklessness, exorbitance, lavishness, improvidence, squandering

profligate *adj.* **1** debauched, vice-ridden, °immoral, unprincipled, °sinful, °shameless, °evil, iniquitous, °wicked, dissipative, °dissolute, °degenerate, °loose, licentious, depraved, °corrupt, °promiscuous, °lecherous, °lascivious, °lewd, °indecent, °perverted, °carnal, °libertine, °wanton, unrestrained, °erotic, sybaritic, °voluptuous, °sensual, °wild, °abandoned **2** °extravagant, °prodigal, °wasteful, °reckless, squandering, °improvident, °spendthrift, °immoderate, °excessive *—n.* **3** debauchee, °sinner, °degenerate, °pervert, sodomite, °reprobate, °rake, rakehell, °libertine, lecher, whoremonger, °roué, °wanton, °sybarite, voluptuary, °sensualist **4** °prodigal, °spendthrift, °wastrel, waster, squanderer

profound *adj.* **1** °deep, unfathomable, abstruse, °recondite, arcane, esoteric, °intricate, knotty, °involved, °tricky, inscrutable, indecipherable, cabalistic, °incomprehensible, °obscure, °subtle, °occult, °secret, °cryptic, °puzzling, enigmatic, mystifying, °mysterious **2** °learned, °scholarly, °intellectual, erudite, discerning, °astute, sagacious, °sage, °wise, °penetrating, °sharp, °keen, insightful, analytical, °knowledgeable, °informed, °well-informed, well-read **3** °deep, °great, °intense, °sincere; °heartfelt, °keen, °acute, utter, °extreme, °overpowering, °overwhelming **4** utter, °complete, °total, °perfect, °absolute, °thorough, thoroughgoing, °out-and-out, °downright, consummate; °awful, °terrible

profoundly *adv.* °very, °extremely, °deeply, greatly, keenly, acutely, intensely, °sincerely; °terribly, °awfully

profundity *n.* **1** °depth, profoundness, abstruseness, reconditeness, arcaneness, intricacy, °subtlety, °complexity, complicatedness, °difficulty, inscrutability, inscrutableness, involvement, involvedness; indecipherability, incomprehensibility, incomprehensibleness, °obscurity **2** erudition, discernment, °scholarship, scholarliness, sagacity, °wisdom, sharpness, keenness, astuteness, acumen, insightfulness, knowledgeableness, knowledgeability

profuse *adj.* **1** °abundant, °ample, °plentiful, copious, unstinting, unsparing, ungrudging **2** °extravagant, °lavish, °bountiful, bounteous, °prolific, °luxuriant, °abundant, °exuberant, superabundant, °lush, °thick, teeming, overflowing, bursting, thriving, °productive, °fruitful, °rich **3** °excessive, copious, °considerable, °prolific, °liberal, °lavish, °free, °abundant, °ample **4** °generous, °abundant, °plentiful, copious, unsparing, °unselfish, unstinting, °exuberant, magnanimous, °liberal

profusion *n.* profuseness, °quantity, °abundance, °plenty, plentifulness, plenteousness, °bounty, copiousness, superabundance; °mass, °host, °hoard, °number, multitude, °lot, °mountain, °load, °mess, °stack, °pile, °heap, agglomeration, conglomeration, °accumulation, °wealth, °glut, °surplus, oversupply, °surfeit, plethora, °superfluity, *Formal* nimiety

progenitor *n.* **1** progenitrix, °ancestor, forefather, forebear **2** °predecessor, °forerunner, °precursor, antecedent, foregoer, °source, originator; °origin, °original, °prototype, archetype, °pattern, °guide

progeny *n.* °offspring, children, descendants, °issue, °young, °posterity, heirs, scions, successors, sons and daughters, *Colloq* kids, °spawn, fry, *US* sprouts

prognosis *n.* °forecast, forecasting, °prediction, °prophecy, prognostication, °projection

prognosticate *v.* **1** °predict, foretell, °prophesy, °forecast, presage, °divine, forebode **2** betoken, augur, herald, °foreshadow, foretoken, °announce, °harbinger, °signal, portend

program *n.* **1** °schedule, °plan, °scheme, agenda, order of the day, °routine, °protocol, slate, °list, listing, °description, °outline, °abstract, °précis, °calendar, menu, bill of fare, curriculum, syllabus, °synopsis, °summary, °prospectus **2** °performance, °production, °show, °presentation, (radio *or* television) play, telecast, °broadcast, °recital, concert **3** °proceedings, events, affairs, activities *—v.* **4** °organize, °arrange, prearrange, °plan, °lay out, map (out), °design, °formulate, °set (up), °schedule, °book, *US* slate

progress *n.* **1** °(forward) movement, going

forward, °progression, °advance, °headway, advancement **2** advancement, °advance, °promotion, °improvement, betterment, °elevation, °rise, °development, °furtherance **3** advancement, °course, °development, °growth, °expansion, °increase, °evolution, maturation, ripening, burgeoning *or* bourgeoning, amplification, enlargement, °spread, °extension, broadening, °promotion, °furtherance, °advance, °encouragement **4** ***in progress.*** °under way, °ongoing, °going on, °happening, occurring, taking place, at work, °in operation, being done, °proceeding, *Colloq* in the works —*v.* **5** °advance, move *or* go (forward(s) *or* onward(s)), °proceed, °continue, go *or* forge ahead, go *or* move along, make (one's) way, °make headway, °travel, go *or* push *or* press on **6** °advance, °improve, get well, get better, °develop, °grow, °expand, °increase, evolve, °mature, °ripen, burgeon *or* bourgeon, °amplify, °enlarge, °spread, °extend, broaden, °rise, move up, upgrade

progression *n.* **1** movement forward *or* forward movement, °advance, advancement, (making *or* gaining) headway, °progress, ascension, °rise, °elevation **2** °progress, °development, °advance, advancement, °spread, spreading, °extension, extending, broadening, enlargement, °headway, intensification, °rise **3** °order, °sequence, °succession, °train, °chain, concatenation, °course, °flow

progressive *adj.* **1** advancing, continuing, developing, increasing, growing, °ongoing, °continuous, °step by step, °gradual **2** reformist, revisionist, °liberal, °radical, °revolutionary, °avant-garde, advanced, °dynamic —*n.* **3** reformist, reformer, revisionist, °liberal, leftist, left-winger

prohibit *v.* **1** °bar, °ban, °forbid, disallow, interdict, °outlaw, °taboo, debar, proscribe **2** °prevent, °stop, °preclude, °rule out, °obstruct, °block, °impede, °hinder, °hamper, °inhibit, °frustrate, °foil, °thwart, °restrain, °check

prohibition *n.* **1** forbiddance, °barring, °bar, banning, °ban, disallowance, disallowing, interdiction, interdicting, outlawing, outlawry, °taboo, debarment, debarring, proscription, proscribing **2** °bar, interdict, °injunction, debarment, °embargo, proscription, °ban

prohibitive *adj.* **1** discouraging, suppressive, °repressive, restrictive, prohibitory, inhibitory, restraining **2** °excessive, °exorbitant, °outrageous, °dear, °high, °outlandish, °abusive, extortionate, insupportable, °criminal

project *n.* **1** °proposal, °plan, °scheme, °design, layout **2** °activity, °enterprise, °program, °undertaking, °venture, °assignment, commitment, °obligation, °contract, °engagement; °occupation, °job, °work —*v.* **3** °plan, °scheme, °prepare, °devise, conjure up, concoct, °think up, °contemplate, contrive, °invent, work up *or* out, °propose, °present, °outline, °design, °draft, °draw up, delineate, °describe, put forth *or* forward, *Colloq* cook up **4** °cast, °hurl, °fling, °throw, °toss, °launch, °propel, °discharge; °shoot, °transmit; *Colloq* chuck, °lob **5** jut out, °stick out, °protrude, °stand out, °bulge (out), °extend (out), poke out, beetle (out), °overhang **6** °estimate, °reckon, °calculate, °predict, °forecast

projectile *n.* °missile, °shell, bullet, °rocket

projection *n.* **1** °protrusion, protuberance, °bulge, °extension, °overhang, °ledge, flange; °ridge, eminence, °prominence, °spur, °crag, outcropping **2** °proposal, outlining, mapping, mapping-out, presenting, °presentation **3** °plan, °scheme, blueprint, °program, °design, °proposal, °outline, diagram, map, °representation, planning **4** °estimate, prognostication, °forecast, °prediction, °calculation, °reckoning

proliferate *v.* °grow, °increase, burgeon *or* bourgeon, multiply, mushroom, snowball; °breed, °reproduce

proliferation *n.* °growth, °increase, burgeoning *or* bourgeoning, °expansion, °spread, escalation, buildup, °rise

prolific *adj.* **1** °fertile, fecund, °productive, °fruitful, °abundant, copious, °bountiful, bounteous, °profuse, °plentiful, plenteous, °lush, °rich, rife **2** °productive, °creative, °fertile

prolong *v.* °extend, °lengthen, elongate, °stretch (out), draw *or* drag out, °drag (on), keep up, °string out, protract

promenade *n.* **1** °walk, °parade, esplanade, boulevard **2** °walk, °stroll, °saunter, °ramble, °turn, constitutional, airing, —*v.* **3** °walk, °stroll, °saunter, amble, °ramble, °parade, perambulate, take a walk *or* stroll **4** °flaunt, °show (off), °display, °parade, °strut

prominence *n.* **1** °celebrity, eminence, °fame, °distinction, notability, °reputation, °preeminence, °standing, °position, °rank, °prestige, °renown, repute, °importance, °weight, °influence, °account, °name, consequence **2** °hill, hillock, °rise, hummock, outcrop, outcropping, °spur, tor, °crag, arête, °spine, °ridge, °peak, °mount, °pinnacle; headland, °point, promontory **3** protuberance, °projection, °protrusion, °growth, excrescence, °swelling, tumefaction, tumescence, extrusion, outshoot, outgrowth, °spur, °bulge

prominent *adj.* **1** °conspicuous, °obvious, °evident, recognizable, °pronounced, °discernible, distinguishable, identifiable, °noticeable, °remarkable, °noteworthy, eye-catching, °striking, °outstanding, °chief, °main, °principal, °significant, °important; °apparent, unmistakable *or* unmistakeable, °patent, °glaring, °salient, °flagrant, egregious **2** °eminent, °preeminent, °distinguished, °notable, °noteworthy, °noted, °leading, °foremost, °first, °outstanding, °well-known, famed, °illustrious, °famous, °celebrated, °renowned, acclaimed, honored, °honorable, respected, °well-thought-of, °prestigious, °reputable, creditable **3** °protuberant, protruding, protrusive, projecting, jutting (out); excrescent, bulging, raised, °elevated

promiscuous *adj.* **1** °indiscriminate, undiscriminating, unselective, nonselective, nondiscriminatory, unconscientious, °heedless, °haphazard, °indifferent, uncaring, uncritical, unfussy, unfastidious, disregardful, neglectful, negligent, °slipshod, slovenly, °irresponsible, °careless, °cursory, °perfunctory, °unthinking, °thoughtless, unconsidered **2** °lax, °loose, °unchaste, °wanton, °wild, °uninhibited, unrestrained, ungoverned, °uncontrolled, unbridled, uncurbed, °immoderate, °abandoned, amoral, °immoral, °indecent, °libertine, licentious, dissipated, °dissolute, depraved, °profligate, debauched, °fast; unfaithful, °faithless, °dishonorable **3** °mixed, °miscellaneous, heterogeneous, °random, intermixed, jumbled, °disorderly, disordered, °confused, °chaotic, motley, intermixed, intermingled, scrambled, unorganized, disorganized, unsystematic, unsystematized, °helter-skelter, higgledy-piggledy, hotchpotch *or US also* hodgepodge

promise *n.* **1** °assurance, °(solemn) word (of honor), °pledge, °vow, °oath, °undertaking, °engagement, °bond, commitment, guaranty, °guarantee, °warranty; °agreement, °contract, covenant, °compact **2** °expectation, °potential, °capability; °likelihood, °probability —*v.* **3** °assure, give one's word (of honor), °pledge, °swear, °vow, take an oath, °undertake, °engage, °commit oneself, guarantee *or* guaranty, °warrant, cross one's heart (and hope to die) **4** give indication of, hint at, °suggest, foretell, augur, °indicate, show signs of, be in store for, look like, seem *or* appear likely *or* probable, *Brit* be on the cards, *US* be in the cards, *Literary* bid fair, betoken, bespeak

promising *adj.* °hopeful, encouraging, °favorable, auspicious, °positive, °rosy, °optimistic, °propitious, cheering, full of promise, reassuring, heartening

promote *v.* **1** °help, °further, °encourage, °assist, °advance, °support, °forward, °back, °sanction, °abet, °aid, °boost, °foster, °patronize, nurture, °develop, inspirit, °strengthen, °stimulate, °inspire **2** °advance, move up, °raise, upgrade, elevate, °exalt, *Colloq* kick upstairs **3** °recommend, °endorse, °sponsor, °support, espouse, commend, °advocate, °advance, °champion, °speak for, °side with, °present, call attention to **4** advertise, °publicize, °push, °sell, *Colloq* beat the drum for, °plug, *Slang* hype, *Chiefly US* ballyhoo

promotion *n.* **1** °furtherance, advancement, °advance, °encouragement, °support, °backing, °sanction, sanctioning, abetting, aiding, °helping, assisting, boosting, fostering, nurturing, cultivation, °development, developing, °improvement, improving, °inspiration, inspiriting, strengthening, stimulation, °stimulating **2** advancement, °advance, upgrading, upgrade, °rise, °elevation, preferment, exaltation **3** promoting, °recommendation, °presentation, espousal, commendation, advocacy, championing **4** advertising, publicity, public relations, °propaganda, selling, hard *or* soft sell, °fanfare, plugging, *Colloq* puffery, *Slang* (media) hype, *Chiefly US* ballyhoo, hoopla **5** °advertisement, advertising, °circular, °brochure, handbill, °bill, handout, °leaflet, °poster, *affiche,* placard, publicity, °space, °(publicity) release, *US and Canadian* flier *or* flyer, billboard, broadside, *Colloq US* puff piece, poop sheet

prompt *adj.* **1** °quick, °ready, °immediate, instantaneous, °unhesitating, °rapid, °fast, °swift, °speedy, °punctual, °timely, °on time, °instant, °summary, °brisk, alacritous **2** °alert, °eager, °ready, °quick, °expeditious, ready and willing, °disposed, predisposed, °unhesitating, °keen, avid —*v.* **3** °urge, egg (on), °prod, °nudge, °spur, exhort, °incite, °induce, impel, °provoke, °rouse, °arouse, °encourage, work *or* stir *or* fire up, °move, °motivate, °cause, °influence, put (someone) up to (something), °coax, °persuade, °cajole, prevail upon *or* on, talk (someone) into (something) **4** °cue, °remind, feed lines (to), °help **5** °bring about, °inspire, °occasion, °give rise to, °elicit, °evoke, °provoke, °call forth, °stimulate, °awaken —*n.* **6** °reminder, °cue, °hint, stimulus

promptly *adv.* °quickly, °at once, straightaway *or* straight away, °directly, right away, °immediately, without delay *or* hesitation, unhesitatingly, °swiftly, speedily, °readily, instantly, °instantaneously, punctually, expeditiously, with celerity, with alacrity, *Colloq US and Canadian* momentarily

prone *adj.* **1** face down *or* downward(s), °prostrate, lying down, reclining, °recumbent, °horizontal, procumbent, *Formal or technical* decumbent, accumbent **2** °inclined, apt, °likely, °liable, °disposed, predisposed, of a mind, °subject, °given, tending, °leaning

pronounce *v.* **1** °declare, utter, °say, °voice, °express, articulate, °enunciate, vocalize, put into words **2** °declare, affirm, °proclaim, °announce, °decree, °judge, aver, °state, asseverate, assert, say to be **3** °announce, °proclaim, promulgate, °publicize, °publish, °deliver, °broadcast, °make known, let (something) be known, put out *or* forth, °set forth; °pass

pronounced *adj.* **1** definite, °clear, °plain, well-defined, °decided, °conspicuous, °noticeable, recognizable, identifiable, °obvious, °striking, °prominent, °notable, °distinct, unmistakable *or* unmistakeable, °marked, strong **2** definite, °distinct, unequivocal, unambiguous, °specific, °unqualified, °undisguised, °downright, °outright, °out-and-out, °decided, °complete, °total, °unmitigated, °strong, utter, unalloyed, unmixed, °clear, clear-cut, unmistakable *or* unmistakeable

pronouncement *n.* **1** °statement, °assertion, °observation, °comment, °opinion, °announcement, °proclamation, pronunciamento, manifesto, °declaration, avowal, affirmation, asseveration, averment, promulgation 2 °judgment, °decree, edict, °proclamation, dictum, °command, ukase, (papal) bull, °imperative, °order, ordinance

pronunciation *n.* enunciation, articulation, elocution, °diction, °speech, speech pattern, manner of speaking, °delivery, °accent, accentuation, °intonation, inflection, modulation

proof *n.* **1** °evidence, verification, corroboration, confirmation, validation, authentication, ratification, substantiation; documentation, °document, °facts, °data, certification, °testimony, *Colloq* ammunition **2** °test, °trial, measure, °standard, °touchstone, criterion *—adj.* **3** impervious, impenetrable, able to withstand *or* resist, °protective, °strong, °tough, °impregnable, °resistant, tempered

prop *v.* **1** Often, ***prop up.*** °support, °brace, °hold (up), °buttress, °stay, °bolster, °uphold, °bear, °sustain, shore up, keep up **2** °lean, °stand, °rest *—n.* **3** °support, °brace, truss, °stay, °buttress, °mainstay, °upright, vertical, shore

propaganda *n.* **1** agitprop, disinformation, newspeak, rumors, lies **2** advertising, °promotion, publicity, public relations, °puff, °fanfare, *Colloq* puffery, ballyhoo, *Slang* hype, *US* hoopla, whoop-de-do *or* whoop-de-doo

propagate *v.* **1** °breed, °generate, °reproduce, multiply, °proliferate, °deliver, °bring forth, °bear, procreate **2** multiply, °increase, °spread, °grow, °develop **3** °publicize, °promote, disseminate, °dispense, °distribute, °spread, °publish, °broadcast, °circulate, °make known, °transmit, °disperse, propagandize, °proclaim, promulgate, bruit about, noise abroad, herald

propel *v.* °drive, impel, °move, actuate, set in motion, get moving, °push, °thrust, °force, °send, °launch, °start

proper *adj.* **1** °right, °appropriate, apropos, apt, °suitable, °fit, °fitting, °befitting, °becoming, suited, apposite, *de rigueur, comme il faut,* adapted, *Literary* °meet **2** °correct, °accurate, °exact, °right, °precise, °orthodox, °formal, expected, °normal, °usual, accepted, established, *Old-fashioned Brit* tickety-boo **3** °decorous, °dignified, °genteel, °fitting, °right, *de rigueur,* °appropriate, °becoming, suitable, °decent, °seemly, °due, °correct, apt, *comme il faut,* conformist; gentlemanly, °ladylike, °polite, °refined, punctilious, °respectable **4** °fitting, °suitable, °correct, °right, °satisfactory, °good, °sensible **5** °complete, °perfect, utter, °thorough, thoroughgoing, °out-and-out, °unmitigated **6** own, °individual, °separate, °distinct, °correct, °specific, °special, °particular, °respective; °characteristic, °distinctive, °peculiar, °singular, °unique *—quasi-adv.* **7** strictly speaking *or* so called, in the strict(est) *or* narrow(est) sense, °only, solely, °alone, on (its *or* someone's) own

properly *adv.* **1** °appropriately, fittingly, correctly, °well, becomingly, suitably, politely, decently, decorously, nicely **2** °duly, °appropriately, °well, suitably, rightly, correctly, aptly

property *n.* **1** °possessions, °belongings, °effects, °gear, °paraphernalia, °goods, chattels **2** °assets, °means, °resources, holdings, °capital (goods), °fortune, °riches, °estate, °worth **3** °land, acreage, realty, real estate *or* property **4** °characteristic, °attribute, °quality, °feature, °trait, °mark, °hallmark, idiosyncrasy, °peculiarity, °oddity, °quirk, *Formal* haecceity, quiddity

prophecy *n.* **1** forecasting, foretelling, °prediction, fortunetelling, divination, soothsaying, augury, prognostication, crystal gazing, *Formal* vaticination **2** °prediction, °forecast, °prognosis, °revelation

prophesy *v.* **1** °predict, foretell, °forecast, forewarn, °prognosticate, vaticinate **2** augur, foretell (of), presage, °foreshadow, portend, °bode, °harbinger, herald, °promise, vaticinate

prophet *n.* prophetess, °oracle, forecaster, °seer, soothsayer, clairvoyant, prognosticator, °fortuneteller, augur, diviner, °witch, warlock, sibyl, haruspex, vaticinator; (of doom) Cassandra

prophetic *adj.* predictive, prognostic, divinatory, oracular, inspired, prescient, sibylline, *Literary* fatidic, vatic

propitiatory *adj.* **1** conciliatory, pacifying, appeasing, expiatory, placative, propitiative, pacificatory, placatory **2** deferential, °ingratiating, °obliging, obeisant, acquiescent, compliant, °tractable

propitious *adj.* °advantageous, °timely, °well-timed, °opportune, °lucky, °fortunate, °happy, °providential, °favorable, °bright, encouraging, auspicious, °promising, °rosy

proponent *n.* proposer, promoter, °supporter, upholder, °backer, subscriber, °patron, espouser, adherent, °enthusiast, °champion, °friend, °partisan, defender, °advocate, exponent, pleader, apologist, spokesman, spokeswoman, spokesperson

proportion *n.* **1** °ratio, °(comparative) relation, °relationship, °comparison **2** °balance, °agreement, concord, °harmony, suitableness, °symmetry, congruity, correspondence, correlation, °arrangement, °distribution **3** °portion, °division, °share, °part, °percentage, °quota, °allotment, °ration, *Colloq* °cut **4** ***proportions.*** °size, °magnitude, dimensions, measurements, °extent; °volume, °capacity, °mass, °bulk, °area, °expanse, °scope, °range, °degree *—v.* **5** °adjust, °modify, °change, °modulate, °poise, °balance, °shape, °fit, °match, °conform, equate

proportional *adj.* proportionate, proportioned, comparable, analogous, analogical, °relative, °related, correlated, balanced, °symmetrical, corresponding, compatible,

°harmonious, °consistent, commensurate, in accordance with

proposal *n.* **1** °offer, °presentation, °bid, °tender, °proposition, °recommendation, °suggestion, *Literary* proffer **2** °plan, °scheme, °outline, °draft, °design, layout; °program, °proposition, °project

propose *v.* **1** °offer, °tender, proffer; °present, °introduce, °submit, °advance, °set forth, °put forward, °propound, °bid, °recommend, °suggest, come up with, call attention to, °broach, *Brit* °table **2** °offer, °mean, °intend, °plan, °expect, °aim **3** °nominate, °name, put forward *or* forth, °suggest, °introduce, °submit, °put up

proposition *n.* **1** See **proposal, 1,** above. **2** See **proposal, 2,** above. —*v.* **3** accost, °solicit, make an indecent *or* sexual advance *or* proposal *or* overture, *Colloq* make a pass at

propound *v.* put *or* set forth *or* forward, °propose, °offer, proffer, °suggest, postulate

proprietor *n.* **1** proprietress, °owner, landowner, °landlady, °landlord, landholder, titleholder, deedholder, property owner **2** °owner, °partner, °landlord, restaurateur, innkeeper, hotelkeeper, hotelier, licensee, °manager, *Brit* publican

propriety *n.* **1** correctness, properness, conformity, suitableness, appropriateness, suitability, aptness, °fitness, seemliness, °decorum; advisability, °wisdom **2** °protocol, good *or* proper form, punctilio, °etiquette, politeness, °courtesy, politesse, °refinement, sedateness, °dignity, modesty, °decorum, decency, °breeding, respectability, gentility, °grace, mannerliness **3** ***the proprieties.*** the social graces, the amenities, the civilities, formality *or* the formalities, social convention *or* the social conventions, social procedure *or* codes, accepted practice, °tradition, °ceremony, °ritual

propulsion *n.* °drive, impulse, °impetus, °thrust, °power, driving *or* propelling *or* propulsive force, °pressure, °momentum, °push

prosaic *adj.* °dull, °banal, overdone, °tedious, clichéd, commonplace, stereotyped, °pedestrian, °flat, stereotypical, hackneyed, °stock, °routine, °everyday, °ordinary, °common, workaday, °mediocre, °undistinguished, °bland, characterless, °homely, °plain, trite, °stale, °threadbare, °tired, °lifeless, °dead, °dry, jejune, °boring, °tiresome, unimaginative, unpoetic, unromantic, uninspiring, uninspired, insipid, uninteresting, °humdrum, °monotonous, *Literary ennuyant, Colloq* ho-hum, °run-of-the-mill, °moldy

prose *n.* °(expository) writing, °text, °language

prosecute *v.* **1** arraign, °indict, °charge, put on *or* bring to trial, °try, take to court, °sue, bring suit *or* action against, °accuse, *Brit* put in the dock **2** °pursue, follow up *or* through, see *or* carry through, °persist, go on with **3** carry on *or* out, °perform, do, °exercise, °conduct, °follow, °engage in, °practice, °continue

prospect *n.* **1** °view, °scene, panorama, °landscape, seascape, °outlook, vista, °sight, °spectacle, °perspective, °aspect **2** °anticipation, contemplation, °outlook, °promise, °plan, °design, °intention, expectancy, °expectation, °thought, °likelihood **3** Often, ***prospects.*** °future, °outlook, chance(s), hope(s), possibility *or* possibilities, °likelihood, opportunity *or* opportunities **4** ***in prospect.*** in sight *or* view, in the offing, on the horizon, in store, °in the wind, projected, °likely, °probable, °possible, *Brit* on the cards, on the table, *US* °in the cards —*v.* **5** Often, ***prospect for.*** °explore, °search (for), °look (for)

prospective *adj.* anticipated, expected, awaited, looked-for, °future, °forthcoming, coming, approaching, °imminent, nearing, °pending, °impending, °destined, °potential, incipient

prospectus *n.* °announcement, °plan, °scheme, °program, °outline, conspectus, °description

prosper *v.* °flourish, °thrive, °succeed, fare well, °progress, °get ahead, °grow, °develop; °profit, °gain, become wealthy, grow rich, make one's fortune, °make good, *Colloq* °make it, make one's pile

prosperity *n.* °success, °(good) fortune, °wealth, °riches, affluence, °money, °luxury, °plenty, prosperousness, opulence, °bounty, *Colloq* life of Riley

prosperous *adj.* **1** °rich, °wealthy, moneyed *or* monied, affluent, well-to-do, °well-off, *Colloq* well-heeled, °loaded, °flush, °in the money, rolling in it *or* wealth *or* money, in clover, on Easy Street, *Slang* stinking rich **2** °successful, thriving, °flourishing, booming, prospering

prostitute *n.* **1** whore, call girl, streetwalker, strumpet, trollop, harlot, lady of the night *or US also* evening, fallen *or* loose woman, demimondaine, cocotte, *fille de joie,* painted woman, woman of ill repute, camp follower, *Archaic* catamite, *Literary* hetaira *or* hetaera, courtesan *or* courtezan, *Brit* rent boy, toy boy, *US* boy toy, *Archaic* bawd, quean, trull, cotquean, *Colloq* °tart, hustler, *Slang* pro, moll, *Brit* °brass, hooker, *US* bimbo, working girl, chippy *or* chippie, roundheels —*v.* **2** Often, ***prostitute oneself.*** °degrade, demean, °lower, cheapen, °debase, °profane, defile, °desecrate, °pervert, °abuse, °misuse, devalue, *Colloq* °sell out

prostitution *n.* **1** whoredom, harlotry, the oldest profession, Mrs. Warren's profession, streetwalking, °vice **2** °degradation, debasement, profanation, defilement, desecration, °misuse, °abuse, devaluation, lowering, °perversion, corruption

prostrate *v.* **1** Usually, ***prostrate oneself.*** lie down, °kowtow, °bow (down), °bow and scrape, grovel, kneel, fall to *or* on one's knees, °truckle, °crawl, °cringe, °submit, abase oneself **2** °overwhelm, °overcome,

°overpower, °crush, lay *or* bring low, °paralyze, °fell, bowl over, °floor, bring down, °humble, make helpless, °ruin; °exhaust, °fatigue, °weary, wear down *or* out, °tire (out) *—adj.* **3** °prone, °horizontal, lying down, laid low, stretched out, procumbent, °recumbent, *Formal or technical* accumbent, decumbent **4** overwhelmed, °overcome, overpowered, crushed, brought *or* laid low, paralyzed, felled, bowled over, brought down, humbled, °helpless, ruined, brought to one's knees, °powerless, °impotent, °defenseless, disarmed, *Colloq* floored **5** °exhausted, drained, °fatigued, °spent, worn-out, wearied, °weary, °tired (out), dead tired, dog-tired, played out, *Colloq* fagged out, knocked out, all in, °beat, bushed, *US* wiped out, *Slang* shagged out, *US and Canadian* pooped (out)

prostration *n.* **1** genuflection *or Brit also* genuflexion, kowtowing, °kowtow, kneeling, bowing, °bow, salaaming, salaam, °submission **2** °servility, °veneration, °worship, °humiliation, °respect, adulation, °deference, °obeisance, °homage **3** °despair, °misery, °desolation, °desperation, dejection, °depression, despondency, wretchedness, unhappiness, °grief, °woe, woefulness **4** weariness, °exhaustion, °weakness, debility, feebleness, enervation, lassitude, paralysis, °collapse, °breakdown

protagonist *n.* **1** °hero, °heroine, antihero, antiheroine, °principal, leading character; °lead, leading role, title role **2** °leader, °supporter, °advocate, °backer, prime mover, moving spirit, °champion, °mainstay, standard-bearer, exponent

protean *adj.* °variable, ever-changing, multiform, mutable, °changeable, labile, polymorphous *or* polymorphic, kaleidoscopic

protect *v.* **1** °defend, °guard, °safeguard, keep safe, °shield, °cover, °screen **2** °care for, °preserve, °keep, °shelter, watch over, °safeguard, °take care of, °conserve, take under one's wing, °foster, nurture, °tend, °mind

protection *n.* **1** °defense, °screen, °shield, °barrier, °guard, °safeguard, °immunity, °bulwark, buffer, °shelter, °refuge, haven, °sanctuary, °security, °safekeeping, °safety, °preservation **2** °care, guardianship, aegis, °custody, °charge, °safekeeping, °patronage, sponsorship, keeping **3** extortion, °blackmail, protection money

protective *adj.* defensive, °jealous, °vigilant, watchful, heedful, °careful, °possessive; preservative, shielding, sheltering, safeguarding

protector *n.* protectress, defender, °benefactor, benefactress, °patron, patroness, °guardian (angel), °champion, knight in shining armor, paladin, bodyguard, *Slang Brit* °minder

protégé *n.* protégée, °ward, °charge, dependant; °discovery, °student, °pupil

protest *n.* **1** °objection, °opposition, °complaint, grumble, °grievance, dissent, °disapproval, protestation, °exception, °disagreement, demur *or* demurral, demurrer, disclaimer, °denial, °scruple, °compunction, °qualm, *Colloq* °gripe, grouse, °squawk, *US* °kick, *Slang* beef, °bitch **2** ***under protest.*** unwillingly, reluctantly, involuntarily *—v.* **3** °object, °oppose, °complain, grumble, dissent, °disapprove, take exception, take issue with, °disagree, demur, disclaim, °deny, °scruple, *Colloq* °gripe, grouse, °squawk, *Brit* °kick (against), *US* °kick, *Slang* beef, °bitch **4** assert, °confirm, °declare, aver, asseverate, affirm, °announce, °profess, insist on, avow, avouch

protocol *n.* **1** rule(s) *or* code(s) *or* standard(s) of behavior *or* conduct, convention(s), custom(s), °diplomacy, °formality, formalities, °form, °etiquette, politesse, °manners, °practice, °usage, °authority **2** °treaty, °pact, °compact, covenant, °agreement, concordat; °memorandum, °minute, °note, °draft, °outline

prototype *n.* **1** °model, archetype, °first, °original, °pattern, exemplar, °precedent, °mold **2** °example, °instance, °illustration, °sample, °norm, °paragon, °epitome, °model, °standard, analogue, referent, °metaphor

protracted *adj.* °long, long-drawn-out, interminable, prolonged, overlong, never-ending, extended, stretched-out, marathon, °endless, °everlasting, long-winded

protrude *v.* °stick out, °jut (out), °project, °extend, poke out, °stand out, thrust out *or* forward, °start (from), exsert, *Rare* extrude; °bulge, balloon, °bag (out), belly (out); °(of the eyes) pop, goggle, *Colloq US* °bug (out)

protrusion *n.* °projection, protuberance, °prominence, °swelling, excrescence, tumescence, °bump, °lump, °knob, °bulge; (condition of the eyes) *Technical* exophthalmic goiter

protuberant *adj.* protrusive, protruding, bulging, gibbous, jutting, bulbous, °swelling, °swollen, turgid, tumescent, distended, tumid, extrusive, excrescent, extruding, projecting, beetling, overhanging, °prominent

proud *adj.* **1** Often, ***proud of.*** pleased (with), satisfied (with), contented (with), °glad (about), happy (with *or* about), delighted (with *or* about), elated (with *or* about); honored, gratified **2** °conceited, °boastful, self-satisfied, narcissistic, °self-important, °egotistical, °vain, vainglorious, prideful, self-centered, complacent, °snobbish, °haughty, °supercilious, °smug, °arrogant, °cocky, cocksure, °boastful, °braggart, *Colloq* high and mighty, snooty, stuck-up, *Slang* snotty, *Brit* toffee-nosed **3** °lofty, °dignified, lordly, °noble, °great, respected, honored, °honorable, °important, °glorious, august, °illustrious, °estimable, creditable, °eminent, °prominent, °distinguished, °reputable, °worthy, °notable, °noted, °noteworthy **4** °stately, °majestic, °magnificent, °splendid, °grand

prove *v.* **1** °verify, °authenticate, °confirm, °make good, corroborate, °demonstrate,

°show, validate, °establish, °substantiate, °certify, affirm; °support, °sustain, °back (up), °uphold **2** °try, °test, °examine, °check, °analyze, assay **3** °turn out, be found, be shown, be established, end up; °develop, °result **4** °show, evince, °demonstrate

provender *n.* **1** °provisions, °food, supplies, victuals, °rations, foodstuffs, groceries, eatables, edibles, comestibles, aliment, °nourishment, °sustenance, *Colloq* grub, eats **2** fodder, forage, °feed, hay, silage, corn, °grain

proverb *n.* saying, °maxim, aphorism, °saw, adage, apophthegm *or* apothegm, axiom, °moral, moralism, homily, dictum, gnome, °epigram; commonplace, platitude, °truism, °cliché, chestnut, bromide

proverbial *adj.* **1** axiomatic, aphoristic, °epigrammatic, apophthegmatic *or* apothegmatic, homiletic, moralistic; acknowledged, °well-known, accepted, °time-honored, °traditional **2** °typical, archetypal, °exemplary

provide *v.* **1** °supply, °furnish, °equip, °outfit, fix up (with) provision, °contribute, °accommodate, purvey, °cater, °stock (up), victual, °provender **2** °produce, °yield, °afford, °lend, °give, °present, °offer, °accord **3** °stipulate, °lay down, °require, °demand, °specify, °state **4** ***provide for.*** °look after, °care for, °support, °take care of, take under one's wing, °minister to, °attend (to) **5** ***provide for or against.*** arrange for, prepare for, °anticipate, forearm, make *or* get ready for, plan for, take precautions, take measures

providence *n.* **1** °foresight, °forethought, °preparation, °anticipation, °readiness, farsightedness, °caution, °precaution, °discretion, °prudence, °care; °thrift, frugality, husbandry, thriftiness, °conservation, °economy **2** Usually, ***(divine) Providence.*** °protection, °care, °concern, beneficence, °direction, °control, divine intervention, °guidance; °destiny, °fate, °lot, °fortune, karma, kismet

provident *adj.* **1** °cautious, °wary, °discreet, canny, °prudent, °careful, °vigilant, °prepared, °farsighted, °thoughtful, °wise, °shrewd, sagacious, °sage, °judicious **2** °frugal, economic(al), °thrifty, °prudent

providential *adj.* °fortunate, °lucky, blessed, felicitous, °happy, °opportune, °timely

providing *conj.* Sometimes, ***providing that.*** provided (that), on (the) condition (that), if (only), only if, as long as, °in the event (that), with the proviso (that), °in case, with the understanding (that)

province *n.* **1** °territory, °state, °zone, °region, °quarter, °area, °district, °domain, dependency *or US also* dependancy, °division, °section, °district **2** °country, °territory, °region, °dominion, °realm, strand, °tract **3** sphere *or* area (of responsibility), °responsibility, bailiwick, °concern, °function, °charge, °business, °field; *Colloq* °thing, °headache, °worry **4** ***provinces.*** outlying districts, countryside, hinterland(s), *Chiefly US* exurbia, *Slang US and Canadian* boondocks, boonies, hicksville

provincial *adj.* **1** °local, regional **2** uncultured, uncultivated, °unsophisticated, °limited, °uninformed, naive *or* naïve *or* naïf, °innocent, °ingenuous, unpolished, °unrefined, °homespun, °rustic, °rude, °country, °parochial, insular, °narrow-minded, °boorish, loutish, cloddish, °awkward, °ungraceful, oafish, backwoods, *Brit* parish pump, *US* small-town, *Colloq US and Canadian* hick, hick-town —*n.* **3** °rustic, country cousin, (country) bumpkin, yokel, *US and Canadian* out-of-towner, hick, hayseed

provincialism *n.* **1** dialectalism, localism, regionalism; °idiom, patois, °dialect **2** narrow-mindedness, insularity, parochialism, narrowness, benightedness; unsophisticatedness, °simplicity, lack of awareness, naivety *or* naiveté *or* naïveté, ingenuousness, innocence, °inexperience

provision *n.* **1** °providing, supplying, furnishing; catering, victualing, provisioning, purveyance, purveying, furnishing, equipping, fitting out, outfitting, accoutrement *or US also* accouterment, °equipment **2** °stipulation, °proviso, °condition, °restriction, °qualification, clause, °term, °exception, °demand, °requirement, °prerequisite, *Colloq* °catch, °string, *US* hooker **3** °preparation, prearrangement, °arrangement, °measures, °steps **4** Usually, ***provisions.*** supplies, stores, stockpile, stock(s), °quantity; °food, foodstuffs, eatables, edibles, drinkables, potables, victuals, viands, comestibles, °rations, groceries, °provender, °staples —*v.* **5** stockpile, °stock, °supply, victual, °cater, purvey

provisional *adj.* **1** °temporary, interim, provisionary, transitional, °stopgap, *Colloq* pro tem **2** conditional, contingent, provisory, °qualified, stipulatory, provisionary, probationary

proviso *n.* See **provision, 2,** above.

provocation *n.* **1** °grounds, °reason, °cause, justification, instigation, °initiation, °incitement, stimulus, °incentive, motivation, °motive, °inducement **2** °insult, °offense, °taunt, irritation

provocative *adj.* **1** °inviting, alluring, °tempting, charming, tantalizing, teasing, intriguing, fascinating, °seductive, °stimulating, °voluptuous, °sensual, °sensuous, °suggestive, °erotic, arousing, °exciting, entrancing, °irresistible, bewitching, *Colloq* °sexy **2** irritating, annoying, galling, °irksome, nettlesome, harassing, plaguing, exasperating, infuriating, angering, incensing, maddening, enraging, vexing, vexatious, disquieting, challenging, upsetting, distressing, °disturbing, °outrageous, wounding, stinging, °offensive, humiliating, mortifying

provoke *v.* **1** °stir (up), °stimulate, °move, °motivate, °push, impel, °drive, °get, °spur (on), egg on, goad, °force, compel, °prompt,

°rouse, °arouse, waken, °awaken, °enliven, °animate, °activate, °induce, °encourage **2** °start, °incite, instigate, °produce, °promote, °foment, °kindle, °work up **3** °irritate, °annoy, °irk, °pester, vex, pique, °anger, °enrage, °madden, incense, °infuriate, °gall, rile, nettle, °harass, hector, °plague, badger, °exasperate, get on one's nerves, try one's patience, °frustrate, °upset, °disturb, °perturb, °distress, °outrage, °offend, °insult, affront

prowess *n.* **1** °ability, °skill, skillfulness, °aptitude, adroitness, °dexterity, dexterousness, adeptness, °facility, °finesse, °expertise, mastery, °genius, °talent, know-how, °ingenuity, °capability, °proficiency **2** °bravery, valor, °courage, boldness, °daring, intrepidity, dauntlessness, mettle, stoutheartedness, valiance, lionheartedness, fearlessness, gallantry, doughtiness, °fortitude

prowl *v.* **1** °lurk, °sneak, skulk, °steal, °slink **2** °scour, scavenge, range over, rove, °roam, °patrol, °cruise, °cover —*n.* **3** *on the prowl.* lurking *or* sneaking *or* skulking *or* stealing *or* slinking about *or* around, searching, seeking, hunting, tracking, stalking

proximity *n.* nearness, closeness, adjacency, °neighborhood, °vicinity, vicinage, contiguity, contiguousness, propinquity

proxy *n.* °substitute, °agent, °delegate, surrogate, °representative, °factor

prude *n.* °prig, °puritan, Mrs. Grundy, *Colloq* °goody-goody, *US* bluenose

prudence *n.* **1** °discretion, °wisdom, sagacity, °judgment, °discrimination, common sense, canniness, °presence of mind, awareness, wariness, °care, °tact, carefulness, °caution, cautiousness, circumspection, watchfulness, °vigilance, heedfulness **2** planning, °preparation, °preparedness, foresightedness, °forethought, °foresight, °providence, °precaution, farsightedness; °economy, husbandry, °thrift, (good *or* careful) management

prudent *adj.* **1** °careful, °cautious, °discreet, discerning, °wise, °sage, sagacious, °politic, °judicious, °discriminating, °sensible, °reasonable, canny, °shrewd, circumspect, watchful, °vigilant, heedful, °wary, °attentive, °alert, °guarded **2** °provident, °thrifty, economic(al), °frugal, prudential

prudery *n.* prudishness, priggishness, puritanicalness, puritanism, squeamishness, Grundyism, primness, stuffiness, oldmaidishness, precisianism

prudish *adj.* °priggish, puritanical, oldmaidish, °prissy, prim, °fussy, °squeamish, °strait-laced, °stiff, °rigid, overnice, overmodest, overcoy, °proper, demure, °decorous, °formal, *Colloq* oldmaidish

prune *v.* °clip, °cut back, °lop, °dock, °pare (down), °trim

prurient *adj.* **1** libidinous, °lecherous, °lascivious, °lewd, lubricious *or* lubricous, salacious, °lustful, concupiscent, licentious, °carnal, debauched, rakehell, °sensual, °randy, °voluptuous, °loose, goatish, ruttish, *Literary* Cyprian, Paphian, *Archaic* lickerish *or* liquorish, *Slang* horny, °hot **2** °dirty, °lewd, °filthy, °pornographic, smutty, °obscene, °foul, °scurrilous, °vile, °indecent, °gross, °lurid, °blue, °bawdy, ribald, titillating, °suggestive, °coarse, °vulgar, °low, °crude, *Literary* Fescennine

pry *v.* **1** °investigate, ferret about, °examine, °peer, °peek, be inquisitive, inquire *or* enquire **2** °intrude, °meddle, °interfere, *Colloq* poke *or* stick one's nose in *or* into, °snoop, be nosy, nose about *or* around, poke about *or* around

pseudonym *n.* nom de plume, nom de guerre, alias, pen name, stage name, °incognito

psyche *n.* °soul, °spirit, °mind, *élan vital,* divine spark, life force, anima, self, °subconscious, °unconscious, °personality, °(essential) nature, inner man *or* woman *or* person, *Philosophy* pneuma

psychic *adj.* **1** psychical, °mental, °spiritual, psychologic(al), °subjective, psychogenic, cognitive, metaphysic(al), °intellectual, cerebral; philosophic(al) **2** psychical, extrasensory, °supernatural, °occult, magical, telepathic, telekinetic, preternatural, spiritualistic, °unearthly, extramundane, supermundane —*n.* **3** °medium, spiritualist, clairvoyant, mindreader, telepathist, °seer, seeress, crystal gazer, soothsayer, astrologer, °fortuneteller, °prophet, prophetess, sibyl

psychological *adj.* °mental, °intellectual, cerebral, cognitive, psychic(al), °spiritual, °subjective, °subconscious, °unconscious, °subliminal, psychogenic; philosophic(al)

psychology *n.* °(mental) makeup, constitution, °attitude, °behavior, thought processes, °thinking, °psyche, °nature, feeling(s), emotion(s), °rationale, °reasoning

psychotic *adj.* **1** °mad, °insane, psychopathic, °deranged, demented, lunatic, paranoiac *or* paranoid, °abnormal, °unbalanced, (mentally) ill *or esp. US* sick, °disturbed, *non compos mentis,* of unsound mind, °exceptional, certifiable, °daft, unhinged, °raving, *Slang* °crazy, nuts, nutty, loony *or* looney *or* luny, off one's rocker *or* trolley *or* chump *or* head, cracked, crackbrained, °mental, out to lunch, batty, bats, having bats in one's belfry, having a screw loose, not all there, touched (in the head), bonkers —*n.* **2** °madman, madwoman, °maniac, psychopath, lunatic, paranoid *or* paranoiac, schizophrenic, bedlamite, *Slang* nut, nutter, screwball, crackpot, °crazy, loony *or* looney *or* luny, schizo, *US* kook

pub *n.* public house, alehouse, tavern, inn, °bar, cocktail lounge, saloon, taproom, hostelry, *Brit* saloon *or* lounge bar, *US* barroom, *Colloq Brit* °local, *Slang* boozer, watering hole, °joint, °dive, *Chiefly Brit* gin palace, *US* barrelhouse, gin mill, honky-tonk

puberty *n.* pubescence, sexual maturity, adolescence, juvenescence, teens; nubility

public *adj.* **1** communal, community, °common, °general, collective, °universal, °catholic, °popular, worldwide **2** °civil, civic, °social, societal, community, communal **3** °accessible, °open, °free, unrestricted, nonexclusive, communal, community, °available **4** °open, °manifest, exposed, °overt, projected, °plain, °obvious, °apparent, °patent, °clear, clear-cut, acknowledged, known, admitted, °visible, viewable, °conspicuous **5** °visible, viewable, °conspicuous, unconcealed, unshrouded, °flagrant, °blatant **6** °well-known, °prominent, °eminent, °celebrated, °famous, °renowned, °noted, °notable, °influential, °illustrious; °notorious, °disreputable, °infamous **7** ***make public.*** See **publish.** —*n.* **8** community, people (at large *or* in general), citizenry, citizens, °nation, °populace, °population, °society, masses, multitude, °hoi polloi, bourgeoisie, plebeians, proletariat, °rank and file, middle class, third estate, commonalty, voters, man *or* woman in the street, *Brit* admass, *US* John Q. Public, Mr. *or* Mrs. Average, *Colloq* (any *or* every) Tom, Dick, and Harry **9** clientele *or Brit also* clientage, customers, °custom, patrons, followers, supporters, buyers, consumers, purchasers, following, °business, °trade **10** sector, °segment, special-interest group, °portion **11** ***in public.*** publicly, °openly, in the open, *Colloq* out of the closet

publication *n.* **1** dissemination, promulgation, publicizing, publishing, °proclamation, issuance, reporting, °announcement, °advertisement, advertising, °pronouncement, airing, putting out, °revelation, °declaration, °appearance **2** °book, booklet, °pamphlet, °brochure, °leaflet, broadside *or* broadsheet, flier *or* flyer, handbill, handout; °periodical, °magazine, °journal, newsletter, newspaper, °paper, tabloid; annual, semiannual, °quarterly, bimonthly, monthly, semimonthly, fortnightly, biweekly, weekly, hebdomadal *or* hebdomedary, semiweekly, °daily

publicize *v.* °promote, advertise, give publicity to, *Colloq* beat the drum for, °plug, °puff, *US* °push, *Slang* hype

publish *v.* °make public, °put out, °broadcast, spread (about *or* around), advertise, °make known, let (something) be known, °announce, °publicize, °report, °proclaim, promulgate, bruit about, °reveal, divulge, °disclose, break the news (about), *Colloq* °leak

pucker *v.* **1** °gather, draw together, compress, °purse, crinkle, ruck, shirr, °ruffle, corrugate, °furrow, °wrinkle, crease, °screw up, °tighten, °contract, °squeeze —*n.* **2** °gather, tuck, pleat, pleating, shirr, shirring, °ruffle, ruck, ruche, ruckle, °wrinkle, wrinkling, °fold, crinkle, crinkling

puerile *adj.* °childish, °immature, babyish, °infantile, °juvenile, °silly, asinine, °foolish, trivial, °ridiculous, °irresponsible, °shallow, °inconsequential, °insignificant, *US* sophomoric

puff *n.* **1** °blow, °breath, °wind, whiff, °draft, °gust, °blast, °huff **2** °draft, °draw, °pull, *Colloq* °drag **3** °praise, commendation, favorable mention *or* review *or* notice, publicity, puffery, *Colloq* °plug, blurb, *Slang* hype —*v.* **4** °blow, °breathe, °huff, °pant, °gasp, wheeze **5** °draw, pull (at *or* on), °inhale, suck, smoke, *Colloq* °drag **6** Usually, ***puff up or out.*** °inflate, distend, bloat, swell (up *or* out), °stretch, balloon, °expand, °pump up, °enlarge **7** °publicize, advertise, °promote, °push, trumpet, ballyhoo, °extol, commend, °praise, *Colloq* °plug, beat the drum (for)

pugilism *n.* boxing, prizefighting; the manly art of self-defense, fisticuffs; *Colloq* the boxing *or* fight game

pugilist *n.* boxer, prizefighter, fighter, contender, °contestant, battler, combatant, *Colloq* °bruiser, scrapper, champ, *Slang* slugger, pug

pugnacious *adj.* °aggressive, °belligerent, combative, °quarrelsome, bellicose, antagonistic, °argumentative, °hostile, litigious, contentious, disputatious, °disagreeable, fractious, °petulant, °testy, irascible, hot-tempered, choleric, unfriendly, curmudgeonly, °irritable, °short-tempered

puling *adj.* whining, wailing, °querulous, whimpering, sniveling, weeping, caterwauling

pull *v.* **1** °draw, °haul, °drag, °lug, °tow, °trail **2** °tug, °jerk, °yank, °wrench, °pluck **3** Sometimes, ***pull out or up.*** °pluck (out), °withdraw, °extract, °uproot, pick (up *or* out), snatch out *or* up, tear *or* rip out *or* up, cull, °select, °draw out, °take out, °remove **4** Often, ***pull apart.*** tear *or* rip (up *or* apart), °rend, pull asunder, °wrench (apart), °stretch, °strain **5** Often, ***pull in.*** °attract, °draw, °lure, °entice, allure, °catch, °captivate, °fascinate, °capture **6** ***pull apart.*** pull to pieces *or* shreds, °criticize, °attack, pick *or* take apart *or* to pieces, flay, °run down, *Colloq* °put down, °pan, °knock, °devastate, °destroy, slate, *Slang* °slam **7** ***pull away.*** °withdraw, draw *or* drive *or* go *or* move away; outrun, outpace, draw ahead of **8** ***pull back.*** **(a)** °withdraw, °draw back, back off *or* away, °recoil, shrink (away *or* back) from, °shy, °flinch (from), °jump, °start **(b)** °withdraw, °(beat a) retreat, °take flight, °flee, °turn tail, drop *or* fall back, back out **9** ***pull down.*** **(a)** °demolish, °raze, °level, °destroy, °wreck **(b)** °draw, °receive, °get, be paid, °earn **(c)** °lower, °debase, °diminish, °reduce, °degrade, °dishonor, °disgrace, °discredit, °humiliate **10** ***pull for.*** hope *or* pray for, be enthusiastic for, be supportive of, °support, campaign for, cheer for, °encourage, °boost, *US* root for **11** ***pull in.*** **(a)** drive up, °arrive, °come, draw up *or* in, °reach **(b)** °arrest, apprehend, take into custody, *Colloq* °pinch, °nab, collar, °nail, *Brit* °nick, *Slang* bust **12** ***pull off.*** **(a)** °detach, rip *or* tear off, °separate, wrench off *or* away **(b)** °accomplish, do, °complete, °succeed, °carry out, °bring off, °manage,

°perform **13** ***pull oneself together.*** °recover, get a grip on oneself, get over it, °recuperate, *Colloq* °snap out of it, buck up **14** ***pull out.*** **(a)** °uproot, °extract, °withdraw **(b)** °withdraw, °retreat, beat a retreat, °recede, °draw back, °leave, °depart, go *or* run away *or* off, °evacuate, *Colloq* °beat it, do a bunk, *Brit* do a moonlight flit **(c)** °leave, °go, °depart, °take off **(d)** °withdraw, °quit, °abandon, °resign (from), °give up, °relinquish **15** ***pull someone's leg.*** °tease, °chaff, rib, °have on, °rag, °twit, °poke fun at, °make fun of, °hoodwink, °ridicule **16** ***pull strings.*** use influence *or* connections, *US* use pull, °pull wires **17** ***pull through.*** °survive, °recover, °improve, get better, get over (it *or* some affliction), °rally; °live **18** ***pull up.*** **(a)** °stop, °halt, come to a standstill **(b)** °uproot, °root out, °dig out, deracinate, eradicate **(c)** draw even *or* level with, come up to, °reach —*n.* **19** °draw, °tug; °yank, °jerk **20** °attraction, °draw, °magnetism, °appeal, drawing *or* pulling power, seductiveness, seduction, °lure **21** °influence, °authority, °connections, °prestige, °weight, leverage, *Colloq* clout, muscle **22** °puff, °draw, inhalation, *Colloq* °drag

pulley *n.* sheave, °block

pulp *n.* **1** marrow, °pith, °heart, soft part, °flesh **2** mush, paste, mash, pap, pomace, °mass, *Technical* triturate —*v.* **3** mash, squash, °pulverize, °destroy, *Technical* levigate, triturate —*adj.* **4** °lurid, °sensational, trashy, °cheap

pulsate *v.* °beat, °pulse, throb, °pound, thrum, drum, thump, °thud, reverberate, hammer, palpitate, °vibrate; °oscillate, °quiver

pulse *n.* **1** °beat, beating, throb, throbbing, pulsing, pulsating, pulsation, pounding, thrumming, drumming, °thumping, thudding, reverberation, reverberating, hammering, palpitation, palpitating, vibration, vibrating —*v.* **2** See **pulsate,** above.

pulverize *v.* **1** °powder, comminute, °grind, °crush, °mill, granulate, °crumble, °break up, bray, °pound, *Technical* triturate, levigate **2** °devastate, °destroy, °demolish, °crush, smash, °shatter, °ruin, °wreck, annihilate

pump *v.* **1** °send, °force, °deliver, °push **2** interrogate, °question, °examine, cross-examine, °quiz, °probe, *Colloq* grill, give (someone) the third degree **3** ***pump out.*** pump dry *or* empty, °empty, °drain, bail out, draw *or* drive *or* force out, siphon (out) **4** ***pump up.*** **(a)** °inflate, °blow up; dilate, °swell, bloat, °expand, puff out *or* up **(b)** °excite, °inspire, °stimulate, °animate, inspirit, °electrify, galvanize, °energize, °motivate, *Colloq* enthuse **(c)** °intensify, °concentrate, °emphasize, °stress, °increase

pun *n.* play on words, °quip, (bon) mot, °witticism, double entendre, *Literary* equivoque, *Technical* paronomasia

punch[1] *v.* **1** °hit, °clip, °jab, whack, thwack, °knock, smack, °box, pummel, °strike, cuff, *Colloq* clout, bop, slug, wallop, thump, lambaste *or* lambast, °slam, *Slang* sock, biff, °plug, °belt, °lace (into), *US* paste —*n.* **2** °clip, °jab, whack, thwack, °knock, smack, °box, cuff, uppercut, left *or* right, *Colloq* clout, bop, slug, wallop, thump, °slam, *Slang* sock, °belt, biff, haymaker, °plug, paste **3** °effect, °impact, effectiveness, °force, forcefulness, °power, °vitality, °gusto, °vigor, °life, vim, °zest, ginger, *Colloq* it, oomph, what it takes, *Slang* zing, zip

punch[2] *n.* **1** awl, auger, bodkin, perforator; °drill, brace and bit —*v.* **2** °pierce, °stab, °puncture, °perforate; °bore, °drill

punctual *adj.* °on time, °timely, °prompt, *Colloq* °on the dot

punctuate *v.* **1** °interrupt, °break, intersperse; °pepper, sprinkle **2** °accent, accentuate, underline, underscore, °emphasize, °stress, °mark

puncture *n.* **1** °hole, perforation, °opening, °leak; °flat (tire) **2** perforation, perforating, holing, puncturing, °piercing, stabbing, punching —*v.* **3** °perforate, °hole, °pierce, °stab, °penetrate, °go through, °prick, °nick, °rupture **4** deflate, °disillusion, bring up short, °discourage, °humble, °dash, °destroy, °ruin

pungent *adj.* **1** °spicy, °hot, °sharp, °strong, °penetrating, °aromatic, °seasoned, peppery, piquant, tangy, flavorful, °tasty, sapid **2** °sharp, °biting, stinging, °caustic, °severe, astringent, °stern, acrid, °harsh, °sour, acid, °tart, acrimonious, °bitter, °cutting, °keen, barbed, °trenchant, °scathing, °incisive, mordant, °sarcastic **3** distressing, upsetting, °poignant, °painful, °hurtful, °penetrating, °piercing, stabbing, °intense, °severe, °acute, °agonizing, °oppressive, °excruciating, racking, consuming

punish *v.* **1** °penalize, °chastise, °castigate, °discipline, °chasten, °scold, °rebuke, °take to task, °reprove, °dress down, admonish, °correct, teach someone a lesson, give a lesson to, throw the book at, rap someone's knuckles, slap someone's wrist, have *or* *US* call on the carpet, *Colloq* take it out on (someone) **2** °imprison, jail *or* *Brit also* gaol, incarcerate, °lock up; °fine, mulct, amerce; °lash, °flog, °beat, °scourge, °spank, °whip, cane, birch, put across *or* *US also* turn over (one's) knee, *US* °paddle; pillory, crucify; tar and feather, °exile, °banish, excommunicate, cashier, drum out of the corps; °hang, °execute, electrocute, draw and quarter, send to the gas chamber, *Colloq* °put away, *Slang Brit* °send down, *US* °send up **3** °hurt, °harm, °injure, °damage, °abuse, maltreat, °rough up, knock about *or* around, maul, thrash, °beat, trounce, °manhandle, °batter, *Slang* beat up

punishing *adj.* grueling, °hard, °arduous, °strenuous, °laborious, °exhausting, tiring, wearying, fatiguing, wearing, taxing, °demanding, °burdensome, backbreaking, torturous

punishment *n.* **1** chastisement, chastising,

castigation, castigating, °discipline, disciplining, chastening, scolding, °rebuke, °reproof, dressing-down, admonishment, admonition, °correction, punitive measures **2** °penance, °penalty, °sentence, sentencing, just deserts; °imprisonment, incarceration, jailing *or Brit also* gaoling; lashing, flogging, beating, °whipping, scourging, °spanking, caning, birching, *US* paddling; °exile, banishment, excommunication, cashiering; hanging, °execution, electrocution, drawing and quartering **3** °injury, °harm, °damage, °abuse, maltreatment, mauling, beating, °thrashing, trouncing, manhandling, battering, torture

punitive *adj.* chastening, castigatory, disciplinary, retributive, punitory, retaliatory, correctional

punk *n.* **1** ruffian, °hoodlum, hooligan, °delinquent, °tough, °thug, vandal, °yahoo, °barbarian, *Colloq* goon, °mug *—adj.* **2** °inferior, °rotten, unimportant, °worthless, °bad, °poor, °awful, *Colloq* °lousy

puny *adj.* **1** °small, °little, °insignificant, °petty, unimportant, °inconsequential, °paltry, trivial, °trifling, °minor, °negligible, nugatory, of little *or* no account, °inferior, °worthless, °useless, *Colloq* piddling, *Slang Brit* not much cop **2** °small, °little, °diminutive, °tiny, °minute **3** °weak, °feeble, °frail, °sickly, weakly, underfed, undernourished, °undersized, underdeveloped, °stunted, °dwarf, midget, pygmy

pup *n.* puppy, whelp, °upstart, whippersnapper, popinjay, cub, jackanapes, °showoff, °braggart

pupil *n.* °student, °learner, °scholar, schoolchild, schoolgirl, schoolboy, °disciple, °apprentice; beginner, °novice, neophyte, tyro *or* tiro, *Chiefly ecclesiastical* catechumen

puppet *n.* **1** hand puppet, finger puppet, glove puppet, doll; marionette, string puppet **2** °figurehead, cat's-paw, °pawn, °dupe, °tool, hireling, yes man, *Colloq* front (man), *Slang* stooge, °sucker, patsy

purchase *v.* **1** °buy, °acquire, °procure, °obtain, °get, °secure, °pay for **2** °win, °gain, °achieve, °realize, attain, °obtain *—n.* **3** °acquisition, acquiring, buying, purchasing, obtaining, securing, procurement **4** °buy, °acquisition **5** °grip, °hold, °support, toehold, foothold, °grasp; leverage, °position, °advantage, °edge

pure *adj.* **1** unmixed, unadulterated, unalloyed, simon-pure; 24-karat, °sterling, °solid; °real, °genuine, °authentic, °flawless, °faultless, °perfect, °natural, °true, °simple **2** uncontaminated, °clear, °clean, °wholesome, °sanitary, uninfected, disinfected, pasteurized, sterilized, °sterile, antiseptic, unpolluted, °spotless, °immaculate, unsullied, unbesmirched, unblemished, unmarred, unstained, untainted **3** °chaste, virginal, virgin, °intact, maidenly, vestal, undefiled, °innocent, guileless, °virtuous, °modest, °moral, °correct, °proper, °decent, °decorous, uncorrupted, °blameless, sinless, °impeccable **4** °theoretical, °hypothetical, conjectural, °speculative, °abstract, conceptual, notional, °philosophical, academic(al) **5** unalloyed, °simple, °unmitigated, °sheer, utter, °absolute, °unqualified, °complete, °total, °perfect, °thorough, °outright, °downright, °out-and-out, °mere **6** °honorable, °(highly) principled, °righteous, °upright, °honest, straightforward, high-minded, °pious, °worthy, °good, °ethical, °virtuous, °sincere, above suspicion, above reproach, like Caesar's wife

purebred *adj.* full-blooded, thoroughbred, pedigreed

purgative *n.* **1** laxative, cathartic, aperient, °purge, physic, depurative *—adj.* **2** laxative, cathartic, aperient, evacuant, diuretic, depurative; abstergent

purge *v.* **1** °cleanse, °purify, °clean (out), °clear, °scour (out), depurate, deterge, °wash (out) **2** °eject, eradicate, °expel, °eliminate, °get rid of, °dismiss, clear out *or* away, sweep away *or* out, oust, °remove, rout out, weed out, °root out; do away with, °exterminate, liquidate, °kill, °destroy **3** °clear, exonerate, absolve, °forgive, °purify, °pardon, exculpate *—n.* **4** °ejection, eradication, °expulsion, elimination, °dismissal, clearing out *or* away, ousting, ouster, °removal, routing out, weeding out, rooting out, unseating; defenestration; extermination, liquidation, °killing, °murder, °slaughter **5** See **purgative, 1,** above.

purify *v.* **1** °cleanse, °clean, °clarify, °wash, sanitize, depurate, decontaminate, °freshen, °disinfect; °fumigate **2** exonerate, exculpate, absolve, °clear, °redeem, shrive, lustrate, acquit, °pardon, °forgive, °excuse

purist *n.* pedant, precisian, formalist, stickler, bluestocking, dogmatist, °pharisee, °fanatic, *Colloq* diehard, stuffed shirt

puritan *n.* **1** moralist, pietist, religionist, °fanatic, °zealot, °purist *—adj.* **2** °prudish, puritanical, prim, °proper, °strait-laced, ascetic, austere, moralistic, pietistic, °intolerant, disapproving, °bigoted, °narrow-minded, °stuffy, stiff-necked, °rigid, uncompromising, hardline, °stern, °severe, °strict, *Colloq* uptight, hard-nosed

purity *n.* **1** pureness, faultlessness, correctness, flawlessness, °perfection, spotlessness, cleanness, cleanliness, °clarity; healthfulness, wholesomeness, salubrity; innocuousness, harmlessness **2** °chastity, chasteness, virginity, virtuousness, °virtue, °morality, °propriety, °honesty, °integrity, °rectitude, properness, innocence, guilelessness, decency, decorousness, modesty, blamelessness, sinlessness

purpose *n.* **1** °object, °intention, °intent, °end, °goal, °ambition, °objective, °target, °aim, °principle, °point, °rationale, °reason; °scheme, °plan, °design, °motive, motivation, °view **2** °resolution, firmness, °determination, °persistence, °drive, single-mindedness, deliberation, deliberateness, purposefulness, steadfastness, °tenacity, doggedness, °will, °resolve, resoluteness, °perseverance, stubbornness **3** °use, practicality, avail, °effect, utility, °usefulness, °outcome, °result; °advantage, °profit, °gain, °good, °benefit **4** ***on purpose.*** **(a)** purposely, intentionally, °deliberately, willfully, by design, consciously, knowingly, designedly, wittingly **(b)** °especially, °specially, °expressly, °exactly, °precisely, specifically, °in particular —*v.* **5** °plan, °intend, °design, °resolve, °mean, °aim, have in mind *or* view, have a mind, °propose, °consider, °contemplate, °aspire, °long, °yearn

purposeful *adj.* °intentional, intended, planned, °deliberate, resolved, settled, °determined, °resolute, °decided, confirmed, affirmed, °sure, °certain, °positive, °definite, °staunch, °steadfast, °persistent, strong-willed, dogged, °tenacious, pertinacious, unfailing, unfaltering, °firm, °fixed

purposeless *adj.* °pointless, °bootless, °meaningless, °empty, vacuous, °senseless, °aimless, °rambling, °discursive, wandering, disorganized, unorganized

purse *n.* **1** °pouch, (money-)bag, °wallet, °pocket, *Dialect* °poke, *Highland dress* sporran, *US and Canadian* (woman's) handbag, pocketbook, °bag **2** °money, °wealth, °resources, °funds, °finances, exchequer, °treasury, °capital, °revenue, °income, °means, °cash, °riches; dollars, shekels, *Derogatory* mammon, pelf, (filthy) lucre, *US* almighty dollar, *Slang* ready *or* readies, *US and Canadian* °scratch, *Brit* lolly **3** °prize, °reward, °award, °present, °gift —*v.* **4** °pucker (up), °contract, °wrinkle, compress, press together

pursue *v.* **1** °follow, °chase, go *or* run after, hunt (after *or* down *or* for *or* up), °trace, °trail, °track, °run down, take off after, dog, °stalk, °shadow, *Brit* chivy *or* chivvy *or* chevy, *Colloq* °tail **2** follow (up *or* on with), °trace, carry on with, °continue, °conduct, devote *or* dedicate oneself to, °cultivate, °undertake, practice, persist *or* persevere in, °maintain, °exercise, °proceed with, adhere to, stay with, apply oneself to, *Colloq* °stick with **3** °aspire to, aim for, work for *or* toward(s), try *or* strive for, °purpose, °seek, °search for, go in search of, quest after *or* for, be intent on, be bent upon *or* on **4** woo, (pay) court (to), seek the hand of, *Formal* press (one's) suit with, pay suit *or* court *or* (one's) addresses to, *Colloq* set one's cap for, *Slang* °chase (after)

pursuit *n.* **1** pursuing, chasing, following, hunting, °hunt, going *or* running after, tracing, trailing, tracking, running down, dogging, stalking, shadowing, *Brit* chivy *or* chivvy *or* chevy, *Colloq* tailing **2** pursuance, striving after, seeking, searching, °search, looking for **3** °work, °line (of work), °employment, °field, °area, °specialty, specialization, °business, °profession, °trade, °vocation, °calling, °career, lifework, °activity; °hobby, °pastime, avocation, °interest; *Slang* °racket

push *v.* **1** °thrust, shove, °drive, °move, set in motion, get moving, °propel; °press **2** °press, °depress **3** shove, °thrust, elbow, °shoulder, °force, jostle, °nudge **4** °urge, °encourage, °press, °induce, °ask, °persuade, °get, egg on, °prod, °spur, goad, °rouse, °prompt, °incite, °move, °motivate, °stimulate, °influence, impel, °make, compel, °force, dragoon, coerce, constrain; badger, °hound, °pester, °harass, °plague, °nag, °browbeat; °beg, importune, entreat **5** °force, °strain, overstrain, °tax, overtax, °burden, overburden **6** °promote, °publicize, advertise, °boost, propagandize, °puff, *Colloq* °plug, *Slang* ballyhoo, hype **7** ***push about or around.*** °intimidate, °bully, cow, domineer, °tyrannize, bullyrag, °torment, °force, coerce **8** ***push away.*** °reject, °deny, brush off *or* aside, give (someone) the cold shoulder, °rebuff, distance oneself from **9** ***push off.*** **(a)** shove off, sail away *or* off **(b)** °leave, °depart, °go away, *Colloq* light out, °take off, hit the road, skedaddle, scram, make oneself scarce, *Slang* °beat it **10** ***push on or forward or along.*** move onward(s) *or* ahead *or* forward, °continue, °proceed, °advance, press on *or* onward(s) **11** ***push through.*** °force, °press, *Colloq* °railroad **12** ***push (up) daisies.*** be dead (and buried), be six feet under —*n.* **13** shove, °thrust, °nudge **14** °effort, °energy, °dynamism, °drive, °force, °enterprise, °ambition, °vigor, °determination, °initiative, °eagerness, °spirit, °enthusiasm, zeal, °verve, *Colloq* get-up-and-go, zing, zip, °gumption, °go **15** °campaign, °attack, °assault, °advance, °offensive, °charge, onslaught, foray, sortie, °invasion, incursion, °raid, sally, blitzkrieg, blitz, °strike **16** ***the push.*** °dismissal, °notice, *Colloq* one's marching orders, *Chiefly Brit* °the sack, the boot, *Chiefly US and Canadian* one's walking papers, a pink slip

pushover *n.* **1** sure thing, *Colloq* °piece of cake, child's play, °snap, °picnic, walkover, *US* °breeze, *Slang* cinch, *Brit* doddle, *US* lead-pipe cinch **2** *Colloq* walkover, chump, soft touch, soft *or* easy mark, easy prey *or* game, *Slang* patsy, °sucker, stooge, °sap, *Brit* °mug, *US and Canadian* milquetoast

pushy *adj.* °forward, (self-)assertive, °forceful, °aggressive, °obnoxious, °arrogant, bumptious, °brassy, °brazen, °impertinent, °insolent, pushing, °presumptuous, °officious, °loud, °showy, °cocky, °brash, °offensive, °bold, *Colloq* °cheeky

pussyfoot *v.* **1** °sneak, °creep, °slink, °prowl, °steal, tiptoe **2** beat about *or* around the bush, hem *or* hum and haw, °equivocate, °hesitate, be evasive, evade the issue, prevaricate, tergiversate, be noncommittal, be *or* sit on the fence, °blow hot and cold

put *v.* **1** °place, °position, °situate, °set, °lay, °station, °stand, °deposit, °rest, °settle; °locate **2** °assign, °commit, °cause, °set, consign, °subject **3** °subject, cause to experience *or* undergo *or* suffer, consign, °send **4** °express, °word, °phrase; °say, utter, °write **5** °offer, °advance, bring forward, °present, °propose, °submit, °tender, set before **6** °bet, °gamble, wager, °stake, °play, °chance, °risk, °hazard **7** °throw, °heave, °toss, °fling, °cast, °pitch, °bowl, °lob, °send, °shy, °shoot, °snap, catapult **8** °place, °assign, °attribute, °lay, °pin, °attach, °fix **9** ***put about.*** °broadcast, °publish, °make known, °publicize, °announce, spread about *or* around **10** ***put across or over.*** make clear, °get across, make (something *or* oneself) understood *or* understandable, °explain, °spell out, convey, °communicate **11** ***put aside.*** set *or* lay aside, °ignore, °disregard, pay no heed to, push aside, shrug off **12** ***put aside or by or away.*** lay aside *or* by, °set aside; °save, °store, stow *or* store *or* salt *or* squirrel away, lay away, °cache, bank **13** ***put away.*** **(a)** See **12,** above. **(b)** jail *or Brit also* gaol, °imprison, incarcerate, *Colloq* °send, °jug, confine, °commit, institutionalize, remand, *Brit* °send down, *US* °send up **(c)** See **16 (d),** below. **(d)** °consume, °gorge, gormandize *or US also* gourmandize **14** ***put back.*** °return, °replace, °restore **15** ***put by.*** See **12,** above. **16** ***put down.*** **(a)** °record, °register, °write down, °set down, °enter, °list; log, °note (down), °jot down, make a note *or* notation of **(b)** depose, put an end to, °topple, °crush, °overthrow, °subdue, °suppress, °check, °quash, °quell **(c)** ascribe, °assign, °attribute **(d)** °kill, °exterminate, °destroy, put to death, put to sleep, °put away, do away with **(e)** abash, °humiliate, °crush, °silence, °mortify, °lower, take down (a peg *or* a notch), °shame, snub, deflate, °slight, °reject, °dismiss **(f)** take for, °reckon, °account, °count, °categorize, °regard **(g)** °belittle, °diminish, °disparage, deprecate, °depreciate, °criticize, disdain, °look down on, °despise, contemn **17** ***put forth.*** **(a)** °propose, °offer, °set forth, °advance **(b)** °grow, °produce, send out *or* forth, bud, °flower **(c)** °begin, °set out, °set forth, °start **(d)** promulgate, °issue, °publish, °make known, °make public **18** ***put forward.*** **(a)** °propose, °present, °tender, °nominate, °name; °recommend **(b)** °suggest, °offer, °propose, °set forth, °put forth, °present, °submit, °tender, proffer, °introduce, °advance, °propound, °air, °make known, °announce **19** ***put in.*** **(a)** °insert, °introduce **(b)** °spend, °devote **(c)** °make **20** ***put in for.*** **(a)** apply for, °request, °ask for, petition for **(b)** °seek, apply for, °pursue, °file **21** ***put off.*** **(a)** °postpone, °delay, °defer, °put back, °stay, °hold off, °shelve, put *or* set aside, *Chiefly US* °put over, °table, put on hold **(b)** °dismiss, °get rid of, send away, turn away; °discourage, *Colloq* give (someone) the brushoff, *US* °brush off **(c)** °dismay, disconcert, °upset, °confuse, °disturb, °perturb, abash, °distress, *Colloq* °throw, °rattle **(d)** °repel, °disgust, °sicken, °revolt, °nauseate **(e)** °leave, °depart, °go (off), °set off **22** ***put on.*** **(a)** don, clothe *or* attire *or* dress (oneself) in, get dressed in, change *or* slip into **(b)** °assume, °take on, °pretend, °affect, feign, °bluff, make a show of **(c)** °add, °gain **(d)** °stage, °mount, °produce, °present, °perform **(e)** °tease, °mock, *Colloq* kid, pull (someone's) leg, rib, °rag, *Brit* °have on **23** ***put out.*** **(a)** °inconvenience, discommode, °disturb, °embarrass, °trouble, °bother, impose upon *or* on, *Colloq* put on the spot **(b)** °annoy, vex, °irritate, °anger, °exasperate, °irk, °perturb, °provoke, *Slang* °bug **(c)** snuff out, °extinguish, °blow out, douse, °quench, °smother **(d)** °exert, °put forth, °expend, °use, °exercise **(e)** °publish, °issue, °broadcast, °make public, °circulate, °spread, °make known, °release **24** ***put out of (one's) misery.*** °release, °relieve, °free, °deliver, °rescue, °save, °spare **25** ***put over.*** **(a)** put *or* get across, convey, °communicate, set *or* put forth, °relate **(b)** See **21 (a),** above. **26** ***put (one or something) over on (someone).*** °fool (someone), pull (someone's) leg, °deceive (someone), °mislead (someone), pull the wool over (someone's) eyes, °trick (someone), °hoodwink (someone) **27** ***put through.*** **(a)** carry out *or* through, °execute, °(put into) effect, °bring off, °accomplish, °complete, °finish, conclude, *Colloq* °pull off **(b)** °process, °handle, °organize, °see to, °follow up on **(c)** °connect, hook up **28** ***put up.*** **(a)** °erect, °build, °construct, °raise, °set up, put together, °fabricate **(b)** °accommodate, °lodge, °board, °house, °take in, °quarter, *Chiefly military* billet **(c)** °preserve, can; °cure, pickle **(d)** °contribute, °pledge, °offer (as collateral), °stake, mortgage, °post **(e)** °contribute, °give, °supply, °donate, ante (up), °advance, °pay, °invest **(f)** °increase, °raise, °boost, elevate **(g)** See **18 (a),** above. **(h)** °offer, °tender, put *or* place on the market **29** ***put up to.*** °incite, °urge, goad, °spur, egg on, °encourage, °prompt, instigate **30** ***put up with.*** °tolerate, °abide, °take, °brook, °stand (for), °stomach, °accept, °resign oneself to, °bear, °endure, °swallow

put-down *n.* °dig, °sneer, snub, disparaging *or* denigrating remark, °slight, °offense, °insult

put-on *n.* **1** °deception, °hoax, °trick, leg-pull, jest, °(practical) joke, °prank, °pretense, *Colloq* spoof **2** °takeoff, °parody, °satire, °burlesque, °caricature, °act, *Brit* sendup, *Colloq* spoof

putrefy *v.* °rot, °decompose, °decay, molder, go bad, °spoil, °deteriorate, °go off

putrid *adj.* °rotten, rotting, decomposed, decomposing, decayed, decaying, °moldy, moldering, spoilt *or* spoiled, putrefied, putrescent, putrefying, °foul, fetid, °rank, tainted, °corrupt

putter *v.* Usually, ***putter around or about.***

dabble (in *or* with), °toy with, °trifle with, fribble, fool (with *or* about *or* around), °fritter (away), mess (about *or* around *or* with), °tinker (with), °meddle (with), monkey (about *or* around *or* with), °fidget (with), *Colloq* fiddle (about *or* around *or* with), footle (around *or* about)

put-up *adj.* °(secretly) preconceived, prearranged, plotted, preconcerted

put-upon *adj.* imposed upon, inconvenienced, put-out, taken advantage of, exploited, °abused

puzzle *v.* **1** baffle, °bewilder, °confuse, confound, °mystify, °flummox, °perplex, °nonplus, °stymie, °stump **2** Usually, ***puzzle***

over. °study, °ponder (over), mull over, °contemplate, meditate on *or* upon *or* over, °consider, muse over *or* on, reflect on *or* over, think about *or* over *or* on **3** ***puzzle out.*** °solve, °decipher, °crack (the code), unravel, °work out, °figure out, think through, °sort out, unlock —*n.* **4** °enigma, °problem, °question, °paradox, poser, °mystery, °riddle, conundrum, *Colloq* brain-teaser

puzzling *adj.* mystifying, enigmatic(al), bewildering, baffling, confounding, °perplexing, confusing, °ambiguous, °contradictory, abstruse

Q

quack *n.* **1** charlatan, °impostor, °pretender, fake(r), °fraud, *Colloq* phoney *or US also* phony —*adj.* **2** °fake, °fraudulent, °sham, °counterfeit, *Colloq* phoney *or US also* phony

quaint *adj.* **1** °curious, °odd, °strange, °bizarre, °peculiar, °unusual, °queer, uncommon, °singular, °unorthodox, °eccentric, °whimsical, °offbeat, °fanciful, °outlandish, unconventional, °fantastic **2** °old-fashioned, archaic, °antiquated, outdated, °picturesque, °antique

quake *v.* **1** °tremble, °shake, °quiver, °shudder; °vibrate, °stagger **2** earthquake, tremor, temblor *or* trembler *or* tremblor, seismic(al) activity, *Rare* seism

qualification *n.* **1** Often, ***qualifications.*** °fitness, °ability, °aptitude, °capability, competence *or* competency, °capacity, suitableness, suitability, eligibility, °proficiency, °skill, °knowledge, *Colloq* know-how **2** limitation, °restriction, modification, °reservation, caveat, °condition, °stipulation, °proviso, °prerequisite, °requirement

qualified *adj.* **1** °able, °suitable, °capable, °competent, °fit, °fitted, equipped, °prepared, °ready, trained, °proficient, °accomplished, °expert, °talented, °adept, °skillful, skilled, °experienced, °practiced, °knowledgeable, °well-informed **2** contingent, conditional, restricted, modified, °limited, °provisional

qualify *v.* **1** °equip, °fit (out), °ready, °prepare, °condition, make eligible; °certify **2** be eligible, meet the requirements, be fit *or* suitable *or* equipped *or* ready *or* prepared, °make the grade **3** °temper, °mitigate, °modify, °moderate, °modulate, °restrict, °limit

quality *n.* **1** °property, °attribute, °characteristic, °mark, °distinction, *je ne sais quoi,* °trait **2** °grade, °caliber, °rank, °status, °importance, value, °worth **3** *Old-fashioned* eminence, °prominence, °importance, °excellence, °superiority, °distinction, °standing, °supremacy, °dignity, °grandeur, °nobility, blue blood

qualm *n.* second thought, °doubt, uncertainty, °misgiving, hesitation, °scruple, uneasiness, °compunction, °reluctance, disinclination, queasiness, apprehension, apprehensiveness, °twinge, °pang, °worry, °concern, *Colloq* funny feeling, sinking feeling

quandary *n.* °dilemma, °predicament, °difficulty, °plight, cleft stick, uncertainty

quantity *n.* °amount, °extent, °volume; °sum, °number, °total; °weight, °measure

quarrel *n.* **1** °dispute, °argument, °disagreement, °debate, °controversy, °discord, °difference (of opinion), contention, °misunderstanding; wrangle, °tiff, °row, squabble, altercation, set-to, scuffle, °feud, °fight, °fray, °fracas, °brawl, donnybrook, melee *or* mêlée, °riot, °battle (royal), *Colloq* dust-up, barney, °scrap, *US* spat —*v.* **2** °argue, °disagree, °dispute, altercate, have an altercation, °differ, wrangle, be at odds *or* loggerheads, °clash, squabble, °feud, °fight, °brawl, °battle, *Colloq* °fall out, °scrap

quarrelsome *adj.* °testy, °petulant, irascible, °irritable, °disagreeable, fractious, °querulous, °peevish, °cross, choleric, curmudgeonly, °contrary, dyspeptic, °cranky, grouchy, °argumentative, combative, squabbling, disputatious, °hostile, antagonistic, dissentious, dissentient, °dissident, °pugnacious, bellicose, °belligerent, contentious

quarry[1] *n.* °prey, °game, °prize, °object

quarry[2] *n.* **1** °mine, °pit, °excavation —*v.* **2** °mine, °extract, °obtain, °get

quarter *n.* **1** fourth **2** three-month period, three months, ninety days, thirteen weeks; fifteen minutes; °phase (of the moon), quadrature **3** °area, °region, °part, °section, °district, °zone, °division, °territory, °place, °neighborhood, locality, °locale, °location, °point, °spot; °direction **4** °mercy, compassion, mercifulness, clemency, leniency, °forgiveness, °favor, °humanity, °pity **5** ***quarters.*** living quarters, lodging(s), dwelling place, °dwelling, accommodation(s), °rooms, chambers, °residence, °shelter, habitation, °domicile, °home, °house, °abode; *Military* billet, barracks, cantonment, casern *or* caserne —*v.* 6 °lodge, °accommodate, °house, °board, °shelter, °put up; *Military* billet, °post, °station

quarterly *adj.* 1 trimonthly, three-monthly —*adv.* 2 every three months, every ninety days, every thirteen weeks, four times a year

quash *v.* 1 annul, nullify, °void, declare *or* render null and void, invalidate, °revoke, °vacate, °set aside, rescind, °cancel, °reject, °throw out, °reverse, °overthrow, °discharge, overrule 2 °suppress, °subdue, °quell, °put down, °squelch, °repress, °overthrow, °crush, °overwhelm

quasi *adv.* 1 Sometimes, ***quasi-***. as if, as it were, °seemingly, °apparently, °partly, to some extent, °to all intents and purposes, more or less, °virtually, °almost —*adj.* 2 °so to speak, kind of, °sort of; °pretended, °fake, pseudo, °so-called, °supposed, °artificial, °mock, °sham, *Colloq* phoney *or US also* phony

quaver *v.* 1 °tremble, °quiver, °shake, °shiver, °vibrate, waver, °shudder, °fluctuate, °oscillate, °flutter —*n.* 2 trembling, °tremble, °quiver, quivering, tremor, shaking, vibration, wavering, °break, °fluctuation, oscillation

queasy *adj.* 1 uncomfortable, uneasy, °nervous, apprehensive, °ill at ease, troubled, °worried, discomfited; °doubtful, °hesitant 2 °sick, °nauseous, °nauseated, °ill, °bilious, °queer, *Colloq* green around *or* about the gills, °groggy, woozy

queen *n.* 1 °sovereign, °monarch, ruler; empress; queen consort; queen mother; queen dowager 2 beauty queen, movie queen, °star, prima donna, diva; °epitome, °model, °idol, leading light, cynosure, °leader

queer *adj.* 1 °odd, °strange, °different, °peculiar, °funny, °curious, uncommon, unconventional, °unorthodox, atypical, °singular, °exceptional, anomalous, °extraordinary, °unusual, °weird, °bizarre, uncanny, °unnatural, freakish, °remarkable, °offbeat, °irregular, °unparalleled, °incongruous, °outlandish, °outré, °exotic, °eccentric, fey, °quaint, °absurd, °ridiculous, °ludicrous, unexampled 2 °questionable, dubious, °suspicious, °suspect, °doubtful, °puzzling, °mysterious, *Colloq* °fishy, °shady 3 °(slightly) ill, °queasy, °sick, unwell, °poorly, °faint, uneasy, °dizzy, °giddy, vertiginous, lightheaded 4 °mad, °unbalanced, unhinged, demented, °deranged, °insane, °daft, touched, *Colloq* dotty, potty, nutty, nuts, loony, batty, cracked —*v.* 5 °ruin, °spoil, °bungle, °botch, °muddle, muff, °mar, °wreck, °destroy, *Colloq* make a hash *or* mess of, gum up (the works), *Slang* °muck up, °screw up, louse up, *US* ball up

quell *v.* 1 °suppress, °put down, °repress, °subdue, °quash, °overcome, °crush, °squelch 2 °moderate, mollify, soothe, assuage, alleviate, °mitigate, allay, °quiet, °calm; pacify, °tranquilize, °compose

quench *v.* 1 °satisfy, °slake, sate, °surfeit, °satiate, allay, appease 2 °put out, °extinguish, douse, °smother, snuff out, °stifle, °kill, °destroy, °suppress, °squelch, °repress, °overcome, °subdue

querulous *adj.* complaining, carping, °critical, criticizing, hypercritical, °faultfinding, °finicky, finical, °fussy, overparticular, censorious, °petulant, whining, murmuring, grumbling, °peevish, °testy, °touchy, °irritable, irritated, annoyed, piqued, in a pique, irascible, fractious, °perverse, °quarrelsome, ill-natured, ill-humored, °cantankerous, curmudgeonly, crusty, crotchety, °fretful, bad-tempered, ill-tempered, °waspish, crabby, °cross, splenetic, choleric, °sour, dyspeptic, grumpy, *Colloq* grousing, pernickety *or US also* persnickety, *Slang* bitching

query *n.* 1 °question, inquiry *or* enquiry 2 °doubt, uncertainty, °skepticism, °reservation, °problem —*v.* 3 °ask (about), inquire *or* enquire (about), °question; °challenge, °doubt, °dispute

quest *n.* 1 °search, °pursuit, °exploration, °expedition, voyage (of discovery), °pilgrimage, °mission, °crusade; °chase, °hunt —*v.* 2 Usually, ***quest after*** *or* ***for.*** seek (after *or* for), search after *or* for, °hunt (for), °track down, °pursue, °stalk

question *n.* 1 °query, inquiry *or* enquiry 2 °problem, °difficulty, °confusion, °doubt, dubiousness, uncertainty, °query, °mystery, °puzzle 3 °matter, °issue, °point, °subject, °topic, °theme, °proposition 4 ***beyond (all or any) question.*** beyond (the shadow of) a doubt, °without question, without a doubt, indubitably, °undoubtedly, doubtlessly, °definitely, certainly, assuredly 5 ***call in or into question.*** °doubt, °query, °challenge, °dispute, harbor *or* entertain *or* have doubts *or* suspicions about, °suspect, cast doubt *or* suspicion on 6 ***in question.*** (a) under discussion *or* consideration (b) °questionable, °debatable, °at issue, °in doubt, °doubtful, open to debate 7 ***out of the question.*** °unthinkable, °impossible, °absurd, °ridiculous, °preposterous, °inconceivable, beyond consideration, insupportable 8 ***without question.*** See 4, above. —*v.* 9 °ask, °examine, interrogate, °query, °interview, °sound out, °quiz, *Colloq* °pump, grill, *Slang* give (someone) the third degree 10 call in *or* into question, °doubt, °query, °mistrust, °distrust, cast doubt upon, °dispute, °suspect

questionable *adj.* °doubtful, dubious, °debatable, °moot, °disputable, borderline, °suspect, °suspicious, °shady; open to question, °in question, in dispute, problematic(al), °uncertain, arguable, unsure, °unreliable, °ambiguous

queue *n.* pigtail, °braid, plait; °tail, ponytail

quibble *v.* 1 °equivocate, split hairs, °evade, be evasive, palter, chop logic, bandy words, °cavil, pettifog, *Colloq* nitpick —*n.* 2 quibbling, equivocation, hair-splitting, splitting hairs, °evasion, paltering, sophistry, *Colloq* nitpicking 3 °cavil, sophism, °subtlety, nicety

quick *adj.* 1 °rapid, °fast, °speedy, °swift, °fleet; °expeditious, °express 2 °sudden, °precipitate, °hasty, °brisk, °short, °abrupt, °hurried, °perfunctory, °summary; °immediate, °prompt, °timely, instantaneous 3 °agile, °lively, °nimble, °energetic, °vigorous, °alert, °animated, °keen, °sharp, °acute, spry, °spirited, °vivacious, °rapid, °swift 4 °intelligent, °bright, °brilliant, facile, °adept, adroit, °dexterous, apt, °able, °expert, °skillful, deft, °astute, °clever, °shrewd, °smart, °ingenious, °perceptive, perspicacious, discerning, °far-sighted, °responsive; nimble-witted, °quick-witted 5 °excitable, °touchy, °testy, °petulant, irascible, °irritable, °impatient

quicken *v.* 1 accelerate, °hasten, °speed up 2 °expedite, °hurry, accelerate, °hasten, °speed (up) 3 °stimulate, °arouse, °kindle, °spark, invigorate, °excite, °animate, °vitalize, vivify, galvanize, °enliven, °awaken, °energize, °revive, resuscitate, reinvigorate

quickly *adv.* 1 °rapidly, °swiftly, speedily, °fast 2 °rapidly, °swiftly, speedily, °fast, with dispatch *or* despatch, apace, °posthaste, at *or* on the double, with all speed, °quick, *Colloq US and Canadian* lickety-split 3 instantly, °promptly, °hastily, °at once, °immediately, *Brit* °straightaway, *US* right away, °shortly, without delay, °(very) soon, hurriedly, °quick, *Colloq* pronto

quick-tempered *adj.* °excitable, °impulsive, °temperamental, hot-tempered, °waspish, choleric, splenetic, °impatient, °short-tempered, °touchy, irascible, °irritable, °snappish, °abrupt, °short, short-spoken, °quarrelsome, °testy, °volatile, hot-blooded, bad-tempered, ill-tempered, churlish, highly strung, *US* high-keyed

quick-witted *adj.* °acute, °sharp, °clever, °smart, nimble-witted, °alert, °keen, °astute, °perceptive, perspicacious

quiet *adj.* 1 °silent, soundless, °noiseless, hushed, °still 2 °still, °serene, °silent, °peaceful, unperturbed, °calm, °tranquil, placid, pacific, °smooth, °mild, °restful, unagitated 3 °dormant, quiescent, °inactive, retired, °withdrawn, °unobtrusive 4 °still, motionless, unmoving, °fixed, stationary, at rest, °inactive, composed, °temperate, unexcited, °calm —*n.* 5 °silence, stillness, soundlessness, noiselessness, °hush, quietness, quietude, °ease, °rest, calmness, °serenity, tranquility, °peace, peace of mind, °repose —*v.* 6 Often, ***quiet down.*** °still, °silence, °hush, °calm, °tranquilize, °lull, *Brit* quieten (down)

quietly *adv.* 1 °silently, soundlessly, noiselessly, inaudibly, in silence, softly 2 in hushed tones, in whispers 3 peacefully, calmly, serenely, peaceably, meekly, mildly 4 modestly, humbly, demurely, unpretentiously, unostentatiously, unobtrusively, unassumingly, sedately

quintessence *n.* °essence, °heart, °core, quiddity, essentialness, essentiality, °pith, marrow, sum and substance, °epitome, °nonpareil, °embodiment, personification, °model, °prototype, exemplar, °ideal, ***beau idéal***, °paragon

quip *n.* 1 (bon) mot, °witticism, sally, jest, ad lib, °joke, °gibe, barb, aphorism, °epigram, apophthegm *or* apothegm, °pun, double entendre, equivoque *or* equivoke, *Colloq* °gag, one-liner, °crack, °wisecrack, wheeze, chestnut —*v.* 2 °joke, jest, °gibe, *Colloq* °wisecrack, *US* crack wise

quirk *n.* °peculiarity, caprice, vagary, °eccentricity, °fancy, °twist, °warp, aberration, idiosyncrasy, °oddity, °kink, °characteristic, crotchet, whim, °trick

quit *v.* 1 °leave, °depart from, go (away) from, get away from, decamp, °exit, °desert, °flee, °forsake, °abandon, *Colloq* °take off, °beat it, °skip 2 °resign, °give up, °relinquish, °leave, °renounce, retire from, withdraw from 3 °cease, °stop, °discontinue, °leave off, desist from —*adj.* 4 °free, °clear, discharged, °rid of, released (from), °exempt (from)

quite *adv.* 1 °completely, °very, °totally, °utterly, °entirely, from head to toe, from A to Z, fully, °wholly, °thoroughly, unequivocally, °absolutely, °perfectly, °altogether, unreservedly 2 °rather, °fairly, °moderately, °somewhat, °relatively, to some *or* a certain extent *or* degree, noticeably 3 °rather 4 very much, °totally, °entirely, °wholly, °altogether; °really, °actually, °truly, °definitely, °positively, °undoubtedly, indubitably, °absolutely, unequivocally, certainly, °surely, unreservedly, °honestly

quiver *v.* 1 °shake, °tremble, °vibrate, °shiver, °quaver; °shudder, tremor, °oscillate, °fluctuate, wobble —*n.* 2 °tremble, °quaver, °shudder, °spasm, °shake, tremor, °shiver

quixotic *adj.* °idealistic, °impractical, °impracticable, °unrealistic, unrealizable, °visionary, °romantic, °fantastic, chimerical, °fanciful, °dreamlike, °dreamy, nephelococcygeal, starry-eyed, °optimistic, °rash, °absurd, °mad, °foolhardy, °reckless, °wild, °preposterous, °ridiculous

quiz *n.* 1 °examination, °test, *Colloq* exam —*v.* 2 °question, interrogate, °ask, °examine, *Colloq* grill, °pump

quizzical *adj.* °curious, °queer, °odd, inquiring *or* enquiring, questioning, puzzled

quota *n.* apportionment, °portion, °allotment, allocation, °allowance, °ration, °share, °part, °proportion, °percentage, °equity, °interest, *Colloq* °cut

quotation *n.* 1 °quote, °passage, citation, °reference, allusion, °extract, °excerpt, °selection 2 °quote, (bid *or* asking *or* offer *or* market) price, °charge, fixed price, °rate, °cost; value

quote *v.* 1 cite, °mention, °recite, °repeat, retell, °reproduce, °duplicate, °call up, °bring up, °bring in, °instance, °exemplify, °refer to, °reference, °extract, °excerpt —*n.* 2 See **quotation,** above.

R

rabble *n.* **1** °mob, °crowd, horde, °throng, °swarm, °gang **2** ***the rabble.*** ***Contemptuous*** masses, proletariat, °hoi polloi, commoners, peasantry, ragtag and bobtail, vermin, outcasts, °riffraff, scum, °dregs (of society), lower classes, *canaille,* commonalty, *Colloq* °trash, °the great unwashed

rabble-rouser *n.* °agitator, demagogue, instigator, inciter, firebrand, incendiary, °radical, °troublemaker, *agent provocateur,* °revolutionary, insurrectionist, *Colloq* hell-raiser

rabid *adj.* **1** °unreasonable, unreasoning, °extreme, °fanatical; raging, °furious, °violent, crazed, frenzied, °maniacal, °wild, °mad, infuriated, frenetic, °berserk **2** hydrophobic, °mad

race[1] *n.* **1** footrace, horse race, marathon, rally *or* rallye; °competition, °contest, °rivalry, contention **2** sluice, flume, °chute, watercourse, °course, °channel, bed, millrace, raceway, spillway; °track **3** ***the races.*** horse races, dog races, the dogs, the track, °the turf, *Brit* racecourse, race meeting, *US* racetrack —*v.* **4** °speed, °hurry, °hasten, °dash, sprint, °fly, °rush, °scramble, highball, step lively, *Colloq* °tear, °rip, zip, step on the gas, °step on it, hop to it, °get a move on, *Brit* hare, *US* get a wiggle on **5** °compete (with)

race[2] *n.* **1** °stock, °line, °lineage, °type, °tribe, °nation, °people, °folk, °clan, °family **2** blood, descent, °breed, °kin, °family, °stock, °line, °lineage

racial *adj.* ethnic, genetic, genealogical, ethnological, °folk; tribal; °national

rack *n.* **1** framework, °frame, trestle, holder, °support; °stand, scaffold, scaffolding, °structure, hatrack, hat stand, coat rack, *Technical* stretcher, tenter, *US* hat tree **2** °suffering, °torment, torture, °agony, °anguish, °pain, °misery, °distress, °affliction, °scourge, adversity —*v.* **3** °distress, °torment, torture, agonize, °oppress, °pain, °persecute, °anguish, beleaguer, °plague, °harass, harrow, °hurt **4** °beat, °strain, °wrench, tear at, °lash (at), °batter, °shake, °damage

racket *n.* **1** °noise, °din, °uproar, °disturbance, clamor, hubbub, °row, °rumpus, hullabaloo, °fuss, ado, commotion, to-do, hue and cry, °outcry, brouhaha, °tumult, babel, °pandemonium, *Archaic* alarms *or* alarums and excursions, *Colloq* ballyhoo **2** °(organized) crime, criminal *or* illegal activity *or* enterprise, °trickery, °trick, °dodge, °scheme, °swindle, °stratagem, °artifice, °game, °ruse, *Slang* °caper, scam, gyp **3** °business, °line, °profession, °occupation, °trade, °vocation, °calling, °job, °employment, livelihood

racketeer *n.* mobster, °gangster, mafioso

raconteur *n.* storyteller, anecdotalist *or* anecdotist, °narrator, relater *or* relator, *Colloq* spinner of yarns

racy *adj.* **1** °fresh, °lively, °animated, °spirited, °sprightly, °buoyant, °vivacious, °energetic, °vigorous, °dynamic, zestful, °stimulating, mettlesome *or* mettled, *Colloq* full of vim and vigor, peppy, full of pep, full of beans **2** °risqué, ribald, °bawdy, °naughty, °lusty, °earthy, °gross, °off-color, salty, °suggestive, °sexual, °immodest, indelicate, °indecent, °blue, smutty, °lewd, salacious, °vulgar, °dirty, °filthy, °pornographic, °obscene, sex-oriented, °adult, °rude, °crude, °coarse, *Colloq* raunchy, °sexy, °spicy, °hot **3** °spicy, piquant, °tasty, flavorful, °pungent, °strong, °savory, °sharp, zesty, tangy, °tart, °hot

radiance *n.* **1** radiancy, °splendor, brightness, °brilliance, resplendence, luminosity, luminousness, °dazzle, °sparkle, coruscation, scintillation, °twinkle, effulgence, refulgence, incandescence, °glow, phosphorescence, °gleam, °luster, °shimmer, °shine **2** °warmth, gladness, °joy, °pleasure, °happiness, cheeriness, °delight

radiant *adj.* **1** shining, °bright, beaming, °burning, °ablaze, blazing, °brilliant, °luminous, resplendent, °splendid, splendorous *or* splendrous, °lustrous, gleaming, °glowing, phosphorescent, shimmering, °shiny, °glossy, glistening, °incandescent, alight, effulgent, refulgent, sparkling, °dazzling, glittering, coruscating, °scintillating, °twinkling; aglow **2** °happy, °overjoyed, °ecstatic, °rapturous, °delighted, °joyful, °blithe, blithesome, blissful, beatific, °glad, °gleeful, joyous, °gay, bubbling, °bubbly, jubilant, °elated, °rhapsodic, °exultant, exhilarated, in seventh heaven, in heaven, *Colloq* on cloud nine, *Brit* over the moon

radiate *v.* **1** °shine, °beam, °burn, °blaze, °gleam, °glow, °shimmer, °glisten, °sparkle, °dazzle, °glitter, coruscate, scintillate, °twinkle **2** °emanate, disseminate, °disperse, °spread, °diffuse, °shed, °send out, °emit, give off *or* out, *Rare* irradiate

radiation *n.* emission, emanation, diffusion, dispersal, shedding

radical *adj.* **1** °basic, °fundamental, °elementary, °inherent, constitutional, °elemental, °essential, °cardinal, °principal, °primary, °deep, deep-seated, °profound, underlying, °organic, °natural, °rudimentary **2** °thorough, thoroughgoing, °complete, °entire, °total, °exhaustive, °sweeping, (all-) inclusive, °comprehensive, all-embracing, °out-and-out, °drastic, °severe, °extreme, extremist, °revolutionary **3** extremist, °revolutionary, fanatic(al), °militant, anarchist(ic), °immoderate —*n.* **4** extremist, °revolutionary, °fanatic, °zealot, °immoderate, anarchist, °militant **5** communist, leftist, left-winger, red, Bolshevik, Bolshevist, °pink, *Slang US* pinko

radio *n.* 1 receiver, °portable (radio), *Old-fashioned* crystal set, *Brit and US old-fashioned* wireless, *Colloq* transistor, *Slang* ghetto blaster, *Brit* trannie *or* tranny, *US* boom box —*v.* 2 °transmit, °broadcast, °air, disseminate, °announce, °present

raffle *n.* °lottery, °draw, sweepstake *or US* sweepstakes, sweep *or US* sweeps

rag[1] *n.* 1 °tatter, °piece, °shred, °scrap, °fragment, °bit, *Dialect* clout 2 newspaper, °periodical, °magazine, °publication, °journal 3 *rags. Facetious* °clothes, clothing, attire, °dress, °garments, *Old-fashioned* duds 4 ***rag trade.*** garment industry, clothing business, fashion industry 5 ***chew the rag.*** (a) °converse, °talk, °gossip, °chat (b) *Brit* °argue, wrangle

rag[2] *v.* °tease, °taunt, °belittle, °twit, °ridicule, °mock, °make fun of, pull (someone's) leg, *Brit* °rally, *Colloq* kid

ragamuffin *n.* (street) urchin, street arab, waif, mudlark, gamin, little lost lamb, babe in the wood, °stray, °guttersnipe, scarecrow

rage *n.* 1 °anger, °fury, wrath, ire, high dudgeon, exasperation, vehemence, °passion 2 °fury, °passion, °frenzy, hysterics, °tantrum, °fit, °temper, *Brit* paddy *or* paddywhack *or* paddywack, *Colloq Brit* wax 3 °fashion, °craze, °vogue, the (latest *or* newest) thing, last word, *dernier cri,* °mode, *Colloq* °fad —*v.* 4 °rant, °rave, °storm, go mad *or* crazy *or* bonkers *or* wild *or* out of one's mind, go berserk, run amok *or* amuck, behave *or* act *or* be like one possessed, °fret, be beside oneself (with anger *or* fury), lose one's temper, have a tantrum, fulminate, °explode; °fume, foam at the mouth, °stew, °smolder, °boil, °seethe, °simmer, *Colloq* have kittens, lose one's cool, °fly off the handle, go off the deep end, *Slang* get into *or* work oneself up into a lather *or* stew *or* sweat, get all worked up, blow one's top, blow a gasket, °blow up, flip one's top *or* lid, hit the ceiling *or* roof, freak out, be fit to be tied, be ready for a straitjacket, *Brit* throw a wobbly, *US and Canadian* °blow one's stack, flip one's wig, blow a fuse, have a hemorrhage, go ape, do a slow burn, have a conniption fit

ragged *adj.* 1 °rough, °shaggy, °shabby, °seedy, °tattered, °unkempt, scraggy, torn, °rent, ripped, frayed, °worn (out), °threadbare, patched, patchy, raveled, *Chiefly Brit* tatty, *Brit* down at heel, *US* down at the heel(s), *Colloq US* frazzled, beat-up 2 °rough, uneven, °irregular, nicked, °jagged; °serrated, sawtooth(ed), zigzag, °notched, toothed, denticulate(d), ridged 3 worn-out, °tired, °exhausted, °on one's last legs, the worse for wear, dead tired, overtired, °fatigued, °weary, fagged out, °spent, *Colloq* all in, dog-tired, *Slang* °dead (on one's feet), °(dead) beat, *Brit* knackered, *US and Canadian* pooped (out) 4 °bad, °rough, patchy, °imperfect, °shabby, messy, disordered, °disorderly, °run-down, battered, broken-down, neglected, deteriorated, °dilapidated, *Colloq* beat-up 5 °rough, °harsh, °discordant, °grating, rasping, hoarse, °scratchy, croaking 6 uneven, °bad, °poor, °shabby, patchy

ragman *n.* rag dealer, ragpicker, scrap dealer, *US* junk dealer, junkman, *Brit* rag-and-bone man, knacker

raid *n.* 1 °(surprise) attack, incursion, °invasion, °onset, onslaught, blitz, sortie, sally, °expedition, *Slang* (police) bust —*v.* 2 °attack, invade, °assault, °storm, °set upon, descend upon, swoop down upon, °pounce upon, *Military* forage; °sack, °plunder, °pillage, °loot, °ransack, °rifle, °strip, maraud, depredate, *Slang* bust

rail[1] *n.* 1 °bar, °rod, handrail, footrail, towel rail; railing, banisters, balustrade, baluster, °fence 2 ***by or via rail.*** by train, by railway *or US also* railroad

rail[2] *v.* Usually, ***rail at or against.*** vituperate, vociferate, fulminate, be *or* become abusive, revile, °attack, °berate, °scold, °upbraid, °criticize, censure, decry, °condemn, °denounce

raillery *n.* °banter, badinage, persiflage, °repartee, frivolity, joking, jesting, chaffing, teasing, °ridicule, *Colloq* kidding

railroad *n.* 1 railway, °train, °rail, rolling stock, *Archaic* iron horse —*v.* 2 °force, compel, °expedite, coerce, °intimidate, °push (through), *Brit* pressurize, *US* °pressure, °bully, hector, °tyrannize, dragoon, °browbeat, bullyrag, *Colloq* bulldoze, °squeeze, °lean on

rain *n.* 1 °precipitation, drizzle, sprinkle, °downpour, °shower, thundershower, cloudburst, rainstorm, squall, deluge, *US* sunshower 2 rainfall, °precipitation 3 °flood, °torrent, °shower, °volley, °stream, °outpouring —*v.* 4 come down, °pour, °teem, sprinkle, drizzle, °spit, *Brit dialect* mizzle, *Colloq* come down in buckets, rain cats and dogs 5 °trickle, °pour, °run, °fall 6 °descend, °shower 7 °bestow, °lavish, °shower

raise *v.* 1 °lift (up), elevate; °hoist, °pull up, haul up, run up, *Literary* upraise 2 °erect, °put up, °construct, °build, °produce, °create, put together, °assemble, °frame 3 °farm, °grow, °cultivate, °plant, °bring up, nurture, °harvest, °propagate 4 °bring up, nurture, °rear; °mother, °father, °parent 5 °assemble, °gather, bring *or* gather *or* get together, °muster, °mobilize, °round up, °rally, °collect, convene, °recruit, *Colloq* pull together 6 °increase, °boost, °advance, °put up, jack up, run up, °inflate, escalate 7 °cultivate, °foster, nurture, °heighten, °stimulate, °buoy, °lift, uplift, °boost, °arouse, °quicken, °encourage, °develop 8 °open, °introduce, °initiate, °broach, °bring up, bring *or* put forward, °present, °suggest, °mention, °moot 9 °remove, °relieve, °lift, °abandon, °eliminate, °discontinue, °(bring to an) end, °terminate 10 °cause, °provoke, °evoke, °occasion, put *or* set in motion, °institute, °prompt, engender, °stir up, instigate, °inspire, °give rise to, °bring about, °arouse, °originate 11 utter, °express, °bring up, °put forward, °shout,

°call **12** °assemble, °obtain, °get, °collect, °amass, °solicit **13** invigorate, °animate, °vitalize, vivify, °buoy, °lift, uplift, °cheer (up), exhilarate, elate

rake[1] *v.* **1** Often, ***rake up.*** °scrape together, gather (together *or* up), °collect, draw together **2** °scrape, comb, °scratch, °grate, graze **3** ***rake in.*** °collect, gather (up *or* in), °pull in, °make **4** ***rake it in.*** °coin money, make money (hand over fist), *Brit* coin it in **5** ***rake out.*** °sift (out), °screen, °remove, °clear, °eliminate **6** ***rake over or through.*** °search, °probe, °ransack, °scour, comb, rummage through, pick through *or* over, go through *or* over (with a fine-tooth(ed) comb), °rifle (through) **7** ***rake up.*** **(a)** See **1**, above. **(b)** °revive, resuscitate, °resurrect, °raise, °bring up, °recall **8** ***rake up or together.*** °gather, scrape up *or* together, °collect, drag together, °pick up, °dig up, dredge up, °find, °unearth

rake[2] *n.* °libertine, womanizer, lecher, °roué, °playboy, ladies' man, Don Juan, Casanova, Lothario, debauchee, voluptuary, °profligate, °prodigal; °scoundrel, °rascal, cad, *Archaic* rakehell, masher; *Colloq* lady-killer, *Colloq old-fashioned* wolf, *Brit* bounder

rake-off *n.* °kickback, commission; °discount, markdown, °rebate, *Colloq* °cut, °piece

rakish *adj.* °dashing, °jaunty, °dapper, °spruce, °debonair, raffish, °smart, °breezy, °flashy, °chic, °fashionable, °elegant; °dandy, foppish

rally *n.* **1** °gathering, °(mass) meeting, °meet, convocation, °convention, assemblage, °assembly, °muster **2** °recovery, °improvement, °revival, turn for the better, recuperation, renewal —*v.* **3** Often, ***rally around.*** bring *or* call *or* get together, °round up, °assemble, convene, °group, congregate, °organize, come together, troop; marshal, °mobilize, °summon, °gather, °muster **4** °revive, °rouse, °recover, °improve, get better, take a turn for the better, °recuperate, °perk up, °pick up, *Colloq* °snap out of it, make a comeback

ram *v.* **1** °jam, °force, °drive, °cram, °crowd, °pack, compress, °stuff, °squeeze, °thrust, tamp, °pound, hammer **2** °butt, °bump, °strike, °hit, °collide with, °dash, °crash, °slam

ramble *v.* **1** amble, °wander (off), °stroll, °saunter, °walk, perambulate, go (off *or* away), °travel, °drift, °range, rove, go *or* move about, hike, trek, *Colloq* mosey **2** °meander, °wander, digress, maunder **3** Sometimes, ***ramble on.*** °babble, °chatter, gibber, °rave, °go on (and on), °rattle on, *Colloq Brit* witter on, rabbit on *or* away —*n.* **4** °stroll, amble, °saunter, °walk, °promenade, constitutional, walkabout, °tour, °tramp, hike, trek

rambling *adj.* **1** °discursive, °roundabout, circuitous, °tortuous, °incoherent, °diffuse, °unsettled, °disconnected, °disjointed, disorganized, unorganized, illogical, maundering, °aimless, °confused, muddled, jumbled, scrambled, unintelligible, °inarticulate, periphrastic, circumlocutory, circumlocutional, circumlocutionary, ambagious, °wordy, verbose, prolix, °endless, interminable **2** unplanned, straggling, °irregular, sprawling, spread-out, spreading, straggly **3** roving, wandering, °traveling, peripatetic, itinerant, wayfaring, migratory, nomadic

ramification *n.* **1** consequence, °result, °effect, °upshot, °implication, °subtlety; °complication, °difficulty **2** °branch, °extension, outgrowth, subdivision, °offshoot

ramp *n.* °slope, °grade, gradient, °incline; °rise, ascent, acclivity; descent, °dip, declivity

rampage *n.* **1** °excitement, °agitation, recklessness, °riot, °tumult, °uproar, °frenzy, °fury, °rage, °furor, turmoil **2** *US* ***on a rampage,*** *Brit* ***on the rampage.*** °berserk, °mad, °crazy, amuck *or* amok, °wild, out of control —*v.* **3** °storm, °rage, °rant, °rave, go berserk, run amok *or* amuck

rampant *adj.* **1** unchecked, °uninhibited, unrestrained, °wild, °uncontrolled, out of control, out of hand, frenzied, unbridled, uncontrollable, °violent **2** °profuse, unbounded, abounding, °flourishing, rife, widespread, °everywhere, °epidemic, pandemic, °prevalent, unrestrained, unchecked, running wild, °uninhibited, °indiscriminate, °wild, °uncontrolled; in control, holding sway, in full sway, °dominant, °predominant; °exuberant, °rank, °luxuriant

rampart *n.* °defense, bastion, °guard, fortification, °security, °stronghold, °bulwark, barricade, °wall; earthwork, breastwork, parados, gabion

ramshackle *adj.* °dilapidated, tumbledown, crumbling, broken-down, °rickety, unsteady, jerry-built, °decrepit, °flimsy, °shaky, °unstable, tottering, unsubstantial *or* insubstantial, ruined, in disrepair, beyond repair, °rundown, neglected, °derelict

rancid *adj.* stinking *or* reeking (to high heaven), foul-smelling, ill-smelling, evil-smelling, noisome, mephitic, miasmic *or* miasmal *or* miasmatic(al), °smelly, °rank, malodorous, fusty; °nasty, °disagreeable, odious, fetid *or* foetid, °rotten, decayed, spoiled, turned, °bad, °awful, °sour, tainted, °high, gamy, °ripe, °putrid, °corrupt, °stale

rancor *n.* hatred, °hate, antipathy, °spite, °resentment, resentfulness, °antagonism, °hostility, malignity, °bitterness, malevolence, malice, venomousness, °venom, vindictiveness, vengefulness, spleen, acrimony, animus, °animosity, enmity, bad feeling, bad blood

rancorous *adj.* °hateful, °spiteful, °resentful, °hostile, malign, °malignant, °bitter, malevolent, malicious, °venomous, °vindictive, vengeful, splenetic, acrimonious

random *adj.* **1** °haphazard, °chance, fortuitous, serendipitous, aleatory, °arbitrary, °casual, °stray, °occasional, °indefinite, °indiscriminate, nonspecific, unspecific, unspecified, unordered, unorganized, undirected, °unpremeditated, unplanned, °accidental, uncalculated, unsystematic, adventitious, °incidental, hit-or-miss **2** ***at random.*** randomly, haphazardly, fortuitously, °by chance, serendipitously, arbitrarily, casually, °occasionally, °(every) now and then, °(every) once in a while, irregularly, indefinitely, erratically, indiscriminately, unsystematically, adventitiously, °incidentally, unpremeditatedly

randy *adj.* aroused, °lustful, °lecherous, *US* in heat *or Brit* on heat, *US* in estrus *or Brit* on oestrus, *Slang* °hot, horny, in rut, rutting, at stud

range *n.* **1** °scope, °sweep, °reach, °limit, °extent, °span, °area, radius, °distance, compass, latitude, °stretch, °sphere, °orbit **2** °assortment, series, °collection, °lot, °spread, °selection, °choice, °number, °variety, °kind, °sort, °scale, °gamut, °register **3** °rank, °row, °tier, °line, °file, series, °string, °chain **4** kitchen range, (cooking) stove, *Chiefly Brit* cooker, *Brit trademark* Aga, *US* cookstove —*v.* **5** °line up, °rank, °order, align, array **6** °vary, °fluctuate, °spread, run the gamut, °extend, °stretch, °run, °go **7** °organize, °categorize, catalogue, °arrange, classify, °sort, °class, °group, °rank, °bracket, pigeonhole, °file, °index, °break down, °grade, °distribute **8** °cover, °traverse, °roam, rove, travel over *or* across, go *or* pass over, °drift, °migrate, °wander, °move, °extend

rank[1] *n.* **1** °status, °standing, °position, °place, °level, °stratum, °class, °caste, °circumstances, echelon, °grade **2** °weight, °authority, °power, °superiority, seniority, ascendancy, °priority, °influence, eminence **3** °nobility, °title, high birth, aristocracy, °dignity, °prestige, (blue) blood; peerage **4** °line, °row, column, °queue, series, °formation; °sequence **5** ***ranks.*** soldiers, workers, °staff, employees —*v.* **6** °grade, °rate, classify, °class, °categorize; °dispose, °organize, °order, °sort, assort, °arrange, array, align, °range, °graduate **7** °rate, °count, °stand, have standing *or* value *or* prestige, be important *or* distinguished

rank[2] *adj.* **1** °lush, °luxuriant, °abundant, °flourishing, °profuse, °prolific, °dense, superabundant, °exuberant, °fertile, °productive, fructuous **2** °corrupt, °foul, °low, °base, °gross; °downright, utter, °sheer, °absolute, °complete, °out-and-out, °blatant, °flagrant, unalloyed, °unmitigated, °undiluted **3** °offensive, °loathsome, °disgusting, °gross, °foul, °corrupt, °indecent, °shocking, °immodest, indecorous, °shameless, °risqué, °lurid, °off-color, °outrageous, °blue, °nasty, °vulgar, °vile, °dirty, °filthy, smutty, scatological(al), °pornographic, °obscene **4** °offensive, °loathsome, °disgusting, °gross, °foul, foul-smelling, °smelly, °rancid, noisome, °stinking, reeky, reeking, mephitic, miasmic *or* miasmal *or* miasmatic(al), fetid *or* foetid, noxious, °rotten, °putrid, °musty, °stale, °disagreeable, °strong, °pungent

rank and file *n.* (general) membership, members, °majority

rankle *v.* °gall, °fester, °irk, vex, °plague, °chafe, °grate, nettle, °torment, °pain, °hurt, °provoke, °anger, °exasperate, °get (to), °upset

ransack *v.* **1** °search, °examine, go through *or* over (with a fine-tooth(ed) comb), comb, rake *or* rummage through, °scour, °explore, °scrutinize, turn inside out **2** °rob, °plunder, °pillage, °sack, despoil, °loot, °strip; burgle, *US and Canadian* burglarize

ransom *n.* **1** redemption, °rescue, deliverance; °release, °liberation **2** °payment, payout, °payoff, °price —*v.* **3** °redeem, °rescue, °release, °deliver

rant *v.* **1** declaim, °hold forth, expound, expatiate, orate, perorate, pontificate, trumpet, °preach, °harangue, °lecture, deliver (oneself of) a tirade *or* diatribe *or* speech, °speak **2** vociferate, °bluster, °rave, rant and rave, °bellow, °rage —*n.* **3** °tirade, philippic, °bluster, flatulence, °rhetoric, °bombast, pomposity, turgidity, gasconade, rodomontade, theatrics, histrionics, °act

rap *v.* **1** °knock, °strike, °tap, °hit **2** °criticize, °rebuke, °scold, °reprimand, rap over the knuckles, *Colloq* °knock, *Brit* tick off **3** °converse, °talk, °chat, °gossip, *Colloq* °gab, *Slang* chew the fat *or* the rag —*n.* **4** °knock, °tap, °hit, °blow, °crack, °stroke, cuff, whack, thwack, °punch, *Colloq* °belt, clout, *Slang* sock, slug, biff **5** °conversation, °discussion, °chat, confabulation, °talk, °dialogue, discourse, colloquy, *Colloq* confab, *Slang chiefly US and Canadian* bull session, rap session **6** °responsibility, °blame; °punishment, °sentence; °charge, °accusation, indictment

rapacious *adj.* °greedy, covetous, °grasping, °avaricious, °mercenary, usurious, acquisitive, °predatory, predacious, °ravenous, ravening, °voracious, insatiable, insatiate, wolfish, wolflike, lupine, vulturine, raptorial

rapacity *n.* °greed, greediness, cupidity, covetousness, °avarice, acquisitiveness, predaciousness, ravenousness, voracity, voraciousness, insatiability, insatiableness, rapaciousness

rape *n.* **1** ravishment, defloration, deflowering, °violation, sexual assault, defilement **2** rapine, despoliation, spoliation, despoilment, °pillage, °depredation, ravagement, ravaging, °plunder, plundering, °sack, sacking, looting, ransacking **3** abduction, carrying-off, kidnapping, °seizure, °capture, snatching —*v.* **4** °violate, °ravish, assault sexually, deflower, defile, force to submit to sexual intercourse, have one's way with, take advantage of **5** despoil, spoliate, °pillage, depredate, °ravage, °plunder, °sack, °loot

rapid *adj.* °quick, °fast, °swift, °speedy, high-speed, °brisk, °expeditious, °prompt, °express, °fleet, lightning(-fast), alacritous;

°hurried, °hasty, °precipitate, °impetuous, °immediate, instantaneous, °instant, °sudden

rapidity *n.* quickness, swiftness, °speed, speediness, briskness, expeditiousness, promptness, promptitude, alacrity, celerity, immediateness, dispatch *or* despatch, instantaneousness

rapidly *adv.* **1** °quickly, °fast, °swiftly, speedily, briskly, expeditiously, °like a shot, at the speed of light, double-quick, at full speed, like one possessed, at a gallop, tantivy, *Colloq* like blazes, like (greased) lightning, *US* lickety-split, *Slang* like a bat out of hell, °like mad **2** °promptly, instantly, °instantaneously, instanter, without delay, °at once, *Brit* °straightaway, *US* right away, in a moment, in a trice, °like a shot, in a wink, in (less than) no time, double-quick, in a flash, at the speed of light, before one can turn around, *Colloq* in a jiffy, in two shakes (of a lamb's tail), like (greased) lightning, before one can *or* could say "Jack Robinson," *US and Canadian* (right) off the bat, lickety-split, *Slang* like a bat out of hell

rapport *n.* empathy, °relationship, °sympathy, °harmony, °affinity, °accord, °bond, °relationship, °(mutual) understanding, camaraderie

rapprochement *n.* °reconciliation, °understanding, °settlement

rapt *adj.* **1** entranced, fascinated, spellbound, mesmerized, hypnotized, engrossed, enthralled, bewitched, °absorbed, transported, captivated, °delighted **2** enraptured, °rapturous, °delighted, °elated, °happy, °ecstatic, blissful, °overjoyed, joyous, °joyful, beatific

rapture *n.* °ecstasy, °delight, °joy, joyfulness, joyousness, °pleasure, exaltation, elation, °thrill, °enchantment, euphoria, beatitude, °transport

rapturous *adj.* °ecstatic, °delighted, °joyful, joyous, °elated, thrilled, °enchanted, euphoric, in seventh heaven, °overjoyed, °rhapsodic, *Colloq* on cloud nine, *Brit* over the moon

rare[1] *adj.* **1** uncommon, °unfamiliar, °unusual, °exceptional, °out of the ordinary, °extraordinary, atypical; °scarce, °unparalleled, °choice, recherché, °phenomenal, infrequent, few and far between, °sparse, °scanty, °limited, seldom encountered *or* met with *or* seen; °unique, °singular, one of a kind; *Chiefly Brit* °thin on the ground **2** °fine, °good, °admirable, °excellent, °choice, °select, °special, °first-rate, first-class, °exquisite, °superior, °superlative, °peerless, unequaled, °matchless, °incomparable, in a class by itself *or* herself *or* himself *or* themselves, *sui generis*, °outstanding; collectible *or* collectable

rare[2] *adj.* underdone, undercooked, *bleu(e)*, *saignant(e)*

rarefied *adj.* **1** °thin, °lean, attenuated, diluted, °sparse, scant, °scanty **2** °exalted, °lofty, °elevated, °high, °sublime, °noble, **3** cliquish, clannish, °exclusive, °private, °select, esoteric

rarely *adv.* °seldom, °infrequently, on rare occasions, °hardly (ever), °scarcely (ever), almost never, *Colloq* once in a blue moon

rarity *n.* **1** °curiosity, °oddity, curio, collector's item, °find, °treasure, conversation piece, *Brit* one-off, *Colloq Brit* oner **2** unusualness, uncommonness, rareness, uniqueness, °scarcity

rascal *n.* °imp, °devil, scamp, mischief-maker; rapscallion, °rogue, °scoundrel, cad, °villain, blackguard, knave, °good-for-nothing, ne'er-do-well, °wastrel, scapegrace, dastard, °wretch, *Colloq* scallywag *or* scalawag, *Brit* rotter, blighter, bounder

rash[1] *adj.* °impetuous, °impulsive, °unthinking, °thoughtless, °foolhardy, unconsidered, ill-considered, °ill-advised, injudicious, °imprudent, °indiscreet, °precipitate, °hasty, °careless, °heedless, °reckless, headlong, °wild, madcap, °harebrained, °hot-headed, °adventurous, °quixotic, °venturesome, °audacious, °bold, °dashing, °brash, devil-may-care

rash[2] *n.* **1** °eruption, eczema, redness, efflorescence, dermatitis **2** number(s), °quantity, lot(s), multitude, °profusion, outbreak, series, °succession, °spate, °wave, °flood, deluge, °plague, °epidemic

rasp *n.* **1** °grating, °scrape, scraping, °scratch, scratching, grinding, stridulation **2** °file, grater —*v.* **3** °scrape, abrade, °grate, °file **4** °irritate, °jar (upon), grate upon *or* against, rub (someone) (up) the wrong way, nettle, °irk, °annoy, vex, wear on, °get, *Literary* gride **5** croak, °squawk, screech

rate[1] *n.* **1** °measure, °pace, gait, °speed, °velocity, *Colloq* °clip **2** °charge, °price, °fee, °tariff, °figure, °amount; °toll **3** °percentage, °scale, °proportion **4** Usually, *-rate.* °rank, °grade, °place, °standing, °status, °position, °class, classification, °kind, °sort, °type, rating, °status, °worth, value, valuation, °evaluation **5** *at any rate.* °in any case, °in any event, anyway, °at all events, anyhow, under any circumstances, °regardless, °notwithstanding —*v.* **6** °rank, °grade, °class, classify, °evaluate, °estimate, °calculate, °compute, °count, °reckon, °judge, °gauge, assess, appraise, °measure **7** °merit, be entitled to, °deserve, be worthy of, have a claim to **8** °count, °place, °measure

rate[2] *v.* °scold, °berate, °reprimand, °rebuke, reproach, °reprove, °take to task, °upbraid, censure, *Colloq* °bawl out, °dress down, *US and Canadian* °chew out

rather *adv.* **1** °quite, °very, °somewhat, °fairly, °moderately, to a certain extent *or* degree *or* measure, to some extent *or* degree *or* measure, more or less, °pretty, °slightly, *Colloq* °sort of, kind of **2** preferably, sooner, °instead, more readily *or* willingly **3** *would or US Colloq had rather.* °prefer, °choose

ratify *v.* °approve, °sanction, °endorse, °support, corroborate, °uphold, °back (up), °sustain, °establish, validate, °substantiate, °verify, °authenticate, °guarantee, °warrant, °certify, affirm, °ensure, °clinch, °settle

ratio *n.* °proportion, °relationship, correlation, correspondence

ration *n.* **1** °share, °quota, °allotment, °portion, °helping, °part, °provision, °measure, °dole, °percentage, °amount **2** ***rations.*** supplies, °provisions, °food, °provender, victuals, viands, eatables, edibles, comestibles, *Brit* commons —*v.* **3** Often, ***ration out.*** °allot, apportion, °dole (out), °give out, °distribute, deal out, mete out, °parcel out, °measure out, °hand out **4** budget, °schedule, °restrict, °control, °limit

rational *adj.* **1** °well-balanced, °sane, °sound, °normal, °reasonable, °reasoning, °logical, ratiocinative, clearheaded, cleareyed, °sober; of sound mind, *Colloq* all there **2** °discriminating, °intelligent, °thinking, °enlightened, °prudent, °wise, °knowledgeable, °informed **3** °sensible, common-sense, commonsensical, °practical, pragmatic, down-to-earth, °everyday, °acceptable, °reasonable, °logical

rationale *n.* °reason, °explanation, logical basis, °grounds, °logic, °reasoning, °philosophy, °principle, theory

rationalize *v.* **1** make plausible *or* believable *or* understandable *or* acceptable *or* reasonable, make allowance(s) *or* excuses for, °vindicate, °account for, °justify, °excuse, reason away, °explain away **2** think through, reason out; apply logic to, ratiocinate

rattle *v.* **1** clatter **2** °shake, °vibrate, °jar, joggle, °jiggle **3** °unnerve, disconcert, °discomfit, °disturb, °perturb, °shake, discountenance, °upset, °agitate, °put off, *Chiefly US and Canadian* faze **4** jounce, °bounce, °bump, °jolt, °speed, °hurtle **5** ***rattle off.*** °recite, °list, utter, °reel off, °run through, °enumerate, °call off **6** ***rattle on.*** °chatter, °babble, °jabber, gibber, prate, °prattle, blabber, cackle, blather, °ramble, *Chiefly Brit* witter, natter, *Slang US* run off at the mouth —*n.* **7** clatter, °racket, °noise; rale *or* râle, crackle, crackling; death rattle **8** °clapper, sistrum, *US* noisemaker

rattletrap *n.* flivver, rattler, *Colloq* jalopy *or* jaloppy, tin lizzie, *US* Model T

ratty *adj.* **1** °irritable, °cross, °testy, °touchy, annoyed, crabbed, irritated, °angry, °short-tempered, °impatient, °disagreeable **2** °dirty, °greasy, straggly, °unkempt, matted

raucous *adj.* °harsh, rasping, °rough, °husky, hoarse, °grating, scratching, °scratchy, °discordant, dissonant, jarring; °strident, °shrill, °noisy, °loud, earsplitting, °piercing

ravage *v.* **1** °lay waste, °devastate, °ruin, °destroy, °demolish, °raze, °wreck, wreak havoc on, °damage **2** °pillage, °plunder, despoil, °ransack, °sack, °loot —*n.* **3** Usually, ***ravages.*** °destruction, °damage, depredation(s), devastation, wrecking, °ruin, demolition

rave *v.* **1** °rant, °rage, °storm, fulminate, °roar, °thunder, °howl, °yell, caterwaul, yowl, °bellow, °shout, °scream, °fly off the handle, *Slang* flip one's lid *or Brit* top, raise hell **2** ***rave about.*** °praise, °laud, rhapsodize over, °applaud, gush over —*n.* **3** °praise, acclaim, °favor, enthusiastic reception, °tribute, °testimonial, encomium, °bouquet, plaudits, accolade, °admiration, *US* hosanna **4** °rage, °fashion, °vogue, °trend, °thing, last word, *dernier cri*, °craze, °mania, *Colloq* °fad

ravenous *adj.* **1** °hungry, °famished, starving, °starved **2** °voracious, °gluttonous, °greedy, insatiable, ravening, swinish, piggish, °hoggish, edacious, wolfish

ravine *n.* °gorge, canyon *or* cañon, °pass, cleft, defile, gully *or* gulley, °valley, *Dialect Brit* clough, *Scots* linn, *US* °gap, gulch, arroyo

raving *adj.* **1** °mad, °insane, °berserk, raging, °crazy, crazed, irrational, manic, °maniacal, °frantic, frenzied, °delirious, °hysterical; out of one's mind *or* head **2** °extraordinary, °outstanding, °unusual, °rare, uncommon, °phenomenal, °great, °striking, °ravishing, *Colloq* °stunning —*n.* **3** Often, ***ravings.*** °rant, ranting, °bombast, pomposity, grandiloquence, magniloquence, rodomontade, °rhetoric, °bluster, blustering, claptrap, balderdash, puffery, bunkum, flatulence, hyperbole, vaporing, fustian, *Colloq* °hot air, bunk **4** gabble, °babble, babbling, °gibberish, *Colloq* °gab

ravish *v.* **1** °enrapture, °delight, °captivate, enthrall, °fascinate, °charm, °entrance, spellbind, °bewitch, °transport **2** °rape, °violate, have one's way with, deflower, defile

ravishing *adj.* °dazzling, °beautiful, °gorgeous, °striking, °radiant, charming, alluring, °attractive, entrancing, captivating, °enthralling, bewitching, °spellbinding, *Colloq* °stunning

raw *adj.* **1** uncooked, °unprepared, °fresh **2** unprocessed, untreated, °unrefined, unfinished, °natural, °crude **3** °new, °inexperienced, unseasoned, °immature, °green, °untried, °fresh, untrained, unskilled, untested **4** exposed, unprotected, uncovered, °open; °sore, °tender, °inflamed, °painful, °sensitive **5** °chill, °chilly, chilling, °cold, °damp, °frigid, °freezing, °biting, stinging, nippy, nipping, °sharp, °keen, °piercing, °penetrating **6** °brutal, °frank, °candid, °blunt, °direct, °unvarnished, unmollified, unembellished, °realistic, °honest, °plain, unreserved, unrestrained, °uninhibited, °bluff, straightforward —*n.* **7** ***in the raw.*** °naked, stark-naked, undressed, unclothed, °nude, in the nude, *Brit* starkers, *Colloq* in the buff, in the altogether, in one's birthday suit

rawboned *adj.* °gaunt, °lean, gangling, °thin, °skinny, °spare, °meager, °scrawny, underfed, bony, °emaciated, half-starved, wasted, hollow-cheeked, cadaverous

ray *n.* **1** °beam, °shaft, °bar, °streak, pencil, °gleam, °flash **2** glimmer, °trace, °spark, scintilla, °flicker

raze *v.* tear *or* pull *or* bring *or* knock *or*

throw down, °demolish, °destroy, °level, °flatten, bulldoze

reach *v.* **1** Often, ***reach out.*** °hold out, °extend, °stretch (out), °stick out, thrust out, outstretch, outreach **2** °arrive at, °get to, °come to, go to, end up at *or* in; land at *or* in, *Colloq* °make (it to) **3** °get, get in touch with, °communicate with, establish *or* make contact with, get through to, get (a) hold of **4** attain, °achieve, °accomplish, °make, get *or* go to, get *or* go as far as **5** come *or* go *or* get up to, °amount to, attain, climb to, °rise to, run to, °equal, °match **6** get through *or* across to, °register with, °communicate with, reach into the mind of, °impress, °influence, °sway, °move, °stir, carry weight with —*n.* **7** °range, ambit, °scope, °orbit, compass, °sphere, °territory **8** °capability, °capacity

react *v.* **1** °act, °behave, °conduct oneself, °proceed; °retaliate, °reciprocate, get even **2** °respond, °answer, °reply, °retort

reaction *n.* **1** °response, °reply, °answer, °effect, feedback **2** repulsion, °resistance, counteraction, counterbalance, compensation **3** retaliation, reciprocation, °reprisal, °revenge

reactionary *adj.* **1** °conservative, ultraconservative, °right, rightist, right-wing; traditionalist; *Chiefly Brit* blimpish, *South African* verkrampte —*n.* **2** °conservative, ultraconservative, rightist, right-winger; traditionalist; *Brit* Colonel Blimp, *South African* verkrampte

read *v.* **1** °peruse, °scan, °skim, °review, °study, °look over, °pore over **2** °understand, °know, be familiar with, °comprehend, °interpret, °decipher **3** °announce, °present, °deliver **4** ***read into.*** assign to, °impute (to), °infer (from), °assume (from), °presume (from), conclude (from)

readable *adj.* **1** °intelligible, comprehensible, understandable, easy to understand, easily understood, °plain **2** °entertaining, easy to read, enjoyable, °pleasurable, °absorbing, °interesting, °engaging, °stimulating, °worthwhile **3** °legible, decipherable, °distinct

readily *adv.* **1** cheerfully, °willingly, eagerly, ungrudgingly, unhesitatingly, °freely, °gladly, °happily, agreeably, graciously, charitably **2** effortlessly, °easily, smoothly, without difficulty **3** °promptly, °quickly, speedily, °swiftly, apace, °at once, without delay, °in no time, °immediately, instantly, °instantaneously, instanter, *Brit* °straightaway, *US* right away, at *or* on short notice, *Colloq* pronto

readiness *n.* **1** willingness, cheerfulness, goodwill, °eagerness, agreeableness, graciousness **2** promptness, quickness; °facility, °ease, °skill, adroitness, expertness, °proficiency **3** ***in readiness.*** See **ready, 1,** below.

ready *adj.* **1** °prepared, °(all) set, °in readiness, in (proper) shape; up, primed, °ripe, °fit, in condition; *Colloq* psyched (up) **2** °agreeable, consenting, acquiescent, °willing, °content, °eager, °keen, °happy, °cheerful, °genial, °gracious, °cordial, °friendly, well-disposed, °enthusiastic, *Colloq* °game **3** apt, °likely, °inclined, °disposed, °given, °prone **4** °about, °liable, °likely, apt; °on the verge of, °subject to, °in danger of, on the brink of, on the point of, °close to **5** °prompt, °rapid, °quick, °immediate, °speedy, °swift, °punctual, °timely **6** °clever, °keen, °sharp, °agile, deft, °skillful, adroit, °alert, °bright, °intelligent, °perceptive, °quick **7** on *or* at *or* to hand, °handy, °available, °accessible, at (one's) fingertips, °at the ready, close at hand, °convenient —*n.* **8** ***readies.*** °money, °cash, wherewithal **9** ***at the ready.*** **(a)** waiting, °on tap, °expectant, in position, °poised **(b)** See **8,** above. —*v.* **10** °prepare, make *or* get ready, °set, fit out, °equip, °organize, psych up

ready-made *adj.* **1** ready-to-wear, finished, prefabricated, *Brit* off-the-peg **2** °convenient, °expedient, °serviceable, usable, °handy, °useful, °suitable, °adaptable; °plausible, credible, believable **3** stereotyped, stereotypic(al), hackneyed, time-worn, trite, °stale, °conventional, unoriginal, °stock, °pedestrian, °routine, °run-of-the-mill

real *adj.* **1** °genuine, °true, °actual, °authentic, verified, verifiable, °legitimate, °right, °bona fide, °official; °legal, °legitimate, licit, °natural, valid, °veritable **2** °genuine, °actual, °true, existent, °authentic, °natural; °material, °physical, °tangible, palpable, corporeal **3** °genuine, °sincere, °heartfelt, °true, °actual, unfeigned, °unaffected, °earnest, °honest, °truthful, °legitimate, valid **4** °genuine, °actual, °true, °loyal, °trustworthy, trusted, °honest **5** °intrinsic, °actual, °true, °genuine, °proper, °essential —*adv.* **6** See **really,** below.

realistic *adj.* **1** practical, °matter-of-fact, down-to-earth, pragmatic, commonsense, °sensible, reasonable, °levelheaded, °rational, °sane, hardheaded, businesslike, °nononsense, unromantic, unsentimental, °tough, tough-minded, *Colloq* hard-nosed, hard-boiled **2** °natural, °lifelike, true-to-life, naturalistic, °vivid, °genuine, °real, °graphic

reality *n.* **1** actuality, °fact, °truth, genuineness, authenticity, *Aristotelianism* entelechy **2** ***in reality.*** See **really,** below.

realization *n.* **1** °conception, °understanding, comprehension, apprehension, awareness, °appreciation, °perception, °recognition, °cognizance **2** actualization, °consummation, °accomplishment, °achievement, °establishment, °fulfillment, materialization, effectuation

realize *v.* **1** make real, °effect, °bring about, make happen, make a reality, actualize, °accomplish, °produce, °achieve, °fulfill, °materialize, °effectuate **2** °understand, °appreciate, °comprehend, be aware of, conceive of, °grasp, °perceive, discern, be *or* become conscious *or* aware *or* appreciative of, °recognize, °see, *Colloq* °catch on (to), cotton (on) to, *Brit* °twig **3** °return, °gain, °clear,

°profit, °make, °earn, bring *or* take in, °net, °produce, °get

really *adv.* **1** genuinely, °actually, °truly, °honestly, °in reality, in actuality, in (point of) fact, as a matter of fact, °surely, °indeed, °absolutely, °definitely **2** °indeed, °actually, °absolutely, unqualifiedly, °positively, categorically, unquestionably, °definitely, undeniably **3** °in effect, °in reality, °actually, °in fact, de facto, in the end, °at bottom, in the final analysis, at the end of the day, *Colloq* deep down **4** °very, °extremely, °quite, exceptionally, remarkably, unusually, uncommonly, extraordinarily, °exceedingly, *Nonstandard* °real

realm *n.* **1** °domain, °kingdom, empire, °monarchy, principality, palatinate, duchy *or* dukedom **2** °territory, °area, bailiwick, °department, °responsibility, °jurisdiction **3** °area, confines, °sphere, °limits

ream *v.* °drill (out), °bore (out), open up, °tap

reap *v.* **1** °harvest, °garner, glean, °gather (in), °mow, take in *or* up **2** °profit, °bring in, °gain, °procure, °acquire, °get, °obtain, °take in

rear[1] *n.* **1** °back (part), °end, hind part, *Nautical* °stern, *Colloq* °tail (end), fag end, *US and Canadian* tag end **2** hindquarters, °posterior, rump, °buttocks, *Colloq* °bottom, behind, backside, rear end, *Slang Brit* arse, °bum, *US and Canadian* ass, tokus, toches; *Babytalk US and Canadian* tushie *or* tushy *or* tush, hinie —*adj.* **3** °back, °last, °end, rearmost, *Nautical* aft, after, °stern

rear[2] *v.* **1** °raise, °bring up, °care for, nurture, °nurse; °cultivate, °educate, °train; °breed, °produce **2** °erect, °raise, °build, °put up, °construct, °fabricate, °create **3** °raise, °lift, °put up, upraise, uplift, °hold up

reason *n.* **1** justification, °argument, °case, °explanation, °rationale, ground(s), °pretext, vindication, °defense, why (and wherefore), *Literary* apologia, apology **2** °judgment, common sense, °intelligence, °sanity, sense(s), saneness, °insight, perspicacity, percipience, °understanding, rationality, °reasoning, °mind, °intellect **3** °purpose, °aim, °intention, °object, °objective, °goal, °motive, °end, °point **4** °excuse, rationalization **5** ***by reason of.*** because of, on account of, °owing to, °by virtue of, as a result of; due to **6** ***within or in reason.*** °reasonable, °sensible, justifiable, °rational, °fitting, °proper, °acceptable —*v.* **7** °think, conclude, °calculate, °reckon, °estimate, °figure (out), °work out, °deduce, act *or* think rationally *or* logically, ratiocinate, use (one's) judgment *or* common sense, use (one's) head, put two and two together **8** ***reason with.*** argue with, remonstrate with, debate with, discuss with, talk over with, °plead with, °convince; °persuade, dissuade, °urge, °prevail upon

reasonable *adj.* **1** °sensible, °rational, common-sense, commonsensical, °sane, °logical, °sober, °sound, °judicious, °wise, °intelligent, °thinking **2** credible, believable, °plausible, °tenable, reasoned, arguable, well-thought-out, well-grounded **3** °moderate, °tolerable, °acceptable, °within reason, °equitable, °fair; °inexpensive, unexcessive, unextravagant, °economical, °conservative **4** °appropriate, °suitable, °proper, °sensible, °right

reasoning *n.* **1** °thinking, °logic, °analysis, rationalization **2** reasons, arguments, premises, °rationale, postulate, °hypothesis, theory, °explanation, explication

reassure *v.* °comfort, °encourage, hearten, °buoy (up), °bolster, °cheer, uplift, inspirit, °brace, °support, restore confidence to, set *or* put (someone's) mind at rest, set *or* put (someone) at ease, settle (someone's) doubts

rebate *n.* **1** °discount, reduction, °deduction, °allowance, markdown, cutback, refund, repayment, *Colloq US* °rake-off **2** °kickback, °percentage, °rake-off, commission, °cut, °bribe, °graft, *Colloq chiefly US* payola, *US* plugola —*v.* **3** °discount, °reduce, °deduct, °mark down, refund, °repay; kick back

rebel *v.* **1** °revolt, °mutiny, rise up **2** Often, ***rebel against.*** °defy, °flout, °dare, °challenge; °disobey, dissent —*n.* **3** °revolutionary, revolutionist, insurgent, insurrectionist, mutineer, resister, resistance fighter, freedom fighter **4** heretic, °nonconformist, apostate, dissenter, recusant, °schismatic

rebellious *adj.* **1** °insubordinate, °defiant, °mutinous, °revolutionary, contumacious, insurgent, insurrectionary, °seditious **2** unmanageable, °disobedient, °incorrigible, °ungovernable, °unruly, °difficult, refractory, °stubborn, °obstinate, °recalcitrant

rebirth *n.* renaissance *or* renascence, °revival, renewal, reawakening, °resurgence, revitalization, resurrection, regeneration, rejuvenation, °restoration, new beginning, reincarnation; metempsychosis, palingenesis

rebound *v.* **1** spring back, °bounce, °recoil, ricochet, resile —*n.* **2** °bounce, °recoil, ricochet, °return, comeback, °repercussion, °backlash, reflex

rebuff *n.* **1** °rejection, snub, °check, °denial, °repulse, °refusal, °dismissal, °defeat, repudiation, °slight, discouragement, *Colloq* cold shoulder, °cut, °put-down, °brushoff, *Slang US* °brush —*v.* **2** °reject, snub, °check, °deny, °repel, drive away, °spurn, °repulse, °refuse, °dismiss, °defeat, °repudiate, °slight, °ignore, *Brit* send (someone) to Coventry, *Colloq* give (someone) the cold shoulder, °cut, put (someone) down, brush (someone) off, give (someone) the brushoff, tell (someone) where to go *or* get off, tell (someone) where to get lost, *Slang* hand (someone) his *or* her *or* their walking papers, freeze (someone) out, *US* give (someone) the brush, show (someone) the door

rebuke *v.* **1** scold, reproach, admonish, °reprove, °reprimand, °lecture, censure, chide, reprehend, °berate, °castigate, °criticize, °take to task, °upbraid, revile, *Colloq* °dress down, °bawl out, give (someone) a piece of one's mind, haul (someone) over the coals, let (someone) have it, give (someone) hell *or* what for, tell (someone) off, tell (someone) where to get off, *Brit* carpet, tear (someone) off a strip, tick (someone) off, wig, blow (someone) up, give (someone) a wigging, *US and Canadian* rake (someone) over the coals, give (someone) the business, chew out —*n.* **2** scolding, reproach, admonition, °reproof, °reprimand, °lecture, censure, chiding, reprehension, berating, castigation, °criticism, upbraiding, revilement, °tongue-lashing, *Colloq* dressing-down, what for, *Brit* wigging, blowup *or* blowing up, *Slang* hell

rebut *v.* refute, °deny, °disprove, confute, invalidate, negate, °discredit, belie, °contradict, controvert, °puncture, °expose, °destroy, °ruin, °devastate, *Colloq* shoot full of holes, knock the bottom out of, shoot down, blow sky-high

rebuttal *n.* °answer, °reply, °retort, °response, rejoinder, counter-argument, riposte, retaliation, °denial, refutation, contradiction, confutation, *Colloq* comeback

recalcitrant *adj.* °stubborn, °obstinate, °willful, °defiant, refractory, headstrong, °perverse, °contrary, contumacious, °mutinous, °rebellious, fractious, °unruly, unmanageable, °ungovernable, uncontrollable, wayward, °insubordinate, intractable, unsubmissive, unyielding, unbending, adamant, °immovable, °inflexible, °stiff, °firm

recall *v.* **1** °remember, °recollect, think back to, reminisce over *or* about, call to mind **2** °withdraw, °retract, call back, °summon **3** rescind, °cancel, annul, nullify, °retract, °withdraw, °revoke, °recant, °take back, call back; disavow, disown, °deny —*n.* **4** °memory, °recollection, remembering, °remembrance **5** withdrawal, recantation, °cancellation, revocation, annulment, nullification, recision, rescission, retraction, °repeal, disavowal, °denial **6** withdrawal, retraction, °return

recant *v.* °recall, forswear, °deny, rescind, °repudiate, disavow, disclaim, °withdraw, °revoke, °retract, °forsake, °abandon, apostasize, °renounce, abjure, °take back

recapitulate *v.* summarize, °sum up; °repeat, °go over (again), °reiterate, restate, °review; °recount, °enumerate, °recite, °relate, °list, *Colloq* recap

recede *v.* **1** °ebb, °subside, fall *or* go *or* move back, abate, °return, °withdraw, °retreat, °back up **2** °diminish, lessen, °decline, °dwindle, °shrink, °wane, °fade, become more distant *or* less likely

receipt *n.* **1** sales receipt, register receipt, sales slip, ticket, °stub, counterfoil, proof of purchase, voucher **2** °delivery, acceptance, °reception, °arrival **3** ***receipts.*** °income, °proceeds, °gate, takings, gains, °return, *Colloq* °take

receive *v.* **1** °get, °obtain, °come by, °collect, °take (into one's possession), °accept, be given, °acquire, come into, °inherit, °gain, °profit, °make **2** °earn, be paid, °make, °draw, °gross, °net, °clear, °pocket, *Colloq* take home, walk off *or* away with, *US* °pull down **3** °greet, °meet, °welcome; show in, give entrée, °let in, °admit **4** °experience, °undergo, °endure, °suffer, °bear, °sustain, be subjected to, °meet with **5** °gather, °hear, °learn, ascertain, be told, be informed *or* notified of, °find out, °pick up

recent *adj.* °late, °latest, °new, just out, °brand-new, °fresh; °current, °modern, up-to-date, late-model

receptacle *n.* container, holder, repository; °box, tin, can, °case, °casket, °chest, reliquary, °vessel, °bag, basket

reception *n.* **1** °welcome, °greeting, °treatment, °reaction, °response **2** °party, levee, °social, soirée, °function; °opening, °preview, vernissage, *Colloq* do

receptive *adj.* **1** °open, °hospitable, amenable, pervious, persuasible, °tractable, °flexible, pliant, °interested, °willing, °responsive **2** °quick, °alert, °perceptive, °astute, °intelligent, °keen, °sharp, °bright, °sensitive

recess *n.* **1** alcove, °niche, °nook, °cranny, bay, °hollow **2** °respite, °rest, °interlude, time off, °break, °intermission, breather, breathing spell, °pause; °holiday, vacation **3** ***recesses.*** innermost reaches, corners, secret places, °depths, penetralia

recession *n.* °setback, (economic) downturn, °slump, °decline, °dip, °depression

recipe *n.* **1** °formula, °prescription **2** °plan, °procedure, °method, °approach, °technique, °way, °means, °system, °program, modus operandi, *Colloq US* MO (= 'modus operandi')

recipient *n.* receiver, beneficiary, heir *or* heiress, legatee

reciprocal *adj.* °mutual, exchanged, returned, complementary, correlative, °common, shared, °joint, requited

reciprocate *v.* °repay, recompense, °requite, °exchange, °return, °trade, °match, °equal, °correspond

recital *n.* **1** (solo) concert, °performance, musicale, °presentation, °show, °entertainment **2** °report, °narration, °account, °recitation, °description, °relation, °telling, recounting, °narrative, °rendition, °interpretation, °version, recapitulation, °rehearsal, °repetition, *Colloq* recap

recitation *n.* **1** reciting, °performance, reading, monologue **2** See **recital, 2,** above.

recite *v.* **1** °quote, °repeat, °present **2** °report, °narrate, °recount, °relate, °tell, °describe, °detail, °chronicle, °list, °share, °recapitulate, °repeat, *Colloq* recap

reckless *adj.* °careless, °rash, °thoughtless, incautious, °heedless, °foolhardy, °imprudent, unwise, injudicious, °impulsive, °irresponsible, negligent, unmindful, °foolish, devil-may-care, °daredevil, °wild, °breakneck, °dangerous, madcap, °mad, °harebrained

reckon *v.* **1** Often, ***reckon up.*** °calculate,

°compute, °add (up), °figure (up), °tally (up), °sum up, °total (up), work out *or* up **2** °include, °count, °number, °enumerate, °list, °name, °consider, °account, °judge, deem, look upon, °regard, °view, °think of, °hold, °gauge, °estimate, appraise, value, °rank, °rate, °class **3** °suppose, °think, °assume, °presume, daresay, °venture, °imagine, °fancy, °consider, conclude, be of the opinion, *US or Colloq* °guess **4** ***reckon on or upon.*** °count on, °rely on, °depend on, °lean on, trust in, take for granted, *Colloq* bank on **5** ***reckon with.*** **(a)** settle (accounts) with, °take care of, °look after, see *or* attend to, °deal with, °handle, pay attention to, °think about **(b)** take into account *or* consideration, °consider, °contemplate, °account for, °remember, °bear in mind

reckoning *n.* **1** counting, °calculating, °calculation, computation, enumeration, °addition **2** °bill, °account, invoice, *US* °check, *Colloq chiefly US and Canadian* °tab **3** °(last) judgment, °retribution, final account(ing) *or* settlement, °doom

reclaim *v.* °restore, °recover, °rescue, °redeem, °salvage, °save, regain, °retrieve, regenerate, °rejuvenate

recline *v.* °lie (down), lie back, lean back, °lounge, °rest, °repose, °sprawl, loll, stretch out

recluse *n.* °hermit, anchorite *or* anchoress, monk *or* nun, eremite

reclusive *adj.* °solitary, lone, °secluded, °isolated, eremitic(al), hermitic, anchoritic, monastic, cloistered, sequestered, °retiring, °shut off

recognition *n.* **1** °identification, detection **2** °acknowledgment, °notice, °attention, °cognizance, acceptance, awareness, °perception, °admission; °honor, °appreciation

recognize *v.* **1** °identify, °detect, °place, °recall, °remember, °recollect, °know (again) **2** °acknowledge, °perceive, °understand, °realize, °see, °admit, °accept, own, °concede, °allow, °grant, °appreciate, °respect, be aware of **3** °approve, °sanction, °endorse, °accept, validate, °ratify **4** °honor, give recognition to, °salute, show gratitude *or* appreciation, °reward, °distinguish, pay respect, do homage

recoil *v.* **1** jerk *or* jump *or* spring back, °start, °flinch, wince, °shrink, blench, balk *or* baulk, shy (away) (from) **2** °rebound, bounce back, resile, kick back —*n.* **3** °kick, °rebound, °repercussion, °backlash

recollect *v.* °recall, °remember, call to mind

recollection *n.* °memory, °recall, °remembrance, °impression, °reminiscence

recommend *v.* **1** °counsel, °advise, °guide, °urge, exhort, °suggest, °advocate, °propose, °(put) forward, °propound, °persuade **2** °endorse, °praise, commend, mention favorably, vouch for, °second, °subscribe to, °back, °push, °favor, °approve, °underwrite, °stand up for, °support, °promote, *Colloq* °tout, °plug **3** make attractive *or* advisable *or* interesting *or* acceptable

recommendation *n.* **1** °counsel, °advice, °guidance, urging, exhortation, °direction, °encouragement, °suggestion, prompting, advocacy, °proposal **2** °endorsement, °praise, commendation, favorable mention, °backing, °blessing, °approval, approbation, °support, °promotion, good word, °testimonial, °say-so

reconcile *v.* **1** get *or* bring (back) together, °unite, reunite, settle *or* resolve differences between, restore harmony between, make peace between, placate, make compatible **2** °resign, °submit, °accommodate, °adjust

reconciliation *n.* **1** conciliation, appeasement, propitiation, pacification, placation, °rapprochement, reconcilement, °understanding, détente, reunion, °harmony, concord, °accord, amity, °rapport **2** compromise, °settlement, °agreement, arbitration, conformity, compatibility, °adjustment

recondite *adj.* abstruse, arcane, °obscure, esoteric, °deep, °profound, °incomprehensible, unfathomable, impenetrable, undecipherable, °opaque, °dark, °occult, cabbalistic *or* cabalistic *or* kabbalistic *or* kabalistic, °inexplicable, enigmatic

reconnaissance *n.* °survey, °examination, scouting, °exploration, reconnoitering, °investigation, inspection, °scrutiny, *Slang Brit* recce

reconnoiter *v.* °survey, °examine, °scout (out), °scan, °explore, °investigate, °inspect, °scrutinize, °check out, check up (on), *Slang Brit* recce

record *v.* **1** °write (down), °transcribe, °document, °register, °note, make a notation (of), °take down, put *or* set down, log, °chronicle, °report, °itemize, °list, °enumerate, catalog **2** °tell of, °relate, °recount, °narrate, °recite —*n.* **3** recording, °report, °document, log, °journal, °memorandum, °note, °notation, minute(s), °transactions, archive(s), annal(s), °chronicle, °diary, °account, dossier, °register, °list, catalog **4** documentation, °data, °information, °evidence; °memorial, °memento, souvenir **5** °(best) performance, track record, °accomplishment; °time; °distance; °height **6** accomplishment(s), deed(s), °history, °reputation, curriculum vitae, CV, *Colloq* track record **7** disk *or* disc, recording, album, °release, LP (= 'long playing'), 78, 33, 45, EP (= 'extended play'), maxisingle, CD (= 'compact disk *or* disc'), *Brit* gramophone record, *US* phonograph record, *Colloq* °single, *Slang US* °platter **8** ***off the record.*** confidential(ly), private(ly), not for publication, secret(ly), °in confidence, unofficial(ly), sub rosa —*adj.* **9** record-breaking, °extreme

recount *v.* **1** °relate, °narrate, °tell, °recite, °report, °communicate, °impart, °unfold **2** particularize, °review, °detail, °describe, °enumerate, °specify

recoup *v.* regain, °make good, °make up, recompense, °repay, °recover; refund, °redeem, °reimburse, remunerate

recourse *n.* **1** °resort, access, entrée, °admittance, availability **2** °resource, backup, °reserve, °refuge, place to turn, °alternative, °remedy

recover *v.* **1** regain, get *or* take *or* win *or* make back (again), °recoup, repossess, retake, recapture, °restore, °retrieve, °reclaim, °redeem **2** get well *or* better, °recuperate, °convalesce, °mend, return to health, regain one's strength *or* health, be on the mend, °heal, °improve, °revive, °rally, take a turn for the better, get back on one's feet, °pull through **3** °save, °salvage, °deliver, °rescue, °return, bring back, °reclaim, °retrieve

recovery *n.* **1** recuperation, convalescence, °restoration, °improvement, healing, °rally, turn for the better; °rise, °revival, °increase, amelioration, bettering, betterment, °advance, °gain, advancement, *Colloq* pickup, comeback **2** retrieval, recouping, repossession, retaking, °restoration, reclamation; recapture, redemption **3** °salvage, °delivery, deliverance, °rescue, °return, °saving, reclamation, retrieval

recreation *n.* °entertainment, °amusement, °enjoyment, °diversion, °distraction, fun and games, °leisure (activity), °pastime, °relaxation, °sport, °play

recrimination *n.* counter-accusation, countercharge, retaliation, counterattack, blaming, °aspersion, °reprisal

recruit *v.* **1** °draft, °induct, °enlist, °enroll, °muster, °raise, °call up, conscript, °mobilize, °impress, levy *—n.* **2** conscript, trainee, beginner, °apprentice, °initiate, °novice, neophyte, tiro *or* tyro, *US* draftee, enlistee, *Colloq* °greenhorn, rookie

rectify *v.* °correct, °revise, redress, put *or* set right, °cure, °repair, °remedy, °improve, emend, °fix, °adjust, °square, ameliorate

rectitude *n.* °propriety, correctness, °morality, uprightness, °probity, °virtue, decency, goodness, °honesty, °integrity, incorruptibility, righteousness, °principle, good character, respectability, unimpeachability

recumbent *adj.* reclining, lying down, flat on one's back, °horizontal, °lying, reposing, accumbent, decumbent, °supine, stretched out; °leaning (back)

recuperate *v.* °improve, °recover, °convalesce, get better, °rally, °revive, °mend, °heal, get back on one's feet, regain one's health, °pull through, °survive, take a turn for the better

recur *v.* °return, happen *or* occur again, reoccur, °repeat, come (back) again, reappear

recurrent *adj.* repeated, recurring, returning, reoccurring, reappearing, °frequent, °periodic, cyclical, °regular, °repetitive, °repetitious, °persistent, incessant, °continual, °intermittent, °habitual, iterative

redeem *v.* **1** °reclaim, °recover, regain, repossess, °retrieve, °get back, buy back, repurchase; °pay off, *Brit* °clear **2** °rescue, °ransom, °deliver, °free, °save, °liberate, set free, °emancipate, °release **3** °exchange, °cash (in), collect on, trade in **4** °rehabilitate, °save, °reform, °convert, absolve, restore to favor, reinstate **5** make amends for, °make up for, atone for, redress, compensate for, °offset, make restitution for **6** °perform, °fulfill, °keep, °make good (on), °discharge, °satisfy, °abide by, keep faith with, be faithful to, hold to, °carry out, °see through

red-handed *adj.* in the (very) act, (in) *flagrante delicto*, *Colloq* with one's hand in the till, *US* with one's hand in the cookie jar

redolent *adj.* **1** °fragrant, sweet-smelling, °aromatic, perfumed, odorous, scented, °savory **2** ***redolent with or of.*** reminiscent of, °suggestive of, evocative of, remindful of, characteristic of, having the earmarks *or* hallmark of

reduce *v.* **1** °cut (back), °cut down (on), °decrease, °diminish, °moderate, abate, lessen, °shorten, truncate, °abbreviate, °abridge, °curtail, crop, °trim, compress, °restrict, °limit, °stunt **2** °ease (up on), °let up (on), °decrease, °mitigate, °tone down, °slacken up (on) **3** lose weight, °slim (down), °diet, trim down, *Chiefly US* slenderize **4** °change, °modify, °adjust, °turn, °convert; break down *or* up, °grind, °rub, triturate, °pulp, °powder **5** °cut, °decrease, °trim, bring down, °lower, °drop, °mark down, °slash, *Colloq* °knock down **6** demote, °degrade, °lower, °downgrade, °break; °humble; *Military US and Canadian* bust **7** °diminish, lessen, bring down, °depreciate, °subdue, °belittle, °minimize **8** *Medicine* °set, °adjust, reset

redundant *adj.* **1** °superfluous, °unnecessary, °surplus, inessential *or* unessential, °nonessential, unneeded, unwanted, *de trop*, in excess, °excessive **2** °wordy, verbose, prolix, overlong, long-winded, °repetitious, tautologic(al) *or* tautologous, circumlocutory, °roundabout

reek *v.* **1** stink *or* smell (to high heaven), *Slang Brit* pong, °hum **2** smoke, steam *—n.* **3** stink, °stench, fetor *or* foetor, miasma, mephitis, °odor, °smell, *Slang Brit* °hum, pong **4** °fumes, smoke, steam, °vapor, °exhalation, cloud, °mist

reel *v.* **1** °stagger, °totter, waver, °stumble, °lurch, falter, °roll, °rock, °sway, °flounder, °pitch **2** ***reel off.*** °list, °recite, °rattle off, °enumerate, °review, °itemize, °name, read off, °call off, °run through, °run over

refer *v.* **1** Often, ***refer to.*** allude to, make reference to, °mention, make mention of, °touch on, °bring up, advert to, °speak of, turn *or* call *or* direct attention to, direct to, °point to, °indicate, advert to, °specify, °name, °concern, °quote, cite, make a note of, take note of, °note **2** °assign, °hand over, pass on *or* over, °send, °direct, °commit **3** Usually, ***refer to.*** °look at, °use, °study, °check, °consult, °resort to, have recourse to, °turn to, appeal to, confer with; °talk to, °ask, inquire *or* enquire of, apply to **4** Usually, ***refer to.*** °mean, °signify, °denote, °say

reference *n.* **1** allusion, °mention, °remark,

referral, °direction, °indication, °specification, naming, °quotation, citation, °note, °notation, notification, °hint, intimation, °innuendo, insinuation **2** °regard, °concern, °connection, °respect, °relation, °relevance, pertinence **3** °endorsement, °recommendation, °testimonial, certification; credentials

refine *v.* **1** °purify, °cleanse, °clear, °clarify, decontaminate **2** °cultivate, °civilize, °polish, °improve, elevate, °perfect **3** hone, °sharpen, °concentrate, °focus, subtilize

refined *adj.* **1** °cultivated, cultured, civilized, °polished, °sophisticated, urbane, °elegant, °well-bred, °genteel, courtly, °ladylike, gentlemanly, polite, °courteous, mannerly, well-mannered, °gracious, °gentle, °noble, aristocratic, °dignified, °elevated, *Colloq* °posh **2** °subtle, °discriminating, discerning, °sensitive, °fastidious, °nice, °precise, °exacting, cultured, °educated, °cultivated, °knowledgeable, advanced, °sophisticated **3** °exact, °precise, °fine, °subtle, °sensitive, °nice, °sophisticated **4** purified, clarified, cleansed, °pure, °clean; distilled

refinement *n.* **1** °culture, °polish, °elegance, °sophistication, urbanity, urbaneness, °breeding, cultivation, gentility, °propriety, courtliness, °civility, politeness, politesse, °delicacy, °tact, °diplomacy, °finesse, suavity, suaveness, °taste, tastefulness, °discrimination, discernment, °sensitivity **2** °subtlety, nicety, nuance, °distinction, °detail, fine point, °delicacy, minutia; fastidiousness, finickiness **3** refining, purification, purifying, clarification, clarifying, cleaning, cleansing; filtration, distillation **4** °improvement, betterment, bettering, enhancement, °development, °perfection

reflect *v.* **1** °mirror, send *or* throw back, °reproduce, °return; °echo **2** °show, °demonstrate, °exhibit, °illustrate, °exemplify, °reveal, °lay bare, °expose, °display, °disclose, °bring to light, uncover, °point to, °indicate, °suggest, °evidence **3** Often, ***reflect about or on.*** think (about *or* over *or* on), °contemplate, muse (about *or* on), °consider, ponder (about *or* over *or* on), deliberate (on *or* over), ruminate *or* meditate (about *or* on *or* over), cogitate (about *or* on *or* over); mull over, °weigh, °evaluate, °examine **4** ***reflect on or upon.*** °result in, end in, °bring, °attract, °cast, °throw

reflection *n.* **1** °image, °echo, *Brit* reflexion **2** °thought, °thinking, meditation, meditating, °consideration, cogitation, rumination, deliberation, deliberating, pondering, °study, cerebration **3** °aspersion, °imputation; °effect **4** °result, °sign, °token, °symbol, °mark; °evidence, °testimony, testament, °proof, substantiation, corroboration

reflective *adj.* reflecting, °thoughtful, °pensive, contemplative, meditating, musing, °meditative, cogitating, cogitative, ruminating, deliberative, deliberating, pondering

reform *v.* **1** °improve, °better, ameliorate, meliorate, emend, °rectify, °correct, °mend, °repair, °fix, °remedy, redo, °revise, revolutionize, °rehabilitate, remodel, refashion, °renovate, reorganize, rebuild, °recover **2** mend one's ways, turn over a new leaf, *Colloq* go straight —*n.* **3** °improvement, betterment, amelioration, melioration, emendation, rectification, °correction, rehabilitation, °change, modification, perestroika, reorganization, renovation, °recovery

reform school *n.* *US* reformatory, *Brit* youth custody center, CHE (= 'community home (with education on the premises)'), *Brit formerly* borstal, approved school

refrain[1] *v.* **1** Usually, ***refrain from.*** °keep (from), forbear, abstain (from), eschew, °avoid **2** °stop, °cease, °give up, °discontinue, desist, °quit, °leave off, °renounce

refrain[2] *n.* °melody, °song, °tune, chorus, °burden, reprise

refresh *v.* **1** °enliven, °renew, °revive, °freshen (up), resuscitate, bring back to life, breathe new life into, invigorate, °vitalize, °energize, °brace, °fortify, exhilarate, revitalize, reinvigorate, reanimate **2** °arouse, °rouse, °awaken, waken, reawaken, °stimulate, °jog, °prod, °activate **3** °fix up, °repair, redo, °revamp, °overhaul, °spruce up, recondition, °renovate, °refurbish, refurnish; °renew, restock, °restore

refreshing *adj.* °invigorating, °stimulating, °bracing, °exhilarating, °fresh, inspiriting, fortifying, °tonic, like a breath of fresh air, rejuvenating, enlivening, vitalizing, revitalizing; cooling, thirst-quenching, slaking

refreshment *n.* **1** Usually, ***refreshments.*** °nourishment, nutriment, °sustenance, restorative, °food, drink(s), edibles, eatables, °bite, snack(s), tidbit(s), *Brit* titbit(s), *Slang* grub, eats, chow, nosh **2** stimulation, invigoration, exhilaration, °tonic, rejuvenation, enlivenment, °revival, °restoration, renewal, resuscitation, fortification, °reinforcement

refrigerate *v.* °cool, °chill, keep cool *or* cold *or* chilled, ice, °freeze

refuge *n.* **1** °sanctuary, °shelter, haven, asylum, °protection, °cover, °retreat, °harbor, °security, safe house, °stronghold, citadel, bolt-hole, hideaway, hide-out, *Colloq* hideyhole **2** °excuse, °pretext, °resort, °recourse, °ruse, °trick, °stratagem, °subterfuge, °dodge, °evasion, °expedient

refugee *n.* °fugitive, °runaway, escapee, displaced person, DP, °exile, émigré

refurbish *v.* °restore, refurnish, redecorate, °clean (up), °polish, °renew, °renovate, °spruce up, remodel, refit, °overhaul, °repair, recondition, °revamp, rebuild, *Colloq* do up, *US* °fix up

refusal *n.* **1** °denial, °rejection, °disapproval, turndown **2** °option, °choice, °privilege, disposal

refuse[1] *v.* **1** °decline, °reject, °spurn, °repudiate, °turn down, °rebuff, give (something) the thumbs down, *US* turn thumbs down on, *Colloq* pass by *or* up **2** °deny, °deprive (of), °withhold, disallow, not allow *or* permit

refuse[2] *n.* °rubbish, sweepings, °waste, °litter, dust, °dirt, °dregs, dross, °garbage, debris, detritus, castoffs, °junk, *Chiefly US* °trash

regal *adj.* **1** °royal, kingly, queenly, °princely, fit for *or* befitting a king *or* queen, °noble, lordly, °sovereign, °majestic, °imperial, °stately, °splendid, °magnificent, °grand, resplendent, °palatial, °exalted **2** °disdainful, °haughty, °proud, °scornful, contumelious, °contemptuous, °derisory, derisive, °pompous, lordly

regale *v.* °entertain, °amuse, °delight, °divert, °indulge, please, °gratify, °captivate, °fascinate, °entrance, °enchant, spellbind, °bewitch, °charm, °enrapture

regalia *n.* °finery, decorations, insignia, emblems, accouterments *or* accoutrements, furnishings, °apparatus, °gear, °paraphernalia, °trappings, °tackle, appurtenances, °equipment, equipage

regard *v.* **1** °view, look at *or* upon *or* on, °observe, °note, °notice, °watch, °eye, keep an eye on, gaze at *or* upon, stare at **2** °contemplate, °consider, °perceive, °view, look upon *or* on, °treat **3** °respect, °esteem, value **4** °consider, °view, look upon *or* on, °think (of), °judge, deem, °rate, °believe (to be), °gauge, °see, pay heed *or* attention to, °esteem, °account, °take into account, °imagine, °reckon, °evaluate **5** °concern, °relate to, be relevant to, pertain to, apply to, °refer to, °affect, have (a) bearing on, bear on *or* upon, °involve, have to do with, °go for —*n.* **6** °reference, °relation, °relevance, relevancy, °association, pertinence, °application, °bearing, °connection, °link, °tie-in **7** °respect, °consideration, °attention, °reverence, °veneration, awe, °deference, °honor, °favor, °esteem, high opinion, °approval, approbation, °appreciation, °admiration, °affection, fondness **8** °point, °particular, °respect, °aspect, °detail, °matter **9** °care, °concern, °thought, °consideration, °respect, °sympathy, °feeling, °sentiment; °heed, °attention, °notice, °mind **10** ***regards.*** best wishes, good wishes, °compliments, °greetings, °respects, salutations, *Archaic* devoirs

regarding *adj.* °concerning, °about, respecting, with regard to, with respect to, with reference to, on *or* in the matter of, pertaining to, on the subject of, apropos, re, *Law* in re, *Archaic or Scots* anent, *Dialectal* anenst

regardless *adj.* **1** Sometimes, ***regardless of.*** °despite, °notwithstanding; °in spite of, heedless of, *Nonstandard* irregardless —*adv.* **2** °notwithstanding, °nevertheless, no matter what, °in any event, °in any case, °at all events, anyway, anyhow, *Nonstandard* irregardless

regime *n.* régime, regimen, °reign, °government, °rule, °regulation, °administration, °direction, °order, °leadership, °management, °system, °discipline

regiment *v.* °discipline, °order, °organize, systematize, whip into shape, °standardize, °regulate, °control

region *n.* **1** °district, °area, °zone, °territory, °division, locality, sector, °section, °tract, °part, °dominion, °precinct, °province, °quarter, °department **2** °sphere, °territory, °domain, °province, °field, ambit, °pale, °jurisdiction, bailiwick

register *n.* **1** °record, °roll, roster, rota, catalogue, annal(s), archive(s), °journal, daybook, °diary, appointment book, °calendar, °chronicle, °schedule, °program, directory, ledger, °file, °index, inventory, °list, listing, °poll, °tally **2** cash register, °till, money box, cashbox —*v.* **3** °record, write *or* jot *or* take *or* put *or* set down, °list, °enroll, sign in *or* on *or* up, °enter, catalog, log, °index, °chronicle, °note, make *or* take note (of) **4** °show, °display, °express, °indicate, °manifest, °reveal, °betray, divulge, °record, °reflect **5** °make known, inform of, °advise, °transmit, °communicate, °record, °note, make note of, °report, °write down, °minute **6** °check in, sign in *or* on, log in **7** Sometimes, ***register with or on.*** °sink in, °impress, become apparent (to), make an impression (on), come home (to), °get through (to); dawn on *or* upon, °occur to **8** °indicate, °read, °mark, °represent, °measure, °point to, °specify, °exhibit, °show, °manifest

regret *v.* **1** rue, °mourn, °lament, °bemoan, °bewail, °repent, be *or* feel sorry for, feel remorse for, feel *or* be remorseful over, be *or* feel upset, never forgive oneself, deplore, deprecate, weep *or* cry over —*n.* **2** Sometimes, ***regrets.*** repentance, °guilt, °sorrow, °disappointment, contrition, °remorse, regretfulness, (pang *or* pangs of) conscience, self-reproach, self-condemnation, °qualm, second thoughts, rue, ruefulness, °grief, °woe, °sadness, mournfulness, *Literary* dolor **3** ***regrets.*** °refusal, nonacceptance, nonconsent, *US* turndown

regretful *adj.* rueful, °mournful, °sad, °repentant, °guilty, °sorry, °sorrowful, °disappointed, contrite, °remorseful, °apologetic, °penitent

regrettable *adj.* °lamentable, °deplorable, woeful, °sad, distressing, upsetting, °unhappy, °unfortunate, unlucky, too bad, °awful, °terrible, execrable, reprehensible, °wrong, °shameful, shaming, *Colloq* °tough, °rough

regular *adj.* **1** °routine, °ordinary, °common, °everyday, °customary, °accustomed, wonted, commonplace, °normal, °usual, °traditional, °time-honored, °conventional, °typical, °habitual, °natural, °familiar, °standard, °predictable, scheduled, °fixed, unvarying, °invariable, °methodical **2** scheduled, °routine, °systematic, ordered, °steady, °consistent, rhythmic(al), °automatic, °uniform, °periodic, cyclic(al); hourly, °daily, weekly, hebdomadal, semiweekly, biweekly, fortnightly, semimonthly, monthly, bimonthly, seasonal, °quarterly, semiannual, annual **3** °symmetrical, °uniform, °even, even-sided, equal-sided, equilateral, equal-angled, equiangular; °harmonious **4** undistorted, °even, well-proportioned, °proportional, °symmetrical, °classic **5** °even, °smooth, °level, °straight, °uniform, uninterrupted, unvarying, °continuous, °flat, °plane, °plumb **6** dependable, °methodical, (well-)regulated, (well-)ordered, °orderly; °proper, °correct, °legal, °official, °bona fide, °legitimate, established, recognized, °orthodox, approved, *Colloq* kosher, O.K. *or* OK *or* okay **7** °usual, expected, °normal, °habitual, °accustomed, °familiar **8** °acceptable, accepted, °estimable, °fine, °good, °likable, °popular, °pleasant **9** °complete, utter, thoroughgoing, °unmitigated, unalloyed, °unqualified, consummate, °perfect, °thorough, °absolute, °well-known, acknowledged **10** °permanent, °career **11** °conventional, °usual, °common, conformable, °ordinary, °systematic, *Colloq US* ruly —*n.* **12** °fixture, °habitué, °(steady) customer, °patron, °client, frequenter

regularity *n.* **1** consistency, constancy, °uniformity, evenness, sameness, °symmetry, °balance, °harmony, harmoniousness, orderliness, °order, °stability, predictability **2** °routine, reliability, dependability, steadiness, invariability; °pace, °rhythm, °cadence

regulate *v.* **1** °adjust, °modify, °modulate, °control, °balance, °set, °fix, °order, °govern, °organize, °maintain, °manage **2** °control, °monitor, °govern, °run, °operate, °administer, °handle, °guide, °steer, °conduct, °direct, °supervise, superintend, °oversee, °manage

regulation *n.* **1** °adjustment, modification, modulation, °control, °balance, balancing, °setting, fixing, °organization, °maintenance **2** °rule, ruling, °law, °code, bylaw *or* byelaw, edict, °order, ordinance, statute, °decree, directive, °dictate **3** edict, ukase, °pronouncement, fiat, (papal) bull, °proclamation —*adj.* **4** °standard, accepted, °official, required, prescribed, °mandatory **5** °usual, °normal, °ordinary, °customary, °typical

regurgitate *v.* °vomit, disgorge, return one's dinner, °spew up, °(of birds of prey) cast; retch, °gag; *Colloq* °throw up, upchuck, *Slang* puke, *US* spiff one's biscuits, barf

rehabilitate *v.* **1** °restore, °save, °reclaim, °rescue, °redeem, reestablish, reinstate, reeducate, reorient, °reform, *US* °straighten out, *Colloq US* rehab **2** °renew, redecorate, °renovate, °refurbish, °restore, °fix (up), °repair, reconstruct, rebuild, °change, °transform

rehash *v.* **1** rework, go over again, restate, redo, rearrange, reshuffle, reuse —*n.* **2** reworking, restatement, redoing, rearrangement, reshuffle, reshuffling, reuse, rewording

rehearsal *n.* **1** °practice, °exercise, dry run, °drill, °run-through, read-through, dress rehearsal, *Technical* undress rehearsal **2** °narration, recounting, °relation, °recital, °telling, °description, enumeration, °account, °repetition, °repeat

rehearse *v.* **1** °practice, °exercise, °run through, read through, °study, °repeat **2** °repeat, °relate, °recite, °tell, °describe, °recount, °review, go through *or* over, °review, °report, °recapitulate, *Colloq* recap

reign *n.* **1** °rule, °sovereignty, ascendancy, °power, hegemony, °influence, °command, suzerainty, °administration, °jurisdiction, °leadership, °government, °direction, °control, °domination, mastery; °kingdom, °monarchy, empire —*v.* **2** °rule, °control, °command, °govern, °lead, °direct, °dominate, °supervise, °manage, hold sway, wear the crown, wield the scepter, occupy the throne, *Colloq* run the show, rule the roost, *Slang* °call the shots **3** °prevail, be *or* become prevalent, °predominate, hold sway, °obtain, be *or* become rampant, be *or* become universal

reimburse *v.* °repay, recompense, refund, °pay back, °compensate, remunerate, indemnify

rein *n.* **1** °check, °curb, °control, °restraint, constraint, limitation, harness, °bridle, °brake **2** ***reins.*** °control, °command, °administration, °running, °leadership, °power, °rule, tiller, °helm —*v.* **3** ***rein in.*** °check, °curb, °control, °restrain, °limit, harness, °bridle, °restrict, pull back on

reinforce *v.* °strengthen, °buttress, °bolster, °support, °fortify, °prop (up), shore up, augment, °brace, °stay, °steel

reinforcement *n.* **1** °buttress, °support, °prop, °brace, °stay, °bolster **2** strengthening, buttressing, bolstering, shoring (up), augmentation, °bracing **3** ***reinforcements.*** °reserves, auxiliaries, men, soldiers, forces, personnel

reiterate *v.* °repeat, restate, iterate, °labor, harp on, °dwell on, °rehash, °recapitulate, *Colloq* recap

reject *v.* **1** °decline, °refuse, disallow, °spurn, °veto, °turn down, give the thumbs-down (on *or* to), °set aside, *US* turn thumbs down (on); °deny, °repudiate, °renounce, °rebuff, °shun, °brush aside, turn a deaf ear to, will not hear of **2** °refuse, °repel, °repulse, °spurn, °rebuff, say no to, °turn down, °decline, °brush aside; °jilt, °drop, °dismiss, °throw over, give (someone) the cold shoulder, show (someone) the door, send (someone) away *or* on his *or* her *or* their way, °turn one's back on, *Slang* give (someone) the brushoff *or US also* the brush, give (someone) his *or* her *or* their walking papers, *Brit* give (someone) the boot **3** throw away *or* out, °discard, disown, jettison, °eliminate, °scrap, *Colloq* °junk, °scratch —*n.* **4** °second, °irregular, °discard, castoff

rejection *n.* °refusal, °denial, repudiation, °rebuff, °dismissal, spurning, renunciation, turndown; cold shoulder, *Slang* brushoff *or US also* brush, the (old) heave-ho

rejoice *v.* °delight, °exult, °glory, °celebrate, °revel, be happy *or* delighted *or* pleased *or* overjoyed *or* elated *or* glad, *Colloq* be tickled (pink)

rejuvenate *v.* °restore, °refresh, reinvigorate, revitalize, revivify, °renew, reanimate, regenerate, recharge, breathe new life into

relapse *v.* **1** °get back, backslide, °fall back, °lapse, slip back, regress, retrogress, recidivate; go back, °return, °retreat, °revert **2** °decline, °deteriorate, °weaken, °degenerate, °fail, °fade, °sink, °sicken, °worsen, get *or* become worse —*n.* **3** backsliding, falling *or* going back, °lapse, lapsing, °return, returning, reversion, reverting, regression, regressing, retrogression, retrogressing, recidivism, apostasy **4** °decline, deterioration, weakening, degeneration, °failing, °failure, fading, °sinking, worsening

relate *v.* **1** °associate, °connect, °couple, °link, °tie, °ally, correlate, °coordinate **2** °recount, °narrate, °tell, °report, °present, °describe, °recite, °detail, °set forth, °communicate, divulge, °impart, °reveal, delineate, °make known, give an account of, °rehearse **3** apply to, coordinate with, °respect, °regard, bear upon *or* on, have a bearing on, have reference to, have to do with, pertain to, °refer to, appertain to, belong with *or* to **4** Often, ***relate to.*** be in *or* en rapport with, °understand, empathize, °sympathize, °communicate with, °identify with, °grasp, °comprehend, be in tune with, °deal with, °handle, °cope with, *Colloq* °dig, tune into, be hip to, be turned on to, be *or* get into

related *adj.* **1** associate(d), affiliate(d), connected, coupled, linked, tied up, allied, correlated, coordinate(d), interconnected, interrelated, interdependent, °mutual, °reciprocal, °common, °joint, cognate **2** °kin, °kindred, consanguineous, cognate, agnate; °akin

relation *n.* **1** °relationship, °connection, affiliation, °association, °bearing, °link, °tie, °tie-in, °reference, pertinence, interconnection, interdependence, correspondence, °kinship **2** °kinship, °relationship **3** °relative, kinsman *or* kinswoman, blood relative, in-law, family member **4** °narration, °narrative, °telling, recounting, °description, °report, °recital, °recitation, delineation, portrayal, °story, recapitulation **5** ***in relation to.*** °concerning, °about, °regarding, respecting, pertaining to, with regard to, with respect to, referring to, with reference to, on *or* in the matter *or* subject of, apropos, re, *Archaic or Scots* anent, *Dialectal* anenst **6** ***relations.*** **(a)** sexual intercourse, coitus, °sex, criminal conversation; carnal knowledge of **(b)** °dealings, °intercourse, link(s), association(s), °liaison, °relationship, *Colloq* doings, °truck

relationship *n.* See **relation, 1, 2,** above.

relative *adj.* **1** °related, connected, associated, allied, °affiliated, interconnected, interrelated, °pertinent, °relevant, germane, °applicable; apropos **2** Sometimes, ***relative to.*** comparative, comparable, proportionate, °proportional, commensurate; analogous to, contingent on, dependent on, reliant on, conditioned by, °subject to, attendant on, correspondent *or* corresponding to, provisional on, appurtenant to; °subordinate to, ancillary to —*n.* **3** See **relation, 3,** above.

relatively *adv.* more or less, °somewhat, comparatively, °rather, to some degree *or* extent

relax *v.* **1** °loosen, let go, °release, °let up (on), °relieve, °ease, °reduce, °moderate, slacken, °remit, *Colloq* ease up on, slacken up on **2** °diminish, °decrease, lessen, °reduce, abate, °weaken, °mitigate, °modify, °tone down, °moderate, °modulate, °lighten (up on), °check, °temper, °curb **3** ease up, °slow down, loosen up, put one's feet up, °rest, unbend, *Colloq* take it easy, unwind **4** °calm down, cool down, °quiet down, stay calm, cool, and collected, *Colloq* take it easy, *Slang* cool it

relaxation *n.* **1** °ease, °repose, °rest, °leisure, °recreation, °amusement, °entertainment, °fun, °pleasure, °diversion, *Colloq* R and R (= 'rest and relaxation') **2** easing (up *or* off), °relief, alleviation, abatement, diminution, lessening, mitigation, moderation, slackening, °remission, weakening, letting up, *Colloq* °letup

relaxed *adj.* °nonchalant, easygoing, °calm, °peaceful, °tranquil, °serene, pacific, °carefree, insouciant, °blasé, languorous, languid, devil-may-care, free and easy, happy-go-lucky, °mellow, at ease, composed, °cool

release *v.* **1** let go, °(set) free, °liberate, (set *or* let *or* turn) loose, unloose, untie, unchain, unfetter, unshackle, °deliver, °let out, disenthrall, °discharge, °let off, °emancipate, manumit, °rescue, °save **2** °issue, °publish, make available, °put out, °pass out, °hand out, come out with, °circulate, °distribute, disseminate; °launch, °unveil, °present —*n.* **3** freeing, releasing, liberating, loosing, unloosing, delivering, emancipating, manumitting, rescuing, °saving, °freedom, °liberation, deliverance, °discharge, emancipation, manumission, °rescue, °remission, salvation **4** press *or* publicity release, °announcement, publicity, °notice, °story, °report

relegate *v.* **1** consign, °banish, °exile, °transfer, dispatch *or* despatch **2** °downgrade, demote **3** °assign, °commit, °hand over, °refer, °transfer, °pass on

relent *v.* °relax, °soften, °yield, °give, give way *or* ground, °bend, °comply, acquiesce, compromise, °capitulate, come round, be merciful, show pity *or* compassion, °melt, show mercy, °succumb

relentless *adj.* **1** unyielding, inexorable, unstoppable, unrelenting, dogged, °implacable, °inflexible, unbending, unmoving, °unmoved, unrelieved, °stiff, °hard, stiff-necked, °rigid, °obstinate, adamant, obdurate, intransigent, °determined, unswerving, undeviating, intractable, persevering, °steely, °tough, intransigent, unsparing, uncompromising, pitiless, unforgiving, °ruthless, °merciless, °cruel, °unmerciful, °remorseless **2** °nonstop, °persistent, incessant, unrelenting, unremitting, unstoppable, °perpetual, unfaltering, unfailing, unflagging, unrelieved, unabated, unrelieved, unbroken, °continual, °continuous, ceaseless, °constant, unceasing, °steady, °habitual, °regular

relevance *n.* relevancy, appropriateness, aptness, pertinence, °bearing, °connection, °affinity, °tie-in, °relation, °significance, suitability, suitableness, applicability, °application, applicableness

relevant *adj.* °pertinent, °appropriate, apt, °related, °relative, °significant, suited, °applicable, °fitting, °proper, germane, °akin, allied, associated, apposite, °to the point

reliable *adj.* dependable, °trustworthy, °honest, trusty, trusted, °principled, °conscientious, punctilious, °honorable, credible, believable, °safe, °sure, °certain, °secure, °sound, °responsible, °predictable, °stable, unfailing, °infallible, °reputable

reliance *n.* °confidence, °trust, °faith, dependence

relic *n.* **1** °memento, °keepsake, °memorial, °remembrance, souvenir, heirloom, °token, artifact **2** °remains; °fragment, °trace, °scrap, shard *or* sherd, °remnant

relief *n.* **1** °ease, easing, abatement, easement, deliverance, °remedy, redress, alleviation, °release, °remission, assuagement, °liberation, °recess **2** °aid, °help, °support, °assistance, succor; °comfort **3** °elevation, °projection, °contrast, °prominence; bas-relief *or* basso rilievo (= 'low relief'), mezzo-rilievo (= 'medium relief'), alto-rilievo (= 'high relief') **4** °substitute, surrogate, replacement, °alternate, locum (tenens), °stand-in; °understudy, °double

relieve *v.* **1** °ease, lessen, °reduce, °diminish, abate, °lift, °raise, alleviate, °mitigate, palliate, °soften, soothe **2** disburden, °free, °rid, °liberate, disencumber, unburden, °rescue, °save, °release **3** °help, °aid, °assist, °support, succor, °rescue, save, °deliver **4** °stand in (for), °replace, °substitute for, take over for *or* from, *US* °spell, *Colloq* sub for

religion *n.* °creed, °belief, °faith; °doctrine, dogma

religious *adj.* **1** °devout, churchgoing, °pious, god-fearing, °holy, spiritual-minded **2** °scrupulous, °exact, °precise, °conscientious, rigorous, °strict, °fastidious, °meticulous, °faithful, punctilious, unerring, unswerving, undeviating

relinquish *v.* **1** °yield, °give up, °cede, °waive, °leave, °quit, °abandon, °drop, °forsake, forswear, °desert, °abdicate, °resign, °renounce, let go, °surrender, °vacate, retire from **2** let go, °give up, °release, unloose, °loose, °free

relish *n.* **1** °enjoyment, °pleasure, °delight, °gusto, °eagerness, avidity, °anticipation, °taste, °appetite, °zest, °liking, °appreciation, fondness, °fancy, °partiality, °preference —*v.* **2** °enjoy, °delight in, take pleasure in, °fancy, be partial to, °appreciate, °savor, °look forward to, °anticipate

reluctance *n.* unwillingness, disinclination, °aversion, °dislike, disrelish, hesitancy

reluctant *adj.* unwilling, °disinclined, °averse, °hesitant, °loath, °unenthusiastic, °indisposed, °opposed, antagonistic; °cautious, chary, °wary, °leery, circumspect, °careful

rely *v.* ***rely on or upon.*** depend on *or* upon, lean on *or* upon, count on *or* upon, bank on *or* upon, have confidence in, bet on, trust in, °swear by, be sure *or* certain of

remain *v.* **1** °stay (behind), be left, °tarry, °linger, °wait, *Colloq* stay put **2** be left, be there **3** °stay, °continue, °carry on, °abide; °endure, °persist, °last, °persevere —*n.* **4** ***remains.*** **(a)** leavings, remnants, crumbs, debris, detritus, °remainder, °balance, °residue, leftovers, °scraps, vestiges, °traces, °fragments, oddments, °odds and ends **(b)** °body, °cadaver, °corpse; carcass

remainder *n.* **1** °rest, °balance, °remains, °residue **2** °excess, overage, °surplus, °residue, residuum, leftovers

remaining *adj.* **1** °left (over), extant, °outstanding **2** °leftover, surviving, °residual; °unused, uneaten, unconsumed

remark *n.* **1** °note, °notice, °observe, °perceive, °regard, °look at, take notice *or* note of **2** comment (on *or* upon), °say, °observe, °reflect, °mention, °declare, °state, assert

remarkable *adj.* **1** °extraordinary, °unusual, °singular, °exceptional, °noteworthy, °notable, uncommon, °incredible, °unbelievable, °impressive, °phenomenal, astonishing, astounding, surprising **2** °striking, °distinguished, °signal, °special, wonderful, °marvelous, out-of-the-ordinary, °unique, °significant, °outstanding, °rare, °memorable, unforgettable, never-to-be-forgotten **3** °strange, °different, °odd, °peculiar, °curious

remedy *n.* **1** °cure, °treatment, °therapy, °antidote, counteractant, countermeasure, medication, medicament, °medicine, °prescription, °drug, pharmaceutical, cure-all, panacea, nostrum, restorative, °specific **2** °cure, °antidote, cure-all, panacea, nostrum, countermeasure, °relief, redress, °answer, °solution —*v.* **3** °cure, °treat, °heal, °mend, °restore, °relieve, soothe, °control, °ease, °mitigate, alleviate **4** °correct, °rectify, °reform, °improve, ameliorate, redress, °repair, put *or* set right, °straighten out

remember *v.* **1** call to mind, °bear in mind; °recall, °recollect **2** muse (on *or* about), °reminisce over *or* about, think back on *or* about, °memorialize, °commemorate, °recognize **3** °retain, °keep in mind, °recall **4** °tip, °reward

remembrance *n.* **1** °memory, °recollection; °reminiscence **2** °memento, °reminder, souvenir, °keepsake, °memorial

remind *v.* °prompt, °cue, cause to remember, jog the memory, put in mind of

reminder *n.* mnemonic, refresher; °cue, °prompt

reminisce *v.* Sometimes, ***reminisce about.*** °remember, °recollect, think back, look back, turn one's mind *or* thoughts back; call to mind, hark back, °return

reminiscence *n.* Usually, ***reminiscences.***

anecdote(s), °memory *or* memories, °reflection(s), °memoir(s)

reminiscent *adj.* Usually, ***reminiscent of.*** recalling, °redolent of, evocative of, °indicative of, °suggestive of, °similar to, comparable with *or* to

remiss *adj.* °slack, °careless, negligent, neglectful, °heedless, unheeding, °inattentive, unmindful, °thoughtless, °forgetful, °unthinking, °slow, °indolent, °lazy, dilatory, °delinquent

remission *n.* **1** °forgiveness, °pardon, deliverance, amnesty, °reprieve, exoneration, °release, absolution, exculpation, °indulgence, °excuse, °exemption, acquittal **2** diminution, abatement, °decrease, lessening, subsidence, alleviation, mitigation, assuagement, ebbing, °relaxation, easing

remit *v.* **1** °send, °transmit, °forward, dispatch *or* despatch; °pay, °compensate, °settle, liquidate **2** abate, °diminish, slacken, °decrease, lessen, °subside, alleviate, °mitigate, assuage, °ebb, °dwindle, °reduce, °relax, ease (up *or* off), °fall off

remittance *n.* °payment, °settlement, °allowance, °consideration

remnant *n.* **1** °scrap, °shred, °fragment, °end, °bit, °piece, °trace, °vestige, °relic **2** °leftover, °remainder, °residue, °rest, °remains, °part

remorse *n.* °regret, repentance, ruefulness, °sorrow, °woe, °anxiety, guilty *or* bad conscience, pangs of conscience, °humiliation, °embarrassment, °guilt, self-reproach, mortification, °shame, contrition, contriteness, °penitence, °compunction, °bitterness

remorseful *adj.* °regretful, °repentant, rueful, °sorry, °apologetic, °sorrowful, woeful, °anxious, °guilty, °bad, conscience-stricken, guilt-ridden, humiliated, humbled, °embarrassed, mortified, °shamefaced, °shameful, °ashamed, shamed, contrite, °penitent, °bitter

remorseless *adj.* **1** °cruel, °heartless, °callous, °harsh, hardhearted, stonyhearted, °savage, °merciless, °unmerciful, pitiless, °ruthless **2** °relentless, unrelenting, unremitting, unstoppable, inexorable, °implacable

remote *adj.* **1** °distant, °faraway, far-off, removed, °outlying, °inaccessible **2** °lonely, °isolated, godforsaken, °secluded, °out-of-the-way, sequestered, tramontane, ultramontane **3** °unfamiliar, °obscure, arcane, °recondite, °subtle, °alien, °far-fetched, °unusual, °unlikely **4** °unrelated, °irrelevant, °inappropriate, unconnected, °outside **5** °slight, °faint, foggy **6** °slight, °faint, °slender, °insignificant, °slim, °small, °meager, °outside, °poor, inconsiderable, °negligible, °improbable, °unlikely, °implausible **7** °aloof, °detached, °withdrawn, °reserved, °indifferent, °standoffish, abstracted **8** °early, °ancient, far-removed, °distant

removal *n.* **1** elimination, removing, eradication, taking away **2** extermination, °murder, elimination, °killing, slaying, assassination, °execution, liquidation, eradication, °massacre, °slaughter, °purge, doing away with, *Slang* bumping off, rubbing out, doing in, *US* rubout, wasting **3** °dismissal, °transfer, transference, transferal, shifting, °discharge, throwing over, throwing out, deposition, unseating, dethroning, dethronement, displacement, °expulsion, ouster, ousting, riddance, °purge, *Colloq* firing, sacking **4** °move, °transfer, departure, °moving

remove *v.* **1** °take off, doff, °shed, °cast off **2** take away, °get rid of, carry away *or* off, °shift; °transfer **3** °obliterate, °delete, °erase, expunge, eradicate, efface, °eliminate, °take off, wipe *or* rub out, wipe *or* rub off, °get rid of **4** °murder, assassinate, °kill, slay, °execute, °exterminate, °eliminate, liquidate, eradicate, °massacre, °slaughter, do away with, °dispose of, °get rid of, °purge, *Slang* rub *or* wipe out, do in, °bump off, *US* °waste **5** °discharge, °dismiss, depose, unseat, °displace, °expel, oust, °turn out, °get rid of, °purge, *Colloq* °fire, °sack, kick out **6** relocate, °move, °transfer, °shift **7** °take out, unfasten, °detach, °disconnect, °separate, °undo —*n.* **8** °distance, °space, °interval, °separation

remuneration *n.* **1** °payment, compensation, °salary, °wages, °earnings, emolument, °income, °pay, °stipend, °consideration, °reward **2** recompense, repayment, reimbursement, °restitution, reparation(s), °damages, °indemnity, indemnification, redress

renaissance *n.* renascence, °rebirth, °revival, reawakening, °restoration, resumption, renewal, °resurgence, °return, regeneration, rejuvenation, new dawn, new birth

rend *v.* **1** rip *or* tear *or* pull (to pieces *or* apart *or* asunder), °wrench, °mangle, °shred **2** °split, °tear, °rip, °rupture, °cleave, rive, °separate, °slice, °lacerate **3** °pain, °distress, °pierce, °stab, smite, °wound, °afflict, °torment, wring, °hurt

render *v.* **1** depict, °picture, °represent, °reproduce, °portray, °create, °produce, do, °execute, °make, °accomplish, °achieve **2** °make, cause to be *or* become **3** °give (up), °yield (up), °surrender, °relinquish, °resign, °cede, °deliver, °hand over, °tender, °offer, proffer, °present, °furnish, °provide **4** °play, °perform **5** °deliver, °return **6** °translate, decode, °decipher, °transcribe, °convert, °explain, °interpret, °put, restate, °reword, rephrase **7** °deliver, °hand in, °present, °offer, proffer, °furnish, °provide, °tender **8** °melt, °clarify, °extract, *Brit* render down

rendering *n.* depiction, showing, °presentation, °interpretation, °conception, °version, °rendition, °representation, delineation, portrayal, °picture

rendition *n.* **1** °performance, °interpretation, °execution, °conception, concept, °understanding, construction, reading, °rendering **2** See **rendering,** above.

renegade *n.* **1** °deserter, °turncoat, heretic, °defector, °traitor, apostate, *Archaic* renegado —*adj.* **2** °traitorous, treacherous, °perfidious, treasonous, apostate, °heretical, °disloyal

renege *v.* **1** *Cards* °revoke **2** °go back on, back out, °default, °repudiate, go back on *or* break (one's) promise *or* word, °recant, abrogate, abjure, *Slang* welsh (on)

renew *v.* **1** °restore, °refresh, °rejuvenate, revitalize, reinvigorate, resuscitate, °revamp, redo, °rehabilitate, °transform, regenerate, °refurbish, refurnish, °renovate, refit, °overhaul, recondition, °modernize, redecorate, do over **2** °resume, °resurrect, restart, pick *or* take up again, recommence, return to, reopen **3** °restore, °replace, restock, °replenish **4** °repeat, °reiterate, reaffirm, °confirm, reconfirm, restate, reassert

renounce *v.* °give up, forswear, °surrender, °abandon, °desert, abjure, °reject, °repudiate, °spurn, °swear off, abstain from, °deny, °forgo, °forsake, eschew, disown, throw off *or* out, °shun, °avoid

renovate *v.* redecorate, °modernize, do over, °refurbish, refurnish, refit, remodel; recondition, °rehabilitate, °restore, °repair, °revamp, °overhaul, °patch up, *Colloq* do up, *US* °fix up

renown *n.* °fame, °celebrity, °glory, °distinction, °esteem, acclaim, °reputation, °prominence, eminence, °note, °mark, °honor, °prestige, repute, éclat, °luster, illustriousness, stardom

renowned *adj.* °famous, famed, °celebrated, °distinguished, acclaimed, °prominent, °eminent, °well-known, °noted, °notable, honored, °illustrious

rent[1] *v.* **1** °let (out), °lease, °hire (out), °charter (out), °farm out —*n.* **2** rental, °hire, °lease, °fee

rent[2] *n.* °tear, °rip, °split, °gash, °slash, °hole, °slit

repair *v.* **1** °mend, °patch (up); °renew, put *or* set right, °restore, °fix (up), °service, put (back) in *or* into working order, vamp, °revamp, °adjust —*n.* **2** °mend, °patch; °restoration, fixing (up), servicing, °improvement, °adjustment, renovation, revamping, renewal **3** °form, °condition, fettle, °state, working order, *Colloq* °shape, *Brit* °nick

repartee *n.* °banter, badinage, persiflage, °patter, °(witty) conversation, wordplay, °raillery, °give-and-take, *Literary* deipnosophy

repay *v.* °pay back, recompense, °compensate, °requite, °reciprocate, return the favor *or* compliment, °reward, °square with, settle (up) with; refund, give back, °return, °reimburse, °restore

repeal *v.* **1** °revoke, °recall, rescind, °reverse, °cancel, annul, nullify, invalidate, °void, °set aside, °abolish, abrogate, *Law* °vacate —*n.* **2** revocation, °recall, rescission, rescindment, °reversal, °cancellation, annulment, nullification, invalidation, voiding, °abolition, abrogation

repeat *v.* **1** °reiterate, restate, °echo, retell, °recite, °quote, °rehearse, °recount, °recapitulate, *Colloq* recap **2** °duplicate, °reproduce, replicate —*n.* **3** °repetition, °duplicate, °copy, duplication, replication, °reproduction, °replica, rerun, rebroadcast, replay, encore, reprise

repeatedly *adv.* again and again, over again, over and over, °frequently, °often, time and (time) again, time after time, recurrently, repetitively, repetitiously

repel *v.* **1** °repulse, drive back *or* away *or* off, °reject, °fend off, parry, °ward off, °hold off, °rebuff, °resist, °withstand, keep at bay *or* arm's length **2** °revolt, °offend, °disgust, °sicken, °nauseate, turn one's stomach, make one's skin crawl, *Colloq* give one the creeps, turn one off

repellent *adj.* °repulsive, repelling, °revolting, °disgusting, nauseating, °nauseous, stomach-turning, sickening, °offensive, °loathsome, °repugnant, °distasteful, vomit-provoking, sick-making, °disagreeable, °obnoxious, off-putting

repent *v.* °regret, feel contrition, °lament, °bemoan, °bewail, be sorry, rue, feel remorse, feel remorseful *or* penitent, show penitence

repentant *adj.* °regretful, contrite, rueful, °remorseful, °apologetic, °sorry, °ashamed, °embarrassed, °penitent

repercussion *n.* Often, ***repercussions.*** reaction, °response, °effect, °outcome, consequence, reverberation, °result, aftermath, aftereffect, °upshot, fallout, °backlash, °echo

repertory *n.* repertoire, °store, reservoir, °collection, °hoard, °cache, repository, °stock, °supply, inventory, stockpile

repetition *n.* **1** Often, ***repetitions.*** reiteration(s), duplication(s), redundancy *or* redundancies, repeats, tautology *or* tautologies **2** reiteration, °repeat, °echo, echoing, repeating, duplication, duplicating, °rehearsal, recapitulation, restatement, replication, rereading, retelling, relisting, °recital, reprise, rerun, rerunning

repetitious *adj.* °tiresome, °tedious, °boring, °redundant, prolix, °windy, long-winded, °wordy, tautological, pleonastic

repetitive *adj.* iterative, °repetitious, incessant, °monotonous, repeated, °redundant, °humdrum, unceasing, ceaseless, °relentless, unremitting, °persistent, °recurrent, °nonstop, uninterrupted, °continual, °constant, °continuous

replace *v.* **1** °change, put in place of, °substitute, °supplant, °renew **2** °succeed, °supersede, °substitute for, take over from, °supplant **3** °restore, °return, °put back, °make good (on), °repay, refund, make restitution for

replenish *v.* refill, restock, °restore, °renew, °replace, °fill, °top up; °furnish, °provide

replete *adj.* **1** Often, ***replete with.*** °full (of), filled up (with), overflowing (with), well-supplied *or* well-provided *or* well-stocked (with), chock-full (of), crammed *or* jammed *or* jampacked (with), brimful (with), chockablock, bursting, teeming, °loaded, overloaded (with), gorged (with), stuffed (with), *Colloq* up to the eyes *or* ears (in), up to here *or* there (in), *US* up to the old wazoo (in), *Slang* °lousy (with), *Taboo slang* up to the *Brit* arse (in) *or US* ass (in) **2** satisfied, sated, satiated

replica *n.* °copy, °duplicate, °facsimile, °reproduction, °likeness, °imitation, carbon copy, photocopy, duplication, *Colloq* °dupe, *US* °knockoff

reply *v.* **1** °answer, °respond, rejoin, °retort, °return, come back, °acknowledge —*n.* **2** °answer, °response, rejoinder, °retort, comeback, riposte, °reaction, *US* °rise

report *n.* **1** °account, °description, °story, article, write-up, °piece, °statement, dispatch *or* despatch, communication, communiqué, °announcement, °narrative, °record; °news, °information **2** °explosion, bang, °boom, °shot, gunshot, gunfire, backfire, °discharge, °crack, °blast, detonation —*v.* **3** °relate, °recount, °describe, °narrate, °tell of, °detail, give an account of, write up, °document **4** °publish, promulgate, °publicize, °put out, °announce, °set forth, °reveal, °disclose, divulge, °announce, °circulate, °make public, °broadcast **5** °arrive, °appear, °surface, °check in, sign in, clock in *or* on, °turn up, °come in, *US* report in **6** ***report on.*** °investigate, °cover, °examine, °explore, °look into, °inquire into, check into *or* on, check (up) on, °research, °study, °probe, °scrutinize, *Slang* °check out, *Brit* suss out

reporter *n.* °journalist, newspaperman, newspaperwoman, newsman, newswoman, °correspondent, columnist, newswriter, gentleman *or* lady of the press, gentleman *or* lady of the fourth estate, *Brit* press man *or* presswoman; newscaster, news presenter, commentator, broadcaster, anchorman, anchorwoman, anchorperson, anchor, photojournalist, cameraman *or* -woman, *Colloq* newshound, newshawk, newshen, stringer

repose *n.* **1** °rest, °inactivity, °calm, °respite, tranquillity, °quiet, restfulness, °peace, °relaxation **2** °sleep, °nap, °doze, catnap, siesta, slumber, *Colloq* forty winks, snooze, *Slang* zizz, shuteye **3** composure, calmness, °calm, °serenity, equanimity, °poise, self-possession —*v.* **4** °lie, °abide, be, °lodge, °rest

represent *v.* **1** °substitute for, stand (in) for, °replace, act for **2** Often, ***represent oneself as.*** °present (oneself), depict (oneself), put *or* set (oneself) forth, °masquerade as, take (on) *or* assume the guise *or* role *or* part of, characterize as, impersonate, pretend to be, °pose as, °imitate, °mimic **3** °describe, delineate, °reproduce, °report, assert, °state, put *or* set forth, °show, °reflect, °mirror, °characterize, °define, °note, °outline, sketch, depict, °picture, °portray, °draw, °paint; °pretend **4** °symbolize, °stand for, °typify, °exemplify, °embody, epitomize; °illustrate

representation *n.* **1** °reproduction, °image, °likeness, °portrait, °picture, depiction, portrayal, °semblance, °model, °manifestation **2** °agency **3** °statement, °account, °exposition, °declaration, deposition, °assertion, °presentation, °undertaking **4** °replica, °reproduction, °figure, figurine, °statue, statuette, bust, °head, °model, effigy

representative *adj.* **1** °symbolic, °typical, °characteristic, °emblematic, archetypal, evocative, illustrative **2** elected, chosen, °democratic —*n.* **3** °agent, °deputy, legate, °ambassador, (papal) nuncio, spokesman *or* -woman, °proxy, °delegate, envoy, emissary, °missionary, commissioner; councillor, congressman *or* -woman, assemblyman *or* -woman, *New England* selectman *or* -woman, *Brit* member of parliament, MP **4** °agent, (traveling) salesman *or* -woman, *Colloq* rep

repress *v.* °suppress, °put down, °(keep in) check, °curb, °quash, °stifle, °overcome, °squelch, °(keep under) control, °contain, °restrain, constrain, °limit, keep back, °quell, hold back *or* in, °subdue, °inhibit, °hamper, °hinder, °deter, °frustrate, °discourage, disallow

repression *n.* **1** °restraint, °suppression, subjugation **2** °check, squelching, °control, °inhibition, hampering, hindering, °hindrance, stifling, deterring, frustration, frustrating

repressive *adj.* °tyrannical, °oppressive, °dictatorial, °despotic, °brutal, suppressive, °authoritarian, °totalitarian; fascist(ic), Nazi

reprieve *v.* **1** °respite, °rescue, °save; °let off, °spare —*n.* **2** °delay, °postponement, °suspension, °remission, °respite, °stay, amnesty

reprimand *n.* **1** scolding, °reproof, °rebuke, admonition, upbraiding, castigation, reproach, °lecture, censure, °criticism, °disapproval, remonstrance, remonstration, reprehension, °tongue-lashing, *Colloq* dressing-down, talking-to, telling-off, ticking-off, rap on the knuckles, slap on the wrist, *Brit* slating, *US and Canadian* chewing-out, *Slang Brit* wigging —*v.* **2** °scold, chide, °reprove, °rebuke, admonish, °upbraid, °castigate, reproach, °berate, °lecture, censure, °criticize, find fault with, °attack, flay (alive), reprehend, read the riot act to, slap on the wrist, rap over the knuckles, °take to task, *Colloq* °bawl out, °dress down, give a dressing-down, °tell off, tick off, haul over the coals, give (someone) a piece of (one's) mind, *Brit* slate, give (someone) a row, send (someone) away with a flea in his *or* her *or* their ear, tell (someone) a thing or two, carpet, wig, °skin (alive), *US and Canadian* °chew out, rake over the coals, call on the carpet, pin (someone's) ears back

reprisal *n.* retaliation, °revenge, °retribution, redress, °requital, °vengeance, repayment, recompense, vindication, getting even, °indemnity

reproachful *adj.* °faultfinding, °critical, censorious, disapproving, disparaging, upbraiding, reproving, scolding, admonitory, condemnatory, hypercritical

reprobate *adj.* **1** unprincipled, °immoral,

amoral, °abandoned, depraved, °despicable, °dissolute, °low, lowlife, °base, °mean, debased, damned, accursed, cursed, °degenerate, °profligate, °shameful, °shameless, °vile, °evil, °wicked, °villainous, °sinful, irredeemable, °foul, iniquitous, reprehensible —*n.* 2 °scoundrel, blackguard, °miscreant, °rake, °profligate, °roué, °villain, °wastrel, °wretch, °degenerate, unprincipled person, evildoer, debauchee, °libertine, °good-for-nothing, ne'er-do-well, cur, rapscallion, scamp, knave, °rascal, *US* lowlife, *Colloq* scallywag *or* scalawag

reproduce *v.* 1 °duplicate, °copy, replicate, °match, recreate, °repeat, °imitate, simulate 2 °breed, multiply, °propagate, procreate, °spawn, produce *or* bring forth *or* beget young; regenerate

reproduction *n.* 1 duplication, copying, printing 2 °duplicate, °copy, °print, clone, carbon (copy), °facsimile, °replica, °lookalike, °double, °twin, °imitation 3 propagation, °breeding, spawning, °proliferation, °production

reproof *n.* See **reprimand, 1,** above.

reprove *v.* See **reprimand, 2,** above.

repudiate *v.* °reject, °scorn, °turn down, °renounce, °retract, rescind, °reverse, °abandon, abrogate, forswear, °forgo, °deny, disown, °discard

repugnant *adj.* °repulsive, °abhorrent, °disgusting, off-putting, °offensive, °repellent, °revolting, °vile, °abominable, °loathsome, °foul, °distasteful, °unpalatable, °unsavory, execrable, intolerable, °obnoxious, noisome, nauseating, °nauseous, sickening, unpleasant, objectionable

repulse *v.* 1 °repel, °rebuff, drive back, °ward off, fight *or* beat off, °check 2 °refuse, °spurn, snub, °reject, °rebuff, °fend off, °resist, °turn down, give the cold shoulder to —*n.* 3 °rejection, °rebuff, °refusal, °denial, snub, cold shoulder, spurning

repulsive *adj.* °disgusting, °revolting, °abhorrent, °loathsome, °repugnant, °repellent, °offensive, °obnoxious, objectionable, °gross, °unsavory, °distasteful, °nasty, unpleasant, displeasing, °disagreeable, °ugly, off-putting, sickening, nauseating, °nauseous, °beastly, °vile, °dreadful, °awful, °rotten, feculent, °foul, odious, °horrible, horrid, °abominable, execrable, fulsome

reputable *adj.* °respectable, °honorable, °well-thought-of, °estimable, respected, °trustworthy, trusted, °honest, °reliable, dependable, °principled, °virtuous, °good, °worthy

reputation *n.* 1 repute, °name, °standing, stature, °position, °status 2 ***have a reputation for.*** be known *or* noted *or* notorious *or* famous for

reputed *adj.* °alleged, purported, °supposed, °assumed, presumed; rumored, said, deemed, held, regarded, viewed, looked on *or* upon, judged, considered, °thought, believed

request *v.* 1 °ask for, °seek, °plead for, apply for, °put in for, °requisition, °call for, °demand, insist on, °solicit, °beg, entreat, °beseech, importune —*n.* 2 °plea, °petition, °application, °requisition, °call, °demand, solicitation, entreaty

require *v.* 1 °order, °command, °ask (for), °call (for), °press (for), °instruct, coerce, °force; °insist, °demand; °make 2 °need, °want, °lack, be lacking, be missing, be short (of); °desire

requirement *n.* 1 requisite, °prerequisite, °demand, °precondition, °condition, °qualification, °stipulation, sine qua non, °provision, °proviso, °demand, °necessity, °essential, desideratum, °must 2 °need, °want, °demand

requisition *n.* 1 °request, °order, °demand, °call, authorization, mandate, voucher —*v.* 2 °request, °order, °demand, °call, °authorize, mandate 3 °seize, °appropriate, commandeer, °confiscate, °take possession of, °take (over), °occupy; expropriate

requital *n.* 1 repayment, °return, recompense, redress, °restitution, reparation, °remuneration, quittance, °amends, °satisfaction, compensation, °payment 2 °revenge, retaliation, °retribution, °reprisal, °vengeance; quid pro quo, *Brit or literary* Roland for an Oliver

requite *v.* 1 °repay, °reward, °reciprocate, recompense, compensate for, °respond to 2 retaliate for, °revenge, avenge, make restitution for, redress, pay back for, give tit for tat for, make amends for

rescue *v.* 1 °save, °deliver, °(set) free, °liberate, let go (free), °release, °(let) loose —*n.* 2 deliverance, °saving; freeing, liberating, °release

research *n.* 1 °investigation, investigating, °exploration, delving, digging, enquiry *or* inquiry, fact-finding, scrutinization, °scrutiny, °examination, inspection, probing, °analysis, experimentation —*v.* 2 °investigate, °explore, delve into, °dig into, enquire *or* inquire into, °scrutinize, °examine, °study, °analyze, °inspect, check in *or* into *or* (up) on, °probe, °experiment with, *Colloq* °check out

resemblance *n.* °likeness, similarity; correspondence, congruity, °coincidence, conformity, °accord, °agreement, equivalence, comparableness, comparability, °comparison

resemble *v.* look *or* sound *or* taste *or* seem *or* be like *or* similar to, bear (a) resemblance to, °approximate, smack of, correspond to, have (all) the hallmarks *or* earmarks of, °take after, *Colloq* °favor

resent *v.* feel embittered *or* bitter about, feel °envious *or* °jealous of, °begrudge, have hard feelings about, be displeased *or* disgruntled at, be angry about

resentful *adj.* °embittered, °bitter, acrimonious, °spiteful, °envious, °jealous, begrudging, °vindictive, °indignant, displeased, °disgruntled, °dissatisfied, unsatisfied, °unhappy, peeved, irritated, irked, annoyed, provoked, riled, °angry, piqued, irate, °furious, incensed, °agitated, °upset, worked up, antagonistic, °hostile

resentment *n.* °bitterness, acrimony, °rancor, °envy, jealousy, °grudge, °indignation, °displeasure, °dissatisfaction, unhappiness, irritation, °annoyance, °provocation, pique, °anger, ire, °fury, °agitation, °upset, °anxiety, °ill will, malice, °antagonism, °hostility, °animosity, enmity, antipathy, °hate

reservation *n.* **1** keeping *or* holding back, withholding, reticence, °reluctance, hesitation, hesitancy, hedging **2** °qualm, °scruple, °qualification, hesitancy, limitation, °exception, °objection, demur *or* demurral *or* demurrer, °condition, °proviso, °provision **3** booking, °appointment, °arrangement **4** °preserve, °sanctuary, °reserve, °area, °tract, °territory, °region, °section, °plot

reserve *v.* **1** keep *or* hold (back), °withhold, °save, set *or* put aside, °conserve, °preserve, °retain, keep (to *or* for oneself), °hold over, °postpone, °delay, °put off, °defer **2** °hold, °keep, °book, °register, °save, put *or* set aside, °charter, °engage, °secure, contract for —*n.* **3** Often, ***reserves.*** °store, °stock, stockpile, inventory, °supply, nest egg, reservoir, °fund, °hoard, °cache **4** reticence, (self-)restraint, (self-)control, taciturnity, aplomb, °formality, coolness, aloofness, guardedness, standoffishness, remoteness, °detachment **5** Often, ***reserves.*** °auxiliary, °alternate, °substitute, °reinforcements, backup, °spare **6** See **reservation, 4,** above. **7** °reservation, °restriction, °restraint, hesitancy, hesitation, °limit, limitation, hedging, avoidance, °evasion, dodging, fudging **8** ***in reserve.*** °ready, °in readiness, on hand, °available, °on call, °accessible, as backup, in store, °on tap, at (one's) fingertips

reserved *adj.* °reticent, restrained, unresponsive, controlled, °silent, °taciturn, uncommunicative, unforthcoming, close-mouthed, unresponsive, undemonstrative, unemotional, poker-faced, °cool, °formal, °aloof, °guarded, °standoffish, °unsocial, antisocial, °distant, °remote, °detached, °retiring, °withdrawn, °sedate, demure, °dignified, °guarded, prim, °rigid, °strait-laced, °icy, °frigid, ice-cold

residence *n.* **1** °abode, °home, °domicile, °dwelling, dwelling place, °place, °house, habitation, °(living) quarters **2** residency, °stay, °sojourn, °visit, °tenancy **3** mansion, villa, manor (house), stately home, °estate, chateau, °castle, °palace, *Brit* °hall

resident *adj.* **1** in residence, residing, living, staying, °abiding, °dwelling, °remaining **2** °local, °neighborhood, °district, regional, °neighboring —*n.* **3** °denizen, dweller, °inhabitant, °citizen, householder, homeowner, °tenant, °local

residual *adj.* °remaining, °leftover, °surplus, °spare, °extra, residuary

residue *n.* °remainder, °leftover, °surplus, °remains, °rest, °excess, °dregs, residuum

resign *v.* **1** °quit, °leave, °go, °abdicate, °give notice; °retire (from), °abandon, °give up, °forsake, °hand over, yield up, °renounce, °relinquish, let go, °release, °vacate, °surrender, deliver up, °turn over **2** ***resign (oneself) (to).*** reconcile (oneself) (to), be *or* become resigned *or* reconciled (to), accommodate (oneself) (to), adjust (oneself) (to), adapt (oneself) (to), acclimatize *or* acclimate (oneself) (to), submit (oneself) (to)

resignation *n.* **1** °notice; abandonment, abdication, resigning, renunciation, forgoing, relinquishment **2** °reconciliation, reconcilement, °adjustment, °adaptation, acclimatization *or* acclimation, °submission, acceptance, compliance, capitulation, abandonment, acquiescence, passivity

resilience *n.* °rebound, °recoil, °bounce, °elasticity, springiness, °spring, buoyancy, °flexibility, suppleness, ability to recover

resist *v.* **1** °stop, °hinder, °prevent, °hold out (against), be proof (against), keep *or* hold at bay, hold the line (against), °thwart, °impede, °block, °obstruct, °inhibit, °restrain, °preclude, °check, °control, °curb, °stem, °bridle, °hold back, °withstand, °weather, °last (against), °endure, °outlast, stand up (to *or* against); °combat, °fight (against), °battle, countervail (against), °counteract, °oppose, °rebuff, °defy **2** °refuse, °deny, °turn down, °forgo

resistance *n.* **1** °opposition, defiance, °refusal, °denial, °obstruction, intransigence, rebelliousness, recalcitrance, stubbornness **2** defenses **3** ***Resistance.*** °underground, partisans, freedom fighters, guerrilla *or* guerilla movement, guerrillas *or* guerillas, irregulars, Maquis, *US* resisters

resistant *adj.* **1** °opposed, against, °defiant, °averse, unsubmissive; impervious, °unaffected **2** °recalcitrant, °stubborn, °obstinate, intransigent, °rebellious, °immovable, intractable, refractory, °willful, °ungovernable, unmanageable, °unruly, uncompliant, uncooperative **3** Often, ***resistant to.*** impervious (to), impenetrable (to), °repellent (to); °proof (against); shedding

resolute *adj.* resolved, °determined, °purposeful, °steadfast, °firm, °stubborn, adamant, °set, °decided, °staunch, °bold, dogged, undaunted, °dauntless, persevering, persisting, °persistent, perseverant, pertinacious, °tenacious, °single-minded, dedicated, °devoted, bulldog, purposive, °deliberate, °inflexible, unwavering, unshakable *or* unshakeable, unshaken, unflagging, °untiring, indefatigable, °tireless, unfaltering, °unhesitating, unhesitant, unswerving, °irreversible, undeviating, unchanging, °changeless, unchangeable, immutable, unalterable

resolution *n.* **1** °resolve, resoluteness, °determination, °purpose, purposefulness, steadfastness, firmness, decidedness, °decision, staunchness, boldness, doggedness, dauntlessness, stubbornness, °obstinacy, °perseverance, °persistence, relentlessness, pertinacity, °tenacity, single-mindedness, °dedication, °devotion, constancy, devotedness, deliberation, deliberateness, inflexibility, inflexibleness, unshakability *or* unshakeability, fixedness, indefatigability, indefatigableness, irreversibility, changelessness, unchangeability, immutability, immutableness, unalterability, *Colloq US* stick-to-itiveness **2** °promise, commitment, °pledge, °word (of honor), °oath, °vow, °undertaking, °obligation; °intention **3** °motion, °resolve, °proposal, °proposition, °plan, °suggestion, °idea, °notion; °determination, verdict, °decision, °judgment **4** °answer, answering, °solution, solving, unraveling, disentanglement, sorting out, explication; °outcome, °issue, °result, °end (result) **5** acutance, sharpness, °precision, °accuracy, exactness, exactitude, fineness, °discrimination, detailing, distinguishability

resolve *v.* **1** °determine, °decide, make up one's mind, °agree, °undertake, °settle, °fix, conclude **2** °work out, °figure out, °solve, °clear up, °answer **3** °adopt, °pass, °approve, °decide **4** ***resolve into.*** °change into, convert into, alter into, transform into, transmute into, metamorphose into, be convert(ed) into, °become, dissolve into, break down into, liquefy into, disintegrate into, reduce to *or* into —*n.* **5** See **resolution, 1,** above. **6** See **resolution, 2,** above

resonant *adj.* vibrating, vibrant, resounding, (re)echoing, reverberating, reverberant, pulsating, ringing, booming, thundering, °thunderous, °loud

resort *n.* **1** spa, °retreat, *Chiefly Brit* watering place **2** °resource, backup, °reserve, °refuge, place to turn, °alternative, °remedy —*v.* **3** ***resort to.*** have recourse to, °turn to, look to, °fall back on, repair to, °take to, °frequent, °patronize, °attend; °visit, °haunt, hang out in

resound *v.* °boom, resonate, °ring (out), °boom (out), (re)echo, reverberate, °pulsate, °thunder

resource *n.* **1** Often, ***resources.*** °initiative, °ingenuity, °talent, inventiveness, °imagination, imaginativeness, cleverness, quick-wittedness, °capability, resourcefulness, °aptitude, °qualifications, °strength, °quality, °forte, *Colloq Brit* °gumption, *Slang* °guts **2** Often, ***resources.*** °capital, °assets, °money, °possessions, °wealth, °property, °cash, °funds

resourceful *adj.* °ingenious, inventive, °imaginative, °clever, Daedalian, °creative, °skillful, °smart, °slick

respect *n.* **1** °regard, °consideration, °admiration, °esteem, °(high) opinion, °appreciation **2** °regard, °consideration, °courtesy, politeness, °civility, attentiveness, thoughtfulness, °etiquette, °deference, °reverence, °veneration **3** °reference, °relation, °connection, °comparison, °regard, °bearing **4** °detail, °point, °element, °aspect, °characteristic, °feature, °quality, °trait, °particular, °matter, °attribute, °property **5** ***respects.*** °regards, good *or* best wishes, °greetings, °compliments, *Formal* salutations, *Formal or archaic* devoirs —*v.* **6** °consider, °admire, °esteem, °honor, °appreciate, value, defer to, pay homage to, think highly *or* well of, °look up to, °revere, °reverence, °venerate **7** °heed, °obey, show consideration *or* regard for, pay attention to, °attend to, be considerate *or* polite *or* courteous to, defer to

respectable *adj.* **1** °proper, demure, °decorous, °seemly, °estimable, °worthy, °dignified, °decent, °upright, °honest, respected, °genteel, °refined, °reputable, °aboveboard, unimpeachable, law-abiding **2** °moderate, appreciable, °goodly, °reasonable, °fair, not inconsiderable, °considerable, °tolerable, °satisfactory, sizable, good-sized, °substantial, not insignificant, °significant, *Colloq* °tidy **3** °presentable, °moral, °decent, °proper, °modest, °chaste, °innocent, °pure, °clean

respectful *adj.* °courteous, °polite, well-mannered, well-behaved, mannerly, °civil, °cordial, gentlemanly, °ladylike, °gracious, °obliging, °accommodating, °considerate, °thoughtful

respective *adj.* °separate, °individual, °particular, °pertinent, °specific, °special, °personal, own, °relevant, corresponding, °several

respectively *adv.* °separately, °individually, °singly, severally, ***mutatis mutandis,*** each to each

respite *n.* **1** °interval, °intermission, °break, °interruption, °recess, breather, °rest; °holiday, *Chiefly US and Canadian* vacation **2** °pause, °delay, hiatus, °stay, °extension, °reprieve, °postponement

respond *v.* **1** °answer, °reply, come back, °return, °react, °reciprocate, °counter; rejoin, °retort **2** Often, ***respond to.*** be responsive (to), °react (to), empathize (with), °sympathize (with), commiserate (with), °feel for, °pity, be affected *or* moved *or* touched (by)

response *n.* °answer, °reply, °retort, rejoinder; °reaction, °effect, feedback, °return, *Colloq* comeback

responsibility *n.* **1** °accountability, °liability, chargeability, answerability, °obligation **2** °charge, °duty, onus, °burden, °trust, °job, °role, °task **3** °blame, °guilt, °fault, culpability **4** dependability, reliability, trustworthiness, °stability, °accountability, creditability

responsible *adj.* **1** °accountable, answerable, °liable, chargeable **2** °reliable, °trustworthy, dependable, °stable, creditable, °accountable, °ethical, °honest **3** °executive, °leading, °authoritative, administrative, °important, decision-making, managerial, directorial, °principal, °chief, °top, *US* front-office **4** °guilty, to blame, °at fault, culpable

responsive *adj.* °alert, °alive, (wide-)awake, reactive, communicative, °sharp, °keen, °receptive, °sensitive, °open, °sympathetic

rest[1] *n.* **1** °repose, °sleep, °nap, °doze, siesta, slumber, *Chiefly Brit* lie-down, *Colloq* forty winks, zizz, snooze; shuteye **2** °relaxation, °intermission, °interval, °interlude, entr'acte, rest period, cessation, (tea *or* coffee) break, °recess, breather, breathing spell, °respite, time off, °holiday, *Chiefly US and Canadian* vacation **3** °ease, °relaxation, °leisure, °indolence, °idleness, °inactivity, loafing, dozing **4** °prop, °support, holder, °brace, trestle, shelf, °bracket **5** ***come to rest.*** °stop, end up, °turn up, °arrive —*v.* **6** °(go to) sleep, °doze, °relax, take a rest, °(take one's) repose, lie down, °recline, go *or* take to one's bed, take one's ease, unwind, loll, languish, laze about, be idle, idle about, °lounge, °(take a) nap, put one's feet up, *Colloq* take it easy, snooze, count sheep, have a zizz, catch *or* grab some shuteye, get *or* take forty winks, *US* catch *or* log some Z's, *Slang Brit* kip, doss down, °hit the sack, hit the hay, *US* sack out **7** reside, be situated, be lodged, °lie, be placed, hinge, be found, °remain, °stay **8** °place, °position, °put, °lay, °set, °lean, °prop **9** °lie, °remain, °stay **10** allay, °calm, °quiet, °still, °stay

rest[2] *n.* **1** °remainder, °balance; °remains, remnants, leftovers, °residue, residuum, °excess, °surplus, overage —*v.* **2** (continue to) be, °remain, keep on being

restful *adj.* **1** relaxing, °soothing, comforting, tranquilizing, °sedative, calming, sleep-inducing, hypnotic, soporific, somnolent **2** °tranquil, °calm, °peaceful, °quiet, °still, °serene, pacific, °comfortable, °relaxed, reposeful

restitution *n.* **1** °amends, compensation, redress, recompense, °remuneration, reparation, °requital, indemnification, °indemnity **2** °restoration, °return, reestablishment, reinstatement, °recovery

restive *adj.* See **restless,** below.

restless *adj.* °restive, uneasy, edgy, °on edge, on tenterhooks, fidgety, °nervous, skittish, °excitable, highly strung, high-strung, worked up, °agitated, °fretful, °jumpy, apprehensive, itchy, *Colloq* jittery, *Slang* uptight, *US* antsy, hyper

restoration *n.* **1** See **restitution, 2,** above. **2** renovation, refurbishment, rehabilitation, renewal, °repair, rejuvenation, reconstruction, resurrection, reconversion, °revival

restore *v.* **1** give *or* hand back, °return, make restitution, bring back **2** °revive, °rejuvenate, reestablish, °renew, bring back, give (someone) back, resuscitate, °resurrect, rekindle, reinvigorate, °refresh, °stimulate, revitalize, °strengthen **3** °renovate, °refurbish, °renew, °repair, °rejuvenate, °resurrect, °revive, reconstruct, °rehabilitate, rebuild; °mend, °fix, °retouch, °touch up; *Colloq US* °fix up **4** °replace, reinstate, °put back; °return, bring back **5** °replace, °reimburse, °repay, °return, pay *or* put *or* give back

restrain *v.* **1** (keep under *or* in) control, (keep *or* hold in) check, hold (back *or* in), °curb, °govern **2** °limit, °restrict, °inhibit, °regulate, °suppress, °repress, °bar, debar, °curtail, °stifle, °hinder, interfere with, °hamper, °handicap **3** °(place under) arrest, confine, °imprison, incarcerate, detain, °hold, °lock up, jail *or Brit also* gaol, shut in *or* up

restraint *n.* **1** °control, °check, °curb, °rein, °bridle, °restriction, constraint, °limit, limitation, curtailment, °taboo, °ban, interdict *or* interdiction, proscription, delimitation, bound(s), °embargo **2** °control, °restriction, constraint, confinement; °bondage, bonds, fetters, °shackles, °handcuffs, gyves, bilboes, pinions, °manacles, ball and chain, straitjacket, *Colloq* cuffs, bracelets **3** °control, °reserve, °self-control, self-possession, °poise, equanimity, self-discipline, self-restraint

restrict *v.* °limit, confine, °bound, circumscribe, delimit, mark off, demarcate, °regulate; °qualify, °restrain, °impede

restriction *n.* **1** °condition, °provision, °proviso, °qualification, °stipulation **2** See **restraint, 1,** above.

result *n.* **1** °outcome, consequence, °effect, °end (result), °fruit; conclusion, °upshot, °issue, °development, °sequel, °follow-up, denouement *or* dénouement —*v.* **2** Often, ***result from.*** °develop, °emerge, °follow, °happen, °occur, °come (about), °come to pass, °arise, evolve, be produced **3** ***result in.*** °end, conclude, culminate, °terminate

resume *v.* °continue, °carry on, take up again, °pick up (where one left off)

résumé *n.* **1** °summary, °digest, °abstract, °synopsis, °précis, °outline, °review, recapitulation, °epitome, *Colloq* °rundown, recap **2** curriculum vitae, CV, °summary, biography, work *or* job history, career description, *Formal* prosopography, *Colloq* bio, *US* vita

resurgence *n.* °renaissance, renascence, °rebirth, °revival, reawakening, °restoration, renewal, resumption, °return, resurrection, regeneration, rejuvenation, new dawn, new birth

resurrect *v.* °revive, bring back, °return, reawaken, °restore (to life), reintroduce, °renew, regenerate, °rejuvenate, °raise (from the dead), resuscitate, breathe new life into, reanimate, reincarnate

retain *v.* **1** °keep (possession of), °hold (on to), °save, °preserve, *Colloq* hang on to **2** °engage, °hire, °employ, commission, °take on **3** °hold, absorb, °contain, °soak up, °preserve **4** °remember, keep *or* bear *or* have in mind, °recall, remain aware of, °memorize, impress on the memory, °recollect

retaliate *v.* °repay, °pay back (in kind), °counter, strike back (at), take revenge (on), wreak vengeance (on), revenge oneself (on), avenge, °reciprocate, settle *or* even a score (with); give tit for tat, take an eye for an eye (and a tooth for a tooth), give as good as one gets, give (someone) a taste of his *or* her *or* their own medicine, pay (someone) back in his *or* her *or* their own coin, *Brit or literary* give a Roland for an Oliver; *Colloq* get even (with), °get back (at)

retard *v.* **1** slow (down *or* up), hold up *or*

back, °set back, °hinder, °impede, °delay, keep back, °stall, °thwart, balk, °block, °restrict, hold in check, °frustrate, interfere with —*n.* 2 *Offensive and derogatory* idiot, moron, °fool, imbecile, dunce, *Slang chiefly US and Canadian* °jerk

reticent *adj.* °quiet, °shy, °timid, °retiring, °reserved; °taciturn, °silent, unresponsive, °tight-lipped, unforthcoming

retinue *n.* entourage, °escort, convoy, cortège, °company, °train, °suite, followers, attendants, following, hangers-on, *Colloq* groupies

retire *v.* **1** °withdraw, rusticate, go off *or* away, °take off, °retreat; hibernate, estivate *or Brit* aestivate, seclude *or* sequester *or* cloister oneself **2** stop *or* give up work(ing), be pensioned off, (be) put out to grass *or* pasture, take the golden handshake, be given the gold watch, go on Social Security, go on a pension, be superannuated, go out of circulation **3** go *or* take to (one's) bed *or* bedroom, °(go to) sleep, lie down, °(take one's) repose, °(take a) nap, put one's feet up, *Colloq* take it easy, snooze, count sheep, have a zizz, catch *or* grab some shuteye, get *or* take forty winks, *US* catch *or* log some Z's, *Slang* °hit the sack, sack out, hit the hay, *Brit* kip, doss down

retiring *adj.* °shy, °bashful, °coy, demure, °modest, diffident, °timid, unpretentious, unassuming, °humble, self-effacing, timorous, °meek, °reticent, °reserved, °unsocial, unsociable, °aloof, removed, °standoffish, °distant, °reclusive, eremitic(al)

retort *n.* **1** °response, °reply, rejoinder, °answer, riposte, °rebuttal, *Colloq* comeback —*v.* **2** fling *or* hurl back, rejoin, °answer back, riposte, °rebut, °counter, come back with, °return, °respond, °answer, °reply, °retaliate

retouch *v.* °touch up, °correct, °restore, °repair, recondition, °refresh, brush up, °adjust, °improve, °finish, put the finishing touches on

retract *v.* **1** °withdraw, pull *or* draw back **2** °take back, °withdraw, rescind, °revoke, °repeal, °deny, disavow, °recant, °renounce, abjure, °cancel, forswear, °repudiate, disclaim, disown, °reverse

retreat *n.* **1** retirement, withdrawal, pulling *or* falling *or* drawing back, giving ground, evacuation, °flight **2** retirement, °seclusion, withdrawal, isolation, °solitude, rustication **3** °sanctuary, °sanctum (sanctorum), °refuge, °shelter, den, haven, asylum, °resort, °hideaway, hide-out —*v.* **4** °withdraw, decamp, °run (away), °turn tail, °depart, give *or* lose ground, pull *or* fall *or* draw back, °retire, °evacuate, °flee, °take flight **5** °ebb, draw *or* move back, °recede

retribution *n.* °vengeance, °revenge, °reprisal, retaliation, °requital, redress, quid pro quo, °satisfaction, °punishment, °justice, just deserts, recompense, compensation

retrieve *v.* **1** bring *or* get (back), °fetch, come back with **2** °recover, °save, °rescue, °take back, °recoup, regain, °reclaim **3** °make up, make amends for, °recover, °cover, °redeem, °repay, °pay for, °return, °get back, regain, be repaid *or* reimbursed for

retrospect *n.* hindsight, reconsideration, °review, remembering, afterthought, °recollection, looking back

return *v.* **1** come *or* go back, °revert, °turn back **2** come back, reappear, resurface, crop up again, turn *or* show up again, put in an appearance again; °recur, reoccur, *Colloq* pop up again **3** °replace, °put back, °restore, give back, bring *or* carry back **4** °exchange, bring *or* carry *or* send back **5** °yield, °earn, °gain, °profit, °benefit **6** °deliver, °render, °give, °offer, °turn in, proffer, °report —*n.* **7** recurrence, reappearance, °repetition, renewal, recrudescence, resurfacing, reemergence **8** replacement, replacing, °restoration, restoring, °restitution **9** Sometimes, ***returns.*** °yield, °earnings, °profit, °gain, °benefit, °income, °revenue, °proceeds, °interest, takings, results **10** °arrival, advent, coming, homecoming **11** reciprocity, reciprocation, repayment, recompense, reimbursement, compensation, °payment, reparation, °indemnity, indemnification, °consideration, °amends, redress, °requital

revamp *v.* °overhaul, redo, recondition, °renovate, °repair, °fix, do up, refit, °refurbish, °restore, °rehabilitate, *US* °fix up

reveal *v.* °expose, °display, divulge, °disclose, °show; °make known, °let on, °let out, let be known, °let slip, °communicate, °give vent to, °air, ventilate, °leak (out)

revel *v.* **1** Usually, ***revel in.*** °(take) delight (in), take pleasure (in), °rejoice (in), °luxuriate (in), bask (in), °wallow (in), °lap up, crow (about *or* over), °glory (in), °savor, °relish **2** °make merry, °carouse, °celebrate, cut loose, go on a spree, *Colloq* live it up, make whoopee, whoop it up, °paint the town red, °party, *Brit* push the boat out, *Slang Brit* have a rave *or* rave-up —*n.* **3** °spree, °party, merrymaking, debauch, °carouse, °festival, °fête, carousal, °celebration, °gala, ball, romp, °fling, carnival, °jamboree, bacchanal, saturnalia

revelation *n.* °news, °information, °proclamation, °publication, °bulletin, communiqué, °announcement, °pronouncement, °declaration, °statement, °leak; °admission, confession; °discovery, unveiling, uncovering, °exposure, disclosure, exposé

revelry *n.* merrymaking, °fun, reveling, carousal, carousing, °gaiety, °festivity, jollity, °mirth, °celebration, ball, high jinks *or* hijinks, °spree, *Colloq* partying, *Slang Brit* rave *or* rave-up

revenge *n.* **1** °vengeance, retaliation, °reprisal, °retribution, vindictiveness, spitefulness, repayment, °satisfaction —*v.* **2** avenge, get even for, take revenge for, make reprisal for, exact retribution *or* payment *or* repayment for **3** ***revenge oneself (on).*** settle a score *or* an old score (with), pay (someone) back in his *or* her *or* their own coin, give tit for tat, take an eye for an eye (and a tooth for a tooth), °punish, *Colloq* °get, get even (with), give (someone) his *or* her *or* their comeuppance, give (someone) a taste of his *or* her *or* their own medicine, *Brit or literary* give a Roland for an Oliver

revenue *n.* °(gross) income, °proceeds, °receipts, return(s), °yield, °interest, takings, °net (income), °gate; °profits, °gain, *Colloq chiefly US* °take

revere *v.* °adore, adulate, °reverence, °venerate, °worship, °idolize, enshrine, °sanctify, beatify, °glorify, °esteem, °admire, °respect, °honor

reverence *n.* **1** °honor, °respect, °esteem, °admiration, glorification, beatification, sanctification, idolization, °worship, °veneration, adulation, adoration, °homage, fealty, °obeisance, °deference, awe —*v.* **2** See **revere,** above.

reverie *n.* °daydream, °fantasy, brown study, woolgathering, absent-mindedness; meditation, °thought

reversal *n.* **1** °reverse, °turnabout, turnaround, U-turn, °change, volte-face, °(complete) switch, *Brit* about-turn, *US* °about-face **2** See **reverse, 8,** below. **3** annulment, nullification, nulling, °cancellation, revocation, °repeal, rescission

reverse *adj.* **1** °opposite, °contrary, inverse, °converse; inverted, upside-down, °mirror, reversed, backward(s) —*v.* **2** invert, °overturn, turn upside down, turn topsy-turvy, °turn over, upend; °exchange, °change, interchange, °transpose **3** °overturn, °overthrow, °upset, °set aside, °quash, override, annul, nullify, °vacate, °abandon, °revoke, negate, °veto, declare null and void, disaffirm, invalidate, °cancel, °repeal, rescind, overrule, countermand, °undo **4** °alter, °change, °modify; °renounce, °recant, °take back **5** °back up, move *or* go backward(s), backtrack, *Nautical* make sternway —*n.* **6** °opposite, °contrary, °converse, antithesis **7** °back, °rear, wrong side, verso, underside; flip side, B-side *or* side B; tail side **8** °setback, °disappointment, °misfortune, °reversal, °mishap, misadventure, °trouble, °problem, °difficulty, °vicissitude, adversity, °defeat; °disaster, °catastrophe, débacle, °rout, *Colloq* °washout

revert *v.* °return, come *or* go back, take *or* pick up again, °lapse, backslide, regress, °relapse, °retreat

review *v.* **1** °survey, °examine, °regard, °look at, °study, con, °consider, °weigh, °inspect, °look over, °scrutinize **2** reexamine, reconsider, go over again, look at *or* over again, reassess **3** °criticize, critique, assess, °judge, °evaluate, give one's opinion of, comment on *or* upon, °discuss —*n.* **4** °criticism, critique, review article, assessment, °judgment, °evaluation, commentary, °study, °comment, °notice **5** °survey, °examination, °study, °consideration, inspection, °scrutiny, °analysis; reviewing, reading **6** reexamination, reconsideration, rehashing *or* rehash, °post-mortem, reassessment, rethinking, rethink **7** °periodical, °journal, °magazine **8** °parade, °procession, array, cavalcade, marchpast, flypast *or chiefly US* flyover

revise *v.* **1** °edit, emend, °improve, °correct, °rectify, °modify, °revamp, redact, rework, °overhaul, update; rewrite **2** °alter, °change, °amend

revision *n.* editing, revising, emendation, °improvement, °correction, rectification, modification, revamping, reappraisal, reexamination, reinterpretation, reassessment, redaction, reworking, °overhaul, overhauling, updating, update; rewrite, °edition, °version, °rendition

revival *n.* **1** resurrection, resuscitation, renewal, °restoration, revitalization, resurfacing, °return, returning **2** °rebirth, renaissance *or* renascence, °resurgence, awakening, quickening, reanimation **3** °recovery, °improvement, °increase, upsurge, upturn, °boost, upswing, °advance, advancement, °progress, °rise, escalation, *Colloq* pickup, comeback

revive *v.* **1** (re)awaken, °wake (up), come *or* bring (a)round, waken, resuscitate; °recover, (re)gain consciousness **2** reawaken, stir up again, °renew, °resume, reopen, °refresh **3** bring back, reactivate, °renew, °resurrect, reestablish, °resume, reopen, revitalize, breathe life into, reinvigorate, °rejuvenate

revoke *v.* °cancel, °deny, invalidate, annul, declare null and void, °void, nullify, negate, °repudiate, °renounce, rescind, °repeal, °recall, °recant, °quash, °veto, °set aside, abrogate, °abolish, °withdraw, °take back, °retract

revolt *n.* **1** rebellion, °revolution, °uprising, °mutiny, insurrection, coup d'état, putsch, takeover —*v.* **2** °rebel, rise up, °mutiny; °protest, dissent **3** °repel, °offend, °disgust, °shock, °horrify, °repulse, °nauseate, °sicken

revolting *adj.* °disgusting, sickening, nauseating, °nauseous, stomach-turning, stomach-churning, vomit-provoking, sick-making, °foul, °loathsome, °abhorrent, horrid, °horrible, °nasty, °vile, °obnoxious, °repulsive, appalling, °abominable, °repellent, °offensive, objectionable, off-putting, °beastly, °gross, °rotten, °rancid, inedible, °disagreeable, unpleasant, *Slang* icky, yukky

revolution *n.* **1** °mutiny, °revolt, rebellion, coup (d'état), °uprising, insurgency, insurrection, putsch, takeover, °overthrow **2** °upheaval, cataclysm, °transformation, (drastic *or* radical *or* major) change, sea change, metamorphosis **3** rotation, °turn, °orbit, °circuit, °spin, °lap, °round, °cycle, °circle, gyration; °wheel, whirl, °pirouette

revolutionary *adj.* **1** °mutinous, °rebellious, insurgent, insurrectionist, insurrectionary, °radical, °rebel, °seditious, °subversive **2** °novel, innovative, °creative, °new, °different, °original, °avant-garde —*n.* **3** °rebel, mutineer, insurgent, insurrectionist, insurrectionary, revolutionist, sans-culotte *or* sans-culottist, anarchist, °radical, extremist, °terrorist, °rabble-rouser

revolve *v.* **1** °spin, °turn, °pivot, °rotate, °gyrate, whirl, °twirl, °reel, °wheel, go (a)round, °circle, °cycle, °orbit; °swivel **2** °turn, °depend, °pivot, °rely **3** °turn over (in one's mind), °ponder, °weigh, °consider, meditate upon *or* on, °think about, reflect upon *or* on, ruminate over *or* on, °chew over, °contemplate

revolver *n.* °pistol, gun, sidearm, firearm, *Chiefly US and Canadian* handgun, *Colloq US* six-gun, six-shooter, *Slang US* °rod, gat, roscoe, °piece, Saturday night special, shooting iron

revulsion *n.* °loathing, detestation, °disgust, repugnance, abomination, abhorrence, °aversion, hatred, antipathy, odium, execration

reward *n.* **1** °award, °favor, recompense, compensation, °return, °payment, °pay, °requital **2** °prize, °award, °tribute, °honor, *Literary* guerdon **3** °retribution, °punishment, just deserts, *Colloq* comeuppance —*v.* **4** recompense, °compensate, °pay, °repay, remunerate, redress, °requite, make (something *or* it) worth someone's while

rewarding *adj.* °satisfying, gratifying, °worthwhile, enriching, enriched, °fruitful; °profitable, °advantageous, °productive, °gainful

reword *v.* °paraphrase, rephrase, put into different words, put another way, express differently, °revise, recast, rewrite

rhapsodic *adj.* rhapsodical, °ecstatic, °enthusiastic, °elated, °overjoyed, °effusive, °rapturous, thrilled, blissful, transported, orgasmic, intoxicated, euphoric, walking on air, °delighted, happy as a sand boy, happy as a pig in clover, °(sitting) on top of the world, *Brit* in the seventh heaven, *US* in seventh heaven, happy as a cow in clover, *Taboo slang US* happy as a pig in shit

rhetoric *n.* **1** eloquence, expressiveness, elocution, way with words, *Colloq* gift of the gab **2** °bombast, °bluster, fustian, rodomontade, grandiloquence, magniloquence, °oratory, windiness, high-flown poppycock, wordiness, sesquipedality, verbosity, prolixity, long-windedness, turgidity, flatulence, gasconade, *Colloq* °hot air, puffery

rhetorical *adj.* **1** stylistic, linguistic, °poetic, °expressive, oratorical **2** °artificial, contrived, for effect, unanswerable, not literal **3** °pretentious, °bombastic, °flamboyant, °extravagant, florid, fustian, high-flown, °inflated, °grandiose, euphuistic, turgid, grandiloquent, magniloquent, long-winded, °windy, orotund, °wordy, prolix, sesquipedalian, *Colloq* highfalutin *or* hifalutin *or* highfaluting

rhyme *n.* **1** rime, °poem, °poetry, verse, versification, metrical composition, °song **2** ***rhyme or reason.*** °(common) sense, °logic, °intelligence, °meaning, °wisdom, rationality, °rationale, soundness, °organization, °structure

rhythm *n.* °tempo, °beat, cadence *or* cadency, throb, throbbing, °accent, accentuation, °time, timing, stress *or* rhythmic(al) pattern, °measure, meter, °pulse, lilt, *Music* downbeat, °thesis, °upbeat, arsis

rhythmic *adj.* rhythmical, °measured, cadenced, throbbing, pulsing, pulsating, °regular, °steady, beating

ribaldry *n.* °vulgarity, immodesty, °indelicacy, indecency, coarseness, bawdiness, earthiness, wantonness, raciness, naughtiness, shamelessness, lustfulness, rakishness, rascality, dissoluteness, lubricity, lasciviousness, looseness, scurrility *or* scurrilousness, lewdness, salaciousness, licentiousness, grossness, offensiveness, rankness, rudeness, smuttiness, smut, °dirt, °filth, foulness, obscenity

rich *adj.* **1** °wealthy, affluent, °prosperous, well-to-do, °well-off, well-provided-for, °opulent, moneyed, in clover, on velvet, *Colloq* °flush, °loaded, on Easy Street, rolling in it *or* money *or* wealth, in the chips *or* the dough *or* the money, well-heeled, *US* well-fixed **2** Sometimes, ***rich in.*** °abundant (in), overflowing (with), °fertile (in), fecund (in), °productive (of), copious (in), abounding in, well-supplied (with), well-stocked (with), rife (with), °replete (with), profuse (in *or* with) **3** valuable, °precious, °invaluable, °priceless **4** costly, °expensive, °dear, valuable, °invaluable, °precious, °priceless, °lavish, °sumptuous, °lush, °luxurious, °palatial, °elaborate, °splendid, °exquisite, °superb, °elegant **5** °intense, °dark, °deep, °warm, vibrant, °strong, °lustrous **6** °fat, fattening, °heavy, creamy, °succulent, °savory, mouthwatering, °luscious, sapid, °delicious **7** °mellow, mellifluous, °resonant, sonorous, °full **8** °aromatic, ambrosial, °savory, °fragrant, °redolent, °pungent, °strong **9** °productive, °plentiful, °abundant, °ample, °bountiful, °prolific, °fruitful, °fertile, fecund, copious, °profitable, °potent **10** laughable, °funny, °hilarious, comic(al), °humorous, amusing, *Colloq* sidesplitting **11** °ridiculous, °preposterous, °outlandish, °ludicrous, °absurd, °nonsensical

riches *n. pl.* wealth, affluence, opulence, °plenty, °prosperity, °abundance, °fortune, °means, °resources; lucre, pelf

richly *adv.* **1** sumptuously, lavishly, luxuriously, splendidly, elaborately, exquisitely, elegantly, superbly **2** °well, °thoroughly, °amply, fully, °appropriately, fittingly, condignly

rickety *adj.* wobbly, unsteady, broken-down, °decrepit, °shaky, tottering, teetering, °ramshackle, °flimsy, °frail, °precarious, °dilapidated, in disrepair, tumbledown, unsecure

rid *v.* **1** ***rid of.*** deliver from, relieve of, free from *or* of, °rescue, °save —*adj.* **2** ***be or get rid of.*** °banish, °exile, °eject, °expel, °dispose of, throw out *or* away, °eliminate,

°dispense with; °refuse, °reject, °dismiss, shrug off

-ridden *adj.* afflicted *or* harassed *or* affected *or* dominated by, infected *or* infested with

riddle[1] *n.* conundrum, °puzzle, °enigma, poser, °question, °mystery, °problem, brainteaser *or Brit* brain-twister

riddle[2] *v.* **1** °perforate, °pepper, °puncture, °pierce, honeycomb **2** °penetrate, °infest, infect, pervade, °permeate, °fill, °spread —*n.* **3** sieve, colander *or* cullender, strainer, °grating, °screen, sifter, °filter

ride *v.* **1** sit on *or* in, travel *or* journey *or* go *or* proceed on *or* in, be borne *or* carried *or* conveyed (on *or* in), °take; propel *or* control *or* drive (a horse *or* a bicycle *or* a motorcycle) **2** °float, °lie **3** °tyrannize, terrorize, °intimidate, °dominate, °oppress; °bully, °rag, harry, °harass, hector, °nag, °provoke, °heckle, badger, °plague, °pester, °annoy, °irritate, *Colloq* hassle —*n.* **4** °drive, °journey, °trip, °excursion, °tour, jaunt, °outing, °expedition, *Colloq* °spin **5** ***take for a ride.*** **(a)** delude, °swindle, °trick, °deceive, °defraud, humbug, gull, °take in, °cheat, bamboozle **(b)** (kidnap and) murder *or* kill *or* execute *or* do in, *Slang* °bump off, *US* (snatch and) rub out *or US* waste

ridge *n.* °crest, °line, °strip, top edge, arête

ridicule *n.* **1** °derision, deriding, °jeer, jeering, °taunt, taunting, °mockery, mocking, °gibe *or* jibe, gibing *or* jibing, °raillery, *Colloq* ribbing, *US and Canadian* razzing, joshing —*v.* **2** °deride, °jeer at, °taunt, °tease, °mock, °gibe *or* jibe, °guy, °chaff, °laugh at, °caricature, °poke fun at, make fun *or* sport of, °lampoon, °burlesque, travesty, °parody, make a laughingstock (of), *Colloq* rib, roast, *Brit* °send up, take the mickey out of, *US and Canadian* razz, josh

ridiculous *adj.* °absurd, laughable, °preposterous, °weird, comical, °funny, °humorous, °ludicrous, °farcical, droll, amusing, mirthful, °hilarious, sidesplitting, risible; °silly, °inane, °nonsensical, °foolish, °stupid, °outlandish, °bizarre, °grotesque, °queer, °crazy, °insane, °zany, °wild, *Slang* far-out

riffraff *n.* °rabble, °hoi polloi, ragtag and bobtail, scum, *canaille*, masses, °dregs (of society), *Colloq* great unwashed

rifle *v.* **1** °rob, °loot, °ransack, °plunder, despoil, burgle, °pillage, *US* burglarize **2** °search, °ransack, °go through, rummage through

rift *n.* **1** °separation, °break, °split, °schism, cleft, °gulf, °gap; °disagreement, °conflict, disruption, °difference, °breach, breakup, °division, °distance, alienation **2,** tear, rent, opening, hole, crack, chink, crevice, cleavage, fracture, flaw, fault

rig *v.* **1** Often, ***rig out or up.*** fit (out *or* up), °equip, °set up, °outfit, °supply, °provision, accoutre *or US also* accouter, caparison, °set up, *Chiefly Brit* kit out **2** °falsify, °manipulate, °doctor, °juggle, °fix, tamper with, °fake, *Colloq* °fiddle (with), cook —*n.* **3** °equipment, equipage, °gear, °tackle, °apparatus, °outfit, °kit, accoutrements *or US also* accouterments, °paraphernalia, appurtenances, *Colloq* °things, °stuff

right *adj.* **1** °just, °moral, °good, °proper, °correct, °legal, °lawful, licit, °honest, °upright, °righteous, °virtuous, °ethical, °fair, °true, °honorable, right-minded, °principled, °open, °aboveboard, °legitimate, *Colloq* legit **2** °correct, °fitting, °suitable, °proper, °accurate, °exact, °precise, °perfect; °factual, °truthful, veracious, valid, °sound, *Colloq Brit* bang on, spot on **3** °propitious, °convenient, °strategic, °advantageous, °beneficial, °favorable, auspicious, preferred, preferable, °promising **4** °sound, °sane, °normal, °rational, lucid, °healthy **5** right-hand, dextral, dexter, *Nautical* starboard **6** rightist, right-wing, °conservative, °reactionary, Tory **7** °face, °upper, °principal, °front **8** utter, °complete, °perfect, °unmitigated, unalloyed, °out-and-out, °thorough, thoroughgoing, 24-karat, dyed-in-the-wool, °pure, °absolute, °real, *Brit* °proper —*n.* **9** °privilege, °prerogative, °license, °power, °claim, °title, °freedom, °liberty **10** °justice, °reason, °fact, °truth, fairness, °equity, °good, goodness, °integrity, °virtue, virtuousness, °honesty, honorableness, °morality, °propriety, °rectitude, right-mindedness, high-mindedness, °nobility, uprightness **11** right side *or* hand *or* fist, *Nautical* starboard **12** ***by rights.*** °properly, °fairly, justly, to be just, to be fair, in fairness, °honestly, in all honesty, to be honest —*adv.* **13** °directly, °straight, °straightaway, right away *or* off, in a beeline, as the crow flies, forthwith; unhesitatingly, °immediately, °promptly, °at once, instantly, without hesitating *or* hesitation, without delay, °quickly, °swiftly, speedily, *Colloq* pronto, °straight off **14** °exactly, °precisely, unerringly, accurately; °just **15** °just, °only **16** °well, satisfactorily, advantageously, profitably, °favorably, opportunely **17** correctly, accurately, °properly, °precisely, °well, sensibly, fittingly, suitably, aptly —*v.* **18** straighten (up *or* out), set upright *or* aright **19** put *or* set *or* make right, put *or* set to rights, °correct, °straighten out, redress, °amend, °make up for, °rectify, °sort out, °repair, °fix **20** avenge, retaliate for, °vindicate, °repay, °revenge, °settle, *Colloq* get even for

righteous *adj.* **1** °moral, °just, °virtuous, upstanding, °upright, °good, °honest, °ethical, °honorable, °fair, °reputable, °trustworthy **2** °right, °correct, justifiable, justified, °appropriate, condign, °fitting, apt, °self-righteous

rightful *adj.* **1** °legal, °lawful, °legitimate, licit, de jure, °correct, °proper, °bona fide, valid, °true, authorized, °right **2** °just, °fair, °equitable, °right

rigid *adj.* **1** °stiff, unbending, unbendable, °firm, °hard, °strong **2** °inflexible, inelastic, unyielding, undeviating, unalterable, °set, °firm, °hard, hard-line, unbending, adamant(ine), °steely, iron, °strong, uncompromising, rigorous, unrelenting, intransigent, stringent, °severe, °strict, rigorous, °stern, °harsh, austere **3** rigorous, °exact, °precise, unwavering, °unqualified, unswerving, undeviating, °demanding, °strict, hard and fast, °literal, °nice, °close, °thorough, °scrupulous, °careful, °conscientious, °painstaking, °meticulous, punctilious, °exacting, °strait-laced **4** °obstinate, °stubborn, pigheaded, °inflexible, °immovable, adamant, adamantine, °fixed, °set, obdurate, °willful, headstrong, dogged, persevering, °determined, °resolute, °steadfast, resolved, °tenacious, °relentless, unrelenting, uncompromising, unadaptable, mulish, close-minded

rigmarole *n.* rigamarole, motions, complication(s), formalities, red tape, °bureaucracy, punctilio, ceremoniousness, °ceremony, °ritual, °procedure, °mess, °mumbo jumbo, gobbledygook *or* gobbledegook, bunkum *or* buncombe, °bother, balderdash, °rubbish, °nonsense, foolishness, *Colloq* hassle, bunk, *Slang* crap, *US* meshugaas *or* mishegaas

rigor *n.* **1** Usually, ***rigors.*** °severity, harshness, °hardship, inhospitableness, bleakness, inclemency *or* inclementness, °bitterness, °cold **2** strictness, rigidity, °precision, preciseness, punctilio, literalness, exactness, meticulousness, stringency, inflexibility, rigorism, harshness, °severity, °hardship, asperity, austerity, sternness

rim *n.* °edge, °brim, lip, °border, °periphery, °perimeter

rind *n.* °peel, °skin, husk

ring[1] *n.* **1** °loop, hoop, °band, °circle, ringlet, circlet, annulus, grommet, eyelet, quoit, noose, cincture, °belt, girdle, cestus *or* cestos, °border, °halo, aureole, nimbus, corona, cuff, collar, necklace, neckband, bandeau, fillet, bracelet, armlet, torque *or* torc, °crown, coronet, tiara, diadem, (laurel) wreath, °garland, *Mechanics* gland, °bearing, *US and Canadian* bushing *or Brit also* bush, washer, O-ring, *Nautical* thimble, *Architecture and heraldry* annulet, *Literary* roundlet, *Anatomy* cingulum **2** rink, °enclosure, arena, circus, bullring, *Spanish plaza de toros,* boxing ring **3** °circle, °organization, °gang, °band, °pack, °cell, °team, °crew, confederacy, confederation, °combination, cartel, °mob, bloc, coterie, °set, °clan, °clique, °fraternity, °brotherhood, sorority, sisterhood, guild, °(secret) society, junta *or* junto, °cabal, °faction, °group, °league, °alliance, °federation, coalition, °union, affiliation, camorra, camarilla, Bund —*v.* **4** °encircle, °surround, °bind, gird, girt, °circle; °loop, compass, °envelop, encompass, °embrace

ring[2] *v.* **1** °peal, °chime, °toll, knell, tintinnabulate, ding-dong, gong, °sound, resonate, °resound, °echo, reecho, reverberate; clang, °jangle; tinkle, clink, °jingle, ding-a-ling, ring-a-ding-ding, *Archaic and dialectal* °knoll **2** °telephone, ring up, phone, °call, give (someone) a ring, *Colloq* (give (someone) a) buzz, give (someone) a tinkle, get (someone) on the blower *or* horn, *US* (give (someone) a) jingle —*n.* **3** ringing, °peal, pealing, °chime, chiming, °toll, tolling, tintinnabulation, knell, sounding, resonating, °echo, echoing, reecho, reechoing, reverberation, reverberating; clang, clanging, °jangle, jangling; tinkle, tinkling, clink, clinking, °jingle, jingling, ding-a-ling, ring-a-ding-ding, *Archaic and dialectal* °knoll **4** (telephone *or* phone) call, *Colloq* °buzz, tinkle, *US* °jingle

rinse *v.* **1** wash (out *or* off), wash up, °clean, °cleanse, bathe, °drench, °flood, °flush, irrigate, *Chiefly Brit* °swill (out), *Literary* lave **2** °tint, dye, °touch up, highlight —*n.* **3** rinsing, °wash, washing, bath, bathing, cleaning, cleansing, ablution, drenching, °flood, flushing, irrigation, *Medical* lavage, *Literary* laving **4** °tint, dye

riot *n.* **1** rioting, riotous behavior, °disturbance, °uproar, °tumult, turmoil, °(civil) disorder, lawlessness, hubbub, °rumpus, turbulence, °fracas, °fray, affray, melee *or* mêlée, °pandemonium, donnybrook, °brawl, °row, °unrest, commotion, °bother, imbroglio, °outburst, anarchy, disruption, °violence, °strife, *Colloq* ruckus, ruction, to-do, do, *Brit* bovver, punch-up **2** funny person *or* woman *or* man, comedian *or* comedienne, hilarious event *or* bit *or* shtick *or* thing *or* piece of business, *Colloq* gas, *US* °panic, laugh-riot —*v.* **3** mount the barricades, take to the streets, °rebel, °revolt, create *or* cause a disturbance, °brawl, °fight, (go on the *or US also* a) °rampage, run riot, °storm

riotous *adj.* **1** °tumultuous, unrestrained, °wild, °noisy, °uncontrolled, uncontrollable, unmanageable, °chaotic, °disorderly, disordered, °lawless, turbulent, °violent, brawling, °obstreperous **2** °rowdy, °boisterous, °unruly, °uproarious, rollicking, roisterous, °wild, rumbustious, unrestrained, °uninhibited, *Archaic* robustious, *Colloq* rambunctious, no-holds-barred

rip *v.* **1** tear (apart *or* asunder), °rend, be torn *or* rent, °split, °cut (apart) **2** ***rip off.*** **(a)** °steal, purloin, °rob, °snatch, °pilfer, filch, °take, shoplift, *Colloq* °pinch, *Brit* °nick, *Slang* °lift, °swipe, *US* °boost, °promote **(b)** °cheat, °swindle, °trick, °fleece, bilk, °dupe, °deceive; °defraud, °embezzle, *Colloq* con, bamboozle, *Slang* °skin, gyp, rook —*n.* **3** °tear, °rent, °split, °gash, °slash; °rift, cleft, °rupture

ripe *adj.* **1** °mature, matured, °seasoned, (fully) grown, (well-)ripened, developed, °mellow, °ready, °fit, *US* °(fully) aged, well-aged **2** °prepared, °ready, °fit, °appropriate, °experienced, °veteran, °seasoned, °sage, °wise, °sophisticated, °mature, °informed, °qualified, dependable, °reliable **3** ***ripe for.*** **(a)** °timely, °opportune, °propitious, °favorable, auspicious, °ideal, °right, °suitable, apt, °proper, suitably advanced **(b)** °ready, °eager, °enthusiastic, °prepared, °fit, °in readiness

ripen *v.* °develop, °mature, °age, °season, maturate, bring *or* come to maturity; °perfect

rip-off *n.* **1** °stealing, purloining, robbing, pilfering, °taking, filching, pilferage, °theft, °robbery, larceny; shoplifting, *Colloq* pinching, *Brit* nicking, *Slang* lifting, swiping, *US* boosting **2** °swindle, confidence trick, swindling, cheating, °cheat, °fraud, °deception, defrauding, defalcation; °embezzlement, *Colloq* con (job *or* trick) **3** overcharging, exploitation, *Colloq* highway *or chiefly Brit* daylight robbery

ripping *adj. Somewhat archaic* °fine, °splendid, °marvelous, °excellent, °exciting, °thrilling, °stirring, spine-tingling

ripple *n.* **1** wavelet, °wave, °ruffle, ruffling, cat's-paw, purl, purling, undulation, *US* riffle, riffling **2** °(slight) disturbance, °upset, perturbation, °agitation, °flurry, °flutter, °suggestion, °hint, soupçon *—v.* **3** °ruffle, purl, undulate, °wave; °splash, °wash, *US* riffle

rise *v.* **1** °get up, °arise, °stand (up), get to one's feet, *Brit* be upstanding **2** °get up, °arise, °awaken, waken, °wake up, start *or* begin the day, *Nautical or colloq* hit the deck, *Colloq* °turn out **3** ascend, be elevated, °arise, °climb, °lift, °go up, °mount **4** Often, ***rise (up) (against)***. °rebel, °revolt, °mutiny, kick over the traces, take up arms, mount the barricades, take to the streets **5** °swell, °flood, °increase, °grow; wax **6** slant *or* incline *or* slope (upward(s)), ascend, °climb, go uphill **7** °fly, °take flight, take wing, take to the air, °take off, °arise, °lift, °climb, °soar, °mount **8** °advance, improve one's lot *or* position, progress, °get ahead, go *or* get somewhere, °succeed, make something of oneself, be promoted, °prosper, °thrive, °make good, *Colloq* °make it, °make the grade, °go places **9** °start, °begin, °originate, °arise, °occur, °happen, °take place **10** °increase, be elevated *or* lifted *or* boosted, °grow, °go up, move upward(s), °climb, escalate, ascend, snowball **11** °arise, be nurtured, be produced, be generated, be created, °spring up, be engendered **12** ***rise to.*** **(a)** °arise, °come up, °meet, be equal to, prove adequate to **(b)** come to get, °take, °swallow, react to, °respond to, succumb to, be tempted by *—n.* **13** ascent, °hill, hillock, °knoll, eminence, °prominence, °elevation, upland, highland, (upward) slope *or* incline, acclivity, *US* upgrade **14** °increase, °increment, °gain, °addition **15** ascent, ascension, °elevation, °flight, °climb, °takeoff **16** ***get or Brit also take a rise out of (someone).*** °provoke, °stimulate, °incite, instigate, °foment, goad, °encourage, °press, °push, °shake up, waken, °awaken, °move, °motivate, °activate, °agitate, °stir (up), °inflame, impassion **17** ***give rise to.*** °start, engender, °generate, °begin, °commence, °produce, °bring out, °cause, °bring about, bring into being

risk *n.* **1** °danger, °peril, °jeopardy, °hazard, °chance, °gamble *—v.* **2** °endanger, imperil, °jeopardize, °hazard, °chance, °gamble

risky *adj.* °dangerous, °perilous, °hazardous, chancy, touch-and-go, °precarious, *Colloq* iffy, °dicey, °dodgy, °touchy

risqué *adj.* indelicate, °unrefined, indecorous, °indecent, °improper, °broad, °naughty, °spicy, salty, °off-color, °racy, °bawdy, °erotic, °suggestive, °wicked, °blue, ribald, °daring, salacious, °gross, *Colloq Brit* near the knuckle

rite *n.* °ceremony, °ritual, °ceremonial, °observance, °formality, °custom, °practice, °routine, °procedure, °solemnity, solemnization, liturgy

ritual *adj.* **1** °ceremonial, °ceremonious, sacramental **2** procedural, °formal, °conventional, °customary, °habitual, °routine, prescribed, °usual, °automatic, °perfunctory *—n.* **3** °formality, °routine, °custom, °practice, °convention, °protocol **4** See **rite,** above.

rival *n.* **1** °competitor, °opponent, contender, challenger, °antagonist, °adversary; °opposition *—v.* **2** compete with *or* against, contend with *or* against, °oppose, °challenge, °contest, struggle with *or* against, vie with, °combat, °compare with, °equal, °measure up to, °(be a) match (for)

rivalry *n.* °competition, competitiveness, contention, vying; °dispute, °feud, feuding, °conflict, °struggle, °strife, °controversy, °dissension, °discord, difference(s)

river *n.* **1** watercourse, °branch, °tributary, °stream, waterway, estuary, rivulet, °creek, °brook, streamlet, runnel, rill, *Scots and Northern England* °burn, *Brit* beck, *US* °kill **2** °stream, °flood, °torrent, °quantity, cataract, °flow, cascade

riveting *adj.* °spellbinding, engrossing, hypnotic, hypnotizing, transfixing, fascinating, °enthralling, gripping, captivating, °absorbing

road *n.* **1** °way, °means, °approach, °route, °procedure, °technique, °method, °passage, °street, avenue, °course, °track, entrée, access, °direction **2** thoroughfare, °way, byway, highway, roadway, highroad, lowroad, avenue, boulevard, °street, lane, alley(way), *Brit* motorway, carriageway, *US* turnpike, expressway, freeway, parkway, throughway *or* thruway, *German Autobahn, Italian autostrada, French autoroute, Colloq US* pike

roam *v.* °wander, rove, °ramble, °range, °walk, °drift, dally, °dawdle, °cruise, °stroll, amble, °meander, °saunter, °stray, °prowl, perambulate, °travel, voyage, peregrinate, circumambulate, traipse, gallivant, jaunt, *Colloq* mosey, swan

roar *v.* **1** °bellow, °thunder; °howl, °bawl, squall, °cry, °yell, yowl; bay, °snarl, growl **2** °laugh, guffaw, °howl (with laughter), hoot *—n.* **3** roaring, °bellow, °thunder, rumble, °boom; °howl, °bawl, squall, °cry, °yell, yowl, clamor, °outcry; °snarl, snarling, growl, growling **4** guffaw, °outburst, °howl, hoot

rob *v.* **1** burgle, °loot, °rifle, °ransack, °plunder, depredate, °raid; hijack; °pillage, °sack; *US* burglarize, *Colloq* °hold up, *Slang* °stick up, knock off *or* over, °rip off **2** prey upon *or* on, *Colloq* °hold up, °mug, *Slang chiefly*

US °stick up, °rip off, *Chiefly US and New Zealand* °roll **3** ***rob (someone) (of).*** °deprive (of), cheat *or* swindle (out of), °defraud (of), °strip (of), °fleece (of), bilk (of), °victimize, mulct (of), *US* euchre (out of), *Colloq* rook (out of), do *or* diddle (out of), gyp (out of), *Slang Brit* nobble (of)

robber *n.* °thief, pickpocket, shoplifter, °burglar, bandit, housebreaker, sneak thief, cat burglar, safe-breaker, highwayman, gentleman of the road, brigand, °pirate, freebooter, buccaneer, privateer, corsair, *Colloq* mugger, holdup man, *Slang* cracksman, rip-off artist, safecracker, safe-blower, *Chiefly US* stickup man, *US* second-story man

robbery *n.* robbing, °theft, thievery, thieving, burglary, burgling, pilfering, pilferage, °stealing, plundering, °plunder, looting, °sack, sacking, ransacking, °depredation, °pillage, pillaging, hijacking, hijack, larceny, breaking and entering, *Colloq* pinching, °holdup, holding-up, mugging, *Slang* °rip-off, ripping-off, *Chiefly US* stickup, sticking-up, *Brit* nicking, *US* heist

robe *n.* **1** °cloak, °dress, garment, vestment, °habit, frock, cassock, caftan, muumuu, surplice, bathrobe, dressing gown, lounging robe, housecoat, kimono, housedress, peignoir, °wrapper, *French robe de chambre,* °costume **2** ***robes.*** °costume, °habit, °uniform, garb, attire, vestments, °apparel, raiment, livery, clothing, °garments, °outfit, accoutrements *or US also* accouterments, °regalia, °finery, °trappings, panoply, °gear, °paraphernalia, appurtenances, equipage, °rig, *Archaic* vesture —*v.* **3** °cloak, garb, °dress, °cover, enrobe, °clothe

robot *n.* **1** automaton, mechanical man *or* monster, android **2** drudge, °clod, °tool, °puppet, cat's-paw, myrmidon, mechanical man, automaton

robust *adj.* **1** °healthy, °fit, °sound, °hale (and hearty), °sturdy, °hardy, °hearty, °strong, °stout, °tough, able-bodied, strapping, °brawny, °sinewy, °rugged, °muscular, °powerful, well-knit, athletic, °staunch, °vigorous; in fine *or* good fettle, *Colloq* °husky **2** °pungent, °strong, flavorful, sapid, °rich, full-bodied, nutty, fruity

rock[1] *n.* **1** stone; boulder **2** °crag, tor, escarpment, scarp, *Brit* outcrop, *US* outcropping **3** ***on the rocks.*** **(a)** on ice **(b)** in (a) shambles, destroyed, in ruins, ruined, finished, °broken down, beyond repair **(c)** °destitute, poverty-stricken, °indigent, penniless, bankrupt

rock[2] *v.* **1** °sway, °swing, °lull **2** °roll, °reel, °lurch, °toss, °swing, °sway, wobble **3** °astound, °astonish, °shock, °surprise, °jar, °stagger, °amaze, °stun, dumbfound *or* dumfound, °daze, stupefy, °overwhelm, disconcert, °unnerve, *Colloq* set (someone) back on his *or* her *or* their heels, °throw, °rattle, °shake up

rocket *v.* zoom, °take off, skyrocket, shoot up, °climb, rise rapidly, °soar, spiral upward(s), *Colloq* go through the roof

rocky[1] *adj.* **1** °stony, pebbly, shingly, boulder-strewn, craggy; °bumpy, °difficult, °hard, uncomfortable, °arduous **2** °stony, adamant(ine), °firm, unyielding, rocklike, °tough, unbending, flinty, °firm, °solid, °steadfast, °steady, unfaltering, °staunch, unflinching, °determined, °resolute, unwavering, unchanging, unvarying, invariant, °invariable, °reliable, dependable, °sure, °certain **3** °stony, flinty, unfeeling, °unsympathetic, unemotional, emotionless, °impassive, °cold, °cool, apathetic, °indifferent, uncaring, °detached, *dégagé,* °callous, °thick-skinned, °tough, °hard

rocky[2] *adj.* °unstable, tottering, teetering, unsteady, °shaky, °rickety, unsure, °uncertain, °unreliable, °weak, °flimsy, wobbly, wobbling, vacillating, dubious, °doubtful, °questionable, *Colloq* iffy

rod *n.* **1** °bar, °pole, baton, °wand, °staff, °stick, dowel, cane, °shaft **2** cane, birch, °switch, °scourge, °lash; °punishment, chastisement, castigation, °discipline, chastening, °correction

rogue *n.* **1** trickster, °swindler, °cheat, cad, ne'er-do-well, °wastrel, °good-for-nothing, °miscreant, *Rather old-fashioned* scamp, °scoundrel, blackguard, knave, °rascal, rapscallion, scapegrace, dastard, cur, churl, °wretch, °villain, charlatan, mountebank, *Brit* bounder; *Colloq* louse, °stinker, rat, °creep, *Brit* rotter, blighter, *Chiefly US and Canadian* son of a gun, *Slang* bastard, *Chiefly US and Canadian* son of a bitch, s.o.b. *or* SOB, °bum —*adj.* **2** °independent, °undisciplined, uncontrollable, °ungovernable, unmanageable, unpredictable, °disobedient, °incorrigible, fractious, °self-willed, °unruly, intractable, unrestrained, °wild, °lawless, strong-willed, headstrong, refractory, contumacious, °recalcitrant, cross-grained, rampageous

role *n.* **1** rôle, °part, °character, impersonation; °lines **2** °function, °position, °situation, °place, °post, °capacity, °job, °duty, °task, °responsibility

roll *v.* **1** °rotate, °cycle, turn (over (and over)), °wheel, trundle; °revolve, go (a)round, °orbit, °tumble, somersault *or* somerset *or* summersault *or* summerset **2** °pass, °go, °flow, °slip, °flit, °glide, °slide, °move (on); °expire, °elapse, °disappear, vanish, °evaporate **3** °move, °drive, °bowl, be carried *or* conveyed, °cruise, °sail, °coast, °ride, °float, °fly **4** undulate, billow, rise and fall **5** °roar, °echo, reecho, rumble, reverberate, °resound, °sound, °boom, °peal, resonate, °thunder **6** °rob, steal from **7** Often, ***roll out.*** °flatten, level (off *or* out), °smooth (out), °even (out), °grade **8** Usually, ***roll over.*** °turn (over), °rotate, °spin **9** Usually, ***roll up.*** furl, °coil, curl, °wind (up), °wrap (up); enwrap, °swathe, enfold, °envelop, °shroud, enshroud **10** ***roll in.*** **(a)** °arrive, °come in, pour in, flow in, °turn up, °show up **(b)** °luxuriate in, °revel in, °wallow in, °savor, bask in, °delight in, take pleasure in, °indulge in, rejoice in, °relish **11** ***roll out.*** unroll, unfurl, °spread (out), °unfold, uncoil, uncurl, unwind, °open (out) **—*n.* 12** °reel, spool, cylinder, scroll; tube **13** °list, rota, °register, °record, directory, listing, roster, slate, docket, catalogue, inventory, °muster, °index, census, annal(s), °schedule, chronicle(s), *Sports* lineup **14** rolling, billowing, waving, wave action, °wave, billow, °swell, undulation, pitching, rocking, tossing **15** °peal, rumble, reverberation, °boom, °echo, °thunder, °roar **16** rotation, °spin, °toss, whirl, °twirl **17** bun; scone, croissant; *Brit* breadroll **18** bankroll, °money, °wad, °bundle

roller *n.* **1** drum, cylinder, barrel, calender; tube; windlass; rolling pin; °mangle, wringer **2** billow, °wave, comber, breaker, °swell

romance *n.* **1** °(love) affair, amour, affair of the heart, *affaire de coeur, affaire d'amour,* °liaison, °relationship, dalliance, °intrigue **2** °(true) love **3** °novel, °narrative, fiction, °story, °mystery, thriller, horror story, ghost story, science fiction, °fantasy, Western, melodrama, gothic *or* Gothic *or* Gothick novel *or* tale, °(fairy) tale, love story, idyll, epic, °legend **4** °sentiment, nostalgia, °mystery, °intrigue, °fantasy, °imagination, imaginativeness, °adventure, °excitement, °fascination, exoticism, °glamour, °color, colorfulness **5** tall tale *or* story, °fantasy, °fabrication, fairy tale, °exaggeration, prevarication, concoction, flight of fancy, °fib, °(white) lie, balderdash, fiction, °nonsense, °imagination **—*v.* 6** °make love to; woo, court **7** °pander to, °flatter, curry favor with, toady (up) to, *Colloq* butter up, soft-soap, *Taboo slang* brown-nose

romantic *adj.* **1** °imaginary, imagined, °fictitious, °fictional, °ideal, idealized, °fancied, °fabulous, made-up, dreamed-up, dreamt-up, fantasized, °fanciful, fairy-tale, °mythical, °idyllic, utopian, °illusory **2** °impractical, °visionary, °fictitious, unpractical, °unrealistic, °ideal, °abstract, °quixotic, chimerical, °absurd, °extravagant, °wild, crackpot, °mad **3** nostalgic, °sentimental, °emotional, °sweet, °tender, °picturesque, °exotic, °glamorous; mawkish, °maudlin, saccharine, *Colloq* soppy, sugary, °mushy, °sloppy **4** °amorous, °affectionate, aroused, °impassioned, °passionate, libidinous, °lustful, overfriendly, *Colloq* lovey-dovey; °fresh **—*n.* 5** romanticist, °dreamer, Don Quixote, °visionary, idealist, sentimentalist

room *n.* **1** °space, °area, °scope, °extent, °allowance, latitude, elbowroom, °range, °leeway, °margin **2** °chamber, apartment, °compartment, °office, °cell, cubicle **3** ***rooms.*** °quarters, lodgings, °accommodation, apartment, °dwelling, *Chiefly Brit or old-fashioned US* °flat **—*v.* 4** °live, °lodge, °dwell, °abide, reside, °stay

roomy *adj.* °spacious, capacious, commodious, °large, sizable, °big, °ample

root[1] *n.* **1** °base, °basis, °foundation, °source, °seat, °cause, fountainhead, °origin, fount, wellspring **2** rootstock, rootstalk, taproot, rootlet; tuber; *Technical* radix, radicle, radicel, rhizome, rhizomorph **3** ***root and branch.*** radically, °completely, °utterly, °entirely, °wholly, °totally **4** ***roots.*** °origins, °heritage, °family, °lineage, °house, antecedents, forefathers, foremothers, descent, genealogy, family tree, forebears, ancestors, predecessors, °stock, °pedigree; birthplace, motherland, °fatherland, native land *or* country *or* soil, cradle **5** ***take root.*** become set *or* established *or* settled, germinate, °sprout, °grow, °develop, °thrive, burgeon, °flourish, °spread **—*v.* 6** °plant, °set, °establish, °found, °fix, °settle, embed *or* imbed; entrench, °anchor **7** ***root out.*** **(a)** Sometimes, ***root up.*** uproot, eradicate, °eliminate, °destroy, extirpate, °exterminate **(b)** °find, uncover, °discover, dig up *or* out, °unearth, °turn up, °bring to light

root[2] *v.* rootle, forage, °dig, °pry, nose, °poke, ferret, °burrow, °rummage, delve, °search, °ransack

root[3] *v.* Usually, ***root for.*** cheer (for), °applaud (for); °boost, °support, °encourage, urge on

rooted *adj.* °firm, established, °set, °fixed, °fast, settled, deep-rooted, deep-seated, °entrenched, ingrained *or* engrained, (firmly) embedded *or* imbedded, implanted, instilled; °chronic, inbred, °inherent, °intrinsic, °essential, °fundamental, °basic, °radical

rope *n.* **1** °line, °cord, °cable, hawser; strand, °string **2** ***the ropes.*** the routine, the procedure, one's way around, the ins and outs; the truth, the (real) situation; *Colloq* what's what, the score, *Brit* the gen **—*v.* 3** °tie, °bind, °lash, °hitch, °fasten, °secure; °tether, °attach **4** ***rope in.*** °attract, °draw (in), °tempt, °entice, °lure, °persuade

ropy *adj.* **1** ropey, viscous, °stringy, viscid, glutinous, mucilaginous, gluey, gummy, thready, fibrous, filamentous **2** questionable, °inadequate, °inferior, °deficient, °indifferent, °mediocre, substandard, °unsatisfactory, °poor, °sketchy

rostrum *n.* °platform, °stage, dais, podium, pulpit, °pedestal, lectern, (reading) stand

rosy *adj.* **1** °pink, rose-colored, red, roseate, reddish, pinkish, cherry, cerise, ruddy, flushed, °glowing, blushing, ruby, rubicund, florid; rose-red **2** °optimistic, °promising, °favorable, auspicious, °hopeful, encouraging, °sunny, °bright

rot *v.* **1** °decay, °decompose, °fester, °spoil, go bad *or* off, be tainted, be ruined, °mold, molder, °putrefy; corrode, rust, °disintegrate, °deteriorate, crumble *or* go *or* fall to pieces **2** °waste away, wither away, languish, °die, molder, °decline, °deteriorate, °degenerate, °decay, atrophy **—*n.* 3** °decay, decomposition, °mold, putrefaction, putrescence, °blight, corrosion, corruption, disintegration, deterioration **4** °(stuff and) nonsense, balderdash, °rubbish, bunkum, tommyrot, twaddle, °drivel, hogwash, eyewash, °trash, *Colloq* claptrap, bunk, boloney *or* baloney, bosh, malarkey, °moonshine, poppycock, tosh, *Slang* crap, bull, codswallop, *Brit* (a load of (old)) cobblers, *Taboo* balls, bullshit

rotary *n.* traffic circle, *Brit* °roundabout, mini-roundabout

rotate *v.* **1** °turn, °revolve, go round, °spin, °gyrate, °pirouette, whirl, °twirl, °wheel, °pivot, °reel **2** °change, °exchange, °alternate, interchange, °switch, trade places; °take turns, *Colloq* swap *or* swop

rote *n.* **1** °routine, °ritual **2** ***by rote.*** **(a)** by heart, from memory **(b)** unthinkingly, automatically, mechanically

rotten *adj.* **1** rotted, decayed, decomposed, decomposing, °putrid, putrescent, putrescing, °moldy, moldering, spoilt *or* spoiled, mildewed, °rancid, fetid *or* foetid, °stale, °rank, °foul, feculent, tainted, contaminated, festered, festering, °corrupt, °bad, °off, turned, overripe, soured, °sour **2** rotted, rusted, corroded, deteriorating, disintegrating, crumbling, crumbly, falling to pieces, friable **3** °immoral, °corrupt, °dishonest, °deceitful, °venal, °shameless, °degenerate, °villainous, iniquitous, °evil, °wicked, °vile, debased, °base, °perverted, depraved, °unscrupulous, unprincipled, amoral, warped, *Slang* °bent **4** heinous, °evil, °vile, °base, °miserable, °despicable, °wretched, °awful, °terrible, °horrible, horrific, °nasty, °contemptible, °filthy, °mean, °low, *Colloq* °lousy, °stinking, °lowdown, dirty-rotten **5** °ill, unwell, °sick, °nauseated, °awful; hung over, *Colloq* °lousy, ropy *or* ropey, °rough

rotund *adj.* **1** round(ed), °circular, orbicular, globular, °spherical **2** °full, full-toned, °deep, °resonant, reverberant, reverberating, sonorous, °rich, °round, °mellow; pear-shaped **3** °chubby, podgy *or US chiefly* pudgy, °(pleasingly) plump, portly, tubby, °heavy, fleshy, corpulent, °stout, °fat, °obese, overweight, *Colloq* roly-poly

roué *n.* °playboy, womanizer, ladies' man, °rake, lecher, Lothario, Don Juan, Romeo, Casanova, °charmer, °flirt, °libertine, debauchee, *Old-fashioned* masher, gay dog, *Colloq* wolf, lady-killer, dirty old man, *Taboo slang* gash-hound

rough *adj.* **1** uneven, °irregular, °coarse, °jagged, °rugged, °bumpy, °lumpy, °broken **2** °agitated, turbulent, choppy, °stormy, storm-tossed, °tempestuous, roiled **3** °brusque, °bluff, °curt, °short, °abrupt, unpleasant, churlish, °discourteous, °impolite, rough-spoken, °ungracious, °surly, °disrespectful, °rude, uncouth, loutish, °unrefined, uncivil, °uncivilized, uncultured, °vulgar, unladylike, ungentlemanly, °coarse, °ill-mannered, ill-bred, °inconsiderate **4** °tough, rough-and-tumble, roughneck, °rowdy **5** °harsh, °violent, unfeeling, unjust, °severe, °cruel, °tough, °hard, °brutal, °extreme; ungentle **6** °dirty, °obscene, smutty, °pornographic, °vulgar, °crude, °raw, °rude **7** °hard, °tough, °Spartan, °difficult, °arduous, °laborious, °rugged, unpleasant **8** °harsh, °grating, cacophonous, °discordant, jarring, °strident, °raucous, rasping, unmusical, inharmonious, °gruff, °husky **9** unfinished, °incomplete, uncompleted, °imperfect, °rudimentary, °crude, °rude, formless, unformed, °raw, rough-and-ready, rough-hewn, roughcast, °undeveloped, unshaped, unworked, unwrought, unprocessed, °unrefined; uncut, unpolished; °shapeless, unshaped, undressed **10** °general, °approximate, °inexact, °cursory, °quick, °hasty, °sketchy, °vague, °hazy; foggy, *Colloq* ballpark **11** unfair, unjust, °bad, °tough; unlucky, °unfortunate **12** See **rotten, 5,** above. —*n.* **13** °rowdy, °tough, hooligan, ruffian, °thug, brawler, °yahoo, *Slang* roughneck, *Australian* larrikin, *US* °mug **14** sketch, °(rough) draft, mock-up, °outline —*v.* **15** ***rough out or in.*** sketch, °draft, mock up, °outline, mark out, °trace, °block out **16** ***rough up.*** °beat (up), thrash, °attack, °batter, °assault, pummel *or* pommel, °lay on, °knock about, °belabor, lambaste *or* lambast, *Colloq* wallop —*adv.* **17** violently, savagely, brutally, brutishly

roughhouse *n.* **1** boisterousness, rowdiness, °rowdyism, °violence, brawling, disorderliness, disorderly conduct, ruffianism —*v.* **2** °brawl

roughly *adv.* **1** °approximately, °around; °about, °nearly **2** harshly, unkindly, °severely, sternly, unsympathetically, brutally, violently, savagely, inhumanly, mercilessly, unmercifully, ruthlessly, pitilessly, cruelly, heartlessly **3** clumsily, rudely, crudely, awkwardly, primitively, inexpertly, amateurishly, maladroitly, heavy-handedly, ineptly, inefficiently, unskillfully, inartistically

round *adj.* **1** °circular; disk-shaped *or* disc-shaped, discoid, disklike *or* disclike **2** ring-shaped, annular, hoop-shaped, hooplike **3** °spherical, ball-shaped, ball-like, globular, spheroid, spheroidal, globe-shaped, globelike, globate, orb-shaped, orblike, orbicular **4** curved, curvilinear, rounded, arched **5** °exact, °precise, °complete, °entire, °full **6** °approximate, °rough, rounded (off *or* up *or* down), °whole **7** rounded, °mellow, °full, vibrant, reverberant, reverberating, sonorous, °rich, mellifluous, orotund, pear-shaped **8** °plain, °honest, straightforward, °direct, °unvarnished, unembellished, unelaborated, °outspoken, °candid, °truthful, °frank, °open, °blunt, *Colloq* upfront **9** *Chiefly Brit* °return —*n.* **10** °circle, disk *or* disc; °ring, hoop, annulus; ball, °sphere, °globe, °orb, bead **11** °cycle, series, °sequence, °succession, °bout, °spell **12** Often, ***rounds.*** °beat, °route, °routine, °circuit, °course, °tour, °turn, ambit **13** °heat, °stage, °level, °turn **14** °spell, °period, °run, °spate, °bout, °outburst, °burst, °volley **15** bullet, cartridge, °charge, °shell, °(single) shot —*v.* **16** °turn, go (a)round **17** °orbit, circumnavigate, go (a)round, °circle, °encircle **18** ***round off or out.*** °complete, °close, °end, bring to an end *or* completion *or* a close, °finish **19** ***round up.*** °gather, °assemble, °muster, draw *or* pull *or* get together, °collect, °herd, marshal, *US and Canadian* (of cattle *or* horses) corral, wrangle —*prep.* **20** See **around,** *prep.* —*adv.* **21** See **around,** *adv.*

roundabout *adj.* **1** circuitous, °circular, °indirect, °long **2** °devious, circuitous, °evasive, °indirect, °oblique

roundup *n.* **1** °gathering, °assembly, °rally, °collection, herding, *US and Canadian* (of cattle *or* horses) corralling, wrangling **2** °summary, °synopsis, °digest, °outline, recapitulation, °review, °survey, *Colloq* recap

rouse *v.* **1** °arouse, °call, waken, °awaken, °wake (up), °get up, °arise **2** °stir (up), °arouse, bestir, °stimulate, inspirit, °animate, invigorate, °electrify, °excite, °provoke, °prompt, goad, °prod, galvanize, °incite, °whet, °move, °work up, fire up

rousing *adj.* °stimulating, inspiriting, animating, enlivening, energizing, inspiring, °invigorating, vitalizing, electrifying; °fervent, °vigorous, °energetic, °enthusiastic, °spirited, °brisk, °lively, °animated, *Colloq* peppy

rout *n.* **1** °defeat, trouncing, °ruin, °overthrow, subjugation, vanquishment, debacle, °conquest, °thrashing, drubbing, beating; dispersal, °retreat, °collapse; *Colloq* licking, hiding, *US and Canadian* shellacking —*v.* **2** °defeat, win (out) over, trounce, °ruin, °overthrow, bring down, °subjugate, °subdue, °suppress, vanquish, °conquer, °overwhelm, °overpower, put to rout *or* flight, worst, °best, °trample, °overrun, thrash, °trim, °whip, drub, °beat, °crush, °batter, smash, °shatter, cut to pieces *or* ribbons *or* shreds, °destroy, °devastate, °wipe out, °eliminate, °put down, seal the doom *or* the fate of, eradicate, °obliterate, *Colloq* lick, wipe the floor with, °polish off, °knock off, *Hyperbolic sports jargon* °pulverize, make mincemeat of, ride roughshod over, °demolish, °mangle, °ravage, °mutilate, °flatten, squash, °topple, °lay waste, wreak havoc on, °ravage, °massacre, °murder, °exterminate, annihilate, liquidate, °smother, °stifle, do away with, *Slang* clobber, do in, *US* skunk, *Chiefly US and Canadian* cream

route *n.* **1** °way, itinerary, °course, °direction, °path, °road, avenue —*v.* **2** °direct, convey, °carry

routine *n.* **1** °custom, °habit, °procedure, °practice, °method, °schedule, °plan, °program, °formula, °pattern, °way, °usage, wont, *Colloq chiefly Brit* °drill **2** °act, °piece, °bit, °performance, °number, °part, *Colloq* °thing, shtick —*adj.* **3** °customary, °habitual, °usual, °rote, °accustomed, °familiar, °conventional, °regular, °ordinary, °everyday; programmed, assigned, designated, scheduled **4** °boring, °tedious, °tiresome, unimaginative, uninteresting; hackneyed, trite, stereotypic(al), clichéd, °run-of-the-mill, °ordinary; unvaried, unvarying, unchanging, °monotonous, uneventful, °rote, °automatic, °mechanical, °perfunctory

rover *n.* wanderer, bird of passage, itinerant, °traveler, rolling stone, nomad, gypsy *or chiefly Brit also* gipsy, wayfarer, gadabout, sojourner, °tourist; °drifter, °tramp, °vagabond, vagrant, *US* hobo, °bum

row[1] *n.* °line, °rank, °tier, bank, °string, series, °file

row[2] *n.* **1** altercation, °argument, °dispute, °quarrel, °disagreement, squabble, spat, °tiff, °conflict, °fracas, *Colloq* shouting match, °scrap, falling-out, *Brit* slanging match **2** commotion, °disturbance, clamor, hubbub, °racket, °din, °rumpus, °tumult, °uproar, brouhaha, °fuss, °stir, turmoil, hullabaloo; °bedlam, °pandemonium, °chaos; *US* foofaraw, *Colloq* ruckus —*v.* **3** °dispute, °quarrel, °argue, °disagree, wrangle, cross swords, have words, °bicker, °tiff, *Colloq* °scrap, °fall out

rowdy *adj.* **1** °boisterous, °uproarious, °disorderly, °noisy, °loud, °obstreperous, °unruly —*n.* **2** ruffian, °tough, hooligan, °yahoo, brawler, lout, *Brit* lager lout, skinhead, *Chiefly US and Canadian* °hoodlum, hood, *Slang Brit* bovver boy

rowdyism *n.* rowdiness, ruffianism, hooliganism, roughhousing, barbarism, troublemaking, brawling, unruliness, boisterousness, *Slang Brit* bovver

royal *adj.* **1** queenly, kingly, queenlike, kinglike, °regal, °imperial, °sovereign, °princely, °majestic **2** °grand, °splendid, °stately, °impressive, august, °imposing, °superior, °superb, °magnificent, °majestic —*n.* **3** °king, °queen, prince, princess, duke, earl, duchess, viscount, viscountess, baron, baroness, °noble, nobleman, noblewoman, °peer **4** ***the royals.*** °royalty, °nobility, nobles, peerage

royalty *n.* **1** queenship, kingship, royal house *or* line *or* family, °sovereignty **2** °percentage, commission, °share, °payment, compensation **3** °nobility, nobles, peerage, *Colloq Brit* royals

rub *v.* **1** °massage, knead, °stroke; °scour, °scrub, °scrape, abrade, °chafe, °clean; °wipe, °smooth, °polish, °shine, buff, burnish **2** ***rub in or on.*** °apply, °smooth, °smear, °spread, °put **3** ***rub (it or something) in.*** °emphasize, °stress, make an issue of, harp on, °reiterate, °dwell on, hammer away, °dramatize **4** ***rub off or out.*** expunge, °erase, °remove, °delete, °cancel, °eliminate, eradicate **5** ***rub off (on).*** °affect, be transferred (to), be communicated *or* transmitted (to), be passed on *or* along (to), be imparted to **6** ***rub out.*** °murder, °kill, °execute, slay **7** ***rub shoulders with.*** rub elbows with, °associate with, socialize with, mix with, fraternize with, keep company with, consort with, *Colloq US* run *or* pal *or* chum around with **8** ***rub (someone) (Brit up) the wrong way.*** °annoy, °irritate, °irk, °anger, °provoke, go against the grain, *Colloq* °bug, get under one's *or* someone's skin, peeve —*n.* **9** °wipe, °stroke, rubbing **10** °massage, rubdown **11** ***the rub.*** the *or* a catch *or* hitch *or* snag *or* hindrance *or* setback, the *or* an obstacle *or* impediment, the *or* a difficulty *or* problem *or* trouble

rubberneck *v.* **1** °gape, °stare, goggle, °gawk —*n.* **2** °tourist, °sightseer, rubbernecker, *US* out-of-towner

rubbish *n.* **1** °refuse, °waste, debris, rubble, detritus, °litter, °garbage, sweepings, dross, °dregs, °residue, leftovers, remnants, lees, °scraps, °fragments, leavings, residuum, °junk, rejects, *Chiefly US* °trash, *Slang chiefly US* dreck **2** °(stuff and) nonsense, balderdash, °moonshine, °gibberish, gobbledygook *or* gobbledegook, tommyrot, bunkum, °trash, °garbage, twaddle, *Colloq* °rot, flapdoodle, crap, hokum, codswallop, bosh, piffle, hooey, bunk, malarkey, poppycock, boloney *or* baloney, eyewash, hogwash, bilgewater, bull, *Scots* havers, *Brit* tosh, gammon, *US* a crock, horsefeathers, gurry, *Slang* °rot, *Brit* (a load of (old)) cobblers, *Taboo slang* bullshit, horseshit, *US* a crock of shit —*v.* **3** °criticize, °attack, °destroy, *Colloq* clobber, °pan, *Chiefly US* °trash, *Slang* °jump on, *Chiefly US and Canadian* badmouth, jump all over

rude *adj.* **1** °impolite, °discourteous, °disrespectful, °ungracious, ungallant, unmannerly, °ill-mannered, uncivil, bad-mannered, ungentlemanly, unladylike, ill-bred, °unrefined, unpolished, uncouth, °boorish, churlish, oafish, loutish, °coarse, °uncivilized, uncultured, unceremonious **2** °impertinent, °impudent, °discourteous, insulting, °insolent, °offensive, saucy, °bold, °disrespectful, uncivil, °flippant, °brusque, °curt, °gruff, °tactless, °outrageous, *Colloq* °fresh **3** °naughty, °unrefined, ribald, °bawdy, °indecent, indelicate, °vulgar, °obscene, °dirty, °filthy, lubricious *or* lubricous, °lewd, °gross, smutty, °taboo, °pornographic **4** °crude, °rough, °clumsy, °awkward, unskillful, unskilled, °artless, inartistic, °imperfect, unpolished, °inaccurate, gauche, bumbling, °raw, inelegant, °makeshift, °homespun, °primitive, °misshapen, ill-formed, unfinished, rough-hewn, °simple, °basic, °bare

rudimentary *adj.* **1** °basic, °essential, °elementary, °fundamental, rudimental, °primary, °introductory, abecedarian, formative, °first, °initial, °elemental, primal, °seminal **2** °crude, °coarse, unshaped, unfinished, °imperfect, °primitive, °undeveloped, °vestigial, embryonic, primordial, °immature

rudiments *n. pl.* basics, °elements, essentials, fundamentals, first principles

ruffle *n.* **1** trimming, °flounce, °frill, ruff, peplum, °flare, smocking, ruche, ruching, °gather, °gathering **2** °ripple, wavelet, °disturbance, °flurry, bustle, °stir, perturbation, °wrinkle —*v.* **3** °agitate, disconcert, °confuse, discompose, °discomfit, °upset, °disturb, °stir up, °perturb, unsettle, disorient, °unnerve, °fluster, °affect, °bother, °intimidate, unstring, °put out, vex, °trouble, °worry, *Colloq* °rattle, °throw, °shake up, *Chiefly US and Canadian* discombobulate, voodoo, hex, psych out, *Slang chiefly US and Canadian* get (someone) all shook up, spook **4** disarrange, dishevel, °disorder, °rumple, °mix up, °tousle, °tangle, °disorder, *Colloq* mess *or* muss (up)

rugged *adj.* **1** °rough, uneven, °broken, °stony, °rocky, °irregular, °bumpy, °pitted, °jagged, °ragged **2** °tough, °rough, °severe, °hard, °harsh, °difficult, °arduous, °Spartan, rigorous, onerous, °stern, °demanding, °burdensome **3** °hardy, °durable, °strong, °sturdy, °hale, °robust, °tough, °vigorous, °hard, rough-and-ready, °stalwart; °independent, individualistic, self-reliant, °self-confident, °self-sufficient, °bold **4** °rude, uncouth, uncultured, °uncivilized, °unrefined, unpolished, °crude, °ungraceful, churlish

ruin *n.* **1** °downfall, °destruction, devastation, °havoc, °breakdown, breakup, debacle, °collapse, °fall, disintegration, ruination, °dissolution, wiping out, °failure, °decay, °undoing, °end; °conquest, °defeat, °overthrow; bankruptcy, liquidation, °failure **2** °degradation, °dishonor, debasement, defilement, corruption, vitiation, seduction, °degrading, dishonoring, debasing, defiling, corrupting, vitiating, seducing; deflowering, defloration **3** nemesis, °end, bane, °curse **4** gin, mother's ruin, blue ruin, *Slang* rotgut **5** °hag, °witch, crone, beldam; dotard, (old) fogy *or* fogey, fossil, fuddy-duddy, °antique, *Brit* OAP (= 'old-age pensioner'), *Chiefly US* retiree, *Colloq* (old) geezer, °wreck, *Slang* dodo **6** ***ruins.*** debris, °wreckage, °fragments, rubble, °remains —*v.* **7** °destroy, °devastate, °demolish, annihilate, °dissolve, °wipe out, °undo, °overthrow, °lay waste, °raze, °shatter, °wreck, °crush, °flatten, wreak havoc upon *or* on, reduce to nothing *or* naught, °pulverize, smash, bring to ruin **8** °spoil, disfigure, °damage, °botch, °mess up, make a mess of, °mar, uglify **9** °spoil, °destroy, °wreck, nullify, °damage, °harm, °hurt, °impair, °poison, *Slang* louse up, °screw up, put the kibosh on, *US* bollix up, *Taboo slang chiefly Brit* make a balls-up of **10** bankrupt, pauperize, impoverish, reduce to penury *or* poverty *or* destitution *or* indigence **11** °violate, deflower, °ravish, °seduce, °lead astray, °dishonor, defile, °corrupt, °debase, defile

ruinous *adj.* °disastrous, °destructive, catastrophic, °calamitous, deleterious, pernicious, crippling, cataclysmic, baleful, °fatal, toxic, °poisonous, noxious, °harmful, °injurious, °nasty, *Archaic* baneful

rule *n.* **1** °regulation, °order, °law, ordinance, ruling, °decree, ukase, statute, °principle, °direction, °guide, guideline, °precept **2** °dominion, °authority, °control, °sovereignty, °sway, °command, ascendancy, °direction, °oversight, supervision, mastery **3** °fact, °standard, °customs, °practice, °form, °routine, °convention, °policy, way things are **4** ***as a rule.*** °generally, °usually, normally, customarily, °for the most part, mostly, °ordinarily, °mainly, °in the main, °chiefly, °on the whole, commonly, more often than not —*v.* **5** Sometimes, ***rule over.*** °reign (over), °govern, be in control *or* charge *or* command (of *or* over), be in power (over), hold sway (over), wield the scepter, wear the crown, °run; °prevail, hold sway, °dominate, °predominate, °control **6** °direct, °guide, °manage, °control, °lead, °head (up), °preside (over), superintend, °oversee, °supervise, °regulate, °govern, °run **7** °decide, °judge, hand down a judgment *or* decision, °decree, deem, °resolve, °settle, °determine, °find, °declare, °pronounce **8** ***rule out.*** °ban, °bar, °prohibit, °exclude, °eliminate, °forbid, °preclude, proscribe, negate, °dismiss, °disregard, °bypass, °ignore

rummage *v.* **1** °search, °hunt, comb, °scour, scrabble, look through, sift through, turn inside out *or* upside down, °examine, *Colloq* °scrounge —*n.* **2** °jumble, miscellanea, °miscellany, knickknacks, °odds and ends, hotchpotch *or US also* hodgepodge

rumor *n.* **1** °news, °gossip, hearsay, °information, °scoop, tidings, °chat, chitchat, tittle-tattle, *on dit*; °grapevine, jungle telegraph, *Colloq* °lowdown, info, *US and Canadian* poop, *Slang chiefly US nautical* scuttlebutt —*v.* **2** bruit about, noise abroad, °circulate, pass around, °intimate, °breathe, °suggest, °whisper, °leak, °reveal, °make known, °put about, °say, °report, °tell

rumple *v.* Sometimes, ***rumple up.*** wrinkle, °crumple, °crush, crease, °fold, crinkle, dishevel, °ruffle, °tousle, scrunch (up), °pucker, muss (up), °mess (up)

rumpus *n.* commotion, °disturbance, °fuss, °confusion, °uproar, °tumult, to-do, ado, °mayhem, °bedlam, brouhaha, °stir, pother, affray, °fracas, °row, melee *or* mêlée, °roughhouse, °brawl

run *v.* **1** sprint, °race, scamper, °scurry, °scud, dart, °bolt, °dash, °flit, °tear (along), scoot, scuttle, zip, whiz *or* whizz, gallop, °jog, °trot, lope; °rush, °hurry (up), °hasten, °scramble, °hustle, step lively, hop (to) it, °step on it, put on some speed, *Archaic* hie, *Colloq* °get a move on, hoof it, °leg it, hotfoot (it), stir one's stumps, *Brit* hare, *US* step on the gas, °hump (it), *Slang* get cracking, *US* get the lead out (of one's pants *or taboo* ass), *Chiefly US* get a wiggle on **2** run away *or* off, °flee, °escape, °take flight, °take to one's heels, °bolt, decamp, °make off, °clear out, show a clean pair of heels, abscond, cut and run, °(beat a (hasty)) retreat, °retire, make a getaway, (make a) run for it, *Colloq* °beat it, scram, skedaddle, °take off, °skip (out), take French leave, fly the coop, *Slang* head for the hills, *Brit* scarper, do a bunk, *US and Canadian* take a (runout) powder, lam out of (somewhere), take it *or* go on the lam, *US* vamoose **3** °go, °cover, °pass over, sprint, °race **4** °wander, rove, °roam, °meander, °drift **5** Often, ***run for.*** °compete (for), be a candidate (for), °vie, °struggle, contend, °fight (for), °stand (for) **6** °pass, °flow, °pour, °stream, °flood, °gush, °spill, dribble, °spurt, °issue, °move, °trickle, seep, °discharge, cascade, °spout **7** °flow, °diffuse **8** °melt, liquefy, °dissolve, °fuse **9** °keep, °maintain, °support, °sustain, °manage **10** °operate, °manage, °direct, °supervise, °oversee, °conduct, superintend, °control, °handle, °manipulate, °head, °carry on, °lead, °regulate, °take care of, °look after, °administer, be in charge of, °coordinate **11** °operate, °perform, °function, °work, tick, °go **12** °extend, °stretch, °reach; °amount, add up, total up, °come (up) **13** convey, °transport, give (someone) a lift, °drive, °take, °bring **14** bootleg, smuggle, deal *or* traffic in, *Chiefly US and Canadian* °rustle **15** be in effect *or* force, be effective, have force *or* effect **16** °incur, invite, °encourage, °attract, be subjected to **17** °propel, °drive; °steer, °guide, °navigate **18** unravel, come undone, *Chiefly Brit* ladder **19** Sometimes, ***run off.*** °print, °offset, lithograph, °reproduce, °publish, °display; imprint, °position, °place, °locate, °lay out **20** ***run across.*** °meet (up with), °run into, °come across, °find, stumble on *or* upon, hit *or* chance *or* happen upon, *Colloq* °bump into **21** ***run after.*** °chase, °pursue, go after, court, woo, *Colloq* set one's cap for **22** ***run along.*** °go away, °leave, *Slang* get lost **23** ***run around.*** philander, be unfaithful, gallivant, *Colloq* sleep around, play the field **24** ***run around with.*** °associate with, spend time with, dally with, consort with **25** ***run away.*** See **2,** above. **26** ***run down.*** **(a)** °trace, °track, °hunt, °stalk, °follow, °pursue, dog, °shadow; °find, °locate, °track down, °discover **(b)** °criticize, decry, defame, °vilify, °disparage, deprecate, °depreciate, denigrate, *Colloq* °knock, °pan **(c)** °weaken, °tire, °expire, play (itself) out, burn out, °run out, °fail, *Colloq* °peter out **(d)** °strike, °hit, smash *or* crash *or* slam into, °run over, knock over *or* down, °collide with **27** ***run in.*** °arrest, take into custody, °jail, apprehend, take *or* bring in, *Colloq* °pinch, °nab, °pull in, bust, collar, *Brit* °nick **28** ***run into.*** See **20,** above. **29** ***run off.*** **(a)** See **2,** above. **(b)** °duplicate, °print, °copy, °turn out, °produce, °make, °manufacture, °generate, *Colloq* do, churn out **30** ***run out.*** **(a)** be exhausted, °expire, °terminate, (come *or* draw to a) close, °end, °cease **(b)** °finish, °go, be exhausted, be used up, *Colloq* °peter out **31** ***run out of.*** °use up, °consume, eat up, °exhaust, be out of **32** ***run out on.*** °desert, °abandon, leave high and dry, °forsake, °leave in the lurch, leave holding the baby **33** ***run over.*** **(a)** See **26 (d),** above. **(b)** °read (through), °(copy) edit, °study, °scan; go over *or* through **(c)** overflow, °spill (over), brim over, slosh over, pour over; °extend, °reach, spread over, stretch over; °exceed, go beyond, overreach, overshoot, °surpass, °transcend **(d)** °rehearse, °run through, °repeat, °practice, °review, °go over, °study, °learn,

°memorize **34** ***run through.*** **(a)** °pierce, °stab, °transfix, °stick, °spit **(b)** squander, °consume, °use up, °waste, °fritter away, °exhaust, deplete, °spend, °dissipate, °throw away, *Slang* °blow **(c)** See **33 (b),** above. ***—n.*** **35** sprint, °dash, °race, °jog, °trot **36** °trip, °journey, °visit, °drive, °expedition, trek, °outing, °excursion, jaunt, junket, °sojourn, *Colloq* °spin, joy ride **37** °route, °routine, °circuit, °passage, °trip, °cycle, °round; °beat **38** °period, °spate, °interval, °time, °spell, °stretch, °course; °engagement, booking, *Colloq* °patch **39** access, °freedom, °liberty **40** °return, °satisfaction, °reward, recompense, compensation, °requital, expiation, °atonement, repayment, °remuneration **41** series, °sequence, °stream, °spate, °string, °succession, °progression **42** °stream, °brook, runnel, °creek, rill, rivulet, *Brit* beck, *Scots* °burn, *US* °branch, °kill **43** °demand, °call, °request **44** °type, °category, °class, °kind, °sort **45** °trail, °track, piste, °path, °slope; °way, runway **46** °enclosure, yard, °pen, °compound, runway; paddock; °pound **47** *Music* roulade, cadenza, arpeggio, riff **48** ***in the long run.*** °eventually, °finally, after all, °ultimately, in (due) time, in due course, in fine, in the end, at the end of the day, in the final analysis, all things considered, when all is said and done **49** ***on the run.*** **(a)** °hastily, in haste, hurriedly, while under way, in a hurry, at speed, in a rush **(b)** on the loose, fleeing, escaping, in flight, °running (away), *Slang US* on the lam **(c)** °running, retreating, on the move *or* the go **50** ***the runs.*** diarrhea, dysentery, upset stomach, *Jocular* tummy rot, Delhi belly, Aztec hop, tourista *or* turista, Mexican fox-trot *or* two-step *or* toothache, Montezuma's revenge, curse of Montezuma, Rangoon runs, Tokyo trots, Lambeth run(s)

runaround *n.* evasive treatment; °slip

runaway *n.* **1** °fugitive, escapee, °refugee, °deserter, °truant, absconder *—adj.* **2** °wild, °uncontrolled, unchecked, °rampant, °renegade, unsuppressed; driverless, riderless, °loose; escaped **3** °easy, °effortless, °overwhelming, uncontested

run-down *adj.* **1** wearied, °exhausted, debilitated, weakened, worn-out, °peaked, °fatigued, enervated, °tired, drained, °spent, out of shape *or* condition, °below par, in bad shape; °unhealthy, °sickly, °ill **2** °ramshackle, °dilapidated, tumbledown, °decrepit, °rickety, broken-down

rundown *n.* °run-through, °synopsis, °summary, °survey, °précis, °résumé, (thumbnail) sketch, °outline, rough idea, °review, recapitulation, briefing; highlights, high points

run-in *n.* °disagreement, °argument, °dispute, altercation, °quarrel, confrontation, contretemps

runner *n.* **1** sprinter, racer, jogger, hurdler, miler **2** °messenger, courier, errand boy *or* girl, messenger boy *or* girl, °page, dispatch-bearer *or* despatch-bearer, dispatch-rider *or* despatch-rider, *Colloq US* gofer **3** °sucker, tendril, creeper, °shoot, °branch, °stem **4** °blade

running *n.* **1** °operation, °management, °direction **2** °competition, °contest, °meet, °tournament, °race, °match; °event, °game *—adj.* **3** °continuous, °ongoing, °continual, °perpetual, °sustained, °constant, uninterrupted, ceaseless, unceasing

runt *n.* °dwarf, pygmy, midget

run-through *n.* **1** °rehearsal, °practice, °trial, °test **2** See **rundown,** above.

rupture *n.* **1** °break, °rift, °split, fissure, °fracture, cleavage, bursting; breaking, splitting, breakup, °breach, °schism, disunity, breaking up, severance, °division, °separation **2** hernia *—v.* **3** break (up *or* apart), °split, °fracture, °cleave, °divide, °breach, °separate; °disrupt, °part, sunder

rural *adj.* **1** °country, °pastoral, sylvan, bucolic, °rustic, Arcadian, exurban; agricultural, agrarian, *Literary* georgic **2** See **rustic, 2,** below.

ruse *n.* °trick, °device, °deception, °maneuver, °dodge, °pretense, °pretext, °subterfuge, °stratagem, ploy, °hoax, °wile, °artifice, imposture

rush *v.* **1** °hurry (up), °hasten, °run, °race, °hustle, bustle, make haste, °dash, °speed, °scurry, °scramble, scoot, °jump, sprint, scamper, scuttle, *Colloq* °move (it), hotfoot (it), skedaddle, °step on it, make it snappy, *US* hightail (it), step on the gas, *Slang* get moving, get cracking, get a wiggle on, go like a bat out of hell, °shake a leg **2** °attack, °assault, °charge, °storm, blitz *—n.* **3** °hurry, °haste, °hustle, bustle, °dash, °speed, turmoil, turbulence, °flurry, commotion, °ferment, pother, ado, to-do, °excitement, °pell-mell, harum-scarum **4** °surge, °sensation, °thrill, °charge *—adj.* **5** °urgent, hurry-up, exigent, high-priority, top-priority, °emergency

rustic *adj.* **1** See **rural, 1,** above. **2** °peasant, °plain, °simple, uncomplicated, °unsophisticated, naive *or* naïve *or* naïf, °ingenuous, guileless, °artless, °unrefined, unpolished, countrified, uncultivated, uncultured, °boorish, °crude, °rough, unmannerly, hillbilly, backwoods, °awkward, ungainly, cloddish, plodding, oafish, gawky, lumpen, loutish *—n.* **3** °peasant, bumpkin, °boor, yokel, hillbilly, countryman, countrywoman, country boy *or* girl, oaf, country cousin, *Colloq* clodhopper, *Brit derogatory and offensive* bogtrotter, *US and Canadian* hayseed, hick

rustle *v.* **1** °whisper, °swish, sibilate, susurrate *—n.* **2** °whisper, whispering, rustling, °swish, swishing, sibilation, sibilance, susurration, susurrus

rut *n.* **1** °groove, °furrow, wheelmark, °track, trough **2** °pattern, °habit, °routine, °groove, °grind, treadmill, dead end, *Colloq* rat race

ruthless *adj.* pitiless, unpitying, °cruel, °unsympathetic, °merciless, °unmerciful, °harsh, °fierce, °remorseless, uncompassionate, °vicious, °savage, °ferocious, hardhearted, °callous, unfeeling, °tough, °severe, °heartless, °inhuman, °brutal, brutish, unrelenting, °relentless, *Chiefly US and Canadian* °mean

S

sabotage *n.* **1** °destruction, °damage, wrecking, °impairment **2** °subversion, treachery, treason *—v.* **3** °undermine, °subvert, °disrupt, °spoil, °ruin, °cripple; °damage, °incapacitate, disable, °destroy, °wreck, *Colloq US* throw a monkey wrench into the machinery, *Brit* throw a spanner in the works, *Slang Brit* °queer (someone's pitch)

sack *n.* **1** °pouch, °bag, *Scots and US Dialectal* °poke; *Technical* sac **2** ***hit the sack.*** °retire, °turn in, go to bed *or* to sleep, *Slang* hit the hay, *Brit* kip (down), *US* sack out **3** ***the sack.*** °dismissal, °discharge, firing, *Colloq* heave-ho, the ax, marching orders, *US* pink slip, °bounce, *Chiefly US and Canadian* walking papers, *Slang Brit* the boot, the chop, °the push *—v.* **4** °dismiss, °discharge, °fire, let go, °lay off, *Brit* make *or* declare redundant, *Colloq* give (someone) the ax *or* the (old) heave-ho, give (someone) his *or* her *or esp Brit* their marching orders, *Brit* give (someone) the sack, *US* °bounce, *Slang Brit* give (someone) the boot *or* the chop *or* the push

sacred *adj.* **1** consecrated, dedicated, hallowed, °holy, blessed, blest, sanctified, revered, °divine, awe-inspiring, °venerable, venerated, sainted, heaven-sent **2** inviolable, inviolate, untouchable, protected, sacrosanct **3** °religious, °spiritual, °ceremonial, church(ly), ecclesiastical, °priestly, hieratic, °ritual, °solemn, sacramental, liturgical

sacrifice *n.* **1** immolation, °surrender, forfeiture, forgoing, giving up, yielding up, °offering (up), °offer, *Christianity* oblation **2** forfeiture, forgoing, giving up, relinquishment, °loss *—v.* **3** immolate, °offer (up), °yield (up), °give up **4** °give up, °forgo, °forfeit, °relinquish, °surrender, let go, °lose, °yield, °renounce, forswear; forbear, desist, °cease, °stop, °refrain from

sacrificial *adj.* **1** sacrificed, immolated, surrendered, given up, yielded **2** atoning, expiatory, °propitiatory, conciliatory

sacrilege *n.* **1** desecration, profanation, debasement, °violation, °prostitution, dishonoring, vitiation, defilement, befouling, fouling, contamination, befoulment, °misuse, °abuse, °perversion, maltreatment **2** impiety, heresy, profanation, °outrage, °violation, °profanity, blasphemy, impiousness, irreverence, °disrespect, secularization

sacrilegious *adj.* °profane, °impious, °heretical, °blasphemous, °irreverent, °disrespectful

sad *adj.* **1** °unhappy, °melancholy, downcast, °dejected, depressed, °low, °sorrowful, °gloomy, morose, °glum, lugubrious, °mournful, heartsick, crestfallen, chapfallen, disheartened, °downhearted, °blue, °despondent, °brokenhearted, °heartbroken, °woebegone, °miserable, °wretched **2** depressing, °gloomy, disheartening, °dreary, °dismal, °funereal, °somber, lugubrious, saddening, heartbreaking, °bleak, distressing, dispiriting, °calamitous **3** °unfortunate, °unsatisfactory, °awful, °bad, °shabby, °dirty, °lamentable, °miserable, °sorry, °wretched, °pathetic, °pitiful, °pitiable, °deplorable, °terrible, *Colloq* °lousy, °rotten

sadden *v.* °depress, deject, °sorrow, dishearten, °distress, dispirit, °discourage, °grieve, aggrieve

sadistic *adj.* °cruel, °monstrous, °brutal, brutish, °beastly, °ruthless, °perverse, *Technical* algolagnic

sadly *adv.* **1** unfortunately, alas, unhappily, unluckily, lamentably, regrettably, deplorably, sad to relate **2** unhappily, gloomily, morosely, mournfully, despondently, miserably, wretchedly, dejectedly, dismally, somberly, lugubriously

sadness *n.* unhappiness, dolor, °misery, °sorrow, dispiritedness, °grief, °depression, dejection, dejectedness, sorrowfulness, despondency, °melancholy, °gloom, gloominess

safe *adj.* **1** unharmed, °whole, uninjured, unhurt, °(safe and) sound, °secure, protected, shielded, sheltered, out of harm's way, all right, *Colloq* O.K. *or* OK *or* okay **2** °harmless, nontoxic, nonpoisonous, innocuous; unpolluted **3** °sure, °secure, °sound, protected, risk-free, riskless, safe as the Bank of England, °reliable, dependable, °solid, °bona fide, °conservative, tried and true, *Brit* safe as houses **4** all right, allowable, °permissible, °acceptable, °satisfactory, °appropriate, °suitable, °timely, °right, °correct, °proper, justifiable, justified, *Colloq* OK *or* O.K. *or* okay **5** secured, protected *—adv.* **6** safely, securely *—n.* **7** vault, °crypt, strongbox, safe-deposit *or* safety-deposit box, coffer, °chest, repository

safeguard *n.* **1** °protection, °defense, °security *—v.* **2** °protect, °defend, °shield, °shelter, keep safe, °guard; °conserve, °save, °keep, °care for, °look after

safekeeping *n.* °charge, °protection, keeping, °custody, °care, guardianship

safety *n.* safeness, °protection, aegis, °cover,

°shelter, °security, °refuge; °sanctuary, °safekeeping

sag *v.* **1** °droop, °sink, °slump, °bend, °dip; swag, °bag **2** °drop, °decrease, °decline, go *or* come down, °fall, °slide, °slip, °weaken, °slump, °descend, °diminish, lessen, °droop, °subside, °flag, falter, °wilt *—n.* **3** sagging, °drop, °droop, °sinking, sinkage, subsidence, °dip; reduction, °decrease, °decline, °fall, °slide, weakening, °slump, lessening, flagging, faltering

saga *n.* °(heroic) legend, °narrative, epic, edda, °chronicle, °romance, *roman-fleuve,* °story, °tale, °adventure

sage *adj.* **1** °wise, sagacious, °prudent, °sensible, perspicacious, °profound, °intelligent, discerning, °reasonable, °logical, °judicious, common-sense, common-sensical *—n.* **2** wise man, savant, °expert, °elder, guru, Nestor, pundit, Solomon, philosopher, °oracle, °authority

sail *v.* **1** °navigate, °pilot, °steer **2** go sailing *or* boating *or* yachting, °cruise, set sail, put (out) to sea **3** °drift, move lightly, °breeze, °flow, °waft, °sweep, °coast, °float, °scud, °glide, °slide, °slip, °plane, °skim, °fly, °flit *—n.* **4** canvas

sailor *n.* seaman, seafarer, seafaring man *or* woman, seagoing man *or* woman, mariner, °(old) salt, seadog, bluejacket, shellback, yachtsman, yachtswoman, boatman, boatwoman, deck hand, captain, °skipper, *Old-fashioned or literary* Jack Tar, *Colloq old-fashioned* tar, *Naval US* swab, swabbie, °gob

saintly *adj.* °holy, blessed, blest, beatific, °godly, sainted, angelic, °seraphic, °pure, °righteous, °virtuous, °blameless

sake *n.* **1** °benefit, °welfare, well-being, °good, °advantage, °behalf, °profit, °gain, °account **2** purpose(s), reason(s), objective(s)

salary *n.* °income, °pay, °earnings, compensation, °remuneration, emolument; wage(s)

sale *n.* **1** selling, °traffic, vending, marketing, trafficking, trading; °trade, °exchange, °transaction **2** °trade, °purchase; trading, buying, purchasing **3** sales event, markdown, white sale, jumble sale, *Brit* boot sale, *US* rummage sale, garage sale, tag sale, yard sale, *Colloq* sell-a-thon, sales marathon **4** °transaction **5** *on sale. US* marked down, cut-price, bargain-priced; reduced (in price) **6** *(up) for sale.* on the market, °available, in stock, *Chiefly Brit* °on sale, on offer, *US* on the block

salesperson *n.* salesman, saleswoman, saleslady, salesgirl, salesclerk, clerk, *Chiefly Brit* shopgirl, *Brit* shop assistant, *Old-fashioned* counter-jumper

salient *adj.* °conspicuous, °outstanding, °pronounced, °noticeable, °prominent, °significant, °important, °marked, °impressive, °striking, °remarkable, distinguishing, °distinctive, °unique, °eminent, °noteworthy, °notable, °principal, °chief, °primary

salt *n.* **1** common *or* table salt, sodium chloride, sea salt, rock salt **2** °spice, spiciness, °zest, zestiness, pungency, °vigor, °vitality, liveliness, °pep, °pepper, poignancy, piquancy, °relish, °bite, °savor, °seasoning, °taste, *Colloq* zip, zing, °punch **3** °(Attic) wit, Attic salt, dry humor, °sarcasm **4** See **sailor,** above. **5** *with a grain or pinch of salt. cum grano salis,* warily, cautiously, qualifiedly, qualifyingly, doubtfully, skeptically, suspiciously, reservedly, with reservation(s) *or* qualification(s) *—v.* **6** °season, °spice, °flavor, °pepper **7** pickle, cure, °preserve, corn, marinate, souse **8** *salt away.* °save (up), °hoard, put *or* lay *or* set by *or* aside, squirrel away, store up, stockpile, °amass, °accumulate, °pile up, *Colloq* stash away, *US and Canadian* sock away *—adj.* **9** salty, saline, brackish, briny **10** pickled, kippered, marinated, soused; corned; cured

salute *v.* **1** °greet, °hail, °address, accost **2** pay respects *or* homage *or* tribute to, °honor, °recognize, °acknowledge *—n.* **3** °greeting, °address, salutation

salvage *v.* **1** °save, °recover, °rescue, °redeem, °deliver, °retrieve, °reclaim *—n.* **2** °recovery, °rescue, retrieval, redemption, deliverance, reclamation, salvation

salve *n.* **1** balm, °ointment, unguent, dressing, cream, °lotion, demulcent, embrocation, liniment **2** emollient, balm, palliative, °tranquilizer, opiate, anodyne, °narcotic, °relief, assuagement *—v.* **3** °mitigate, °relieve, °ease, alleviate, assuage, palliate, soothe, mollify, °comfort, appease

same *adj.* **1** °identical, °exact (same), selfsame; °very **2** unchanged, unchanging, °changeless, unmodified, unaltered, °constant, °uniform, unvaried, unvarying; word-for-word, °verbatim **3** *all the same.* °at the same time, °nevertheless, °nonetheless, °even so, °yet, but, anyway, anyhow, °in any case, °in any event, °at any rate, °regardless, °still (and all), in spite of *or* despite the fact, °notwithstanding, for all that, that (having been) said, having said that, after all is said and done, just the same

sample *n.* **1** °specimen, °example, °representative, °representation, °illustration, sampling, sampler, cross section; swatch; °bite, nibble, °taste *—v.* **2** °test, °try, °taste, °experience *—adj.* **3** °representative, °specimen, illustrative, representational, °trial, °test

sanctify *v.* **1** consecrate, °hallow, make sacred *or* holy, °glorify, °exalt, canonize, enshrine; *Roman Catholic Church* beatify **2** °purify, °cleanse **3** °confirm, °sanction, °ratify, °justify, °legitimate, legitimatize *or* legitimize, legalize, °license

sanctimonious *adj.* °hypocritical, °self-righteous, canting, °mealy-mouthed, holier-than-thou, pharisaical, pietistic, unctuous, Tartuffian, *Colloq* °goody-goody, *Chiefly Brit* smarmy, *Slang Brit* pi

sanction *n.* **1** confirmation, ratification, secondment, authorization, legalization, legitimatization *or* legitimization, validation, °license, certification, °approval, °permission, imprimatur, seal *or* stamp (of approval), signet **2** °help, °aid, °encouragement, °support, advocacy, °backing, sponsorship, °favor, countenance 3 °agreement, concurrence, acceptance, affirmation, assent, acquiescence, compliance, °approval, OK *or* O.K. *or* okay 4 °ban, °penalty, °punishment, °retribution, °discipline, retaliation, redress —*v.* 5 °confirm, °ratify, °second, °authorize, legalize, legitimatize *or* legitimize, validate, °license, °certify, °approve, °permit, °allow, notarize, °vouchsafe, °subscribe to, commission, °consent to 6 °support, °encourage, °advocate, °back, °sponsor, °favor, countenance, °help

sanctity *n.* °piety, holiness, saintliness, divinity, °grace, sacredness, godliness, °devotion, °dedication

sanctuary *n.* 1 °sanctum, shrine, chapel, °temple, church, house of worship, house of God; synagogue, mosque, pagoda 2 asylum, °refuge, °retreat, °protection, °shelter, °safety 3 (nature *or* wildlife) reserve *or* preserve, °reservation, conservation area, national park

sanctum *n.* 1 °sanctuary, holy of holies, shrine 2 sanctum sanctorum, den, °study, °retreat; hiding place, hide-out, °hideaway, cubbyhole

sane *adj.* °normal, of sound mind, °rational, *compos mentis,* °well-balanced, right-minded, °levelheaded, °rational, °reasonable, °sensible, °judicious, *Colloq* right in the head, all there

sang-froid *n.* coldbloodedness, coolness, coolheadedness, °indifference, composure, phlegm, self-possession, °self-control, °poise, imperturbability, equanimity, *Colloq* unflappability, °cool, coolth

sanguinary *adj.* 1 °bloodthirsty, °cruel, °brutal, brutish, °gory, °merciless, °remorseless, °ruthless, pitiless, °heartless, °savage, barbarous, slaughterous, °grim, °fell, °murderous, °homicidal 2 bloody, sanguineous, sanguinolent

sanguine *adj.* °optimistic, °rosy, °confident, °hopeful, forward-looking, anticipatory, °expectant, °enthusiastic, fervid, zealous

sanitarium *n.* rest home, convalescent home, nursing home, clinic, health farm, sanatorium

sanitary *adj.* °clean, °sterile, °hygienic, antiseptic, disinfected, aseptic, germ-free, bacteria-free; °healthy, unpolluted, salubrious, healthful, salutary, °wholesome

sanity *n.* saneness, °reason, mental health *or* soundness, normality, rationality, °reason, reasonableness, °stability, °balance

sap[1] *n.* 1 (vital) juice *or* fluid, bodily *or US also* body fluid, lifeblood, °essence, *Literary* ichor 2 °fool, idiot, nincompoop, ninny, ninnyhammer, simpleton, ignoramus, nitwit, dimwit, dunce, ass; °dupe, gull, *US* thimblewit; *Colloq* chump, °drip, *Brit* (right) charlie, noddy, noodle, °wet, *Chiefly Brit* °twit, *Slang* patsy, °sucker, °(easy) mark, °pushover, saphead, *Brit* muggins, *US* schnook, schlemiel *or* schlemihl *or* shlemiel, fall guy —*v.* 3 bleed, °drain, °draw, °tap, °rob, °milk

sap[2] *v.* °undermine, °sabotage, °weaken, °cripple, °wreck, devitalize, deplete, °drain, °erode, °enervate, debilitate

sarcasm *n.* °scorn, contumely, °derision, °ridicule, °bitterness, acrimony, acrimoniousness, acerbity, harshness, acridity, acridness, asperity, °venom, °poison, venomousness, poisonousness, °virulence, °spite, spitefulness, malice, maliciousness, malevolence, °satire, irony, cynicism, disdain

sarcastic *adj.* °scornful, contumelious, derisive, °derisory, ridiculing, °bitter, °biting, °cutting, °trenchant, °incisive, acrimonious, acerbic, acid, acidic, acidulous, °harsh, acrid, aspersive, °venomous, °poisonous, °virulent, °spiteful, malicious, malefic, malevolent, satiric(al), ironic(al), cynical, °disdainful, mocking, °contemptuous, °critical, censorious, captious, carping, caviling, °sardonic, °scathing, °caustic, °nasty

sardonic *adj.* ironic(al), derisive, °derisory, mocking, cynical, °sarcastic

satanic *adj.* 1 diabolic(al), °fiendish, °devilish, Mephistophelian, demonic, demoniac(al), cacodemonic, °ghoulish, hellish, °infernal, °evil, °wicked, iniquitous, °corrupt, depraved, °perverted, °perverse, °godless, °ungodly, °impious, unholy, °sinister, °dark, °black, °immoral, amoral 2 dire, °monstrous, heinous, °atrocious, °hideous, °horrible, horrendous, horrid, horrifying, °loathsome, °vile, °abhorrent, unspeakable, unutterable, °damnable, °despicable, °abominable

satellite *n.* 1 moon, spacecraft, *Old-fashioned* sputnik 2 °follower, °attendant, retainer, °disciple, acolyte, °aide, aide-de-camp, minion, lieutenant, °assistant, helper, °hanger-on, dependent, °shadow, right-hand man, vassal, °parasite, sycophant, *Colloq* sidekick

satiate *v.* 1 °stuff, °glut, °gorge, cloy, °surfeit, overfill, overstuff, °glut, °pall, overindulge, °saturate, °choke, deluge, °flood, suffocate, °weary, °exhaust, °bore, °tire, °jade 2 °slake, °satisfy, °quench, °content, °gratify, sate

satiety *n.* °surfeit, °glut, superabundance, overindulgence, saturation, nimiety, °excess, °superfluity

satire *n.* 1 °ridicule, irony, °sarcasm, °mockery, spoofing, °exaggeration, °caricature 2 °burlesque, °lampoon, °parody, travesty, pasquinade, spoof, cartoon, °caricature, *Colloq* °takeoff, *Chiefly Brit* sendup

satirical *adj.* satiric, ironic, °sarcastic, mocking, spoofing, °irreverent, exaggerating, Hudibrastic, derisive, disparaging, °abusive, °scornful, °flippant, ridiculing, chaffing

satirize *v.* °lampoon, °burlesque, °parody, °caricature, travesty, °poke fun at, °(hold up to) ridicule, make fun *or* sport of, pillory, °deride, °mock; °mimic, °imitate; *Colloq* °take off, °put down, *Brit* °send up

satisfaction *n.* 1 °gratification, °comfort, °fulfillment, contentment, °delight, °joy, °enjoyment, °pleasure, °happiness **2** °payment, °requital, repayment, compensation, recompense, °remuneration, reparation, °indemnity, indemnification, °restitution, vindication, °damages, °amends, redress, °atonement, expiation

satisfactory *adj.* °adequate, °sufficient, °acceptable, °passable, all right, not bad, good enough, °fair, *Colloq* OK *or* O.K. *or* okay

satisfy *v.* **1** °gratify, °fulfill, °comfort, please, °content, placate, appease, pacify **2** °fill, °meet, °fulfill, °provide for, look after *or* to, °serve, °answer, comply with, °resolve, °solve, °gratify, °indulge; °slake, °quench, sate, °satiate **3** °convince, °persuade, °reassure, °assure, put (someone's) mind at rest, °content **4** °pay, °repay, redress, °make good, indemnify, °write off, liquidate

satisfying *adj.* gratifying, °satisfactory, fulfilling, °filling, satiating; comforting, °pleasing, pacifying, °pleasurable

saturate *v.* °soak, °wet, °drench, °steep, °fill, imbue, souse, °suffuse, °impregnate, °permeate; waterlog; *Technical* ret

sauce *n.* **1** gravy, condiment **2** °impertinence, sauciness, °impudence, audacity, insolence, brazenness, pertness, °disrespect, disrespectfulness, *Colloq* cheek, cheekiness, lip, back talk, backchat, °brass, °nerve, °gall, *Slang* crust, *US and Canadian* sass, sassiness

saunter *v.* °walk, °stroll, amble, °meander, °ramble, °wander, *Colloq* mosey, traipse

savage *adj.* **1** °wild, °untamed, undomesticated, feral, unbroken **2** °vicious, °ferocious, °fierce, °beastly, bestial, brutish, °bloodthirsty, °brutal, °cruel, °ruthless, pitiless, °merciless, °harsh, bloody, °unmerciful, °fell, barbarous, barbaric, °murderous, demonic, demoniac, °sadistic **3** °wild, °uncivilized, uncultivated, °primitive, °inhuman, bestial, barbaric, barbarous, °untamed, °rude —*n.* **4** wild man *or* woman, °brute, °barbarian; Caliban

save *v.* **1** °(come to someone's) rescue, °deliver; °(set) free, °liberate, °release, °redeem, bail (someone) out; °recover, °salvage, °retrieve **2** °keep, °preserve, °guard, °safeguard, °protect, °conserve, °secure, °shelter, °shield **3** lay *or* put aside, lay *or* put by, lay *or* put away, °keep, °retain, °set apart, °hold, °reserve, °preserve, °conserve; °economize, scrimp, °scrape **4** obviate, °preclude, °spare, °prevent

saving *adj.* **1** redeeming, redemptory *or* redemptive *or* redemptional, compensating, °compensatory, qualifying, °extenuating, extenuatory **2** parsimonious, °economical, °thrifty, °provident, °frugal, °sparing, °prudent —*n.* **3** economizing, economization, °economy, °thrift, °providence, frugality, °prudence, scrimping, scraping, sparingness **4** ***savings.*** °resources, °reserve, °cache, °hoard, nest egg

savior *n.* **1** rescuer, salvation, friend in need, Good Samaritan, liberator, redeemer, deliverer, emancipator, °champion, knight-errant,

knight in shining armor **2** ***the or our Savior or Saviour. Christian religion*** Christ (the Redeemer), Jesus, the Messiah, Lamb of God, Our Lord, Son of God, King of Kings, Prince of Peace, *Islam* Mahdi.

savoir-faire *n.* °tact, tactfulness, °sophistication, °finesse, urbanity, °discretion, knowledgeability, °diplomacy, urbanity, smoothness, °polish, suavity *or* suaveness, °poise, °grace, °style, °skill, adroitness, °knowledge, comprehension, *Slang* savvy

savoir-vivre *n.* °breeding, °upbringing, comity, °knowledge, °sophistication, °polish

savor *n.* **1** °taste, °flavor, °zest, °tang, smack, piquancy **2** °hint, °suggestion, °odor, °scent, °fragrance, °smell, °perfume, redolence, °bouquet, °breath, °trace, °quality, *soupçon*, °dash —*v.* **3** °taste, °sample, °perceive, °detect, °sense, discern, °mark, descry, °observe, °notice, °note, °identify; °enjoy, °luxuriate in, °relish, °indulge in, bask in, °appreciate, °revel in, °delight in, value, °cherish, *Colloq* lick *or* smack one's lips *or* chops over

savory *adj.* **1** palatable, °delicious, delectable, °tasty, toothsome, appetizing, flavorful, flavorous, flavorsome, ambrosial, °luscious **2** °tasteful, °honest, °proper, °decent, °reputable, °respectable, °honorable, creditable, °upright, °decorous, °seemly, °wholesome, °innocent —*n.* **3** appetizer, °hors d'oeuvre; °dessert, °sweet; °morsel, °dainty, tidbit *or Brit* titbit, *Chiefly Brit* starter, *Archaic* warner

saw *n.* °proverb, °maxim, (old) saying, aphorism, apophthegm *or* apothegm, axiom, adage, °epigram, gnome; °slogan, °motto, catchword, catch phrase, °byword; dictum, platitude, °truism, °cliché, commonplace

say *v.* **1** °state, affirm, °declare, °maintain, °hold, aver, °remark, assert, °claim, asseverate, °announce **2** assert, °allege, °report, °mention, °rumor, °reveal, bruit about, °disclose, divulge, °bring to light, °put about, noise abroad, °suggest, °hint, °whisper **3** °pronounce, articulate, utter; °phrase, rephrase, °translate **4** °tell, °put, °express, verbalize, °communicate, °explain, °reveal, °bring up, °break, °impart **5** °reply, °respond, °answer **6** °guess, °estimate, conjecture, °venture, °judge, °imagine, °believe, °think **7** mean *or* intend *or* try to say, °think, °contemplate, °imply, °suggest **8** °predict, °prognosticate, foretell **9** °signify, °denote, °symbolize, °communicate, °indicate, convey, °suggest, °imply, °mean **10** °order, °require, °demand, °bid, °stipulate, °command, give the word **11** °deliver, utter, °speak —*n.* **12** °voice, °authority, °influence, °power, °weight, °sway, clout **13** °turn, °chance, °opportunity, °vote —*adv.* **14** °approximately, °about, °roughly, circa; °nearly **15** °for example, °for instance, as *or* for an illustration, e.g.

say-so *n.* °authority, °word, °say, °order, dictum; authorization

scale[1] *n.* Often, *scales.* °balance
scale[2] *n.* 1 °flake, imbrication; scurf, dandruff; *Technical* squama, °plate, scute *or* scutum, lamina, lamella 2 coating, encrustation *or* incrustation, crust, overlay, layer, °cake, caking, tartar, °plaque
scale[3] *n.* 1 °range, compass, °rank, ranking, gradation, graduation, °register, spectrum, calibration, °progression, hierarchy, °scope, °gamut 2 °proportion, °ratio —*v.* 3 °climb, ascend, °mount, clamber up, surmount, °go up, escalade 4 °regulate, °adjust, °proportion, *Chiefly US and Canadian* prorate 5 *scale up or down.* °increase, °enlarge, °raise; °decrease, °reduce, °diminish, °lower
scaly *adj.* 1 °rough, imbricated, shingly, flaky, *Technical* lamellar, laminar, lamellate, scutate 2 scabby, scabrous, squamous, squamulose, squamosal, squamose, scurfy, furfuraceous, scruffy
scan *v.* 1 glance at *or* through, °look over, °skim, read over, flip *or* thumb *or* leaf through 2 °study, °pore over, °examine, °investigate, °scrutinize, °inspect, delve into, °research, °explore (in depth), °sweep, *Archaic* con —*n.* 3 °examination, °investigation, °scrutiny, inspection, °research, °exploration
scandal *n.* 1 °shame, °disgrace, °embarrassment, °sin, °outrage 2 °discredit, °damage, calumny, ignominy, obloquy, °dishonor, °degradation, disrepute, °infamy 3 °slander, °libel, °aspersion, °innuendo, insinuation, °abuse, °dirt, defilement, defamation, °slur, °smear, °taint, °blemish, °spot, °stigma, smirch, black mark *or* spot, °blot (on the escutcheon), °(badge of) infamy, skeleton in the cupboard, *Brit* blot on one's copybook
scandalize *v.* appall *or* appal, °shock, °outrage, affront, °offend, °horrify, °upset, °disturb; °rankle, stick in (someone's) craw *or* throat, °gall
scandalous *adj.* 1 °shocking, °disgraceful, ignominious, °improper, indecorous, °unseemly, °infamous, °outrageous, °shameful, °immodest, °dishonorable, °disreputable, °sordid, °despicable, flagitious, °wicked, °sinful, °evil, iniquitous, °profligate, °immoral, °indecent, °lewd, °lascivious, °lustful, licentious, °lecherous, °atrocious, heinous, °disgusting, fulsome, °taboo, °unmentionable, unspeakable 2 defamatory, libelous, °slanderous, calumnious, calumniatory, aspersive, °abusive, °scurrilous, °injurious
scanty *adj.* 1 scant, °sparse, °scarce, °little, °meager, °minimal; barely adequate *or* sufficient, °limited, restricted, *Colloq* °measly 2 skimpy, °short, °small, °sparse, °minimal, °meager, °in short supply, *Colloq chiefly Brit* °thin on the ground
scapegoat *n.* °victim, °front, °dupe, gull, cat's-paw, whipping boy, *Brit* man of straw, Aunt Sally, *US* straw man, *Colloq* fall guy, *Slang* °sucker
scar *n.* 1 °blemish, °mark, °damage, disfigurement, °wound, °injury, °scratch, °mar, °cut, °burn, °brand, cicatrix —*v.* 2 °blemish, °mark, °damage, disfigure, °wound, °injure, °scratch, °mar, °cut, °burn, °brand; dent
scarce *adj.* °scanty, scant, °insufficient, °inadequate, °deficient, °wanting, lacking, °rare, °unusual, °at a premium, °in short supply, °meager, few and far between, seldom met with, hard to come by, *Chiefly Brit* °thin on the ground
scarcely *adv.* 1 °hardly, °barely, °(only) just, not quite 2 (probably *or* certainly *or* surely *or* definitely) not, in no way, not at all, not in the least, °by no means, on no account, under no circumstance, nowise, *Colloq US* noway
scarcity *n.* °lack, °want, °need, paucity, °dearth, insufficiency, °shortage, inadequacy, inadequateness
scare *v.* 1 °frighten, °alarm, °startle, °shock, °dismay, °daunt, °appall, give (someone) a shock *or* a fright, °terrify, terrorize, °threaten, °menace, cow, °intimidate, °horrify, *US and Canadian* spook, *Colloq* scare the pants off, scare the life *or* the living daylights *or* the hell out of, scare out of one's wits, make one's hair stand on end, make one's flesh creep *or* crawl, give one goose bumps *or* goose pimples, *US* scare the bejesus out of, *Taboo slang* scare *or* frighten the shit out of, scare shitless, *US* scare shitty 2 *scare up.* scrape together *or* up, °find, °gather, °collect, °raise, °dig up, °get, °come by, °scrounge (up) —*n.* 3 °fright, °shock, °surprise, °start
scared *adj.* frightened, alarmed, °afraid, appalled, shocked, terrified, horrified, startled
scary *adj.* °frightening, °eerie, °terrifying, °frightful, hair-raising, unnerving, bloodcurdling, horrifying, spinechilling, intimidating, daunting; horrendous, horrid, °horrible, creepy, crawly, *Colloq* spooky
scathing *adj.* searing, °withering, damaging, °harmful, °severe, °harsh, °stern, °nasty, °biting, acrid, acrimonious, mordant, °incisive, °cutting, °sharp, °keen, °virulent, vitriolic, acid, °scorching, °burning, °fierce, °savage, °ferocious
scatter *v.* 1 °spread, °diffuse, °shower, °litter, sprinkle, °strew, °circulate, °distribute, disseminate, °sow, °broadcast 2 °disperse, °separate, °dissipate, dispel, °disband, °break up, °go off
scatterbrained *n.* °harebrained, rattleheaded, rattlebrained, °frivolous, flibbertigibbet, °giddy, dazed, °flighty, woolgathering, *Colloq* dippy, °dizzy, dopey *or* dopy, slaphappy
scattering *n.* smattering, sprinkling, °trifle, °bit, °suggestion, soupçon, °hint
scenario *n.* 1 (master *or* ground *or* floor) plan, °(grand) scheme, °plot, schema, °design, °outline, layout, framework, °structure; sequence of events, °routine 2 °(plot) summary, °précis, °résumé, °synopsis; (working *or* shooting) script, screenplay
scene *n.* 1 °location, °site, °place, °area, °locale, °spot, locality, °whereabouts,

°sphere, °milieu, backdrop, °background 2 °action, °episode, °part, chapter, °section, °segment; °(stage) setting, *mise en scène;* scenery 3 commotion, °upset, °exhibition, °display, °row, brouhaha, °disturbance, °furor, °tantrum, °argument, altercation, uncomfortable *or* disagreeable situation, °episode, °incident 4 °view, scenery, °sight, °landscape, seascape, panorama, vista, °picture, °view, °prospect 5 ***behind the scenes.*** °secretly, privately, clandestinely, confidentially, surreptitiously, sub rosa, on the Q.T. 6 ***make*** *or* ***do the scene.*** °socialize, °appear, get around *or* about, °go out, °participate

scenic *adj.* °picturesque, °panoramic, °pretty, °beautiful, °grand, °awesome, awe-inspiring, °impressive, °striking, spectacular, breathtaking

scent *n.* 1 °fragrance, °aroma, °perfume, redolence, °smell, °odor, °bouquet, whiff, °trace 2 °trail, spoor, °track —*v.* 3 °perceive, °detect, °find out, °determine, discern, °distinguish, °recognize, °sense, °smell, °sniff (out), °get wind of, learn *or* hear about 4 °perfume

schedule *n.* 1 °program, °timetable, °plan, °calendar, agenda, °outline, °list, listing, °record, °register —*v.* 2 °program, °organize, °plan, °outline, °list, °record, °register, °arrange, °book, °time, slate, °appoint, °assign, °allot, °dedicate, earmark

schematic *adj.* 1 diagrammatic(al), representational, °graphic, charted —*n.* 2 diagram, blueprint, layout, (floor *or* game) plan, °scheme, °design, °representation, graph, (flow *or* PERT) chart

scheme *n.* 1 °plan, °plot, °design, °program, °system, °course (of action), schema, °outline, °exposition, °projection, °draft, °method, °technique, °approach, game plan, °scenario 2 °pattern, °arrangement, layout, °design, diagram, blueprint, °chart, map, °drawing, °schematic, °disposition, °order, °organization, schema 3 °plot, °plan, ploy, °maneuver, °strategy, °stratagem, °tactic, °machination, °subterfuge, °trick, °device, °dodge, °wile, °ruse, °intrigue, *Colloq* °racket, °game, °move —*v.* 4 °plan, °plot, °devise, contrive, °intrigue, °organize, °formulate, °hatch, conspire, machinate, °maneuver, connive, concoct, *Colloq* cook up

scheming *adj.* conniving, plotting, nefarious, treacherous, °crafty, cunning, °artful, °sly, °wily, °devious, Machiavellian, intriguing, °slick, °calculating, °tricky, °foxy, °slippery, underhanded, duplicitous, °deceitful

schism *n.* °split, °rift, °break, °breach, °division, °rupture, °separation, disunion

schismatic *adj.* schismatical, separatist, breakaway, divisive, °dissident, °heretical

scholar *n.* 1 °academic, professor, °teacher, pedagogue, °authority, °expert, pundit, savant, bookman, bookwoman, man *or* woman of letters, °intellectual, °highbrow, °bookworm, *Colloq* egghead, °brain, *US* longhair 2 °student, °pupil, schoolboy, schoolgirl, undergraduate

scholarly *adj.* °learned, erudite, °lettered, scholastic, °profound, °deep, °intellectual, °academic, highbrow(ed), ivory-tower(ed), *Colloq* egghead, brainy, *US* longhair(ed)

scholarship *n.* 1 °learning, erudition, °knowledge, °lore, °education, °schooling, training, °preparation, *Colloq* know-how 2 °grant, °endowment, °award, °fellowship, *Brit* °exhibition, *Chiefly Scots and New Zealand* bursarship, bursary

school *n.* 1 °(educational) institution, kindergarten, nursery school, primary *or* grammar *or* secondary *or* high school, °institute, college, university, °seminary; *US* alma mater; boarding school, day school; public school, private school, *Brit* state school; *lycée;* Lyceum, first *or* middle school, *US* junior high school 2 °set, coterie, °circle, °clique, °group, °denomination, °faction, °sect, followers, devotees, adherents, votaries, disciples; °style, °kind, °form, °manner, °fashion 3 °philosophy, °principles, °creed, set of beliefs, way of life, °persuasion, credo, dogma, teaching, °view, °opinion, °faction, °approach —*v.* 4 °teach, °educate, °drill, inculcate, °instill, °indoctrinate, °instruct, °tutor, °train, °discipline, °coach, °prepare, °prime, °equip, °ready; °mold, °shape, °form; school in, imbue with, infuse with

schoolbook *n.* text(book), primer, grammar (book), reader, °manual, handbook, exercise book, notebook, copybook, *Rare* enchiridion, *Old-fashioned* hornbook, abecedarium

schooling *n.* °education, teaching, °instruction, tutelage, °tuition, °guidance, training, °preparation, indoctrination, °edification, enlightenment; °learning, °study, °research

schoolteacher *n.* °teacher, professor, °instructor, °tutor, pedagogue, schoolmaster, schoolmistress, *Scots* dominie, *Colloq* schoolmarm

science *n.* 1 (body of) knowledge *or* information, (body of) laws *or* principles, °discipline, °study, °branch, °field, °area, °subject, °realm, °sphere 2 °skill, °art, °technique, °expertise, °proficiency, °method, °system

scientific *adj.* (well-)organized, (well-)regulated, (well-)controlled, (well-)ordered, °orderly, °systematic, °methodical, °precise, °meticulous, °thorough, °painstaking, °detailed

scintillating *adj.* 1 sparkling, coruscating, flashing, °dazzling, gleaming, glittering, °twinkling, shimmering, glistening, shining, °lustrous, °radiant, effulgent, °brilliant, *Literary* nitid 2 °exciting, °engaging, °lively, °effervescent, fascinating, entrancing, °stimulating, °invigorating, °dynamic, °vivacious

scoff *v.* Often, ***scoff at.*** deride, °belittle, °dismiss, °disparage, °mock, °make light of, °sneer (at), poke fun (at), °ridicule, spoof, °lampoon, °jeer (at), °chaff, °tease, °twit, rib, kid, *Brit* °rag

scold *v.* 1 °reprimand, chide, °reprove, °upbraid, °criticize, censure, °find fault (with),

°rebuke, reproach, °lecture, °berate, °rate, °castigate, take (someone) to task, find fault with, rap someone's knuckles, slap someone's wrist, *Colloq* °bawl out, °dress down, give (someone) hell, give (someone) what for, °jump on (someone), jump down (someone's) throat, call (someone) to account, bring (someone) to book, let (someone) have it with both barrels, give (someone) a piece of (one's) mind, give (someone) a tongue-lashing *or* a talking-to, give (someone) a hard time, rake *or* haul (someone) over the coals, tell (someone) off, tick (someone) off, skin (someone) alive, call *or* have (someone) on the carpet, light *or* rip *or* tear *or* lace *or* sail into (someone), *US* °chew out, jump all over (someone), *Brit* carpet —*n.* **2** °nag, °shrew, termagant, virago, fishwife, beldam, harridan, hellcat, °fury, amazon, tigress, Xanthippe, *Colloq* battle-ax

scoop *n.* **1** ladle, dipper, bailer, spoon **2** °exclusive **3** °(latest) news, °(inside) story, °revelation, °truth, *Colloq* °latest, °lowdown, info, °dope, *Brit* gen, *US* poop —*v.* **4** Often, ***scoop up.*** bail, °dip, ladle, spoon **5** ***scoop out.*** gouge out, °excavate, spoon out, hollow out, °dig, °cut **6** ***scoop up.*** °pick up, °gather (up), sweep up *or* together, take up *or* in

scope *n.* **1** °range, °reach, °field, °area, °extent, compass, °expanse, °breadth, °sphere, °orbit, °span **2** °leeway, °space, °room, elbowroom, °freedom, °opportunity, °capacity, °stretch, latitude, °spread

scorch *v.* sear, °blacken, °burn, roast, °singe, char

scorching *adj.* **1** °hot, °torrid, searing, parching, shriveling, tropical, hellish, sizzling, broiling, boiling, °sweltering **2** °critical, °caustic, °scathing, mordant, °vituperative, excoriating, °harsh, acrimonious, °bitter

score *n.* **1** °record, °account, °reckoning, °register, °tally, °amount, °number, °count, °sum, °total; °mark, °grade **2** °nick, °groove, °scratch, °line, °mark, °stroke, °notch, °cut, *Archery* nock **3** twenty **4** Often, ***scores.*** dozens, hundreds, (tens *or* hundreds of) thousands, millions, number(s), drove(s), horde(s), host(s), multitude(s), herd(s), legion(s), lot(s), mass(es), myriad(s), shoal(s), pack(s), covey(s), bevy *or* bevies, swarm(s), flock(s), army *or* armies, crowd(s), throng(s) **5** music, accompaniment, *Technical* full *or* short *or* vocal score **6** °situation, °story, °news, °status (quo), °condition, °word, *Colloq* °latest, °scoop, *US* poop **7** °dupe, gull, °victim, °greenhorn, *Colloq* fall guy, chump, goat, sitting duck, *Slang* °sucker, patsy, °mark, *Brit* °mug **8** ground(s), °basis, °account, °reason, °rationale, °provocation, °cause **9** ***settle or pay off or even a score or the score or old scores.*** get revenge, °retaliate, get even, avenge, °repay, get an eye for an eye, give tit for tat, give measure for measure, pay (someone) back in his own coin, give (someone) a taste *or* a dose of his *or* her *or* their own medicine, *Colloq* get one's own back —*v.* **10** °mark, °line, incise, °scratch, °nick, °notch, °cut, °groove, °graduate; °scrape, °deface, °mar, °gouge, °slash **11** gain *or* make a point *or* points, °record, °tally, °account for **12** °count (for), reckon for *or* as **13** °succeed, be successful, °triumph, °win, make an impression, have an impact, *Colloq* make a hit **14** succeed in seducing, *Slang* °make out, get laid

scorn *n.* **1** contumely, °contempt, contemptuousness, disdain, deprecation; °rejection, °dismissal **2** °mockery, °derision, derisiveness, sneering, °ridicule, scoffing, jeering, taunting —*v.* **3** °reject, °rebuff, disown, disavow, °disregard, °ignore, °shun, snub, °flout, contemn, treat with *or* hold in contempt, °have no use for, disdain, °spurn, °despise, turn up one's nose at, curl one's lip at, look down on *or* upon, look down one's nose at, °thumb one's nose at, *Colloq* pooh-pooh, °put down, *Brit* cock a snook at **4** °mock (at), °deride, sneer at, °ridicule, scoff at, °jeer at, °taunt, °poke fun at, °make fun of, °laugh at

scornful *adj.* contumelious, °contemptuous, °disdainful, deprecative, disparaging, °derisory, derisive, snide, °supercilious, mocking, sneering, scoffing, °haughty, overweening, highhanded, °superior, *Colloq* snooty, *Slang* snotty

scoundrel *n.* °villain, °rogue, °wretch, °good-for-nothing, scapegrace, blackguard, °rascal, scamp, cur, *Old-fashioned* bounder, cad, knave, *Colloq* °heel, *Slang* louse, *Brit* rotter

scour *v.* **1** °scrub, °clean, °cleanse, °wash, °rub, abrade, °polish, burnish, buff, °shine **2** scrape (about *or* around), °rake, comb, turn upside down, °search, °ransack

scourge *n.* **1** °curse, °misfortune, bane, °evil, °affliction, °plague, adversity, °torment, °misery, °woe **2** °whip, °lash, cat-o'-nine-tails, knout, quirt, horsewhip, bullwhip —*v.* **3** °whip, °flog, °beat, °lash, horsewhip, whale, °belt, flagellate **4** °punish, °castigate, °chastise, °discipline, °afflict, °torment

scout *v.* **1** Often, ***scout about or around.*** °reconnoiter, °investigate, °study, °research, °examine, °explore, °spy, search *or* look (about *or* around) (for), hunt (about *or* around) (for), cast around *or* about (for), *Colloq* check (about *or* around) **2** ***scout up or out.*** °discover, °find, °locate, uncover, *Colloq* °dig up

scowl *v.* **1** glower, °frown, grimace, °glare, look daggers, lower *or* lour —*n.* **2** °frown, grimace, °glare, dirty look

scramble *v.* **1** °climb, clamber, °crawl, scrabble, °struggle **2** °rush, °hurry, scamper, °run, °hasten, °race, °scurry, scoot, scuttle, °dash, hotfoot (it), °hustle, *Chiefly US and Canadian,* hightail (it), *Colloq* skedaddle **3** Often, ***scramble up.*** °mix up, °confuse, °jumble, intermingle, °mingle, commingle —*n.* **4** °scrimmage, °struggle, tussle, contention, °clash, °competition, °contest, °race, °rush, °clash, °conflict, °disorder, commotion, °riot, melee *or* mêlée, °pandemonium, *Colloq* free-for-all, hassle, *Brit* scrum *or* scrummage **5** °struggle, °climb

scrap[1] *n.* **1** mite, °bit, °shred, °bite, °morsel, °piece, °fragment, shard *or* sherd, °particle, °sliver, snippet, °snip, °crumb, whit, iota, jot *or* tittle, °snatch, °drop, °drip, °grain, °speck, molecule, atom, °dab, °trace, scintilla, °hint, °suggestion **2** ***scraps.*** remnants, °remains, leftovers, leavings, °residue, vestiges, °traces, scrapings, discards, rejections, rejects **3** °waste, debris, °rubbish, *Colloq* °junk —*v.* **4** °discard, °throw away, °reject, °abandon, °give up, consign to the scrapheap, °forsake, °forget, °get rid of, °dispose of, °dispense with, *Colloq* °junk, *US* °trash

scrap[2] *n.* **1** °fight, °brawl, °fracas, °fray, affray, °rumpus, scuffle, donnybrook, °battle (royal); °row, °dispute, °argument, °quarrel, °disagreement, wrangle, squabble, °tiff, spat, *Colloq* ruckus, set-to, dust-up —*v.* **2** °fight, °brawl, °spar, scuffle, °battle, °row, wrangle °argue, °disagree, squabble, °bicker

scrapbook *n.* album, portfolio, °collection

scrape *v.* **1** abrade, graze, °scratch, bark scuff, °skin, °bruise, °damage, °injure **2** Often, ***scrape off or away or out.*** °remove, rub off *or* away, scour *or* scrub *or* clean (off *or* away), scratch off *or* away, claw (at *or* away *or* out), gouge out, scrabble (at), dig out *or* away at **3** skimp, scrimp (and scrape), °save, °stint, be frugal *or* stingy *or* parsimonious *or* thrifty, pinch and save *or* scrape, °economize; °struggle, *US* scrabble **4** ***bow and scrape.*** make obeisance, °kowtow, salaam, genuflect, kiss the feet *or* hem *or* ring, grovel, demean *or* lower oneself, °prostrate oneself, toady, *Colloq* bootlick **5** ***scrape by or through.*** °get by, °cope, °(barely) manage, °survive, scrape *or* get along, *Colloq* squeak by, barely make it **6** ***scrape together or up.*** glean, °garner, scratch *or* get *or* rake together *or* up, dredge up, scrabble for, °gather, °save (up), get hold of, marshal, °amass, °muster, °accumulate, aggregate, °compile, °pile up, °stack up, °assemble, *Colloq* °scrounge (up) —*n.* **7** abrasion, °bruise, °scratch, graze, scuff, °damage, °injury **8** °predicament, °difficulty, °quandary, °dilemma, °plight, (fine) kettle of fish, °muddle, °stew, °situation, °position, °pinch, *Colloq* pickle, °fix, °mess, the crunch, (tight *or* tough) spot

scratch *v.* **1** °mar, °mark, °gouge (out), °gash, abrade, graze, scuff, grate against, °bruise, °damage, °injure; °claw **2** °chafe, °rub **3** Often, ***scratch out or off.*** °erase, °obliterate, rub out *or* off, °cross out, °delete, strike out *or* off, expunge; °exclude, °eliminate, *US* x out —*n.* **4** °mark, °gouge, °gash, abrasion, °scrape, graze, scuff, °bruise, °damage, °injury; °line **5** ***up to scratch.*** up to standard *or* par, °adequate, °sufficient, good enough, °competent, °satisfactory, competitive, *Colloq* up to snuff —*adj.* **6** °hasty, °hurried, impromptu, unplanned, °haphazard, °rough, °casual, °informal, °unprepared, °unpremeditated, °makeshift, extempore, *Colloq* off the cuff, *US* pickup

scratchy *adj.* **1** itchy, irritating, °prickly **2** °rough, hoarse, °raw, °grating, °sore, raspy, °dry

scrawl *n.* **1** scribble, *Colloq* squiggle, *US* hen-scratch, chicken-scratch —*v.* **2** scribble, °scratch, doodle

scrawny *adj.* bony, °skinny, °spare, °drawn, reedy, °haggard, °lean, lank(y), scraggy, °gaunt, °rawboned, angular, °emaciated, cadaverous; anorectic *or* anorexic

scream *v.* **1** °shriek, screech, squeal, yowl, wail, caterwaul, °howl, °cry **2** °laugh, °roar, hoot, °howl, guffaw —*n.* **3** °shriek, screech, squeal, yowl, wail, caterwaul, °howl, °cry **4** *Colloq* °card, °panic, °riot, thigh-slapper

screen *n.* **1** °partition, (room) divider, paravent, °wall; *Theater* tormentor **2** °shelter, °protection, °shield, °cover **3** curtain, °blind, °shroud, °cloak, °cover; concealment, °camouflage **4** sieve, °mesh, strainer, °filter, colander, °riddle **5** motion pictures, °movies, silver screen; °television, small screen, home screen, *Colloq* °box, telly, *US* boob tube —*v.* **6** °partition (off), °separate, °divide, °wall off **7** °shelter, °protect, °shield, °cover, °guard, °conceal, °camouflage, °mask, °veil, °hide **8** °sift, °separate (out), °sort (out), °filter, °select, cull, °process, °interview, °evaluate, °grade, °gauge, °qualify, °examine, °scan, *Chiefly Brit* °vet

screw *n.* **1** °bolt, screw bolt, machine screw, lag bolt, lag screw **2** helix, °spiral, corkscrew **3** sexual intercourse; sexual partner, *Slang* °lay, *Taboo slang* fuck **4** ***put the screws on (someone).*** °pressure, °influence, °force, constrain, °press, °oblige, °require, °demand, coerce, compel, apply pressure, bring pressure to bear (on); °insist; *Chiefly Brit* pressurize, *Colloq* twist (someone's) arm, °put the squeeze on (someone) —*v.* **5** °twist, °turn, °rotate **6** Often, ***screw out of.*** °defraud, °cheat, °swindle, gull, bilk, do out of, *Slang* °take, °clip, °fleece **7** ***screw up.*** **(a)** °raise, °increase, °stretch, °strain; °summon, °call up, °call upon, °tap, draw on *or* upon **(b)** °ruin, °destroy, make a mess of, °botch, °bungle, °muddle, mismanage, °mishandle, *Colloq* make a hash of, *Slang* louse up, *US* bollix up, *Brit* make a muck-up of, *Taboo slang* fuck up, *Brit* °bugger up, ballocks *or* bollocks up, make a balls-up of **(c)** contort, °twist, deform, °warp

scribe *n.* **1** copyist, copier, transcriber, *Archaic* scrivener; amanuensis, clerk, secretary **2** °writer, °author, penman, scrivener, wordsmith, scribbler, °hack, penny-a-liner; °dramatist, dramaturge, °playwright, °poet, novelist, essayist, columnist, technical writer; °journalist, gentleman *or* lady of the press, newspaperman, newspaperwoman, °reporter, rewrite man *or* woman *or* person, °editor, reviewer, commentator, newswriter, sob sister, agony aunt *or* uncle, Miss Lonelyhearts, gossip columnist, member of the fourth estate, *Brit* paragraphist, leader writer, *US* Grubstreeter, *Colloq Brit* journo —*v.* **3** inscribe, incise, °etch, °engrave, °mark, °scratch, °score, °grave, scrimshaw, °carve, chase *or* enchase

scrimmage *n.* °skirmish, scuffle, °fray, affray, °disturbance, brouhaha, melee *or* mêlée, °riot, °row, °brawl, °struggle, °scramble, tussle, °fracas, °rumpus, donnybrook, °battle, °fight, *Colloq* ruckus, set-to, dust-up, free-for-all, °scrap, *Brit* scrum *or* scrummage, *Slang Brit* (bit of) bovver

script *n.* **1** handwriting, °hand, °(cursive) writing, °penmanship; calligraphy **2** manuscript, °scenario, °book, °play, screenplay, teleplay, libretto, continuity —*v.* **3** °write, °pen, °prepare, °create **4** °plan, °organize, °design, °arrange, °lay out, °order, configure, °pattern

Scripture *n.* Scriptures, sacred writings, Bible, Good Book, Holy Writ *or* Scripture(s), Word of God, Gospel(s); Book of Mormon; Koran; Upanishad(s), Bhagavad-Gita

scrounge *v.* **1** ferret out, seek out, nose *or* smell out, come up with, scrape together *or* up, scratch up; importune, cadge, °beg, (borrow, or steal), *Colloq US* freeload, °bum —*n.* **2** scrounger, cadger, °parasite, *Colloq* sponger, *US* freeloader

scrub *v.* **1** See **scour, 1,** above. **2** °cancel, °call off, abort, °scratch, °drop, °terminate, °give up, °end, °abandon, °stop, °cease, °discontinue, do away with

scruple *n.* **1** °compunction, °qualm, °reluctance, °misgiving, second thoughts, °doubt, °(twinge of) conscience, hesitation, uneasiness, °discomfort, squeamishness —*v.* **2** °pause, falter, °hesitate, vacillate, have doubts *or* compunctions (about), demur, waver, shrink from *or* at, have misgivings *or* qualms (about *or* over), be loath *or* loth (to), think twice (about), °stick at, be reluctant, balk (at), have scruples (about)

scrupulous *adj.* **1** °careful, °cautious, °meticulous, °exacting, °precise, overnice, °strict, °rigid, rigorous, °severe, °critical, °fastidious, °neat, °conscientious, finicky *or* finical, °fussy, °painstaking, punctilious **2** °ethical, °honorable, upstanding, °moral, °righteous, °principled, high-minded, °just

scrutinize *v.* °examine, °analyze, dissect, °investigate, °probe, °study, °inspect, °sift, go over *or* through, °check

scrutiny *n.* °examination, °analysis, °investigation, °probe, probing, °study, inspection, sifting, inquiry *or* enquiry, °exploration, °check

scud *v.* °fly, °skim, °race, scoot, °speed, °shoot

sculpture *n.* **1** °figure, figurine, °statue, statuette, °group, °head, bust, °relief; bronze, marble —*v.* **2** sculpt *or* sculp, °model, °chisel, °carve, °cast, °form, °fashion

scurrilous *adj.* foulmouthed, thersitical, °gross, °indecent, °profane, Fescennine, °vulgar, °obscene, licentious, Sotadean *or* Sotadic, °foul, °vituperative, °low, °coarse, scabrous, °vile, °nasty, defamatory, °derogatory, disparaging, vilifying, calumnious *or* calumniatory, malign, aspersive, opprobrious, °offensive, °abusive, insulting

scurry *v.* °dash, °scramble, scamper, scoot, dart, °fly, °race, sprint, scuttle, °hurry, °hasten, °speed, °hustle, °rush, °tear, zoom, zip, °bolt, °rip, °scud

scurvy *adj.* °low, °miserable, °contemptible, °vile, °base, °despicable, °rotten, °sorry, °bad, ignoble, °dishonorable, °mean, °worthless, °shabby

sea *n.* **1** °ocean, deep blue sea, high seas, *Literary* °(briny) deep, °(bounding) main, Neptune's *or* Poseidon's kingdom *or* domain, *Nautical* blue water, Davy Jones's locker (= 'bottom of the sea'), *Colloq* briny, °drink, pond (= 'Atlantic Ocean') **2** °swell, breaker, °wave **3** plethora, °quantity, °abundance, °surfeit, °profusion, °flood, multitude, °spate, legion, °mass, *Colloq* lot(s), heap(s), pile(s), ton(s), mountain(s), load(s), oodles, gobs, scads **4** ***(all) at sea.*** °confused, disoriented, at sixes and sevens, bewildered, perplexed, baffled, mystified, °lost, adrift

seacoast *n.* seashore, shore, °coast, seaside, seaboard, shoreline, coastline, littoral, sand(s), °beach, strand

seafaring *adj.* maritime, °nautical, naval, °marine

seal *n.* **1** °symbol, °token, °mark, insigne (*plural* insignia), °sign, signet, °crest, °bearing, coat of arms, escutcheon, °emblem, badge, monogram, °identification, cartouche, °design, imprint, °stamp **2** authentication, confirmation, verification, validation, affirmation, attestation, ratification, corroboration, °assurance, guarantee *or* guaranty, °endorsement, substantiation, °evidence, °notice, notification —*v.* **3** Sometimes, ***seal off or up.*** close (off *or* up), °shut (off), zip up, °plug (up), °stop (up), °lock, °bolt, °secure, batten down, make airtight *or* waterproof; cork **4** °authenticate, °confirm, °verify, validate, affirm, °attest, °ratify, °clinch, corroborate, °assure, °ensure, °guarantee, °endorse

seam *n.* **1** °junction, °juncture, °joint, suture, *Technical* commissure; °scar, °ridge, °line, cicatrix **2** lode, °vein, °stratum, bed, layer, thickness

seamy *adj.* °sordid, °nasty, °dark, °disreputable, °shameful, °unwholesome, °unpalatable, °unsavory, °distasteful, °unseemly, squalid, °low, depraved, °degenerate, degraded, °foul, °vile, odious, °abhorrent, °contemptible, °scurvy, °rotten, unattractive. °ugly, °repulsive, °repellent

search *v.* **1** Often, ***search through.*** °examine, °scrutinize, °check, comb (through), °explore, °go through, °investigate, °scout out, °inspect, look at *or* into, °probe, °scour, sift through, pry into, hunt *or* rummage through; inquire *or* enquire of, *Colloq* plow through **2** Often, ***search for.*** look (about *or* around), cast about, °seek, leave no stone

unturned —*n.* 3 °hunt, °pursuit, °quest 4 researching, °analysis; °exploration, °examination, °scrutiny, °probe, °study, °perusal, sifting, inspection, scouring, inquiry *or* enquiry
searchingly *adv.* penetratingly, piercingly, °intently, °deeply, fixedly, concentratedly, eagerly
season *n.* 1 °time, °period, °occasion, °opportunity 2 ***in season.*** °ripe, °ready, °edible, °seasoned, °seasonable, °available —*v.* 3 °spice, °salt, °flavor, °pep up, °enliven 4 °ripen, °mature, °age, °condition, °mellow
seasonable *adj.* °appropriate, °opportune, °suitable, apt, °timely, °fitting, °providential, °well-timed, °proper, °fit, °propitious, °welcome, well-suited, °happy, °lucky, °fortunate, °convenient, auspicious, °favorable, °advantageous, °expedient
seasoned *adj.* °experienced, trained, long-standing, long-serving, practiced, well-versed, habituated, acclimatized *or* acclimated, °accustomed, familiarized, °prepared, established, °veteran, tempered, hardened, toughened, inured
seasoning *n.* °spice, °zest, °flavor, °relish, °sauce
seat *n.* 1 °place, °chair, bench, sofa, settee, °settle, stool, throne 2 °focus, °base, °center, °heart, °hub, °site, °capital, cradle, headquarters, fountainhead 3 membership, °position, incumbency 4 °bottom, °buttocks, posterior(s), rump, hindquarters, fundament, derrière, *Colloq* behind, °butt, backside, °rear (end), *Brit* °bum, *US* fanny, tushie, tush, tokus, hinie, *Slang* °tail, *Brit* arse, *US* ass 5 °abode, °residence, °home, °domicile, °estate, mansion —*v.* 6 °hold, °accommodate, have room *or* space *or* capacity for, °contain, °sit 7 install *or* instal, enthrone, ensconce, instate, °invest, °establish, °place, swear in
seating *n.* °accommodation, °capacity, °space, °room
secede *v.* withdraw *or* resign *or* retire (from), °abandon, °forsake, apostasize, break with *or* away (from), drop *or* pull out (of), turn one's back to *or* on, °quit, separate from, °leave, °wash one's hands of, have nothing further to do with
secession *n.* withdrawal, seceding, defection, °break, breaking, disaffiliation, retirement, °separation, splitting off *or* away, apostasy
secluded *adj.* 1 °private, °separate, °isolated, °lonely, cloistered, sequestered, °detached, °solitary, retired, eremitic, monastic 2 off-the-beaten-track, °out-of-the-way, °remote, °faraway, far-off, °separate, segregated, °private
seclusion *n.* °privacy, °private, °separation, isolation, loneliness
second[1] *adj.* 1 °subsequent, following, next 2 °subordinate, next 3 °alternative, second-best 4 °alternate, other 5 other, later, younger, newer, more recent 6 another, °duplicate —*n.* 7 defective *or* imperfect *or* damaged *or* faulty *or* deficient *or* flawed *or* impaired *or* marred *or* blemished *or* bruised *or* inferior merchandise 8 °subordinate, °assistant, number two, lieutenant, aide-de-camp, man Friday, girl Friday, right hand; °understudy, °stand-in, °substitute, surrogate, °double, °alternate, °backer, °supporter; *Colloq US* gal *or* guy Friday —*v.* 9 °support, °back, °aid, °help, °assist, °approve (of), °advance, °promote, °subscribe to, espouse, °sponsor, °patronize, °favor, °encourage, °go along with 10 °transfer, °move, °assign, °shift, relocate —*adv.* 11 secondly, in the second place, secondarily, (number) two, b *or* B
second[2] *n.* °moment, °instant, °flash, °minute, twinkling *or* wink *or* bat (of an eye), split second, *Colloq* sec, jiffy, two shakes (of a lamb's tail), *Brit* tick, half a mo
secondary *adj.* 1 less important, unimportant, inessential *or* unessential, °nonessential, noncritical, °subsidiary, ancillary, °minor, °inferior, °subordinate 2 °derivative, derived, °indirect, °secondhand, unoriginal, not original; copied, imitated 3 °auxiliary, second-line, backup, °extra, °reserve, °spare, °provisional, supporting, °supportive, °alternate, °alternative
secondhand *adj.* °used, °old, °worn, *Colloq* hand-me-down
secrecy *n.* 1 °mystery, concealment, confidentiality, °stealth, secretiveness, surreptitiousness, °privacy, furtiveness, covertness, clandestineness 2 ***in secrecy.*** °secretly, mysteriously, confidentially, stealthily, secretively, surreptitiously, privately, furtively, covertly, clandestinely, sneakily
secret *adj.* 1 concealed, °hidden, °private, covert, shrouded, clandestine; °confidential, °quiet, under cover, °secretive, unpublishable, unpublished, *Colloq* hush-hush 2 °cryptic, °private, arcane, °mysterious, °incomprehensible, esoteric, °recondite, abstruse; cryptographic, encrypted, encoded —*n.* 3 private *or* confidential matter *or* affair, °mystery 4 ***in secret.*** privately, confidentially, °secretly, on the Q.T.; surreptitiously, under cover, by stealth, stealthily, furtively, °quietly, °on the sly, clandestinely
secrete[1] *v.* °hide, °conceal, °cache, °bury, °cloak, °shroud, enshroud, °camouflage, °mask, °disguise, *Slang* stash away
secrete[2] *v.* °yield, excrete, °pass, °generate, °release, °ooze, seep, exude, °discharge, °leak, °drip, °drop, dribble, °trickle, °run, °drain, °emit, °give off, °emanate, transude, *Technical* extravasate
secretion *n.* secreting, °release, °escape, oozing, seeping, seepage, °discharge, discharging, °leak, leaking, leakage, °drip, dripping, °drop, dropping, dribbling, trickling, °trickle, °running, °drain, draining, emission, emitting, giving off, exudation, transudation, excretion, excreting, emanation, emanating, °generation, *Technical* extravasation; transudate, excreta, *Technical* extravasate

laced, °prudish, °fussy, prim, °conventional, °old-fashioned

secretive *adj.* °reticent, °silent, close-mouthed, °taciturn, uncommunicative, °reserved, °tight-lipped, °close, *Colloq* °mum

secretly *adv.* surreptitiously, °quietly, privately, covertly, on the Q.T., furtively, stealthily, mysteriously, clandestinely, °in secret, confidentially, °on the sly, slyly, sub rosa, sub sigillo

sect *n.* **1** religious order *or* group *or* denomination *or* body *or* cult *or* persuasion *or* subdivision **2** °school (of thought), °faction, ism, °set, °clique, °cabal

sectarian *adj.* **1** cultist, cultish, clannish, cliquish, °partisan, °partial, °dogmatic, doctrinaire, factional **2** °parochial, °narrow, °narrow-minded, °limited, insular, °provincial, °rigid, fanatic(al), °prejudicial, °prejudiced, °bigoted —*n.* **3** adherent, °member, sectary, votary, cultist, °partisan **4** (true) believer, dogmatist, °fanatic, bigot, °zealot, extremist, *Slang* nut, °bug, °fiend

section *n.* **1** °part, °division, °department, °branch, sector, °group, °detachment, °segment, °portion, subdivision, component, °element **2** °sample, °slice, cross section, fraction **3** °part, °stage, °segment, °portion, °leg —*v.* **4** °cut (up), °divide (up), °segment, °split, °cleave, °measure out, apportion, °allot, allocate

secular *adj.* °worldly, °terrestrial, mundane, °temporal, °material, °lay, laic *or* laical, nonclerical, nonecclesiastic(al), nonspiritual, nonreligious, °civil, °state

secure *adj.* **1** °safe, shielded, sheltered, protected, °immune, unthreatened, unexposed, unimperiled, °snug, °cozy **2** °firm, °steady, °stable, °fixed, °fast, moored, anchored, °immovable, closed, °shut, fastened, locked (up), °tight, °sound, °solid, °sturdy, °strong **3** °reliable, °safe, °good, °profitable, °healthy, °solid **4** °sure, °certain, assured, ensured, °definite, °inevitable, °assumed, °evident, °obvious, °unquestionable, established, °probable, °easy —*v.* **5** °obtain, °get (hold of), °come by, °acquire, °procure, °win; °gain, get *or* take possession of, arrogate **6** °guarantee, °underwrite, hypothecate, collateralize **7** °protect, °shelter, °shield, °defend, °guard, °safeguard, °preserve **8** °fasten, make fast, °fix, affix, °attach, °anchor

security *n.* **1** °safety, °shelter, °protection, fastness, °refuge, °safekeeping, °sanctuary, asylum **2** °confidence, °certainty, surety, °assurance, °conviction **3** guarantee *or* guaranty, collateral, °deposit, gage, °pledge, °insurance **4** °surveillance, safeguarding, guarding, °safekeeping, °protection, °custody, custodianship, °care

sedate *adj.* **1** composed, °serene, °peaceful, °calm, °tranquil, °cool, °collected, even-tempered, °detached, imperturbable, unruffled, undisturbed, unperturbed, controlled, placid, °grave, °serious, °sober, °solemn, *Colloq* unflappable **2** °dignified, °decorous, °refined, °formal, °stiff, °staid, °proper, °strait-laced, °prudish, °fussy, prim, °conventional, °old-fashioned

sedative *n.* **1** °narcotic, °tranquilizer, opiate, sleeping pill, soporific, calmative, anodyne, depressant, hypnotic, barbiturate, lenitive, *Colloq* downer, knockout drop, *Slang* Mickey (Finn) —*adj.* **2** °narcotic, tranquilizing, relaxing, °soothing, calming, allaying, opiate, soporific, sleep-inducing, calmative, anodyne, lenitive, depressing, hypnotic

sedentary *adj.* seated, sitting, stationary, °fixed, immobile, unmoving, house-bound, desk-bound

sediment *n.* lees, °dregs, °deposit, °grounds, °precipitate, °remains, °residue, settlings, residuum, detritus

sedition *n.* °agitation, °incitement (to riot), rabble-rousing, fomentation, instigation, firing-up, stirring-up, whipping-up; °mutiny, insurrection, insurgency *or* insurgence, rebellion; treason, treachery

seditious *adj.* °rebellious, °mutinous, °revolutionary, insurgent, °inflammatory, rabble-rousing, insurrectionist, insurrectionary, refractory, °subversive, treacherous, °dissident, °disloyal, °turncoat, unfaithful

seduce *v.* **1** °lure, °entice, °attract, allure, °tempt, °mislead, °beguile, °deceive, °decoy, °draw on, °charm, °captivate, vamp, entrap, ensnare, °trap, *Colloq* sweet-talk **2** °dishonor, °ruin, °corrupt, °lead astray, defile, debauch, deflower, °violate, °ravish

seducer *n.* See also **seductress,** below. °rake, °libertine, °roué, °playboy, lady-killer, lecher, debauchee, debaucher, °lover, *cicisbeo,* Don Juan, Lothario, Casanova, *Colloq* wolf

seductive *adj.* alluring, °attractive, °tempting, tantalizing, enticing, °inviting, seducing, °enchanting, entrancing, bewitching, fascinating, °flirtatious, coquettish, captivating, beguiling, °provocative, °siren, °irresistible, °winning, appealing, °prepossessing, *Colloq* °sexy

seductress *n.* See also **seducer,** above. °temptress, °siren, *femme fatale,* enchantress, Circe, Lorelei, Jezebel, vamp

see *v.* **1** °perceive, °note, °notice, °mark, °spot, °watch, °witness, °recognize, °behold, discern, °distinguish, °observe, °look at, °regard, °sight, °catch sight of, descry, espy, °spy, °make out, look upon, °view, glimpse, catch a glimpse of, *Slang* get a load of, *US* glom **2** °understand, °comprehend, apprehend, °perceive, °appreciate, °fathom, °grasp, °take in, °realize, °know, be aware *or* conscious of, get the idea *or* meaning of, *Colloq* °dig, °get, get the drift *or* the hang of **3** °foresee, foretell, °imagine, °envisage, °envision, visualize, °picture, °divine, °conceive (of), dream of, conjure up, °accept **4** °determine, ascertain, °find out, °investigate, °discover, °learn **5** Often, *see to it.* °ensure, °assure, make sure *or* certain, °mind, be vigilant **6** °accompany, °escort, °show, °lead, °conduct, usher, °take, convoy, °bring, °walk, °drive **7** go out with, socialize with, keep company with, consort with, °associate with; court, woo; *Colloq* go steady with, *Chiefly US* °date **8** make up one's mind, think over, mull over, °consider, ponder (on *or* over), °contemplate, °decide, °reflect (on), meditate (on *or* over *or* about), ruminate (on *or* over), °brood over **9** °receive, °meet (with), talk *or* speak with, confer with, °consult (with), have a word with, sit down with, visit with, °interview; °welcome, °greet **10** °undergo, °experience, °go through, °endure, °survive **11** °help, °aid, °assist, °support, °finance, pay the way for; °guide, °shepherd **12** ***see about.*** **(a)** °see to, °attend to, °look after, take care *or* charge of, look to, °organize, °manage, do, °undertake, °sort out; °think about, °consider, give some thought to, pay attention *or* heed to **(b)** °investigate, °study, °probe, °look into, make enquiries *or* inquiries, enquire *or* inquire about **13** ***see off.*** bid adieu *or* bon voyage **14** ***see through.*** **(a)** °penetrate, °detect, °perceive, *Slang* be wise to **(b)** ***see (something) through.*** °persevere, °persist, °manage, °survive, °last, ride out, *Colloq* °stick out **(c)** ***see (someone) through.*** provide with help *or* aid *or* assistance, °help, °aid, °assist, °last **15** ***see to.*** See **12 (a),** above.

seed *n.* **1** °grain, spore, °kernel, °pit, tuber, bulb, corm, *Technical* ovum, ovule, embryo, egg, °germ **2** °origin, °source, °cause, °root, °provocation, °reason, °basis, °grounds; °motive, motivation, motivating factor **3** °offspring, children, °progeny, °young, °issue, descendants, heirs, successors **4** ***go or run to seed.*** °run down, become dilapidated *or* worn out *or* shabby, °decay, go downhill, °decline, °degenerate, °deteriorate, go to rack and ruin, *Colloq* go to pot —*v.* **5** °scatter, °sow, °distribute

seedy *adj.* **1** °shabby, °dilapidated, °worn (out), decayed, deteriorated, °run-down, broken-down, °mangy, grubby, decaying, tatty, scruffy, squalid, °sleazy, *Colloq* °ratty **2** °tired, °weary, wearied, °run-down, worn-out, unwell, °out of sorts, ailing, °ill, °sickly, *Colloq* °poorly, °under the weather, off one's feed

seeing *conj.* °in view of (the fact that), whereas, in (the) light of, inasmuch as, since, °considering

seek *v.* **1** °look (for), °search (for), °hunt (for), go *or* be after, °quest after, °pursue **2** °hope, °aim, °aspire, °try, °essay, °endeavor, °undertake **3** °ask for, °request, °beg, °solicit, invite; °demand

seem *v.* °appear, look (as if *or* ***nonstandard in*** *US* like), °sound, °feel, have (all) the hallmarks *or* earmarks of, give every indication *or* appearance of

seeming *adj.* °apparent, °evident, ostensible, °outward, °superficial, °surface, °assumed, feigned, °pretended, °false, °so-called, °alleged, °specious, purported, °professed

seemingly *adv.* °apparently, °evidently, °ostensibly, °outwardly, superficially, falsely, allegedly, speciously, purportedly, professedly, °on the face of it, °possibly, feasibly, conceivably, plausibly, believably

seemly *adj.* **1** °proper, °fitting, °appropriate, °becoming, suited, °suitable, °fit, °befitting, apt, *comme il faut,* °right, apropos, apposite, °characteristic, °meet, °reasonable, °sensible **2** °decent, °decorous, °proper, °dignified, °genteel, gentlemanly, °ladylike, °diplomatic, °discreet, °prudent, °politic

seer *n.* soothsayer, °fortuneteller, sibyl, °oracle, °prophet, prophetess, augur, vaticinator, prophesier, clairvoyant, °psychic, crystal gazer, stargazer

seesaw *n.* **1** °teeter —*v.* **2** °teeter, °totter, waver, °vary, vacillate, °oscillate, °alternate, °fluctuate, °swing, °switch

seethe *v.* **1** °boil, °stew, °simmer, °foam **2** °stew, °simmer, °foam (at the mouth), °fume, °smolder, °burn, °rage, °rant, °rave, become livid *or* feverish, be in ferment, be furious *or* incensed, *Colloq* blow one's stack *or* top, °carry on, °take on, get hot under the collar, get red in the face, get all steamed up

see-through *adj.* °sheer, diaphanous, gauzy, °transparent, translucent, gossamer, °filmy, peekaboo

segment *n.* **1** °section, °part, °division, °portion, component, °element; °piece, fraction, °fragment, °length, °joint, °slice, °wedge —*v.* **2** °divide, °partition, °section, °separate, °part, °cleave, °split, subdivide, °fragment

segregate *v.* °separate, °segment, °partition, °isolate, seclude, sequester, °set apart, compartmentalize, °exclude, °ostracize, discriminate against

segregation *n.* °separation, segmentation, °partition, isolation, °seclusion, sequestration, setting apart, compartmentalization, °exclusion, ostracism, °discrimination, apartheid, *US* Jim Crowism

seize *v.* **1** Sometimes, ***seize on.*** °grab, °grasp, °clutch, °take (hold of), °grip, °snatch **2** °capture, °catch, °arrest, take into custody, take prisoner, apprehend, °round up, *Colloq* °pinch, °nab, collar, °pick up, *Brit* °nick, *Slang* bust **3** °catch, °transfix, °stop, °hold, °possess, °take possession of, °afflict, °beset, °visit, °subject **4** take advantage of, make good use of **5** °confiscate, °take (away), commandeer, °appropriate, °capture, °take possession of, impound **6** seize up, °bind, °jam, °stop, °lock (up), °stick, °freeze (up)

seizure *n.* **1** seizing, confiscating, confiscation, appropriation, impounding, commandeering, °capture, °taking, °possession, annexation, sequestration, usurpation **2** °spasm, °attack, °fit, °paroxysm, convulsion, *Technical* ictus

seldom *adv.* °rarely, °infrequently, not often, hardly ever, very occasionally

select *v.* **1** °choose, °pick, show (a) preference for, °prefer, opt for, °single out, handpick, °distinguish —*adj.* **2** selected, chosen, handpicked, °choice, °special, preferred, preferable, °favored, °favorite, °exceptional.

°excellent, °first-rate, first-class, °superior, °supreme, °prime, °better, °best, finest, tip-top **3** °limited, restricted, restrictive, °exclusive, °privileged, élite *or* elite, closed

selection *n.* **1** °choice, °pick, °preference, °option **2** °assortment, °variety, °collection, °range, °batch, °number, °set, series, °group **3** selecting, choosing, picking, singling out, electing, settling on, voting for, opting for, °choice, °pick, °election **4** °extract, °quotation, °excerpt, °abstract, °passage, °piece, °quote

selective *adj.* °particular, discerning, discriminative, °discriminating, discriminatory, eclectic, °exacting, °demanding, °choosy, *Colloq* picky

self-abuse *n.* masturbation, onanism, self-gratification, autoeroticism *or* autoerotism, self-stimulation, self-manipulation, self-pollution, self-defilement, self-contamination, *Technical* manustrupation

self-confidence *n.* °confidence, self-assurance, °self-respect, °self-esteem, °assurance, °poise, *armour-propre*, aplomb, self-reliance, self-sufficiency

self-confident *adj.* °confident, self-assured, assured, °poised, self-reliant, °secure, sure of oneself, °positive, °definite, °assertive, °independent

self-conscious *adj.* °embarrassed, °coy, diffident, °shy, °modest, self-effacing, °sheepish, shrinking, °retiring, unsure, apprehensive, °reserved, insecure, °affected, °awkward, °nervous, uncomfortable, °hesitant, °timid, timorous

self-contained *adj.* **1** °self-possessed, unemotional, self-controlled, in control, composed, °serene, °peaceful, °calm, °tranquil, °cool, °collected, even-tempered, °detached, imperturbable, unruffled, undisturbed, unperturbed, controlled, placid, °grave, °serious, °sober, °solemn, *Colloq* unflappable **2** °reserved, controlled, °distant, °aloof, °formal, °withdrawn, °reticent, °standoffish **3** °whole, °entire, °complete, stand-alone, unitary

self-control *n.* **1** self-discipline, self-restraint, °restraint, °self-denial, °control, willpower, strength (of character *or* of mind *or* of will), mettle, °fortitude, moral fiber, °determination, self-possession, resoluteness, °resolve, °will, constancy, steadfastness, °perseverance, doggedness, obduracy, °persistence, *Facetious US* won't-power **2** calmness, tranquillity, °serenity, placidity, imperturbability, coolheadedness, coolness, °poise, levelheadedness, °patience, aplomb, °dignity, equanimity, forbearance, °control, °restraint, self-restraint, even temper

self-denial *n.* **1** self-sacrifice, self-abnegation, renunciation, selflessness, °altruism, unselfishness, magnanimity **2** °hardship, °suffering, self-mortification, asceticism, °privation, renunciation, renouncing, abstemiousness, abstinence, abstention, self-deprivation, keeping away from, °refusal, refusing, giving up, desisting, *Colloq* swearing off **3** See **self-control, 1,** above.

self-esteem *n.* **1** °conceit, °vanity, egoism, narcissism, self-centeredness, egotism, *amour-propre*, self-approbation, self-satisfaction, self-admiration, self-love, self-adulation, self-idolatry, smugness, self-importance, self-regard **2** See **self-confidence,** above.

self-evident *adj.* °evident, °obvious, °patent, °clear, °incontrovertible, °definite, °express, °distinct, clear-cut, °apparent, unmistakable *or* unmistakeable, undeniable, inescapable, incontestable, °plain, axiomatic, °proverbial, °manifest, °true, palpable, °tangible

self-government *n.* **1** self-rule, °independence, self-determination, home rule, autonomy, °freedom **2** See **self-control, 1** above.

self-important *adj.* °conceited, self-centered, self-seeking, self-absorbed, °vain, egotistic(al), self-satisfied, °smug, °pompous, swollen-headed, swellheaded, °arrogant, overweening, °overbearing, vainglorious, self-glorifying, self-engrossed, °presumptuous, °snobbish, °haughty, *Colloq* snooty, *Slang* snotty, stuck-up

self-indulgent *adj.* self-gratifying, °selfish, self-gratifying, °extravagant, °sensual, intemperate, overindulgent, °greedy, °immoderate, hedonistic, sybaritic, °epicurean, °gluttonous, gormandizing, pleasure-bound, pleasure-seeking, °dissolute, dissipating, licentious, °profligate, debauching

selfish *adj.* **1** °greedy, covetous, °grasping, °avaricious, °self-indulgent, self-aggrandizing, acquisitive, self-seeking, self-loving, self-centered, self-absorbed, self-interested, self-serving, egotistic(al), egoistic(al) **2** stingy, °mean, °mercenary, °tight, tightfisted, °narrow, °penurious, parsimonious, °miserly, niggardly, penny-pinching, cheeseparing, ungenerous, illiberal, grudging, uncharitable, °possessive, °inconsiderate, °thoughtless

selfless *adj.* °open, °charitable, °unselfish, self-denying, °generous, altruistic, ungrudging, magnanimous, °considerate, °thoughtful; self-sacrificing

self-made *adj.* °independent, self-reliant, entrepreneurial, °self-sufficient

self-possessed *adj.* composed, °cool, °serene, placid, °collected, self-assured, °peaceful, °calm, °tranquil, even-tempered, °detached, imperturbable, unruffled, undisturbed, unperturbed, controlled, °dignified, °refined, *Colloq* unflappable

self-respect *n.* °honor, °dignity, °integrity, self-regard, °self-esteem, °pride, *amour-propre*, °morale

self-righteous *adj.* pharisaic(al), °sanctimonious, holier-than-thou, pietistic, °mealy-mouthed, °hypocritical, complacent, °smug, self-satisfied, °priggish, °superior, tartuffian, canting, *Colloq* °goody-goody, *Slang Brit* pi

self-styled *adj.* would-be, self-called, *soi-disant*, °professed, self-appointed, self-christened, °so-called, °quasi

self-sufficient *adj.* °independent, self-reliant, self-supporting, self-sustaining

self-willed *adj.* headstrong, °determined, °forceful, refractory, °stubborn, °obstinate, pigheaded, °willful, °ungovernable, uncontrollable, °unruly, unmanageable, intractable, °contrary, °perverse, uncooperative, contumacious, °recalcitrant, stiff-necked, vexatious, °difficult, °incorrigible, °disobedient

sell *v.* **1** vend, °transfer, convey (title), °trade, barter, °exchange, °dispose of **2** °market, deal in, °merchandise, trade in, traffic in, °peddle, vend, hawk, °handle, retail, °carry, °stock, °furnish, °supply, °offer, *Colloq* °push, *Slang* °flog **3** Often, ***sell out.*** °betray, °inform against, deliver up, °give away, *Slang* rat on, grass on, °tell on, tattle on, sell down the river, blow the whistle on, °double-cross, *Brit* °shop **4** °promote, °push, put across *or* over **5** ***be sold on.*** persuaded, convinced, won over

seller *n.* °dealer, vendor, °merchant, retailer, shopkeeper, °salesperson, salesman, saleswoman, saleslady, sales agent, °representative, °traveler, traveling salesman, °peddler, hawker, colporteur, sutler, chandler, *Old-fashioned* counter-jumper, *Brit* shop assistant, -monger (*as in* costermonger, ironmonger, fishmonger, etc.), *US and Canadian* salesclerk, clerk, shopgirl, *Colloq* rep, *US* drummer

semblance *n.* **1** °appearance, °image, °likeness, °resemblance, °form, °figure, °bearing, °aspect, °air, °look, mien, °exterior, °mask, façade, °front, °face, °show, °veneer **2** °guise, °face, °front, façade, °air, °show, °veneer, °look, °pretense, °show, °cloak, simulation, °impression, °affectation, *Rare* °superficies

seminal *adj.* **1** °original, °basic, °creative, °primary, °prime, formative, °imaginative, innovative, °new, unprecedented, precedent-setting, °landmark, bench mark, °important, °influential, °telling **2** embryonic, germinal, °potential, °undeveloped, incipient

seminary *n.* academy, °school, °institute, °institution, college, university, training ground

send *v.* **1** Sometimes, ***send off.*** dispatch *or* despatch, commission, °charge, depute, °delegate, °assign **2** °communicate, °transmit, convey, °deliver, consign, address to, °mail, °post, fax, °remit, °ship, °forward; °broadcast, telecast, televise, °radio, telegraph **3** °release, °discharge, °shoot, °propel, °fire, °fling, °project, °hurl; °cast, °throw, °toss, °let fly **4** °delight, please, °charm, °enrapture, °stir, °thrill, °move, °electrify, *Slang* turn (someone) on **5** ***send down.*** °imprison, incarcerate, send away, jail *or Brit also* gaol, *Slang US* °send up (the river) **6** ***send for.*** °call for, °summon, °order, °request, °ask for **7** ***send forth or out.*** °emit, °radiate, °discharge, °give off, exude, °grow **8** ***send off.*** send (someone) away (with a flea in his *or* her *or* their ear), °dismiss, °discharge, send (someone) packing, send (someone) (on) about his *or* her *or* their business, *Colloq* give (someone) his *or* her *or* their walking papers, *Slang* give (someone) the brushoff, *US* give (someone) the brush **9** ***send up.*** **(a)** °lampoon, °satirize, °burlesque, °parody, °make fun of, *Colloq* °take off, spoof, *Brit* take the mickey out of **(b)** °imprison, incarcerate, send away, jail *or Brit also* gaol, *Slang US* °send up (the river)

senile *adj.* (of a woman) anile; senescent, °decrepit, declining, °failing, in one's dotage, doting, °doddering, in one's second childhood, dotty, °simple, °feebleminded; °forgetful, *Colloq* past it

senility *n.* (of a woman) anility; senile dementia, Alzheimer's disease, senescence, °decrepitude, °decline, dotage, second childhood, loss of one's faculties

senior *adj.* °elder, older, *Brit* (*postpositive*) °major; (higher) ranking, °superior, °chief

senior citizen *n.* elderly person, retired person, °pensioner, *Chiefly US* retiree, golden ager, *Brit* OAP (= 'old age pensioner'), gray panther

sensation *n.* **1** °feeling, °sense, °impression, °perception, °foreboding, presentiment, prescience, awareness, °suspicion, *Colloq* sneaking suspicion, funny feeling, °hunch **2** commotion, °stir, °thrill, °furor; °excitement **3** °hit, *coup de théâtre*, °success, *Colloq* show-stopper, crowd-puller, crowd-pleaser

sensational *adj.* **1** °exciting, °stimulating, electrifying, galvanizing, °shocking, hair-raising, spine-tingling, °thrilling, °stirring, breathtaking, °amazing, astonishing, astounding, staggering, mind-boggling, °unbelievable, °incredible, spectacular, *Slang* mind-blowing **2** °lurid, °vivid, overdone, overdrawn, °extreme, °melodramatic, exaggerated, °dramatic, °extravagant **3** °(very) good, °great, °marvelous, wonderful, °superior, °superb, °matchless, °peerless, unequaled, °nonpareil, °extraordinary, °terrific, °phenomenal, °splendid, °fabulous, °fantastic, stupendous, *Colloq* °super, smashing, *Slang* far-out

sense *n.* **1** °faculty **2** common sense, °intelligence, °perception, quick-wittedness, quickness, °(mother) wit, °judgment, °reason, °wisdom, sagacity, °discrimination, discernment; °sanity, *Colloq* brains, *Slang Brit* nous **3** See **sensation, 1,** above. **4** °meaning, intelligibility, coherence, head or tail, °drift, °gist, °import, purport, nuance, °significance, °message, °substance **5** °sentiment, °atmosphere, °impression, °intuition, °sensation —*v.* **6** °feel, °perceive, °detect, °divine, intuit, have a hunch *or* feeling, have *or* get *or* be under the impression that, °suspect, *Colloq* have a funny feeling that, feel (something) in one's bones, °pick up

senseless *adj.* **1** °insensible, °unconscious, °(knocked) out (cold), stunned, insensate, comatose **2** numb(ed), insensate, unfeeling, benumbed, °insensible, anesthetized, °dead, deadened, insentient **3** °pointless, °purposeless, °ridiculous, °ludicrous, unintelligent, illogical, irrational, °incongruous, °meaningless, °absurd, °wild, °mad, °crazy, demented, °insane, asinine, °nonsensical, imbecilic *or* imbecile, idiotic, moronic, simple-minded, fatuous, °stupid, °foolish, °silly, °dizzy, °half-witted, °mindless, brainless, witless, empty-headed, thimble-witted, pea-brained, birdbrained, °harebrained, featherheaded, rattlebrained, addlepated, muddle-headed, *Colloq* °daft, *US* daffy, nutty, batty, *Slang* wacky, dippy

sensibility *n.* **1** See **sensitivity, 3,** below. **2** Often, ***sensibilities.*** °feelings, responsiveness, responsivity, emotions, °sentiments

sensible *adj.* **1** °reasonable, °realistic, °logical, common-sense, common-sensical, °rational, reasoned, °sound, °practical, °prudent, °judicious, °discreet, °intelligent, °sage, °wise, °sane; down-to-earth, °matter-of-fact, well-thought-out **2** perceivable, °perceptible, detectable, °evident, °discernible, recognizable, ascertainable, apprehensible, cognizable, °manifest, palpable, °physical, °tangible, corporeal, substantive, °material, °visible, °observable, seeable **3** sentient, °feeling, °sensitive, °live, °conscious, °aware **4** Usually, ***sensible of or to.*** °conscious (of), °aware (of), °acquainted (with), cognizant (of), °sensitive (to), °alive to, °mindful (of), °understanding (of), in touch (with), °observant (of), °awake (to), °alert (to), *Slang* °wise (to), hip *or old-fashioned* hep (to) **5** appreciable, °significant, °considerable, °substantial, substantive, °noticeable

sensitive *adj.* **1** °delicate, °tender, °sore, °susceptible **2** °touchy, °susceptible, susceptive, reactive, °responsive, attuned, °impressionable, °emotional, thin-skinned, °vulnerable, supersensitive, hypersensitive, °testy, irascible, °quarrelsome, °irritable, °volatile, °excitable, °temperamental, °petulant, hot-tempered, °quick-tempered **3** finely tuned, °delicate, °responsive, °subtle, °acute, reactive, °receptive

sensitivity *n.* **1** sensitiveness, °delicacy, touchiness, oversensitivity, hypersensitivity, supersensitivity; soreness, irritability **2** compassion, °concern, °sympathy, tenderness, tenderheartedness, kindheartedness, kindliness, °warmth, °feeling **3** awareness, consciousness, acuteness, °perception, °understanding, °intuition, °feeling, °sense, °sensitivity, sensitiveness, receptivity *or* receptiveness, receptibility, °appreciation, appreciativeness, susceptibility, susceptivity *or* susceptiveness

sensual *adj.* °physical, appetitive, °voluptuous, °carnal, bodily, fleshly, °erotic, °sexual, °lustful, °unchaste, °abandoned, °dissolute, °profligate, dissipated, licentious, °lewd, °lascivious, lubricious *or* lubricous, goatish, hircine, °lecherous, libidinous, salacious, °prurient, °rakish, °wanton, debauched, Cyprian, °loose, °dirty, *Slang* °randy

sensualist *n.* lecher, °profligate, °wanton, debauchee, °roué, °rake, Romeo, Don Juan, Casanova, Lothario, °libertine; voluptuary, hedonist, °sybarite, *bon viveur, bon vivant,* °epicure, °epicurean, °gourmet, gourmand, gastronome, pleasure-seeker

sensuous *adj.* sensory, sybaritic, °epicurean, hedonist(ic), °sumptuous, °luxurious, °rich

sentence *n.* °judgment, °decision, ruling, verdict, °decree, °determination; °punishment, *Slang* °rap

sentiment *n.* **1** °attitude, °feeling, °sensibility, °emotion, susceptibility, tenderness, tender-heartedness, °sentimentality, sentimentalism **2** Often, ***sentiments.*** °view, °outlook, °opinion, °position, °attitude, °judgment, °thought, °belief, °feeling, °emotion

sentimental *adj.* **1** °emotional, °sympathetic, compassionate, °tender, warmhearted, tenderhearted **2** °romantic, nostalgic, °emotional, °maudlin, mawkish, overemotional, °tender, °tearful, weepy, sickening, nauseating, simpering, °sweet, saccharine, *Colloq* °sloppy, °gooey, °sticky, °tacky, °mushy, slushy, °gushy, soppy, drippy, tear-jerking, ill-making, sick-making, *Slang* corny, schmaltzy, icky, yucky *or* yukky

sentimentality *n.* romanticism, nostalgia, pathos, emotionalism, maudlinism, bathos, mawkishness, overemotionalism, tenderness, tearfulness, weepiness, sweetness, *Colloq* sloppiness, gooeyness, mushiness, slushiness, gushiness, soppiness, drippiness, *US* stickiness, tackiness, *Slang* corn, corniness, schmaltz, schmaltziness, ickiness, yuckiness *or* yukkiness

sentinel *n.* sentry, °guard, °watchman, °watch, °picket, °lookout, °patrol

separable *adj.* distinguishable, segregable, detachable, divisible, severable, removable, fissile, scissile

separate *v.* **1** disjoin, pull *or* take *or* break apart, come *or* fall apart, fall *or* take *or* break to pieces, split *or* divide *or* break (up), split *or* break (off *or* away), °disconnect, °disengage, °part, °partition, °sort (out), uncouple, disarticulate, disassemble, unhook, °detach, disunite, unyoke, disentangle, unravel **2** °distinguish, °discriminate, °analyze, °sort, °break down, classify, °segregate, °single out, sequester, °type, codify, °organize, °split up; °group, collate **3** split *or* break up, °part (company), °divide (up), °disband, °divorce **4** fork, split (up *or* off), bifurcate, °diverge, °branch —*adj.* **5** divided, separated, disjoined, °disconnected, °detached, °isolated, °discrete, °distinct, °individual, °independent, °solitary, °different **6** °different, °independent, °unrelated, other **7** °withdrawn, °solitary, °alone, shut *or* closed off *or* away, °apart, °detached, removed, cloistered, °secluded, sequestered, °isolated, separated

separately *adv.* °individually, independently, °singly, one by one, one at a time, °personally, °alone, severally

separation *n.* 1 °rift, °break, °split, split-up, °divorce, breakup, disunion, estrangement 2 °partition, °division, °split, °schism, dividing line, dissociation, disassociation, severance 3 disintegration, shattering, breakup, fragmentation, dismemberment, taking *or* keeping apart, °segregation, °division, disjoining, disjunction, fission, scission, °rupture, °schism, splitting, °split, fracturing, °fracture, °break

sepulcher *n.* °tomb, mausoleum, burial vault, °grave, °crypt, pyramid, burial-place

sequel *n.* °follow-up, °upshot, °issue, °result, consequence, °development, °supplement

sequence *n.* °succession, °progression, °order, series, °chain, °string, °course, °cycle, °arrangement, °organization, °train, °line, °set, °run, concatenation, °system

sequential *adj.* °successive, ordered, °orderly, serial, °progressive, organized, °systematic, cyclic, °continuous

seraphic *adj.* angelic, °celestial, °divine, °heavenly, blissful, °sublime, empyrean, elysian, ethereal, °holy, °saintly, °godly

serene *adj.* 1 °peaceful, °tranquil, °calm, pacific, °peaceable, °restful, halcyon, °idyllic, bucolic, °pastoral, undisturbed, unruffled, imperturbable, unperturbed, untroubled, °quiet, °still 2 °calm, °cool, °collected, placid, composed, °self-possessed, °poised, unexcitable, even-tempered, °temperate, °nonchalant, easygoing, coolheaded, °easy, *Colloq* unflappable

serenity *n.* 1 peacefulness, °peace, tranquillity, °calm, calmness, restfulness, °quiet, stillness 2 tranquillity, peacefulness, peaceableness, unexcitability, calmness, °calm, composure, self-possession, °poise, aplomb, even-temperedness, °temperance, nonchalance, coolheadedness, placidity, *Colloq* unflappability

serious *adj.* 1 °grave, °solemn, °earnest, unsmiling, poker-faced, straight-faced, °sedate, °sober, °pensive, °thoughtful; humorless, °somber, °grim, °dour, °severe 2 °grave, °important, °vital, °dangerous, °weighty, °significant, °momentous, °crucial, consequential, life-and-death, °urgent, °pressing; no laughing matter, of consequence *or* moment *or* importance 3 °sincere, straightforward, not joking *or* fooling, °genuine, °honest 4 °acute, °critical, life-threatening, °bad, °dangerous, °nasty, °perilous, alarming, °grave, °severe, °precarious

seriously *adv.* 1 gravely, °badly, °severely, critically 2 °really, °honestly, scout's honor, °sincerely, °truly, candidly, °openly, *Colloq* joking *or* kidding aside, no joking *or* kidding *or* fooling, cross one's heart (and hope to die) 3 soberly, earnestly, unquestioningly, without a doubt, at face value

sermon *n.* 1 °lecture, °lesson, preaching, °reprimand, reproach, °reproof, remonstration, remonstrance, scolding, °harangue, *Colloq* talking-to, dressing-down 2 homily, °address, exhortation, °lesson, °lecture, °speech, °talk, discourse

serpentine *adj.* 1 °evil, °bad, diabolical, °satanic, Mephistophelian, reptilian, °devilish, °wily, cunning, conniving, °sneaky, °shrewd, °artful, °crafty, °slick, °sly, insidious, °shifty, °tricky, °scheming, plotting, Machiavellian 2 twisting, winding, °tortuous, snaking, snakelike, sinuous, anfractuous, °roundabout, °meandering, ambagious, °indirect, °devious, °crooked, °labyrinthine, vermicular, vermiculate, complex, °complicated, Byzantine

serrated *adj.* sawlike, sawshaped, sawtoothed, toothed, °notched, zigzag, °jagged, serrate, serriform, serratiform, serrulate(d), crenelated, crenulate, crenate, denticulate

serried *adj.* ranked, tiered, row on row, ranged, assembled, °packed, °close, compacted, °compact

servant *n.* 1 °domestic (servant), °help, retainer, servitor; °maid, maidservant, parlor maid, upstairs maid, lady's maid, cleaner, cleaning man, cleaning woman, amah; housekeeper, chatelaine, major-domo, factotum, steward, seneschal, butler, houseman, houseboy, °boy, °page; valet, °man, gentleman's gentleman, manservant, serving-man, footman, footboy, chauffeur, driver, °attendant, °groom; governess, au pair (girl), °nurse, nursemaid, ayah; cook, chef, °waiter, waitress, stewardess, wine steward, sommelier (des vins); °menial, lackey, dogsbody, *Archaic* servitor, *Historical* coachman, postillion, serving-woman, serving-girl, servant-girl, serving-wench, scullery maid, scullion, *Literary* cupboy, Ganymede, *Chiefly Brit* nanny, *Brit* boots, charwoman, charlady, °daily, tweeny, *US* scrubwoman 2 ***civil servant.*** civil-service employee *or* worker, public servant, (government *or* state) official, officeholder, government worker

serve *v.* 1 °attend (to), wait on *or* upon, °minister to, °look after (the needs of), be at (someone's) beck and call, °assist, °help, be of assistance *or* help, be in the service of, °oblige, °accommodate, °gratify 2 fulfill *or* carry out *or* perform *or* discharge (a function *or* a duty *or* one's duty), °work (for), do (duty) (as *or* for), do one's part, °suffice, be used *or* of use *or* useful (to *or* for), function (as *or* to), act (as *or* to), fill the bill, be serviceable (as *or* for), be available (for), °answer (for), be sufficient *or* adequate *or* suitable, °suit, be advantageous *or* of advantage (to); °fight (for), be obedient (to), take one's part 3 °distribute, deal out, dole out, °give out, °present, °set out, °provide, °supply, °offer, pass out *or* about *or* around, make available, come (a)round with, dish up *or* out 4 be convenient *or* opportune *or* favorable (to) 5 not fail, not play tricks (on), work *or* function (for), be accurate *or* correct 6 °go through, °complete, °spend, °last, °endure, °survive

service *n.* **1** °help, °assistance, °aid, °use, °usefulness, utility, °benefit, °advantage **2** °maintenance, °overhaul, servicing, checking, °repair, mending **3** serving, °accommodation, amenities, waiting, °care **4** °employment, °employ **5** °use, utilization, °usage, handling **6** °assignment, °post, °appointment, *Military Brit* secondment **7** °rite, °ceremony, °ritual, °worship **8** Often, ***services.*** army, °navy, air force, marines; armed forces *or* services, °military **9** Often, ***services.*** talents, °help, professional care, °work, °advice **10** °serve, serving; putting into play

serviceable *adj.* **1** workable, working, °functional, functioning, usable, °useful, °operative, operating **2** hard-wearing, long-wearing, °durable, utilitarian, long-lasting, °tough, wear-resistant

servile *adj.* °submissive, subservient, °menial, craven, acquiescent, abject, cringing, slavish, °mean, fawning, deferential, mean-spirited, °vile, °low, °base, °ingratiating, °groveling, °obsequious, toadying, toadyish, sycophantish, sycophantic, truckling, wheedling, unctuous, °slimy, °flattering, °time-serving, bootlicking, *Colloq chiefly Brit* smarmy, *US and Canadian* apple-polishing, *Slang Brit* arse-kissing, *US* ass-kissing, *Taboo slang* brown-nosing, *Brit* arse-licking, *US* ass-licking

servility *n.* submissiveness, °submission, subservience, servileness, acquiescence, abjectness, abjection, cringing, slavishness, meanness, fawning, mean-spiritedness, vileness, baseness, °groveling, obsequiousness, obsequence, toadying, toadyism, sycophancy, sycophantism, truckling, wheedling, unctuousness, sliminess, °flattery, bootlicking, *Colloq chiefly Brit* smarminess, *US and Canadian* apple-polishing, *Slang Brit* arse-kissing, *US* ass-kissing, *Taboo slang* brown-nosing, *Brit* arse-licking, *US* ass-licking

servitude *n.* °bondage, °slavery, thralldom, serfdom, subjugation, enslavement, °subjection, vassalage

session *n.* **1** sitting, °seating, °assembly, °conference, °meeting, hearing **2** °term, °period

set *v.* **1** °set down, °place, °put, °situate, °locate, °site, °plant, °position, °station, °stand, °lay, install *or* instal, °lodge, °mount, °park, °deposit, °plump, °drop, plunk *or* plonk (down) **2** °go down, °sink, °decline, °subside **3** jell *or* gel, congeal, °freeze, °solidify, °stiffen, °harden, clot, °coagulate, °thicken, °cake **4** °establish, °fix, fasten on, °appoint **5** focus on, home *or* zero in on, pinpoint, °pin down **6** °adjust, °regulate, °turn, synchronize, °fix, °calibrate, °coordinate **7** °present, °introduce, °establish, °determine, °stipulate, °lay down, °define, °indicate, °designate, °specify; set *or* mark off, delineate **8** °prepare, °set up, concoct, °lay, °arrange, °fix **9** °set forth, °propound, °present, °devise, work out *or* up, °make up, °select, °choose, °decide, °settle, °establish **10** °arrange, °lay, °spread **11** °adjust, °move, °tilt, °fix, °place, °position, °lodge **12** ***set about.*** **(a)** get *or* make ready, °start, °begin, get to work, set in motion, get under way, start the ball rolling, °break the ice, °undertake, °launch, °tackle, °address oneself to, enter upon, *Colloq* get cracking **(b)** °attack, assail, °assault, beat up **13** ***set against.*** **(a)** °compare, °evaluate, °rate, °balance, °weigh, juxtapose, °contrast **(b)** antagonize, set at odds, °alienate, °divide, disunite **14** ***set apart.*** **(a)** °distinguish, °separate, °differentiate **(b)** °reserve, put *or* set aside, °store, earmark, °put away, lay away, set by, °save, keep back **15** ***set aside.*** **(a)** See **14 (b)**, above. **(b)** annul, °cancel, nullify, declare *or* render null and void, °reverse, °repudiate, abrogate, °quash, °overturn, overrule, °discard **16** ***set back.*** °put back, °hinder, °slow, °hold up, °retard, °delay, °impede, °obstruct, °stay, °thwart, °frustrate, °inhibit **17** ***set down.*** **(a)** °write (down), put in writing, °put down, °record, °register, mark *or* jot down, °list **(b)** ascribe, °assign, °attribute, °impute, °charge **(c)** °put down, °land **18** ***set forth.*** **(a)** °express, °voice, °propose, °propound, °state, °offer, °submit, °suggest, °broach, make a motion, °move **(b)** set out *or* off, put forth *or* out, °begin, °start (out), get under way, °go, °embark, sally forth, °push off, °depart, °leave **(c)** °set out, °present, °declare, °describe, °propose, °state, articulate, °enunciate **19** ***set in.*** °begin, become established, °arrive, °come **20** ***set off.*** **(a)** ignite, °kindle, detonate, °light, °touch off, trigger, °trip **(b)** °dramatize, °enhance, highlight, throw into relief, °show (off), °display **(c)** See **18 (b)**, above. **21** ***set on.*** °set upon, °attack, °assault, pounce on *or* upon, fall on *or* upon, fly at **22** ***set out.*** **(a)** See **17 (b)** and **(c)**, above. **(b)** °put out, °lay out, °arrange, °dispose, °display **23** ***set up.*** **(a)** °build, °put up, °erect, °assemble, °construct, °raise, elevate, put together, °arrange, °prepare **(b)** °start, °begin, °initiate, °organize, °establish, °found; °finance, °fund, invest in, °back, °subsidize **24** ***set upon.*** °attack, °assault, °ambush, beat up, °fall upon, set about *Colloq* mug —*n.* **25** °collection, °group, °combination, °number, grouping, °assortment, °selection, °arrangement, series **26** °clique, coterie, °group, °company, °circle, °ring, °crowd, °faction, °sect, °gang **27** °kit, °outfit, °rig; °equipment, °apparatus **28** °setting, stage set *or* setting, °scene, *mise en scène,* mounting, scenery —*adj.* **29** °fixed, established, °determined, °predetermined, arranged, prearranged, °decided, °customary, °usual, °normal, °regular, agreed, °conventional, °habitual, °definite, defined, °firm, unvarying, unvaried, unchanging, wonted, °rigid, °strict, settled, scheduled **30** stereotyped, trite, hackneyed, °routine, °standard, °traditional, unchanged, unvaried, °invariable **31** °prepared, °ready, °fit, primed

setback *n.* °hindrance, °hitch, °check, °reverse, °reversal, °impediment, °block, °obstruction, °defeat, °holdup, °delay, °check, °rebuff, °upset; °relapse; *Colloq* hiccup
setting *n.* mounting, scenery, °background, backdrop, °locale, °location, surroundings, °habitat, °home, environs, °environment, °milieu, °frame, °context, °site, °placement; stage set *or* setting, *mise en scène,* °scene
settle *v.* **1** °arrange, °order, °dispose, °organize, °straighten out, put in *or* into order, °compose, °sort out, classify, °coordinate, °resolve, set to rights, °reconcile **2** Often, ***settle on or upon.*** °fix (on), °decide (on), °establish, °appoint, °set, °confirm, affirm, conclude, make sure *or* certain (of), °determine, agree (upon *or* on), °pick, °choose, °select **3** °decide, °reconcile, °resolve, put an end to, conclude, °clear up, °patch up, °adjust, °negotiate, mediate **4** Often, ***settle down.*** take up residence, go *or* come *or* move to, °dwell, reside, make one's home, °abide, °remain, °stay, °live, set up home *or* house, put down roots, °locate, °inhabit, *US* set up housekeeping, **5** Sometimes, ***settle down.*** °light, alight, °land, come down, °put down, °set down, (come to) rest *or* (roost), °descend, °perch **6** °populate, °people, colonize, °pioneer **7** Usually, ***settle down.*** °calm down, °subside, °quiet down, be *or* become tranquil, *Chiefly Brit* quieten (down) **8** °calm, °quiet, soothe, °tranquilize, °relax, *Chiefly Brit* quieten **9** °subside, °sink, °decline, °fall **10** Often, ***settle up.*** °pay, °square, °dispose of, °clear, °balance, liquidate, °discharge **11** Often, ***settle out.*** gravitate, °sink, °fall, °precipitate (out) **12** °clarify, °clear
settlement *n.* **1** colony, outpost, °post, °camp, community, encampment, village, hamlet **2** colonization, settling, populating, **3** °agreement, °rapprochement, °resolution, °adjustment, elimination, °reconciliation, working out, °accommodation, arbitration, °arrangement **4** °payment, defrayal, °discharge, liquidation, °satisfaction, settling, quittance, clearing, °clearance **5** deciding, settling, °setting, °decision, conclusion, confirmation, affirmation, °establishment, stabilization, °determination, °agreement, °choice, °selection
settler *n.* colonist, frontiersman, frontierswoman, °pioneer, °immigrant
setup *n.* **1** °arrangement, °system, °organization, layout, °regime, °structure, °makeup, °composition, framework, °frame, construction; °conditions, °circumstances **2** prearrangement, °trap, *Slang* put-up job
sever *v.* **1** cut off *or* apart *or* in two, lop *or* chop *or* hew *or* hack off, slice *or* shear off, °cleave, °dock, bob, dissever, °split, °separate, °divide, disjoin, °detach, °disconnect **2** °separate, disunite, °dissolve, break off *or* up, °terminate, °end, °cease, °stop, °discontinue, °suspend, °abandon, put an end to
several *adj.* **1** some, a few, not too *or* very many, a handful *or* a sprinkling *or* a number (of) **2** °various, °sundry, a variety of, °diverse, °divers, °different, °respective, °individual, °distinct, disparate, °particular, °certain, °specific, °discrete, °dissimilar
severe *adj.* **1** °strict, °harsh, rigorous, austere, °hard, °stony, stonyhearted, hardhearted, flinty, inexorable, ironhanded, °oppressive, unbending, °rigid, uncompromising, °relentless, unyielding, obdurate. pitiless, °punitive, °merciless, °unsympathetic, unfeeling, °cruel, °brutal, °mean, °savage, °inhuman, °beastly, °ruthless, °despotic, °dictatorial, °tyrannical, autocratic, °demanding, °exacting, °painstaking, °fastidious, exigent, taxing **2** °stern, °forbidding, °dour, glowering, °grave, °grim, °stiff, °straitlaced, °serious, unsmiling, °sober, °cold, °frigid, °aloof, austere **3** °dangerous, °critical, °dreadful, °awful, life-threatening, °acute, dire; °mortal, °fatal, °terminal **4** stringent, °punitive, °harsh, °punishing, °burdensome, °tough, onerous, °grievous, °painful, Draconian *or* Draconic **5** °harsh, °bitter, °cold, °inclement, °keen, °violent, °stormy, °intense, turbulent, °fierce, °wicked **6** °stark, °bare, °plain, austere, °Spartan, ascetic, °primitive, °simple, °sparse, °spare, monastic, °modest, °unadorned, unembellished, °crude, undecorated, unembroidered
severely *adv.* **1** acutely, °seriously, °badly, °dangerously, dreadfully; °permanently, fully, °entirely **2** strictly, harshly, rigorously, austerely, oppressively, relentlessly, mercilessly, cruelly, brutally, savagely, inhumanly, tyrannically **3** sternly, forbiddingly, dourly, gloweringly, gravely, °seriously, grimly, unsmilingly, soberly, coldly, coolly, austerely **4** stringently, punitively, harshly, onerously, grievously, °painfully **5** °dangerously, acutely, critically, dreadfully, °awfully; mortally, fatally, terminally **6** starkly, plainly, °barely, modestly, austerely, ascetically, monastically, primitively, °simply, crudely, sparsely, sparely
severity *n.* **1** strictness, harshness, °rigor, rigorousness, austerity, hardness, flintiness, inexorability, inexorableness, stringency, °oppression, oppressiveness, rigidity, inflexibility, relentlessness, obduracy, obdurateness, pitilessness, mercilessness, coldbloodedness, abusiveness, cruelty, brutality, meanness, savagery, inhumanity, beastliness, ruthlessness, °despotism, °tyranny, fastidiousness, exigency **2** coldness, aloofness, sternness, °gravity, grimness, frigidity, austerity, °solemnity **3** dangerousness, acuteness, seriousness, °gravity, ferocity, fierceness, °virulence, °violence, °intensity **4** stringency, punitiveness, °punishment, harshness, onerousness, grievousness, painfulness, burdensomeness, oppressiveness **5** harshness, inclemency, °violence, storminess, °intensity, ferocity, fierceness, °fury, furiousness, tempestuousness **6** plainness, starkness, austerity, asceticism, bareness, modesty, °simplicity, primitive-

ness, spareness, sparseness, monasticism, crudeness

sew *v.* sew up, stitch, darn, °mend, °repair; sew on, °attach, °fasten; °tack, baste, hem

sex *n.* **1** gender **2** sexual intercourse *or* relations, coitus, coition, mating, copulation, (sexual) congress *or* union, intimacy, lovemaking, making love, coupling, *Colloq* making out, going to bed, shacking up, *Slang* having it away, *Taboo slang* screwing, shafting, shagging, fucking, *Chiefly Brit* bonking

sexual *adj.* **1** °sex, reproductive, genital, procreative *or* procreant, progenitive, propagative **2** °sensual, °sensuous, °erotic, °carnal, fleshly, °voluptuous, libidinous, °earthy, bodily, °physical, °lustful, °animal, *Colloq* °sexy

sexy *adj.* **1** °erotic, arousing, °exciting, °sensual, °sensuous, °seductive, °suggestive, °provocative, °inviting, alluring, bedroom, °flirtatious, appealing, fascinating, °striking, °tempting, captivating, °enchanting, °stunning, *Colloq* come-hither **2** °sex, °dirty, °pornographic, °obscene, °filthy, smutty, °lewd, °foul, °lascivious, °indecent, °explicit, °gross, X-rated, °vulgar, °rude, °coarse, °off-color, °risqué, titillating, °bawdy, ribald, °lusty, °immodest, °rough, indelicate, °suggestive, °unseemly, °improper, indecorous, °naughty, °shameless, *Slang* raunchy

shabby *adj.* **1** °worn, °dingy, faded, worn-out, °threadbare, tatty, °tattered, frayed, raggedy, °ragged, scruffy, °dilapidated, °ratty, °dirty, °bedraggled, °mangy, °run-down, °seedy, (much) the worse for wear, *Brit* down at heel, *US* down at the heel(s), *Colloq* grubby, scrubby, °tacky, *US* grungy **2** °poor, °peremptory, unpleasant, °nasty, °disagreeable, °mean, °contemptuous, demeaning, grudging, ungenerous, °impolite, °rude, unfriendly, unhelpful, °shoddy, ungentlemanly, unladylike, °dishonorable, °unworthy, °scurvy, *Colloq* °rotten **3** °dilapidated, tumbledown, broken-down, shattered, battered, °run-down, °ramshackle, °seedy, neglected, °dirty, squalid, slumlike, slummy, *Colloq* beat-up, crummy **4** °mean, stingy, ungenerous, niggardly, °contemptible, °low, °lowly, °base, mean-spirited, °despicable, °vile, uncouth, discreditable, °inferior, °disreputable, °infamous, °abominable, °dishonorable, ignoble, °atrocious, ignominious, odious, detestable, opprobrious

shack *n.* °hut, °hovel, shanty, °cabin, lean-to, *Colloq* °dump

shackle *n.* **1** Often, ***shackles.*** fetter(s), leg iron(s), chains, iron(s), bilboes, gyve(s), ball and chain, manacle(s), handcuff(s), restraint(s), bond(s), trammel(s), *Colloq* cuff(s), *Slang* bracelet(s), *Brit* darbies **2** Usually, ***shackles.*** °restriction, °restraint, °deterrent, °impediment, °check, °obstacle, °obstruction, °barrier, °hindrance, °bar, °encumbrance —*v.* **3** °chain, fetter, °manacle, handcuff, °bind, °restrain, °tie, °secure, truss, pinion, °tether **4** °restrain, °hold back, °check, °deter, °hinder, °discourage, °hobble, °handicap, °restrict, °curb, °rein, °bridle, °control, fetter, °inhibit, °limit

shade *n.* **1** °shadow, shadiness, dimness, duskiness, semidarkness, gloominess, murkiness, °dusk, °gloom, murk, darkness, °obscurity, *Literary* °shades **2** °tint, tinge, °tone, °color, °hue, °intensity **3** °hint, intimation, tinge, °suggestion, °modicum, sprinkling, soupçon, °trace, °suspicion, undertone, °overtone, °touch, °speck, °dash, nuance, atom, °grain, scintilla, iota, jot *or* tittle **4** °ghost, °specter, apparition, °phantom, phantasm, °spirit, wraith, °vision, banshee, *Colloq* spook **5** °blind, window blind, curtain, Venetian blind; lampshade; °screen, °cover, covering, °protection, °veil, awning, canopy, °shield, °shelter, °umbrella, parasol **6** fraction, hairsbreadth, °bit, °hair, *Colloq* smidgen **7** °variation, °variety, nuance, °degree **8** ***put (someone) in or into the shade.*** °overshadow, °exceed, °surpass, °outstrip, outclass, °eclipse, outshine, °best, °better, °beat, °put to shame, outplay, outperform, °outdo, *Colloq* run rings *or* circles around, °show up **9** ***shades.*** sunglasses —*v.* **10** °screen, °protect, °shield, °shelter, °cover **11** darken, °opaque, black out, °blacken **12** °dim, °shadow, °veil, °blot out, cloud, °conceal, °hide, °obscure, °shroud, °screen, °mask, °camouflage, °disguise

shadow *n.* **1** darkness, °gloom, dimness, °dusk, °obscurity **2** °cover, °screen, covering, °shield, °veil, curtain, °protection, concealment **3** °hint, intimation, °suggestion, °suspicion, °trace, °vestige; °remnant **4** cloud, °blight, °curse **5** See **shade, 4,** above. **6** °companion, alter ego, °comrade, *Colloq* sidekick, crony, °chum, °(bosom) pal, *US* (bosom) buddy —*v.* **7** °follow, °trail, °track, dog, °stalk, °pursue, °trace, *Colloq* °tail, *US and Canadian* bird-dog

shadowy *adj.* **1** °dark, °shady, bowery, °leafy, shaded, °gloomy, °dusky, °dim, *Literary* bosky **2** °vague, °dim, °dark, °obscure, °faint, °indistinct, °indefinite, °hazy, ill-defined, unclear, indeterminate **3** °spectral, °ghostly, °phantom, phantasmal, wraithlike, phantasmagoric(al), °illusory, °dreamlike, °imaginary, °visionary, chimerical, hallucinatory, °unreal, unsubstantial, °fleeting, impalpable, transitory, ethereal, °immaterial **4** See **shady, 2,** below.

shady *adj.* **1** See **shadowy, 1,** above. **2** °indistinct, °indefinite, °questionable, °doubtful, °uncertain, °unreliable, °suspicious, °suspect, dubious, °shifty, °disreputable; °devious, °tricky, °slippery, underhand(ed), unethical, °unscrupulous, °dishonorable, °dishonest, *Colloq* °fishy, °crooked, °bent, not (strictly) kosher

shaft *n.* **1** °pole, °rod, °staff, °stick, °stem, shank, °handle, helve; °pillar, column, °post, stanchion, °upright **2** °beam, °ray, °gleam, °streak, pencil **3** °thrust, barb, °sting, dart, gibe *or* jibe, *Colloq* °slap (in the face),

°knock, °put-down 4 mineshaft, °tunnel, adit, °well, °pit; airshaft, duct, flue

shaggy *adj.* °hairy, °woolly, °unkempt, unshorn, uncut, hirsute, disheveled, matted, °untidy

shake *v.* 1 °quiver, °quake, °shudder, waver, wobble, °tremble, °shiver 2 wiggle, °wriggle, °squirm, shimmy, twitch, joggle, °jiggle, waggle, °sway, °swing, °roll, °bump, °grind, °vibrate, °oscillate, °pulsate, °gyrate 3 °weaken, undermined, °impair, °harm, °damage, °discourage; disenchant, °disappoint, disaffect 4 °wave, brandish, °flourish, °display, °show off, °parade, °exhibit, vaunt, waggle, °flap, °flutter 5 Often, ***shake up.*** °agitate, °stir (up), °mix (up); °upset, °distress, °frighten, °scare, °shock, °disturb, °unnerve, unsettle, disconcert, °discomfit, °worry, °fluster, disquiet, confound, °confuse, °perplex, °puzzle, *Colloq* °rattle, °get to, *US* °throw (for a loop) 6 ***shake down.*** (a) °break in, °condition, °test, °prove, *Colloq* debug (b) °blackmail, extort *or* extract *or* squeeze *or* wrest money from, °hold up, °squeeze, °threaten 7 ***shake off.*** °get rid of, °discard, dislodge, °drop, °brush off, °elude, °evade, °lose, °throw off, rid oneself of, give the slip to —*n.* 8 shaking, quivering, quaking, shuddering, wavering, wobbling, trembling, shivering, °quiver, °quake, °shudder, waver, wobble, °tremble, °shiver, wiggle, °wriggle, twitch, joggle, °jiggle, °sway, °swing, °roll, gyration 9 agitating, °agitation, shaking, °stirring (up), °jolt, °jar, jarring, jounce, jolting, jouncing 10 ***the shakes.*** trembling, tremors, delirium tremens, *Colloq* D.T.'s

shake-up *n.* reorganization, rearrangement, °overhaul, °revamp, restructuring, rehabilitation, make-over, realignment

shaky *adj.* 1 °uncertain, wobbly, °unstable, °precarious, °unsound, °flimsy, °weak, unsteady, unsupported, unsubstantiated, undependable, °unreliable, °tenuous, untrustworthy, dubious, °questionable, °doubtful, *Colloq* iffy 2 wobbly, wobbling, °unstable, °precarious, °dilapidated, °ramshackle, °on its last legs, °decrepit, falling down *or* apart, °rickety, °flimsy, unsteady, °insecure, °unsound, unsubstantial, °insubstantial, °feeble

shallow *adj.* 1 °surface, °skin-deep, °superficial, °thin, °empty, °flimsy, trivial, unimportant, °slight, °frivolous, °idle, °foolish 2 Often, ***shallows.*** shoal(s), sandbar, sandbank, bank, shelf

sham *n.* 1 °fake, °fraud, °counterfeit, °imitation, °hoax, humbug, °pretense, °forgery, °copy, imposture, *Colloq* phoney *or US also* phony —*adj.* 2 °fake, °fraudulent, °counterfeit, °imitation, paste, simulated, °false, make-believe, °fictitious, made-up, °bogus, °spurious, °mock, ersatz, °artificial, °synthetic, *Colloq* phoney *or US also* phony, pseudo

shambles *n.* °chaos, devastation, °mess, °disaster, Augean stables, pigsty, °muddle, pigpen

shambling *adj.* shuffling, lumbering, dragging, scuttling, °awkward, °clumsy, lurching, unsteady, faltering

shame *n.* 1 °embarrassment, °humiliation, mortification, chagrin, ignominy, shamefacedness, loss of face, abashment 2 °disgrace, ignominy, °dishonor, disrepute, °degradation, opprobrium, vilification, calumniation, °infamy, obloquy, odium, °contempt, °scandal, denigration, loss of face, defamation, °discredit, disesteem, °disfavor, derogation, disparagement 3 °pity, °calamity, °disaster, °catastrophe; °outrage 4 °humility, modesty, (sense of) decency *or* decorum *or* propriety, respectability, decorousness, diffidence, shyness, coyness, prudishness, timidity, shamefacedness 5 ***put to shame.*** (a) °surpass, °eclipse, outclass, °overshadow, cast into the shade, °outdo, °outstrip, outshine, °show up (b) See **8**, below. —*v.* 6 °embarrass, °humiliate, °mortify, °humble, chagrin, disconcert, discountenance, °put down, bring down, abash, °chasten, *Colloq* bring (someone) down a peg, °suppress, °subdue 7 coerce, °force, °drive, °bully, °push; °embarrass, °humiliate, °mortify, °humble 8 °disgrace, °embarrass, °dishonor, °scandalize, calumniate, °degrade, °debase, defame, °discredit, °stigmatize; °smear, °blacken, °stain, °taint, besmirch, °tarnish

shamefaced *adj.* 1 °bashful, °shy, °modest, self-effacing, diffident, °timid, °meek, °coy, °sheepish, timorous 2 °ashamed, shamed, abashed, °embarrassed, humiliated, dishonored, mortified, humbled, chastened, chagrined, uncomfortable, discomfited, °remorseful, red-faced

shameful *adj.* °disgraceful, °dishonorable, °base, °low, °mean, °vile, °degrading, °indecent, inglorious, °deplorable, discreditable, °corrupt, °disreputable, °infamous, ignominious, humiliating, °embarrassing, mortifying, humbling, chastening, discomfiting, shaming, blameworthy, °scandalous, °outrageous, unprincipled

shameless *adj.* °wild, °flagrant, unreserved, °uncontrolled, °immodest, °wanton, indecorous, °indecent, °rude, °improper, °forward, °bold, unembarrassed, unblushing, °audacious, °brazen, °brash, °unabashed, unashamed, °impudent, °shocking, °outrageous

shape *n.* 1 °form, °figure, °build, °body, °physique; °lines, °profile, °silhouette, contours 2 °form, °pattern, configuration, °structure, °aspect 3 °form 4 °state, °condition, fettle, °status, °(state of) health, °order, °trim 5 °guise, °disguise, °form, °appearance, °likeness, °image —*v.* 6 °form, °fashion, °mold, °cast, °make, °model, °sculpture, sculpt; °cut, °carve, hew, °hack, °trim 7 °determine, give form to, °control, °govern, °regulate, °affect, °condition, °influence, °decree, °frame, °define 8 °word, °express, embody in words, °put, °formulate, °form 9

°change, °modify, remodel, °accommodate, °fit, °adapt, °adjust **10** ***shape up.*** **(a)** take form, take shape, °develop, evolve, °proceed **(b)** °conform, °improve, °progress, go *or* move *or* come along, show improvement, come up to snuff; behave better

shapeless *adj.* **1** amorphous, formless, °nebulous, unformed, °indefinite, unstructured, °vague **2** unshapely, °deformed, °misshapen, distorted, twisted, °bent, battered

shapely *adj.* curvaceous, °comely, well-proportioned, °graceful, °neat, well-turned-out, good-looking, °pleasing; °voluptuous, *Colloq* °sexy

share *n.* **1** °portion, °allotment, °division, apportionment, allocation, °ration, appropriation, dispensation, °allowance, °part, °due, °percentage, °interest, dividend, °quota, °portion, °helping, serving, *Colloq* °cut **2** °interest, °piece, °part, °stake, °equity, °slice —*v.* **3** share out, °divide up, °allot, apportion, allocate, °ration, °appropriate, share in, °split, °partition, parcel *or* deal *or* dole out, °pay out

sharp *adj.* **1** °acute, °keen, edged, razor-sharp, knifelike, knife-edged, sharpened; °pointed, needle-sharp **2** °abrupt, °sudden, °precipitous, °sheer, vertical, °marked **3** °keen, keen-witted, keen-minded, sharp-witted, °shrewd, °intelligent, °smart, °alert, °bright, °quick, °agile, °astute, °clever, on the qui vive, °penetrating, °observant **4** °caustic, °bitter, °biting, acrid, °hot, °spicy, °pungent, piquant, tangy, °harsh, °sour, acid, acidulous, °tart **5** acid, acidulous, acerbic, vitriolic, acrimonious, °cutting, piquant, °biting, °bitter, °unkind, °strict, °hurtful, °spiteful, °virulent, °sarcastic, °sardonic, °trenchant, °severe, °scathing, malicious, °nasty, °malignant, °venomous, °poisonous **6** °clever, °shrewd, °artful, °crafty, °sly, cunning, °foxy, °calculating, °unscrupulous, °dishonest, *Colloq* °sneaky, °fly **7** high-pitched, °shrill, °penetrating, °piercing, °strident, °harsh, earsplitting, °loud **8** °poignant, °severe, °cutting, °intense, °sudden, °piercing, °extreme, °acute, °fierce **9** °chic, °dapper, °spruce, °stylish, °smart, °fashionable, °dressy, *Colloq* °snappy, natty, classy, °nifty, °swell, °swanky —*adv.* **10** °sharply, °precisely, °exactly, punctually, °on the dot, *Colloq* on the button, *US* on the nose **11** °sharply, °suddenly, abruptly **12** °sharply, alertly, attentively, vigilantly, watchfully, carefully

sharpen *v.* hone, °grind, strop, °whet

sharp-eyed *adj.* sharp-sighted, °eagle-eyed, hawk-eyed, lynx-eyed, gimlet-eyed, keen-sighted, wide-awake, °wakeful, watchful, °observant, °(on the) alert, on the qui vive, °wary, circumspect, Argus-eyed, °cautious, °careful

sharply *adv.* **1** °severely, sternly, harshly, cuttingly, acerbically, peremptorily, angrily, strictly, °firmly **2** °suddenly, °quickly, abruptly, precipitously, precipitately **3** acutely, distinctly, °definitely, definitively

shatter *v.* **1** °disintegrate, °burst, °pulverize, °shiver, smash, °demolish, °break (to smithereens), °splinter, °fragment, °fracture, dash to pieces **2** °destroy, °ruin, °devastate, °wreck, °dash, °crush, °demolish, torpedo, °undermine, °blast **3** °upset, °disturb, °perturb, °trouble, °unnerve, °overcome, °overwhelm, °crush, °devastate, °depress, deject, °rattle, °shake (up), unsettle, °agitate, confound, °confuse, stupefy, °daze, °stun, °paralyze, *Colloq* °throw

shave *v.* **1** shear (off), °cut (off), °trim, °clip, crop, snip off, °remove **2** °pare, °scrape, °plane, °whittle —*n.* **3** ***close shave.*** narrow escape, *Colloq* narrow *or* near squeak, *US* squeaker

shed[1] *n.* lean-to, °shelter, °structure, °addition, penthouse, °hut, °shack, °stall, °booth, °pen, cote, hutch

shed[2] *v.* **1** °spill **2** °shine, °spread, °scatter, °throw, °cast, let fall, °impart, °release, °focus, pour forth, °radiate **3** pour *or* stream *or* flow *or* surge *or* spill (out *or* forth), °discharge, °emanate, °emit, °drop; exude, °ooze, °weep **4** °cast off, doff, °drop, °abandon; molt, defoliate, desquamate, °peel (off), °flake (off)

sheen *n.* °shine, °gleam, °polish, °luster, shininess, burnish, brightness, °gloss, °glow, glimmer, °shimmer, °radiance, glint, °dazzle

sheepish *adj.* **1** °timid, °withdrawn, °passive, docile, °obedient, compliant, sheeplike, manipulable, °tractable, °pliable, °meek, amenable **2** See **shamefaced,** above.

sheer *adj.* **1** °steep, °precipitous, °abrupt, °perpendicular, °bluff, vertical **2** °absolute, °unmitigated, °unqualified, °downright, °out-and-out, unalloyed, unadulterated, °pure, unmixed, °plain, °simple, °rank, °total, °complete, arrant, °thorough, thoroughgoing, utter **3** °transparent, °see-through, °thin, diaphanous, °filmy, gauzy, gossamer, translucent, peekaboo

sheet *n.* **1** bedsheet, cribsheet, fitted sheet, flat sheet, *US* contour sheet **2** leaf, folio, °page **3** °pane, panel, °plate, °slab **4** lamina, lamination, layer, °stratum, °veneer, membrane **5** °area, °expanse, °stretch, layer, °film, °coat, coating, covering, blanket, °cover, °surface, °skin, °veneer **6** newspaper, °journal, °paper, tabloid, gazette, °daily, weekly, monthly, *Colloq* °rag

shell *n.* **1** cartridge, °projectile, °shot **2** °exterior, °outside, façade, framework, °frame, chassis, externals, skeleton, °hull —*v.* **3** shuck, husk, °peel, °hull, excorticate, decorticate **4** fire on *or* upon, °bombard, barrage, °attack, °bomb, blitz, cannonade, *Slang Brit* prang **5** ***shell out.*** °pay out, °give out, disburse, pend, °expend, °hand over, °hand out, *Colloq* °lay out, fork out, dish out, *Chiefly US* ante up

shelter *n.* **1** °protection, °cover, °refuge, asylum, °sanctuary, haven, °safety, °security **2** °cover, covering, concealment, °screen, °umbrella 3 dwelling place, habitation, °home, °dwelling, °housing, °accommodations —*v.* 4 °protect, °screen, °shield, °safeguard, °guard, °keep, °secure, °harbor 5 seek *or* take refuge *or* shelter, hole up, *Colloq* lie *or* lay low

shelve *v.* °postpone, °defer, put off *or* aside *or* on ice *or* on the shelf, pigeonhole, lay aside, hold in abeyance, *US* °table

shepherd *v.* °lead, convoy, °escort, °conduct, °guide, usher, °take, °pursue

shibboleth *n.* °password, catchword, catch phrase, buzzword, °byword, watchword, °jargon

shield *n.* 1 °protection, °guard, °safeguard, °defense, °screen, °bulwark, °shelter —*v.* 2 °protect, °guard, °safeguard, °keep, °defend, °screen, °shelter

shift *v.* 1 °move, change position; °edge, budge, relocate, rearrange, °transpose, °switch 2 Usually, ***shift for (oneself).*** °manage, °succeed, °make do, °look after, °take care of, get *or* scrape by *or* along, fend for (oneself), °make it, paddle one's own canoe 3 °sell, °market, °move —*n.* 4 hours, °stint, °schedule; work force, relay, °crew, cadre, °staff, workers, °squad, °team, °corps, °group, °party, °gang 5 °change, °movement, °switch, °transfer, °swerve, deflection, veer 6 smock, chemise, muumuu; kaftan *or* caftan

shiftless *adj.* unambitious, °lazy, °indolent, uninspired, unmotivated, °idle, °lackadaisical, °irresponsible, uncaring, unenterprising, °aimless, °slothful, otiose, °ineffective, ne'er-do-well, °good-for-nothing, fainéant, pococurante

shifty *adj.* °tricky, °artful, °shrewd, canny, cunning, °foxy, °wily, °sharp, °devious, °slick, °evasive, °smooth, °slippery, °scheming, °designing, conniving, °calculating, underhand(ed), conspiratorial, treacherous, °traitorous, °deceitful, deceiving, duplicitous, °two-faced, Janus-faced, °dishonest, untrustworthy, °crooked, *Colloq* °bent

shilly-shally *v.* hem and haw, dillydally, teeter-totter, °seesaw, yo-yo, vacillate, waver, °alternate, °fluctuate, dither, falter, tergiversate, *Brit* haver, hum and haw, *Scots* swither; °delay, °hesitate, °dawdle

shimmer *v.* 1 °shine, °gleam, °glow, glimmer, glint, °glisten, °ripple, °flicker —*n.* 2 shimmering, °shine, °gleam, °glow, glimmer, glint, °gloss, °flicker, °light

shin *v.* Usually, ***shin up.*** climb, clamber up, °scramble up, °scale, *US* shinny up

shine *v.* 1 °gleam, °glow, °shimmer, °radiate, °beam, °glare, °flare, °glisten, °glitter, coruscate, °twinkle, °sparkle, scintillate, glint, °flash, °flicker 2 °polish, burnish, rub (up *or* down), buff, °brush, °brighten 3 °excel, °surpass, °stand out, outshine, be outstanding *or* preeminent *or* excellent *or* prominent *or* conspicuous —*n.* 4 °gleam, °glow, °shimmer, °sparkle, brightness, °radiance, °gloss, °luster, °sheen, °glaze, patina 5 ***take a shine to.*** °like, be attracted to, take a fancy to, °fancy

shiny *adj.* gleaming, °glowing, shimmering, °glossy, shimmery, °lustrous, °glassy, °radiant, °bright, beaming, glistening, °polished, burnished, glittering, °dazzling, coruscating, °twinkling, sparkling, °scintillating, glinting, flashing, °flashy, flickering, lambent, fulgent

ship *n.* 1 °vessel, (ocean *or* passenger) liner, steamer, windjammer, cutter —*v.* 2 °send, °move, ferry, °transport, °deliver, °carry, dispatch *or* despatch, °freight, °haul, °truck, °cart 3 ***ship out.*** °leave, °depart, °embark, set sail, °take off, get out, °quit, *Slang* scram

shipshape *adj.* °neat, °trim, °spotless, °orderly, Bristol fashion, spick-and-span *or* spic-and-span, °tidy

shirk *v.* °avoid, °evade, °shun, °dodge, °get out of, °shrink from, *Colloq* °duck (out of), *Brit* skive, *Military Brit* scrimshank, *US* goldbrick

shiver[1] *v.* 1 °shake, °quake, °tremble, °shudder, °quiver 2 °vibrate, luff, °flap, °flutter, °chatter, °rattle, °shake, wallop —*n.* 3 °shake, °quake, °tremble, °shudder, °quiver, °thrill, *frisson*, trembling, tremor, °flutter 4 ***the shivers.*** trembling, shivering, goose pimples *or* bumps, *Colloq* °the shakes, *US* the chills

shiver[2] *v.* °shatter, °fragment, °splinter, °disintegrate, °rupture, °explode, implode, smash (to smithereens), °crash

shock *v.* 1 °startle, °surprise, °stagger, °jar, °jolt, °shake (up), °stun, °numb, °paralyze, °daze, stupefy, dumbfound *or* dumfound, bowl over, °appall, °astonish, °astound, °frighten, °scare, °petrify, traumatize, °horrify, °outrage, °disgust, °nauseate, °repel, °revolt, °sicken, °upset, disquiet, °disturb, °perturb, discompose, unsettle, *Colloq* °throw, *US* throw for a loop, flabbergast, give (someone) a turn —*n.* 2 trauma, °stupor, paralysis, °prostration, °breakdown, °collapse, nervous exhaustion 3 °surprise, thunderbolt, bolt from the blue, °bombshell, °revelation, shocker, eye-opener, °jolt 4 tingle, °jolt, °impact

shocking *adj.* 1 surprising, astounding, astonishing, °amazing, °striking, stupefying, numbing, °sudden, unexpected, electrifying, °startling, *Colloq* mind-boggling, mind-blowing 2 °disgusting, °revolting, nauseating, °nauseous, sickening, °repulsive, °abominable, °hideous, °horrible, horrifying, horrific, horrid, °foul, °loathsome, °abhorrent, °ghastly, °hideous, °dreadful, unspeakable, distressing, °outrageous, appalling, °monstrous, °scandalous

shoddy *adj.* °shabby, tatty, °inferior, °poor, rubbishy, °cheap, pinchbeck, meretricious, °tawdry, °gaudy, brummagem, °plastic, °artificial, tinsel, tinselly, second-rate, trashy, junky, *Colloq* crappy, cheap-jack, °tacky, *US* chintzy

shoo *interj.* 1 Scat!, Go away!, Away with you!, Be off!, Get out!, Begone!, *Colloq* Get lost!, Beat it!, Scram! —*v.* 2 Often, ***shoo***

away or off. scare off, frighten away, drive away, force to leave

shoot *v.* **1** scoot, dart, °whisk, °speed, °bolt, °run, °race, °rush, °flash, °fly, °dash, °hurtle, °streak, scuttle, °bound, °leap, °spring, *Colloq* zip, whiz **2** °discharge, °fire, open fire; °let fly, °launch, °propel, °project, °fling, °hurl, °throw, °toss **3** °wound, °hurt, °harm, °injure; °kill, slay, assassinate, °execute, *Slang* fill *or* pump full of lead, °plug, °blast, °zap, °knock off, snuff (out) **4** °sprout, germinate, burgeon, °flourish, °grow, °spring up, mushroom, °develop —*n.* **5** °sprout, °stem, bud, °branch, °offshoot, °slip, scion, °sucker

shop *n.* **1** °store, boutique, department store **2** workshop, machine shop —*v.* **3** °betray, inform on *or* against, *Slang* peach on, rat on, snitch on, blow the whistle on **4** ***shop for.*** °buy, °purchase, °seek, °look for, °research

short *adj.* **1** °small, °little, °slight, °petite, °diminutive, °wee, °tiny, °elfin, minuscule; midget, dwarfish, squat, °dumpy, runty, stubby, °stunted, *Colloq* pint-sized, knee-high to a grasshopper, sawn-off **2** shortened, °brief, °concise, compressed, compendious, °compact, °pocket, *US* vest-pocket; °abbreviated, abridged, °cut **3** laconic, °terse, °succinct, pithy, sententious, °epigrammatic **4** °abrupt, °curt, °terse, °sharp, °blunt, °bluff, °brusque, °sharp, °offhand, °gruff, °testy, °snappish, °discourteous, uncivil, °impolite **5** °direct, °straight, straightforward, short and sweet **6** Usually, ***short of.*** °deficient (in), lacking (in), needful (of), °wanting, °inadequate, °shy (of), °low (on) **7** °brief, °limited; transitory, °temporary, °short-lived, °momentary, °quick, °transient **8** impecunious, °straitened, pinched, underfunded, °poor, penniless, °deficient **9** ***in short supply.*** °rare, °scarce, °scanty, unplentiful, °meager, °sparse, *Colloq chiefly Brit* °thin on the ground **10** ***short of.*** °before, °failing, excluding, °exclusive of, °barring, eliminating, precluding, excepting, °except for, leaving out, °apart from, setting aside —*adv.* **11** abruptly, °suddenly, peremptorily, without warning, instantly, unexpectedly, hurriedly, °hastily, °out of the blue **12** ***cut short.*** **(a)** °trim, °curtail, °shorten, °abbreviate, °cut **(b)** °stop, °cut off, °terminate, cut in on, break in on, °interrupt; °butt in **13** ***fall or come short.*** °fail, be *or* prove inadequate *or* insufficient —*n.* **14** ***in short.*** °briefly, °in a word, all in all, to make a long story short, in a nutshell **15** ***shorts.*** Bermuda shorts, knee breeches, knee pants, hot pants

shortage *n.* °deficit, deficiency, shortfall, °dearth, °scarcity, °lack, °want, paucity

shortcoming *n.* °failure, °defect, deficiency, °weakness, °frailty, °drawback, °liability, °imperfection, °weak point, °flaw

shorten *v.* **1** °cut, °curtail, cut off *or* down *or* short, °reduce, °diminish, °trim; lop off, °dock, °prune; hem **2** condense, °abridge, °abbreviate, °digest, compress

short-lived *adj.* ephemeral, evanescent, °temporary, °fleeting, transitory, °transient, °passing, fugacious, °volatile

shortly *adv.* **1** °soon, °presently, anon, before long, in a (little) while, by and by, *Archaic* ere long **2** °just, °immediately, °soon, °right **3** abruptly, °briefly, peremptorily, curtly, brusquely, °sharply, tersely, testily, gruffly, rudely, tartly

shortsighted *adj.* **1** °nearsighted, myopic, dim-sighted **2** unimaginative, unprogressive, °improvident, °imprudent, injudicious, °rash, °brash, °impulsive, °reckless, impolitic, °limited, °unwary, incautious, °careless, °thoughtless, unmindful

short-staffed *adj.* undermanned, shorthanded, understaffed

short-tempered *adj.* °testy, irascible, °short, °curt, °abrupt, °gruff, °peremptory, °bluff, °rude, °tart, acid, acidulous, °terse, °brusque, crabbed, crabby, °irritable, °touchy, °petulant, °peevish, bearish, °snappish, °waspish, shrewish, curmudgeonly, crusty, °surly, °discourteous, grouchy, °disagreeable, °caustic, acrimonious, acerbic

short-winded *adj.* short of *or* out of breath, winded, °breathless, panting, huffing (and puffing), gasping (for air *or* for breath), *Technical* dyspnoeal

shot *n.* **1** °discharge, shooting **2** bullet, ball, slug, cannonball, buckshot, pellet, °projectile, °missile **3** °attempt, °try, °opportunity, °chance, °go, °essay, °endeavor, °guess, conjecture, *Colloq* °stab, °crack, whack **4** marksman, markswoman, sharpshooter, sniper, rifleman **5** °photograph, snapshot, °picture, *Colloq* °snap, photo **6** injection, inoculation, vaccination **7** °drink, jigger, °tot, dram, °nip, °spot, °swallow, *Colloq* °finger, swig, slug, snort **8** (space) launch *or* launching **9** ***call the shots.*** run *or* direct *or* manage *or* administer *or* control things *or* affairs *or* matters, run the show, rule the roost, be in command *or* the driver's seat **10** ***like a shot.*** °quickly, °swiftly, °rapidly, speedily, hurriedly, °hastily, °at once, like a flash, °immediately, instantly, °instantaneously, *Colloq* in two shakes of a lamb's tail, like greased lightning, before you can say Jack Robinson **11** ***(not) by a long shot.*** no way, under no circumstances, °by no means, on no account, by no chance, °never **12** ***shot in the arm.*** °boost, stimulus, °encouragement, °incentive, °inducement, °provocation, motivation

shoulder *n.* **1** °side, °edge, °verge, °margin; breakdown lane **2** ***give (someone) the cold shoulder.*** °rebuff, snub, °ostracize, *Chiefly Brit* send (someone) to Coventry, cold-shoulder, put (someone) down, °reject, °exclude, freeze (someone) out, °shun, °avoid, *Colloq* °cut (dead) **3** ***put (one's or the) shoulder to the wheel.*** make every effort, make an effort, °strive, work hard, °pitch in, apply oneself, roll up one's sleeves, set *or* get to work, *Colloq* knuckle down, buckle down **4** ***rub shoulders (with).*** °associate (with), °hobnob (with), °socialize (with), consort (with), °mix (with), °fraternize (with), keep company (with) **5** ***shoulder to shoulder.*** °side by side, °united, as one, cooperatively, jointly, arm in arm, °hand in hand, in partnership **6** ***straight from the shoulder.*** °directly, straightforwardly, candidly, frankly, °honestly, °openly, unabashedly, unashamedly, unambiguously, unequivocally, plainly, bluntly, man to man, (with) no holds barred, °outright, *Colloq* without beating about the bush, without pulling (any) punches —*v.* **7** °push, shove, jostle, °hustle, thrust aside, elbow, °force **8** °support, °carry, °bear, take upon oneself, °take on, °accept, °assume

shout *v.* **1** °yell, °scream, °bellow, °bawl, °howl, °roar, °cry (out), °call (out), °whoop, *Colloq* holler —*n.* **2** °yell, °scream, °bellow, °howl, yelp, °roar, °cry, °call, °whoop, *Colloq* holler

show *v.* **1** °display, °present, °expose, °demonstrate, °indicate, °exhibit, °manifest, °(lay) bare, °disclose, °reveal, °betray, °make known, divulge, °register, °express, make clear *or* plain *or* manifest, elucidate, °clarify, °explain **2** °escort, °accompany, °conduct, usher, °lead, °guide, °direct; °steer **3** °prove, °demonstrate, °confirm, corroborate, °verify, °substantiate, °bear out, °certify, °authenticate **4** °teach, °instruct, °tell, °inform, let (someone) in on, give (someone) an idea of **5** °appear, become *or* be visible, peek through, can *or* may be seen **6** °exhibit, °reveal, °indicate, °display, °register **7** make an appearance, °appear, °show up, °arrive, °come, *Colloq* °surface **8** °represent, °symbolize, depict, °portray, °picture, °illustrate **9** °present, °play, °put on, °stage, °screen; be (being) presented *or* played *or* playing *or* put on *or* staged *or* screened **10** °grant, °accord, °bestow **11** ***show off.*** make an exhibit *or* a spectacle of, °flaunt, advertise, °display, °parade; °pose, °swagger, °posture, °boast, °brag, *US and Canadian* grandstand **12** ***show up.*** **(a)** °expose, °give away, °reveal **(b)** °stand out, be conspicuous, be noticeable, °contrast **(c)** °embarrass, °(put to) shame, °mortify, upstage, °overshadow, outshine, °eclipse **(d)** See **7,** above. —*n.* **13** °display, °demonstration, °exhibition, °exposition, °fair, °presentation, *Colloq* expo **14** °production, °presentation, °drama, °musical, °entertainment **15** °ostentation, °display, °appearance, pretentiousness, °pretension, °affectation

showdown *n.* confrontation, °climax, moment of truth, final settlement, moment of decision, *US* face-off

shower *n.* **1** sprinkle, sprinkling, drizzle **2** deluge, °torrent, °flood, °stream, barrage, overflow, °abundance, °profusion —*v.* **3** sprinkle, °rain, °pour, °spray, °bombard, °fall, °descend, °drop **4** °lavish, inundate, °overwhelm, °heap, °load (down)

showman *n.* °producer, impresario, °director

showoff *n.* °braggart, exhibitionist, swaggerer, egotist, boaster, *Colloq* blowhard, windbag

showy *adj.* °flashy, °garish, °flamboyant, °conspicuous, °ostentatious, °pretentious, bravura, °gaudy, *US* °showoff; °elaborate, °fancy, florid, °ornate, °fussy, °intricate, baroque, rococo, Byzantine, arabesque

shred *n.* **1** °scrap, °fragment, °bit, °tatter, °sliver, snippet, °rag, °remnant, °chip, °piece; atom, °trace, whit, °grain, jot *or* tittle, scintilla, °trace, °hint, °suggestion, iota, °speck —*v.* **2** °fragment, °tear (up), °tatter, °rip (up); °destroy, °demolish; °throw away, °dispose of, °scrap, *US* °trash

shrew *n.* harridan, virago, termagant, vixen, °scold, fishwife, °nag, °fury, spitfire, maenad, harpy, °witch, °hag, crone, hellcat, beldam, °bitch, banshee, Xanthippe, Thyiad *or* Thyad, *Colloq* battle-ax, dragon

shrewd *adj.* °clever, °smart, °astute, cunning, canny, °acute, °sharp, keen-minded, °keen, °quick-witted, °crafty, °artful, manipulative, °calculating, °calculated, °foxy, °sly, °wily, °perceptive, percipient, perspicacious, discerning, °wise, °sage, sagacious, long-headed, °intelligent, °ingenious, Daedalian, inventive, °resourceful

shriek *n.* **1** °scream, °cry, screech, squeal, °squawk, squall —*v.* **2** °scream, °cry, screech, squeal, °squawk, squall

shrill *adj.* high-pitched, earsplitting, °piercing, ear-piercing, °sharp, piping, screeching, screechy, °penetrating

shrink *v.* **1** wither, °shrivel (up), °contract **2** Often, ***shrink from.*** °withdraw (from), °draw back, °recoil (from), back away (from), °retreat (from), cower, °cringe, °flinch, shy away (from), wince, balk (at)

shrivel *v.* Often, ***shrivel up.*** shrink, °wrinkle, °pucker (up), curl (up), wizen, °contract; wither, °wilt, dry up, desiccate, dehydrate

shroud *v.* **1** °screen, °veil, °mask, °disguise, °camouflage, °cover, °shield, blanket, °shade, °hide, °conceal, °protect, °cloak, °swathe, °wrap, °envelop —*n.* **2** winding sheet, cerement, cerecloth, graveclothes **3** °veil, °cover, °shield, °cloak, blanket, °mask, °mantle, °pall, °screen, covering, cloud

shrubbery *n.* shrubs, planting(s), hedge(s), hedging, hedgerow, °thicket, underbrush, °brake, bracken, undergrowth, coppice *or* copse

shudder *v.* **1** °quiver, °shake, °tremble, °shiver, °jerk, convulse, °quaver, °quake; °vibrate, °rattle —*n.* **2** °quiver, °shake, °tremble, twitch, °shiver, convulsion, °paroxysm, °spasm, °quaver, °quake; vibration, °rattle

shuffle *v.* **1** °mix (up), intermix, disarrange, rearrange, interfile, intersperse, °jumble, °confuse; °shift (about), °mess up, turn topsy-turvy, °scatter, disorganize **2** scuff *or* drag (one's feet), scrape along, shamble **3** °equivocate, hem and haw, bumble, °shift, °cavil, °fence, be evasive *or* shifty, °dodge,

°niggle, split hairs, °quibble, prevaricate, *Brit* hum and haw, *Colloq* °waffle —*n.* **4** shamble, °shambling, scuffling, scraping **5** °sidestep, °evasion, °subterfuge, °trick, °dodge, °shift, prevarication, °quibble, shuffling

shun *v.* °avoid, keep *or* shy away from, °steer clear of, eschew, °shrink from, °fight shy of, run *or* turn (away) from, flee *or* escape from; °forgo, °give up; disdain, °spurn, °rebuff, °reject, cold-shoulder, give the cold shoulder to

shut *v.* **1** °close, °fasten, °secure, °shut up; °lock, °bolt, °seal **2** ***shut down.*** °close down, °discontinue, °cease, °suspend, °halt, °leave off, °shut up; switch *or* turn *or* shut off, °stop **3** ***shut in.*** **(a)** confine, seclude, °keep in, °pen, fence in, °secure **(b)** See **6(a),** below. **4** ***shut off.*** **(a)** switch *or* turn off, °shut down, *Colloq* °kill, douse, °cut (off) **(b)** °separate, °isolate, seclude, °segregate, sequester, °bar, °shut out, °cut off, *Chiefly Brit* send to Coventry **(c)** °close (off), °shut (down) **5** ***shut out.*** **(a)** °exclude, °eliminate, °bar, debar, °lock out, °ban, keep out *or* away, disallow, °prohibit **(b)** keep out, °screen, °exclude, °block out, °cut out **(c)** °screen, °mask, °hide, °conceal, °veil, °cover **6** ***shut up.*** **(a)** confine, °shut in, coop (up), °cage (in), °bottle up, °box in; °imprison, °jail, incarcerate, intern, immure **(b)** °silence, keep quiet, °stifle, °mute, °gag, shush, *Chiefly Brit* quieten **(c)** See **1,** above. **(d)** See **2,** above. —*adj.* **7** closed (up), sealed (up), locked (up), bolted, fastened

shuttle *v.* commute, °alternate

shy *adj.* **1** diffident, °coy, °bashful, °retiring, °withdrawn, withdrawing, °reserved, °timid, °meek, °modest, °sheepish, unconfident, °self-conscious, introverted, °nervous, apprehensive, timorous, *Rare* verecund **2** timorous, °cautious, °wary, chary, °leery, °guarded, °afraid, °fearful, frightened, °anxious, °worried, °suspicious, °distrustful, °cowardly, craven, uncourageous **3** missing, lacking, deficient in, °short of —*adv.* **4** ***fight shy of.*** °avoid, be unwilling *or* reluctant *or* averse *or* loath *or* loth *or* disinclined *or* not disposed; be wary *or* cautious *or* watchful

sick *adj.* **1** °nauseated, °queasy, sick to one's stomach, °squeamish, qualmish; seasick, carsick, airsick, *Colloq* green around the gills **2** °ill, unwell, °unhealthy, °sickly, °indisposed, °infirm, ailing, °diseased, afflicted, *Colloq* °under the weather, on the sick list, °poorly, laid up, not (feeling) up to snuff **3** °affected, troubled, °stricken, heartsick, °wretched, °miserable, burdened, weighed down **4** °mad, °crazy, °insane, °deranged, °disturbed, °neurotic, °unbalanced, psychoneurotic, °psychotic, *Colloq* °mental, *US* off ((one's) rocker *or* trolley) **5** °peculiar, unconventional, °strange, °weird, °odd, °bizarre, °grotesque, °macabre, °shocking, °ghoulish, °morbid, °gruesome, stomach-turning, °sadistic, masochistic, sadomasochistic, *Colloq* °kinky, °bent, far-out, *US* °off **6** sickened, shocked, °put out, °upset, appalled, °disgusted, revolted, repulsed, offended, repelled, °nauseated; annoyed, chagrined, irritated **7** Sometimes, ***sick of.*** °(sick and) tired, bored, °weary, *Colloq* fed up with

sicken *v.* **1** fall ill, take sick, °contract, be stricken by, come down with *or* catch something *or* a bug, °fail, °weaken **2** make ill *or* sick, °afflict, °affect, °disgust, °nauseate, turn one's stomach, °upset, appall *or* appal, °shock, °repel, °revolt, °repulse, °offend, make one's gorge rise; °put out

sickly *adj.* **1** See **sick, 2,** above. **2** ailing, °feeble, °delicate, °wan, °weak, pallid, °pale, °drawn, °peaked, peaky, peakish **3** °mushy, mawkish, °maudlin, cloying, insipid, °weak, °watery

side *n.* **1** Sometimes, ***sides.*** flank(s), edge(s), °verge, margin(s), °rim, °brim, °brink, border(s); bank; boundary *or* boundaries, °perimeter, °periphery, limit(s) **2** °surface, °face, °plane; facet **3** °faction, °interest, °party, °part, °sect, °camp, °(point of) view, °viewpoint, °aspect, °opinion, °standpoint, °stand, °cause, °angle, °position, °attitude, °school, °philosophy **4** °team; °string, °squad; ***American football*** and ***Association Football*** or ***Soccer*** and ***Cricket*** and ***Field Hockey*** eleven, ***Australian Rules football*** eighteen, ***Baseball*** nine, ***Basketball*** five, ***Gaelic football*** and ***rugby union*** fifteen, ***Rugby league football*** thirteen, ***Ice hockey*** six **5** °affectation, °pretension, haughtiness, °arrogance, insolence, pretentiousness, °airs **6** ***side by side.*** together, jointly, cheek by jowl **7** ***take sides.*** show preference, be partial, show favoritism —*adj.* **8** °secondary, °incidental, °subordinate, °tangential, °subsidiary, °indirect, ancillary, °marginal, lesser, °minor, unimportant, °inconsequential, inconsiderable, °insignificant **9** °auxiliary, °secondary —*v.* **10** ***side with.*** take sides with, show preference for, be partial to, show favoritism to *or* for, °support, °favor, °prefer, go in *or* along with, join ((up) with), ally with, be *or* become allied with, *Colloq US* throw in with, team up with

sidelong *adj.* °oblique, °indirect, °sideways, covert, °surreptitious

sidestep *v.* °avoid, °dodge, circumvent, skirt, °evade, °shun, °steer clear of, *Colloq* °duck

sidetrack *v.* °divert, °deflect, draw off *or* away, °distract, °turn aside; shunt

sidewalk *n.* °walk, *Chiefly Brit* pavement, footpath, footway

sideways *adv.* obliquely, laterally, edgeways, edge on, °sidelong, crabwise, indirectly, ***US and Canadian*** edgewise

sidle *v.* °edge

siege *n.* **1** blockade, encirclement, beleaguerment, besiegement —*v.* **2** lay siege to, °besiege, blockade, beleaguer, cordon off, °encircle, box *or* pen *or* shut in, °bottle up

sift *v.* **1** °strain, sieve, °riddle, °filter, °screen,

°bolt; winnow, °separate, weed out, °sort out, °select, °choose, °pick 2 °examine, °analyze, °study, °probe, °screen, °scrutinize, °investigate

sigh *v.* 1 °breathe, sough; suspire 2 ***sigh for.*** °bemoan, lament *or* mourn *or* grieve *or* weep for, °bewail; yearn *or* pine for —*n.* 3 °murmur, °exhalation, °sound; suspiration

sight *n.* 1 eyesight, °vision, eyes 2 field of view *or* of vision, range of vision, ken, °perception, °view, eyeshot, °gaze 3 °spectacle, °scene, °show; °rarity, °marvel, °wonder, °phenomenon; °pageant 4 °mess, °disaster, eyesore, °monstrosity, *Colloq* °fright, °atrocity 5 ***catch sight of.*** °spot, °notice, descry, °spy, espy, glance at, (catch a) glimpse (of), (get a) look *or* peep *or* peek at, *Colloq* take a gander at, get a look-see at, *Slang* get a load of, *US* glom, °pipe 6 ***out of sight.*** **(a)** °remote, °distant, far away, unseeable, °imperceptible, °invisible **(b)** °unusual, °rare, °extraordinary, °outrageous, °imaginative, awe-inspiring, °incredible, °shocking, °unreal, °moving, jolting, *Colloq* °neat, °cool, *Brit* °brilliant, brill —*v.* 7 °look, °view, °(take) aim, °peer, °peek, °peep, draw a bead 8 °spot, °see, °catch sight of, °mark, °observe, °behold, °view, °distinguish, discern, °identify, °note, °notice, °remark, glimpse, descry, espy, °spy

sightseer *n.* °tourist, °traveler, globe-trotter, *Colloq* rubberneck(er), *Brit* tripper, day-tripper

sign *n.* 1 °token, °symbol, °indication, °mark, °signal, °indicator; °notice 2 °movement, °gesture, °motion, °signal, °cue, gesticulation 3 °trace, °indication, °evidence, °mark, °clue, °hint, °suggestion, °vestige 4 °device, °mark, °symbol, °representation, °emblem, trademark, badge, °brand, °stamp, °seal, ideogram, ideograph, lexigram, phonogram, grapheme, hieroglyph, cartouche, rebus, logo(type), colophon, ensign, °standard, °banner, °flag; monogram, initials, cipher *or* cypher 5 signboard, °advertisement, placard, °poster, *US* broadside; shingle, °notice, °announcement 6 °omen, augury, °warning, forewarning, °foreboding, portent, °indication, (hand)writing on the wall, °prophecy, prognostication, foreshadowing —*v.* 7 autograph, put one's signature on *or* to, inscribe, countersign, °endorse, °witness, put *or* set one's hand to, °mark; sign on the dotted line; *Colloq US* put one's John Hancock on *or* to 8 ***sign away.*** °forgo, °relinquish, °give up, °abandon, abandon *or* quit claim to, °waive, °release, °surrender, °dispose of, °sacrifice, °get rid of 9 ***sign off.*** °close down, °discontinue (broadcasting, writing a letter, etc.) 10 ***sign on or up.*** **(a)** °enroll, °enlist, °sign up (for), °register, volunteer, °join (up), °contract **(b)** °enroll, °enlist, °hire, °employ, put under contract, °retain, °engage, °take on, *Colloq* take on board, bring aboard 11 ***sign over.*** °assign, consign, °transfer, °make over, °deliver, °give, °donate, present, °dispose of, °turn over

signal *n.* 1 See **sign, 1,** above. 2 °incitement, stimulus, °spur, °impetus, goad, °prick —*adj.* 3 °remarkable, °conspicuous, °striking, °extraordinary, °unusual, °unique, °singular, °special, °noteworthy, °notable, °exceptional, °significant, °important, °outstanding, °momentous, consequential, °weighty —*v.* 4 °motion, °indicate, °gesture, gesticulate, °communicate, °announce, °notify; whistle, wink, °blink, °nod, °beckon, °wave, °sign

significance *n.* 1 °meaning, °sense, signification, denotation, °message, °idea, °point, °import, purport, °implication, portent, °content, °pith, °essence; °gist, °drift, °vein, °impression, connotation 2 °importance, °weight, weightiness, consequence, °moment, °relevance, value

significant *adj.* 1 °important, °weighty, °momentous, consequential, °critical, °substantial, substantive, °noteworthy, °notable, valuable, valued, °meritorious, °outstanding, °impressive, °historic, °relevant, °signal 2 °meaningful, °eloquent, pithy, °expressive, °pregnant, °suggestive, °informative

signify *v.* 1 °sign, °signal, °indicate, °communicate, °make known, convey, °symbolize, betoken, °represent, °express, °announce, °declare, °denote, °say, °mean, °specify; connote, °intimate, °suggest, °reveal, °disclose, °impart 2 °matter, °count, be significant *or* important *or* consequential, be of significance *or* of importance *or* of consequence, carry weight, °impress, °stand out, deserve *or* merit consideration

silence *n.* 1 °quiet, quietness, stillness, soundlessness, noiselessness, °calm, calmness, °hush, quietude, tranquillity, °peace, peacefulness, °serenity 2 speechlessness, muteness, dumbness, reticence, taciturnity, uncommunicativeness —*v.* 3 °quiet, °mute, °hush, °still, shush, °calm, °tranquilize, soothe, *Chiefly Brit* quieten 4 °mitigate, °temper, mollify, take the sting out of, propitiate, pacify, °blunt, °suppress, °repress, °restrain, °subdue, draw the fangs *or* teeth of, °inhibit, °put down, °damp, °mute, °squelch, °quash, emasculate, muzzle, °muffle, °shut off, °gag, °stifle, °smother, °deaden (the effect of)

silent *adj.* 1 °quiet, °still, soundless, °noiseless, °tranquil, hushed, shushed, °mute; °calm, °serene, placid, °peaceful, pacific, unagitated, unruffled, untroubled, undisturbed, *Literary* stilly 2 uncommunicative, °mute, closemouthed, °taciturn, °reticent, °reserved, °mum, °tight-lipped, °secretive 3 unspeaking, unspoken, °mute, unexpressed, °tacit, °understood, °implicit, implied, unstated, unsaid 4 °inactive, nonparticipating, °passive, quiescent, *Brit* sleeping 5 unpronounced, unuttered, not sounded, *Technical* aphonic

silently *adv.* °quietly, soundlessly, noiselessly, with catlike tread, as quietly as a mouse, stealthily; wordlessly, speechlessly, mutely

silhouette *n.* °outline, °profile, contour, °form, °figure, °shape, °shadow, configuration, °periphery, °perimeter

silky *adj.* silken, silklike, °delicate, °sleek, °soft, °smooth, satiny, °shiny, °glossy, °lustrous, *Technical* sericeous

silly *adj.* **1** °senseless, °nonsensical, °absurd, °ridiculous, °ludicrous, laughable, risible, asinine, °inane, °preposterous, idiotic, °childish, °puerile, °foolish, °foolhardy, °irresponsible, °unreasonable, illogical, irrational, °pointless, fatuous, °stupid, unwise, imbecilic, °crazy, °mad, °insane **2** stunned, stupefied, °dazed, °giddy, °dizzy, muzzy, benumbed —*n.* **3** °fool, nincompoop, idiot, dunce, ninny, °half-wit, simpleton, numskull *or* numbskull, dimwit, booby, °dolt, jackass, °twit, blockhead, bonehead, nitwit, ignoramus, °clod, *US* thimble-wit, *Colloq* °dope, °dummy, knucklehead, goose, °drip, silly-billy, *Brit* clot, *Slang US and Canadian* °jerk, nerd

silt *n.* **1** °deposit, °sediment, alluvium, °ooze, °sludge —*v.* **2** Usually, ***silt up or over.*** become clogged *or* choked *or* obstructed *or* dammed *or* congested

silver *n.* **1** silverware, °sterling, °(silver) plate; cutlery, *US* flatware; holloware **2** °white, grayish, whitish-gray, grayish-white, °gray —*adj.* **3** silvery, °shiny, shining, °polished, burnished, °lustrous, °pearly, nacreous, °bright, gleaming, *Literary and heraldry* argent; °white **4** silvery, silver-toned, silver-tongued, °sweet, °pretty, euphonious, °melodious, mellifluous, mellifluent, dulcet, °musical

similar *adj.* **1** °like, almost identical, comparable, °equivalent, nearly the same; °alike **2** ***be similar to.*** °resemble, be like, correspond to, compare favorably with

simmer *v.* **1** °seethe, °stew, cook, °boil, °bubble **2** °chafe, °seethe, °stew, steam, °smolder, °fume, °rage, °burn, *Colloq US* do a slow burn **3** ***simmer down.*** calm *or* cool down, cool off, calm oneself, become quiet, control oneself, get control of *or* over oneself, *Chiefly Brit* quieten down, *Slang* cool it

simple *adj.* **1** uncomplicated, °plain, uninvolved, °unsophisticated, understandable, °intelligible, °(easily) understood, comprehensible, °clear, lucid, straightforward, °easy (as ABC), °elementary, °basic **2** °plain, °unadorned, undecorated, unembellished, °basic, °fundamental, °elementary, °elemental, °mere, unostentatious, unassuming, unpretentious, °modest, °classic, uncluttered, °stark, °clean, °severe, austere, °Spartan, °homely; °unvarnished, °naked, °honest **3** °sincere, °frank, °candid, °open, °unaffected, uncomplicated, unpretentious, straightforward, °aboveboard, simple-hearted, uncontrived, °direct, °upright, °square, °forthright, foursquare, °righteous, °honest, naive *or* naïve *or* naïf, guileless, °artless, undesigning, °childlike, °ingenuous, °unsophisticated, °innocent, °green **4** °unsophisticated, naive *or* naïve *or* naïf, °slow, slow-witted, °stupid, °thick, thick-headed, simple-minded, °feebleminded, oafish, bovine, °dense, °obtuse, °dull, dull-witted, witless, °half-witted, brainless, °backward, imbecilic *or chiefly Brit* imbecile, cretinous, *Colloq* °dumb, moronic **5** °lowly, °humble, °inferior, °mean, °base, subservient, °common, °subordinate

simplicity *n.* **1** uncomplicatedness; understandability, comprehensibility, lucidity, straightforwardness, °clarity, intelligibility, decipherability **2** plainness, cleanness, °clarity, °severity, starkness, austereness, asceticism, °restraint, bareness, °purity **3** °sincerity, openness, artlessness, °candor, guilelessness, frankness, unsophisticatedness, ingenuousness, straightforwardness, forthrightness, unaffectedness, unpretentiousness, modesty, naivety *or* naiveté *or* naïveté; plainness, directness, inelegance, rusticity, pastoralism **4** °stupidity, slow-wittedness, thickheadedness, simple-mindedness, feeblemindedness, oafishness, cloddishness, obtuseness, dullness, dull-wittedness, witlessness, half-wittedness, imbecility, brainlessness

simplify *v.* °clarify, °clear up, make easy, °paraphrase, °explain, explicate, disentangle, untangle, unravel, streamline

simply *adv.* **1** °merely, °barely, purely, °only, solely, °just, °entirely, fully, °totally, °wholly, °altogether, °absolutely, °really **2** °totally, °completely, °altogether, °entirely, °just, plainly, °obviously, °really, unreservedly, unqualifiedly **3** naively *or* naïvely, artlessly, guilelessly, °openly, innocently, ingenuously, unaffectedly, unpretentiously, plainly, °naturally **4** plainly, modestly, starkly, °severely, sparely, sparsely, austerely, ascetically **5** distinctly, unambiguously, plainly, °obviously, unmistakably *or* unmistakeably

simultaneous *adj.* coincident, coinciding, concurrent, contemporaneous, synchronous; °contemporary

sin *n.* **1** trespass, °transgression, °offense, °wrong, impiety, °misdeed, profanation, desecration, iniquity, °evil, °devilry, °sacrilege, °crime, infraction, °misdeed, dereliction, °infringement, °violation, misdemeanor, °fault, °foible, °peccadillo **2** wickedness, sinfulness, °vice, corruption, ungodliness, badness, °evil, wrongfulness, iniquity, iniquitousness, immorality, depravity, impiety, irreverence, impiousness, °sacrilege —*v.* **3** °transgress, °offend, °fall (from grace), °lapse, °go wrong, °stray, go astray, °err, *Biblical or archaic* trespass

sincere *adj.* °honest, °truthful, °true, veracious, °genuine, °heartfelt, true-hearted, undissembling, unfeigned, °open, °(open and) aboveboard, straightforward, °direct, °frank, °candid, guileless, °artless, *Colloq* upfront, °on the level, on the up and up

sincerely *adv.* °truly, °honestly, °really, wholeheartedly, candidly, frankly, unequivocally, °seriously, earnestly, genuinely, °deeply, fervently

sincerity *n.* °honesty, truthfulness, straightforwardness, openness, forthrightness, frankness, °candor, candidness, seriousness, genuineness, uprightness

sinew *n.* **1** ligament, tendon; muscle, thew **2** Usually, ***sinews.*** °strength, °force, °power, °energy, °brawn, °vigor, °might, °stamina, °vitality

sinewy *adj.* °strong, °powerful, °muscular, °mighty, °stout, °wiry, °robust, °tough; strapping, °brawny, °burly

sinful *adj.* °corrupt, °evil, °wicked, °bad, °wrong, wrongful, iniquitous, °vile, °base, °profane, °immoral, °profligate, depraved, °criminal, °sacrilegious, °ungodly, unholy, demonic, irreligious, piacular, °impious, °irreverent

sing *v.* **1** °chant, intone, carol, vocalize, trill, croon, °pipe, °chirp, warble; chorus; yodel **2** whistle, °pipe, °peep **3** °tell, °tattle, °name names, *Slang* rat, snitch, squeal, blow the whistle, peach, °spill the beans

singe *v.* char, °blacken, sear, °scorch, °burn

singer *n.* °vocalist, soloist, songster, crooner, chanteuse, nightingale, °minstrel, troubadour, balladeer, caroler, chorister, choir boy *or* girl *or* member, chorus boy *or* girl *or* member, *Colloq* songbird, canary, thrush

single *adj.* **1** °unmarried, unwed, °unattached, °free; °celibate **2** °singular, °individual, °distinct, °solitary; °one, °only, °sole, lone, °unique, °isolated **3** °separate, °distinct, °individual, °solitary —*v.* **4** ***single out.*** °select, °choose, °pick, °separate, take *or* put *or* set aside *or* apart, °distinguish, cull, °segregate, fix *or* fasten on

single-handed *adj.* **1** °solo, lone, °solitary, °independent, unaided, unassisted —*adv.* **2** single-handedly, by oneself, °alone, °solo, on one's own, independently

single-minded *adj.* dedicated, °devoted, °resolute, °steadfast, persevering, °firm, °determined, dogged, unswerving, unwavering, °tireless, °purposeful

singly *adv.* one at a time, °separately, °individually, one by one, successively, one after the other, seriatim

singular *adj.* **1** °unusual, °different, atypical, °eccentric, °extraordinary, °remarkable, °special, uncommon, °strange, °odd, °peculiar, °bizarre, °outlandish, °curious, °queer, *outré*, °offbeat, *Colloq* far-out **2** °outstanding, °prominent, °eminent, °preeminent, °noteworthy, °significant, °important, °conspicuous, °particular, °notable, °signal, °exceptional, °superior **3** lone, °isolated, °single, °separate, uncommon, °rare, °unique, °distinct, one-of-a-kind

singularity *n.* **1** individuality, distinctiveness, uniqueness, idiosyncrasy **2** °eccentricity, °peculiarity, strangeness, oddness, queerness, outlandishness, uncommonness **3** *Technical* black hole

sinister *adj.* **1** °fateful, °inauspicious, unfavorable, °foreboding, °threatening, °menacing, minacious, minatory *or* minatorial, °portentous, °ominous, unpropitious, °disastrous, °dark, °gloomy **2** °evil, °bad, °corrupt, °base, malevolent, °malignant, malign, °harmful, pernicious, treacherous, nefarious, °wicked, diabolic(al), baleful, °villainous, insidious, °sneaky, furtive, underhand(ed)

sink *v.* **1** °founder, °submerge, °go down, °go under, °plunge, °descend, be engulfed **2** °subside, °cave in, °collapse, °settle, °drop, °fall in, °go down, °slip away **3** °descend, °go down, °drop, °fall, move down *or* downward(s), go down to *or* on **4** °decline, °weaken, °worsen, °degenerate, °subside, °deteriorate, °flag, °fail, °diminish, °die, °expire; languish; *Colloq* go downhill **5** °disappear, vanish, fade away, °evaporate; °set, °go down, °descend, °drop **6** °settle, °precipitate, °descend, °drop **7** °bore, °put down, °drill, °dig, °excavate, °drive **8** °submerge, °immerse, °plunge **9** °stoop, °bend, °get, °go, lower *or* humble oneself **10** °invest, °venture, °risk, °put **11** ***sink in.*** be understood, °penetrate, °register, make an impression on, get through to —*n.* **12** basin, washbasin, washbowl, lavabo; *Church* font, stoup, piscina **13** cesspool, cesspit, °pit, hellhole, den of iniquity, sinkhole, *Colloq* °dive

sinking *adj.* **1** °queasy, °nervous, uneasy, °tense, apprehensive, unquiet, °fretful, °shaky, jittery, °jumpy, °anxious **2** depressed, °dejected, °miserable, dolorous, °doleful, °mournful, °forlorn, woeful, °desolate, despairing, °stricken, heavy-laden

sinner *n.* °transgressor, wrongdoer, °miscreant, °offender, evildoer, malefactor, °reprobate, *Biblical or archaic* trespasser

sip *v.* **1** °taste, °sample, sup —*n.* **2** °taste, °sample, ***soupçon,*** °drop, °bit, °swallow, °mouthful, spoonful, thimbleful, °nip, dram, *Colloq* swig

siren *n.* **1** whistle, warble, wailer, horn, foghorn; °signal, °alarm, °warning, °alert, tocsin **2** °temptress, °seductress, enchantress, °charmer, sorceress, *femme fatale*, Circe, Lorelei, *Colloq* vamp, *US* mantrap

sissy *n.* °milksop, mama's boy, mummy's boy, namby-pamby, °weakling, °baby, crybaby, mollycoddle, *US* milquetoast, *Colloq* softy, *Brit* °wet

sit *v.* **1** be seated, °settle, sit down, take a seat, °rest, *Colloq* take the weight *or* a load off one's feet **2** hold a session, be in session, °assemble, °meet, convene; °gather, °get together **3** Often, ***sit on.*** have *or* hold *or* occupy a seat (on), °participate (in), be a member (of) **4** °remain, °stay, °lie, °rest; °relax, mark time, °abide, °dwell **5** °seat, °contain, °hold, °accommodate, have seats *or* seating for, have room *or* space *or* capacity for seating **6** ***sit in.*** **(a)** Often, ***sit in on.*** play, °join (in), °participate (in), take part (in); °observe, °watch **(b)** °substitute, °fill in, °stand in, °double, *Colloq* °cover, sub,

US pinch-hit **7** ***sit out.*** wait out, outwait, outstay, °outlast, outlive, last through, live through **8** ***sit tight.*** °wait, hang back, °hold back, be patient, bide (one's) time, play a waiting game, take no action, °delay, temporize, *Colloq* hold (one's) horses **9** ***sit up.*** °awaken, pay attention, °notice, become alert *or* interested *or* concerned **10** ***sit (with).*** Often, ***sit well or right (with).*** agree with, be agreeable to; °seem, °appear, °look

site *n.* **1** °location, °place, °plot, plat, °spot, °locale, °area, °milieu, °neighborhood, locality, purlieus, °placement, °position; °situation, °orientation —*v.* **2** °locate, °position, °place, °put, °situate, install *or* instal

situate *v.* place in a position *or* situation *or* location, °place, °position, °locate, °set, °spot, °put, install *or* instal

situation *n.* **1** °place, °position, °location, °spot, °site, °locale, °setting **2** °state (of affairs), °condition, °circumstances, °case, °status (quo), lay of the land, °picture; °plight, °predicament; *Colloq* ball game; kettle of fish **3** °position, °place, °job, °employment, °post, *Colloq* berth

size *n.* **1** °magnitude, largeness, bigness, °bulk, °extent, °scope, °range, dimensions, °proportions, measurement(s), °expanse, °area, square footage, °volume, °mass, °weight; hugeness, immensity, greatness, vastness, °enormousness —*v.* **2** dimension, °measure **3** ***size up.*** assess, °judge, °evaluate, °measure, take the measure of, appraise, assay, make an estimate of, °estimate, value, °gauge, °rate

skeptic *n.* doubter, questioner, doubting Thomas, disbeliever, nullifidian, agnostic, scoffer, cynic

skeptical *adj.* doubting, dubious, °doubtful, questioning, disbelieving, °incredulous, agnostic, scoffing, cynical, mistrustful, °distrustful

skepticism *n.* °doubt, dubiety, dubiousness, doubtfulness, disbelief, incredulity, incredulousness, agnosticism, cynicism, °mistrust, °distrust, mistrustfulness, distrustfulness

sketchily *adv.* cursorily, superficially, incompletely, patchily, °roughly, perfunctorily, skimpily, °vaguely, imperfectly, crudely, °hastily, hurriedly

sketchy *adj.* °cursory, °superficial, °incomplete, patchy, °rough, °perfunctory, skimpy, °imperfect, °crude, °hasty, °hurried, °vague, ill-defined, °fuzzy, °indistinct, °inexact, °imprecise, °unrefined, unpolished, rough-hewn, unfinished

skill *n.* **1** °talent, °ability, °aptitude, expertness, °expertise, °facility, skillfulness, °art, artistry, cleverness, adeptness, adroitness, mastery, °dexterity, handiness, °ingenuity, °experience, °proficiency, °finesse, °knack, quickness, deftness, °technique **2** °accomplishment, °forte, °strength, °gift, °capability, know-how, °faculty

skillful *adj.* skilled, °accomplished, °adept, adroit, °dexterous, °expert, °proficient, masterly, °masterful, °gifted, apt, °able, °clever, °talented, °capable, °professional, trained, °qualified, °experienced, °practiced

skim *v.* **1** Often, ***skim off.*** °separate, cream, scoop *or* ladle off, °take off, °remove **2** Often, ***skim through or over.*** °scan, flip *or* thumb *or* leaf through, skip through, glance at *or* through, °dip into **3** °soar, °glide, skate, °slide, °sail, °fly

skin *n.* **1** epidermis, derma, integument, °hide, °pelt, °fleece, °fell **2** °coat, °film, coating, crust, incrustation, husk, °peel, °rind, °outside, °shell, pellicle, °veneer, outer layer, lamina, overlay —*v.* **3** flay, °strip, decorticate, excoriate **4** °peel, °hull, husk, °shell **5** abrade, °scrape, graze, bark

skin-deep *adj.* °superficial, °shallow, °surface, °slight, °external, unimportant, trivial, unprofound, °insubstantial

skinny *adj.* °thin, underweight, °gaunt, bony, scraggy, lank, °lanky, gangly, gangling, °rawboned, °meager, °spare, °emaciated, half-starved, undernourished, pinched, hollow-cheeked, wasted, shrunken

skip *v.* **1** °leap, °cavort, °caper, gambol, °frisk, °prance, °jump, °hop, romp, °bound, °dance **2** °omit, °leave out, °pass by, °overlook, °pass over, °avoid, °ignore, °disregard, °steer clear of, °cut —*n.* **3** °leap, °cavort, °caper, gambol, °frisk, °prance, °jump, °bound, °dance, °hop, romp **4** lacuna, °gap, °omission, avoidance, °disregard; °miss, *Colloq* go-by

skipper *n.* captain, °master, commander; °boss, °leader, °chief

skirmish *n.* **1** °fight, °encounter, °fray, °brush, °clash, °engagement, confrontation, °showdown, °combat, °battle, °conflict, °struggle, set-to, °contest, °scrimmage, °fracas, tussle, melee *or* mêlée, *Law* affray, *Colloq* °scrap, dust-up, *Brit* scrum —*v.* **2** °fight, °clash, °struggle, °battle, tussle

sky *n.* **1** heaven(s), skies, arch *or* vault of heaven, °firmament, °(wild) blue (yonder), ether, *Literary or archaic* welkin, empyrean, azure **2** ***to the skies.*** °overly, excessively, extravagantly, fulsomely, profusely, inordinately, °highly

slab *n.* °slice, °wedge, °piece, hunk, chunk, tranche, *Colloq Brit* wodge

slack *adj.* **1** °remiss, °careless, °indolent, negligent, °lax, °lazy, °idle, neglectful, °delinquent, °inattentive, otiose, dilatory, cunctatory, °laggard, easygoing, °slothful, sluggish, °lethargic, °shiftless, do-nothing, fainéant, *Colloq* asleep at the switch *or* the wheel, asleep on the job **2** °loose, °flabby, flaccid, °soft, °limp, baggy, drooping, droopy, bagging, sagging, floppy —*v.* **3** Often, ***slack or slacken off or up.*** **(a)** let go, let run, °let loose, °release, slacken, °loose, °loosen, °relax, ease (out *or* off), °let up (on) **(b)** slow (down *or* up), °delay, reduce speed, °tire, °decline, °decrease, °diminish, °moderate, abate, °weaken **4** °neglect, °shirk, *Colloq Brit* skive (off), *US* goof off, *Chiefly*

military goldbrick, *Taboo slang US* fuck the dog —*n.* 5 °lull, °pause, °inactivity, cutback, lessening, reduction, abatement, drop-off, downturn, diminution, °decline, falloff, °decrease, dwindling 6 °room, looseness, slackness, °play, °give
slacker *n.* shirker, °loafer, °idler, *Slang Brit* skiver, *Military* scrimshanker, *US* goldbrick, goof-off
slake *v.* °satisfy, °quench, °gratify, allay, assuage, °ease, °relieve
slam *v.* 1 °shut, fling closed, bang 2 °crash, smash, smack, °dash, °ram, bang, °slap 3 °criticize, °attack, °vilify, pillory, °run down, °disparage, denigrate, °denounce, °put down, flay, pounce on *or* upon, *Colloq* shoot down, °pan, *Chiefly Brit* slate
slander *n.* 1 defamation (of character), calumny, obloquy, misrepresentation, °slur, vilification; °libel —*v.* 2 defame, calumniate, °disparage, °slur, traduce, malign, °smear, °vilify, decry; °libel
slanderous *adj.* defamatory, calumnious, disparaging, °smear, deprecatory, depreciative, discrediting, decrying; libellous *or* libelous
slant *n.* 1 °angle, °viewpoint, °(point of) view, °standpoint, °approach, °twist, °idea, °aspect, °attitude 2 °bias, °prejudice, °partiality, one-sidedness, °turn, °bent 3 °slope, °incline, °tilt, °ramp, gradient, °pitch, °lean, °leaning, deflection, °angle, °rake, °cant, camber —*v.* 4 °tilt, °angle, °incline, °pitch, °cant, °slope, °bend, °lean, °list, °tip, bevel, °shelve 5 °bend, °distort, °deviate, °twist, °warp, °color, °weight, °bias
slap *v.* 1 smack, cuff, whack, °rap; °spank; *Colloq* clout, wallop 2 °flap, slat, °whip, °beat, bat 3 °fling, °toss, °splash, °hurl, °throw, °sling —*n.* 4 smack, °blow, cuff, whack, °rap, *Colloq* clout, wallop 5 Often, ***slap in the face.*** °reprimand, °reproof, °rebuff, °criticism, censure, °rebuke, °shot, °thrust, °attack, °put-down, °insult, °offense, smack in the eye —*adv.* 6 ***slap on.*** °exactly, °directly, °precisely, °straight, °point-blank, °right, squarely, °plumb, smack, bang
slash *v.* 1 °cut, °gash, °hack, °score, °slit, °knife, °lacerate; °wound; °scar 2 °lash, °whip, °scourge, °flog, °beat, horsewhip, flail, flagellate, flay, thrash, *Colloq* lambaste *or* lambast 3 °cut, °reduce, °decrease, °drop, °mark down, °trim, °lower —*n.* 4 °cut, °gash, °incision, °slit, °slice, °gouge, °rent, °rip, °score, laceration 5 °cut, reduction, °decrease, markdown
slattern *n.* slut, °tramp, sloven, trollop, hussy, °wanton, whore, °prostitute, harlot, streetwalker, lady of the evening, woman of ill repute, loose *or* fallen woman, *trottoise, Colloq* call girl, pro, *Slang* °tart, hooker, hustler, *US* roundheel(s), bimbo
slaughter *n.* 1 butchery, butchering, *Rare* abattage 2 °massacre, °killing, °bloodshed, blood bath, °murder, homicide, manslaughter, °carnage, extermination, °execution, liquidation, slaying, bloodletting, butchery, pogrom, genocide, mass murder *or* execution *or* extermination, °sacrifice, hecatomb —*v.* 3 °butcher, °kill, °murder, slay, °execute, °exterminate, °massacre, put to the sword, put to death, liquidate, °destroy 4 °defeat, °beat, win (out) over, vanquish, °overcome, °overwhelm, smash, °crush, thrash, °destroy, °rout, °upset, trounce, *Colloq* clobber
slave *n.* 1 lackey *or* lacquey, scullion, serf, slave girl, slaveling, odalisque *or* odalisk, bondservant, bondslave, bondsman *or* bondman, bondswoman *or* bondwoman, bondmaid, vassal, thrall, *Disparaging chiefly Brit* skivvy, *Archaic* esne, helot, hierodule, *Colloq Brit* slavey 2 drudge, workhorse, °hack, °grind, toiler, °laborer, *Chiefly Brit* °fag, dogsbody, *Colloq US* gofer —*v.* 3 °labor, toil, moil, °grind, grub, drudge, °sweat, burn the midnight oil, lucubrate, work one's fingers to the bone, work like a Trojan *or* a horse, *Brit* skivvy
slaver[1] *v.* 1 drool, salivate, slobber, °drivel, dribble, °spit, *Dialect* slabber —*n.* 2 drool, saliva, °drivel, dribble, °spit, spittle, *Dialect* slabber 3 °nonsense, °drivel, °rubbish, twaddle, piffle
slaver[2] *n.* 1 slave ship, slave trader 2 blackbirder, slave trader; white slaver, °pimp, panderer
slavery *n.* 1 enslavement, °bondage, thralldom, thrall, enthrallment, °servitude, serfdom, vassalage, yoke; subjugation, °captivity, *Historical US* peculiar institution 2 slave trade, blackbirding 3 toil, moil, °drudgery, travail, °grind, °strain, °(hard) labor
sleazy *adj.* 1 unsubstantial *or* insubstantial, °flimsy, °slight, °shabby, °poor, gimcrack, jerry-built, °tawdry, °cheap, tatty, °ramshackle, °rickety, °slipshod, *Colloq US* chintzy 2 °disreputable, low-class, low-grade, squalid, °dirty, °base, °seedy, °sordid, °contemptible, trashy, °run-down, °mean, °cheap, *Colloq* crummy, slummy, *Slang* crappy, cheesy
sleek *adj.* 1 °smooth, °slick, velvety, °lustrous, °shiny, shining, °glossy, °silky, silken 2 °graceful, °trim, °streamlined 3 °suave, unctuous, °slimy, fawning, °oily, °specious, °hypocritical, *Chiefly Brit* smarmy
sleep *v.* 1 °doze, °(take a) nap, catnap, °rest, °repose, slumber, drowse, drop *or* nod off, be in the Land of Nod, be in the arms of Morpheus, snore, *Colloq* snooze, saw wood, catch a few Z's, take *or* have a zizz, catch forty winks —*n.* 2 °nap, °doze, slumber, °rest, siesta, *Colloq* forty winks, snooze, zizz, beauty sleep
sleepless *adj.* 1 °restless, °wakeful, insomniac, °disturbed 2 °alert, watchful, °vigilant, unsleeping
sleepwalking *n.* 1 noctambulism, somnambulism, noctambulation, somnambulation —*adj.* 2 noctambulant, somnambulant
sleepy *adj.* 1 °drowsy, somnolent, °tired, °nodding, dozy, °lethargic, °torpid, slumberous, sluggish, oscitant; °weary, °fatigued, °exhausted, *Colloq* dead on one's feet,

°(knocked) out, °beat, *US and Canadian* pooped **2** °boring, °inactive, °dull, °quiet, soporific, °slow, sluggish

slender *adj.* **1** °slim, °lean, °willowy, sylphlike, svelte, lissom *or* lissome, lithe, °graceful, snake-hipped, °thin, °spare, °slight, °lanky **2** °slim, °narrow, °slight, °poor, °unlikely, °small, °little, °scanty, °remote, °meager, °weak, °feeble **3** °slim, °slight, °little, °scanty, °inadequate, °insufficient, °insignificant, °trifling

sleuth *n.* °(private) detective, (private) investigator, *US* P.I., *Colloq* private eye, sherlock, °snoop, *Brit* tec *or* 'tec, *US* hawkshaw, *Slang US* dick, shamus, *US and Canadian* gumshoe

slice *n.* **1** °slab, °piece, rasher, collop, shaving, layer, *Cookery* scallop, escalope, scaloppine (*pl. of scaloppina*) *or* scaloppini (*pl.*) **2** °portion, °piece, °part, °wedge, °share, °sliver, °helping **3** spatula; slicer —*v.* **4** °cut, °carve, °divide

slick *adj.* **1** °smooth, °sleek, °glossy, °silky, silken, °shiny, shining, °glassy, °slippery **2** °smooth, urbane, °suave, smooth-spoken, °glib, °smug, °plausible; sycophantic, unctuous, *Colloq* smarmy **3** °smooth, °clever, °skillful, adroit, °dexterous, °professional, °ingenious, °imaginative, inventive, °creative, *Colloq* °neat **4** °superficial, °shallow, meretricious, °specious, °glib —*v.* **5** Often, ***slick down.*** °smooth, plaster down, grease, °oil

slicker *n.* **1** confidence man *or* woman, °cheat, °swindler, mountebank, *Colloq* con man, city slicker **2** oilskin (raincoat)

slide *v.* **1** °glide, °slip; °coast, °skim, glissade, skate, °plane, skid, toboggan, °slither **2** °creep, °steal, °slip, °slink, °move **3** °decline, °decrease, °drop, °fall **4** ***let slide.*** °forget, °ignore, °neglect, gloss *or* pass over, pay no heed *or* mind (to) —*n.* **5** landslide, earthslip, avalanche, mudslide

slight *adj.* **1** °small, °little, °minor, °negligible, °unlikely, °insignificant, °inconsequential **2** °trifling, °tiny, °slender, °minute, infinitesimal; °trace, °perceptible **3** °small, °short, °petite, °thin, °slim, °slender, °delicate, °diminutive, °tiny, °miniature, bantam, °wee, °pocket, pocket-sized, *US* vest-pocket, *Colloq* pint-sized **4** insubstantial *or* unsubstantial, °weak, °feeble, °delicate, °dainty, °frail, °unstable, °fragile, °flimsy, lightly made *or* built, °precarious, °inadequate, °rickety, °insecure —*v.* **5** °disregard, °ignore, disdain, °scorn, snub, °rebuff, °cut, °disrespect, cold-shoulder **6** °insult, °offend, affront, °mortify, °diminish, °minimize, °depreciate, °disparage —*n.* **7** °insult, affront, °slur, °indignity, °outrage, offense, °disrespect **8** inattention, °neglect, °disregard, °indifference, snub, cold shoulder, coldness, ill-treatment

slightly *adv.* a little, °somewhat, to a certain *or* slight *or* minor extent *or* degree *or* measure, marginally

slim *adj.* **1** See **slender, 1,** above. **2** See **slender, 2, 3,** above. —*v.* **3** °reduce, lose *or* shed weight, °diet, *Chiefly US* slenderize

slimy *adj.* **1** oozy, °slippery, mucky, squashy, squishy, viscous, °sticky, gluey, mucilaginous, uliginous, °oily, oleaginous, glutinous, mucous, °clammy, °mushy, *US* squushy *or* squooshy, *Colloq* °gooey, gunky, *US* gloppy **2** °slippery, unctuous, °obsequious, sycophantic, toadying, °servile, creeping, °groveling, abject, *Colloq* smarmy

sling *v.* **1** °toss, °throw, °cast, °propel, °hurl, °shy, °fling, °fire, °shoot, °pitch, °let fly, °launch, °heave, °lob, *Colloq* chuck —*n.* **2** slingshot, catapult, trebuchet *or* trebucket **3** °support, strap, °band; °belt

slink *v.* °sneak, °creep, °steal, °prowl, skulk

slip[1] *v.* **1** °slide, skid, °glide, °slither **2** °stumble, lose one's footing *or* balance, miss one's footing, °trip; °fall, °tumble **3** Often, ***slip up.*** °err, °blunder, make a mistake, °miscalculate, °go wrong, °botch (up), *Slang* °screw up **4** ***let slip.*** °reveal, divulge, °blurt out, °leak, °let out, °disclose, °expose, *Colloq* come out with, °blab **5** ***slip away or by.*** °pass, °elapse, vanish, °go by **6** ***slip away or off or out.*** °escape, °disappear, °leave, vanish, °steal, go *or* run away *or* off *or* out, °break away, °get away, give (someone) the slip; sneak away *or* off *or* out **7** ***slip in.*** °enter, °get in, sneak in; °put in —*n.* **8** °blunder, °error, °mistake, °fault, °oversight, slip of the tongue *or* pen, inadvertence, °indiscretion, °impropriety, °transgression, °peccadillo, faux pas, *Colloq* slip-up, *Chiefly US* blooper, *Slang Brit* boob, bloomer

slip[2] *n.* **1** °piece, °scrap, °strip, °sliver; °paper, °note, chit, °permit, °permission, °pass, °document **2** °shoot, scion, °cutting, sprig, °twig, °sprout, °runner, °offshoot

slippery *adj.* **1** °slick, °sleek, °slimy, °icy, °glassy, °smooth, °greasy, °oily, lubricated, *Colloq* skiddy **2** °evasive, °devious, °shifty, °unreliable, undependable, °questionable, untrustworthy, °dishonest, treacherous, °disloyal, °perfidious, °slick, °crafty, °sly, °foxy, cunning, °tricky, °sneaky, °false, reptilian, °faithless, *Colloq* °shady

slipshod *adj.* °careless, slovenly, slapdash, °haphazard, messy, °untidy, disorganized, °lax, unorganized, *Colloq* °sloppy

slit *v.* **1** °split, °cut, °slash, °gash, °knife, °slice —*n.* **2** °split, °cut, °gash, °incision, fissure, °groove, °slash, cleft, °aperture, °opening

slither *v.* °slide, worm, °snake, °slip, °slink, °glide, skitter, °creep, °crawl

sliver *n.* °fragment, °piece, shard, °shred, °splinter, °slip, shaving, paring, °flake, °chip, °bit, °scrap, snippet, °snip

slob *n.* oaf, °boor, pig, lout, churl, °yahoo, *Archaic* slubberdegullion, *Slang Brit* yob, yobbo, *Chiefly US* galoot *or* galloot, slobbovian

slogan *n.* war cry, battle cry, rallying cry, catchword, watchword; °motto

slope *v.* **1** °incline, °decline, ascend, °descend, °rise, °fall, °dip, °sink, °drop (off),

°angle, °slant, °pitch, °tilt, °tip —*n.* **2** °incline, °decline, ascent, descent, acclivity, declivity, °rise, °fall, °ramp, °dip, °sink, °drop, °angle, °slant, °pitch, °tilt, °rake, °tip, camber, °cant, °grade, bevel, °hill, bank, °mount, gradient, *US* °grade, upgrade, °downgrade

sloppy *adj.* **1** messy, °dirty, slovenly, °careless, °slipshod, °untidy, disordered, °disorderly; draggletailed, °bedraggled, disheveled, °unkempt, °dowdy, frumpish, °shabby, scruffy, *Colloq US* grungy **2** °wet, slushy, °watery, soggy, soppy, sopping, sodden, sloshy, °muddy, rainy **3** °sentimental, °gushy, gushing, mawkish, °maudlin, °mushy, overemotional, *Colloq* slushy, *Brit* °wet, soppy

slot *n.* **1** °groove, fissure, °notch, °slit, °opening, °hollow, °depression, °channel, sulcus **2** °opening, °position, °vacancy, °job, °place, °assignment, °niche, °space, °spot, pigeonhole —*v.* **3** °groove, fissure, °notch, °slit, hollow out **4** °assign, °schedule, °place, °position, pigeonhole, °fit

sloth *n.* °idleness, laziness, °indolence, slothfulness, °inertia, apathy, °indifference, accidie, °torpor, faineance, pococurantism, torpidity, °sluggishness, languor, languidness, °lethargy, phlegm, *Rare* hebetude

slothful *adj.* °idle, °lazy, °indolent, apathetic, °indifferent, °torpid, °inert, pococurante, °slack, °lax, °shiftless, fainéant, °inactive, do-nothing, sluggish, sluggard(ly), °slow, °laggard, languorous, languid, °lethargic, °lackadaisical, °phlegmatic, hebetudinous

slouch *v.* **1** °droop, °sag, °stoop, loll, °slump, °hunch —*n.* **2** °stoop, °sag, °droop, °slump, °hunch **3** Usually, ***no slouch.*** sloven, °loafer, sluggard, °laggard, °idler, malingerer, lazybones

slow *adj.* **1** lagging, °laggard, dawdling, sluggish, sluggard(ly), slow-moving, °leaden, °ponderous, °unhurried, plodding, snaillike, tortoiselike, °torpid, leaden-footed, creeping, crawling; °deliberate, slow-paced, leisurely, °gradual, °easy, °relaxed, °lax, °lackadaisical, °lazy, *US* lallygagging *or* lollygagging **2** °gradual, °progressive, °moderate, °perceptible, almost imperceptible, measurable **3** °unhurried, slow-moving, slow-paced **4** behindhand, unpunctual **5** °late, °tardy, behindhand, dilatory, delayed, unpunctual **6** °slack, °inactive, °quiet, sluggish, unproductive **7** °dense, °dull, slow-witted, dull-witted, °obtuse, °backward, bovine, °dim, dimwitted, °stupid, unresponsive, blockish, cloddish, unintelligent, doltish, °simple, °stolid, unimaginative, Boeotian, *Colloq* slow on the uptake, °thick, °dumb **8** °conservative, unprogressive, °old-fashioned, out-of-date, °backward, old-fogyish, °behind the times, *Colloq* °square, not with it, past it, *US* out of it **9** °boring, °dull, °tiresome, ennuyant, °tedious, °dead, °sleepy, somnolent, °torpid, soporific, wearisome, dryasdust, uninteresting, °monotonous, °tame, uneventful, °humdrum, *Colloq* ho-hum, °dead, *Brit* dead-and-alive **10** °reluctant, not quick, unwilling, °hesitant, °disinclined, °averse, loath *or* loth, °indisposed —*adv.* **11** slowly, °unhurriedly, cautiously, carefully, circumspectly **12** behindhand, tardily, °late, unpunctually **13** slowly, °easy, leisurely, °easily —*v.* **14** Often, ***slow down or up.*** slack *or* slacken off, reduce speed, °hold back, put on the brakes, take it easy **15** °relax, take it easy, *Colloq* ease up

sludge *n.* °muck, °mire, °ooze, °mud, slime, °dregs, °silt, °residue, °precipitate, *Colloq* goo

sluggishness *n.* °sloth, laziness, slothfulness, languor, lassitude, °lethargy, languidness, laggardness, °torpor, phlegm, lifelessness, stagnation, shiftlessness, pococurantism, fainéance, accidie, *Rare* hebetude

slum *n.* Often, ***slums.*** ghetto, warren, shantytown, *US* skid row *or* Skid Road

slump *n.* **1** °dip, trough, depreciation, °decline, downturn, downslide, °recession, °depression, falling-off, falloff, °fall, °drop, °plunge, descent, °crash, °collapse, °failure; nose dive, tailspin —*v.* **2** °decline, °slip, °recede, °fall (off), °drop, °plunge, °descend, °sink, °crash, °collapse, °dive, °plummet, take *or* go into a nosedive *or* tailspin **3** See **slouch, 1,** above.

slur *n.* **1** °smear, °insult, calumny, °aspersion, affront, °stigma, °stain, °blot, °spot, °(black) mark, °discredit, insinuation, °innuendo, °imputation, °slander, °libel, °slight, *Colloq* °put-down —*v.* **2** °mumble, misarticulate, °garble, stutter, lisp **3** ***slur over.*** °gloss over, °pass over, °disregard, give short shrift to, °ignore

sly *adj.* **1** cunning, °artful, °crafty, °clever, °wily, guileful, underhand(ed), °deceitful, treacherous, °foxy, °scheming, plotting, °designing, conniving, furtive, °shrewd, °sneaky, °stealthy, insidious, °devious, °disingenuous, °tricky, °shifty, °sharp, canny, *Colloq* °shady **2** impish, elfish, roguish, °mischievous, puckish, °devilish, scampish, °naughty, °arch, waggish —*n.* **3** ***on the sly.*** slyly *or* slily, °quietly, surreptitiously, covertly, stealthily, furtively, sneakily, underhandedly, clandestinely, *Colloq* on the Q.T., on the side

small *adj.* **1** °little, °tiny, °short, °diminutive, °petite, mignon(ne), °wee, teeny, °elfin, Lilliputian, midget, °miniature, °minute, minuscule, °baby, bantam, pocket(-sized), mini; °undersized, °immature, °young, underage; *Colloq* pint-sized, *US* peewee **2** °slight, °secondary, °insignificant, trivial, °inconsequential, lesser, °puny, °negligible, °minor, °trifling, unimportant, °paltry, nugatory **3** unimaginative, °shallow, unoriginal, mundane, °everyday, °limited, unprofound, uninspired, commonplace, °matter-of-fact, °flat, two-dimensional **4** skimpy, niggardly, stingy, uncharitable, ungenerous, °scanty, °meager, °cheap, °petty, parsimonious, grudging, stinting, °selfish, °miserly, °tight, tightfisted, closefisted, °close; °poor, °insignificant, °inadequate, °insufficient, °unsatisfactory, °negligible, °trifling, °humble, small-scale, °modest, unpretentious, *Colloq* piddling, °measly **5** °insignificant, °limited, °negligible, °trifling, °tiny; °little, °minor, diminished, reduced, °slight **6** ***feel small.*** feel embarrassed *or* ashamed *or* shamed *or* humiliated *or* foolish, feel discomfited *or* disconcerted *or* uncomfortable, feel mortified *or* chagrined, *Colloq* feel put down

small-minded *adj.* °small, °petty, °selfish, stingy, grudging, niggardly, ungenerous, °mean, °narrow-minded, °narrow, close-minded, uncharitable, °hidebound, °rigid, °intolerant, unimaginative, °shortsighted, °nearsighted, myopic

small-time *adj.* °small, small-scale, unimportant, °petty, piddling, °minor, °insignificant, °trifling, trivial

smart *adj.* **1** °intelligent, °clever, °bright, °brilliant, °quick-witted, °sharp, °acute, °astute, °capable, °adept, apt, °quick, °ingenious **2** canny, perspicacious, °perceptive, percipient, discerning, °knowledgeable, *au fait*, well-educated, well-read, erudite, °learned, well-versed, °aware, °shrewd, streetwise, *Slang* °hip, tuned-in, *US* savvy **3** °elegant, °chic, °fashionable, °stylish, modish, à la mode, °well-groomed, °trim, °neat, °dapper, °spruce, soigné(e), *Colloq* °snappy, natty **4** °pert, °pointed, saucy, °witty, nimble-witted, °poignant, °trenchant, °effective **5** °brisk, °vigorous, °animated, °active, °energetic, °spirited, °lively; °quick, °alert, °jaunty, °perky, °breezy **6** °quick, °swift, °stiff, smarting, stinging, °sharp, °severe —*v.* **7** °sting, °hurt, °pinch, °pain, °ache, tingle, °prickle, °burn, throb, °stab, °pierce —*n.* **8** °injury, °harm, °pain, °pang, °twinge, °affliction, °suffering, smarting

smear *v.* **1** daub, °rub, anoint, °spread, °cover, °coat, °wipe, °plaster, bedaub; besmirch, °dirty, smudge, °stain, °soil, begrime **2** °blacken, besmirch, °soil, °sully, calumniate, °slander, °discredit, °tarnish, defile, °vilify, °scandalize, °stigmatize, *Colloq* drag through the mud —*n.* **3** smudge, daub, °stain, splodge *or chiefly US* splotch, °blot, °taint, °spot **4** °slander, °scandal, °libel, vilification, mudslinging, defamation, calumny, °aspersion, °reflection

smell *n.* **1** °odor, °scent, °aroma, °perfume, °fragrance, °bouquet, °breath, whiff **2** stink, °stench, fetor *or* foetor, fetidness, mephitis, effluvium, *Colloq Brit* pong —*v.* **3** °scent, °sniff, *Colloq* get a whiff of **4** stink, °reek, *Colloq Brit* pong, °hum

smelly *adj.* malodorous, evil-smelling, foul-smelling, °foul, mephitic, fetid, °putrid, reeky, °stinking, noisome, °rank, °offensive, miasmic *or* miasmatic *or* miasmatical *or* miasmal, odoriferous, °rancid, °high, gamy, *Slang Brit* whiffy

smile *v.* **1** grin, °beam —*n.* **2** grin

smirk *n.* **1** °leer, °sneer, grin, grimace, simpering smile —*v.* **2** °sneer, grimace, °leer

smitten *adj.* **1** °affected, afflicted, °beset, °stricken, troubled, distressed, burdened, crushed, plagued, haunted, °worried, bothered, vexed **2** captivated, enthralled, struck, bewitched, °enchanted, beguiled, °charmed, enraptured, °infatuated, enamored, ensorcelled, swept off one's feet, *Colloq* bowled over, gaga

smolder *v.* °burn; °seethe, °simmer, °chafe, °rage, °fume, °foam, °boil, °stew, °fester, *Colloq* get hot under the collar, get (all) steamed up, see red, *US* do a slow burn, get (all) burnt up

smooth *adj.* **1** °regular, °even, °flush, °flat, °level, °plane, unruffled, unbroken, unwrinkled, undisturbed, °tranquil, °peaceful, °calm, °serene, °glassy **2** °slick, °sleek, °shiny, °glossy, °glassy, mirrorlike, °uniform, °polished, burnished; °silky, silken, velvety, satiny **3** unobstructed, °easy, °effortless, °free, uncluttered, °even, °orderly, well-ordered, uneventful, flowing, °fluent, unconstrained, uninterrupted **4** °hairless, bald, °bare, °naked, cleanshaven, smooth-shaven, depilated, glabrous **5** °soothing, °mellow, °pleasant, °bland, °mild, °soft **6** °suave, °slick, °slippery, unctuous, silken, °silky, °glib, urbane, soigné(e), °agreeable, °winning, °plausible, facile, °nonchalant, courtly, °eloquent, honey-tongued, smooth-spoken, °persuasive, °oily, °slimy, syrupy, *Colloq chiefly Brit* smarmy **7** °sweet, dulcet, pear-shaped, °mellow, well-modulated, silver-tongued **8** °slick, °scheming, conniving, °crafty, °shrewd, cunning, °tricky, °shifty, °sly, °foxy, Machiavellian, sophistic(al), °plausible, credible, believable, *Colloq* cagey —*v.* **9** Often, ***smooth out or away.*** °flatten, °even, °level, iron, °press, °mangle, calender **10** °prepare, °lay, °pave, °ease, °ready, °clear, °open, °prime, lubricate, °facilitate **11** sand, °plane, °polish, buff, burnish **12** Often, ***smooth over.*** ameliorate, assuage, allay, °calm, °gloss over, °minimize, °mitigate, lessen, soothe, °reduce, °temper, mollify, smoothen, °soften, palliate, appease

smother *v.* **1** suffocate, °stifle, °choke, asphyxiate; throttle, strangle, snuff (out), °kill **2** be suffocated *or* stifled *or* asphyxiated, be choked *or* strangled, be killed **3** °overwhelm, °overcome, blanket, inundate, °cover, °shower; °envelop, °wrap, enshroud, °surround **4** °repress, °subdue, °suppress, °conceal, °hide, keep *or* hold back, °cover up, °mask, choke back *or* down, °check; °stifle, °muffle, blanket, blank out **5** °extinguish, °put out, snuff out

smug *adj.* self-satisfied, complacent, holier-than-thou, °self-important, °overconfident, °conceited

snack *n.* **1** °bite, nibble, °morsel, tidbit *or Brit also* titbit, refreshment(s), *Brit* elevenses, *Anglo-Indian* tiffin, *Colloq* nosh —*v.* **2** °bite, nibble, *Colloq* nosh

snag *n.* **1** °hitch, °catch, °problem, °(stumbling) block, °stricture, bottleneck, °complication, °obstacle, °impediment, °obstruction, °hindrance, °difficulty, *US* hang-up —*v.* **2** °catch, °tear, °rip

snake *n.* **1** reptile, serpent, ophidian, viper **2** snake in the grass, °traitor, °turncoat, Judas, quisling, betrayer, double-crosser, °informer, rat, *US* Benedict Arnold, *Slang chiefly US and Canadian* fink, rat fink —*v.* **3** °slither, °glide, °creep, °crawl, worm **4** °twist, °wind, curve, °bend, °turn, zigzag, worm, °wander, °loop, crook, °meander

snap *v.* **1** °break (off), °separate, °crack; °cleave, °split, °fracture, °give way, °part **2** click; °pop; °crack **3** Often, ***snap at.*** **(a)** °bite (at), °nip, gnash *or* snatch at **(b)** °attack, lunge at, °lash out (at), snarl at, growl (at), bark (at), be brusque *or* short *or* curt (with), *Colloq* jump down (someone's) throat, °fly off the handle (at) **4** Usually, ***snap up or US also off.*** °grab (up), °snatch (up), °seize, °pluck, pounce on *or* upon, °make off with, °take (away), °capture, °catch, °get, °secure **5** °shoot, snapshoot, snapshot, °photograph, click, °catch **6** ***snap one's fingers at.*** disdain, °scorn, °flout, °dismiss, contemn, °disregard, °ignore, °defy, °mock, °deride, °thumb one's nose at, *Brit* cock a snook at **7** ***snap out of it.*** °recover, come round *or* around, °revive, °awaken, °wake up, °perk up, liven up, cheer up; get a grip *or* (a) hold on *or* of oneself, °pull oneself together, (re)gain control of oneself —*n.* **8** °crack, °pop, click **9** °spell, °period, °interval, °wave **10** °catch, spring-catch, (snap) fastener, °fastening, °clasp **11** °energy, °vigor, °animation, liveliness, °vitality, °bounce, alertness, sprightliness, élan, °dash, °sparkle, °verve, *Colloq* zip, zing, get-up-and-go, °pep, pizazz **12** easy job, *Slang* °picnic, *US and Canadian* °breeze —*adj.* **13** °abrupt, °sudden, °precipitate, °hurried, °hasty, incautious, °rash, °unpremeditated, unplanned, not well-thought-out, °quick, instantaneous, °instant

snappish *adj.* **1** °short-tempered, °testy, °petulant, °peevish, °irritable, °prickly, °touchy, irascible, quick to anger, °quick-tempered, hot-tempered, °waspish, *Brit* °snappy, *US* on a short string *or* tether **2** °curt, °short, °abrupt, °brusque, curmudgeonly, °cantankerous, °sharp, °cross, grouchy, °gruff, °cranky, crusty, crabby, crabbed, acid, °tart, acerbic, churlish, dyspeptic, choleric, splenetic, ill-humored, ill-tempered, °temperamental, °moody, *Brit* °snappy

snappy *adj.* **1** °quick, °sharp, °brisk, °smart, °crisp, °lively, °rapid, °speedy **2** °fashionable, °chic, °sharp, °smart, °stylish, °dapper, modish, *Colloq* natty, *Brit* °trendy

snare *n.* **1** °trap, °net, springe, noose, gin —*v.* **2** °trap, °catch, entrap, °seize, °capture, ensnare

snarl[1] *v.* **1** growl; °snap —*n.* **2** growl

snarl[2] *v.* **1** Often, ***snarl up.*** °tangle, °entangle, °complicate, °confuse, °scramble, °muddle, °twist, mix *or* mess up, *Colloq* ball up, °screw up **2** °tangle, °entangle, °knot, °twist, ravel, °jam, °kink —*n.* **3** °tangle, entanglement, °complexity, °snag, °problem, °difficulty, °complication, °muddle, °mess, °predicament, °fix, °quandary, °dilemma, *Colloq* snarl-up, tight spot, pickle **4** jungle, °maze, labyrinth, °knot

snatch *v.* **1** °grab, °grasp, °seize, °clasp, °clutch, °pluck, °take (hold of), °catch, °lay hold of, wrest, latch onto, °capture, °snap up, °win, °get, lay *or* get one's hands on **2** *Chiefly US* °kidnap, °abduct **3** °save, °rescue, °deliver, °remove —*n.* **4** °grab, °clutch, °grasp **5** °scrap, °bit, °fragment, snippet, °segment, °morsel, °specimen, °sample

sneak *v.* **1** °lurk, °slink, °steal, °creep, skulk, cower, °pad, °prowl, °sidle, *Colloq* °pussyfoot —*n.* **2** °informer, *Colloq* tattletale, *Brit* grass, *Slang* stool pigeon, snitch, *Brit and Australian* nark, *US* stoolie, *Chiefly US and Canadian* fink, rat fink, *US* shoofly

sneaking *adj.* **1** °persistent, °lingering, lurking, °nagging, worrying, worrisome, °niggling, intuitive, deep-rooted, deep-seated, *Slang* °gut **2** innate, intuitive, °inherent, °private, °secret, suppressed, °hidden, unexpressed, undeclared, unvoiced, unavowed, unconfessed, unrevealed, unadmitted, undivulged, undisclosed, covert

sneaky *adj.* underhand(ed), °devious, furtive, °sly, °slippery, °disingenuous, °deceitful, °dishonest, °unscrupulous, °shifty

sneer *v.* **1** °smirk, curl one's lip, °sniff **2** °scorn, disdain, °despise, contemn, turn up one's nose (at), °sniff (at), °jeer (at), °laugh (at), °deride, °mock, °ridicule; underrate; *Colloq* °sneeze at, *Slang* °knock —*n.* **3** °scorn, °jeer, disdain, °contempt, °derision, °mockery, °ridicule; sneering, jeering

sneeze *v.* **1** sternutate **2** ***sneeze at.*** See **sneer, 2,** above. —*n.* **3** sternutation; sneezing

snicker *v.* **1** snigger, °chuckle, °giggle, °titter, laugh up one's sleeve, °mock, °scorn, °laugh (at), °jeer (at) —*n.* **2** snigger, °chuckle, °giggle, °titter

sniff *n.* **1** whiff, °breath, °odor, °scent **2** °hint, °spirit, °feeling, °suggestion —*v.* **3** °smell, snuffle, snuff **4** ***sniff (at).*** See **sneer, 2,** above.

snip *v.* **1** °nip, °clip, crop, °cut, °lop, °prune, °dock —*n.* **2** °cut, °slit, °gash, °slash, °incision, °nick **3** °bit, °scrap, °shred, snippet, °fragment, °cutting, clipping, °remnant, °morsel **4** ***snips.*** scissors, shears, tin snips

snipe *v.* Usually, ***snipe at.*** shoot at, fire at; °attack, °criticize, °deride, find fault with, carp at, pick apart

snivel *v.* sniffle, snuffle, blubber, whimper, whine, mewl, pule; °cry, *Colloq Brit* whinge

snobbery *n.* snobbism, snobbishness, pretentiousness, °pretension, hauteur, haughtiness, superciliousness, condescension, loftiness, contemptuousness, presumptuousness, lordliness, disdainfulness, disdain, pompousness, pomposity, °affectation, inflatedness, self-importance, °conceit, vainness, °vanity, narcissism, self-admiration, self-centeredness, egotism, smugness, *Colloq* uppishness, uppitiness, snootiness, snottiness

snobbish *adj.* °condescending, °superior, patronizing, °arrogant, °haughty, lordly, °lofty, putting on airs, °disdainful, °supercilious, °contemptuous, °pretentious, °smug, °scornful, °self-important, °affected, °conceited, egotistic(al), °vain, self-satisfied, complacent, °pompous, *Colloq* snooty, snotty, highfalutin *or* hifalutin *or* highfaluting, on one's high horse, uppity, °hoity-toity, high and mighty, stuck-up, *Brit* °uppish, *Chiefly US* high-hat, *Slang Brit* toffee-nosed

snoop *v.* **1** °pry, °spy, °interfere, °meddle, °intrude, butt in(to), *Colloq* stick *or* poke one's nose; be nosy, nose around *or* about —*n.* **2** °busybody, meddler, °spy, °intruder, snooper, peeper; private detective *or* investigator, *Brit* Paul Pry; *Colloq* Nosy Parker, *US* buttinsky *or* buttinski; private eye, shamus

snug *adj.* °cozy, °comfortable, °intimate, relaxing, °restful, °warm, sheltered, °friendly, °easy, °homely, °casual, *Colloq* comfy

snuggle *v.* °cuddle, snug down, °nestle, nuzzle

soak *v.* **1** °drench, °saturate, °wet, °immerse, souse, douse *or* dowse, bathe, °steep, inundate, ret **2** ***soak up.*** absorb, °take in, sponge up; assimilate, °learn —*n.* **3** °alcoholic, drunkard, °drunk, dipsomaniac, drinker, tippler, toper, sot, *Slang* sponge, souse, boozer, *US* °dip, °lush, juicer

soaking *n.* **1** drenching, wetting, dousing *or* dowsing, immersing, saturating —*adj.* **2** °wet, sopping, drenched, dripping, saturated, soaked, wringing wet, streaming, sodden, waterlogged

soar *v.* **1** °rise, °fly, °hover, °float, °hang **2** °rise, °increase, escalate, °climb, spiral upward(s), shoot up *or* upward(s), °rocket, skyrocket

sob *v.* °cry, °weep, blubber, shed tears, °snivel, whimper, °sniff, snuffle, pule, wail, °moan, boohoo, mewl, °bawl, °howl, yowl

sober *adj.* **1** teetotal, °temperate, *US* °dry, *Colloq* on the (water) wagon **2** °serious, °solemn, °earnest, °dispassionate, unruffled, unflustered, unexcited, unperturbed, °steady, °sedate, °staid, composed, °dignified, °cool, °calm, °serene, °tranquil, °collected, coolheaded, °levelheaded, °sane, balanced, °practical, °realistic, °rational, clearheaded, *Slang* together **3** °sedate, °somber, °plain, °simple, °subdued, °quiet, repressed, °dreary, °dark, °drab, °colorless, °neutral —*v.* **4** ***sober up.*** detoxify, °recover, *Colloq* dry out

sobriety *n.* **1** teetotalism, abstemiousness, abstention, abstinence, nonindulgence, °temperance **2** seriousness, soberness, °solemnity, staidness, °gravity, temperateness, sedateness, °formality, °dignity

so-called *adj.* **1** styled, °self-styled, designated, *soi-disant,* called, °professed **2** °alleged, °pretended, °supposed, ostensible, misnamed, misdesignated; °suspect

sociable *adj.* °friendly, affable, approachable, °social, gregarious, °outgoing, extrovert(ed) *or* extravert(ed), companionable, °accessible, °amiable, °amicable, °genial, congenial, convivial, °warm, °cordial, °neighborly, hail-fellow-well-met, *Colloq* °chummy, °cozy

social *adj.* **1** communal, community, °common, collective, °group, °public, °popular, societal **2** °sexual, sexually transmitted, °venereal **3** See **sociable,** above.

socialize *v.* °mix, °get together, °fraternize, keep company, °go out, get out; °associate

society *n.* **1** °fellowship, °brotherhood, °association, °intercourse, °companionship, °company, camaraderie, °friendship **2** mankind, °people, the public **3** °culture, °civilization, community, way of life, °world; °organization, °system **4** high society, ***haut monde, beau monde,*** upper classes, polite society, elite *or* élite, °gentry, *Colloq* °upper crust **5** °organization, °club, °association, °circle, °league, °institute, academy, °alliance, guild, °group, °fraternity, sorority, °brotherhood, sisterhood, °fellowship, °union, consociation, sodality, *Verein,* bund *or* Bund

soft *adj.* **1** °yielding, cushiony, plushy, spongy, squeezable, compressible, squashy, squashable, °flexible, °plastic, °pliable, pliant, °supple, flexile, flexuous, unstarched **2** °easy, °comfortable, undemanding, *Colloq* cushy **3** °gentle, °mild, balmy, °pleasant, °moderate, °warm, halcyon, springlike, summery, °restful, °tranquil, relaxing, °lazy **4** °subdued, toned *or* turned down, muted, °low, °quiet, °melodious, mellifluous *or* mellifluent, °mellow, °gentle, °faint, softened, °soothing, °smooth **5** easygoing, °tolerant, °kind, compassionate, °gentle, °merciful, °lenient, °indulgent, °permissive, °liberal, °lax, °easy, docile, °tame, °submissive, deferential, °benign, tenderhearted, °sympathetic, kindhearted, °kind **6** Usually, ***soft in the head.*** °foolish, °silly, °simple, *Colloq chiefly Brit* °daft, *US* °off **7** depressed, declining, in decline, in recession, °slow, °unprofitable, borderline, °questionable, °weak **8** downy, °silky, silken, satiny, furry, °fluffy, feathery, fleecy, °fuzzy, velvety, °smooth (as a baby's bottom) **9** pastel, °pale, °delicate, °fine, °subdued, °light, matte *or* matt, °quiet, diffuse(d), °soothing **10** °harmless, nonaddictive **11** °fuzzy, °woolly, blurred, blurry, foggy, diffuse(d) **12** °weak, °feeble, °frail, effete, °delicate, nonphysical, nonmuscular, °puny, °flabby, out of training *or* condition *or* shape, pampered; namby-pamby, °effeminate, unmanly, unmanful, *Colloq* sissified, °sissy **13** °easy, °luxurious, pampered, °rich, °opulent, °plush, °posh, *Colloq* ritzy, swank(y)

soften *v.* **1** Often, ***soften up.*** °melt, °affect, mollify, °mellow, palliate, soothe, °relax, appease **2** °mitigate, assuage, °diminish, °moderate, °reduce, °cushion, lessen, °weaken, allay, °ease, °lighten, abate, °temper, °relieve **3** °muffle, °deaden, °damp, soft-pedal, °lower, °still, °quiet, °tone down, lessen, °diminish, °lighten, °turn down, °quell, *Chiefly Brit* quieten **4** °give in, °succumb, °surrender, °yield, °agree, °consent, concur, assent, °give way, °relax, °ease (up), °let up

softhearted *adj.* tenderhearted, compassionate, °tender, warmhearted, °sentimental, °charitable, °generous, giving, °sympathetic, °indulgent, °kind, kindhearted, °responsive

soil[1] *v.* **1** °dirty, °stain, begrime, °muddy, °smear, °spot **2** °pollute, °contaminate, °sully, defile, °foul, befoul, °tarnish, besmirch, °disgrace, °muddy, °smear, °blacken; °blot —*n.* **3** °dirt, °filth, °muck, °mire, °mud, °sludge, °dregs, °refuse; excrement, °waste (matter)

soil[2] *n.* °earth, loam, °dirt, °ground, °turf, humus; clay

sojourn *n.* **1** °stay, °stop, stopover, °visit, °rest, °holiday, vacation —*v.* **2** °stay, °stop (over), °visit, °rest, °holiday, vacation, °tarry

solace *n.* **1** °comfort, consolation, condolence, °relief, balm, °support, °help, succor; reassurance, °cheer —*v.* **2** °comfort, °console, condole, °support, °help, succor, soothe, allay, alleviate, ameliorate, °mitigate, assuage, °relieve; °cheer (up), °reassure, hearten

soldier *n.* **1** serviceman, servicewoman, °recruit, fighter, infantryman, foot soldier, trooper, warrior, military man, man-at-arms, *Brit* Tommy (Atkins), *US* enlisted man *or* woman, *Colloq Brit* squaddie, *US* GI *or* G.I. (Joe), *Old-fashioned* (*WWI*) doughboy **2** fighter, °stalwart, °supporter, °militant —*v.* **3** °serve (in the army) **4** ***soldier on.*** °continue, °persist, °persevere, °endure, °drive, keep going, keep on *or* at, °grind, drudge

sole *adj.* lone, °only, °singular, °unique, °solitary; °particular, °exclusive, °individual, °personal

solecism *n.* °error, °slip, °impropriety, °fault, °breach, °violation, °lapse, °mistake, misusage, incongruity, inconsistency, barbarism, °blunder, gaffe, °bungle, °fumble, gaucherie, faux pas, botch *or* botch-up, *Colloq* boo-boo, *US* flub, *Slang* boner, *Brit* boob, bloomer, *Chiefly US and Canadian* blooper

solemn *adj.* **1** °serious, °sober, °reserved, °grave, °earnest, °sedate, °staid, °taciturn; morose, °morbid, mirthless, unsmiling, °gloomy, °somber, °grim; °glum, long-faced, saturnine **2** °ceremonial, ritualistic, liturgical, °religious, ecclesiastical, °holy, °divine, °sacred, hallowed, sacramental, reverential, devotional **3** °ceremonious, °ritual, °formal, °dignified, °stately, °grand, august, °imposing, °impressive, awe-inspiring, °awesome, °important, °momentous

solemnity *n.* solemnness, °gravity, seriousness, soberness, °reserve, sedateness, taciturnity, staidness, earnestness, impressiveness, °grandeur, °importance, momentousness, consequence

solicit *v.* **1** entreat, °beseech, °ask (for), implore, °petition, importune, appeal for *or* to, call on *or* upon, °beg, supplicate, °pray, crave **2** accost, °approach, °entice, °lure, °pander to, *Slang* °hustle

solicitous *adj.* **1** °concerned, caring, °considerate, uneasy, troubled, °anxious, apprehensive, °worried **2** °eager, °earnest, zealous, °keen, °anxious, °desirous, °ardent, avid

solicitude *n.* °concern, °consideration, °regard, disquiet, disquietude, uneasiness, °anxiety, apprehension, °worry, nervousness, °fear, fearfulness, °alarm

solid *adj.* **1** three-dimensional, cubic **2** filled (in *or* up), °packed, jammed, crowded, teeming, °congested, crammed, swarming, compressed, concentrated, *Colloq* chockablock, jampacked, chock-full **3** °compact, °firm, °hard, °stable; unshakable *or* unshakeable, unshaky, °substantial, °concrete, °sturdy, °sound, °stout, °strong **4** °consistent, °homogeneous, °uniform, unalloyed, unmixed, °pure, °continuous, unbroken, °real, °authentic, °true, °genuine, 24-karat, unadulterated, *Slang* honest-to-God **5** law-abiding, upstanding, °upright, °decent, °stout, °substantial, °powerful, °reliable, °regular, °steady, °steadfast, °stalwart, °straight, °estimable, °sure, trusty, °trustworthy, trueblue, °worthy, dependable, °sober **6** °steady, °stable, °stalwart, dependable, °sturdy, °strong, °substantial, °sound, °firm, well-built, well-constructed, well-made, °tough, °durable, °rugged, °stout **7** cogent, °sound, °concrete, °weighty, proved, provable, valid, °reasonable, °sensible, °rational, °sober, well-founded, °authoritative, °indisputable, °incontrovertible, irrefutable, incontestable, °good, °powerful, °potent, °forceful, convincing, °persuasive **8** °firm, °downright, °vigorous, °telling, °effective, °forceful, °potent, °powerful, °mighty, °dynamic, °thorough, through and through, °intensive **9** See **solvent, 1,** below. **10** °entire, °complete, °whole, °continuous; uninterrupted, °undivided, unbroken, unrelieved, °blank, windowless

solidarity *n.* °unity, unanimity, unification, °accord, concord, concordance, °harmony, concurrence, like-mindedness, °agreement, mutuality, single-mindedness, singleness (of purpose), community of interest, esprit de corps, camaraderie, comradeship, sodality, *Solidarność*

solidify *v.* **1** °harden, °freeze, °set, °cake, °compact, compress, crystallize; jell *or* gel, clot, congeal, °coagulate, °thicken, *Technical* inspissate; °sublime **2** consolidate, °unite, °unify, pull *or* draw together

solitary *adj.* **1** lone, °single, °sole, °individual; unattended, °solo, companionless, friendless, °lonesome, °lonely, °unsocial, cloistered, °secluded, °reclusive, °separate, eremitic(al), hermitic(al), °remote, °withdrawn, °distant, °out-of-the-way, unfrequented, °desolate —*n.* **2** solitary confinement

solitude *n.* **1** solitariness, aloneness, isolation, °seclusion, °privacy **2** loneliness, remoteness; °emptiness, wilderness

solo *adv.* **1** °alone, °unaccompanied, on one's own *—adj.* **2** °individual, °unaccompanied, °solitary

solution *n.* **1** solving, working *or* figuring out, °discovery, finding out, unraveling, explication, deciphering, decipherment, elucidation, °revelation, clarification, °explanation; °answer, °key **2** °settlement, settling, °resolution, °result, denouement *or* dénouement, °outcome, conclusion **3** °mixture, °blend, °compound, infusion; °liquid, °fluid; *Technical* emulsion, °suspension, colloid *or* colloidal solution *or* colloidal suspension **4** dissolving, °dissolution, mixing, °mixture

solve *v.* work *or* figure out, unravel, disentangle, untangle, °clarify, °clear up, make plain *or* clear, °interpret, explicate, °decipher, °crack, °explain, elucidate, °reveal, °answer, °resolve

solvent *adj.* creditworthy, °(financially) sound, °solid, °reliable; debt-free; °profitable

somber *adj.* **1** °gloomy, morose, lugubrious, °funereal, °morbid, lowering *or* louring, °melancholy, °sad, °dismal, °unhappy, cheerless, °joyless, °serious, °sober, °doleful, dolorous, °mournful, depressed, depressing, °grave, °grim, grim-faced, grim-visaged, *Literary* melancholic, darksome **2** °dark, °gloomy, °foreboding, °bleak, depressing, °shadowy, °murky, °leaden, °gray, °black, °dismal, °dreary, °overcast, °dusky, °dim, °dingy, darkling, °dull, subfusc *or* subfuscous **3** °staid, °sedate, °sober, °solemn, °dark, °dull, subfusc

somebody *pron.* **1** °one, someone, some person *—n.* **2** °personage, °celebrity, °dignitary, VIP, luminary, °notable, °star, superstar, *Colloq* hotshot, °bigwig, big wheel, big gun, big noise, big White Chief, big Daddy, big Chief, big-timer; hot stuff; *Old-fashioned* big cheese; *US* Mr. Big

somehow *adv.* someway, in one way or another, in some way, somehow or other, °by hook or by crook, by fair means or foul, *Colloq* come hell or high water

sometime *adj.* **1** °former, erstwhile, °past, °recent, one-time, quondam *—adv.* **2** at some time or other, someday, one day, any time, on a future occasion, when *or* if the opportunity arises, °soon, by and by, one of these days **3** °sooner or later, in (due) time, in the fullness of time, °in the long run, one fine day, *Un bel di,* °eventually, when all is said and done, before long, before you know it

sometimes *adv.* °occasionally, °on occasion, °(every) now and then, °now and again, off and on, °at times, from time to time, every so often, °(every) once in a while

somewhat *adv.* °rather, °quite, °relatively, more or less, °moderately, °pretty, °fairly, to some *or* a certain extent *or* degree *or* measure, °slightly, a bit, a little, *Colloq* °sort of, kind of

song *n.* **1** °tune, °air, °melody, ditty, °number **2** ***for a song.*** cheaply, inexpensively, at a bargain price **3** **(*old*)** ***song and dance.*** **(a)** °fuss, to-do, commotion, °bother, ado, *Colloq* °flap, °performance, *Brit* kerfuffle **(b)** °evasion, °tale, prevarication, °(long) story, °(long) explanation

soon *adv.* **1** before long, °presently, ere long; in the near future, any minute (now), before you know it, in good time, in a little while, in a minute *or* a moment, momentarily, °shortly, anon, in a second, *Colloq* in a jiffy **2** °quickly, speedily, °at once, °promptly, °immediately, °directly, without delay, straightway, *Brit* °straightaway, *US* right away, forthwith, in short order, °on the double, in two shakes (of a lamb's tail), in a wink, *tout de suite,* without delay, *Colloq* pronto, *US and Canadian* lickety-split **3** °quickly, speedily, °promptly, °swiftly **4** °willingly, lief, °gladly, °happily, °readily **5** ***sooner or later.*** at some time or other, some time, one day, °in time, in due course, °eventually, °ultimately, in the end, when all is said and done, at the end of the day, in the last *or* final analysis, °at bottom

soothing *adj.* **1** relaxing, °restful, °serene, °peaceful, pacifying, °calm, calming, °quiet, °soft, quieting **2** mollifying, comforting, palliative, lenitive, demulcent, balsamic, emollient

sophistic *adj.* sophistical, °specious, fallacious, °deceptive, °hypocritical, °false, °unsound, baseless, °groundless, casuistic(al), jesuitic(al), captious, misleading, °bogus, °sham, °untenable

sophisticated *adj.* **1** °cultivated, cultured, °refined, °experienced, °worldly, cosmopolitan, °polished, °elegant, urbane, worldly-wise, °knowledgeable, °knowing, °suave, soigné(e), °blasé, chi-chi, °slick, *Slang* hip *or* hep, °cool, with it **2** advanced, complex, °complicated, °intricate, °elaborate, °subtle, °refined, multifaceted

sophistication *n.* **1** worldliness, urbanity, °culture, °refinement, °knowledge, knowledgeability, cosmopolitanism, °polish, °elegance, °poise, suavity *or* *suaveté,* °savoir-faire, °savoir-vivre, °finesse, °discrimination, discernment, awareness, °taste, tastefulness, °style **2** °complexity, intricacy, °subtlety, °refinement

sorcerer *n.* sorceress, magus, necromancer, wizard, °witch, warlock, enchanter, enchantress, °magician, thaumaturgist, shaman, witch doctor, medicine man

sorcery *n.* witchcraft, °enchantment, sortilege, necromancy, wizardry, (black *or* white) magic, shamanism, black art, diabolism

sordid *adj.* **1** °base, °vile, °corrupt, °low, ignoble, debased, degraded, abased, °mean, ignominious, °dishonorable, °despicable, °disreputable, °shabby, °shameful, °scurvy, °rotten, execrable **2** °avaricious, °greedy, °grasping, °mercenary, piggish, °hoggish, °selfish, °rapacious, money-grubbing, stingy, parsimonious **3** °dirty, °foul, °filthy, squalid, unclean, °untidy, °mean, slummy, °seamy, °seedy, °wretched, unsanitary, insanitary, °offensive, defiled, polluted, fetid, feculent, mucky, maggoty, °putrid, flyblown, °slimy **4** °wretched, °miserable, °poor, poverty-stricken, °down-and-out, °impoverished, °ramshackle, hovel-like, tumbledown, °dingy, °seamy, °seedy, slummy, deteriorated, °sleazy, back-alley

sore *adj.* **1** °painful, °sensitive, °tender, °raw, °angry, °burning, stinging, smarting, hurting; irritated, °inflamed, chafed **2** °sensitive, °delicate, °tender, °embarrassing, °awkward, °ticklish, °touchy, °thorny, °prickly **3** dire, °serious, °acute, °extreme, °critical, °urgent, °pressing, °desperate **4** °angry, angered, annoyed, irritated, vexed, irked, °upset, *Colloq* peeved **5** °painful, °troublesome, °grievous, aggrieved, distressing, distressful, °harrowing, °severe, °agonizing, °bitter, °fierce, °burdensome, onerous, °heavy, °oppressive **6** ***sore straits.*** °difficulty, °trouble, °distress, °danger, dangerous *or* precarious condition —*n.* **7** °injury, °damage, °swelling, rawness, infection, °inflammation, °bruise, abrasion, °cut, laceration, °scrape, °burn, canker, °ulcer

sorrow *n.* **1** °sadness, heartbreak, °grief, unhappiness, dolor, °misery, °woe, °anguish, °distress, °suffering, °torment, °agony, wretchedness, heartache, °desolation, desolateness **2** °affliction, °trouble, °trial, tribulation, °misfortune, °hardship, adversity, bad *or* hard luck, cares, °pressure, °strain, travail —*v.* **3** °grieve, °lament, °mourn, °regret, °keen, °bemoan, agonize, °moan, °bewail

sorrowful *adj.* **1** °sad, °unhappy, °regretful, °sorry, depressed, °dejected, crestfallen, chapfallen, °gloomy, downcast, °blue, dispirited, °melancholy, in the doldrums, °wretched, °woebegone, °miserable, heartsick, disheartened, °piteous, heavy-hearted, °brokenhearted, rueful, woeful, °tearful, disconsolate, °inconsolable, grief-stricken, *Colloq* °down in the mouth, down in the dumps **2** distressing, °lamentable, °doleful, °unfortunate, °bitter, distressful, troublous, °grievous, unlucky, hapless, afflictive

sorry *adj.* **1** °regretful, °penitent, °remorseful, contrite, conscience-stricken, guilt-ridden, °repentant, °apologetic, penitential **2** abject, °miserable, depressing, °wretched, °pitiful, °pitiable, °pathetic, °deplorable, °stark, °grim, °sordid, °dismal, °base, star-crossed, ill-starred **3** See **sorrowful, 1,** above

sort *n.* **1** °kind, °variety, °type, °class, classification, °group, °category, °brand, °make, °mark, °stamp, °description, °mold, °stripe, ilk, feather, kidney, °character, °nature; °manner, species **2** °kind, °type, °manner **3** species, genus, °family, phylum, subgenus, subspecies, °race, °breed, °strain, °stock, °kind, °variety, °type **4** °person, °individual, °lot; °thing **5** ***of sorts.*** of a sort, of a mediocre *or* passable *or* admissible *or* not (too) bad *or* fair *or* sufficiently good *or* adequate *or* undistinguished *or* indifferent kind *or* quality *or* proficiency **6** ***out of sorts.*** not oneself, not up to snuff, unwell, ailing, °indisposed, °(slightly) ill, °low, *Colloq* off one's feed, °under the weather **7** ***sort of.*** See **somewhat,** above. —*v.* **8** assort, classify, °file, °order, °rank, °grade, °class, °categorize, °separate, °divide, °combine, °merge, °arrange, °organize, systemize, systematize, catalogue, °group, °sort out **9** °describe, °characterize, °categorize, °cast, °throw, °combine, °mold, °type **10** ***sort out.*** **(a)** °organize, set *or* put straight, °straighten out, °resolve, °tidy (up), °clarify, °clear up, °solve; °decide **(b)** °choose, °select, °separate, °divide

so-so *adj.* °mediocre, all right, °average, °undistinguished, °passable, not (too) bad *or* good, °adequate, °fair (to middling), middling, °indifferent, °ordinary, °tolerable, *comme ci, comme ça,* °modest

soul *n.* **1** (vital) spirit *or* force, being, (inner *or* true) self, °essence, °psyche, °heart, °mind, °intellect, °reason, anima **2** °person, °individual, °man, °woman, °mortal, (human) being **3** incarnation, °embodiment, personification, typification, °essence, °quintessence **4** °emotion, °feeling, °sentiment, °sincerity, °fervor, °ardor, °warmth, °dynamism, vivacity, °energy, °spirit, °vitality, °force

soulful *adj.* °sincere, °deep, °profound, °moving, °emotional, °warm, °ardent, °intense, °fervent, °expressive

sound[1] *n.* **1** °tone; °noise; °din; cacophony; °report **2** °ring, °tone, °impression, °characteristic, °quality, °effect, °aspect, °look **3** hearing, °range, earshot —*v.* **4** °resound, reverberate, °echo, resonate **5** °seem, °appear, °look; strike one, give one the impression *or* feeling *or* sense (that); °resemble, sound *or* seem *or* look like **6** °ring, (be) activate(d), (be) set *or* touch(ed) off, °signal **7** Sometimes, ***sound out.*** articulate, °pronounce, °enunciate, utter; °voice, vocalize **8** Sometimes, ***sound out or off.*** °shout (out), cry out, °yell (out) **9** ***sound off.*** °vituperate, °complain, °bluster, grumble, *Slang* °bitch

sound[2] *adj.* **1** undamaged, uninjured, °whole, unmarred, in good condition *or* shape, °intact, unimpaired, °unscathed **2** °healthy, °hale (and hearty), °fit (as a fiddle), °robust, °vigorous, blooming, °rosy, ruddy **3** °firm, °solid, °substantial, °strong, °sturdy, °tough, °rugged, °durable, well-built, well-constructed, dependable **4** °sane, balanced, °normal, °rational, °wholesome, °reasoning, °reasonable, clearheaded, lucid, right-minded, °responsible, °practical, °prudent, °politic, °wise, °sensible, °logical, commonsense, common-sensical, °astute, °far-sighted, °perceptive, perspicacious, percipient; valid, °good, °judicious, °reliable, °useful **5** °safe, °secure, °good, °conservative, nonspeculative, °solid, riskless; °profitable **6** unbroken, uninterrupted, undisturbed, untroubled, °peaceful, °deep

sound[3] *v.* 1 Often, ***sound out.*** °plumb, °probe, °test, check (out *or* into), °fathom, inquire *or* enquire of, °question, °poll, °canvass, °investigate, °examine, °survey 2 °dive, °plunge, °submerge

sound[4] *n.* inlet, strait(s), fjord, bight, (sea) loch, bay, arm of the sea, cove, *Scots* firth

sour *adj.* 1 acid, acidic, °tart, vinegary, lemony, acidulous *or* acidulent, acidulated, acescent, acerbic 2 turned, °bad, °(gone) off, fermented, curdled, °rancid, spoilt *or* spoiled 3 °disagreeable, unpleasant, °distasteful, °bad, °nasty, °bitter, °terrible 4 acrimonious, °bitter, °embittered, unpleasant, churlish, ill-natured, ill-tempered, bad-tempered, crusty, curmudgeonly, crabbed, crabby, grouchy, °cross, °cranky, °testy, °petulant, °impatient, °abrupt, °nasty, °curt, °caustic, °brusque, °peevish, °snappish, edgy, °sullen, morose, °gloomy, °discontented —*v.* 5 °turn, °spoil, curdle, go bad *or* off, °ferment 6 embitter, acerbate, disenchant, °exasperate, vex, *Colloq* peeve

source *n.* 1 fountainhead, wellspring, °origin, provenance, provenience, inception, °start, °outset, °beginning, root(s), commencement, °rise 2 originator, °author, °creator, begetter 3 °authority, documentation; informant, *Colloq* horse's mouth

sovereign *n.* 1 °monarch, ruler, emperor, empress, °king, °queen, prince, princess, potentate, °chief, °master, °mistress, shah, sultan; Akund (of Swat), Gaekwar (of Baroda), Nizam (of Hyderabad), Mehtar (of Chitral), Nucifrage of Nuremberg, Sheik of Araby, *Colloq* supremo —*adj.* 2 °supreme, °paramount, highest, °principal, °foremost, greatest, °predominant, °dominant, ranking, °leading, °chief, °superior, °preeminent, ruling, regnant, reigning, governing, all-powerful, °absolute, °unlimited 3 °royal, °regal, °majestic, °noble, lordly, aristocratic, kingly, queenly

sovereignty *n.* suzerainty, hegemony, °dominion, °rule, °preeminence, °power, °jurisdiction, °authority, °leadership, °command, °sway, °supremacy, ascendancy, primacy

sow *v.* °seed, disseminate, °broadcast, °plant

space *n.* 1 spaciousness, °room, °place, °expanse, elbowroom, °leeway, °margin, latitude, °play 2 °blank 3 °interval, °lapse, °period, °time, hiatus, lacuna, °span, while, duration, °extent, °spell, °stretch, °pause, °wait, °intermission, °gap, °break, °interruption 4 °accommodation, °seat, berth, °room, °place —*v.* 5 °arrange, °organize, array, °set out, align, °range, °order, °rank, °lay out, °measure (out)

spacious *adj.* °vast, °large, °extensive, °enormous, °wide, °broad, commodious, °ample, °expansive, °roomy, °huge, sizable, °large, capacious, °great, °immense, outsize(d), °voluminous, oversize(d)

span *n.* 1 °bridge, °link, °stretch, overpass, *Chiefly Brit* flyover 2 °course, °extent, °interval, °stretch, °period, °time, °term, °spell —*v.* 3 °cross, stretch over, reach over, extend over, °go over, °bridge

spank *v.* °slap, smack, put *or* take over one's knee, thrash, °paddle; °chastise, °punish, °castigate; *Colloq* wallop, tan (someone's) hide, paddywhack *or* paddywack, whack, give (someone) a (good) licking *or* hiding

spanking *adj.* 1 spick-and-span *or* spic-and-span, °smart, °bright, °snappy, gleaming, °brand-new, °fine, °remarkable, °outstanding, °big, °large, °great 2 °brisk, °lively, °crisp, °bracing, °fresh, freshening, rattling, °strong, °invigorating, blustery 3 °quick, °rapid, °swift, °lively, °snappy, °fast, °smart, °energetic, °vigorous, °brisk

spar[1] *n.* Nautical mast, yard, yardarm, °boom, boomkin, gaff, jigger, mizzen, *Colloq* °stick, °pole

spar[2] *v.* 1 °fight, °box, exchange blows; shadowbox 2 °dispute, °argue, °bicker, squabble, wrangle, bandy words, have words; °fight, *Colloq* °scrap

spare *adj.* 1 °extra, °surplus, supernumerary, °auxiliary, °supplementary, additional; °odd, °leftover; °in reserve, °in addition 2 unoccupied, °leftover, °leisure, °free, °surplus, °extra; not spoken for 3 °thin, °skinny, °scrawny, cadaverous, °gaunt, °rawboned, °meager, gangling, lank(y), °wiry, °slim, °slender; all skin and bones 4 See **sparing,** below. 5 °meager, °frugal, °small, skimpy, °modest, °scanty —*v.* 6 °save, °rescue, °deliver, °redeem 7 °pardon, let go, °release, have mercy on, °let off, °free, °liberate 8 °allow, °relinquish, let go (of), °give, °award, °bestow, let have, °donate, °part with, °give, °yield 9 °avoid, °dispense with, manage *or* do without, °give up, °forgo, °forsake, °surrender, °sacrifice

sparing *adj.* 1 °thrifty, °saving, °frugal, °spare, °careful, °prudent, parsimonious, °economical, °penurious, °mean; penny-pinching, stingy, niggardly, °miserly, °close, closefisted, tightfisted, °cheap, *Colloq* °tight, *Brit* mingy 2 See **sparse, 2** below.

spark *n.* 1 scintilla, °flicker, glimmer, glint, °sparkle, °speck, °hint, °suggestion, °vestige, atom, whit, °jot (or tittle), iota —*v.* 2 Often, ***spark off.*** set *or* touch off, ignite, °kindle, enkindle, °electrify, °animate, trigger, °energize, galvanize, °activate, °excite, °stimulate, set in motion, °bring about, °start (up), °begin, °initiate, °inspire, inspirit, °provoke, °precipitate

sparkle *v.* 1 °glitter, scintillate, glint, °flicker, °shine, °twinkle, wink, °blink, glimmer, °flash, coruscate, °blaze, °burn, °flame 2 effervesce, °fizz, °bubble —*n.* 3 °glitter, scintillation, °twinkle, coruscation, °dazzle, °spark, °gleam, brightness, °brilliance, °radiance 4 vivacity, liveliness, °fire, brightness, wittiness, effervescence, ebullience, °excitement, °animation, °vigor, °energy, °spirit, °cheer, °joy, lightheartedness, élan, zeal.

°gusto, °dash, °life, °gaiety, °cheer, cheerfulness; certain something; *Colloq* vim, zip, zing, pizazz, oomph

sparse *adj.* **1** °thin (on the ground), °few (and far between), °meager, °scanty, (widely) dispersed *or* scattered, °spread out, °spotty, °in short supply, °scarce **2** °little, °limited, °meager, scant, °sparing, inappreciable, not much, °insignificant

Spartan *adj.* austere, °strict, °severe, °harsh, °hard, °stern, rigorous, °rigid, ascetic, stringent, controlled, disciplined, self-denying, abstinent, abstemious

spasm *n.* **1** convulsion, °throe, °fit, twitch, °paroxysm **2** °fit, °seizure, convulsion, °paroxysm, °spell, °outburst, °burst, °eruption

spasmodic *adj.* **1** spasmodical, paroxysmal, convulsive, jerky, jerking, °sudden, *Technical* spastic **2** °fitful, °irregular, °intermittent, arrhythmic, °random, interrupted, °sporadic, °erratic, °occasional, °periodic, unsustained, discontinuous, pulsating, cyclic(al), °broken

spate *n.* °flood, inundation, onrush, °onset, °rush, deluge, °outpouring, outflow, outflowing, °flow

spatter *v.* °splash, splatter, speckle, bespatter, °spray, °dabble, daub, bedaub, sprinkle, besprinkle, *Brit* splodge, *US* splotch

spawn *v.* give birth to, °yield, °bear, °bring forth, °breed, beget, °create, °father, sire, °produce, °generate, engender, °give rise to, °bring about, °cause

speak *v.* **1** °talk, °converse, discourse **2** °talk to, converse *or* discourse with, °address, say (something *or*) anything to **3** °talk, communicate in, discourse *or* converse in, utter in, articulate in, °use **4** °express, utter, °say, °state, °tell, °pronounce, °enunciate, °voice; articulate, °make known, °communicate, °reveal, °indicate **5** °symbolize, betoken, °signify, °communicate, convey, °indicate **6** ***so to speak.*** as it were, in a manner of speaking, figuratively *or* metaphorically (speaking) **7** ***speak for.*** **(a)** °support, °uphold, °defend, °stand up for, °plead for, make a plea for, °recommend, *Colloq* °stick up for **(b)** act on *or* in behalf of, act for, °represent, act as agent for **(c)** °demand, °require, °beg, °request, °ask for **8** ***speak for itself.*** be self-evident, be obvious, be significant **9** ***speak of.*** °mention, advert to, allude to, °refer to, make reference to, °comment on, speak *or* talk about **10** ***speak on.*** °discuss, °address, discourse upon *or* on, °speak to, °treat (of), °deal with, °examine, touch upon *or* on **11** ***speak out or up.*** **(a)** talk (more) loudly *or* clearly, make oneself heard **(b)** talk freely *or* unreservedly, express one's opinion, speak one's mind, °declare, °come out, state one's position, take a stand **12** ***speak to.*** **(a)** °reprove, °scold, °reprimand, °rebuke, admonish, °warn, °lecture **(b)** be meaningful to, appeal to, °influence, °affect, °touch **(c)** accost, °address, °talk to, *Formal* apostrophize **(d)** See **10,** above. **13** ***spoken for.*** °reserved, °engaged, bespoke, °set aside, accounted for, chosen, selected

speaker *n.* orator, lecturer; keynoter; °rabble-rouser, demagogue, *Colloq* tub-thumper, spieler

spearhead *v.* **1** °launch, °initiate, °lead (the way), take the initiative, °pioneer, blaze the trail, °break the ice, take the lead, be in the van *or* vanguard —*n.* **2** vanguard, advance guard, van, forefront, cutting edge

special *adj.* **1** °particular, °specific, °exceptional, uncommon, especial, °rare, °unusual, out-of-the-ordinary, °extraordinary, °different, °unorthodox, unconventional, °unique, °precise, °individual, °singular, °distinctive, specialized, °certain, °remarkable, inimitable, idiosyncratic, °curious, °peculiar, °odd, °strange, °bizarre, °weird, one-of-a-kind; °distinguished, °notable, °noteworthy **2** °significant, °important, °momentous, earth-shaking, °memorable, red-letter; °gala, festive, celebratory **3** °pointed, concerted, °deliberate, °particular, °extra, °determined **4** °exclusive, °express, °individual, °extra **5** °dear, °intimate, °particular, °good, °close, °bosom, °staunch, °loyal, °faithful, °devoted, °steadfast; dearest, °best, closest; esteemed, valued **6** °prime, °primary, °major, °prominent, °paramount —*n.* **7** See **specialty, 2** below.

specialist *n.* °expert, °authority, °professional, °master, connoisseur, maestro, artist, °adept, *Chiefly Brit* artiste

specially *adv.* °especially, °particularly, °custom, °expressly, exclusively

specialty *n.* **1** °expertise, °talent, °genius, °gift, °skill, °aptitude, °trade, °craft, °accomplishment, °ability, °strength, °forte, strong point, °capability, adeptness, °art, °sphere, °field, °area, °subject, concentration, specialization, métier, *Chiefly Brit* speciality, *Colloq* °bag, °thing, cup of tea, °baby, claim to fame **2** ***pièce de résistance, spécialité de la maison,*** °special, *Chiefly Brit* speciality, *US* blueplate special

specific *adj.* **1** °definite, °precise, °exact, °particular, °explicit, °express, unambiguous, °definitive, clear-cut, unequivocal, (well-)defined, °determined, specified, °individual, °peculiar, °certain, °limited, indicated, °predetermined, established, spelled out, delineated, °set, °distinct, °fixed, circumscribed, restricted **2** Often, ***specific to.*** °characteristic (of), unique to, °individual (to), sui generis, °proper (to), °typical (of), °peculiar to, identified with, °personal (to), °discrete (to), °special (to), associated with

specification *n.* **1** °identification, identifying, °description, describing, particularization, particularizing, specifying, naming **2** itemization, itemizing, °list, listing, checklist, inventory, list of particulars, °detail, enumeration **3** °requirement, qualification, °condition, °restriction, °stipulation, °consideration

specify *v.* particularize, °enumerate, °itemize, °name, denominate, °list, °indicate,

°mention, °identify, cite, °define, °detail, °stipulate, °spell out, set out *or* forth, individualize, be specific about, delineate, °determine, disambiguate, °establish

specimen *n.* °sample, °example, °instance, exemplar, °representative, °representation; °illustration, °case (in point), °type, °model, °pattern

specious *adj.* °deceptive, °superficial, casuistic, ostensible, misleading, °apparent, °seeming, fallacious, sophistic(al), °plausible, °likely, conceivable, °possible, °supposed, purported, presumed, presumable, °alleged, °so-called

speck *n.* °spot, °dot, fleck, mote, speckle, °mark, °bit, °particle; °crumb, iota, °jot (or tittle), whit, atom, molecule, °touch, °hint, °suggestion, °suspicion, tinge, °modicum, °amount, °grain, smidgen

speckled *adj.* spotted, °mottled, dotted, sprinkled, °flecked, stippled, dapple(d), freckled, brindle(d); discolored, spattered, bespattered

spectacle *n.* **1** °show, °display, °sight, °performance, °event, °presentation, °exhibition, °exhibit, °exposition, °demonstration, °extravaganza, °marvel, °wonder, °sensation **2** °fool, laughingstock, °curiosity **3** ***spectacles.*** eyeglasses, °glasses, *Colloq* specs

spectator *n.* °witness, °eyewitness, °observer, viewer, °onlooker, looker-on, beholder, watcher

specter *n.* **1** °ghost, °phantom, wraith, apparition, °vision, °spirit, °shade, revenant, doppelgänger, chimera, *Colloq* spook, bogeyman *or* bogyman **2** °image, °vision, °(mental) picture

spectral *adj.* °ghostly, ghostlike, °phantom, °eerie, wraithlike, incorporeal, °unearthly, °supernatural, °weird, *Colloq* spooky

speculate *v.* **1** Often, ***speculate on or upon or about or over.*** reflect (on *or* about *or* over), °consider, muse (on *or* about *or* over), meditate (on *or* over *or* about), contemplate (on *or* about), cogitate (on *or* about), think (about *or* over *or* on), ponder (over *or* about), mull over, chew on *or* over, ruminate (on *or* over *or* about), °wonder (about), deliberate (over *or* on *or* about), °weigh, °judge, °evaluate, theorize (on *or* about), conjecture (on *or* about), postulate, hypothesize **2** °gamble, wager, take a chance, *Colloq* have a flutter, play the market, take a plunge

speculation *n.* **1** conjecture, °guess, °hypothesis, theory, guesswork, postulation, °surmise, °supposition, °opinion **2** °thinking, rumination, cogitation, °reflection, meditation, contemplation, °consideration, cerebration, pondering, wondering, deliberation, °evaluation **3** gambling, °gamble, wagering, wager, taking (a) chance(s) *or* risk(s), chance-taking

speculative *adj.* **1** °intellectual, ideational, °abstract, cogitative, notional, °theoretical, °hypothetical, conjectural, suppositional, supposititious *or* suppositious, suppositive, °rational, ratiocinative, °ideal, idealized, °idealistic, °unrealistic, unpractical, °impractical, analytical **2** °risky, °hazardous, °uncertain, °unreliable, untrustworthy, °doubtful, dubious, untested, unproven, unproved, *Colloq* iffy, chancy, *Slang* °dicey

speech *n.* **1** speaking, talking, articulation, °diction, °language, °expression, enunciation, elocution, speech pattern; communication **2** °oration, °address, °lecture, °talk, discourse, disquisition, °sermon, homily; °tirade, °harangue, philippic; °(sales) pitch, °line, song and dance; *Colloq* spiel, °blast **3** °dialect, idiolect, °jargon, °parlance, °idiom, *façon de parler,* °language, °tongue, *Colloq* °lingo

speechless *adj.* **1** °mute, °dumb, voiceless **2** dumbfounded *or* dumfounded, dumbstruck *or* dumbstricken, wordless, struck dumb, °tongue-tied, °thunderstruck, shocked, dazed, °inarticulate, paralyzed, nonplussed

speed *n.* **1** °rapidity, fleetness, quickness, speediness, swiftness, °velocity, dispatch *or* despatch, °hurry, hurriedness, °haste, hastiness, celerity, alacrity, expeditiousness, °expedition, briskness, promptness, timeliness; suddenness, precipitateness, precipitousness, abruptness —*v.* **2** Often, ***speed up.*** accelerate, °move, °expedite, °forward, °advance, °facilitate, °boost, °further, °promote, °help, °assist, °aid, *Colloq* give a leg up **3** °hasten, make haste, °hurry, °rush, °charge, dart, °bolt, °shoot, °run, °race, sprint, °fly, °streak, °scurry, °tear, °hustle, °scramble, scamper, °career, highball, bowl along, go *or* fly like the wind, *Colloq* go hell for leather, go like a bat out of hell, belt along, °step on it, put one's foot down, zip, zoom, skedaddle, go like a shot, *US* hightail it, step on the gas, go like greased lightning, make tracks, *Slang US* burn rubber

speedy *adj.* **1** °quick, °rapid, °swift, °brisk, °expeditious, °fast, °immediate, °prompt **2** °hasty, °precipitate, °precipitous, °hurried, °summary **3** °fleet, °nimble, wing-footed, winged, °fast, °quick, °rapid, °swift

spell[1] *n.* **1** °period, °interval, °time, °term, °season; °stint, °turn, °run, °course, °shift, °tour (of duty), °watch, °round —*v.* **2** °relieve, °replace, °substitute for, take over for

spell[2] *n.* **1** °enchantment, allure, °charm, °magic, witchcraft, witchery, °fascination, captivation, enthrallment **2** incantation, °formula, °charm **3** °attraction, °lure, allure, °appeal, °draw, °pull, °magnetism, °fascination, °influence, mesmerism, hypnotic effect

spell[3] *v.* **1** augur, portend, presage, °promise, hold promise of, °signify, °point to, °indicate, °omen, °bode, look like, °amount to, °mean **2** ***spell out.*** °specify, delineate, make clear *or* plain *or* explicit, °clarify, elucidate

spellbinding *adj.* fascinating, °enchanting, °enthralling, captivating, enrapturing, bewitching, mesmerizing, charming, °overpowering

spend *v.* **1** °pay out, disburse, °expend, °lay

out, *Colloq* fork out, dish out, °shell out, *Brit* splash out **2** squander, °throw away, °fritter away, °waste, °go through, °splurge, °lavish, °dissipate **3** °devote, °allot, °assign, °invest, °put in, °pass

spendthrift *n.* **1** °profligate, °wastrel, (big) spender, squanderer, °prodigal —*adj.* **2** °wasteful, free-spending, °prodigal, °profligate, squandering, °extravagant, °improvident

spent *adj.* **1** drained, °exhausted, °prostrate, °tired, °fatigued, fagged out, °weary, wearied, worn-out, *Colloq* °(dead) beat, done in, done for, all in, dog-tired, played out, burnt *or* burned out, used up, *Brit* knackered, done up, *US* pooped **2** °exhausted, used up, emptied, gone, expended, finished, *finis*, consumed, depleted

spew *v.* Often, ***spew forth or out or up.*** belch (up *or* out *or* forth), vomit (up *or* forth), °regurgitate, spit up *or* out, °spout, °discharge, °emit, °eject, °send forth, °spurt, °gush, throw up *or* out, disgorge, *Slang* puke

sphere *n.* **1** °globe, °orb, globule, spherule; °drop, droplet, °bubble **2** °society, °class, °level, °caste, °rank, °domain, walk of life, °station, °stratum, °position **3** °area, °field, °province, °subject, °discipline, °range, °specialty, °forte, *Colloq* bailiwick, °territory, °department, °thing, °bag

spherical *adj.* spheric, globular, °round, ball-shaped, ball-like, globelike, globe-shaped, globose *or* globous, globoid, globate(d), spheroid(al)

spice *n.* **1** condiment, °relish, °seasoning, flavor(ing); herb **2** °zest, spiciness, piquancy, °tang, pungency, °bite, sharpness, poignancy, °gusto, °excitement, °seasoning, °dash, élan, °color, °life, °vigor, °interest, stimulation, °stimulant, °spirit, *Colloq* vim, zip, °pep, °kick, pizazz, °punch, ginger, °pepper —*v.* **3** °season, °flavor **4** Often, ***spice up.*** °enliven, inspirit, °stimulate, invigorate

spicy *adj.* **1** zesty, zestful, piquant, tangy, (well-)spiced, (well-)seasoned, °hot, peppery, °sharp, °pungent, °snappy, °biting, full-bodied, °aromatic, °savory, flavorsome, flavorful **2** °off-color, indelicate, °suggestive, °risqué, °improper, °indecent, indecorous, ribald, °racy, °bawdy, °unseemly, °offensive, titillating, °sexy, *Colloq* °hot **3** °scandalous, °sensational, °outrageous, °notorious, revealing, revelatory, °intimate

spike *n.* **1** skewer, °stake, prong, treenail, °nail, °peg, °picket, °pin, pike, °spine —*v.* **2** °impale, °stab, °stick, spear, °pierce, °spit, °lance **3** disable, °thwart, nullify, °disarm, °block, °frustrate, °foil, °void, balk, °check, °cancel, annul **4** °strengthen; °drug, °poison, *Slang* slip in a Mickey (Finn)

spill *v.* **1** pour (out *or* over), overflow, slop *or* run *or* brim over **2** °waste, °throw out, °lose **3** ***spill the beans.*** reveal *or* tell *or* disclose *or* divulge all *or* everything, °blab, °tattle, let the cat out of the bag, °confess, *Slang* squeal, be a stool pigeon *or* stoolie, spill one's guts, °sing (like a canary), *Brit* blow the gaff —*n.* **4** °outpouring, °flood, °leak, leakage **5** °fall, °tumble, °accident, *Colloq* cropper, header

spin *v.* **1** °revolve, °turn, °rotate, °gyrate, °twirl, whirl, °twist, °reel, °pirouette, °pivot **2** °invent, concoct, °make up, °devise, °produce, °fabricate; °weave, °relate, retail, °recount, °narrate, °tell, °unfold **3** be dizzy, suffer vertigo, swim, whirl, be giddy **4** ***spin off.*** °separate, °derive **5** ***spin out.*** °prolong, protract, drag *or* draw out, stretch out, °perpetuate, °continue, °extend, keep alive, keep going —*n.* **6** whirl, whirling, °twirl, twirling, °turn, turning, gyration, °reel, °pirouette, °revolution, revolving, rotation, rotating **7** °drive, whirl, joy ride, °ride, °tour, °excursion, °outing, jaunt

spine *n.* **1** °backbone, spinal column, vertebrae **2** °thorn, needle, barb, °spike, °spur, prong, quill, °ray, barbel, °bristle, °prickle, *Technical* barbule, spicule *or* spiculum *or* spicula

spineless *adj.* **1** *Technical* invertebrate **2** °weak, °feeble, °flabby, °irresolute, weak-willed, °indecisive, °ineffectual, °ineffective, °impotent, °powerless **3** °cowardly, dastardly, pusillanimous, timorous, lily-livered, white-livered, craven, °fearful, °timid, spiritless, °squeamish, *Colloq* yellow, chicken-hearted, chicken, yellow-bellied, wimpish

spiral *n.* **1** helix, °coil, corkscrew, °screw, scroll; whorl, volute, °turn, curl —*adj.* **2** helical, coiled, °screw, corkscrew, cochlear *or* cochleate; scrolled, volute(d), whorled

spire *n.* **1** column, °tower, belfry; steeple, flèche **2** °top, °pinnacle, apex, °peak, °summit, °acme, °tip, °crest, °crown, °vertex

spirit *n.* **1** anima, °breath, °life, °vitality, vital spirit, pneuma, °soul, consciousness, °psyche, self, °heart, °essence **2** °character, temperament, °temper, °persona, °disposition, °mind, °will, willpower, °attitude, °bent, °inclination, °energy, °ardor, °desire, °impetus, °drive, °urge, °eagerness, °zest, zeal, zealousness, °fire, passion(s), °enthusiasm, motivation, mettle, °resolution, °resolve, °intention, °enterprise **3** °zest, pungency, piquancy, °warmth, °fire, °animation, °life, liveliness, vivacity, vivaciousness, °panache, élan, °dash, °spice, *Colloq* °sauce, °pepper **4** See **specter, 1,** above. **5** °bravery, °courage, °grit, °backbone, valor, °pluck, °daring, stoutheartedness, manfulness, manliness, gameness, resoluteness, °will, willpower, *Colloq* vim, °spunk, get-up-and-go, °(right) stuff, °guts, *US* sand **6** °meaning, °sense, °tenor, signification, purport, °intent, °intention, °purpose, °aim, °implication, °message, °essence, °quintessence, °core, °heart, °meat, °pith, °substance, marrow **7** °attitude, °principle, °thought, °idea, °inspiration, °notion, °feeling, °inclination, impulse **8** Often, ***spirits.*** °temper, °mood, °sentiments, °feelings, °cheer, °humor, °frame of mind; °morale **9** ***spirits.*** **(a)** °feelings, °mood, °temper, °sentiments; °morale, esprit de corps, team spirit **(b)** °alcohol, °liquor,

°whiskey, strong drink, *Colloq* °booze, firewater, *Slang chiefly US and Canadian* hooch *or* hootch —*v.* **10** ***spirit away or off.*** °abduct, make off *or* away with, °carry off, °transport, take away, °kidnap, steal (off *or* away with), whisk away, abscond with; make disappear

spirited *adj.* °lively, °sprightly, °energetic, °vigorous, °animated, sparkling, °dynamic, °buoyant, °effervescent, °vivacious, °ardent, mettlesome

spiritual *adj.* **1** °sacred, ecclesiastic(al), churchly, °clerical, °priestly, devotional, °holy, °divine, sacerdotal, °religious, nonsecular **2** nonmaterial, incorporeal, psychic(al), °mental, °psychological, inner

spit *v.* **1** expectorate; dribble, salivate, drool, °slaver, sputter, splutter; °discharge, °spew (forth), °eject **2** ***spitting image or spit and image.*** °twin, °duplicate, clone, °image, counterpart, °likeness, °copy —*n.* **3** spittle, saliva, drool, *Technical* sputum

spite *n.* **1** spitefulness, maliciousness, malice, malevolence, malignity, °ill will, °venom, spleen, °rancor, °animosity, °gall (and wormwood), °resentment, °bitterness, °hostility, °antagonism, hatred, °hate, *Colloq* bitchiness **2** ***in spite of.*** °despite, °notwithstanding, °regardless of, ignoring, in defiance of —*v.* **3** °annoy, °irritate, vex, °upset, disconcert, °offend, °provoke, °discomfit, pique, °put out, °hurt, °injure, °wound, *Colloq* peeve, get under (someone's) skin, needle, *US* do a number on

spiteful *adj.* °rancorous, °bitter, acrimonious, malevolent, malicious, °venomous, °hateful, invidious, °hostile, antagonistic, unfriendly, unforgiving, retaliative *or* retaliatory, °punitive, retributive *or* retributory

splash *v.* **1** °spatter, bespatter, splatter, °shower, °spray, sprinkle, besprinkle, *Brit* splodge *or US also* splotch; mottle, °spot **2** blazon, °spread, °plaster —*n.* **3** °spatter, °spray, splatter, sprinkle, °spot, °stain, °smear, smudge, *Brit* splodge *or US also* splotch **4** °impression, °show, °uproar, ado, brouhaha, °sensation, commotion, °excitement, *US* foofaraw, *Colloq* to-do

splendid *adj.* **1** splendorous, °magnificent, resplendent, °dazzling, °gorgeous, °showy, °dashing, °marvelous, spectacular, °grand, °glorious, °lavish, °ornate, °sumptuous, °majestic, °brilliant, °extraordinary, °exceptional, °superb, °supreme, °imposing, °impressive, awe-inspiring, °awesome, °lush, °plush, °rich, °luxurious, *Colloq* splendiferous, °posh, swank(y), ritzy **2** °impressive, °marvelous, °brilliant, °eminent, °prominent, °superior, °noteworthy, °notable, °celebrated, °illustrious, °famous, °distinguished, °exemplary, °remarkable, °admirable, °conspicuous, °outstanding, °sublime, °striking, °extraordinary, °successful, °admirable, °meritorious, creditable **3** °excellent, °superior, °preeminent, °fine, °marvelous, °extraordinary, °exceptional, °unbelievable, °incredible, first-class, unequaled, unsurpassed, °fabulous, °peerless, °matchless, °nonpareil, °superlative, °praiseworthy, °laudable, *Brit* °brilliant, *Colloq* °great, °colossal, supercolossal, stupendous, fab, °fantastic, °super, smashing, A-1 *or* A-one, tiptop, °capital, *Brit* brill, *Slang* far-out, °way-out, °dandy, °cool, °keen, *US* °solid, out-of-sight, fantabulous, °boss, °neat, °major

splendor *n.* **1** magnificence, °grandeur, °brilliance, °display, °radiance, resplendence, sumptuousness, stateliness, majesty, panoply, °spectacle, °show, °glory, °pomp, gorgeousness, °dazzle, refulgence, °beauty, splendidness, exquisiteness, luxuriousness, richness, lavishness, °luxury, *Colloq* swankiness, poshness, swank, ritziness **2** °brilliance, °shine, °luster, °light, effulgence, brightness, °glitter, °dazzle, refulgence, luminosity, luminousness, °gloss

splice *v.* **1** °join, °unite, °marry, °bind, conjoin; °knit, °entwine, intertwine, °braid, plait, °twist, interlace —*n.* **2** joining, °union, splicing, °joint, connection *or Brit* connexion, °tie, °bond, binding, °fastening, linking, linkage

splinter *n.* **1** °sliver, °fragment, °piece; °scrap, shard *or* sherd, °shred, °chip —*v.* **2** °shatter, °break, °fragment, °split, °disintegrate, smash into smithereens

split *v.* **1** Often, ***split up or apart.*** °divide, °separate, °cleave, cut *or* chop apart, cut *or* chop in two, pull *or* tear apart, °rend, break *or* snap apart *or* in two, °break up, °come apart, °rupture, °partition, °detach, become detached; bisect, dichotomize **2** Often, ***split up.*** °divorce, °separate, go separate ways, °break up, part company **3** Often, ***split up.*** °branch, fork, °diverge, °separate **4** Often, ***split up.*** °divide (up), apportion, deal out, dole out, °distribute, °allot, share *or* parcel out, °carve up **5** °burst, crack *or* break up, fall apart *or* about, *Slang* bust **6** °leave, °depart, °go, *Slang* take a (runout) powder, take it on the lam, °beat it, scram, skedaddle —*n.* **7** °crack, cleft, fissure, °chink, °cranny, °slit, °slot, °crevice, °groove, °furrow, °channel, sulcus; °gap, hiatus, lacuna, °opening, °separation, °division, chasm; °rift, °break, °rupture, °fracture; °slash, °gash, °tear, °rip, °rent **8** °division, dichotomy, °schism, °breach, °rupture, °partition, disunion, °discord; °break, °separation —*adj.* **9** divided, separated; halved, bisected, cleft; °cut, °broken, fractured

splurge *n.* **1** °display, °show, ostentatiousness, °extravagance, °indulgence, access, °splash, °burst, °outburst, °spree —*v.* **2** Often, ***splurge on.*** squander *or* dissipate *or* waste *or* burn (up) *or* throw away money (on), show off *or* flaunt one's money, *Slang* blow everything (on)

spoil *v.* **1** °ruin, °destroy, °wreck, °queer, °mess up, °upset, °demolish, °harm, °damage, *Colloq* °kill **2** °damage, °mar, °injure, °harm, °deface, disfigure, °scar, °blemish **3** °baby, mollycoddle, °coddle, °indulge, °pamper, dote on, spoon-feed, *Rare* cocker **4**

°turn, go off *or* bad, curdle, molder, °decay, °decompose, become addle(d), °rot, °putrefy, mildew **5** ***be spoiling for.*** itch (for *or* after), °yearn (for), be eager (for), be keen (for), °look for, be bent on, be desirous of, crave, be after —*n.* **6** ***spoils.*** °loot, °booty, °plunder, °pillage, prizes, pickings, *Slang* swag, °take, °goods, boodle

spoilsport *n.* °killjoy, damper, dog in the manger, *Colloq* wet blanket, *US* party pooper

spoken *adj.* **1** °oral, vocal, °verbal, viva voce **2** ***spoken for.*** See **speak, 13,** above.

sponsor *n.* **1** °backer, °supporter, promoter, angel, °patron, Maecenas, subsidizer **2** (radio *or* television) advertiser —*v.* **3** °back, °support, °promote, °fund, °patronize, °subsidize, °finance, °underwrite

spontaneous *adj.* **1** unannounced, °unpremeditated, unplanned, impromptu, °extemporaneous, extempore, °unprepared, unrehearsed, °offhand, ad-lib, spur-of-the-moment, *Colloq* off the cuff **2** °natural, unforced, unbidden, °instinctive, instinctual, °unconscious, reflex, °automatic, °mechanical, °immediate, °offhand, °unguarded, °unthinking, unwitting, °involuntary, °impetuous, °impulsive, *Slang* knee-jerk

sporadic *adj.* °occasional, °intermittent, °random, °irregular, uneven, °erratic, °chance, unexpected; spasmodic(al), °fitful, periodic(al)

sport *n.* **1** °recreation, °diversion, °pastime, °amusement, °entertainment, °play, °distraction, °relaxation, divertissement, °pleasure, °enjoyment, °fun **2** jest, °humor, °fun, °mockery **3** ***make sport of.*** °tease, °deride, make a laughingstock, °(hold up to) ridicule, make a fool of —*v.* **4** °frolic, gambol, °cavort, romp, °caper, °play, °frisk, °lark, rollick, skip about **5** °show off, °exhibit, °flaunt, °display, °wear

sportive *adj.* °frisky, gamboling, cavorting, frolicking, romping, capering, rollicking, °sprightly, coltish, °spirited, °frolicsome, °buoyant, gamesome, °gay, °kittenish, °merry, °playful, °gleeful, lighthearted, °blithe, prankish, waggish

sportsmanship *n.* fair play, sportsmanliness, fairness, honorableness, °honesty, °honor, °probity, scrupulousness, °integrity, uprightness, °justice, justness

sporty *adj.* °informal, °casual; °stylish, °chic, °smart, °trendy, °fashionable, modish, à la mode, up-to-date, °showy, °rakish, *Colloq* swank(y), °loud, *Slang* classy, °swell, °flashy, snazzy, °sharp, *US and Canadian* spiffy

spot *n.* **1** °mark, °patch, °speck, °blot, blotch, °blemish, speckle, fleck, °particle, mote, macula, smudge, °stain, °stigma, discoloration, *Brit* splodge *or US also* splotch **2** °site, °place, °locale, °location, locality, °scene, °setting, °section, °area, °neighborhood, °quarter **3** °morsel, °bit, °bite, *Colloq* smidgen **4** °predicament, °situation, °quandary, °mess **5** ***spots.*** eruptions, pimples, acne, pustules, blackheads, comedos *or* comedones, whiteheads; boils, blains, wens; pockmarks; *US and Canadian old-fashioned* zits, hickeys —*v.* **6** °see, °catch sight of, glimpse, discern, °identify, °pick out, °distinguish, °single out, °detect, °sight, °recognize, °make out, descry **7** °mark, °stain, fleck, speckle, °spray, °splash, °spatter, bespatter, °sully, °soil, °dirty, °taint, besmirch, smudge

spotless *adj.* **1** °immaculate, °clean, gleaming, °shiny, °polished, unspotted, spick-and-span *or* spic-and-span **2** °pure, unsullied, unassailable, °flawless, °faultless, °untarnished, °blameless, °irreproachable

spotlight *n.* **1** arc light, searchlight, *US* pin spotlight, *Colloq US* °(pin) spot **2** °focus (of attention), limelight, public eye —*v.* **3** °light (up), °illuminate, focus (light) upon *or* on, shine *or* shed *or* throw *or* cast light upon *or* on, °emphasize, highlight, draw attention to, °feature, give prominence to, °stress, accentuate, °accent, °point up, underscore, underline

spotty *adj.* **1** spotted, dotted, °speckled, freckled, °flecked, blotched, blotchy, stained, °marked, pied, piebald, brindle(d), skewbald, °mottled, motley, dapple(d), macular, foxed; soiled, °dirty; *Brit* splodgy, splodged *or US also* splotchy, splotched **2** pimply, pimpled, blotched, blotchy, acned, pockmarked, pocky, °bad, *Scots* plouky *or* plooky **3** patchy, °irregular, uneven, °erratic, °sporadic, °capricious, °fitful

spout *v.* **1** °discharge, °emit, squirt, °spurt, jet, °shoot, °gush, °erupt, spew (up *or* out *or* forth), °spit, °eject, disgorge, vomit (up *or* forth), pour (out *or* forth), °flow, °stream **2** °ramble on, °rant, °rave, °carry on, pontificate, orate, declaim, °hold forth, maunder (on), witter on, expatiate, speechify, °talk, *Colloq* °go on, *Brit* rabbit on —*n.* **3** waterspout, gargoyle, downspout, duct, °drain, °outlet, conduit **4** ***up the spout.*** gone, °lost, destroyed, beyond hope *or* recovery, to be written off *or* abandoned

sprawl *v.* **1** °spread (out), °stretch (out), straddle, °ramble, °meander, °wander, °straggle, branch out **2** °spread out, stretch out, loll, °lounge, °slouch, °slump, °recline, lie about *or* around —*n.* **3** °spread, °stretch, °expansion, °extension

spray[1] *v.* **1** sprinkle, °spatter, °scatter, °shower, °disperse, °diffuse, atomize, °spread —*n.* **2** °shower, sprinkling, drizzle, °mist, sprinkle, spindrift *or* spoondrift **3** atomizer, sprayer, sprinkler, vaporizer, aerosol

spray[2] *n.* flower *or* floral arrangement, nosegay, posy, °bouquet, sprig, °branch, bough

spread *v.* **1** Often, ***spread out.*** °diffuse, °distribute, °disperse, disseminate, °broadcast, °sow, °scatter, °strew, °shed, dispel, °dissipate **2** Often, ***spread about*** *or* ***around.*** °broadcast, °publicize, °make known, bruit about, °air, televise, °circulate, °publish, °distribute, disseminate, trumpet, °announce, °pronounce, promulgate, advertise, enounce, °make public, tell the world, herald, °repeat, °recite 3 Often, *spread out.* °unfold, °draw out, °display, stretch out, open out, °extend, °lay out, fan out, unroll, unfurl 4 Often, *spread out.* °stretch (out), °extend, protract, °prolong, drag out, °distribute, °disperse 5 Often, *spread out.* °stretch, °extend, °separate, put apart *or* out, °part 6 °grow, °develop, °increase, broaden, °expand, °extend, °widen, °enlarge, mushroom, °proliferate, °sprawl, branch out; metastasize 7 °smear, °apply, °smooth, °put, °rub, °cover, layer, °plaster, °plate, °coat, °wash, °glaze, °paint, varnish, overlay, overspread; °cloak, °mantle, swaddle, °wrap, blanket —*n.* 8 spreading, °extension, extending, °expansion, expanding, enlargement, enlarging, °development, developing, °increase, increasing, °proliferation, proliferating, broadening, °growth, widening, mushrooming, dispersion, dispersal, dispersing, dissemination, disseminating, °distribution, distributing, dispensation, dispensing 9 °extent, °expanse, °area, °span, °sweep, vastness, °stretch, °reach, °breadth, °depth, °size, dimensions, compass, °limits, °bounds, boundary *or* boundaries 10 °range, °extent, °scope, °span, °difference 11 °feast, °banquet, °meal, dinner, repast, barbecue; °table; *Colloq* °feed 12 butter, margarine, °jam, jelly, °preserve, °conserve, confiture, paste, *US old-fashioned* oleo 13 ranch, landholding, holding, °property, °place, plantation, °farm, homestead 14 bedspread, counterpane, coverlet, bedcover, °cover, quilt, eiderdown, duvet, afghan, *US* comforter, *US and Canadian* °throw

spree *n.* °frolic, romp, °lark, °outing, escapade, °revel, wild party, °fling, debauch, °orgy, bacchanalia; drinking bout, carousal, *Colloq* °bender, binge, °jag

sprightly *adj.* °lively, chipper, spry, °vivacious, °cheerful, °gay, °brisk, °animated, °sportive, °active, °alert, °nimble, °agile, °energetic, °jaunty, °perky, °playful, °spirited

spring *v.* 1 °leap, °bound, °jump, °hop, vault, dart, °fly, °bounce 2 °arise, °appear, °grow, °come up, °rise, come into being *or* existence, be born, °emerge, °sprout, shoot up, burst forth 3 Often, *spring up or from.* °originate, °begin, °start, evolve; °proceed from, stem from, descend from, derive from, come from, develop from 4 start *or* begin *or* experience *or* cause to occur *or* appear *or* happen suddenly *or* unexpectedly, °broach, °pop, introduce *or* divulge *or* reveal *or* disclose suddenly *or* unexpectedly 5 *spring for.* °pay for, treat (someone) to, assume the expense(s) of —*n.* 6 °leap, °bound, °jump, °hop, vault, °bounce, °skip 7 bounciness, °bounce, resiliency, °resilience, springiness, buoyancy, °elasticity, sprightliness, airiness, °flexibility 8 °source, fount, fountainhead, wellspring, °well, °origin, °beginning, °root 9 springtime, Eastertide, Maytime —*adj.* 10 vernal

sprout *v.* bud, germinate, °come up, °arise, °begin, bloom, blossom, °flower

spruce *adj.* 1 °neat, °dapper, °smart, °trim, well-turned-out, °well-groomed, °elegant, *Colloq* natty —*v.* 2 *spruce up.* °tidy (up), °neaten (up), °primp, °clean (up), straighten out *or* up, smarten (up), titivate *or* tittivate

spunk *n.* °nerve, °courage, °pluck, °spirit, gameness, °resolve, °resolution, mettle, °heart, °grit, spunkiness, °backbone, marrow, *Colloq* °guts, °gumption, *Brit* °bottle, *US* sand

spur *n.* 1 goad, °prod, urging, impulse, °incitement, instigation, prompting, °pressure, stimulus, stimulation, °incentive, °provocation, °inducement, °encouragement, °motive, motivation 2 °projection, prong, °spike, °spine, gaff, barb, quill, tine, barbel, barbule, °process 3 *on the spur of the moment.* impetuously, impulsively, unthinkingly, unpremeditatedly, impromptu, on the spot; rashly, thoughtlessly, recklessly, °hastily, brashly, incautiously, unexpectedly, °suddenly —*v.* 4 goad, °prod, °urge, egg on, impel, °incite, °prompt, press, °push, pressure *or Brit* pressurize, °stimulate, °drive, °provoke, °induce, °encourage, °motivate, °excite, °animate

spurious *adj.* °false, °counterfeit, °sham, °fake, °fraudulent, °bogus, °mock, °imitation, simulated, unauthentic, ungenuine, forged, feigned, °pretended, °deceitful, meretricious, contrived, °factitious, °artificial, ersatz, °synthetic, *Colloq* pseudo, *Brit* phoney, *Chiefly US* °phony

spurn *v.* °reject, disdain, °scorn, contemn, °despise, °rebuff, °repudiate, °refuse, sneer at, snub, °brush off, °turn down, turn one's back on *or* upon, look down on *or* upon, *Colloq* cold-shoulder, turn one's nose up at, °sneeze at

spurt *n.* 1 °burst, access, °effort, outbreak, °spell, °interval, °spate, °moment, °instant 2 °increase, °advance, acceleration, °rise, °improvement —*v.* 3 °gush, °spew, squirt, jet, °shoot, °erupt, °burst, °surge

spy *n.* 1 double agent, foreign agent, secret (service) agent, intelligence agent, undercover agent, mole, fifth columnist, CIA man *or* woman *or* agent, *Brit* MI5 *or* MI6 man *or* woman *or* agent; °informer, informant, *Colloq* mole, *Slang* stool pigeon, stoolie, fink, rat fink —*v.* 2 Usually, *spy on or upon.* °follow, °shadow, °trail, °watch, °observe, °reconnoiter, keep under surveillance, *US* surveil, *Colloq* °tail, °check out, °case 3 espy, glimpse, °spot, catch sight *or* a glimpse of, descry, °note, °notice, °see, discern

spying *n.* espionage, undercover work, secret service; detection, °intelligence, °surveillance

squad *n.* °unit, °team, °band, °company, °crew, °force, troop, cadre, °gang, °section, °group, squadron, °platoon, °party

square *adj.* 1 equilateral, quadrangular, rectangular, right-angled, quadrilateral, four-sided, cubic, cubed, six-sided, boxy 2 °equal, on a par, °even, on equal terms, settled, balanced **3** °even, °true, °exact, °straight, °accurate, °precise, °correct **4** °honorable, °upright, °honest, straightforward, °fair (and square), °decent, °ethical, °open, (open and) above board, °right, °(right and) proper, °clean, °just, °equitable, *Colloq* °on the level, on the up and up **5** healthful, °healthy, °nutritious, °substantial, °solid, °full, °generous, °satisfying, °filling, unstinting **6** naive *or* naïve *or* naïf, °innocent; °bourgeois, °conservative, °conventional, °unsophisticated, °provincial, °old-fashioned, conformist, °strait-laced, unimaginative, °predictable, *Colloq* antediluvian, up tight, out of it, not with it, not in the know, not hip *or* hep, unhip, °stuffy, °behind the times, °straight —*n.* **7** rectilinear figure, rectangle; cube, °block **8** plaza, piazza, °place, °park, °(village) green, marketplace, °market (square), agora, quadrangle **9** °bourgeois, °conservative, conformist, traditionalist, (old) fogy *or* fogey, diehard; °outsider; *Colloq* stuffed shirt, fuddy-duddy, *US* longhair, *Slang US* nerd, dweeb —*v.* **10** °stiffen, throw back, °straighten (up), °tense **11** Usually, ***square with.*** °meet, °match (with), conform to *or* with, °obey, correspond to *or* with, tally with, accord with, °agree with, reconcile with *or* to **12** °adapt, °adjust, °change, °modify, harmonize, °accommodate, °arrange, comply with, °fit **13** °settle, °arrange, °come to terms, °patch up, °clear up, °satisfy, °fix

squawk *v.* **1** cackle, screech, °shriek, °yell, yowl, °whoop, hoot, °scream, °call, °cry **2** °complain, grumble, whine, grouse, °protest, °object, °(make a) fuss, °yap, yowl, *Slang* bellyache, °bitch, °kick, beef, °gripe, kick up a fuss —*n.* **3** °complaint, grouse, grumble, °protest, *Colloq* °kick, beef, °gripe

squeamish *adj.* **1** °dainty, °delicate, °prudish, punctilious, °demanding, °critical, °exacting, °difficult, °fussy, °scrupulous, °fastidious, °meticulous, °painstaking, finicky *or* finical, *Colloq* persnickety *or* pernickety, fuddy-duddy **2** °nauseous, qualmish, easily disgusted *or* revolted *or* nauseated

squeeze *v.* **1** °press, compress, °compact, °crush, squash, wring, °pinch, °nip, °grip, °tweak **2** °extract, wrest, °exact, °extort, °milk, °wrench, °pry (out), °tear, *Colloq* bleed **3** °milk, *Colloq* °shake down, bleed, °lean on, put the screws to, °put the squeeze on, twist (someone's) arm, *US* put the arm on **4** °ram, °jam, °pack, °stuff, °cram, °crowd, °force, °press, °wedge **5** °clasp, clench, °embrace, °hug, °hold, enfold, °fold, °clutch, *Archaic* °clip **6** ***squeeze through or by.*** get through *or* by, °pass, °(barely) succeed, *Colloq* squeak through *or* by, °(barely) make it —*n.* **7** °clasp, °embrace, °hug, °clutch, *Colloq* °clinch **8** °pressure **9** °crush, °jam, °crowd, squash, °press **10** girl friend, °mistress, °sweetheart, *Colloq* sweetie, *Slang* moll, °broad, *Archaic* doxy **11** ***put the squeeze on.*** °press, bring pressure to bear on, °urge, °influence, *Brit* pressurize, *US* °pressure

squelch *v.* **1** °suppress, °subdue, °put down, °quell, °quash, °defeat, °overcome, °outdo, °humiliate, *Colloq* shoot *or* slap down, take down a peg (or two), take the wind out of (someone's) sails, settle (someone's) hash —*n.* **2** riposte, °retort, comeback, °quip, sally, jibe, barb, *Colloq* °wisecrack, °put-down

squire *v.* **1** °escort, °accompany, °conduct, °go with, °take; convoy —*n.* **2** esquire, gentleman, landowner, landholder, landed proprietor

squirm *v.* °wriggle, writhe, °twist, °flounder, °shift, °fidget, be (very) uncomfortable, agonize, *Colloq* °sweat

stab *v.* **1** °stick, °puncture, °prick, °lance, °jab, °pierce, °run through, °impale, °gore, °transfix, °knife, bayonet, skewer, °spike, °spit, spear, °pin; °plunge, °poke, °thrust **2** ***stab in the back.*** °harm, °betray, °sell out, °double-cross, give the Judas kiss, play false with —*n.* **3** °puncture, °jab, °thrust, °(stab) wound **4** °attempt, °try, °essay; °guess, conjecture **5** °pang, °twinge, °pain, °ache, °hurt, stitch **6** ***stab in the back.*** treachery, °betrayal, °double-cross, Judas kiss, kiss of death, duplicity

stability *n.* **1** steadiness, solidity, firmness, soundness, sturdiness, °strength **2** steadfastness, constancy, dependability, reliability, °tenacity, °resolve, resoluteness, °perseverance, °determination, °persistence, durability, lasting quality, solidity, °permanence

stable *adj.* **1** °steady, °solid, °firm, °sound, °sturdy, °strong, °durable, well-founded, °fast, °sure, established, deep-rooted, °stout **2** °lasting, °enduring, long-lasting, long-standing, °secure, °steadfast, °steady, °strong, unchanging, unchanged, unchangeable, unalterable, °fixed, °invariable, unwavering, immutable, °permanent **3** °sane, (well-)balanced, °responsible, °reasonable, °sensible, °competent, °accountable

stack *n.* **1** °pile, °heap, °mound, °mass, °accumulation, °hill, °mountain, °store, °stock, bank, °deposit, °supply, stockpile, °hoard, °load, °bundle, bale, *Colloq US and Canadian* stash **2** haystack, cock, haycock, rick, rickle, hayrick, *Brit* °clamp **3** °collection, aggregation, °accumulation, agglomeration, amassment, °mass, °load, °pack, °amount, °abundance, °plenty, °profusion, °volume, array, °sea, °throng, multitude, °swarm, °host, °number, °quantity, °pileup **4** smoke stack, chimney, chimney stack, funnel; *Building* soil stack **5** ***blow one's stack.*** °anger, become angry, become furious *or* infuriated, °rage, °rant, lose one's temper, *Slang* blow *or* lose one's cool, get hot under the collar, blow one's top —*v.* **6** Often, ***stack up.*** °pile (up), °heap, °accumulate, °amass, °store, °stock, stockpile, °hoard, °collect, aggregate, agglomerate, *Colloq* stash (away), squirrel away **7** ***stack up.*** **(a)** make sense, add up, °agree, jibe, be verifiable, *Colloq* °check out **(b)** °compare, measure up, hold a candle to, be on a par (with), be as good as

stadium *n.* arena, °ground, amphitheater, hippodrome, coliseum *or* colosseum, circus

staff *n.* **1** °stick, °pole, °standard, baton, °rod, pikestaff, pike, °stake, cane, stave, °shaft, alpenstock, shillelagh, °club, truncheon, mace, crook, crozier, scepter, °wand, caduceus **2** personnel, employees, °help, work force, °crew, °team, °organization

stage *n.* **1** °position, °situation, °grade, °level, °stratum, °tier, echelon, °step, °station, °place, °point, °spot, °juncture, °division, °phase, °lap; °status, °condition **2** °platform, dais, podium; °rostrum **3** ***the stage.*** show business, °the theater, the boards, the footlights, Broadway, *Chiefly Brit* the West End; acting, thespianism; *Colloq* show biz —*v.* **4** °put on, °produce, °present, °mount, °exhibit **5** °put on, contrive, °organize, °originate, °devise, °make up, concoct, °fake, trump up, stage-manage, °manipulate, °maneuver

stagger *v.* **1** °totter, °reel, °lurch, °teeter, °sway, walk unsteadily *or* shakily, °pitch, °rock, wobble **2** °surprise, °amaze, °astound, °astonish, °overwhelm, °overcome, dumbfound *or* dumfound, °shock, stupefy, °stun, °nonplus, °floor, confound, °bewilder, °startle, °jolt, °shake (up), °take one's breath away, make one's head swim, take (someone) aback, throw (someone) off balance, °tax, °burden, *Colloq* flabbergast, °flummox, bowl over, *Slang* blow (someone's) mind **3** °alternate, °space (out), °vary, rearrange, zigzag, *US* change off

stagnant *adj.* motionless, °standing, °still, °quiet, sluggish, unmoving, immobile, °flat; °stale, °foul, °putrid, putrescent, putrefied, polluted, °dirty, contaminated, °filthy

stagnate *v.* languish, °idle, vegetate, °deteriorate, °degenerate, °decline, go to seed *or* pot, °decay, rust, molder, °decompose, °spoil, °rot

staid *adj.* °sedate, °rigid, °stiff, prim, °dignified, °sober, °calm, composed, °quiet, restrained, °solemn, °serious, serious-minded, °grave, sober-sided

stain *n.* **1** °blot, °mark, °spot, discoloration, blotch, smutch, smirch, °speck, *Brit* splodge *or US also* splotch **2** °mark, °blot (on the escutcheon), °stigma, °blemish, *Brit* blot on one's copybook, *Colloq US* black eye **3** dye, °color, coloring, °tint, tinge, pigment —*v.* **4** °blot, °mark, °spot, discolor, blotch, speckle, dye, °spatter, splatter, tinge, smudge, smutch, °splash **5** °spoil, defile, °ruin, smirch, besmirch, °taint, °tarnish, °stigmatize, °shame, °disgrace, °sully, °contaminate, °soil, °corrupt

stake[1] *n.* **1** °stick, °post, °spike, °picket, paling, °pale, °pole, pike, stave; palisade, °upright, °pillar, column **2** ***pull up stakes.*** °move (house), resettle, move on, °migrate, °emigrate, °leave, °depart —*v.* **3** °tether, °tie (up), °secure, °fasten, °picket, °lash, leash, °hitch, °chain **4** Usually, ***stake out.*** **(a)** fence (in *or* off), confine, °pen, °enclose, close in *or* off, hem in, °shut in, impound, °enclose, °cage, wall in **(b)** mark off *or* out, °define, delimit, °outline, demarcate, delineate, circumscribe

stake[2] *n.* **1** °bet, wager, ante, °risk, °hazard **2** investment, °interest, °share, involvement, °concern **3** ***at stake.*** at hazard, hazarded, at risk, risked, on the table, in jeopardy, jeopardized, °concerned, °involved —*v.* **4** °risk, °jeopardize, °venture, put (money) on, °chance, °hazard, °gamble, wager, °bet

stale *adj.* **1** °old, past its prime, unfresh, °dry, dried-out, hardened, °limp, wilted, withered, °flat, °sour, turned, °(gone) off, °moldy, °musty, spoiled, °rotten **2** °old, °banal, overused, °antiquated, °old-fashioned, °threadbare, trite, clichéd, unoriginal, hackneyed, stereotyped, °tired, °weary, °boring, °tiresome, warmed-over, shopworn, °familiar, °stock, °well-known, *Colloq* hand-me-down, *Brit* reach-me-down

stalemate *n.* °impasse, °deadlock, standoff, °standstill, (dead *or* full) stop, °tie; °check, checkmate, °mate; *US* Mexican standoff

stalk[1] *v.* °follow, dog, °haunt, °shadow, °trail, °track (down), °hunt (down), °pursue, °hound, °chase, *Colloq* °tail

stalk[2] *n.* °stem, °trunk, cane, main axis, leafstalk, °shaft, °spike

stall[1] *v.* **1** °stop, °halt, °die, °quit, °shut down, °fail, cease operating, come to a standstill, *Colloq* conk out —*n.* **2** °compartment, °stand, °booth, cubicle, alcove, °section, °space, °area, °slot, °enclosure, °quarters; °counter, °table **3** °shed, °pen, cote, °fold, coop, sty, corral, °enclosure, cowshed, barn, °stable

stall[2] *v.* **1** °delay, °dawdle, dillydally, dally, loiter, °linger, temporize, °equivocate, °hesitate, prevaricate, °play for time, waste time, stonewall, be obstructive, put (someone *or* something) off; vacillate, dither, hedge, °procrastinate; *Brit* haver, *Colloq* beat about *or* around the bush, °drag one's feet, give (someone) the runaround —*n.* **2** stalling, °delay, hedge, hedging, °pretext, °subterfuge, °wile, °trick, °ruse, °artifice, °stratagem, °maneuver, °move, stonewalling, obstructionism, playing for time, procrastination, procrastinating, *Colloq* beating about *or* around the bush, °runaround, foot-dragging

stalwart *adj.* **1** °robust, °stout, °strong, °mighty, °powerful, °rugged, °staunch, °hardy, °sturdy, °vigorous, °lusty, °indomitable, °solid, able-bodied, °brawny, °sinewy, °muscular, °fit, °healthy, °hale, °(hale and) hearty, *Colloq* °husky, °hefty, beefy **2** redoubtable, °intrepid, undaunted, °resolute, °firm, °determined, unbending, °steadfast, °tenacious, unswerving, unwavering, unfaltering, unflinching, uncompromising, unyielding, persevering, °persistent, unflagging, °relentless, °tireless, °untiring, indefatigable **3** °brave, °courageous, °daring, °intrepid, valiant, °heroic, °manly, manful,

°fearless, °indomitable, stouthearted, °bold, °audacious, °game, red-blooded, plucky, mettlesome, lionhearted, °spirited —*n.* 4 °supporter, upholder, sustainer, °partisan, loyalist, °(party) faithful, trouper, °hero, °heroine

stamina *n.* ruggedness, °vigor, vigorousness, °(intestinal) fortitude, robustness, indefatigability, staying power, °endurance, °energy, °power, °might, mettle, °(inner) strength, staunchness, stalwartness, °courage, indomitability, *Colloq* °grit, °guts, starch, *US* stick-to-itiveness, sand, *Taboo slang* balls

stammer *v.* 1 stutter, °hesitate, hem and haw, °stumble, falter, °pause, *Brit* hum and haw —*n.* 2 stutter

stamp *v.* 1 °trample, bring down one's foot; tread, °step, °tramp; *Colloq* stomp (on) 2 °impress, °mark, imprint, °print, °record, °document, °register, log; °engrave, emboss, inscribe; °sign, °initial 3 °brand, °label, °mark, °tag, °term, °name, °style, °identify, °categorize, classify, °characterize, °designate, denominate, show to be 4 ***stamp out.*** °eliminate, eradicate, °abolish, °get rid of, annihilate, °exterminate, °kill, snuff out, °terminate, °end, put an end to, °destroy, °put down, °put out, °extinguish, extirpate; °quell, °subdue, °suppress, °squelch, °repress —*n.* 5 °mark, °sign, °hallmark, earmarks, traits, °features, characteristics 6 °die, °block, °punch, °seal, matrix, °plate, die stamp, stereotype, °mold; signet (ring) 7 °seal, (trade *or* service) mark, °brand, logo, logotype, °symbol, °representation, colophon, imprint, °emblem, insigne (*singular of* insignia), °label, monogram, °sign, °crest, coat of arms, escutcheon, cartouche, signature, initials 8 °character, °kind, °sort, °make, °fashion, °type, °cast, °mold, °grade, °style, °cut, °genre, °class, °level, kidney, feather, °stripe, classification, species, genus, °variety, °description

stampede *n.* 1 °rout, °flight, °scattering, °panic, °rush, °dash —*v.* 2 °panic, °frighten, °rush, °scatter, °rout 3 °rush, °run, °race, °charge, °take to one's heels, °flee, °take flight

stance *n.* °carriage, °bearing, deportment; °position, °posture, °attitude, °standpoint, °stand, °viewpoint, °point of view

stanch *v.* °staunch, °stop, °stem, °halt, °check, °arrest, °stay, °end, °cease; °prevent

stand *v.* 1 °rise, °arise, °get up, *Brit* be upstanding 2 Sometimes, ***stand up.*** (a) °set, °place (upright), °position, °put, °move; upend (b) °stay, °remain (standing) 3 °endure, °survive, °tolerate, °brook, countenance, °face, confront, last through, °abide, °allow, °accept, °take, °suffer, °bear, °withstand, °undergo, °experience, °cope with, °brave, stand *or* bear up under, °stand for, °withstand, °stomach, °weather, °handle, *Colloq* °put up with 4 °continue, °remain, °persist, be *or* remain in effect *or* in force, °prevail, °obtain, °apply, °exist 5 ***stand by.*** (a) °support, °defend, °back, stand *or* stick up for, stand behind, be *or* remain loyal *or* faithful to, °uphold, take the side of, °side with, °sympathize with, *US* go to bat for (b) °wait (in the wings), stand *or* wait *or* stay *or* remain on the sidelines, be *or* stand ready *or* available *or* accessible, be *or* stand in readiness (c) stick to, adhere to, °support, °maintain, °persist in, affirm, reaffirm, °confirm, °abide by 6 ***stand down.*** °resign, °quit, step aside, °withdraw 7 ***stand for.*** (a) °symbolize, betoken, °represent, °signify, °mean, be emblematic of, °exemplify, epitomize, °illustrate, °typify, °refer to, allude to (b) °support, °advocate, °favor, °sponsor, °promote, espouse (the cause of), °subscribe to, °back, °champion, lend support *or* one's name to, °second (c) campaign for, be *or* present (oneself) as a candidate for, *US* stump for, °run for (d) See 3, above. 8 ***stand in.*** °substitute (for), °understudy (for), °replace, °relieve, double for, take the place of, *US and Canadian* pinch-hit (for), *Colloq* cover for 9 ***stand out.*** (a) be prominent *or* conspicuous *or* noticeable, be notable *or* noteworthy (b) °protrude, °project, °stick out, jut out, °bulge, °obtrude, beetle, °overhang, °extend 10 ***stand up.*** (a) °stand, °rise, °arise, get to one's feet, °get up (b) °endure, °last, °wear (well), °survive (c) °jilt, break *or* fail to keep an appointment with 11 ***stand up for.*** °support, °defend, take the side of, °side with, °champion, °uphold, *Colloq* °stick up for 12 ***stand up to.*** (a) confront, °brave, °challenge, °encounter, °dispute, °question, °resist, °defy, °withstand (b) °resist, °defy, °withstand, °endure, °outlast, last through, °suffer —*n.* 13 °position, °attitude, °stance, °posture, °policy, °philosophy, °point of view, °viewpoint, °standpoint, °belief, °opinion, °sentiment, °feeling, °line 14 °defense, °resistance, °effort 15 °stop, stopover, °halt, °stay; °performance, °show 16 °counter, °booth, °stall, °table; wagon *or* *Brit also* waggon, barrow, °cart 17 °rack, °frame, °bracket; hat stand, coat rack 18 staging, °platform, dais, °stage, bandstand, summerhouse 19 copse, grove, wood, °thicket, °brake, wood, *Brit* spinney, coppice

standard *n.* 1 criterion, °measure, bench mark, °model, °pattern, archetype, °touchstone, °yardstick, °gauge, °guide, guideline, paradigm, °paragon, exemplar, °example, °sample, °type, °ideal, *beau idéal,* °rule, canon, °law, °requirement, °precept, °principle 2 °mean, °average, °norm, °par, °level, rating 3 °flag, °banner, ensign, °emblem, °pennant, burgee, insigne (*singular of* insignia), guidon, gonfalon *or* gonfanon, labarum 4 °pole, °post, stanchion, lamppost, column, °pillar, °support, °pedestal, °pier, °footing, (upright) bar *or* rod *or* timber —*adj.* 5 accepted, approved, °definitive, defined, °authoritative, °official, required, regulative, regulatory, textbook 6 recognized, °prevailing, °prevalent, °usual, °customary, °habitual, °orthodox, °set, established, °regular, °familiar, °ordinary, °traditional, °classic, °stock, °typical, °normal, °staple, °conventional, °universal

standardize *v.* °regiment, systematize, codify, °normalize, homogenize

standby *n.* **1** °supporter, defender, °backer, upholder, °partisan, °sympathizer, adherent, °stalwart **2** °substitute, surrogate, replacement, backup, °understudy, °second, *US and Canadian* °alternate **3** °resource, °support, replacement

stand-in *n.* °double, °substitute, stunt man *or* woman; surrogate, replacement, °standby, backup, °understudy, °second, *US and Canadian* °alternate

standing *adj.* **1** established, °set, °standard, °conventional, °customary, °usual, °normal, °regular, °fixed, °permanent, continued, continuing, °regular **2** °stagnant, motionless, unmoving, stationary, °still, °static **3** °continuous, °fixed, °ongoing, °perpetual, unbroken **4** °erect, °upright, on one's feet, vertical, unseated —*n.* **5** °status, °rank, °station, °position, °place, °grade, °order, °level, °stratum **6** eminence, °prominence, repute, °reputation **7** Usually, ***long standing.*** (considerable) age *or* longevity *or* experience *or* seniority *or* duration

standoffish *adj.* °aloof, °haughty, °unsocial, °reserved, °cool, frosty, °withdrawn, °remote, removed, °distant, °detached, °unapproachable, °inaccessible, uncongenial, unfriendly, unsociable; Olympian, lordly, °pompous, *Colloq* highfalutin *or* hifalutin *or* highfaluting, snooty

standpoint *n.* °viewpoint, °point of view, vantage point, °perspective, °position, °angle, °view

standstill *n.* (dead *or* full) stop, °halt

staple *adj.* **1** °basic, °elementary, °essential, °necessary, requisite, required, °vital, °indispensable, °critical, °fundamental, °primary, °principal, °main, °chief **2** °standard, °usual, °habitual, °ordinary, °customary, °prevailing, °normal, °conventional, °universal —*n.* **3** Often, ***staples.*** necessities, essentials, basics, fundamentals

star *n.* **1** celestial *or* heavenly body; evening star, morning star, falling star, shooting star, comet; nova, supernova **2** °celebrity, °personage, °dignitary, VIP, °name, °somebody, luminary, leading light, leading man *or* woman *or* lady, °lead, °principal, diva, prima donna, °hero, °heroine, °idol, superstar, *Technical slang* top banana, headliner, *Colloq* big shot, °(big) draw, celeb, big name —*adj.* **3** °principal, °major, °leading, °important, °celebrated, °famous, famed, °prominent, °eminent, °preeminent, °distinguished, °brilliant, °illustrious, unequaled, °peerless, °matchless, °incomparable, unrivaled, inimitable, unmatched, °unparalleled, °top, °foremost —*v.* **4** feature *or* be featured; play *or* act *or* take the lead *or* the leading part *or* role

stare *v.* **1** °gaze, °gape, goggle, °gawk, °watch, *Colloq* °rubberneck, *Slang Brit* gawp —*n.* **2** fixed *or* blank look; goggle, °gaze

stark *adv.* **1** °completely, °utterly, unqualifiedly, °wholly, °absolutely, °entirely, °totally, fully, °altogether, plainly, °obviously, °clearly, certifiably —*adj.* **2** °plain, °simple, °Spartan, °severe, unembellished, °unadorned, °cold, °bare, °harsh, °hard, °grim, bald, °blunt **3** °harsh, °severe, °bleak, austere, °barren, °desolate, °dreary, °gray, depressing, ravaged, °empty, °vacant, *Literary* drear, *Colloq US* spooky **4** °sheer, °complete, utter, °absolute, °perfect, °pure, °thorough, thoroughgoing, arrant, °unmitigated, °out-and-out, °downright, °outright, °total, unconditional, °unqualified, °clear, °plain, °evident, °obvious, °patent, °flagrant, °gross, °rank

start *v.* **1** Often, ***start off or up.*** °begin, °commence, get (something) going, get off the ground, °originate, °initiate, °open, set in motion, °activate, °embark on; turn *or* switch on, crank up, *Colloq* kick off **2** Often, ***start off or up or in.*** °arise, °come up, come to be *or* into being, °emerge, crop up, °develop, °begin, °commence, get under way, °originate **3** Often, ***start off or up or in.*** °go, °leave, °depart, get going, move (off *or* out *or* on), get under way, set off *or* out *or* forth, *Colloq* hit the road, get the show on the road **4** Often, ***start in.*** °begin, °commence, get *or* start the ball rolling, get things under way, be on one's way, get going **5** °jump, °flinch, blench, quail, °shy, °recoil, wince, °shrink, °draw back **6** cause to spring *or* leap *or* dart *or* jump *or* bound **7** °establish, °found, °begin, °set up, °initiate, °institute, °create, °father, give birth to, beget **8** °bulge, °protrude, °stick out; *Colloq US* bug out —*n.* **9** °beginning, °opening, °move **10** °beginning, commencement, °opening, °outset, °onset, inception, startup **11** beginning(s), inception, °birth, °initiation, °onset, °rise, genesis, °creation, °emergence, °origin **12** °opportunity, °chance, °beginning; °help, °assistance, °aid, °backing, financing, sponsorship, °encouragement, *Colloq* °break **13** head start, °advantage, °edge, °lead, *Colloq* °(the) jump, *US and New Zealand* °drop (on someone) **14** inauguration, °opening, °beginning, °initiation, *Colloq* kickoff **15** beginning(s), founding, °foundation, °establishment, inception, °birth, °origin

startle *v.* °frighten, °surprise, °scare, °disturb, unsettle, °upset, discompose, make (someone) jump, °jolt, °jar, °dismay, °perturb, °stun, take (someone) aback, °shock, °astound, °astonish, *Colloq* °shake up, give (someone) a turn, *US* discombobulate

startling *adj.* °shocking, °terrifying, °frightening, astounding, astonishing, °awesome, staggering, jarring, °disturbing, °unsettling, upsetting, °amazing, surprising

starved *adj.* **1** starving, °(extremely) hungry, °famished, °ravenous **2** ***starved or starving for.*** yearning for, dying for, hankering for, hungry *or* hungering for, pining for, longing for, burning for, craving, thirsting for *or* after, desirous of, aching for, *Colloq* hurting for **3** ***starved of.*** deprived of, in need *or* want of, lacking, bereft of

state *n.* **1** condition(s), circumstance(s), °situation, state of affairs, °status, °shape, °position **2** °structure, °form, constitution, °shape, °phase, °stage **3** °grandeur, °pomp, °style, °splendor, magnificence, °glory, °brilliance **4** °nation, °country, °land, body politic *—adj.* **5** governmental, °government, °national, federal **6** °ceremonial, °formal, °dignified, °stately, °solemn, °official; °royal, °regal, °imperial, °majestic *—v.* **7** aver, assert, asseverate, °declare, affirm, °express, °report, articulate, °voice, °specify, delineate, °claim, °maintain, °allege, °submit, °confirm; °say, °testify, °hold, °have

stately *adj.* °dignified, august, °solemn, °distinguished, °impressive, °striking, °imposing, °awesome, °grand, °lofty, °elevated, °noble, °majestic, °regal, °royal, °imperial

statement *n.* °assertion, °allegation, °declaration, °expression, °report, °account, affirmation, asseveration, averral, °announcement, annunciation, °proclamation, utterance, communication, communiqué, disclosure

static *adj.* **1** °immovable, immobile, unmoving, motionless, stationary, °fixed, °stagnant, °inert, °still, unchanging, unchanged, °changeless, unvarying, °invariable, °constant *—n.* **2** °interference, °noise, atmospherics; difficulty *or* difficulties, °trouble, problem(s), *Colloq* °flak

station *n.* **1** °place, °position, °spot, °post, °site, °location **2** °position, °place, °status, °rank, °caste, °standing, °class, °level **3** railway station, train station, passenger station, bus station, *US and Canadian* depot *—v.* **4** °position, °place, °spot, °post, °site, °locate, °assign, °appoint, garrison, °install, *Colloq* billet

stationery *n.* writing paper, letterhead(s), paper and envelopes, writing implements *or* supplies; office supplies *or* equipment

statue *n.* °sculpture, °figure, figurine, statuette, carving, casting, °model, bronze, °image, icon *or* ikon, effigy, °representation; bust, atlas, caryatid, colossus, °figurehead, *Bible* graven image

statuesque *adj.* °imposing, °impressive, °majestic, °regal, °stately, °magnificent, °noble, °dignified, august, °grand, well-proportioned, °comely, °handsome, queenly, Junoesque

status *n.* **1** eminence, °prominence, °preeminence, °standing, stature, °importance, °significance, repute, °reputation, °rank, °station **2** See **standing, 5,** above.

staunch *adj.* **1** °steadfast, °loyal, °firm, unflinching, °steady, unshrinking, unswerving, dependable, °reliable, °(tried and) true, °devoted, trueblue, trusty, trusted, °faithful, unfaltering, undeviating, unwavering **2** °strong, °solid, °sturdy, °sound, well-built, °stout, °substantial, well-constructed, well-made, °tough, °rugged, long-lasting; °watertight, seaworthy

stay[1] *v.* **1** °remain, °stop, °continue, °tarry, °wait, °stand, *Colloq* °freeze **2** °remain, °stop, °lodge, °sojourn, °abide, reside, °dwell, °live, °visit **3** °keep, °remain, continue to be **4** °stop, °arrest, °thwart, °prevent, put an end to, °halt, °interrupt, °block, °check; °curb, °retard, °slow, °impede, °foil, °obstruct, °hamper, °hinder, °discourage, °deter; °delay, °postpone, °put off, °discontinue, °defer, *Technical* prorogue **5** °linger, loiter, °wait, °tarry, °stop, °remain, *Archaic* bide *—n.* **6** °stop, stoppage, °arrest, °setback, °check, °halt, °prevention, discontinuance, discontinuation, °interruption, blockage, °delay, °postponement, deferment, deferral, °reprieve **7** stopover, °sojourn, °visit, °stop

stay[2] *n.* **1** °guy, °line, °rope, °cable, °chain, °support, °brace, °reinforcement; *Technical* headstay, (running) backstay, forestay, °mainstay, mizzenstay *—v.* **2** °support, °strengthen, °secure, °reinforce, °brace, °buttress, gird, shore (up)

steadfast *adj.* °resolute, °determined, persevering, resolved, °single-minded, °steady, unflinching, unfaltering, unwavering, unswerving, indefatigable, dependable, °immovable, °stable, °firm, °fixed, °constant, °persistent, unflagging, °tireless, °enduring, dedicated, deep-rooted, °faithful, °true, °loyal, °staunch

steady *adj.* **1** °stable, °firm, °solid, °substantial, °sound, °stout, °strong **2** °even, °regular, °uniform, °habitual, °invariable, unvarying, unfluctuating, unwavering, undeviating, °changeless, unchanging, °continuous, °constant; °perpetual, °nonstop, around-the-clock *or* round-the-clock, °persistent, uninterrupted, unbroken, unrelieved, unceasing, ceaseless, incessant, °relentless, unremitting, never-ending, unending, °endless **3** unflinching, unblinking, °fixed, °constant, unfaltering, °continuous, °direct **4** °calm, °cool, balanced, °equable, controlled **5** °devoted, °firm, °staunch, °faithful, °loyal, longstanding, inveterate, °consistent, confirmed, °persistent **6** °staid, °sedate, °sober, °dignified, °poised, °sophisticated, civilized, °sensible, down-to-earth, settled, °serious, °levelheaded, °reliable, *Colloq* unflappable *—adv.* **7** °firmly, solidly **8** ***go steady.*** keep company, °date, °socialize *—n.* **9** boyfriend, girlfriend, (regular) fellow *or* girl, °sweetheart, *Colloq* °guy, gal, °woman, °man **10** °regular, °habitué, °customer, frequenter, familiar face *—v.* **11** stabilize, hold fast; °brace, °secure, °support, °strengthen

steal *v.* **1** °take (away), °appropriate, filch, shoplift, °pilfer, purloin, make *or* walk off *or* away with, get away with; °embezzle, °misappropriate, peculate; *Colloq* °lift, °pinch, °hook, snitch, °borrow, *US* °boost, °liberate, heist, hijack *or* highjack, *Slang* °swipe, *Brit* °nick, °prig, *US* °hoist **2** plagiarize, °pirate, °copy, °imitate, °appropriate, usurp, °take **3** °sneak, °creep, °slip, tiptoe, °prowl, °lurk, skulk, *Colloq* °pussyfoot —*n.* **4** °bargain, °(good) buy, *Colloq* giveaway

stealing *n.* °theft, °robbery, robbing, larceny, pilferage, shoplifting, poaching, °embezzlement, peculation, thievery, thieving, filching, burglary, °plagiarism, plagiarizing, piracy, pirating

stealth *n.* furtiveness, °secrecy, clandestineness, surreptitiousness, sneakiness, slyness, underhandedness

stealthy *adj.* stealthful, furtive; °secretive, °secret, °sly, clandestine, °surreptitious, °sneaky, °sneaking, skulking, covert, °undercover, underhand(ed), backstairs, huggermugger, closet

steamy *adj.* **1** °humid, steaming, °damp, °moist, °muggy, °sticky, dank, sweaty, °sweltering, sodden, °sultry, boiling, °wet **2** steamed (up), fogged (up), befogged, °misty, misted, °hazy, clouded, cloudy, beclouded, °dim, blurred **3** °erotic, °passionate, °(sexually) exciting, arousing, °hot, *Colloq* °sexy, *Slang* horny

steel *n.* **1** sword, °dagger, °blade, °knife, dirk, stiletto —*v.* **2** °brace, °nerve, °stiffen, °fortify, grit one's teeth, °bear up, bite the bullet, screw up one's courage (to the sticking point); inure, °insulate, °protect

steely *adj.* **1** grayish, °gray **2** iron, °tough, indurate, adamant(ine), °hard, °strong, °rugged, unyielding, flinty, °sturdy

steep[1] *adj.* **1** °sheer, °abrupt, °precipitous, °bluff, °sharp, nearly vertical *or* perpendicular *or* upright **2** °expensive, °dear, °high, overpriced, °exorbitant, °excessive, °extravagant, extortionate, *Colloq* °stiff

steep[2] *v.* **1** °soak, °submerge, souse, °drench, °immerse, °saturate, douse, °wet, ret; pickle, marinate **2** imbue, °fill, °saturate, °immerse, inundate; °bury

steer *v.* **1** °guide, °pilot, °conduct, °direct; °manage, °control, °channel **2** ***steer clear of.*** °avoid, °dodge, keep away from, °shun, circumvent, give (something *or* someone) a wide berth —*n.* **3** Usually, ***bum steer.*** (bad *or* poor) tip *or* suggestion *or* hint; (bad *or* poor) guidance *or* advice *or* information

stellar *adj.* **1** astral, °star, sidereal **2** °chief, starring, °principal, °leading, °main, headlining

stem[1] *n.* **1** °trunk, °stalk, °stock; *Technical* peduncle, pedicel, petiole, °shoot **2** bows, prow, stempost —*v.* **3** °come, °arise, °develop, °derive, °issue, °flow, °generate, °originate, °spring, °emanate, °sprout, °grow, °descend, °result, °proceed

stem[2] *v.* **1** °check, °stop, °halt, stanch *or* staunch, °arrest, °stay, °curb, °control, °quell, °suppress; °retard, °slow, lessen, °diminish, °reduce, cut (back (on)) **2** ***stem the tide (of).*** °resist, °withstand, go *or* make headway *or* advance *or* make progress against, prevail over *or* against

stench *n.* stink, °reek, noisomeness, mephitis, fetor *or* foetor, foul odor, effluvium, *Colloq Brit* pong

stenographer *n.* secretary, amanuensis, stenotypist, tachygrapher, phonographer

stenography *n.* shorthand, stenotypy, tachygraphy, speed writing

step *n.* **1** °movement, °move **2** footfall, °footstep, tread **3** °footstep, footprint, °trace, spoor, °track, °mark, °impression; imprint, °vestige **4** °action, °initiative, °measure, °activity, °procedure, °move, °motion **5** °stage, °move, gradation, °degree, °progression **6** °pace, °footstep, stride **7** ***in step (with).*** in keeping (with), in harmony *or* agreement (with), °harmonious (with), °agreeable (with), according (with *or* to), concordant (with), attuned (to), in tune (with), consonant (with), °consistent (with), °appropriate (to), °fitting (for); °conventional, °traditional, °routine **8** ***out of step (with).*** out of keeping (with), out of *or* not in harmony *or* agreement (with), not harmonious (with), not agreeable (with), not according (with *or* to), °discordant (with), not concordant (with), not attuned (to), out of tune (with), not consonant (with), °inconsistent (with), °inappropriate (to), not fitting (for); °offbeat, unconventional, °eccentric, *Slang* °kinky **9** ***step by step.*** °gradually, a step at a time, slowly, steadily **10** ***steps.*** **(a)** °course, °way, °route, °direction, °path, °movement, °passage; °journey, journeying, °travels, °traveling **(b)** stairway, stairs, stair, staircase, stepladder, *US and Canadian* °stoop **11** ***take steps.*** °proceed, °move, begin *or* start *or* commence to act *or* to take action, do something **12** ***watch one's step.*** tread carefully *or* cautiously, be cautious *or* careful, exercise care *or* caution, be wary *or* discreet, be on the qui vive, be *or* remain alert, be on one's guard, have *or* keep one's wits about one, take care *or* heed, *Colloq* pussyfoot about —*v.* **13** °move, °walk, °look; °pace, stride **14** ***step down.*** **(a)** °resign, °abdicate, °quit, bow out, °retire **(b)** °decrease, °diminish, °reduce **15** ***step in.*** °intervene, °interfere, intercede, become involved **16** ***step on it.*** °hurry (up), make haste, °hasten, °speed up **17** ***step out.*** **(a)** go outside *or* out of doors, °leave **(b)** °go out, °socialize **(c)** become disinvolved, °withdraw, °secede **18** ***step up.*** **(a)** °improve, °progress **(b)** °increase, accelerate, °raise, °intensify, °boost, escalate, up, °speed up

sterile *adj.* **1** °barren, °fruitless, unfruitful, childless, unproductive, °infertile, infecund **2** °pure, aseptic, uninfected, unpolluted, uncontaminated, disinfected, °sanitary, sterilized, germ-free, antiseptic **3** °barren, unproductive, °stale, effete

sterilize *v.* **1** °purify, °disinfect, °cleanse, °clean, °fumigate, depurate, *Technical* autoclave **2** castrate (males), emasculate (males), geld (horses), spay (female animals), °alter (animals), °neuter (animals), caponize (male fowl), eunuchize (males), *Technical* ovariectomize (females), vasectomize (males), *Colloq* °fix (animals), °cut (male animals), *Slang* tie (someone's) tubes

sterling *adj.* **1** °genuine, °authentic, °real, °true, °pure **2** °excellent, °superior, °superb, °superlative, first-class, °exceptional, °matchless, °peerless, unequaled, °nonpareil, °incomparable, °fine, very good, °worthy, °estimable, °admirable

stern *adj.* **1** austere, °severe, °strict, stringent, °demanding, °critical, °rigid, rigorous, flinty, °steely, °authoritarian, uncompromising, °hard, °tough, °inflexible, °firm, °immovable, °unmoved, unrelenting, unremitting, °steadfast, °resolute, °determined, unyielding, adamant, adamantine, obdurate, hard-hearted, °stony, stonyhearted, unsparing, unforgiving, °unsympathetic, °harsh **2** °serious, frowning, °grim, °forbidding, °grave, °gloomy, °dour, °somber, saturnine, lugubrious, °gruff, °taciturn, crabby, crabbed, crusty, churlish, °sour

stew *n.* **1** gallimaufry, goulash, salmagundi, °hash, °mess, olla podrida, olio, °mixture, °mishmash, *Brit* hotchpotch, *US also* °hodgepodge **2** state of excitement *or* alarm *or* anxiety, dither, pother, °bother, °lather, °sweat, *Colloq* tizzy, °state —*v.* **3** °simmer, °seethe, agonize, °fret, dither, °chafe, °burn, °smolder, *Colloq* get steamed (up) (about *or* over), work (oneself) (up) into a sweat *or* lather *or* state (over)

stick[1] *v.* **1** °pierce, °thrust, °stab, °transfix, °pin, °spike, °impale, spear, °spit, °run through, °poke, °gore, °jab, °prick, °puncture, °punch, °penetrate, °drill, °bore, °riddle, °perforate **2** °put, °drop, °place, °deposit, *Colloq* shove, plonk, plunk, plop **3** °put, °poke, °push, °thrust, °prod, °dig; °insert **4** °attach, °fasten, affix, °fix, °nail, °pin, °tack; °glue, °cement, paste, gum, °weld, solder, °bind, °tie, °tape, wire; °bond, °melt, °fuse, °unite, °join **5** Often, ***stick together.*** cohere, adhere, stay *or* remain *or* cleave *or* cling together **6** °hold, °last, °endure, °go through, be upheld, be *or* remain effective, remain attached **7** °linger, °dwell, °remain (fixed), °continue, °stay; be *or* become lodged *or* stopped *or* fixed *or* fast *or* immovable *or* stationary, be *or* become entangled *or* enmired *or* bogged down **8** °burden, °weigh down, °encumber, saddle with, °charge, °impose on, force on **9** baffle, °puzzle, °bewilder, °perplex, °confuse, °stump, °stop, °nonplus **10** °stand, °abide, °tolerate, °endure, °bear **11** ***stick around or about.*** °wait, °tarry, °linger, °stay, °stand by, °remain, *Colloq* hang around *or* about *or* on **12** ***stick at.*** stop at, hesitate at, pause at, scruple at, be deterred *or* put off by, °take exception to, shrink from *or* at, balk at **13** ***stick by.*** °support, be loyal *or* faithful to, °stand by **14** ***stick it (out).*** °persevere, °persist, stand fast, bear it, be resolute, °soldier on, hold (one's) ground, grin and bear it, see it through, weather it, *Colloq US* tough it out **15** ***stick out or up.*** °protrude, °jut (out), °extend, °project, °poke (out); °bulge, °obtrude, °stand out, °overhang, beetle **16** ***stick together.*** **(a)** °unite, °unify, °join (forces), consolidate, °merge, confederate, °amalgamate, °cooperate, work together **(b)** See **5,** above. **17** ***stick up.*** **(a)** °rob, °mug, *Colloq* °hold up, *US* heist **(b)** °put up, °post, affix, °display **18** ***stick up for.*** rally to the support of, °support, stand by *or* up for, °defend, speak for *or* in behalf of, take up the cudgels for **19** ***stick with.*** °persevere, °persist, stay *or* remain *or* continue with, not change one's mind about

stick[2] *n.* **1** °stake, °twig, °branch, baton, °wand, °staff, °rod, cane, °pole, pike, walking stick **2** °person, °man, °fellow, °chap, *Colloq* °guy, *Brit* geezer, bloke **3** ***the sticks.*** the country, the provinces, the countryside, the backwoods, the bush, *Brit* the hinterland *or US* the hinterlands, *Australian* the outback, *US* the boondocks, the boonies **4** ***wrong end of the stick.*** °misunderstanding, misreading, misconstruction, misinterpretation

stick-in-the-mud *n.* (old) fogy *or* fogey, °conservative, °anachronism, *Colloq* fuddy-duddy, fossil, °square, back number

sticky *adj.* **1** gluey, gummy, viscous, °tacky, glutinous, viscid, *Colloq* °gooey **2** °awkward, °ticklish, °tricky, °sensitive, °delicate, uncomfortable, discomfiting, discomforting, °embarrassing, *Slang* °hairy **3** °humid, °clammy, dank, °damp, °muggy, °close, °sultry, °oppressive, °sweltering

stiff *adj.* **1** °firm, °rigid, inelastic, unbending, °inflexible, °hard, unbendable, °tough, °solid, solidified, stiffened, unyielding, °brittle **2** °severe, °harsh, °punitive, °hurtful, °punishing, °abusive, torturous, distressing, afflictive, °painful, °overwhelming, °unbearable, tormenting, °merciless, °excruciating, °cruel, °drastic, *US* cruel and unusual **3** °strong, °potent, °powerful, °overpowering, °alcoholic **4** °vigorous, °energetic, °staunch, dogged, °tenacious, °resolute, resolved, °determined, °stubborn, °obstinate, unyielding, °indomitable, °relentless **5** °strong, °steady, °powerful, °fresh, °brisk, °spanking, gusty, °forceful, howling **6** °excessive, °exorbitant, °high, °steep, °expensive, °dear **7** °cool, °haughty, °rigid, °wooden, °stuffy, °aloof, °tense, °intense, unrelaxed, °forced, °pompous, °stilted, °mannered, °ceremonious, austere, °formal, °chilly, °cold, unfriendly, °standoffish, °reserved, °snobbish, *Colloq* snooty, *Slang* uptight **8** °stilted, unrelaxed, °wooden, °forced, °artificial, °labored, °pedantic, turgid, °formal, prim, *Colloq* °stuffy **9** °difficult, °hard, °steep, uphill, °laborious, °arduous, tiring, fatiguing, °exhausting, °harrowing, °toilsome, rigorous, challenging, *Colloq* °rough, °tough **10** °solid, semisolid, °firm, °hard, °thick, °dense, °compact —*n.* **11** °corpse, °body, °cadaver **12** skinflint, °miser, *Colloq* cheapskate, *Slang* piker, *US and Canadian* tightwad

stiffen *v.* **1** °thicken, °coagulate, clot, °harden, °jell, °set, °solidify, congeal, crystallize 2 °brace, °reinforce, tauten, rigidify, toughen, °strengthen

stifle *v.* 1 suffocate, °smother, °choke, strangle, throttle, asphyxiate 2 °choke back, keep *or* hold back, °withhold, °repress, °suppress, °hold in, °restrain, °prevent, °curb, °cover up, °control 3 °destroy, °crush, °demolish, °extinguish, °stamp out, °kill, °quash, °silence, °stop, °check

stigma *n.* °brand, °(bad) mark, °blot, smirch, °stain, °spot, °taint, °blemish, demerit, blot on the escutcheon, *Brit* blot in one's copybook

stigmatize *v.* °brand, °mark, °scar, °blemish, besmirch, °sully, °disparage, °depreciate, °denounce, °condemn, calumniate, defame, pillory, °slander

still *adj.* 1 °quiet, °serene, placid, °calm, °tranquil, motionless, unmoving, °peaceful, pacific, at rest, quiescent, °even, °flat, °smooth, °inert, stationary, undisturbed, unruffled 2 °silent, °quiet, °noiseless, soundless; hushed, °restful, *Literary* stilly —*n.* 3 stillness, °hush, °quiet, °silence, tranquillity, noiselessness, peacefulness, °calm —*adv.* 4 even now, to *or* till *or* until this *or* that time, (up) till *or* until now, °yet 5 °even, °in addition 6 °notwithstanding, °yet, even then 7 motionless(ly), quiet(ly), silent(ly), stock-still —*conj.* 8 °however, but, °notwithstanding, °nevertheless, °even so, °in any event, °in any case —*v.* 9 °calm, allay, assuage, alleviate, °relieve, °silence, °lull, quiet *or chiefly Brit* quieten, pacify, soothe, mollify, appease, °subdue, °suppress

stilted *adj.* °awkward, °ungraceful, graceless, °clumsy, °wooden, °stiff, turgid, °affected, °artificial, °unnatural, °mannered, °labored; °pretentious, °formal, °pompous, °lofty, °bombastic, grandiloquent, high-flown, °inflated

stimulant *n.* 1 stimulus, °incentive, °provocation, °spur, °prompt, goad, °urge, °prod, fillip, °impetus, °incitement, °drive, impulse, °push, °pull, °draw 2 energizer, antidepressant, °tonic, restorative, *Colloq* bracer, pick-me-up, °shot in the arm, *Slang* pep pill, °upper, bennie, °speed

stimulate *v.* 1 °rouse, °arouse, waken, °awaken, °wake up, °excite, °incite, °inspire, °encourage, °spur, °quicken, °fire, °fuel, °nourish, °activate, whip *or* stir up, goad, galvanize, °jolt, inspirit 2 °increase, °encourage, °prompt, °provoke, °quicken

stimulating *adj.* °exciting, inspirational, inspiring, arousing, °stirring, animating, °exhilarating, °provocative, thought-provoking

sting *v.* 1 °prick, °stab, °pierce, °stick; °bite 2 °hurt, °wound, °pain, °injure, °distress, nettle, cut to the quick 3 See **stimulate, 1,** above 4 °cheat, overcharge, °swindle, °fleece, °defraud, *Slang* °rob, °soak, °rip off, °take for a ride

stinker *n.* °wretch, °villain, °scoundrel, cad, °heel, °beast, cur, viper, snake in the grass, skunk, swine, polecat, *Somewhat old-fashioned* blackguard, °rogue, *Archaic* knave, varlet, dastard, (base) caitiff, *Colloq* stinkpot, louse, °creep, rat, *Brit* nasty piece of work, sod, *Old-fashioned* rotter, bounder, blighter, *Slang* (rotten) bastard, son of a bitch, *Brit* toerag, °bugger, *US* SOB, °bum, stinkeroo *or* stinkaroo, *Taboo slang* shit, *Brit* arse-hole, *US* asshole

stinking *adj.* 1 foul-smelling, °smelly, fetid *or* foetid, mephitic, °rank, noisome, malodorous, reeking, °putrid, miasmal *or* miasmatic(al) *or* miasmic, °rancid, gamy, *Colloq Brit* pongy, whiffy 2 °wretched, °villainous, °beastly, °vile, °contemptible, °low, °despicable, °mean, °nasty, °disgusting, °rotten, °terrible, °awful, *Old-fashioned* dastardly, *Colloq* °lousy, *Taboo slang* shitty 3 drunken, drunk (as a lord *or US also* a skunk), intoxicated, inebriated, (be)sotted, °under the influence, over the limit, °high, °maudlin, tipsy, woozy, *Colloq* pie-eyed, °loaded, in one's cups, °under the weather, three sheets to the wind, *Slang* sozzled, soused (to the gills), potted, plastered, smashed, bombed, pissed, boozed, boozy, tanked, stoned, canned, *US* in the bag

stint *n.* 1 °share, °quota, °allotment, °bit, °assignment, °stretch, °shift, °term, °time, °job, chore, °task, °routine, °turn, °tour, °duty, °responsibility, °obligation, °charge 2 °control, °curb, °limit, limitation, °restriction, °check, °restraint, constraint, °condition, °qualification, °reservation —*v.* 3 °control, °curb, °limit, °restrict 4 skimp, scrimp, be stingy *or* cheap *or* penurious *or* parsimonious *or* sparing *or* cheeseparing *or* frugal, °hold back (on), °withhold, °economize, °pinch (pennies), cut corners, *Colloq Brit* be mingy

stipend *n.* °pay, °salary, °payment, °remuneration, °remittance, recompense, compensation, °reward, emolument, °earnings, °income; °grant, subvention, °scholarship, °subsidy, °allowance, °allotment, °(financial) support

stipulate *v.* °specify, °demand, °require, covenant, °set forth, °agree (to), °provide (for), °guarantee, °warrant, °promise, insist (upon *or* on); °call for

stipulation *n.* °condition, °demand, °essential, °given, °requirement, requisite, °prerequisite, °specification, °undertaking, °obligation, covenant, clause, °proviso, °term, °agreement, °provision, °guarantee, °warranty, °promise

stir *v.* 1 Often, ***stir up.*** °agitate, °shake (up), °mix (up), °scramble, °amalgamate, °mingle, commingle, intermingle, °merge, °blend, °fold (in), churn (up), °beat, °whip (up) 2 °move, °rise, °arise, °get up, bestir (oneself), be up and about, *Colloq* °get a move on, get moving, get a wiggle on, °shake a leg, look *or* step lively, look alive, stir one's stumps 3 °disturb, °trouble, °affect, °upset, °stimulate, °activate 4 Often, ***stir up.*** °motivate, °encourage, °stimulate, °energize, galvanize, °electrify, °animate, °excite, °inspire, °provoke, °move, °rouse, °arouse, °get, °prompt,

°urge, °incite, °spur, °prod, °induce, °persuade, °convince **5** Often, ***stir up.*** °awaken, °rouse, (cause to) recall *or* call to mind, °revive, resuscitate —*n.* **6** bustle, °activity, °movement, °stirring, °action, commotion, °flurry, °confusion, °tumult, ado, to-do, °fuss, °disturbance, °excitement, hubbub, *Colloq Brit* kerfuffle **7** °prison, jail *or Brit also* gaol, jailhouse, clink, penitentiary, lockup, *Military Brit* glasshouse, *US* brig, *Slang chiefly Brit* quod, *US* big house, °pen, slammer, can, calaboose

stirring *adj.* °moving, °telling, °emotional, emotive, emotion-charged, °rousing, °stimulating, inspiring, gripping, evocative, °exciting, °thrilling, °melodramatic, °dramatic, heady, °intoxicating, °spirited, inspiriting, °exhilarating, awe-inspiring

stock *n.* **1** °supply, °store, inventory, stockpile, °reserve, reservoir, °cache, °hoard; °wares, °merchandise, °goods, °selection, °assortment, °range, °variety, array **2** °pedigree, bloodline, °house, °dynasty, (line of) descent, genealogy, °extraction, °roots, °lineage, °family, ancestry, °parentage, °breeding, °heritage **3** °source, °progenitor, °creator, °father, begetter, forefather, °ancestor, °precursor, °forerunner, forebear; °founder **4** livestock, (domestic *or* farm) animals, °cattle, beasts; horses, cows, oxen, sheep, goats **5** °share, ownership, investment, °capital, °funds; °property, °assets **6** ***take stock.*** °weigh (up), °estimate, °review, appraise, °look at, *Colloq* °size up —*adj.* **7** °routine, stereotyped, °banal, clichéd, commonplace, °usual, hackneyed, °ordinary, °stale, °staple, °run-of-the-mill, °tired, °old, °everyday, °customary, °set, °standard, °traditional, trite, worn-out, *Colloq* corny **8** °standard, °ordinary, °regular, °routine, °staple —*v.* **9** °carry, °have, have *or* make available, °handle, deal in, °market, °sell, °supply, °furnish, °provide, °offer, trade in, °keep **10** Often, ***stock up (on).*** °accumulate, °amass, °pile up, stockpile, °hoard, °store (up), °cache, °lay in, inventory

stocky *adj.* thickset, °sturdy, chunky, °dumpy, °solid, stumpy, °burly, beefy, heavyset, squat, pyknic, mesomorphic

stodgy *adj.* °stuffy, °dull, °heavy, °ponderous, elephantine, °boring, °tedious, °humdrum, °tiresome, turgid, uninteresting, unimaginative, dryasdust, jejune, °vapid, °dreary, °flat, °colorless, °bland, *Colloq* ho-hum, blah, °deadly

stoical *adj.* stoic, °impassive, resigned, apathetic, °cool, unemotional, emotionless, °frigid, imperturbable, °calm, °dispassionate, °indifferent, °phlegmatic, long-suffering, °stolid, disciplined, °self-possessed, (self-) controlled, *Colloq* unflappable

stoicism *n.* °indifference, self-possession, austerity, °self-control, °fortitude, calmness, °calm, coolness, imperturbability, longanimity, forbearance, °patience, fatalism, °resignation, *Colloq* unflappability

stole *n.* tippet, scarf, boa, shawl

stolid *adj.* °impassive, °dull, doltish, °obtuse, °thick, °dense, bovine, °wooden, °slow, lumpish, unemotional, clodlike, °phlegmatic, °lethargic, apathetic, °indifferent, uninterested

stomach *n.* **1** abdomen, belly, °gut, potbelly, °pot, °paunch, *Colloq* corporation, bay window, tummy, breadbasket, spare tire **2** °tolerance; °taste, °appetite, °desire, °hunger, °thirst, craving, °need, °inclination, °relish, °longing, yearning, hankering —*v.* **3** °abide, °tolerate, °endure, °stand, °bear, °suffer, °take, °accept, °swallow, resign *or* reconcile oneself to, °put up with, countenance, °brook, *Brit* °stick

stony *adj.* **1** stoney, °rocky, pebbly, shingly, shingled **2** stoney, °hard, obdurate, adamant(ine), °heartless, stonyhearted, hardhearted, °indifferent, °unsympathetic, °implacable, intractable, °heartless, insensitive, °insensible, unfeeling, unsentimental, °merciless, pitiless, °cold, °coldhearted, °chilly, °frigid, °icy, °tough, °callous, °steely, °inflexible, unresponsive, *Colloq* hard-boiled

stoop *v.* **1** Sometimes, ***stoop down.*** °bend (down), °bow, °duck (down), °lean (down), °hunch (down), hunker (down), °crouch (down), scrunch down **2** Often, ***stoop low.*** °condescend, °deign, lower *or* abase *or* degrade oneself, °sink, humble oneself; be demeaned *or* diminished —*n.* **3** °hunch, °slouch, scrunch, °crouch, stooping, slouching, *Technical* lordosis, curvature of the spine, torticollis, wryneck

stop *v.* **1** °discontinue, °halt, °terminate, °cease, °break off, °end, put an end *or* a stop to, bring to a stop *or* a halt *or* an end *or* a close, °give up, °quit, °leave off, °finish, conclude, desist (from), °refrain (from), °abandon; draw to a close, be over, come to a stop *or* a halt *or* an end *or* a close; *Colloq* °cut (out), °lay off, *Brit* °pack in **2** bring to a stop *or* a halt *or* a standstill, °check, °cut off; °arrest, °suppress, °restrain, °thwart; °block, °bar, °obstruct, dam, keep *or* hold back, °prevent, °hinder; °slow, °impede, °stem, stanch *or* staunch **3** Often, ***stop up.*** °obstruct, °block (up), °jam (up), °plug (up), °clog (up), °choke (up), °stuff (up), °fill (up), close (up *or* off) **4** °peter out, be over, °end **5** °pause, °break, take a break, °interrupt, °tarry; °sojourn, °rest, °stay, °put up, °lodge, °visit, stop off *or* in *or* over; pull over, °pull up —*n.* **6** °halt, °end, cessation, °termination, °ban, °prohibition; °close, °standstill, conclusion **7** °stay, °sojourn, °visit, °break, °rest, stopover, *US* layover **8** stopping place, °station, °terminal, °stage, terminus, *US and Canadian* depot **9** blockage, blocking, stopping(-up), stoppage, closing up, °obstruction, °block

stopgap *n.* **1** °makeshift, improvisation, °substitute —*adj.* **2** °makeshift, °temporary, improvised, impromptu, °substitute, °emergency, °provisional, °standby; jury-rigged

stopper *n.* stopple, cork, °plug, bung

store *v.* **1** °stock, °collect, °accumulate, °put

by, lay away, °set aside, °pile (up), aggregate, °amass, cumulate; °hoard; °assemble **2** °keep, °hold, °stow (away), °preserve, °warehouse, stockpile —*n.* **3** °supply, inventory, °collection, °accumulation, °stock, stockpile, reservoir, °cache, °fund **4** °shop, department store, °market, retailer, °outlet, cooperative (store), *Colloq* co-op **5** ***set or lay store by.*** give credence to, °believe (in), have faith *or* trust in, °trust (in), bank *or* rely on, depend on *or* upon, °count on, value

storehouse *n.* °warehouse, depository *or* depositary, repository, storeroom, bank, °store, (*in Asia*) godown; arsenal, °magazine, armory

storm *n.* **1** °tempest, °disturbance, turbulence; windstorm, mistral, °gale, °whirlwind, °hurricane, tornado, typhoon, cyclone, *US and Canadian* williwaw; °shower, cloudburst, °downpour, rainstorm, deluge, monsoon, thundershower, thunderstorm, electrical storm; dust storm, sandstorm, simoom *or* simoon *or* samiel, harmattan, khamsin, sirocco; snowstorm, blizzard; hailstorm, ice storm **2** °outburst, °outcry, °explosion, °eruption, °outpouring, furor *or Brit* furore **3** °disturbance, °rumpus, °stir, commotion, °agitation, furor *or Brit* furore; turbulence, °strife, turmoil, °disorder —*v.* **4** °rage, °rant, °rave, °bluster, °fume, °explode, °thunder, °roar, raise the roof, raise hell, raise Cain, *Colloq* °fly off the handle, blow one's top, *US* °blow one's stack **5** °blow, °rain, °hail, snow, sleet, °rage, °bluster, squall, °howl **6** °attack, °assault, assail, °raid, blitz, blitzkrieg, °bombard, barrage, fire upon *or* on, °shell; °besiege, lay siege to, °siege

stormy *adj.* **1** °violent, °tempestuous, blustery, turbulent, °wild, howling, raging, roaring, °foul, °nasty, °bad, not fit for man or beast, °inclement **2** °violent, °tempestuous, turbulent, °fierce, °fiery, °frantic, frenetic, °nerve-racking, frenzied, °feverish, °raving, °wild

story[1] *n.* **1** °narrative, °tale, recounting, anecdote, °yarn; °account, °recital, °chronicle, °record, °history; °legend, °myth, fairy tale *or* story, °romance, gest *or* geste, fable, fabliau; epic, °saga, edda; °joke, *Colloq* °gag; °mystery, detective story, whodunit, thriller; horror story; allegory, °parable; °piece, article **2** contention, °testimony, °assertion, °version, °statement, °representation, °allegation **3** °fib, confabulation, (white *or* black) lie, °alibi, °excuse, untruth, °falsehood; tall tale, fishing *or* fish story **4** article, °item, °report, °dispatch, °news, tidings, °release, °information, °copy, °feature; °scoop, °exclusive **5** story line, °plot, °scenario, °(plot) outline, °summary, °book **6** biography, curriculum vitae, °life (story); °facts, experiences, adventures, °fortunes

story[2] *n.* storey, °floor, °level, °tier

stout *adj.* **1** °fat, °obese, tubby, overweight, thickset, heavyset, °big, °burly, corpulent, fleshy, °heavy, °plump, portly **2** valiant, °brave, undaunted, °dauntless, °hardy, °courageous, °gallant, plucky, valorous, °staunch, °resolute, doughty, °bold, °gallant **3** °strong, °tough, °substantial, °durable **4** °brawny, °sturdy, °healthy, °robust, strapping, °stalwart, °lusty, °hulking, athletic, *Colloq* beefy, °husky

stow *v.* °pack, °store, °load, °deposit, °put (away), °place; °cram, °stuff, °wedge, °bundle, °jam; °hide, °secrete, °conceal, °cache, *Colloq* stash (away)

straggle *v.* °stray, °ramble, loiter, rove, °prowl, °range, °drift, °wander, °meander, °(be) spread, *Colloq* mosey

straight *adj.* **1** °direct, unbending, undeviating, uncurved, °regular, linear **2** °erect, vertical, °upright, upstanding, °perpendicular; °plumb **3** °even, °square, °true, °right, °flat, °smooth, °horizontal, °level **4** °honest, °frank, straightforward, °direct, °forthright, °legitimate, °(fair and) square, °fair, °equitable, °just, °aboveboard, °upright, °respectable, °decent, °trustworthy, °honorable, dependable, °reliable, *Colloq* °up front **5** unequivocal, unambiguous, straightforward, °candid, °plain, °simple, °explicit, °blunt, unembellished, unelaborated, °unqualified, °outright, °accurate **6** °direct, °point-blank, straightforward, straight-from-the-shoulder, °candid, °outright, °plain, °frank, °no-nonsense **7** °shipshape, °orderly, °neat, °tidy, °in order, arranged, organized, sorted out, °spruce, straightened out **8** °sober, °staid, °sedate, °serious, unsmiling, unemotional, °impassive, emotionless, °taciturn, composed, masklike **9** °undiluted, °neat, unmixed, °pure, unadulterated, uncut, unmodified, unaltered, unalloyed **10** °even, °square, settled, straightened out, agreed **11** heterosexual, *Slang* hetero —*adv.* **12** °directly, °right, undeviatingly, unswervingly; as the crow flies, in a beeline **13** °(straight) ahead **14** Sometimes, ***straight out.*** °directly, unequivocally, unambiguously, forthrightly, straightforwardly, °point-blank, candidly, plainly, °simply, in plain *or* simple English, explicitly, °outright, °honestly, accurately **15** Often, *Brit* ***straightaway or straight off.*** °immediately, °at once, without delay, instantly, °summarily, °directly, right off the bat, °promptly, *US* right away, *Brit* right off, *Colloq* PDQ (= 'pretty damned quick') **16** ***straight up.*** without ice

straighten *v.* **1** Often, ***straighten out.*** uncurl, untangle, disentangle, unsnarl, unravel, unkink; °clear (up), °settle, °resolve, °sort out, set *or* put straight *or* right *or* to rights, °correct, °adjust, °rectify **2** Often, ***straighten out.*** °reform, °rehabilitate, °organize, reorganize **3** Often, ***straighten out or up.*** °tidy (up), °arrange, rearrange, °neaten, °spruce up, put in order, °clean (up)

strain[1] *v.* **1** °stretch, °force, °tax, overtax, °burden, overburden, °overwork, °push; °exceed, °surpass **2** °push, °pull, °tug, °heave, °stretch, °twist, °wrench, °struggle **3** °injure, °hurt, °harm, °impair, °damage, °overwork, °tax, °pull, °tear, °twist, °wrench 4 °stretch, crane, °twist; °try (hard), °struggle, °strive, °labor, toil, °push, make an effort, °exert oneself 5 °filter, °sift, °drain, °screen, sieve; winnow, °draw off, °separate; °purify, seep, °percolate —*n.* 6 sprain, °injury, °damage, °harm, °wrench 7 °anxiety, °worry; °effort, °exertion, °stress, °tension, °pressure, °burden; °tax, °demand, °obligation 8 Often, ***strains.*** °air, °melody, °tune, °song, °sound, music 9 °tenor, °tone, °drift, °inclination, °tendency, °quality, °spirit, °mood, °humor, °character, complexion, °cast, °impression, °thread, °vein, °theme

strain[2] *n.* 1 °family, °stock, ancestry, °roots, °extraction, °derivation, °(family) background, °heritage, descent, °parentage, °lineage, °pedigree, bloodline, °race, °line, descendants 2 °trace, °hint, °suggestion, °suspicion, *soupçon*, °streak, °trait, °mark, °indication, °vestige, °evidence, °sign

strained *adj.* °labored, °forced, °artificial, °stiff, °tense, °awkward, uneasy, uncomfortable, °difficult, tension-ridden, °self-conscious, °unnatural, °insincere, °put-on

strait *adj.* 1 °narrow, °tight, constricted, constricting, confining, confined, restricting, restricted, °limited, limiting, rigorous, °demanding, °exacting; °difficult, °straitened —*n.* 2 Usually (except in gazetteers), ***straits.*** °narrows, °channel 3 ***dire or desperate or sore straits.*** bad *or* poor state *or* condition, °trouble, °predicament, °plight, °mess, °dilemma, tight spot, hot water, *US* bind *Colloq* pickle, °jam, °scrape, pretty *or* fine kettle of fish, *US* °box

straitened *adj.* °inadequate, °insufficient, reduced, oppressed, distressed, °needy, necessitous, °poor, poverty-stricken, °indigent, °impoverished, °destitute, penniless, °insolvent, *Colloq* °hard up, *US* strapped

strait-laced *adj.* °priggish, prim, °conservative, °old-fashioned, Victorian, oldmaidish, °proper, °prudish, puritanical, moralistic, °strict, °narrow-minded, (over)scrupulous, °fussy, *Colloq* pernickety *or US also* persnickety, °stuffy, °goody-goody

strange *adj.* 1 °odd, °peculiar, °bizarre, °weird, °curious, uncommon, °unusual, °rare, °singular, exceptional, °eccentric, °weird, °funny, °quaint, °fantastic, out-of-the-ordinary, °extraordinary, °out-of-the-way, °queer, °outlandish, °unheard-of, °grotesque, °abnormal, °remarkable, surprising, °inexplicable, °unaccountable, uncanny, *Colloq* °offbeat, far-out, *Slang* °kinky, *Brit* rum, *US* kooky 2 °unfamiliar, °unknown, °unaccustomed

stranger *n.* °foreigner, outlander, °alien, °newcomer, °visitor

stratagem *n.* °trick, °artifice, °device, °dodge, °subterfuge, °lure, °wile, °ruse, °plan, °scheme, °plot, °intrigue, °maneuver, ploy, °tactic

strategic *adj.* °tactical, °key, °crucial, °principal, °cardinal, °critical, °vital, °key

strategy *n.* °plan, tactic(s), °design, °policy, °procedure, °scheme, blueprint, *Colloq* game *or* master plan, °scenario

stratum *n.* 1 layer, °level, stratification, °table, °vein, °seam; °plane 2 °level, °caste, °class, °rank, °station, °standing, °status, °bracket, °group, °estate

stray *v.* 1 °wander, °roam, rove, °range, °straggle, °drift, °meander 2 °deviate, °diverge, °wander, digress, °ramble, divagate, get *or* go off the track *or* subject, go off on *or* at a tangent, get sidetracked —*n.* 3 straggler, vagrant, waif, *US* dogie —*adj.* 4 vagrant, °lost, roving, roaming, wandering, °homeless, °derelict, °abandoned 5 °random, °casual, °chance, °accidental, °haphazard, °singular, °freak, unexpected 6 °isolated, separate(d), lone, °odd, °single

streak *n.* 1 °stripe, striation, °strip, °stroke, °bar, °band, °line, °mark, °smear, °slash, °dash, °touch, daub, fleck, °trace; °vein, layer, °seam, °stratum 2 °flash, °bolt 3 °spell, °spate, °period, °stretch, °run —*v.* 4 °stripe, striate, °line, °bar, °mark, °smear, daub, °slash 5 °race, °run, °rush, °dash, sprint, dart, °hurtle, °fly, scoot, °speed, °hasten, °hurry, °tear, whistle, zip, zoom, *Colloq* whiz *or* whizz

stream *n.* 1 °brook, brooklet, streamlet, rivulet, °tributary, °river, freshet, °run, watercourse, waterway, °channel, *Chiefly literary* rill, runnel, *Literary or N Brit dialect* beck, °burn, *Archaic NE US except in place names* °kill, *US* °creek, °branch 2 °flow, °current, °outpouring, effluence *or* efflux, effusion, °rush, °spurt, °surge, °fountain, geyser, °torrent, °flood, deluge, cataract, cascade 3 °flow, °rush, °swarm, tide, °flood, deluge, °succession, series, °row, °line, °string, °chain, barrage, *Brit* °queue —*v.* 4 °run, °flow, °course, °glide, °rush, °slide, °slip, °surge; °pour, °issue, °emanate, °gush, °flood, °spout, well up *or* out *or* forth, squirt, °spurt, °shoot, jet; cascade 5 °issue, °emanate; °rush, °surge, °pour, °flood, °file, °proceed, °march, °walk, °move

streamer *n.* °pennant, °banner, pennon, °flag, bannerette *or* banneret, banderole *or* bannerol, gonfalon *or* gonfanon, jack, burgee

streamlined *adj.* 1 aerodynamic, hydrodynamic, curved, curvilinear; °smooth, flowing 2 °modern, ultramodern, modernistic, modernized, up-to-date, timesaving, labor-saving, °compact, (well-)organized, °efficient, automated 3 well-run, °smooth, °efficient, automated, labor-saving, timesaving, °profitable, °productive, simplified

street *n.* 1 thoroughfare, °way, °road, roadway, highroad, avenue, concourse, boulevard, lane, °drive, terrace, °circle, °row, °passage, alley, byway 2 ***up (someone's)*** *Brit* ***street or US alley.*** (someone's) cup of tea, in (someone's) bailiwick, suiting (someone) to a T

strength *n.* 1 °power, °might, °force, mightiness, robustness, toughness, stoutness, sturdiness, °brawn, brawniness, muscle, °sinew **2** °fortitude, °backbone, °stamina, °tenacity, tenaciousness, willpower, °perseverance, °persistence, resoluteness, °resolution, pertinacity, °nerve, °grit, °pluck, °determination, gameness, intrepidity, firmness, °stability, *Colloq* °guts, gutsiness, °spunk, *US* intestinal fortitude, stick-to-itiveness **3** °talent, °ability, °aptitude, °gift, strong point, °asset **4** concentration, concentratedness, °intensity, potency **5** °vigor, °force, °energy, °power, potency, °intensity **6** durability, °power, toughness, °stability, reliability, °resistance, solidity, °stamina, ruggedness, °endurance, soundness **7** persuasiveness, cogency, °weight, °force, convincingness, incisiveness, soundness

strengthen *v.* **1** °reinforce, °renew, °bolster, °fortify, °support, °confirm, corroborate, °substantiate, °buttress, °step up, °boost **2** °encourage, hearten, invigorate, °fortify, °rejuvenate, °nourish, °energize, °vitalize, toughen, °brace (up), °steel, innervate, °stiffen

strenuous *adj.* **1** °demanding, taxing, °tough, °arduous, °laborious, °toilsome, °burdensome, tiring, °exhausting, °difficult, °hard, uphill **2** °energetic, °active, °vigorous, °enthusiastic, zealous, °earnest, °dynamic, °intense, indefatigable, °tireless, °persistent, dogged, °determined, °tenacious, pertinacious, °resolute, °sincere, °eager

stress *n.* **1** °emphasis, °force, °pressure, forcefulness, °accent, accentuation, °prominence, *Technical* ictus **2** °emphasis, °significance, °importance, °weight, °force, insistence, °urgency **3** °(stress and) strain, °burden, °anxiety, °worry, °distress, °pain, °grief, °suffering, °anguish, °pressure, tenseness, °tension —*v.* **4** °emphasize, °accent, accentuate, lay stress *or* emphasis on, underscore, underline, °mark, °note, °make a point of, °bring home, focus on, bring into prominence, °spotlight, °feature, highlight **5** °strain, put under strain *or* stress, °upset, °disturb, °burden, °worry, °distress, *Brit* pressurize *or US* pressure

stretch *v.* **1** °extend, °reach; °span, °spread **2** distend, °lengthen, elongate, °widen, broaden, °swell, draw *or* pull out, balloon, °inflate, °enlarge, °expand, °increase, dilate, °blow up **3** overtax, overextend; °warp, °strain, °distort, °bend, °break —*n.* **4** °elasticity, °give, °resilience, resiliency, stretchability, stretchiness **5** °extent, °reach, °span, °spread, °expanse, °sweep, °area, °tract, *US* °section **6** °time, °stint, °period, °spell, °term, °tour (of duty), *Colloq US and Canadian* °hitch

strew *v.* °scatter, bestrew, sprinkle, °disperse, °spread, °toss, °distribute; °litter

stricken *adj.* **1** Usually, ***stricken by.*** struck (down) (by), °hit (by), laid low (by *or* with), affected (by *or* with), afflicted (with), wracked (by *or* with) **2** Often, ***struck.*** °affected (by), °smitten (by), overwhelmed (by *or* with), overcome (by *or* with), plagued (by *or* with), tormented (by); °broken, crushed, demoralized, °brokenhearted, grief-stricken

strict *adj.* **1** rigorous, °narrow, °close, undeviating, confining, constricting, constrictive, °rigid, defined, °precise, °exact, °exacting, stringent, °meticulous, °compulsive, punctilious, finicky *or* finical, °scrupulous, °attentive, °conscientious, °faithful, °thorough, °complete **2** °severe, austere, °authoritarian, autocratic, °stern, °firm, °hard, °tough, uncompromising, °inflexible, °coldblooded, ironfisted, °tyrannical, °harsh, °ruthless, pitiless, °unsympathetic

stricture *n.* **1** interdiction, blockage, °restriction, °restraint, constraint, °deterrent, °impediment **2** °criticism, censure

strident *adj.* °shrill, °raucous, °harsh, °loud, °grating, stridulous, stridulant, scraping, scratching, °scratchy, grinding, hoarse, °rough, guttural, °husky, gravelly, rasping, jarring, °discordant, unharmonious, unmelodious, unmusical, cacophonous, croaking, creaking

strife *n.* **1** °discord, disharmony, °disagreement, °difference, °conflict, °rivalry, °competition, contention, °dispute, °dissension, °struggle, squabbling, bickering, arguing, quarreling **2** °animosity, °friction, hard feelings, bad feeling(s), bad blood, °antagonism, °ill will, hatred, enmity, °hostility, unfriendliness

strike *v.* **1** °hit, deal a blow to, °knock, smack, thump, thwack, °crown, cuff, °punch, smite; °beat, hammer, °belabor, °batter, pummel *or* pommel, °pelt, buffet, thrash; cudgel, bludgeon, °club, °whip, horsewhip, °scourge, °lash, cane, °flog, birch, °slap, *Colloq* wallop, slug, whack, clout, sock, conk, °belt, bash, lambaste *or* lambast, bop **2** °deliver, °deal, °aim, °direct **3** °hit, °collide with, land on *or* in *or* against, smash *or* bump *or* bang *or* crash *or* dash into, go *or* run into, °impact **4** °remove, take away, take apart, dismantle, °knock down; take *or* pull *or* haul down **5** Usually, ***strike off*** *or* ***from*** *or* ***out.*** °obliterate, expunge, °erase, eradicate, °blot out, °delete, °scratch, °eliminate, °rub out, °cross (out), °cancel, °wipe out, *US* x out **6** °light, ignite **7** °affect, °impress, °influence, °afflict, *Colloq* °hit **8** °make, °reach, attain, conclude; agree *or* settle (on *or* upon), °ratify, °confirm **9** occur *or* come to, dawn on *or* upon, *Colloq* °hit, °register (with) **10** °impress, °print, °stamp, °punch, °mint, °make **11** °instill, °implant, °induce **12** °assume, °adopt, °put on, °display, °affect, °take on, feign **13** Often, ***strike down.*** °afflict, °affect, °attack, indispose, °incapacitate, disable, °cripple, °invalid **14** °encounter, come *or* happen *or* hit upon, °come across, chance upon, °discover, °stumble on, °find **15** °revolt, °rebel, °mutiny, walk out (of *or* off the job) **16** ***strike on*** *or* ***upon.*** dream up, °devise, conjure up, °improvise, °work out, °invent, contrive, come up with, hit on *or* upon, °arrive at **17** ***strike out.*** (a) °fail, get nowhere, *Colloq US* miss the boat, °flop, come a cropper, *Slang US* blow it, blow the gaff, come to nothing *or* naught *or* nought **(b)** See **5**, above. **18** ***strike up.*** (cause to) begin *or* start *or* commence **—*n.* 19** °attack, °assault **20** walkout, sit-down (strike), job action, slowdown, go-slow, work-to-rule

striking *adj.* °remarkable, astounding, astonishing, °amazing, wondrous, awe-inspiring, °awesome, °stunning, °impressive, °imposing, °fabulous, out-of-the-ordinary, °unusual, °rare, °exceptional, °marvelous, °extraordinary, °magnificent, °superb, °splendid, stupendous, *Colloq* °great, smashing, *Slang old-fashioned Brit* °ripping, rip-snorting, top-hole, topping

string *n.* **1** °line, °cord, °thread, °twine, °fiber, °rope, °cable, ligament, strand, filament **2** leash, °lead, °leader **3** °line, °row, series, °sequence, °succession, °chain, °procession, °stream, °train, °file, *Chiefly Brit* °queue **4** necklace, °chain, °loop, strand, dog-collar, choker, chaplet, wreath, rivière, *Archaic* carcanet **5** ***pull strings or wires.*** use *or* exert influence, *Colloq* throw one's weight around **6** ***pull the strings.*** be in control, °control, °run, °operate, °dominate, be in command, be in the driver's seat, hold the reins, °manipulate **7** ***strings.*** °conditions, stipulations, provisos, °qualifications, requirements, prerequisites, °terms, obligations, limitations, °provisions, musts, *Colloq* catches **—*v.* 8** °thread, °join **9** Often, ***string together or up.*** °loop, festoon, °link, °drape, °suspend, °sling, °hang, array, concatenate, chain together **10** ***string along.*** **(a)** °follow, go along (with), °agree, concur, °collaborate **(b)** keep waiting *or* dangling, keep on a string, keep on tenterhooks, *Colloq* play fast and loose with (someone) **(c)** °fool, °deceive, °bluff, °dupe, °cheat, °trick, °hoax, *Colloq* take someone for a ride, put one *or* something over on (someone) **11** ***string out.*** **(a)** °stretch, °reach, °extend **(b)** °delay, °postpone, drag out, protract, °spin out **12** ***string up.*** °hang, lynch

stringy *adj.* fibrous, chewy, °sinewy, gristly, °ropy, leathery, °tough

strip[1] *n.* °band, ribbon, fillet, °belt, swath *or* swathe, °stripe

strip[2] *v.* **1** °peel, °skin, °bare, uncover, denude, °lay bare, decorticate, excoriate, flay **2** °disrobe, undress, get undressed, unclothe, strip down to nothing *or* to the skin *or* to the buff *or* to (one's) birthday suit, take off *or* peel off *or* divest (oneself) of *or* shed (one's) clothes *or* clothing, get naked **3** (do a) striptease, *US* work the runway **4** °remove, take away, °confiscate, °seize, expropriate, *Slang* °rip off **5** °rob, °pillage, despoil, °plunder, °ransack, °loot, °sack

stripe *n.* **1** °band, °bar, striation, °strip, °streak, °line, °stroke, °slash, °length **2** °style, °kind, °sort, °class, °type, complexion, °character, °nature, °description, °persuasion, kidney, feather

striped *adj.* streaked, lined, striated

stripling *n.* °lad, °boy, °adolescent, °juvenile, °minor, schoolboy, youngster, °teenager, °youth, young fellow *or* man, fledgling, *Dialect* gossoon, young 'un, *Archaic* hobbledehoy

strive *v.* **1** °endeavor, °strain, °struggle, make every effort, °attempt, °try (hard), do one's best *or* utmost, °exert oneself, work at, *Colloq* give (it) one's all, go all out **2** °compete, contend, °fight

stroke *n.* **1** °blow, °rap, °tap, thump, °knock, smack, whack, °swipe, °slam, °strike, *Colloq* wallop **2** °action, °motion, °go, °move, °movement, °feat, °achievement **3** °flourish, °movement, °gesture; °mark, °dash, *Colloq* °splash **4** °beat, throb, °pulse, pulsation, thump **5** °attack, °seizure, °fit, apoplexy, apoplectic fit, °spasm, paralytic attack *or* fit; *Technical* embolism, thrombosis, cerebrovascular accident, aneurysm **6** °pat, °touch, °caress **7** °achievement, °accomplishment, °feat, °act, °action, °work; °example; °touch **8** °bit, jot or tittle, °scrap, iota, °touch, stitch, °hint, °suggestion **9** °occurrence, °happening, °matter **—*v.* 10** °caress, °pet, °pat, °fondle; °massage, °rub, soothe

stroll *v.* **1** amble, °saunter, °ramble, °walk, °wander, °promenade, °meander, °stray, *Colloq* mosey **—*n.* 2** amble, °ramble, °saunter, °walk, °wander, °promenade, °meander, constitutional

strong *adj.* **1** °powerful, °muscular, °mighty, °brawny, strapping, °robust, °sturdy, °stalwart, °burly, °stout, °sinewy, athletic, °wiry, *Colloq* beefy, °hefty, °husky **2** °powerful, concentrated, °intense, °pungent, °potent, °sharp, piquant, acrid, heady, °penetrating, °aromatic, °fragrant, °hot, °spicy **3** °smelly, odoriferous, noisome, °stinking, °foul, mephitic, miasmic, °putrid, putrescent, °rotten **4** concentrated, °undiluted, °potent, intensified **5** °vigorous, °active, °dynamic, °energetic, °eager, unflagging, °tireless, unfailing, °diligent, indefatigable, °staunch, true-blue, °steadfast, dedicated, °enthusiastic, °ardent, °fervent, fervid, vehement, °rabid, zealous, °resolute, °determined, unwavering, unswerving, °firm, uncompromising, °regular, °persistent, °tenacious, sedulous, assiduous, hard-working **6** °competent, °talented, skilled, °qualified, °knowledgeable, °able, °experienced, well-versed, trained, °efficient, °capable **7** °influential, °persuasive, convincing, compelling, °trenchant, unmistakable *or* unmistakeable, °telling, °great, °profound; °effective, °efficacious, °effectual, °powerful, °formidable **8** well-supported, irrefutable, well-substantiated, cogent, °forceful, °substantial, convincing, conclusive **9** °well-established, well-founded, redoubtable, °substantial, °powerful, °formidable **10** °likely, °definite, °substantial, °good, better than average, °reasonable, sizable **11** °stable, °sound, °solvent, °prosperous, °flourishing, thriving, affluent **12** °solid, °sturdy, °substantial, °tough, well-built, reinforced, heavy-duty, °durable; hard earing **13**

°drastic, °extreme, Draconian, highhanded, °severe, °forceful, rigorous, °harsh, stringent, °aggressive, °strenuous, °stiff, °tough, *Colloq* hard-nosed **14** numerous, °large, °considerable, °great; numerically, in number, in strength **15** °vivid, °graphic, etched, engraved, imprinted, impressed; °definite, clear-cut, °clear, °pronounced, °distinct, °striking, °marked **16** °willful, °aggressive, combative, defensive, °difficult, °assertive, °incisive, °dogmatic, doctrinaire, °opinionated, °self-willed, hard-headed, °strong-minded, °recalcitrant, °stubborn, °obstinate, °emphatic, *Colloq* °pushy **17** °vigorous, °forceful, °powerful, °heavy **18** °rugged, craggy, °rough, weather-beaten **19** °dazzling, °glaring, °bright, °garish, °brilliant, °vivid, °bold, blinding **20** °urgent, strongly worded, °emphatic, °assertive **21** unvarying, the same, °steady, °stable, °firm, balanced **22** °emotional, deep-felt, deep-rooted, °basic, °intense, °fervent, °passionate, °deep, °earnest *—adv.* **23** overbearingly, overenthusiastically, offensively, aggressively, antagonistically, truculently

strong-arm *adj.* °threatening, °menacing, bullying, high-pressure, thuggish, °violent, °brutal, brutish, °aggressive, terrorizing, °terrorist, intimidating, minacious

stronghold *n.* fortress, °bulwark, bastion, fastness, fortification, citadel

strong-minded *adj.* strong-willed, °obstinate, °firm, °determined, uncompromising, °resolute, resolved, °independent

structure *n.* **1** °form, °shape, configuration, °organization, °arrangement, °makeup, framework, °order, °design, °formation, °system, °nature, °character **2** °building, edifice, °house, construction *—v.* **3** °construct, °build, °organize, °design, °form, °shape, °arrange, systematize

struggle *v.* **1** °strive, °strain, expend energy, °exert oneself, °endeavor, °try, °attempt **2** contend, °fight, °wrestle, °battle **3** °wriggle, wiggle, °squirm, writhe, °twist, worm *—n.* **4** °effort, °exertion, °strain; toil, °work, travail, °labor, °drudgery, striving, struggling **5** contention, °competition, °contest, °battle, °fight, tussle, °match, °clash, °encounter, °strife

strut *v.* °swagger, °parade, °promenade, peacock, °prance

stub *n.* **1** °butt, °end, °stump, °tail (end), °remnant, *Colloq Brit* fag end **2** counterfoil; °receipt

stubborn *adj.* °obstinate, unyielding, °inflexible, intransigent, intractable, uncompromising, mulish, pigheaded, refractory, wayward, adamant(ine), °recalcitrant, bullheaded, °persistent, °tenacious, pertinacious, unrelenting, dogged, °determined

student *n.* **1** °pupil, °learner, °scholar, undergraduate, schoolboy, schoolgirl, schoolchild, trainee, °apprentice, °disciple; *Colloq Brit* swot *or* swotter *or* swat, *US* °grind **2** °devotee, °follower, °admirer, °observer, evaluator, commentator, critic

studied *adj.* °premeditated, °deliberate, °calculated, planned, °intentional, °willful, well-thought-out, °conscious, contrived, feigned, °forced, °labored

studious *adj.* **1** assiduous, sedulous, °diligent, °industrious, °attentive, °careful, °painstaking, °thorough, °tireless **2** °scholarly, bookish, °academic

study *v.* **1** °learn (about), °read, con, °memorize, burn the midnight oil, lucubrate, *Colloq* bone up (on), °cram, *Brit* swot *or* swat, mug up **2** °contemplate, °consider, °reflect on, think over *or* about, ruminate on, °chew over, °turn over, °weigh, °ponder, deliberate over *or* on *or* about, muse about *or* on, mull over, meditate on *or* about *or* over **3** look *or* go into *or* over, °look at, °scan, °examine, °analyze, °inspect, °investigate, °scrutinize, °survey, °observe *—n.* **4** °analysis, °review, °examination, °survey, inquiry *or* enquiry, °investigation, °scrutiny, °research, °exploration **5** °learning, lessons, bookwork, °work, reading, contemplation, °investigation, *Colloq* boning up, cramming, *Brit* swotting *or* swatting **6** library, reading *or* writing room, °sanctum (sanctorum), °haunt, studio, °retreat, den, workroom, °office

stuff *n.* **1** °substance, °material, °matter, °fabric, ingredients, °essence, essentials, fundamentals, building blocks, makings **2** °equipment, °goods, °gear, °trappings, °kit, °tackle, accessories, °paraphernalia, accoutrements *or US also* accouterments, °effects, °belongings, °possessions, °things, bits and pieces, impedimenta, baggage, °property, chattels, °furniture, *Brit* °lumber, *Colloq* °junk, °rubbish, crap, *Brit* clobber, *Taboo slang* shit **3** °spirit, °attitude, °grit, °substance, makings, talent(s), °abilities, capabilities, qualities, attributes **4** °nonsense, °trash, °rubbish, stuff and nonsense, twaddle, humbug, bunkum, tommyrot, balderdash, *Colloq* °rot, °garbage, bunk, tripe, poppycock, crap, malarkey, baloney *or* boloney, bosh, hogwash, °swill, claptrap, piffle, °hot air, flapdoodle, fiddle-faddle, codswallop, bull, *US* horsefeathers, *Taboo slang* bullshit, horseshit **5** creations, accomplishments, °things, °works, materials, °matter *—v.* **6** °jam, °ram, °cram, °crowd, compress, °pack, °press, °squeeze, squash, shove, °thrust, °force **7** °line, °fill, °pack **8** °overeat, °gorge, overindulge, gormandize *or US also* gourmandize, gluttonize, *Colloq* make a pig *or* a hog of oneself **9** *stuff up.* °clog, °plug, °obstruct, °choke, °block (up), stop *or US also* pack up

stuffy *adj.* **1** °close, airless, unventilated, °oppressive, stifling, suffocating, °stale, °musty, fusty, °moldy, mildewy, °muggy, fetid *or* foetid, frowzy *or* frowsy, *Brit* frowsty **2** °pompous, °pedantic, self-important, self-centered, °stodgy, old-fogyish *or* old-fogeyish, °old-fashioned, °strait-laced, °staid, °conventional, prim (and proper), °priggish, niminy-piminy, °stilted, °stiff, °rigid, *Colloq* fuddy-duddy, uptight

stumble *v.* 1 falter, °blunder, °slip, °trip, miss one's footing, °stagger, °lurch, °flounder 2 falter, °pause, °hesitate, °trip, °slip, °blunder 3 ***stumble on or upon.*** chance *or* come *or* happen on *or* upon, °hit upon, come *or* run across, °find, °discover, °encounter, *Colloq* °bump into

stumbling block *n.* °impediment, °obstacle, °bar, °block, °obstruction, °hurdle, °hindrance, °barrier, °difficulty, °snag

stump *n.* 1 °stub, °butt, °end —*v.* 2 °mystify, °confuse, °perplex, °bewilder, °flummox, °foil, °puzzle, baffle, confound, dumbfound *or* dumfound, °stop, °stymie, °nonplus, bring up short 3 °campaign, °electioneer, °canvass, ***US and Canadian*** barnstorm 4 ***stump up.*** pay up *or* out, °contribute, °donate, *Colloq* cough up, °chip in, shell *or* fork out

stun *n.* 1 °daze, °numb, benumb, °knock out 2 °astonish, °daze, °paralyze, °stagger, stupefy, °overcome, °overwhelm, °astound, °jar, °shock, °jolt, strike dumb, °amaze, confound, °bewilder, take (someone's) breath away, *Colloq* °shake up, bowl over, discombobulate, flabbergast

stunning *adj.* 1 stupefying, paralyzing, staggering, benumbing, numbing; °knockout 2 °beautiful, °dazzling, °brilliant, °gorgeous, spectacular, °ravishing, °sensational, °extraordinary, °remarkable, °marvelous, stupendous, °fabulous, wonderful, °superb, °grand, °divine, °heavenly, °sublime, °lovely, °exquisite, °glorious, astonishing, astounding, °amazing, °striking, °splendid, staggering, °overpowering, mind-boggling, earthshaking, °magnificent

stunt[1] *n.* °caper, °act, °deed, °feat, tour de force, °exploit, °trick, *US* dido

stunt[2] *v.* °stop, °limit, delimit, °restrict, °check, °arrest, put an end to, °end; °impede, °hamper, °hinder, °slow, °retard

stunted *adj.* dwarfed, shrunken, °undersized, °small, °tiny, °diminutive, °little, °wee

stupid *adj.* 1 unintelligent, fatuous, °obtuse, bovine, °dull, °dense, lumpish, doltish, °simple, simple-minded, moronic, imbecilic, cretinous, Boeotian, subnormal, °feebleminded, weak-minded, °stolid, dull-witted, °dim, dimwitted, °half-witted, °thick, thick-witted, thickheaded, slow-witted, witless, brainless, °mindless, empty-headed, birdbrained, featherbrained, featherheaded, rattlebrained, rattleheaded, oxlike, boneheaded, addlepated, addle-headed, addled, *Chiefly Brit* imbecile, *Chiefly US* °dumb, jerky, thimble-witted, *Colloq* dopey, *Brit* dozy 2 °foolish, °silly, °frivolous, asinine, °harebrained, °crazy, °insane, °mad, crackbrained, °scatterbrained, °absurd, °inane, idiotic, °ridiculous, risible, laughable, °ludicrous, °nonsensical, °senseless, °bootless, °irresponsible, irrational, °ill-advised, °foolhardy, half-baked, *Colloq* cuckoo, balmy, cockeyed, damnfool, *Chiefly Brit* °daft, barmy, *US* cockamamie *or* cockamamy 3 insipid, °dull, °tedious, °boring, °tiresome, °humdrum, °prosaic, °monotonous, unimaginative, uninspired, uninteresting, °vapid, vacuous, *Colloq* ho-hum

stupidity *n.* 1 fatuity, obtuseness, dullness, denseness, lumpishness, doltishness, °simplicity, simplemindedness, imbecility, cretinism, feeblemindedness, weak-mindedness, stolidity, dull-wittedness, dimness, dimwittedness, half-wittedness, thick-wittedness, slow-wittedness, thimble-wittedness, witlessness, brainlessness, mindlessness, empty-headedness, featherheadedness, rattleheadedness, boneheadedness 2 foolishness, °folly, asininity, craziness, °insanity, °madness, °absurdity, absurdness, inanity, idiocy, ridiculousness, risibility, ludicrousness, °nonsense, senselessness, bootlessness, irresponsibility, irrationality, foolhardiness

stupor *n.* insensibility, stupefaction, °torpor, °lethargy, listlessness, languor, laziness, lassitude, lifelessness, supineness, °inertia; inertness, coma, °trance, unconsciousness, numbness

sturdy *adj.* 1 °strong, °solid, °stout, °rugged, °tough, well-built, °substantial; strapping, °muscular, °powerful, °brawny, °burly, °robust, well-muscled, athletic, °hardy, *Colloq* °husky, °hefty 2 °stalwart, °staunch, °steadfast, °resolute, °firm, °vigorous, °determined, uncompromising, unyielding, unwavering, unswerving, unfaltering, °enduring, °indomitable

style *n.* 1 °type, °kind, °variety, °category, °genre, °sort, °manner, °mode, °make, °design, °fashion, °look, °period, °pattern, configuration, °line, °cut, °shape, °form 2 °fashion, °trend, °vogue, °mode, °look, °rage, °craze, *Colloq* °fad, °(latest) thing 3 °luxury, high style, °comfort, opulence, °splendor, °elegance 4 °chic, stylishness, °taste, smartness, °flair, °dash, élan, °panache, °cachet, tastefulness, fashionableness, °elegance, °refinement, °polish, °sophistication, sophisticatedness, cosmopolitanism, *Colloq* pizazz; ritziness 5 °quality, °character, mode of expression, °approach, °treatment, °vein, coloring, °spirit, °mood, °form, °technique; °tenor, °tone, °wording, phraseology, phrasing, °language, vocabulary, word choice, °diction, sentence structure 6 ***in style.*** See **stylish,** below. —*v.* 7 °characterize, °designate, denominate, °call, °name, °term, °label, °tag, °brand 8 °fashion, °design, °arrange, °set, do, °cut, °tailor, °shape, °form

stylish *adj.* °chic, °fashionable, °smart, à la mode, modish, in style *or* fashion *or* vogue, °elegant; chi-chi; *Colloq* in, with it, °swanky, *Chiefly Brit* °trendy, *Slang* °swell, °neat, classy, snazzy, *US* spiffy

stymie *v.* °thwart, °obstruct, °block, °frustrate, snooker, °defeat, °spike, °ruin, °foil, confound, °stump, °nonplus, °hinder, °impede, *Colloq* °flummox

styptic *adj.* astringent

suave *adj.* °debonair, °sophisticated, urbane, cosmopolitan, °worldly, °smooth, °gracious, °nonchalant, civilized, °cultivated, °courteous, °diplomatic, °polite, charming, °agreeable, affable, °bland

subconscious *adj.* 1 °subliminal, °unconscious, suppressed, °hidden, latent, repressed, inner, innermost, underlying, deep-rooted, *Colloq* Freudian —*n.* 2 °(collective) unconscious, inner self; °heart

subdue *v.* 1 put *or* beat down, °quell, °repress, °suppress, °quash, °crush, °control, °master, °overpower, gain mastery *or* control *or* the upper hand over, get the better of, °dominate, °triumph over, hold *or* keep in check, °bridle, °tame 2 °conquer, vanquish, °defeat, °overcome 3 quiet *or* tone down, *Chiefly Brit* quieten down, °moderate, °mellow, °temper, °soften, soft-pedal, °check, °curb, °control

subdued *adj.* 1 °quiet, mellow(ed), toned-down, moderate(d), tempered, hushed, muted, low-key, °unenthusiastic, repressed, restrained, °peaceful, °tranquil, placid, calm(ed), °temperate, °reserved 2 chastened, °sober, sobered, °solemn, saddened, °dejected, °sad, °down in the mouth, crestfallen, downcast, °grave, °serious

subject *n.* 1 °(subject) matter, °topic; °issue, °theme, °angle, °thesis, °gist, °substance, °business, °affair, °point 2 °course (of study), °field, °area, °discipline, branch of knowledge 3 °cause, ground(s), °motive, °reason, °basis, °source, °rationale; °excuse 4 °participant, °case, guinea pig, testee 5 °citizen, °national; taxpayer, voter; liegeman, vassal —*adj.* 6 Usually, ***subject to.*** exposed (to), °open (to), °vulnerable (to), °susceptible (to), °prone (to), °disposed (to), at the mercy (of), liable (to suffer *or* undergo) 7 discussed, under discussion, referred to, °above 8 ***subject to.*** (a) answerable to, responsible for, bound by, obedient to, subservient to, submissive to, controlled by, under the control of (b) dependent on, conditional on, contingent on —*v.* 9 ***subject to.*** °expose, lay open, °submit, °put through, °impose on, cause to undergo 10 °conquer, °subjugate, °dominate, °subdue, °enslave, °crush, °humble, *Archaic* enthrall

subjection *n.* subordination, °domination, °conquest, subjugation, enslavement, enthrallment, humbling, °humiliation

subjective *adj.* 1 °personal, °individual, idiosyncratic; °prejudiced, °biased 2 self-centered, °egoistic, egocentric, °selfish, self-serving —*n.* 3 *Technical* nominative

subjugate *v.* °dominate, °enslave, °crush, °humble, °subject, °oppress, °suppress, °put down, °tyrannize, °subdue, °reduce, °quell, °overcome, °overpower, make subservient *or* submissive, °humble, °humiliate, *Archaic* enthrall

sublimate *v.* transmute, °alter, °transform; °channel, °divert

sublime *adj.* 1 °lofty, °high, °supreme, °exalted, °elevated, empyrean *or* empyreal, °heavenly, °noble, °glorious, °grand, high-minded; °honorable, ennobled, °eminent, °glorified, beatified, canonized, sanctified, °great, °good 2 °awesome, °overwhelming, inspiring, mind-boggling, °overpowering, humbling, awe-inspiring, °majestic, °splendid, empyrean

subliminal *adj.* °subconscious, °unconscious, °suggestive

submerge *v.* 1 °plunge, submerse, °immerse, inundate, °dip, °wash, °soak, °drench, °saturate, °wet, douse, *Colloq* dunk 2 °dive, °plunge, °go down, °descend, °sink, °sound, °plummet 3 °flood, °immerse, inundate, °swamp, °bury, engulf, °overwhelm, deluge, °drown; °conceal, °hide, °camouflage, °obscure, °cloak, °veil, °shroud

submission *n.* 1 concession, acquiescence, capitulation, °surrender, °yielding, °deference, giving in, °obedience, compliance, °resignation, submissiveness, tractability; meekness, docility, passivity, timidity, unassertiveness 2 submittal, °offering, °tender, contribution, °entry

submissive *adj.* 1 °yielding, acquiescent, deferential, compliant, °obedient, °tractable, amenable, °agreeable, °accommodating, °passive, unresisting, pliant, °flexible, °manageable, unassertive, docile, °meek, °timid, resigned, uncomplaining 2 °obsequious, abject, subservient, °servile, °humble, deferential, slavish, °ingratiating, truckling, biddable, sycophantic, toadying, *Colloq* bootlicking, *Taboo slang* brown-nosing, *Brit* arse-kissing, arse-licking, *US* ass-kissing, ass-licking

submit *v.* 1 Often, ***submit to.*** °surrender (to), °yield (to), °capitulate (to), give in *or* up (to), °comply (with), °agree (to), °concede (to), °consent (to), accede (to), °defer (to), bow *or* bend (to), °succumb (to), °truckle (to), knuckle under (to), resign (oneself) (to), be *or* become resigned (to); °respect, °accept, *Colloq* °put up with 2 °offer, proffer, °tender, °enter, °propose, °present

subordinate *adj.* 1 Often, ***subordinate to.*** °minor; °inferior (to), °lower (than), lesser (than), °secondary (to), °second (to), °junior (to), °subsidiary (to); next to, °below, °beneath, °under —*n.* 2 °assistant, °aide, °junior, subaltern, staff member; underling, hireling, °inferior, lackey, °servant, °slave, vassal; *Colloq US* staffer —*v.* 3 make (something) secondary

subscribe *v.* 1 Often, ***subscribe to.*** °endorse, °support, °underwrite, °advocate, °back (up), °approve (of), agree (with *or* to), °accept, °consent (to), assent (to), countenance, °tolerate, condone, °allow, °permit, °brook 2 Often, ***subscribe to.*** °contribute (to), °support, °give (to), °donate (to), °pledge, °promise, sign (up) (for), *Colloq* chip in (to *or* for)

subscription *n.* 1 °payment, °remittance, investment; commitment, °dues, °fee, °price, °cost 2 °obligation, °pledge, °promise, underwriting

subsequent *adj.* 1 succeeding, following, ensuing, next, °future, later, °successive; resultant, resulting, consequent —*prep.* 2 ***subsequent to.*** after, following, succeeding, in the wake *or* aftermath of

subsequently *adv.* later (on), afterward(s)

subside *v.* 1 °sink (down), °drop (down), °go down, °recede, °descend, °decline; °lower, °settle 2 abate, quiet *or chiefly Brit* quieten (down), °calm (down), °moderate, °let up, °decrease, °diminish, lessen, die (down *or* off *or* out), °pass (away), °wear off

subsidiary *adj.* Often, ***subsidiary to.*** ancillary (to), °secondary (to), °auxiliary (to), lesser (than), additional (to), supplementary *or* supplemental (to), complementary (to), °accessory (to), °subordinate (to), adjuvant (to)

subsidize *v.* °fund, °finance, °support, °aid, °sponsor, subvene, °maintain, °underwrite; capitalize, *Slang US and Canadian* bankroll

subsidy *n.* funding, financing, subsidizing, sponsoring, sponsorship, °assistance, °aid, contribution, °support, °grant, subvention, °maintenance, underwriting, capitalization

subsistence *n.* 1 °existence, living, survival, subsisting, being 2 °food, °rations, victuals, °provision, °sustenance, °board, °nourishment, nutriment, aliment; °maintenance, °keep, °upkeep

substance *n.* 1 °material, °matter, °stuff; °fabric, °composition, °makeup 2 °essence, °pith, °heart, °core, °gist, °burden, °theme, °meat, °kernel, °nub, crux, sum total, sum and substance, °point, gravamen, haecceity, °quintessence, quiddity 3 °meaning, °import, °significance, purport, signification, °point 4 °reality, corporeality, solidity, actuality, concreteness 5 °means, °wealth, °property, °possessions, °riches, °resources, affluence, °assets

substantial *adj.* 1 °material, °considerable, °significant, °great, °worthwhile, consequential, °ample, °goodly, °respectable, °abundant, °generous, °big, °large, sizable, °major, *Colloq* °tidy, °healthy 2 °strong, °solid, well-built, °durable, °sound, °stout, °sturdy; °big, °large, °massive, °huge, sizable, °impressive, °vast; numerous, °numberless 3 well-founded, °sound, °weighty, °solid, °well-established, °telling, °good, valid, °actual 4 °wealthy, well-to-do, °rich, affluent, °prosperous, °profitable, °successful; landed, propertied

substantially *adv.* in substance, essentially, °at bottom, fundamentally, basically, °in essence, intrinsically, °in reality, at heart, °sincerely, °truly, °actually, °in truth, veritably, °indeed, °in fact, as a matter of fact; °largely, to a large extent, in large measure, °materially, °practically, °in the main, °for the most part, mostly, °virtually, °to all intents and purposes; *Archaic* verily

substantiate *v.* °confirm, affirm, corroborate, °support, °sustain, °back up, °bear out, °authenticate, °show (clearly), °prove, °document, °verify, °certify, validate

substitute *v.* 1 Sometimes, ***substitute for.*** °replace, °exchange, °displace, °relieve, °supplant; °switch; take the place of, stand in for, double for, *Colloq* sub for, cover for, swap *or* swop, *US and Canadian* pinch-hit for —*n.* 2 °substitution, replacement, °alternative, °relief, °representative, °deputy, °delegate, °stand-in, °standby, °understudy, surrogate, succedaneum, *Brit* locum (tenens), *US and Canadian* °alternate

substitution *n.* 1 °exchange, exchanging, °change, changing, replacement, replacing, supplanting, °switch, switching, interchange, interchanging, *Colloq* swap *or* swop, swapping *or* swopping 2 See **substitute, 2,** above.

substratum *n.* substrate, °foundation, underlayer, °basis, fundament, °base, substructure, °groundwork

subterfuge *n.* °artifice, °trick, °device, °stratagem, °maneuver, ploy, °evasion, °deception, °dodge, °feint, °shift, °excuse, °expedient, contrivance, °intrigue

subtle *adj.* 1 °delicate, °fine, °refined, °exquisite, °nice, *Archaic* subtile 2 abstruse, arcane, °recondite, °remote, °deep, °profound, concealed, °hidden, °shadowy, °nebulous, °vague, °obscure, °veiled, °thin, airy, °insubstantial, °elusive, °faint; sophistic(al) 3 °tricky, °shrewd, cunning, °wily, °sly, °devious, °crafty, °smart, °clever, °foxy, °artful, °scheming, °designing, underhand(ed), °deceptive, jesuitical, Machiavellian, °ingenious, °skillful, °strategic, insidious, casuistic, °shifty, °slick, °slimy, *Chiefly Brit* smarmy

subtlety *n.* 1 °refinement, nicety, °delicacy, exquisiteness, intricacy, fineness, acuteness, °elegance, °sophistication 2 treachery, guile, insidiousness, casuistry, cunning, artfulness, craftiness, deviousness, slyness, deceptiveness

subtract *v.* 1 °deduct, take away, °take off, take (something) from 2 Sometimes, ***subtract from.*** °detract (from), °diminish, take away (from)

subversion *n.* °overthrow, °ruin, °destruction, undermining, °upheaval, displacement

subversive *adj.* 1 subversionary, °seditious, seditionary, treasonous, treacherous, °traitorous, °revolutionary, insurrectionary —*n.* 2 °traitor, insurgent, saboteur, fifth columnist, collaborator, collaborationist, quisling, °radical, °revolutionary, insurrectionist, insurrectionary; °dissident, °defector

subvert *v.* °overthrow, °ruin, °destroy, °undermine, °topple, °demolish, °wreck, °sabotage

subway *n.* 1 *Brit* °underground (railway), tube 2 *US* °tunnel, underpass

succeed *v.* 1 °follow, come after, supervene 2 Often, ***succeed to.*** be successor (to), °follow, be heir (to), °replace, take the place of, inherit *or* take over from 3 Often, ***succeed in or at.*** °make good, °thrive, °prosper, °flourish, be a success, be successful, °progress, °advance, get ahead *or* on, attain *or* gain *or* achieve success, °win, °triumph, *Colloq* °make it, °arrive, get to the top

success *n.* **1** good *or* happy result *or* outcome, good fortune, °achievement, °triumph, attainment, ascendancy, °prosperity **2** °star, °celebrity, °(big) name, °sensation

successful *adj.* **1** °wealthy, °rich, °prosperous, °fortunate, °lucky, °flourishing, thriving, prospering, well-to-do, affluent, *Colloq* °loaded, well-heeled, °flush, °in the money, *US* well-fixed **2** lucrative, booming, °profitable, °fruitful, moneymaking, remunerative **3** °famous, °well-known, famed, °celebrated, °renowned, °eminent; °prominent, °preeminent, °popular, °leading, °top, best-selling **4** °victorious, °triumphant; °first; °winning

succession *n.* **1** °passing (on), handing down *or* on, transmittal, °transmission, °transfer, transferal, °shift, conveyance, conveyancing **2** °sequence, °progression, °order, series, °turn, °course, °flow, °chain, °train, °procession **3** accession, assumption, attainment, °elevation, °promotion; °inheritance **4** °lineage, descent, birthright, °dynasty, ancestry, descendants, bloodline **5** ***in succession.*** one after *or* behind the other, at intervals, successively, consecutively, in a row, °running, without interruption, uninterruptedly, °in order, °in line

successive *adj.* uninterrupted, °continuous, unbroken, °continual, consecutive, succeeding

succinct *adj.* °compact, °brief, °concise, pithy, °terse, °short, compressed, condensed, °epigrammatic

succulent *adj.* °juicy, °rich, °luscious, mouthwatering, toothsome

succumb *v.* °yield, °give up, °give way, °surrender, accede, °submit, °capitulate

sucker *n.* °dupe, goat, gull, °victim, °butt, cat's-paw, °fool, *Colloq* °(easy) mark, easy *or* fair game, chump, °pushover, soft touch, *Chiefly US and Canadian* fall guy, *Slang* °sap, pigeon, *Brit* °mug, *Chiefly US and Canadian* patsy

sudden *adj.* unexpected, unannounced, unanticipated, °unforeseen; °unwonted, surprising, °startling; °precipitate, °abrupt, °quick, °immediate, °rapid, °swift, °brisk; °impetuous, °hasty, °rash, °impulsive

suddenly *adv.* **1** in a flash *or* a moment *or* a split second, all at once, instantly, °instantaneously, momentarily, fleetingly, in the twinkling of an eye, in a trice; °quickly, abruptly, °swiftly, speedily, °rapidly **2** all of a sudden, °out of the blue, unexpectedly, without warning, °on the spur of the moment, °hastily, hurriedly, feverishly

sue *v.* **1** proceed *or* move *or* act (against), take (legal) action *or* bring suit *or* prefer charges (against); summon(s), °charge, °accuse **2** °petition, °beg, °plead, entreat, °pray, °request, °solicit, °apply, °beseech, implore, supplicate

suffer *v.* **1** Sometimes, ***suffer from or with.*** agonize, °smart, °hurt, writhe, °sweat, °ache **2** °endure, °undergo, °experience, °bear, live *or* go through, °tolerate, °withstand, °sustain, °take, °submit to, °abide, *Colloq* °put up with **3** °allow, °tolerate, °permit, °let, °admit °humor, °indulge **4** °deteriorate, °diminish °decline, °go down, °fall off, be reduced *or* diminished

suffering *n.* °pain, °agony, °distress, °misery, °affliction, °hardship, °torment, torture tribulation, °trial

suffice *v.* °satisfy, °serve, do, be sufficient *or* enough *or* adequate, °answer, sate, °satiate °quench

sufficient *adj.* °adequate, °enough

suffix *n.* **1** ending, desinence, °addition affix —*v.* **2** °add (on), °join, fasten to, subjoin, °amend, *Colloq* °tack on

suffrage *n.* °(right to) vote, voting right(s) franchise, °voice, °say, ballot, °option °choice

suffuse *v.* overspread, imbue, pour *or* spread over, bathe, °cover, °permeate, pervade, °flood, °flush, °penetrate, °saturate °mantle, infuse, °transfuse, imbrue *or* embrue

suggest *v.* **1** °propose, °advance, °recommend, °urge, °advocate, °support, °offer proffer, put *or* set forward, °present, °mention, °introduce **2** call to mind, °bring up °hint (at), °imply, °insinuate, °intimate, make one think, lead one to believe, °indicate

suggestible *adj.* °impressionable, °susceptible, °receptive, impressible, susceptive °open, moldable, fictile

suggestion *n.* **1** °proposal, °proposition °recommendation, °plan, °advice, °counsel, °idea, °notion, °opinion; prompting, urging **2** °indication, °trace, °whisper, insinuation, °innuendo, °implication, intimation, °hint *soupçon*, °touch, tinge, °suspicion, °breath, iota, jot or tittle

suggestive *adj.* **1** Often, ***suggestive of*** °reminiscent (of), evocative (of), indicative (of) **2** °provocative, °naughty, °risqué, ribald, °off-color, °racy, °bawdy, °earthy, °lusty, °rude, indelicate, °unseemly, °immodest °improper, °indecent, °prurient, °blue, °offensive, °vulgar, smutty, °dirty, °pornographic, °lewd, salacious, *Colloq* °sexy, °spicy, *Slang* raunchy

suit *v.* **1** °adapt, °accommodate, °fit, °adjust, °tailor, make appropriate *or* suitable **2** please, °satisfy, fill (someone's) needs, °gratify, be acceptable *or* suitable *or* convenient to *or* for, befit; conform to —*n.* **3** jacket and trousers *or* skirt, °outfit, °uniform, °ensemble, °costume, °habit; garb, clothing, °clothes, livery **4** lawsuit, °action, °case °proceeding, °process, °cause, °trial; °litigation **5** °petition, °plea, °request, entreaty, °prayer, solicitation, °application, °appeal, °supplication; courtship

suitable *adj.* °appropriate, apt, °fit, °fitting, °befitting, °becoming, °right, °proper, °correct, °acceptable, °satisfactory, °applicable, °meet, °seemly; °timely, °opportune

suitcase *n.* °bag, valise, overnight bag,

holdall, grip *or Brit* handgrip, *Brit formerly* portmanteau

suite *n.* 1 °set, series, °collection, °number 2 °set 3 following, °retinue, entourage, °train, cortège, convoy, °escort; followers, attendants, retainers

suitor *n.* °admirer, beau, wooer; boyfriend, °paramour, °lover, inamorato, *cicisbeo,* °escort, *Archaic* swain

sulk *v.* mope, °brood, °pout, be sullen *or* moody *or* ill-humored

sullen *adj.* sulky, sulking, morose, brooding, pouting, °gloomy, °moody, °temperamental, °dour, lugubrious, °funereal, °dismal, °dreary, °grim, depressing, depressed, churlish, ill-humored, °glum, grumpy, °somber, out of humor, antisocial, unsociable, °cross, °petulant, °perverse, crusty, crotchety, choleric, crabby, ill-natured, ill-tempered, bad-tempered, splenetic, °peevish, dyspeptic, °out of sorts, *US* °cranky

sully *v.* besmirch, °stain, smirch, °blemish, °mar, defile, °soil, °disgrace, °dirty, °tarnish, °pollute, °spoil, °ruin, °destroy, °wreck

sultry *adj.* 1 °hot, °humid, °sticky, °stuffy, stifling, °oppressive, °close, °muggy, °steamy, steaming, °moist, °damp, °sweltering, suffocating 2 °lusty, °lustful, °passionate, °erotic, °seductive, °voluptuous, °provocative, °sensual, *Colloq* °sexy, °hot

sum *n.* 1 °total, aggregate, grand total, sum total, °whole, °totality; °amount, °quantity —*v.* 2 ***sum up.*** (a) °recapitulate, summarize, encapsulate, synopsize, °digest, °abridge, condense, consolidate, epitomize, °review (b) °reckon, add up, °calculate, °total, tot up, °measure (up), take the measure of (c) °estimate, °evaluate, °size up, assess

summarily *adv.* 1 °immediately, °at once, °straightaway, °directly, °quickly, without delay, unhesitatingly, without hesitation, forthwith, °promptly, °swiftly, speedily, expeditiously, instantly, *Colloq* PDQ (= 'pretty damn(ed) quick(ly)') 2 °suddenly, without warning, abruptly, peremptorily, precipitately

summary *n.* 1 summarization, recapitulation, encapsulation, compendium, °synopsis, °digest, °abridgment, condensation, shortening, consolidation, °epitome, epitomization, °review, distillate, conspectus, °brief, °outline, °précis, °résumé —*adj.* 2 °abrupt, °peremptory, °short, °quick, °brief, laconic, °perfunctory, °curt, °terse

summit *n.* °peak, °top, apex, °acme, °pinnacle, °zenith, °crown; culmination, °climax

summon *v.* 1 °call, °assemble, convoke, convene, °send for, invite, °muster, °get together, °arouse, °rouse 2 Often, ***summon up.*** call *or* draw on *or* upon, °draw up, °mobilize, °muster (up), °work up, °gather, invoke

sumptuous *adj.* °expensive, costly, °extravagant, °exorbitant, °dear, °rich; °lavish, °luxurious, de luxe, °opulent, °palatial, °royal, °majestic, °regal, °magnificent, °dazzling, °splendid, °showy, *Colloq* °posh, °plush, ritzy

sun *n.* 1 (old) Sol, Helios, Phoebus (Apollo), Ra, Sunna, daystar —*v.* 2 tan, suntan, sunbathe, bask, bake, brown, bronze

sundries *n. pl.* knickknacks *or* nicknacks, trinkets, small items, notions, miscellanea, °miscellany, kickshaws, brummagem, frippery, °bric-a-brac, °odds and ends

sundry *adj.* °various, °varied, °miscellaneous, assorted, °different, °mixed, diversified, °divers

sunken *adj.* 1 °hollow, hollowed-out, °haggard, °drawn 2 submerged, undersea, underwater, submersed 3 buried, °underground, in-ground, below-ground, settled, lowered

sunless *adj.* °dark, °grim, cheerless, °unhappy, °joyless, °funereal, depressing, °dreary, drear, °somber, °gloomy, °gray, Stygian, °black, pitchy, inky, °shadowy, tenebrous, unlit, unlighted, °dusky, subfusc *or* subfuscous, darkling

sunny *adj.* 1 sunlit, sunshiny, °brilliant, °bright, °radiant, °fair, °fine, cloudless, °clear, unclouded 2 °cheerful, cheery, °happy, joyous, °joyful, lighthearted, smiling, beaming, °buoyant, °blithe, °gay, mirthful, °jolly, °bubbly, °ebullient, °genial, °warm, °friendly, °outgoing

super *adj.* wonderful

superb *adj.* wonderful, °marvelous, °excellent, °superior, °gorgeous, °glorious, °magnificent, °outstanding, °exquisite, °fine, °splendid, unequaled, °sensational, °noteworthy, °admirable, °peerless, °matchless, unrivaled, °first-rate, °superlative, °perfect, °classic, °exceptional, °extraordinary, °striking, °brilliant, °dazzling, °miraculous, °incredible, °unbelievable, °fantastic, °fabulous, stupendous, staggering, mind-boggling, breathtaking, *Woman's dialect* °divine, *Colloq* °great, °super, smashing, °magic, °terrific, fantabulous, °unreal, °out of this world, mind-blowing, °super, far-out, *Slang* °out of sight, °boss, °solid, °cool, °hot, °bad

supercilious *adj.* °haughty, °contemptuous, °superior, °snobbish, °disdainful, °arrogant, °condescending, patronizing, °overbearing, °scornful, lordly, high and mighty, °pompous, °lofty, °stuffy, °pretentious, *Colloq* °hoity-toity, highfalutin *or* hifalutin *or* hifaluting, uppity, snooty, stuck-up, *Brit* toffee-nosed, °uppish, la-di-da *or* lah-di-dah *or* la-de-da

superficial *adj.* 1 °surface, °external, °exterior, °shallow, °skin-deep, °slight, °outside 2 °surface, °slight, °external, °apparent, °skin-deep, °outward, °cursory, °insignificant, °passing, unimportant, trivial, °empty, °insubstantial; paying lip-service, for appearances' sake, cosmetic 3 °cursory, slapdash, °quick, °hurried, °hasty, °perfunctory, °nominal, °meaningless, °passing

superficies *n.* °(outer) surface, façade, °face, externals, °outside

superfluity *n.* °excess, superabundance, overabundance, °surplus, oversupply, °surfeit, °glut, superfluousness, °profusion, plethora, oversupply, supersaturation

superfluous *adj.* °excessive, °excess, superabundant, overabundant, supererogatory, °surplus, unneeded, uncalled-for, °unnecessary, °redundant, °extra; °needless, °dispensable, °gratuitous

superhuman *adj.* **1** °heroic, herculean, °godlike, °legendary, valiant, °courageous, °brave, °daring, °dangerous, death-defying, °extraordinary, °miraculous, °phenomenal, °incredible, °fabulous, °fantastic, °unbelievable, °amazing —*n.* **2** superman, °hero, superhero, *Übermensch*, Hercules

superintendent *n.* °supervisor, °foreman, °overseer, °manager, administrator, °chief, °head, °boss; governor, controller, °director, conductor

superior *adj.* **1** higher, higher-ranking, higher-level, higher-class, higher caliber, °upper, upper-level, °upper-class, loftier, nobler, °better; of a higher order *or* status *or* standing, *Colloq* classier, tonier **2** °high-class, °elevated, °first-rate, °distinguished, °exceptional, °excellent, preferred, choice, °select, élitist, °outstanding, °superlative, °matchless, unequaled, °peerless, °nonpareil, °sterling, °supreme, °fine, °noteworthy, °notable, °worthy, °estimable **3** See **supercilious,** above. —*n.* **4** See **supervisor,** below.

superiority *n.* **1** ascendancy, °preeminence, °supremacy, °leadership, °lead, dominance, °predominance, primacy, hegemony **2** °excellence, greatness, peerlessness, matchlessness, inimitability, superlativeness, °prominence, eminence, °importance, °distinction, °prestige, °renown

superlative *adj.* unsurpassed, °paramount, °supreme, consummate, °superior, °best, choicest, finest, °matchless, °peerless, unequaled, unrivaled, °singular, °unique, °incomparable, °excellent, °superb, °sterling, °dazzling, °first-rate, °exceptional, °extraordinary, °marvelous, spectacular, °capital, *Colloq* tip-top, °super, smashing, °great, ace, °terrific, °fantastic, *Slang* °crack

supernatural *adj.* preternatural, °unusual, °extraordinary, °exceptional, °unnatural, °miraculous, °remarkable, °fabulous, preterhuman, °ghostly, °spectral, °abnormal, °inexplicable, unexplainable; metaphysical, otherworldly, °unearthly, ultramundane, supramundane, extramundane, °occult, mystic, paranormal, °psychic, uncanny, °weird, °mysterious, arcane, °unreal, magical, °dark

supersede *v.* °replace, °succeed, °displace, °supplant, oust, take the place of, °substitute for

supervise *v.* °oversee, °overlook, °watch (over), °manage, °run, °control, superintend, °govern, °direct, be in *or* have charge (of), °handle, keep an eye on, °administer

supervisor *n.* °overseer, °foreman, °manager, controller, °superintendent, °superior, governor, °director, °boss, °chief, °head, administrator

supervisory *adj.* managerial, administrative, °executive

supine *adj.* **1** °flat (on one's back), °lying (down), °prostrate, °recumbent, *Formal or technical* procumbent, accumbent, decumbent **2** °indolent, °lazy, °lethargic, °idle, °listless, °indifferent, apathetic, unconcerned, uninterested, °torpid, languid, languorous, sluggish, °slothful, °phlegmatic, lymphatic, °lackadaisical, °inert, °inactive, °passive, motionless, °inanimate, spiritless, abject

supplant *v.* °replace, °displace, oust, °turn out, °eject, °remove, °expel, °dismiss, unseat, °supersede, °substitute, °exchange

supple *adj.* **1** °flexible, flexile, pliant, bendable, °elastic, resilient, °pliable, tractile, fictile **2** °willowy, lithe, limber, °nimble, pliant, lissom *or* lissome, °graceful, athletic **3** °tractable, compliant, °yielding, °accommodating, °obliging, complaisant, acquiescent, °submissive, unresistant, unresisting, °servile, °obsequious, °ingratiating, fawning, toadying

supplement *n.* **1** addendum, °addition, appendix, epilogue, endpiece, postscript, appendage, °extension, continuation, adjunct, annex, appurtenance, °accessory, codicil, °insert, °sequel; supplementation; *Technical* suppletion —*v.* **2** add (on *or* to), °extend, augment; °complement

supplementary *adj.* **1** additional, added, annexed, adjunct, °new **2** supplemental, °supportive, contributory, ancillary, °secondary, °subordinate, annexed, additional, °attached, added, appended, °subsidiary, adscititious; °extraneous, adventitious, supervenient, °extra, °excess; *Technical* suppletive

supplicant *adj.* **1** suppliant, supplicating, entreating, petitioning, supplicatory, beseeching, praying, imploring, °solicitous, importunate, begging, mendicant —*n.* **2** suppliant, applicant, petitioner, beseecher, °suitor, pleader, aspirant, appellant, plaintiff, °beggar, mendicant

supplication *n.* **1** entreaty, °petition, °prayer, °appeal, pleading, °plea, °suit, solicitation, obsecration, obtestation, impetration **2** supplicating, begging, pleading, soliciting, petitioning, entreating, beseeching

supply *v.* **1** °furnish, °provide, °give, endow, present, purvey, °deliver, come up with, °contribute, °distribute, °sell; °stock, °accommodate, °afford, °equip, °outfit, °gear (up), °rig (out), °fit (out), °provision, °cater to, *Chiefly Brit* kit out *or* up; victual **2** °yield, °give, °contribute, come up with, °deliver, °provide, °furnish **3** °satisfy, °fulfill, °replenish, °fill —*n.* **4** °stock, stockpile, °store, inventory, °quantity, reservoir, °reserve, °cache, °hoard, °accumulation, °fund **5** furnishing, °provision, °providing, purveying, supplying, °distribution, equipping, outfitting, provisioning, °delivery, stocking, stockpiling

support *v.* **1** °back (up), °stand by, °help,

bolster, °uphold, °brace, °strengthen, °fortify, °buttress, °prop (up), shore up, °reinforce, °boost, °champion, °assist, take up the cudgels for, °aid, °promote, °forward, °second, °advance, °advocate, °stand up for, be supportive (of *or* in), *Colloq* °stick up for **2** °brace, °hold up, °carry, °prop (up); °strengthen, shore up, °reinforce, °fortify, °buttress **3** °tolerate, °bear, °stand (for), °suffer, °submit to, °undergo, °brook, °stomach, °endure, °abide, countenance, °face, *Brit* °stick, *Colloq* °put up with **4** °pay for, °fund, °maintain, °keep, °finance, °subsidize, °underwrite, °sponsor, *Colloq US* bankroll **5** °sustain, °withstand, °stand, °take, °bear, °tolerate, hold up under, °weather **6** °verify, corroborate, °authenticate, vouch for, °endorse, °confirm, affirm, °bear out, attest to, °certify, °substantiate, validate, °ratify —*n.* **7** °help, °backing, backup, °reinforcement, bolstering, °encouragement, reinforcing, fortifying, °assistance, °aid, succor, °sustenance **8** °brace, °prop, °stay, °frame, °foundation, underpinning, substructure, truss, °beam, column, °pillar, °strut, °guy, guywire, °mainstay, °buttress, °bolster, °reinforcement, °supporter **9** °sustenance, °(living) expenses, °keep, °maintenance, °subsistence, °upkeep; °finances, funding

supportable *adj.* **1** °tolerable, °bearable, endurable, °acceptable, sufferable **2** defensible, confirmable, verifiable, °demonstrable, °tenable, believable

supporter *n.* **1** °enthusiast, °champion, promoter, °fan, aficionado, °devotee, °admirer, °backer, °follower, °support, °advocate, exponent, adherent, °aid, °assistant, helper **2** See **support, 8,** above.

supportive *adj.* °helpful, sustaining, supporting, encouraging, °sympathetic, °understanding, reassuring

suppose *v.* **1** °assume, °presume, °presuppose, °surmise, °take, take as given *or* as read, take for granted; °believe, °think, °fancy, °imagine; *Colloq* °take it **2** hypothesize, °theorize, postulate, °posit, °assume

supposed *adj.* **1** °alleged, °assumed, putative, °reputed, presumed, °hypothetical, °theoretical, theorized, imagined, suppositious, supposititious **2** °obliged, expected, required; meant, intended

supposedly *adv.* allegedly, reputedly, theoretically, hypothetically, °presumably; rumor has it

supposing *conj.* if, even if, in the event that, despite the fact that, although, °though

supposition *n.* assumption, °presumption, °surmise, °belief, °thought, °fancy, theory, °hypothesis, postulate, °proposal, °proposition

suppress *v.* **1** °end, °discontinue, °cut off, °cease, °stop, °terminate, put an end to, °halt, °prohibit, °preclude, °prevent, °repress, censor, °forbid, interdict, °block, °obstruct, °withhold, °stifle, °inhibit, °hinder, °arrest **2** °put down, °quell, °crush, °squelch, °quash, °subdue, °check, °stamp out, snuff out, °smother, °extinguish, °quench, crack down on **3** keep down, °control, keep under control, keep *or* hold in check, °restrain, hold in *or* back, °repress, °cover up, °conceal, °hide, keep quiet *or* secret, °mute, °muffle, °quiet, °silence

suppression *n.* suppressing, ending, °end, discontinuation, discontinuing, cutting off, cutoff, cessation, ceasing, surcease, stopping, °stop, terminating, °termination, °halting, °halt, prohibiting, °prohibition, preclusion, precluding, preventing, °prevention, repressing, °repression, censoring, censorship, °forbidding, forbiddance, interdicting, interdiction, blocking, obstructing, °obstruction, withholding, stifling, hindering; putting down, °put-down, quelling, crushing, squelching, quashing, subduing, checking, °check, stamping out, smothering, snuffing out, extinguishing, extinction, elimination, quenching, cracking down on, crackdown; °control, controlling, restraining, °restraint, concealing, concealment, hiding, muting, muffling, quieting, silencing

supremacist *n.* supremist, bigot, racist, racialist, dogmatist, °zealot, °fanatic

supremacy *n.* **1** transcendency, °preeminence, °superiority, ascendancy, °excellence, primacy, peerlessness, matchlessness, incomparability, inimitability **2** °sovereignty, °dominion, °sway, mastery, °control, dominance, (supreme *or* absolute) rule *or* authority, autarchy, omnipotence, hegemony

supreme *adj.* **1** highest, loftiest, topmost, greatest, °first, °foremost, °principal, unsurpassed, °top, °uppermost, °chief, °paramount, °sovereign **2** greatest, °maximum, °extreme, uttermost, utmost, °ultimate **3** °best, greatest, °first, °outstanding, °preeminent, °first-rate, °prime, °primary, unexcelled, °leading, crowning, consummate **4** °superb, °marvelous, °excellent, °outstanding, °superlative, °matchless, °peerless, °incomparable, °unparalleled, °masterful, masterly, °sublime, °brilliant, °transcendent, inimitable, °choice

supremely *adv.* °very, °extremely, °completely, °perfectly, superlatively, sublimely, transcendently

sure *adj.* **1** °certain, assured, convinced, persuaded, °positive, °definite, unwavering, unswerving, unflinching, °steadfast, °steady, unshakable *or* unshakeable, °confident, satisfied, undeviating, unfaltering **2** established, °firm, °solid, trusty, °stable, °steadfast, °secure, °safe, °trustworthy, °reliable **3** °accurate, °reliable, dependable, tried and true, unfailing, °infallible, °foolproof, °effective, *Colloq* sure-fire **4** °certain, °inevitable, indubitable, °unavoidable, ineluctable, inescapable, guaranteed

surely *adv.* **1** certainly, to be sure, °positively, °absolutely, °definitely, °undoubtedly, indubitably, unquestionably, beyond the shadow of a doubt, beyond question, °doubtless, doubtlessly, assuredly, *Colloq* °sure, *US* absotively-posolutely **2** °firmly, solidly, confidently, unfalteringly, steadily, unswervingly, unhesitatingly, determinedly, doggedly, securely

surface *n.* **1** °exterior, covering, °outside, °top, °skin, integument, façade, °face, °boundary, interface, °superficies; °side, °plane **2** ***on the surface.*** superficially, to all appearances, at first glance, °outwardly, to the casual observer, extrinsically, °ostensibly —*v.* **3** °appear, °show up, °emerge, °materialize, °arise, °rise, °come up, *Colloq* pop up, crop up **4** °pave, °concrete, tarmac

surfeit *n.* overabundance, superabundance, plethora, °glut, °excess, °surplus, oversupply, overdose, °satiety, overflow, °flood, deluge, °superfluity, nimiety

surfeited *adj.* gorged, overfed, satiated, sated, stuffed, glutted, °jaded

surge *v.* **1** °swell, °wave, billow, °bulge, °heave, °roll, undulate, well forth *or* up, rise and fall, ebb and flow, °pulsate; °rush, °gush, °pour, °flood, °stream, °flow —*n.* **2** °swell, °wave, billow, °roller, whitecap, white horse, breaker, comber, upsurge, °eddy, °rush, °gush, °flood, °stream, °flow

surly *adj.* unpleasant, °rude, crusty, °cantankerous, curmudgeonly, churlish, crabby, crabbed, choleric, splenetic, dyspeptic, °bilious, °temperamental, °cross, crotchety, grouchy, grumpy, bearish, °testy, °touchy, °short-tempered, ill-tempered, bad-tempered, ill-natured, bad-natured, ill-humored, °peevish, °quarrelsome, °argumentative, °obnoxious, uncivil, °rough, °obstreperous

surmise *v.* **1** °imagine, °guess, conjecture, °speculate, °suppose, hypothesize, °theorize, °assume, °presume, conclude, °gather, °infer, °understand, °fancy, °suspect, °feel, °sense —*n.* **2** °guess, conjecture, °speculation, °notion, °hypothesis, theory, °supposition, assumption, °presumption, conclusion, °understanding, °fancy, °suspicion, °feeling, °sense

surpass *v.* °exceed, °excel, go *or* pass beyond, °outdo, °beat, worst, °better, °best, °outstrip, outdistance, outperform, outclass, outshine, °eclipse, °overshadow, °top, °cap, °transcend, prevail over, leave behind

surpassing *adj.* °excessive, °extraordinary, °great, °enormous, unrivaled, °matchless, °peerless, unmatched, unequaled, unsurpassed

surpassingly *adv.* °exceedingly, extraordinarily, incomparably, *Literary* °surpassing

surplus *n.* **1** surplusage, overage, °excess, leftover(s), °surfeit, overabundance, oversupply, overdose, °glut —*adj.* **2** °excess, °leftover, °extra, °spare, overabundant, °superfluous, °unused, °redundant

surprise *v.* **1** °shock, °astound, °astonish, °amaze, disconcert, °nonplus, dumbfound *or* dumfound, °stagger, °take aback, °strike, °hit, *Colloq* °floor, bowl over, flabbergast, rock *or* set (someone) back on his *or* her *or chiefly Brit* their heels, *Brit* knock (someone) for six, *US* knock (someone) for a loop **2** take *or* catch unawares, catch red-handed *or* in the act *or* in flagrante delicto, catch napping *or* off-guard, °discover —*n.* **3** °shock, °astonishment, °amazement, stupefaction, °wonder, incredulity **4** °blow, °jolt, shocker, bolt from *or US also* out of the blue, °bombshell, eyeopener

surrender *v.* **1** °give up, °yield, let go (of), °relinquish, °deliver (up), °hand over, °forgo, °forsake, °turn over, °turn in, °part with, °cede, °concede **2** °give up, °yield, °quit, cry quits, °capitulate, throw in the sponge *or* the towel, raise the white flag, throw up one's hands, °succumb, °submit, °give way, acquiesce, °comply, °give in, °concede, °crumble —*n.* **3** °submission, capitulation, °yielding, renunciation, relinquishment, transferal, °transfer, transference, handing *or* turning over, conveyancing, ceding, cession, concession

surreptitious *adj.* furtive, °secret, clandestine, °stealthy, underhand(ed), covert, °(on the) sly, °secretive, °private, concealed, °hidden, °veiled, *Colloq* °sneaky

surround *v.* **1** encompass, °encircle, °envelop, °enclose, hem in, °ring —*n.* **2** environs, °environment, surroundings, °atmosphere, ambiance *or* ambience, °setting

surrounding *adj.* °nearby, °neighboring, °local, °adjoining, °neighborhood, adjacent, bordering, abutting, circumambient, circumjacent

surveillance *n.* °observation, °watch, °scrutiny, °reconnaissance

survey *v.* **1** °examine, appraise, °evaluate, take the measure of, °inspect, °study, °scan, °scrutinize, °measure, °size up, assess, °investigate, look into *or* over, °review **2** °view, °look at, get a bird's eye view of, °contemplate —*n.* **3** surveying, °examination, appraisal, °evaluation, °measure, °study, °scan, scanning, °scrutiny, inquiry *or* enquiry, °measurement, °investigation, inspection

survive *v.* **1** °continue, °last, °live (on), °persist, subsist, °pull through, °endure; remain solvent, keep one's head above water **2** °outlast, outlive

susceptible *adj.* **1** Often, ***susceptible of or to.*** °open (to), °prone (to), °subject (to), °disposed (to), predisposed (to), °receptive (to), affected by, °responsive (to) **2** °impressionable, influenceable, °vulnerable, reachable, °accessible, credulous, °suggestible, °gullible, naive *or* naïve *or* naïf

suspect *v.* **1** disbelieve, °doubt, °mistrust, °distrust, harbor *or* have suspicions about *or* of, be suspicious of **2** °feel, °think, °believe, °sense, have a feeling, °fancy, °imagine, °theorize, °guess, °surmise, have a sneaking suspicion, think it likely *or* probable, *Colloq* °expect —*adj.* **3** °suspicious, °questionable, °doubtful, dubious, °shady, °shadowy; suspected

suspend *v.* **1** hold up *or* off (on), °withhold, °put off, put in(to) *or* hold *or* keep in abeyance, °shelve, °postpone, °delay, °defer, °interrupt, stop *or* check *or* cease *or* discontinue temporarily, *US* °table **2** °hang, °attach, °fasten, °dangle, °swing **3** debar, °exclude, °eliminate, °reject, °expel, °eject, °evict; deprive the rights of, deny the privileges of; blackball

suspense *n.* **1** uncertainty, indefiniteness, insecurity, °doubt, irresolution, expectancy, °indecision, not knowing **2** °anxiety, °tension, apprehension, nervousness, °agitation, anxiousness, °anticipation, °expectation, °excitement

suspension *n.* **1** debarring, disbarment, °exclusion, elimination, °rejection, °expulsion, °ejection, °eviction, deprivation, °denial **2** °intermission, °moratorium, deferment, °holdup, °delay, delaying, °interruption, °postponement, postponing, discontinuing, discontinuation, °stay

suspicion *n.* **1** °doubt, dubiousness, dubiety, °misgiving, °mistrust, °distrust, °skepticism, °qualm, wariness, apprehension, apprehensiveness, cautiousness, hesitation, second thought(s), uncertainty, leeriness, *Colloq* funny feeling, bad vibes **2** °notion, °inkling, °suggestion, °hint, °trace, °flavor, soupçon, °taste, °dash, glimmer, tinge, °touch, °shadow, °shade, scintilla, *Colloq chiefly US and Canadian* tad

suspicious *adj.* **1** °doubtful, °in doubt, dubious, °questionable, °debatable, suspect(ed), under suspicion, open to doubt *or* question *or* misconstruction, *Colloq* °shady, °fishy **2** mistrustful, °distrustful, °doubtful, °in doubt, °skeptical, suspecting, disbelieving, °unbelieving, °leery, apprehensive, °wary, °uncertain, uneasy

sustain *v.* **1** °uphold, °support, keep up, °maintain, °continue, keep (someone *or* something) going, keep alive, °preserve; °prolong, °persist in **2** °support, °carry, °bear, °bolster, °buoy (up), °reinforce, keep (someone) going, °strengthen, shore up, underpin, °prop up, °buttress **3** °endure, °stand, °withstand, bear up under, °put up with, °suffer, °undergo, °experience, °tolerate, °weather, °brave **4** °bear, °carry, °support **5** °uphold, °recognize, °allow, °admit, °approve, °ratify, °sanction, °authorize, °endorse, validate

sustained *adj.* continued, °continuous, °continual, prolonged, unremitting, °steady, ceaseless, unceasing, incessant, interminable; °uniform, °even, °level, unchanged, unchanging

sustenance *n.* **1** nutriment, °nourishment, °food (and drink), daily bread, °rations, victuals, °provisions, °provender, groceries, aliment, edibles, eatables, foodstuff(s), viands, °meat, *Colloq* grub, eats, chow, nosh, *Slang Brit* prog, °scoff **2** livelihood, °support, °maintenance, °upkeep, °keep, °subsistence, living

swagger *v.* **1** °strut, °prance, °parade, *Archaic* swash, *Colloq US* sashay, cut a swath **2** °boast, °brag, °show off, vaunt, crow, *Colloq Brit* swank —*n.* **3** °strut, °prance, strutting, swaggering, °show, °display, showing off, °ostentation, braggadocio, °arrogance, boastfulness

swallow *v.* **1** °eat, °consume, °devour, ingest, dispatch *or* despatch; °drink, °gulp, guzzle, down, *Colloq* put *or* pack away, swig, °swill **2** °accept, °allow, °credit, °believe, °take, *Colloq* °buy, °fall for **3** Often, ***swallow up.*** absorb, make disappear, engulf, °consume, assimilate **4** Sometimes, ***swallow back.*** keep *or* choke back *or* down, °repress, °suppress, °control, °stifle, °smother, °overcome, °conquer —*n.* **5** °bite, nibble, °morsel, °mouthful; °drink, °gulp, guzzle, *Colloq* swig

swamp *n.* **1** °bog, fen, °marsh, quagmire, °morass, °moor, *Chiefly literary* slough, *Scots and northern English dialect* moss, *Southern US* everglade —*v.* **2** °overwhelm, °overcome, °flood, inundate, °submerge, °immerse, deluge, °overload, overtax, overburden, *Colloq* snow under **3** scuttle, °sink, °founder

swanky *adj.* °smart, °stylish, °fashionable, °chic, chi-chi, °fancy, °luxurious, °grand, °elegant, *Colloq* swank, snazzy, °neat, °nifty, °plush, °posh, ritzy, *Brit* °swish

swarm *n.* **1** °throng, horde, army, °host, multitude, hive, °herd, °mob, °mass, drove, °flood, °stream, cloud, °flock, °pack, shoal, °bunch —*v.* **2** °throng, °mass, °crowd, congregate, °flock, °gather, °flood, °stream, °flow **3** ***swarm with.*** Often, ***be swarming with.*** crawl with, abound in *or* with, throng with, °teem with, burst with, bristle with, be overrun with

swarthy *adj.* swart, °black, ebon, ebony, sable, °pitch-black, jet-black, coal-black, raven, °dark

swashbuckling *adj.* °adventurous, °daring, °daredevil, swaggering, roisterous, °bold, °dashing, °flamboyant

swath *n.* °swathe, °path, °belt, °strip

swathe *v.* °tie, °bind, bandage, °wrap, enwrap, swaddle, °bundle (up), °envelop, °shroud, °muffle (up)

sway *v.* **1** °wave, waver, °swing, °sweep, °oscillate, undulate, °reel, °totter, swing *or* move to and fro *or* back and forth *or* from side to side *or* backward(s) and forward(s), °rock, °fluctuate; °bend, °lean **2** °move, °incline, °divert, °tend, veer, °tilt, °lean, °slant, °bias; °influence, °persuade, °impress, °win over, °bring around, °convince, °talk into —*n.* **3** °sweep, °wave, °swing, (period of) oscillation, libration **4** °influence, °control, °power, °command, °authority, °dominion, °rule, °sovereignty, °leadership, mastery; °grip, °clutches, °grasp

swear *v.* **1** depose, aver, asseverate, °declare, °insist, assert, solemnly affirm *or* state, °testify, °promise, take an oath, °undertake, °vow, avow, °vouchsafe, °warrant, °pledge, give one's word, °agree **2** °curse, °blaspheme, imprecate, use profanity, utter profanities, execrate, *Colloq* cuss **3** ***swear by.*** °trust (in), °believe in, °rely on, have confidence in, °count on **4** ***swear off.*** forswear, °renounce, abjure, °go off, °forgo, °shun, °avoid, °give up, eschew, °forsake, °throw over

sweat *v.* **1** perspire, °glow **2** Often, ***sweat out.*** °worry, be anxious, agonize, °anguish, bite (one's) nails, be on pins and needles, °fret, °fuss, °stew, torture *or* torment oneself, lose sleep (over), *Colloq* sweat blood, be in a tizzy, *US* sweat bullets **3** °slave (away), °labor, drudge, °grind, toil and moil, slog, work like a Trojan *or* a horse, *Slang Brit* swot *or* swat **4** °ooze, exude, squeeze out, transude **—*n.*** **5** °perspiration, *Technical* diaphoresis, sudor **6** °(hard) work, °labor, laboriousness, °grind, toil, °drudgery, slogging, sweating, *Slang Brit* swotting *or* swatting **7** state of confusion *or* upset *or* excitement *or* distraction *or* agitation *or* anxiety *or* distress *or* worry; pother, *Colloq* dither, tizzy, °lather **8** ***No sweat!*** No problem!, Don't worry!, Everything is taken care of!, All is well!, That presents no difficulty!

sweep *v.* **1** °brush, °whisk, °clean, °clear, °tidy up **2** Often, ***sweep away.*** carry *or* take (away *or* off), °destroy, °wipe out, °demolish, °remove, °wash (away); °blow (away) **3** °swoop, °flounce, °glide, °sail, °march, °parade, °skim, °tear, °dash, zoom **4** curve, arc, °arch, °bend, °bow, °circle, °turn **—*n.*** **5** °pass, °clearance, °stroke; °purge **6** curve, arc, °arch, °bow, °bend, curvature, flexure **7** °range, °extent, compass, °reach, °stretch, °scope, °swing, °span

sweeping *adj.* **1** °comprehensive, (all-)inclusive, °general, °extensive, °universal, all-embracing, °broad, widespread, wide (-ranging), far-ranging, blanket, °umbrella, °catholic, °exhaustive, °radical, thorough(going), °out-and-out, across-the-board, wholesale, *Colloq* wall-to-wall **2** °complete, °total, °overwhelming, decisive

sweet *adj.* **1** sugary, honeylike, honeyed, sweetened **2** °fragrant, perfumed, scented, °aromatic, ambrosial, sweet-smelling, sweet-scented, balmy, °redolent **3** °harmonious, °melodious, sweet-sounding, euphonious, dulcet, °musical, °tuneful, euphonic, mellifluous, °mellow, °lyric, silvery, bell-like, °golden **4** °gentle, °amiable, °agreeable, °genial, °warm, °friendly, °kind, °nice, unassuming, easygoing; °attractive, appealing, charming, °winning, °pleasant, °pleasing, °lovely; °cute, °pretty **5** °dear, °beloved, °precious, prized, treasured, wonderful, °marvelous, °splendid, *Colloq* °great **6** °considerate, °attentive, °solicitous, °thoughtful, °sympathetic, compassionate, °kind, kind-hearted, °generous, °gracious, °accommodating **7** cloying, °sentimental, syrupy, saccharine, treacly, °precious, honeyed, sickening, *Colloq* gushing, °gushy, °sloppy, soppy, °maudlin, °sticky, *Brit* twee, *Colloq* icky **8** ***sweet on.*** °fond of, taken with, °keen on, devoted to, enamored of, infatuated with, (head over heels) in love with, *Colloq* wild *or* mad *or* crazy about, nuts about *or* over, *Slang* gone on, stuck on, batty about **—*n.*** **9** Often, ***sweets.*** bonbon, chocolate, confection, sweetmeat, *Old-fashioned* comfit, *US* °candy **10** °dessert, *Brit* pudding, afters

sweeten *v.* **1** sugar, sugar-coat **2** °dress up, make more attractive *or* agreeable, sugar-coat, °embellish, embroider; make less painful, °mitigate, alleviate, assuage, °lighten, °soften, palliate, mollify, °ease, allay, °moderate, °temper

sweetheart *n.* girlfriend, boyfriend, °friend, °admirer, beau, °darling, °dear, °love, °beloved, °lover, °paramour, inamorato, inamorata, ladylove, betrothed, intended, fiancé(e), *Archaic* swain, *Colloq* heartthrob, °flame, sweetie, °steady

swell *v.* **1** Often, ***swell out or up.*** °grow, °increase, °enlarge, °expand, blow *or* puff up *or* out, distend, °inflate, dilate, wax; mushroom, belly, balloon, bloat, °bulge, billow, fatten, °rise, tumefy **2** °grow, °increase, mushroom, snowball, °accumulate, °mount **3** °increase, °raise, augment, °enlarge, °boost, °step up **—*n.*** **4** enlargement, broadening, °increase, °extension, °spread, °swelling, inflation, °expansion, °rise, °surge **5** °wave, °surge, billow **6** fop, °dandy, gay blade, fashion plate, Beau Brummell, *Archaic* coxcomb, *Historical* macaroni, *Colloq* clotheshorse, *US* fancy Dan, *Slang* nob, *Archaic* lounge lizard, *Brit* toff **—*adj.*** **7** °smart, °chic, °stylish, °fashionable, modish, °grand, °luxurious, deluxe, °elegant, °first-rate, first-class, top-grade, *Colloq* °posh, swank, °swanky, ritzy **8** °marvelous, °thrilling, °splendid, spectacular, °first-rate, °fine, *Colloq* °great, °super, °terrific

swelling *n.* enlargement, distension, tumescence, protuberance, °bump, °prominence, °bulge, °lump, excrescence, °protrusion, °tumor, node, nodule

sweltering *adj.* °hot, °torrid, steaming, °sultry, °steamy, °muggy, °sticky, °oppressive, stifling, °stuffy, suffocating, °clammy, °humid, °wet, broiling, boiling, °scorching, roasting, baking, wilting, melting, tropical, *Colloq* °close

swerve *v.* veer, °career, °swing, °diverge, °deviate, sheer off, skew, °stray, °turn (aside)

swift *adj.* °fleet, °fast, °rapid, °speedy, °hasty, °lively, °nimble, °expeditious; °quick, °brisk, °sudden, °abrupt

swiftly *adv.* °fast, °quickly, speedily, °rapidly, expeditiously; briskly, hurriedly, °hastily, °suddenly, abruptly, in a flash, in a trice, in the wink of an eye, before one can *or* could say "Jack Robinson," before you can say "knife," like a shot, in an instant, in (less than) no time, precipitately, unexpectedly, *Colloq* like greased lightning, *US* lickety-split, in a jiffy, *Slang* pronto, like a bat out of hell

swill *n.* **1** hogwash, pigswill, °refuse, pigwash, slop(s), °garbage, °waste **2** °nonsense, °rot, °rubbish, *Slang* crap **—*v.*** **3** °drink, guzzle, quaff, °swallow, *Colloq* swig, toss off *or* down, throw down, °polish off, knock back *or* off, *US* chug-a-lug

swimmingly *adv.* smoothly, °easily, effortlessly, °well, successfully, without a hitch *or* a problem, like a dream, cozily, like clockwork, without difficulty, °handily, °readily

swindle *v.* **1** °cheat, cozen, bilk, °defraud, °deceive, °hoodwink, °take in, °fleece, °dupe, °fool, mulct, gull, make a fool *or* sucker (out) of, °victimize, °exploit, °trick, *Old-fashioned or literary* euchre, *Archaic* chouse, *Colloq* bamboozle, °chisel, diddle, pull a fast one on, flimflam, °pluck, °burn, take (someone) for a ride, *Brit* °fiddle, *US* buffalo, *Slang* con, °sting, °screw, rook, gyp, rip (someone) off —*n.* **2** °fraud, confidence game *or* trick, cheating, swindling, defrauding, °deception, °racket, °trickery, sharp practice, thimble-rigging, °chicanery, knavery, *US* shell game, three-card monte, *Colloq Brit* °fiddle, swizzle *or* swizz, *Slang* °rip-off, scam, con (game), gyp, *US* bunco

swindler *n.* °cheat, confidence man *or* woman, hoaxer, mountebank, charlatan, knave, °scoundrel, sharper, °fraud, trickster, thimblerigger, °villain, *Technical* defalcator, *Colloq* flimflam man, *Slang* con man *or* woman, *US* bunco artist, fourflusher

swing *v.* **1** °sway, move *or* go to and fro *or* back and forth *or* backward(s) and forward(s), come and go, °wave, °fluctuate, °flap, °oscillate, °vibrate, librate, waver, wobble, waggle, zigzag, wigwag, °flourish **2** °hang, °dangle; be hanged, be suspended —*n.* **3** °swinging, °sway, swaying, to-ing and fro-ing, coming and going, waving, °fluctuation, fluctuating, flapping, °flap, oscillation, oscillating, vibration, vibrating, libration, waver, wavering, wobble, wobbling, waggle, waggling, zigzag, zigzagging, wigwag, wigwagging, °flourish, °flourishing, °stroke **4** °sweep, °scope, °range, °trend, limit(s); °change, °switch, °shift **5** °pace, °routine, °groove, °pattern **6** *in full swing.* in (full) operation, °under way, in business, °animated, °lively, °on the move, °moving, °going, *Colloq* on the hop, cooking

swinging *adj.* °fashionable, °chic, up-to-date, °modern, *Colloq* à-go-go, in the swim, with it, *Chiefly Brit* °trendy, *Slang* °hip, groovy, in the groove

swipe *v.* **1** Usually, *swipe at.* swing at, strike at, hit at, lash out at **2** °steal, filch, °pilfer, purloin, *Colloq* °pinch, °lift, snitch, *Chiefly Brit* °nick, °whip, snaffle —*n.* **3** °swing, °strike, °clip

swirl *v.* **1** whirl, °spin, °eddy, churn, °circulate, °gyrate, °surge, °boil, °seethe **2** °twist, whirl, whorl, curl, °roll, furl, °spin, curve, °spiral, °twirl, °wind (round) —*n.* **3** °twist, whirl, curl, °roll, °twirl, °spiral

swish *v.* **1** °hiss, °whisk, °rustle, °whisper, susurrate —*n.* **2** °hiss, hissing sound, whoosh, swoosh, °rustle, whistle —*adj.* **3** °elegant, °fashionable, °stylish, de rigueur, °smart, *Colloq* °posh, °plush, ritzy, °swell, swank(y) **4** °homosexual, °effeminate, camp(y), °gay, *All of the following are offensive and derogatory* swishy, *US* fruity, limp-wristed, *Colloq* °queer, *Chiefly Brit* °bent, *US* faggy, *Slang* °kinky

switch *n.* **1** twitch, °lash, °rod, °whip, birch (rod), °scourge **2** °change, °alteration, °exchange, °shift, changeover, °reversal, deflection, °trade, swap *or* swop —*v.* **3** twitch, °lash, °whip, birch, °beat, °strike, thrash, °scourge, °flog **4** °change, °shift, °exchange, °divert, °deviate **5** °divert, °turn, rechannel, redirect, °direct

swivel *v.* **1** °pivot, °turn, °rotate, °spin, °revolve, °pirouette, move freely —*n.* **2** °pivot, elbow joint, gimbal, ball-and-socket joint

swollen *adj.* enlarged, distended, °inflated, °bloated, bulging, puffed-up *or* -out, tumid, tumescent, expanded, turgid, puffy, oversized, outsized, *Technical* dropsical, hypertrophied, °proud

swoop *v.* **1** °descend, °dive, sweep down, °pounce, °stoop —*n.* **2** descent, °dive, °sweep, °pounce, °stoop, °stroke, °blow, °rush

sybarite *n.* °epicure, °epicurean, hedonist, voluptuary, °sensualist, °aesthete, gastronome, °gourmet, *bon vivant, bon viveur,* pleasure-seeker, °playboy, jet-setter

symbol *n.* °representation, °figure, °metaphor, allegory, insigne (*singular; plural is* insignia), °token, °sign, °emblem, badge, °image, logotype, °mark, trademark, colophon, °brand, °code, °abbreviation, phonogram, initialism, cryptogram, acronym, monogram, °password, °shibboleth, watchword, codeword; arms, °bearing, armorial bearing, °crest, escutcheon, coat of arms, °banner, °flag, °pennant, °standard, *Colloq* logo

symbolic *adj.* Often, *symbolic of.* symbolical (of), tokening, betokening, °emblematic (of), figurative, allegoric(al), °typical (of), °representative (of), °symptomatic (of), °characteristic (of), metaphoric(al), allusive (of), denotative (of), connotative (of), mnemonic (of)

symbolize *v.* °represent, °stand for, °denote, connote, °suggest, °express, °imply, °signify, °mean, °typify, °exemplify, betoken, °illustrate, °embody, epitomize

symmetrical *adj.* symmetric, (well-) balanced, proportionate, °proportional, well-proportioned, °orderly, (well-)ordered, in proportion, °even, °regular, congruous, congruent, °uniform, °harmonious; °equal, mirror-image, mirrorlike

symmetry *n.* °balance, °proportion, evenness, °order, orderliness, °regularity, °uniformity, congruity, congruousness, correspondence, °agreement, °harmony, consistency, °equality

sympathetic *adj.* **1** Often, *sympathetic to or toward(s).* compassionate (to *or* toward(s)), commiserating (with), commiserative (with), °understanding (of), °supportive (of), caring (to *or* toward(s)), concerned (about *or* with), solicitous (of *or* to *or* toward(s)), warmhearted (to *or* toward(s)), kind-hearted (to *or* toward(s)), responsive (to *or* toward(s)), well-meaning, well-intentioned, good-natured (to *or* toward(s)), considerate (of *or* to *or* toward(s)), empathetic *or* empathic (with *or* to *or* toward(s)); sympathizing, °kindly, comforting, consoling **2** Often, ***sympathetic to** or **toward(s)***. °agreeable, °pleasant, °friendly, well-disposed, favorably disposed, encouraging, like-minded, °responsive, congenial, ***en rapport***, simpatico

sympathize *v.* **1** Often, ***sympathize with***. suffer *or* grieve *or* mourn (with), feel (sorry) (for), have pity (for), empathize (with), condole (with), commiserate (with) **2** Often, ***sympathize with***. harmonize (with), °get along (with), °relate (to), °identify (with), go along (with), see eye to eye (with), °agree (with), °side (with), °understand, be ***en rapport*** (with), be in sympathy (with), be simpatico (with), have (a) rapport (with), *Colloq* be *or* vibrate on the same frequency *or* wavelength (with), *Slang* °dig

sympathizer *n.* condoner, approver, conspirator, coconspirator, collaborator, °accomplice, °accessory, °supporter, fellow traveler, °ally

sympathy *n.* **1** compassion, commiseration, °pity, °concern, tenderness, empathy, °understanding, solicitousness, °warmth, tenderheartedness, warmheartedness, *Archaic* ruth **2** °agreement, °harmony, compatibility, °rapport, concord, °accord, fellow feeling, congeniality, °affinity, closeness, °unity, communion, °fellowship, camaraderie

symptom *n.* °manifestation, °evidence, syndrome, °mark, °token, °indication, °cue, °clue, °(warning) sign, °characteristic, °trait, °feature, earmark, marker

symptomatic *adj.* Often, ***symptomatic of***. indicative (of), °representative (of), °suggestive (of), °characteristic (of), °emblematic (of), °symbolic (of), °peculiar (to), °specific (to), idiosyncratic (of); indicating, suggesting

syndicate *n.* **1** °trust, monopoly, bloc, cartel, syndication **2** °(crime) family, cosa nostra, mafia —*v.* **3** affiliate, °ally, °associate, °amalgamate, consolidate, °league, confederate, synthesize **4** serialize, °distribute

synonymous *adj.* Often, ***synonymous with** or **to***. °equal (to), °equivalent (to), tantamount (to), identified (with), corresponding (to *or* with); transposable (with), exchangeable (with), identical (to *or* with), interchangeable (with), the same (as)

synopsis *n.* °summary, condensation, °abridgment, epitomization, °outline, °abstract, °digest, °précis, °epitome, compendium, conspectus, ***aperçu***, °résumé

synthesis *n.* °blend, °compound, °merge, °union, °amalgamation, coalescence, integration, unification, composite, °composition, °mixture, °combination; compounding, combining, blending, merging, integrating, mixing, fusing, fusion, unifying

synthetic *adj.* °artificial, human-made, manufactured, ersatz; °fake, °false, °counterfeit, °sham, °bogus, °spurious, °mock, °imitation, pseudo, °plastic, *Colloq* phoney *or US also* phony

system *n.* **1** organized whole, °organization, °set, °group, °combination; °structure, °arrangement, °pattern, °setup **2** °scheme, °method, °approach, modus operandi, °way, °procedure, methodology, °technique, °plan, °process, °practice, °routine

systematic *adj.* organized, systematized, planned, °methodical, businesslike, °orderly, well-organized, well-ordered, °regular, °routine, standardized, °standard

T

tab *n.* **1** °flap, °tag, °loop, ticket, sticker, °label, °flag, lappet, strap, °handle **2** °charge, °bill, °account, °reckoning, *Chiefly US* °check

table *n.* **1** °food, victuals, °provender, comestible, edibles, eatables, °fare, °board, °provisions **2** °plain, flatland, mesa, tableland, °plateau, steppe **3** (tabular *or* columnar) list *or* listing, °register, °record, tabulation, °chart, catalogue, °index, inventory, itemization, °précis, table of contents —*v.* **4** °submit, °present, °offer, proffer, bring forward, °bring up, °propose **5** °shelve, °postpone, °defer, °suspend, °put off, °stay, pigeonhole, mothball, *Colloq* put on ice

tableau *n.* °scene, °sight, °spectacle, °picture, °image; °composition, °arrangement, grouping, °effect

tablet *n.* **1** (scribbling *or* writing *or* note *or* memo) pad, (spiral(-bound)) notebook, *US* scratch pad **2** °slab, °plaque, °plate, panel, plaquette **3** stone, gravestone, headstone, °tombstone, °memorial **4** °pill, capsule, troche, pellet, pastille, °drop, lozenge, bolus

taboo *adj.* **1** tabu, anathema, forbidden, interdicted, off limits, out of bounds, ***verboten***, proscribed, banned, prohibited, restricted, °unmentionable, unspeakable; censored, censorable, °unacceptable, °rude, °impolite, indecorous, °dirty, °explicit; outlawed, °illegal, °illicit, °unlawful —*n.* **2** tabu, anathema, interdict, interdiction, proscription, °ban, °prohibition, °restriction —*v.* **3** tabu, °forbid, interdict, proscribe, °ban, °prohibit

tabulate *v.* systematize, °organize, °order, °group, °list, °arrange, classify, °categorize,

°rate, °grade, catalog, codify, pigeonhole, °sort, assort, °index, °itemize; °record, °note

tacit *adj.* unspoken, undeclared, unsaid, unstated, unvoiced, unuttered, °silent, °understood, unexpressed, implied, °implicit

taciturn *adj.* °silent, uncommunicative, °mum, °mute, °reticent, °reserved, unforthcoming, °tight-lipped, close-lipped, untalkative, °quiet

tack *n.* **1** °pin, pushpin, °nail, *Brit* drawing pin, tintack, *US* thumbtack **2** °fastening, stitch, baste **3** °direction, °bearing, heading, °course, °approach; °way, °path, °procedure, °method, °technique, °attack, °line **4** °tackle, °gear, °equipment, equipage, harness, saddlery, °fittings, fitments, °kit, °outfit, °rig, rigging, accoutrements *or US also* accouterments —*v.* **5** °pin, °attach, °fasten, °secure, °join, °couple, °unite, °combine, °stick, °fix, affix, °staple, °nail, skewer, °peg, °screw, °bolt, rivet; baste, stitch, °sew, °bind, °tie; paste, °glue, °cement, solder, braze, °weld **6** change direction *or* heading *or* course, *Nautical* go *or* come about; zigzag, veer off *or* away, *Nautical* °beat **7** ***tack on.*** °add (on), append, annex, °attach, tag on

tackle *n.* **1** °gear, °rig, °fittings, °equipment, equipage, rigging, °paraphernalia, °outfit, tools, °apparatus, °trappings, accoutrements *or US also* accouterments, *Colloq Brit* clobber **2** °block (and tackle), °fall, hoisting gear, °pulley, sheave —*v.* **3** °come to grips with, °grapple with, °approach, °take on, try to solve, (try to) deal *or* cope with, stand *or* face up to, °face, confront, °address oneself to, °attend to, °set about, °pursue, *Colloq* take a crack at, have a go at **4** °attack, °fall upon, °devour, °consume, °demolish, °destroy

tacky[1] *adj.* °sticky, gluey, gummy, adhesive, °ropy, viscous, viscid, *Colloq* °gooey

tacky[2] *adj.* °tawdry, °cheap, brummagem, °gaudy, °tasteless, °vulgar, °shabby, tatty, °sleazy, chintzy, °shoddy, °seedy

tact *n.* °discretion, °diplomacy, °sensitivity, °savoir-faire, °judgment, politesse, °delicacy, °finesse, cleverness, °prudence, °care, carefulness, °dexterity, dexterousness, discernment, judiciousness, adroitness, °skill, acumen, acuteness, °perception, °understanding, °consideration, thoughtfulness, politeness

tactful *adj.* °discreet, °diplomatic, °sensitive, °politic, °judicious, °delicate, °clever, °prudent, °careful, °dexterous, discerning, adroit, °skillful, °acute, °perceptive, °considerate, °understanding, °thoughtful, °polite

tactic *n.* **1** °move, °maneuver, ploy, °caper, °plan, °strategy, °stratagem, °device, °ruse, °plot, °scheme, °design **2** ***tactics.*** maneuvers, °strategy, plans, °campaign, generalship, military science, military operation(s), orchestration, engineering, masterminding

tactical *adj.* °artful, °clever, cunning, °shrewd, adroit, °strategic, °skillful, °adept, °politic, °smart, °tactful

tactician *n.* strategist, campaigner, °mastermind, intriguer, plotter, planner, schemer, manipulator, maneuverer, orchestrator, *Colloq* °operator

tactless *adj.* °coarse, °boorish, °uncivilized, °unsophisticated, °rough, °rude, uncouth, °discourteous, ungentlemanly, unladylike, °crude, °gruff, °bluff, °abrupt, °blunt, °brusque, °impertinent, °disrespectful, uncivil, °impolite, insensitive, °awkward, bungling, °clumsy, maladroit, °inept, undiplomatic, °thoughtless, gauche, unskillful, impolitic, °imprudent, °inconsiderate, injudicious, °indiscreet, unwise

tag *n.* **1** °label, name *or* price tag, °mark, marker, °tab, ticket, sticker, °stub, docket **2** °name, epithet, °label, designation, °title, appellation, °nickname, *Slang* °handle, moniker —*v.* **3** °label, °mark, ticket, °identify, earmark **4** °label, °name, °call, dub, °nickname, °style, °entitle, °christen, baptize **5** ***tag along.*** °follow, trail (along) after, °tail, °shadow, °attend, °accompany, drag along with *or* after

tail *n.* **1** appendage, °brush (of a fox), scut (of a hare, rabbit, deer), °dock, caudal fin (of a fish), uropygium (of a bird), pope's *or* parson's nose, tailpiece, °flag **2** rear end, tail end, backside, °buttocks, croup, rump, posterior(s), °bottom, *Colloq* behind, hinie, *Taboo slang Brit* °bum, arse, *US* ass **3** °reverse —*v.* **4** dog, °follow, °trail, °stalk, °shadow, °track

tailor *n.* **1** couturier, couturière, costumier, °dressmaker, modiste, clothier, garment maker, outfitter, seamstress —*v.* **2** °fit, °adapt, °suit, °adjust, °alter, °accommodate, °modify, °change, °convert, °cut, °fashion, °mold, °stretch, °accustom

tailor-made *adj.* **1** °fitted, custom-made, made-to-order, bespoke; made-to-measure **2** °ideal, °perfect, customized, made-to-order, custom-made, suited, °suitable, °(just) right, *Colloq* right up one's *Brit* street *or US* alley

taint *n.* **1** °stain, °blot, °blemish, °slur, tinge, tincture, (black *or* bad) mark, °stigma, °imperfection, °flaw, °scar, °defect; °discredit, °dishonor —*v.* **2** °sully, °tarnish, °stain, °stigmatize, °smear, °harm, °hurt, °damage, °debase, °vitiate, °blacken, °foul, °contaminate, °pollute, °dirty, °muddy, smirch, besmirch, °blemish, °soil, °corrupt, °spoil, defile, °ruin, °destroy

take *v.* **1** °grip, °seize, °grasp, °clasp, °get, get *or* take hold of, °grab, °snatch, °clutch, °catch, °capture, °obtain, °lay hold of, lay (one's) hands on, °procure, °acquire, °gain (possession of), °take possession of, °secure, °win, °carry off, °abduct, *Colloq* °nab **2** °pick, °select, °choose, opt for, settle *or* decide *or* fasten on *or* upon **3** °appropriate, arrogate, °extract, carry off *or* away, °steal, purloin, °pilfer, filch, palm, °rob, shoplift, °pocket, °remove, walk off *or* away with, run *or* make off *or* away with; °embezzle,

°misappropriate, peculate; plagiarize, °pirate; *Colloq* °lift, °swipe, snitch, *Chiefly Brit* °pinch, °nick, *Slang* °knock off, °hook, °rip off, °liberate, *US* °boost, crook **4** °reserve, °book, °engage; °hire, °rent, °lease **5** °acquire, °get, °adopt; °assume, °derive, °obtain, °draw, °receive, °inherit **6** °accept, °receive, °bear, °withstand, °stand, °endure, °weather, °tolerate, °abide, °brave, °go through, °undergo, °suffer, °submit to, °swallow, *Colloq* °put up with, °brook, °stomach, *Brit* °stick **7** °assume, °bear, °undertake, °adopt, arrogate; °acknowledge, °accept **8** °believe, °think, °judge, deem, °hold, °feel; take for, assess (as), °consider (as), °regard (as), °view (as), °accept (for) **9** °carry, convey, °bear, °transport, °bring, °deliver, ferry; °haul, °cart **10** °take up, °study, be involved *or* occupied in *or* with, apply oneself to, °learn; °read, *Colloq* °tackle **11** prove *or* be effective *or* efficacious *or* operative *or* functional, °take effect, take hold, °operate, °function, °work, °perform, *Colloq* °do the trick **12** °exact, °extract, °get **13** °swallow, °eat, °consume, ingest, °devour, gulp down, gobble up *or* down, wolf, °bolt; °drink, imbibe, quaff; °inhale **14** °subtract, °deduct, °remove, take away, take from, °take off **15** °end, °terminate, annihilate, °wipe out; °kill **16** °require, °demand, °need, necessitate, °call for **17** °hold, °contain, °accommodate, °accept, fit in **18** convey, °lead, °conduct; °escort, convoy, °guide, °accompany **19** °understand, °gather, °interpret, °perceive, apprehend, °deduce, conclude, °infer, °judge, deem, °assume, °suppose, °imagine, °see **20** °charm, °captivate, °capture, °attract, °lure, allure **21** °use, °employ, make use of, °establish, put in(to) place, °adopt, put into effect, °effect, °apply; °resort to, have recourse to, °turn to **22** °clear, get *or* go over *or* past *or* round *or* through **23** °experience, °entertain, °feel **24** °express, °voice, °raise, °put forth **25** cause *or* make *or* induce *or* drive *or* persuade (someone) (to) go *or* be **26** °act, °assume, °play, °perform **27** bilk, °cheat, °swindle, °defraud, *Colloq* con, *Brit* °fiddle **28** ***take aback.*** °astound, °astonish, °surprise, °startle, °shock **29** ***take after.*** **(a)** °resemble, look like, be the spit and image *or* the spitting image of, °favor, remind one of, *Colloq* be a chip off the old block **(b)** Sometimes, ***take off after.*** chase, °follow, °run after, °pursue **30** ***take back.*** °retract, °withdraw, °recant, disavow, °repudiate **31** ***take down.*** **(a)** °note, make a note *or* memo *or* memorandum of, °write down, °record, put *or* set down, put in writing, °document, °transcribe, °chronicle **(b)** °debase, deflate, °lower, °diminish, °belittle, °depreciate, deprecate, °humble, °humiliate, °shame, °disparage, °degrade, °disgrace **32** ***take in.*** **(a)** °accommodate, °receive, °let in, °quarter, °board, °lodge **(b)** °deceive, °fool, °trick, °impose upon, overcharge, °cheat, mulct, °defraud, cozen, bilk, °dupe, gull, °hoodwink, °swindle, *Colloq* bamboozle, con, pull the wool over (someone's) eyes, *Slang Brit* do **(c)** °include, subsume, °embrace, comprise, °cover, encompass, °contain **33** ***take it.*** **(a)** withstand *or* tolerate *or* survive punishment *or* abuse, °survive **(b)** See **19**, above. **34** ***take off.*** **(a)** °remove, doff, strip *or* peel off, °discard, divest (oneself) of **(b)** °satirize, °lampoon, °caricature, °mock, °parody, travesty, °burlesque, °mimic, °imitate, *Colloq* spoof, *Brit* sendup **(c)** °depart, °leave, °go (away), decamp; °fly off, become airborne, lift off, blast off; *Colloq* skedaddle, make (oneself) scarce, *Slang* hit the road, scram, °beat it, °split **35** ***take on.*** **(a)** °hire, °engage, °employ, °enroll, °enlist, °retain **(b)** °challenge, °rival, °face, contend against, °oppose, match *or* pit (oneself) against, vie with, °fight **(c)** °assume, °accept, °undertake, °tackle **36** ***take out.*** °entertain, °escort, invite out; court, woo **37** ***take over.*** assume *or* take *or* usurp *or* gain control *or* possession *or* command of **38** ***take to.*** **(a)** °like, find pleasant *or* pleasing, feel affection *or* liking *or* affinity for, find suitable **(b)** leave *or* depart *or* take off for, °run for, head for, flee to, °make for **39** ***take up.*** **(a)** °pick up, °accept, °agree to, acquiesce to, accede to **(b)** °assume, °resume, °carry on, °continue, go on with, follow on with, °pick up **(c)** espouse, °embrace, become interested *or* involved in, °support, °sponsor, °advocate **(d)** °occupy, °cover, °use (up), °fill (up) **(e)** °deal with, °treat, °consider, °bring up, °raise —*n.* **40** °revenue, takings, °yield, °return, °receipts, °proceeds, °gain, profit(s); °gate, box office

taken *adj.* captivated, entranced, °enchanted, °charmed, bewitched, °infatuated

takeoff *n.* **1** °flight, flying, taking off, departure, leaving, °going; °launch, liftoff **2** °satire, °lampoon, °caricature, °mockery, °parody, travesty, °burlesque, °imitation, *Colloq* spoof, *Brit* sendup

taking *adj.* °attractive, alluring, °engaging, captivating, °winning, winsome, charming, entrancing, °enchanting, bewitching, °fetching, fascinating, °delightful, °irresistible, compelling, intriguing, °prepossessing

tale *n.* **1** °story, °narrative, °report, °account, °record, °chronicle, °history, °narration, °recital, anecdote **2** °falsehood, °lie, fiction, °fib, °fabrication, untruth, falsification, °exaggeration, *Colloq* tall tale *or* story, °(cock-and-bull) story, *US* fish story **3** °rumor, °gossip, °slander, °allegation, tittle-tattle, °libel, °story, *US chiefly naval* scuttlebutt

talebearer *n.* °gossip, rumormonger, gossipmonger, taleteller, talemonger, scandalmonger, telltale, °troublemaker, quidnunc, tattler, °informer, sieve, *Chiefly US and Canadian* tattletale, *Slang* bigmouth, °blabbermouth, squealer, stool pigeon, stoolie, rat, *Brit* °sneak, nark, *US* fink, rat fink

talent *n.* **1** °ability, °power, °gift, °faculty,

°flair, °genius, °facility, °aptitude, °capacity, °knack, °ingenuity, °forte, °strength; °endowment **2** °tendency, proclivity, propensity, °penchant, predilection, predisposition, °bent, °inclination

talented *adj.* °gifted, °accomplished, °brilliant, skilled, °skillful, °masterful, °expert, °adept, adroit, °dexterous, deft, °clever, °good, °polished, °proficient, °first-rate, top-drawer, °excellent, *Colloq* ace, °crack, top-notch, *Brit* wizard, whizzo, *US* crackerjack

talisman *n.* °amulet, °charm, tiki, fetish *or* fetich, juju, periapt, abraxas; wishbone, rabbit's foot, *Brit* merrythought

talk *v.* **1** Sometimes, ***talk in.*** °speak (in), °use, communicate in, converse in, express (oneself) in, discourse in **2** °confer, °consult, °parley, have a (little) talk, °(have a) chat, confabulate, *Colloq* confab, *Slang US* °rap **3** °chatter, prate, °prattle, °jabber, blather *or* blether, gibber, gibber-jabber, cackle, °babble, °patter, °rattle on, °go on, *Brit* natter, witter, rabbit on, *Colloq* °gab, *Slang* gas, jaw, *US* run off at the mouth **4** °chat, °gossip, °palaver, *Slang* chew the fat *or* the rag, shoot the breeze, *US* chin, schmooze, °rap, have a bull session, bat the breeze, shoot the bull **5** °inform, °confess, give the game away, °blab, *Colloq* °come clean, *Slang* rat, squeal, °sing, °spill the beans, *Brit* grass **6** °speak, give *or* deliver a speech *or* a talk *or* an address, °lecture **7** ***talk about or over or of.*** °discuss, confer about *or* on, parley about **8** ***talk big.*** °boast, °brag, vaunt, crow, °bluster, °exaggerate, blow *or* toot (one's) own horn **9** ***talk down.*** **(a)** °depreciate, deprecate, denigrate, °disparage, °belittle, °minimize, °diminish, °criticize, *Colloq* °knock, °pan, °put down **(b)** Usually, ***talk down to.*** condescend to, °patronize **10** ***talk into.*** °convince, °bring around, °sway, °persuade **11** ***talk over.*** °discuss **12** ***talk to or with.*** speak to *or* with, °communicate with, converse with **13** ***talk up.*** °promote, °support, °sponsor, advertise, °publicize, °push, *Colloq* °plug, hype, ballyhoo **—*n.*** **14** °oration, °lecture, °address, °presentation, °speech, discourse, °report, disquisition, dissertation; °sermon; °harangue, °tirade, *Colloq* spiel **15** °conversation, °conference, °discussion, °meeting, consultation, °dialogue, colloquy, °parley, °palaver, °chat, °tête-à-tête, confabulation, *Colloq* confab, pow-wow, *Slang* chinwag, head-to-head, *US* one-on-one, rap session **16** subject *or* topic of conversation *or* gossip *or* rumor **17** °gossip, °rumor, hearsay, °information, °news, °report, *Colloq* info, *Slang* °dope **18** °palaver, °gossip, claptrap, °prattle, prattling, °chatter, verbiage, cackle, bunk, °nonsense, °rubbish, balderdash, poppycock, °hot air, stuff and nonsense, twaddle, *Colloq* malarkey, piffle, hooey, hokum, bunkum, bosh, hogwash, horsefeathers, *Slang* bilge (water), crap, bull, tripe, *Brit* tosh, balls, *US* applesauce, *Taboo slang* horseshit, bullshit **19** °dialect, °speech, way *or* manner of speaking, ***façon de parler,*** °language, °jargon, argot, °cant, patois, °accent, *Colloq* °lingo

talkative *adj.* garrulous, loquacious, verbose, long-winded, °voluble, prolix, °wordy, chatty, gossipy, °effusive, talky, logorrhoeic *or* logorrhoeal, *Colloq* gabby, blabby, *Slang* big-mouthed; *US* running off at the mouth

talker *n.* **1** °speaker, lecturer, orator, speechmaker, keynoter, spellbinder, tub-thumper, °rabble-rouser, demagogue, haranguer, ranter, speechifier **2** blusterer, blatherskite, swaggerer, °showoff, *Slang* windbag, gasbag, lot of hot air, blowhard

tall *adj.* **1** °high, °towering, °big, soaring, °lofty, °giant, °gigantic; multistory **2** °lanky, gangling, rangy, leggy, long-legged, °big, °giant, °huge, °gigantic, °large **3** exaggerated, overblown, °far-fetched, °improbable, °unbelievable, °incredible, °preposterous, °outrageous, overdone, °absurd, *Colloq Brit* °steep

tally *v.* **1** °agree, °coincide, °accord, °correspond, °fit, °compare, °match (up), °square, °conform, concur, harmonize, *Colloq US* jibe **2** Sometimes, ***tally up.*** count (up *or* out), °enumerate, °record, °register, °reckon, °add (up), °total (up), °tabulate, °itemize, °list, °calculate, °compute **—*n.*** **3** °count, enumeration, °record, °register, °reckoning, °addition, °total, tabulation, itemization, listing, °calculation, computation **4** ticket, °label, °mark, marker, °tag, °tab **5** counterfoil, °stub, counterpart, °duplicate, °mate

tame *adj.* **1** tamed, docile, disciplined, °obedient, domesticated, housebroken, trained, °broken **2** °mild, °gentle, °fearless, unafraid **3** °tractable, pliant, compliant, °meek, °submissive, °mild, under (someone's) control *or* thumb, °subdued, suppressed; unassertive, °feeble, °ineffectual, °timid, timorous, °cowardly, pusillanimous, chicken-hearted, °faint-hearted, white-livered, lily-livered, yellow, *Colloq* wimpish **4** °boring, °tedious, °tiresome, °dull, insipid, °bland, °lifeless, °flat, °vapid, °prosaic, °humdrum, °bland, unexciting, uninspired, uninspiring, °run-of-the-mill, °ordinary, uninteresting, °dead, *Colloq* °wishy-washy **—*v.*** **5** °break, domesticate, °train, house-train, °gentle, °master, °subdue, °subjugate **6** °calm, °subdue, °control, mollify, pacify, °mute, °temper, °soften, °curb, °tone down, °moderate, °mitigate, °tranquilize

tamper *v.* °interfere, °meddle, intermeddle, °intrude, °tinker, mess (about *or* around), *Colloq* fiddle *or* fool (about *or* around), °monkey (around), °muck (about)

tang *n.* **1** pungency, piquancy, °bite, °zest, zestiness, sharpness, poignancy, spiciness, °nip, °edge, °spice, °taste, °flavor, °savor, °aroma, °smell, °odor, *Colloq* zip, °kick **2** tinge, °flavor, °hint, °suggestion, ***soupçon,*** °trace, °dab, smack, °touch, smattering **3** prong, °tab, °projection, °tongue, °strip, tine, shank, °pin, °spike

tangential *adj.* °divergent, digressive, off

or beside the point, °peripheral, °irrelevant, °extraneous, °unrelated

tangible *adj.* °material, °real, °physical, corporeal, bodily, somatic, °solid, °concrete, touchable, tactile, °manifest, palpable, °evident, °actual, °substantial, °visible, seeable, °discernible, °perceptible, ponderable, °objective, ostensive

tangle *n.* **1** °confusion, °knot, gnarl, °mesh, °snarl, °twist, °kink, entanglement, °jam, °snag, °jumble, °mess, skein, °web, °coil **2** °muddle, °complication, °jumble, °puzzle, °medley, °complexity, °complication, °scramble, °mishmash, °mix-up, hotchpotch *or US and Canadian also* hodgepodge, jungle, °maze, labyrinth —*v.* **3** Often, ***tangle up.*** °confuse, °knot, °mesh, °snarl, gnarl, °twist, °kink, ravel, °entangle, °jam, °snag, intertwist, intertwine, interlace, interweave, °jumble, °mess up, °scramble, °shuffle, °muddle **4** Often, ***tangle with.*** wrangle (with), contend (with), fight (with *or* against), °(come into) conflict (with), come *or* go up against, lock horns (with), °dispute, cross swords (with), °disagree (with)

tantalize *v.* °tease, °taunt, °provoke, °torment, torture, bait, °tempt, °plague, °frustrate

tantamount to *adj.* amounting to, as good as, virtually the same as, (pretty) much the same as, °equal to, equivalent to, °like, °of a piece with, comparable to, commensurate with

tantrum *n.* fit (of anger *or* of passion), °outburst, °eruption, blowup, °explosion, flare-up, °storm, °rage, °fury, *Colloq Brit* paddy, wax

tap[1] *v.* **1** °rap, °knock, °dab, °strike, peck; drum, °beat —*n.* **2** °rap, °knock, °dab, °strike, peck, °pat; tapping, tap-tap, rapping, knocking, pecking, °beat, beating, °patter, pattering

tap[2] *n.* **1** cock, stopcock, petcock, sillcock, seacock, spigot, °spout, valve, *US* faucet **2** bung, °stopper, cork, spile, °plug, stopple, °peg **3** wiretap, °bug, listening device, electronic eavesdropper **4** ***on tap.*** **(a)** on draft, out of the barrel *or* keg **(b)** °ready, °available, on *or* at hand, waiting, °in reserve, °on call —*v.* **5** °drain, °draw (off), siphon off *or* out, °extract, °withdraw **6** °open, °drain, unplug, °sap, bleed, °milk, °broach, °mine, °use, utilize, make use of, put to use, draw on *or* upon, turn to account **7** °bug, eavesdrop on, wiretap

tape *n.* **1** °strip, °band, fillet, °stripe, strap, °belt, ribbon **2** (tape) recording, °reel, spool, cassette, video —*v.* **3** strap, °band, °bind; °seal, °stick **4** °record; tape-record, video

taper *v.* **1** °narrow (down), °thin, °diminish, come *or* go down **2** Often, ***taper off.*** °diminish, °reduce, °thin out, °wind down, °decrease, °fade, lessen, °peter out, °wane, °subside, °let up, slacken, die away *or* down *or* off *or* out, °decline, slow (down *or* up), °weaken, abate, °ebb, °slump, °drop (off), °fall (off), °plummet

tardy *adj.* **1** °late, unpunctual, behind schedule, °overdue, behindhand **2** °slow, dilatory, °belated, °slack, retarded, sluggish, °reluctant, °indolent, °lackadaisical, °listless, °phlegmatic, °slothful, °lethargic, languid

target *n.* °goal, °object, °objective, °aim, °end; °butt, °quarry

tariff *n.* **1** °tax, assessment, °duty, excise, levy, impost, °toll, *Brit* °rate **2** °schedule (of charges), price list; bill of fare, menu

tarnish *v.* °sully, °disgrace, °taint, °blacken, °blemish, °stain, °blot, °soil, °spot, °dirty, °contaminate, defame, °injure, °spoil, °ruin, °damage, °harm, °hurt, °stigmatize, °debase, °degrade, denigrate, °dishonor, asperse, calumniate

tarry *v.* **1** °delay, °pause, °wait, °linger, loiter, °stall, °procrastinate, °dawdle, bide one's time, temporize, hang back, *Colloq* hang on *or* about *or* around **2** °remain, °sojourn, °stay, °stop, °rest, °dwell, bide (one's) time, °settle

tart[1] *adj.* **1** °sour, acidic, acidulous, acidulated, lemony, citrusy, vinegary, acetous, acescent; °sharp, tangy, astringent, acerb, acerbic, acrid, °bitter, °pungent, piquant, °harsh **2** °biting, °bitter, °caustic, acid, corrosive, mordant, astringent, acrimonious, °trenchant, °harsh, °scathing, stinging, acerbic, °incisive, °cutting, °keen, barbed, °nasty, curmudgeonly, °testy, crusty, °abusive, °virulent, °sarcastic, °sardonic, satiric(al), °vicious, cynical

tart[2] *n.* **1** pie, tartlet, pastry, °turnover, flan, quiche, patty, *Brit* °pasty **2** strumpet, streetwalker, °prostitute, whore, harlot, fallen woman, trollop, °wanton, working girl, *fille de joie,* call girl, loose woman, slut, °drab, °jade, demimondaine, courtesan, woman of ill repute, hussy, doxy, camp follower, piece of baggage, lady of the evening *or* the night, woman of easy virtue, *Slang* floozy, hooker, *US* chippy *or* chippie, roundheel(s), bimbo

task *n.* **1** °duty, °assignment, °business, °job, °charge, °stint, °mission, °work, chore, °undertaking **2** °(major) effort, °test (of strength), piece of work, °struggle, °strain **3** ***take to task.*** °scold, °reprimand, call to account, °blame, censure, recriminate, reproach, °reprove, °rebuke, °criticize, °lecture, °upbraid, chide, reprehend

taste *n.* **1** °drop, *soupçon,* °dash, °pinch, °touch, °hint, °suggestion, °grain, °trace, °bit; °flavor, °savor, °relish, °tang **2** °sample, °morsel, °bite, °mouthful, °sip, °nip, °swallow **3** palate, °desire, °inclination, °leaning, °partiality, °disposition, °penchant, °liking, °fancy, °preference, fondness, °appetite, °relish, °stomach, °tolerance **4** discernment, °discrimination, °perception, °judgment, cultivation, °refinement, stylishness, °grace, °polish, °elegance **5** °style, °mode, °fashion, °manner, °form, °design, °motif **6** °decorum, °discretion, tactfulness, °delicacy, °refinement, politesse, politeness, correctness, °propriety, tastefulness —*v.* **7** °savor, °sample, °examine, °try, °test **8** °experience, °sample, °know, have knowledge of, °undergo, °encounter, °meet (with), come up against

tasteful *adj.* in good taste, °decorous, °refined, finished, °tactful, °polite, °polished, restrained, °correct, °harmonious, °fitting, °fit, °proper, °discriminating, °aesthetic, discriminative, °fastidious, °cultivated, ***comme il faut***, °elegant, °graceful, charming

tasteless *adj.* **1** in bad *or* poor taste, °garish, °gaudy, °loud, °tawdry, meretricious, °cheap, °flashy, °unrefined, inelegant, unesthetic; °improper, °wrong, indecorous, indelicate, uncultivated, uncouth, uncultured, gauche, °boorish, maladroit, °distasteful, °unsavory, °coarse, °crude, °gross, °vulgar, °base, °low **2** insipid, °bland, °dull, °flat, °watery, °vapid, flavorless, °unsavory, *Colloq* °wishy-washy

tasty *adj.* °delicious, delectable, °luscious, flavorous, flavorsome, flavorful, °savory, toothsome, palatable, appetizing, sapid, mouthwatering, ambrosial, *Colloq* °yummy, scrumptious

tatter *n.* **1** Often, ***tatters.*** scrap(s), rag(s), shred(s), bit(s), piece(s) **2** ***in tatters.*** in ruins, in shreds, destroyed, ruined, shattered, in disarray, demolished

tattered *adj.* °ragged, torn, shredded, °rent, °threadbare

tattle *v.* **1** °blab, °tell, reveal *or* divulge *or* give away secrets, *Slang* squeal **2** °gossip, °prattle, prate, °babble, °chatter, °jabber, blather *or* blether, *Brit* natter, witter, *Slang* yak

taunt *v.* **1** °tease, °jeer (at), °flout, °twit, °mock, °torment, °annoy, make fun *or* sport of, °poke fun at, °deride, °sneer (at), °scoff (at), °insult, °ridicule, °burlesque, °lampoon, *US* °ride, *Colloq* kid, rib, roast, °put down, *Brit* °guy, *Slang* °bug, °rag, hassle, *US* get on (someone's) case —*n.* **2** °jeer, °gibe, brickbat, °insult, °scoff, °derision, °sneer, °slap (in the face), raspberry, *Colloq* °dig, *US* Bronx cheer

taut *adj.* **1** °tight, °tense, °strained, stretched, °rigid, °stiff **2** *Nautical* °neat, °tidy, Bristol fashion, °shipshape, °spruce, °(in) trim, °smart, °orderly, well-organized; well-disciplined

tautology *n.* °repetition, redundancy, battology, pleonasm, iteration, tautologism; repetitiousness, repetitiveness, wordiness, prolixity, verbiage, verbosity, long-windedness

tawdry *adj.* °gaudy, °cheap, °flashy, brummagem, °showy, meretricious, °garish, °loud, tatty, tinsel, tinselly, °plastic, °tinny, °shabby, *US* °tacky, *Colloq* cheapjack

tax *n.* **1** levy, impost, °duty, °tariff, assessment, °tribute, °toll, excise, °customs, °charge, contribution, *Archaic* scot, tithe, *Brit* octroi, cess, rate(s), °dues **2** onus, °burden, °weight, °load, °encumbrance, °strain, °pressure —*v.* **3** assess, °exact, °demand, °charge, impose *or* levy a tax (on), *Archaic* tithe **4** °burden, °strain, put a strain on, °try; °load, °overload, °stretch, °exhaust; °encumber, °weigh down, saddle, *Brit* pressurize, *US* °pressure

taxi *n.* **1** taxicab, °cab, hackney, *Colloq* °hack —*v.* **2** °drive, °ride (on the ground)

teach *v.* °instruct (in), °inform (about), °communicate (to), °educate, °guide, °train, °tutor, °coach, °enlighten, edify, °indoctrinate, inculcate, °instill, school in, °demonstrate, °show, familiarize *or* acquaint with, give lessons (in) (to); °drill, °discipline

teacher *n.* °schoolteacher, educator, °instructor, professor, °doctor, °tutor, °fellow, lecturer, °master, °mistress, schoolmaster, schoolmistress, °coach, trainer, °guide, mentor, guru, cicerone, °counselor, °adviser; educationist; *Brit* don, *Scots* dominie, *US* docent, *Colloq* schoolmarm

team *n.* **1** °side, line-up, °group, °band, °gang, °body, °crew, °party, troupe **2** °pair, yoke, °span, duo, °set, °rig, tandem —*v.* **3** Often, ***team up.*** join (up *or* together), band *or* get *or* work together, °unite, °combine, °link (up), °cooperate, °collaborate; conspire

tear *v.* **1** °rip, °rend, rive, °rupture, °pull apart, °shred, °mutilate, °mangle, °claw, °split, °divide, °separate, °sever **2** °pull, °snatch, °wrench, **3** °dash, °fly, °run, gallop, °race, sprint, °rush, scoot, °shoot, sprint, °speed, °bolt, dart, °flit, °scurry, scuttle, °career, zoom, °hurry, °hasten, *Colloq* zip —*n.* **4** °rip, °rent, °rupture, °hole, °split, °slash, °gore, °cut, °score, °slit, °gash, fissure, °rift, laceration

tearful *adj.* weeping, crying, in tears, sobbing, whimpering, dewy-eyed, blubbering, sniveling, lachrymose, *Colloq* weepy

tease *v.* **1** bait, °taunt, °torment, °harass, bedevil, °bother, nettle, °plague, °chaff, °pester, °annoy, °irritate, needle, goad, badger, °provoke, vex, °twit, °tantalize, °frustrate, *Nonstandard* °aggravate, *Colloq* °guy, °pick on, rib, drive mad *or* crazy, °drive up the wall, *Brit* take the mickey out of, *Slang* °rag **2** °coax, °worry, winkle, °work, °manipulate

technical *adj.* **1** complex, °complicated, °detailed, °intricate, specialized **2** °mechanical, applied, industrial, polytechnic, technologic(al)

technique *n.* **1** technic, °method, °approach, °manner, °mode, °fashion, °style, °procedure, °system, °tack, °line, modus operandi, standard operating procedure, *Colloq* MO (= 'modus operandi'), SOP (= 'standard operating procedure') **2** technic, °art, craftsmanship, artistry, °craft, °knack, °touch, °skill, skillfulness, adroitness, adeptness, dexterousness, °facility, competence, °faculty, °ability, °aptitude, °performance, °proficiency, °talent, °gift, °genius, know-how, °knowledge, °expertise

tedious *adj.* overlong, long-drawn-out, prolonged, °endless, unending, °monotonous, unchanging, °changeless, unvarying, °laborious, long-winded, wearing, wearying, wearisome, tiring, °exhausting, fatiguing, °tiresome, °boring, °dreary, °dull, dryasdust,

°drab, °colorless, °vapid, insipid, °flat, uninteresting, °banal, unexciting, °prosaic, prosy, soporific, °humdrum, °routine, °repetitious, °repetitive, °mechanical, automatonlike, °automatic, *Colloq* ho-hum, *Slang* °dead, *US* blah

tedium *n.* tediousness, monotony, changelessness, invariability, long-windedness, wearisomeness, tiresomeness, °boredom, ennui, dreariness, dullness, drabness, colorlessness, vapidity, insipidity, insipidness, two-dimensionality, banality, °routine, repetitiousness

teem[1] *v.* Usually ***teem with.*** °proliferate (with), be prolific (with), °abound, be abundant, °swarm (with), be alive (with), °crawl (with), °bristle (with), overflow (with), °overrun (with), be full (of), °brim (with)

teem[2] *v.* °pour, °rain, °stream (down), *Colloq* come down (in buckets), bucket down, rain *or* pour cats and dogs

teenager *n.* °adolescent, °youth, °boy, °girl, young man, young lady, °juvenile, °minor, *Colloq* kid

teeter *v.* °balance, wobble, °rock, °sway, °totter, waver, °tremble, °stagger

telegram *n.* °cable, cablegram, radiogram, radiotelegram, wire, telex, (In France) *bleu, pneu, US trademark* Mailgram, *Brit trademark* Telemessage

telephone *n.* **1** handset, phone, *Colloq* blower, *Chiefly US* horn, *Slang Brit* dog (and bone) —*v.* **2** phone, °ring (up), °call (up), give (someone) a ring *or* a call, *Colloq* get (someone) on the blower *or chiefly US* the horn, give (someone) a tinkle *or* a buzz, °buzz

telescope *n.* **1** spyglass, *Old-fashioned* °glass; refracting telescope, reflecting telescope, radiotelescope —*v.* **2** °shorten, compress, °abbreviate, °curtail, condense, summarize, °précis, °digest, °tighten (up), boil down, °abridge, truncate, °abstract **3** concertina, squash, °crush

television *n.* TV, video (receiver), small screen, *Colloq* °box, idiot box, *Brit* telly, *US* boob tube, *Slang* tube, *Brit* gogglebox

tell[1] *v.* **1** °relate, °narrate, °recount, °recite **2** Sometimes, ***tell of.*** °say, °mention, hint at, °refer to, °touch on, utter, °state, °declare, °proclaim, °announce, °publish, °broadcast, °communicate, °make known, °report, °impart, °indicate, °release, °break, let (something) be known, advertise, trumpet, herald, °bring to light, °disclose, divulge, °intimate, °leak, °admit, °betray, °acknowledge, °confess, disbosom, get (something) off (one's) chest, unburden *or* disburden (oneself), °blab, °tattle, *Colloq* °talk, let the cat out of the bag, °spill the beans, °let out, °let slip, blow the whistle on, give away the (whole) show, *US* pull the plug on, *Slang* squeal, squeak, rat, peach, *US* spill (one's) guts **3** apprise, °advise, °inform, let (someone) know, °notify, acquaint (someone) with (something) **4** °recount, °describe, delineate, °outline, °portray, depict, °express, °put, °word, °explain **5** °order, °command, °require, °demand (that), °charge, °direct, °dictate (that), °instruct, °bid **6** carry weight, be influential, be effective, have (an) effect **7** °determine, °say, °confirm, aver, assert, asseverate, °swear, take an oath, be sure *or* certain *or* positive, know (for sure *or* for certain) **8** ascertain, °determine, °perceive, °understand, °make out, discern, °identify, °recognize, °distinguish, °discriminate, °differentiate **9** °predict, °prophesy, °forecast, foretell, °foresee, °determine, ascertain, °know **10** ***tell off.*** °scold, °reprimand, °berate, chide, °castigate, censure, °take to task, °rebuke, °lecture, reproach, °reprove, *Colloq* give (someone) a tongue-lashing, rake *or* haul (someone) over the coals, give (someone) a piece of (one's) mind, tick off, *Slang* tear a strip off, *US* °chew out **11** ***tell on.*** tattle on, blab about, *Brit* grass on

tell[2] *n.* tumulus, °mound, barrow, hillock

telling *adj.* **1** °effective, °effectual, °influential, °weighty, °important, °powerful, °forceful, °potent, °significant, °considerable, °striking —*n.* **2** tattling, (too) revealing, *Colloq* letting the cat out of the bag, giving away the whole show

temper *n.* **1** °mood, °disposition, temperament, °humor, state *or* frame of mind, °character, °personality, °nature, °makeup, constitution **2** composure, °self-control, self-possession, calmness, equanimity, °balance, °sang-froid, coolness, *Colloq* °cool **3** ill humor, ill temper, foul temper, irascibility, irritability, petulance, volatility, peevishness, huffishness, surliness, churlishness, hot-headedness, hot-bloodedness **4** °(temper) tantrum, °fury, °fit (of pique), °rage, °passion, *Colloq Brit* wax, paddy —*v.* **5** °modify, °moderate, assuage, mollify, °soften, °cushion, °tone down, allay, soothe, °mitigate, palliate, °reduce, °relax, slacken, °lighten, appease **6** anneal, toughen, °strengthen, °harden

temperamental *adj.* **1** °moody, °sensitive, °touchy, hypersensitive, °volatile, irascible, °irritable, °petulant, °testy, °short-tempered, hot-tempered, hotheaded, hot-blooded, °excitable, °explosive, on a short fuze *or Brit* fuse, °capricious, °impatient, bad-humored, °curt, °brusque, °short, °gruff, °bluff, curmudgeonly, °waspish, °snappish, °peevish, crabby, crabbed, grumpy, huffish, huffy, crotchety, *US* °cranky, *Colloq* grouchy **2** °erratic, uneven, °unreliable, °inconsistent, undependable, unpredictable

temperance *n.* **1** (self-)restraint, moderation, (self-)control, forbearance, (self-) discipline, continence **2** abstemiousness, teetotalism, abstinence, °sobriety, Rechabitism; °prohibition

temperate *adj.* **1** °moderate, °reasonable, (self-)restrained, disciplined, controlled, forbearing, °reasonable, °sensible, °sane, °rational, not excessive, composed, °steady, °stable, even-tempered, °equable, °sober, sober sided, sober-minded, °mild, °dispassionate, unimpassioned, °cool, coolheaded, unexcited, °calm, unruffled, °tranquil, imperturbable, unperturbed, °self-possessed, °quiet, °serene **2** abstemious, teetotal, abstinent, continent, °moderate, °sober; °chaste, °celibate, austere, ascetic, self-denying, puritanical

tempest *n.* **1** °storm, windstorm, hailstorm, rainstorm, °hurricane, typhoon, tornado, cyclone, squall, thunderstorm **2** °storm, commotion, °disturbance, °upheaval, disruption, °furor, turbulence, °ferment, °tumult, °agitation, perturbation, hurly-burly, °disorder, outbreak, °unrest, °riot, °chaos, °uproar, brouhaha, *Colloq* hoo-ha

tempestuous *adj.* °stormy, °wild, °uncontrolled, uncontrollable, disrupting, disruptive, turbulent, °tumultuous, °riotous, °chaotic, °uproarious, °boisterous, °frantic, frenzied, frenetic, °furious, wrathful, vehement, °fiery, °impassioned, °fierce

template *n.* templet, °pattern, °mold, °guide, °model, °die

temple *n.* place *or* house of worship, holy place, house of God, church, synagogue, mosque, pagoda, cathedral, °sanctuary, chapel, shrine, *Yiddish* shul *or* schul

tempo *n.* °cadence, °rhythm, °beat, °time, °pulse, meter, °measure; °pace, °speed, °rate

temporal *adj.* **1** °earthly, °terrestrial, terrene, mundane, °worldly, nonspiritual, nonclerical, °lay, laic(al), °secular, nonreligious, nonecclesiastic, °material, °civil, °profane, fleshly, °mortal **2** See **temporary**, below.

temporarily *adv.* **1** °for the time being, in the interim, pro tem, in *or* for the meantime *or* the meanwhile, for now **2** °briefly, fleetingly, for a (short *or* little) while *or* time, for the moment

temporary *adj.* impermanent, °makeshift, °stopgap, °standby, °provisional; pro tem, transitory, °transient, °fleeting, °fugitive, °passing, ephemeral, °temporal, evanescent, °short-lived, °momentary

tempt *v.* **1** °attract, °entice, °lure, allure, °draw (in), invite, °lead on, whet (one's) appetite, °seduce, °captivate, °persuade, °coax, °cajole **2** °lead, °induce, °persuade, °prompt, °move, °incline, °dispose **3** °provoke, °dare, °(put to the) test

temptation *n.* **1** °tempting, enticing, leading on, seducing, captivating, persuading, coaxing, cajoling **2** °enticement, seduction, captivation, °persuasion, allurement, °invitation, °attraction, °draw, °lure, °inducement, °snare, *Colloq* °pull, °come-on

tempting *adj.* **1** °seductive, enticing, °inviting, alluring, captivating, °attractive, tantalizing, appealing, °irresistible, titillating; °fetching, winsome, °prepossessing, °ravishing, °voluptuous, °sensuous, *Colloq* °sexy, *US* °foxy **2** appetizing, mouthwatering, °delicious, °savory, delectable, °succulent, °luscious, toothsome

temptress *n.* °seductress, vamp, °siren, *femme fatale*, coquette, °flirt, enchantress, sorceress, Circe, *Slang* sexpot, man-eater, *US* foxy lady, fox, mantrap

tenable *adj.* defensible, °supportable, justifiable, maintainable, workable, °viable, defendable, °plausible, °reasonable, °rational, arguable, believable, credible, creditable, imaginable, conceivable, °possible

tenacious *adj.* **1** °persistent, dogged, unfaltering, pertinacious, unswerving, °determined, °diligent, °resolute, °staunch, °stalwart, °steadfast, °strong, °sturdy, unwavering, strong-willed, °strong-minded, unshaken, unshakable *or* unshakeable, °obstinate, intransigent, °stubborn, adamant, obdurate, refractory, °immovable, °inflexible, °rigid, °firm, unyielding, uncompromising **2** cohesive, °strong, °tough; adhesive, °sticky, clinging; gummy, gluey, mucilaginous, glutinous, viscous, viscid **3** Often, *tenacious of.* clinging (to), °grasping, maintaining, keeping (up), staying with, retentive (of), persisting *or* persistent (in), retaining **4** retentive, °good

tenacity *n.* **1** tenaciousness, °persistence, doggedness, °perseverance, pertinacity, °determination, °grit, diligence, resoluteness, °resolution, purposefulness, °resolve, staunchness, steadfastness, °stamina, assiduity, sedulousness, °strength, strong-mindedness, unshakability *or* unshakeability, °obstinacy, intransigence, stubbornness, obduracy, inflexibility, rigidity, firmness, uncompromisingness, *Colloq US* sand, stick-to-itiveness **2** tenaciousness, cohesiveness, °strength, °power, toughness, °resilience; adhesiveness, stickiness, gumminess, glueyness, mucilaginousness, glutinousness, viscousness, viscidity, *US* °cling

tenancy *n.* occupancy, °occupation, °possession, °tenure

tenant *n.* °occupant, lessee, renter, leaseholder, occupier, °resident, °inhabitant

tend¹ *v.* be inclined *or* disposed, be liable *or* apt *or* likely, °incline, °lean, have *or* show *or* exhibit *or* demonstrate a tendency, °favor, °verge, gravitate, be biased; be prone

tend² *v.* °care for, °take care of, °look after, look out for, watch over, °see to, keep an eye on, °attend (to), °wait on, °cater to, °minister to, °serve, °nurse, nurture

tendency *n.* °inclination, °bent, °leaning, °disposition, propensity, predisposition, proclivity, predilection, susceptibility, proneness, °readiness, °partiality, °affinity, °bias, °drift, °direction, °trend, °movement

tender¹ *adj.* **1** °sensitive, °delicate, °fragile, °frail, °infirm, °unstable, °shaky, °weak, °feeble, unwell, °sickly, ailing, °unsound **2** chewable, °edible, eatable, °soft **3** °young, youthful, °immature, °juvenile, °inexperienced, °impressionable, °vulnerable, °green, °new, °raw, °undeveloped, untrained, uninitiated, °callow **4** °sensitive, °touchy, °ticklish, °dangerous, °troublesome, °provocative, °difficult, °tricky **5** °gentle, °soft, °delicate, °light, °sensitive, °soothing **6** °kind, kindhearted, loving, °affectionate, °fond, °gentle, °mild, compassionate, °considerate, humane, °benevolent, °sympathetic, °feeling, °thoughtful, °softhearted, °warm, caring, °merciful, °solicitous, tenderhearted, warmhearted, °good-natured **7** °touching, °emotional, °moving, °stirring, soul-stirring, °heart-rending, °heartfelt, °passionate, °impassioned, impassionate, °poignant, °sentimental, mawkish, °maudlin **8** °sore, °raw, °painful, °sensitive, °inflamed; smarting, °burning, hurting, aching, °agonizing **9** loving, °affectionate, amatory, amorous, adoring, °romantic

tender[2] *v.* **1** °offer, proffer, °present, °propose, °put forward, °extend, °hold out, °submit, °advance, °put up, set before —*n.* **2** °offer, °bid, °presentation, °proposal, °proposition **3** currency, °money, specie, °(bank) notes, °cash, bills; °payment, compensation

tender[3] *n.* **1** dinghy, gig, skiff, °launch, °boat, rowboat *or* rowing boat, jollyboat **2** wagon, °truck, °vehicle

tenet *n.* °belief, credo, °creed, article of faith, °ideology, °precept, °conviction, °principle, dogma, °idea, °opinion, °position, °view, °viewpoint, °maxim, axiom, canon, teaching, °doctrine

tenor *n.* °drift, °tone, °spirit, °essence, °character, °gist, °bias, °import, °substance, °effect, °significance, °meaning, °sense, connotation, °theme, °thread, °implication, °inference, °intent, °purpose, °tendency, purport, °direction

tense *adj.* **1** °taut, °strained, °stiff, under tension, °rigid **2** °intense, °nervous, °anxious, under (a) strain, highly strung, highstrung, °strained, °on edge, wrought up, keyed up, worked up, °taut, on tenterhooks, apprehensive, distressed, °upset, °disturbed, °worried, edgy, on pins and needles, °jumpy, fidgety, °overwrought, *Colloq* wound up, jittery, having a case of the jitters, *Brit* strung up, *US* strung out, *Slang* uptight, *US* antsy **3** °nervous, °anxious, worrying, worrisome, distressing, °disturbing, stressful, °nerveracking, °fraught, disquieting —*v.* **4** °tighten, °stretch, °strain, tauten, °tension

tension *n.* **1** °stress, tightness, tautness, °strain, °pull, °traction, °pressure, tenseness, °force **2** nervousness, °anxiety, anxiousness, °strain, edginess, apprehension, °suspense, tautness, °distress, °upset, °worry, jumpiness, fidgetiness, *Colloq* jitteriness, (a case of) the jitters

tentative *adj.* **1** °experimental, °speculative, exploratory, probative, °trial, °provisional **2** unsure, °hesitant, °uncertain, °indecisive, °cautious, °timid, °shy, diffident, uneasy, apprehensive

tenuous *adj.* **1** °thin, °slender, °fine, attenuated, °delicate, gossamer, diaphanous, °fragile **2** °flimsy, insubstantial *or* unsubstantial, °paltry, °weak, °feeble, °frail, °meager, °vague, °negligible, °insignificant, °trifling, °sketchy, °hazy, °nebulous, dubious, °doubtful, °shaky

tenure *n.* **1** °possession, holding, occupancy, incumbency, tenantry, °tenancy, °occupation, residency, °residence **2** °(job) security, °permanence, permanency

tepid *adj.* **1** °lukewarm, warmish **2** °lukewarm, °unenthusiastic, °cool, °indifferent, apathetic, uninterested, unconcerned, °nonchalant, uncaring, °neutral, °blasé

term *n.* **1** °name, °title, designation, appellation; °word, °expression, locution, °phrase **2** semester; °time, °period (of time), °interval, length of time, °span (of time), duration, °spell, °stretch, while **3** sitting, °stint, °session, °course; incumbency, °administration **4** Often, ***terms.*** condition(s), provision(s), article(s), clause(s), proviso(s); stipulation(s), qualification(s), assumption(s) **5** ***come to terms.*** °agree, come to *or* reach an agreement *or* an arrangement *or* an understanding, °reconcile, °arrange, °settle, compromise **6** ***in terms of.*** °concerning, °regarding, as regards, with regard to, °in relation to, °relative to, relating to, in the matter of **7** ***terms.*** **(a)** °payment, °schedule, rates **(b)** °standing, °position, °basis, °relationship, °relations, °footing —*v.* **8** °call, °name, °label, °designate, denominate, °entitle, °title, °style, dub; °nickname

terminal *adj.* **1** closing, concluding, terminating, ending, °final, °ultimate, °extreme; °maximum, greatest **2** °deadly, °mortal, °fatal, °lethal, °incurable —*n.* **3** terminus, °(terminal) station, end of the line, depot **4** keyboard, °monitor, °position, °station, VDU (= 'visual display unit'), VDT (= 'visual display terminal'), PC (= 'personal computer'), module, CRT (= 'cathode ray tube'), °screen, (control) panel **5** °connection, wire, connector, coupler, coupling, conductor

terminate *v.* °stop, °end, come to an end, °finish; put an end to, °cease, conclude, °discontinue, °drop, abort, bring to an end *or* a close, wind up *or* down, °sign off, °cut off

termination *n.* **1** °end, ending, °stop, stopping, stoppage, ceasing, cessation, discontinuation, abortion, *Colloq* windup, winding-up, °close, °finish, finishing, conclusion **2** °suffix, desinence, ending

terminology *n.* nomenclature, vocabulary, °language, °words, locutions, °wording, °terms, phraseology, phrasing, °jargon, shoptalk, argot, °cant, *Colloq* °lingo

terrain *n.* topography, °landscape, °ground, °territory

terrestrial *adj.* **1** °earthly, earthbound, °worldly, terrene, tellurian *or* telluric, °global, sublunary, subastral; mundane —*n.* **2** earthman, earthwoman, earthperson, earthling, °mortal, °human

terrible *adj.* **1** °bad, °serious, °grave, °severe, °acute, distressing, °disagreeable, °nasty, °foul, °unbearable, °dreadful, °loathsome, °hideous, °vile, intolerable, °awful, *Colloq* °rotten, °lousy, °beastly **2** °bad, °remorseful, °regretful, rueful, °sorry, contrite, °ashamed, conscience-stricken, °guilty, distressed, °dreadful, °awful, *Colloq* °rotten, °lousy, °beastly **3** °unhappy, unpleasant, °disagreeable, °awful, °miserable, °joyless, °wretched, °unfortunate, *Colloq* °rotten, °lousy, °beastly **4** °gruesome, °grisly, °macabre, °gory, °grotesque, °brutal, °savage, °horrible, horrendous, °terrifying, °terrific, °harrowing, horrid, horrifying, °ghastly, °frightening, °frightful, unspeakable, °monstrous, °dread, °terrible, appalling, °shocking, alarming, °awful, °foul **5** °disgusting, °revolting, nauseating, °nauseous, °offensive, vomit-provoking, °obnoxious, stomach-turning, stomach-churning, °abominable, mephitic, noisome, noxious, °loathsome, °horrible, °hideous, °terrific, °evil, °vile, °rotten, °awful **6** °terrifying, °frightening, °frightful, °fearsome, °formidable, redoubtable, °awesome, awe-inspiring, °terrific

terribly *adv.* °very, °extremely, °exceedingly, °thoroughly, decidedly, unbelievably, incredibly, monumentally, outrageously, °awfully, fabulously, *Colloq* °frightfully

terrific *adj.* **1** See **terrible, 4, 5, 6,** above. **2** wonderful, °marvelous, °splendid, breathtaking, °extraordinary, °outstanding, °magnificent, °exceptional, °unbelievable, °incredible, mind-boggling, stupendous, °superb, °excellent, first-class, °superior, *Colloq* °great, ace, °fantastic, °fabulous, °sensational, smashing, °super

terrify *v.* °alarm, °frighten, °scare, terrorize, °shock, make one's flesh crawl *or* creep, °horrify, make one's blood run cold, make one's hair stand on end, °stun, °paralyze, °petrify

terrifying *adj.* alarming, °frightening, °scary, °shocking, horrifying, paralyzing, petrifying

territory *n.* **1** °area, °region, °district, °neighborhood, °zone, sector, °tract, °land, °precinct, °quarter, vicinage, °vicinity, purlieu **2** °area, bailiwick, °domain, °province, haunts, °patch, *Colloq* stamping ground, *US* °turf

terror *n.* **1** °fright, °dread, °fear, °horror, °panic, °shock, °alarm, °anxiety, °dismay, consternation, intimidation, awe **2** °scourge, °demon, °brute, °monster, °fiend, °devil, *US* mad dog

terrorist *n.* °subversive, °radical, insurgent, °revolutionary, anarchist, nihilist; bomber, arsonist, incendiary; desperado, gunman, °thug, °felon, °criminal

terse *adj.* **1** °concise, °brief, °short, °compact, pithy, °succinct, °summary, laconic, short and sweet, °to the point, sententious, °crisp, °epigrammatic, aphoristic; distilled, condensed, compendious, °abbreviated, abridged, shortened, concentrated **2** °abrupt, °curt, °short, °brusque, °blunt, °gruff, °bluff, °ungracious, °petulant, °tart, °rude

test *n.* **1** °trial, °examination, exam, °proof, °evaluation, assay, °check, checkup, °investigation, °study, °analysis —*v.* **2** °try (out), check (up) (on), °examine, °evaluate, assess, assay, °prove, °probe

testify *v.* °state, aver, assert, °attest, °swear, °say, affirm, °declare, give evidence *or* testimony, °bear witness, avow, °vouchsafe, °proclaim, °announce

testimonial *n.* °endorsement, certification, commendation, °(letter of) recommendation, °reference, *Colloq* blurb

testimony *n.* °evidence, attestation, affirmation, confirmation, verification, authentication, corroboration, avowal, deposition, °statement, affidavit, °declaration, °assertion, °claim, averral, asseveration, °information

testy *adj.* °irritable, bad-tempered, irascible, °short-tempered, °petulant, °touchy, tetchy, °querulous, °peevish, hot-tempered, crusty, °cross, grumpy, grouchy, bearish, crabby, crabbed, °fretful, captious, °waspish, °snappish, °quarrelsome, fractious, contentious, choleric, splenetic, ill-humored, °disagreeable, ill-tempered, edgy, °on edge, °quick-tempered, crotchety, °cantankerous, *US* °cranky, *Colloq or dialectal US and Canadian* ornery

tête-à-tête *n.* **1** (cozy *or* personal) chat, °dialogue, causerie, pillow talk, private talk *or* word, °parley, °interview, *Colloq* confab, *US* one-on-one —*adv.* **2** intimately, privately, °in private, °face to face, confidentially, °secretly, *à deux,* °in secret, *Colloq US* one on one —*adj.* **3** °intimate, °private, intime, °cozy

tether *n.* **1** °lead, leash, °rope, °cord, fetter, °restraint, halter, °tie, °chain —*v.* **2** tie (up *or* down), °restraint, fetter, chain (up *or* down), leash, °manacle, °secure, °shackle, °fasten, °picket, °stake

text *n.* **1** °wording, °words, °content, °(subject) matter; printed matter, °(main) body (text), °contents **2** °extract, °abstract, °section, °quotation, °part, paragraph, °passage, verse, °line **3** °subject (matter), °topic, °theme, °motif, °issue, °focus **4** textbook, °schoolbook, reader, °manual, primer, workbook, exercise book, *Archaic* hornbook

texture *n.* °feel, °surface, °character, °grain, °features, consistency, °weave; configuration, °nature, °structure, °fabric, constitution, °substance

thank *v.* **1** express *or* show (one's) gratitude *or* thanks *or* appreciation, say "Thank you" *or* "Thanks," give *or* offer *or* tender thanks **2** °blame, hold responsible, °credit, °acknowledge —*n.* **3** ***thanks.*** °gratitude, °appreciation, gratefulness, °acknowledgment, °recognition, thanksgiving **4** ***thanks to.*** °owing to, because of, as a result of, thanks be given to, in consequence of, as a consequence of, °by reason of, °through, *Sometimes nonstandard* due to

thankful *adj.* °grateful, appreciative, °indebted, pleased, °glad, °obliged, obligated, under obligation, beholden to

thankless *adj.* unappreciated, unacknowledged, °useless, unrewarding, °fruitless, °unprofitable, profitless, unrequited, °vain, °futile, °bootless

thaw *v.* **1** Sometimes, ***thaw out.*** °melt, de-ice, liquefy, defrost, °warm (up), °heat (up), unfreeze **2** °soften, °warm, become (more) cordial *or* friendly, °relax, °yield, °relent, °bend, unbend, let (oneself) go

theater *n.* **1** playhouse, °(opera) house, °(music) hall, auditorium, amphitheater, theater in the round, coliseum, hippodrome, arena (theater) **2** °drama, stagecraft, dramaturgy, melodrama, theatrics, histrionics, staginess, acting, performing, °performance **3** ***the theater.*** °drama, °the stage, dramaturgy, dramatic *or* thespian *or* histrionic art, the boards, show business, *Colloq* show biz **4** °area, arena, °scene, sphere *or* place *or* field of action, °setting

theatrical *adj.* **1** theatric, °dramatic, °stage, histrionic, °thespian; °repertory **2** stagy, overdone, °camp, campy, °melodramatic, °overwrought, exaggerated, °forced, overacted, overacting, °sensational, sensationalistic, °fake, °false, °mannered, °affected, °unnatural, °artificial, °showy, °ostentatious, spectacular, °extravagant, *Colloq* phoney *or US also* phony, ham *or* hammy, grandstand

theft *n.* °robbery, °stealing, pilferage, pilfering, filching, shoplifting, thievery, purloining, °embezzlement, hijacking, larceny, *Colloq* lifting, appropriation, pocketing, pinching, swiping, snitching, *Chiefly Brit* nicking, *US* boosting, *Slang* heist, knocking off, °rip-off

theme *n.* **1** °subject (matter), °topic, °idea, °notion, concept, °thesis, °text, °thread, keynote, °gist, °core, °substance, °point, °essence **2** °essay, °paper, °composition, °review, article, °story, °piece, °exposition, °study, °exercise, °monograph, °tract, °thesis, dissertation, disquisition, treatise

theorem *n.* **1** °hypothesis, °proposition, assumption, conjecture, °thesis, postulate **2** °statement, dictum, °rule, °deduction, °formula, axiom, °principle

theoretical *adj.* **1** °hypothetical, conjectural, °speculative, untested, unproved, unproven, °moot, putative, °debatable, suppositious, suppositional **2** °impractical, °unrealistic, °pure, °ideal, °abstract, °academic

theorist *n.* theoretician, speculator, hypothecator, hypothesizer, theorizer, philosopher, °dreamer

theorize *v.* °guess, hypothesize, conjecture, °speculate

therapeutic *adj.* therapeutical, healing, curative, remedial, restorative, salutary, health-giving, °healthy, °beneficial, corrective, salubrious, medical, °medicinal

therapist *n.* psychotherapist, psychologist, analyst, therapeutist, psychiatrist, psychoanalyst, °counselor, °adviser, *Colloq* °shrink

therapy *n.* **1** °remedy, °treatment, remedial program; °cure **2** psychotherapy, psychoanalysis, °analysis, group therapy

therefore *adv.* °consequently, so, °thus, as a result *or* consequence, °hence, ergo, for that reason, wherefore, °accordingly, that being so *or* the case

thesaurus *n.* **1** °treasury, treasure trove, °storehouse, armory, arsenal, repository, °cache **2** synonym dictionary, synonymy, °dictionary, lexicon

thesis *n.* **1** °argument, theory, °proposition, °point, contention, °belief, °idea, premise *or* premiss, assumption, °view, °assertion, °precept, °opinion, °notion, °theorem, axiom, postulate **2** See **theme, 2,** above.

thespian *adj.* **1** °dramatic, theatrical *or* theatric, histrionic, acting, performing; *Colloq* ham, hammy —*n.* **2** actor, actress, °performer, trouper, °player; supernumerary; matinee idol, °star; *Colloq* ham

thick *adj.* **1** °broad, °wide, °solid, thickset, °burly, °ample, °solid, °bulky, °substantial, °beamy **2** Usually, ***thick with.*** °dense, °solid, °compact, concentrated, condensed, °packed, close-packed, compressed, crowded, choked, filled, °full, °deep, clotted, chock-full *or* choke-full *or* chuck-full, chockablock, teeming, swarming, °alive, bristling, crawling, bursting, crammed, jammed, brimming, *Colloq* °lousy with **3** °compact, condensed, compressed, choking, °packed, impenetrable, impassable, °dense; pea-soup, soupy, °murky, °misty, foggy, smoggy, smoky, °opaque, °obscure, obscuring, °hazy **4** °abundant, °plentiful, bushy, °luxuriant **5** °dense, viscid, viscous, gelatinous, mucilaginous, gluey, glutinous, °ropy, coagulated, clotted, congealed, jelled, jellied, inspissated, stiffish; °stiff, °firm, °rigid, °solid **6** thickheaded, thick-witted, thick-skulled, °dense, °stupid, °slow, slow-witted, °dull, dull-witted, °stolid, °obtuse, gormless, boneheaded, fat-headed, pinheaded, woodenheaded, addlepated, °half-witted, blockheaded, doltish, Boeotian, cretinous, imbecilic, moronic, *US* thimble-witted; insensitive, °thick-skinned; *Colloq* dimwitted, *Slang* dopey **7** guttural, hoarse, throaty, raspy, rasping, °rough, °husky, °grating, gravelly, °indistinct, distorted, °inarticulate; °gruff, °raucous **8** °close, °friendly, like that, inseparable, °devoted, °hand in glove, on good terms, on the best (of) terms, °intimate, *Colloq* °chummy, pally, (as) thick as thieves, *Brit* matey, well in, *US* palsy-walsy **9** °marked, °pronounced, °strong, °decided, °obvious, °typical —*n.* **10** °core, °heart, °center, °middle, °focus, °midst

thicken *v.* °coagulate, clot, congeal, °jell, gel, °set, °solidify, °stiffen, °harden, °firm up, °cake, incrassate, inspissate

thicket *n.* copse, °brake, grove, covert, wood, *Brit* spinney

thick-skinned *n.* insensitive, insensate, °dull, °obtuse, °stolid, °callous, numb(ed), steeled, hardened, toughened, °tough, unsusceptible, inured, unfeeling, case-hardened, impervious, pachydermatous, *Colloq* hard-boiled

thief *n.* **1** °robber, °burglar, cat burglar,

housebreaker, picklock, sneak thief, safecracker, pilferer, shoplifter, purloiner; embezzler, peculator; pickpocket, cutpurse, purse snatcher, mugger, highwayman, footpad, brigand, bandit, °thug, dacoit, ruffian, °outlaw, desperado, hijacker, gunman, plunderer; poacher; *Technical* kleptomaniac, *Australian* bushranger, *US* road agent, *Colloq* holdup man, crook, *US* second-story man, bandito *or* bandido, *Slang* cracksman, box man, °dip, stickup man **2** °cheat, °swindler, confidence man, mountebank, charlatan, sharper, trickster, flimflam artist *or* man, thimble-rigger, *Colloq* con man, con artist, shell game artist, *US* highbinder **3** °pirate, °(sea) rover, picaroon *or* pickaroon, corsair, freebooter, buccaneer, marauder, filibuster, privateer

thin *adj.* **1** °slim, °slender, °lean, °spare, °slight, °lanky, spindly, °skinny, thin as a rail *or* reed *or* rake, wispy, twiggy, skeletal, °gaunt, gangling, bony, °emaciated, cadaverous, °meager, °scrawny, all skin and bones, scraggy, undernourished, underfed, underweight, °undersized, °puny, °sparse, hollow-cheeked, (half-)starved, pinched, withered, shrunken, shriveled (up) **2** °sparse, unsubstantial, °poor, scant, °insufficient, °inadequate, °slight, °worthless, unimportant, °deficient, skimpy, unplentiful, °paltry, piddling **3** attenuated, threadlike, stringlike, pencil-thin, °fine; °narrow **4** °flimsy, °weak, °feeble, °slight, unsubstantial, °insubstantial, °fragile, °frail, °poor, °lame; °unbelievable, unconvincing **5** airy, °filmy, diaphanous, gossamer, °sheer, °light, °delicate, chiffon, °silky, silken, gauzy, translucent, °see-through, °transparent **6** °watery, watered-down, dilute(d), °weak, unsatisfying **7** ***thin on the ground.*** °rare, uncommon, °scarce, °few (and far between), °unusual, hard to come by *or* find, scant, °scanty —*v.* **8** Often, ***thin down.*** °draw out, attenuate, °reduce, °trim, °cut down, °prune; °sharpen **9** Often, ***thin down or out.*** °dilute, °water (down), °decrease, °reduce, °diminish

thing *n.* **1** °item, °(inanimate) object, article, °possession **2** °item, °subject, °matter, °detail, °feature, °aspect, °affair, constituent, °element, °factor, °point **3** °fad, °trend, °fashion **4** °feeling, °reaction, °attitude, °sentiment, emotional attachment; °quirk, °fixation, preoccupation, °obsession; fetish *or* fetich, *idée fixe*, °affection, °liking, °partiality, predilection, °fancy, °love, °passion, °mania; °phobia, °fear, °terror, °aversion, °loathing, °horror, detestation, °dislike, *Colloq* hang-up **5** °device, °item, °gadget, °object, °entity, °mechanism, contrivance, °apparatus, °instrument, utensil, *Colloq* dingus, doodad, whatchamacallit, thingumajig, whosis, whatsis, thingummy, thingumabob, *Chiefly US and Canadian* gizmo *or* gismo **6** chore, °task, °responsibility, °matter; °act, °action, °deed, °activity, °proceeding **7** °opportunity, °chance, °possibility **8** ***things.*** **(a)** affairs, matters, °business, concerns **(b)** °circumstances, events, happenings **(c)** °belongings, °luggage, baggage, impedimenta, °possessions, °paraphernalia, °effects, °clothes, clothing, °goods; °equipment, tools, utensils, implements, °apparatus, *Colloq* °gear, °stuff, *Slang Brit* clobber, *US* crap, °junk, *Taboo slang US* shit

think *v.* **1** °believe, °imagine, °expect, °dream, °fantasize, °suppose **2** °judge, °reckon, °consider, deem, °regard (as), °characterize (as), °believe, °assume, °mark **3** °contemplate, cogitate (on *or* over *or* about), ruminate (over *or* about), °reflect (on), meditate (on *or* over *or* about), muse (on *or* over *or* about), deliberate (on *or* over *or* about), think about *or* of *or* over **4** Often, ***think of.*** °recall, °remember, °recollect, call to mind **5** ***think of or about.*** **(a)** °consider, °ponder, °weigh, °contemplate, muse over, have in mind, mull over, entertain the idea *or* notion of, °intend, °propose **(b)** assess, °evaluate, value, °judge **6** ***think up or of.*** °devise, concoct, contrive, come up with, °invent, °conceive (of), dream up, °create, °make up, °improvise

thinkable *adj.* conceivable, °possible, imaginable, °feasible, °reasonable, °tenable, not unlikely, °plausible, believable, credible

thinker *n.* °sage, wise man, savant, Nestor, Solomon, pundit, °mastermind, philosopher, °scholar, learned person, mentor, °expert

thinking *adj.* **1** °rational, °sensible, ratiocinative, °intelligent, °reasoning, °reasonable; °meditative, contemplative, °reflective, °philosophical, cogitative, °pensive, °thoughtful, °intellectual —*n.* **2** °opinion, °judgment, °belief, °thought, °point of view, °viewpoint, assessment, °evaluation, theory, °reasoning, conclusion, °idea, °philosophy, °outlook

thirst *n.* **1** craving, °desire, °appetite, °hunger, °eagerness, avidity, ravenousness, voracity, voraciousness, °lust, °passion, °enthusiasm, °fancy, hankering, °longing, yearning, *Colloq* °itch, yen —*v.* **2** Often, ***thirst for or after.*** crave, °desire, hunger for *or* after, lust for *or* after, °fancy, hanker for *or* after, long for, yearn for, wish for

thirsty *adj.* **1** parched, °dry, dehydrated; arid **2** °desirous, °hungry, avid, °eager, °ravenous, °voracious, °burning, °greedy, °avaricious, hankering, yearning, craving, *Colloq* itching

thorn *n.* **1** barb, °spine, °spike, °prickle, °bristle, brier, bur *or* burr, °point, bramble, cocklebur **2** Often, ***thorn in (one's) side.*** °bother, irritation, °annoyance, °nuisance, vexation, °torment, torture, °scourge, °plague, °affliction, irritant, bane, *Colloq* pain in the neck, *Taboo slang* pain in the *Brit* arse *or US* ass

thorny *adj.* **1** °prickly, barbed, spiny, spiked, brambly, spinous, *Technical* spinose, acanthoid, spiculose, spiculate, spinulose, aciculate, muricate, barbellate, setigerous, setaceous, setiferous, setose **2** °difficult, °hard, °tough, °prickly, nettlesome, °painful, °ticklish, °delicate, °intricate, °critical, complex, °complicated, °problematic, vexatious, knotty, tangled, °involved, °troublesome, °controversial, °nasty, worrying, *Colloq* °sticky, *Slang* °hairy

thorough *adj.* 1 thoroughgoing, °complete, °downright, °perfect, through and through, °total, °unmitigated, °undiluted, unmixed, unalloyed, °out-and-out, °unqualified, °sheer, utter, arrant, °absolute, °proper 2 °exhaustive, °extensive, °painstaking, °meticulous, assiduous, °careful, °scrupulous, °particular, °conscientious, °methodical 3 °extensive, °exhaustive, °detailed, in-depth, °comprehensive, °full, °complete, (all-)inclusive, °total, all-embracing, °encyclopedic, °universal, A-to-Z, *Colloq* all-out

thoroughly *adv.* 1 °completely, °downright, °perfectly, °totally, unqualifiedly, °utterly, °absolutely, °entirely, °extremely, unreservedly, °wholly, fully, °positively, °definitely, °quite 2 carefully, painstakingly, exhaustively, extensively, assiduously, sedulously, methodically, conscientiously, scrupulously, meticulously, intensively, comprehensively, °completely, °throughout, from top to bottom, from stem to stern, backward(s) and forward(s), in every nook and cranny

though *conj.* 1 although, °even though, while, in spite of *or* despite the fact that, notwithstanding that, albeit, granted, granting *or* conceding that, allowing *or* admitting that, even if, °supposing —*adv.* 2 °however, °nonetheless, °nevertheless, °yet, but, °still, °even so, be that as it may, °all the same, °notwithstanding, for all that

thought *n.* 1 °thinking, °reflection, reflecting, meditation, meditating, contemplation, contemplating, cogitation, cogitating, musing, pondering, rumination, ruminating, brooding, mental activity, mentation, brown study; brainwork, cerebration, deliberation, deliberating, °consideration, °considering 2 °idea, °notion, brainstorm, °observation 3 °consideration, contemplation, planning, °plan, °scheme, °design, °intention, °expectation, °hope, °prospect, °anticipation, °dream, °vision 4 thoughtfulness, °consideration, kindliness, kindheartedness, °concern, compassion, tenderness, °kindness, °sympathy, attentiveness, °regard, °solicitude 5 Often, *thoughts.* recollection(s), memory *or* memories, remembrance(s), reminiscence(s) 6 °intellect, °intelligence, °reasoning, rationality, ratiocination, °reason 7 °bit, °trifle, °touch, small amount, °trace, *soupçon*, °little, tinge

thoughtful *adj.* 1 °considerate, °kind, °kindly, kindhearted, compassionate, °tender, °sympathetic, °attentive, °solicitous, °helpful, °charitable 2 contemplative, °pensive, °reflective, musing, in a brown study, pondering, °meditative, engrossed, introspective, °rapt, °wistful, brooding, woolgathering, daydreaming 3 °prudent, °wary, °cautious, °mindful, heedful, °thinking, °attentive, circumspect, °careful, caring

thoughtless *adj.* 1 °inconsiderate, °rude, °impolite, insensitive, °tactless, undiplomatic, untactful, °unthinking 2 °rash, °imprudent, negligent, °foolish, °stupid, °careless, neglectful, °reckless, °silly, °unthinking, unreflective, °absent-minded, °forgetful, °remiss, ill-considered, °heedless, °inadvertent, °inattentive

thrashing *n.* 1 beating, drubbing, °whipping, flogging, °assault, caning, belting, mauling, lashing, trouncing, basting, battering, pounding, *Colloq* hiding, tanning, lambasting, hammering, pasting 2 °punishment, chastisement, disciplining, °discipline, castigation

thread *n.* 1 °fiber, filament, strand, °(piece of) yarn; °string, °line, °cord, °twine 2 °theme, °plot, story line, °subject, °motif, °thesis, °course, °drift, °direction, °tenor, °train (of thought), sequence *or* train *or* chain of events —*v.* 3 °string 4 °file, °wind, °pass, °squeeze (through), pick *or* make (one's) way (through), inch, °ease

threadbare *adj.* 1 frayed, °worn (out), worn to a frazzle, °ragged, moth-eaten, °tattered, tatty, scruffy, °shabby, °seedy, torn, °wretched, °sorry, slovenly 2 trite, hackneyed, overused, overworked, reworked, °stale, °tired, stereotyped, commonplace, clichéd, cliché-ridden, °banal, °prosaic, °dull, °monotonous, °tedious, °tiresome, °boring, played out, *Colloq* old hat

threat *n.* 1 intimidation, °menace, commination, °warning, °peril, °risk, °danger, Damoclean sword 2 °omen, presage, portent, °foreboding, forewarning, intimation

threaten *v.* 1 °intimidate, °menace, terrorize, °daunt, cow, °bully, °browbeat, °warn, °caution 2 imperil, put at risk, °endanger, °jeopardize, put in jeopardy 3 impend, °loom; augur, portend, presage, forebode

threatening *adj.* °ominous, °menacing, °portentous, °sinister, looming, °inauspicious, minatory, minacious, comminatory, intimidating, °foreboding, °imminent, °impending

threshold *n.* 1 sill, doorsill, doorstep; doorway, °entrance 2 °brink, °verge, °edge, °beginning, commencement, °outset, °start, °dawn

thrift *n.* °economy, husbandry, °care, carefulness, °prudence, parsimony, frugality, thriftiness, sparingness, scrimping, skimping; penuriousness, closefistedness, tightfistedness, niggardliness, stinginess, miserliness

thrifty *adj.* °economical, °careful, °prudent, parsimonious, °frugal, °sparing, scrimping, skimping; °penurious, closefisted, tightfisted, niggardly, stingy, °miserly, penny-pinching, °cheap

thrill *n.* 1 °excitement, titillation, frisson, tingle, tingling (sensation), stimulation, *Colloq* °kick, bang, °charge, °buzz 2 tremor, °quiver, quivering, °shudder, shuddering, °tremble, trembling, °flutter, throb, throbbing, tremor, pulsation, vibration —*v.* **3** °excite, °stimulate, °animate, °electrify, galvanize, enliven, °stir, titillate, °touch, °strike, °move, impassion, °arouse, *Slang* °send, give (someone) a kick

thrilling *adj.* °exciting, °stimulating, animating, electrifying, galvanizing, enlivening, °stirring, titillating, °striking, °moving, arousing, °rousing, gripping, °sensational, °riveting, spine-tingling, soul-stirring

thrive *v.* °succeed, °prosper, °boom, °advance, °flourish, °grow, bloom, burgeon, °develop, wax, °increase, fructify, °ripen

throe *n.* Usually, ***throes.*** pang, °anguish, °struggle, °chaos, turmoil, °tumult, °paroxysm, °spasm, °fit, °seizure, convulsion, *Technical* ictus

throng *n.* **1** horde, °crowd, °host, assemblage, °assembly, °gathering, °mass, °crush, °jam, multitude, congregation, °press, °swarm, °herd, °flock, bevy, drove —*v.* **2** °crowd (into), °fill, °pack (into), °cram (into), °crush (into), °jam (into), °press (into), °swarm (into), °herd (into), flock (into *or* to); assemble (in *or* at), gather (in *or* at), mass (in *or* at), congregate (in *or* at)

through *prep.* **1** because of, on account of, °owing to, as a consequence *or* result of, °by virtue of, via, °by means of, °by way of, with the aid *or* help of, under the aegis *or* auspices of, *Sometimes nonstandard* due to **2** during, °throughout, in the course *or* middle of **3** °inclusive of, including **4** to; into —*adj.* **5** Often, ***through with.*** done (with), finished (with); at the end of one's tether (with), washing (one's) hands (of) —*adv.* **6** °by, °past **7** °entirely, through and through, °completely, °thoroughly, °totally, °wholly, °utterly, fully, to the core, from head to foot *or* toe, from top to bottom, from stem to stern, from one end to the other, in every way, in all respects

throughout *prep.* **1** during, all (the way) through, from the beginning to the end of **2** everywhere in, all over, in every part of, in every nook and cranny of, from one end to the other of —*adv.* **3** all (the way) through, °everywhere, from one end to the other, °wholly, °entirely, °completely, fully

throw *v.* **1** °toss, °cast, °hurl, °fling, °sling, °pitch, °dash, °propel, °project, °shy, °bowl, °send, °launch, *Colloq* chuck **2** °cast, °shed, °project **3** throw *or* bring down, °floor, °fell, knock down *or* over, °overthrow, °upset, °overturn **4** °dismay, confound, °confuse, dumbfound *or* dumfound, baffle, disconcert, °unnerve, throw off *or* out, unsettle, °put off, put (someone) off his *or* her *or* their stride *or* pace *or* stroke, *Colloq* discombobulate **5** ***throw away.*** **(a)** °discard, °cast off, °dispose of, jettison, °get rid of, °scrap, °throw out, °dispense with, *Colloq* °dump, °trash, chuck out, *Slang* ditch **(b)** °waste, squander, °lose, °forgo, °fritter away, fail to exploit *or* take advantage of, *Slang* °blow **6** ***throw off.*** **(a)** °eject, °expel, °emit, throw up *or* out **(b)** °shake off, rid *or* free (oneself) of, °get rid of, °reject, °renounce, °repudiate **(c)** °deceive, °mislead, °decoy, misguide, °misdirect, °distract, °divert, °bewilder, confound, °confuse, *Colloq* °flummox, bamboozle **(d)** See **3**, above. **7** ***throw out.*** **(a)** °radiate, °emit, °send forth, give out *or* off, °diffuse, put out *or* forth, disseminate **(b)** °expel, °eject, force out, °evict, *Colloq Brit* turf out, *Slang* °bounce **(c)** See **5 (a),** above. **(d)** See **6 (a),** above. **8** ***throw over.*** °jilt, °leave, °abandon, °desert, °forsake, break *or* split up with, *Colloq* walk out on, chuck, °drop **9** ***throw up.*** **(a)** °vomit, spit up, puke, °spew up, be sick; °regurgitate, disgorge, *Colloq* °heave (up) **(b)** °abandon, °quit, °leave, °throw over, °give up, °relinquish, °resign, °renounce, *Colloq* chuck **(c)** °reveal, bring out *or* up, bring to the surface *or* the top, bring forward *or* forth, bring to light *or* to notice **(d)** throw *or* slap *or* knock together, jerry-build **(e)** See **5 (a),** above.

thrust *v.* **1** °push, shove, °drive, °force, impel, °ram, °jam, °butt, °propel, °prod, °urge, °press; °shoulder, jostle, elbow **2** °stab, °plunge, °stick, °jab, °poke; °lunge **3** Usually, ***thrust upon.*** press (upon *or* on), impose (upon *or* on), force (upon *or* on), urge (upon *or* on) —*n.* **4** shove, °push, °drive, °lunge, °poke, °prod, °stab **5** °propulsion, °force, °power, °energy

thud *n.* clunk, thump, whomp, wham, clonk, °bump

thug *n.* hooligan, °gangster, desperado, gunman, °terrorist, °hoodlum, °robber, assassin, °murderer, °killer, °cutthroat, ruffian, mafioso, (*in Paris*) *apache*, °tough, mugger, *Technical* p'hansigar, *Brit* °rough, *Slang* °tough, hood, crook, hit man, °heavy, *US* goon, *Australian* larrikin

thumb *n.* **1** *Technical* pollex. **2** ***all thumbs.*** °awkward, °clumsy, maladroit, *Colloq* butter-fingered, ham-fisted, cack-handed **3** ***turn or give thumbs down (to).*** °disapprove (of), °reject, °rebuff, °turn down **4** ***turn or give thumbs up (to).*** °approve (of), °accept, °welcome, *Colloq* O.K. *or* OK *or* okay **5** ***under (one's) thumb.*** under (one's) control, wrapped (a)round (one's) little finger, in the palm of (one's) hand, eating out of (one's hand), at (one's) beck and call —*v.* **6** hitchhike, *Colloq* °hitch, *US* hook a ride **7** Often, ***thumb through.*** leaf (through), flick *or* flip (through), riffle (through), °skim (through), °browse (through) **8** ***thumb (one's) nose at.*** scoff at, °deride, °jeer at, °mock, °dismiss, °scorn, °flout, be contemptuous of, show contempt for, exhibit defiance for, be defiant of, contemn, *Brit* cock a snook at

thumbnail *adj.* °rough, undetailed, °cursory, °sketchy, °superficial; °brief, °short, °quick; °compact, °concise, pithy, °succinct

thumping *adj.* **1** °great, °huge, °colossal, stupendous, °gigantic, °enormous, °immense, °monumental, °massive, titanic, elephantine, behemoth, gargantuan, mammoth, °jumbo, *Colloq* °whopping, thundering, walloping **2** °complete, utter, °unmitigated, 24-karat, °perfect

thunder *n.* **1** °roll, reverberation, °boom, booming, °roar, roaring, pealing, rumble, rumbling; °crash, crashing, °crack, cracking, °explosion, °blast —*v.* **2** °roll, reverberate, °boom, °roar, rumble, °resound; °explode, °crash, °crack, °blast **3** °shout, °yell, °scream, °bellow, bark, °roar; °denounce, fulminate against, °swear (at), °rail (at), °curse (at), execrate; °threaten, °intimidate, °menace

thunderous *adj.* roaring, booming, thundering, °tumultuous, °noisy, °loud, earsplitting, deafening

thunderstruck *adj.* dumbfounded *or* dumfounded, astonished, astounded, awestruck, awed, °speechless, struck dumb, amazed, taken aback, staggered, stunned, shocked, dazed, °numb, paralyzed, aghast, open-mouthed, nonplussed, *Colloq* flabbergasted, floored, bowled over, *Brit* knocked for six

thus *adv.* **1** so, in this manner *or* way *or* fashion *or* wise, as follows, *Nonstandard* thusly **2** °therefore, ergo, °consequently, as a consequence, as a result, °accordingly, (and) so, then, for this *or* that reason, °hence, in which case *or* event, that being the case, that being so

thwart *v.* **1** °frustrate, °impede, °check, °stymie, baffle, °stop, °foil, °stump, °hinder, °obstruct, balk, °block, °oppose, negate, nullify, *Colloq* short-circuit —*n.* **2** °brace, cross brace; °(rowing) seat, bench

tickle *v.* titillate, °delight, please, °gratify, °amuse, °entertain, °divert, °captivate, °thrill, tickle pink *or* to death

ticklish *adj.* **1** °uncertain, unsteady, unsure, °unstable, °unsettled, °fickle, touch-and-go, °touchy **2** °delicate, °precarious, °risky, °hazardous, °dangerous, °critical, °thorny, °fragile, °awkward **3** °delicate, °sensitive, hypersensitive, °difficult, °touchy, °prickly

tidbit *n.* °delicacy, °(dainty) morsel, °treat, choice item, ***bonne bouche, Chiefly Brit*** titbit, *Colloq* goody

tidy *adj.* **1** °neat, °orderly, °trim, °shipshape, °spruce, spick-and-span *or* spic-and-span, °clean, well-kept, °well-groomed **2** well-organized, organized, well-ordered, °methodical, °systematic, °trim **3** °respectable, sizable, °significant, °considerable, °substantial, °good, °goodly, good-sized, °ample, °large, °big, °fair, °generous, not insignificant; *Colloq* not to be sneezed at —*v.* **4** Often, ***tidy up.*** °neaten (up), straighten (out *or* up), °clean (up), put in order, *Colloq* °fix (up), °spruce up, °organize, reorganize, °arrange, rearrange

tie *v.* **1** °bind, °fasten, make fast, °tie up, °lash, °secure, truss, °attach, °tether, °rope, °chain, °moor; °connect, °join, °knot, °link, °couple, °splice, °unite **2** °bind, truss (up), °tie up, °lash, pinion, °restrict, confine, °restrain; °limit, °tie down, °curtail, °curb, cramp, °hamper, °hinder **3** °connect, °associate, °unite, °join, °link, °bind (up), affiliate, °ally, °league, °team (up) **4** °equal, °even, be equal *or* even (with), °match, be neck and neck (with) **5** ***tie down.*** **(a)** °clinch, °secure, °confirm, *Colloq* °nail down **(b)** °restrict, °restrain, constrain, confine, °curtail **6** ***tie in.*** **(a)** be consistent, make sense, °correspond, °coincide, °fit (in), be logical, °coordinate **(b)** °relate, °connect, °link, °associate, °coordinate **7** ***tie up.*** **(a)** °occupy, °engage, °(keep) busy **(b)** °use, °take up, encroach on, °impose on **(c)** °stop, °halt, bring to a standstill **(d)** °commit, °oblige, °obligate, °bind **(e)** See **1,** above. **(f)** See **2,** above. —*n.* **8** °link, °fastening, °bond, °band, °connection, °tie-up, °relationship, affiliation, °liaison, involvement, entanglement **9** °string, °cord, °lace, °rope, thong, ribbon, °band, ligature, shoelace, °line, leash, °stop **10** °equality, dead heat, °deadlock, °draw, °stalemate **11** cravat, *US* necktie **12** railway tie, sleeper

tie-in *n.* °tie-up, °relationship, °relation, °association, °connection, °link, linkage

tier *n.* °row, °line, °level, °order, °range, °course, series, °stratum, layer, echelon, °file, °rank, °story

tie-up *n.* **1** slowdown, slowup, entanglement, stoppage, °jam, logjam, traffic jam, °delay, congestion **2** See **tie-in,** above.

tiff *n.* °(petty) quarrel, °disagreement, °misunderstanding, °dispute, °argument, °difference (of opinion), squabble, °bicker, °row, wrangle, *US* spat

tight *adj.* **1** °secure, °firm, °fast, °fixed, secured, close-fitting, °snug, sealed, hermetically sealed, leak-proof, °hermetic, impervious, impenetrable, °impermeable, airtight, °watertight, waterproof, **2** °taut, stretched, °tense, constricting, °(too) small, ill-fitting **3** °strict, binding, restrictive, stringent, °severe, °tough, uncompromising, unyielding, rigorous, °stern, austere, autocratic, °harsh, hard and fast, °inflexible **4** ***Chiefly nautical*** °taut, (well-)disciplined, °orderly, °neat, well-organized, °trim, °tidy, °smart **5** stingy, niggardly, °mean, °penurious, °miserly, parsimonious, penny-pinching, tightfisted, close-fisted, *Colloq Brit* mingy **6** °close, °(almost) even, (highly) competitive, neck and neck, evenly matched **7** °difficult, °trying, °dangerous, °perilous, °risky, °hazardous, °touchy, °problematic, °sticky, °tricky, °ticklish, °precarious, touch-and-go **8** tipsy, °drunk, intoxicated, *Colloq* °high, woozy, °under the influence, *Brit* tiddly **9** °scarce, °scanty, hard to find *or* come by, °rare; °dear, °expensive —*adv.* **10** °tightly, securely, °firmly; closely **11** compactly, densely, solidly, °firmly, closely

tighten *v.* **1** Sometimes, ***tighten down or up.*** °anchor, °fasten, °fix, °tense, °secure **2** make tighter *or* tenser *or* stronger, °strengthen **3** Sometimes, ***tighten up.*** make more rigorous *or* strict *or* stringent *or* severe *or* restrictive, close gaps in **4**

Sometimes, ***tighten up.*** tauten, °stiffen, °tense, °close

tight-lipped *adj.* close-mouthed, °silent, °quiet, °mum, °mute, close-lipped, °noncommittal, °reticent, °secretive, °taciturn, unforthcoming, uncommunicative, °reserved

tightly *adv.* closely, tensely, °vigorously, rigorously

tights *n. pl. US and Canadian and New Zealand* pantyhose, *Australian also* pantihose

till[1] *v.* plow *or* plough, °cultivate, °farm, °work, °dig, hoe, harrow, manure, *Literary* delve

till[2] *n.* money *or* cash drawer, cash box *or* register

tilt *v.* **1** °lean, °slant, °incline, °slope, °angle, °tip, heel over, °pitch, °list, °cant **2** ***tilt at.*** joust with, compete with, °battle against, contend with, spar with, cross swords with, °attack —*n.* **3** °lean, °slant, °incline, °slope, °angle, °tip, °heel, °list, °pitch, °cant, °inclination **4** joust, tourney, °tournament, °meeting, tilting, °engagement, °encounter, °match, °contest, °test, °trial, °fight, °combat; °dispute, °argument, °difference, °quarrel, altercation, squabble, °tiff, *US* spat, *Colloq* set-to

timber *n.* **1** trees, forest, woodland **2** wood, beams, boards, planks, *US and Canadian* °lumber **3** °material, °potential, °stuff, °character, °quality, °talent, °prospect

timbre *n.* tone (color *or* quality), tonality, °color, resonance

time *n.* **1** °period, °interval, °stretch, °spell, °patch **2** °period, °interval, °stretch, while, °span, °space, °term, duration **3** hour; °point, °moment **4** °age, °period, epoch, °era, lifetime, heyday, day(s) **5** °opportunity, °chance, °occasion **6** °experience **7** °tempo, °beat, °rhythm, meter, °measure **8** °ease, °leisure; convenience **9** Often, ***times.*** °life, °things, °circumstance, °conditions, °everything, °culture, mores, habits, values **10** ***ahead of time.*** °(bright and) early, °prematurely, beforehand, in good time **11** ***all the time.*** °always, °ever, constantly, continuously, continually, perpetually, at all times, without surcease, unceasingly **12** ***at one time.*** **(a)** °once, once upon a time, on one occasion, °previously, in days of yore, °formerly, heretofore, in the (good) old days **(b)** simultaneously, °(all) at once, °at the same time, together, all together, in unison **13** ***at the same time.*** **(a)** °all the same, °nonetheless, °yet, °even so, but, °however, be that as it may, °nevertheless, °notwithstanding, just the same **(b)** See **12 (b),** above. **14** ***at times.*** from time to time, °occasionally, °(every) now and then, °once in a while, °on occasion, every so often, at intervals, °sometimes, *Colloq* every so often **15** ***behind the times.*** °old-fashioned, outdated, dated, outmoded, °antiquated, °passé, °obsolescent, °obsolete, *Colloq* old hat, °dead **16** ***for the time being.*** for now, for the present, for the moment, °meanwhile, °temporarily, pro tempore, pro tem, *Archaic* for the nonce **17** ***in no time.*** °at once, forthwith, °straightaway, °immediately, °quickly, speedily, without delay, °swiftly **18** ***in time.*** **(a)** in timely fashion, °early, in good time, in the nick of time **(b)** °soon, one of these days, °sometime, someday, one day, °eventually, °sooner or later, anon **19** ***on time.*** **(a)** punctually, °on the dot, in good time **(b)** in installments, on terms, on account, on credit, *Colloq Brit* on the never-never, on hire-purchase *or* h.p. **20** ***take (one's) time.*** °dawdle, dillydally, °shilly-shally, °delay, °linger, loiter **21** ***time and again.*** again (and again), °repeatedly, (over and) over again, time and time again, time after time, °frequently, °often, many times, on many occasions —*v.* **22** °schedule, °set, °regulate, °control **23** °schedule, °set, °organize, °adjust, °fix

time-honored *adj.* established, °traditional, °habitual, °customary, °rooted, °conventional, age-old, °set, °fixed; °venerable, venerated, respected, revered, honored

timeless *adj.* °eternal, °everlasting, °immortal, undying, °endless, unending, ceaseless, °abiding, °deathless, ageless, °changeless, unchanged, immutable, unchanging, °permanent, °indestructible

timely *adj.* °punctual, °prompt, °well-timed, °propitious, °opportune, °convenient, °favorable, auspicious

timeserving *adj.* self-seeking, self-serving, °selfish, °self-indulgent, °ambitious, °mercenary, °venal, °greedy, profit-oriented, fortunehunting, gold-digging, °opportunistic, °hypocritical, °obsequious, sycophantic, toadying, toadeating, bootlicking, subservient, *Colloq* °on the make, on the take, *Slang US* out for numero uno, *Taboo slang* brown-nosing

timetable *n.* °schedule, °calendar, curriculum, °program, agenda, *Chiefly Brit* °diary

timeworn *adj.* aging *or* ageing, °old, °tired, °worn, time-scarred, °decrepit, °dilapidated, tumbledown, °ramshackle, °run-down, dog-eared, °ragged, moth-eaten, °threadbare, °seedy, °shabby, archaic, °antique, well-worn, worn-out, °passé, broken-down, °old-fashioned, out-dated, dated, °antiquated, °ancient, °obsolescent, °obsolete, stereotyped, stereotypic(al), hackneyed, °stale, trite, overused, *Colloq* old hat

timid *adj.* °shy, °retiring, °modest, °coy, °bashful, diffident, timorous, °fearful, apprehensive, °mousy, °scared, frightened, °nervous, °cowardly, pusillanimous, craven, *Colloq* chicken-hearted, yellow, yellow-bellied, chicken, chicken-livered, lily-livered, gutless

tinker *v.* °trifle, °dabble, °meddle, mess (around *or* about), °toy, fool *or* play (around *or* about), putter *or Brit* potter (about *or* around), *Colloq* fiddle *or* monkey *or* muck (about *or* around)

tinny *adj.* **1** °shabby, °flimsy, flimsily *or* poorly made, °shoddy, °inferior, °cheap, °tawdry **2** metallic, °harsh, twangy

tint *n.* **1** tincture, °wash, °hue, °color, °cast; tinge, °touch, °hint, °trace, °dash, coloring, °shade, °tone, °suggestion **2** dye, °rinse, °wash, °stain, tincture, colorant, coloring, touchup —*v.* **3** dye, °stain, °color, °rinse, tinge, °touch up **4** tinge, °color, °influence, °affect, °taint, °stain

tiny *adj.* microscopic, infinitesimal, °minute, minuscule, °diminutive, °wee, °small, °little, °miniature, micro, mini, °pocket, pocket-sized, bantam, pygmy *or* pigmy, midget, Lilliputian, °petite, °delicate, °dainty, °elfin, °slight, °insignificant, °negligible, °trifling, °paltry, °inconsequential, °puny, *Colloq* pint-sized, teeny, teeny-weeny, teensy-weensy, itty-bitty, itsy-bitsy

tip [1] *n.* **1** °end, °extremity, °peak, apex, °summit, °vertex, °cap, °top, °pinnacle, tiptop, °crown, °head, °terminal, ferrule *or* ferule, finial, nib *or* neb, °point —*v.* **2** °top, °cap, °crown, surmount

tip [2] *v.* **1** Often, ***tip over.*** °upset, °overthrow, knock *or* cast *or* throw down, upend, knock over, °overturn, °topple (over), °capsize **2** °slant, °lean, °incline, °tilt, °cant **3** °empty, °unload, °dump, °deposit, *Slang Brit* ditch

tip [3] *n.* **1** gratuity, baksheesh, *pourboire, douceur,* lagniappe *or* lagnappe, °present, °gift, *Colloq* little something **2** tip-off, °(inside) information, °warning, °advice, °suggestion, °clue, °hint, °pointer, °forecast, °prediction, *Colloq Brit* gen —*v.* **3** °reward **4** Usually, ***tip off.*** °advise, °warn, °caution, °alert, forewarn, °notify, let (someone) know, *Colloq* let (someone) in on

tirade *n.* declamation, °harangue, diatribe, philippic, °outburst, onslaught, screed, jeremiad, denunciation, stream of abuse, invective

tire *v.* **1** °weary, tire out, °fatigue, °exhaust, °wear out, °drain, °sap, °enervate, debilitate, °weaken, *Colloq* take it out of, °fag (out) **2** °bore, °exasperate, °weary, °irk, °irritate, °annoy, °bother

tired *adj.* **1** °exhausted, tired out, worn-out, °weary, °fatigued, °spent, drained, *Colloq* all in, °(dead) beat, knocked out, fagged (out), dog-tired, ready to drop, dead tired, done in, *Brit* knackered, whacked, *US* bushed, pooped, wiped out **2** Usually, ***tired of.*** bored with, exasperated by, °weary of, irked *or* irritated *or* annoyed *or* bothered by, sick (and tired) of, *Colloq* fed up (to here) with **3** overworked, overused, clichéd, stereotyped, stereotypic(al), hackneyed, unimaginative, trite, °stale, worn-out, unoriginal, commonplace, *Colloq* bromidic

tireless *adj.* °energetic, °vital, °vigorous, °dynamic, °spirited, °lively, indefatigable, hardworking, °industrious, °untiring, unflagging, unfaltering, unfailing, °persistent, dogged, °tenacious, pertinacious, persevering, °staunch, sedulous, unwavering, unswerving, undeviating, °steady, °steadfast, °resolute, °determined

tiresome *adj.* **1** °boring, °dull, fatiguing, °humdrum, °monotonous, °flat, °tedious, wearisome, tiring, uninteresting, insipid, °bland, dryasdust, fatiguing, soporific, hypnotic **2** irritating, °irksome, vexing, vexatious, annoying, bothersome, exasperating, °trying, °disagreeable, °troublesome, unpleasant

tissue *n.* °fabric, °network, °web, interweaving, °combination, °chain, series, °accumulation, conglomeration, concatenation, °pile, °mass, °pack

title *n.* **1** °name **2** designation, appellation, epithet **3** caption, inscription, headline, °head, subtitle, °legend, subhead, rubric **4** championship, °crown **5** °right, °interest, °privilege, entitlement, ownership, °possession, °tenure; °(title) deed, documentation of ownership —*v.* **6** °name, °call, °designate, °style, °label, °term, °entitle, °christen, baptize, °nickname, denominate, °tag, dub

titter *v.* **1** °chuckle, °snicker, chortle, °giggle; snigger —*n.* **2** °chuckle, °snicker, °giggle, °(suppressed) laughter, chortle, snigger

titular *adj.* °nominal, °so-called, so-designated, so-styled, °self-styled, ***soi-disant,*** °token, putative, °theoretical

toast *n.* **1** °tribute, °pledge, salutation(s), greeting(s), felicitations, °honor, good wishes, °appreciation, remembrance(s), cheers **2** °heroine, °hero, °favorite, °darling, °idol —*v.* **3** pay tribute to, °salute, °drink to, °honor, °greet, °congratulate, felicitate

toilet *n.* **1** (water) closet, W.C. *or* WC, men's (room), ladies' (room), (public) convenience, facility *or* facilities, washroom, bathroom, °lavatory, °privy, outhouse, urinal, (in France) ***pissoir, vespasienne***; ***Nautical*** °head, ***Chiefly military*** latrine, ***Chiefly US*** rest room, ***New England*** °necessary, *Colloq* gents', ladies', powder room, little girls' room, little boys' room, *Brit* loo, *Military* ablutions, *Slang Brit* °bog, karzy, *US and Canadian* john, can, crapper **2** *Formal or literary* grooming, dressing, making up, *Brit* toilette

toilsome *adj.* °arduous, °laborious, °tough, hard, °difficult, °strenuous, °burdensome, onerous, backbreaking, °exhausting, fatiguing, tiring, enervating, wearying, draining

token *n.* **1** °coin, disk *or* disc **2** °symbol, °sign, °mark, marker, badge, °emblem, °indication, °proof, °evidence **3** souvenir, °memento, °keepsake, °reminder, °remembrance, *Archaic* remembrancer —*adj.* **4** °symbolic, °emblematic, °representative **5** °superficial, cosmetic, °surface, °perfunctory, °minimal, °slight, °nominal

tolerable *adj.* **1** °bearable, °supportable, allowable, endurable, °acceptable, sufferable **2** °acceptable, unexceptional, °common, °fair, common-or-garden variety, middling, °ordinary, °average, °so-so, °mediocre, °adequate, °run-of-the-mill, °passable, °indifferent, *Colloq* O.K. *or* OK *or* okay, not (too) bad, pretty *or* fairly good

tolerance *n.* **1** open-mindedness, toleration, forbearance, broad-mindedness, permissiveness, magnanimity, °indulgence, sufferance,

°patience, freedom from bigotry *or* prejudice **2** °play, °clearance, °allowance, °variation **3** toleration, °resistance, °endurance, imperviousness; °immunity, insensitivity

tolerant *adj.* open-minded, °objective, forbearing, °unprejudiced, unbigoted, °dispassionate, broad-minded, °indulgent, magnanimous, °patient, °generous, °charitable, °catholic, latitudinarian, °permissive, °liberal, bighearted, °fair, evenhanded, °considerate

tolerate *v.* **1** °stand (for), °allow, °permit, °bear, °suffer, °brook, countenance, °abide, °admit, °indulge, °concede, °sanction, °swallow, °stomach, turn a blind eye to, *Colloq* °put up with, *Brit* °stick **2** °bear, °stand, °submit to, °endure, °weather, °take, °accept, °undergo

toll[1] *v.* **1** °ring, °peal, °chime, °strike, °sound —*n.* **2** °ring, ringing, °peal, pealing, °chime, chiming, °striking, °sound, sounding, tolling, knell

toll[2] *n.* **1** °charge, °fee, °dues, assessment, °tariff; excise, °duty, impost, levy, °tribute **2** °loss, °penalty, °cost, damage(s); exaction

tomb *n.* °sepulcher, °crypt, vault, mausoleum, °grave, catacomb, burial chamber, last resting place

tombstone *n.* gravestone, headstone, marker, °monument, cenotaph

tone *n.* **1** °sound, °note **2** °stress, °emphasis, °force, °accent, °intonation, modulation, phrasing, inflection, °pitch, tonality, °timbre, °sound (color), tone color *or* quality, color *or* coloring, resonance, sonorousness, sonority, fullness, richness **3** °manner, °style, °attitude, °air, °aspect, °approach, °note, °tenor, tone of voice, mode of expression, °temper, °vein, °spirit, °air **4** °tint, tinge, °shade, °hue, °color, coloring, °cast —*v.* **5** ***tone down.*** °temper, °modify, °reduce, °moderate, °modulate, °soften, quiet *or Brit* quieten (down), °dampen, °dull, °subdue, °mute, soft-pedal **6** ***tone up.*** (re)invigorate, °tune (up), °brighten (up), (re)vitalize, °freshen (up), limber up, get into condition *or* shape

tongue *n.* **1** °language, °speech; °dialect, patois, creole, °idiom, °parlance, argot, °talk, °vernacular, *façon de parler* **2** °(verbal) expression, utterance, °voice, articulation **3** ***hold (one's) tongue.*** be *or* remain *or* keep silent, keep mum, say nothing *or* nought, not breathe a word, keep (one's) counsel, not say a word, *Slang* °shut up **4** ***slip of the tongue.*** °slip, °mistake, gaffe, °blunder, faux pas, Freudian slip, *Colloq Brit* boob **5** ***with (one's) tongue in (one's) cheek.*** facetiously, whimsically, ironically, jocularly, jokingly, not seriously, in jest, jestingly, °in fun, to be funny, *Colloq* kiddingly

tongue-lashing *n.* scolding, berating, °reproof, °rebuke, °reprimand; °(verbal) abuse, castigation, chastisement, vituperation, revilement, *Colloq* dressing-down, telling-off, talking-to, *Brit* slating, ticking-off, wigging

tongue-tied *adj.* °speechless, at a loss for words, struck dumb, dumbfounded *or* dumfounded, °mute, °inarticulate

tonic *n.* **1** °stimulant, restorative, invigorant, °boost, refresher; *Obsolete or literary* ptisan *or* tisane, *Technical* roborant, analeptic, *Colloq* bracer, pick-me-up, pickup, °shot in the arm, *US* picker-upper —*adj.* **2** °stimulant, °stimulating, restorative, °invigorating, fortifying, °bracing, strengthening, reviving, enlivening, °refreshing, *Technical* analeptic, roborant

tool *n.* **1** utensil, °implement, °instrument, °device, °apparatus, appliance, contrivance, °aid, °machine, °mechanism, °gadget, *Colloq* °contraption, °gimmick, *Chiefly US and Canadian* gizmo *or* gismo **2** °means, °way, °agency, weapon, °medium, °vehicle, instrumentality, avenue, °road **3** °puppet, cat's-paw, °pawn, °dupe, *Slang* stooge, °sucker —*v.* **4** °work, °carve, °cut, °embellish, °decorate, °ornament, °dress, °shape

top *n.* **1** °summit, apex, °peak, °acme, °crest, °head, °pinnacle, °vertex, °zenith, meridian, °crown, culmination, high point, °height, apogee **2** lid, °cover, °cap, covering, °stopper, cork —*v.* **3** °surpass, °better, °best, °outstrip, °exceed, °outdo, °excel, °beat, °transcend **4** surmount, °cover, °cap, °crown, °tip; °finish, °complete, garnish **5** °trim, crop, lop *or* cut off, °clip, °prune, °nip, °pinch (back) **6** °scale, °climb, ascend, surmount **7** ***top up.*** °fill (up), °refresh, refill, °replenish, *US* °freshen (up) —*adj.* **8** °best, greatest, °foremost, °leading, °preeminent, °eminent, °first, °first-rate, °principal, °prime, finest, choicest, topmost; °excellent, °superior, °superb, top-drawer, top-grade, topnotch, °supreme, °peerless, unequaled, °incomparable, *Colloq* °crack, ace, A-1 *or* A-one **9** °uppermost, topmost, highest

topic *n.* °subject (matter), °matter, °issue, °question, °point, °thesis, °theme, °text, keynote, field *or* area of study *or* of inquiry

topical *adj.* **1** °contemporary, °current, up-to-date, °timely **2** °local, °superficial

topple *v.* **1** °upset, upend, knock down *or* over, bring down, °fell, °capsize, °collapse **2** bring *or* throw down, °overthrow, °defeat, vanquish, °overcome, °overturn, unseat, oust **3** fall (over *or* down), °drop, °collapse, keel over, tumble down

topsy-turvy *adj.* **1** upside down, wrong side up, °head over heels, inverted, reversed, backward(s), °vice versa **2** °chaotic, muddled, jumbled, °disorderly, disordered, disorganized, °confused, mixed-up, messy, °untidy, in a muddle, higgledy-piggledy, *Colloq* arsy-varsy, every which way

torment *v.* **1** torture, °abuse, maltreat, °mistreat, °distress, agonize, excruciate, crucify, harrow, °rack, °pain **2** °worry, °trouble, °plague, °annoy, bedevil, vex, harry, badger, hector, °harass, °pester, °nag, °persecute, needle, nettle, °irk, °irritate, °bother, torture, °afflict, *Brit* chivy *or* chivvy *or* chevy —*n.* **3** °agony, wretchedness, °anguish, °distress,

°misery, °pain, °woe, painfulness, torture, °suffering, °curse, °hell **4** °worry, vexation, °annoyance, harassment, °ordeal, °persecution, needling, °nuisance, bane, irritation, °bother, °affliction, °scourge, torture

torpid *adj.* sluggish, °slow, slow-moving, slow-paced, tortoiselike, °lethargic, apathetic, °indolent, °passive, °slothful, °dull, stupefied, °sleepy, somnolent, °inactive, °inert, languid, languorous, °phlegmatic, spiritless, °lifeless, °listless, fainéant, °lackadaisical, pococurante, °indifferent, uncaring, unconcerned, insouciant

torpor *n.* °sluggishness, °sloth, °lethargy, apathy, °indolence, passivity, slothfulness, dullness, stupefaction, drowsiness, sleepiness, somnolence, °inactivity, °inertia, inertness, languor, laziness, phlegm, lifelessness, listlessness, °idleness, fainéance, pococurantism, °indifference, unconcern, insouciance

torrent *n.* °stream, °rush, °flood, deluge, effusion, gushing, °outburst, °outpouring, °spate, inundation, °flow, overflow, tide, cascade

torrential *adj.* rushing, streaming, copious, °profuse, teeming, °relentless, °violent; °fierce, vehement, vociferous, °ferocious

torrid *adj.* **1** °hot, °fiery, °sultry, stifling, °sweltering, broiling, sizzling, roasting, blazing, °burning, baking, cooking, boiling, blistering, blistery, °scorching, scorched, parched, parching, arid; °humid, °steamy, steaming, °muggy; tropical **2** °fervent, fervid, °passionate, °intense, °ardent, °inflamed, °impassioned, °lustful, amorous, °erotic, *Colloq* °sexy, °hot

tortuous *adj.* **1** twisted, twisting, winding, wandering, °serpentine, turning, °crooked, sinuous, °bent, curled, curling, curved, curvy, curvilinear, flexuous, anfractuous, convoluted, involuted, zigzag, mazelike, mazy, °labyrinthine **2** °roundabout, °indirect, °devious, °intricate, °involved, unstraightforward, °complicated, °ambiguous, ambagious, circuitous, warped, °crooked, °tricky, misleading, °deceptive

toss *v.* **1** °throw, °cast, °lob, °pitch, °fling, °hurl, °heave, °shy, °launch, °send, °let fly, °propel, catapult, °sling, °bowl, *Colloq* chuck **2** °shake, °jerk, °stir up, °agitate, °fling **3** °shake (up), °stir (up), °agitate, °jiggle, °tumble, joggle; °wave, °lash, thrash **4** writhe, °wriggle, °squirm, toss and turn, thrash **5** °pitch, yaw, °wallow, °roll, °lurch, undulate, °plunge —*n.* **6** °throw, °lob, °pitch, °heave, °shy

tot *n.* °child, toddler, infant, °baby

total *n.* **1** °sum (total), °totality, aggregate, °whole, °amount, total number —*adj.* **2** °whole, °entire, °complete, °full, °gross, °overall, °comprehensive **3** °complete, unalloyed, °unmitigated, °unqualified, unconditional, utter, °out-and-out, °thorough, thoroughgoing, °perfect, °outright, °downright, all-out, °absolute —*v.* **4** °add (up), tot up, °sum up, °reckon, °compute **5** °amount to, add up to, °come to, mount up to

totalitarian *adj.* °absolute, absolutist, °arbitrary, °authoritarian, autocratic, °dictatorial, fascist(ic), undemocratic, illiberal, °monolithic, Nazi, °oppressive, °despotic, °tyrannical

totality *n.* °total, aggregate, °sum (total), °whole, °entirety, beginning and end, alpha and omega, be-all and end-all

totally *adv.* °completely, °utterly, °entirely, fully, unqualifiedly, unconditionally, °perfectly, °absolutely, °thoroughly, °wholly, consummately

totter *v.* waver, °topple, falter, °tremble, °teeter, °sway, °rock, °stagger, °stumble, wobble, °quiver, °shake, °quake, °shiver, dodder

touch *v.* **1** put (one's) hand on, °feel, °handle **2** bring into contact with, °apply, °put, °set **3** Sometimes, ***touch (up) against.*** be in contact (with), °border, adjoin, °meet, come up *or* be (up) against, push *or* press *or* lean (up) against, brush *or* rub (up) against, come *or* be together, abut **4** lay a hand *or* finger on; meddle with, have to do with, interfere with, come near, °approach **5** °drink, °eat, °consume, °partake of, °take, °use, °taste, have to do with **6** °affect, °impress, °influence, °disturb, °move, °stir, °arouse, °excite, impassion, °stimulate, °strike, *Colloq* °get to **7** °rival, °match, °equal, °compare with, come up to, be on a par with, be a match for, be in the same league *or* class as *or* with, be on an equal footing with, °reach, come *or* get near *or* close to, hold a candle to, measure up to *or* against, *Colloq US* stack up to *or* with *or* against **8** Usually, ***touch on or upon.*** °refer to, have reference to, pertain to, °relate to, have a bearing on, °regard, °mention, allude to, speak *or* write of, °tell of, bring up *or* in, °raise, °deal with, °cover **9** have access to, access, °use, °employ, make use of, put to use, avail (oneself) of, °take, °get, take advantage of **10** ***touch down.*** °land, alight, come to earth **11** ***touch off.*** **(a)** detonate, °spark (off), set alight, °set off, ignite, °light, °fire, put a match to **(b)** instigate, °initiate, °begin, °start, set in motion, ignite, °set off, trigger, °provoke, °foment, °cause, °give rise to **12** ***touch up.*** °retouch, °patch up; °beautify, °enhance, titivate *or* tittivate, °renovate, °spruce up —*n.* **13** °feeling, °feel, °texture **14** °pat, °tap, °blow, °hit, °stroke, °brush, °caress **15** °dash, °hint, intimation, °suggestion, *soupçon*, °bit, intimation, °pinch, °jot, °spot, °trace, tinge, °taste, °suspicion, smattering, coloring, smack, °speck, °drop, whiff, °odor, °scent, °smell **16** °ability, deftness, °expertise, °dexterity, adroitness, °facility, °skill, skillfulness, °knack, °capability, °genius, °talent, °gift, °flair **17** °response, °feel, responsiveness, °feeling, °movement, °operation, performance level **18** signature, trademark, °characteristic, °influence, °approach, °style, °manner, °technique, °execution, °method

touching *adj.* °moving, °stirring, °emotional, °tender, °poignant, °pathetic, soul-stirring, °heart-rending, heartbreaking, °sad, °pitiful, distressing, distressful

touchstone *n.* °standard, °yardstick, criterion, °reference, benchmark, °test, °norm, °measure

touchy *adj.* **1** (over)sensitive, supersensitive, hypersensitive, highly strung, °tense, thin-skinned, crabby, crabbed, °testy, irascible, °irritable, tetchy, °temperamental, grouchy, °peevish, °querulous, °petulant, pettish, splenetic, captious, bad-tempered, °short-tempered, hot-tempered, °quick-tempered, crusty, °cross, curmudgeonly, grouchy, °cantankerous, choleric, dyspeptic, °waspish, bearish, snarling, °snappish, °argumentative, disputatious, contentious, *US* high-strung, °cranky **2** °critical, touch-and-go, °sensitive, °ticklish, °risky, °precarious, °hazardous, chancy, unsure, °uncertain, °close, hairsbreadth *or* hairbreadth, °dangerous, hair-raising, °frightening, °terrifying, °nerve-racking, *Jocular* °parlous, *Colloq* °hairy

tough *adj.* **1** °hard, °firm, °durable, long-lasting, wear-resistant, °substantial, °strong, °stout, °rugged, °sturdy, °sound, well-built **2** °stiff, °hard, leathery, °inflexible, chewy, fibrous, cartilaginous, °sinewy, °ropy, °wiry, °stringy **3** °strong, °stalwart, °brawny, °burly, °muscular, °powerful, virile, °manly, °sturdy, doughty, °intrepid, °stout, °rough, °vigorous, strapping, athletic **4** °difficult, °demanding, °exacting, °hard, °troublesome; °laborious, taxing, °strenuous **5** baffling, °thorny, °puzzling, °perplexing, mystifying, knotty, °irksome, °difficult **6** °stubborn, hardened, inured, °obstinate, obdurate, °hard, °harsh, °severe, °stern, °inflexible, refractory, intractable, adamant, unyielding, ungiving, °rigid, unbending, unsentimental, unfeeling, °unsympathetic, °callous, hard-boiled, uncaring, °cold, °cool, °icy, °stony, *Colloq* hard-nosed *—interj.* **7** *Colloq* Too bad!, Tough luck!, Hard luck!, *Brit* Hard cheese!, *Slang* Tough titty!, *Taboo slang* Tough shit! *—n.* **8** °bruiser, hooligan, °bully (boy), °rowdy, °thug, ruffian, *Colloq* roughneck, tough guy, gorilla

tour *n.* **1** °journey, °trip, °excursion, °outing, °expedition, voyage, trek, peregrination, jaunt, junket **2** °stroll, perambulation, walkabout, °ramble, °walk, °drive; °round, °circuit, ambit **3** °spell, °shift, °assignment, °turn, *Military* period of service *or* enlistment *—v.* **4** °journey, °travel, voyage, °visit, °trip, trek, sight-see, °cruise; *Colloq* globetrot

tourist *n.* °traveler, voyager, °visitor, °sightseer, *Colloq* rubberneck(er), out-of-towner, *Brit* tripper, day-tripper, holiday-maker

tournament *n.* tourney, °competition, °contest, °match, °meeting, °event, °meet

tousle *v.* dishevel, °disorder, °ruffle, disarrange, °tangle (up), °mess (up), °rumple, disarray, *US* muss (up)

tout *v.* **1** hawk, °peddle, °sell, °promote, °talk up, *Colloq* °push, °plug *—n.* **2** tipster

tow *v.* °pull, °drag, °draw, °haul, °lug, °trail, °tug, trawl

toward *prep.* **1** towards, in the direction of, to; °for, so as to approach *or* near, on the way *or* road to **2** towards, to, °for, as a help to, supporting, promoting, assisting **3** towards, °near, nearing, °close to, approaching, shortly before

tower *n.* **1** belltower, campanile, minaret, pagoda, obelisk; belfry, °spire, turret, steeple, flèche **2** fortress, citadel, °stronghold, °castle, fastness; °keep, °dungeon, °prison *—v.* **3** Often, ***tower over or above.*** °loom, °soar, °rise, ascend, °rear

towering *adj.* **1** °lofty, °tall, °high, soaring, °outstanding, °elevated, skyscraping, sky-high, °great, °impressive, °imposing, °huge, °gigantic, °supreme, °superior, °paramount, °extraordinary, unmatched, unequally, unrivaled, °unparalleled, unsurpassed **2** °violent, °fiery, °burning, °passionate, °excessive, vehement, °intense, consuming, °mighty, °overwhelming, unrestrained, °immoderate, °inordinate, intemperate, °extreme, °colossal, °enormous

town *n.* township, village, hamlet, community; °municipality, °city, °metropolis, borough, burgh

toy *n.* **1** °plaything **2** °trifle, trinket, °bauble, °gewgaw, gimcrack, knickknack *or* nicknack, bagatelle, kickshaw, bit of frippery *—v.* **3** Usually, ***toy with.*** °trifle (with), dally (with), °play (with), °sport (with), °fool (with), °fiddle (with), °tinker (with) **4** Usually, ***toy with.*** °flirt (with), dally (with), dilly-dally (with), °play (with), deal with carelessly, amuse oneself with *—adj.* **5** °miniature, °tiny, °diminutive, °small, °dwarf **6** °imitation, °fake, phoney *or US also* phony, simulated, °artificial

trace *n.* **1** °hint, intimation, °sign, °token, °suggestion, °touch, °vestige, °indication, °mark, °record, °evidence, °clue **2** °bit, °spot, °speck, °jot, °drop, °dash, °suspicion, °remnant, tinge, *soupçon*, iota, whiff, °suggestion, °trifle **3** Often, ***traces.*** track(s), °trail, spoor, footprint(s), print(s), footmark(s) *—v.* **4** dog, °pursue, °follow (in the footsteps of), °stalk, °track (down), °shadow, °trail, *Colloq* °tail **5** °investigate, °discover, ascertain, °detect, °determine, °find, °seek, °search for, hunt down *or* up, °unearth, °track **6** delineate, °outline, °copy, °draw, map, °chart, °mark (out), °record, °reproduce, sketch

track *n.* **1** °line, rail(s), °way, railway, *US* °railroad **2** °path, °trail, °route, footpath, °course, °road, °street, alley **3** spoor, °trail, footprint(s), print(s), trace(s), footmark(s), °scent, °slot, °wake **4** ***keep track of.*** °trace, keep an eye on, °follow, °pursue, °monitor, °supervise, °oversee, keep up with *or* on, °watch, keep a record of *or* on, °record **5**

lose track of. °lose, misplace, °mislay, lose sight of, °forget —*v.* **6** °follow, dog, °pursue, °trace, °stalk, °shadow, °trail, hunt down, °chase, *Colloq* °tail **7** See **4,** above. **8** ***track down.*** °find, seek out, ferret out, hunt down, °trace, °catch, apprehend, °capture, smell *or* sniff out, run to earth *or* ground, *Colloq* °run down

trackless *adj.* °empty, pathless, untrodden, unexplored, °uncharted, virgin, untrod

tract[1] *n.* °region, °area, °stretch, °territory, °expanse, °zone, °portion, °section, sector, °quarter, °district, °patch, °plot, °parcel, *US* °lot

tract[2] *n.* treatise, °monograph, °essay, article, °paper, dissertation, disquisition, homily, °sermon, critique; °pamphlet, booklet, °brochure, °leaflet

tractable *adj.* **1** docile, amenable, °tame, °manageable, biddable, persuadable *or* persuasible, compliant, easygoing, °willing, °submissive, °obedient, governable, °yielding **2** °manageable, handleable, workable, °adaptable, malleable, °pliable, °plastic, ductile, fictile

traction *n.* °grip, gripping power, °drag, °purchase, °friction, adhesion

trade *n.* **1** °commerce, °business, °traffic, °exchange, barter, dealing(s), buying and selling, merchandising, marketing, mercantilism, °truck **2** °calling, °occupation, °pursuit, °work, °business, °employment, °line (of work), métier, °job, °vocation, °craft, °career, °profession **3** swap *or* swop, °exchange, interchange, barter **4** customers, °clientele, °custom, patrons, following, °patronage, shoppers —*v.* **5** transact *or* do business, °buy, °sell, °deal, °traffic, °merchandise, have dealings **6** °exchange, swap *or* swop, interchange, °switch, barter; °return

trader *n.* °dealer, °merchant, businessman, °broker, merchandiser, distributor, °seller, salesman, saleswoman, °salesperson, vendor, °buyer, purchaser, retailer, wholesaler

tradesman *n.* **1** °merchant, °dealer, shopkeeper, retailer, vendor, °seller **2** artisan, craftsman, journeyman, handicraftsman

tradition *n.* °custom, °practice, °habit, °usage, °convention, °ritual, °rite, unwritten law, °institution, °form, praxis, °lore

traditional *adj.* °customary, °usual, °routine, °habitual, °standard, household, °stock, °time-honored, established, °well-known, °conventional, °ritual, unwritten, °accustomed, °historic, °old, ancestral

traffic *n.* **1** °movement, conveyance, shipping, °transport, °freight, *Chiefly US* transportation **2** See **trade, 1,** above —*v.* **3** See **trade, 5,** above

tragedy *n.* °catastrophe, °calamity, °disaster, °misfortune, adversity, °blow

tragic *adj.* °sad, depressing, °lamentable, °unhappy, °funereal, °forlorn, °melancholy, cheerless, °mournful, lachrymose, dolorous, °grievous, morose, lugubrious, °dismal, °piteous, °pitiable, °pitiful, pathetic(al), appalling, °wretched, °dreadful, °awful, °terrible, °horrible, °deplorable, °miserable, distressing, °disturbing, upsetting, °shocking, unlucky, °unfortunate, hapless, ill-fated, °inauspicious, star-crossed, ill-omened, ill-starred, °calamitous, catastrophic, crushing, °disastrous; tragical

trail *n.* **1** °(beaten) path, °way, footpath, °route, °track, °course **2** °track, spoor, °scent, °smell, °trace, °footsteps, footprints, °path, °wake **3** See **train, 2,** below —*v.* **4** °tow, °draw, °drag (along), °haul, °pull, °tag along, trawl, bring along (behind), carry along (behind) **5** °drag, °pull, °move, be drawn, °stream, °sweep, °dangle **6** °lag (behind), °dawdle, loiter, °linger, °follow, °straggle, bring up the rear, hang back, fall *or* drop behind **7** °follow, °pursue, dog, °trace, °shadow, °stalk, °track, °chase, °hunt, *Colloq* °tail **8** ***trail off or away.*** °diminish, °decrease, fade away *or* out, °disappear, °dwindle, lessen, die out *or* away, °peter out, °subside, °taper off, °weaken, grow faint *or* dim

train *n.* **1** °carriage, °coach, *Babytalk* choo-choo **2** °retinue, entourage, cortège, °suite, following, °escort, °guard, attendants, retainers, followers, °trail; °staff, court, household **3** °line, °queue, °procession, °succession, °string, °set, °sequence, °chain, °progression, caravan, cavalcade, °parade, column, °file —*v.* **4** °discipline, °exercise, °tutor, °teach, °coach, °drill, °school, °instruct, °prepare, °educate, edify, °guide, °bring up, °indoctrinate, °rear, °raise **5** °work out, °exercise, practice

trait *n.* °feature, °characteristic, °attribute, °quality, °peculiarity, idiosyncrasy, °quirk, lineament, °mark, °property

traitor *n.* °turncoat, Judas, quisling, betrayer, °renegade, fifth columnist, *US* Benedict Arnold, *Colloq* double-crosser, snake in the grass, double-dealer, two-timer

traitorous *adj.* treacherous, °perfidious, °seditious, °subversive, insurrectionist, °renegade, insurgent, °disloyal, °deceitful, °untrue, unfaithful, °faithless; treasonable, *Colloq* double-crossing, double-dealing, two-timing

trajectory *n.* flight path, °course, °track

tram *n.* tramcar, trolleybus, *US and Canadian* streetcar, trolley (car)

trammel *n.* **1** Usually, ***trammels.*** impediment(s), hindrance(s), shackle(s), handicap(s), check(s), restriction(s), restraint(s), curb(s), deterrent(s), constraint(s), snag(s), hitch(es), (stumbling) block(s), obstacle(s), °bar —*v.* **2** °impede, °hinder, °handicap, °check, °restrain, °curb, °deter, constrain, °block, °obstruct, fetter, confine

tramp *v.* **1** °march, hike, trudge, °plod, slog, plough, tread, trek, °walk, *US* mush **2** Usually, ***tramp on or upon.*** See **trample, 1,** below. —*n.* **3** °march, trudge, °plod, slog, trek, hike, °walk **4** °derelict, °vagabond, vagrant, °drifter, °rover, gypsy *or* gipsy, beachcomber, *Brit* dosser, °down-and-out,

Australian swagman, *US* hobo, °bum, down-and-outer 5 °step, tread, footfall, °footstep

trample *v.* 1 trample on *or* upon, tramp (on *or* upon), °stamp (on), tread (on), step on, °crush, press, squash, °flatten, *Colloq* stomp (on *or* upon), squish, squush *or* squoosh 2 Often, ***trample on or upon.*** °violate, °damage, °harm, °hurt, infringe *or* encroach on, ride roughshod over, set at naught, °scorn, contemn, disdain, °defy, °disregard, °ignore, °fly in the face of, fling *or* cast *or* throw to the winds 3 Usually, ***trample out.*** trample down, trample under foot, °stamp out, °extinguish, °put out, °destroy, °crush, °break down

trance *n.* °daze, °stupor, semiconscious *or* half-conscious *or* hypnotic *or* cataleptic *or* dream state, state of semiconsciousness *or* half-consciousness *or* catalepsy *or* suspended animation *or* stupefaction *or* abstraction *or* (complete) absorption *or* exaltation *or* rapture *or* ecstasy; brown study

tranquil *adj.* °calm, °serene, placid, °quiet, °peaceful, °still, °smooth, unagitated, halcyon, °relaxed; unruffled, °sedate, °steady, °regular, °even, °dispassionate, °self-possessed, °cool, self-controlled, cool-headed, unexcited, undisturbed, untroubled, unperturbed

tranquilize *v.* °calm, soothe, pacify, °still, °quiet, °relax, °lull, °compose, °sedate

tranquilizer *n.* bromide, barbiturate, opiate, °sedative, antipsychotic, antianxiety drug, *Slang* downer, red

transact *v.* do, carry on *or* out, °conduct, °manage, °handle, °negotiate, °transact, °administer, °discharge, °perform, °enact, °settle, conclude, °complete, °finish

transaction *n.* 1 °deal, dealing, °negotiation, °matter, °affair, °business, °action, °proceeding, °agreement, °arrangement, °bargain 2 ***transactions.*** °proceedings, record(s), acta, °minutes, annals, *Colloq* goings-on, doings

transcend *v.* °surpass, °outstrip, °exceed, go beyond, outdistance, °overstep, °outdo, °excel, °overshadow, °top, outdistance, outvie, rise above, outshine, °beat

transcendent *adj.* °peerless, °incomparable, unequaled, °matchless, unrivaled, °unparalleled, °unique, consummate, °paramount, °superior, °surpassing, °supreme, °preeminent, °sublime, °excellent, °superb, °magnificent, °marvelous; transcendental

transcribe *v.* 1 °copy, °reproduce, replicate, °duplicate 2 °translate, transliterate, write out, °render, °represent, °show, °interpret

transcript *n.* 1 transcription, °translation, transliteration, °rendering, °interpretation, °representation 2 (carbon *or* machine *or* Xerox *or* photostatic *or* xerographic) copy, carbon, °duplicate, duplication, photocopy, °reproduction, Photostat, *Colloq* °dupe

transfer *v.* 1 °move, °transport, convey, °remove, °carry, °take, °deliver, °bring, °transmit, °cart, °haul, °shift, hand (on *or* over), °turn over, °give, pass (on *or* along *or* over) —*n.* 2 °move, conveyance, transmittal, °transmission, °delivery, °change

transfix *v.* 1 °pin, °fix, °impale, skewer, °nail, °pierce, spear, °spike, °spit, °stick 2 °enrapture, galvanize, °electrify, °hypnotize, mesmerize, rivet, °fascinate, °bewitch, °enchant, ensorcell, engross, root to the spot, °stun, °paralyze, *Colloq* stop dead (in one's tracks)

transform *v.* °change, °modify, transfigure, °alter, transmute, metamorphose, °turn into, °convert, transmogrify, mutate, permute

transformation *n.* °change, modification, transfiguration, transfigurement, °alteration, transmutation, metamorphosis, conversion, transmogrification, °mutation, permutation

transfuse *v.* 1 °instill, °transmit, °transfer, °inject 2 infuse, °permeate

transgress *v.* 1 °sin, trespass, °offend, °err, °lapse, fall from grace, °disobey, °misbehave, go wrong *or* astray, do wrong 2 break *or* violate *or* contravene *or* go beyond *or* exceed *or* overstep *or* infringe *or* defy *or* disobey (the law)

transgression *n.* °sin, trespass, °offense, °error, °lapse, fall from grace, disobedience, °misbehavior, °wrong, °violation, °fault, °misdeed, misdemeanor, °crime, wrongdoing, infraction

transgressor *n.* °sinner, °offender, °criminal, °felon, °culprit, lawbreaker, trespasser, wrongdoer, evildoer, °villain, °miscreant, malefactor, °delinquent

transient *adj.* transitory, °temporary, °brief, °fleeting, °momentary, °passing, ephemeral, fugacious, °fugitive, evanescent, °short-lived, short-term, impermanent, °fly-by-night, °volatile

transit *n.* 1 °moving, °movement, °travel, °traveling, °motion, °passing, °progress, °progression, °transition; °passage, °traverse, traversal, traversing 2 °transport, transportation, °carriage, haulage, cartage, conveyance, °transfer, transference, transferal, transmittal —*v.* 3 °cross, °traverse, go *or* move *or* pass *or* travel across *or* over *or* through

transition *n.* 1 °change, °alteration, metamorphosis, changeover, °transformation, transmutation, °mutation, °development, °evolution, conversion, modification, metastasis 2 See **transit, 1,** above.

translate *v.* 1 °convert, °paraphrase, °change, rewrite, °interpret, °transcribe, °render, decode, °decipher, metaphrase 2 °transform, °convert, °change, mutate, °turn, transmute, metamorphose, transubstantiate, °alter, transmogrify 3 °interpret, rewrite, °explain, °reword, elucidate, °spell out 4 °transfer, convey, °carry, °move, °transport, °forward, °ship, °send, dispatch *or* despatch

translation *n.* 1 conversion, °paraphrase, °interpretation, transcription, transliteration, °rendering, °rendition, metaphrase, °gloss, decipherment, decoding 2 metamorphosis, °change, °alteration, transmutation, transfiguration, °transformation, transmogrification, transubstantiation, conversion **3** °interpretation, rewriting, rewrite, °explanation, rewording, elucidation **4** °transfer, transference, transferal, conveyance, carrying, °moving, °movement, transportation, °transport, forwarding, shipping, shipment, sending, °transmission, dispatch *or* despatch

transmission *n.* **1** °transfer, transference, transferal, transferring, conveyance, carrying, °moving, °movement, transportation, °transport, transporting, forwarding, shipping, shipment, sending, transmittal, transmitting, dispatch *or* despatch, dispatching *or* despatching **2** °broadcast, broadcasting, sending, telecasting, dissemination, communication

transmit *v.* **1** °send, °transfer, convey, °communicate, °pass on, °deliver, °forward, dispatch *or* despatch; °post, °ship, °cable, °radio, telegraph, fax, telex, °telephone, phone, *Chiefly US and Canadian* °mail, *Colloq* wire **2** pass *or* go through, °pass on, °send, °put, °direct, °conduct, °channel

transparent *adj.* **1** °(crystal) clear, pellucid, diaphanous, °see-through, limpid, crystalline, °sheer, transpicuous **2** °plain, °apparent, °obvious, °evident, unambiguous, °patent, °manifest, unmistakable *or* unmistakeable, °(crystal) clear, as plain as day, as plain as the nose on (one's) face, °undisguised, recognizable, understandable, transpicuous **3** °candid, °open, °frank, plainspoken, °direct, unambiguous, unequivocal, straightforward, °ingenuous, °forthright, °aboveboard, °artless, guileless, °simple, naive *or* naïve *or* naïf, undissembling, *Colloq* °on the level, °up front

transpire *v.* **1** become known, be rumored, be revealed, °come to light **2** *Sometimes nonstandard* °happen, °occur, °take place, °come about, °come to pass, °materialize, °arise, °turn out

transplant *v.* °displace, °move, °remove, relocate, °shift, °uproot, resettle, °transfer

transport *v.* **1** °carry, °bear, convey, °move, °remove, °transfer, °deliver, °fetch, °bring, °get, °take, °ship, °haul, °transmit, °send, °forward **2** °exile, °banish, deport, send away **3** °carry away, °enrapture, °captivate, °delight, °charm, spellbind, °bewitch, °fascinate, °enchant, °entrance, °hypnotize, mesmerize, °electrify, °ravish —*n.* **4** transportation, °carrier, conveyance, shipping, °transfer, transferal, shipment, haulage, cartage, °carriage, °moving **5** Usually, ***transports.*** °rapture, °ecstasy, exaltation, exultation, euphoria, °delight, °(seventh) heaven, °happiness, °bliss, elation, exhilaration, °thrill, Elysium, °paradise; Elysian Fields, *Colloq* cloud nine

transpose *v.* °exchange, interchange, metathesize, °switch, swap *or* swop, °trade, commute, °transfer

trap *n.* **1** °snare, °pitfall, gin, springe, deadfall, booby trap **2** °trick, °subterfuge, °wile, °ruse, °stratagem, °ambush, °deception, °device, °artifice, ploy **3** °mouth, *Slang* °yap, °gob, mush, °face —*v.* **4** °snare, ensnare, entrap, °catch, °net **5** °imprison, confine, °lock, °hold, °keep **6** °trick, °deceive, °fool, °dupe, °beguile, inveigle

trappings *n. pl.* accoutrements *or US also* accouterments, panoply, caparison, equipage, °apparatus, °equipment, °paraphernalia, appointments, furnishings, °furniture, °gear, °rig, habiliments, decoration(s), embellishment(s), accessories, frippery *or* fripperies, adornment(s), trimmings, raiment, °fittings, °finery

trash *n.* **1** °rubbish, °(stuff and) nonsense, balderdash, °moonshine, °gibberish, gobbledygook *or* gobbledegook, tommyrot, bunkum, °garbage, twaddle, *Colloq* °rot, flapdoodle, crap, codswallop, bosh, piffle, hooey, bunk, malarkey, poppycock, boloney *or* baloney, eyewash, hogwash, bilgewater, bull, *Scots* havers, *Brit* tosh, gammon, *US* a crock, hokum, gurry, horsefeathers, *Slang Brit* (a load of (old)) cobblers, *Taboo slang* bullshit, horseshit, *Brit* balls, *US* a crock of shit **2** °junk, brummagem, knickknacks *or* nicknacks, gewgaws, trifles, °bric-a-brac, frippery *or* fripperies, bits and pieces, °odds and ends, trinkets, tinsel **3** (*In the US and Canada*) °rubbish, °litter, °garbage, °waste, °refuse, °junk, debris, rubble, °dregs, dross, scoria, slag, offscourings, °dirt, sweepings, *Slang* crap —*v.* **4** *Slang chiefly US* °destroy, °ruin, °wreck, vandalize, °deface

traumatic *adj.* °shocking, upsetting, °disturbing, °painful, °agonizing, distressing, °harmful, °hurtful, °injurious, damaging, wounding, traumatizing

travel *n.* **1** °traveling, tourism, touring, globe-trotting **2** ***travels.*** trips, expeditions, journeys, excursions, tours, voyages, touring, treks, trekking, °traveling, wanderings, peregrinations, junkets, pilgrimages —*v.* **3** °journey, °go, °move, °proceed, °roam, rove, °traverse, °tour, take *or* make a trip *or* tour *or* excursion *or* junket *or* journey, trek, voyage **4** °go, °move, °socialize, °fraternize, °associate, *Colloq* hang around *or* about

traveler *n.* °tourist, voyager, °sightseer, globe-trotter, gypsy, wanderer, hiker, °rover, wayfarer, *Jocular* bird of passage, *Colloq* rubberneck(er), jet-setter, *Chiefly Brit* tripper, day-tripper, holiday-maker

traveling *adj.* itinerant, wandering, peripatetic, roving, °mobile, nomadic, touring, wayfaring, migratory, °restless

traverse *v.* **1** °cross, crisscross, travel *or* pass *or* move over *or* through, °walk, °cover, °roam, °wander, °range, °tramp, °tour **2** °cross, crisscross, go across; lie *or* extend across *or* athwart, °bridge, intersect **3** °oppose, °cross, °thwart, go *or* act against, go *or* act in opposition *or* counter to, °conflict (with), controvert, contravene, °counter, °obstruct, °contradict, gainsay, °deny **4** °examine, °look into, °scrutinize, °inspect, °investigate, °review, °study, °look at, °consider,

°contemplate, °scan, °look over, °check, °survey, °reconnoiter, °observe

treasure *n.* **1** °wealth, °riches, °money, °fortune, valuables, °cash, °cache, °hoard **2** °pride (and joy), °delight, °joy, °darling, °ideal, apple of (someone's) eye, *Colloq* °jewel, °gem, °prize, °find, °catch —*v.* **3** hold dear, °cherish, value, °prize, °esteem, rate *or* value highly

treasury *n.* exchequer, bank, °cache, °resources, °funds, money(s)

treat *v.* **1** °handle, °manage, behave *or* act toward(s), °deal with; °use **2** °handle, °manage, °deal with, °discuss, touch on *or* upon, °consider, °take up, °study, °examine, °explore, °investigate, °scrutinize, °analyze, °go into, °probe, °survey, expound (on), °criticize, °review, critique **3** °nurse, °doctor, °attend, °care for, °look after, prescribe for, medicate **4** °entertain, °take out, °pay for, °regale, play host to; wine and dine **5** ***treat (someone) to (something).*** pay (the bill) for, buy (something) for —*n.* **6** °favor, °gift, °present, °boon, °bonus, °premium, *Colloq US and Canadian* freebie

treatment *n.* **1** Often, ***treatment of.*** behavior (toward(s)), conduct (toward(s)), action (toward(s)), handling (of), °care (of), °management (of), dealing(s) (with), manipulation (of), °reception (of); °usage (of) **2** °therapy, °care, curing, remedying, healing

treaty *n.* °pact, °agreement, °alliance, concordat, entente, covenant, °deal, °contract, °compact, °accord

tremble *v.* **1** °quiver, °shake, °quake, °shiver, °shudder, °quaver, quail; °vibrate, °rock —*n.* **2** °quiver, °shake, °quake, °shiver, °shudder, °quaver, tremor; vibration

tremulous *adj.* **1** trembling, atremble, quivering, shaking, quaking, shivering, shuddering, quavering, °hesitant, wavering, unsure, unsteady, faltering, °doubtful, °nervous, °shaky, palpitating, °jumpy, *Colloq* jittery **2** °timid, °shy, °bashful, °anxious, °worried, timorous, °fearful, °afraid, frightened, °scared

trenchant *adj.* °cutting, °keen, °acute, °sharp, °pointed, °poignant, °penetrating, °incisive, °biting, mordant, mordacious, °sarcastic, °bitter, acerbic, acid, vitriolic, °tart, acrid, acrimonious, acidulous, corrosive, °caustic

trend *n.* **1** °tendency, °leaning, °bias, °bent, °drift, °course, °inclination, °direction **2** °fashion, °style, °vogue, °mode, °look, °rage, *Colloq* °fad, °craze, °thing —*v.* **3** °tend, °lean, be biased, °bend, °drift, °incline, veer, °turn, °swing, °shift, °head

trendy *adj.* **1** °fashionable, °stylish, à la mode, °modern, °up to date, up to the minute, in vogue, voguish, all the rage, *Slang* °hot, °now, with it, groovy, in the groove, in, °flash —*n.* **2** °showoff, clotheshorse, coxcomb, exhibitionist, *Slang Brit* pseud, grandstander

trial *n.* **1** °test, testing, °experiment, °proof, tryout, trying out, trial run, °examination, °check, checking, *Colloq* dry run **2** hearing, enquiry *or* inquiry, °examination, inquisition, °litigation, judicial proceeding, lawsuit, °contest **3** °try, °attempt, °endeavor, °effort, °venture, °essay, *Colloq* °go, °shot, °stab, °fling, whirl, °crack, whack **4** °trouble, °affliction, tribulation, °hardship, adversity, °suffering, °grief, °woe, °misery, °distress, bad *or* hard luck, °misfortune, hard times **5** °nuisance, irritation, °bother, bane, °annoyance, °pest, irritant, thorn in the flesh *or* side, *US* bur *or* burr under the saddle, *Colloq* °plague, hassle, °pain (in the neck), °headache, *Taboo slang* pain in the *Brit* arse *or US* ass —*adj.* **6** °sample, °experimental, exploratory, °provisional, probationary, °tentative, conditional, °pilot

tribe *n.* °race, °stock, °strain, °nation, °breed, °people, °seed, °(ethnic) group, gens, °clan, blood, °pedigree, °family, sept, °dynasty, °house; °caste, °class

tribunal *n.* court (of justice), °bar, bench, judiciary, Inquisition, Star Chamber

tributary *n.* °branch, °offshoot, streamlet, feeder, °brook, rivulet, °run, rill, runnel, runlet, streamlet, *Scots and Northern England* °burn, *Northern England* beck, *US* °creek, *Northeastern US* °kill

tribute *n.* **1** °honor, °homage, °recognition, °celebration, °respect, °esteem, °testimonial, °compliment, encomium, °acknowledgment, acclaim, acclamation, commendation, °praise, °kudos, laudation, panegyric, °eulogy, glorification, exaltation **2** °tax, exaction, impost, °duty, excise, levy, °dues, assessment, °tariff, °charge, surcharge, °payment, contribution, °offering, °gift; °ransom; tithe, Peter's *or* Peter pence

trick *n.* **1** °ruse, °artifice, °device, °stratagem, °wile, °deception, °maneuver, °deceit, °fraud, °hoax, imposture, °intrigue, °machination, °conspiracy, °subterfuge, °dodge, confidence trick, °sham, *Slang* con **2** °prank, °frolic, antic, °(practical) joke, °hoax, tomfoolery, °caper, jape; °sport, horseplay, °mischief; *Scots* cantrip, *Colloq* leg-pull, °gag, shenanigans, *US* dido **3** °art, °knack, °technique, °skill, °secret, °gift, °ability, *Colloq* °hang **4** Usually, ***no + (adj.) + trick.*** °feat, °accomplishment, °deed **5** sleight of hand, legerdemain, °magic, °stunt **6** °trait, °characteristic, °peculiarity, idiosyncrasy, °eccentricity, °quirk, °practice, °habit, °mannerism, crotchet, °weakness, °foible **7** ***do the trick.*** °work, °answer, fulfill the need, °suffice, be effective, solve *or* take care of the problem, do *or* accomplish the necessary, *US* turn the trick, *Colloq* fill the bill —*v.* **8** °fool, °hoodwink, °dupe, °mislead, °outwit, outmaneuver, °deceive, misguide, °misinform, gull, bilk, °cheat, °defraud, cozen, °take in, °swindle, humbug, *Colloq* bamboozle, °take, put something over on (someone), pull the wool over (someone's) eyes, *Brit* gammon, *Slang* rook —*adj.* **9** See **tricky, 3,** below.

trickery *n.* °chicanery, °deception, °deceit,

guile, shrewdness, craftiness, slyness, shiftiness, evasiveness, artfulness, °artifice, °craft, imposture, swindling, knavery, duplicity, double-dealing, °fraud, cheating, *Colloq* °hanky-panky, skulduggery, funny *or* monkey business, jiggery-pokery

trickle *v.* **1** °drip, °drop, dribble, drizzle, °run, °flow, °spill; °ooze, seep, °leak, exude —*n.* **2** °drip, seepage, °spill, dribble, runnel, runlet, rivulet

tricky *adj.* **1** °deceitful, °shady, °deceptive, °shifty, °dodgy, °artful, guileful, °crafty, duplicitous, °shrewd, cunning, °dishonest, °devious, °sly, °wily, °slippery, °foxy, double-dealing, cheating **2** °ticklish, °risky, °hazardous, °sensitive, °delicate, touch-and-go, °thorny, °difficult, °awkward, complex, °complicated, knotty, °uncertain, °debatable, *Colloq* iffy, °sticky **3** unfair, unjust, unsportsmanlike, °deceptive, *Colloq* °trick

trifle *n.* **1** knickknack *or* nicknack, trinket, °bauble, bagatelle, °toy, °gewgaw, °nothing, °plaything, bêtise, *Colloq* doodah **2** °little, °bit, °drop, iota, scintilla, °suggestion, °dash, °dab, °pinch, whiff, mite, whit, °jot, tittle, *Colloq* smidgen, *US* tad —*v.* **3** Usually, ***trifle with.*** dally (with), °flirt (with), °wanton (with), mess about (with), °toy (with); °play (with), °fiddle (with), dandle, °tinker (with), °fidget (with)

trifling *adj.* trivial, °insignificant, unimportant, °puny, °minor, °paltry, °slight, °petty, °inconsequential, °frivolous, °superficial, °incidental, °negligible, commonplace, inconsiderable, °shallow, valueless, °worthless, *US and Canadian* picayune, *Colloq* piddling

trim *adj.* **1** °neat, °tidy, °orderly, well-ordered, °well-groomed, well-turned-out, well-kempt, °smart, °crisp, °dapper, spick-and-span *or* spic-and-span, °spruce, °shipshape (and Bristol fashion), *Archaic or dialectal* trig, *Colloq* natty, *US* spiffy **2** in good *or* fine fettle, °fit (as a fiddle), athletic, °slim, °slender, clean-cut, °shapely, °streamlined, °compact —*v.* **3** °curtail, °shorten, °prune, °pare, °lop (off), crop, bob, °clip, °cut, °shave, shear, °snip, °dock; barber **4** °decorate, °embellish, °dress up, embroider, adorn, °ornament, deck out, caparison, °beautify —*n.* **5** trimming, edging, piping, purfling, rickrack, embroidery, °border, hem, °frill, °fringe, °ornament, ornamentation, °decoration, °embellishment, adornment **6** °condition, °state, fettle, °health, °form, °order, °fitness, °repair, *Colloq* °shape

trio *n.* threesome, trilogy, triad, triplex, triple, troika, triptych, triumvirate, triplet, trine, triune, trinity, three

trip *n.* **1** °stumble, °slip, °blunder, false step, °misstep, °fall **2** °stumble, °slip, °blunder, false step, °misstep, faux pas, °error, °mistake, °indiscretion, °lapse, °slip of the tongue, *lapsus linguae,* erratum, °oversight; Freudian slip; *Slang Brit* boob **3** °tour, °journey, °excursion, °outing, °expedition, voyage, trek, peregrination, jaunt, junket, °drive —*v.* **4** °dance, °caper, °skip, °cavort, gambol, °frisk, °hop, °spring **5** °stumble, °slip, °blunder, °misstep, °fall (down), °tumble, °topple, °dive, °plunge, °sprawl, °lurch, °flounder, °stagger, falter **6** Often, ***trip up.*** °trap, °trick, catch out, unsettle, °throw off, disconcert **7** °journey, °travel, voyage, °visit, °tour, trek, sightsee, °cruise; *Colloq* globe-trot **8** detonate, °set off, trigger, °operate, °release, °explode, °spark off **9** Often, ***trip out.*** hallucinate, *Slang* freak out, °turn on

triumph *n.* **1** °victory, °conquest, °success, °achievement, °accomplishment, attainment, coup, ascendancy **2** exultation, rejoicing, exulting, elation, °delight, °rapture, exhilaration, jubilation, °happiness, °joy, °celebration, °glory —*v.* **3** Often, ***triumph over.*** °win, °succeed, carry the day, be victorious, gain a victory, take the honors, °thrive, °dominate, °prevail; °defeat, °beat, °rout, vanquish, °best, °conquer, °overcome, °overwhelm, °subdue

triumphal *adj.* celebratory, °rapturous, jubilant, °joyful, °glorious, °exultant; commemorative

triumphant *adj.* °victorious, °successful, conquering, °winning; undefeated

triviality *n.* **1** smallness, unimportance, insignificance, meaninglessness, inconsequentiality *or* inconsequentialness *or* inconsequence *or* inconsequentness, trivialness, pettiness, paltriness **2** °trifle, technicality, °nonessential, small matter, unimportant *or* insignificant *or* inconsequential *or* trivial *or* petty detail, bêtise

trivialize *v.* °belittle, denigrate, lessen, °minimize, undervalue, °depreciate, °underestimate, underrate, °make light of, laugh off, underplay, °dismiss, °disparage, misprize, °beggar, deprecate, °slight, scoff at, °scorn, °run down, decry, *Colloq* °put down, °play down, pooh-pooh

trophy *n.* **1** °prize, laurel(s), wreath, cup, °award, °reward, honor(s), medal, citation, palm, bays; °booty, °spoils, *Colloq* gold, °silver, silverware **2** °memento, souvenir, °token, °record, °reminder, °remembrance, °keepsake

trot *v.* **1** °jog, °run; bustle, °hustle, °hurry, °hasten, scamper, scoot, *Colloq* skedaddle **2** ***trot out.*** °bring out, °show, °display, °exhibit, °flaunt, come out with; dredge up, drag out; °recite, °repeat —*n.* **3** °jog, lope, single-foot, °pace; °run **4** °translation, °gloss, °interpretation, crib, *Colloq US* pony, horse

trouble *v.* **1** °bother, °upset, °anguish, °alarm, °worry, °afflict, °agitate, disquiet, °discomfit, make uncomfortable, °grieve, °perturb, discommode, °inconvenience, discompose, discountenance, °put out, °burden, °encumber, °weigh down **2** °annoy, °irritate, °irk, vex, °bother, °plague, °pester, °torment, °harass, hector, harry, °provoke, nettle, °exasperate, °ruffle, *Colloq* get *or* grate on (someone's) nerves, give (someone) a hard time, get under (someone's) skin **3** discommode, incommode, °impose on, °inconvenience, °put out, °thank 4 °care, be concerned, take the trouble *or* the time, go to the trouble, °bother, °exert (oneself), °concern (oneself), take pains —*n.* 5 °distress, °worry, °concern, °difficulty, °discomfort, unpleasantness, °inconvenience, vexation, °grief, °woe, °affliction, disquiet, °suffering, tribulation, °anxiety, °torment, °anguish, °strife 6 °annoyance, °bother, tormentor, irritation, °nuisance, °nag, heckler, °pest, *Slang US* nudnik 7 °disorder, °agitation, °row, °disturbance, turbulence, °tumult, °upset, °dissatisfaction, °unrest, °discord, °dispute, turmoil, rebellion, °revolt, °uprising, outbreak, fighting, °fight, skirmishing, °skirmish 8 °affliction, °defect, °disability, °disease, °ailment, °illness, sickness, °disorder, °complaint 9 ***in trouble.*** **(a)** in deep trouble, in a mess, in a predicament, in dire straits, *Colloq* in a pickle, in hot water, on the spot, in a scrape, *Slang Brit* in shtuk *or* shtuck *or* schtuck, *Taboo slang* in deep shit, up shit creek (without (the vestige of) a paddle) **(b)** unmarried *or* unwed and impregnated *or* pregnant *or* with child *or* expecting *or* in a delicate condition *or Colloq* in a family way

troublemaker *n.* mischief-maker, °rabble-rouser, gadfly, firebrand, *agent provocateur*, stormy petrel, incendiary, gossipmonger, scandalmonger, malcontent, instigator, meddler, °agitator

troublesome *adj.* worrisome, worrying, annoying, °irksome, irritating, vexatious, bothersome, distressing, °difficult, °burdensome, *Colloq* pestiferous, *US and Canadian* pesky

truant *n.* 1 malingerer, °runaway, absentee, °delinquent, dodger, shirker, °idler, °loafer, layabout, *Slang Brit* skiver, *Brit military* scrimshanker —*adj.* 2 malingering, °runaway, °absent, absentee, °delinquent, shirking, loafing, *Slang Brit* skiving

truce *n.* 1 armistice, cease-fire, suspension of hostilities, °lull, °moratorium, °respite, °letup, °intermission, °interval, °interlude 2 °pact, °treaty, °compact, °agreement, cease-fire, armistice

truck *n.* 1 °merchandise, commodities, °goods, °stock, °wares, °stuff, °odds and ends, °sundries, °junk, °rubbish, *US* °trash 2 dealing(s), °traffic, °business, °transaction, °trade, °commerce, communication, °contact, °connection, (business *or* social) relations

truckle *v.* °kowtow, be obsequious, toady, °defer, °bow, °scrape, genuflect, salaam, drop to the ground *or* to (one's) knees *or* down on (one's) knees, °submit, °yield, cower, °cringe, grovel, °crawl, quail, fawn (on *or* upon), *Colloq* butter up, fall all over, lick (someone's) boots, bootlick, *US* apple-polish, *Slang* suck up to, *Taboo slang* brown-nose, kiss (someone's) *Brit* arse *or US* ass

truculent *adj.* °surly, °sullen, bad-tempered, ill-tempered, unpleasant, °nasty, °obstreperous, °rude, unpleasant, °ferocious, °fierce, °savage, feral, barbarous, °harsh, °scathing, °virulent, combative, °belligerent, antagonistic, bellicose, °hostile, contentious, °warlike, °violent, °pugnacious, *Colloq* scrappy

true *adj.* 1 °accurate, °correct, °truthful, °faithful, °literal, °authentic, veracious, °actual, °factual, °realistic, °genuine, °right, valid, unelaborated, °unvarnished, unadulterated, verified, verifiable 2 °staunch, °faithful, °devoted, dedicated, °loyal, °fast, °firm, unswerving, °steady, °steadfast, °trustworthy, trusty, °dutiful, °upright, °honorable, °constant, unwavering, °stable, dependable, °sincere, °reliable, trueblue 3 °proper, °exact, °accurate, unerring, °correct, °precise, °right, *Slang Brit* spot on —*adv.* 4 °truly, truthfully, °honestly, accurately, candidly, frankly, °sincerely, straightforwardly 5 °exactly, correctly; geographically 6 ***come true.*** °come to pass, °occur, °take, °place, °happen, be realized, become a reality, be fulfilled

truism *n.* commonplace, platitude, bromide, axiom, °cliché, °maxim

truly *adv.* 1 truthfully, °actually, °really, °honestly, °in fact, °in truth, in actuality, °in reality, in all honesty, °sincerely, genuinely 2 °properly, rightly, rightfully, justly, legitimately, justifiably, °duly, well and truly, accurately 3 °definitely, °really, °actually, °undoubtedly, indubitably, beyond (the shadow of) a doubt, beyond question, without a doubt, °indeed, unquestionably, °absolutely, °positively, decidedly, certainly, °surely 4 °in truth, °indeed, °really, °honestly, °sincerely, genuinely, *Archaic* (yea), verily, *Usually ironic* forsooth

trunk *n.* 1 main stem, °stalk, °stock, *Technical* bole 2 torso, °body 3 °chest, locker, footlocker, °box, °case, bin, coffer, °casket 4 snout, proboscis 5 (*In the US and Canada*) luggage compartment, *Brit* °boot

trust *n.* 1 °confidence, °reliance, °faith, °conviction, certitude, °certainty, sureness, positiveness, °assurance, °belief 2 °credit, reliability, dependability, credibility, trustworthiness 3 °custody, °care, keeping, °charge, guardianship, °protection, °safekeeping, trusteeship 4 monopoly, cartel; °group, corporation, conglomerate —*v.* 5 rely (on *or* upon), have faith *or* confidence (in), confide (in), depend *or* bank *or* count (on *or* upon), pin (one's) faith *or* hopes on *or* upon 6 °entrust, °commit, °give, °delegate, make *or* turn *or* sign *or* hand over, depute, °assign, empower, consign

trusting *adj.* trustful, unsuspicious, confiding, °confident, °unsuspecting; naive *or* naïve *or* naïf, °innocent, °gullible, incautious, credulous

trustworthy *adj.* °reliable, trusty, dependable, °accurate; °responsible, °steady, °steadfast, °loyal, °faithful, °(tried and) true, °honorable, °honest, °ethical, °principled, °moral, incorruptible

truth *n.* 1 genuineness, °reality, actuality,

correctness, °accuracy, °fact **2** fact(s) **3** ***in truth.*** °in fact, °truly, °actually, °really

truthful *adj.* °true, °accurate, °factual, veracious, true-to-life, °honest, °realistic, °reliable, °faithful, °trustworthy, straightforward, °candid, °frank, °sincere, °earnest, °forthright, °unvarnished, unembellished

try *v.* **1** °attempt, °endeavor, °essay, °seek, °undertake, °venture, °strive, °struggle, make an effort, try (one's) hand at, *Colloq* have a stab *or* go *or* whack (at), take a shot *or* crack (at) **2** °test, try out, °prove, °evaluate, °examine, °inspect, °check out, °sample, appraise, assay, °look over, °analyze, °scrutinize, assess, °judge **3** °test, °prove, °strain, °tax **4** °hear, °sit on, adjudicate, °judge, adjudge —*n.* **5** °attempt, °endeavor, °essay, °undertaking, °venture, °struggle, °effort, °turn, *Colloq* °go, °stab, whack, °fling, °shot, °crack

trying *adj.* irritating, exasperating, frustrating, annoying, °irksome, infuriating, maddening, bothersome, °tiresome, vexing, °troublesome, worrying, worrisome, distressing, disquieting, upsetting, dispiriting, taxing, °demanding, °tough, stressful, °difficult, tiring, fatiguing

tug *v.* **1** °pull, °tow, °yank, °jerk, °draw, °drag, °haul, °wrench —*n.* **2** °pull, °tow, °yank, °jerk, °drag, °haul, °wrench

tuition *n.* °education, teaching, tutelage, training, °schooling, °instruction, °guidance, °preparation

tumble *v.* **1** °fall (down), °pitch, turn end over end *or* head over heels, °roll, °drop **2** °drop, °toss, °dump, °jumble **3** ***tumble to.*** °understand, apprehend, °perceive, °comprehend, see the light, *Colloq* get the signal *or* message, °catch on, *Brit* twig to, *Slang* get wise, wise up, °dig —*n.* **4** °fall, °slip, °stumble, *Colloq* header, °spill

tumble-down *adj.* °ramshackle, °dilapidated, ruined, in ruins, °decrepit, °rickety, °shaky, falling apart *or* to pieces, disintegrating, tottering, broken-down, crumbling, gone to rack and ruin

tumor *n.* neoplasm, cancer, melanoma, sarcoma, malignancy, carcinoma, °growth, °lump, °swelling, protuberance, excrescence

tumult *n.* commotion, °disturbance, °upset, °uproar, °riot, °disorder, disquiet, insurrection, °agitation, °bedlam, °chaos, brouhaha, °fracas, hubbub, °stir, °pandemonium, hullabaloo, °furor, °brawl, donnybrook, affray, °row, melee *or* mêlée, turbulence, °ferment, ado, turmoil, °confusion, °rampage, °frenzy, °rage, °excitement, °rumpus, *Colloq US* ruckus

tumultuous *adj.* clamorous, °noisy, °boisterous, °disorderly, turbulent, °violent, °uproarious, °chaotic, frenzied, °furious, °excited, °agitated, °hectic, °riotous, °rowdy, °unruly, unrestrained, °fierce, °savage, °wild, °hysterical, °frantic, rumbustious, °obstreperous, °tempestuous, °stormy

tune *n.* **1** °melody, °air, °song, °strain, °motif, °theme **2** euphony, °pitch, °harmony, °accord, accordance, consonance, °unison, correspondence, conformity —*v.* **3** tune up, °calibrate, °adjust, °regulate, °coordinate, °adapt, attune, align, °set **4** ***tune in (on).*** °attend (to), pay attention (to), °listen (to), °understand, be aware (of), be on the qui vive, be alert (to), *Slang* be on the same wavelength *or* frequency (with) **5** ***tune out.*** °ignore, °disregard, turn a blind eye to, be blind to, °turn one's back on, turn a deaf ear to

tuneful *adj.* melodic, °musical, sweet-sounding, °melodious, euphonious, dulcet, mellifluent, mellifluous, harmonic, catchy, °mellow, °smooth, °rich, °rhythmic, *Colloq* easy on the ear(s)

tunnel *n.* **1** °shaft, °subway, (underground) passage(way), underpass; °burrow, °hole; *Colloq* Chunnel (= 'Channel Tunnel') —*v.* **2** °burrow, °dig, °hole, °excavate, °penetrate, °mine

turf *n.* **1** sod, sward, °green, grass, greensward, °lawn **2** °territory, bailiwick, °area, °neighborhood, back yard, *Colloq* stamping ground, home ground, °(personal) space **3** ***the turf.*** horse-racing, racing, the racing world, racecourse, racetrack

turn *v.* **1** °rotate, °revolve, °spin, °roll, °reel, °circle, °gyrate, whirl, °wheel, go (a)round *or* about, °pivot, °swivel **2** °move, °shift, °wheel, veer, °swing, °face **3** °reverse, turn (a)round, °alter, °change, °adapt, reorganize, remodel, °modify, refashion, reshape, °reform, °transform, °make over, °convert, bring over **4** go *or* pass *or* move (a)round, veer, °drive, °walk **5** go bad, become rancid, °spoil, curdle, addle, °sour, °decay, molder, °rot, °putrefy, *Colloq* °go off **6** °apply, °put, °use, °employ **7** Sometimes, ***turn aside or away.*** °block, avert, °thwart, °prevent, balk *or* baulk, parry, °deflect, °fend off, °check **8** °form, °make up, °fashion, °formulate, °construct, °cast, °create, °coin, concoct, °express **9** °direct, °aim, °point **10** °twist, sprain, °wrench **11** °twist, °wind, °snake, curve, °bend, arc, °coil, °loop, °meander, zigzag **12** ***turn against.*** °defy, °mutiny, °rebel, °revolt, rise (up) against **13** ***turn back.*** **(a)** °reverse, °repulse, °repel, °rebuff, drive back, beat back **(b)** go back, retrace (one's) steps, °return **14** ***turn down.*** **(a)** °refuse, °reject, °rebuff, °decline, °deny **(b)** decrease *or* diminish *or* lessen *or* lower *or* soften the sound of **15** ***turn in.*** **(a)** go to bed *or* sleep, °retire, °withdraw, call it a day, *Slang* hit the sack *or* the hay **(b)** hand in *or* over, °turn over, °deliver, °give in, °submit, °offer, proffer, °tender, give back, °return, °surrender, °yield **(c)** °turn over, °deliver (up), °inform on, °betray, *Colloq* squeal on, rat on, °finger, °tell on **16** ***turn into.*** **(a)** °turn to, °become, change into *or* to, metamorphose into *or* to **(b)** go *or* come into, drive into, pull into, walk into **17** ***turn off.*** **(a)** °stop, switch off, deactivate, °discontinue; °extinguish **(b)** °disillusion, °depress, °cool (off), disenchant, disaffect, °alienate, °repel, °repulse, °bore, °offend, °put off, displease, °sicken, °nauseate, °disgust **(c)** °deviate, °diverge **18** ***turn on.*** **(a)** °start (up), switch on, °energize, °activate, set in motion, cause to function *or* operate **(b)** depend on *or* upon, be contingent upon *or* on, hinge on *or* upon, be subject to **(c)** °excite, °thrill, °arouse, °stimulate, titillate, °work up, impassion **19** ***turn on or upon.*** **(a)** °concern, revolve about, °relate to **(b)** be hostile to, °attack, assail, °set upon, *Colloq* tear into **20** ***turn out.*** **(a)** °make, °form, °shape, °construct, °build, °fabricate, put together, °assemble, °manufacture, °produce, °put out, °bring out **(b)** °develop, evolve, eventuate, °happen, °result, °prove, °occur, end up, °arise **(c)** °eject, °evict, °throw out, °expel, oust, °dismiss, °terminate, cashier, *Colloq* °fire, °sack, kick out, ax, *Brit* turf out **(d)** °dress, fit out, °equip, °rig out, accoutre *or US also* accouter **(e)** °come, °arrive, °appear, °attend, °assemble, °meet, *Colloq* °show (up), °surface **21** ***turn over.*** **(a)** °consider, muse *or* ruminate over *or* about, °revolve, °ponder (over) **(b)** °reverse, invert, turn upside down **(c)** °overturn, °upset, knock over **(d)** °sell, °merchandise **22** ***turn tail.*** °run away, °flee, °bolt, scoot, show a clean pair of heels, cut and run, take to (one's) heels, beat a hasty retreat, *Colloq* °take off, °beat it, scram, skedaddle **23** ***turn to.*** **(a)** appeal to, apply to, °resort to **(b)** advert to, °refer to, pick *or* take up, have recourse to **(c)** get to work, °pitch in, buckle *or* knuckle down **(d)** °turn into, °change to, convert to, °become **24** ***turn turtle.*** °capsize, °overturn, keel over, °upset, upend, *Colloq* go bottoms up **25** ***turn up.*** **(a)** °surface, °appear, °arrive, *Colloq* °show (up), °show one's face **(b)** °come up, °arise, *Colloq* crop up, pop up **(c)** uncover, °discover, °find, °unearth, °come across, °hit upon, °dig up, °expose, °disclose, °reveal, °bring to light **(d)** increase *or* raise *or* amplify *or* intensify the sound of —*n.* **26** °revolution, rotation, °cycle, °spin, whirl, °circuit, °round, °roll, °twirl; °pirouette **27** curve, °bend, turning, corner, sinuosity, dogleg, hairpin bend *or* curve, irregularity, °meander, °twist, zigzag, *Colloq* to-ing and fro-ing **28** °loop, °coil, °spiral, °twist **29** deviation, turning, °detour, °shift, change of direction *or* course **30** opportunity, °chance, °say, °round, °spell, °time, °watch, °shift, °stint, °tour (of duty), °move, °trick, *Colloq* whack, °crack, °shot, go **31** °drive, °spin, °ride; airing, constitutional, °ramble, °saunter, °stroll, °walk, °promenade, amble **32** °trend, °direction, °drift **33** °change, °alteration, °switch **34** Usually, ***bad turn.*** °disservice, °harm, °injury, °wrong **35** Usually, ***good turn.*** °favor, °(good) deed, °act (of kindness), °courtesy, °boon, °mercy **36** °shock, °fright, °surprise, °start, °scare **37** °form, °style, °manner, °mode **38** °disposition, °inclination, °bent, °bias, °leaning, °tendency **39** ***at every turn.*** °everywhere, constantly, °always, °all the time **40** ***by turns.*** alternately, reciprocally, in rotation, successively, °in succession **41** ***in turn.*** sequentially, one after the other, °in succession, successively, in (proper) order **42** ***out of turn.*** **(a)** out of sequence, °out of order **(b)** imprudently, indiscreetly, improperly, disobediently, inappropriately **43** ***take turns.*** °alternate, °vary, °rotate, °exchange

turnabout *n.* reciprocity, °exchange

turncoat *n.* °renegade, °traitor, betrayer, °deserter, fifth columnist, double agent, apostate, tergiversator, °defector, backslider, Vicar of Bray, *US* Benedict Arnold, *Colloq* snake in the grass

turnoff *n.* **1** °exit, side road, feeder (road), °auxiliary (road), °ramp, *Brit* slip road, *US* (exit *or* entrance) ramp **2** damper, °killjoy, *Colloq* wet blanket, *Slang US* freeze-out

turnout *n.* **1** assemblage, °muster, °attendance, audience, °crowd, °gate, °throng, °gathering **2** °output, °production, outturn, °volume; gross national product, GNP, gross domestic product, GDP **3** °gear, °outfit, clothing, °apparel, °apparatus, °equipment, °trappings, °fittings, equipage

turnover *n.* °gross (revenue), °(total) business, °volume

tutor *n.* **1** °teacher, °instructor, educator, °coach, mentor, guru —*v.* **2** °teach, °instruct, °coach, °educate, °school, °train, °indoctrinate, °drill, °enlighten, °advise, °direct, °guide, °prepare, °ground

tweak *v.* **1** °pinch, °nip, twitch, °squeeze, °jerk, °grip —*n.* **2** °pinch, °nip, twitch, °squeeze, °jerk, °grip

twiddle *v.* **1** °play with, °twirl, °fiddle (with), wiggle, °juggle, °toy with, fidget with, *Colloq* °fool with, °mess with, monkey with **2** ***twiddle (one's) thumbs.*** do nothing, be idle, idle *or* while away (the) time, waste time, bide (one's) time

twig[1] *n.* sprig, °stem, °shoot, °offshoot, branchlet, °stick, °sucker, °sprout, withe *or* withy, tendril

twig[2] *v.* °understand, °grasp, °fathom, °get, °comprehend, °see, °know, °sense, °divine, *Colloq* °catch on, be *or* get *or* become wise to, °tumble to, *Slang* rumble, °dig

twilight *n.* **1** °dusk, sunset, gloaming, sundown, half-light, crepuscule *or* crepuscle **2** °decline, °wane, waning, °ebb, downturn, downswing, °slump, °decay, weakening, declination, diminution **3** ***Twilight of the Gods.*** Götterdämmerung, Ragnarök *or* Ragnarok —*adj.* **4** °evening, crepuscular, dimming, darkening, darkish, darksome, °shadowy, °shady, °dim, °dark, °obscure, °somber, °gloomy, *Literary* darkling **5** ***twilight zone.*** °limbo

twin *n.* **1** °double, clone, °duplicate, °lookalike, counterpart, *Slang* ringer —*adj.* **2** °identical, °matching, matched, °duplicate, corresponding, °lookalike —*v.* **3** °pair,

°match, yoke, °join, °link, °couple, °combine, °connect, °associate

twine *n.* **1** °cord, °string; °rope, °cable, °yarn —*v.* **2** °entwine, °braid, °twist, intertwine, curl, wreathe, °spiral, °wind, °weave, interweave, °encircle, °wrap

twinge *n.* **1** °stab, °pang, cramp, °spasm, °pinch, stitch, °(sharp) pain, °prick, °bite, °gripe **2** °pang, °pain

twinkle *v.* **1** scintillate, °sparkle, coruscate, °glitter, °shimmer, wink, °flicker, °glisten, glint, °flash, fulgurate, °spark, °dance, °blink, °shine, °gleam —*n.* **2** °twinkling, scintillation, °scintillating, °sparkle, sparkling, coruscation, coruscating, °glitter, glittering, °shimmer, shimmering, winking, °flicker, flickering, glistening, glint, °flash, flashing, fulguration, °spark, sparking, dancing, blinking, °shine, shining, °gleam, gleaming, °dazzle, °dazzling

twinkling *n.* **1** °(split) second, °flash, twinkling *or* wink of an eye, °instant, trice, *Colloq* jiffy, two shakes (of a lamb's tail), tick **2** See **twinkle, 2,** above.

twirl *v.* **1** °spin, whirl, °rotate, °revolve, °wheel, °turn, °gyrate, °twist, wind (about *or* around) —*n.* **2** twirling, °spin, spinning, whirl, whirling, °turn, turning, °revolution **3** whorl, winding, convolution, °spiral, helix, °coil, volute

twist *v.* **1** plait, °braid, °weave, °entwine, intertwine, °twine, interweave, pleach, °splice, wreathe, interlace **2** °distort, °warp, contort, °pervert, °alter, °change, °slant, °bias, °color, °falsify, misquote, misstate, °garble, miscite, °misrepresent, °violate; °misinterpret, mistranslate, °misunderstand, misconstrue **3** °wriggle, worm, °squirm, writhe, wiggle **4** °wind, °snake, °meander, °turn, zigzag, worm, °bend, curve **5** °wrench, °turn, sprain, rick *or* wrick **6** ***twist (one's or someone's) arm.*** °force, coerce, °make, °persuade, °bully, *Brit* pressurize, *US* °pressure —*n.* **7** °coil, °spiral, skew, zigzag, dogleg, °turn, curve, °angle, °bend, °bow, °meander **8** °interpretation, °analysis, °understanding, °slant, °angle, construction, construal; °treatment, °approach, °version, °variation **9** distortion, misinterpretation, contortion, °perversion, warping, °alteration, °change, departure, °bias, coloring, falsification, misquotation, °misstatement, garbling, misrepresentation; mistranslation, °misunderstanding, misconstrual, misconstruction **10** °quirk, idiosyncrasy, crotchet, °peculiarity, °oddity, °trick, °eccentricity, incongruity, inconsistency, irregularity; °weakness, °flaw, °fault, °foible, °failing **11** ***round the twist.*** °mad, °crazy, °insane, °eccentric, *Colloq* °daft, balmy, *Brit* round the bend, *Slang* nuts, nutty, bonkers, cuckoo, batty, off (one's) rocker, *Brit* barmy

twister *n.* tornado, cyclone, typhoon, °hurricane, °whirlwind; waterspout

twit[1] *v.* °tease, °cajole, °taunt, °jeer (at), °make fun of, °banter, °tweak, gibe *or* jibe, °chaff, °ridicule, °mock; °blame, °berate, °deride, °scorn, contemn, censure, revile, reproach, °upbraid; *Colloq* kid, pull (someone's) leg

twit[2] *n.* nitwit, nincompoop, ass, ninny, ninnyhammer, °fool, imbecile, blockhead, °halfwit, idiot, simpleton, *Colloq* chump, moron, *Brit* silly-billy, *Slang* °dope, *US and Canadian* °jerk

twitter *v.* **1** °peep, cheep, tweet, °chirp, warble, trill, chirrup, °chatter **2** °chatter, °prattle, °gossip, °giggle, prate, °titter, °snicker, snigger, simper —*n.* **3** °peep, peeping, cheep, cheeping, twittering, tweet, tweeting, chirrup, chirruping, °chirp, chirping, warble, warbling, trill, trilling **4** ado, bustle, °excitement, °flutter, dither, whirl, °agitation, *Colloq* °stew, tizzy

two-faced *adj.* double-dealing, °hypocritical, duplicitous, dissembling, °deceitful, Janus-faced, treacherous, °dishonest, untrustworthy, °insincere, °scheming, °designing, °crafty, Machiavellian, °sly, °perfidious, °lying, mendacious

tycoon *n.* °mogul, magnate, baron, °financier, (multi)millionaire, billionaire, merchant prince, potentate, *Colloq* big shot, °(big-time) operator, wheeler-dealer, big-timer, *US* big wheel, big cheese

type *n.* **1** °class, °category, classification, °kind, °sort, °genre, °order, °variety, °breed, species, °strain, °group, genus, ilk, kidney **2** typeface, *Brit* fount, *US* font **3** °prototype, paradigm, archetype, °epitome, exemplar, °model, °specimen, °pattern, personification, °standard, °quintessence —*v.* **4** typewrite; keyboard; °transcribe

typical *adj.* **1** °representative, °characteristic, °conventional, °normal, °standard, °ordinary, °regular **2** °orthodox, °classic, °conventional, °in character, in keeping, °usual, commonplace, °run-of-the-mill, °natural, °customary, °common, to be expected, °ordinary

typify *v.* °exemplify, °instance, epitomize, °personify, °represent, °characterize, °embody, evince, °symbolize, °suggest

tyrannical *adj.* tyrannous, °oppressive, °dictatorial, fascistic, °despotic, autocratic, °authoritarian, °arbitrary, imperious, °overbearing, unjust, highhanded, °severe, °harsh, ironhanded, °heavy-handed

tyrannize *v.* Often, ***tyrannize over.*** domineer over, °bully, °subjugate, °enslave, °dominate, °intimidate, dictate to, order about *or* around, ride roughshod over, °browbeat, keep under (one's) thumb, °oppress, °subdue, °suppress, keep down, *Archaic* enthrall

tyranny *n.* autocracy, fascism, authoritarianism, absolutism, °despotism, dictatorship, Stalinism, Nazism; arbitrariness, °oppression, °suppression, subjugation, enslavement, enthrallment, °domination

tyrant *n.* °dictator, °despot, autocrat, martinet, Hitler, °bully, °oppressor, °authoritarian, hard taskmaster, slave driver, Simon Legree, overlord

U

ugly *adj.* **1** unattractive, unlovely, unprepossessing, °unsightly, °hideous, °grotesque, °gruesome, °ghastly, °offensive, repulsive-looking, °plain, plain-looking, plain-featured, bad-featured, ill-favored, dreadful-looking, awful-looking, terrible-looking, horrible-looking, frightful-looking, monstrous-looking, *US and Canadian* °homely **2** objectionable, °disagreeable, unpleasant, °offensive, °nasty, °loathsome, °repellent, °repugnant, °repulsive, noisome, nauseating, nauseous, °revolting, sickening, °disgusting, °obnoxious, mephitic, °rotten, °corrupt, °filthy, °vile, heinous, °bad, °sordid, °evil, °foul, °perverted, °immoral, depraved, °degenerate, °base, debased, detestable, °hateful, °abominable, execrable, °despicable, odious **3** disquieting, uncomfortable, discomforting, °troublesome, °awkward, disadvantageous, °ominous, °dangerous, °perilous, °hazardous **4** unpleasant, °disagreeable, °surly, °hostile, °nasty, °spiteful, bad-tempered, ill-tempered, currish, irascible, curmudgeonly, °cantankerous, crabby, crabbed, crotchety, °cross, °cranky, °mean

ulcer *n.* **1** °sore, lesion, abscess, ulceration, canker, chancre, °boil, gumboil, °eruption, carbuncle, °inflammation **2** cancer, canker, festering spot, °blight, °scourge, °poison, °disease, °pestilence, °curse, bane, °plague

ulcerous *adj.* ulcerative, cancerous, cankerous, festering, ulcerated, ulcerative, suppurating, suppurative, gangrenous, septic, *Technical* furuncular, furunculous, necrotic, necrosed, sphacelated

ulterior *adj.* **1** °hidden, concealed, covert, °secret, unrevealed, undisclosed, unexpressed, °private, °personal, underlying, °surreptitious, underhand(ed) **2** °outside, beyond, °further, °remote, remoter

ultimate *adj.* **1** °final, °last, terminating, °terminal, °end, °eventual, conclusive, concluding, decisive, deciding **2** °final, °maximum, highest, greatest, °supreme, utmost, °paramount **3** °elemental, °basic, °fundamental, underlying, °primary, °essential, °final **4** remotest, farthest, °extreme, uttermost, °last, °final

ultimately *adv.* °finally, at long last, in the final *or* last analysis, in the end, at the end of the day, after all is said and done, at (the) last, °in the long run; fundamentally, essentially, basically, °at bottom

ultimatum *n.* demand(s), term(s), condition(s), stipulation(s), requirement(s)

ultra- *adj.* °extreme, °immoderate, °excessive, °drastic, °radical, fanatic(al), °unmitigated, °outrageous, °unqualified, °sheer, °blatant, °out-and-out, °complete, °thorough, thoroughgoing, dyed-in-the-wool, diehard, °rabid, °opinionated, unregenerate, °unrepentant, unreformed, fundamentalist, °prejudiced, °bigoted, *Colloq* hard-nosed

umbrage *n.* Usually, ***take umbrage.*** feel *or* be offended, °take offense, feel displeasure *or* annoyance *or* exasperation *or* indignation *or* vexation *or* bitterness *or* resentment, be piqued *or* displeased *or* annoyed *or* exasperated *or* indignant *or* vexed *or* resentful, harbor a grudge

umbrella *n.* **1** parasol; *Colloq chiefly Brit* gamp, *Brit* brolly, *US* bumbershoot **2** °protection, °cover, coverage, aegis, °shield, °screen, °patronage, °agency

umpire *n.* **1** referee, arbiter, °judge, °moderator, adjudicator, arbitrator; °official; *Colloq* ref, *Australian* umpy, *US* ump —*v.* **2** referee, arbitrate, °judge, °moderate, adjudicate; °officiate

umpteen *adj.* a lot of, °many, innumerable, unnumbered, countless, a huge number of, very many, numerous, hundreds of, thousands of, millions of, billions of, trillions of

unabashed *adj.* unashamed, unblushing, unembarrassed, °brazen, °blatant, °bold, undaunted, unawed, undismayed, unconcerned

unable *adj.* not able, °powerless, unfit, °unqualified, °impotent

unabridged *adj.* **1** uncut, °whole, full-length, °entire, °complete, °intact, uncondensed, unshortened; unbowdlerized, unexpurgated **2** °extensive, °thorough, °comprehensive, °exhaustive, all-encompassing, (all-)inclusive

unaccented *adj.* unstressed, unemphasized, unaccentuated, °weak, *Technical* lenis

unacceptable *adj.* °unsatisfactory, objectionable, °wrong, °bad, °improper, unallowable, °undesirable, not *de rigueur*, °distasteful, °disagreeable, unsuitable, °inappropriate, unpleasant, °tasteless

unaccompanied *adj.* °alone, °solo, on (one's) own, unescorted, unchaperoned, unattended, *Music* a cappella, *Colloq* stag

unaccountable *adj.* **1** unexplained, °inexplicable, unexplainable, °mysterious, inscrutable, °incomprehensible, unintelligible, °strange, °puzzling, baffling, °peculiar, °odd, °bizarre, unfathomable **2** not answerable, not responsible **3** °weird, °unheard-of, °extraordinary, °unusual, °unorthodox, uncanny

unaccustomed *adj.* **1** °unfamiliar, °unusual, °rare, unexpected, uncommon, unprecedented, unanticipated, °curious, °peculiar **2** ***unaccustomed to.*** °unused to, inexperienced in *or* at, amateurish at, unpracticed in *or* at, °unfamiliar with, uninitiated in

unadorned *adj.* °plain, °simple, unembellished, undecorated, unornamented, °stark, °bare, austere

unaffected[1] *adj.* °genuine, °real, °sincere, °natural, °simple, °plain, unpretentious, unassuming, °ingenuous, °unsophisticated, unstudied, °honest, guileless, °artless, unartificial, straightforward, unfeigned

unaffected[2] *adj.* Usually, ***unaffected by.*** impervious (to), °immune (to), untouched (by), °unmoved (by), unresponsive (to), aloof (to *or* from), uninfluenced (by), unimpressed (by), remote (to *or* from), cool *or* cold (to), unconcerned (by), unstirred (by)

unapproachable *adj.* **1** °distant, °remote, °aloof, °reserved, stand-offish, austere, °withdrawn, unfriendly, °forbidding, °chilly, °cool, °cold, °frigid **2** °inaccessible, °remote, unreachable, °out-of-the-way, out of reach, beyond reach

unarmed *adj.* unprotected, °defenseless, weaponless

unasked *adj.* uninvited, unrequested, undemanded, °unsolicited, unsought, unwanted, unprompted, °gratuitous, unbidden, °spontaneous, °unwelcome, unasked-for

unattached *adj.* **1** °separate, unconnected, °detached, °independent, unaffiliated, self-governing, self-regulating, self-regulated, autonomous, self-reliant, self-sustaining, self-sustained **2** °single, °unmarried, uncommitted, unengaged, on (one's) own, unspoken for

unauthorized *adj.* unsanctioned, unapproved, °unofficial, °unlawful, °illegal, °illicit, °illegitimate

unavoidable *adj.* inescapable, ineluctable, °inevitable, °irresistible, inexorable, °sure, °certain, °fated, °destined, predestined, °determined, °predetermined, unchangeable, unalterable, settled, °fixed, °definite

unaware *adj.* °ignorant, °oblivious, unknowing, °unsuspecting, °unconscious, °uninformed, unenlightened, incognizant, inobservant, °insensible, °heedless, unmindful, °unsuspecting

unawares *adv.* **1** unexpectedly, abruptly, by surprise, °suddenly, off (one's) guard **2** inadvertently, unconsciously, unintentionally, unknowingly, unwittingly, by mistake, mistakenly, by accident, accidentally, in an unguarded moment

unbalanced *adj.* **1** uneven, asymmetric(al), unsymmetric(al), °lopsided, unequal, overbalanced, °unstable, wobbly, °shaky, unsteady **2** °mad, demented, certifiable, °crazy, °insane, °eccentric, ***non compos mentis,*** touched (in the head), °unstable, unhinged, °deranged, °disturbed, of unsound mind, out of (one's) head, *Colloq* daffy, °dizzy, *Chiefly Brit* °daft, *Slang* nuts, batty, off (one's) rocker, *Chiefly Brit* bonkers, *US* out of one's gourd, loco

unbearable *adj.* intolerable, unsupportable, unendurable, °insufferable, °unacceptable, too much

unbeatable *adj.* unsurpassable, undefeatable, °excellent, unexcelled, °incomparable, °matchless, unrivaled, °peerless, °unparalleled, °superlative, °supreme

unbecoming *adj.* **1** unsuited, unsuitable, °inappropriate, ill-suited, unfitting, unfit, inapt, unapt, °out of character, °out of place **2** indecorous, °unseemly, indelicate, °improper, ungentlemanly, unladylike, °offensive, °tasteless

unbelievable *adj.* °incredible, °preposterous, °inconceivable, unimaginable, mind-boggling, °implausible, °unthinkable

unbelieving *adj.* °incredulous, disbelieving, nonbelieving, doubting, mistrusting, distrusting, mistrustful, °distrustful, °suspicious, °skeptical, unpersuaded, unconvinced

uncertain *adj.* **1** unsure, indeterminate, unpredictable, undeterminable, unforeseeable, unascertainable, °haphazard, °chance, °arbitrary, °random, aleatory, serendipitous, hit-or-miss, °casual **2** unsure, in *or* of two minds, vacillating, undecided, unclear, ambivalent, °irresolute, °indecisive, °hesitant, hesitating, undetermined, shilly-shallying, *Brit* °at a loose end, *US* °at loose ends **3** unsure, indeterminate, up in the air, °indefinite, unpredictable, °unresolved, °unsettled, in the balance, conjectural, °speculative, °debatable, touch-and-go, °unreliable, °doubtful, dubious, °questionable, °vague, °hazy **4** °variable, °changeable, °inconstant, unfixed, °unsettled, °irregular, °fickle, °erratic, °fitful, unsteady, wavering, °unreliable, °sporadic, °occasional; unmethodical, unsystematic

uncharted *adj.* unmapped, °unknown, unexplored, undiscovered, °strange, °unfamiliar, virgin, °trackless

unchaste *adj.* °impure, °wanton, °immoral, unvirtuous, °promiscuous, °immodest, Cyprian, debased, °lecherous, °lewd, °lascivious

uncivilized *adj.* **1** barbarous, °savage, °wild, uncultivated, °barbarian, barbaric, °crude, °primitive, brutish **2** °unrefined, uncultured, uncouth, loutish, °coarse, °uneducated, untutored, unpolished, churlish, °boorish, °philistine, °provincial, °rough, °rude, unlearned, °ill-mannered, incondite, unmannerly, °unsophisticated, inelegant, °gross, gauche

unconscionable *adj.* **1** conscienceless, °unscrupulous, amoral, unprincipled, °immoral, unethical, °evil, °criminal, unjust, °wicked, arrant **2** °excessive, extortionate, egregious, °extreme, °unwarranted, °unreasonable, °outrageous, °inordinate, °immoderate, °exorbitant, indefensible, unpardonable, °inexcusable, unforgivable

unconscious *adj.* **1** °insensible, °out (cold), knocked out, °senseless, °numb, stunned, comatose, dead to the world, *Colloq* blacked-out **2** Often, ***unconscious of.*** heedless (of *or* to), unheeding, unheedful (of), insensitive (to), °mindless, unmindful (of), reflex, °automatic, °involuntary, unintentional, °instinctive, °subliminal, °unthinking, °unpremeditated, °subconscious, unwitting; °blind (to), °unaware (of), oblivious (to *or* of), °deaf (to)

uncontrolled *adj.* unrestrained, ungoverned, unchecked, untrammeled, °undisciplined, °wild, °unruly, °boisterous, °riotous, out of hand *or* of control, °rampant, frenzied,

°frantic; going berserk, running amok *or* amuck

under *prep.* **1** °beneath, °below, underneath, covered by **2** °subordinate to, answerable to, inferior to, second to, secondary to, subservient to, °below, °beneath, underneath, junior to, directed *or* supervised *or* controlled by, under (the) control of, at the mercy of, at the beck and call of **3** included *or* comprised in *or* under, subsumed under **4** under the aegis *or* protection *or* eye *or* guardianship *or* care of **5** less than, lower than **6** ***under the influence.*** °drunk, tipsy, °high, impaired —*adv.* **7** °below, underneath, °beneath **8** underwater, beneath the waves, down, °out of sight

underclothes *n.* underclothing, underwear, undergarments, lingerie, *Old-fashioned* °unmentionables, *Colloq* underthings, undies, *Brit* smalls, *Old-fashioned Brit* small clothes, *US* skivvies

undercover *adj.* °secret, °private, clandestine, °confidential

undercurrent *n.* **1** undertow, crosscurrent, riptide, °rip (current), underflow **2** undertone, subcurrent, °trend, °tendency, °overtone, °tenor, °suggestion, °murmur, °implication, connotation, °sense, °feeling, °aura, tinge, °flavor, °atmosphere, ambiance *or* ambience; vibrations, *Colloq* °vibes

undercut *v.* **1** °undermine, °excavate, hollow out, cut out *or* away, gouge out **2** underprice, undercharge, °sacrifice, sell cheaply *or* at a loss, undersell

underdog *n.* °loser, °scapegoat, °victim; vanquished, °defenseless; *Colloq* fall guy, little fellow *or* guy

underestimate *v.* undervalue, underrate, °discount, misjudge, °miscalculate, misprize, °minimize, °depreciate, °belittle, not do justice to, fail to appreciate, set (too) little store by, think (too) little of

undergo *v.* °suffer, °bear, °endure, °experience, live *or* go through, be subjected to, subject oneself to, °sustain, °submit to, °weather, °stand, °withstand

underground *adj.* **1** subterranean, buried, below-ground, °sunken, covered **2** °secret, clandestine, concealed, °hidden, covert, °undercover, °surreptitious, °stealthy, °private **3** °alternative, °radical, °experimental, °avant-garde, °nonconformist, °revolutionary —*n.* **4** tube, metro, underground railway, *US* °subway **5** °resistance, partisans *or* partizans, freedom fighters, (in France) Maquis, insurgents, seditionaries *or* seditionists, insurrectionists, guerrillas *or* guerillas, extremists, revolutionaries; fifth columnists, fifth column, saboteurs, subversives

undermine *v.* **1** °sap, °drain, disable, °weaken, debilitate, °threaten, °sabotage, °subvert, °damage, °hurt, °harm, °impair, °ruin, °dash, °wreck, °spoil, *Slang* °queer, °bugger (up) **2** See **undercut, 1,** above.

undersized *adj.* undersize, °little, °short, °small, °petite, °tiny, °elfin, bantam, °slight, mignon; °stunted, underdeveloped, runty, runtish, dwarfish, dwarfed, pygmy, squat; underweight, °undeveloped

understand *v.* **1** °grasp, °comprehend, °see, °perceive, discern, °make out, get the drift *or* the hang of, °appreciate, °interpret, take cognizance of, °recognize, be aware *or* conscious of, be conversant with, °know, °realize, conceive of, be aware (of), apprehend, °penetrate, *Colloq* °get (it), °dig, °catch on (to), °tumble to, cotton on (to), *Brit* °twig **2** °accept, °agree, °arrange, convenant, °take **3** °interpret, °take, °read, gather from, construe, surmise from, assume from, infer from, °view, °see **4** °hear (of), °gather, get wind (of), °take it, be told *or* informed *or* advised, have found out *or* learned, *Colloq* hear tell **5** sympathize *or* empathize (with), be in sympathy (with), show compassion (for), commiserate (with); °accept, °tolerate, °allow, °forgive

understanding *n.* **1** °agreement, °contract, °arrangement, °bargain, covenant, concession, °pact, °compact, °accord, °treaty, concordat, entente, °alliance, °truce, armistice, °reconciliation, °settlement **2** discernment, °sensitivity, sensitiveness, °sympathy, empathy, °perception, °insight, good sense, °intuition, enlightenment, percipience, sagacity, sageness, sapience, °wisdom, *Colloq* savvy **3** Usually, ***understanding of.*** comprehension *or* awareness *or* grasp *or* control *or* idea *or* conception *or* knowledge *or* mastery (of), acquaintance *or* familiarity *or* intimacy *or* dexterity *or* skillfulness *or* deftness *or* adroitness *or* adeptness (with), competence *or* skill *or* expertness *or* know-how *or* proficiency *or* expertise (in), *Colloq US* °fix (on), °handle (on) **4** reading, °interpretation, °opinion, °judgment, °estimation, °notion, °view, °perception, apperception, apprehension **5** °intellect, °intelligence, °mind, °brain, brainpower, °sense, °reason, reasoning power, °wisdom, *Colloq* brains

understated *adj.* °subtle, restrained, low-key, °simple, °basic, unembellished, °unadorned

understood *adj.* accepted, agreed, arranged, °given, covenanted, settled, conceded

understudy *n.* **1** °second, °substitute, °stand-in, °alternate, backup, °double, sub, °reserve, *US* pinch hitter —*v.* **2** °substitute for, stand in for, °back up, double for, °second, °replace, *US* pinch-hit for

undertake *v.* **1** °assume, take on *or* upon (oneself), °accept, take *or* assume *or* bear the responsibility for, enter upon, °begin, °start, °set about, °embark on, °tackle, °try, °attempt **2** °promise, covenant, °agree, °contract, °pledge, °vow, °swear, °warrant, °guarantee, °bargain, °commit (oneself), °stipulate, °engage

undertaker *n.* mortician, funeral director

undertaking *n.* **1** °enterprise, °affair, °business, °project, °task, °effort, °venture, °work, °feat **2** doing, performing, °performance,

°realization, °achievement **3** °promise, °pledge, commitment, °assurance, °contract, °agreement, °vow, guarantee *or* guaranty, °warranty

underworld *n.* **1** Usually, ***the underworld.*** organized crime, the syndicate, the Mafia, the mob, Cosa Nostra, criminals, the criminal element, *Colloq* gangland **2** nether regions, abode of the dead, Hades, Hell, Avernus, Dis, Orcus, *Facetious* Egyptian underground

underwrite *v.* **1** °back (up), °finance, °support, invest in, °subsidize, subvene, °sponsor, °uphold, °approve, insure, °guarantee, *US* subvene **2** °subscribe to, endorse *or* indorse, °sign, countersign, °consent to, °agree to, °confirm, accede to, °sanction, °ratify, °approve, validate, *Colloq* OK *or* O.K. *or* okay

undesirable *n.* **1** *persona non grata,* pariah, °outcast, °exile, °reject, leper *—adj.* **2** unwanted, objectionable, °offensive, °unacceptable, °obnoxious, °unsavory, °unwelcome, disliked, °distasteful, °repugnant, unfit, °unbecoming, unsuitable

undeveloped *adj.* embryonic, °premature, °immature, incipient, inchoate, °potential, latent

undiluted *adj.* °pure, °neat, °straight, unmixed, uncut, unblended, unadulterated, unwatered, unalloyed

undisciplined *adj.* untrained, unschooled, °unprepared, untutored, °uneducated, untaught, unpracticed, °uncontrolled, °disobedient, °naughty, °bad, °willful, wayward, unrestrained, °erratic, unpredictable, °unruly, °wild

undisguised *adj.* °open, °out-and-out, unmistakable *or* unmistakeable, °overt, unconcealed, unreserved, unrestrained, unfeigned, unpretended, obvious, °evident, °patent, °clear, °explicit, °transparent, °sincere, °heartfelt, unalloyed, °unmitigated

undisputed *adj.* unquestioned, °unquestionable, beyond question, accepted, acknowledged, admitted, °indisputable, indubitable, undoubted, °certain, °sure, unmistakable *or* unmistakeable, °definite, °explicit, °clear, (self-)evident, °obvious, uncontested, unchallenged, incontestable, irrefutable, °incontrovertible, undeniable, conclusive

undistinguished *adj.* °ordinary, commonplace, °common, °everyday, °run-of-the-mill, °pedestrian, unexceptional, °plain, °homespun, °simple, °prosaic, unremarkable; °mediocre, middling, °indifferent, unexciting, unimpressive, unpretentious, *Brit* °homely, *Colloq* °so-so, no great shakes, no big deal, nothing to write home about, nothing special *or* unusual *or* extraordinary

undivided *adj.* **1** °whole, °entire, unbroken, uncut, °intact, unseparated, °complete, unsplit **2** undiverted, °whole, °entire, °devoted, concentrated, °full, °complete, °exclusive, undistracted

undo *v.* **1** °loosen, °loose, °open, unfasten, unhook, unlace, unzip, unsnap, unbutton, untie, unpin; unlock, unbolt **2** unwrap, uncover, °open, untie, unbind **3** °cancel, annul, rescind, nullify, °void, declare null and void, °reverse, invalidate

undoing *n.* **1** °ruin, ruination, °destruction, devastation, °defeat, °downfall, °overthrow, °fall, °collapse, descent, debasement, °degradation, abasement, mortification, °humiliation, °shame, °disgrace **2** °curse, °misfortune, bane, °affliction, °trouble, °blight

undone [1] *adj.* **1** ruined, °lost, wrecked, crushed, destroyed, devastated, shattered, brought to ruin, defeated, prostrated, °overcome **2** °open, °loose, loosened, untied, unfastened, °detached, unhooked, unlaced, unzipped, unsnapped, unbuttoned, unpinned, unstuck

undone [2] *adj.* unaccomplished, uncompleted, °incomplete, unfinished, omitted, neglected, °left (out), skipped, missed, passed over, forgotten, unattended to

undoubtedly *adv.* indubitably, without (a) doubt, indisputably, unquestionably, beyond *or* without (a *or* the shadow of) (a) doubt, certainly, °definitely, °surely, assuredly, unmistakably *or* unmistakeably, explicitly, °clearly, °obviously, incontestably, irrefutably, incontrovertibly, undeniably

unduly *adv.* **1** disproportionately, excessively, °overly, unnecessarily, inordinately, unreasonably, irrationally, unjustifiably, improperly, inappropriately **2** immoderately, lavishly, profusely, extravagantly

unearth *v.* °dig up, disinter, exhume; °excavate, dredge up, °mine, °quarry, °find, pull *or* root out, °come across, °discover, °turn up, °expose, uncover

unearthly *adj.* **1** °supernatural, °unnatural, preternatural, unworldly, otherworldly, psychic(al), extramundane, extraterrestrial, extrasensory, supersensory, out-of-(the)-body, asomatous, incorporeal, °sublime, °celestial, astral **2** °weird, °bizarre, °macabre, °nightmarish, uncanny, °eerie, °strange, °ghostly, °spectral, °unreal, *Literary* eldritch, *Colloq* spooky, creepy **3** °strange, °odd, °peculiar, °unusual, °abnormal, °absurd, outof-the-ordinary, °extraordinary, °outrageous; °unheard-of, °unreasonable, *Colloq* °ungodly

uneducated *adj.* unschooled, untaught, uncultivated, unread, uncultured, °illiterate, unlettered, °ignorant, unenlightened

unemployed *adj.* °out of work, jobless, °idle, laid off, out of a job, °out of work, unoccupied, °inactive, *Facetious* resting, °at liberty, °at leisure, *Brit* °redundant, *Colloq Brit* on the dole

unenthusiastic *adj.* °lukewarm, °cool, °cold, uninterested, °indifferent, °blasé, unresponsive, apathetic, unexcited, unimpressed

unenviable *adj.* uncoveted, °undesirable, unwished-for, unattractive

unfamiliar *adj.* **1** °new, °novel, °unknown, unconventional, °unusual, °different, uncommon, °strange, °odd, °peculiar, °bizarre **2**

Usually, ***unfamiliar with.*** unacquainted with, °unaccustomed to, inexperienced in *or* with, °unused to, unconversant with, uninformed about, ignorant of, unpracticed *or* unskilled in, unskilled at, uninitiated in, unversed in

unflattering *adj.* **1** °harsh, °unsympathetic; °realistic, °stark, °candid **2** uncomplimentary, insulting, unfavorable

unfledged *adj.* °undeveloped, °immature, unmatured, °inexperienced, °green, °callow, °young, °raw, ungrown

unfold *v.* **1** open (out *or* up), °spread (out), unfurl, stretch out, °expand, uncoil, unwind, °straighten out **2** °develop, evolve, °happen, °take place, °occur, be divulged, be disclosed *or* revealed

unforeseen *adj.* unexpected, surprising, unanticipated, unpredicted, unlooked-for, unsought, unhoped-for, undreamt-of *or* undreamed-of, unthought-of, °startling, °surprise, °chance, fortuitous

unfortunate *adj.* **1** unlucky, luckless; cursed, out of luck, unblessed, *Colloq* down on (one's) luck **2** °poor, °miserable, °wretched, °woebegone, °pathetic, °dismal, °unhappy, °forlorn, °pitiable, °doomed, ill-starred, star-crossed, ill-fated **3** °deplorable, °terrible, °awful, catastrophic, °disastrous, °calamitous, °tragic, °lamentable, °regrettable, distressing, upsetting, °disturbing, °inauspicious, °grievous, °ruinous

unfounded *adj.* baseless, °groundless, °unwarranted, unjustified, unsupported, unsupportable, °unsound, unjustifiable, unattested, unproven

ungodly *adj.* **1** °wicked, °sinful, °impious, °blasphemous, °heretical, irreligious, iconoclastic, atheist(ic), antireligious, °sacrilegious, demonic, demoniac(al), diabolic(al), °satanic, °fiendish, hellish, °infernal; depraved, °godless, °corrupt, °immoral, °evil, iniquitous, °bad, °villainous, heinous, flagitious, °profane, °vile **2** °awful, °outrageous, °indecent, °monstrous, °nasty, °dreadful, °terrible, appalling, °frightful, °shocking, *Colloq* god-awful, °unearthly, *Brit* °beastly

ungovernable *adj.* °unruly, refractory, intractable, unmanageable, uncontrollable, °rebellious, °wild, °disobedient, unrestrainable, °incorrigible

ungraceful *adj.* **1** °awkward, °clumsy, ungainly, lubberly, *Colloq* °all thumbs, butter-fingered, *Slang US and Canadian* klutzy **2** inelegant, graceless, °coarse, °crude, inartistic, °vulgar, °tasteless, unesthetic, °unrefined, barbarous, unlovely, °ugly, unharmonious, unattractive, ill-proportioned, unsymmetric(al), asymmetric(al)

ungracious *adj.* °discourteous, °overbearing, churlish, gauche, °rude, uncivil, °impolite, ill-bred, bad-mannered, unmannerly, ungentlemanly, unladylike, °gruff, °bluff, °brusque, °abrupt, °surly, curmudgeonly

ungrateful *adj.* unthankful, unappreciative, °rude; °selfish, °heedless

unguarded *adj.* **1** incautious, °unwary, °careless, °inattentive, °heedless, inobservant, °inadvertent, °unthinking, unwatchful, unvigilant **2** °defenseless, unprotected, undefended, unfortified, °open, uncovered, exposed, °vulnerable **3** °indiscreet, °careless, °imprudent, unwise, °hasty, °unthinking, °thoughtless; guileless, incautious

unhappy *adj.* **1** °sad, depressed, °blue, °dejected, °melancholy, °despondent, downcast, °gloomy, °downhearted, dispirited, heavy-hearted, long-faced, disconsolate, °sorrowful, °miserable, crestfallen, cheerless, °forlorn, low-spirited, °glum, distressed, °tearful, *Formal* lachrymose, *Colloq* down, *Slang US* bummed out **2** unlucky, °unfortunate, unpropitious, °inauspicious, unfavorable, luckless, hapless, cursed, °wretched, ill-omened, ill-fated, ill-starred, star-crossed, jinxed, °disastrous **3** infelicitous, unfitting, °inappropriate, unsuitable, unsuited, °wrong, inexpedient, °ill-advised, °poor, °unfortunate

unhealthy *adj.* **1** ailing, unwell, °ill, °sickly, °infirm, °feeble, °frail, debilitated, °unsound, °sick, in poor *or* delicate health *or* condition, °indisposed, °invalid, valetudinary **2** °unwholesome, °harmful, noxious, °detrimental, insalubrious, damaging, °injurious, °destructive, malign **3** °risky, °dangerous, °perilous, life-threatening, touch-and-go

unheard-of *adj.* **1** °unknown, °unfamiliar, °obscure, °unidentified, °nameless, °unsung **2** unimaginable, undreamed-of *or* undreamt-of, unprecedented, unimagined, °unbelievable, °inconceivable, °unusual **3** °shocking, °offensive, °outrageous, °disgraceful, °extreme, °unthinkable, °outlandish

unheralded *adj.* unannounced, unpublicized, unadvertised; unexpected, °surprise, unanticipated, °unforeseen, unpredicted

unhesitating *adj.* **1** °swift, °rapid, °quick, °immediate, instantaneous, °prompt, °ready, unhesitant **2** unfaltering, unwavering, °wholehearted, °unqualified, unswerving, undeviating, °staunch, °steadfast, °implicit, °resolute

unhurried *adj.* leisurely, unrushed, °easy, easygoing, °casual, °gradual, °deliberate, °steady, °sedate, °calm

unidentified *adj.* °nameless, anonymous, °unknown, unmarked, unnamed, °unknown, °unfamiliar, unrecognized, °mysterious

uniform *adj.* **1** °homogeneous, °consistent, unvaried, unchanged, unaltered; unvarying, unchanging; °invariable, unchangeable, unalterable, regimented, °standard; ordered, °orderly, °equal, °even, °like, °identical; °alike **2** °even, unbroken, °smooth, °regular, °flat —*n.* **3** livery, °habit, °regalia, °costume, °outfit; regimentals

uniformity *n.* **1** °regularity, similarity, sameness, homogeneity, consistency, °symmetry, evenness, invariability, unchangeability, similitude, conformity, °agreement, concord, °accord, harmoniousness; °harmony, concordance, accordance, conformance, correspondence **2** dullness, monotony, drabness, sameness, °tedium, featurelessness, flatness, invariability, lack of variety, changelessness

unify *v.* consolidate, °unite, °combine, °amalgamate, coalesce, bring together, °fuse, °join, °weld, °merge, confederate, °integrate

unimpeded *adj.* unblocked, unchecked, °free, unconstrained, unrestrained, unhindered, unhampered, unencumbered, °open, untrammeled, unrestricted

unimposing *adj.* unimpressive, nugatory, trivial, °trifling, °minor, unimportant, °puny, inconsiderable, °negligible

uninformed *adj.* °ignorant, nescient, unknowledgeable, unenlightened, °uneducated, unschooled, untutored, untaught, uninstructed, °unaware, incognizant

uninhabited *adj.* °desolate, °empty, °abandoned, °deserted, unoccupied, °vacant, vacated, tenantless, untenanted; °desert, unpopulated, unpeopled, °trackless, depopulated, °waste, °barren

uninhibited *adj.* °wild, unchecked, unbridled, uncurbed, intemperate, °boisterous, unrepressed, unconstrained, unrestrained, °uncontrolled, unself-conscious, unreserved, °relaxed, °casual, easygoing, °free (and easy), °open, °frank, °candid, °outspoken, *Colloq* °up front

uninviting *adj.* °repulsive, °repellent, °offensive, unappealing, unattractive, unpleasant, °disagreeable, °distasteful, unappetizing, °unsavory, sickening, °revolting, °obnoxious, °nasty, °disgusting, *Brit* off-putting

union *n.* **1** uniting, °unity, combining, °combination, joining, °junction, conjoining, conjunction, allying, °alliance, associating, °association, coalition, amalgamating, °amalgamation, fusing, fusion, marrying, °marriage, confederating, confederation, confederacy, synthesizing, °synthesis, mixing, °mixture, °federation, togetherness **2** °alliance, °association, °organization, °society, °circle, °fraternity, °club, °fellowship, °team, °ring, °gang, °syndicate, coalition, °party, confederation, confederacy, °federation, Bund, °league, consortium, bloc, cartel, °trust **3** °joint, °seam, °splice, °junction, conjunction, °graft, °weld; coupling **4** °agreement, °accord, °harmony, harmoniousness, congruity, coherence, compatibility, unanimity, °unity

unique *adj.* **1** °single, lone, °(one and) only, °solitary, one of a kind, sui generis **2** unequaled, °unparalleled, unrivaled, °incomparable, inimitable, °peerless, unmatched, unsurpassed, unexcelled, second to none

unison *n.* ***in unison (with).*** in harmony, together, corresponding exactly, in (perfect) accord, consonant, °harmonious

unit *n.* °element, component, °entity, °part, °item, constituent, °piece, °portion, °segment, °section, module

unite *v.* **1** °combine, °unify, °merge, coalesce, °amalgamate, °mix, °mingle, commingle, intermix, °blend, consolidate, °fuse **2** °join (forces), °unify, °wed, °marry, °link, °connect, °merge **3** °bond, fuse *or* weld *or* solder *or* glue *or* stick *or* tie *or* bind *or* fasten *or* fix *or* fit (together)

united *adj.* **1** unified, °common, °mutual, combined, merged, coalesced, pooled, shared, collective, °joint, amalgamated, connected **2** °joint, cooperative, °common, communal, collaborative, synergetic *or* synergistic, collective, concerted, coordinated, allied; partnership **3** agreed, unanimous, in agreement, of one mind, of like mind *or* opinion, like-minded, in accord, in harmony, °harmonious

unity *n.* **1** consistency, unanimity, constancy, °uniformity, sameness, consensus, °agreement, concord, concordance, °accord, °solidarity, compatibility, concurrence, continuity, consentaneousness, °rapport, °sympathy, like-mindedness **2** oneness, °singularity, °integrity, singleness, congruity, °uniformity, congruousness, homogeneity, °identity, sameness, °resemblance, °likeness, similarity, similitude **3** unification, uniting, °combination

universal *adj.* **1** °prevalent, °prevailing, °general, worldwide, widespread, ubiquitous, omnipresent, °limitless, °unlimited, °common, pandemic, °epidemic **2** cosmic, infinite, °boundless, °limitless, °unlimited, measureless, °endless, uncircumscribed, (all-)inclusive, all-embracing, all-encompassing, wide-ranging, °comprehensive

universally *adv.* in every case *or* instance, in all cases *or* instances, unexceptionally, without exception, uniformly, °always, invariably

universe *n.* **1** cosmos, °creation, macrocosm **2** °world, bailiwick, °sphere, °province, °domain, °circle, °milieu, °territory, corner, °quarter, microcosm

unkempt *adj.* disheveled, uncombed, tousled, disarranged, ungroomed, windblown, °untidy, disordered, mussed (up), messy, messed up, °bedraggled, °shaggy, scruffy, rumpled, slovenly, frowzy, blowzy, *Archaic* draggletailed, *Colloq* °sloppy

unkind *adj.* °inconsiderate, unthoughtful, °thoughtless, unfeeling, unconcerned, insensitive, unkindly, °unsympathetic, uncharitable, unchristian, uncaring, hardhearted, °heartless, flinty, hard, °rigid, °callous, °tough, °inflexible, unyielding, unbending, °severe, °harsh, °stern, °cruel, °mean, °inhuman

unknown *adj.* **1** unrecognized, °unfamiliar, °strange, unnamed, anonymous, °nameless, °unidentified; °obscure, °unheard-of, little-known, °humble, °undistinguished, °unsung **2** °unfamiliar, unexplored, uninvestigated, unresearched, unrevealed, °mysterious, °uncharted, °unidentified, °dark **3** unbeknownst, °untold, unrevealed

unlamented *adj.* unmissed, unmourned, unbemoaned, unbewailed, unloved

unlawful *adj.* °illegal, °illicit, against the

law, °illegitimate, under-the-table, under-the-counter, °criminal, felonious; outlawed, banned, prohibited, forbidden, interdicted, disallowed, proscribed, *verboten;* °unauthorized, unlicensed, unsanctioned

unlike *adj.* **1** °different (from), °dissimilar (to), unalike, °distinct (from), opposite (from *or* to), contrasting *or* contrastive (with *or* to), °separate (from), °divergent (from), °incompatible (with), distinguishable (from), far apart (from), °far (from), °distant (from), ill-matched (with), unequal (to), unequivalent (to) **2** atypical, uncharacteristic, untypical —*prep.* **3** different from, differing from, in contradistinction to, in contrast with *or* to, dissimilar to, distinct from, opposite from *or* to, contrasting with *or* to, divergent from, incompatible with, distinguishable from, ill-matched with, unequal to, unequivalent to

unlikely *adj.* **1** °improbable, °doubtful, dubious, °remote, °unthinkable, unimaginable, °inconceivable, °implausible **2** °unseemly, °inappropriate, unfit, unfitting, unsuitable, uncongenial, objectionable, °unbecoming, °unacceptable, unattractive, °distasteful **3** unpropitious, °unpromising, °inauspicious

unlimited *adj.* **1** unrestricted, unrestrained, °limitless, unconstrained, °unqualified, °full, °absolute, unconditional, far-reaching, unchecked, °uncontrolled **2** °limitless, °boundless, °endless, °vast, unbounded, °immense, °immeasurable, measureless, °numberless, innumerable, °inexhaustible, interminable, never-ending, °infinite, myriad, °extensive

unload *v.* °empty, °dump, unpack, off-load, °discharge; disburden, unburden

unmarried *adj.* °single, unwed(ded), bachelor, spinster, old-maid, °maiden, °unattached, unengaged, unbetrothed, unplighted, unpromised, °free, uncommitted

unmentionable *adj.* **1** unspeakable, unutterable, °ineffable, °taboo, °scandalous, forbidden, interdicted; °inexpressible **2** °disgraceful, °indecent, °immodest, °shameful, °shocking, appalling, °dishonorable, indescribable, °obscene, °filthy —*n.* **3** *unmentionables.* °underclothes, underclothing, underwear, undergarments, lingerie, *Archaic* small clothes, *Colloq* underthings, undies, *Brit* smalls, *US* skivvies

unmerciful *adj.* °merciless, pitiless, unsparing, °unkind, °relentless, unpitying, °heartless, stonyhearted, hardhearted, flinty, unfeeling, °unsympathetic, unforgiving, °mean, °cruel, °savage, °brutal, brutish, °vicious, barbarous

unmitigated *adj.* °undiluted, unalloyed, unmixed, untempered, unmoderated, unmodified, unabated, unlessened, undiminished, unreduced, unrelieved, °oppressive, unalleviated, unmollified, unsoftened, °relentless, °unqualified, °out-and-out, °thorough, thoroughgoing, °outright, °downright, °categorical, °absolute, °immoderate, °sheer, °complete, consummate, °total, °perfect, °true, °pure, arrant, utter, °plain

unmoved *adj.* °cool, °aloof, °calm, °col-

lected, °unaffected, untouched, °unsympathetic, unstirred, undisturbed, apathetic, stoic(al), °impassive, °dispassionate, unemotional, unfeeling, unconcerned, °indifferent, unreactive, unresponsive, °stolid, °stony, adamant, stonyhearted, hardhearted

unnatural *adj.* **1** uncharacteristic, °out of character, °odd, °peculiar, °strange, unexpected, °abnormal, unusual **2** °labored, °forced, °stilted, °stiff, restrained, °artificial, °false, °insincere, feigned, contrived, °affected, °mannered, °self-conscious, °theatrical, stagy **3** °outlandish, °weird, uncanny, °strange, °odd, °unaccountable, °supernatural, preternatural, °queer, °grotesque, °bizarre, °extraordinary, °eccentric, freakish

unnecessary *adj.* unneeded, °needless, unrequired, °dispensable, °disposable, °expendable, unwanted, °surplus, °superfluous, supererogatory, inessential, unessential, °nonessential

unnerve *v.* °upset, °agitate, °perturb, °ruffle, °fluster, °rattle, °discomfit, unsettle, disconcert, °dismay, °intimidate, °stun, stupefy, *Colloq* °shake (up), faze

unnoticed *adj.* unnoted, overlooked, unobserved, undiscovered, unremarked, unmarked, unperceived; unseen, unheard

unobtrusive *adj.* °inconspicuous, unostentatious, low-key, °retiring, °modest, self-effacing, unpresuming, unpretentious, unassuming, °quiet, °humble, unaggressive, unassertive, nonassertive, °subdued, °reserved, °reticent, suppressed

unofficial *adj.* °informal, °unauthorized, undocumented, °off the record, °private, °secret, unpublicized, unannounced

unopened *adj.* closed, °shut

unorthodox *adj.* °irregular, unconventional, °nonconformist, unconforming, nonconforming, aberrant, aberrational, °deviant, heteroclite, °unusual, °abnormal, uncustomary, uncommon

unpaid *adj.* **1** °payable, °outstanding, owed, owing, °due, °unsettled **2** unsalaried, °voluntary, volunteer, °honorary, *US* dollar-a-year

unpalatable *adj.* °distasteful, °disagreeable, unpleasant, °unsavory, unappetizing, unattractive, °repugnant, °nasty, °offensive; °rancid, °sour, °off, turned, °bitter, inedible, uneatable

unparalleled *adj.* unequaled, °incomparable, °matchless, °peerless, unrivaled, unmatched, inimitable, unexcelled, °superior, °supreme, °superlative, unsurpassed, °unusual, °special, °singular, °rare, °unique, °exceptional, consummate

unperfumed *adj.* unscented, °plain, °natural

unpopular *adj.* out of favor, in bad odor, unliked, disliked, shunned, avoided, snubbed, ignored, unsought-after, unaccepted, unwanted, rejected, °unwelcome, °undesirable; unloved, friendless

unprejudiced *adj.* unbigoted, unbiased,

°impartial, unjaundiced, °just, °fair, °objective, °disinterested, fair-minded, °nonpartisan, °liberal, open-minded, undogmatic

unpremeditated *adj.* °unprepared, unplanned, unarranged, uncontrived, unstudied, °coincidental, °spontaneous, spur-of-the-moment, last-minute, impromptu, extemporaneous *or* extemporary, extempore, ad-lib, °offhand, °casual, °impulsive, °natural, °involuntary, °automatic, °unconscious, *Colloq* off the cuff

unprepared *adj.* **1** unready, surprised, taken aback, (caught) napping *or* off guard, dumbfounded *or* dumfounded, at sixes and sevens, *Colloq* (caught) with (one's) pants down, *Brit* caught on the hop, *US* asleep at the switch **2** unfinished, °incomplete, uncompleted **3** unwarned, unreadied, not set up, not forewarned **4** See **unpremeditated,** above.

unprofessional *adj.* **1** °unbecoming, °improper, unethical, unprincipled, °unseemly, undignified, unfitting, unbefitting, °unworthy, unscholarly, negligent, °lax **2** amateurish, °amateur, inexpert, °inexperienced, untrained, untutored, unschooled, °incompetent, unskilled, unskillful, °inferior, second-rate, °inefficient, °poor, °shoddy, low-quality, °sloppy **3** nontechnical, unspecialized, nonspecialized, nonspecialist, °lay, °everyday, °ordinary, °plain (English), understandable

unprofitable *adj.* **1** profitless, ungainful, unremunerative, unfruitful, non-profit-making; breaking even; losing, loss-making **2** °bootless, °pointless, °purposeless, unavailing, °futile, °useless, unproductive, °worthless, °ineffective, °inefficient

unpromising *adj.* °inauspicious, unpropitious, unfavorable, °gloomy, °ominous, adverse, °portentous, baleful, °hopeless

unqualified *adj.* **1** °ineligible, unfit, untrained, ill-equipped, unsuited, unequipped, °unprepared **2** unrestricted, unreserved, unconditional, °categorical, °outright, °unmitigated, °downright, °out-and-out, °pure (and simple), °true, °perfect, utter, °absolute, consummate

unquenchable *adj.* insatiable, unslakable *or* unslakeable, unsatisfiable; °inextinguishable, unsuppressible, °irrepressible, °indestructible

unquestionable *adj.* unexceptionable, indubitable, undoubted, °indisputable, incontestable, unimpeachable, undeniable, °certain, °sure, °positive, irrefutable, °manifest, °obvious, °patent, °clear, °definite, °incontrovertible, unequivocal, unmistakable *or* unmistakeable, conclusive

unreal *adj.* **1** °imaginary, °fantastic, chimeric(al), °fanciful, °fancied, °illusory, make-believe, phantasmagoric(al), phantasmal, °spectral, figmental, °unrealistic, °nonexistent **2** °theoretical, °hypothetical, °mythical, °imaginary, made-up, °fictitious, make-believe, °fanciful **3** °artificial, °synthetic, synthesized, °mock, °false, fake(d), °counterfeit, °fraudulent, °dummy, °spurious, falsified, pretend(ed), °sham, pseudo, make-believe

unrealistic *adj.* **1** °impractical, illogical, °unreasonable, unworkable, unrealizable, °quixotic, °romantic, °fanciful, °visionary, delusional, delusive, delusory **2** °unreal, unlifelike, °unnatural, unauthentic, nonrepresentational, unrepresentative, °inaccurate

unreasonable *adj.* **1** irrational, illogical, °unthinking, °absurd, °foolish, °senseless, °nonsensical, °mindless, brainless, °thoughtless, °silly, °mad, °crazy, °insane, idiotic, moronic, imbecilic, °stupid, fatuous, °ridiculous, °ludicrous, laughable, °preposterous, °far-fetched, °shortsighted, unperceptive, unperceiving, undiscerning, myopic, °blind **2** °excessive, °outrageous, °exorbitant, °extravagant, °immoderate, extortionate, °inordinate, °unconscionable, unjust, °unwarranted, inequitable, unfair, unequal, °improper, unjustified, unjustifiable, uncalled-for **3** °inappropriate, unapt *or* inapt, unsuitable, unbefitting, °impractical, °unrealistic

unrefined *adj.* **1** °coarse, °rude, °rough, °unsophisticated, uncultured, °uncivilized, uncultivated, unpolished, inelegant, ill-bred, °impolite, °discourteous, unmannerly, °ill-mannered, bad-mannered, ignoble, °plebeian, undignified, unladylike, ungentlemanlike, ungentlemanly, uncourtly, °ungracious, °boorish, loutish, °gross, °vulgar, uncouth, cloddish, bumbling, °awkward, gauche **2** °impure, unpurified, unclarified, °raw, °crude, °coarse, untreated, unfinished, °natural, unprocessed

unrelated *adj.* °independent, °separate, °distinct, °different, °dissimilar, °incompatible, °inappropriate, °foreign, °alien, unassociated, unaffiliated, unconnected, uncoupled, unlinked, unallied, uncoordinated

unreliable *adj.* °irresponsible, °disreputable; untrustworthy, undependable, °uncertain, °unstable, treacherous, °flimsy, °weak

unrepentant *adj.* unrepenting, unremorseful, impenitent, unapologetic, unregretful, unashamed, unembarrassed, unself-conscious, °remorseless, unreformed, unrehabilitated, unregenerate, recidivist *or* recidivistic *or* recidivous

unresolved *adj.* °unsettled, °open, up in the air, °moot, °pending, °debatable, arguable, problematic(al), °indefinite, °vague, open to question, °questionable, unanswered, unsolved; undetermined, undecided, °uncertain, unsure, ambivalent, wavering, vacillating, °irresolute

unrest *n.* disquiet, uneasiness, °distress, °anxiety, anxiousness, nervousness, °anguish, unease, °worry, °concern, °agitation, turmoil, °disturbance, °trouble, °strife, °agony

unruly *adj.* unmanageable, °ungovernable, uncontrollable, °undisciplined, unregulated, °lawless, °disobedient, °insubordinate, °rebellious, °mutinous, fractious, refractory, contumacious, °obstreperous, °willful, headstrong, °stubborn, °recalcitrant, intractable, °defiant, uncooperative, wayward, °disorderly, turbulent, °riotous, °tumultuous, °violent, °stormy, °tempestuous

unsatisfactory *adj.* °insufficient, °inadequate, °inferior, °poor, °unacceptable, displeasing, °disappointing, °unworthy, °inappropriate, °deficient, °weak, °wanting, lacking, unsuitable, °imperfect, °flawed, °defective, °faulty

unsavory *adj.* °distasteful, objectionable, unpleasant, °disagreeable, unappetizing, °unpalatable, °offensive, °repugnant, °obnoxious, °repellent, °nasty, °repulsive, °revolting, °disgusting, nauseating, sickening

unscathed *adj.* unharmed, unhurt, uninjured, unmarked, untouched, undamaged, unscarred, unscratched, safe and sound, in one piece, as new, *Archaic* scatheless, *Colloq* like new

unscrupulous *adj.* °unconscionable, conscienceless, unprincipled, amoral, unethical, °immoral, °dishonorable, °corrupt, °dishonest, °deceitful, °sly, cunning, °artful, insidious, °shifty, °sneaky, °slippery, roguish, knavish, °disingenuous, treacherous, °perfidious, °faithless, °false, untrustworthy, °wicked, °evil, *Colloq* °crooked

unseasonable *adj.* unsuitable, °inopportune, °inappropriate, untimely, ill-timed, inexpedient

unseemly *adj.* **1** °improper, °unrefined, °unbecoming, indecorous, indelicate, unladylike, ungentlemanly, undignified, in poor *or* bad taste, °disreputable, discreditable, °risqué, °naughty, °indecent, °shameful, °offensive, °lewd, °lascivious, °obscene, °rude, °coarse **2** impolitic, unwise, °imprudent, inapt, °inappropriate, °inopportune, °inconvenient, uncalled-for, unsuitable, °improper, inadvisable, °ill-advised, unbefitting, unfitting, out of place *or* keeping, °awkward, °inauspicious, inexpedient, °unfortunate, ill-timed, untimely

unselfish *adj.* °generous, °charitable, openhanded, ungrudging, unstinting, unsparing, giving, magnanimous, °philanthropic, °humanitarian, °free, °liberal, altruistic, °selfless, self-sacrificing

unsettled *adj.* **1** unfixed, °unstable, changing, varying, °variable, °changeable, °inconstant, ever-changing, °protean, unpredictable, °uncertain **2** °disturbed, turbulent, riled, °agitated, disquieted, °upset, perturbed, ruffled, rattled, flustered, °restive, °restless, unnerved, *US* roiled **3** disoriented, °confused, mixed up, unorganized, disorganized, °disorderly, disordered, °tumultuous **4** See **unresolved,** above

unsettling *adj.* unnerving, upsetting, °disturbing, perturbing, discomfiting, °disconcerting

unsightly *adj.* °ugly, °hideous, awful-looking, °horrible, frightful-looking, unattractive, unprepossessing, unlovely, unpretty, °plain, *US and Canadian* °homely

unsocial *adj.* unsociable, unfriendly, °cool, °cold, °chilly, °aloof, uncongenial, unamiable, unforthcoming, °standoffish, °inhospitable, °withdrawn, °reserved, °solitary, °retiring, °distant, °detached, °reclusive, hermitic(al), eremitic(al), anchoritic *or* anchoretic; antisocial, °misanthropic, °hostile

unsolicited *adj.* unlooked-for, unsought, unsought-after, unrequested, unasked-for, uncalled-for, °gratuitous, uninvited; *Colloq US* over-the-transom

unsophisticated *adj.* **1** naive *or* naïve *or* naïf, °inexperienced, °simple, °childlike, unworldly, °innocent, °ingenuous, °artless, guileless **2** °simple, °plain, uncomplicated, undetailed, uninvolved, °unrefined

unsound *adj.* **1** °weak, °feeble, °frail, °rickety, °shaky, °ramshackle, °infirm, °unstable, wobbly, tottering, unsteady, broken-down, crumbling, disintegrating, °dilapidated, °defective, °imperfect, °faulty, decayed, °rotten **2** °unhealthy, °diseased, °ill, afflicted, in poor health, ailing, °sickly, °sick, unwell, °delicate, injured, wounded **3** °insane, °mad, °psychotic, °unbalanced, °unstable, demented, °deranged **4** illogical, °faulty, °flawed, fallacious, °untenable, °invalid, °groundless, °unfounded, °erroneous, °defective, °specious

unspoiled *adj.* unspoilt, unsullied, °pristine, virgin, °whole, untainted, unstained, °immaculate, uncorrupted, unpolluted, °spotless, stainless

unstable *adj.* **1** °changeable, °variable, unsteady, °inconstant, °inconsistent, °insecure, °capricious, °fickle, °irregular, unpredictable, °unreliable, °erratic, °volatile, fluctuating, °flighty, mercurial, vacillating, tergiversating, °indecisive, undecided, °irresolute, °indefinite, °unsettled **2** See **unsound, 1,** above.

unsuccessful *adj.* **1** °unfortunate, unavailing, °vain, abortive, °useless, °bootless, °fruitless, unfruitful, unproductive, °ineffective, °ineffectual, °inefficacious, °worthless, °unprofitable, °sterile **2** unlucky, hapless, °unfortunate, luckless, defeated, beaten, jinxed, cursed, foiled, frustrated, balked

unsung *adj.* uncelebrated, unrecognized, unglorified, unexalted, unpraised, unhonored, °unnoticed, disregarded, °unknown, anonymous, °unidentified, °nameless, °obscure, °insignificant, °inconspicuous

unsuspecting *adj.* unsuspicious, °unwary, unknowing, °ignorant, °unconscious, °gullible, credulous, naive *or* naïve *or* naïf, °ingenuous, °innocent, °trusting; °unaware, off guard

unsympathetic *adj.* uncaring, unconcerned, °callous, unfeeling, °unaffected, untouched, °unmoved, °indifferent, unemotional, °dispassionate, uncompassionate, unreactive, unresponsive, °impassive, °stolid, °cold, °cool, °aloof, unstirred, apathetic, insensitive, stoic(al), °stony, adamant, stonyhearted, hardhearted, unpitying, pitiless, °ruthless

untamed *adj.* undomesticated, °wild, unbroken, unsubdued, uncontrollable, °savage, °fierce, feral, °ferocious

untarnished *adj.* unsoiled, unsullied, °immaculate, °spotless, unspotted, untainted, °faultless, uncorrupted, unfouled, °chaste, lily-white, undefiled, virginal

untenable *adj.* insupportable *or* unsupportable, indefensible, unsustainable, unmaintainable, unjustified, unjustifiable, baseless, °groundless, °unfounded, °flawed, °faulty, °weak, illogical, °specious, °implausible, °unreasonable, °unsound

unthinkable *adj.* **1** °inconceivable, °unbelievable, unimaginable, °incredible, °incomprehensible, beyond belief, °extraordinary, *Colloq* mind-boggling, *Slang* mind-blowing **2** °unacceptable, °absurd, illogical, °impossible, °improbable, °unlikely, °out of the question, °preposterous, °ridiculous, laughable, °ludicrous, *Colloq* not on

unthinking *adj.* **1** °thoughtless, °mindless, undiscriminating, unconsidered, unwitting, unreflecting, unthoughtful, irrational, °unreasonable, illogical, unperceptive, unperceiving, undiscerning, witless, brainless, °foolish, °senseless, °nonsensical, °rash, °stupid, °silly, °mad, °crazy, °insane, idiotic, moronic, imbecilic, °hasty, °shortsighted **2** °inconsiderate, °impolite, °tactless, °rude, °thoughtless, undiplomatic, °discourteous, uncivil, °imprudent, unwise, °indiscreet, neglectful

untidy *adj.* °disorderly, messy, disheveled, °unkempt, slovenly, slatternly, °bedraggled, rumpled, frowzy, °sloppy, °dirty; littered, cluttered, °chaotic, °helter-skelter, jumbled, *Archaic* draggletailed, *Colloq US* mussy, mussed up

untiring *adj.* unflagging, °determined, indefatigable, dogged, persevering, perseverant, °tireless, unwearying, unwearied, dogged, dedicated, unfailing, unfaltering, °steady

untold *adj.* **1** countless, uncounted, uncountable, unnumbered, °numberless, innumerable, myriad, incalculable; °immeasurable, measureless, °unlimited **2** unrecounted, unnarrated, undescribed, unpublished, unrevealed, undisclosed, undivulged, unreported, °private, °hidden, °secret **3** °inexpressible, unutterable, indescribable, unimaginable, °inconceivable, °unthinkable, unspeakable

untoward *adj.* **1** adverse, unfavorable, unpropitious, discouraging, °inopportune, °unpromising, °bleak, °inauspicious, °bad, °unfortunate **2** °unbecoming, unfitting, °awkward, °inappropriate, unapt, unsuitable, °improper, °impolite, °rude, °boorish, ungentlemanly, unladylike, indecorous, indelicate, °unwarranted, uncalled-for, °unrefined, °unseemly, unwise, °imprudent, undiplomatic, °tactless, untactful, ill-conceived, °silly, °foolish, °stupid; ill-timed, vexatious, vexing, irritating, annoying

untried *adj.* untested, unproved *or* unproven, °new

untrue *adj.* **1** unfaithful, °faithless, °disloyal, °fickle, °capricious, undependable, °unreliable, °dishonorable, untrustworthy, °false, °hypocritical, °dishonest, °insincere, °two-faced, duplicitous, °devious, °deceitful, treacherous, °perfidious **2** °wrong, °false, °inaccurate, °incorrect, °erroneous, misleading, °mistaken, distorted **3** °inexact, nonstandard, substandard, °imprecise, °imperfect

unused *adj.* **1** °(brand) new, untouched, °pristine, °original, °intact, °fresh, first-hand **2** °disused, °abandoned, °derelict, neglected, given up **3** unconsumed, °left (over), °remaining **4** ***unused to.*** °unaccustomed to, °unfamiliar with, inexperienced in *or* at, amateurish at, unpracticed in *or* at, uninitiated in

unusual *adj.* uncommon, °exceptional, atypical, untypical, °different, unexpected, °singular, °out of the ordinary, °extraordinary, °odd, °peculiar, °curious, °bizarre, °strange, °queer, °remarkable, °unique, freakish, unprecedented, unconventional, °unorthodox, *Slang* off the wall

unvarnished *adj.* °plain, °simple, °pure, unembellished, straightforward, °straight, °direct, °honest, unelaborated, °naked, °stark, °sincere, °frank, °candid, °outspoken

unveil *v.* °reveal, °expose, uncover, lay bare *or* open, °bare, °bring to light

unwarranted *adj.* uncalled-for, °unasked, unasked-for, unjustified, indefensible, unjust, unfair, °unconscionable, °unworthy, °improper, °inexcusable, °gratuitous, unmerited, undeserved, unprovoked, °outrageous, °excessive, °unreasonable, unrestrained, intemperate, untempered, °immoderate, undue, °unnecessary

unwary *adj.* °heedless, °careless, °hasty, incautious, °unguarded, °imprudent, °rash, °foolhardy, °reckless, °thoughtless, °indiscreet, °unthinking, °mindless, unwise

unwashed *adj.* **1** °dirty, uncleaned, unclean, uncleansed —*n.* **2** ***the (great) unwashed.*** *Derogatory* °the rabble, °the masses, the mob, the plebs, people (at large *or* in general), the population, the populace, the man *or* woman in the street, Mr. (& Mrs.) Average, the working class(es), most people, the (silent) majority, *US* John Q. Public

unwelcome *adj.* **1** uninvited, unsought-for, unwished for, undesired, °undesirable, displeasing, unpleasing, °distasteful, unpleasant **2** unwanted, rejected, unaccepted, excluded; *persona non grata*, anathema

unwholesome *adj.* **1** °unhealthy, unhealthful, °detrimental, deleterious, pernicious, insalubrious, unhygienic, insalutary, °harmful, noxious, toxic, °injurious, °destructive **2** °corrupt, °immoral, °bad, °wicked, °evil, °sinful, °perverted; demoralizing, depraved, °degrading, corrupting, perverting **3** °ill, ailing, °sickly, °sick, °pale, °wan, anemic, pallid, °pasty

unwieldy *adj.* °awkward, °clumsy, °bulky, oversized, cumbersome, ungainly, unmanageable, unhandy, unmaneuverable

unwonted *adj.* infrequent, °unusual, uncustomary, uncommon, °unfamiliar, unprecedented, °rare, °singular, atypical, °abnormal, °peculiar, °odd, °strange, °irregular, unconventional, °unorthodox

unworthy *adj.* **1** unequal, meritless, unmerited, substandard, °inferior, second-rate, °menial, °puny, °petty, °paltry, °unprofessional, °mediocre, °despicable, °contemptible, °dishonorable, ignoble, °disreputable, discreditable, °unqualified, °ineligible, unfit, undeserving **2** ***unworthy of.*** unbecoming to, inappropriate to, unsuitable for, unfit for, out of character for, inconsistent with *or* for, out of place with *or* for, incongruous with *or* for

upbeat *adj.* °positive, °optimistic, °sanguine, °favorable, °cheerful, encouraging, heartening, °buoyant, lighthearted

upbraid *v.* °scold, °rebuke, °reprimand, reproach, °berate, °castigate, °chastise, °reprove, chide, censure, °take to task, *Colloq* °tell off, tick off, °dress down, give a dressing-down, give (someone) a piece of (one's) mind, tell (someone) a thing or two, rake (someone) over the coals, jump on *or* all over, °bawl out, *US* °chew out

upbringing *n.* rearing, raising, training, °education, cultivation, nurture, °breeding

upheaval *n.* °upset, °unrest, commotion, °change, cataclysm, disruption, °disturbance, °disorder, °confusion, °chaos, °furor

uphold *v.* °support, °maintain, °sustain, °preserve, °hold up, °defend, °protect, °advocate, °promote, espouse, °embrace, °endorse, °back, °champion, °stand by

upkeep *n.* **1** °maintenance, °repair, °support, °sustenance, °preservation, °conservation, °subsistence, °running, °operation **2** (operating) costs, °(running) expenses, °outlay, °expenditure, *Brit* °overheads, oncosts, *US* °overhead

upper *adj.* **1** higher (up), loftier, topmost, more elevated, °uppermost **2** higher, upland, more elevated; (more) northerly, northern **3** later, more recent **4** ***upper case.*** capital letter(s), capital(s), large letters, majuscule (letters *or* characters) **5** ***upper crust.*** upper class, elite *or* élite, aristocrats, nobles, blue bloods, °wealthy, *US* Four Hundred **6** ***upper hand.*** °advantage, °control, °authority, °power, °sway, °superiority, °supremacy, °command, dominance, ascendancy, *Colloq* °edge —*n.* **7** ***on (one's) uppers.*** °poor, °indigent, °destitute, poverty-stricken, *Colloq* °broke

upper-class *adj.* **1** elite *or* élite, aristocratic, blueblooded, well-born, °noble, highborn, patrician, *Colloq* upper-crust **2** °high-class, °elegant, °fancy, °luxurious, °first-rate, deluxe, °royal, °regal, °sumptuous, *Colloq* swank(y), ritzy, °posh

uppermost *adj.* **1** highest, topmost, loftiest, °top **2** °foremost, °first, most important *or* prominent *or* influential *or* telling, °principal, °paramount, °preeminent, °predominant

uppish *adj.* °affected, putting on airs, °snobbish, °conceited, overweening, °self-important, *Colloq* uppity, snooty, high and mighty, °hoity-toity, highfalutin *or* hifalutin *or* highfaluting, stuck-up, on (one's) high horse, *Slang* snotty, *Brit* toffee-nosed

upright *adj.* **1** °erect, °perpendicular, vertical, °on end, straight up and down, °plumb, standup, °standing (up), *Brit* upstanding **2** °moral, °principled, high-minded, °ethical °virtuous, upstanding, °straight, °righteous, straightforward, °honorable, °honest, °just, °trustworthy, unimpeachable, uncorrupt(ed), incorruptible, °decent, °good —*n.* **3** °post, °pole, column, vertical, °perpendicular —*adv.* **4** perpendicularly, vertically, upward(s), °straight up (and down) **5** right side up

uprising *n.* rebellion, °revolt, °mutiny, °revolution, insurrection, rising, putsch, coup (d'état)

uproar *n.* clamor, hubbub, °disturbance, commotion, hullabaloo, brouhaha, °din, °racket, °pandemonium, °tumult, turmoil, pother, °outcry, °outburst, °bedlam, °agitation, °frenzy, °broil, °rumpus, °fuss; affray, °fracas, °brawl; *Colloq* hoo-ha, to-do, *US* hoopla, *Brit* kerfuffle *or* carfuffle *or* kurfuffle

uproarious *adj.* **1** clamorous, °noisy, deafening, °tumultuous, turbulent, °tempestuous, °excited, frenzied, °rowdy, °riotous, °disorderly, °wild **2** °hilarious, °hysterical, °(screamingly) funny, sidesplitting, *Colloq* too funny for words, °killing

uproot *v.* **1** °transfer, °transplant, °move, °displace; °exile, °banish **2** deracinate, extirpate, °root out, °dig out, pluck out, tear out; °destroy, °demolish, °ruin, eradicate, annihilate, °kill, °devastate, °ravage

upset *v.* **1** °disturb, °agitate, °distress, unsettle, °put off, °put out, °perturb, disquiet, °fluster, °ruffle, °frighten, °scare, disconcert, °dismay, °trouble, °worry, °bother, discompose, make (someone) nervous **2** °overturn, °capsize, °topple, upend, °tip over, knock over *or* down, invert, turn topsy-turvy *or* upside down, °spill **3** °disturb, derange, °disrupt, disarrange, °mess up, disorganize, °snarl up, °jumble, °muddle, *Colloq Scots* kerfuffle *or* carfuffle *or* kurfuffle **4** °overthrow, °defeat, °beat, worst, thrash, °rout, °conquer, °overcome, win out over, get the better of, get *or* gain the advantage over, °triumph over, be victorious over, vanquish **5** °defeat, °ruin, °spoil, °thwart, interfere with, °destroy, °demolish, °mess up, °disturb, *Colloq* throw a *Brit* spanner in *or US* monkey wrench into (the works), *US* discombobulate, *Slang* °screw up, gum up, put the kibosh on, *Taboo slang* fuck up, *Brit* °bugger up —*adj.* **6** capsized, overturned, upside down, bottom side up, inverted, reversed, toppled, tipped over, °topsy-turvy **7** °sick, °queasy **8** perturbed, °disturbed, disquieted, °disconcerted, °agitated, distressed, °worried, troubled, unnerved, distracted, apprehensive, °nervous, frightened, °scared, °afraid **9** disordered, °confused, disorganized, messed up, jumbled, muddled, °disturbed, disarranged **10** °angry, irate, °furious, °beside oneself, °mad, *Colloq* fit to be tied, *Slang* freaked out —*n.* **11** °defeat, upsetting, °conquest, °overthrow, °rout, °thrashing, °triumph, °victory **12** °surprise, unexpected event *or* occurrence **13** °reversal, °overthrow, °overturn, bouleversement

upshot *n.* °result, °end (result), °outcome, ending, conclusion, °termination, °effect, aftereffect, fallout, °wake, backwash, °repercussion, afterclap, feedback, °resolution, culmination, denouement *or* dénouement, °issue, *Colloq* °payoff, *US* wrap-up

upstart *n.* parvenu(e), arriviste, nouveau riche, (social) climber, status seeker, °pretender, °nobody

uptake *n.* comprehension, °understanding, apprehension, °grasp, °perception, °insight, perspicaciousness, perspicacity, perceptiveness, °sensitivity

urge *v.* **1** °press, °push, °drive, °force, impel, °speed, accelerate, °hurry, °rush, °hustle, °move, goad, °prod, egg on, °spur **2** °press, goad, °prod, egg on, °spur, °prompt, °induce, °incite, constrain, exhort, °encourage, °demand, °request, °ask, °plead (with), °beseech, °beg, entreat, importune **3** °coax, °persuade, °induce, °prevail upon, °campaign (with), °sway, °influence, °talk into, °advise, °suggest, °counsel **4** °argue, °set forth, affirm, °state, °allege, assert, °hold, °advise, °advocate, °demand —*n.* **5** °pressure, °impetus, °desire, compulsion, impulse, °itch, °longing, yearning, °drive, °fancy, °hunger, °thirst, craving, *Colloq* yen

urgency *n.* imperativeness, °pressure, °stress, °extremity, °importance, seriousness, importunity, °necessity, °need, insistence, exigency, °emergency

urgent *adj.* **1** °immediate, °instant, °imperative, °pressing, compelling, °vital, life-and-death, °important, °serious, °necessary, exigent, °rush, °emergency, °pressing, high-priority **2** supplicative, begging, °solicitous, °earnest, importunate, °insistent, °loud, clamorous, °active, °energetic, pertinacious, °tenacious, °forceful, °firm

urinate *v.* pass *or* make water, *Technical* micturate; *Babytalk* °(make a) wee, (go) wee-wee, (have a *or US also* take a) pee, (make) pee-pee, do number one, tinkle, piddle; *Euphemistic* go to the men's *or* ladies' (room), go to the lavatory, °excuse (oneself), wash (one's) hands, go to the bathroom, go to the powder room; *Mincing* go to the little boys' *or* girls' room; *Colloq Brit* spend a penny, go to the loo, *Slang* (take *or* have a) piss, *Brit* have a *or* go for a slash

usage *n.* **1** °use, °custom, °habit, °practice, °routine, °convention, °form, °tradition **2** °treatment, °use, °management, handling, °operation, manipulation

use *v.* **1** °employ, make use of, put into practice *or* operation, practice, utilize, °exercise, bring into play, have recourse to, °resort to, put *or* press into service, put to use, avail (oneself) of; °say, utter, °speak **2** capitalize on, turn to account, profit by *or* from, °exploit, utilize, make use of, take advantage of, °manipulate, °maneuver, °handle, °abuse, °misuse, °play, °work **3** °consume, °eat, °drink, smoke, °take, °partake of, ingest, °inject, *Slang* °shoot (up) **4** °consume, °buy, °purchase, °employ, utilize **5** ***use up.*** °consume, °exhaust, °expend, °run through, °run out of, deplete; °waste, squander, °fritter away, pour down the drain, °throw away —*n.* **6** °usage, °application, °employment, utilization; using **7** °function, utility, °application; °advantage, °benefit, °good, °service, °interest, °profit, avail **8** °wear (and tear), utilization, °treatment, °usage, handling **9** usability, °usefulness, utility, utilization, °usage, °function, functioning, service(s), serviceability, °power **10** °license, °permission, °permit, °privilege **11** consumption, purchases, buying, °acquisition **12** °advantage, °purpose, °point, °end, °object, °reason, °basis, °ground **13** °demand, °need, °necessity, °urgency, exigency **14** See **usage, 1,** above. **15** ***have no use for.*** execrate, °detest, °abhor, °hate, °despise, °scorn, contemn, °spurn, °reject, °dislike

used *adj.* **1** °secondhand, castoff, °old, °worn, *Euphemistic* preowned, *Colloq* hand-me-down, *Brit* reach-me-down **2** utilized, employed, occupied; in use **3** ***used to.*** accustomed to, habituated to, acclimatized *or* acclimated to, adapted to, hardened *or* toughened *or* inured to *or* against, tempered to, tolerant of; familiar *or* acquainted with

useful *adj.* utilitarian, °functional, °serviceable, °practical, usable, of use, °beneficial, salutary, °advantageous, °expedient, °profitable, valuable, °gainful, °helpful, °fruitful, °productive, °effective, °worthwhile

usefulness *n.* utility, applicability, practicability, °purpose, purposefulness, °point, practicality, °benefit, °advantage, expediency, °profit, profitability, value, °gain, °help, fruitfulness, effectiveness, °worth

useless *adj.* **1** °ineffective, °ineffectual, unserviceable, °impractical, °impracticable, unpractical, unavailing, °vain, °pointless, °purposeless, °idle, °futile, unproductive, °unsuccessful, °impotent, effete, °sterile, °barren, abortive, unusable, °bootless, °worthless, *Rare* inutile **2** °inefficient, °incompetent, unproductive, °ineffectual, °ineffective, °hopeless, °inept

user *n.* **1** consumer, °buyer, purchaser, °owner; °operator **2** alcohol *or* drug *or* narcotic addict

user-friendly *adj.* °simple, °practicable, usable, °explicit, °accommodating, understandable

usual *adj.* °same, °customary, °habitual, °accustomed, °familiar, °well-known, °common, °everyday, established, °traditional, °set, °time-honored, °old, °conventional, workaday, °stock, wonted, °regular, °ordinary, °normal, expected, °routine, °typical, °run-of-the-mill, stereotypic(al), hackneyed, trite, °prosaic, worn-out, shop-worn, °predictable, unexceptional, unoriginal, unremarkable, unimaginative

usually *adv.* customarily, °as a rule, °generally (speaking), most of the time, °for the most part, most often, mostly, almost always, inveterately, °on the whole, normally, commonly, regularly, predominantly, °chiefly, all things considered, °in the main, °mainly, by and large, as usual, *Colloq* as per usual

utopia *n.* Utopia, °paradise, °heaven, seventh heaven, (Garden of) Eden, °bliss, Cloud-Cuckooland, Nephelococcygia, never-never land, Shangri-La, Cockaigne *or* Cockayne, heaven on earth, °perfection

utterly *adv.* °completely, °perfectly, °absolutely, °thoroughly, fully, °entirely, °wholly, unreservedly, °totally, unqualifiedly, °out-and-out, °altogether, overwhelmingly, unequivocally, categorically, °definitely, °properly; °extremely, *Brit dialect* °proper; no holds barred, body and soul

V

vacancy *n.* **1** °emptiness, °void, °gap, lacuna, hiatus, °blank, deficiency, °opening, °breach, vacuum **2** °(job) opening, °slot, °position, °post, °situation **3** blankness, °emptiness, vacuity, absent-mindedness, inanity, vacuousness, incomprehension, fatuity, unawareness

vacant *adj.* **1** °empty, °void, °hollow, unoccupied, untenanted, °uninhabited, °abandoned, °deserted **2** °blank, expressionless, deadpan, °empty, vacuous, °dull, °absent-minded, °inane, uncomprehending, fatuous, °unaware **3** unoccupied, °free, °unused, unutilized, °spare, °extra, °idle, unfilled, unengaged, unspoken-for

vacate *v.* **1** °leave, °depart (from), withdraw from, °quit, °evacuate, get *or* go out of; °desert, °abandon **2** °give up, °relinquish, °sacrifice, °renounce, let go, °resign, °abdicate, °cede, give up right *or* claim to, °abandon **3** annul, declare null and void, nullify, °void, °repudiate, override, overrule, rescind, °revoke, °recall, °quash, °set aside, invalidate

vade mecum *n.* handbook, °manual, ready reference, °book, °guide

vagabond *n.* **1** gypsy *or* gipsy, °tramp, vagrant, wayfarer, °rover, wanderer, itinerant, °migrant, bird of passage, rolling stone, beachcomber, °derelict, *Chiefly US and Canadian* hobo, *Australian* swagman, *Colloq US* °bum, *Slang US* bindle-stiff —*adj.* **2** vagrant, wayfaring, roving, wandering, itinerant, °migrant, °derelict, nomadic, gypsy *or* gipsy, °rambling, roaming, drifting, peripatetic, °transient, peregrinating

vague *adj.* **1** °indefinite, °indistinct, °imprecise, °inexact, unclear, °confused, unspecified *or* nonspecified, °general, generalized, unspecific *or* nonspecific, inexplicit *or* unexplicit, ill-defined, °hazy, °fuzzy, °ambiguous, °obscure, amorphous; °shapeless, blurred, blurry, °filmy, °dim, °shadowy, °veiled, bleary, foggy, °misty, cloudy, clouded, hardly *or* barely distinguishable *or* discernible **2** undetermined, indeterminate, unfixed, °indefinite, °inexact, unspecified *or* nonspecified, unspecific *or* nonspecific, °ambiguous, °doubtful, °in doubt, °uncertain, °equivocal, °ambiguous **3** °veiled, concealed, °hidden, shrouded, °obscure, ill-defined, unspecific *or* nonspecific, inexplicit *or* unexplicit, °ambiguous **4** °subliminal, °subconscious, indefinable, unexplained **5** °indefinite, °ambiguous, °wishy-washy, undecided, °indecisive, °irresolute, vacillating, wavering, °inconstant, °unsettled, °uncertain, °nebulous, up in the air **6** °vacant, °empty, °blank, expressionless, vacuous, °dull; puzzled

vaguely *adv.* **1** distantly, remotely, indefinitely, dimly, subliminally, subconsciously, inexplicably **2** ambiguously, imprecisely, inexactly, unclearly, confusedly, confusingly, hazily, fuzzily, nebulously, obscurely **3** °idly, vacantly, detachedly, absent-mindedly, dreamily, absently, distractedly

vain *adj.* **1** °proud, °conceited, °haughty, °arrogant, °boastful, °egotistical, °cocky, °self-important, vainglorious, narcissistic, *Colloq* bigheaded, swell-headed, stuck-up, swollen-headed **2** °worthless, profitless, °bootless, °pointless, °unsuccessful, °empty, °futile, °useless, unavailing, unproductive, °fruitless, °ineffective, abortive **3** ***in vain.*** **(a)** vainly, futilely, unsuccessfully, fruitlessly, bootlessly **(b)** irreverently, blasphemously, disrespectfully, improperly

valley *n.* glen, dale, dell, vale, dingle, °hollow, coomb *or* coombe *or* combe *or* comb, *Northern Brit and Welsh* cirque *or* corrie *or* cwm, *Scots* strath

vanity *n.* **1** °conceit, conceitedness, egotism, narcissism, °arrogance, cockiness, self-importance, vainglory, haughtiness, °pride, self-admiration, self-worship, *Colloq* swell-headedness, bigheadedness **2** vainness, °emptiness, hollowness, worthlessness, futility, unreality, bootlessness, pointlessness, uselessness, °folly, vapidity, silliness, vacuousness, vacuity, foolishness, fatuity, frivolousness

vapid *adj.* insipid, flavorless, °tasteless, °bland, °watery, watered-down, °wishy-washy, jejune, °colorless, °unpalatable, °flat, °tame, °lifeless, °boring, °tedious, °tiresome, uninteresting, trite, wearisome, wearying, °humdrum, *Colloq* blah, ho-hum

vapor *n.* **1** °mist, °fog, steam, cloud, smoke, smog, °exhalation **2** ***the vapors.*** morbidity, hypochondria, hysteria, nervousness, °depression, rheuminess, *Archaic* distemper, *Colloq* the pip

variable *adj.* °changeable, °protean, changing, °inconstant, varying, wavering, mercurial, °fickle, °capricious, unsteady, unfixed, °unstable, °uncertain, undependable, unpredictable, fluctuating, vacillating, mutable, chameleonic, chameleon-like

variance *n.* **1** °variation, °difference, °disparity, °discrepancy, °disagreement, deviation, inconsistency, divergence, incongruity **2** °disagreement, °misunderstanding, °discord, °difference (of opinion), °dissension, contention, °dispute, dissent, °controversy, °quarrel, °conflict, °argument, °debate, lack of harmony, falling-out, °schism, °rift **3** ***at variance.*** in dispute, in disagreement, quarreling, in contention, in conflict

variant *n.* **1** °alternative, modification, °variation —*adj.* **2** varying, °variable, changing, altering, °unstable, °deviant, deviating, °different, differing; °separate, °distinct

variation *n.* **1** °change, changing, °alteration, altering, °variety, varying, modification, modifying, °difference, differing, diversification, °diversity, diversifying, modulation, modulating, conversion, converting, permutation, permuting **2** °variety, °choice, °novelty, °diversity, departure (from the norm *or* usual), change of pace, divergence, variegation, deviation (from the norm)

varied *adj.* **1** °diverse, diversified, °mixed, °miscellaneous, assorted, heterogeneous **2** See **various,** below. **3** See **variegated,** below.

variegated *adj.* multicolor(ed), particolor(ed), varicolored, many-colored, motley, pied, piebald, brindled, °mottled, polychrome, polychromatic; nacreous, changeant, °opalescent, opaline

variety *n.* **1** °diversity, diversification, multifariousness, multiplicity, °number, °range, °assortment, °medley, °mixture, °mix, °miscellany, heterogeneity, °choice, °selection, °collection **2** °difference, heterogeneity, °discrepancy, °diversity, °disparity, °variation, °contrast **3** °sort, °brand, °make, °mark, °kind, °class, °category, °breed, °type, °order, °genre, species, genus, classification, °strain

various *adj.* **1** °different, a number of, a variety of, diversified, °diverse, °several, °many, numerous, °sundry, heterogeneous, °miscellaneous, *Literary* °divers **2** °different, °distinct, °individual

vary *v.* **1** °change, °alter, °diversify, °transform, reshape, remodel, restyle, °modify, reorganize **2** change off, °switch, °alternate, °fluctuate, vacillate **3** °depart, °deviate, °differ, °diverge, °shift, veer

vast *adj.* °infinite, °unlimited, °boundless, °limitless, unbounded, interminable, °endless, never-ending, °inexhaustible, indeterminate, °immeasurable, incalculable, measureless; °immense, °enormous, °huge, tremendous, °great, °prodigious, stupendous, °gigantic, °massive, °voluminous, capacious, °colossal, °monumental, mammoth, °jumbo, elephantine, behemoth, cyclopean, Brobdingnagian, titanic, *Literary* vasty, *Colloq US* ginormous, humongous

vastly *adv.* immensely, greatly, hugely, enormously, considerably, °substantially, °(almost) entirely, infinitely, °exceedingly, °extremely, very much, *Colloq* worlds

vehicle *n.* **1** conveyance **2** °means, °channel, °mechanism, °carrier, conduit, °agency, °instrument

veil *n.* **1** covering, °cover, °screen, °camouflage, °cloak, curtain, °mask, °shroud —*v.* **2** °cover, °conceal, °hide, °camouflage, °cloak, °mask, °disguise, °shroud, °shield, °obscure

veiled *adj.* concealed, °hidden, masked, °obscure, unrevealed, covert, disguised, °secret, sub rosa, °subtle

vein *n.* **1** blood vessel; nervure **2** °streak, °seam, °stripe, striation, stria, °thread, °line **3** °seam, lode, °stratum, °course, °deposit, bed **4** °thread, °hint, °suggestion, °touch, °trace, °streak, °line, °strain, °mood, °spirit, °tone, °note, °tenor, °feeling, °attitude, °disposition, °humor, °temper; tendency *or* inclination *or* proclivity toward(s) **5** °way, °manner, °course, °fashion, °style, °mode, °pattern

velocity *n.* °speed, swiftness, °rapidity, fleetness, quickness, briskness, alacrity, celerity, °pace, rate of speed, miles per hour, mph, kilometers per hour, km/hr

venal *adj.* °corrupt, corruptible, bribable, buyable, purchasable, °mercenary, unprincipled, °dishonorable, °rapacious, °avaricious, °greedy, simoniacal, *Colloq* °crooked, *Slang* °bent

vendetta *n.* °(blood) feud, °quarrel, °dispute, °conflict, °rivalry, enmity, °bitterness, hatred, °ill will, bad blood

veneer *n.* °gloss, façade, °finish, °pretense, °(false) front, (outward) show *or* display, °appearance, °mask, °guise, °aspect, °superficies

venerable *adj.* °respectable, °honorable, °estimable, respected, honored, esteemed, august, °sedate, °impressive, revered, reverenced, worshiped

venerate *v.* °respect, °honor, °esteem, °revere, °reverence, °worship, °hallow, °adore, °admire, °look up to

veneration *n.* °respect, °honor, °esteem,

°reverence, °deference, °homage, °devotion, °worship, °admiration, adoration, idolization, awe

venereal *adj.* °sexual; genital; °social, sexually transmitted, gonorrheal *or* gonorrheic, syphilitic

vengeance *n.* **1** °revenge, retaliation, °retribution, °requital, °reprisal **2** ***with a vengeance.*** **(a)** violently, °fiercely, ferociously, wildly, vehemently, furiously, forcefully **(b)** energetically, to the fullest extent, to the utmost *or* the fullest *or* the limit, (with) no holds barred, enthusiastically, wholeheartedly

venial *adj.* forgivable, excusable, pardonable, °tolerable, tolerated, °minor, °petty, °insignificant, unimportant, remittable *or* remissible

venom *n.* **1** °poison, toxin **2** malice, maliciousness, malevolence, °ill will, malignity, °animosity, °hate, hatred, °hostility, °antagonism, °spite, spitefulness, spleen, °rancor, °bitterness, embitteredness, °gall, °poison, poisonousness, °virulence

venomous *adj.* **1** °poisonous, °deadly, toxic, °dangerous, life-threatening, °lethal **2** °poisonous, °virulent, malicious, malevolent, malign, °malignant, °savage, baleful, envenomed, °hostile, antagonistic, °spiteful, splenetic, acerbic, °rancorous, °bitter, °embittered, °mean, °vicious

vent *n.* **1** °opening, °slit, °slot, °hole, °aperture, air hole, blow-hole, spiracle, orifice, °outlet, inlet, funnel, flue, duct, °passage; fumarole, fissure, °pipe, mofette *or* moffette **2** ***give vent to.*** See **3,** below. —*v.* **3** °give vent to, °express, verbalize, °air, articulate, °enunciate, °declare, °voice, °announce, °communicate, °pronounce, °proclaim, °reveal, °release, let go, °let loose, allow to become known, °make known, °blurt out, °make public, °broadcast **4** °discharge, °release, °emit, °eject, °issue, °empty, °dump, °expel, send *or* pour out *or* forth, °throw out

venture *n.* **1** °risk, °chance, hazardous undertaking, °experiment, °speculation, °gamble, °plunge, °fling —*v.* **2** dare(say), make bold, °hazard, volunteer, °tender, °offer, °broach, °advance, proffer, °put forward **3** °jeopardize, °risk, °endanger, °hazard, imperil; °gamble, °bet, wager, °plunge, °put down

venturesome *adj.* **1** °daring, °bold, °intrepid, °adventurous, °courageous, plucky, adventuresome, °audacious, °fearless, doughty, °brave, °spirited **2** °risky, °rash, °reckless, sporting, °game, °daredevil

verbal *adj.* **1** °spoken, °oral, vocal, said, uttered, expressed, enunciated, articulated, colloquial, conversational, viva voce, word-of-mouth, unwritten **2** word-for-word, °verbatim, °literal **3** °word, lexical, vocabulary

verbatim *adj.* **1** word-for-word, verbatim et literatim (= 'word-for-word and letter-for-letter'), °literal, °exact, °precise, °accurate, °faithful, °strict —*adv.* **2** word-for-word, verbatim et literatim, °literally, °exactly, °precisely, accurately, faithfully, °to the letter, strictly

verge[1] *n.* **1** °edge, °border, °boundary, °margin, °brink, °threshold, °brim **2** ***on the verge of.*** about to, ready to, on the (very) point of, preparing to, soon to —*v.* **3** Often, ***verge on.*** °border (on), °approach, come close *or* near (to), *Technical* be asymptotic to

verge[2] *v.* °incline, °lean, °tend, °extend, °stretch, °turn; °approach, °draw, °move

verify *v.* affirm, °confirm, testify to, °attest (to), bear witness to, vouch for, corroborate, °support, °substantiate, clinch *or* clench, °prove, °demonstrate, °show, °bear out, °authenticate, validate, °certify, °guarantee, °back up, °warrant

veritable *adj.* °real, °true, °virtual, °genuine, °actual, °legitimate, °authentic

vernacular *adj.* **1** °native, °local, regional, °indigenous, autochthonous **2** °popular, °informal, colloquial, conversational, °ordinary, °familiar, °everyday, °spoken, °vulgar, vulgate; °plain, °simple, straightforward, °easy —*n.* **3** °jargon, patois, argot, °cant, °idiom, phraseology, °language, °talk, °speech

versatile *adj.* **1** °adaptable, °resourceful, all-round, all-purpose, many-sided, multipurpose, multifaceted, °flexible, adjustable, °protean, °dexterous, °handy, facile **2** °variable, °changeable, °protean, changing, °flexible, fluctuating

versed *adj.* Usually, ***well-versed in.*** well-read *or* (well-)informed in *or* (well-)trained *or* (well-)grounded *or* (well-)schooled *or* (well-)educated *or* (well-)tutored *or* learned *or* cultured *or* lettered *or* cultivated *or* literate *or* competent *or* accomplished *or* skilled in, (well-)posted on, knowledgeable in *or* about, proficient *or* experienced *or* practiced *or* expert *or* good in *or* at, conversant *or* familiar *or* (well-)acquainted with

version *n.* **1** °form, °variant, °variation, °type, °model, °style, °kind, °variety, °manifestation, portrayal, °adaptation, °rendition, °interpretation, °construct, construction, °conception, °idea **2** °story, °account, °rendering, °rendition, °translation, °interpretation, reading, °understanding, °view, °side

vertex *n.* °top, °tip, °extremity, °zenith, meridian, apogee, °peak, apex, °acme, °summit, °pinnacle, °crest, °crown, °cap, height(s)

vertigo *n.* dizziness, lightheadedness, giddiness, instability, *Colloq* wooziness

verve *n.* °spirit, vivacity, vivaciousness, °vitality, °life, liveliness, °animation, °sparkle, °energy, °vigor, °exuberance, briskness, brio, esprit, élan, °dash, °flair, °panache, °flourish, °enthusiasm, zeal, °zest, °gusto, *Colloq* pizazz, zip, vim, get-up-and-go, zing, oomph

very *adv.* **1** °extremely, °truly, °really, to a great extent, °exceedingly, greatly, (very) much, °profoundly, °deeply, acutely, unusually, extraordinarily, uncommonly, exceptionally, remarkably, °absolutely, °completely, °entirely, °altogether, °totally, °quite, °rather, hugely, °vastly, *Dialectal* °right, *Brit* °jolly, *Colloq* damn(ed), °terribly, °awfully, darned, *US dialectal* danged, °plumb, *Slang Brit* bleeding, *Chiefly Brit* bloody **2** most, °extremely, certainly, °surely, °definitely, decidedly, unequivocally, unquestionably, °quite, °entirely, °altogether —*adj.* **3** °exact, °precise, °perfect; °same, selfsame, °identical, °particular **4** least, °mere, merest, °bare, barest, °sheer, sheerest; utter, °pure, °simple

vessel *n.* **1** container, °receptacle, utensil, holder **2** °craft, °boat, °ship, ark, *Literary* barque *or US also* bark

vestige *n.* °trace, °suggestion, ***soupçon,*** °hint, glimmer, °inkling, °suspicion, °sign, °evidence, °mark, °token, °scent, whiff, tinge, °taste; °remnant, °scrap, °fragment, °memorial, °residue, °relic, °remains

vestigial *adj.* °imperfect, °undeveloped, underdeveloped, °rudimentary, °incomplete

vet *v.* °examine, °review, °investigate, °scrutinize, °inspect, °check (out), °look over, °scan; validate, °authenticate; *Colloq* give (something *or* someone) the once-over, °size up

veteran *n.* **1** old hand, past master, old-timer, trouper, *Colloq* warhorse —*adj.* **2** °experienced, °practiced, °seasoned, °mature, long-serving, battle-scarred

veto *v.* **1** °stop, °block, °deny, °ban, °turn down, °reject, disallow, °rule out, °quash, °prevent, °prohibit, interdict, °taboo, °outlaw, proscribe, °preclude, *Colloq* put the kibosh on, °kill, nix —*n.* **2** °denial, °ban, stoppage, °block, °embargo, turndown, °rejection, disallowance, quashing, °prevention, °prohibition, interdiction, °taboo, proscription, preclusion, vetoing, *Colloq* °killing, nixing

viable *adj.* sustainable, °supportable, °sensible, °reasonable, °practical, °practicable, °applicable, workable, °feasible, °possible

vibes *n. pl.* vibrations, °feelings, sensations, resonance(s), °rapport, empathy, °sympathy

vibrate *v.* °quiver, °shiver, °shudder, °fluctuate, °quake, °shake, °tremble, throb, °pulsate, °oscillate, °pulse, reverberate, resonate, *Brit* judder

vicarious *adj.* surrogate, delegated, deputed, commissioned, assigned, °indirect, substituted

vice *n.* **1** immorality, corruption, °evil, badness, depravity, °degradation, degeneracy, iniquity, villainy, venality, evildoing, wickedness, °profligacy, °sin, sinfulness, °transgression **2** °flaw, °defect, °fault, °imperfection, °blemish, °shortcoming, °failing, °weakness, °frailty, °foible, °infirmity, deficiency

vice versa *adv.* conversely, contrariwise, to *or* on the contrary, reversed, the other way around

vicinity *n.* °area, °neighborhood, °locale, vicinage, environs, locality, °precincts, purlieus, °territory

vicious *adj.* **1** °immoral, unprincipled, amoral, barbarous, °corrupt, °evil, °bad, °base, depraved, °vile, °atrocious, execrable, degraded, °degrading, °degenerate, °venal, iniquitous, heinous, odious, °perverted, nefarious, °wicked, flagitious, °devilish, diabolic(al), °fiendish, °monstrous, °profligate, °shameful, °shameless, °abominable, °sinful **2** malicious, °spiteful, °mean, °nasty, °hateful, malevolent, °malignant, °bitter, acrimonious, °rancorous, °venomous, °vindictive, defamatory, °slanderous, °scandalous, *Slang* °rotten, bitchy **3** °savage, °wild, °untamed, °ferocious, °fearful, °brutal, °fierce, °fiendish, bestial, feral, brutish, ravening, *Literary* °fell

vicissitude *n.* **1** °change, °mutation, °alteration, changeability, mutability, °variation, variability, °variety, °alternation, °flux, °fluctuation, unpredictability **2** ***vicissitudes.*** fluctuations, changes, variations, contrasts, °inconstancy, unpredictability, uncertainties, *Colloq* ups and downs, flukiness

victim *n.* **1** sufferer, martyr, °casualty, °scapegoat, sacrificial lamb, injured party **2** °dupe, gull, °fool, °butt, fair game, *Colloq* chump, fall guy, *Slang* °sucker, °sap, *Chiefly US and Canadian* patsy, *US* schnook, schlemiel *or* schlemihl *or* shlemiel

victimize *v.* **1** °prey on, °pursue, go after, °pick on, °bully, take advantage of, °persecute, °exploit, °use **2** °cheat, °swindle, bilk, °defraud, °dupe, °hoodwink, °deceive, gull, °fool, °trick, °outwit, °outsmart, outfox, *Colloq* snooker, flimflam, *Slang* suck *or* sucker in, °screw, °shaft, °take (in), rook

victor *n.* °winner, °champion, conqueror, prizewinner

victorious *adj.* °triumphant, °successful

victory *n.* °triumph, °conquest, °supremacy, °superiority, °success, overcoming, mastery, °winning, quelling, crushing

vie *v.* °compete, contend, °struggle, °strive

view *n.* **1** °outlook, °aspect, °prospect, °scene, °perspective, vista, panorama, °spectacle, °picture, °tableau; °landscape, seascape, cityscape **2** °opinion, °point of view, °approach, °position, °judgment, °belief, way of thinking, °conception, °understanding, °impression, °feeling, °sentiment, °notion **3** °aspect, °angle, °position, °prospect, °perspective, °vision, °representation, °projection **4** inspection, °survey, °vision, °sight, °observation, °scrutiny, °examination, contemplation, °study **5** °aim, °direction, °intent, °intention, °purpose, °objective, °object, °expectation, °prospect, °vision, °hope, °dream **6** ***in view of.*** °in light of, °considering, in consideration of, because of, on account of —*v.* **7** look at *or* upon *or* over, °see, °take in, °watch, °observe, °scrutinize, °examine, °regard, °behold **8** °witness, °see, °watch, °observe, °take in **9** °regard, °consider, °think of, look on *or* upon, °judge, deem, °believe, °hold, °estimate, °rate, °gauge, assess

viewpoint *n.* °standpoint, °(point of) view, °attitude, °angle, °slant, °position, °stance, vantage point, °perspective, frame of reference, way of thinking, °context

vigilance *n.* watchfulness, alertness, °observance, guardedness, circumspection, attentiveness, °caution

vigilant *adj.* watchful, °alert, °sharp, °observant, °guarded, circumspect, °attentive, °wakeful, °cautious, °careful, °wary, chary, on one's guard, on the alert, on the lookout, °eagle-eyed, hawk-eyed, Argus-eyed, on the qui vive, on one's toes, with one's eyes open, *Colloq* with one's eyes skinned *or* peeled

vigor *n.* °vitality, °resilience, °strength, °power, °energy, forcefulness, °force, °stamina, °endurance, mettle, mettlesomeness, °pith, °dynamism, °spirit, liveliness, °animation, °verve, vivacity, °exuberance, brio, briskness, °zest, zealousness, °enthusiasm, °gusto, °eagerness, *Colloq* °spunk, °pep, pizazz, vim, oomph, zing, get-up-and-go

vigorous *adj.* °energetic, °active, °vivacious, °dynamic, °brisk, °lively, °spirited, °robust, °strong, °hardy, °hale, °hearty, °vital, °fit, °lusty, °stalwart, in good *or* fine fettle, spry, °sprightly, resilient, *Colloq* peppy, full of pep, full of get-up-and-go, full of beans

vigorously *adv.* energetically, actively, vivaciously, dynamically, briskly, spiritedly, robustly, strongly, hardily, heartily, lustily, stalwartly, eagerly, with might and main, °with a vengeance, strenuously, *Colloq* °like mad, like crazy, hammer and tongs

vile *adj.* **1** °base, abject, °contemptible, debased, °degenerate, depraved, °bad, iniquitous, execrable, °atrocious, °sordid, °immoral, amoral, °wicked, °evil, °sinful, hellish, °fiendish, ignoble, °revolting, °despicable, horrid, °horrible, °dreadful, °terrible, °corrupt, °mean, °wretched, °miserable, °degrading, ignominious, °disgraceful, °shameful, °shameless **2** °disgusting, °nasty, sickening, °nauseous, nauseating, °foul, °loathsome, °offensive, noxious, °repulsive, °repellent, °repugnant

vilify *v.* °depreciate, devalue, deprecate, °debase, °disparage, denigrate, °diminish, traduce, defame, speak ill of, revile, °slander, °libel, °abuse, defile, °sully, °smear, °tarnish, malign, calumniate, asperse, °run down, decry, *Rare* vilipend, *Colloq US* bad-mouth

villain *n.* °wretch, evildoer, °criminal, °miscreant, blackguard, °rogue, °rascal, cad, scallywag *or* scalawag, malefactor, °scoundrel, dog, cur, viper, reptile, snake in the grass, rat, *Archaic* rapscallion, *Literary* knave, caitiff, *Colloq Brit* bounder, blighter, *Slang* bastard, son of a bitch, *Brit* rotter, *US* s.o.b *or* S.O.B. *or* SOB (= 'son-of-a-bitch')

villainous *adj.* **1** treacherous, °perfidious, °dishonest, °unscrupulous, °traitorous, °corrupt, °faithless, °criminal, felonious, °murderous, *Colloq* °crooked, °bent **2** See **vile, 1,** above.

vindicate *v.* **1** °clear, exonerate, absolve, acquit, exculpate, °excuse **2** °justify, °support, °uphold, °prove

vindictive *adj.* avenging, vengeful, vindicatory, revengeful, retaliatory, °spiteful, unforgiving, splenetic, °resentful, °rancorous, °implacable

vintage *n.* **1** year, crop, °harvest, °origin, °generation —*adj.* **2** °quality, °choice, °superior, °better, °good, °select, °best, °classic; °aged, °seasoned, mature(d), mellow(ed) **3** °antiquated, °old-fashioned, old-fogy(ish), °antique, °bygone, old-time, collector *or* collector's, *Colloq* over the hill

violate *v.* **1** °break, °breach, °disobey, °disregard, contravene, °infringe, °ignore **2** °dishonor, °desecrate, °profane, defile, °degrade, °debase, treat irreverently **3** °rape, debauch, °ravish, °ravage, °molest, °attack, °assault, °outrage

violation *n.* **1** °infringement, °breach, °disregard, disobedience, contravention, °abuse; ignoring, infringing, breaching, disregarding, disobeying, contravening, abusing, violating **2** profanation, profaning, °sacrilege, desecration, desecrating, defilement, defiling, °degradation, °degrading, °dishonor, dishonoring, debasement, debasing, violating **3** °rape, ravishment, molestation, °attack, °outrage, °assault, violating

violence *n.* **1** (brute *or* physical) force, °might, mightiness, °power, °strength, °severity, °intensity, °energy, vehemence, ferocity, ferociousness, fierceness, °fury, °vigor; destructiveness, °virulence **2** bestiality, brutality, °barbarity, savagery, cruelty, bloodthirstiness, wildness, ferocity, °frenzy, °fury, °passion, fierceness, vehemence, murderousness **3** ***do violence to.*** **(a)** °harm, °damage, °injure **(b)** °warp, °twist, °distort

violent *adj.* **1** °wild, °physical, °destructive, vehement, °brutal, brutish, °beastly, °nasty, °cruel, °mean, barbarous, °inhuman, °savage, °fierce, °ferocious, °furious, frenzied, uncontrollable, °untamed, °ungovernable, raging, °raving, irrational, °insane, crazed, *Colloq* fit to be tied **2** °harmful, °injurious, damaging, °detrimental, °destructive, deleterious, catastrophic, cataclysmic, °ruinous, °devastating **3** °acute, °serious, °severe, °extreme, °harsh, °trenchant, °virulent, °intense, °energetic, °forceful, vehement, °passionate, °impetuous, °tempestuous

virtual *adj.* °effective, °essential; °practical, °understood, accepted

virtually *adv.* essentially, effectively, °practically, °almost, °to all intents and purposes, for all practical purposes, more or less, °nearly, as good as, °substantially, °in effect, °in essence

virtue *n.* **1** °morality, high-mindedness, °honor, goodness, justness, righteousness, fairness, °integrity, right-mindedness, °honesty, °probity, uprightness, °rectitude, decency, °worth, worthiness, °nobility, °character, respectability **2** virginity, °chastity, chasteness, °honor, innocence, °purity **3** °quality, °credit, °strength, good point, °asset **4** ***by virtue of.*** by dint of, °owing to, °thanks to, °by reason of, because of, on account of

virtuosity *n.* °(technical) skill, °technique, °ability, °expertise, mastery, °excellence, °brilliance, craftsmanship, °craft, °flair, °dash, élan, éclat, °panache, pyrotechnics, showmanship, °show, staginess, *Colloq* razzle-dazzle

virtuoso *n.* **1** °master, maestro, °expert, °genius, °talent, °prodigy, old hand, *Colloq* wizard, whizz *or* whiz *or* wiz, whizz-kid *or* whiz-kid *or* wiz-kid, *Chiefly Brit* °dab hand, *US* maven *or* mavin *or* mayvin —*adj.* **2** °masterful, masterly, °expert, °talented, °brilliant, °dazzling, bravura, prodigious, °excellent, °superb, °extraordinary, °exceptional, °superior, °first-rate, °superlative, °matchless, °peerless, °sterling, °marvelous, °remarkable

virtuous *adj.* **1** °moral, °honorable, °ethical, °honest, °good, upstanding, high-principled, °upright, °righteous, °pure, uncorrupted, incorruptible, °just, °fair, right-minded, fair-minded, high-minded, °scrupulous, °trustworthy **2** °chaste, °innocent, virginal, virgin; °decent, °proper, unsullied, °faithful, °true, uncorrupted

virulence *n.* **1** virulency, poisonousness, venomousness, toxicity, noxiousness, deadliness, perniciousness, injuriousness, destructiveness, malignity, malignancy, °violence, balefulness **2** virulency, acrimony, acrimoniousness, °bitterness, acerbity, °rancor, spleen, °poison, poisonousness, °venom, venomousness, malignity, malevolence, maliciousness, malice, °spite, °hostility, °resentment, °antagonism, hatred

virulent *adj.* **1** °lethal, life-threatening, °deadly, °fatal, pernicious, septic, °poisonous, toxic, baleful, noxious, °dangerous, °harmful, °injurious, °detrimental, deleterious, °destructive, °unhealthy, °unwholesome **2** °vicious, °venomous, °bitter, °spiteful, °malignant, malign, malicious, malevolent, °poisonous, splenetic, acrimonious, acerbic, acid, mordant, °sarcastic, °nasty, °trenchant, °caustic, antagonistic, °hateful, °hostile

visible *adj.* **1** seeable, perceivable, °perceptible, °discernible, detectable, discoverable, °noticeable, unmistakable *or* unmistakeable, °clear, °obvious, °observable; visual **2** °obvious, °conspicuous, °evident, °apparent, °prominent, °manifest, °distinct, °patent, well-defined, identifiable

vision *n.* **1** eyesight, acutance, °perception, °sight **2** farsightedness, °understanding, °imagination, °foresight, foresightedness, °insight **3** °view, °perspective, °perception, envisioning, envisaging, °dream, °idea, °plan, °scheme **4** °phantom, apparition, chimera, °delusion, °hallucination, mirage, °specter, °shade, eidolon, revenant, phantasm, materialization, °illusion, °ghost, wraith **5** sight for sore eyes, °(welcome) sight, °dream, °epitome

visionary *adj.* **1** °dreamy, °speculative, unpractical, °impractical, °fanciful, °imaginary, °unrealistic, °unreal, °romantic, °idealistic, unworkable, utopian —*n.* **2** °dreamer, idealist, °romantic, fantast, wishful thinker, Don Quixote

visit *v.* **1** (go *or* come to) see, call (in *or* on *or* upon), look in on, stop in *or* by, *Colloq* pop in *or* by, drop in (on), °take in **2** °afflict, °attack, befall, °fall upon, assail, °seize, smite, °scourge, descend upon, °inflict, °affect —*n.* **3** °stay, °call, °sojourn, °stop, stopover

visitation *n.* **1** staying, °calling, visiting, sojourning, stopping (over) **2** °affliction, °ordeal, °trial, °punishment, °disaster, °catastrophe, cataclysm, °calamity, °tragedy, °curse, °scourge, °blight, °plague, °pestilence

visitor *n.* caller, °guest, °company; visitant

vital *adj.* **1** °imperative, °essential, °necessary, needed, requisite, required, °indispensable, °mandatory, compulsory, °cardinal, °fundamental, °basic, °critical, °crucial, °central, °pivotal **2** °important, °key, °central, °critical, °crucial, life-or-death, °pivotal, °paramount, °main **3** °lively, full of life, °vivacious, °spirited, °vigorous, °dynamic, °alive, °animated, °brisk, °energetic **4** °invigorating, quickening, life-giving, animating, vitalizing, reviving, vivifying, enlivening, rejuvenating

vitality *n.* **1** °energy, °life, life force, °vigor, °power, °intensity, °force, liveliness, vivacity, vivaciousness, °animation, °sparkle, spiritedness, °exuberance, *Colloq* zing, °pep, pizazz, oomph, get-up-and-go, zip, vim **2** °stamina, hardiness, °endurance, °energy, °strength, robustness

vitalize *v.* °stimulate, °activate, °arouse, vivify, °animate, °awaken, inspirit, invigorate, °enliven, °inspire, °revive, °rejuvenate, innervate, °energize, °fortify, reinvigorate, °renew, °refresh, °charge (up)

vitiate *v.* **1** °spoil, °ruin, °harm, °impair, °mar, °sully, °corrupt, °pervert, °contaminate, °adulterate, °weaken, °degrade, °downgrade, °depreciate, °diminish, °depress, vulgarize, °lower, °reduce, °undermine **2** °debase, deprave, °pervert, °corrupt, °demoralize, defile **3** invalidate, °destroy, °delete, °cancel, nullify, annul, °revoke, °void, abrogate, °abolish, °withdraw, °quash, °suppress

vituperate *v.* °berate, °rate, reproach, revile, °vilify, execrate, °abuse, °denounce, decry, deprecate, °disparage, devalue, °diminish, °put down, °run down, devaluate, °depreciate, °blame, inculpate, censure, find fault with, °attack, assail, °castigate, °scold, °reprimand, °upbraid, °rebuke, chide, °chasten

vituperative *adj.* °abusive, calumniatory, calumnious, °scurrilous, °derogatory, belittling, depreciatory, depreciative, detractory, °contemptuous, damning, denunciatory, denigrating, deprecatory, censorious, aspersive, defamatory, °slanderous, libelous, castigatory, condemnatory, malign, °scornful, °withering, °harsh, °sardonic, °sarcastic, °biting, acid, contumelious, opprobrious, insulting, *Formal* vilipenditory, *Colloq* downputting

vivacious *adj.* °lively, °spirited, °sprightly, °energetic, °animated, °brisk, °ebullient, °effervescent, °bubbly, °gay, °cheerful, °happy, °blithe, °jaunty, lighthearted, °sunny, °merry, high-spirited, °buoyant, chipper, *Colloq* up, peppy, full of pep, full of beans, zippy

vivid *adj.* **1** °intense, °strong, °brilliant, °fresh, °bright, °dazzling, lucid, °rich, °clear, colorful, °glowing **2** °clear, °detailed, °sharp, °realistic, °graphic, true to life, °lifelike, °distinct, °powerful, °strong, °memorable, °dramatic, °striking **3** °prolific, °fruitful, °fertile, fecund, inventive, °creative

vocalist *n.* °singer, soloist, choir boy *or* girl, choir member, chorus boy *or* girl, chorus member, chorister, caroler; diva, prima donna, chanteuse; cantor, crooner; *Colloq* songbird, canary, thrush, nightingale

vocation *n.* °calling, °trade, métier, °business, °profession, °occupation, °career, °employment, °job, °pursuit, lifework, °line (of work), *Slang* °bag, °thing

vogue *n.* **1** °fashion, °mode, °style, °look, °taste, °trend, °rage, °craze, last word, *dernier cri*, °(latest) thing, *Colloq* °fad, the latest **2** °popularity, °favor, °preference, acceptance, currency, °prevalence, fashionableness

voice *n.* **1** °speech, utterance, articulation, °words, °expression **2** °share, °part, °vote, participation, °say, °decision, °option, °turn, °chance **3** spokesman, spokeswoman, spokesperson, °representative, °agent, °agency, °instrument; °organ, °medium, °vehicle, forum, °publication —*v.* **4** °express, utter, articulate, °enunciate, °present, verbalize, put into words, give utterance *or* voice *or* expression *or* vent to, °communicate, convey, °declare, assert, °make known, °reveal, °disclose, °raise, °bring up, °air

void *adj.* **1** null and void, °invalid, not (legally) binding, inoperative, unenforceable, °ineffectual, °futile, °ineffective, °vain, unavailing, °idle, °useless, °pointless, °bootless **2** °empty, °vacant, unoccupied, °unused, unutilized, unfilled, °blank, °clear; °deserted **3** *void of.* devoid of, without, lacking, °destitute of —*n.* **4** °emptiness, vacantness, vacuum, blankness, nothingness **5** °space, °niche, °slot, °opening, °place, °vacancy, °gap, °emptiness —*v.* **6** nullify, annul, °cancel, °delete, disannul, declare *or* render null and void, invalidate, °quash, °vacate, °discharge, °abandon, disestablish, °neutralize, disenact, set *or* put aside, rescind, °reverse, abnegate, abrogate **7** °evacuate, °discharge, °expel, °emit, °purge, °clear, °empty, °drain, °eject; °pass, excrete, °urinate, °defecate

volatile *adj.* **1** vaporizing, evaporable, evaporative **2** °changeable, °fickle, °flighty, °inconstant, °erratic, °restless, °unstable, °variable, mercurial, °capricious **3** °explosive, hair-trigger, °sensitive, charged, eruptive, °tense, tension-ridden

volition *n.* °(free) will, °choice, °option, choosing, °discretion, °preference

volley *n.* **1** salvo, bombardment, barrage, cannonade, fusillade, °discharge, °hail, °shower **2** °outpouring, °torrent, °flood, deluge, inundation, °burst, °storm, outbreak **3** °give-and-take, to-and-fro, interaction, reciprocity, °exchange, volleying, crossfire, badinage, bantering

voluble *adj.* °talkative, °glib, °fluent, loquacious, garrulous, chatty, °profuse, gossipy, °exuberant, long-winded, °bombastic, °windy, °wordy, *Colloq* blessed with the gift of the gab

volume *n.* **1** °amount, °quantity, °supply, °mass, °bulk, °abundance, sum total, aggregate **2** °capacity, °size, °measure **3** loudness **4** °book, tome

voluminous *adj.* **1** °large, °extensive, °great, °spacious, capacious, °expansive, °roomy, °loose, °ample, °big, °bulky, cavernous, copious, °massive, °huge, °substantial, tremendous, °enormous, °gigantic, mammoth, °vast **2** oversized, outsized, °ample, billowing

voluntarily *adv.* °freely, °willingly, spontaneously, of (one's) own free will, on (one's) own (initiative *or* recognizance *or* responsibility), without prompting, without being prompted *or* asked, gratis, gratuitously; by choice, intentionally, purposely, °on purpose, °deliberately

voluntary *adj.* **1** °free, elective, °willing, °spontaneous, °unsolicited, unbidden, °unasked, °gratuitous, contributed **2** discretionary *or* discretional, unconstrained, °intentional, °willful, °deliberate, intended, °premeditated, planned, volitional, °optional

voluptuous *adj.* **1** °sensual, sensualistic, °sensuous, °luxurious, voluptuary, sybaritic(al), hedonist(ic), pleasure-seeking, pleasure-loving, luxury-loving, (self-) indulgent **2** °seductive, °attractive, °desirable, °beautiful, °tempting, °inviting, appealing, enticing, alluring, °ravishing, °luscious, °delicious, °gorgeous, °shapely, °buxom, well-proportioned, well-endowed, well-built, *Colloq* curvaceous, °sexy, eye-filling, *Slang* (well-)stacked, busty, *US* built

vomit *v.* spew out *or* up, spit up, belch forth; °regurgitate, °throw up, °gag, retch, °heave, *US* keck, *Colloq* puke, °return (food), *Brit* sick up, *Slang chiefly Australian* chunder, *US* barf, upchuck, toss (one's) cookies, spiff (one's) biscuits

voracious *adj.* **1** insatiable, °gluttonous, °ravenous, ravening, °rapacious, piggish, °hoggish, cormorant, predacious, edacious, devouring, °greedy, °avaricious, esurient, uncontrollable, °uncontrolled, °unquenchable, °enormous, °prodigious, *US* cormorant

2 °thirsty, °hungry, °desirous, avid, °eager, zealous, °enthusiastic, °fervent, fervid, °ardent, °earnest, °passionate, °devoted

vote *n.* 1 ballot, ticket, show of hands; referendum, °plebiscite 2 °suffrage, franchise 3 °opinion; voter, elector —*v.* 4 opt, °choose, come out (for *or* against), express *or* signify (one's) opinion *or* preference *or* desire

vouch *v.* Usually, ***vouch for.*** support, °guarantee, °back (up), °endorse, °certify; °uphold, °sponsor, °bear witness, attest to

vouchsafe *v.* 1 °offer, °give (up), °yield, °accord, °supply, °grant, °impart, °bestow, deign *or* condescend to give 2 °permit, °allow, °suffer

vow *v.* 1 °swear, °pledge, °promise, °assure, °state, °declare, give (one's) (solemn) word (of honor) —*n.* 2 °oath, °pledge, °promise, °agreement; °(solemn) word (of honor)

vulgar *adj.* 1 indelicate, °boorish, uncultured, uncultivated, °low, °unrefined, °common, °plebeian, inelegant, unladylike, ungentlemanly, gauche, uncouth, °coarse, °tasteless, °ostentatious, ignoble, low-class, *Colloq* °flash 2 °tasteless, indelicate, °indecent, °rude, °crude, °naughty, °dirty, °improper, °off-color, °risqué, ribald, °blue, indecorous, °nasty, °offensive, °gross, °lustful, °obscene, °lewd, °lascivious, licentious, smutty, salacious, scatologic(al), °filthy, °pornographic, *Slang US* raunchy 3 °popular, °vernacular, °ordinary, °everyday, °general, °homespun, commonplace, household, °average

W

wad *n.* 1 °pad, °mass, °lump, °clod, ball, °plug, chunk, hunk, °block, °pack 2 °roll, pocketful, °heap, °quantity, °load, *Colloq US* bankroll

waddle *v.* toddle, °shuffle, wobble *or* wabble, °totter, °paddle, °pad, waggle, duckwalk, *Brit dialect* wamble

wade *v.* 1 ford, °cross, °traverse, °walk, make one's way 2 °paddle, °play, °splash 3 ***wade in or into.*** **(a)** °enter, get in (*or* into), °join (in) **(b)** °attack, °approach, get *or* set to work, plunge *or* dive into 4 ***wade through.*** plow *or* plough through, work (one's) way through, hammer *or* pound away at, plod through, peg away at

waffle *v.* 1 Often, ***waffle on.*** °carry on, °jabber (on), °prattle (on), prate, blather (on *or* away), *Colloq* run on, *Brit* witter (on), natter (on), rabbit on, *Slang* run off at the mouth 2 °equivocate, hedge, °quibble, °shuffle, tergiversate, hem and haw, prevaricate, beat about *or* around the bush, *Colloq* fudge —*n.* 3 °talk, °palaver, verbiage, °prattle, twaddle, blather, prolixity, wordiness, °jabber, gibber-jabber, *Colloq* °hot air

waft *v.* 1 °drift, °float, °blow, whiff, be borne *or* carried *or* transported —*n.* 2 °breath, °suggestion, °puff, whiff, °hint

wag[1] *v.* 1 °wave, waggle, °oscillate, °fluctuate, °sway, undulate, °flutter, °flap, °flip, °flicker, °shake, °vibrate, °quiver, °nod, °rock, °dance, wobble, bob, bobble, waver, *Rare* vellicate —*n.* 2 °wave, waggle, oscillation, °fluctuation, °sway, undulation, °flutter, vellication, °flap, °flip, °flicker, °shake, vibration, °quiver, °nod, wobble, bobble, waver

wag[2] *n.* °comedian, °wit, punster, pundit, °joker, jester, °comic, jokester, droll, merry-andrew, °clown, *Colloq* °card

wage *n.* 1 Often, ***wages.*** °pay, compensation, emolument, °remuneration, °payment, °fee, °salary, °stipend, recompense, °reward, °earnings; °honorarium —*v.* 2 °carry on, °pursue, °conduct, °engage in, °undertake, practice, °prosecute, °proceed with

wait *v.* 1 °tarry, °linger, °hold on, °stay, bide (one's) time, mark time, °stand by, *Colloq* cool (one's) heels, °stick around, °sit tight, °hang on, *Brit* °hang about, *US* °hang around 2 be delayed *or* postponed *or* deferred *or* shelved *or* put off, *US* be tabled, *Colloq* be put on ice *or* on the back burner 3 ***wait on or upon.*** °serve, °attend (to), °minister (to) —*n.* 4 °delay, °pause, °stay, °holdup, °interval, °halt, °stop, stoppage, °break, hiatus, lacuna, °gap, °respite, °rest (period), °intermission, discontinuation, °recess

waiter *n.* waitress, headwaiter, ***maître d'hôtel,*** °host, hostess, ***sommelier*** (***des vins***), wine steward, stewardess; cupbearer, Ganymede, Hebe

waive *v.* 1 °give up, °relinquish, °renounce, °resign, °forsake, °forgo, °cede, °sign away, °surrender, °abandon, °yield, °dispense with 2 set *or* put aside, °except, °ignore, °disregard, °overlook, °abandon, °defer, °postpone

waiver *n.* renunciation, relinquishment, forgoing, ceding, cession, °resignation, °surrender, abandonment, setting *or* putting aside, deferral, °remission, °postponement

wake[1] *v.* 1 Often, ***wake up.*** °awaken, °awake, °rouse, waken, °bring around; °stir, bestir (oneself), °get up, °come to, get going 2 °awake, waken, °awaken, °animate, °stimulate, °enliven, galvanize, °fire, °quicken, inspirit, °inspire, °activate, liven up, vivify, °kindle, °vitalize, °stir, °arouse, get (someone) going, bring to life —*n.* 3 vigil, °watch, deathwatch, °funeral

wake[2] *n.* 1 °track, °trail, aftermath, °path, backwash, °wash, bow wave; °trace, spoor, °scent 2 ***in the wake of.*** following (on *or* upon), after, °subsequent to; as a result *or* consequence of, on account of, because of, °owing to, °by virtue of

wakeful *adj.* **1** °awake, °sleepless, waking, unsleeping, °restless, °restive, insomniac **2** watchful, °(on the) alert, on the qui vive, °sharp, °attentive, °vigilant, °wary, °cautious, °observant, heedful, on the lookout

walk *v.* **1** °advance, °proceed, °move, °go, wend, go *or* make (one's) way by foot, tread, °step, perambulate, °stalk, stride, °tramp, °stroll, amble, °ramble, ambulate, shamble, °pad, °shuffle, °saunter, trudge, trek, °plod, slog, hike, °parade, °promenade, °strut, °swagger, °prance, °march, goose-step, °pace, °trip, °sidle, tiptoe, sashay, °flounce, °stagger, °lurch, °limp, °waddle, °stamp, mince, °slink, °steal, °prowl, skulk, °sneak, °creep, *Colloq* go by *or* ride by shanks' *or* shanks's pony *or* mare, hoof it, foot it, traipse, °pussyfoot, *Slang US* boogie **2** °take, convoy, °accompany, °escort, °go with; °conduct, °lead; °empty **3** °patrol, trace out, °stalk, °cover, °haunt, °prowl, °wander, °roam, rove *or* range about in *or* on, °frequent **4** ***walk out.*** **(a)** °leave, °depart, °desert; walk out on **(b)** °strike, go (out) on strike, °protest, take industrial action, *Brit* down tools **—*n.*** **5** °path, lane, pathway, pavement, footpath, °promenade, esplanade, boardwalk, *Brit* footway, *US* °sidewalk **6** gait, °step, °carriage, °bearing, stride **7** constitutional, °stroll, amble; slog, °tramp, hike

wall *n.* **1** °screen, °partition, divider, °enclosure, separator, bulkhead, °barrier, °obstruction, °obstacle, °impediment, °block, °fence **2** barricade, fortification, °protection, °bulwark, breastwork, embankment, °rampart, palisade, stockade **3** ***drive up the wall.*** drive crazy *or* insane *or* mad, °madden, °exasperate, derange, °try, °irritate, °infuriate, °enrage **4** ***go to the wall.*** °fail, °collapse, be ruined, face ruin, go bankrupt, lose everything, *Colloq* go broke, °go under, °fold (up), *Slang* go bust **—*v.*** **5** Often, ***wall up or off.*** °enclose, °partition (off), °close (off), brick up, immure

wallet *n.* °purse, pocketbook, *Brit* notecase, *US* billfold

wallow *v.* **1** roll *or* loll about *or* around, °welter, writhe, °tumble, splash *or* plash **2** Usually, ***wallow in.*** °luxuriate in, bask in, °revel in, glory in, indulge (oneself) in, give (oneself) up to, succumb to, °take to, °appreciate, °fancy, °enjoy, °like, °love, °savor, *Slang* get a kick *or* a bang *or* a boot from *or* out of **3** °stumble, °stagger, °lurch, °flounder, °teeter, °totter, falter, °pitch

wan *adj.* **1** °white, °sickly, °pale, pallid, livid, °pasty, ashen, bloodless, waxen, wheyfaced, sallow, °colorless, deathly, °ghostly, °ghastly, cadaverous **2** °weary, °weak, °hollow, °feeble, °frail, °ineffectual, °sorry, °pitiful

wand *n.* baton, °staff, °stick

wander *v.* **1** °walk, °go, °roam, rove, °range, °stray, °ramble, °stroll, °saunter, °meander, °drift, °cruise, °prowl, *Colloq* mosey **2** °wind, °meander, zigzag, turn this way and that **3** digress, °go off, become absent-minded, go woolgathering, lose concentration *or* focus **4** °deviate, digress, °turn, divagate, °stray, °drift, °depart, go off at a tangent, lose (one's) train of thought, °lapse

wane *v.* **1** °decrease, °diminish, grow less, lessen, °decline, °die out, abate, °ebb, °subside, °fade (away), °dim, °taper off, °peter out, °wind down, °weaken **2** draw to a close, °end, °terminate **—*n.*** **3** °decrease, diminution, lessening, °decline, abatement, °ebb, subsidence, fading, tapering off, petering out, winding down, weakening, deterioration, degeneration **4** ***on the wane.*** on the decrease *or* decline *or* ebb, diminishing, decreasing, declining, abating, subsiding, fading, tapering off, petering out, winding down, weakening, deteriorating, degenerating

wangle *v.* °scheme, °plot, °work out, contrive, °maneuver, °engineer, °manage, °manipulate, machinate, *Colloq* °fix, °fiddle, °work, °pull off, finagle, °swing

want *v.* **1** °desire, crave, °wish (for), long for, pine for, °hope (for), °fancy, covet, °hanker after, °lust after, hunger for *or* after, thirst for *or* after, yearn for, *Colloq* have a yen for **2** °need, °lack, °miss, °require, °call for, °demand, be deficient in, be *or* stand in want *or* in need of, necessitate; be *or* fall short of **—*n.*** **3** °need, °lack, °shortage, deficiency, °dearth, °scarcity, scarceness, insufficiency, scantiness, inadequacy, paucity **4** °appetite, °hunger, °thirst, craving, °desire, °fancy, °wish, °longing, yearning, hankering, °demand, °necessity, °requirement, requisite, °prerequisite, *Colloq* yen **5** °poverty, °need, indigence, homelessness, destitution, °privation, pauperism, penury, neediness, impecuniousness

wanting *adj.* **1** °deficient, °inadequate, not up to par *or* expectations, °insufficient, leaving much to be desired, °unsatisfactory, unsatisfying, °disappointing, second-rate, °inferior, °poor, °shabby, °shoddy, °flawed, °faulty, °imperfect, °incomplete, unfinished, °defective, patchy, impaired, damaged, °broken, °unsound **2** °absent, missing, lacking, °short (of), *US and Canadian* °shy (of)

wanton *adj.* **1** °immoral, °dissolute, °profligate, dissipated, depraved, °loose, °promiscuous, °lustful, licentious, °lecherous, °wild, libidinous, °lewd, °lascivious, °unchaste **2** °abandoned, unrestrained, °undisciplined, ungoverned, °ungovernable, unmanageable, °outrageous, °immoderate, intemperate, untempered **3** °reckless, °rash, uncaring, °lavish, °extravagant, °willful, °heedless, °irresponsible, °careless **4** °wicked, °evil, malevolent, malicious, °merciless, inhumane, °vicious, °cruel, °violent, unjustified, unprovoked, uncalled-for, °purposeless, motiveless, unjustifiable, °arbitrary, °gratuitous **—*n.*** **5** vamp, strumpet, whore, harlot, loose woman, °prostitute, voluptuary, slut, trollop, Jezebel, *Colloq* °tart, *Slang* hooker, working girl, call girl

war *n.* **1** warfare, °combat, °conflict, fighting, °clash, °hostilities, °battle, °struggle, °engagement, °encounter, °strife, contention **2** ***at war.*** fighting, battling, in combat, in conflict; in disagreement, in dispute, in contention, struggling, antagonistic, at daggers drawn —*v.* **3** do battle *or* fight *or* struggle *or* (engage in) combat with *or* against, make *or* wage war with *or* against, take up arms *or* strive *or* campaign *or* tilt against, cross swords *or* contend *or* joust with

ward *n.* **1** °district, °division, °precinct, °section, °zone, °quarter **2** °minor, dependent —*v.* **3** ***ward off.*** °fend off, °repel, avert, °avoid, °block, °thwart, keep away *or* off *or* at bay *or* at arm's length, °check, °repulse, chase away *or* off, °forestall

wardrobe *n.* **1** (collection *or* stock of) clothing *or* clothes *or* attire *or* apparel **2** clothespress, closet, clothes cupboard

warehouse *n.* °storehouse, °store, storeroom, depository, stockroom, depot, godown

wares *n. pl.* merchandise, °goods, commodities, manufactures, °produce, °stock (in trade), supplies, °lines

warlike *adj.* combative, °belligerent, bellicose, °aggressive, °pugnacious, °hostile, °bloodthirsty; hawkish, militaristic, jingoistic, warmongering

warm *adj.* **1** °heated, °tepid, °lukewarm, °cozy, °comfortable, not uncomfortable, balmy **2** passionate, °impassioned, °excited, °animated, °fervent, fervid, °spirited, °lively, °ardent, zealous, °keen, °eager, °emotional, °heated, °intense, irritated, annoyed, vexed, °angry, irate, °furious, °testy, short-tempered, °touchy, °quick-tempered, irascible, °irritable, °stormy, turbulent, °vigorous, °violent, *Colloq* worked up, hot under the collar, steamed up **3** °amiable, °friendly, °cordial, affable, °pleasant, °genial, °cheerful, °kindly, °hospitable, °hearty; °affectionate, °tender, °mellow, loving, amorous **4** °ardent, °enthusiastic, °earnest, °eager, °sincere **5** uncomfortable, °awkward, unpleasant, °strained, °tense **6** Often, ***getting warm.*** close *or* near to making a discovery, about to make a discovery —*v.* **7** °heat (up), warm up *or* over **8** Often, ***warm to.*** become less antagonistic *or* hostile to *or* toward(s), become enthusiastic *or* supportive of, become excited *or* animated about *or* over, be attracted to *or* toward(s), °like, feel affection for **9** °stir, °move, please, °delight, make (one *or* someone) feel good

warm-blooded *adj.* **1** *Technical* homoiothermic *or* homoiothermal *or* homoeothermic *or* homoeothermal *or* homeothermic *or* homeothermal **2** °passionate, °ardent, fervid, hot-blooded, °impetuous, *Colloq* °randy

warmly *adv.* **1** affectionately, tenderly, °fondly, lovingly **2** cordially, amiably, amicably, solicitously, warmheartedly **3** earnestly, eagerly, fervently, enthusiastically, °well, °kindly **4** °vigorously, intensely, °fiercely, intensively, °intently, energetically, doggedly, persistently, zealously, fervently, fervidly, °hotly, ardently, enthusiastically **5** heatedly, vehemently, vociferously, forcefully, energetically, °vigorously, feverishly, frantically, furiously, angrily, violently

warmth *n.* **1** °heat **2** cordiality, heartiness, friendliness, geniality, amiableness, kindliness, tenderness, affability, °love **3** °ardor, effusiveness, °enthusiasm, zeal, excitedness, °fervor, vehemence, °vigor, ebullience, °passion **4** irritation, °annoyance, pique

warn *v.* **1** °caution, admonish, °advise, °notify, apprise, °inform, give (fair) warning, °alert, give (prior) notice, put (someone) on notice *or* on guard *or* on the alert, make (someone) aware (of), forewarn, °tip off, *Rare* premonish **2** °advise, °counsel, °caution

warning *n.* **1** °caution, admonition, °advice, °counsel, caveat, °word (to the wise), °tip, notification, °notice, °threat; °lesson, °example **2** °omen, °sign, °signal, °indication, augury, foretoken, portent, foreshadowing, forewarning, °prophecy

warp *v.* **1** °twist, contort, °distort, deform, bend out of shape, °wrench, °pervert, misshape —*n.* **2** °twist, contortion, distortion, °bias, deformity, deformation, °bend, °wrench, °perversion, °kink, idiosyncrasy, °quirk, deviation

warrant *n.* **1** authorization, °sanction, °reason, justification, °approval, validation, °license, °right, certification, entitlement, °grounds, °cause, °rationale, °basis, °assurance, °carte blanche, °guarantee, °pledge, °security, °charter, °warranty **2** writ, °order, affidavit, °paper, °document, credential, °permit, entitlement, °license, summons, subpoena, mandate, °decree, fiat, edict, ukase —*v.* **3** °guarantee, °promise, °assure, ensure *or* insure, °answer for, be answerable for, °certify, vouch for, °underwrite, °back up, °uphold, stand by *or* behind **4** °authorize, °sanction, °justify, °explain, °approve, °verify, validate, °permit, °allow, provide *or* offer grounds *or* justification *or* cause *or* reason for, °call for, necessitate, °entitle, empower, °excuse, °license

warranty *n.* °guarantee, °assurance, °promise, commitment, covenant, °undertaking, °agreement, °pledge, °bond

wary *adj.* °cautious, °careful, on (one's) guard, circumspect, °prudent, apprehensive, chary, watchful, °vigilant, on the qui vive, heedful, °observant, on (one's) toes, *Colloq* cagey, *Slang* °leery (of)

wash *v.* **1** wash up, °clean (up), °cleanse, bathe, °shower, douche, douse, °scrub (up), shampoo, soap up, °lather, °launder, °scour, °soak, °rinse, °flush, °wet, °drench, deterge, sponge (off), *Facetious* perform (one's) ablutions, *Archaic* absterge, *Formal or literary* lave, *Brit* bath **2** Sometimes, ***wash away or out or off.*** °remove, °move, °transport, °carry, °bear, convey, °deliver, °deposit, °drive, °sweep **3** °splash, °spatter, splatter, plash, °dash, °beat, °pound, thrash, °break, °toss, °surge, undulate, °rush, °run, °lap, °ripple, °roll, °flow **4** Usually, ***wash away or off.*** °erode, wear off *or* away, °remove, °delete, °erase, expunge, °destroy, eradicate, °obliterate, °extinguish, °blot out, °wipe out **5** Often, ***wash away or out.*** °erode, cut *or* dig *or* wear *or* eat *or* dredge (away *or* out), °excavate, °channel **6** decontaminate, °purify, °sift, °filter, depurate **7** overlay, °film, °coat, °paint, °glaze; °plate **8** °hold up, °stand up, stand the test of time, carry weight, bear scrutiny, prove true, make sense, be believable *or* credible, *Colloq* hold water **9** ***wash down.*** °swallow **10** ***wash (one's) hands of.*** stay *or* keep away from, disown, °repudiate, turn (one's) back on, have nothing more *or* further to do with, °get rid of, rid (oneself) of, °desert, °abandon, °leave —*n.* **11** washing, cleaning, cleansing, scrubbing, °scrub, scouring, shampoo, shampooing, bath, bathing, °shower, sponge bath, tub bath; laundering; *Facetious* ablutions; *Colloq Brit* tub, tubbing **12** °wave, °wake, °surge, backwash **13** °lotion, °rinse, liniment, °salve, embrocation, emulsion, °preparation; mouthwash, gargle; eyewash, collyrium **14** °flow, °wave, °swell, welling, °sweep, °sweeping, ebb and flow, °surge, surging, undulation, rise and fall **15** °coat, coating, °film, overlay, °glaze; plating

washed-out *adj.* **1** °wan, °pale, pallid, °colorless, faded, °lackluster, °flat; blanched, bleached, etiolated **2** °exhausted, °spent, °tired, tired-out, °weary, worn-out, °fatigued, drained, *Colloq* dog-tired, bone-tired, done in, all in, fagged out, bushed, *Brit* knocked up, *US* knocked out, *Slang* °beat, *US and Canadian* tuckered out, pooped

washed-up *adj.* finished, °through, failed, done for, played-out, °over (and done with), *Slang* kaput, *fini*

washout *n.* °failure, °disaster, debacle, °(total) loss, °fiasco, °disappointment, *Colloq* °flop, °dud, *Brit* damp squib, *US* lead balloon

waspish *adj.* irascible, bad-tempered, foul-tempered, °temperamental, °testy, grouchy, °sensitive, °volatile, °querulous, edgy, °petulant, °spiteful, °peevish, °cantankerous, curmudgeonly, °cross, crabby, crabbed, crotchety, splenetic, grumpy, captious, °cranky, crusty

waste *v.* **1** squander, °misuse, °throw away, °fritter away, misspend, °splurge, °dissipate, *Slang* °blow **2** Often, ***waste away.*** °diminish, °deteriorate, °dwindle, °decline, °decay, atrophy, wither, °shrink, °weaken, become debilitated, °fade, become enervated *or* enfeebled, regress, °ebb, °sink **3** °enervate, enfeeble, emaciate, °gnaw, °destroy, °consume, debilitate, °exhaust, disable **4** assassinate, °murder, °kill, *Slang* °put away, °rub out, *US* ice —*n.* **5** °misuse, misapplication, squandering, °dissipation, misemployment, °abuse, °neglect **6** wasting, °extravagance, °prodigality, wastefulness, squandering, °indulgence, lavishness, °profligacy, dissoluteness, improvidence, overindulgence **7** °refuse, °rubbish, °garbage, °dregs, debris, leavings, °scrap, offscourings, sweepings, °litter, *Archaic* orts, *US and Canadian* °trash **8** wasteland, °desert, wilderness, barrens, °wilds, °emptiness, vastness —*adj.* **9** °extra, °leftover, °unused, °superfluous, °worthless, °useless **10** °barren, unproductive, unusable, unsalvageable, °useless, unrecyclable, °unprofitable, °worthless **11** ***lay waste.*** °devastate, °destroy, °demolish, despoil, °ruin, °wreck, °ravage, °pillage, °sack, °plunder, °loot, °rob, °strip, °spoil, °gut, °ransack, wreak havoc upon *or* on, °crush, °raze, annihilate, eradicate, extirpate, °wipe out

wasteful *adj.* °extravagant, °spendthrift, °profligate, °prodigal, °lavish, °improvident, unthrifty, uneconomical, overindulgent, openhanded, freehanded, penny-wise and pound-foolish

wastrel *n.* **1** °spendthrift, °profligate, waster, °prodigal, big spender, squanderer **2** °idler, layabout, malingerer, °loafer, shirker, °good-for-nothing, ne'er-do-well, *Chiefly Brit* drone, *Slang Brit* skiver

watch *v.* **1** °observe, °regard, °look at, gaze at *or* on, °take in, °contemplate **2** °look after, °tend, °mind, keep an eye on, watch over, °guard, °care for, °take care of, °safeguard, °protect, °shield, keep safe, °supervise, superintend; chaperon, °accompany, °attend; *Colloq* baby-sit (for), °sit (with) **3** °observe, °note, °notice, make *or* take note of, °see, pay attention (to), °attend (to), °follow, °(take) heed (of), °examine, °inspect, °scrutinize, °pore over; °eye, peer at; °ogle, make eyes at **4** Often, ***watch (out) for.*** °look for, be on the watch *or* lookout *or* alert *or* qui vive (for), °guard (against), keep an eye open (for), be watchful (for), °note, take note *or* notice of, be vigilant (for *or* of), keep (one's) eyes open (for), keep a (sharp) lookout (for), be prepared *or* ready for, be careful of, °anticipate, await, °wait (for), °look for, *Colloq* keep (one's) eyes peeled *or* skinned (for), keep a weather eye open (for) —*n.* **5** vigil, °surveillance, °observation, °lookout **6** clock, timepiece, pocket watch, wristwatch; chronometer **7** sentry, °sentinel, °guard, °watchman **8** ***on the watch (for).*** on the alert (for), on the lookout (for), on (one's) guard (for), on the qui vive (for), alert (for *or* to), °awake (to), °observant (of), watchful (of), °cautious (of), °wary (of), °vigilant, circumspect

watchman *n.* °(security) guard, °sentinel, sentry, °watch, night watchman, custodian, caretaker; watchdog

water *n.* **1** H_2O; distilled water, tap water, drinking water, bottled water, spa water, still water, soda (water), effervescent water, mineral water; sea water, salt water; ditchwater, dishwater, bathwater, *US* branch water, *Facetious* Adam's ale, *Technical and Latin* aqua; *Technical* heavy water *or* deuterium oxide *or* D_2O; *Brit* fizzy water **2** ***not hold water.*** be illogical *or* unsound *or* invalid, not be sensible, be inconsistent, not make sense, be unbelievable *or* incredible, be indefensible, be unfeasible *or* unworkable, not work, not function, not hold up under *or* bear scrutiny *or* examination, not ring true, ring false, *Colloq* not wash **3** ***like water.*** lavishly, extravagantly, °freely, wastefully, profligately, openhandedly, liberally, excessively, copiously, unstintingly, unreservedly **4** ***make water.*** °urinate, pass water, *Colloq* pee, piss **5** ***of the first water.*** of superior *or* excellent *or* first *or* top *or* A-one *or* the finest *or* the highest *or* the best quality *or* grade; first-grade, top-grade —*v.* **6** inundate, °flood, °drench, °saturate, °soak, douse, irrigate, hose, °wet, °shower, °splash, °spray, sprinkle, moisten, °damp, °dampen, bedew **7** Often, ***water down.*** °dilute, °weaken, °thin out, °adulterate; °cut; mollify, °modify, °soften, °tone down, °qualify

watercolor *n.* aquarelle

waterfall *n.* cascade, cataract, fall(s), °chute, Niagara, *Northern Brit* °force, *Scots* linn

watertight *adj.* **1** sealed, waterproof **2** unassailable, °impregnable, °solid, airtight, °flawless, °faultless, °incontrovertible; without loopholes

watery *adj.* **1** °weak, dilute(d), watered-down, °tasteless, insipid, flavorless, °bland, °flat, °dull, °thin, runny, pallid, anemic, *Colloq* °wishy-washy **2** weeping, teary, °tearful, °running, weepy, lachrymose, rheumy **3** °wet, swampy, boggy, marshy, aqueous, squelchy; soggy, °moist, °damp, °humid; *Colloq* squushy *or* squooshy

wave *n.* **1** °swell, undulation, billow, °sea, °heave, °roller, whitecap, white horse; °ripple, wavelet, breaker, comber **2** °surge, °swell, welling up, ground swell, °movement, °flood, upsurge, °uprising, °current, tide **3** °signal, °sign, gesticulation, °gesture —*v.* **4** undulate, billow, move to and fro, °flap, °flutter, °quiver, flip-flop, °swing, °sway, °ripple, °oscillate, zigzag, °fluctuate, °shake; °wag, whiffle, wigwag, wiggle, waggle, brandish **5** °signal, °sign, °indicate, °signify; °gesture, gesticulate

way *n.* **1** °manner, °method, °mode, °fashion, °means, °system, °course (of action), °procedure, °approach, °scheme, °technique, °practice, modus operandi, *Colloq* MO (= 'modus operandi') **2** °manner, °spirit, °feeling, °sense, °character, °approach, °personality, temperament, °disposition, modus vivendi (= 'lifestyle'), °nature, °technique, °style, °conduct, °habit, behavior pattern, °custom **3** °path, °road, °street, avenue, °course, °route, °trail, °direction **4** °distance; °route, °trail, °course, °road **5** °progress, °passage, °advance, °headway; °speed, °velocity, °motion, °(forward) movement **6** °aspect, °respect, °particular, °detail, °point, °sense, °feature **7** °clearance, pathway, avenue, °scope, °freedom, °opportunity **8** °condition, °situation **9** ***by the way.*** °incidentally, °moreover, by the by, parenthetically **10** ***by way of.*** **(a)** via, °through, °by means of **(b)** (functioning) as, in (the) way of, in the capacity of, equivalent to, more or less, something like **11** ***give way.*** **(a)** °collapse, °break (down), °fail, °cave in, °fall (down), °crumble, °crumple, °disintegrate, °go to pieces **(b)** °yield, °surrender, °retreat, °concede, °withdraw, accede, make concessions, acquiesce, °acknowledge **12** ***under way.*** °proceeding, progressing, °on the move, °moving, advancing, °going, begun, started, °in progress, operating, functioning, at work, *US* °in work, *Colloq* in the works, *US* °in the pipeline

waylay *v.* **1** °ambush, lie in wait for, await, °intercept, pounce upon *or* on, swoop down upon *or* on, accost **2** °attack, °mug, °seize, °assault, accost, °set upon

way-out *adj.* **1** °bizarre, °mad, °weird, °crazy, °strange, °odd, °peculiar, freakish, freaky, °eccentric, °queer, °abnormal, °offbeat, °outrageous, °wild, °exotic, esoteric, *Colloq* °kinky, *Slang* kooky, off the wall, far-out, screwy, nutty, *US* flaky, screwball **2** °avant-garde, advanced, °original, innovative, °unorthodox, unconventional, °experimental, precedent-setting, °progressive, exploratory, ground-breaking, *Slang* far-out

weak *adj.* **1** °feeble, °frail, °fragile, unsubstantial, °flimsy, breakable, frangible, °delicate, °rickety, unsteady, °unsound, °decrepit, °shaky, °infirm **2** °frail, °infirm, debilitated, enervated, °delicate, °sickly, anemic, wasted, °decrepit, °puny, effete, worn-out, °tired, °exhausted **3** unassertive, °retiring, namby-pamby, °spineless, °irresolute, °impotent, °ineffectual, °ineffective, °incompetent, feckless, °inept, °wishy-washy, °timid, °meek, craven, timorous, °cowardly, pusillanimous, lily-livered, chicken-hearted, *Colloq* chicken, yellow **4** °feeble, °lame, half-baked, °poor, °miserable, unconvincing, unpersuasive, °empty, °shallow, °flimsy, °hollow, °pathetic, °pitiful, °unbelievable, °untenable **5** weak-minded, dimwitted, dull-witted, slow-witted, °foolish, °feebleminded, °simple, simple-minded, softheaded, °stupid, °dull, moronic, imbecilic, *Colloq* °dumb **6** °faint, °dim, °poor, °dull, °pale, faded, °indistinct, °vague, °hazy, °imperceptible, indiscernible, unclear, blurred, blurry, muzzy, wavering, faltering, ill-defined, °feeble, flickering, °subdued **7** °feeble, °subdued, °low, °soft, hushed, muffled, muted, almost inaudible, stifled, °indistinct **8** See **watery, 1,** above. **9** ***weak point.*** See **weakness, 3,** below.

weaken *v.* **1** debilitate, enfeeble, °enervate, emasculate, °mitigate, °moderate, °dilute, deplete, °diminish, lessen, °depress, °lower, °reduce, °sap, °undermine, °exhaust, impoverish **2** °fade, °dwindle, °tire, °droop, °sag, °fail, °give way, °crumble, °flag **3** °give in, °relent, acquiesce, °give way, °yield, accede, °consent, °agree, assent, °soften, °bend, ease up, °let up, ease off, °relax **4** °water (down), °dilute, °thin (out)

weakling *n.* °milksop, °baby, mollycoddle, lightweight, namby-pamby, *US and Canadian* milquetoast, *Colloq* sissy *or Brit also* cissy, °loser, cream puff, jellyfish, °pushover, softy *or* softie, *Slang* wimp, twirp, *US* weak sister, schnook, schlemiel *or* schlemihl *or* shlemiel

weakness *n.* **1** feebleness, °frailty, fragility, °delicacy, delicateness, vulnerability, °infirmity, °decrepitude **2** incapacity, irresolution, irresoluteness, °impotence, powerlessness, puniness **3** °weak point, °foible, °failing, °fault, °shortcoming, °flaw, Achilles' heel, °defect, °imperfection, °liability **4** soft spot, fondness, °affection, °liking, °preference, °bent, °leaning, °inclination, °fancy, °penchant, predilection, proneness, proclivity, predisposition, °partiality, °appreciation, °appetite, sweet tooth, °taste, °eye

wealth *n.* **1** affluence, °riches, °money, opulence, °prosperity, °property, holdings, °capital, °assets, wherewithal, °cash **2** °profusion, °abundance, °bounty, plenteousness, bounteousness, copiousness, °mine, plenitude, fullness, °store, cornucopia, richness

wealthy *adj.* °rich, affluent, °well-off, °prosperous, well-to-do, °opulent, °comfortable, moneyed, *Colloq* °in the money, on Easy Street, °flush, well-heeled, in clover, *Slang* °loaded, °stinking (rich), filthy rich, *Brit* quids in, rolling in it

wear *v.* **1** be dressed *or* clothed in, dress in, °put on, don, be in, step *or* get into *or* in, °have on, °sport **2** °display, °show, °exhibit, °have, °adopt, °assume **3** Often, ***wear down or away or off.*** °damage, °impair, °harm, °fray, °erode, abrade, corrode, °rub (off) **4** Often, ***wear well.*** °last, °endure, °survive, °hold up, °bear up, °stand up **5** °drag, pass slowly, creep by *or* along, go by gradually *or* tediously **6** Often, ***wear out.*** °tire, °fatigue, °exhaust, debilitate, °weary, °enervate, °drain, °burden **7** °bore, °exasperate, °harass, vex, °annoy, °irritate, °tax, °strain —*n.* **8** wearing, °use, utilization; attire, garb, clothing, °clothes, °apparel, °dress, °gear **9** wear and tear, attrition, deterioration, °damage, fraying, chafing, abrasion, °erosion, corrosion, °friction

weary *adj.* **1** °tired, °fatigued, °exhausted, worn-out, drained, °spent, *Colloq* all in, ready to drop, fagged (out), done in, dead (on (one's) feet), frazzled, dead beat, dog-tired, *Brit* knocked up, *US* knocked out, *Slang Brit* whacked, knackered, *US* pooped, zonked (out), °shot **2** °boring, °irksome, irritating, °tedious, vexing, annoying, exasperating, °burdensome, wearying, tiring, fatiguing, draining, taxing, wearisome **3** bored, °impatient, °jaded, °blasé, *Colloq* fed up, sick and tired, *Taboo slang* browned off —*v.* **4** Often, ***weary of.*** °tire (of), be *or* become bored (with *or* by) *or* impatient (with) *or* jaded (with *or* by), *Colloq* be *or* become fed up (with) *or* sick and tired (with *or* of) **5** °exhaust, °enervate, °fatigue, °tire, debilitate, °drain, °tax, wear *or* tire out

weather *n.* **1** (meteorological) condition(s), °climate **2** ***under the weather.*** ailing, °ill, °sickly, unwell, °indisposed, °out of sorts, °sick, *Colloq* °poorly, °seedy —*v.* **3** °stand, °survive, °suffer, bear up against, °endure, °withstand, rise above, ride out, live through, °brave

weave *v.* **1** °loom; °braid, plait, °entwine, intertwine, interlace, interweave, °knit (together) **2** °blend, °combine, °fuse, °merge, °unite, intermingle, °mesh, °splice, dovetail, °join **3** °construct, °make, contrive, °build, °create, °fabricate, °compose, °spin, °design **4** zigzag, crisscross, wend *or* make (one's) way, °dodge, bob and weave, °shift **5** ***get weaving.*** get started, °get a move on, °hurry (up), °start, *Colloq* °shake a leg, *Brit* get *or* pull (one's) finger out, *Chiefly US* get a wiggle on

web *n.* spider's web, cobweb; °net, °network, entanglement, °snare, °trap

wed *v.* **1** °marry, espouse, get married, become husband and wife, say *or* take (one's) (marriage) vows, join *or* unite in holy wedlock *or* matrimony; lead down the aisle, lead to the altar, *Archaic* wive; *Colloq* tie the knot, get hitched, get spliced **2** °combine, °unite, °ally, °marry, °blend, °merge, °join, °mingle, intermingle, commingle, coalesce, °mix, intermix, °amalgamate, °compound, °alloy, °fuse, homogenize

wedded *adj.* Usually, ***wedded to.*** intimately *or* obstinately attached *or* connected (to), enamored (of)

wedding *n.* **1** °marriage (ceremony), wedding ceremony, nuptials; confarreation **2** combining, °combination, uniting, °union, joining, °juncture, blending, °blend, allying, °alliance, associating, °association, marrying, °marriage, merging, °merger, mingling, intermingling, commingling, coalescing, coalescence, mixing, °mixture, intermixing, amalgamating, °amalgamation, compounding, °compound, alloying, °alloy, fusing, fusion, homogenizing, homogenization

wedge *n.* **1** °block, chock **2** °separation, separator, °division, °partition, °split, fissure, cleavage —*v.* **3** °ram, °jam, °stuff, °cram, °crowd, °force, °squeeze, °pack, °thrust

wee *adj.* **1** °tiny, °small, °diminutive, °little, minuscule, midget, °minute, °miniature, Lilliputian, microscopic, *Colloq* itty-bitty, itsy-bitsy, teeny(-weeny), teensy(-weensy) **2** unimportant, °insignificant, trivial, °little, °puny

weep *v.* **1** °cry, shed tears, °bawl, blubber, °keen, °sob, °lament, °mourn, °bemoan, °bewail, °moan, °grieve, whine, whimper, mewl, pule, °snivel, *Colloq* blub, boohoo, *Brit and Australian* whinge **2** °ooze, seep, exude, °drip

weigh *v.* **1** Sometimes, ***weigh in at or out at.*** *Colloq* tip the scales at **2** °consider, °ponder, °contemplate, think on *or* over *or* about, mull over, turn over in the *or* (one's) mind, ruminate over, °chew over, reflect on *or* upon, °brood over, °pore over, °study, °examine **3** °judge, °estimate, assess, °evaluate, value, °determine **4** Usually, ***weigh on or upon.*** lie heavy on, °burden, °depress, °prey on, °oppress, °disturb, °perturb, °upset **5** °matter, °count, have (an) effect *or* influence, carry weight, be of value *or* account **6** ***weigh down.*** °burden, overburden, °load, °overload, °encumber, °tax, overtax, °strain, °trouble, °worry, °depress, °oppress

weight *n.* **1** heaviness, avoirdupois, °mass, tonnage, *Dialect* heft **2** °burden, °load, millstone, onus, °pressure, °strain, albatross, °cross **3** °influence, °authority, °power, °substance, °force, °moment, °importance, consequence, °impact, persuasiveness, value, °worth, *Colloq* clout **4** °mass, °majority, preponderance *or* preponderancy, °bulk, °superiority *—v.* **5** °load, °charge, ballast **6** °arrange, °manipulate, °bias, °incline, °slant, *Colloq* °rig

weighty *adj.* **1** °heavy, °ponderous, °massive, °huge, °bulky, °substantial, °ample, °large, mammoth, °colossal, °immense, °enormous, °gigantic, °prodigious; corpulent, °fat, °obese, adipose, *Colloq* °hefty **2** °important, consequential, °significant, °momentous, °grave, °crucial, °portentous, thought-provoking, °provocative **3** °influential, convincing, °persuasive, °impressive, °telling, °powerful, °potent, °leading; °forceful

weird *adj.* °strange, °odd, °peculiar, °bizarre, °unnatural, °eerie, °queer, °grotesque, freakish, °outlandish, uncanny, °unearthly, otherworldly, °supernatural, preternatural, *Literary* eldritch, *Colloq* spooky, freaky, °kinky, *Slang* far-out, °way-out

weirdo *n.* °eccentric, °madman, madwoman, lunatic, °psychotic, *Colloq* °crazy, weirdie, nutcase, oddball, queer fish, °crank, *Slang* °freak, loony, psycho, *Brit* nutter, *US* screwball, nut, kook

welcome *v.* **1** °greet, °hail, °meet, °receive, °accept, offer hospitality (to) *—adj.* **2** accepted, °acceptable, well-received, °desirable, °agreeable, gratifying, appreciated **3** freely permitted *or* allowed, invited, entitled, suffered *—n.* **4** °reception, °greeting, salutation

weld *v.* **1** °unite, °combine, °merge, °fuse, °connect, °link, °join; solder, braze, °cement, °bond *—n.* **2** °seam, °joint, °juncture, commissure

welfare *n.* °benefit, °good, °advantage, well-being, °prosperity, °(good) fortune, °profit, °interest, °(good) health, °happiness, felicity

well[1] *adv.* **1** satisfactorily, sufficiently, adequately, agreeably, nicely, °(well) enough, *Colloq* O.K. *or* OK *or* okay **2** successfully, °famously, marvelously, wonderfully, fabulously, incredibly, splendidly, admirably, spectacularly, excellently, °swimmingly, superbly **3** articulately, understandably, expressively, correctly, accurately, °properly, proficiently, effectively, artistically, poetically; grammatically **4** comfortably, luxuriously, prosperously, extravagantly, showily, pretentiously, ostentatiously, sumptuously, grandly, opulently **5** graciously, °kindly, °highly, °favorably, glowingly, approvingly, °warmly, genially, cordially, amiably, kind-heartedly, warmheartedly, affectionately, lovingly **6** skillfully, expertly, adeptly, proficiently, ably **7** °far, by a long way, immeasurably, (very) much; far and away, °definitely, °positively, °obviously, °clearly, plainly, °manifestly, °evidently, unquestionably, decidedly, beyond (the shadow of a) doubt, *Colloq* by a long chalk **8** good-naturedly, equably, coolly, serenely, calmly, soberly, unexcitedly, sedately **9** °likely, °probably, in all probability, doubtlessly, without doubt, not unexpectedly, °indeed **10** °easily, without difficulty **11** °completely, °entirely, °wholly **12** °thoroughly (cooked), (cooked) through and through, °completely (cooked) **13** intimately, closely, familiarly, °personally; °thoroughly, °profoundly, soundly, fully **14** °fairly, justly, suitably, °properly, adequately, reasonably, fully, generously, °amply **15** °happily, mercifully, fortunately, luckily *—adj.* **16** °healthy, °fit, °hale, °robust, °vigorous, °hearty, in fine *or* good fettle, *Colloq* in good shape **17** °satisfactory, °pleasing, °agreeable, °good, °right, all right, °fine, °proper, *Colloq* O.K. *or* OK *or* okay

well[2] *n.* **1** wellspring, °spring, °fountain, wellhead, fountainhead, fount, °source, reservoir *—v.* **2** Often, ***well up or out or forth.*** °flow, °spring, °surge, °rise, °stream, °trickle, brim over, °swell, °start; °gush, °spurt, jet, °spout; °ooze, seep, °leak

well-advised *adj.* °prudent, °wise, °sensible, °intelligent, °smart

well-balanced *adj.* **1** °rational, °sane, °sensible, °reasonable, °levelheaded, °sober, °sound, well-adjusted, cool(headed), *Slang* together **2** °even, symmetric(al), °harmonious, well-proportioned, °orderly, well-ordered, well-disposed

well-bred *adj.* well-brought-up, well-mannered, °polite, °decorous, mannerly, °refined, °courteous, °cultivated, °polished, cultured, gentlemanly, °ladylike, °elegant, °suave, urbane, °sophisticated, °gracious, courtly, °genteel, °gallant, °chivalrous

well-established *adj.* longstanding, °traditional, °set, °venerable, °well-known, accepted, well-founded

well-fed *adj.* °plump, chunky, thickset, °chubby, rounded, °rotund, portly, °stout, fleshy, overweight, adipose, °fat, °obese, °gross, *Brit* podgy *or US* pudgy

well-groomed *adj.* °neat, °dapper, °fastidious, °tidy, °trim, °smart, clean-cut, °spruce, natty, well-dressed, *Colloq* °nifty, *Slang US and Canadian* spiffy

well-informed *adj.* °knowledgeable, °learned, well-read, well-versed, well-educated, literate, °educated, *Colloq* in the know, °wise, *US* vibrating on the right frequency, *Slang* hip *or* hep

well-known *adj.* **1** known, °familiar, (well-)

established, acknowledged, °customary, °everyday 2 °famous, °noted, °notable, °celebrated, °renowned, °illustrious, famed, °prominent, °eminent, °preeminent

well-off *adj.* °comfortable, °wealthy, °rich, affluent, °prosperous, well-to-do, *Colloq* well-heeled, *US* well-fixed

well-thought-of *adj.* admired, highly regarded, respected, °reputable, venerated, esteemed, revered, looked-up-to, valued

well-timed *adj.* °timely, °seasonable, °opportune, auspicious, °favorable, °advantageous, °beneficial

welsher *n.* nonpayer, °cheat, cheater, °swindler, *Slang* deadbeat, *US also* welcher

welt *n.* 1 bead, °ridge, °seam, °edge, wale, °stripe 2 °bruise, contusion, °bump, °lump, °scar, weal *or* wale *or* wheal

welter *n.* 1 °mass, °mess, °jumble, °tangle, °confusion, °mishmash, °muddle, °clutter, *Brit* hotchpotch *or US also* hodgepodge —*v.* 2 be sunk *or* involved in, °flounder, be bogged down in, be entangled *or* ensnarled in

wet *adj.* 1 °moist, moistened, °damp, dampened, soaked, °soaking, sopping, wringing, dripping, sodden, soppy, saturated, drenched 2 rainy, raining, teeming, pouring, drizzling, showery 3 °feeble, °weak, °irresolute, effete, namby-pamby, °foolish, °ineffectual, °ineffective, °spineless, timorous, °cowardly —*n.* 4 moisture, °water, wetness, dampness, °damp, humidity, °liquid 5 °rain, wetness, °mist, dew, °fog, °damp, humidity 6 °milksop, softy *or* softie, lightweight, *Colloq* °drip, °loser, *Brit* weed, *Slang* wimp, *US* weak sister

wheedle *v.* °coax, °cajole, inveigle, °charm, °beguile, °persuade, °talk; butter up; *Colloq* con, sweet-talk

wheel *n.* 1 disc, °ring, annulus, °circle, hoop —*v.* 2 °spin, °turn, veer, °swivel, °pivot, °swing, whirl

whereabouts *n. pl.* or *sg.* 1 °location, °position, °place, °site, °situation, °locale, °neighborhood, °vicinity —*adv.* 2 where, in *or* at *or* to what place, whither

whet *v.* 1 °sharpen, hone, °grind, °file, put an edge on, strop 2 pique, °sharpen, °awaken, °arouse, °stimulate, °kindle, °fire, °increase, °excite, °enhance

whimsical *adj.* 1 °quaint, fey, °fanciful, °odd, °curious, °unusual, chimeric(al), °queer, °singular, °peculiar, °funny, fantastic(al), pixyish, °playful, puckish, °absurd, °preposterous, *Colloq* °offbeat 2 °capricious, °erratic, °eccentric, wavering, °flighty, °unsettled, °fickle, mercurial, fluctuating, unpredictable, °inconsistent, °volatile, unsteady

whip *v.* 1 °beat, thrash, °lash, °flog, horsewhip, °scourge, °switch, cane, birch, flagellate, leather, °spank, strap; °castigate, °chastise, °punish, °discipline; *Slang* tan, *US* wale 2 trounce, °defeat, °beat, °conquer, °overwhelm, °rout, °overcome, °overpower, °thwart, °check, °best, worst, drub, °stop, °outdo, *Colloq* lick, wipe the floor with, °batter, *Slang* °pulverize, clobber, °destroy, °ruin, °murder, °slaughter, °kill, squash, smash, *US* cream 3 °run, scamper, scoot, °race, °scurry, °scramble, °hurry, °flit, °rush, °dash, dart, *Colloq* zip, zoom, skedaddle 4 °beat, °whisk, °fluff up 5 *Nautical* °seize, °bind, °wind, °fasten, °tie 6 ***whip out.*** yank out, jerk out, °pull (out), whisk out, °present, °exhibit, °flash, °produce 7 ***whip up.*** (a) °stir up, °agitate, °arouse, °rouse, °work up, °excite, °incite (b) °improvise, put together *or* assemble *or* prepare quickly *or* hurriedly, *Colloq* knock together, °knock up, *US* slap together —*n.* 8 °scourge, knout, °lash, cat-o'-nine-tails, rawhide, quirt, horsewhip, bullwhip, cane, birch, °switch, thong, (riding) crop, *Colloq* cat

whipping *n.* 1 beating, °thrashing, lashing, flogging, horsewhipping, scourging, switching, caning, birching, flagellation, °spanking 2 *Nautical* seizing, binding, tying, winding, °fastening

whirlpool *n.* maelstrom, vortex, °eddy, whirl, °swirl, *Heraldry* gurges

whirlwind *n.* 1 waterspout, dust devil, cyclone, typhoon, anticyclone, °hurricane, extratropical cyclone, tropical cyclone, *Nontechnical* tornado, *Nautical* white squall, *Australian* willy-willy, *Colloq US* whirly —*adj.* 2 °speedy, °quick, °swift, °sudden, °precipitous, lightning, headlong, °hasty, °rash, °impetuous

whisk *v.* 1 °rush, dart, °sweep, °brush 2 °speed, °rush, °carry, °whip, °hasten, °hustle, °hurry 3 See **whip, 4,** above. —*n.* 4 °sweep, °wave, °brush, flick 5 °brush, flywhisk 6 beater, °whip

whiskey *n.* whisky, °alcohol, °spirits, John Barleycorn, usquebaugh, Scotch, home brew, mother's ruin (= 'gin'), *Scots* barley-bree, *US* rye, bourbon, white lightning, white mule, °moonshine, *Colloq* °booze, hooch, rotgut, *US* corn, firewater, *Slang US* sneaky pete, smoke

whisper *v.* 1 °breathe, °murmur, °mutter, °mumble, °hiss, speak *or* say softly *or* under (one's) breath, °sigh, susurrate 2 °gossip, bruit about, noise abroad, °murmur, °insinuate, °hint, °rumor, °disclose, divulge, °reveal, breathe a word —*n.* 3 °murmur, undertone, hushed tone(s) 4 °hint, °suggestion, *soupçon*, °suspicion

white *adj.* 1 snow-white, snowy, chalk-white, chalky, ivory, creamy, milky, milk-white, oyster-white, off-white; °silver, hoary 2 °pale, pallid, °pasty, °wan, wheyfaced, ashen, bloodless, drained, whitish, waxen, °ghastly, °ghostly, anemic, dead-white, deathly white, cadaverous, corpselike 3 °innocent, °pure, unsullied, stainless, unblemished, °spotless, °immaculate, virginal, °virtuous, undefiled, °chaste 4 Usually, ***White.*** Caucasian, Caucasoid, light-skinned, fair-skinned, pale-complexioned

whitewash *v.* °gloss over, °cover up, sugarcoat, °hide, °camouflage, °conceal, °qualify,

°minimize, extenuate, °diminish, °play down, downplay, °make light of, °rationalize, °excuse

whittle *v.* **1** pare (down *or* away), °shave, °trim, °cut, °carve, hew, °shape **2** Usually, ***whittle away at or down.*** °pare, °shave, °cut, °trim, °reduce, °diminish, °erode, eat away at

whole *adj.* **1** °entire, °complete, uncut, °full, °intact, unbroken, °total **2** in one piece, °intact, unharmed, undamaged, °unscathed, unimpaired, unhurt, uninjured **3** °well, °healthy, °sound, °fit, °strong —*n.* **4** °everything, aggregate, °(sum) total, °totality, °lot, °entirety; °ensemble; *Colloq* whole kit and kaboodle **5** ***on the whole.*** °largely, mostly, °usually, more often than not, °for the most part, in general, °generally, by and large, with few exceptions, all things considered, all in all, °as a rule, °chiefly, °mainly, °in the main, predominantly

wholehearted *adj.* °devoted, dedicated, committed, °earnest, °sincere, °unqualified, °unmitigated, unreserved, °complete, °entire, unstinting, °real, °true, °genuine, °hearty, °heartfelt, °serious, °enthusiastic, zealous, °warm, °fervent, °ardent, °spirited, °eager, °energetic

wholesome *adj.* **1** healthful, °healthy, health-giving, °nutritious, nourishing, °beneficial, °tonic, salutary, salubrious, strengthening, °bracing, °stimulating **2** °moral, °ethical, °righteous, °upright, °honorable, °decent, °principled, °proper, °fit, °meet

wholly *adv.* **1** °altogether, °entirely, °absolutely, °quite, °totally, °thoroughly, °completely, *in toto,* fully, in all respects, in every way, all in all, °utterly, unqualifiedly, every inch, 100 percent; °lock, °stock, and barrel; °root and branch; backward(s) and forward(s); from the ground up; *Colloq* bag and baggage; °hook, °line, and sinker; to the nth degree; (the) whole hog, *US* up one side and down the other **2** °only, exclusively, solely, unexceptionally, categorically, unequivocally, unambiguously, explicitly

whoop *n.* **1** °shout, °shriek, °yell, °roar, °bellow, hoot, (battle *or* war) cry, war-whoop, °outcry, °scream, screech, squeal, yelp, yowl, °howl, bark; °cheer, hurrah, huzzah; *Colloq* holler —*v.* **2** °shout, °shriek, °yell, °roar, °bellow, hoot, °cry (out), °scream, screech, squeal, yelp, yowl, °howl, bark; °cheer, hurrah, huzzah; *Colloq* holler

whopping *adj.* **1** °huge, °great, °enormous, °colossal, °gigantic, °immense, tremendous, °prodigious, °monstrous, °thumping, mammoth, °massive, Brobdingnagian **2** °flagrant, °outrageous, °extravagant, °terrible, °awful

wicked *adj.* **1** °evil, °bad, °immoral, amoral, unprincipled, °sinful, °impious, piacular, irreligious, °blasphemous, °profane, °sacrilegious, °ungodly, °godless, diabolic(al), °satanic, Mephistophelian, demonic, demoniac(al), hellish, °infernal, accursed, °damnable, °fiendish, °ghoulish **2** depraved, °dissolute, °villainous, blackhearted, iniquitous, °horrible, horrid, °hideous, heinous, °beastly, °base, °low, °vile, debased, °degenerate, °perverse, °perverted, °corrupt, °foul, °offensive, °abominable, °disgraceful, °shameful, °dreadful, °awful, °gross, °gruesome, °grim, appalling, °grisly, °loathsome, °lawless, °unrepentant, unregenerate, °incorrigible, °criminal, felonious, rascally, knavish, °terrible, egregious, execrable **3** °dirty, °pornographic, °filthy, °erotic, °obscene, °lewd, °offensive, °indecent, °prurient, smutty, °rude, °taboo, °blue, °coarse, °bawdy, °vulgar, salacious, licentious, °nasty, X-rated, *Colloq US* raunchy **4** °vicious, °beastly, °savage, °nasty, °bad, °violent, °mean, °cruel **5** °naughty, °mischievous, impish, °sly, °devilish, rascally, roguish, scampish, puckish; vexatious, exasperating, annoying, irritating, °irksome, °trying, galling, bothersome **6** °foul, °offensive, pernicious, baleful, mephitic, °disgusting, °revolting, sickening, °repulsive, °repellent, °nauseous, °repugnant, °rotten, pestilential, noxious **7** °expert, °ingenious, °superior, °superb, °superlative, °outstanding, °masterful, masterly, °skillful, deft, °adept

wide *adj.* **1** °spacious, °roomy, °ample, °extensive, °broad **2** °broad, °extensive, °comprehensive, encyclopedic *or* encyclopaedic, °inclusive, far-reaching, wide-ranging, widespread **3** °extreme, °considerable, °substantial, sizable *or* sizeable, °major, °big, °large; widespread **4** ***wide of the mark.*** off the mark, astray, °deviant, deviating, off (the) target, not on target, °inappropriate —*adv.* **5** astray, afield, °wide of the mark, off the mark, off (the) target, to one side **6** all the way, as much as possible, fully, °completely, to the utmost

widely *adv.* **1** extensively, °thoroughly, °universally, °everywhere, °generally, by many **2** to a large *or* a great extent, greatly, °largely, very much, °extremely, considerably, °substantially

widen *v.* distend, dilate, °spread, °stretch, °enlarge, °increase, °expand; °extend, broaden, °supplement, °add to, augment

width *n.* **1** °breadth, wideness, compass, broadness, °span; diameter, °caliber, °bore; °measure; *Nautical* °beam **2** °reach, °scope, °range, °breadth, °extent, extensiveness

wield *v.* **1** °flourish, °swing, brandish, °wave, °handle, °use, °employ **2** °exercise, °have, °employ, °exert, °use, utilize

wife *n.* °mate, helpmeet, helpmate, spouse, bride, °partner, *Colloq* better half, the little woman, the missus *or* missis, old lady *or* woman, the ball and chain, *Slang* the trouble and strife

wild *adj.* **1** undomesticated, °untamed, unbroken, °savage, feral **2** uncultivated, °uninhabited, °waste, °desert, °desolate, virgin, unpopulated, °empty, °trackless, °barren, °lifeless; °deserted **3** °savage, °uncivilized, barbarous, °primitive, °rude, uncultured, uncultivated, brutish, barbaric, °fierce,

°ferocious **4** °uncontrolled, unrestricted, unrestrained, untrammeled, unbridled, unfettered, unshackled, °free, unchecked, °lively, °impetuous, unconventional, °undisciplined, °disobedient, °insubordinate, °self-willed, wayward, °mutinous, rowdy(ish), °boisterous, °unruly, °tumultuous, turbulent, °tempestuous, °uproarious; uncontrollable, unmanageable, °ungovernable, intractable, unrestrainable **5** °mad, maniac(al), crazed, °crazy, irrational, distracted, frenzied, °frantic, °distraught, °hysterical, °raving, raging, unhinged, demented, °delirious; °berserk; run amok *or* amuck **6** °exciting, °excited, vehement, °passionate, °romantic, turbulent, °chaotic, °tempestuous, °reckless, madcap **7** °absurd, irrational, °unreasonable, °extravagant, °fantastic, °imprudent, °foolish, °foolhardy, °impractical, °impracticable, unpractical, unworkable, °ridiculous, °reckless, °silly, °giddy, °flighty, madcap, °outrageous, °preposterous, °bizarre, °strange, °odd, °peculiar, *Colloq* °offbeat **8** tousled, windblown, °unkempt, disheveled, °untidy, disordered, °disorderly, messed up, *Colloq* mussed up **9** °enthusiastic, avid, °eager, °agog, *Colloq* °crazy, °mad, °daft, dotty, *Brit* potty, *Slang* nutty, nuts *—n.* **10** Usually, ***wilds.*** wasteland, wilderness, °desert, vastness, °emptiness, *Colloq* sticks, middle of nowhere, back of beyond

wile *n.* Often, ***wiles.*** trick, °stratagem, °ruse, °artifice, °subterfuge, °dodge, °trap, °snare, °maneuver, ploy, contrivance, °move, gambit, °plot, °scheme, °machination, *Colloq* °(little) game

will *n.* **1** °desire, °wish, °longing, °liking, °inclination, °disposition, °drive, purposefulness, °purpose, °intent, °intention, °resolve, commitment, °resolution, °determination; willpower **2** °choice, wishes, °desire, °inclination **3** (last will and) testament, last wishes **4** ***at will.*** as *or* when (one) pleases *or* wishes *or* thinks fit(ting), at (one's) desire *or* whim *or* pleasure *or* discretion *—v.* **5** °want, °desire, °wish, °choose, see fit, °make, compel, °force, °command, °order, ordain, °require **6** °leave, °bequeath, °devise, hand down *or* on, °pass on, °transfer; settle upon *or* on

willful *adj.* **1** °intentional, °deliberate, °voluntary, °conscious, intended, °purposeful, °premeditated **2** °stubborn, headstrong, pigheaded, °obstinate, mulish, °inflexible, adamant(ine), obdurate, intransigent, unyielding, °self-willed, °ungovernable, °recalcitrant, °unruly, °immovable, intractable, dogged, °determined, refractory, uncompromising, wayward, °perverse, °contrary

willing *adj.* °agreeable, acquiescent, compliant, amenable, consenting, assenting, °passive, complaisant, docile, °ready, well-disposed, °happy, °content, pleased, °delighted, °enthusiastic, avid, °eager, zealous, *Colloq* °game

willingly *adv.* °readily, °happily, contentedly, °gladly, cheerfully, amenably, agreeably, °freely, passively, docilely, of (one's) own accord *or* free will, on (one's) own, ungrudgingly, by choice, °voluntarily, unhesitatingly, nothing loath, eagerly, enthusiastically, zealously, avidly, *Colloq* at the drop of a hat

willowy *adj.* **1** lissom *or* lissome, pliant, lithe, °flexible, °supple, limber, loose-limbed **2** °slim, °slender, °graceful, sylphlike, svelte, °thin, long-limbed, clean-limbed

willy-nilly *adv.* **1** whether one likes it or not, inevitably, °necessarily, of necessity, perforce, whether or no, like it or not, ***nolens volens, bon gré mal gré*** *—adj.* **2** °necessary, °unavoidable, °inevitable, °involuntary

wilt *v.* **1** °sag, °droop, wither, °shrink, shrivel (up *or* away), °diminish **2** °sag, °droop, °bow, °weaken, °sink, °wane, wither, lose courage *or* nerve, °flag, °dwindle, languish

wily *adj.* °shrewd, cunning, °crafty, °sly, °artful, guileful, °clever, °foxy, vulpine, °disingenuous, °shifty, °scheming, plotting, °calculating, °designing, °sharp, canny, °deceitful, deceiving, °deceptive, treacherous, °perfidious, °false, double-dealing, °dishonest, underhand(ed), °tricky, °smooth, °slick, °slippery, °oily, unctuous, *Scots and North England* pawky, *Colloq* cagey, °crooked, two-timing, *Slang chiefly Brit* °fly

win *v.* **1** come (in *or* out) first, carry the day, °conquer, °overcome; °carry off (the palm), finish first (in), achieve first place (in), °triumph (in), be victorious (in), be the victor (in), gain a victory (in), °prevail (in), °succeed (in), take first prize (in), *Colloq* bring home the bacon **2** °gain, carry off *or* away, attain, °acquire, °get, °obtain, °secure, °procure, °receive, °collect, °net, °bag, °earn, °realize, °pick up, glean **3** ***win over.*** °influence, °sway, °incline, °persuade, °charm, °prevail upon, °convert, °induce, °bring around, °convince *—n.* **4** °victory, °conquest, °triumph, °success

wind[1] *n.* **1** °breeze, zephyr, °puff, °gust, °breath, °draft, light air, °current (of air) **2** puffery, °bombast, rodomontade, °bluster, boasting, braggadocio, vain speech, blather, (idle *or* empty) talk, fustian, °nonsense, twaddle, humbug, °babble, °gibberish, *Colloq* °gab, °hot air, claptrap, hogwash, °rot, hooey, baloney, *Slang Brit* (load of (old)) cobblers **3** gas, flatulence, windiness, flatus, borborygmus, heartburn, *Taboo slang* fart **4** ***before the wind.*** *Nautical* downwind, °off the wind **5** ***break wind.*** *Taboo slang* fart **6** ***get or have wind of.*** °hear of, °learn of, come to know, °pick up, be made *or* become aware of, °gather, °understand, hear on the grapevine, *Colloq* hear tell of **7** ***get or have the wind up.*** take fright, become frightened *or* afraid *or* apprehensive **8** ***in the wind.*** °around, °about, rumored, in the air, detectable, °discernible, discoverable, °imminent, °impending, approaching, °close (at hand), about to happen *or* take place *or* occur, afoot, in the offing, °near, on the way, *Colloq Brit* on the cards, *US* °in the cards **9** ***off the wind.*** See **5**, above. **10** ***on the***

or a wind. Nautical upwind, windward, to the wind, into (the teeth *or* the eye of) the wind; near the wind **11** ***put the wind up.*** °scare, °frighten, °alarm **12** ***sail close or near to the wind.*** take risks, throw caution to the winds, °play with fire, skate on thin ice, take (one's) life in (one's) hands, *Colloq* stick (one's) neck out, *Slang* go for broke **13** ***take the wind out of (someone's) sails.*** deflate (someone), disconcert (someone), destroy (someone's) advantage, ruin (someone's) superiority *or* supremacy *or* ascendancy

wind[2] *v.* **1** °turn, °bend, °twist, °snake, worm, °twine, zigzag, slew, °swerve, °loop, °coil, curve, °meander, °ramble, veer **2** °reel, °roll, °spiral, °turn, °twist, curl, °coil, °wrap, °twine, wreathe; °crank (up), °wind up **3** ***wind down.*** **(a)** °taper off, °slow down, °diminish, °reduce, close out, slacken *or* slack off (on), °ease (up on), °decrease, cut back *or* down (on); °wind up **(b)** °relax, become calm *or* tranquil, °calm down, cool off *or* down, regain (one's) equilibrium, ease up *or* off, *Colloq* unwind, let (one's) hair down, take it easy **4** ***wind up.*** **(a)** °terminate, conclude, come *or* bring to an end *or* a close *or* a conclusion, °end (up), close down *or* up, °finish (up), °wrap up; liquidate, °settle **(b)** end up, °finish (up), become ultimately **(c)** °excite, innervate, °energize, °stimulate, invigorate, °stir up **(d)** °agitate, °fluster, disconcert, °ruffle **(e)** See **3 (a),** above.

windfall *n.* bonanza, °godsend, stroke of (good) fortune, serendipitous find, °boon, piece of (good) luck, jackpot, °(lucky) strike

windy *adj.* **1** blustery, blowing, blowy, °breezy, gusting, gusty, °wild, squally, °tempestuous; windswept **2** °talkative, long-winded, garrulous, °wordy, verbose, prolix, loquacious, °rambling, °voluble, °fluent, °effusive, °glib, turgid, °bombastic, °pompous, longiloquent

winner *n.* °victor, °champion, prizewinner, titleholder, conqueror, conquering hero, *Colloq* champ

winning *adj.* **1** °engaging, °attractive, alluring, captivating, °endearing, °prepossessing, winsome, bewitching, °fetching, °taking, °enchanting, °pleasing, °delightful, charming, °amiable, °friendly, °pleasant, °sweet **2** °triumphant, conquering, °victorious, °successful

wintry *adj.* **1** hiemal, brumal, hibernal; °icy, snowy, °freezing, frozen, frosty, °cold, °frigid, °bitter (cold), °chilly, chilling, °piercing, °cutting, glacial, Siberian, arctic, hyperborean **2** °cold, °frigid, °chilly, °cool, chilling, glacial **3** °forbidding, °bleak, °dismal, cheerless, °dreary, °harsh, unfriendly, °ugly, °menacing, °ominous, °threatening, °dark

wipe *v.* **1** Sometimes, ***wipe off or out or up.*** °rub, clean (off *or* out *or* up), °cleanse; dry (off *or* out *or* up), dust (off), mop (up), swab, sponge (off *or* up) **2** Often, ***wipe off.*** °remove, °erase, take off *or* away, °get rid of **3** ***wipe out.*** °kill (off), annihilate, °massacre, °destroy, °finish (off), °dispose of, eradicate, °obliterate, °exterminate, do away with, °stamp out, °get rid of, °remove, wipe off the face of the earth

wiry *adj.* °muscular, °sinewy, °lean, lank, thin and strong, tough and flexible

wisdom *n.* **1** sagacity, sageness, °judgment, discernment, °reason, °prudence, judiciousness, °(common) sense, °insight, °penetration, sapience, understanding, rationality, clearsightedness, clearheadedness, perspicacity, perspicuity, percipience, °perception, perceptiveness, °intelligence, acuteness, acumen, astuteness, sharpness, shrewdness, longheadedness **2** °knowledge, °learning, erudition, °lore, °scholarship, enlightenment

wise *adj.* **1** °sage, sagacious, °judicious, °reasonable, common-sensical, °prudent, °sensible, insightful, sapient, °understanding, °rational, °sound, clearsighted, clearheaded, discerning, perspicacious, perspicuous, percipient, °perceptive, °intelligent, °acute, °astute, °sharp, °shrewd, °crafty, °clever, °bright, °quick-witted, °smart, °brilliant, longheaded, *Colloq* brainy **2** °knowledgeable, °learned, °enlightened, °informed, erudite; (well-)educated, °knowing, well-read, well-versed, °lettered, °scholarly **3** °well-advised, °advisable, °judicious, °sensible, °expedient, °reasonable, °strategic, °tactful, °tactical, °prudent, °politic, °discreet, °diplomatic, well-thought-out, well-considered, °proper, °fitting, °appropriate, °meet **4** ***put wise (to).*** inform *or* advise *or* warn (of *or* about) **5** ***wise to.*** aware *or* knowledgeable *or* informed of *or* about, sensitive to, on to *or* onto, *Colloq* in the know about —*v.* **6** ***wise up (to).*** become informed *or* aware (of *or* about), °wake up (to), *Colloq* get wise (to) *or* in the know (about)

wisecrack *n.* **1** °joke, °quip, rejoinder, °witticism, °pun, barb, jest, jibe, *Colloq* °gag; °dig —*v.* **2** °joke, °quip, °pun, jibe

wise guy *n.* wiseacre, smart alec *or* aleck, *Archaic* witling, *Colloq* know-all *or* know-it-all, *Brit* Clever Dick *or* cleverdick, *Slang* smartie-pants, smartie, smart-ass, *US* wisenheimer

wish *v.* **1** °desire, °want; °yearn, crave, °long, °hope, °hanker, have a mind, °(have a) fancy, °choose, °care **2** °require, °request, °demand, °order, °specify **3** foist *or* force *or* thrust *or* impose upon, *Colloq* fob off on *or* upon, palm off on —*n.* **4** °desire, °request, whim, °want, craving, °longing, hankering **5** °desire, °longing, craving, °need, yearning, hankering, °passion, keenness, °thirst, °appetite, °hunger, whim, °urge, °liking, fondness, °fancy, °preference, predisposition, °disposition, °inclination, *Colloq* yen, *Slang* °itch

wishy-washy *adj.* **1** neither here nor there, undecided, °indecisive, °irresolute, half-hearted, shilly-shallying, tergiversating, vacillating, °uncertain, of *or* having mixed feelings, °of two minds **2** °feeble, °weak, °watery, watered-down, °thin, °vapid, °flat, °bland, runny, diluted, °tasteless, insipid, flavorless, °stale

wisp *n.* °shred, °scrap, strand, °thread, snippet, tuft, °lock

wistful *adj.* **1** °melancholy, °mournful, °sad, morose, °sorrowful, disconsolate, heartsick, °forlorn, woeful, °woebegone, °desirous, °longing, yearning **2** °thoughtful, contemplative, °pensive, °absent-minded, °detached, °absorbed, in a brown study, °preoccupied, meditating, °meditative, °reflective, ruminating, ruminative, °dreamy, dreaming, daydreaming, musing

wit *n.* **1** °intelligence, brains, °mind, °(common) sense, °judgment, °understanding, discernment, °wisdom, sagacity, °insight, astuteness, cleverness, *Slang* savvy **2** °humor, drollery, °levity, joking, °repartee, °raillery, facetiousness, waggishness, badinage, jocularity, wordplay, paronomasia; °amusement, °entertainment **3** °comedian, comedienne, humorist, °comic, °wag, °joker, *farceur, farceuse,* punster, madcap, °zany; parodist, satirist, caricaturist; *Colloq* pundit, °card, °character

witch *n.* **1** sorceress, enchantress, °magician, sibyl, pythoness; warlock **2** °hag, °fury, battle-ax, crone, gorgon, Medusa, ogress, Xanthippe, °shrew, virago, harridan, fishwife, termagant, *Archaic* beldam *or* beldame, *Slang* old bag, °bitch

withdraw *v.* **1** °draw back, °retract, °pull back, °recoil, shrink back **2** °retract, °recall, °take back, °cancel, rescind, °recant, disavow, disclaim, abjure, °void, annul, °go back on, back out (of), back down (on) **3** °pull out, °extract, °remove, *Technical* retrude **4** °retire, °retreat, °go, °repair **5** °leave, °depart, °go, make (oneself) scarce, °absent (oneself), °retire

withdrawn *adj.* **1** °reserved, °detached, °distant, °standoffish, °aloof, °shy, diffident, °bashful, °timid, timorous, introverted, °taciturn, °reticent, °silent, °quiet, °retiring, shrinking **2** °remote, °distant, °isolated, °solitary, °hidden, °secluded, °private, °out-of-the-way, °reclusive

withering *adj.* °destructive, °devastating, death-dealing, °murderous, °deadly

withhold *v.* **1** hold *or* keep back, °retain, °reserve, °restrain, °control, °repress, °check, °hide, °conceal **2** hold *or* keep back, °deduct, °retain, °reserve

withstand *v.* °resist, °oppose, °stand (up to), °face, °defy, confront, °combat, °grapple with, °fight (against), °cope with, hold out against, °weather, °suffer, °survive, °tolerate, °take, °bear, last through, °endure, °brave, *Colloq Brit* °stick

witness *n.* **1** °observer, °onlooker, °spectator, viewer, °eyewitness, °bystander, watcher, *Rare* earwitness **2** deponent, testifier, corroborating witness, corroborator **3** ***bear witness* (*to or of*).** °testify (to), °attest (to), be *or* give *or* provide *or* furnish *or* constitute evidence *or* proof *or* testimony (of *or* to), °verify, °confirm, corroborate, °show, °prove —*v.* **4** °see, °observe, °watch, look on *or* at, °view, °behold, °mark, °note, °notice, °take in, *Colloq* °spot, °catch **5** countersign, °sign, °certify, °endorse, °substantiate, °document, certificate **6** See **3,** above.

witticism *n.* °pun, °quip, play on words, bon mot, jest, °joke, °epigram, clever remark, sally, *Archaic or literary* conceit, *Colloq* °gag, one-liner

witty *adj.* °ingenious, °subtle, °clever, °humorous, °sarcastic, °sardonic, piquant, comic(al), °farcical, °ludicrous, facetious, amusing, jocular, waggish, droll, °funny

wizened *adj.* wrinkled, shrunken, shriveled (up), withered, °gnarled, dried-up, wilted, faded, wasted

woe *n.* °trouble, °hardship, adversity, °misery, °anguish, tribulation, °calamity, °trial, wretchedness, °grief, unhappiness, °desolation, dolor, °melancholy, °gloom, °depression, °sadness, disconsolateness, °misfortune, °affliction, °sorrow, °distress

woebegone *adj.* troubled, °miserable, anguished, °wretched, grief-stricken, °unhappy, °desolate, °doleful, dolorous, °melancholy, melancholic, °gloomy, °mournful, °sorrowful, depressed, °dejected, °sad, °glum, crestfallen, chapfallen, lugubrious, downcast, disconsolate, °unfortunate, star-crossed, afflicted, distressed, woeful, °forlorn, °downhearted, broken-hearted, °heartbroken, disheartened, *Slang US* bummed out

woman *n.* **1** female, lady; °girl **2** °wife, spouse, bride, ladylove, °sweetheart, lady, °girl, girl friend, °mistress, concubine, °mate, helpmeet, helpmate, °partner, *Colloq* sweetie, better half, little woman, the missus *or* missis, old lady *or* woman, ball and chain, *Slang* trouble and strife **3** °lass, °maid, °maiden, °miss, lassie, *Slang* gal, dame, bird, skirt, chick, °bit of fluff, °broad, °piece (of work), °number, baggage, moll, popsy **4** °domestic, housekeeper, °maid, cleaning woman *or* lady, maidservant, chambermaid, handmaiden, abigail, lady-in-waiting, *Brit* charwoman, *Colloq Brit* char, °daily

wonder *n.* **1** °marvel, °prodigy, °phenomenon, °spectacle, °rarity, °sight, °curiosity, miracle, *Slang* °knockout, stunner, mind-blower, mind-boggler, °trip **2** awe, °astonishment, °admiration, °amazement, wonderment, °surprise, stupefaction, °fascination —*v.* **3** °ponder, °muse, °meditate, °think, °theorize, conjecture, °puzzle, °query, °question, °inquire, be inquisitive, be curious, ask oneself, °speculate, cudgel (one's) brains **4** °marvel (at), goggle, °gawk, °gape, °stare, be awed, be thunderstruck, be amazed, be astonished **5** ***wonder about.*** question *or* doubt the sanity *or* reason *or* reasonableness of

wooded *adj.* sylvan, forested, bosky, tree-covered, woody, timbered

wooden *adj.* **1** wood, woody, ligneous, xyloid **2** °stiff, °rigid, °artificial, °clumsy, °stilted, °unnatural, °awkward, ungainly, spiritless, unanimated, °dead, °lifeless, °dry, passionless, unimpassioned, °impassive, °vacant, °empty, °colorless, expressionless, deadpan **3** unintelligent, blockheaded, °stupid, °dull, insensitive, slow-witted, dull-witted, °obtuse, oafish, doltish, tiny-minded, dimwitted, dunderpated, *Colloq* °thick, wooden-headed, knuckleheaded

woolly *adj.* **1** fleecy, woolen, wool-bearing, laniferous, lanate *or* lanose, lanuginose *or* lanuginous, downy, °fuzzy, °shaggy, flocculent *or* floccose, flocky **2** °hazy, °fuzzy, unclear, obscure(d), foggy, °indistinct, °confused, °vague, cloudy, clouded, °nebulous, ill-defined

word *n.* **1** °(little) talk, °(brief) conversation, °chat, °discussion, consultation, °dialogue, °huddle, °parley, °tête-à-tête, chitchat, confabulation, °conference, °interview, *Colloq* powwow, confab **2** °news, °intelligence, °information, °facts, °data, °report, °story, tidings, °account, communiqué, °bulletin, dispatch *or* despatch, °advice, °message, *Colloq* °lowdown, *Slang* info, °dope, *Brit* gen, *US* poop **3** °name, °term, designation, locution, appellation, °expression, °phrase **4** °promise, °pledge, °vow, °oath, (solemn) word of honor, °undertaking, °assurance, °warrant, guarantee *or* guaranty, °warranty **5** utterance, °expression, °declaration, °statement **6** °suggestion, °hint, scintilla, °bit **7** °command, °order, °signal, °direction, °instruction, *Colloq US* high sign **8** ***in a word.*** succinctly, °briefly, °in brief, in a few words, concisely, °in short, in summary, in sum, not to mince words, to make a long story short, when all is said and done, in the final analysis, not to beat about the bush, *Colloq* in a nutshell **9** ***words.*** **(a)** °quarrel, °dispute, °argument, unpleasantness **(b)** °lyrics, °book, libretto, °text —*v.* **10** °put (forth), °say, °couch, °express, °phrase, utter, °state, °term, °style, °set forth

wording *n.* phraseology, °language, phrasing, choice of words, word choice

wordy *adj.* verbose, prolix, °rambling, long-winded; pleonastic, °redundant, garrulous, °windy, °talkative, loquacious

work *n.* **1** °labor, toil, °effort, °drudgery, travail, °exertion, °industry **2** °employment, °business, °occupation, °vocation, °calling, °profession, °trade, °line, métier, °career, livelihood, °job, °post, °position, °situation **3** °task, °function, °duty, °assignment, °charge, °responsibility, chore, commission, °undertaking, °stint **4** °feat, °achievement, °creation, °accomplishment, °opus, handiwork, *oeuvre,* °production, °composition, °piece, masterwork, °masterpiece, *chef d'oeuvre, magnum opus,* °output **5** ***in work.*** in production, °under way, being done, in the works, being planned, in the planning stage(s) **6** ***out of work.*** °unemployed, °idle, jobless, °at liberty, between engagements, °available, °free, *Brit* °redundant, *Colloq Brit* on the dole, *US* on *or* collecting unemployment —*v.* **7** °labor, toil, °exert oneself, °sweat, moil, °slave (away), °peg away, slog (away) **8** °till, plough, °farm, °cultivate **9** have a job, hold (down) a post *or* position, earn a living, be employed **10** °control, °manage, °manipulate, °maneuver, °wield, °handle, °operate, °use, make use of, utilize, °exploit, °deal with, bring into play **11** °function, °operate, °run, °go, °develop, °turn out, *Colloq* °pan out **12** °function, °operate, °run, °go **13** knead, °mold, °form, °fashion, °shape; °mix, °stir, °incorporate **14** °maneuver, °manipulate, °guide **15** °operate, °use, °employ, put to (good *or* effective) use, °wield, °manipulate, °ply, °apply, °exploit **16** °bring about, °effect, °accomplish, carry out *or* off, °make, °produce, °achieve, engender, beget, °create, do, °put through, °execute, °fulfill, °effectuate, °implement, °realize **17** ***work in.*** find time *or* space for, °include, °insert, °introduce, fit in, squeeze in, °accommodate **18** ***work on.*** °wheedle, °coax, importune, °press, *Brit* pressurize, *US* °pressure; °influence, °persuade, act on, °prevail upon, °induce, °dispose, °urge **19** ***work out.*** **(a)** °exercise, do callisthenics, do aerobics, warm up, do setting-up exercises, do (one's) daily dozen, °jog, lift weights, °train, °drill **(b)** Often, ***work out at or to.*** °equal, °total (up to), °result in, °amount to, °come to **(c)** °clear up, °resolve, °solve, *Slang Brit and New Zealand* suss out **(d)** evolve, °develop, °succeed, °prosper, come out all right, prove satisfactory, go well, be effective, *Colloq* °pan out **(e)** °formulate, °work up, contrive, °draw up, °detail, °plan, °develop, °devise, put together, °elaborate, °expand, °enlarge (on) **20** ***work up.*** **(a)** °excite, make excited, °agitate, °inflame, enkindle, °arouse, °rouse, °stir, °move, °animate, °incite, °spur, *Colloq* °fire (up), get (someone) (all) steamed *or* hopped *or* het up **(b)** °prepare, (make *or* get) ready, whip into shape, °develop, come up with, write up, put together, °produce, °turn out **(c)** °advance, ascend, °rise, move up *or* ahead *or* on **(d)** See **19 (e),** above.

worker *n.* °laborer, working man *or* woman, workman, °hand, °employee, artisan, craftsman, °tradesman, white-collar worker, blue-collar worker, proletarian, breadwinner, wage earner

workmanship *n.* handicraft, °craft, craftsmanship, artistry, °art, °technique, handiwork, °skill, skillfulness, mastery, *US* artisanship

works *n. pl.* **1** °plant, °factory, workshop, °shop, °mill **2** °mechanism, machinery, workings, (moving *or* working) parts; clockwork, *Colloq* innards, °insides, *Slang* °guts **3** ***the works.*** **(a)** °everything, °the lot, *Colloq* the whole kit and caboodle, the whole shooting match, everything but *or* including the kitchen sink, *Chiefly US and Canadian* the whole shebang **(b)** a thrashing, a beating, a drubbing, a battering, a flogging, a lambasting

world *n.* **1** °earth, planet, °sphere, °globe, terra; °universe, cosmos, °existence, °creation, °life **2** °humanity, mankind, °people, the human race, °society, the public, men, humankind, everybody, °everyone, the world at large **3** °area, °sphere, °domain, community, °clique, °crowd, °circle, °fraternity, °faction, °set, coterie **4** °period, °time, °age, °era, epoch, time(s) **5** ***bring into the world.*** **(a)** °deliver, °have, give birth to, beget, *Rare or dialectal* °birth **(b)** °deliver, °midwife **6** ***for all the world.*** °precisely, °exactly, in all respects, in every respect, in every way, °just **7** ***on top of the world.*** °ecstatic, °delighted, °elated, °happy, °exultant, °overjoyed, °rapturous, *US* in seventh heaven, *Brit* in the seventh heaven, *Colloq* on cloud nine, *Brit* over the moon **8** ***out of this world.*** °marvelous, wonderful, °exceptional, °unbelievable, °incredible, °excellent, °superb, *Colloq* °great, smashing, °fantastic, °fabulous, *Slang* °out of sight, far-out, *Brit* °magic, *US* to the max

worldly *adj.* **1** mundane, °earthly, °terrestrial, °temporal, °physical, °carnal, fleshly, corporeal, °human; °lay, nonspiritual, nonreligious, civic, °secular, °profane **2** urbane, °suave, °sophisticated, cosmopolitan, worldly-wise, *Slang* with it, °hip, °cool

worn *adj.* **1** °shabby, °threadbare, tatty, °tattered, °ragged, frayed **2** °haggard, °drawn **3** ***worn out.*** °tired, °fatigued, °exhausted, frazzled, °spent, °jaded, played out, °haggard, °drawn, the worse for wear, *Colloq* dog-tired, all in, done in, *Slang* °dead (on one's feet), °beat, *US* pooped

worried *adj.* °fearful, apprehensive, °anxious, distressed, °nervous, uneasy, anguished, disquieted, agonized, °agonizing, °distraught, °on edge, on tenterhooks, °ill at ease, troubled, °fretful, °agitated, perturbed, °upset, °suffering

worry *v.* **1** be anxious, be fearful, be concerned, °fret, agonize, be distressed, be vexed, *Colloq* °stew, bite *or* chew (one's) nails, go *or* get gray, get gray hair, *Slang* sweat blood, *US* sweat bullets **2** °annoy, °irk, °pester, nettle, harry, °harass, °tease, °bother, °tantalize, °torment, °plague, hector, badger, °gall, peeve, *Colloq* hassle —*n.* **3** °concern, °care, °responsibility; °problem, °bother, °trouble, °affliction, irritation, °annoyance, vexation **4** °anguish, °anxiety, uneasiness, unease, nervousness, °distress, apprehension, disquiet, perturbation, °agitation, °upset, °misgiving

worsen *v.* **1** °increase, exacerbate, °heighten, °intensify, °aggravate **2** °weaken, °deteriorate, °decline, °degenerate, °decay, °slip, °sink, °slide, °fail, °disintegrate, take a turn for the worse, get worse, go from bad to worse, *Colloq* go downhill

worship *v.* **1** °venerate, °revere, °reverence, °extol, °honor, °exalt, °praise, °admire, °adore, adulate, °glorify, deify, °idolize, be devoted to, pay homage to, bow down before, kneel before, °put on a pedestal —*n.* **2** °veneration, °reverence, adoration, °devotion, °homage, °honor, °respect, °esteem, exaltation, °praise, °admiration, adulation, glorification, deification, idolatry

worth *n.* °quality, °merit, value, °advantage, °benefit, °good, °importance, °significance, °usefulness

worthless *adj.* **1** valueless, unimportant, °insignificant, inessential *or* unessential, °dispensable, °disposable, °paltry **2** °pointless, °bootless, °silly, °inane, °vain, unavailing, °useless, °futile, °fruitless, unproductive, °unprofitable **3** °cheap, valueless, °tawdry, °poor, trashy, rubbishy, °shabby, °wretched, *Colloq* °tinny, crappy, cheesy, *Slang* chintzy

worthwhile *adj.* **1** °profitable, justifiable, °productive, °gainful, °rewarding, °fruitful, cost-effective, remunerative **2** °useful, valuable, °good, °helpful, °beneficial, °worthy, beneficent, °desirable, °exemplary, °matchless, °honorable, °upright, °sterling, °irreproachable

worthy *adj.* **1** °worthwhile, °deserving, meriting, °meritorious, °praiseworthy, °good, °estimable, °qualified, creditable **2** See **worthwhile, 2,** above. —*n.* **3** °dignitary, °personage, °notable, eminence, luminary

wound *n.* **1** °damage, °hurt, °injury, trauma, traumatism; laceration, °puncture, °cut, °gash, °slash, lesion, °bruise, contusion **2** °slight, °damage, °injury, °harm, °blow, °distress, mortification, °torment, torture, °anguish, °pain, °insult —*v.* **3** °damage, °harm, °injure, °hurt, traumatize; °cut, °slash, °gash, °lacerate, °slit, °stab, °shoot, *Colloq* wing **4** °slight, °distress, °damage, °mortify, °insult, °hurt, °pain, °grieve, °offend, aggrieve, °wrong

wrap *v.* **1** Sometimes, ***wrap up.*** °swathe, swaddle, °bind, °cover, enwrap, °envelop, °wind, enshroud, °shroud, enfold, °fold, °muffle, °enclose, sheathe, encase; °pack, °package, do up, gift-wrap **2** ***wrapped up in.*** immersed in, submerged in, buried in, absorbed in, engrossed in, bound up in, involved in, occupied with *or* by *or* in, engaged in, dedicated to, devoted to **3** ***wrap up.*** **(a)** °complete, conclude, °finish, °end, bring to a close, °terminate, °wind up, °settle, °tidy up **(b)** ***Wrap up!*** Be silent!, Be quiet!, Stop talking!, Hold your tongue!, *Slang* Shut up!, Shut your face!, Shut your trap!, Shut your mouth!, *Brit* Put a sock in it! —*n.* **4** °stole, shawl, °mantle, poncho, serape, °cloak, °cape

wrapper *n.* **1** housecoat, °robe, dressing gown, bathrobe, kimono, negligee, lounging robe, peignoir, *US* housedress **2** envelope, °package, packing, wrapping, covering, jacket, °case, casing, container

wreak *v.* °inflict, °exercise, °exert, °carry

out, °bring (to bear), °visit, °effect, °work, unleash, °execute, °impose, °force, °vent, let go

wreck *v.* **1** °destroy, °ruin, °devastate, °demolish, smash, °shatter, °spoil, °dash (to pieces), reduce to nothing, turn into scrap, annihilate **2** °sink, scuttle, run aground, °founder, °capsize —*n.* **3** °hulk, shipwreck, °ruins **4** °mess, °disaster, °ruin; °havoc **5** °destruction, °loss, °sinking, devastation, foundering, grounding, °capsize, capsizing, disabling, disablement, wrecking; demolition, demolishing, leveling, tearing down, razing, pulling down, obliteration

wreckage *n.* debris, °fragments, °remains, rubble, ruin(s)

wrench *v.* **1** °yank, °twist, °jerk, °force, °pull, °tug, °tear, wring, °rip, wrest **2** °strain, sprain, °twist, overstrain **3** °extract, wrest, wring, °force, °pry, °draw —*n.* **4** °yank, °twist, °jerk, °pull, °tug, °rip **5** °pang, °pain, °agony, torture, °blow, °ache, °throe, °anguish, °sadness, °grief, heartbreak **6** *Brit* spanner, shifting spanner, adjustable spanner, *US* monkey wrench

wrestle *v.* °battle, °fight, °struggle, tussle, °strive

wretch *n.* **1** °scoundrel, blackguard, worm, °villain, cur, °beast, dog, swine, °rogue, °good-for-nothing, knave, varlet, scalawag *or* scallywag, °rascal, rapscallion, *Archaic* caitiff, whoreson, *Colloq* rat, °stinker, louse, °creep, *Slang* bastard, *Brit* rotter, bounder, blighter, *US* °bum **2** °unfortunate, poor fellow *or* chap, miserable creature, poor devil, pilgarlic, *Slang* poor bastard *or* son-of-a-bitch, *Brit* poor bugger *or* sod, *US* sad sack

wretched *adj.* **1** °miserable, °awful, °terrible, °atrocious, °deplorable, *Colloq* °lousy, °rotten **2** °unhappy, °sad, °miserable, °woebegone, woeful, °dismal, °downhearted, °heartbroken, °brokenhearted, heartsick, °dejected, depressed, melancholic, °melancholy, °mournful, disconsolate, °inconsolable, °doleful, cheerless, crestfallen, °joyless, °desolate **3** °pitiable, °pathetic, °sorry, °pitiful, hapless, °hopeless, °unfortunate, °miserable **4** °vile, °shameful, °scurvy, underhand(ed), treacherous, °contemptible, °despicable, °base, °low, °mean, °paltry, mean-spirited, detestable

wriggle *v.* **1** wiggle, wobble, °shake, °tremble, °quiver, °jiggle, waggle, writhe, °twist, °fidget **2** °twist, °squirm, °snake, worm, writhe, °slither, °crawl —*n.* **3** wiggle, zigzag, wavy line, *Colloq* squiggle, squiggly line **4** wriggling, writhing, °squirm, squirming, wiggle, wiggling, shaking, trembling, °quiver, quivering, shimmying, waggle, waggling, twisting, °twist

wrinkle[1] *n.* **1** crease, °fold, °line, °furrow, crinkle, crow's-foot, corrugation, °pucker, °ridge —*v.* **2** crease, °fold, °line, °furrow, crinkle, corrugate, °pucker, °gather, ruck, crimp, °screw up, °rumple, °crumple

wrinkle[2] *n.* °dodge, °gimmick, °device, ploy, °ruse, °scheme, °trick, °idea, °plan, °plot, °stunt, °way, °approach, °technique, °method, *Slang chiefly Brit* wheeze

write *v.* **1** °pen, scribble, °get off, °dash off; indite, inscribe, °make out **2** °correspond (with), send a letter *or* a note *or* a postcard *or US also* a postal card, °communicate (with) **3** °compose, °create, °make up, °author **4** ***write down.*** **(a)** °register, °list, catalogue, °note, make a note *or* notation, °record, °transcribe, set *or* jot *or* take down, put in writing, put in black and white **(b)** derogate, decry, °disparage, °put down, °minimize, make little of, °play down, °detract, °belittle **5** ***write off.*** °delete, °cancel, °disregard, °ignore, °forgive, °forget (about), annul, eradicate, °erase

writer *n.* °author, novelist, littérateur, essayist, man of letters, °scribe, scribbler, wordsmith, freelancer, penny-a-liner, °hack, Grubstreeter, °journalist, newsman, °reporter, °correspondent, member of the fourth estate, (gossip) columnist, stringer, *Brit* paragraphist, *US* paragrapher, *Colloq* pen pusher, pencil pusher, sob sister, *Brit* journo

writing *n.* **1** handwriting, longhand, °penmanship, °script, calligraphy *or* chirography, scribble **2** Sometimes, ***writings.*** (literary) work(s), °composition, °theme, °book, article, critique, °criticism, °review, °editorial, column, exposé, °essay, °poetry, °poem, °novel, nonfiction, fiction, °document, °letter, correspondence, °publication, *Chiefly Brit journalism* leading article *or* leader, *Chiefly US journalism* op-ed article **3** °literature, belles-lettres, °letters

wrong *adj.* **1** °improper, unjust, unfair, injudicious, unethical, °terrible, °foul, °awful, °bad, °immoral, °sinful, °evil, iniquitous, °villainous, °wicked, °vile, diabolic(al), °infernal, °fiendish, °corrupt, °dishonest, reprehensible, °abominable, °dreadful, °dishonorable, blameworthy, °naughty, °shameful, °disgraceful, opprobrious, °criminal, felonious, °illegal, °illicit, °unlawful, °illegitimate, *Colloq* °crooked **2** °mistaken, °in error, °erroneous, °incorrect, °inaccurate, °imprecise, °inexact, fallacious, askew, °false, °wide of the mark; °strange, °odd, °peculiar, °curious; *Colloq* off target *or US also* off the target, off the beam, *Brit* off beam **3** °incorrect, °improper, unsuitable **4** °inappropriate, inapt, °improper, indecorous, °unseemly, unfitting, °unacceptable, °undesirable, °incongruous, °unbecoming, °out of place, ill-considered, wrongheaded, °imprudent, °misguided, inexpedient, impolitic, infelicitous, *Colloq* out of line **5** °out of order, not working, °faulty, awry, °amiss, the matter, °defective, °imperfect, °unsound, °flawed, °deficient **6** °opposite, °reverse, °incorrect, °improper —*adv.* **7** awry, imperfectly, incorrectly, improperly, inappropriately, °amiss, °badly, wrongly, *Scots and No. England and literary* agley, *Colloq* out of sync

8 *go wrong.* **(a)** go astray, falter, °fail, °lapse, °err, fall from grace, go to the bad, °deteriorate, go downhill, backslide, regress, retrogress, recidivate **(b)** °fail, malfunction, °break down, °miscarry, backfire, °fall through, *Colloq* °flop, °come to grief, go kaput, *Brit* go phut —*v.* **9** °abuse, °mistreat, °injure, °misuse, maltreat, ill-use, °ill-treat, °discredit, asperse, calumniate, malign, °dishonor, °impose upon, take advantage of, °harm, °damage, °oppress

wry *adj.* **1** distorted, contorted, twisted, °lopsided, °deformed, °crooked, aslant, °one-sided, askew, °bent, tilted, off-center **2** °dry, droll, °witty, °sardonic, °sarcastic, ironic(al), amusing; °perverse, fey; *Scots* pawky

Y

yahoo *n.* °boor, °barbarian, °philistine, °savage, churl, °brute, lout, °bourgeois, lowbrow, oaf, °clod, °peasant, *Slang* °slob, *Brit* mucker, yob *or* yobbo, *US* rube

yank *v.* **1** °jerk, °jolt, °tug, °wrench, °snatch, °hitch —*n.* **2** °jerk, °jolt, °tug, °wrench, °snatch, °hitch

yap *v.* **1** bark, yelp **2** gabble, °babble, blither *or* blather, °chatter, °jabber, °tattle, °prattle, prate, *Colloq chiefly Brit* witter, natter, *Slang* jaw, run on, *US* run off at the mouth —*n.* **3** °mouth, *Slang* °trap, °gob, *US* bazoo

yardstick *n.* °measure, bench mark, criterion, °standard, °gauge, °basis, °touchstone, °scale, exemplar

yarn *n.* **1** °thread, °fiber; strand **2** °tale, °story, °account, °narrative, anecdote; tall tale, fable, °fabrication, fiction, cock-and-bull story, *Colloq* whopper, *Brit* fishing story, *US* fish story, fish tale

yearly *adv.* **1** annually, perennially, every year, once a year, year after year, year in (and) year out, regularly **2** per year, per annum, by the year, each year —*adj.* **3** annual, °perennial, once-a-year, °regular

yearn *v.* °long, pine, °ache, °hanker, °itch, °hunger, °thirst, crave, have a craving, °desire, °wish, °want, °fancy, °prefer

yell *v.* **1** °shout, °scream, °bellow, °howl, screech, yowl, °roar, °bawl, caterwaul, squall, yelp, *Colloq* holler —*n.* **2** °shout, °scream, °cry, °bellow, °howl, screech, yowl, °roar, caterwaul, squall, yelp, *Colloq* holler

yeomanly *adj.* yeoman, workmanlike, °useful, °staunch, °courageous, °loyal, dedicated, °faithful, °steadfast, unswerving, unwavering, °firm, °sturdy, °reliable, °solid

yes man *n.* toady, sycophant, toadeater, timeserver, °hanger-on, lickspittle, bootlicker, truckler, °flunky, courtier, jackal, spaniel, lap dog, *Taboo slang Brit* arse-kisser, arse-licker, *US* ass-kisser, ass-licker, *US* brown-noser

yet *adv.* **1** as yet, (up) till *or* until now, °so far, thus far, up hitherto, to the present (time) **2** °still, up to this time, up to now, even now, till *or* until now, to this day **3** °moreover, furthermore, °besides, °further, °still **4** in the future, in time to come, later, °eventually **5** °still, °notwithstanding, anyway, anyhow, °nonetheless, °nevertheless, °regardless, in spite of *or* despite everything, just *or* all the same, °even so, after all, *US* still and all —*conj.* **6** °notwithstanding, in spite of *or* despite it *or* that *or* the fact, °still, °nevertheless, but

yield *v.* **1** °surrender, give up (the fight *or* struggle), °give in, knuckle under, °submit, °cede, cry quits, throw in the towel *or* the sponge, °capitulate, °succumb, raise the white flag **2** °give up, °surrender, °give over, hand in *or* over, °abandon, °relinquish, °renounce, °cede **3** °agree, °consent, °comply, °concede, °relent, assent, °give way, accede, concur **4** °earn, °return, °pay, °bring in, °supply, °generate, °produce, °net —*n.* **5** °return, °production, °output, °revenue, takings, °gate, °earnings, °income, °proceeds, °profit, °gain

yielding *adj.* **1** pliant, flexile, °flexible, °pliable, °soft, °plastic, fictile, °elastic, resilient, °supple, springy, bouncy, spongy, rubbery **2** °accommodating, docile, °submissive, amenable, °tractable, compliant, °obedient, °flexible, acquiescent, °agreeable, °obliging, °manageable, manipulable

young *adj.* **1** youthful, teenage(d), °adolescent, prepubescent, pubescent, °juvenile, °minor, °junior, underage **2** °boyish, girlish; °immature, °callow, °green, °inexperienced, °unfledged, uninitiated, °unsophisticated, °childlike, °innocent, naive *or* naïve *or* naïf **3** °childish, °puerile, °infantile, babyish, *US* sophomoric —*n.* **4** °offspring, babies, °issue, little ones, °progeny, °litter, °brood; children

youth *n.* **1** °childhood, boyhood, girlhood, young manhood, young womanhood, prepubescence, pubescence, adolescence, salad days; immaturity, minority **2** °child, youngster, schoolchild, °teenager, teen, °minor, °juvenile, °adolescent; °boy, schoolboy, °stripling, young boy *or* man, °lad, laddie, whippersnapper; °girl, °lass, lassie, schoolgirl, °maid, °maiden, *Literary* damsel, demoiselle, mademoiselle, *Colloq* kid, (little) shaver, *US and Canadian* tad, *Slang* teenybopper, *Brit* sprog **3** children, youngsters, juveniles, adolescents, young people, °young, *Colloq* kids

yucky *adj.* yukky *or US also* yuchy, °disgusting, °repugnant, °repellent, unappetizing, vomit-provoking, sick-making, ill-making, °nauseous, nauseating, °revolting, °foul, mucky, °beastly, °awful, *Slang Brit* grotty

yummy *adj.* °delicious, mouthwatering, °luscious, appetizing, °tasty, toothsome, °savory, delectable, ambrosial, *Colloq* scrumptious

Z

zany *adj.* **1** clownish, °mad, °wild, °frolicsome, °sportive, °playful, °gay, °merry, slapstick, °crazy, °funny, comic(al), amusing, °hilarious, °absurd, °nonsensical, °ludicrous, °silly, °foolish, °inane, *Colloq* wacky, loony, madcap, crackpot, nutty, goofy, *US* kooky —*n.* **2** °clown, °comic, jester, °fool, °joker, buffoon, °wag, °comedian, merry-andrew, laughingstock, *Slang* nut, *US* screwball

zap *v.* °destroy, °kill, °slaughter, annihilate, °murder, slay, assassinate, liquidate, °erase; °shoot, electrocute, *Slang* °rub out, °polish off, °knock off, °bump off, snuff (out), °waste, °hit, *US* ice

zealot *n.* °fanatic, extremist, °radical, bigot, °maniac, °militant, °terrorist

zealotry *n.* °fanaticism, extremism, radicalism, °bigotry, militantism, terrorism, single-mindedness, monomania, °fervor, °frenzy, hysteria, °obsession, obsessiveness

zenith *n.* meridian, °summit, °acme, apex, °vertex, apogee, high point, °top, °peak, °pinnacle

zero *n.* **1** °none, °nil, null, °nothing, °nought, ought, cipher, *Brit cricket* °duck, *Colloq* nix, *US* goose egg, nada, ***niente***, *Slang US* zilch, *Brit* sweet F.A. *or* Fanny Adams, bugger-all, *Taboo slang* fuck-all **2** °(rock) bottom, nadir **3** °nobody, °nothing, nonentity, *Slang US* nebbish, bupkis —*v.* **4** ***zero in on.*** focus on, pinpoint, °fix on, home in on, concentrate on, bring to bear on

zest *n.* **1** °spice, °relish, °gusto, °tang, °pepper, ginger, piquancy, pungency, °edge, °bite, °flavor, *Colloq* zing, zip, pizazz **2** °eagerness, zestfulness, °exuberance, °appetite, °interest, °enthusiasm, °hunger, °thirst

zone *n.* °area, °quarter, °district, °region, sector, °section, °sphere, °belt, °territory, °province, °realm, °domain, °precinct, bailiwick, °department, °terrain, °circle, locality, °locale, *Slang US* °turf

zoo *n.* **1** zoological garden, menagerie, *Tiergarten*, °(safari) park **2** madhouse, °mess; °chaos, °pandemonium, °bedlam, *Colloq US* three-ring circus, Chinese fire-drill